The Harry S. Truman Encyclopedia

The G.K. Hall
Presidential Encyclopedia Series

Harry S. Truman, thirty-third president of the United States of America. (Library of Congress)

The
Harry S. Truman
Encyclopedia

Edited by
Richard S. Kirkendall

G.K. Hall & Co.
Boston

Chronology © 1989 by William E. Pemberton

Communism and Communists and The Rosenberg Case © 1989 by Ellen
W. Schrecker

Typeset in 9½/11 Sabon by Compositors Corporation.

Library of Congress Cataloging-in-Publication Data

The Harry S. Truman encyclopedia/edited by Richard S. Kirkendall.
   p.   cm.—(The G. K. Hall presidential encyclopedia series)
   ISBN 0-8161-8915-3
   1. Truman, Harry S., 1884-1972—Dictionaries, indexes, etc.
2. United States—Politics and government—1945-1953—Dictionaries.
I. Kirkendall, Richard Steward, 1928-   . II. Series.
E814.H336   1989
973.918′092—dc20
[B]   89-38738
                                                          CIP

CONTRIBUTORS

W. Andrew Achenbaum
The University of Michigan

Howard W. Allen
Southern Illinois University at Carbondale

Stephen E. Ambrose
University of New Orleans

Terry H. Anderson
Texas A & M University

Joseph Preston Baratta
Society for the Study of Internationalism

John Barnard
Oakland University

Clay R. Bauske
Harry S. Truman Library

Michal R. Belknap
California Western School of Law

Larry Berman
University of California, Davis

William C. Berman
University of Toronto

Mary Frances Berry
Howard University

Gary Dean Best
University of Hawaii at Hilo

Ian J. Bickerton
The University of New South Wales

Roger Biles
Oklahoma State University

Monroe Billington
New Mexico State University

Guenter Bischof
Harvard University

Thomas E. Blantz, C.S.C.
University of Notre Dame

Mary H. Blewett
University of Lowell

Harry R. Borowski
United States Air Force Academy

H. W. Brands
Texas A & M University

Charles C. Brown
Columbia, Mo.

D. Clayton Brown
Texas Christian University

William P. Browne
Central Michigan University

Russell D. Buhite
The University of Oklahoma

Robert E. Burke
University of Washington

Betty Boyd Caroli
Kingsborough Community College

Anthony Champagne
The University of Texas at Dallas

James H. Charleton
Department of the Interior

William R. Childs
The Ohio State University

Thomas D. Clark
Lexington, Ky.

Alan Clive
Silver Springs, Md.

Ron Cockrell
United States Department of the Interior

Wayne S. Cole
The University of Maryland, College Park

Paolo E. Coletta
United States Naval Academy

Robert M. Collins
University of Missouri—Columbia

Elmer E. Cornwell, Jr.
State of Rhode Island and Providence Plantations
House of Representatives

Bruce Cumings
The University of Chicago

John T. Curry
Harry S. Truman Library

George H. Curtis
Harry S. Truman Library

Richard M. Dalfiume
State University of New York at Binghamton

Roger Daniels
University of Cincinnati

Richard O. Davies
University of Nevada—Reno

Henry C. Dethloff
Texas A & M University

Leonard Dinnerstein
The University of Arizona

Frederick J. Dobney
Washington State University

Justus D. Doenecke
New College of the University of South Florida

Andrew J. Dunar
The University of Alabama in Huntsville

Charles W. Eagles
The University of Mississippi

Alfred E. Eckes
United States International Trade Commission

Jerome E. Edwards
University of Nevada—Reno

J. Merton England
Washington, D.C.

Ronald T. Farrar
University of South Carolina

Terrence R. Fehner
United States Department of Energy

Sidney Fine
The University of Michigan

Gary M. Fink
Georgia State University

Paul Finkelman
State University of New York at Binghamton

Gilbert C. Fite
Bella Vista, Ark.

Shannon E. Fleming
Chicago, Ill.

George Q. Flynn
Texas Tech University

James L. Forsythe
Fort Hays State University

Steven Fraser
Basic Books, Inc.

Richard M. Fried
The University of Illinois at Chicago

Richard Frucht
Northwest Missouri State University

James N. Giglio
Southwest Missouri State University

Karla A. Goldman
Harvard University

James W. Goodrich
The State Historical Society of Missouri

Candice L. Goucher
Portland State University

Norman A. Graebner
University of Virginia

Dewey W. Grantham
Vanderbilt University

Peter Grose
Council on Foreign Relations

Alonzo L. Hamby
Ohio University

Samuel B. Hand
The University of Vermont

Daniel F. Harrington
Albuquerque, N. Mex.

William H. Harris
Texas Southern University

Susan M. Hartmann
The Ohio State University

Alan Havig
Stephens College

Ellis W. Hawley
The University of Iowa

Richard F. Haynes
Northeast Louisiana University

Jim F. Heath
Portland State University

Thomas J. Heed
Ramapo College of New Jersey

Francis H. Heller
The University of Kansas

Gregg Herken
University of California, Santa Cruz

George C. Herring
University of Kentucky

Richard G. Hewlett
Bethesda, Md.

James W. Hilty
Temple University

Joan Hoff-Wilson
Organization of American Historians

Jack M. Holl
Department of Energy, United States of America

John W. Huston
United States Naval Academy

D. Clayton James
Mississippi State University

John W. Jeffries
The University of Maryland, Baltimore County

Niel M. Johnson
Harry S. Truman Library

Manfred Jonas
Union College

Howard Jones
The University of Alabama

George McT. Kahin
Cornell University

Lawrence S. Kaplan
Kent State University

David A. Kathka
Western Wyoming College

Donald F. Kettl
University of Virginia

Linda R. Killen
Radford University

Elise K. Kirk
Washington, D.C.

Richard S. Kirkendall
University of Washington

Dean W. Kohlhoff
Valparaiso University

Clayton R. Koppes
Oberlin College

Mark Kornbluh
Washington University

Bruce R. Kuniholm
Duke University

Joel Kunze
Iowa State University

Ronald D. Landa
Office of the Secretary of Defense

Fred H. Lawson
Mills College

Linda J. Lear
George Mason University

R. Alton Lee
The University of South Dakota

Francis L. Loewenheim
Rice University

Robert W. Love, Jr.
United States Naval Academy

Richard Lowitt
Iowa State University

David W. Mabon
United States Department of State

Arthur F. McClure II
Central Missouri State University

Donald R. McCoy
The University of Kansas

George T. McJimsey
Iowa State University

Richard D. McKinzie
University of Missouri—Kansas City

Robert J. McMahon
University of Florida

Eduard Mark
Washington, D.C.

Norman Markowitz
Rutgers University

Stephen G. Marshall
Montclair, N.J.

George T. Mazuzan
National Science Foundation

Dennis Merrill
University of Missouri—Kansas City

Robert L. Messer
The University of Illinois at Chicago

Aaron D. Miller
United States Department of State

James Edward Miller
United States Department of State

Franklin D. Mitchell
University of Southern California

William Howard Moore
The University of Wyoming

Anne Hodges Morgan
Robert S. and Grayce B. Kerr Foundation

Paul L. Murphy
University of Minnesota

Frank A. Ninkovich
St. John's University

Keith W. Olson
The University of Maryland, College Park

William L. O'Neill
Rutgers University

Kenneth O'Reilly
University of Alaska, Anchorage

David M. Oshinsky
Rutgers University

David S. Painter
Georgetown University

S. Victor Papacosma
Kent State University

Herbert S. Parmet
Graduate School and University Center of the City
   University of New York

William E. Parrish
Mississippi State University

Thomas G. Paterson
The University of Connecticut

William E. Pemberton
University of Wisconsin—La Crosse

Kenneth R. Philp
The University of Texas at Arlington

Donald K. Pickens
North Texas State University

Allen Howard Podet
State University College of New York at Buffalo

Monte M. Poen
Northern Arizona University

Forrest C. Pogue
George C. Marshall Library

Robert A. Pollard
United States Department of State

David L. Porter
William Penn College

James R. Ralph, Jr.
Harvard University

Julian S. Rammelkamp
Albion, Mich.

Alan R. Raucher
Wayne State University

Linda Reed
University of North Carolina at Chapel Hill

Gary W. Reichard
The University of Maryland, College Park

Glenda Riley
University of Northern Iowa

Donald A. Ritchie
United States Senate Historical Office

Jo Ann Robinson
Morgan State University

Alfred B. Rollins, Jr.
Old Dominion University

Lisle A. Rose
United States Department of State

Mark H. Rose
Michigan Technological University

Richard T. Ruetten
San Diego State University

Lois Scharf
Case Western Reserve University

Ronald Schatz
Wesleyan University

Eugene F. Schmidtlein
Stephens College

Ellen W. Schrecker
Yeshiva University

Robert D. Schulzinger
University of Colorado

Thomas Schwartz
Harvard University

Jordan A. Schwarz
Northern Illinois University

Ingrid Winther Scobie
Texas Woman's University

Bruce E. Seely
Michigan Technological University

Michael Shaller
The University of Arizona

Michael S. Sherry
Northwestern University

Harvard Sitkoff
University of New Hampshire

Robert Sklar
New York University

Gaddis Smith
Yale University

Thomas G. Smith
Nichols College

Thomas F. Soapes
National Archives and Records Administration

Martha H. Swain
Texas Woman's University

Athan Theoharis
Marquette University

Charles E. Timberlake
University of Missouri—Columbia

Gil Troy
Harvard University

John Trumpbour
Harvard University

Nancy Bernkopf Tucker
Georgetown University

Robert Underhill
Iowa State University

Melvin I. Urofsky
Virginia Commonwealth University

Stephen L. Vaughan
University of Wisconsin—Madison

William O. Wagnon, Jr.
Washburn University of Topeka

J. Samuel Walker
United States Nuclear Regulatory Commission

Winifred D. Wandersee
Hartwick College

Gilbert Ware
Drexel University

George M. Watson, Jr.
Office of Air Force History

Richard A. Watson
University of Missouri—Columbia

Donald R. Whitnah
University of Northern Iowa

William M. Wiecek
Syracuse University

William H. Wilson
University of North Texas State

Marshall Windmiller
San Francisco State University

Lawrence A. Yates
United States Army Command and General Staff
  College

Robert L. Zangrando
The University of Akron

Robert H. Zieger
University of Florida

Benedict K. Zobrist
Harry S. Truman Library

TABLES

Chronology of Harry S. Truman's Life   xix

Harry S. Truman's Cabinets   45

Honorary Degrees Conferred upon Harry S.
   Truman   21

Military Spending, 1945–54   237

Party Alignment in Congress during Truman's
   Presidency   75

Presidential Election of 1948, Total Votes and Pollsters'
   Predictions   290

Presidential Election Returns and Distribution of Seats
   in U.S. Congress, 1946–52   118

INTRODUCTION

Since his death in 1972, Harry S. Truman has become a national hero. His life has been portrayed in best-selling books and widely viewed television and stage productions; his image has been displayed in the Oval Office and the cabinet room even when Republicans controlled the White House; and the politicians have competed with one another for recognition as a Truman type. Much of what has been said and written tells us more about our times than about him. In a period of tarnished and failed presidencies, he has looked better than he did to most of his contemporaries. But even Ronald Reagan, the first president since Eisenhower to serve two full terms and a man who left office with a high approval rating in the public opinion polls, found much to praise in the Man from Independence.

By the time Truman became a national hero, scholars had developed several basic interpretations of him. A liberal interpretation had dominated scholarly writing on Truman in its early years. The liberal scholars detected some defects in him but emphasized his accomplishments. He had, they argued, exercised, enlarged, and preserved the powers of the presidency, attacked Jim Crow more vigorously than any president before him, and achieved some significant victories in domestic affairs. Even more important in this view, he had made major and valuable decisions in foreign affairs, responding firmly yet prudently to the powerful aggressive thrust of the Soviet Union. These scholars regarded Truman as underrated and as a great or at least a near-great president.

Several assumptions or themes figured prominently in the liberal interpretation. American history, compared with the history of other nations, is essentially a success story that includes the work of many distinguished men and the selection of some of them for the presidency. The American presidency is an institution of unusual value that should be strong but has limits on its power, and thus a president should try to lead but should not be measured by unreasonable standards. In the Truman period, the United States could not have developed good relations with the Soviet Union and could not have controlled events in Eastern Europe or China, and thus interpreters of the period should emphasize Truman's large accomplishments in Western Europe. His Fair Deal, like the New Deal with which it was linked, was a set of valuable programs and proposals to which Truman was personally committed and which improved American life in important ways and could have improved it even more if opposing forces had not blocked the way. Public opinion, congressional conservatism, and the pressure of foreign affairs, not defects in Truman, were chiefly responsible for his failure to accomplish more at home.

By the late 1960s, the liberal interpretation had run up against a vigorous challenge from revisionists who exerted a large influence on the historical profession. In their overall interpretation of American history, these revisionists emphasized the power and influence of capitalism and capitalists, and in their analyses of the foreign affairs of the Truman administration, they stressed several themes. The United States was more powerful than the Soviet Union at the time and seldom if ever hesitated to use its power. Soviet behavior was largely a reaction to American actions, which threatened the security of the Soviet Union, and would have been different if the United States had acted differently. The United States intervened in the Korean War and invaded North Korea in order to gain support for plans for a military buildup and/or to pacify domestic critics. And the United States (or Truman) was largely to blame for the unhappy course of recent history.

The revisionist challenge extended beyond foreign affairs to include domestic matters as well. Here, revisionists argued that although Truman achieved some victories, his failures and shortcomings were much more meaningful, and his personal defects, not the difficulties of the situation, were chiefly responsible for the failures. He gave too much attention to foreign affairs, appointed too many conservatives and incompetent people to office, exaggerated the strength of the opposition to his proposals, was often timid and weak, and lacked the boldness and strength that the situation demanded. He was dominated by political considerations, did not have strong commitments, and failed to press proposals as vigorously and consistently as possible. He also employed rhetoric and pursued policies that violated civil liberties and led to McCarthyism.

Looking at Truman from the Left, the revisionists often maintained that he represented an ideology—liberalism—that was seriously defective. It did not understand racism, poverty, and corporate power and failed to provide a strong defense of civil liberties during the second red scare. This line of criticism implied that Truman would have failed to achieve greatness even if he had promoted his proposals effectively.

The revisionists were not a solid intellectual bloc, however. They split apart on some major points, including the power of the presidency and the importance of the individual in history. Some argued that Truman was too weak; others objected that he made the presidency too strong. Some saw the substitution of Truman for Henry A. Wallace in 1944 and then Franklin D. Roosevelt in 1945 as changes of great significance, whereas others maintained that the capitalist system dictated the course of American history no matter which individual held office.

By the mid-seventies, reactions to revisionism had gained prominence in historical writing on the Truman presidency. A group of antirevisionists had emerged who found little of value in revisionism. Often insisting that revisionist scholarship was seriously flawed, the antirevisionists admired Truman and his points of view and attacked the assumptions of the revisionists, regarding them as unrealistic as to possibilities at home and abroad. These scholars reasserted the liberal interpretation of earlier years but documented and developed it much more fully.

Another group of scholars found too much of value in revisionism to be labeled antirevisionists yet rejected too much of it to be identified with it. These "postrevisionists" endorsed the conception of America as an expansive, even antirevolutionary nation, agreed that economic factors deserved attention in historical accounts, and shared the revisionists' concern about the power of the presidency, doubts about Truman's motivation and leadership, and criticism of his civil liberties record. Nevertheless, these scholars could not agree that the United States and Truman were chiefly responsible for the course of in-

ternational affairs after 1944. Some argued, for example, that Hitler, not Truman or American capitalism, was responsible for the cold war. Postrevisionists also argued that revisionists made too much of economics and of Truman's contributions to the emergence of McCarthyism and too little of his commitment to principles, his accomplishments, and the difficulties he faced. These scholars emphasized the complexity of influences and motives, called attention to the limits on American power in the Truman years and especially to the administration's view of that power as limited, and argued that domestic political pressures inevitably exerted a powerful influence on foreign policy.

The book that comes after these introductory remarks does not take a stand on the appropriateness of Truman's placement in the galaxy of national heroes or on the strengths of the various scholarly interpretations. Instead, it lets the reader decide. To assist in the move toward appraisal, the book offers the full range and rich diversity of scholarly opinion on Truman. The book is not dominated by one point of view. It offers examples of the several intellectual positions that have been brought to bear upon Truman's life and career. It is controlled only by an assumption that Truman was a person of large historical significance—or at least appeared to be doing things of great importance, though deeper forces may have been responsible for what occurred.

Although it does not offer one interpretation, the book does have one model: the well-received *Franklin D. Roosevelt: His Life and Times, An Encyclopedic View*, edited by Otis L. Graham, Jr., and Meghan Robinson Wander and published by G. K. Hall & Co. in 1985. That book focused on one historically significant person and looked at him from the vantage points occupied by representatives of the community of scholars dedicated to the study of the history and government of the United States in the twentieth century. This new book has similar goals and employs the same means.

Like the earlier book, this one is biographical. Many of the essays focus directly on Truman himself, on his personality, his ideas, and his activities, including his jobs and his hobbies, his politics and his policies. Truman the farmer, Truman the soldier, and Truman the businessman as well as Truman the politician appear in these pages. So do Truman the reader, Truman the piano player, and Truman the walker. Some of the essays take a step or two away from him and look at his family, including his ancestors, his grandfather, his parents, his brother and sister, his wife, Bess, his daughter, Margaret. Other articles move farther away and look at other people who were important in his life, foes as well as friends, those who influenced him as well as people who felt his impact. There are essays on places of importance in the Truman story, such as the state of Missouri, the Missouri River, and the city of Independence. There are articles on other features of the "Truman period" in Missouri and American history, including government policies and agencies, elections, and interest groups. No essay ignores Truman. His presence is at least implied in every one. Most often, the author emphasizes the connection between the man and the subject of the essay.

Although modeled after the Roosevelt encyclopedia, the Truman encyclopedia can also be viewed as a sequel to another book, edited by me, that was published in two quite different editions: *The Truman Period as a Research Field* (1967) and *The Truman Period as a Research Field: A Reappraisal, 1972* (1974). Designed to offer guidance to scholars interested in research in the field, those volumes served their purpose rather well, but they are now seriously out of date. This new work can serve as a fresh guide to research and interpretation. Featuring essays by authors who are heavily involved in research and writing on the Truman period, the encyclopedia supplies a guide to the work that has been done—and the research that remains to be accomplished.

One point that the essays make very clearly is that the literature on Truman and the Truman period has become very rich since the publication of *The Truman Period as a Research Field,* even the second edition. Scholars from many locales have rushed into the field, attracted by the apparent importance of the subject and the opening of sources for study. Two decades ago, it appeared that Truman had not been much of a letter writer. Now we know that he not only wrote many letters over a long life but revealed much about himself in those letters. Two decades ago, scholars had little opportunity to explore the diplomatic and military records of his presidency, two of its most important facets. Now, as many of the articles reveal, scholars have been able to explore many if not all of the most important documents. The bibliographical notes attached to each article, though usually short, can help readers find the publications of greatest interest to them.

Although the encyclopedia can assist scholars interested in research on Truman and his times, it is not written only (or even chiefly) for them. It is written for the history teacher seeking aid in the development of a course in American history or the history of a region or a nation outside the United States that felt the influence of the Truman presidency. The encyclopedia can also serve the history student looking for a topic or engaged in a term paper. Above all, the work should benefit the citizen who has an interest in history, regards historical study as an activity of great value, and is curious about the historical significance of Harry Truman. And the reader need not be an American citizen, for Truman occupied the White House (and Blair House) during a crucial period in the history of the American move onto the world stage. It was a period that included the end of World War II, the dropping of the atomic bomb, the beginnings of the cold war, and the establishment of the containment policy. Truman's times also featured the Marshall Plan, the Berlin airlift, the creation of NATO, and the Korean War, to mention only some of the most prominent features. The volume examines large episodes such as these and also less momentous ones.

A substantial number of people contributed to the development of the book. I owe my thanks not only to the many authors who wrote essays for this volume but also to Meghan Robinson Wander, senior editor at G. K. Hall. The idea for the Truman encyclopedia originated with her, and, drawing upon her rich experience, including her work on the Roosevelt encyclopedia, she worked with me at every stage, always imaginatively and creatively. She also recruited and supervised a series of assistants who moved the project along on a daily basis, and she drew in a group of talented people in the publishing house who strengthened the book in a variety of ways. I am grateful to her and to them.

RICHARD S. KIRKENDALL
Seattle, Washington

CHRONOLOGY OF HARRY S. TRUMAN'S LIFE

8 May 1884	Harry S. Truman born, Lamar, Missouri.
December 1890	Truman family moves to Independence, Missouri.
September 1892	Enters first grade at Noland School in Independence.
May 1901	Graduates from Independence High School.
1901–1906	Enters working world; employed most of this period at a large Kansas City bank.
1906–1917	Works the family farm at Grandview, Missouri.
1917–1919	Serves in World War I as captain in the 129th Field Artillery of the Thirty-fifth Division.
6 May 1919	Receives discharge from army.
28 June 1919	Marries Bess (Elizabeth Virginia) Wallace.
1919–1922	Owns and operates a men's clothing store in Kansas City, Missouri, with partner Edward Jacobson.
7 November 1922	Elected eastern district judge of the Jackson County Court.
17 February 1924	Daughter, Mary Margaret Truman, born.
4 November 1924	Defeated for reelection as eastern district judge.
1925–1926	Works with Kansas City Automobile Club.
2 November 1926	Elected presiding judge, Jackson County Court.
4 November 1930	Reelected presiding judge, Jackson County Court.
7 August 1934	Wins Democratic primary for U.S. Senate.
6 November 1934	Elected to U.S. Senate.
6 August 1940	Wins Democratic primary for reelection to U.S. Senate.
5 November 1940	Reelected to U.S. Senate.
1941–1945	Wins national recognition as chairman of the Special Committee to Investigate the National Defense Program (Truman committee).
21 July 1944	Receives nomination as vice president to run with Franklin D. Roosevelt.
7 November 1944	Roosevelt and Truman win election.
20 January 1945	Takes oath as vice president.
12 April 1945	Takes oath as president, following Roosevelt's death.
8 May 1945	Announces German surrender.
16 July 1945	Successful test of atomic bomb in New Mexico.
17 July–2 August 1945	Presides at Potsdam Conference of the Big Three Allies.
28 July 1945	Senate ratifies the UN charter.
6 August 1945	United States drops atomic bomb on Hiroshima, Japan.
9 August 1945	United States drops atomic bomb on Nagasaki, Japan.
14 August 1945	Announces Japanese surrender.
6 September 1945	Sends Twenty-one Point Address to Congress, containing most of his domestic program later called the Fair Deal.
20 February 1946	Signs the Employment Act of 1946.
25 May 1946	Asks for legislation to draft into the army striking workers under certain conditions.
1 August 1946.	Signs the Atomic Energy Act of 1946.
20 September 1946	Requests Henry Wallace's resignation as secretary of commerce.
5 November 1946	Republicans win control of House and Senate in the Eightieth Congress.
12 March 1947	Delivers the Truman Doctrine speech.

21 March 1947	Establishes federal government loyalty program.
5 June 1947	Secretary of State George C. Marshall outlines what becomes the Marshall Plan.
20 June 1947	Vetoes Taft-Hartley Act.
26 July 1947	Signs National Security Act of 1947, unifying the armed forces.
29 October 1947	Receives report of President's Commission on Civil Rights, *To Secure These Rights*.
2 February 1948	Submits his civil rights program to Congress.
3 April 1948	Signs Foreign Assistance Act, implementing the Marshall Plan.
14 May 1948	Recognizes state of Israel.
June 1948	Berlin blockade and airlift begins, lasting almost a year.
15 July 1948	Accepts nomination as Democratic candidate for president.
26 July 1948	Issues executive orders directing end of discrimination in armed services and federal government.
2 November 1948	Wins 1948 election.
20 January 1949	Inaugurated as president.
4 April 1949	Signs North Atlantic Treaty.
15 July 1949	Signs Housing Act of 1949.
23 September 1949	Announces that an atomic explosion has been detected in the Soviet Union.
6 October 1949	Signs Mutual Defense Assistance Act, providing aid to North Atlantic Treaty members.
December 1949	Nationalist government officials flee from the mainland of China to Formosa.
31 January 1950	Announces order to construct a hydrogen bomb.
9 February 1950	Senator Joseph McCarthy announces that he has a list of names of Communists in the Department of State.
24 June 1950	Learns of North Korean attack on South Korea.
30 June 1950	Commits ground troops to Korea.
15 September 1950	Gen. Douglas MacArthur successfully lands troops at Inchon.
15 October 1950	Meets with MacArthur on Wake Island.
November 1950	Chinese intervention in Korean War shatters UN offensive.
11 April 1951	Relieves General MacArthur of his command.
10 July 1951	Negotiations begin for a truce in Korea.
29 March 1952	Announces he will not run for reelection.
8 April 1952	Issues order seizing steel mills.
2 June 1952	Supreme Court strikes down Truman's seizure of steel mills.
4 November 1952	Dwight D. Eisenhower elected president.
20 January 1953	Attends Eisenhower inaugural and returns with Bess to Independence.
1955-1956	Publishes his two-volume *Memoirs*.
July 1957	Attends dedication of Truman Library.
26 December 1972	Dies at age eighty-eight in Kansas City.

A

Acheson, Dean Gooderham

(11 April 1893–12 October 1971)

Under secretary of state, 1945–47; secretary of state, 1949–53; President Truman's closest and most influential adviser on foreign affairs. Dean Acheson's ideas, diplomacy, and bureaucratic power within the Truman administration significantly shaped all the following: the Baruch Plan for international control of atomic weapons (1946), resistance to Soviet pressure on Iran and Turkey (1946), the Truman Doctrine (1947), the Marshall Plan (1947), the lifting of the Berlin blockade (1949), the negotiation and ratification of the North Atlantic Treaty (1949) and subsequent organization of NATO with a permanent American military presence in Europe, the formation of the West German government and that nation's rearmament (1949 and after), the decision of 1949 not to recognize the People's Republic of China while waiting for an eventual split between Communist China and the Soviet Union, the decision to develop the hydrogen bomb (1950), the writing of National Security Council document 68 (1950), the conduct of the Korean War (1950–53), the Japanese peace treaty (1951), the American response to the nationalization of British oil interests in Iran (1951–53), and aid for the French in Indochina (1950 and after).

Acheson was born in Middletown, Connecticut, son of a British-born Episcopal bishop and a Canadian-born mother. Throughout his life he acted on the belief that Anglo-American cooperation was essential for American and world security. After education at Yale and Harvard Law School and a short stint in the U.S. Navy during World War I, Acheson served as clerk to Supreme Court Justice Louis D. Brandeis and then began the private practice of law in Washington. In 1933 he was under secretary of the treasury in the Franklin D. Roosevelt administration but resigned over a disagreement on monetary policy. With war in Europe in 1939 he emerged as an articulate advocate of American intervention on the side of Britain against Hitler's Germany. In 1941 he rejoined the Roosevelt administration as an assistant secretary of state. He became the number two officer of the State Department in 1945 and was acting secretary of state during extended periods when Secretaries James F. Byrnes and George C. Marshall were abroad. In July 1947 he resumed private law practice until Truman selected him to succeed Marshall as secretary of state in January 1949.

Acheson and Truman worked as well together as any president and secretary of state in American history. Acheson met with the president almost every day and presented issues for decision in a crisp, clear fashion—and then made sure that the president's will was carried out. The president placed full trust in Acheson and supported him without qualification as his senior adviser and principal voice in foreign affairs. Potential rivals either accepted this reality or were fired. Acheson and Truman agreed completely on the necessity of "negotiation from strength" with the Soviet Union and on the primacy of Western

Cloyd J. Sweigert, *San Francisco Chronicle* (1945–52).

Europe for American security. They agreed that the North Korean attack of June 1950 had to be thrown back both for the preservation of the American position in Asia and as a demonstration to European allies of American reliability. The only large issue on which they did not see eye to eye was Israel. Acheson believed that Truman's policies should have taken greater account of American interests in maintaining warm relations with Arab states.

Acheson considered President Truman's conduct of the Korean War to be sound in every essential: prompt resistance to aggression, assertion of his authority as commander in chief through the dismissal of Gen. Douglas MacArthur, careful control to avoid escalation into World War III, acceptance of negotiations for an armistice, but refusal to compromise the principle that no prisoner of war should be returned to the other side against his will.

Acheson's and the administration's greatest failure involved the (Communist) People's Republic of China. It proved impossible for the administration simultaneously to ward off the domestic political attacks of Republicans who wanted unlimited support of the Chiang Kai-shek Nationalist regime on Taiwan (Formosa), to signal to the Chinese Communists that they should worry about the long-term threat from their Soviet ally rather than from a benign United States, to send American troops through North Korea to the border with China, and to keep China from entering the war in response to its own perceived security needs. The enlargement of the Korean War and the failure of China policy embittered relations between Congress and the Truman administration in general and Acheson in particular and also provided fuel for the absurd accusations of Senator Joseph McCarthy that Acheson was protecting communists in the State Department and otherwise abetting the Soviet cause.

The American commitment to provide military aid for the French in their war against the nationalistic communists led by Ho Chi Minh in Vietnam followed Acheson's recommendation. The commitment began on a small scale in May 1950 and increased rapidly after the outbreak of the Korean War in June. Its dual purpose was to contain Communist China and make the French more amenable to American plans for the economic and military revival of West Germany. Acheson was uneasy at the time over the growing American involvement in Indochina, but neither he nor anyone else foresaw its ultimate disastrous consequences.

The relations of the United States with Latin America were quiet during the Truman years. That was fortuitous, because Acheson knew little about the region and did not care deeply, except about Brazil. The continent of Africa in those years was still under European colonial control. In the 1960s Acheson was not a strong supporter for the rapid attainment of independence for Black Africa. He did not see the United Nations, especially the General Assembly, as particularly useful. He was critical of all institutions and situations where power in the material sense was divorced from a voice on decisions.

When the Truman presidency ended in January 1953, Acheson resumed his partnership in the major Washington law firm of Covington and Burling. He corresponded with former president Truman and wrote scores of articles and half a dozen books, all of considerable literary distinction, culminating in the magisterial memoir *Present at the Creation*. He never again assumed full-time public office, but both presidents John F. Kennedy and Lyndon B. Johnson frequently asked his advice

Dean Acheson, 8 March 1947.
(National Archives)

and used him for short special missions. He was a hard-liner during the Cuban missile crisis of 1962, advocating that the United States bomb the Soviet missile installations in Cuba. He deplored every suggestion that Russia and the West could disengage militarily in Europe and develop a pattern of peaceful cooperation. He supported the Vietnam War until early 1968 when he told President Johnson that the cost of the war was disproportionate to any conceivable gains and that the president was not receiving accurate information. That advice was instrumental in Johnson's decision not to run for reelection and to seek a negotiated end of the war. During the final years of his life, Acheson supported the foreign policies of President Richard M. Nixon.

Acheson's own books, *Morning and Noon* (Boston: Houghton Mifflin, 1965) and *Present at the Creation: My Years in the State Department* (New York: W. W. Norton, 1969), provide good accounts of his career. For more information, see also McGeorge Bundy, ed., *The Pattern of Responsibility* (Boston: Houghton Mifflin, 1952), which includes selected speeches; David S. McLellan, *Dean Acheson: The State Department Years* (New York: Dodd, Mead, 1976); David S. McLellan and David C. Acheson, eds., *Among Friends: Personal Letters of Dean Acheson* (New York: Dodd, Mead, 1980); and Gaddis Smith, *Dean Acheson*, vol. 16 of *The American Secretaries of State and Their Diplomacy*, ed. Samuel Flagg Bemis and Robert Ferrell (New York: Cooper Square, 1972). Collections of Acheson manuscripts are in the Harry S. Truman Library and The Archives and Historical Manuscripts Division of the Yale University Library, New Haven, Conn.

GADDIS SMITH

See also Cabinets (photograph); China; Cold War; Indochina; Korean War; Roosevelt, Anna Eleanor (photograph)

Africa

The conventional assessment of U.S. policy toward Africa during the Truman years is that with few exceptions, African issues were largely ignored and consequently Africa figured little in the administration's foreign policy concerns. There was no doubt that African issues were not among the priorities of Truman's foreign policy which was preoccupied with the restoration of a postwar Europe and the containment of a perceived Soviet threat. Relations with Africa, however, demonstrated the overall restraint of U.S. attitudes toward both the Western anticolonialist sentiment and the nationalism that had arisen out of the exigencies and expectations of World War II economic conditions and rhetoric. Even tropical Africa felt the chilling breezes of the cold war.

The Africa of the Truman years was by and large colonial. Despite the fact that American troops had been stationed there during the war, Americans were largely ignorant of the continent. In 1945, only four of its fifty administrative entities were independent states. The remainder of the postwar African population continued under the imperialist control of British, French, Belgian, Spanish, and Portuguese governments into the fifties. More important, the Truman administration continued to relate to Africa through the organizational structure created by the colonial powers themselves.

During World War II, Roosevelt had openly expressed hostility toward European imperialism which he regarded as a threat to world peace. Both race and self-determination were central issues of World War II propaganda. It would be an error, however, to view the subsequent lack of concerted action by Truman's administration against colonial rule in Africa as a true departure from established U.S. policy objectives. The widespread acceptance of the centrality of the strategic and economic interests of the West in Africa remained intact, from the minerals of Rhodesia to the fossil fuels of Libya and the military bases at Freetown, Takoradi, and Mombasa. This ensured the continuity of the overriding policy objective in Africa: maintaining stability. The greater conservatism of Truman's administration, however, also helped create a State Department policy toward colonial Africa in which colonial administrations were accountable to an international authority. Under such a paternalistic program of international trusteeship, the United States could play a key role.

Fears of American interference led to critical accusations that U.S. policy was underwriting colonialism and even that the Americans themselves were acting like a colonial power. Indeed, the sustained military presence on the continent, the repeated efforts to secure commercial privileges in North Africa and elsewhere, and the protection of U.S. business interests totaling $250 million south of the Sahara helped slow the response of the Truman administration to the African cries for independence and the needling by black American and liberal critics of U.S. policy.

The paradoxical and ambivalent character of Truman pol-
icy toward Africa came to full fruition in the relations between the United States and South Africa. The official U.S. assessment of South African issues reveals the assumptions and policy objectives that guided the Truman administration. It is particularly significant that the upgrading of U.S. and South African diplomatic relations including the creation of full embassies in Pretoria and Washington occurred in 1948, following the rise to power of Daniel Malan's National party. During the 1948 election, Nationalists had challenged Jan Smuts in a campaign dominated by emotional attacks against communism and the demands of strengthened protection of exclusive white supremacy. The Nationalist victory in what has come to be known as the "apartheid" election was the twentieth-century turning point in terms of the entrenchment of white minority rule. Following Truman's November 1948 approval of improved diplomatic relations, the Senate confirmed the first U.S. ambassador to South Africa, North Winship, on 1 March 1949.

This was but one indication that relations with South Africa were to be considered outside the broad discussion of eventual self-government. Indeed, policy analysts in 1948 had perceived for South Africa a unique and preeminent position on the African continent by reason of its "large white population." The importance of South Africa as a market for U.S. goods and a supplier of strategic minerals was outweighed only by the consideration of the extent to which the West could count on South Africa's firm opposition to Soviet expansion and communism. The military support given by the South Africans to Truman in Korea in 1950–51 left no doubt as to the status of South Africa as an ally in the containment of communism.

If the sentiments of liberals and black Americans had figured little in the formulation of policy toward Africa, Africans mattered even less. The secret 1950 State Department policy statement on Africa reported that although "Black" Africa was oriented toward the noncommunist world, the continuation of this state of affairs should not be taken for granted. In fact, the report warned that the metropolitan powers required assurances that the United States was "not purposefully working to bring about a premature according of political independence to the peoples of Africa." President Truman had had little to say about Africa since his public assurance in 1945 that the right of self-determination did indeed extend to Africa.

In such a context, the rise of African nationalism was viewed as a problem and an obstacle to the maintenance of order and security on the continent. It would be left to Truman's successors to solve this dilemma and find a realistic policy toward Africa that could encourage eventual self-government. That the United States did not advance such a solution before its European counterparts may be the clearest testimony to the capitalist alliance that emerged as a legacy of the war years.

Owing in part to the low priority given to Africa within foreign policy concerns, there are few studies on the subject during the Truman years. The classic histories of U.S. policy toward Africa such as Rupert Emerson's *Africa and United States Policy* (Englewood Cliffs, N.J.: Prentice-Hall, 1967) have not been satisfactorily supplanted by Peter Duignan and L. H. Gann's more extensive and conservative views in the volume *The United States and Africa: A History* (Cambridge: Cambridge University Press and Hoover Institution, 1984). Thomas Noer's recent book, *Cold War and Black Liberation: The United States and White Rule in Africa,*

1948–1968 (Columbia: University of Missouri Press, 1985), deals expertly with southern Africa, and coverage of the U.S. policy toward North Africa is contained in an article by Paul J. Zing, "The Cold War in North Africa: American Foreign Policy and Postwar Muslim Nationalism, 1945–1962," *Historian* 39 (1976): 40–61. None of the works deals exclusively with Africa during the Truman years.

CANDICE L. GOUCHER

Agriculture

In his *Memoirs*, Harry Truman noted that by 1948 "the American farmer had reached an economic position better than he had ever known before." Heavy World War II and postwar demands for farm products had resulted in higher prices, relaxed government controls, and greater output, creating the belief that American agriculture had achieved stability, if not prosperity.

The Steagall Amendment (1941) to the Agricultural Adjustment Act (AAA) of 1938 sought to stimulate war production and discourage a postwar price slump such as had occurred after World War I by placing a floor on basic farm crops at 90 percent of parity through the war years and for two years after the close

John Churchill Chase, *New Orleans States* (1950–54). Courtesy of the *New Orleans Times-Picayune*.

of hostilities. The AAA of 1938 had established loan rates for cotton, corn, and wheat that varied between 52 and 75 percent of parity. The act had also set marketing quotas for tobacco, corn, wheat, cotton, rice, and peanuts, in addition to acreage allotments for protected farm commodities. Marketing quotas were subject to approval by a two-thirds vote of crop producers. By the end of World War II price guarantees had been extended to cover other essential commodities like eggs, hogs, dairy products, peas, beans, and oil-bearing nuts. Generally, government financial guarantees under the programs were not a great burden on the federal treasury and the taxpayers. Postwar demands continued at record highs and government surpluses declined.

The heavy demand, stimulated by postwar U.S. commitments to feed the war-torn nations of Europe, good prices, and relaxed controls contributed to substantial increases in production by 1948. Wheat acreage expanded from the 1942 level of 53 million acres to 78 million in 1948, and cotton production, which had declined during the war, rose to 23 million acres. Beef cattle and hog production also rose sharply.

After 1948, postwar adjustments and the restoration of European farm production began to sharply reduce the demand for American farm commodities. Government warehouses burgeoned with farm goods committed to surplus storage under the provisions of the AAA of 1938. Nevertheless, the consensus held that American agriculture, especially relating to food production, was not overexpanded, given the full employment economy at home and active world trade. In Congress, the House Committee on Agriculture conducted a study of long-range agricultural policies and concluded that "if we maintain a relatively high and stable level of employment, demand would apparently increase fast enough in relation to available supplies of farm products to maintain the general level of prices received by farmers at parity."

Truman noted in his *Memoirs* that farm income in 1948 had risen to $30 billion a year compared to the 1932 farm income of less than $5 billion. Farm debt had declined by 25 percent and farmer savings were the highest in history. Moreover, many agricultural economists and policymakers believed that farm production was approximately balanced with market demands. Concern, in fact, developed over the necessity of maintaining an "Ever-Normal Granary" in order to ensure ample supplies during poor harvest years. A "farm problem" seemed to be a thing of the distant prewar past.

Not everyone concurred in this analysis, however. Truman appointed the able Charles F. Brannan from the U.S. Department of Agriculture's professional staff as the new secretary of agriculture in 1948. Brannan, and other advisers, believed that high support prices had been translated into declining exports, artificially high consumer prices for farm commodities, and growing surpluses in storage. In addition, the allotments and marketing quotas favored the large producer in preference to the small family farmer, for it had become clear that one of the consequences derivative of a farm program that sought to regulate output by reducing the acreages in cultivation was that farmers, with the assistance of the agricultural sciences, were learning to produce higher yields per acre. For the most part, the benefits appeared to accrue to the larger producer. The secretary sought to grapple with such problems with a farm plan of his own, introduced in 1949.

Congress, however, preferred to retain the basic provisions of the AAA of 1938, rather than establish a new program for price supports and marketing controls. Adjusting to the new circumstances, however, Congress allowed the 1941 Steagall Amendment to expire and passed the Agricultural Act of 1948 which preserved the procedures of the 1938 act while adjusting the parity formula. The following year Congress approved the Agricultural Adjustment Act of 1949. This act revised the formula for allowable acreage allotments and authorized the implementation of marketing quotas in any year when the total supply of produce on hand would exceed the normal annual production, but these were technical adjustments rather than basic changes in the farm programs. The high price support levels at 90 percent of parity were allowed to stand. Farm output continued to rise, and the Commodity Credit Corporation increased the purchase of feed grains, oilseeds, cotton, and wheat from the 1948 and 1949 crops. But despite these heavier government purchases, the supply of stored government-owned surpluses actually declined between 1949 and 1952 as the demands generated by the Korean War absorbed current production and stored surpluses.

With the close of the Truman administration and the end of the Korean War, however, farm income began to decline and government warehouses again bulged with government-held farm surpluses, despite full employment and rising nonfarm incomes. The Truman era had marked a respite in rather than a resolution of the farm problem.

The most useful and pertinent secondary sources relating to agriculture during the Truman administration include J. Allen Matusow, *Farm Policies and Politics in the Truman Years* (Cambridge: Harvard University Press, 1967); Murray R. Benedict, *Farm Policies of the United States, 1790–1950* (New York: Twentieth Century Fund, 1953); and Benedict and Oscar O. Stine, *The Agricultural Commodity Programs: Two Decades of Experience* (New York: Twentieth Century Fund, 1956). Especially relevant are Edward L. and Frederick H. Schapsmeier, *Prophet in Politics: Henry A. Wallace and the War Years, 1940–1965* (Ames: Iowa State University Press, 1970), and Pete Daniel, *Breaking the Land: The Transformation of Cotton, Tobacco, and Rice Culture since 1880* (Urbana: University of Illinois Press, 1985).

HENRY C. DETHLOFF

See also Brannan, Charles; Kline, Allan Blair; Patton, James George

Aiken, George David

(20 August 1892–19 November 1984)

Wildflower enthusiast and commercial cultivator; Republican governor of Vermont, 1937–41; U.S. Senator, 1940–75. George Aiken was one of the few liberal Republican senators in the Eightieth Congress and was ranking Republican on the Senate Committee on Agriculture and Forestry. He successfully supported flexible price supports in the Agricultural Act of 1948 as a means of controlling agricultural productivity, thus backing a position taken by many in the Truman administration. During the struggles in 1949 over the Brannan Plan, he noted similarities between the plan and his act of 1948 but observed that the cost was an unknown.

Projects receiving his support included Truman's food program during the Korean War and the food stamp program, which he thought would help provide an adequate diet for all Americans. He also supported the St. Lawrence Development Project during the Truman years and for the next few decades.

Aiken later became more involved with armament control, foreign relations with Latin America, and the United Nations. He was especially vocal about the Watergate scandal in the early 1970s.

See George David Aiken, *Senate Diary, January 1972–January 1975* (Brattleboro, Vt.: Stephen Green Press, 1976), Allan J. Matusow, *Farm Policies and Politics in the Truman Years* (Cambridge: Harvard University Press, 1976), and Reo M. Christenson, *The Brannan Plan: Farm Politics and Policy* (Ann Arbor: University of Michigan Press, 1959), for further details on Aiken's farm policies.

JAMES L. FORSYTHE

Airlift, Berlin

See Berlin Airlift

Air Power

Air power, specifically strategic bombing, became the centerpiece of U.S. national defense during Truman's presidency. Americans had grown keenly aware of and fully supported military aviation during World War II, but air power presented dilemmas for the president. He appreciated its potential but feared its cost. Truman considered excessive government spending a prelude to depression, but his containment policy demanded power projection overseas. Ultimately, air power seemed to promise the least expensive, if not the only, way to secure America's extensive global interests. Nonetheless, Truman took a tortuous path to this choice.

After playing a key role in Allied victory during World War II, U.S. air power went into eclipse after 1945. Demobilization reduced the Army Air Forces (AAF) from 243 combat groups to 55 by 1947, with only two (atomic) combat-effective. The AAF argued that 70 combat-capable groups were necessary to achieve its assigned missions. The associated costs, however, did not fit with Truman's remainder method of budgeting: projected revenues, less costs of the civilian government, equaled military expenditures. Therefore U.S. Air Force capability declined and prospects looked bleak, despite its newly won independent status in September 1947.

The public and Congress, however, gave strong support to air power. In 1948 two independent commissions issued reports urging more federal support of all aviation. The Finletter Report from Truman's own Air Policy Commission, described American military air power as inadequate and hopelessly wanting for the future and called for a dramatic increase in procurement funds to build a seventy-group air force. The Congressional Aviation Policy Board echoed these concerns and recommendations. Ultimately Congress, by votes of 342–3 and 74–2, appropriated an additional $822 million to permit a seventy-group air force. Truman, however, refused to spend the additional funds until forced by international events.

As the cold war grew in intensity, U.S. military presence in Europe remained minimal. When the Soviet Union imposed the Berlin blockade in June 1948, the president could respond only with air power. He deployed two squadrons of B-29s to England, hinting possible use of atomic bombs, and began a modest airlift into Berlin to supply the city. The airlift, initially a stop-gap measure, proved highly successful, and Stalin abandoned the blockade in May 1949. The deployed B-29s, however, were less important than the cargo planes.

The blockade stirred activity and support within the United States for improved air power. A secret report by Charles A. Lindbergh, commissioned by the air force, assessed the U.S. strategic bombing capability as inadequate, largely because of the Strategic Air Command's (SAC) leadership. National Security Council (NSC) Memorandum 20 outlined U.S. goals in Europe and the deterrent role of strategic bombing forces, and the air force chief of staff, Gen. Hoyt S. Vandenberg, appointed Gen. Curtis E. LeMay to head the SAC.

With strong leadership by Secretary of the Air Force Stuart Symington, Vandenberg, and LeMay, the air force claimed a greater share of the defense dollar, amidst great interservice squabbling, and at the expense of naval aviation and the air force's tactical air arm. By 1950, LeMay had built a credible bombing force, but it still fell short of Truman's containment policy.

Air power grew in importance in early 1950 when Truman elected to proceed with the development of thermonuclear weapons. In April, NSC 68 appeared, recommending a dramatic strengthening of conventional forces and maintaining a strong nuclear deterrent capability. As Truman struggled with a projected $35 million to $50 million defense budget, the Korean War erupted in June, forcing him to place cost considerations aside.

During the Korean War, the United States employed strategic and tactical air power extensively. Gen. Douglas MacArthur credited air power with preventing UN forces from being pushed off the Pusan perimeter. Equipped with conventional bombs, B-29s found only limited strategic targets in North Korea but served in an interdiction role throughout the war. New jet fighters, the F-80, F-84, and F-86, and the Navy F3D, maintained command of the Korean skies. Despite its small budget, tactical air power demonstrated a highly developed combat capability and sustained an eleven-to-one air-to-air kill ratio with enemy fighter aircraft. The strategic nuclear force, where most air resources dollars had gone, was never used.

Led by Col. Charles E. Yeager's 1947 flight that broke the sound barrier, American air power had made important advances by 1953. Despite the Korean War experiences and the obvious need for more tactical air power, the SAC continued to receive a heavy share of the defense budget. The SAC introduced the B-36 bomber and began acquisition of jet aircraft (B-47, B-52, and KC-135) to achieve its long-sought global range. Research and development of intercontinental ballistic missiles began as well during Truman's presidency. Fiscally conservative and mistrustful of the military's spending habits, Truman initially resisted heavy expenditures for air power, but

in the last analysis, he found it more economical to achieve his defense needs through air power, specifically strategic bombing forces. During his administration, aviation made its greatest strides to date and became the foundation of containment, America's new foreign policy.

Harry R. Borowski, in *A Hollow Threat: Strategic Airpower and Containment before Korea* (Westport, Conn.: Greenwood Press, 1982), traces the development of the Strategic Air Command between 1946 and 1950. An excellent treatment of Truman's role as commander in chief is Richard R. Haynes, *The Awesome Power: Harry S. Truman as Commander in Chief* (Baton Rouge: Louisiana State Press, 1973). Robert F. Futrell, in *Ideas, Concepts, Doctrine: A History of Basic Thinking in the United States Air Force, 1907–1964* (Montgomery, Ala.: Air University, 1974), offers a superb discussion of air power development in all phases. The best and most thorough treatment of air power's role during the Korean War is Futrell's *United States Air Force, 1950–1953*, rev. ed. (Washington, D.C.: Office of Air Force History, 1983).

HARRY R. BOROWSKI

See also Berlin Airlift; Military Spending

American Communist Party
See Communism and Communists

American Federation of Labor
See Labor

American Indians
See Indian Policy

Americans for Democratic Action

For nearly all of Truman's presidency Americans for Democratic Action (ADA) was the country's most important liberal political organization. It was fathered by the Union for Democratic Action (UDA), a small body of democratic socialists who had broken with Norman Thomas in 1941 over his support of isolationism. In response to its call some four hundred liberals met on 3 January 1947 to form a group that would be broader and less sectarian than the UDA. They included prominent New Dealers such as Chester Bowles, Elmer Davis, Leon Henderson, John Kenneth Galbraith, and, above all, Eleanor Roosevelt, who became the patron saint of ADA and for many years its honorary chair. Among labor leaders attending were James B. Carey, David Dubinsky, and Walter Reuther. Younger political figures included Richardson Dilworth, Hubert Humphrey, and Franklin D. Roosevelt, Jr. Henderson, formerly head of the Office of Price Administration and Wilson Wyatt, President Truman's housing czar, were ADA's first chairs, serving together at first and then individually.

The organization was created for two reasons; to offer, or find, leadership for liberals superior to that extended by President Truman and to combat the pro-Soviet tendency among liberals embodied by the Progressive Citizens of America (PCA) and its favorite politician Henry A. Wallace. The group would realize only the latter aim, made abundantly clear by its founding statement which rejected "any association with Communists or sympathizers with communism." James Loeb, Jr., who had been the UDA's executive secretary and would serve ADA in the same position for five years, put it even more bluntly. Writing to the *New Republic*, at that time a voice of popular-front liberalism, Loeb said that ADA was "a declaration of liberal independence from the stifling and paralyzing influence of the Communists and their apologists in America."

Although by 1947 American Communists were distrusted by most Americans, they were still important in the trade union movement and among certain liberals, too. This can be established by the names of those associated with the PCA, which was almost a who's who of intellectuals and entertainers. They were united, a historian friendly to them has written, by admiration for Russia as a wartime ally and "as the source of a remarkable and on the whole successful experiment on behalf of human welfare." In exposing the falseness of this view and combating the PCA and its outgrowth the Progressive party, ADA did its most valuable work. Because it was based upon delusions, popular-front liberalism was bound to collapse in any event, but by providing a morally and intellectually superior alternative to it, ADA hastened the process.

The organization was less successful in providing guidance to the Democratic party, mainly because of its doubts about President Truman. Members of ADA shared the belief, common among liberals at the time, that Truman was a small man who could not fill Roosevelt's shoes, and they were distressed by the parade of New Dealers leaving government, not always voluntarily, after he became president. With Democrats generally, they feared that Truman's unpopularity would drag down the entire ticket in 1948. They had no quarrel with Truman programmatically, however. Indeed, when his new agenda was unveiled in the fall of 1947, Senator Robert Taft attacked it, unjustly, as the work of "Leon Henderson and his crowd." Yet despite Truman's liberal proposals ADA leaders sought frantically to nominate someone else in 1948. They tried to draft Dwight D. Eisenhower, whose politics were then a complete mystery, and were embarrassed on the convention's eve when he announced that he would not accept the nomination under any "terms, conditions, or premises." To make matters worse, they then tried to promote the candidacy of Supreme Court Justice William O. Douglas, even though it was probable, as soon happened, that Truman would be nominated on the first ballot.

The group redeemed itself, though not in Truman's eyes, by persuading Democrats to adopt the most liberal civil rights plank ever written into the party's platform. Members of ADA had been laboring to that end since March, and by July they had enlisted the support of some fifty important Democrats. Led by Hubert H. Humphrey, the young mayor of Minneapolis, ADA went to the floor of the convention and persuaded it to substitute ADA's daring plank for the administration's cautious one. The result was what Truman had been seeking to avoid: southern extremists bolted from the convention and, temporarily at least, from the party, too. Their "Dixiecrat" fourth party (Wallace's Progressive party was the third) attracted 1,169,312 votes, most of which would otherwise have gone to Truman. Undaunted at having caused this split, ADA declared the Democratic platform to be "the most forthright and liberal document of its kind ever offered the American people by a major party," and they went on to help elect liberal Democrats in some critical races.

Possibly for this reason Truman seems to have forgiven ADA, and his relations with it were cordial, if not particularly warm, during the remainder of his presidency. For its part, ADA tried to forget its "dump Truman" campaign, which not only failed but deserved to fail since the president, by his championing of liberal causes, had earned ADA's support. On the other hand, ADA never had to apologize for forcing its civil rights plank on Democrats in 1948. Right in principle, ADA's strong attack on racism was good politics, too, and won at least as many votes in the North as were lost in the South to Dixiecrats.

An outstanding history of the complex relations between the president and his natural allies, including ADA, is Alonzo L. Hamby, *Beyond the New Deal: Harry S. Truman and American Liberalism* (New York: Columbia University Press, 1973). The only book on ADA itself is Clifton Brock, *Americans for Democratic Action* (Washington, D.C.: Public Affairs Press, 1962). A leftist critique of ADA and other anti-Communist liberal organizations is Mary Sperling McAuliffe, *Crisis on the Left: Cold War Politics and American Liberals, 1947–1954* (Amherst: University of Massachusetts Press, 1978).

WILLIAM L. O'NEILL

See also Bowles, Chester Bliss; Democratic Party; Dubinsky, David; Election of 1948; Humphrey, Hubert Horatio, Jr.; Liberalism; Reuther, Walter Philip; Roosevelt, Anna Eleanor; Schlesinger, Arthur Meier, Jr.

American Socialist Party
See Thomas, Norman Mattoon

Ancestry

The family background of Harry S. Truman is notably homogenous. Not only is the Truman family English in origin but virtually all their agnates trace their roots to England. There are, however, no demonstrable links between the family and a John de Tremain who was reputed to have come to England from Normandy in approximately 1257 or between a descendant of this Norman who emigrated from Nottingham to New

London, Connecticut, in 1666—although both President Truman and his brother, Vivian, on occasion claimed that these were some of their early ancestors.

The earliest Truman mentioned in any record appears to have been Abraham who died in 1796 in Bedford County, Virginia. Abraham's grandson, William (1783–1863), received a land bounty in Kentucky as a reward for his service in the War of 1812 and moved to Shelby County, Kentucky. There he met and married Emma Grant Shipp, with whom he had twelve children, ten of whom lived to adulthood. One of them, Anderson Shipp Truman (1816–87), would become the grandfather of the thirty-third president of the United States.

The Shipp line can also be traced to the late seventeenth century when Josiah Shipp married Elizabeth Brookes whose father, Thomas, was apparently a prosperous landowner in York County, Virginia. Their grandson, William, was born in Essex County, Virginia, and moved with his wife, Rachel, to Kentucky. The couple (for whom no exact dates are available) were the parents of Emma, the mother of Anderson Truman. Anderson's first name derived from his maternal grandfather, Anderson Doniphan, a Virginia "gentleman," as the family records describe him. Anderson's father, Alexander Doniphan ("Captain" Doniphan, ca. 1653–ca. 1717) had come to North America from Devonshire. Anderson Shipp Truman was a school director and apparently reasonably well off: the 1850 census lists him as owning three slaves. Four years earlier (13 August 1846) he

had married Mary Jane Holmes (1821–78), the ninth of ten children of Jesse and Nancy Holmes.

Jesse Holmes (1808–74) was the son of James Holmes, Jr. (1745–1833), who had seen service as a junior officer in the Revolutionary War and had received a land bounty that enabled him also to move from Virginia to Kentucky. Robert and Margaret Tyler, Nancy's parents, had made the same move somewhat earlier (ca. 1770). The Tyler family, in turn, can be traced back to the late seventeenth century when Robert Tyler married Susanna DuVall, the daughter of a French Huguenot who had emigrated to Maryland in 1660. This French ancestor, six generations removed from President Truman, is one of only two among his forebears who was of non-English birth, the other being Hans Michael Gutknecht who arrived in North America in 1752 and took the name John Goodnight. His daughter Rachel married Jacob Young and they became the parents of Solomon (1815–92), Harry Truman's maternal grandfather.

The Young family appears originally in Mecklenburg County, North Carolina, but moved, as did all the president's ancestors, to Shelby County, Kentucky, where Solomon married Harriet Louisa Gregg (1818–1909), the third of twelve children of David Gregg (ca. 1776–1823) and Sarah Scott (1775–1823). David, in turn, was a son of John Gregg (+1791), and Sarah was the daughter of William Scott "Senor" (Senior?) (1747–ca. 1824). The records of that line of the family do not go beyond these two names, except that, like virtually all of Harry Truman's forebears, they were evidently of English ancestry.

The Harry S. Truman Library has gathered such information as is available. This includes genealogical charts of various branches of the family, correspondence with family members interested in establishing their exact relationship to the president, and newspaper clippings, mainly from Kentucky, discussing the president's forebears. George H. S. King and D. Emerson Miller, "Some Notes Relative to the Virginia Ancestry of Harry S Truman," *Tyler's Quarterly* 28, no. 4 (April 1947) provides a good overview of the Virginia records pertaining to the family. Also useful is a typescript compiled by Elsie Spray Davis, "Forebears of Solomon Young" (1980). A 1901 work by Ebenezer Mack Treman and Murray E. Poole, *The History of the Treman, Tremaine, Truman Family*, appears to be the source of the story about John de Tremain. This book, which provides no information on the Truman ancestry in America, was evidently relied upon by Roland Truman, a Long Beach attorney and distant cousin of President Truman, in the preparation of a typescript on the family's ancestry, a copy of which is also in the files of the Truman library.

FRANCIS H. HELLER

Mary Jane Holmes at sixteen, nine years before her marriage in 1846 to Anderson Shipp Truman. (National Archives)

Anderson, Clinton Presba

(23 October 1895–15 November 1975)

Former reporter, editor, and businessman; congressman and senator from New Mexico; secretary of agriculture, 1945–48. As a Democratic congressman during World War II, Clinton Anderson chaired a special committee on food shortages which criticized some aspects of food policy during the war, especially those that Anderson believed had led to shortages of beef and pork. In May 1945, President Truman named him secretary of agriculture to succeed Claude R. Wickard.

Although Anderson had little background in agriculture, he helped formulate agricultural policy in the immediate postwar years that would return production to normal levels, sustain an abundance of food products, achieve reasonable income levels for America's farmers, reduce their dependence on the federal government for income, and introduce more technology into agriculture production. His efforts resulted in storms of protest at times; nevertheless, they helped develop adequate policy for the years to come.

Anderson created some discomfort for the Truman administration. Criticized for his lack of support for the Office of Price Administration, he was blamed by some for the end of price controls in 1945. Scholars have faulted him for not providing early leadership in the crusade to feed the hungry in Europe in 1945–46, for being too partisan or too narrow in his views on policies concerning trade tariffs and wool, for lacking a sense of social concern for consumers, and for failing to support the Bureau of Agricultural Economics. Nevertheless, some of the most constructive agricultural legislation was passed and policy decisions made while he was secretary of agriculture: the passing of the Agriculture and Marketing Act of 1946, changes in agricultural credit policies the same year, a successful effort to reduce cotton surpluses, enactment of wool legislation, development of a philosophy of abundance for agriculture, and support for a new agricultural bill in 1948.

Anderson advocated flexible price supports, believing that rigid supports led to surpluses, lower farm income, and more government control in agriculture. His proposal for a new flexible program in early 1947 was attacked by some farmers and farm groups who feared a postwar depression, but he pursued bipartisan support for his program. Midwestern Republican and southern Democrats, looking upon his plan as a shift from New Deal agricultural policies, proposed a program with rigid price supports instead; eventually a compromise program was passed. The Agricultural Act of 1948 called for rigid price supports at 90 percent of parity until 1 January 1950, when flexible price supports of 60 to 90 percent on basic crops would become effective. The Hope-Aiken bill was finally passed in the early summer of 1948, as both parties wished to have a farm bill in time for that year's presidential election. Anderson, however, believed that a great opportunity for reform of agricultural legislation related to price supports and production was lost that election year.

While secretary, Anderson also sought to reorganize the Department of Agriculture, and he strongly supported the modernization and mechanization of agriculture. On the other hand, he was admittedly motivated at times by partisan politics, and he never forgot his beef, dairy, and wool constituencies in the Southwest.

Anderson resigned as secretary in 1948 to run for the U.S. Senate. He returned to Washington in 1949 as the Democratic senator from New Mexico and served on the Agriculture and Forestry Committee. He vigorously opposed the farm plan of Charles F. Brannan, his successor as secretary of agriculture, because Brannan abandoned flexible price supports.

Anderson gradually shifted to other interests after his failure to get administrative and congressional backing for flexible price supports in 1949, 1951, and 1952. He continued to serve in the Senate until 1973.

Further discussion of Anderson and his policies can be found in James L. Forsythe, "Clinton P. Anderson: Agricultural Policymaker and Southwesterner," in *Southwestern Agriculture: Pre-Columbian to Modern*, ed. Henry C. Dethloff and Irvin M. May, Jr., 253–72 (College Station: Texas A&M Press, 1982), and Allan J. Matusow, *Farm Policies and Politics in the Truman Years* (Cambridge: Harvard University Press, 1967).

JAMES L. FORSYTHE

See also Agriculture; Brannan, Charles Franklin

Arendt, Hannah

(14 October 1906–4 December 1975)

The political philosopher Hannah Arendt had already contributed to two of the major foreign policy debates during the Truman years—regarding Palestine and anticommunism—by the time she became an American citizen in 1951. Born in Germany, Arendt received her Ph.D. in philosophy from the University of Heidelberg when she was twenty-two. She fled from the Nazis twice, first to Paris in 1933 and then to New York City in 1941. In New York, Arendt worked in Jewish communal affairs and published articles in both scholarly and popular journals. Her involvement with Schocken Books, a major publishing force in the German émigré community, culminated in her tenure as chief editor from 1946 through 1948.

In May 1948, *Commentary* published Arendt's essay, "To Save the Jewish Homeland: There Is Still Time." Arendt feared that Zionism had degenerated into chauvinism. She hoped that President Truman's proposal for an interim trusteeship for Palestine under UN supervision would postpone the partition of Palestine and the inevitable bloodshed between Jews and Arabs. The establishment of Israel shortly after the article's publication made the argument moot. Nevertheless, her call thrilled the few Jews like Judah Magnes still hoping for a binational state. It also outraged the American Jewish community at large, whose emerging consensus in favor of the Jewish state had alarmed the iconoclastic Arendt and had encouraged Truman's recognition of the new country.

By this time, Arendt was deeply involved in the project that would make her an intellectual star, *The Origins of Totalitarianism*. Begun in 1945 and published to wide acclaim in 1951, the book explored the relationships among anti-Semitism, imperialism, and totalitarianism. Arendt believed that the instruments of state terror epitomized by concentration camps distingushed totalitarianism from all other forms of government. She therefore equated the regimes of Hitler and Stalin. Many scholars rejected this parallel and criticized Arendt's superficial treatment of Leninism. Yet this argument probably contributed to the book's popularity in the increasingly anti-Communist atmosphere of Truman's America. Thus, Arendt, an anti-Communist who nevertheless found much of the Communist-bashing during the Truman years unnerving, ultimately provided important theoretical grounding for that movement.

The acerbic, brown-eyed, brown-haired Arendt continued to write controversial books and articles. She became in 1959 the first woman ever appointed a full professor at Princeton University. She also taught at various other universities, including the New School for Social Research, where she was on the faculty from 1967 until her death in 1975.

Hannah Arendt's early career was reviewed in *Current Biography, 1959*, pp. 14–16. One of her former doctoral students, Elisabeth Young-Bruehl, wrote the comprehensive *Hannah Arendt: For Love of the World* (New Haven: Yale University Press, 1982). A "philosophical biography," it provides an excellent analysis of Arendt's thought, but slights the broader social and political context.

GIL TROY

See also Communism and Communists

Armed Forces, Racial Integration of the

Black American outrage against military segregation and discrimination during World War II resulted in some small experiments with integrated units and equal opportunity policies toward the war's conclusion. In each of the services there emerged a small group of officers and civilians convinced that racial segregation was not only unfair to black servicemen but led to major inefficiencies in the training and utilization of manpower. But despite continued attempts of reformers in the immediate postwar period, most influential officers and civilians in the defense establishment contented themselves with the racial status quo on the grounds of racial stereotypes, a belief that the majority of white servicemen would violently resist integration, and a conviction that the military had no role in social reform. In fact, through the use of enlistment quotas for blacks and the reimposition of rigid segregation policies, there was a retreat from gains made at the end of the war.

As civil rights became a major political issue in the postwar years leading up to the 1948 presidential election, military racial policies were too important to be left in the hands of military authorities. Military segregation, a campaign issue in the two previous presidential elections, had by 1948 become an important symbol of President Truman's resolve to use his executive authority to advance civil rights in the face of a recalcitrant Congress. In 1947, the President's Committee on Civil Rights was critical of segregation in general and found military segregation "particularly repugnant"; immediate action to end it was recommended. In his special message to Congress on civil rights in February 1948, Truman noted that he had instructed the secretary of defense to eliminate military segregation. But the services resisted and civil rights activist A. Philip Randolph threatened to lead civil disobedience resistance against implementation of the new draft law unless segregation was ended. Needing to cement the political support of black voters in the closely contested 1948 election, Truman issued Executive Order 9981 in July of that year. The President's Committee on Equality of Treatment and Opportunity in the Armed Forces was thus established.

The President's Committee was chaired by former solicitor general Charles H. Fahy, and its active members included William E. Stevenson, president of Oberlin College; Dwight R. G. Palmer, president of General Cable Corporation; John H. Sengstacke, publisher of the *Chicago Defender*; and Lester Granger, head of the National Urban League. Journalist E. W. Kenworthy played a major role with his critical intelligence and his energetic performance as executive secretary. The committee got underway in 1949 with Truman's firm pledge of support, as well as the active support of Secretary of Defense Louis A. Johnson. The secretary of defense eventually was overwhelmed by interservice rivalries over other matters and weakened on the race issue as the army resisted mightily and the navy talked change but did little to make it reality. Only the air force, under the leadership of its secretary, Stuart Symington, moved enthusiastically to meet the goals of the president's order.

There ensued a process of bitter negotiations between the committee and the army, with the army's leadership intent upon wearing down or outmaneuvering the committee and forcing the administration to accept less than full integration. The committee countered with documented arguments demonstrating that segregated military units inevitably wasted resources and prevented equal opportunity. When the president remained steadfast in support of the committee, the army issued a new personnel policy in January 1950 stipulating that blacks would be utilized according to skills and would be "assigned to any unit without regard to race or color." The army intended to implement this policy over a long period, maintaining control through the existing 10 percent quota on black enlistments. The committee now insisted that the quota be eliminated, and Truman intervened personally with Secretary of the Army Gordon Gray to accomplish this.

The end of the quota and the policy of assigning blacks on the basis of need and training were two key accomplishments of the committee that quickly spurred integration in the Korean War that began in June 1950. Black enlistments expanded beyond the capacity of existing black units to absorb them, and first basic training facilities and then units under fire in Korea were integrated. Despite continued resistance and pleas to reinstate the quota, integration proceeded by its own logical necessity without the dire consequences that had been predicted. A team of social scientists declared the results a success, and the Korean experience added to the pressure for the army to complete the process in U.S. installations and to begin it in Europe. By the end of the Korean War, 90 percent of the army's units were integrated. Problems of discrimination and race would continue to surface in the military for years to come, as in civilian society, but the basic policies of integration and equal opportunity had been established as yardsticks.

Donald R. McCoy and Richard T. Ruetten, *Quest and Response: Minority Rights and the Truman Administration* (Lawrence: University Press of Kansas, 1973), is a detailed account placing military integration in a broad context. Richard M. Dalfiume, *Desegregation of the U.S. Armed Forces: Fighting on Two Fronts, 1939–1953* (Columbia: University of Missouri Press, 1969), analyzes the political and military aspects of the topic. Bernard C. Nalty, *Strength for the Fight: A History of Black Americans in the Military* (New York: Free Press, 1986), is a superb synthesis based upon the secondary literature and primary sources.

RICHARD M. DALFIUME

See also Black Americans; Civil Rights

Armed Forces, Unification of the

Unification of the armed forces was finally if only partly realized in the National Security Act of 1947 and subsequent amendments.

Before 1947, responsibility for national defense had rested with the War and Navy departments and a hodgepodge of other organizations: the State, Treasury, and Justice departments; the wartime Office of Strategic Services; the nonstatutory Joint Chiefs of Staff established in 1942; a complex and shifting apparatus of scientific and industrial mobilization; and lesser agencies like the U.S. Coast Guard. Since World War I, dozens of bills had floated into Congress—but never out of it—to rationalize or unify the ever-growing bureaucratic sprawl. Those bills had been prompted by desires to economize operations, modernize them along lines pursued by other nations, and, most often, liberate military aviation from army and navy control by giving it statutory equality with the older services.

World War II and its aftermath gave fresh impetus to these older impulses and added new ones. The thickening bureaucratic tangle, the colossal scale of wartime expenditures, and the postwar conflict between the needs to combat the Russians and to cut budgets all emboldened proponents of economy. The global war had demonstrated powerfully that war was no longer the business only of the military but of a vast public and private apparatus for mobilizing people, business and industry, scientists, and the academy. And for American strategic leaders, including Gen. George C. Marshall, the army's wartime chief of staff, the war also offered a painful comparison between their confused planning and the concerted, integrated approach to strategy of their British counterparts.

But political calculations prompted unification as much as dispassionate considerations of national need. Politicians and the media repeatedly, if not always accurately, blamed American disaster at Pearl Harbor and elsewhere on the armed services' failure to cooperate. The Army Air Forces' key role in World War II—supported by President Franklin Roosevelt, exploited by the air force's publicists, capped by use of the atomic bomb—made its continued subordination to the army appear foolish and played to a nation eager to see technology replace American men in the nation's defense. In truth, the Army Air Forces was already the near-equal of the other services, although it soft-pedaled its campaign for independence during the war in return for the army's support of its cause when peace came. In turn, the army's acceptance of equality for the air force, and some scheme for unification to go along with it, was politically decisive. Marshall and Secretary of War Henry L. Stimson not only saw the political handwriting on the wall but themselves embraced much of the argument for air power. When Truman became president, only the navy remained adamant against both unification and the air force's equality, fearing deeply its relegation to third place in a unified system, plus the loss of its marines to the army and its aviation to a new air force. Indeed, in public debate "unification" had become a catchword, its virtue almost beyond question even though few truly sought it—if it meant genuine integration into one armed force—and none certainly got it.

In a complex struggle waged for two years after the war's end, Truman, who as senator had investigated costly foul-ups in the machinery of national defense, strongly supported unification and pushed his war and navy secretaries, Robert Patterson

and James Forrestal, toward a compromise on the issue. They, along with key congressmen, largely worked out the delicate compromises and elaborate structure that composed the final legislation. Forrestal was the key player, as he struggled to balance a zealous defense of the navy's interests against his brooding concern over fashioning a modernized apparatus to contest Soviet policy. The National Security Act of 1947 established a nebulous National Military Establishment that embraced three equal and coordinated armed services, each with its own secretary, to be presided over by a secretary of defense with broad but vague duties and by the Joint Chiefs of Staff. Beyond but connected to that establishment were other agencies created by the act, most notably the National Security Council and the Central Intelligence Agency.

The act had its defenders, but two subsequent years of bruising public battles among the services, plus persistent uncertainty about the authority of the secretary of defense and the new agencies, made it clear that neither service unification nor effective coordination of the larger apparatus had been achieved. "Poor Forrestal," Truman once remarked of the new defense secretary, "he never could make a decision." But the problem lay not just with Forrestal, as Truman's disastrous choice of Louis Johnson to succeed him in 1949 made clear. Only Marshall's ascent to the post in 1950 and the necessities of waging the Korean War diminished the turmoil over unification. Truman's unsteady leadership complicated matters, but even with his steadier hand Eisenhower experienced so much conflict among the services that presidential leadership hardly could be regarded as the decisive factor. Amendments in 1949 strengthened the secretary's authority and established the Department of Defense roughly in its current form, but service rivalries and botched coordination of the larger apparatus persisted. At bottom, those problems were less structural than most authorities in the 1940s had wanted to believe or been willing to admit.

Although the unification controversy has yet to find its historian, a large literature treats various aspects of it. Steven L. Rearden, *History of the Office of the Secretary of Defense*, vol. 1, *The Formative Years* (Washington, D.C.: Office of the Secretary of Defense, 1984), is valuable and contains an exhaustive bibliography. Among older studies, see Demetrios Caraley, *The Politics of Military Unification* (New York: Columbia University Press, 1966). Walter Millis, ed., *The Forrestal Diaries* (New York: Viking Press, 1951), is a lively firsthand account. Among the many biographical sources, volumes 3 and 4 of Forrest Pogue, *George C. Marshall* (New York: Viking Press, 1973, 1987), are by far the best.

MICHAEL S. SHERRY

See also Forrestal, James Vincent; Johnson, Louis Arthur; Joint Chiefs of Staff; Marshall, George C., Jr.

Army Corps of Engineers

The Army Corps of Engineers has both military and civil engineering functions. During the Truman years the latter role became increasingly significant, as the corps turned its attention from wartime activities to planning and development of the nation's water resources. Historically, the corps had maintained a closer relationship with Congress than with the president; that would continue to be the case during the Truman administration. When Congress assumed authority for river and harbor work in the early nineteenth century, the Corps of Engineers had been placed in an enviable position—it could offer legislators from every geographical region, regardless of political affiliation, an opportunity to "bring home the bacon" for their districts (critics pointed out that bacon is a kind of pork). Harry S. Truman would run aground on this reality on two major initiatives during his presidency.

Franklin D. Roosevelt had attempted to remove the corps from the congressional orbit by depriving the corps of its jurisdiction over civil works through the Reorganization Act of 1939; he failed. Truman sought similar authority through the Reorganization Act of 1945. Congress, however, was not willing to imperil its mutually beneficial relationship with the Corps of Engineers, and the House specifically excluded it from reorganization planning, saying it had "for over 125 years been an efficient aid to Congress in the solution of the engineering and economic problems involved in river and harbor and flood control work."

Truman persisted, however, and in February 1947 Congress provided legislation allowing him to appoint the Commission on Organization of the Executive Branch of the Government (the first Hoover Commission). Its recommendations led Truman to seek, once again, unlimited authority to reorganize the executive branch through the Reorganization Act of 1949. This time Congress did not exempt the Corps of Engineers, but reserved the right to disapprove of any reorganization. Subsequent testimony at hearings on the act made it clear the corps could muster support nationwide for its civil functions and that Congress was not likely to approve any removal of its civil activities. Ultimately, then, the Hoover Commission findings came to naught; the corps was unassailable behind its phalanx of congressional supporters.

The Corps of Engineers was instrumental in thwarting another Truman initiative on what he called "a subject close to my heart and vital to the future of the nation"—the expansion of regional water power projects. In particular, Truman advocated extending the Tennessee Valley Authority model to the Columbia and Missouri river basins. Although Truman's preference was for a Missouri Valley Authority, he believed that politically the odds for gaining acceptance for a Columbia Valley Authority (CVA) were better. Throughout his first administration, he advocated the new authorities in speeches, letters, and messages to Congress. After carrying ten of eleven western states in the 1948 election, Truman believed he had a mandate to create the Columbia Valley Authority. On 13 April 1949, the president sent a special message to Congress recommending establishment of a Columbia Valley Administration (*Administration* was substituted for *Authority* to imply local rather than centralized control). None of the four bills subsequently introduced to create a CVA was reported out of committee, but Truman continued to lobby for it, telling a crowd in Boise, Idaho, on 10 May 1950, "Don't let anybody tell you that the Columbia Valley Administration is socialistic." He pointed out that "without a Columbia Valley Administration we will continue to have a scatter-shot approach to resource development." The following year, on 3 August 1951, he wrote to CIO president Philip Murray that "too often the right action

has been blocked by shortsighted people who can't see beyond their purely local interests."

A common theme in both Truman's administrative reorganization effort and the attempt to create river valley authorities was the inefficiency and conflict inherent in the blurred relationship between the Corps of Engineers and the Bureau of Reclamation in developing water resources in the western United States. The two agencies frequently assumed a competitive, even adversarial, posture. But the specter of a CVA threatened to take authority away from both the corps and the bureau, and their common peril led to what contemporary observers called "a shotgun marriage." This union played the key role in defeating the president's plan for a CVA. Bureaucratic maneuvering by the corps had begun as early as 1946. Alone, it had been too formidable an opponent for the president on the reorganization issue. When it joined forces with the Bureau of Reclamation, Truman's plan for a CVA was doomed.

Truman's relationship with the Corps of Engineers was not always antagonistic, however. He signed into law a number of acts that expanded the role of the corps in water resource development and provided funds for large-scale construction projects. As he pointed out in an 8 August 1951 letter to Senator Kenneth McKellar, chairman of the Senate Appropriations Committee, "In the four fiscal years 1948 through 1951, Federal expenditures for these essential improvements totaled 2.2 billion dollars. This amount is about equal to the entire Federal investment for river and harbor, flood control, and navigation work during the previous century and a half." Moreover, he actively lobbied for the St. Lawrence Seaway throughout his presidency, to the point of securing the transfer of four anti-seaway representatives from the House Public Works Committee in 1952.

Nevertheless these positive interactions with the corps were more than overshadowed by the corps' sinking of two of his major domestic policy initiatives. Congress might support efficiency in government and rational development of natural resources in the abstract, but that support would stop short of compromising the position of an agency that provided such an extraordinary opportunity for building political capital at home. Harry S. Truman, like presidents before and after him, would fail to curb the congressional appetite for the Corps of Engineers pork barrel.

No single study concentrates on the relationship of Harry S. Truman and the Army Corps of Engineers, but several contain significant sections devoted to some aspect of that relationship. The earliest of these is Arthur Maass, *Muddy Waters: The Army Engineers and the Nation's Rivers* (Cambridge: Harvard University Press, 1951), a stridently anti–Corps of Engineers work, which is nevertheless helpful on organizational issues. A more recent and more balanced work is Elmo Richardson, *Dams, Parks & Politics* (Lexington: University Press of Kentucky, 1973). Richardson is especially useful on the CVA controversy, as is P. R. DeLuna in "Bureaucratic Opposition as a Factor in Truman's Failure to Achieve a Columbia Valley Authority," *Historical Papers, Canadian Historical Association*, 1975, 231–56.

FREDRICK J. DOBNEY

See also Conservation; Missouri River; Reclamation

Assassination Attempt

"The only thing you have to worry about is bad luck," Harry Truman said after two members of the Puerto Rican Nationalist party, the champion of independence for the territory, tried to kill him on 1 November 1950. "I never had bad luck."

The president was napping in Blair House, where he was living while the White House was being renovated. The front door was open, but the screen door was latched. At 2:20 P.M., Oscar Collazo and Griselio Torresola stormed the house. But the president's luck held out—Collazo's pistol misfired. Twenty-seven shots later, Leslie Coffelt, a White House guard, and Torresola were dead. Two other guards and Collazo were wounded.

Truman shrugged off the attack and kept to his schedule. "A president has to expect those things," he said, although he cried when honoring his dead bodyguard. And he resented the subsequent tightened security: "It's hell to be President of the Greatest Most Powerful Nation on Earth," he quipped. The attack unsettled Bess Truman and fueled her desire to go home.

Truman commuted Collazo's death sentence to life imprisonment. In 1979, in a gesture to Latin America, President Jimmy Carter freed Collazo.

Robert J. Donovan carefully chronicles the assassination attempt in the second volume of his definitive account on the Truman presidency, *Tumultuous Years: The Presidency of Harry S Truman, 1949–1953* (New York: W. W. Norton, 1982). Truman talked about the attempt with Merle Miller in *Plain Speaking: An Oral Biography of Harry S. Truman* (New York: G. P. Putnam's Sons, 1973, 1974), and some diary entries and letters capture Truman's reactions in *Off the Record: The Private Papers of Harry S. Truman*, ed. Robert H. Ferrell (New York: Harper & Row, 1980). Margaret Truman describes both her parents' reactions in *Bess W. Truman* (New York: Macmillan, 1986).

GIL TROY

Atomic and Hydrogen Bombs

Although it was Franklin Roosevelt's choice to build the atomic bomb, the wartime decision to use the weapon fell to Harry Truman. It was also Truman who decided, in the course of the ensuing cold war, to embark upon a crash effort to develop a second generation of nuclear weapons—the hydrogen super-bomb, or "Super."

Upon first hearing of the top-secret Manhattan Project as a senator, Truman's initial impulse had been to urge cancelation of the multi-billion-dollar project on the grounds that it constituted an unnecessary drain upon the war effort while promising an unknown and uncertain result. Although dissuaded, Truman apparently did not learn of the atomic bomb itself until shortly after Roosevelt's death.

As president, Truman was briefed on the potential military and strategic significance of the untested weapon by Secretary of War Henry Stimson—who described the fission bomb as potentially "the most terrible weapon ever known in human history"—and army major general Leslie Groves, head of the Manhattan Project, on 25 April 1945. Subsequently, Truman ordered Stimson to form an Interim Committee to advise him on the wartime use of the weapon and its role in the postwar world.

As preparations progressed for the test of the first atomic bomb, scientists working on the weapon at the University of Chicago and Los Alamos—the secret nuclear laboratory established by the army in the New Mexican desert—urged that there be a nonmilitary "demonstration" of the bomb before its use against the enemy in Japan. One such scientist, physicist Leo Szilard, circulated a petition among his colleagues in the summer of 1945 which asked Truman not to use the atomic bomb "unless the terms which will be imposed upon Japan have been made public in detail and Japan knowing the terms has refused to surrender."

Although the Interim Committee's Scientific Panel, headed by physicist Robert Oppenheimer, briefly considered the so-called demonstration option in a climactic meeting in Washington on 31 May, its report to Stimson two weeks later concluded that "no technical demonstration [is] likely to bring an end to the war; we see no acceptable alternative to direct military use." Szilard's petition, sent to Groves, was not forwarded to Truman until after the order to drop the bombs had already been given.

The first test of a nuclear weapon occurred in the early morning hours of 16 July 1945 at a spot in the desert that Oppenheimer had designated "Trinity Site," near Alamogordo, New Mexico. The light from the bomb—compared by one observer to "a close flash of lightning on a dark night"—was visible from nearly two hundred miles away. The force of the explosion—equivalent to some fifteen thousand tons of dynamite—dug a crater twelve hundred feet across and sent a mushroom-shaped cloud of radioactive debris more than forty thousand feet into the atmosphere.

Two days later, Groves's report on the test reached Truman at Potsdam, where the president was attending a summit meeting with Soviet premier Joseph Stalin and British prime minister Winston Churchill. Groves described the experiment as "successful beyond the most optimistic expectations of anyone." The news from Alamogordo left the president "tremendously pepped up," according to Stimson's account. Truman himself admitted the test "gave him an entirely new feeling of confidence."

Even before the Potsdam meeting—which Truman delayed until the atomic test could be conducted—there had been discussion between the president and his aides regarding what to tell the Russians about the bomb. Some advisers—including, at one point, Stimson—argued that informing the Soviets, America's allies in the war, of the bomb might be a way of allaying postwar distrust and perhaps also of heading off a dangerous nuclear arms race. Secretary of State James Byrnes, on the other hand, thought an enduring American atomic monopoly might make the Russians "more manageable" on the diplomatic disputes that were bound to arise after the end of the war over issues like the occupation of Eastern Europe. With the atomic bomb now "a colossal reality," as Stimson said, the United States was no longer eager to have the Soviet Union enter the war against Japan, thereby earning a stake in the postwar Japanese peace settlement.

Perhaps because he feared that the Russians, knowing of the atomic bomb, might then demand a share in its postwar control, Truman ultimately decided to steer a middle course

Maj. Gen. Leslie R. Groves (seated, center) and the Atom Bomb Project Military Advisory Board, 8 January 1946. (National Archives)

between Byrnes and Stimson; he told Stalin at Potsdam, during a break in the negotiations on 24 July, merely that the United States had "a new weapon of unusual destructive force." Stalin—who, unbeknownst to Truman, already knew of the Manhattan Project through espionage and had even ordered work to begin on Russia's own atomic bomb—appeared "unimpressed" to an observer.

That same day, Truman approved an order directing that the first atomic bomb be dropped after 3 August and "as soon as weather will permit" upon one of four cities: Hiroshima, Kokura, Niigata, or Nagasaki. The four had been chosen as targets not only because they were strategically important but because each until then had been left relatively undamaged by conventional bombing. Hiroshima was picked as the target for the first bomb because of its location on flat terrain ringed by mountains—so that "the effects of the bomb would run out," as Groves said. Kyoto, long considered a cultural and religious shrine by the Japanese, had been earlier removed from the target list at Stimson's explicit order.

On 6 August 1945, a B-29 named *Enola Gay* dropped "Little Boy"—a gun-design weapon of enriched uranium that was one of two types of atomic bombs—upon the city of Hiroshima, killing between 78,000 and 100,000 of its inhabitants. Three days later, on the morning of 9 August, the B-29 *Bock's Car* dropped "Fat Man"—an implosion-design plutonium weapon of the kind that had been tested at Alamogordo—upon Nagasaki, where between 60,000 and 70,000 Japanese almost instantly perished. During the following

months, deaths from radiation exposure added to the toll in both cities. A third bomb was being readied for use against Toyko sometime after mid-August when the Japanese emperor, stunned by the attacks and by Russia's invasion of Manchuria a week earlier, surrendered unconditionally on 14 August.

Because Truman's order had specified that atomic "bomb*s*" were to be dropped as soon as they were available and because there was no provision for review of that command after the first strike, some historians have criticized the dropping of the second bomb and the destruction of Nagasaki as "unnecessary." Even had the Japanese not surrendered on the fourteenth, however, it is doubtful that the third bomb would have been used as scheduled against Tokyo. Truman told his cabinet on 10 August, that "he had given orders to stop the atomic bombing. He said the thought of wiping out another 100,000 was too horrible."

Although Truman wrote in his personal journal on 25 July that the "target will be a purely military one and we will issue a warning statement asking the Japs to surrender and save lives," neither the atomic raid upon Hiroshima, the site of an army headquarters, nor the bombing of Nagasaki, an industrial and shipping center, was preceded by warning—in part because the Interim Committee had advised Truman that prior warning might prompt the Japanese to move Allied prisoners-of-war into the target area.

More controversial still is the charge made by some of Truman's critics that the decision to drop the bomb was motivated by considerations of "atomic diplomacy"—specifically, the desire on the part of the president and his advisers to end the war before the Russians could establish a foothold in Asia and to impress the Soviets with the power of a weapon the United States alone possessed. Although there can be little doubt that Byrnes, and perhaps others in the Truman administration, hoped and even expected that the nuclear monopoly might prove to be what Stimson had called a diplomatic "master card" in America's future dealings with the Soviet Union, this motivation probably acted only to reinforce the preexisting, and predominant, military rationale of using the atomic bomb to defeat Japan.

Ironically, the atomic bomb failed to play a major role in postwar diplomacy—where Byrnes discovered that the Russians were, as he later admitted, "stubborn, obstinate, and they don't scare." With Russia's rejection in June 1946 of the so-called Baruch Plan for the international control of atomic energy—an American proposal that would have required the opening up of Soviet territory to Western inspection—the nuclear arms race that Stimson had hoped to avoid began in earnest.

Also in 1946, Congress passed the administration-sponsored McMahon Act, which established the civilian-run Atomic Energy Commission (AEC) and gave it control over both nuclear weapons and atomic energy for civilian uses. Improved weapons technology and the mounting political pressures of the cold war led, during the next few years, to an almost explosive growth in the nation's atomic stockpile—from only 9 bombs in 1946 to approximately 650 by 1951. The result was that nuclear weapons, which had initially been considered only an adjunct of America's strength, quickly became dominant in the nation's military strategy and the centerpiece of U.S. plans for a possible war with Russia. Nonetheless, evidently on only one occasion after 1945 did Truman again give serious consideration to using atomic bombs—in March 1951, when the United States feared that Russia was about to join China in the Korean War. Although that threat failed to materialize, Truman the following month ordered custody of some nine atomic bombs transferred from the AEC to the military.

Midway through his second term, Truman was confronted with another fateful choice affecting the arms race and the development of nuclear weapons: whether to launch an all-out effort to develop the fusion superbomb, or "Super." Although scientists had recognized as early as 1942 that hydrogen bombs were a theoretical possibility, there was little political pressure to develop an American Super until after the detonation of the Soviet Union's atomic bomb, which was detected by the United States in early September 1949 and publicly announced by the president later that month.

Opposing development of the Super on both moral and technical grounds were the scientists of the AEC's General Advisory Committee, headed by Robert Oppenheimer. Promoting its development was a so-called H-bomb lobby consisting of physicist Edward Teller, AEC commissioner Lewis Strauss, and several important congressional and military figures. On 31 January 1950, Truman ordered the AEC to proceed with determining the feasibility of a superbomb. Some six weeks later, the president—advised, incorrectly, that a recently arrested Soviet spy, Klaus Fuchs, had given the Russians vital information pertaining to the Super—secretly approved a crash program to build the H-bomb.

In reality, the secret of how to build a Super continued to elude scientists for more than another year, until the spring of

Art Bimrose, *Oregonian*, 21 September 1952.

1951, when Teller, mathematician Stanislaw Ulam, and other scientists at Los Alamos hit upon the idea of using X rays from an exploding fission bomb to heat and compress a physically distinct core of fusionable fuel, in what became known as the "radiation-implosion" or "staged" Super. The thermonuclear breakthrough achieved by Teller and Ulam allowed the testing of a prototype Super to be scheduled for the summer or early fall of 1952 on the Pacific atoll of Eniwetok.

But in the weeks leading up to that test—code-named Mike—Oppenheimer and other scientists appointed the previous April to a so-called Panel of Consultants on Disarmament recommended that Truman postpone the experiment until after the coming presidential election. They proposed that either he or his successor meanwhile approach the Russians with the offer of a mutual "nuclear stand-still," whereby both sides would agree not to test either nuclear or thermonuclear weapons. The Disarmament Panel also urged Truman to adopt a policy of greater "candor" regarding nuclear weapons—informing the public, for example, of the relative size of Soviet and American nuclear stockpiles, of the much greater destructiveness of superbombs, and of the fact that devastation would inevitably occur on both sides in the event of an unlimited nuclear war.

Although Truman was not attracted to the idea of the stand-still, or any of the other ideas of the Disarmament Panel, he did agree to delay Mike and sent an envoy to the Pacific less than a week before the test to order its postponement. Told that the countdown for Mike was already too far advanced to be interrupted without adversely affecting the development of the

Super and other nuclear weapons, Truman agreed to let the test proceed on schedule.

On 31 October 1952, the world's first superbomb exploded with a force equivalent to 10,400,000 tons of dynamite—reportedly almost half again the yield that scientists expected—excavating a crater two miles wide and a half mile deep out of the ocean floor and obliterating a coral island. (The Russians would not test a multimegaton hydrogen bomb until 23 November 1955.) Truman personally briefed his successor, President-elect Dwight Eisenhower, on the awesome power of Mike in a meeting at the Oval Office just two weeks after the election. On 30 December 1952, Truman rejected a proposal by some of his advisers that he and Eisenhower issue a year-end statement telling in graphic detail of the more dangerous world that superbombs had created, and he also refused a suggestion to make the secret report of the Disarmament Panel public.

Martin J. Sherwin, *A World Destroyed: The Atomic Bomb and the Grand Alliance* (New York: Knopf, 1975) is an excellent history of the political events leading up to Truman's decision to drop the atomic bombs. Richard G. Hewlett and Oscar E. Anderson, Jr., *A History of the United States Atomic Energy Commission*, vol. 1, *The New World, 1939/1946*, and Hewlett and Francis Duncan, vol. 2, *Atomic Shield, 1947/1952* (Washington, D.C.: U.S. Government Printing Office, 1972), offer a comprehensive and exhaustively detailed technical and political history of the atomic and hydrogen bomb projects and the AEC. A popular but extremely well-written and researched account of the people who built and used the atomic bomb, with an epilogue on the making of the hydrogen bomb, is Richard Rhodes, *The Making of the Atomic Bomb* (New York: Simon & Schuster, 1986). Herbert York, in *The Advisors: Oppenheimer, Teller, and the Superbomb* (New York: W. H. Freeman, 1976) gives an accurate insider account of the scientific and political controversy over the Super. Gregg Herken, *The Winning Weapon: The Atomic Bomb in the Cold War, 1945–1950* (New York: Knopf, 1980), is a history of the political, diplomatic, and military roles that atomic bombs played in the early cold war, with a brief section on the origins of the Super.

GREGG HERKEN

See also Atomic Energy Commission; Commander in Chief; Japan; Nuclear Energy; Stimson, Henry L.; World War II

Atomic Energy Commission

A federal agency created during the Truman administration to control the development of atomic energy.

The atomic attacks on Japan in the summer of 1945 not only brought World War II to an abrupt end but also left the United States and the world face to face with a new technology of fearful dimensions. Within weeks President Truman asked Congress to consider legislation to ensure domestic and international control of the new energy source, but congressional hearings soon revealed a host of controversial issues that would take months to resolve. In the course of the protracted public debate, Truman supported a bill introduced by Senator Brien

McMahon, which would establish a civilian Atomic Energy Commission (AEC) with complete control of the production and use of nuclear materials.

The Atomic Energy Act of 1946 (P.L. 585, 79th Cong.), which Truman signed on 1 August, established the principle of civilian control but also created a military liaison committee consisting of officers representing the armed services with official access to the AEC. The act also ensured that scientists would have a direct voice in the AEC's affairs through a general advisory committee. The act placed severe restrictions on the dissemination of atomic information and outlawed private ownership of nuclear materials or facilities for producing or using them.

Truman set out to establish the new commission on a nonpartisan basis; he later claimed that he did not initially appoint even one Democrat as one of the five commissioners. The appointment of David E. Lilienthal, however, as the first chairman of the commission, and J. Robert Oppenheimer as the first chairman of the general advisory committee, brought a decidedly liberal flavor to the new agency. As former chairman of the Tennessee Valley Authority, Lilienthal looked upon the AEC as an opportunity to develop nuclear technology for peaceful purposes, particularly the generation of electric power. Oppenheimer, an influential physicist who had directed the building of the bomb at Los Alamos during the war, was best known for his work in the spring of 1946 on the aborted Acheson-Lilienthal plan for international control of atomic energy.

Art Bimrose, *Oregonian*, 16 February 1952.

In 1947 Truman supported the AEC in its struggle with the military services to maintain control over weapon production facilities and the stockpile of nuclear weapons. The AEC also made some headway in establishing a network of national laboratories to develop nuclear technology for peaceful purposes. But the initial alarms of the cold war in 1948 forced the agency to turn its attention to increasing the production of nuclear materials and developing more reliable nuclear weapons that could be mass-produced.

The AEC launched a series of construction projects that resulted in an enormous increase in production capacity for nuclear weapons. But the armed services, faced with severe financial restraints imposed by Truman on military spending, were placing such heavy reliance on nuclear weapons to counter the Soviet threat in Europe that demand seemed constantly to outrun the capacity to produce—a practice the commission considered a threat to civilian control. To give the AEC a stronger voice in planning, Truman named Lilienthal to a special committee of the National Security Council.

The context for nuclear planning, however, changed dramatically in August 1949, when the Soviet Union tested its first nuclear weapon. The AEC launched still another massive expansion of its production facilities, and Commissioner Lewis L. Strauss demanded a "quantum jump" over the Soviet achievement by accelerating research on a thermonuclear weapon, or hydrogen bomb. The ensuing debate within the administration pitted Lilienthal and most of the AEC and the general advisory committee on one side in opposition to the H-bomb against the Joint Committee on Atomic Energy, the military services, and some influential scientists. Truman ended the debate on 31 January 1950, when he made the decision to accelerate development of the hydrogen bomb. Discouraged and frustrated, Lilienthal resigned as chairman and was replaced by Commissioner Gordon E. Dean, a former law partner of Senator McMahon, who had sided with Strauss on the H-bomb decision.

Although military requirements continued to preoccupy the AEC during the last years of the Truman administration, scientists and engineers in the national laboratories made some progress in developing the peaceful uses of atomic energy. Of most immediate impact were the increasing quantities of a variety of radioactive isotopes produced for distribution to hospitals and industrial laboratories. New research reactors and high-energy accelerators made possible the compilation of vital data on the effects of radiation on materials and biological organisms as well as the exploration of the atomic nucleus. The AEC also began construction of a series of reactor experiments to demonstrate the nuclear generation of electric power. When President Truman left office in January 1953, the Atomic Energy Commission was a mature and effective agency of the federal government.

The first two volumes of *A History of the United States Atomic Energy Commission* cover in detail Truman's role in establishing the commission and in defining atomic energy policy during his administration: Richard G. Hewlett and Oscar E. Anderson, Jr., vol. 1, *The New World, 1939/1946* (University Park: Pennsylvania State University Press, 1962); and Hewlett and Francis Duncan, Vol. 2, *Atomic Shield, 1947/1952* (University Park: Pennsylvania State University Press, 1969). David E. Lilienthal, the first chairman, provides some vivid and valuable insights into Truman's views on atomic energy policy in *The Journals of David E. Lilienthal*, vol. 2, *The Atomic Energy Years, 1945–1950* (New York: Harper & Row, 1964). Candid accounts of the president in action were recorded by Gordon Dean, Lilienthal's successor as chairman, in his diary edited by Roger M. Anders, *Forging the Atomic Shield: Excerpts from the Office Diary of Gordon E. Dean* (Chapel Hill: University of North Carolina Press, 1987).

RICHARD G. HEWLETT

See also Atomic and Hydrogen Bombs; Lilienthal, David Eli; Nuclear Energy

Attlee, Clement Richard

(1 March 1883–10 August 1967)

British prime minister, 1945–51. Harry Truman first met Clement Attlee in summer 1945 at the Potsdam Conference. During the meeting the new president had grown weary of Winston Churchill's pugnacious attitude toward the Soviets and hoped for closer Anglo-American cooperation with the newly elected Attlee. "It is too bad about Churchill," Truman wrote his mother, "but it may turn out to be all right for the world."

Most Americans had a different view; the press had been charmed by Churchill and their editorials were much tougher on Attlee. "Old Sobersides" *Newsweek* labeled him, a "chilly little man who walks with a shuffle." To many Americans Attlee did not look like a prime minister but like "Winston Churchill's butler."

These comments were unfair, for Attlee had an impressive background. After an education at Oxford, he joined the bar and practiced law before moving to a poor district of London where he eventually became a socialist and joined the Labour party. He was commissioned in World War I and served in Gallipoli and France. In 1922 he won a seat in Parliament, and by 1935 he had assumed leadership of his party. He supported Britain's declaration of war on Germany but not the leadership of Prime Minister Neville Chamberlain. Consequently Chamberlain was forced to resign in 1940, and Winston Churchill formed the wartime coalition in which Attlee became deputy prime minister. Labour won the elections at the end of the war, and in July 1945 Attlee became prime minister, a post he held until October 1951.

In contrast to his flamboyant predecessor, Attlee was more comfortable working in the background with cabinet committees on domestic policy than attending conferences with world leaders. He enjoyed the administrative chores of government, once saying that the "job of a prime minister is to lead and coordinate a team, not to seek to be an omnipotent minister." Therefore, personal diplomacy almost ended between Attlee and Truman. The prime minister and president rarely wrote each other and met only a few times during the half dozen years they were in office. This would have been incredible—considering the numerous decisions that both democracies had to make during the cold war era—if it was not for the fact that the prime minister picked an outstanding foreign secretary, Ernest Bevin, who maintained close relations with the Truman administration.

Attlee and Bevin continued policies toward the Truman administration that had been initiated by Churchill. The British aim was to prevent Soviet domination of the Continent and since the U.K. was in economic crisis that meant convincing Americans to take primary responsibility for reviving West Europe. In one of the few letters Attlee wrote Truman he urged continuing defense cooperation in the postwar era, a request he reiterated in November 1945 when he made a rare visit to the White House.

British policy was successful. Fearing Soviet expansion, Truman in 1947 agreed to Anglo-American defense planning, announced the Truman Doctrine and endorsed the Marshall Plan. By 1950 British and American troops were fighting side by side in Korea. What impact Attlee had on Truman is difficult to estimate. Soviet behavior prompted the president to act, and the prime minister chose to play a secondary role, leaving personal negotiations to Ernest Bevin.

Attlee's memoirs, *As It Happened* (London: Heinemann, 1954) are not as revealing as a series of interviews by Francis Williams, *A Prime Minister Remembers: The War and Post-War Memoirs of the Rt. Hon. Earl Attlee* (London: Heinemann, 1961). Also consult Kenneth Harris, *Attlee* (London: Weidenfeld & Nicolson, 1982), and Raymond Smith and John Zametica, "The Cold Warrior: Clement Attlee Reconsidered, 1945–1947," *International Affairs* 61 (Spring 1985): 237–52.

TERRY H. ANDERSON

See also Great Britain

Austria

The planning for postwar Austria had begun with the Moscow Declaration of October 1943, which granted Austria eventual liberated status while calling upon this victim of Nazi aggression to assist in the defeat of the Hitlerites. Moreover, the Allies established the European Advisory Commission (EAC) in London to formulate zones and controls for both Germany and Austria.

When Truman entered the White House in April 1945, Soviet troops had control of eastern Austria, and the EAC had not settled zonal boundaries or occupation procedures. The new president had to tackle several related problems: French control of northwestern Italy, Yugoslav occupation of the Austrian provinces of Carinthia and Styria, and the Soviet Union's delaying tactics in the EAC over the Austrian occupation and the final shape of the zones. The cold war was definitely on.

Truman insisted that the United States not extend the harsh Morgenthau Plan, aimed at Germany, into Austria, but he rejected British suggestions to renege on the final agreements by not removing troops from portions of the agreed-upon Russian zone. The issues of zonal boundaries and occupation procedures were finally decided in July 1945 at the Potsdam Conference. Through it all Truman regarded the Austrian situation as equal in importance to that of Germany. Unhappily the Americans listened to the British in delaying Western recognition of the Soviet-sponsored Karl Renner provisional government until

late autumn, assuming erroneously that anything accepted by the Soviets must be riddled with communism.

As the Allied occupation in Austria settled in—it would last until 1955—Truman paid less attention to the small country. Nevertheless, he consistently bemoaned Russian behavior there. The Soviets delayed the signing of the State Treaty for at least seven years beyond Western wishes and stripped their zone of anything they wanted. Incensed at Soviet kidnappings in Germany and Austria and its actions in Iran, Truman considered major economic aid to Austria, France, and Italy even before the 1947 announcement of the Marshall Plan and thought of calling for UN support against the Russians. Furthermore, he encouraged the use of displaced persons camps in Austria as a conduit to future emigration of Jews to Israel. Later, and consistent with his pro-Austrian beliefs, Truman insisted that the nation be treated favorably in the European Recovery Program.

Diverted by the Korean War, Truman gave the Austrian occupation problem lower priority during the last years of his presidency, but the country was not forgotten. In 1956, while visiting in Salzburg, the former president expressed pleasure upon learning that the Austrians had favorable memories of the American and British occupation. "The Austrians are very lucky that the Russians are gone," he reflected privately. "They robbed the country of everything they could get their hands on."

Primary sources are located in the files of the Army and State departments, National Archives, Washington, D.C.; the papers of Harry S. Truman, Truman Library, Independence, Missouri; Truman's *Memoirs*, vol. 1, *Years of Decision* (Garden City, N.Y.: Doubleday, 1955); and Robert H. Ferrell, ed., *Off the Record: The Private Papers of Harry S. Truman* (New York: Harper & Row, 1980). For detailed secondary books based on the primary materials, see William B. Bader, *Austria between East and West, 1945–1955* (Stanford: Stanford University Press, 1966), and Donald R. Whitnah and Edgar E. Erickson, *The American Occupation of Austria: Planning and Early Years* (Westport, Conn.: Greenwood Press, 1985).

DONALD R. WHITNAH

Aviation, Commercial

As a senator from Missouri, Harry S. Truman became an aviation enthusiast and regarded this revolutionary form of transportation favorably for the rest of his life. He was involved in Senate consideration of the organizational structure of civil aviation's federal watchdog, then the Bureau of Air Commerce, and joined the debate about whether the new Civil Aeronautics Administration (CAA) should be independent of the Department of Commerce. In 1938, Truman chaired the Senate's Interstate Commerce Committee's Aviation Subcommittee. Later he joined Senator Pat McCarran in unsuccessfully fighting Franklin D. Roosevelt's reorganization plan of 1940, which took away the CAA's independent status. Perhaps too critical of the United States, Truman contended that Uncle Sam was merely muddling about in aviation, compared with England, France, Germany, and the Soviet Union.

Throughout World War II, Truman kept abreast of aviation

budgets and problems, making clear his interest in flying by keeping a picture of Orville Wright on his desk. He also lamented the possibility of commercial flight becoming a political pork barrel in the postwar era. Nevertheless, he understood the inevitability of large domestic expenditures being invested in public works projects like highways and airports, for he realized how important the airplane would be to the country's future. Upon President Franklin D. Roosevelt's death and Truman's elevation to the White House in April 1945, commercial aviation experts agreed that a death knell had been struck against those lobbying for combined regulation of air, rail, and ship transportation.

At the end of the war, President Truman fended off criticism of CAA administrator T. P. Wright, who then held the position for three more years. During that period, the CAA had serious morale problems, and internal inquiries revealed that several regional CAA authorities should be fired. The president agreed to a number of top personnel changes within both the CAA and the Civil Aeronautics Board (CAB), the latter agency now charged with economic regulation and safety and accident investigations.

Public faith in flying was boosted when Truman flew home to Independence for Christmas in 1945. Privately his aides questioned the judgment of aviation experts who delivered his new DC-6 airliner only to acknowledge subsequently that four sets of mechanical adjustments had been necessary to render the plane safe. Calling it the "Flying White House," the president often used the plane to crisscross the nation. These trips were not devoid of humor: he reportedly informed the crew to advise him whenever they crossed Ohio so that he could remember his disdain for archrival Senator Robert Taft.

Presidential budget support for civil aviation was consistently forthcoming. For example, CAA appropriations rose from $35,781,478 in fiscal year 1945 to $187,100,000 in 1950. The Korean War exacted its toll, however, and the figures were drastically reduced to $136,400,000 in Truman's last fiscal year, 1953. The reductions prevented Washington from filling the growing need for airways and airports, but both Truman and Congress gave higher priority to the Korean struggle.

The president encountered the usual political opposition to his appointments. In 1947, he weathered a storm of protest, even in his own party, for his refusal to rename FDR brains truster James M. Landis to the CAB. A dynamic but controversial leader, Landis had alienated a portion of the aviation industry as well as the president. The Senate, in a bipartisan vote, then refused to accept the president's choice of a military leader, Maj. Gen. Laurence S. Keuter, for the civilian post.

A series of fatal crashes in 1947 led Truman to appoint the Air Policy Commission to examine current and future needs and to commission a Presidential Board of Inquiry on Air Safety. Larger appropriations for safety devices on the airways followed. Later he appointed an Airport Commission headed by the famous aviator Jimmy Doolittle. But the cold war and Korea diverted attention from the commercial phases of aviation, delaying reforms until later in the fifties. Meanwhile, Truman monitored the activities of the CAA and CAB, intervening at times on behalf of projects he favored. For example, in 1949, he banned airplane flights as of 1951 into wilderness areas of Minnesota's Superior National Forest, becoming the first president to make use of a power granted by the Air Commerce Act of 1926. His aim was to prevent the destruction of wildlife by hunters and fishermen.

Truman was not always successful in his efforts. In 1949, he failed to block acceptance of Baltimore's proposed Friendship Airport as the second Washington, D.C., facility. He personally selected a site at Burke, west of the capital. Nevertheless, Baltimore built its airport, and Congress later overruled Truman's choice of Burke when it decided to build yet another major airport, the present Dulles International.

Overall, commercial aviation in this nation benefited strongly from Truman's support, for his enthusiasm came at a critical juncture—the conversion from wartime to commercial and private uses after 1945.

For primary sources, see the files in Washington, D.C., of the Civil Aeronautics Administration and the Federal Aviation Agency. At the Harry S. Truman Library, Independence, see Truman's papers and the collections of the various aviation inquiry bodies. The secondary literature best representative of the primary data are Donald R. Whitnah, *Safer Skyways: Federal Control of Aviation, 1926–1966* (Ames: Iowa State University Press, 1966, 1967); John R. M. Wilson, *Turbulence Aloft: The Civil Aeronautics Administration amid Wars and Rumors of Wars, 1938–1953* (Washington, D.C.: U.S. Department of Transportation, 1979); and Roger Bilstein, *Flight in America, 1900–1983* (Baltimore: Johns Hopkins Press, 1984).

DONALD R. WHITNAH

See also Landis, James McCauley

Awards

Awards conferred upon Harry S. Truman fall into four categories: honorary degrees from universities and colleges throughout the United States and abroad; miscellaneous certificates, medals, and plaques received primarily during his years as president; honorary chairmanships and memberships in various organizations; and awards relating to his involvement in Masonic work.

Among the schools that bestowed degrees on him were Grinnell College in 1944; Westminster College at Fulton, Missouri, in 1946, upon which occasion Winston Churchill, who also received an honorary degree, delivered his famous "iron curtain" speech; the University of Missouri in 1950; and Oxford University in 1956. A selective list of degrees is given in the accompanying table.

Beginning in 1945, he received a succession of awards in the form of certificates, medals, and plaques, a preponderance of which were presented by foreign or veterans' groups. Included were the Verdun Commemorative Medal from the City of Verdun, France; Grand Cross of the Order of the Sepulchre from the Greek Orthodox Church of Jerusalem; Order of the Haller Sword from the United American and Polish Veterans Club; Medal of Athens from the City of Athens, Greece; Order of the Cross of the Compassionate Heart from the Russian Veterans Society of the World War; Amvets Award of Merit from the American Veterans of World War II; Medal of Honor from the Phalanx of Greek Veterans of America; Certificate of Merit from the American Legion; and the Grand Golden Cross of Merit from the Republic of Austria. The many awards from veterans' organizations indicate the importance of his military background in Truman's life. After serving as commander of Artillery Battery D in World War I, he helped organize the Reserve Officers Association and was honored by that group in 1971 when they presented him with a special Founder's Appreciation Award.

More than two thousand organizations throughout the country elected Truman to honorary memberships during and after his presidency. Just a few of his home area organizations in which he held a lifetime honorary membership were the Kansas City Bar Association, Kansas City Host Lions Club, and the Tirey J. Ford Post Number 21 in Independence, which was the American Legion Post he joined after World War I. He was also honorary chairman of a number of organizations including the American Red Cross, Boy Scouts of America, and Franklin D. Roosevelt Memorial Committee.

A member of the Free and Accepted Masons from 1909, Truman was the only president to hold the 33d degree. He and Andrew Jackson were the only presidents to serve their states as grand master, and he was the only person to serve as president of the United States and master of his lodge at the same time. In 1945, he was awarded the Gourgas Medal of the Supreme Council of the Northern Masonic Jurisdiction of the Scottish Rite, and in 1948 he received the Certificate of Merit from the Knights Templar of Missouri.

Accounts of the conferring of many of Truman's awards, including honorary degrees, appeared in the *New York Times* and may also be found in his papers in the Truman Library.

JOHN T. CURRY

Former president Truman beams during June 1956 ceremonies in which Oxford University conferred upon him an honorary doctor of civil law degree. (Associated Press/Wide World Photos)

Honorary Degrees Conferred upon Harry S. Truman

DATE RECEIVED	INSTITUTION	DEGREE
28 May 1945	Grinnell College, Grinnell, Iowa	LL.D.
28 May 1945	Elon College, Elon, N.C. (received in absentia; Congressman Carl I. Durham represented the president)	LL.D.
17 June 1945	Georgetown University, Washington, D.C. (received in absentia; Senator Dennis Chavez represented the president)	LL.D.
28 June 1945	University of Kansas City, Kansas City, Mo.	LL.D.
6 March 1946	Westminster College, Fulton, Mo.	LL.D.
11 May 1946	Fordham University, New York City	LL.D.
20 May 1946	William Jewell College, Liberty, Mo.	LL.D
29 May 1946	George Washington University, Washington, D.C.	LL.D.
1 June 1946	Washington College, Chestertown, Md.	LL.D.
6 March 1947	Baylor University, Waco, Tex.	LL.D.
17 June 1947	Princeton University, Princeton, N.J.	LL.D.
2 April 1948	William and Mary College, Williamsburg, Va.	LL.D.
12 June 1948	University of California, Berkeley, Calif.	LL.D.
10 June 1948	Olympic Junior College, Bremerton, Wash.	A.A.
8 March 1949	Rollins College, Winter Park, Fl.	L.H.D.
9 June 1950	University of Missouri, Columbia, Mo.	LL.D.
24 April 1953	University of Hawaii, Honolulu, Hawaii	L.H.D.
20 June 1956	Oxford University, England	D.C.L.
9 June 1957	Brandeis University, Waltham, Mass.	LL.D.
25 April 1958	University of the State of New York, Albany, N.Y.	LL.D.
22 February 1960	Jewish Theological Seminary, Miami, Fl.	LL.D.
16 March 1967	Salonika University, Salonika, Greece (received in absentia)	LL.D.

LL.D.: Doctor of Laws
L.H.D.: Doctor of Humanities
D.C.L.: Doctor of Civil Law
A.A.: Associate in Arts

B

Barkley, Alben W.

(24 November 1877–30 April 1956)

Congressman; senator; vice president, 1949–53. When Harry S. Truman reached the Senate in 1935, Alben W. Barkley, a member of Congress from Kentucky since 1912, apparently knew him only through newspaper stories. The two had no more than a passing acquaintance until the death of Senator Joseph Robinson of Arkansas, although Barkley had by then noted that Truman "voted right." In the subsequent contest between Barkley and Pat Harrison of Mississippi for the majority leadership of the Senate, Truman committed his support to Barkley but then told him that he was under great pressure and would have to switch his support to Harrison. Later Barkley wrote, "I have often wondered how I would have felt about Harry Truman if I had lost the majority leadership by one vote."

Barkley was convinced that his highly publicized opposition to Franklin D. Roosevelt's 1944 tax bill kept him from being chosen as vice-presidential candidate that year. At the Democratic convention Robert Hannegan persuaded Barkley to place Roosevelt's name in nomination for a fourth term and left the senator with the impression that he would be nominated for the vice presidency rather than Henry A. Wallace. When Harry S. Truman was nominated instead, Barkley felt he had been deceived by Hannegan. Later he wrote that he did "not want the vice presidency," but he resented Hannegan's manipulating the nomination of Truman. In a subsequent casual conversation, Truman said the "office caught up with him." Barkley replied by telling him a story about an eastern Kentucky Republican who rode a mule to Frankfort to be handy when an office caught up with him. After six months none did, and he saddled his mule and started home. On the road he met a friend and told him if an office came by seeking him, "tell it that I'm riding out the Somerset Pike and ridin' damned slow."

When the press created a modest sensation by publishing a picture of Truman playing a piano with the shapely Lauren Bacall seated on the lid, Barkley spoofed the vice president in a speech, "Advice to Newly Elected Senators." He warned that if there were any piano players among them, they should not try to hold down the lid with the movie actress because there was a "shape which would hew their destinies to an end."

When Truman suddenly became president Barkley commented there was no humor in the man. Truman for his part stressed his extreme humility in assuming the office—his friends thought to an excessive degree. Barkley and others called on him and advised him to strike out boldly as leader of a nation at war—counsel he accepted.

Despite their close association as majority leader and vice president, and subsequently as majority leader and president, Barkley was convinced in 1948 that he would not be named vice-presidential candidate on the Truman ticket. The president favored William O. Douglas, associate justice of the Supreme Court, but noted in his diary that Douglas was wishy-washy about the matter.

When Barkley arrived at the Democratic National Convention in Philadelphia, he observed, "I found the most discouraged and downcast group I had ever seen. You could cut the gloom with a corn knife. The very air smelled of defeat." He said he was approached by several delegates, including governors, urging him to allow his name to be placed in nomination for the presidency. The morning following Barkley's speech to the convention, Truman telephoned to congratulate him. Barkley assured Truman that if he were nominated for president, he would take the floor and renounce it. In the course of the conversation the president said he did not know Barkley wanted to be vice president. Barkley denied he did, but said he would not resist that nomination. In his diary entry of 12 July 1948, Truman wrote, "My 'good' friend, Leslie Biffle, spends all his time as sergeant-at-arms of the Convention running Barkley for President. I watch the demonstration on television. Having been in on numerous demonstrations I'm not fooled. I can see everything taking place on the platform. The 'actors' forget that Barkley in his good speech mentions me only casually by name."

The convention, not the president, chose Barkley for the vice presidency.

Barkley and Truman campaigned hard, with Truman going by special train to engagements, and Barkley reaching his as best he could. They thoroughly relished their victory. Barkley was amused at the glee with which Truman waved a copy of the *Chicago Tribune*, with its famous headline "Dewey Wins," on his arrival back in Washington. From that point on, they worked well together, with Barkley acting as political adviser and performing sensitive missions. "He has made a great Vice President," Truman wrote in his diary late in his presidency. "No President and Vice President have been as cooperative as Barkley and I."

Surprisingly, the collected Barkley correspondence in the University of Kentucky Library contains only a sparse amount of Truman material. The letters for the most part are folksy and chatty. Truman had Barkley's mother flown to Washington aboard the presidential plane and was amused at her reactions. In his diary Truman described a landing of the presidential plane in Paducah to allow Barkley and Noble Gregory, a congressman, to deplane. A large crowd had gathered at the airport to meet the plane. Barkley told Truman it was always so when he came home. On its return trip to pick up the vice president there was an even larger crowd. Truman twitted Barkley that the people were even gladder to see him leave.

Barkley wrote Truman in April 1953 that a writer was preparing an article about him and apologized for imposing on him to answer the man's questions. Truman responded, "It is not imposing on me to answer questions about you. I am in a position to give better answers than anybody alive and that is taking in a lot of territory." In the same letter Truman said he had agreed with *Life* magazine to write a history of the period 1935–53, and he hoped to "give a fair picture of the effort which you and I made to be good public servants."

The Barkley papers are deposited in the Special Collections Division of the University of Kentucky. A revealing personal source is Alben W. Barkley, *That Reminds Me: The Autobiography of the Veep* (Garden City, N.Y.: Doubleday, 1954). In this book Barkley revealed more of his underlying feelings toward Truman and the vice presidency than he possibly realized. Robert H. Ferrell, ed., *Off the Record: The Private Papers of Harry S. Truman* (New York Harper & Row, 1980), gives Truman's views of major incidents in the Truman-Barkley relationship. James K. Libby, *Dear Alben: Mr. Barkley of Kentucky* (Lexington: University Press of Kentucky, 1976), is the most recent full-length biography. A thoroughly researched study is Polly Ann Davis, "Alben W. Barkley: Senate Majority Leader and Vice President" (Ph.D. diss., University of Kentucky, 1963), from which Davis published two excerpts: "Alben Barkley's Public Career in 1944," *Filson Club History Quarterly* 71 (April 1977): 143–77, and "Alben W. Barkley: Vice President," *Register of the Kentucky Historical Society* 76 (April 1978): 112–32. See also George W. Robinson, "Alben W. Barkley and the 1944 Tax Vote," *Register of the Kentucky Historical Society* 67 (July 1969): 197–210.

THOMAS D. CLARK

See also Cabinets (photograph); Election of 1948

Baruch, Bernard Mannes

(19 August 1870–20 June 1965)

Financial speculator, head of the War Industries Board in World War I, and unofficial adviser to presidents. Bernard Baruch began public life as a contributor to the presidential campaign of Woodrow Wilson in 1912 and as a supporter of the preparedness-for-war campaign in 1914–16. Wilson appointed Baruch chairman of the War Industries Board in 1918 and took him to the Paris Peace Conference of 1919 as an economic adviser. During the 1920s Baruch acted as an adviser and financial angel to many Democratic senators, and by the Hoover presidency he had become one of the most powerful Democrats in Washington. The New Deal diminished but did not obscure his influence with conservative southern Democrats in the Senate. Although Baruch was a self-proclaimed expert on war mobilization, President Roosevelt in 1939–41 attempted to exclude his influence in mobilization planning. But Baruch had cultivated in the press and among the public an image of trust as America's "Park Bench Statesman." Moreover, events proved his forecasts accurate, and by 1942 Roosevelt had begun to use his prestige in such roles as chairman of the Rubber Survey Committee, which tackled the controversial problem of gasoline rationing.

Following the war Baruch tried to remain a useful septuagenarian. But, as an "arrogant, opinionated man," Baruch was less welcome at Truman's White House than he had been at Roosevelt's. Although Truman had been the beneficiary of Baruch's generosity in his 1940 primary campaign, Truman resented Baruch's "meddling" in 1945 when he endorsed the Morgenthau Plan for the deindustrialization of Germany and opposed the administration's proposal for a loan to Great Britain. But when the State Department proposed the controversial Acheson-Lilienthal plan for internationalizing the control of atomic energy, Truman bowed to Secretary of State James F. Byrnes's urging that Baruch lead the American delegation to the United Nations when it presented the plan, in order to enhance its acceptance with conservatives in the Senate and with the public. Baruch, however, insisted upon adding his own proposal for abrogating the right of a big power to veto matters of atomic energy in the United Nations—which Truman reluctantly agreed to. When the Soviets rejected the "Baruch Plan," Truman blamed the veto stipulation for incurring the Soviets' hostility, but it is extremely doubtful that Moscow in any event would have approved the international authority called for in the Acheson version.

The experience left Truman bitter toward Baruch. When the president articulated the Truman Doctrine, he balked at consulting Baruch for the sake of public relations. "I'm just *not* going to do it," Truman expostulated. "I'm not going to spend hours and hours on that old goat!" Still, he spent ninety minutes with Baruch in 1948 to assure himself of the old man's support for the Marshall Plan. Publicly Baruch assailed the administration's economic policies, and privately he told a Democrat, "The leadership in our party now amounts to a zero and a very little zero, too." When Baruch refused Truman's 1948 nomination for his election finance committee, Truman accused him of ingratitude. Truman's victory left

Baruch out in the cold, yet even in his eighties he was not a man to be ignored. Following American intervention in the Korean War, Baruch outspokenly insisted that the military buildup be accompanied by a stabilization program reminiscent to that in World War II. A spontaneous flood of letters from the public descended upon the White House to compel Truman's reluctant acquiescence.

In 1952, considering himself a victim of Truman's petty vindictiveness, Baruch refused to endorse Truman's nominee, Adlai Stevenson, and bolted the Democratic party to support Dwight Eisenhower. In 1960 and 1964, aspiring Democrats such as John F. Kennedy and Lyndon B. Johnson still made a show of publicly consulting this ancient Democratic talisman. With the advent of Vietnam, Baruch patriotically endorsed the fifth American war of his lifetime; but he died in June 1965, fearing that if Johnson did not adopt stabilization policies, the cost of war inflation would defeat America, whatever the outcome on the battlefields.

On Baruch and Truman, see Jordan A. Schwarz, *The Speculator: Bernard M. Baruch in Washington, 1917–1965* (Chapel Hill: University of North Carolina Press, 1981), Margaret L. Coit, *Mr. Baruch* (Boston: Houghton Mifflin Co., 1957), and Bernard M. Baruch, *Baruch: The Public Years* (New York: Holt, Rinehart & Winston; 1960).

JORDAN A. SCHWARZ

Battery D

Capt. Harry S. Truman's command of a field artillery battery of nearly two hundred soldiers during World War I was his first opportunity to lead men, and he enjoyed his success in spite of the cultural gap that separated him from most of them. One of six batteries in the 129th Field Artillery Regiment of the thirty-fifth Division, Battery D had a reputation for rebelliousness when Truman took command in July 1918, a month before the battery saw its first combat action in France's Vosges Forest. Irish Catholics from Kansas City composed more than half of the battery. Many were high school graduates; all but a handful were single; and many were athletes—boxers and basketball and football players. Most worked in city jobs as clerks, salesmen, bookkeepers, and laborers; only a few, including Truman, had been farmers.

Truman developed an unusual rapport with his men. His firm leadership inspired loyalty and confidence that outlasted the Meuse-Argonne campaign in September 1918, the battery's major action in World War I. Although the lack of battlefield casualties among battery members testified as much to the relative security of artillery positions as to leadership, his men believed that Truman deserved much of the credit.

After the war, the veterans of Battery D and their regiment would be influential in Truman's Jackson County campaigns. They toasted "Captain Harry" at annual reunions and received national acclaim when they formed an honor guard for the president's automobile in the 1949 inaugural parade.

Jonathan Daniels's *The Man of Independence* (Philadelphia: J. B. Lippincott, 1950) views the battery as Truman saw it. Richard Miller's *Truman: The Rise to Power* (New York: McGraw-Hill, 1986) is more critical.

ANDREW J. DUNAR

See also Military Career

Ben-Gurion, David

(16 October 1886–1 December 1973)
Born David Green at Plonsk, Poland, Ben-Gurion was one of the great figures in twentieth-century Jewish history. He settled in Palestine in 1906 and later was instrumental in organizing both the Labor Federation (the Histadrut) and the Labor party (Mapai). In the 1930s he was the spokesman for the Yishuv. He was chairman of the Jewish Agency for Palestine from 1935 to 1948, and after independence he served as Israel's prime minister and defense minister until 1953, and again from 1955 to 1963. A pronounced hawk in the 1940s and 1950s, Ben-Gurion later modified his views.

Truman generally took a sympathetic approach to the Jewish state. But prior to and just after the establishment of Israel—the period of Ben-Gurion's leadership—the Israeli's attitudes on several matters created problems for the Truman administration, at one point even threatening continued American economic assistance. To Truman, Ben-Gurion's belief that military struggle was the only means to secure Israel, his refusal to repatriate Palestinian war refugees, his view that the state's boundaries were insufficient to fulfill Zionism's aspirations, and his insistence that Jerusalem was an integral part of the Jewish state threatened peace in the region and invited Soviet intervention. Thus accepted historical wisdom notwithstanding, relations between the United States and Israel from 1948 to 1953 were uneasy and frequently strained. This was in no small part due to Ben-Gurion's unwillingness to compromise along lines suggested by the Truman administration.

On a personal level, Ben-Gurion's relationship with Truman was never close. They met only once during Truman's presidency—in May 1951 when Ben-Gurion visited the White House to pay respects to the president on his sixty-seventh birthday. Nevertheless, the gift he bore indicated he was not insensitive in regard to Truman. He gave the president an oil-burning bronze candelabrum (the menorah is the official emblem of Israel) made in 1767. The symbolism was not lost on Truman; he noted that it was made the year his hero Andrew Jackson was born!

A useful introduction to Ben-Gurion's career is Shabtai Teveth, *Ben-Gurion and the Palestinian Arabs: From Peace to War* (New York: Oxford University Press, 1985).

IAN J. BICKERTON

See also Israel (and photograph); Palestine; Zionism

Benton, Thomas Hart

(15 April 1889–19 January 1975)

Painter and friend of Truman during his postpresidential years. Born in Neosho, Missouri, Thomas Hart Benton was the son of a Missouri congressman and the grandnephew and namesake of Missouri's first senator. His interest in art drew him away from Missouri; he studied in Chicago and Paris and then took up residency in New York City. Upon receiving a commission to paint historical murals in Missouri's state capitol building in Jefferson City, as well as an invitation to teach at the Kansas City Art Institute, Benton returned to his native state in 1935 to reside permanently in Kansas City.

Benton was Missouri's most famous twentieth-century artist and was considered by many authorities to be the nation's foremost muralist during his lifetime. He was also controversial, both as an artist and as a social commentator.

Truman was critical of Benton's work. When invited in late 1953 to a small dinner to be attended by Benton, Truman is reported to have said "Well, he's the fellow who made a mistake in painting those murals about Mr. Pendergast [Truman's early political mentor] down at Jefferson City. I got a long memory, you know, and I don't know whether we'll get along or not." In January 1955 Truman declined an invitation to pose for the artist, indicating to Benton's agent that he did not like Benton's style of art: "I won't encourage him to do any more horrors like those in Missouri's beautiful capitol."

But early in his postpresidential years Truman began tentatively to socialize with Benton. They soon became good friends, and Truman often attended public events that focused on Benton and his art. After the completion in 1957 of the Harry S. Truman Library in Independence, Truman selected Benton to paint a mural in that building's museum lobby. Benton started the mural, entitled *Independence and the Opening of the West*, in December 1959 and completed it in 1961. In 1970–71 Benton did a painting of the former president entitled *Portrait of Harry Truman at 86*. This was to be the last portrait for which Truman was to sit.

Benton, commenting on Truman in 1970, stated, "Great individuals are accidents. Only rarely does an Alexander or Shakespeare or Michelangelo turn up. The only individual who stands out in my lifetime is Harry S. Truman. If there is an ounce of vanity in that man, it has yet to show itself."

Thomas Hart Benton in his Kansas City studio, 20 May 1957. The murals he is preparing for the New York State Power Authority depict encounters between the Seneca and the French in 1534–35 along the St. Lawrence River. (Associated Press/Wide World Photos)

There are two autobiographies by Thomas Hart Benton: *An Artist in America*, 4th rev. ed. (Columbia: University of Missouri Press, 1983), and *An American in Art: A Professional and Technical Autobiography* (Lawrence: University of Kansas Press, 1969). Information on the Benton-Truman relationship is contained in Truman Library oral history interviews with Benton and Mr. and Mrs. Randall S. Jesse, as well as in the Papers of Harry S. Truman. Robert Sanford's article "Image Overload" in a January 1971 issue of the *St. Louis Post-Dispatch* tells of Benton's efforts and problems in sketching Truman.

GEORGE H. CURTIS

Berlin Airlift

Harry Truman used the Berlin airlift in 1948 to delay a choice between two unpalatable alternatives: retreating in humiliation from Berlin or starting a war in the name of American rights over the city. To his surprise—and Stalin's—this magnificent improvisation proved so successful he never had to choose at all.

When the Soviets cut surface traffic to and from West Berlin on 24 June 1948, they seemed to confront Western leaders with an agonizing dilemma. As Berliners began to starve, the Western powers would have to challenge the blockade on the ground, probably triggering World War III, or they would have to turn the city over to the Russians, with catastrophic consequences for U.S. credibility and prestige in Germany and throughout Europe. As Truman's advisers saw the situation, the basic question was whether Berlin was worth war or not. If it was, the West should force the blockade with an armed convoy; if not, the British, French, and American garrisons should withdraw.

The president avoided a decision. Although a famous passage in the published diaries of Secretary of Defense James V. Forrestal summed up Truman's stance on 28 June as "we were going to stay period," the president told his chief of staff, William D. Leahy, next day that he had meant that the West should remain "as long as possible"; two days later Leahy told a Pentagon meeting that Truman was not committed to Berlin if "that would start a war." On 19 July, Forrestal recorded a similar statement. "Our policy would remain fixed," Truman had told him. "We would stay in Berlin until all diplomatic means had been exhausted in order to come to some kind of an accommodation to avoid war." And if diplomacy failed? Would the Allies fight or get out? Truman seemed to be saying the latter, but his diary account of the session suggested just the opposite. "I made the decision ten days ago to *stay in Berlin*," he wrote. "I don't pass the buck, nor do I alibi out of any decision I make. . . . We'll stay in Berlin, come what may."

But how could the Allies stay? As Western officials pondered the bleak alternatives in the first months of the blockade, the airlift hardly figured in their calculations. Everyone shared Under Secretary of State Robert A. Lovett's view of it as a "temporary expedient" that bought time but offered no solution to the crisis. Even as he ordered the first U.S. flights into the city, the American military governor in Germany, Gen. Lucius D. Clay, told a friend with a snap of his fingers, "I wouldn't give you *that* for our chances." Berliners would start

to suffer "in a few days," he advised Washington on 25 June, "and this suffering will become serious in two or three weeks." Short-run prospects looked better in July, but the long-run prognosis was the same; National Security Council deliberations rested on the assumption that bad weather would ground the airlift in October. Then, Forrestal told his colleagues, "we will have to face up to the hard decision whether to use armed convoys."

Defying all expectations, the airlift not only survived October but outlasted the winter. The credit belonged to the Berliners, who withstood without complaint new privations so soon after defeat and occupation; the British and American aircrews, who endured an exhausting flying schedule and living conditions that one flight surgeon compared with "those found in concentration camps"; and the airlift commander, U.S. Air Force Maj. Gen. William H. Tunner, who transformed chaotic improvisation into smooth efficiency. Tunner's goal was to reduce the airlift to a "steady, even rhythm with hundreds of planes doing exactly the same thing, every hour, day and night, at the same persistent beat." He was so successful that the Kremlin gave up and lifted the blockade on 12 May 1949. To build up stocks in case the Russians tried again, the airlift continued until 30 September. When it was over, it had delivered 2,325,809 tons of supplies in 277,804 flights. Its unexpected success made Berlin a symbol of the U.S. commitment to defend Western Europe against Soviet expansion.

Two points stand out regarding Truman's handling of the Berlin crisis. First, he was not the impulsive decision maker many people think he was. He relied on an airlift he thought was doomed to fail in order to postpone what appeared to be an inevitable choice between war and surrender. Second, he could not acknowledge to himself that that was what he was doing. There is nothing wrong with waiting until you come to your bridges to cross them, but Harry Truman thought there was; Quintus Fabius Maximus held no honored place in his pantheon of heroes. "The most dangerous course a President can follow in time of crisis," he wrote in *Mr. Citizen*, "is to defer making decisions until they are forced on him. . . . When a President finds himself in that position, he is no longer a leader but an improviser who is driven to action out of expediency or weakness."

Truman's belief that presidents must take charge of events and his deep psychological need to see himself as a strong, decisive leader caused him to exaggerate the firmness of his Berlin policy, then and later. That was unfortunate. He had balanced prudence and resolve during the blockade in a way that could have become a model of crisis management in the nuclear age, had it been properly understood. Instead, Harry Truman's obsession with appearing tough threw away that opportunity and helped enshrine hard-line dogmas in American political culture.

General Tunner's memoirs, *Over the Hump* (New York: Duell, Sloan, & Pearce, 1964), provide an excellent introduction to the airlift; *Bridge in the Sky* (New York: David McKay, 1968), by Frank Donovan, is a colorful anecdotal account. W. Phillips Davison, *The Berlin Blockade: A Study in Cold War Politics* (Princeton: Princeton University Press, 1958), long the standard work on the crisis, has been supplanted in many respects—but not all—by Avi Shlaim's *United States and the Berlin Blockade, 1948–1949: A Study in Crisis Decision-Making* (Berkeley and Los Angeles: University of

California Press, 1983). Shlaim too readily accepts the stereotypical image of Truman as temperamentally unable to put off until tomorrow a decision he could make today.

DANIEL F. HARRINGTON

See also Germany

Biographers and Public Reputation

Until well past his fortieth birthday, Harry Truman was scarcely known outside Jackson County, Missouri, where he had been an unsuccessful businessman and a competent officeholder. Locally, Truman was widely liked and respected. He made friends easily, was devoted to honesty and efficiency in government, and was an active member in fraternal and service organizations. From his first run for office in 1922 through his last local election in 1930, he was a leading vote getter on the Democratic ticket.

As presiding judge of the Jackson County Court (1927–34), he built an impressive network of statewide contacts among other county judges, fellow officers in the U.S. Army Reserve, comrades in the American Legion, and friends in the Masonic Order. These friendships would give him the backing of numerous political influentials when he ran for statewide office. Nonetheless, outside the Kansas City area his name did not evoke widespread recognition when he declared his candidacy for the U.S. Senate in 1934. Instead, he was usually identified with the city's notorious Pendergast machine, and he thereby incurred the reflexive opposition of many reform-oriented elements outside of Kansas City, including the influential *St. Louis Post-Dispatch.*

The Pendergast problem would plague his entire career and would present his biographers with a major analytical difficulty. Some of Truman's private writings make it clear that he personally detested the machine's dishonesty, and his performance as a county administrator exemplifies his determination to run a clean operation. Still, he stubbornly refused to renounce his machine associations, even after they had become more of a liability than an asset. (Even in 1945 as vice president of the United States, he flew to Kansas City to attend the funeral of Tom Pendergast.) Privately, he worked hard to persuade himself that Pendergast and a few other top machine leaders were actually better, more honest men than the reformers who sought to establish in Kansas City a regime not unlike the one Truman had set in motion for the county. The refusal to denounce Pendergast after he had fallen from power earned Truman some praise for his loyalty, but left him vulnerable throughout his life to charges that he had been the tool of an especially corrupt political organization.

The Pendergast association dominated his public identity when he entered the Senate in 1935. The scant attention he received outside Missouri during his first term in the Senate appears usually to have proceeded from the assumption that he was an obscure mediocrity sent to Washington as Boss Pendergast's puppet. Truman possessed neither the public relations skills nor the inclination to forge an independent national identity during these years. Instead, he concentrated on building a reputation as a conscientious, hard-working legislator among his fellow senators and was largely successful in doing so.

It was not until after his upset reelection victory in 1940 that Truman succeeded in building a strong, independent public reputation. In his home state, many Democrats appear to have accepted him as the party's leading figure. In Washington, he emerged as one of the most respected and influential men on Capitol Hill. His new standing was almost wholly attributable to his chairmanship of the Special Committee to Investigate the National Defense Program.

Although (as is invariably the case in congressional investigations) much of the actual work of the committee was done by its staff, Truman was remarkably successful in holding the members of the committee together, maintaining a relatively nonpartisan atmosphere, and providing a constructive critique of the war effort. The group, popularly known as the Truman committee, kept his name constantly in the public eye for more than two years. Still, the chairman, in keeping with the style he had already established, eschewed flamboyance and lacked color. By 1944, his name was well established, but his public image remained indistinct. Americans who followed politics knew him in a general way as a competent, hard-working, but self-effacing legislator.

Harry Truman's nomination for the vice presidency, his role in the 1944 campaign, and his abbreviated tenure as vice president finally brought him fully into the national spotlight. In general, his modesty and hard campaign work seem to have been favorably received by the public. He was especially effective in his denial of charges that he once had been a member of the Ku Klux Klan. His months as vice president, however, were unconstructive. Given little to do by President Roosevelt, he was most often noticed at Washington social gatherings and surely most remembered for a photograph of himself playing a

Charles Werner, *Indianapolis Star,* 30 September 1952.

piano upon which was perched the leggy young actress Lauren Bacall.

During the years that he occupied the presidency, Truman failed to establish a solid, enduring image of leadership. Public opinion survey results measuring overall approval or disapproval of the president have left a rough gauge of the ups and downs of Truman's reputation. Shortly after taking office, he benefited from a vast wave of public sympathy and registered an 87 percent approval rating. The difficulties of postwar reconversion and the beginnings of the cold war took a heavy toll. By the fall of 1946, the president was down to 32 percent and reeling badly from such episodes as the firing of Henry Wallace, the "meat strike," and a perceived inability to handle the problems of the domestic economy.

The election of a Republican Congress in 1946 proved a blessing in disguise, for it allowed Truman to go on the offensive. Casting the opposition party in the role of menacing reactionaries and taking a strong anti-Soviet stand in foreign affairs, he made a substantial comeback. In the spring of 1947, a poll showed a 60 percent approval rating; yet a year later his standing had fallen all the way back to 36 percent, a figure that reflected both widening dissatisfaction with him on both the right and left wings of the Democratic party and also a mounting conviction that he could not possibly be elected president in his own right.

No approval/disapproval polls exist for the last half of that year, but one election survey after another seemed to confirm impressions that he was a certain loser. Truman enhanced his public image and scored an upset victory in 1948 through a strategy that exploited an appealing dimension of his personality and emphasized issues of deep import to the American people.

The exploitation of personality grew out of the president's extensive, hard whistle-stop campaigning. Truman reverted as closely as he could to the kind of folksy campaigning that had characterized his Jackson County political career. Speaking briefly and off-the-cuff to crowds in small towns across America, accompanied by his wife and daughter, he seemed to many undecided voters a gutsy, ordinary "little man," not so different from themselves, and won sympathy for his struggle against the odds.

The exploitation of issues involved a constant assertion that a Republican administration not only would fail to meet pressing public needs but would attempt to repeal the benefits the New Deal had brought to the American people. Truman emphasized different specific issues in different parts of the country, shrewdly speaking to the salient interests of each audience.

His surprising win brought him a new standing with the public. In January 1949, he was riding on the crest of a 69 percent approval rating. As before, however, the road ran steeply downhill. A little more than a year later, he was slightly below 50 percent. During 1951 and 1952, the polls ranged from a high of 37 percent to a low of 23 percent. During his second term, Truman was in large part a victim of foreign policy disappointments (the fall of China, the Soviet atomic bomb, the Korean War), McCarthyism, and petty corruption in his administration.

The polling numbers reveal an extraordinarily fragile public image. An obvious explanation is William Leuchtenburg's observation that Harry Truman languished *In the Shadow of FDR: From Harry Truman to Ronald Reagan* (Ithaca, N.Y.:

Cornell University Press, 1983, 1985). Almost any successor to Roosevelt was bound to appear pale by comparison. Bernard Sternsher, "Harry Truman: The Gallup and Roper Polls," in *Popular Images of the Presidents,* ed. William Spragens (Westport, Conn.: Greenwood Press, forthcoming) has attempted to explain the polls by commenting that Americans were more prone to disapprove of Truman's "management" than of Truman policies or even Truman himself. It is, however, probably simplest and most valid to observe that his weaknesses were the obverse of his strengths. At his most popular when he was imagined an ordinary little man struggling with a difficult situation, he also was at his least popular when considered the little man who had failed to deal with one or more crises. The image of ordinariness cuts both ways in a democracy. The leader who courts it may be liked in certain situations but is not necessarily respected; he may equally be scorned if events seem beyond his grasp.

Truman became increasingly popular as he faded from the active political scene in the years after his presidency. As politics became increasingly dominated by television imagery and public opinion polling, he came to seem an American original who was a refreshing contrast to the synthetic politicians of the sixties and seventies. By the time of the Watergate scandal, he had become celebrated as an American folk hero who in his simple, decisive, plain-speaking ways epitomized the virtues of the common man. The image was not inaccurate, and it was one that Truman himself relished; but it was at best an incomplete characterization of a far more complex and interesting leader.

The first biography of Truman quickly followed his ascension to the presidency. *This Man Truman* (New York: McGraw-Hill, 1945) by Frank McNaughton and Walter Hehmeyer is a short, eulogistic volume designed to promote Truman's virtues with the public. (McNaughton knew Truman well as Senate correspondent for *Time* magazine. Hehmeyer had handled press relations for the Truman committee and thus had been responsible for much of the work done in boosting Truman's reputation during his later years in the Senate.) Although the authors make no acknowledgments, the work was clearly assisted by the White House. The two men quote on numerous occasions from Truman's handwritten 1945 autobiography and appear to have had access to other personal documents. The book also rests on interviews with Truman and numerous other public officials and acquaintances. A rush job, it is thin and factually unreliable, not even conforming in every detail to Truman's own handwritten account. Three years later, the authors produced a follow-up volume, *Harry Truman: President* (New York: McGraw-Hill, 1948); it begins with Truman's assumption of office and follows through with an account of most of his first term.

William P. Helm, *Harry Truman: A Political Biography* (New York: Duell, Sloan & Pearce, 1947) is the work of the Washington correspondent for the *Kansas City Journal-Post* in the 1930s. Helm had known Truman very well before his rise to the presidency and describes him as "my warmest friend and best news source in the Senate." Nonetheless, Helm does not appear to have enjoyed the sort of assistance rendered to McNaughton and Hehmeyer. Mostly on the Senate years, the book is based largely on the author's personal contacts with Truman and on interviews with Victor Messall, Truman's administrative assistant during 1935–41. The tone of the book is one of almost unrelieved praise, although Messall is quoted as saying that Truman had drunk a bit too much on occasions in

HISTORY: "Where were you gentlemen when U.S. power and prestige sank from a high in 1945 to a low in 1952?"

blood, sweat, tears

HST   Acheson   Marshall

Time's Inquisition.

Clarence D. Batchelor, *New York Daily News* (1952). Copyright New York News Inc. Reprinted with permission.

covers the prepresidential period. If more anecdotal than analytical, *Man from Missouri* is solid journalistic biography.

The next full biography of note was Margaret Truman's *Harry S. Truman* (New York: Morrow, 1972). It was, as one expects of books written about fathers by daughters, an admiring work with no pretense at objectivity or academic analysis. As an account of the public events of Truman's life, it leaves much to be desired, but it is very valuable for its personal information and insights. Miss Truman's biography of her mother, *Bess W. Truman* (New York: Macmillan, 1986), delivers a candid and revealing account of the personal lives of her family.

A year after the publication of *Harry S. Truman*, Merle Miller published *Plain Speaking: An Oral Biography of Harry S. Truman* (New York: Berkeley Publishing, 1973). The book consists entirely of excerpts from interviews, done primarily with Truman but also with family, friends, and political associates. They took place in 1961 and 1962, when Miller was doing production work on a proposed documentary television series. Some historians have privately questioned the authenticity of some of Miller's quotations and doubted the existence of the audio tapes he claimed to have used. All the same, the book strikes one as an accurate representation of Harry Truman as he was at the age of seventy-seven. It would be dangerous, however, to read that characterization backward into Truman's earlier life.

The first truly scholarly biography, *Truman's Crises* (Westport, Conn.: Greenwood Press, 1980), was the work of Harold F. Gosnell, one of the most distinguished of American political scientists. Gosnell undertook the project as a career capstone; he was eighty-four the year the book was published. He worked available sources at the Truman Library energetically, but did so just before Truman's confidential correspondence as president (the President's Secretary's File; PSF) was opened for research. The result is a good account of Truman's life with emphasis on the presidency. Gosnell is at times suggestive (as in his remark that Truman possessed an "oral personality") but neither terribly rigorous nor systematic in his analytical framework. Moreover, the accessioning of the PSF and other valuable new material by the Truman Library gave *Truman's Crises* an appearance of instant obsolescence that it did not entirely deserve.

In the meantime, a series of writers had begun to concentrate on the presidential years to the exclusion of the rest of Truman's life. Strictly speaking, none of these works was a biography, but the best contained some biographical insights. The most notable have been Cabell Phillips, *The Truman Presidency* (New York: Macmillan, 1966); Robert J. Donovan, *Conflict and Crisis* (New York: W. W. Norton, 1977) and *Tumultuous Years* (New York: Norton, 1982); and Donald R. McCoy, *The Presidency of Harry S. Truman* (Lawrence: University Press of Kansas, 1984). Phillips and Donovan covered the Truman White House as reporters and write from considerable firsthand experience with their subject; McCoy, an eminent historian who has written biographies of Calvin Coolidge and Alfred Landon, knows the sources at the Truman Library as thoroughly as anyone and comments intelligently on the Truman personality.

Considering that Truman was nearly sixty-one when he became president, it is surprising that only one substantial book has been published on his prepresidential years, and that quite recently. Richard Lawrence Miller's *Truman: The Rise to Power* (New York: McGraw-Hill, 1986) is the work of a Kansas City free-lance writer who did prodigious research in local materials.

the 1930s. In general, the book is worth reading for Truman's Senate service.

The first real breakthrough in Truman biography came with the publication of *Man of Independence* (Philadelphia: J. B. Lippincott, 1950) by Jonathan Daniels. An eloquent writer and political friend of Truman, Daniels received the president's authorization for a biography as a consolation prize of sorts after Truman was unable to appoint him secretary of the navy (a post Daniels's father had held). A liberal-leaning North Carolinian with a sense of history, Daniels understood Truman and the collective experience that had produced him. He had considerable access to the president, his family, friends, and political associates. The book is largely based on interviews, the morgue files of the *Kansas City Star*, and a few published sources and public records. At times, its frankness is limited by the delicacy of Daniels's privileged position; nonetheless, it remains a probing and empathetic exploration of the man and his environment. The first two-thirds of the book are still a good starting point for examining Truman's prepresidential career.

Alfred Steinberg's *The Man from Missouri* (New York: G. P. Putnam's Sons, 1962) is a work very similar to Daniels's in method and conception, and is based on published sources and extensive interviews, including some time with Truman himself. If less insightful than *Man of Independence*, it is franker. Because of the time at which it was written, it is also more thorough, covering Truman's entire presidency and almost the entire active period of his later years. Slightly more than half the book

Perhaps because he is not a trained historian, Miller is not always as discriminating as he might be in his use of sources. Moreover, it is hard to discern a consistent interpretation of his subject, although the book possesses a clear tendency to debunk Truman. As the most complete account of Truman's first sixty-one years, *Rise to Power* should be consulted by all historians with an interest in its topic. Yet it suffers from numerous factual errors that require considerable caution in its use.

The latest full biographies of Truman are notable primarily for their brevity. Robert H. Ferrell, *Harry S. Truman and the Modern American Presidency* (Boston: Little, Brown, 1983), is a volume in the Library of American Biography series. Designed for use in college courses, it manages to compress Truman's life into less than two hundred pages but in the course of doing so yields little in the way of new information or interpretations. Roy Jenkins, *Truman* (New York: Harper & Row, 1986), is of interest mainly for the way in which its author, a shrewd and distinguished representative of the British political center, views an American counterpart of an earlier generation.

ALONZO L. HAMBY

See also Public Opinion Polling; Press, The

Black Americans

In the twentieth century Afro-Americans experienced major changes in their status. Several factors were at work in creating change: the escalation of black migration from the South to the North, the formation of self-help organizations such as the National Association for the Advancement of Colored People (NAACP) and the National Urban League, strong individual black and white leadership, two world wars which bolstered the confidence of black society, and sympathetic national administrations. Harry S. Truman's presidency proved most significant in its demands to secure and sustain policies that would end discrimination and guarantee for blacks the basic rights that America promised its citizens. Accordingly, the Truman administration must be credited with making an interest in civil rights a major priority for the nation. By stressing that he was "dead earnest" about ensuring for all American citizens the guarantees of the Constitution and the promise of a good life, President Truman personalized the fight for an end to discrimination. By virtue of the immense personal and symbolic influence of his office, he made it acceptable for large numbers of black and white citizens to act upon their commitment and push the nation to end discrimination based on race.

As is true of most changes, antecedents lead to gains in later periods. The maxim especially applies to Truman in relation to the Afro-American cause. Truman was in a position to consolidate advances made possible by President Franklin Roosevelt, who unintentionally had shown that racism was the most important factor blocking the industrial and economic development of the South and thereby hampering the advancement of the entire nation. In 1938 the National Emergency Council (NEC), a group established by Roosevelt to study economic conditions in the South, issued a report describing the economic stagnation of the region as the number-one problem facing the nation. Although the South was the poorest region in

the country, the NEC argued that its abundant natural resources gave it the potential to become the richest. Stagnation resulted not from lack of resources but from the region's racist institutions that prevented the utilization of all its human talent. White southerners generally agreed with NEC findings but steadfastly continued the practices of racial separation and discrimination.

To some degree, the economic aspects of Roosevelt's New Deal agencies were influenced by a desire to remedy the problems pointed up by the NEC report and by the principle of equality. If blacks failed to share equally in the relief and reform provided by the New Deal, it was not wholly because of the Roosevelt administration's policy. Rather it was due to the sustained prejudice and community-approved policies of discrimination by local and state authorities, whose fair administration of federal policy was essential to the New Deal's success. Despite southern obstinacy, blacks generally embraced the New Deal and sought ways to make national policy meet their needs. In fact, numerous black leaders became wholly convinced of Roosevelt's commitment to equality and justice for all. They joined in leading a massive shift in political allegiance of black support from the Republican party, "the party of Lincoln," to the Democratic party. Thus, they positioned themselves to wield increased political influence on national economic and human rights issues.

Like the New Deal, World War II also provided an opportunity for Afro-Americans to press forward in demanding an end to official discrimination. During the war, A. Philip Randolph and others loosely aligned in the march on Washington movement pressured President Roosevelt into signing Executive Order 8802, an order that outlawed discrimination in war-related industries and created the Fair Employment Practice Committee (FEPC) to guarantee compliance with the order. The president had forced civil rights leaders to compromise on some of their demands; yet despite his desire to appease conservative politicians, the president gave way on several issues, too. Clearly a war document intended to quiet domestic unrest, Executive Order 8802 marked the first time in the nation's history that the executive office admitted that racial discrimination existed and that its elimination was in the country's best interest. Although several prominent black leaders had criticized the Roosevelt administration for New Deal programs that discriminated against blacks, they applauded him in 1941 for issuing the order. Under the circumstances, Afro-Americans seemed justified in pushing the philosophy that the nation would progress only insofar as all elements of the society were permitted to participate and develop their talents. That ideology prevailed through the highly publicized Double V campaign in which black Americans fought simultaneously against Nazism abroad and racism at home, and that same ideology had advanced so that blacks entered the postwar period with renewed hope.

During the years between 1945 and 1953, President Truman enlarged the expectations World War II had engendered. Truman personally believed in the struggle for justice, and when Congress refused to aid him in his commitment, he used the executive branch to mandate change. Although his actions had an immediate direct impact on only a limited number, they added national prominence to efforts to end racial discrimination. Truman, with personal concern unlike that of his predecessors, made the civil rights struggle a centerpiece of his administration, a crucial point that raised even more the hopes and aspirations of blacks. The Truman period signaled the be-

STILL NO CLUES ON LYNCHERS OF 4 IN GEORGIA

"I see the F.B.I. cleared up another big postage stamp robbery."

By Bill Mauldin. Copyright 1946 by Bill Mauldin.

ginning of changes in attitudes that would result in civil rights gains during the administrations of Dwight D. Eisenhower, John F. Kennedy, and Lyndon B. Johnson.

Truman's support of civil rights becomes all the more important when viewed in the context of the cold war. He established a Committee on Civil Rights in December 1946, and one of the significant assessments that group made dealt with fears of communism in a time of Communist expansion. The committee reported that the reaction to communism had reached "a state of near-hysteria." Hard-line anti-Communists accused more and more Americans of being Communists and generated public opposition to numerous social and economic betterment activities by arguing that the efforts were Communist-inspired. Although conservatives leveled charges of communism against supporters of civil rights, Truman himself escaped the accusation. Aside from being president, itself a shield, he did so largely because several of his policies, notably his loyalty program, the Truman Doctrine, and the Marshall Plan, were clearly anti-Communist.

Upon creating the Civil Rights Committee, the president directed its members to research and report to him on legal safeguards for civil rights. In far too many instances local authorities refused to act while American citizens were killed, maimed, or intimidated. Truman asserted that if local officials failed to do their job, federal ones would not. The committee's report, *To Secure These Rights*, called for a rectification of the U.S. civil rights record. The committee recognized the occurrence of serious civil rights violations in every section of the nation, but emphasized that "much of it ha[d] to do with limitations on civil rights in our southern states."

After giving many examples and analyzing past injustices, the committee called for the end of segregation and a strengthening of equal opportunity for all Americans. It also recommended the establishment of a permanent civil rights commission, the enactment of a federal Fair Employment Practice Act, and passage of federal laws outlawing restrictive housing covenants, lynching, and state poll taxes and protecting suffrage and economic rights. Representing the boldest national administration to that point, Truman set up yet another group, a Commission on Higher Education, which reported in 1947 that "there will be no fundamental correction of the total condition [of Afro-Americans] until segregation legislation is repealed."

During this same period northern groups, such as the Union for Democratic Action, the forerunner of Americans for Democratic Action, worked to raise the consciousness of white Americans concerning the nation's minority populations. Even in the South, white-led liberal organizations, such as the Southern Conference Educational Fund and the Southern Regional Council, achieved wider support as they addressed the needs and concerns of black Americans.

Truman agreed with the committees' reports, but the conservative Congress refused to have any part of them. It was not until July 1948 that President Truman acted on one committee request calling for the government's own internal civil rights campaign. Since ongoing efforts had already begun to show integration as a realistic possibility in the armed services, Truman issued Executive Order 9981 that summer, officially integrating the armed forces. Thus he fulfilled another of A. Philip Randolph's demands made during the march on Washington movement in 1941 and regularly repeated in the years after. When the United States ended the Korean campaign in 1953, its armed forces, segregated during World War II, were almost completely integrated. Of revolutionary proportions in itself, the integrated armed forces set a precedent for future progress toward desegregation among civilians, particularly in education.

In addition to the successful integration of the armed forces, Truman used his executive authority on other occasions to circumvent conservative opposition. His Justice Department sided with the plaintiffs and prepared amici curiae briefs in Supreme Court cases such as the 1948 *Shelley* v. *Kraemer* decision that outlawed restrictive covenants designed to maintain residential segregation. The Truman years also saw three other important Supreme Court decisions: *Henderson* v. *Southern Railway*, *Sweatt* v. *Painter*, and *McLaurin* v. *Oklahoma State Regents for Higher Education*, which established in 1950 the legal framework for outlawing segregation.

Aware of the change in mood of black America after World War II, Truman astutely made it difficult for the northern urban black voters to deny him their support. In contrast to southern blacks, those in the North encountered few obstacles to the exercise of the right to vote. Now a large and growing group, they had been moving away from the Republican party to the Democratic party since 1932. Truman continued the trend Roosevelt had started by recognizing the importance of his black constituency.

The president also affirmed Roosevelt's appointments of President Mary McLeod Bethune of Bethune-Cookman College, President Mordecai W. Johnson of Howard University, and W. E. B. Du Bois and Walter White of the NAACP as delegates to the United Nations. Political scientist Ralph Bunche, a member of the State Department staff, became director of the UN Trusteeship Council and in 1950 became the first black American to win the Nobel Peace Prize for his service as UN mediator in the Palestine dispute. These precedents resulted in blacks becoming a regular part of the American UN delegation. Bunche's selection was all the more outstanding since he served as deputy secretary general of the United Nations until his death in 1971. Outside the United Nations, Truman, in 1946, promoted William H. Hastie, Roosevelt's 1937 choice for federal judge of the Virgin Islands, from that position to governor of the American territory. Three years later the president named Hastie to the Third United States Circuit Court of Appeals. On other occasions, Truman appointed at least a dozen other blacks to judicial posts.

Nationwide, by 1948 six black citizens were serving on city councils; thirty-three, including two senators, were in state legislatures; and two, William L. Dawson from Illinois and Adam Clayton Powell, Jr., from New York, had been elected to Congress. Although the payoff in terms of appointments and elected officials was disproportionately small, black citizens gained renewed hope and maintained their loyalty to the Democratic party.

In 1948, black voters proved that their loyalty was an important factor in American politics. At the Democratic National Convention, convention leaders, such as Mayor Hubert H. Humphrey of Minneapolis and gubernatorial candidate Adlai E. Stevenson of Illinois, pushed through a pro–civil rights, prolabor platform. The civil rights plank was too much for many southerners. Although they had supported Roosevelt's and Truman's internationalist foreign policy and interventionist economic policy, they would not tolerate federal interference in race relations. Disgruntled over Truman's and the party's stand on civil rights, conservative southern Democrats established the Dixiecrat party and selected Governor J. Strom Thurmond of South Carolina as their candidate for president. The Dixiecrat revolt strengthened black allegiance to the Democratic party, and black voters helped Truman win his surprising victory. That victory, despite the controversy created by the civil rights proposals, demonstrated the pivotal place of the black vote in national politics.

This in turn made it possible for civil rights organizations to become more outspoken on the issue of racial equality. They would capitalize on the prestige that the Democratic platform added to the struggle for racial justice and point to the president as a champion of their cause. The liberalism of the national administration improved the atmosphere in which civil rights organizations had to work. These groups recognized that the administration's commitment to social justice, on the one hand, augmented by its determination to establish the United States as the moral leader of the world, on the other, made it all the more difficult for racists to continue to support discrimination in contradiction to the ideals and promises of American democracy.

An economic assessment of the Truman years and their impact on Afro-Americans reveals that for a brief period black workers benefited from changing conditions. The economic boom, especially during World War II and the Korean War, supplied jobs for almost all black workers and improved their position in the American economy. In 1947, wages and salaries of black males averaged 54 percent of those of white males, but by 1951, the figure had climbed to 64 percent. Labor force participation also peaked for young black males. In 1953, 93 percent of black males in their early twenties were in the labor force, compared to 85.6 percent in 1948. The low unemployment rate of 5.4 percent for black Americans in 1947 and the all-time low rate of 4.1 percent in 1953, compared to 3.3 percent and 2.3 percent, respectively, for white Americans, also indicated the relative prosperity blacks enjoyed. In subsequent years black Americans' unemployment rates were always double those of whites and rarely fell below 7.5 percent. Furthermore, unemployment figures reflected only a small part of the plight of black workers. Usually, the black population in general has lived in economic depression, and constantly, white Americans have outstripped blacks economically.

If, in 1950, the Korean War ushered in economic gains for Afro-Americans, it also deflected the Truman administration's attention from civil rights issues and focused it on foreign policy for the remainder of Truman's term. Nonetheless, the Supreme Court would take the cue Harry Truman had given with his own commitment to civil rights, and black Americans successfully sustained attention to racial equality. In 1964 and 1965, after another vice president, Lyndon B. Johnson, had taken office as the result of his predecessor's death, the national mood was such that Congress willingly enacted most of Johnson's civil rights program even though it virtually paralleled the one proposed by Truman that an earlier Congress had refused to endorse.

William C. Berman, in *The Politics of Civil Rights in the Truman Administration* (Columbus: Ohio State University Press, 1970), charts Truman's move from a moderate Missouri senator to a liberal president on the issues of civil rights and the status of blacks within American society. Berman asserts that politics, not humanitarianism, moved Truman. Mary Frances Berry and John W. Blassingame, in *Long Memory: The Black Experience in America* (New York: Oxford University Press, 1982), trace the black experience from precolonial through twentieth-century developments. They are not optimistic about the immediate future of black Americans. Thomas Cripps, in "Movies, Race and World War II: *Tennessee Johnson* as an Anticipation of the Strategies of the Civil Rights Movement," *Prologue* 14 (Summer 1982): 49–67, shows that the national unity dictated by World War II brought about a watershed in American racial politics as blacks, liberals, and governmental agencies cooperated to produce propaganda urging integration in the interest of national security. Richard M. Dalfiume, *Desegregation of the U.S. Armed Forces: Fighting on Two Fronts, 1939–1953* (Columbia: University of Missouri Press, 1969), is a description of the dramatic changes in the military services owing to World War II and Truman's liberal stance; both increased militancy among Afro-Americans. William H. Harris, in *The Harder We Run: Black Workers since the Civil War* (New York: Oxford University Press, 1982), finds that although black workers reached their highest point in economic opportunities between 1947 and 1953, those gains deteriorated in later years. Peter J. Kellog, "Civil Rights Consciousness in the 1940s," *Historian* 42 (November 1979), recounts the sympathetic response of many white Americans to Truman's initiative on civil rights. Richard Kluger, *Simple Justice: The History of Brown v. Board of Education and Black America's Struggle for Equality* (New York: Knopf, 1975), details the Supreme Court cases that immediately preceded the *Brown* decision and traces the change in NAACP strategy as it ended attacks on unequal facilities and set out to dismantle desegregation. Harvard Sitkoff, in *A New Deal for Blacks: The Emergence of Civil Rights as a National Issue* vol. 1, *The Depression Decade* (New York: Oxford

University Press, 1978), outlines Roosevelt's problems in addressing Afro-American concerns but trying to appease conservative congressmen, especially southerners. A reluctant Roosevelt nevertheless provided new opportunities for blacks. *To Secure These Rights: The President's Committee on Civil Rights* (New York: Simon & Schuster, 1947) is the report from Truman's committee which provides details of his charge to the committee and the recommendations it issued.

WILLIAM H. HARRIS AND LINDA REED

See also Armed Forces, Racial Integration of the; Civil Rights; Civil Rights, President's Commission on; Dixiecrats; Fair Employment Practices Committee; Hastie, William Henry; National Association for the Advancement of Colored People

---

Blockade, Berlin

See Berlin Airlift

Bowles, Chester Bliss

(5 April 1901–25 May 1986)
Administrator of the Office of Price Administration, 1943–46; director of the Office of Economic Stabilization, 1946; governor of Connecticut, 1949–51; ambassador to India, 1951–53, 1963–69). Born and raised in Springfield, Massachusetts, and educated at Choate School and Yale, the tall, robust, gregarious Chester Bowles was cofounder of the Benton and Bowles advertising agency and a multimillionaire by the time he was forty. During World War II, he left private business and began a long career of public service by catapulting through a series of offices from head of Connecticut's tire rationing program in December 1941 to administrator of the federal Office of Price Administration (OPA) by October 1943.

Although Bowles enjoyed good wartime relations with Senator Harry Truman, whose understanding cooperation he appreciated, his relations with President Truman were more complicated. As with other highly visible, adamantly liberal, holdover New Dealers in his administration, Truman was somewhat uncomfortable with Bowles and ambivalent about him. Calling the voluble, public relations–minded Bowles a "grand guy," Truman nonetheless complained that "he makes me mad as the devil at times. He has a headline in every Monday morning paper, and I think that he makes entirely too many speeches." Bowles, moreover, an often outspoken man with political ambition and "a feeling for the people's side," aggressively headed an agency that gave Truman great policy and political difficulties in 1945 and 1946, when much of the support for the OPA and its programs evaporated. Although Truman supported extending the Price Control Act, Bowles felt himself a lone wolf in the administration for his insistent public espousal of holding the line on prices. When he angrily resigned in February 1946 after the president and John Snyder (chief of the Office of War Mobilization and Reconversion) approved a steel price hike, Truman, conscious of Bowles's prestige among liberals and many consumers, named him director of the Office of Economic Stabilization. But when Congress in late June 1946 passed a weak extension of price controls, Bowles resigned again, and Truman, who vetoed the bill, accepted the resignation.

In early 1947 Bowles helped found the Americans for Democratic Action (ADA). Believing like others in the ADA that Truman was too conservative and a liability for the Democratic party, he joined the effort to deny him the nomination in 1948. But Bowles was reassured as to Truman's combativeness and liberalism at the national convention, and when Truman campaigned in Connecticut that autumn he greeted Bowles, who narrowly carried the state's gubernatorial race, warmly and without apparent resentment. After Bowles was defeated for reelection in 1950, Truman appointed him ambassador to India in 1951, a post that appealed to his long-standing interest in foreign service and his advocacy of economic and technical assistance abroad.

Subsequently Bowles was elected to Congress in 1958, served as under secretary of state in 1961 and then as President Kennedy's special representative for Asian, African, and Latin American affairs, and concluded his public service as ambassador to India again from 1963 to 1969.

No adequate biography exists for Bowles, but his autobiography, *Promises to Keep: My Years in Public Life, 1941–1969* (New York: Harper & Row, 1971), is useful and engaging.

JOHN W. JEFFRIES

See also Americans for Democratic Action; Fiscal and Monetary Policies; Office of Price Administration

---

Bradley, Omar Nelson

(12 February 1893–8 April 1981)
General of the army; administrator of the Veterans Administration; chief of staff of the army; chairman of the Joint Chiefs of Staff. Omar Bradley was born in Clark, Missouri, of a family he characterized as "farmers, proud, honest, hardworking and . . . desperately poor." Commissioned in the class of 1915 at West Point, Bradley felt frustrated over not serving overseas in World War I. Instead he spent thirteen of his first twenty-three commissioned years as an instructor.

After war erupted in Europe in 1939, he worked closely with Chief of Staff Gen. George C. Marshall during the buildup of American forces and was promoted to brigadier general in 1941, the first of his class to attain that rank. His initial combat experience came in 1943 under his classmate Gen. Dwight D. Eisenhower. Bradley commanded the Second American Army Corps in North Africa and Sicily and then led the First Army in the invasion of Europe in June 1944. Later as commander of the Twelfth Army Group, he participated in the Battle of the Bulge, and he and his troops were the first Allied forces to reach the Elbe. By March 1945 Bradley with four-star rank commanded 1.3 million troops, the largest group force ever led by an American general. Eisenhower praised him as the "best-rounded combat leader I have yet met in our service."

Bradley was "devastated" when asked by General Marshall on behalf of President Truman, ten days after the German surrender, to take over the Veterans Administration (VA). Truman called it the "biggest job we had," but it appeared at the time to Bradley as "inconsequential" and "demeaning." Nevertheless he accepted the job after talks with Truman, who Bradley said was "direct, unpretentious, clear-thinking, and forceful." Bradley witnessed an increase in the veteran population from 5 million to 17 million during his first eight months in office. In the course of his tenure he administered the G.I. bill, decentralized the agency, established a VA medical corps, and concentrated on hospital construction and medical school affiliation programs, which, according to one source, created a "revolution" in VA medicine. Truman kept his promise to Bradley that the agency would not be politicized.

When Eisenhower retired as chief of staff of the army in February 1948, Truman, as he had promised earlier, appointed Bradley to succeed Ike. His years in "the only job I wanted" reflected the tensions of the cold war. Three weeks after the general was sworn in, the Soviet Union took over Czechoslovakia. As chief of staff Bradley had to balance Truman's policy of containment with the weakness of the army, which he said had "almost no combat effectiveness" and only one ready division. The general later thought that his decision to support Truman's reduction of the military budget was "perhaps the greatest mistake I made in my postwar years in Washington." He also

Omar N. Bradley, July 1945. (U.S. Army/National Archives)

supported Truman's policy when the United States removed its troops from Korea following the free elections in the South in 1948. When the Russians blockaded Berlin in June of that year, Bradley counseled caution lest war result and concluded, following the successful airlift, that "we were very, very lucky."

Bradley, however, disagreed with the president's 1948 decision to desegregate the armed forces and said so publicly. He later conceded that he had done his "utmost to discourage" what he perceived to be instant integration of the army. But a letter of explanation to the president about newspaper accounts of his public statements appears to have mollified Truman.

When the United States joined the North Atlantic Treaty Organization (NATO) in April 1949, it affirmed Truman's and Bradley's view that the greatest threat to American security lay in the Soviet Union and Europe rather than that of Gen. Douglas MacArthur and others that America's first line of defense was in the Far East. Arming and equipping NATO became Bradley's major concern during the remainder of his service to Truman.

When appointed in August 1949 by Truman to become the first permanent chairman of the Joint Chiefs of Staff, Bradley was immediately faced with congressional hearings regarding the "revolt of the admirals" over air power expenditures. Normally placid, Bradley found their actions "disgraceful" and in testimony before Congress lashed out at navy supporters for their attacks on the air force B–36 bomber. Although no admirer of the air force, Bradley supported Truman on the emerging "massive retaliation" policy. When informed that Russia had exploded an atomic device in September 1949, he led the Joint Chiefs in urging that the president authorize a program to develop a hydrogen bomb. He was an "active lobbyist" for the new weapon until Truman set the program in motion.

The defeat of the Chinese Nationalist forces and their exile to Formosa in September 1949 came as no surprise to Bradley. He viewed the event as unfortunate but had been unable to convince Truman that military aid to Chiang Kai-shek should be continued at the time.

The day after Bradley returned from a visit to the Far East in June 1950, North Korean forces invaded South Korea. Bradley agreed with Truman that the aggression had to be met by American forces. From then until the close of the Truman administration, Bradley was in daily contact with the president who relied heavily on the advice of the chairman and the Joint Chiefs.

When the war went badly, MacArthur proposed a landing behind enemy lines at Inchon to relieve pressure on his retreating armies. Although this proposal was received coolly by Bradley and the Joint Chiefs, Truman personally approved the landing site. The results of this brilliant action increased MacArthur's already considerable confidence in his own abilities, and from then on he scarcely concealed his contempt for the opinions of the military leadership in Washington.

In dealing with MacArthur on issues of strategy, tactics, and the political implications of his actions in Korea, the Joint Chiefs did not fare well. Secretary of State Dean Acheson's comment that the military in Washington held an "uneasy respect for the MacArthur mystique" is probably not wide of the mark. Among their problems in dealing with MacArthur was the fact that Bradley and the Joint Chiefs leadership, all of whom had been combat commanders in World War II, believed that, rather than a war's being solely directed from the Pentagon, considerable operational latitude should be given to the local commander on the scene. On the other hand, the senior military leaders as well as Truman and Acheson perceived that many of MacArthur's proposals involved strategic and political ramifications that could lead to a third world war. MacArthur's ability to capitalize on his immense popularity in the United States as well as his willingness to exploit the press and appeal to Truman's political opponents complicated an already difficult situation. Truman's promotion of Bradley to five-star rank in September 1950 was not only recognition of his ability and achievements but also a clear message to MacArthur of the president's esteem for the chairman of the Joint Chiefs.

MacArthur's public criticism of Truman's policies, his disregard of written instructions governing release of uncleared information to the press, and his refusal to face the political implications of his actions finally forced Truman, with the concurrence of Bradley and the Joint Chiefs, to relieve MacArthur of his command in April 1951. In the ensuing congressional hearings, Bradley offered his oft-quoted assessment that widening the war to the mainland of Asia would have been the "wrong war, at the wrong place, at the wrong time, and with the wrong enemy." Bradley and the Joint Chiefs recommended to Truman the negotiated settlement that finally concluded the war.

Bradley later recalled finding "little to admire" in the election campaign of 1952 when both candidates, Eisenhower and Stevenson, appeared to run against Truman's "mess" in Washington. But a month after the election Bradley accompanied President-elect Eisenhower on the trip to Korea he had promised to make during the campaign. On this journey Bradley urged Eisenhower not to change the chairman and service chiefs in order to keep these military positions from politicization. Eisenhower followed Bradley's suggestion and normal attrition took place. The death of Stalin in March 1953 was followed by serious negotiations in Korea with the Communists and an armistice was signed in July, just as Bradley's four-year tenure as chairman of the Joint Chiefs was ending. He retired the next month after more than forty-two years in the service and became a corporate executive. He died in 1981 at the age of eighty-eight.

Although Bradley in retrospect was critical of his own and the Joint Chiefs' caution during the Korean War, Truman never voiced any significant criticism of Bradley, his actions, or his counsel. Their relationship was forged of mutual respect: Truman relied heavily on Bradley's professionalism and judgment in military matters, and Bradley had great admiration for Truman. The general always deferred to civilian control of the nation's armed forces.

There are two book-length accounts of Bradley. The first is his own *A Soldier's Story* (New York: Henry Holt, 1951) which he wrote while chairman of the Joint Chiefs. Covering the period from 1943 to the surrender of the Germans in May 1945, it is almost exclusively limited to "how war is waged on the field from the field command post." The second is *A General's Life: An Autobiography* by Bradley and Clay Blair (New York: Simon & Schuster, 1983). In this account of his entire career, Bradley and his collaborator are usually candid, particularly about the caution exhibited by the general and the Joint Chiefs in the Korean War.

JOHN W. HUSTON

See also Joint Chiefs of Staff; Veterans; World War II

Brannan, Charles Franklin

(23 August 1903–)

Secretary of agriculture, 1948–53. Charles F. Brannan was born and raised in Denver, Colorado, the son of Quakers Ella and John Brannan, the latter an electrical engineer. Charles attended the University of Denver, received a law degree in 1929, and practiced law in Denver from 1929 to 1935, specializing in irrigation and mining. A strong supporter of the New Deal, he began his career in government service in 1935 as assistant regional attorney for the Resettlement Administration and became regional attorney in the Office of Solicitor of the Department of Agriculture in 1937. Four years later he was promoted to the position of regional director of the Farm Security Administration (FSA) for the states of Colorado, Montana, and Wyoming and in 1944 became assistant administrator of the FSA, a position based in Washington, D.C. Later that year, President Roosevelt appointed Brannan assistant secretary of agriculture, and in 1946, Secretary of Agriculture Clinton P. Anderson placed Brannan in charge of long-range agricultural planning.

When Secretary Anderson resigned in May 1948 to campaign for the Senate, he recommended Brannan as his successor. This move was fully supported by James Patton, president of the liberal National Farmers Union and Brannan's close friend. Other groups such as the rival American Farm Bureau Federation proposed candidates of their own. Truman, however, decided upon Brannan, whose appointment was confirmed by the Senate on 28 May 1948.

Brannan played an instrumental role in the presidential campaign later that fall. Republicans blamed the Truman administration for farm problems and the Truman campaign had all but conceded the farm vote to Dewey. But beginning in September Brannan forcefully argued that the fault really lay with the Republican-controlled Congress and that the Republicans opposed price supports. He delivered over eighty speeches to help Truman win the farm vote.

Because of his public visibility during the campaign and the key part he played in securing Truman's election, Brannan became one of Truman's most trusted advisers and an architect of the Fair Deal. His main contribution was a proposal for a new farm program, known as the Brannan Plan, which contained several innovative provisions.

The plan's objective was to guarantee farmers a high income without production controls while ensuring consumers a low-cost but nutritious diet. To achieve this goal producers were to be encouraged to grow fewer grain crops and raise more livestock. This would lessen bothersome surpluses of grains and lower prices of meat and dairy products. The plan contained four innovative farm policy recommendations. First, the 1909–14 parity base would be replaced by a ten-year moving average of farm income as the standard for calculating support prices. Thus, the high farm incomes of the prosperous World War II period would be continued. Second, producers of perishable commodities like meat and milk would receive direct government payments to support their incomes. This would enable consumers to pay low prices for perishable goods. The policy of high fixed price supports for other commodities would remain unchanged. Third, the list of commodities eligible for price supports would be revised to include animal products. And fourth, a ceiling would be established on the payment a farmer could receive from the federal government. This limit was based on the production level of a family-sized farm, which was estimated to be about $26,100 in 1949.

The Brannan Plan received endorsements from the liberal National Farmers Union and the Congress of Industrial Organizations, but criticism and objections were more widespread. Objections centered on the plan's potential high cost, the "socialistic tendencies" of direct government payments, the limits on benefits, and the potential threat to Republicans if the plan succeeded in forging a Democratic alliance between farmers and urban workers. For these reasons Republicans, southern Democrats, the American Farm Bureau Federation, the National Grange, the U.S. Chamber of Commerce, and countless other groups, including most of the rural press, opposed the plan. Brannan was thrust into the center of national attention as he tried to defend his proposals in the presence of such a fierce storm of criticism. In July 1949 Congress soundly rejected the plan, and the administration had to settle for legislation that postponed the imposition of flexible price supports.

During the Korean War, Brannan's influence in the Truman administration lessened. It seemed to the secretary that agricultural policy was taken out of his hands and placed under the control of others in the name of checking inflation. Truman ignored suggestions from Brannan because there were more important issues at hand.

Brannan sought to improve his standing in the administration in 1951 through an extensive nationwide review of the impacts of farm policy on family farms. Because of his lifelong commitment to such farms, he wished to make policy more responsive to their needs. This effort, however, was thwarted by the American Farm Bureau Administration, which charged that Communists had instigated the review.

Brannan once again vigorously campaigned in 1952. He toured fourteen farm states in a sixty-day period but was unable to contribute to a Democratic victory as he had in 1948; the midwestern and western states were won by Eisenhower. Since leaving the Department of Agriculture in January 1953, Brannan has practiced law in Denver and served as general counsel of the National Farmers Union. Even though the Brannan Plan was never accepted, a structure similar to the plan's production payments and income standard was finally implemented in 1973.

The most authoritative analysis of farm policy in the Truman administration remains Allen J. Matusow's *Farm Policies and Politics in the Truman Years* (Cambridge: Harvard University Press, 1967). Reo M. Christenson provides the most thorough discussion of the Brannan Plan episode in *The Brannan Plan: Farm Politics and Policy* (Ann Arbor: University of Michigan Press, 1959). Willard W. Cochrane and Mary E. Ryan place the policies of Brannan within a larger context of postwar farm policy in *American Farm Policy, 1948–1973* (Minneapolis: University of Minnesota Press, 1976).

JOEL KUNZE

See also Agriculture; Cabinets (photograph)

Brannan Plan

See Brannan, Charles Franklin

Bretton Woods System

The goal of American policymakers at Bretton Woods was to create a free-trade system immune from the dangers of economic isolationism and protectionism. The July 1944 agreements establishing the International Monetary Fund (IMF) and the World Bank (International Bank for Reconstruction and Development, or IBRD) marked the first major attempt by Washington to restructure the world economy. Although they did not fulfill all their creators' objectives, the Bank and IMF symbolized the U.S. commitment to a world order based upon expanded trade and currency convertibility.

Postwar American leaders believed that the neomercantilism of the 1930s had helped cause World War II. Free traders of the day—not least Senator Harry S. Truman—often quipped, "If goods can't cross borders, soldiers will." In their view, free trade and stable currencies almost by themselves could guarantee world peace.

The new monetary and trade system was meant to be politically neutral. The architects of Bretton Woods—Roosevelt's Treasury Secretary Henry Morgenthau and his chief assistant, Henry Dexter White—sought to discourage autarkic trading practices of all types, whether in the British Commonwealth, Japan's sphere in East Asia, or Stalin's Russia. Yet they specifically designed the system to include the Soviet Union and other "state-trading," socialist countries. In the end, Great Power differences over Eastern Europe, not substantive economic objections, led Stalin to veto the participation of the Soviet Union and the occupied East European countries in Bretton Woods.

Washington also accepted special measures to ease the transition of its hard-pressed allies to a freer trading regime. The "scarce currency" clause of the IMF agreement permitted a country with chronic payments difficulties (such as Great Britain) either to restrict its payments to a surplus country (such as the United States) or to devalue its currency until its trade balance approached equilibrium. This gave the British a breathing spell before they were required to make the pound sterling freely convertible with the dollar.

American leaders, including President Truman, at first put too much trust in Bretton Woods as an antidote to the world's economic ills, hoping that the IMF and Bank could quickly restore balanced patterns of trade and investment without Washington's direct intervention. With Europe teetering on the brink of economic collapse, the administration shifted gears. Beginning in 1946, the World Bank—which Washington controlled as the largest subscriber—served as a conduit for U.S. aid to France, Italy, Greece, and other countries. Although Poland and other Eastern bloc countries received some IBRD assistance, the Truman White House generally used Bank aid before the Marshall Plan to prop up Western countries faced with insolvency or potential Communist takeovers.

Meanwhile, the Bank never lived up to the "development" aim in its title. Third world countries rightfully complained that Washington put a priority on rebuilding Europe and Japan. The World Bank became a instrument of U.S. containment policy, rather than the neutral agent that its founders had anticipated.

If the Bank did not live up to every expectation, the IMF never got off the ground. The severe dollar shortage of the late 1940s and early 1950s meant that the major European countries did not restore currency convertibility until the late fifties. Nonetheless, the IMF established the principle that parties to the new institution should not use currency devaluations to win unfair trading advantages against their rivals, as so many countries had done between the wars.

For all its limitations, Bretton Woods was a resounding success. It committed the United States to restoring world equilibrium through a massive aid program, in sharp contrast to its policy after the First World War. Bretton Woods restrained the major industrial countries from using tariffs and other trade barriers as a weapon against each other in hard times. Currency stability, in the form of a firm dollar-gold ratio, was also reestablished. As part of President Truman's free-trade program, Bretton Woods contributed mightily to the expansion of world trade and prosperity after the war.

On wartime planning, see Richard N. Gardner, *Sterling-Dollar Diplomacy: The Origins and Prospects of Our International Economic Order*, rev. ed. (New York: McGraw-Hill, 1969). On cold war politics, see Robert A. Pollard, *Economic Security and the Origins of the Cold War, 1945–1950* (New York: Columbia University Press, 1985). On operations of the Bank and IMF, see Alfred E. Eckes, Jr., *A Search for Solvency: Bretton Woods and the International Monetary System, 1944–71* (Austin: University of Texas Press, 1979), and Edward S. Mason and Robert E. Asher, *The World Bank since Bretton Woods* (Washington, D.C.: Brookings Institution, 1973).

ROBERT A. POLLARD

See also International Trade; Reciprocal Trade Agreements

Budget, Bureau of the

On 12 April 1945 President Franklin D. Roosevelt died from a massive cerebral hemorrhage while vacationing in Warm Springs, Georgia. The following day Director Harold Smith of the Bureau of the Budget (BOB) wrote President Harry Truman pledging "my support in any way in which you may wish me to serve." Smith added that "few men have been in a better position than I to appreciate the heavy responsibilities and onerous burdens of the Presidency." In a memorandum to the bureau's staff, Smith observed that Roosevelt's reliance on the bureau and "our close appreciation of him makes our sorrow the deeper with his passing." But he reminded his staff that the BOB served the institution of the presidency as well as the president. "The tasks that were dropped remain to be completed. . . . We must now turn the best of our abilities and our energies to performing the tasks required of us by our new President."

President Truman used the Budget Bureau as his personal and institutional staff arm in managing the federal government, viewing the BOB as the key component in an institutional presidency. On 25 July 1946 James Webb was selected by President Truman as the new director of the Bureau of the Budget. At the time Webb was serving as the executive assistant to the under secretary of the Treasury Department and was recommended for the BOB job by Secretary of the Treasury John Snyder. Many Washington observers viewed Webb's selection as subordinating the bureau to Treasury's control. It was generally assumed that the Office of War Mobilization and Reconversion (OWMR), not BOB, would emerge as the president's central staff agency. Whereas OWMR's predecessor, the Office of War Mobilization, had focused almost exclusively on high-priority policy matters, OWMR ventured into the BOB's responsibilities for administrative coordination and legislative clearance.

Webb, it turned out, was an exceptionally imaginative and entrepreneurial bureaucrat whose success rested on his managerial capabilities. He decided that the bureau's institutional staff could help the president by dealing directly with Truman rather than through intermediaries. The White House staff was relatively small and totally dependent upon what the president passed to them rather than being in the mainstream of the relevant documents; as BOB director, Webb was in this flow. The White House soon turned to the bureau for help in its projects and, most significant, borrowed people from the BOB for ad hoc assignments. Webb made the bureau staff available to the White House staff and volunteered to take some of the difficult problems the president faced back to the bureau for analysis. These problems included drafting legislation for labor unions, the Employment Act of 1946, national health insurance, the Fair Employment Practices Committee, unification of the armed services, the National Defense Act, and the harnessing of atomic energy for peaceful purposes.

The most important institutional change of the period concerned the bureau's traditional legislative clearance role. Prior to 1948, legislative clearance had been fundamentally negative in character. But now teams from the BOB and the White House worked long hours to formulate the Housing Act of 1949 and the Social Security Act Amendments of 1950.

By establishing the bureau's Office of Legislative Reference as an extension of the White House, Webb proved that an institutional watchdog was needed. When the White House staff was preparing the president's 1947 State of the Union message, to be delivered at the opening session of the Eightieth Congress, Special Counsel Clark Clifford requested that a BOB group provide him with a draft of their ideas on possible labor legislation. Clifford also requested that the group keep track of the Taft-Hartley legislation, and they later assisted Clifford in drafting the veto message after the bill had been enacted. Webb developed the policy of helping those people on whom President Truman relied most directly, and by 1950 several BOB staffers had crossed the street from the Executive Office Building to work in the White House. He also bridged the gap between the BOB and the White House in the program development area.

Under Webb's directorship as well as those of his successors, Frank Pace, Jr., and Fred Lawton, the bureau's role in congressional relations was vastly expanded. In 1947, through a process of direct referrals, Republican congressional chairmen could inquire what the Democrats' intentions were regarding pending legislation. The opening of channels with the Eightieth

Congress allowed congressional committees to request from the BOB its "views on pending bills, at the same time that requests for views were sent to the agencies." President Truman appointed Roger Jones, a Republican, to serve as liaison with the Eightieth Congress. Jones noted that "President Truman wanted an institutional relationship with an opposition Congress. He wanted them to know what his programs were, how he wanted to go about doing it. We were expositors, explanatory people. We were not peddlers of doctrine."

In summary, the Bureau of the Budget as a general presidential staff thrived during Truman's tenure. The BOB's work load increased in direct proportion to the federal government's growing involvement in the initiation of domestic and foreign policies. This presidential activism created a need for an institutional general staff responsive to the president—a need the Bureau of the Budget helped fill.

For a history of the BOB, see Larry Berman, *The Office of Management and Budget and the Presidency, 1921–1979* (Princeton: Princeton University Press, 1979). For relevant developments during the Truman presidency, see Richard Neustadt, "Presidency and Legislation: Planning the President's Program," *American Political Science Review* 57 (December 1963): 855–64, and Neustadt, "Presidency and Legislation: The Growth of Central Clearance," *American Political Science Review* 49 (December 1954): 980–1021.

LARRY BERMAN

Burton, Harold Hitz

(22 June 1888–28 October 1964)

Supreme Court justice appointed by Truman in 1945. Harold Burton was sworn in as the Republican freshman senator from Ohio in 1941 and quickly developed a reputation as a middle-of-the-road conservative. With the help of his old college roommate, Owen Brewster (R.-Me.), he was appointed on 16 March 1942 to Truman's Special Committee to Investigate the National Defense Program. Through his work on this significant assignment, Burton became one of Truman's trusted cronies, which, in 1945, contributed to the new president's decision to appoint him to the U.S. Supreme Court when Owen J. Roberts retired. Burton's qualifications for the high post were uncontested, but party politics did play a prominent role in Truman's decision. By appointing a Republican, Truman could keep the Senate Democratic; also, all of Roosevelt's appointments had been Democrats, so choosing a Republican candidate was a logical and timely decision. On 17 September 1945, Burton was confirmed by a voice vote as an associate justice of the Supreme Court.

Burton described the transition from the Senate to the Court as "like going from a circus to a monastery." As justice, he consciously attempted to decide questions before the Court on established legal principles alone, but his voting record and opinions exhibit an awareness of politics. His first major case amply illustrates this point. In the Hawaii martial law cases *Duncan v. Kahanamoku*, 327 U.S. 304 (1946), Burton signed on to Felix Frankfurter's dissent and sent it to his old friend.

Truman, thanking him for the opinions, commented, "I think your approach to the situation is much more in line with what is necessary than is the majority opinion, although I am no lawyer, as you know."

During his first term, Burton was the lone dissenter in *Morgan* v. *Virginia*, 328 U.S. 373 (1945), which declared that racial segregation was an unconstitutional burden on interstate commerce. He thereafter reversed field in his opinion for a unanimous Court that the Interstate Commerce Act forbade discrimination in public transportation in *Henderson* v. *U.S.*, 339 U.S 816 (1950). He also joined in the unanimous decision of the Court when it declared school segregation illegal in *Brown* v. *Board of Education*, 344 U.S. 294 (1954). Burton, however, often voted with the anti–civil libertarians. In *American Communication Association* v. *Douds*, 339 U.S. 382 (1949), he, along with newly appointed justices Minton and Clark, concurred in the majority opinion that struck down the "clear and present danger standard" for the First Amendment freedoms.

The widely publicized steel seizure case, *Youngstown Sheet and Tube Co.* v. *Sawyer*, 343 U.S. 579 (1951), brought the issue of presidential powers squarely before the Court. Burton voted eventually with the majority to condemn the president's exercise of powers. Burton questioned whether Truman was correct to act under the authority of the War Production Act instead of the Taft-Hartley Act. Ignoring his political friendship with Truman and turning to established legal principles, Burton in his concurring opinion decided that "the President was without power to seize the steel plants" because Taft-Hartley provided a different procedure.

After the Truman presidency, Burton acted increasingly as the Court's swing vote, gaining respect for his dispassionate manner, his attention to detail, his minimizing of political considerations, and his ability to conciliate conflicting views among his colleagues.

A biographical piece on Burton by Richard S. Kirkendall appears in Leon Friedman and Fred L. Israel, *The Justices of the Supreme Court, 1789–1969: Their Lives and Major Opinions* (New York: Bowker, 1969). See also David N. Atkinson, "Justice Harold H. Burton and the Work of the Supreme Court," *Cleveland Law Review* 27 (1978): 69–83, and "American Constitutionalism under Stress: Mr. Justice Burton's Response to National Security Issues," *Houston Law Review* 9 (November 1971): 271–88. The only book-length biography on Burton is Mary Frances Berry, *Stability, Security, and Continuity: Mr. Justice Burton and Decision-Making in the Supreme Court, 1945–1958* (Westport, Conn.: Greenwood Press, 1978).

MARY FRANCES BERRY

See also Supreme Court, United States

Business-Government Relations

Business-government relations during the Truman administration are best characterized as troubled yet moving toward workable accommodations and in some areas toward collaboration and partnership. On such issues as taxation, economic management, social policy, and labor relations, most business-persons supported the administration's political opponents. But in such areas as developmental activity, antitrust action, and foreign economic policy, sizable elements of the business community could be mobilized in support of administration programs; and in both business and government there were those who envisioned postwar counterparts for the collaborative arrangements of the war period. Furthering these cooperationist initiatives, moreover, were changing business attitudes about government's proper role in a modern economy, changing liberal attitudes about the capacity of corporate power to serve democratic ends, and changing ideas about what was politically possible. Increasingly, activists tended to embrace a pragmatic centrism willing to accept and work within existing structures of power.

The conflictual aspects of these relationships were most evident in battles over reconversion controls and domestic reform. Organized business, speaking through the U.S. Chamber of Commerce, the National Association of Manufacturers, and a variety of trade and industrial associations, was an opponent of continued price controls, especially as administered by the Office of Price Administration. It was also an opponent of Truman's program for improving the welfare system and a supporter of the conservative initiatives producing such measures as the Taft-Hartley Labor Relations Act of 1947 and the Internal Revenue Act of 1948. In business rhetoric, Truman was seeking power for antibusiness bureaucrats, who would end up destroying the very basis of further national progress. And in response, especially in his campaign for reelection in 1948, Truman adopted a neopopulist rhetoric in which corporate power and high finance appeared as unregenerate enemies of a virtuous people.

Adversarial relations were also characteristic of some areas of regulatory activity and especially of that forged by a revival of antitrust litigation. Under Wendell Berge, the Antitrust Division of the Department of Justice attempted, with some success, to fashion a "new Sherman Act" that could be used against the inherent market power of oligopolistic industries. In addition, the government's antitrust lawyers successfully attacked the practice of basing-point pricing in cement and the use of rate-fixing associations by the railroads. And working with antitrusters and small-business champions in Congress, they secured an amendment to the Clayton Act that could be used to prevent anticompetitive mergers. Antimonopoly rhetoric, moreover, helped justify a continuation of special aid to small business; and in a few industries, aluminum being the most publicized case, the disposal of government-built war plants became a means for making market structures more competitive. To some businessmen it seemed that the legal shields against reckless structural reformers and neopopulist politicians were in the process of being removed, and by 1950 some were calling for a new "rule of reason" that would stress market performance rather than structural analysis.

These antitrust activities, however, also produced business-government alliances as well as conflicts. Efforts were made to construct a supporting cast of small business groups, and railroad regulators helped their industry secure special legislation overturning the decision on rate-fixing associations. For numerous officials, moreover, the need to accommodate antitrust principles coexisted with a search for ways to preserve the efficiency and effectiveness of wartime arrangements. There had to be, it was said, a "middle ground," and from the search for one came two kinds of institutional arrangements, both of which the Justice Department found worrisome. One consisted of business councils advisory to relevant parts of the government and attempting in varying degrees to coordinate the use of public and private power. The other consisted of jobs within government that were more or less reserved for businessmen formally or informally on leave from the private sector. With both arrangements Truman seemed comfortable, and both survived periodic charges that government was thus being captured or hamstrung for business purposes.

Such arrangements were particularly noticeable and at times unusually vigorous in the relationships established by the mineral divisions of the Interior Department, the economic branches of the State Department, the trade and efficiency promotion bureaus of the Commerce Department, the procurement agencies of the armed forces, and the foreign aid instrumentalities of the Economic Cooperation Administration. They were noticeable as well in the survival of the Commerce Department's Business Advisory Council and the collaboration of various agencies with big business's Committee for Economic Development, in the elaborate advisory structures used by the National Security Resources Board and the Council of Economic Advisers, and in an industrial cooperation program established under an antiinflation measure passed in late 1947. Movement, moreover, seemed to be in the direction of making them stronger rather than weaker. The year 1949 brought an antirecession program in which properly educated businesspersons were to function as "partners" and act in concert to increase investment spending. It also brought a Committee on Business and Government Relations seeking to develop "cooperative" as opposed to "compulsive" methods of regulation. And with the advent of the Korean War in 1950 came a resurrection, under the auspices of new mobilization agencies, of the structures and practices utilized during World War II.

In 1952 Truman's seizure of the steel industry again alienated most of the business community. But clearly, the collaborative arrangements that became a distinguishing feature of the Eisenhower administration had their roots in the Truman period. By 1950 the antibusiness side of New Dealism—the side that made room for neopopulist formulations, maturity and redistributive concepts, and equations of business-government partnership with fascism—was fading fast; and, as one commentator put it, government and business seemed prepared to "go steady."

A comprehensive history of business-government relations during the Truman era has yet to be written. The most helpful accounts are in the relevant portions of Robert M. Collins, *The Business Response to Keynes* (New York: Columbia University Press, 1981); Crauford Goodwin, ed., *Energy Policy in Perspective* (Washington, D.C.: Brookings Institution, 1981), and *Exhortation and Control* (Washington, D.C.: Brookings Institution, 1975); Kim McQuaid, *Big Business and Presidential Power* (New York: Morrow, 1982); and Richard S. Kirkendall, ed., *The Truman Period as a Research Field* (Columbia: University of Missouri Press, 1967).

ELLIS W. HAWLEY

See also Committee for Economic Development; Economy, The; National Labor Relations Board; Taft-Hartley Act

Business Ventures

During his early years, Harry S. Truman engaged in a number of business ventures, all of them unsuccessful. The failures were due not so much to Truman's mismanagement as to bad luck, inopportune timing, or an unfortunate choice of business associates.

In his first venture, in March 1916, Truman leased and operated for several months a lead and zinc mine in Commerce, Oklahoma, with two of his friends, Tom Hughes and Jerry Culbertson. This was a year when many people expected zinc prices to soar because of the war in Europe. Lead and zinc mines across the nation were rushed into stepped-up production, including many abandoned earlier for poor-quality ore or exhausted veins. But the week Truman and his friends opened their mine the price of ore fell. His partners soon abandoned him, leaving him to manage the mine alone. He had to learn quickly how to rely upon his own resources. At about this time, he wrote to Bess, "You would do better perhaps if you pitch me into the ash heap and pick up someone with more sense and ability and not such a softhead."

Although he mined record ore tonnages each week, it all came to nothing in the end. When TCH Mine had opened, zinc ore sold for $115 a ton; by the time it was closed, ore brought only $45 a ton; TCH Mine's last payroll was 2 September 1916. Within months zinc prices soared to new record highs.

Truman had lost about $7,500 on TCH Mine, but he soon joined Jerry Culbertson in another equally risky venture. On 25 September 1916, the two men and David Morgan started the Atlas-Okla Lands Syndicate, with Morgan serving as president, Culbertson as secretary, and Truman as treasurer. They chartered Morgan & Company Oil Investment Corp. as the sole marketing agent for Atlas-Okla.

With petroleum consumption breaking new records annually, Truman felt confident his new venture would bring him financial success. Early in the effort he wrote to Bess, "People seem to think our promotional project has some merit. . . . We got $225 yesterday and sixty so far today. If it comes at the rate of $50 per day we can pay rent anyway if we never drill a well."

In March 1917 Atlas-Okla was dissolved and a new producing trust was formed, Morgan Oil & Refining Company. David Morgan stayed in the field, locating and leasing oil properties, Culbertson ran the sales force, and Truman received the cash and issued the stock. The company auditor, a Mr. Buford, recalled later, "Harry S. Truman was surrounded by people, people, people. Salesman, leaseman, lease owners, scouts and what have you. Morgan had his duties, but he shoved quite a burden of seeing people over to Truman."

By placing producing lands under a trust umbrella, however, the partners had moved into a gray area of state law. Just four years after Truman severed ties to Morgan Oil, in fact, the state of Missouri made such trusts illegal. Shares in them provided only "beneficial interests" in the properties and "undivided interest in the entire holdings." In these trusts, usually referred to as blue sky trusts, prices of the shares were subject only to a salesman's guile. Morgan shares sold from one dollar to twenty-five dollars a share, for example, depending on the sophistication of the buyer.

There were other ethical problems, too. In April 1917 the Morgan prospectus listed as assets "a thoroughly equipped refinery with a capacity of 400 barrels per 24 hours . . . capable of refining gasoline, kerosene, naphtha, etc.," and pipelines linking the refinery to producing wells in the area. All these statements were false. The refinery was a skimming plant designed only to remove gross impurities from crude; moreover, there was never enough oil in the region to support a real refinery. The prospectus abounded in errors and exaggerations. In late 1917, finally, Morgan and Truman could no longer accept Culbertson's excesses and forced him out.

Around this time Morgan Oil leased 320 acres of oil rights in Greenwood County, Kansas. When the drill reached 900 feet, Truman's partners abandoned the lease; with the nearest producing well thirty miles across the prairie, they had decided to cut their losses. Truman remembered that event all his life, for, as he wrote later, a "well drilled at the other end of it [the area covered by the Greenwood lease] and from one end to another of that 320 acres never had a dry hole. It was worth about seven million dollars when I got home from war."

On 22 June 1917, after the United States declared war on Germany, Truman left Morgan Oil and rejoined the National Guard. On his return from Europe in 1919, he divested all remaining shares in the firm.

In the spring of that year, Truman met Eddie Jacobson, his clerk from the regimental canteen at Camp Donelson, Oklahoma. After discussing old times they decided to open their own haberdashery to be called Truman and Jacobson's. They leased a store at 104 West Twelfth Street in Kansas City for five years. Because it was located directly across from the famous Muehlebach Hotel, Truman and Jacobson anticipated heavy floor traffic. Stocked with expensive silk shirts and ties, hats and spats, and other men's furnishings, the store did very well in the early months.

Truman, however, quickly became bored with the staid life in the shop and spent more and more time in the world of veterans' affairs. Whether helping found American Legion posts and V.F.W. halls, organizing Reserve Officers clubs, or campaigning for new armories, he devoted his evenings and increasingly his days to veterans' activities. Harry Murphy, a Battery D veteran recalled, "I used to go down there [Truman and Jacobson's] every time I was downtown; it was sort of a headquarters."

But in the spring of 1920 the New York Federal Reserve Board, to counter inflationary forces, raised the rediscount rate to a record 7 percent and ignited deflationary moves throughout the economy. In June 1920 farm prices snapped: wheat fell from $2.55 a bushel to $.93; corn from $1.86 to $.41. In just twelve months the farm index slid from 234 to 112. The money supply contracted, bank rates soared, notes were not renewed, inventory values collapsed, and credit costs exploded.

Truman and Jacobson, undercapitalized as they were, could not weather such an assault. One year they had held an inventory valued at $35,000; twelve months later it brought barely $10,000. By 1922 the store had failed. When Mike Pendergast, brother of Thomas, stopped by the store and asked Truman to run for eastern district Jackson County Court judge, Truman welcomed the opportunity. The retail sales business was not for him.

Two years later, on 13 October, Truman joined with other veterans Arthur Metzger, Spencer Salisbury, H. H. Halvorsen, and Rufus Burrus in organizing the Community Savings and Loan Association. Savings and loans were popular in the twenties as "poor men's banks." Customers promised to save small amounts on a regularly scheduled basis, much like today's

Christmas Club accounts. The Community Savings and Loan grew slowly but steadily: after three quarters, assets were $6,613; by 1930 they tallied $457,164.

In January 1926 Truman joined with some friends and purchased the Citizens Security Bank of Englewood. He borrowed $10,000 for his share of the bank, but this investment too turned out badly. When the partners had the books of Citizens audited, they discovered that from the date they had signed the purchase contract, the officers of the bank had made $18,000 in uncollateralized loans. Salisbury quickly bailed out of the deal and once again Truman was stuck.

Little involved in the daily operations of the Community Savings and Loan when he was serving as judge and even less so when he went to the U.S. Senate, Truman permitted Salisbury to take control. In 1934, Truman heard so many complaints about Salisbury's operations of the bank that he reported the conduct to the federal director of Home Loan Banks and an investigation resulted. A federal court found Salisbury guilty of fraudulent foreclosures, and he served six months in Leavenworth Federal Prison.

Truman was not to be a banker either.

Jonathan Daniels, *The Man of Independence* (Philadelphia: J. B. Lippincott, 1950), is among the earliest of Truman's biographies, but it still remains solid on his business activities. Robert H. Ferrell, ed., *Dear Bess: The Letters from Harry to Bess Truman, 1910–1959* (New York: W. W. Norton, 1983), offers fascinating glimpses of Truman's feelings about his business dealings. Richard Lawrence Miller, *Truman: The Rise to Power* (New York: McGraw-Hill, 1986), is flawed in many ways, but Miller has found many sources on Truman's business ventures. See also Thomas J. Heed, "Harry S. Truman: The County Years" (forthcoming). This work on Truman's first fifty years uses extensive sources not previously published. It examines his business years in great depth.

THOMAS J. HEED

See also Jacobson, Eddie; Kansas City, Missouri

Byrnes, James Francis

(2 May 1879–9 April 1972)

Truman's "patient but firm" secretary of state, 1945–47. Years after their first meeting on the Senate floor, President Truman recalled that Jimmy Byrnes had been one of the few members of that exclusive club who from the first treated him as a colleague and not just the "gentleman from Pendergast." Their affinity as senators was both personal and political. Both men had risen from modest backgrounds to positions of national prominence. Self-educated after the age of fourteen, Byrnes had helped support his widowed mother by hawking seafood and newspapers and running errands for local attorneys in his hometown of Charleston, South Carolina. A gregarious, indefatigable go-getter grandson of Irish immigrants, Byrnes rose quickly from court reporter, law clerk, prosecutor, and newspaper editor to candidate for Congress. After seven terms in the House (1910–24) he was disappointed in a bid for the Senate but achieved this goal in 1930. As senator he was an early supporter of

Roosevelt's presidential candidacy. By the time Truman took his seat in the Senate in 1935, Byrnes was already well established as "the New Deal's ball carrier" on Capitol Hill. During their time together in the Senate Byrnes and Truman generally found themselves on the same side of most issues.

In 1941 Byrnes departed the Senate for the Supreme Court bench. But after just one term on the High Court, he resigned to take up a wartime White House post as the nation's inflation fighter. The job of economic stabilizer eventually gave way to even broader responsibilities when Byrnes accepted an appointment as director of the Office of War Mobilization. In this role as "assistant president for the home front" Byrnes again found himself working with the chairman of the Truman committee.

Nearly a decade of friendly personal and professional relations between the two men formed an important part of the background of the 1944 Democratic National Convention. When Byrnes telephoned Truman at home in Independence a few days before the gathering in Chicago and asked him if he would deliver the speech nominating him for vice president, Truman immediately agreed not only to make the speech but to work for Byrnes's nomination at the convention.

Once in Chicago and faced with the growing possibility of his own nomination, Truman was embarrassed by his prior commitment to Byrnes. In the end Byrnes graciously released Truman from his obligation and withdrew from the fight for the vice presidency, leaving only Henry A. Wallace as Truman's major challenger. Bitter toward Roosevelt for having raised false hopes, Byrnes did not blame Truman for his disappointment. Nonetheless he could not escape the feeling that he rather than Truman should have been Roosevelt's chosen successor. The contest for the vice presidency thus complicated relations between Truman and Byrnes.

After Roosevelt's death in April 1945 the legacy of friendship and competition brought Truman and Byrnes together in an alliance that was expedient but inherently unstable. Within hours of taking the oath as president, Truman met with Byrnes and offered him the highest appointment he could give him. Roosevelt's "assistant president" was to become Truman's secretary of state, a position at that time next in line of succession to the presidency.

Truman's first major appointment could not be made public until July after the incumbent secretary, Edward Stettinius, had concluded his work in San Francisco helping establish the United Nations Organization. But even before his swearing in, Byrnes, the master of cloakroom politics, was working behind the scenes in a number of areas. One of these confidential roles was as Truman's personal representative to the top secret Interim Committee, a hand-picked group charged with advising the president on the use of the atomic bomb.

This extraordinary reliance on a man whose credentials, although in many ways impressive, did not include a history of involvement in foreign or military policy is only partly explained by Truman's regard for Byrnes as a legislative leader and his indebtedness because of the 1944 vice-presidential fight. As he later put it, Truman was trying to "balance things up" for what had happened in Chicago. An equally if not more important reason for the appointment, however, was Truman's belief that Byrnes alone held the secret to "what went on at Yalta."

Byrnes's personal shorthand notes were the only verbatim stenographic record of Roosevelt's last and most important summit meeting. Yet Roosevelt had made sure that Byrnes's version of Yalta would reflect only those aspects of

Outgoing secretary of state James F. Byrnes gives his Report from the World, January 1947. (National Archives)

the negotiations most palatable to the domestic American audience. Byrnes's public relations effort as Roosevelt's "Yalta front man" helped sell the agreements to Congress and the folks at home. It also helped make him Truman's secretary of state.

From the outset, then, the Truman-Byrnes partnership was flawed in that it was based in part on a fiction largely of Roosevelt's making. Although he did not expect the "prima donna" Byrnes to be around very long as secretary of state, Truman relied on his "able and conniving" former Senate colleague to help get him through the difficult period of ending the war against Japan and negotiating postwar agreements with the victorious Allies. Both men's first test was the Big Three summit conference at Potsdam.

On the eve of that conference their confidence was bolstered by news of the successful atomic bomb test. Earlier Byrnes had been instrumental in the Interim Committee's decision to continue Roosevelt's policy of keeping the bomb project secret from the Russians. With that project's spectacular success before them, Byrnes and Truman agreed that, although a Soviet declaration of war against Japan was still desirable, the bomb provided an opportunity to end the war quickly on American terms and before, as Byrnes put it, the Russians "could get in so much on the kill."

Byrnes's performance at Potsdam and in the surrender of Japan reinforced Truman's reliance on his chief diplomat. During a series of postwar meetings of the Big Three foreign ministers Byrnes operated essentially on his own with the broadest

possible mandate from the president and apart from the bureaucracy in Washington. As one wag put it, "The State Department fiddles while Byrnes roams." Byrnes's independent improvisatory approach led to swings in policy such as his attempt to use the American atomic monopoly as a stick or threat in dealing with the Russians followed by a more conciliatory carrot approach.

But the latter soon ran afoul of the emerging cold war consensus at home. Truman privately condemned Byrnes's dealings as "appeasement" and reasserted his control over policy. Unwilling to accept his new subordinate status, Byrnes secretly resigned in April 1946. Crises such as the confrontation over withdrawal of Soviet troops from northern Iran and the foreign ministers' ongoing negotiations of peace treaties forced Byrnes to stay on until January 1947. When he was finally able gracefully to depart from the Truman administration, Byrnes was hailed as *Time* magazine's "Man of the Year" for his "patient but firm" diplomacy.

By 1948 Truman and Byrnes had drifted apart personally and politically. By not openly declaring his support for the president, Byrnes implicitly sided with the Dixiecrat revolt against Truman's reelection. In his best-selling memoir, *Speaking Frankly*, published the year before, Byrnes had given Truman little credit as a foreign policy leader. The break was final after 1949 when Byrnes spoke out publicly against Truman's Fair Deal policies. In a terse bitter note Truman told his former friend that he now knew how Caesar felt when he said "Et tu Brute"; to which Byrnes replied, "I am no Brutus, and you are no Caesar."

In 1950 Byrnes returned to politics once again, this time on the state level, as governor of South Carolina. After 1955 he retired from public life. His version of his long, varied, and eventful career, appropriately titled *All in One Lifetime*, appeared in 1958. The former congressman, senator, Supreme Court justice, "assistant president," secretary of state, and governor died in April 1972 just a few months before the death of his one-time friend, rival, and foe, Harry Truman.

Byrnes warrants but has not yet received a full-length biography. He did leave us his political memoir of his involvement in foreign affairs under Roosevelt and Truman, *Speaking Frankly* (New York: Harper & Bros., 1947), as well as his autobiography, *All in One Lifetime* (New York: Harper & Bros., 1958). The James F. Byrnes manuscript collection at Clemson University, Clemson, South Carolina, has yielded a number of scholarly works on particular aspects of Byrnes's long career. His House and Senate years are treated in Winfred B. Moore, Jr., "New South Statesman: The Political Career of James Francis Byrnes, 1911–1941" (Ph.D. diss., Duke University, 1976). His wartime service in Roosevelt's White House is the subject of John W. Partin, "'Assistant President' for the Home Front: James F. Byrnes and World War II" (Ph.D. diss., University of Florida, 1977). The Roosevelt-Byrnes-Truman relationship and its impact on the cold war is analyzed in Robert L. Messer, *The End of an Alliance: James F. Byrnes, Roosevelt, Truman, and the Origins of the Cold War* (Chapel Hill: University of North Carolina Press, 1982). Finally, a useful collection of essays prepared for Byrnes's centennial is Kendrick A. Clements, ed., *James F. Byrnes and the Origins of the Cold War* (Durham, N.C.: Carolina Academic Press, 1982).

ROBERT L. MESSER

See also Potsdam Conference

C

Cabinets

Harry S. Truman, when he succeeded to office upon the death of President Franklin D. Roosevelt, immediately asked all cabinet officers to remain at their posts. Thus his first cabinet was composed of appointees of his predecessor. In his *Memoirs* the new president wrote that "every President must have a cabinet of his own choosing," but he also stressed the importance of continuity in government during wartime and his need to get to know his new colleagues and the problems the United States faced. Thus it was not until May, about a month after his taking office, that Truman made the first of what were to be thirty cabinet appointments by the time he left the White House in 1953.

After discussing in his *Memoirs* his initial cabinet changes, the president noted that "by mid-July [1945] all that remained of the cabinet which had served under President Roosevelt were four men": Wallace at Commerce, Ickes at Interior, Forrestal at Navy, and Stimson at the War Department. Stimson left in the fall of 1945 and Ickes and Wallace the next year. Forrestal stayed on until his resignation from the new office of Secretary of Defense in 1949.

Elected presidents can devote considerable time between election and inauguration considering candidates for cabinet office, but President Truman was in a different position. He had assumed office suddenly, without the relative leisure of a transition period to mull over appointees. Yet in a three-month period he decided upon six of his cabinet officers.

Often he chose people whom he had gotten to know during his Senate career. Four of the first six had served in Congress previously, and another, Hannegan, was an old Missouri friend, as was Snyder who replaced Vinson a year later at the Treasury. The first Truman cabinet was not a stellar group, and some members gave the president serious trouble. Byrnes was replaced after a year and a half in office because of Truman's dissatisfaction with his performance. Wallace, a Roosevelt holdover, was also replaced because of friction with his chief.

Stephen Hess wrote in his book *Organizing the Presidency*

that Truman's cabinet appointments "resulted in a blending of stunningly capable patricians, unimaginative professionals, and incompetent cronies." This overall appraisal is justified.

There were twelve departments (counting Defense and its three components) during most of the Truman years and an average of between two and three appointments for each department. Truman had three secretaries of state of his own choosing, four at the War Department (renamed the Department of the Army), four defense secretaries, three navy secretaries, and two each in the other cabinet chairs.

For his second- and third-round choices, as Hess refers to them, the president tended to make better nominations. Often these were promotions of under and assistant secretaries of proven ability such as Chapman, Brannan, and, in a sense, Acheson, or they were seasoned Washington hands like Robert Lovett and Averell Harriman. Twice Truman called George Marshall out of retirement when he needed a prestigious appointment to restore confidence after a prior one had gone sour.

The cabinet also changed in composition during the Truman years because of the reorganization of the military service departments. The president had inherited a cabinet of ten members; in 1947 that number was reduced to nine when the position of secretary of defense replaced those of secretary of war and secretary of the navy. From then on, only the secretary of defense sat in the cabinet. Initially the three service secretaries—army (formerly war), navy, and air force—were given seats on the National Security Council, but the 1949 amendments to the National Security legislation dropped them from the council as well.

Harry Truman sought to revive the cabinet as an institution from the relative disuse into which it had fallen under his predecessor. In his *Memoirs* he wrote that little of consequence was discussed in the Roosevelt sessions he attended as vice president, and that most of the real business was dealt with at informal meetings or individual conferences with the president. But his initial views on the proper role of the cabinet were not wholly consistent. He talked of making it a "board of directors" for the government, and on occasion, in the early days at least,

The president and his cabinet at Blair House, 1949. Front row, l. to r., Secretary of Defense Louis Johnson, Secretary of State Dean Acheson, President Truman, Vice President Alben Barkley, Secretary of the Treasury John Snyder, Attorney General Tom Clark. Rear, l. to r., Secretary of the Interior Julius Krug, Postmaster General Jesse Donaldson, Secretary of Agriculture Charles Brannan, Secretary of Commerce Charles Sawyer, Secretary of Labor Maurice Tobin. (Abbie Rowe, National Park Service/Courtesy of the Harry S. Truman Library)

he actually took votes on matters of moment. The *Memoirs* record, however, that he also made it clear that he as president was the boss, citing the famous Lincoln story in which the president's "aye" overrode the unanimous "nays" of his cabinet. Truman expected loyalty from his subordinates and took vigorous action when he felt it was not forthcoming, as in the cases of Secretaries Byrnes and Wallace.

Another aspect of his view of the cabinet's role emerged when he wrote, "The cabinet presents the principal medium through which the President controls his administration." Apparently with this in mind, he stressed the importance of the weekly meetings as means of keeping himself informed of important issues in the various departmental areas and the members informed of what the others were doing. He also saw the cabinet as a political sounding board and welcomed the expression of diverse opinions. Some members urged the president to do what Eisenhower was to do later—create a cabinet secretariat and prepare formal meeting agendas. He rejected this idea but decided to have luncheons before each meeting. Richard Fenno in his book *The President's Cabinet* suggests that these gathering offered members the same kind of opportunity for a personal word with the president that individuals had had with Roosevelt after meetings adjourned.

In time the president's enthusiasm for cabinet meetings, and his concern that they entail discussion of important issues,

diminished. Charles Sawyer, one of his secretaries of Commerce, summarized his impressions in his memoirs: "Most cabinet meetings were routine. The President frequently called for comment on some matter, but did not ask for lengthy reports or discussions." He also saw the luncheons as opportunities for a private word and noted that members tended to accompany the president back to his office after meetings to discuss a particular issue.

It is evident that in the long run the Truman cabinets functioned much as had those of his predecessors. Fenno gives an example of an interdepartmental dispute over the postwar sale of surplus tankers which pitted Interior and State against the Navy. Discussion at two cabinet meetings failed to resolve the issue, underlining again the chronic inability of that body to cope with policy differences—much less make policy—even when there was a consensus, as there was in this case, favoring State.

Structurally the cabinet as an institution had changed little from its historic form and operation by the time Truman left office, aside from the creation of the Defense Department and the National Security Council. The latter is actually a cabinet subcommittee, and if put to full use, it can decrease the cabinet's overall role by preempting the areas of security and foreign policy. But the history of the National Security Council, under Truman and his successors, has been no more consistent than that of the cabinet itself.

Harry S. Truman's Cabinets

Vice President
 Alben W. Barkley, Jan. 1949

Secretary of State
 *Edward R. Stettinius, 1944
 James F. Byrnes, July 1945
 George C. Marshall, Jan. 1947
 Dean G. Acheson, Jan. 1949

Secretary of the Treasury
 *Henry Morgenthau, Jr., 1934
 Fred M. Vinson, July 1945
 John W. Snyder, June 1946

Secretary of War
 *Henry L. Stimson, 1940
 Robert P. Patterson, Sept. 1945

Secretary of the Army
 Kenneth C. Royall, Oct. 1947
 Gordon Gray, June 1949
 Frank Pace, Jr., Apr. 1950

Secretary of the Navy
 *James Forrestal, 1944
 John L. Sullivan, Oct. 1947
 Francis P. Matthews, May 1949
 Dan A. Kimball, July 1951

Secretary of the Air Force
 W. Stuart Symington, Oct. 1947
 Thomas K. Finletter, Apr. 1950

Secretary of Defense
 James Forrestal, July 1947
 Louis Johnson, Mar. 1949
 George C. Marshall, Sept. 1950
 Robert A. Lovett, Oct. 1951

Attorney General
 *Francis Biddle, 1941
 Tom C. Clark, June 1945
 J. Howard McGrath, Aug. 1949

Postmaster General
 *Frank C. Walker, 1940
 Robert E. Hannegan, July 1945
 Jesse M. Donaldson, Nov. 1947

Secretary of the Interior
 *Harold L. Ickes, 1933
 Julius A. Krug, Feb. 1946
 Oscar L. Chapman, Dec. 1949

Secretary of Agriculture
 *Claude R. Wickard, 1940
 Clinton P. Anderson, June 1945
 Charles F. Brannan, June 1948

Secretary of Commerce
 *Henry A. Wallace, 1945
 W. Averell Harriman, Oct. 1946
 Charles Sawyer, May 1948

Secretary of Labor
 *Frances Perkins, 1933
 Lewis B. Schwellenbach, July 1945
 Maurice J. Tobin, Aug. 1948

*Roosevelt appointees.

Harry S. Truman's *Memoirs*, vol. 1, *Year of Decisions* (New York: Doubleday, 1955) is valuable for its insights on the president's own view of the cabinet. Stephen Hess, *Organizing the Presidency* (Washington, D.C.,: Brookings Institution, 1976), and Richard F. Fenno, *The President's Cabinet* (Cambridge: Harvard University Press, 1959), provide useful discussions of the Truman cabinet in a comparative context. Wallace, in *The Diaries of Henry A. Wallace: The Price of Vision* (Boston: Houghton Mifflin, 1973), makes frequent mention of cabinet discussions, and Charles Sawyer, in *Concerns of a Conservative Democrat* (Carbondale: Southern Illinois University Press, 1968), provides another participant perspective.

ELMER E. CORNWELL, JR.

See also entries for individual cabinet members

Campaigns, Presidential

See Elections in the Truman Era

Catholics

Postwar American Catholicism has been likened to a sleeping giant. The nation's largest minority, it numbered 24 million in 1946, compared with 15 million black Americans, 14 million Baptists, and less than 10 million Hispanic-Americans. The church conducted ten thousand grade and high schools, with enrollments of 2.5 million, and two hundred colleges and universities. When Harry Truman assumed the presidency, there were eight Catholic governors, nine senators, and seventy-eight congressmen. The American church received international recognition in 1946 when four of its hierarchy—Francis Spellman of New York, Edward Mooney of Detroit, Samuel Stritch of Chicago, and John Glennon of St. Louis—were elevated to the College of Cardinals by Pope Pius XII.

The majority of American Catholics supported the Truman administration. The president had commanded a predominantly Catholic Battery D in World War I, had worked closely with the Catholic Tom Pendergast in Kansas City, spoke out frequently against prejudice and discrimination, and appointed four Catholics to his cabinet—Postmaster General Robert Hannegan, Secretary of Labor Maurice Tobin, and Attorneys General J. Howard McGrath and James McGranery. Most Catholics were middle- or lower-middle-class wage earners and benefited from the president's Fair Deal program. His hardening cold war stance after 1946 also gained support from a Catholic public angered by Soviet domination of heavily Catholic Eastern Europe and by Communist persecution of church leaders Josef Beran, Aloysius Stepinac, and József Cardinal Mindszenty.

The Truman years, however, were not without controversy among Catholics. When Congressman Graham Barden of North Carolina introduced a federal aid to education bill in 1949, expressly excluding private schools from participation, Cardinal Spellman opposed it. An animated exchange took place between the cardinal and Eleanor Roosevelt, during which Spellman spoke of her "record of anti-Catholicism ... unworthy of an American mother." The bill was never brought to a vote.

A second controversy concerned the appointment of an official representative to Vatican City. President Roosevelt had appointed Myron Taylor, former chairman of U.S. Steel, as his personal representative in 1939, and President Truman nominated Gen. Mark Clark to succeed him in 1951. The National Council of Churches with Protestants and Other Americans United for the Separation of Church and State led a strong opposition, and General Clark withdrew his name in early 1952.

A third controversy, with less direct religious overtones, concerned the congressional investigations of Senator Joseph McCarthy of Wisconsin. McCarthy was Catholic, and although there was no official Catholic position on his activities, most of the Catholic press supported him, few in the hierarchy criticized him in public, and polls indicated that most Catholics approved.

By the close of the Truman administration in 1953, the American church had grown to 30 million, its immigrant character continued to recede, and it was poised for even greater national and international prominence with the election of John F. Kennedy in 1960 and the opening of the Second Vatican Council by Pope John XXIII in 1962.

The best general histories of American Catholicism are James Hennesey, S.J., *American Catholics* (New York: Oxford University Press, 1981), and Jay P. Dolan, *The American Catholic Experience* (Garden City, N.Y.: Doubleday, 1985). On specialized topics, the activities of the era's leading Catholic spokesman are examined in Robert I. Gannon, S.J., *The Cardinal Spellman Story* (Garden City, N.Y.: Doubleday, 1962); the General Clark nomination in George J. Gill, "The Truman Administration and Vatican Relations," *Catholic Historical Review* 73 (July 1987): 408–23; and the American church and McCarthyism in Donald F. Crosby, S.J., *God, Church, and Flag* (Chapel Hill: University of North Carolina Press, 1978).

THOMAS E. BLANTZ

ligence services, conduct covert operations, and reach into domestic matters.

Of these issues, the first was the most urgent, although never entirely resolved by Truman or his successors. Viewed jealously by the old-line agencies in State, Treasury, Justice, and the armed services, allegedly weighed down with deadwood when abler personnel hesitated to join the untried agency, and presided over by a naval officer (Rear Adm. Roscoe H. Hillenkoetter) who was competent but lacked political clout, the CIA struggled in its first years to carve out an identity and a commanding position. Lacking also in technical means, it often produced bland and indecisive intelligence analyses.

Nonetheless, the CIA under Truman was already moving into those areas where controversy would later arise. In 1948, it worked behind the scenes to promote anti-Communist politicians in Italy. It contributed analyses during some of the key crises in foreign policy during the Truman years. Covertly, it infiltrated and promoted anti-Communist organizations at home, including the liberal intellectuals' Congress for Cultural Freedom. Truman approved these operations, despite his later condemnation of the CIA's "strange activities." The CIA's most notable triumphs and debacles came after Truman, although there is an element of uncertainty about this judgment since much about its operations under him remains locked up in archives.

Because the CIA's archives remain closed longer than those of other government agencies, scholarly work on the early years is scant. A useful start is William Leary, *The Central Intelligence Agency: History and Documents* (University: University of Alabama Press, 1984). Steven L. Rearden, *History of the Office of the Secretary of Defense*, vol. 1, *The Formative Years* (Washington, D.C.: Office of the Secretary of Defense, 1984), is dispassionate and informative.

MICHAEL S. SHERRY

Central Intelligence Agency

Like many other creations of the National Security Act of 1947, the Central Intelligence Agency (CIA) only slowly found its place in the new system of national security.

The CIA resulted in part from the wartime scandal over disasters—above all, that of Pearl Harbor—which were attributed to rivalry and confusion among several uncoordinated intelligence offices. Institutionally, it was something of a successor to the Office of Strategic Services (OSS), although that office had only added to the hodgepodge rather than coordinating its constituent agencies. The CIA succeeded more directly the Central Intelligence Group, which President Truman established but hemmed in out of fear of creating a "gestapo." Truman's awareness of that group's deficiencies meshed with the desires of Navy Secretary James Forrestal—a key player in all facets of the National Security Act—for a stronger and more centralized intelligence community. Given memories of World War II and congressional preoccupation with other issues, the enabling legislation for the CIA encountered little controversy. The 1947 act placed the agency under the National Security Council and gave its director access to the president, but evaded trickier issues—whether the CIA would control the older intel-

Chambers-Hiss Case

See Hiss-Chambers Case

Chapman, Oscar Littleton

(22 October 1896–8 February 1978)

Secretary of the interior, 1949–53. Oscar Chapman was a bellwether liberal whose career in Washington exemplified the shift in the liberal agenda from the New Deal to the Fair Deal. Born in Halifax County, Virginia, Chapman moved to Denver, Colorado, in 1920 to recover from tuberculosis, which he contracted while serving in the medical corps in World War I. Attracted to social welfare causes, he became an assistant to crusading juvenile court judge Ben Lindsey and advanced to several positions in the state welfare bureaucracy. He also took a degree at a night law school. Drawn into Democratic political circles, Chapman managed liberal attorney Edward P. Costigan's successful campaign for the U.S. Senate in 1930 and the reelection bid of conservative senator Alva Adams in 1932.

The young Coloradoan was rewarded for his efforts on behalf of the Roosevelt ticket with the position of assistant secretary of the interior in 1933, when the president needed a westerner to balance his choice of Harold L. Ickes of Chicago as secretary of the western-oriented department. Chapman's thirteen-year tenure as assistant secretary was largely uneventful, for Ickes entrusted important matters chiefly to other appointees and his personal staff. The Coloradoan positioned himself among the New Deal's left liberals, and possessing a sunny, genial personality, he built a wide circle of political friends in Washington.

When Ickes resigned in a celebrated row with Truman in February 1946, Julius A. Krug was named secretary of the interior. Chapman said he was offered the secretaryship but turned it down because he feared liberals would resent his succeeding Ickes, who embodied the Roosevelt legacy for many of them. Valuing Chapman's knowledge of the department and western politics, Krug elevated him to under secretary. In that thankless position Chapman devoted much of his time to fending off and scaling back programs that aroused the hostility of the Republican-controlled Eightieth Congress.

Chapman was an early Truman loyalist in the seemingly doomed 1948 campaign and worked hard as an advance man throughout the West. When Krug, an indolent secretary who had done little to help the campaign, resigned, Chapman assumed the secretaryship on 1 December 1949. In 1950 he was called before a Senate investigating committee to answer charges of alleged disloyalty propounded largely by Republican Andrew F. Schoeppel of Kansas. The charges against Chapman were even flimsier than most, and he was easily vindicated.

Chapman's secretaryship was stormy and strained his relations with the dwindling remnant of New Deal liberals, who bitterly criticized his efforts to move the department in line with Fair Deal emphases. In environmental issues he stressed the development of natural resources, particularly big dams for hydroelectric power and irrigation, in concert with the Truman administration's strategy of economic growth. With Chapman's support, the Bureau of Reclamation, headed by the aggressive commissioner Michael Straus, consumed more than 60 percent of the department's budget by 1950. The secretary pressed for a Columbia Valley Administration (CVA), a scaled-down version of the river valley authorities typified by the Tennessee Valley Authority; when powerful regional interests blocked authorization of the CVA, however, Chapman readily settled for construction of several dams on the Columbia and Snake rivers by the Reclamation Bureau.

The centerpiece of Chapman's western development program was the Upper Colorado River Basin project, an ambitious string of dams on the Colorado. The program's proposed Echo Park Dam, in the heart of Dinosaur National Monument, touched off a heated controversy with preservationist groups, who pointed out that construction of the dam would destroy the integrity of the national park and monument system and open these reservations to further dam building. Chapman backed down on Echo Park, and in 1955 an alternative site was chosen outside the national monument.

He supported the Bureau of Reclamation's vast extension of its network in the Central Valley of California. Part of the political price of this accomplishment was gutting the 160-acre law, a key provision of reclamation law that was designed to help small farmers by providing water to irrigate no more than a quarter section. Many liberals chastised the department for allowing heavily subsidized water to flow to large growers and agribusiness corporations.

Equally controversial was Chapman's marked change of direction on Indian policy. He appointed Dillon S. Myer, who had supervised the World War II internment camps of the Japanese and Japanese-Americans, as commissioner of Indian affairs. Myer called his policy "termination." In contrast to the New Deal practice of supporting Indian communities and preserving tribal life, he encouraged Indians to leave reservations for jobs in urban areas, abolished some reservations, and reduced federal Indian-support programs.

Liberals, however, applauded Chapman's devotion to the Truman administration's civil rights program. He supervised the desegregation of public facilities controlled by the Interior Department in the District of Columbia, oversaw the transition of Puerto Rico to commonwealth status and the appointment of the first Puerto Rican, Luis Muñoz Marín, as governor, advocated a greater degree of self-government for the Virgin Islands, Guam, Samoa, and the Trust Territory of the Pacific, and supported statehood for the territories of Hawaii and Alaska.

During the Korean War Chapman served as the administrator of several emergency agencies patterned after the World War II experience, most notably the Petroleum Administration for Defense. Upon his retirement from public life, Chapman used his political capital to establish a prosperous Washington law firm that specialized in matters pertaining to the Interior Department and the Federal Power Commission.

The only full study of Chapman's public career is Clayton R. Koppes, "Oscar L. Chapman: A Liberal at the Interior Department, 1933–1953" (Ph.D. diss., University of Kansas, 1974). Essential primary sources for the study of his career, and the many issues in which he was involved, include the Oscar L. Chapman Papers at the Harry S. Truman Library and the Records of the Office of the Secretary of the Interior and Chapman's Office File, both in Record Group 48 in the National Archives. For environmental issues during Chapman's career, see Clayton R. Koppes, "Efficiency, Equity, Esthetics: Shifting Themes in American Environmental History," in *The Ends of the Earth: Essays in World Environmental History*, ed. Donald Worster and Alfred Crosby (New York: Cambridge University Press, 1988): Clayton R. Koppes, "Public Water, Private Land: Origins of the Acreage Limitation Controversy, 1933–1953," *Pacific Historical Review* 47 (November 1978): 607–36; and Elmo Richardson, *Dams, Parks & Politics: Resource Development & Preservation in the Truman-Eisenhower Era* (Lexington: University Press of Kentucky, 1973). On Indian rights, see Clayton R. Koppes, "From New Deal to Termination: Liberalism and Indian Policy, 1933–1953," *Pacific Historical Review* 46 (November 1977): 543–66, and Donald L. Fixico, *Termination and Relocation: Federal Indian Policy, 1945–1960* (Albuquerque: University of New Mexico Press, 1986).

CLAYTON R. KOPPES

See also Conservation; Indian Policy; Reclamation

Chiang Kai-shek

(31 October 1887–5 April 1975)

Leader of the Chinese Nationalist forces. Born in Chekiang, China, Chiang Kai-shek rose quickly through the ranks of the Kuomintang party. His commanding status was recognized in 1938, when he received the long-coveted title of director general. During World War II, President Roosevelt, acting in the vain hope that Chiang would create a major anti-Japanese offensive, bolstered his regime with loans and credits and spoke of China as one of the postwar world's "Four Policemen."

Although Truman never met Chiang, he certainly affected the generalissimo's fortunes. During his first year in office, Truman genuinely believed that Chiang could rejuvenate China by creating an authentic reform movement. In July 1945, at Chiang's request, Truman protested against Stalin's demands to control Manchuria. When the final and more moderate Sino-Soviet Treaty of Friendship and Alliance was signed on 14 August, Madame Chiang was pleased enough to thank Truman personally for his support. Again, at Chiang's bidding, the president ordered over fifty-thousand American marines to North China, ostensibly to facilitate the Japanese surrender but in reality to check any Chinese Communist advance.

Yet Chiang soon met with Truman's opprobrium. Negative reports from Gen. George C. Marshall, the president's special envoy to China, and accounts of Kuomintang repression led Truman to warn Chiang on 10 August 1946 that continued American aid depended upon reform and a quick settlement. In his reply, Chiang simply blamed the Communists for all impediments. Until Chiang fled to Formosa late in 1949, Truman remained disillusioned with his rule. Even a personal visit from Madame Chiang to Truman in December 1948 could not convince Truman to approve the $3 billion in aid, to be extended over three years, that her husband requested.

Cautious while in office, Truman was outspoken about Chiang once he left the presidency. He called the generalissimo "an old-fashioned warlord," whose selfishness and rigidity were responsible for the Nationalists' fall and whose in-laws were "all thieves." Chiang, never able to return to the mainland, died in 1975 ruling a rump Nationalist regime on Formosa.

There is no scholarly biography of Chiang. For two journalistic treatments, see Brian Crozier, *The Man Who Lost China: The First Full Biography of Chiang Kai-shek* (New York: Charles Scribner's Sons, 1976), and Robert Payne, *Chiang Kai-shek* (New York: Weybright & Talley, 1969). Chiang offers his own account, which supplies far more than the title would suggest, in *Soviet Russia in China: A Summing-up at Seventy* (New York: Farrar, Straus & Giroux, 1957). Truman presents his postpresidential views in *Memoirs*, vol. 2, *Years of Trial and Hope* (Garden City, N.Y.: Doubleday, 1956), and Merle Miller, *Plain Speaking: An Oral Biography of Harry S. Truman* (New York: Berkley, 1973).

JUSTUS D. DOENECKE

See also China (and photograph); Formosa; Isolationism; Korean War; Marshall, George C., Jr.; Mao Tse-tung

China

Truman entered the White House lacking both firsthand experience and detailed knowledge of the Far East, and throughout his presidency he was far more attuned to events in Europe. Often turning policy over to such advisers as George C. Marshall and Dean Acheson, he kept only marginally informed. When he did intervene personally, his concern was less centered on China per se than upon a desire to preserve American prestige, protect the United States against partisan encroachments, and defend administration programs against partisan foes. Yet China was a highly explosive issue, causing enough domestic stress to erode his leadership.

When Truman assumed the presidency, he was committed to the unity of China under the aegis of Chiang's Kuomintang, an Open Door that would encompass Manchuria, and the containment of the Soviet Union in Asia. Fearful of Communist insurgents, Truman, on 15 August 1945, issued his General Order No. 1, in which he insisted that the million Japanese troops must surrender only to Chiang's forces. Moreover, he flew half a million Nationalist troops, in what was then the largest airlift in history, to northern areas, a move that allowed them to control major cities and position themselves in the Chinese heartland. The president also told Gen. Albert C. Wedemeyer, commander in chief of U.S. forces in the China theater and chief of staff to Chiang, to secure major ports and communication points until the Nationalists were ready to assume responsibility. Over fifty thousand American marines landed in such places as Tienstin and Tsingtao, although Truman stressed that they could not be used in any civil conflict.

On 27 November, Truman appointed Gen. George C. Marshall his special envoy to China with rank of ambassador. In a public statement, released on 15 December, Truman called Chiang's government the "proper instrument" for developing a democratic nation, but said it must involve "fair and effective representation" of China's "major political elements." He also sought mediation of the ongoing civil war between Nationalists and Communists and integration of all "autonomous armies" into a unified Chinese force. Although Truman indicated that economic and military aid would be contingent upon such moves, a secret codicil indicated otherwise: if Marshall could not secure the generalissimo's cooperation, the United States would nevertheless back the Nationalist regime.

Early in February 1946, Marshall sounded sufficiently optimistic for Truman to expect the removal of American troops before the year was over. In the same month, however, he favored plans, which soon came to fruition, for an American military advisory group that might number a thousand men. By May, Marshall reported that northern China was in chaos, with much fault lying in Chiang's belligerent stance and his overextending Nationalist forces in Manchuria. In May, the United States sold the Nationalist government nearly $1 billion in war surplus, plus $451.7 million in "pipeline" equipment. To establish impartiality between Nationalist and Communist factions, however, it levied an arms embargo in July. In December, Truman called the Chinese conflict "a threat to world stability and peace," but commented, "We are pledged not to interfere in the internal affairs of China."

In January 1947, Truman withdrew a completely frustrated Marshall from China. Not yet giving up on the Nationalists, in

Generalissimo Chiang Kai-shek. (National Archives)

April he ordered the transfer of naval equipment to Chiang's forces and lifted the embargo on arms. Between April and September, as the American marines withdrew from North China, they "abandoned" over sixty-five hundred tons of ammunition to the Nationalists.

In July, Truman made another attempt at salvaging the Nationalist regime, then facing a nationwide Communist offensive, by sending General Wedemeyer to survey "the political, economic, psychological, and military situations" in both China and Korea. In his orders to Wedemeyer, Truman stressed that the United States could "consider assistance in a program of rehabilitation only if the Chinese government presents satisfactory evidence of effective measures looking towards recovery." Wedemeyer reported that the Kuomintang's "reactionary leadership, repression and corruption have caused a loss of popular faith in the Government." Fearful, however, that the Chinese Communists were "bound ideologically to the Soviet Union" and "admittedly" sought "a Communist state in China," the general called for large-scale economic aid to Chiang accompanied by close American supervision, ammunition and technical military assistance, and American supervision of "field forces, training centers and particularly logistical agencies." Another recommendation involved the turning over of Manchuria, then threatened by Communist forces, to an international trusteeship that would include both the United States and the Soviet Union. It was this last recommendation that caused the Truman administration to suppress Wedemeyer's report.

By the beginning of 1948, the China situation had seriously deteriorated. Large areas north of the Yangtse River, south of the Yellow River, and east of the Han River had fallen into Communist hands, and in Manchuria the Nationalists controlled Changchun, Kirin, and Mukden only by flying in supplies. In February, Truman requested $570 million in economic aid for China, to be spent over fifteen months. Knowing that military and economic aid to Europe depended upon support from a Republican-dominated Congress, Truman hoped that relatively small amounts of aid would mollify the China Lobby and other conservatives. Congress trimmed the sum to $463 million and limited the expenditure to twelve months, but—contrary to Truman's request—allowed $125 million of the appropriation for military purposes. In March, Truman denied—in obvious contrast to his statement of 15 December 1945—that he had ever sought Communist participation in the Chinese government.

As 1948 came to a close, the Chinese Communists had gained control of all Manchuria, half of Inner Mongolia, and a large portion of the five northern provinces. Dominating a third of China's territory, they were forcing the Nationalists back to the Yangtze. Most Washington policymakers now viewed Chiang's fall as inevitable, and Truman was no exception. Acting in the belief that American armed forces lacked sufficient manpower to protect the more important fronts of Europe, much less Asia, and that Americans would not approve any campaign in such a remote area, Truman refused to commit American ground troops.

Yet Truman soon took a more active role in China policy. Three weeks after the 1948 presidential elections, he advised against closing the American naval base at Tsingtao, then surrounded by Communists, only relenting when the Nationalists withdrew from the port. In February 1949, he agreed to keep aid flowing to the Nationalists. Aware, however, that it would likely soon fall into the hands of victorious Communist armies, he informally ordered shipments delayed whenever possible. On 3 March, the president agreed to a series of position papers emerging from the National Security Council. These papers stressed the folly of further military aid to Chiang's forces, recommended continued recognition of the Nationalist government "until the situation is further clarified," called for a program of covert aid to pro-Western groups on the mainland, sought to foster rifts between the Soviet and Chinese Communists, suggested carefully controlled trade in nonmilitary goods with a Communist regime, and urged diplomatic and economic support for Formosa.

Such proposals could have given the president some real flexibility, but Mao's stated intent to stand with Soviet policy, combined with congressional and military pressure, caused Truman to become increasingly firm with the budding Communist regime. In July 1949, he vetoed a proposed trip by his ambassador to China, John Leighton Stuart, to Peking, where Stuart could well have established contact with Communist leaders Mao Tse-tung and Chou En-lai. Reasons included Truman's fear that a China bloc on Capitol Hill might withhold support for critical enterprises in Europe and the belief that a positive response would only encourage Chinese aggression.

Yet Truman knew he was on the defense. On 5 August 1949, the State Department released a 1,054-page defense entitled *United States Relations with China with Special Reference to the Period 1944–1949*, informally known as the China White

Chou En-lai, secretary-general of the Communist party in China, party chairman Mao Tse-tung, and U.S. ambassador to China, Patrick J. Hurley, arrive in Yenan, 14 September 1945, en route to Chungking for a "unification" conference with Generalissimo Chiang Kai-shek. (OWI/ National Archives)

Paper, which argued that the United States in no way could have blocked the Communists' impending triumph. Truman was an especially strong backer of this project, assuring his staff that publication would convince the public that his administration had no serious options.

Upon discovering in August that two American oil tankers were heading for Communist-dominated Manchuria, Truman wanted to halt the shipment, and it took the State Department to thwart the proposal on the grounds that the move would harm American shipping while not, in the long run, halting the delivery. In October, he indicated his desire to support the Kuomintang's illegal blockade of mainland ports, and the State Department had to be satisfied with a pro forma protest to the Nationalist government. During the same month, he remarked that the United States was in no hurry to recognize the People's Republic of China, and he kept his options open until the Korean War. He told Senator Arthur H. Vandenberg that eventually "the Russians will turn out to be the 'foreign devils' in China" and that "the situation will establish a Chinese government that we can recognize and support." He also signed a Mutual Defense Assistance Act that included $75 million for use in the "general area of China," a clause that permitted use of the funds elsewhere in Asia.

When, in October 1949, American consul Angus Ward and his staff were interred in Mukden, Truman considered using an

American plane for a rescue mission. He also thought of blockading coal to Shanghai, and if need be, he said, "we should be prepared to sink any vessels which refuse to heed our warning." Fortunately for Truman, Ward was freed in early December and the crisis was over. By the end of the year, the Communists controlled all of China but Tibet, and Truman policies centered on the rump Nationalist government on Formosa. In fact, the administration appeared acquiescent to Chiang's fall when, on 12 January 1950, Dean Acheson publicly put Formosa—and South Korea—outside the American defense perimeter. Although the secretary of state added that the United Nations could well aid endangered regimes, he made it apparent that the United States had no commitment.

On 25 June 1950, North Korea invaded its southern neighbors, and within a week Truman dispatched ground divisions to support Syngman Rhee's forces. At the same time, Truman, concurring with a recommendation of Acheson, sent the Seventh Fleet to the Formosa Straits, for he feared a Communist attack and sought to keep the Far Eastern struggle limited. Also, by this action, both Chiang and Mao would be prevented from invading the other's nation. The war triggered a major exodus of Americans living in China, and on 16 December Chinese Communist assets in the United States were frozen.

Although the administration lacked any evidence of Chinese Communist involvement, it assumed that Peking had connived with North Korea in the assault. The Sino-Soviet Friendship Treaty, signed on 14 February 1950, had implied mutual assistance in case of American attack; thus, the administration suspected the worst, and Truman and his advisers abandoned whatever thoughts of recognition they might have had. In the late fall of 1950, in response to Gen. Douglas MacArthur's crossing of the thirty-eighth parallel, massive Chinese Communist ground forces engaged American troops in North Korea. The move came as a surprise to the administration, which had thought that mainland China lacked the capacity to fight and moreover had no material interest at stake. Truman had felt personally reassured after conferring on 15 October with MacArthur at Wake Island.

Although the British sought to open relations between the West and Mao's regime, the administration balked. Recognition, it believed, would reward aggression and invite further right-wing attack. In April 1951, Truman removed MacArthur from his command, in part because the general openly recommended "unleashing" Chiang's forces on Formosa and bombing "privileged sanctuaries" in Manchuria. On 1 February 1951, however, the administration secured a resolution from the UN General Assembly branding Communist China guilty of aggression. Truman personally believed, as he noted in his *Memoirs*, that the Chinese Communists were "Russian satellites." Nevertheless, by the time Truman left the presidency, both Communist China and the United States were seeking to end the conflict and, since July 1951, had engaged in negotiations.

Despite the author's outdated claim that pressure upon Chiang would well have retained China for the West, Tang Tsou, *America's Failure in China* (Chicago: University of Chicago Press, 1963), contains enough detail to remain a classic. Also rich in research is Nancy Bernkopf Tucker's provocative *Patterns in the Dust: Chinese-American Relations and the Recognition Controversy, 1949-1950* (New York: Columbia University Press, 1983), which argues that Truman would have been willing to consider recognition of the Peking regime if the Communists had taken Formosa. William Whitney Stueck, Jr., *The Road to Confrontation: American Policy toward China and Korea, 1947-1950* (Chapel Hill: University of North Carolina Press, 1981), offers a fine narrative. Robert M. Blum, *Drawing the Line: The Origin of the American Containment Policy in East Asia* (New York: W. W. Norton, 1982), contains much more on China than its title might suggest. For a superb anthology, see Dorothy Borg and Waldo Heinrichs, eds., *Uncertain Years: Chinese-American Relations, 1947-1950* (New York: Columbia University Press, 1980). Ernest R. May, *The Truman Administration and China, 1945-1949* (Philadelphia: Lippincott, 1975), makes telling comparisons to America's later involvement in Vietnam. For the argument that Truman, whose China policy originally was governed by wise caution, permitted the extreme Right to turn it into an ideological crusade, see Lewis McCarroll Purifoy, *Harry Truman's China Policy: McCarthyism and the Diplomacy of Hysteria, 1947-1951* (New York: New Viewpoints, 1976). Superior memoirs and biographies include Gary May, *China Scapegoat: The Diplomatic Ordeal of John Carter Vincent* (Washington, D.C.: New Republic, 1979); John F. Melby, *The Mandate of Heaven: Record of a Civil War, China 1945-1949* (Toronto: University of Toronto Press, 1968); Albert C. Wedemeyer, *Wedemeyer Reports!* (New York: Henry Holt, 1958); John Leighton Stuart, *Fifty Years in China* (New York: Random House, 1954); and Forrest C. Pogue, *George C. Marshall: Statesman, 1945-1959* (New York: Viking, 1987). Robert J. Donovan, *Conflict and Crisis: The Presidency of Harry S Truman, 1945-1948* (New York: W. W. Norton, 1977), and Robert J. Donovan, *Tumultuous Years: The Presidency of Harry S Truman, 1949-1953* (New York: W. W. Norton, 1982), retain their excellence on this as on many other subjects.

JUSTUS D. DOENECKE

See also Acheson, Dean Gooderham; Chiang Kai-shek; Formosa; Isolationism; Korean War; Marshall, George C., Jr.; Mao Tse-tung

Churchill, Winston S.

(30 November 1874–24 January 1965)

When Winston Churchill learned of President Roosevelt's sudden death on 12 April 1945, he considered immediately flying to Washington to meet his successor. But the war was in its critical final stage, and it was not until 16 July that the prime minister and the new president met on the eve of the Potsdam Conference.

Like most Americans, Truman greatly admired Churchill, but that did not mean that he was uncritically prepared to follow the political and diplomatic course the prime minister would urge on him. In the spring of 1945, for instance, Truman was determined to carry out the commitments FDR had made at and before Yalta, and he therefore refrained from embarking on the sharply differing policy toward the Soviet Union that Churchill soon proposed.

On 15 May, the prime minister sent the president one of his most toughly worded messages, elaborating the hard-line policy he had repeatedly urged on President Roosevelt in the last weeks of FDR's life. "An iron curtain is drawn down upon their front," Churchill telegraphed Truman. "We do not know what is going on behind. There seems little doubt that the whole of the regions east of the line Lübeck-Trieste-Corfu will soon be completely in their hands. . . . Surely, it is vital now to come to an understanding with Russia, or see where we are with her, before we weaken our armies mortally or retire to the zones of occupation. This can only be done by a personal meeting. I should be most grateful for your opinion and advice. Of course we may take the view that Russia will behave impeccably, and no doubt that offers the most convenient solution. To sum up, this issue of a settlement with Russia before our strength has gone seems to me to dwarf all others."

For his part, Truman had no soft spot in his heart for the Soviet Union. Before and during the war, he had often been highly critical of Stalin and Stalinism. But the president was continuing to feel his way, and so he turned aside the prime minister's urgent counsel, a fact Churchill still deplored many years later.

Indeed Truman's initial view of the prime minister was far from supportive. Talking with Joseph E. Davies, the former U.S. ambassador to Moscow, in mid-May 1945, Truman remarked he was "having as much difficulty with Prime Minister Churchill as I was having with Stalin—that it was my opinion that each of

Sir Winston S. Churchill, 1946. Artist: Douglas Chandor. (National Portrait Gallery, Smithsonian Institution)

them was trying to make me *the paw of the cat* that pulled the chestnuts out of the fire ..."

On 27 May, Davies met with Churchill in London, and the prime minister lost no time reiterating his idea of a special Anglo-American relationship: "The Prime Minister cannot readily bring himself to accept the idea that the position of the United States is that Britain and Soviet Russia are just two foreign Powers, six of one and half a dozen of the other, with whom the troubles of the late war have to be adjusted. Except in so far as force is concerned, there is no equality between right and wrong. The great causes and principles for which Britain and the United States have suffered and triumphed are not mere matters of the balance of power. They in fact involved the salvation of the world."

Such arguments carried little weight with Truman, who likewise declined to meet with Churchill before their summit with Stalin at Potsdam, so as not to give the Soviet leader ground for believing that there was secret collaboration between Washington and London.

Churchill, Truman wrote in his diary on 22 May, has "been importuning me to urge Stalin to come to a meeting. But Churchill wanted me to meet with him first—which I do not want to do. Stalin already has an opinion we're ganging up on him."

One result of the president's circumspection was that there was little advance planning for Potsdam between Washington and London, and Churchill was highly displeased with what he regarded as a serious lack of Anglo-American coordination at the conference.

On the other hand, at Potsdam, the prime minister was far from being as diametrically anti-Soviet as he often liked to represent himself. No one realized this better than his foreign secretary, Anthony Eden. As he noted in his conference diary on 17 July: "have never seen [Winston] worse. Dined alone with him and again urged him not to give up our few cards without return. But he is again under Stalin's spell. He kept repeating 'I like that man' and I am full of admiration of Stalin's handling of him. I told him I was hoping that would move him. It did a little!"

Eden spoke too soon. The next night Churchill and Stalin dined together and the prime minister came away singing his praises. Stalin, he told his physician, Lord Moran, "gave me his word there will be free elections in the countries set free by his armies. You are sceptical, Charles? I don't see why. We must listen to these Russians. They mobilized twelve million men, and nearly half of them were killed or are missing. I told Stalin Russia has been like a giant with his nostrils pinched. I was thinking of the narrows from the Baltic and the Black Sea. If they want to be a sea power, why not?"

It has recently been contended that, following his defeat in the 1945 general election, Churchill busied himself trying to persuade Truman to adopt a much stronger stand against the Soviet Union. The published and still unpublished record does not support that conclusion. It is true that the President was on the podium when Churchill delivered his famous "iron curtain" address at Westminster College at Fulton, Missouri, on 5 March 1946, but Truman had no advance knowledge of Churchill's remarks, nor did he specifically endorse them later.

As the president put it in a letter to his mother and sister on 11 March, "I think [the speech] did some good, although I am not yet ready to endorse Mr. Churchill's speech." The following day, Truman repeated his circumspect view in a letter to "My dear Winston": "The people in Missouri," he wrote, "were highly pleased with your visit and enjoyed what you had to say." But beyond that, he was clearly unwilling to go.

As Britain's economic and international situation deteriorated dramatically in 1946–47, Churchill made no personal effort to alert the president to what loomed ahead in Greece and Turkey, though he warmly applauded Truman's address to the Congress on 12 March 1947, in which the president set forth what soon became known as the Truman Doctrine. As Churchill put it in a two-page long-hand letter—addressed "My dear Harry"—on 24 September 1947: "I cannot resist ... [telling] you how much I admire the policy into which you have guided your great country, and to thank you from the bottom of my heart for all you are doing to save the world from famine and war."

For his part, the president was far from certain that the new U.S. interventionist course would suffice to deter a possible Soviet move in central or southern Europe. As he wrote Mrs. Truman back in Independence on 30 September 1947: "here is a situation fraught with terrible consequences. Suppose, for instance, that Italy should fold up and that Tito then would march into the Po Valley. All the Mediterranean coast of France then is open to Russian occupation and the iron curtain comes to Bordeaux, Calais, Antwerp, and The Hague. We withdraw from Greece and Turkey and *prepare for war*."

While Truman was busy trying to stabilize postwar Europe,

Churchill was occupied writing his multivolume history of the Second World War. When the State Department objected to the former prime minister publishing the verbatim texts of his wartime messages to Roosevelt, on 5 May 1948, Churchill appealed directly to Truman, noting, "I cannot myself see anything in them, the publication of which would be harmful or embarrassing to the United States, but if there is any passage in them which you would prefer should be deleted, pray let me know."

Truman at once directed the State Department to "make an examination of the whole matter," and, on 18 May he wrote Churchill that "there seems to have been a misunderstanding as to what you had proposed to do." In any case, the president added, "I am more than happy that the publication will not come out until January first, 1949 because, as you know, we are in the midst of a very bitter political presidential election in this country and it will be better for all concerned if this publication comes out after that election is over."

Although undoubtedly Governor Thomas E. Dewey and the Republican party supported continued close relations with Great Britain, there was nothing neutral about Churchill's position during the 1948 campaign, and following Truman's victory, Churchill sent him a warm message of congratulations.

"I felt keenly," Churchill wrote, "the way you were treated by some of your party and in particular [Henry A.] Wallace who seemed to us over here to be a greater danger than he proved. But all this has now become only the background of your personal triumph. Of course it is my business as a foreigner or half a foreigner to keep out of American politics, but I am sure I can now say what a relief it has been to me and most of us here to feel that the long continued comradeship between us and also with the Democratic Party in peace and war will not be interrupted. This is most necessary and gives the best chance of preserving peace."

Truman's victory did not, however, significantly reduce Churchill's gloom about the prevailing international prospect. He remained concerned that World War III was a serious possibility and that only their possession of the atom bomb gave the Western democracies a measure of reassurance. As Churchill wrote the president on 29 June 1949: "I was deeply impressed by your statement about not fearing to use the atomic bomb if the need arose. I am sure this will do more than anything else to ward off the catastrophe of a third world war. . . . I remain under the impression of the fearful dangers which impend upon us. Complete unity, superior force and the undoubted readiness to use it, give us the only hopes of escape. Without you nothing can be done."

Having just experienced the perilous Soviet blockade of West Berlin, a move that brought East and West dangerously close to a military showdown, Truman seemed unwilling to share Churchill's gloomy forebodings. On 2 July the president replied: "I am not quite so pessimistic as you are about the prospects for a third world war. I rather think that eventually we are going to forget that idea, and get a real world peace. I don't believe even the Russians can stand it to face complete destruction, which certainly would happen to them in the event of another war."

When the Korean War broke out in June 1950, Churchill was still in opposition, but when he returned to office in October 1951, the prime minister lost no time seeking to restore something like his old wartime relationship with FDR. That effort, assiduously pursued for the remainder of Truman's term, did not, however, meet with much success. For although he was far too discreet to say so, Truman recognized only too well that circumstances had radically changed since 1945, and, rightly or wrongly, he was determined to steer a largely independent American course in international affairs.

The president had never been an exponent of summitry, and he did not share Churchill's enthusiasm for another early meeting with Stalin. The president was likewise dubious about joining the British government in establishing a united policy toward Iran, at a time when its radical new prime minister Dr. Mohammad Mossadegh had recently directed the nationalization of the Anglo-Iranian Oil Company in May 1951, a move Churchill rightly considered a serious blow to Britain's declining international position.

In January 1952, Churchill traveled to Washington for what proved to be his last extended sessions with Truman. The visit was to cover both general and concrete questions. There was the present and future state of Anglo-American relations. There was Britain's policy toward the proposed European army (EDC), and the maintenance of U.S. air bases in the United Kingdom. There was the increasingly turbulent Iranian situation, threatening long-standing Anglo-American oil interests, for which the British wanted a specific expression of U.S. support. There was the identity of the future NATO naval commander. Over six years after the end of the war, Churchill did not need to be told that his hand was considerably weaker than when he had arrived for his first wartime visit with President Roosevelt in late December 1941.

Probably the most sensitive question was the identity of the future head of the new NATO Atlantic Command. It had previously been agreed that it should be an American. Not surprisingly, Churchill was strongly—almost pathologically—opposed to that decision. But after extended and sometimes heated discussion at the highest level, the earlier agreement was allowed to stand.

In addition, the prime minister hoped to use the opportunity to learn where the president seemed headed in world affairs and to contribute his views to the continued shaping of American policy. But unknown to Churchill, Truman had long decided not to seek another term in the White House. His overriding concern was the interminable Korean War. Long-range foreign policy planning he would leave to his eventual successor.

Undoubtedly, the highlight of the prime minister's visit was his third address to Congress. Churchill's speech frankly recognized Britain's decline since the era of the Second World War but at the same time placed renewed emphasis on a broader Anglo-American relationship. "Bismarck," he concluded, "once said that the supreme fact of the nineteenth century was that Britain and the United States spoke the same language. Let us make sure that the supreme fact of the twentieth century is that they tread the same path."

Whatever its limited success, Churchill's visit marked the beginning, not the end, of an active period of Anglo-American diplomacy, especially as it related to the volatile Iranian oil situation. On 16 August—while Anthony Eden was on his honeymoon with Lady Clarissa—the prime minister initiated a personal exchange on the subject with Truman, looking toward a joint U.S.-British message to the Iranian leader.

"If it came about," he telegraphed the president, "that American oil interests were working to take our place in the Persian oil fields after we have been treated so ill there, this might well raise serious controversy in this country. . . . We are also helping all we can in Korea. No country is running voluntarily the risks which we are, should atomic warfare be started by Soviet Russia.

"I hope," Churchill continued, "you will do your best to prevent American help for Musaddiq, either Governmental or commercial, from becoming a powerful argument in the mouths of those who care little for the great forward steps towards Anglo-American unity in the common cause which you and I have worked for so long."

Truman replied at once. Supporting Churchill's "offer" in principle, he cautioned the prime minister, "I am concerned lest the enemies of the West in their propaganda seize on such an approach as evidence that our two nations are 'ganging up' on Iran. The most logical procedure seems to me to have each of us send a message to Mosadeq but so drafted as to clearly indicate consultation and agreement between us."

On 22 August, Churchill responded: "I thought that it might do good if we had a gallop together such as I often had with F.D.R. There is little doubt that a brief cogent, joint telegram would be far more effective than a continuance of the futile parleying which has got us no further in all these months."

Two days later, the president agreed: "In view of your strong feelings on the matter, and the fact that we are in agreement that this approach limits neither you nor me nor our governments to particular courses of action in the future, I agree to join with you in a common message to the Prime Minister of Iran."

In his diary, John Colville, Churchill's joint principal private secretary, recorded with much satisfaction, "It is the first time since 1945 that the Americans have joined with us in taking joint action against a third power."

The Truman-Churchill collaboration was drawing to a close. On 12 November, the president summed up his feelings about the recent Eisenhower-Stevenson campaign: "The whistle stop tour on my part didn't work out as well this time as it did before. I think the people were voting for their great military hero because the majority in the House and Senate is very narrow and a great many members of the House and Senate were elected in the states that went for the General."

The last official Truman-Churchill meeting took place at the White House on 8 January 1953. The prime minister had come over mostly to confer with the president-elect. "The meeting," Secretary of State Dean Acheson's memorandum of conversation declared, "was a social and mostly friendly one. ... The President and the Prime Minister recalled their meeting at Potsdam and the next meeting, which was the trip to Fulton, Missouri, for Mr. Churchill's speech."

That night Churchill gave a formal dinner for the president. Colville's diary reported how it ended: "After dinner Truman played the piano. Nobody would listen because they were all busy with post-mortems on a diatribe in favor of Zionism and against Egypt which W. had delivered at dinner (to the disagreement of practically all the Americans present, though they admitted that the large Jewish vote would prevent them disagreeing publicly). However, on W.'s instructions, I gathered all to the piano and we had a quarter of an hour's presidential piano playing before Truman left. He played with quite a nice touch and, as he said himself, could probably have made a living on the stage of the lesser music-halls."

Not surprisingly, following the president's retirement from the White House, relations between the two men gradually ebbed. On 24 June 1956 Truman, on a trip to Europe, visited Churchill—himself retired since April 1955—at his country home, and he recorded in his diary: "Sir Winston and I had a most pleasant conversation about Potsdam, its agreements and Russian perfidy. . . . Mr. Churchill is as keen mentally as ever. . . . But his physical condition shows his 82 years. . . . He remarked that it would be a great thing for the world if I should become President of the United States again. I told him there was no chance of that."

In his memoirs, published in 1969, Dean Acheson wrote that "President Truman often spoke of Mr. Churchill as the greatest public figure of our time." Churchill warmly reciprocated the president's sentiment. "You, more than any other man, have saved western civilization," he told Truman on board the *Williamsburg* in January 1952. The president might have agreed that they did their damnedest.

Copies of the complete Truman-Churchill correspondence are located at the Harry S. Truman Library. Churchill's *Triumph and Tragedy*, vol. 6 of his World War II memoirs (Boston: Houghton Mifflin, 1953), contains a diplomatic introduction to their relationship in 1945. Churchill's far less diplomatic comments, then and later, are recorded in his physician's extraordinary account *Churchill: The Struggle for Survival, 1940–1965, Taken from the Diaries of Lord Moran* (Boston: Houghton Mifflin, 1966), with some additional details in John Colville, *The Fringes of Power: 10 Downing Street Diaries 1939–1955* (New York: Norton 1985). Truman gave a brief account of their relations in his *Memoirs*, and perceptive reflections are contained in Margaret Truman's *Harry S. Truman* (New York: Morrow, 1972). There are some interesting details in Anthony Eden, *The Reckoning* (Boston: Houghton Mifflin, 1965). Richard A. Best, *Co-operation with Like-Minded Peoples: British Influences on American Security Policy, 1945–1949* (Westport, Conn.: Greenwood Press, 1986), and Henry B. Ryan, *The Vision of Anglo-America: The US-UK Alliance and the Emerging Cold War, 1943–1946* (Cambridge: Cambridge University Press 1987), are useful introductions to contemporary Anglo-American relations in the Truman-Churchill era, and so is Robin Edwards, *Setting the Mold: The United States and Britain, 1945–1950* (Oxford: Oxford University Press, 1986). William Roger Louis and Hedley Bull, eds., *The Special Relationship: Anglo-American Relations since 1945* (New York: Oxford University Press, 1986), supplies additional perspective. Martin Gilbert's volumes 7 and 8 of the official Churchill biography *Winston S. Churchill* (London: Heineman, 1986, 1988) are important. Fraser J. Harbutt, *The Iron Curtain: Churchill, America, and the Origins of the Cold War* (New York: Oxford University Press, 1986), significantly overestimates Churchill's influence on Truman.

FRANCIS L. LOEWENHEIM

See also Great Britain; Potsdam Conference; Soviet Union (photograph)

Civil Liberties

The history of civil liberties during the Truman presidency is paradoxical. Truman's early political battles with the Ku Klux Klan and his personal sense of fair play made him sympathetic to civil liberties. He was elected to the Senate with important support from labor unions and civil rights groups. Yet, although he was unalterably opposed to the demagoguery of Joseph McCarthy, Carl Mundt, Richard Nixon, and other red-baiters, Truman as president was unable to stop the growing hysteria. Moreover, his Justice Department and four Supreme Court appointees showed little sympathy for the cause of civil liberties. Thus, overall, the Truman years were particularly bleak for civil liberties.

All three branches of the federal government followed policies that restricted and undermined civil liberties during Truman's presidency. In addition, many states repressed dissent, labor unions, and free political expression. The strongest assault on civil liberties at the national level came from the conservative Congress, dominated by Republicans and southern Democrats, which passed restrictive legislation, conducted repressive investigations, and pressured the executive branch to root out subversives, even where none existed. Congressional investigators rarely respected civil liberties and due process. Both the Senate Internal Security Committee and the House Committee on Un-American Activities were notorious for their arbitrary procedures, bullying of witnesses, and extreme hostility to First and Fifth Amendment rights. Some media commentators compared these committee investigations to the Salem witch trials of 1692. A similar comparison appeared in an important literary work, Arthur Miller's *The Crucible*.

The executive branch was more sensitive to constitutional rights but nevertheless undermined civil liberties through prosecutions of political radicals, immigration and visa restrictions, limitations on foreign travel, and internal government investigations of civil servants suspected of disloyalty. Prosecutions and investigations begun by Truman's Justice Department added to the postwar red scare and the rising tide of McCarthyism. The courts abetted these investigations, which were often carried out with little regard for due process. For example in *Bailey* v. *Richardson* (1951) the Supreme Court upheld the firing of a federal employee even though the allegation of her disloyalty was based on the accusations of witnesses who were never revealed to her.

Bailey was one of many Truman era cases in which the Supreme Court upheld arbitrary procedures, vague statutes, and apparent denials of free speech or due process by the executive and legislative branches of the government. Truman's appointees to the Court were far less sensitive to civil liberties concerns than the Roosevelt appointees they replaced. When Truman left office, civil liberties in America were far less secure than when he entered the White House.

Truman had become president four months before the end of World War II. During this period the Supreme Court gradually moved away from the expansion of civil liberties begun in the mid-1930s. In *Cramer* v. *United States* (1945) the Court strictly defined treason and overturned the conviction of a citizen who had done nothing more than meet with a Nazi saboteur. But in 1947 the Court used a far less precise standard of treason in upholding the conviction in *Haupt* v. *United States*, even though the accused had not actually participated in any acts of sabotage.

Similar changes took place in immigration law. In 1945 the Court prevented the deportation of an Australian-born labor leader who the government claimed was a Communist. Similarly, in 1946 the Court upheld the right of a pacifist to be naturalized, even though the 1940 Naturalization Act required a willingness to bear arms in defense of the nation. A year later, however, the Court sustained the revocation of American citizenship for a naturalized pro-Nazi German-American. This decision effectively meant that naturalized citizens would have different civil liberties than native born Americans.

As the war came to an end the Truman administration dismantled the internment camps set up in 1942 for over 110,000 Japanese-Americans and Japanese resident aliens. But in 1950 Congress passed, over President Truman's veto, the Emergency Detention Act allowing for the detention of citizens at the authorization of the president during an "emergency."

The end of the war also led to war crimes trials in Europe and Japan. The United States vigorously took part in these trials, with Supreme Court Justice Robert Jackson serving on the Nuremberg Tribunal. Although some Americans raised questions about the propriety of these trials, on the grounds that they were ex post facto proceedings, the Supreme Court refused to hear appeals from the various war crimes trials.

On the labor front, immediately after World War II, unions sought higher wages, which reflected postwar economic realities. In 1946 the United Mine Workers went on strike after contract negotiations broke down. Using his war powers Truman seized the coal mines, but the miners still refused to work. Despite his previous prolabor stance, Truman then sought an injunction against the strike. The Supreme Court, ignoring the Norris–La Guardia Act, upheld large fines against the United Mine Workers and union president John L. Lewis. The opinion in this case was written by Chief Justice Fred Vinson, a recent Truman appointee.

In 1947 Congress passed the Taft-Hartley Act over Truman's veto. An amendment to the Wagner Act, it took power away from organized labor while strengthening management. The law undermined the civil liberties of unions by prohibiting union donations to political campaigns, limiting the closed shop, and forcing union officials to sign affidavits that they were not Communists and that they did not subscribe to Communist ideas. In a series of decisions in 1949 and 1950 the Supreme Court upheld the Taft-Hartley Act and limited the rights of picketers and strikers. Significantly the Court gradually removed Bill of Rights protections from picketers. In *Thornhill* v. *Alabama* (1940), the Court had held that "the dissemination of information concerning the facts of a labor dispute must be regarded as within the area of free discussion that is guaranteed by the Constitution." But in *Giboney* v. *Empire Storage and Ice Co.* (1949) the Court held that picketing was not always protected by the First Amendment. The Court declared that picketers were "doing more than exercising a right of free speech of press" and were actually "exercising their economic power." The removal of constitutional protection for picketing was taken a step further in *International Brotherhood of Teamsters* v. *Hanke* (1949), which involved peaceful picketing for a totally lawful purpose. Nevertheless, the Court held, by a vote of 5 to 3, that "while picketing has an ingredient of communication it cannot dogmatically be equated with the constitutionally protected freedom of speech." Three of the five majority votes came from Truman appointees. In *American Communication Association* v. *Douds* (1950) the Court further limited the freedom of expression of unions by upholding the anti-Communist provisions of the Taft-Hartley Act. Chief Justice Vinson declared that this was not a restriction on free speech, but a legitimate commercial regulation. In dissent Justice Hugo Black

"Loyalty tests? Essential to security. Movie censorship? Of course! Should left-wingers be jailed? Naturally. What's that? Should food be rationed? RIDICULOUS! WHO WANTS TO LIVE IN A POLICE STATE?"

By Bill Mauldin. Copyright 1947 by Bill Mauldin.

complained that the commerce clause did not "restrict the right to think."

Limiting the rights of workers did not, however, carry over to management. During the Korean War Truman ordered the seizure of the nation's steel mills to maintain production during a strike. But in *Youngstown Sheet and Tube* v. *Sawyer* (1952) the Court ordered Truman to relinquish the mills. Here the Court protected the Fifth Amendment property rights of the factory owners. Although two Truman appointees, Chief Justice Vinson and Sherman Minton, dissented in this case, two others, Tom Clark and Harold Burton, sided with the majority.

The postwar anti-Communist crusades got underway in 1947 when the Republican-controlled House of Representatives resurrected the House Committee on Un-American Activities (HUAC). Under the Republican chairman, J. Parnell Thomas, HUAC began to investigate the spread of communism in America. In 1947 ten screen writers and directors, known as the "Hollywood Ten," were jailed for contempt of Congress for refusing to answer questions at a HUAC hearing. They were later blacklisted by Hollywood studios, as were scores of other actors, writers, and film professionals who refused to cooperate with congressional investigations. One actor who cooperated fully was the president of the Screen Actors Guild, Ronald Reagan. In 1948 HUAC committee activities led to the investigation of Alger Hiss, a State Department official accused of having once been a Communist. Although the charges of Communist affiliation were never proved, Hiss was eventually convicted of perjury. These hearings catapulted an obscure

California congressman, Richard Nixon, into the national limelight.

Pressure from Congress and newspapers led Truman to institute his own loyalty investigations. In 1946 Truman established a Temporary Commission on Employee Loyalty, which was followed in 1947 by the Federal Loyalty and Security Program. By 1951 the Civil Service Commission had investigated and cleared over 3 million federal employees, and the FBI had investigated another 14,000. Only 212 federal employees were dismissed because their loyalty was in doubt, but another 2,000 left government service, although few, if any, were disloyal. In 1947 Attorney General Clark issued a list of "subversive groups." This led to investigations of thousands of Americans with only the most tangential connections to these organizations. The careers and lives of those examined were often destroyed in the process.

In 1950 Congress passed the Internal Security Act, or McCarran Act. Title I of this act required that all Communist organizations register with the attorney general and provide a full list of their members. Title II, the Emergency Detention Act, allowed for the incarceration of civilians without formal charges. The act also created the Subversive Activities Control Board. Truman vetoed this bill, calling it "the greatest danger to freedom of speech, press, and assembly since the Alien and Sedition Laws of 1798," but Congress overrode the veto.

Although Truman opposed much of the era's red scare mentality, his administration's implementation of immigration policies probably exacerbated the hysteria. Before 1952 the Truman administration arbitrarily deported immigrants, refused others entry to the nation, and confined some without charges. Persons who had joined a Communist party in their native lands twenty or thirty years earlier were deported in the early 1950s. In *Shaugnessy* v. *U.S. ex rel Mezei* (1953) the Supreme Court upheld the incarceration, without formal charges, of an immigrant on the basis of an anonymous charge that he was a threat to national security. While deporting persons who had long ago renounced their Communist affiliations, the Truman administration allowed former Nazis to enter the nation and even helped some Nazi war criminals relocate in the United States and elsewhere. In 1952 Truman vetoed the Walter-McCarren Immigration Act because he thought it too repressive. The new law, passed over Truman's veto, relaxed some of the nation's racist immigration quotas while creating ideological restrictions.

The Truman administration also devoted its energies to prosecuting native-born Communists. In 1948 the government prosecuted eleven leaders of the American Communist party, who were convicted in a sensational nine-month trial in New York City before a judge blatantly hostile to the defendants. These Communist party leaders were not charged with any overt acts against the national interest, but only with a conspiracy to teach and advocate the overthrow of the government. In *Dennis* v. *United States* (1952) the Supreme Court upheld these convictions. Speaking for the Court, Chief Justice Vinson admitted that the Communist party did not pose any immediate danger to the nation, but nevertheless upheld the suppression of advocacy as a clear and present danger to the nation. The Court adopted the reasoning of Chief Judge Learned Hand, who had upheld the convictions in the Court of Appeals. Hand had asserted that the court "must ask whether the gravity of the 'evil,' discounted by its improbability, justifies such invasion of free speech as is necessary to avoid the danger." Despite the Communist party's minuscule size and lack of both resources and public support, the Court found this test sufficient to uphold the convictions. In dissent Justice Black noted that the party officials had been convicted of using speech and press "to teach and advocate" their ideas. He concluded, "No matter how it is worded, this is a virulent form of prior censorship of speech and press, which I believe the First Amendment forbids." Black understood that "few will protest the conviction of these Communist petitioners," and he could only express his hope "that in calmer times, when present pressures, passions, and fears subside, this or some later Court will restore the First Amendment liberties to the high preferred place where they belong in a free society."

In *Dennis* Vinson's majority opinion was joined by two other Truman appointees, Harold Burton and Sherman Minton, and by Stanley Reed, a Roosevelt appointee. Two other Roosevelt appointees, Felix Frankfurter and Robert Jackson, wrote concurring opinions, while two others, Black and William O. Douglas, dissented. Tom Clark, who had been Truman's attorney general when the *Dennis* prosecutions began, did not participate in the case. Had he voted, Clark would have undoubtedly upheld the conviction. This voting pattern indicates the nature of the Court that Truman helped create. On free speech and national security issues it was conservative, with a narrow view of the meaning of the First and Fifth Amendments. In a number of decisions during the period the court limited freedom of speech and the press in political matters.

The Court during the Truman administration also weakened the First Amendment's requirement of a prohibition on the separation of church and state. In *Everson* v. *Board of Education of the Township of Ewing* (1947) the Court upheld the use of tax dollars to fund transportation to religious schools. Although the Court did not allow the use of public property for religious education (*McCollum* v. *Board of Education*, [1951]), in *Zorach* v. *Clauson* (1952) it did allow the release of students from the public schools for religious education. Even though school officials played an active role in guaranteeing the attendance of the students in the church school programs, the Court allowed such practices. In a bitter dissent Justice Jackson complained that this decision left the wall of separation between church and state "warped and twisted."

Thus, although Truman opposed the hysterical nature of the Communist witch-hunts of these years and vetoed some repressive legislation, he nevertheless abetted the hysteria in two important ways. First, his administration conducted its own investigations and prosecutions. The Justice Department and the Immigration and Naturalization Service were particularly insensitive to civil liberties issues. As he knew when he adopted the slogan "the buck stops here," Truman was ultimately responsible for the actions of subordinates in executive branch departments. Second, Truman appointed four men to the Supreme Court who were generally unconcerned about civil liberties, especially in national security cases.

For good discussions of the fate of civil liberties in these years, see Alfred H. Kelly, Winfred A. Harbison, and Herman Belz, *The American Constitution*, 6th ed. (New York: W. W. Norton, 1983); Richard Kirkendall, "Tom C. Clark," in *The Justices of the United States Supreme Court, 1789–1978*, ed. Leon Friedman and Fred L. Israel, 2665–95 (New York: Chelsea House, 1980); Paul Murphy, *The Constitution in Crisis Times* (New York: Harper & Row,

1972); and C. Herman Pritchett, *Civil Liberties and the Vinson Court* (Chicago: University of Chicago Press, 1954).

PAUL FINKELMAN

See also Japanese-Americans; Labor; Loyalty Program; Red Scare; Supreme Court, United States

Civil Rights

Following the death of Franklin Roosevelt many newspaper articles likened the new president, Harry S. Truman, to Abraham Lincoln's successor, Andrew Johnson. It was not a comparison to buoy the hopes of civil rights advocates. Indeed, the partisans of black rights had been disheartened by the "second Missouri Compromise" which resulted in Truman replacing Henry Wallace on the Democratic ticket in 1944; and the Republicans that year circulated a rumor in Harlem—"Roosevelt is old and may die and you will have a Ku Klux Klansman in the White House."

Although Truman, as a successful candidate of the Pendergast machine in Missouri, had done nothing to alienate the 130,000 black voters in his constituency and, as a loyal New Dealer, had voted for appropriations for the Fair Employment Practices Committee (FEPC) and for passage of anti–poll tax and antilynching legislation, he had never expressed enthusiasm for any civil rights measure. "Everything is going to be all right," commented one southern senator on Truman's racial views. "The new president knows how to handle the niggers." And little that Truman did in his first year in the White House altered the perception of him as a border-state moderate anxious to please the southern whites in his party.

The pressures for racial reforms, however, continued to build. The New Deal and, especially, the Second World War had quickened the expectations of those insisting that the national government do more and had emboldened Negro organizations to demand and threaten more. The revulsion against Nazi racism had spurred increased rhetorical denunciations of southern discrimination, and the wartime economic gains of blacks had galvanized their determination to secure a permanent FEPC, outlaw lynching, and abolish the poll tax. At the same time, the accelerating northward migration of blacks made the Negro vote increasingly important to urban politicians in both parties and to all potential presidential candidates. The emerging cold war—as well as the establishment of the United Nations with its promise of human rights for all and the struggle for independence of the nonwhite nations of Africa and Asia—tied civil rights issues to those of national security and made the struggle against racial discrimination part of the battle against communism.

Over a million blacks who had served in the armed forces returned from the war eager to challenge the institutions and practices of white supremacy. But their demands for first-class citizenship, particularly their attempts to register to vote, led to a revived Ku Klux Klan and the widespread use of violence to maintain the segregated southern way of life. The murders of several blacks and the brutal repression of others in 1946 prompted the creation of new progressive organizations like the National Committee for Justice in Columbia, Tennessee, and hastened some forty religious and civil liberties groups to join the National Association for the Advancement of Colored People (NAACP) in a National Emergency Committee against Violence. They pleaded with the president to act to protect the physical security of defenseless southern blacks.

Genuinely shocked by the gruesome racial murders and fearful of the grist they provided for Communist propaganda mills, Truman established a Committee on Civil Rights in December 1946, with a mandate to investigate law enforcement procedures and to recommend measures to safeguard minorities. The extremely liberal and independent-minded members of the committee, however, chose to range far beyond their specific instructions. They surveyed the entire spectrum of race relations and presented the president in October 1947 with a report, *To Secure These Rights*, that boldly advocated passage of laws to end lynching and the poll tax, establishment of a permanent FEPC, home rule for the District of Columbia, desegregation of the armed forces, creation of a permanent civil rights division of the Justice Department, elimination of grants-in-aid from the federal government to segregated institutions, and support for a legal assault on segregation in education, housing, and interstate transportation. The president heralded the report as "an American charter of human freedom," but avoided any commitment to implement it.

A month later Truman received a confidential memorandum, "The Politics of 1948," from Clark Clifford, his special counsel and administrative assistant. Clifford believed that the 1948 presidential election would hinge on winning the support of urban minorities. In such states as New York, New Jersey, Pennsylvania, Ohio, Illinois, and Michigan the black vote constituted a potential balance of power, and unless Truman championed civil rights, Clifford warned, this essential constituency would go either to the Progressive Henry Wallace or the Republican Thomas Dewey. Confidently predicting that the espousal of civil rights would not cost Truman his southern support, Clifford urged the president to steal Wallace's thunder and to outbid the GOP by calling upon Congress to enact the recommendations of the Committee on Civil Rights.

In a special message to Congress on 2 February 1948, Truman strongly endorsed most of the proposals in *To Secure These Rights*. Although he did not issue the executive orders the committee had urged and did not submit the report's more controversial recommendations, such as withdrawing federal grants from state institutions that practiced racial discrimination, civil rights leaders hailed Truman's message as "Lincolnesque," the greatest freedom document since the Emancipation Proclamation. Southern segregationists, however, accused Truman of "a stab in the back" and threatened to bolt the Democratic party in protest. The president quickly backtracked. Eager to conciliate the conservative Democrats in the South, Truman refused to send the omnibus civil rights bill that had been drafted in the White House to the Hill, would not comment publicly on the issue, and let the Democratic National Convention know that he favored readoption of the vague, noncommittal 1944 civil rights plank in the party platform rather than the uncompromising amendment supported by black, liberal, and labor delegates that pledged the party to support the president's February recommendations to Congress. To hold the Negro vote, which they needed to win their local and state elections, the urban Democrats defied the president and succeeded in adopting a platform that thrust Truman into the role of civil rights tribune.

Edwin Marcus, *New York Times*, 20 March 1949. Copyright 1949 by The New York Times Company. Reprinted by permission.

When few southern Democrats deserted the party for the segregationist States' Rights Democratic, or Dixiecrat, party, Truman was able to turn his attention to winning as large a plurality of Negro votes as possible in his campaign against Dewey and Wallace. In July he issued executive orders against racial discrimination in federal employment and in the armed forces, establishing a fair employment board within the Civil Service Commission and a President's Committee on Equality of Treatment and Opportunity in the Armed Services. Then, in October, Truman became the first president to speak in Harlem. He expressed pride in his antidiscrimination executive orders, warmly praised the Committee on Civil Rights, and, for the first time since his February message to Congress, strongly endorsed the civil rights program charted by the committee. The extreme closeness of the 1948 election enabled various groups to claim that they provided the margin of victory. Truman's plurality of Negro votes in California, Illinois, and Ohio, however, were as decisive to his triumph as any other single factor. Some civil rights leaders believed that this would bring the speedy enactment of the president's civil rights program.

They were mistaken. Truman dutifully submitted legislative proposals to establish a permanent FEPC and to outlaw lynching and the poll tax, but the conservative coalition in Congress effectively blocked their enactment. In 1950, following House approval of an FEPC bill and a measure to grant suffrage and self-government to residents of the District of Columbia, southern senators filibustered the legislation to death. Then the Korean War put an end to Truman's efforts to press Congress on civil rights. Needing the support of southerners for his military and foreign policies, the president repeatedly demurred at black demands for a Korean War Fair Employment Practices Committee. Finally, in December 1951, with black unemployment more than twice as great as white, Truman established an ineffective Committee on Government Contract Compliance. Lacking presidential support, an adequate budget, the right to hold public hearings, and powers of enforcement, the committee failed to halt job discrimination against blacks.

More successfully, the Justice Department in the Truman administration filed briefs as a friend of the court to aid black plaintiffs seeking to overturn racial restrictive covenants in housing and segregation in public education. In *Shelley* v. *Kraemer* (1948) the Supreme Court unanimously held that no court could enforce agreements that prevented minorities from acquiring real estate in certain areas; and, in two key 1950 decisions, *Sweatt* v. *Painter* and *McLaurin* v. *Oklahoma Board of Regents*, the Court ruled that a separate law school for blacks violated the Fourteenth Amendment's requirement for equality in education and that graduate schools could not segregate students according to race. These decisions pointed the way to *Brown* v. *Board of Education* (1954), which declared all segregated educational facilities inherently unequal and, therefore, unconstitutional. In addition, Truman was the first president to appoint a black to a federal judgeship and to the post of governor of the Virgin Islands.

Some historians have criticized Truman for being, at best, a "reluctant tribune" of civil rights. They are dismayed by the gap between presidential promise and performance. They blame him for giving the civil rights cause a low priority, for deferring too often to southern Democrats, for failing to stimulate public support for his civil rights program, and for lacking the commitment necessary to see his reforms through. Other historians claim Truman was not primarily responsible for his administration's failure to achieve more. They emphasize the conservative coalition's veto power over the president's legislative proposals, the necessity of Truman giving priority to foreign and military policies, and the general conservatism of the American people on racial matters. Most Americans evidenced no enthusiasm to go further than Truman on the civil rights issue. In the North as well as the South, popular opposition to racial equality remained firm. When the Democrats in 1952 approved a party platform that retreated from the bold stand on civil rights it had taken four years earlier and left unspecified the steps necessary to end racial discrimination, it went largely unnoticed.

Yet, whatever the reasons for white America's lack of commitment to equality for blacks, the Truman administration brought civil rights squarely into the political arena. Because of new pressures, Truman moved well beyond Franklin Roosevelt and any previous twentieth-century president in furthering the cause of racial justice. Truman was the first American president to proclaim the equality of blacks, to assail discrimination and violence against them, to appoint a commission on civil rights, to present Congress with a comprehensive legislative program on civil rights, and, most significant, to identify his office and administration with the broad goals of the movement for black equality. These actions helped legitimize the campaign for civil rights, increase white awareness of the harms done by racial discrimination, and raise the expectations of blacks that they would soon share the American Dream.

The two most comprehensive accounts of Truman and civil rights are the favorable Donald R. McCoy and Richard T. Ruetten, *Quest and Response: Minority Rights in the Truman Administration*

(Lawrence: University of Kansas Press, 1973), and the much more critical William C. Berman, *The Politics of Civil Rights in the Truman Administration* (Columbus: Ohio State University Press, 1970). The leading revisionist critique is Barton J. Bernstein, ed., "The Ambiguous Legacy: The Truman Administration and Civil Rights," in *Politics and Policies of the Truman Administration*, 269–314 (Chicago: Quadrangle Books, 1970). On what Truman called "the greatest thing that ever happened to America," see Richard M. Dalfiume, *Desegregation of the U.S. Armed Forces; Fighting on Two Fronts, 1939–1953* (Columbia: University of Missouri Press, 1969). See also the relevant chapters in Steven F. Lawson, *Black Ballots: Voting Rights in the South, 1944–1967* (New York: Columbia University Press, 1976), and Doug McAdam, *Political Process and the Development of Black Insurgency, 1930–1970* (Chicago: University of Chicago Press, 1982), as well as Harvard Sitkoff, "Harry Truman and the Election of 1948: The Coming of Age of Civil Rights in American Politics," *Journal of Southern History* 37 (November 1971): 597–616.

HARVARD SITKOFF

See also Armed Forces, Racial Integration of the; Black Americans; Civil Rights, President's Commission on; Dixiecrats; Fair Employment Practices Committee; National Association for the Advancement of Colored People; Supreme Court, United States

Civil Rights, President's Committee on

By Executive Order 9808 issued on 5 December 1946, President Truman established the President's Committee on Civil Rights (PCCR). Chaired by Charles E. Wilson, president of General Electric, and consisting of fourteen other distinguished Americans (including two blacks, Mrs. Sadie T. Alexander and Dr. Channing Tobias), the committee was to examine ways "to safeguard the civil rights of the people." Meeting with committee members at the White House on 15 January 1947, the president gave them a broad charge: "I want our Bill of Rights implemented in fact."

The committee had its origin in the wave of racial violence that followed the Second World War—the war that had promised freedom from fear and oppression. As the incidence of brutality mounted, especially against southern blacks, the National Association for the Advancement of Colored People (NAACP) and the American Council on Race Relations enlisted the support of some forty organizations to create the National Emergency Committee against Mob Violence, which dispatched a delegation to meet with President Truman on 19 September 1946. There, Walter White of the NAACP recounted the acts of savagery, especially the blinding of a black former serviceman, Isaac Woodard. Visibly disturbed, the president rose from his chair and exclaimed: "My God! I had no idea that it was as terrible as that! We've got to do something!" That "something" was the PCCR, the brainchild primarily of White House assistant David Niles.

Over the next six months, the committee elicited information and recommendations from government agencies and private organizations; 141 of the latter responded. On 29 October 1947, the committee presented its report, *To Secure These Rights*, to the president. Consisting of thirty-five recommendations—based on moral, economic, and international considerations—the report was in essence a clarion call of the legitimate grievances of America's minorities, especially those of blacks, and urged citizens, organizations, and government at all levels to work to achieve the "democratic ideal" and "the elimination of segregation, based on race, color, creed, or national origin, from American life."

If the committee's recommendations went beyond what the administration had wanted or anticipated, Truman gave no indication, endorsing the report as "a charter of human rights for our time." With the support of the White House, *To Secure These Rights* received widespread distribution; in the process, it became the most significant educational instrument on racism by any administration to that time.

The report also served as the basis of the president's special message on civil rights to Congress on 2 February 1948—a historic first. In that message, the president observed that *To Secure These Rights* illuminated a "serious gap between our ideals and some of our practices," which "must be closed." He then outlined a ten-point program, which advocated abolition of the poll tax, federal protection against lynching, a fair employment practice committee and a permanent commission on civil rights, a civil rights division in the Department of Justice, stronger civil rights statutes, home rule for the District of Columbia and, for its residents, the right to vote in presidential elections, statehood for Alaska and Hawaii and more self-government for other territories, elimination of segregated facilities in interstate transportation, removal of inequities in naturalization laws, and settlement of the evacuation claims of Japanese-Americans.

In his message, the president also promised executive action that ultimately materialized on 26 July 1948 with Executive Order 9980, which created the Fair Employment Board in the Civil Service Commission, and Executive Order 9981, which established the Committee on Equality of Treatment and Opportunity in the Armed Services. Of course, Truman ignored several of the committee's recommendations, especially "the elimination of segregation . . . from American life," if only because some were politically impossible in the America of the 1940s and 1950s.

In presenting his civil rights program to Congress, Truman had described it as the "minimum," but it was actually bold for its time. And some of that boldness may have been an attempt to undermine the appeal of Henry A. Wallace's Progressive party in the campaign of 1948. In any event, primarily because of a coalition of southern Democrats and midwestern Republicans, much of the president's program failed of legislative enactment. But the PCCR's report and Truman's special message established the agenda for political, judicial, and private action on civil rights for the next generation.

The most thorough account of the PCCR is Donald R. McCoy and Richard T. Ruetten, *Quest and Response: Minority Rights and the Truman Administration* (Lawrence: University Press of Kansas, 1973). For a slightly more critical version of Truman's motives and actions, see William C. Berman, *The Politics of Civil Rights in the Truman Administration* (Columbus: Ohio State University Press, 1970). See also the President's Committee on Civil Rights, *To Secure These Rights: The Report of the President's Committee on Civil Rights* (Washington, D.C.: U.S. Government Printing Office, 1947).

RICHARD T. RUETTEN

See also Civil Rights

Clark, Bennett Champ

(8 January 1890–13 July 1954)

Lawyer, U.S. senator, author, federal judge. Bennett Clark was born in Bowling Green, Missouri, to James Beauchamp ("Champ") and Genevieve Bennett Clark. His father was a prominent Democratic congressman from Missouri (1893–95, 1897–1921), and Speaker of the House from 1911 to 1919. Young Clark attended public schools in Bowling Green and Washington, D.C., and then graduated Phi Beta Kappa from the University of Missouri in 1912. He earned the LL.B. degree from George Washington University in 1914.

Clark became interested in politics at an early age. A local precinct captain at fourteen, he campaigned tirelessly during the 1912 Democratic convention for his father's unsuccessful presidential bid. He was named parliamentarian of the House of Representatives in 1913 and served in that position through 1917. An expert on House procedures, he wrote a useful manual on the subject.

Like his father, Clark was an isolationist. When the United States entered World War I, however, he joined the army, transferred to the Missouri National Guard, and served in France. There he became acquainted with an artillery officer named Harry S. Truman.

After the war, Clark first practiced law in Missouri and then in 1932 entered and won the Democratic primary for the U.S. Senate by defeating a candidate backed by Kansas City boss Tom Pendergast; he then won the general election. In the 1934 Democratic primary, Truman (Pendergast's choice, not Clark's) won the nomination and the general election to become Missouri's junior senator. Throughout their senatorial careers the two Missourians often tangled over patronage and governmental programs. Clark constantly spoke out against New Deal measures. He opposed Roosevelt's Court-packing plan, and the formation of the National Recovery and the Agricultural Adjustment administrations. Clark's political stances, one historian wrote "stemmed from his sense of independence, his identification with the 'old' Democratic party, his lifelong respect for congressional prerogatives and, finally, his commitment to international neutrality." Despite their differences, President Roosevelt asked him to play a part in his 1936 reelection campaign. That same year, at the Democratic National Convention, Clark successfully led the forces to abolish the "two-thirds rule" which had denied his father a presidential nomination.

Clark won reelection in 1938 and continued to try to restrict military spending, curtail the expansion of executive powers, and stymie interventionism. After Pearl Harbor, he abandoned these positions, but by then his political prominence had begun to wane. Clark also had displayed a flaw that would hurt his quest for a third term: Truman said that Clark "never had time to see ordinary customers from Missouri." His neglect of his constituency, his prewar isolationist stance, and opposition from internationalists and labor combined to defeat Clark in the 1944 Democratic primary. His return to private practice was short-lived, however. President Truman appointed him to the Circuit Court of Appeals for the District of Columbia in 1945, on which he served for nine years.

Clark was married twice—first to Miriam Marsh in 1922 (with whom he had three sons) and then, after her death in

1943, to Violet Heming, an English actress. In the summer of 1954, the judge, suffering from poor health, was vacationing in Gloucester, Massachusetts, where on 13 July he died from a cerebral hemorrhage.

Clark's papers are located in the Joint Collection, University of Missouri Western Historical Manuscript Collection–State Historical Society of Missouri Manuscripts. Other papers in the collection also include information about him. No major biography of Clark has been written, although Edward A. Purcell, Jr., recounts his career in John A. Garraty, ed., *Dictionary of American Biography, supp. 5, 1951–1955* (New York: Scribner, 1977). Thomas T. Spencer's "Bennett Champ Clark and the 1936 Presidential Election," *Missouri Historical Review*, January 1981, is a useful study. Books about Truman's political career include information about Clark; see, in particular, Harold F. Gosnell, *Truman's Crises: A Political Biography of Harry S. Truman* (Westport, Conn.: Greenwood, 1980). Most general histories of Missouri mention Clark's political role. Of particular note is Richard S. Kirkendall's *A History of Missouri*, vol. *5, 1919 to 1953* (Columbia: University of Missouri Press, 1986).

JAMES W. GOODRICH

Clark, Tom Campbell

(23 September 1899–13 June 1977)

Attorney general, 1945–49; associate justice, U.S. Supreme Court, 1949–67. Educated at the University of Texas (B.A., 1921; LL.B., 1922), Tom C. Clark practiced law in his native Dallas until 1937 when he became a special assistant to the attorney general. In 1942 Clark worked closely with the military in developing and implementing the internment of the Japanese-Americans, despite Attorney General Francis Biddle's opposition to the program.

In 1943 Clark became an assistant attorney general in the Antitrust Division and then in the Criminal Division. As head of the Criminal Division Clark worked with Senator Truman's special investigating committee, which uncovered frauds against the United States. In 1944 Clark worked with Truman to unseat Henry Wallace as the Democratic party's vice-presidential nominee. Attorney General Biddle supported Wallace in this intraparty struggle, and when Truman succeeded Roosevelt to the presidency, he replaced Biddle with Clark.

As attorney general Clark supported a strong national government. He vigorously enforced antitrust laws and also prosecuted labor leader John L. Lewis for violating an injunction prohibiting the coal strike of 1946. Clark was also a strong advocate of the use of wire taps in criminal and national security cases. He supported loyalty oaths and issued the first attorney general's list of subversive organizations. He worked with Truman in establishing a loyalty program for federal employees and then persuaded Truman to allow the FBI, an arm of the Department of Justice, to administer the program. Clark's policies toward dissent were reminiscent of his attitudes during the wartime internment of Japanese-Americans. He believed national security was far more important than individual rights, civil liberties, or constitutional protections. Under him the Justice Department prosecuted numerous aliens, immigrants, and American-born radicals, including the leaders of the American Communist party in *United States* v. *Dennis, et al.* (1951).

Although willing to suppress civil liberties, Clark was more moderate on civil rights issues. Since he was a southerner, his advocacy of Truman's civil rights programs was particularly important. Under Clark the Justice Department initiated its first modern amicus brief on behalf of a black plaintiff, successfully arguing in *Shelley* v. *Kramer* (1948) that racially restrictive covenants were unconstitutional. This marked the beginning of Justice Department support of civil rights litigation which continued through the next six administrations, until stopped under President Ronald Reagan.

In 1949 Truman rewarded Clark's loyalty by appointing him to replace Justice Frank Murphy on the U.S. Supreme Court. Murphy, a northern urban Catholic and firm supporter of civil liberties, due process, and labor, was a polar opposite of the conservative Texan. Clark's role in implementing the Japanese-American internment program contrasted with Murphy's vigorous condemnation of the program in *Hirabayashi* v. *United States* (1943) and the subsequent internment cases. Organized labor, civil rights groups, and civil libertarians actively opposed Clark's confirmation, but hard lobbying by Senators Lyndon Johnson and Tom Connally, as well as support from the American Bar Association and numerous jurists, led to his confirmation by a vote of 73–8.

On the Court Clark continued to support black civil rights. In *Sweatt* v. *Painter* (1950) he voted with a unanimous Court in ordering the integration of his alma mater, the University of Texas School of Law. Clark was also part of the unanimous Court in *Brown* v. *Board of Education* (1954), and in *Heart of Atlanta Motel, Inc.* v. *United States* (1964), he spoke for a unanimous Court in upholding a key provision of the Civil Rights Act of 1964.

Clark's southern and conservative background would later give some authority to his opinion striking down school prayer in *Abington* v. *Schempp* (1963). Speaking as a native of America's 'Bible Belt,' Clark affirmed that "we are a religious people," but asserted that prayer had no place in the public schools. Clark's conservatism also strengthened the force of his opinion in *Mapp* v. *Ohio* (1961), applying the exclusionary rule to the states, and concurrence in *Baker* v. *Carr* (1962), which undermined states' rights by requiring massive electoral reapportionment.

On other issues Clark was far more conservative. He had restrictive notions of freedom of speech and the press in nonpolitical areas, and he almost always supported the McCarthy era prosecutions on the Court, just as he had in the Justice Department. He invariably supported the military in cases brought by soldiers or civilians.

Although generally supportive of national power and the presidency, Clark did not back the president in the steel seizure case, *Youngstown Sheet and Tube Co.* v. *Sawyer* (1952). Clark was not opposed to the federal seizure of private property during strikes. He had helped implement the seizure of the coal mines in 1946 and had prosecuted the United Mine Workers and union president John L. Lewis when the miners struck the federally operated mines. But he thought that President Truman should have ordered the steelworkers back to work under the Taft-Hartley law before seizing the mills. Truman felt betrayed by his appointee on this issue, just as many other presidents have felt betrayed by their judicial appointees. Clark's vote was predictable, however. He was a "law and order" man who opposed labor. Here he favored use of an existing law, the Taft-Hartley Act, while Truman refused to use the law because he felt it was antilabor.

Clark remained on the bench until 1967, when he left the court because his son, Ramsey, had been appointed attorney general by President Lyndon Johnson. Clark was the only one of Truman's four appointees to have an important impact on the Court.

For further information on Clark and the events he was part of, see Roger Daniels, *The Decision to Relocate the Japanese-Americans* (Philadelphia: J. B. Lippincott, 1975); Alfred H. Kelly, Winfred A. Harbison, and Herman Belz, *The American Constitution*, 6th ed. (New York: W. W. Norton, 1983); Richard Kirkendall, "Tom C. Clark," in *The Justices of the United States Supreme Court, 1789–1978*, edited by Leon Friedman and Fred L. Israel, 2665–95 (New York: Chelsea House, 1980); and C. Herman Pritchett, *Civil Liberties and the Vinson Court* (Chicago: University of Chicago Press, 1954).

PAUL FINKELMAN

See also Cabinets (photograph); Civil Liberties; Civil Rights; Japanese-Americans; Labor; Loyalty Program; Supreme Court, United States (and photograph)

Capt. Clark Clifford, naval aide to President Truman, testifies before Congress, 25 March 1946. (Associated Press/Wide World Photos)

Clifford, Clark McAdams

(25 December 1906–)

Adviser to the president; Washington attorney; secretary of defense under President Johnson. Born in Fort Scott, Kansas, to railroad auditor Frank Andrew Clifford and writer Georgia McAdams Clifford, Clark M. Clifford moved with his family to Saint Louis where he was raised and educated, attending Washington University and its law school. Upon graduating in 1928, he entered private practice in Saint Louis. While on a trip to Europe he met Margery Pepperell Kimball, and they were married on 3 October 1931; the Cliffords had three daughters.

Although married and a father, Clifford asked for and received a commission in the Naval Reserve in 1944 and was assigned as a lieutenant, j.g., to the staff of the Pacific Naval Supply Offices. When the war ended, he had been promoted to lieutenant commander and was serving as assistant to an old acquaintance from Saint Louis, Comm. James K. Vardaman, President Truman's naval aide. When Vardaman resigned in early 1946, Clifford (now a captain) took his place.

Clifford had first met Truman at a dinner in Saint Louis in 1938, and they met again in Washington in 1944. The two men hit it off well, and when Samuel I. Rosenman, who had stayed on from the Roosevelt administration as presidential counsel, resigned in February 1946, Truman began assigning some of Rosenman's former responsibilities to Clifford. At the end of Clifford's term of military service in June 1946, Truman named him to the counsel's post, and he soon became one of the president's closest advisers.

One of Clifford's first tasks involved the railway labor dispute of 1946, when two railway unions struck, despite the government's seizure of the roads. The strike threatened relief shipments to Europe and also imperiled the postwar economic recovery. An angry Truman drafted an intemperate speech which Clifford and Charles Ross toned down somewhat, although it still contained a strong condemnation of the workers; soon after Truman asked Congress for authority to draft the strikers. Later in the year when John L. Lewis threatened to take the United Mine Workers out on strike, Clifford devised the legal strategy that led to the contempt conviction of Lewis and heavy fines on the union.

At the same time the Truman administration was rethinking American foreign policy. The Grand Alliance of World War II between the Soviet Union and the Western democracies had begun to crumble almost as soon it had defeated Germany. By early 1946 people within the government were exploring the alternatives for the administration in its dealings with Russia. Clifford undertook the task of synthesizing these suggestions, and on 24 September 1946 he submitted a seventy-page memorandum to the president. Clifford pictured a Soviet Union bent on expansion. Ready to use any means at its disposal (including espionage and subversion), the country could not be trusted to keep its diplomatic word. The appropriate American response, he suggested, should be an unyielding diplomatic posture, military preparedness, and a determination to resist Soviet pressures, even if that meant war. Clifford himself should not, however, be seen as a hard-liner or "Cold Warrior." His memorandum summed up a process of rethinking that had been going on since the Potsdam and Foreign Ministers' conferences of the year before. But the fact that he wrote it lent credence to Washington speculation that the young aide was emerging as one of the top advisers in the White House.

Clifford's foreign policy responsibilities involved him in drafting Truman's important State of the Union address for 1947, which signaled the change in American policy, and also the message to Congress in March of that year which launched the Truman Doctrine. Initially limited to aid to Greece and Turkey, the doctrine stated that the United States would provide assistance to any country threatened by Communist subversion. Sometime earlier Truman had ordered a review of the country's military organization, and now Clifford was the principal draftsman of the 1947 National Security Act, which brought some unity to the military establishment, and the 1949 amendments that created the Department of Defense as an executive agency with a cabinet-level secretary (a position Clifford later held in the Johnson administration). He also played a key role in convincing Truman to recognize, against the recommendations of the State Department, the new state of Israel shortly after it declared independence in May 1948.

Liberal columnists who believed they saw Truman abandoning the New Deal intimated that this "new conservatism" emanated from Clifford's influence. Although not a knee-jerk liberal, Clifford could hardly be characterized as a conservative at a time when Robert A. Taft epitomized that term. The nature of Clifford's liberalism can be seen in his key role in crafting Truman's 1948 presidential campaign strategy.

A few weeks after the Republicans captured Congress in the 1946 mid-term election, a group of administration officials began a series of informal weekly meetings designed primarily to move the administration in a more liberal direction and to recapture lost political ground for the president. The "progressive caucus" included Oscar Ewing, Leon Keyserling, and Charles Murphy among others, but no one doubted that the key member was Clifford, who had the most direct access to the president. The group did not try to pressure Truman in a particular direction; rather, it presented options to him, pointing out the political and moral advantages of a liberal policy.

In the summer of 1947 Clifford, with the president's approval, began preparing an analysis of the political situation. On 19 November, he submitted a forty-three-page memorandum, which has been termed a "classical political document." Clifford urged Truman to identify himself as a liberal and to do so by openly wooing such traditional Democratic constituencies as labor, intellectuals, and minority groups. Former vice president Henry A. Wallace was already courting these groups, and Truman would have to discredit Wallace and claim for himself the mantle of liberal Democratic leadership. Clifford also recommended that Truman take the offensive and, after capturing the party's nomination, barnstorm the country, traveling coast to coast and delivering two speeches a day. The president adopted the strategy his counsel had suggested, and Clifford accompanied Truman on part of the twenty-two-thousand-mile campaign trail.

Political professionals within the party were impressed not only by Clifford's obvious political savvy but by the man himself. Tall, handsome, and self-assured, he seemed an obvious prospect for elective political office, and they urged him to run for the U.S. Senate from Missouri. But with growing family responsibilities, Clifford decided to opt for the certainties of a law practice. On 1 February 1950, he resigned as special counsel and opened a law office in Washington. Over the next two decades, Clifford & Miller became one of the most prestigious and influential law firms in the capitol. He continued to advise Democratic politicians, although resisting repeated invitations to enter the government. The crisis in Vietnam finally led him to take a cabinet position, succeeding Robert S. McNamara as secretary of defense on 1 March 1968. In that role he is credited with

convincing Lyndon Johnson to begin winding down American involvement in Indochina. At the end of the term he returned to private practice.

Clifford's influence over the years has derived from a number of factors, not the least of which are his open-mindedness, political savvy, and loyalty. From the beginning, he seemed destined for success, and succeed he did, in college, law school, private practice, and the navy. Truman immediately liked his young aide and, according to several sources, enjoyed Clifford's Missouri colloquialisms, his hardheaded approach to problems, and above all, the fact that Clifford spoke to the president without any intimation that Truman was a poor substitute for Franklin Roosevelt. His liberalism, derived from an uncle who had been editor of the *St. Louis Post-Dispatch*, was generally sympathetic to New Deal ideas, but unlike some Roosevelt holdovers, he did not want Truman to carry New Deal measures to an extreme. He believed that at heart the country wanted moderate, not sweeping, reform, and like Truman, he saw the liberal agenda for the late forties as codifying rather than extending the New Deal. It was an approach that greatly appealed to the president.

Clifford Papers relating to the Truman administration are in the Truman Library. There are no formal biographies of Clifford, although countless newspaper and magazine articles have appeared. A good profile is in *Current Biography 1968*, 90–93. One should also see political histories of the Truman administration, such as Alonzo L. Hamby, *Beyond the New Deal: Harry S. Truman and American Liberalism* (New York: Columbia University Press, 1973).

MELVIN L. UROFSKY

See also Armed Forces, Unification of the; Cold War; Election of 1948

Cold War

The cold war between the United States and the Soviet Union emerged from a dense tapestry of events and developments between 1944 and 1947 resulting from the collapse of Europe as World War II ended. The subsequent political, military, and economic division of the Continent into Soviet and U.S. spheres of influence and occupation led to a perpetual competition between the Kremlin and the West. In the late 1940s and early 1950s this competition expanded to global proportions and deeply affected U.S. domestic politics.

The development and growth of the cold war during Truman's presidency can be divided into five stages. Stage 1, a time of continued hope but fraying alliances, began with Truman's first interview with Soviet foreign minister Vyaschlev Molotov on 23 April 1945, only nine days after the Missourian assumed the presidency. As the Red Army occupied Eastern Europe on its way to victory in Berlin, Truman "talked tough" to Molotov about alleged Soviet failures to carry out the Yalta European accords. Truman particularly stressed Soviet delays in the reorganization of the Polish Lublin government to allow sufficient representation in London by the Polish government-in-exile. Truman's objective was to win Soviet respect, but

Molotov's response was that he had never been talked to like that before (a questionable statement, given whom he worked for). Thus, Truman's effort to appear strong and confident may have boomeranged.

Truman's blunder (if such it was) was compounded several weeks later, on 8 May, when the official end of the war in Europe led to the president's accepting doubtful counsel and cutting off Lend-Lease supplies to U.S. Allies. This move actually hurt the British more than the Soviets, but Stalin apparently interpreted the president's move as another unfriendly signal from the new administration in Washington. Subsequent partial restoration of Lend-Lease supplies to both Britain and Russia (to support the final push to end the war against Japan) failed to mollify Stalin completely or allay his suspicions.

These inauspicious beginnings of Truman administration diplomacy toward the Soviets were soon largely offset, however, by more favorable developments in East-West relations. First, Truman dispatched Roosevelt's close confidant and de facto foreign minister, Harry Hopkins, to Moscow in late May to work out a solution to the Polish government crisis. In two extensive talks, Hopkins and Stalin worked out a mutually satisfactory formula for including elements of the London Polish government-in-exile in the new Polish government sponsored and promoted by Stalin.

Second, despite inevitable tensions and strains in negotiating a major international treaty, the United Nations charter was completed at San Francisco in June of 1945, only one month after the fall of Nazi Germany and with U.S. and some British forces preparing for the final battle against Japan. The inclusion of all the major Allied combatants of World War II in the new United Nations reflected hope for an era of general international cooperation after Japan's inevitable defeat.

Third, at the Potsdam Conference in July 1945 Truman got most of what he wanted from Stalin. The Soviet leader confirmed his determination to enter the war against Japan within weeks and relieve the United States of the need to subdue Japanese forces on the Asian mainland after an expected bloody invasion of the home islands. Stalin shared intelligence information with his U.S. colleagues about frantic efforts of the Japanese to convince their leaders to sue for peace. Moreover, James Byrnes, Truman's new secretary of state, was successful in organizing the four-power occupation of Germany, emphasizing centralized administration and accepting Soviet rights to substantial reparations from the Western zones. Byrnes also obtained Soviet acquiescence in the establishment of a Council of Foreign Ministers, consisting of the United States, the Soviet Union, Great Britain, France, and Nationalist China, to write peace treaties with Italy and with Hitler's former allies in Eastern Europe.

Finally, Stalin acceded to U.S. wishes and agreed to negotiate a treaty with Nationalist China that would define Soviet and Chinese territories and spheres of influence in East Asia. At Potsdam Stalin obtained not only a highly favorable agreement on reparations from the Allied zones of Germany but also vague promises of possible Soviet UN mandates over former Italian colonies and revision of the 1923 Montreux Convention, which had granted Turkey the right to regulate shipping through the Dardanelles.

The one issue unresolved at Potsdam was, of course, the atomic bomb. Critics then and now have always assumed that Truman "had it" and that his lack of candor in telling Stalin about it justified subsequent Soviet cold war distrust and suspi-cion. Those familiar with standard diplomatic practice, however, can understand that one never mentions something that is not certain. No atomic bomb had ever been tested or used; an atomic "device" had been set off in the New Mexico desert. Whether that device would translate into a deliverable weapons system of revolutionary proportions was quite uncertain during the Potsdam Conference. Truman obviously realized this. Stalin, also a good diplomat when he wanted to be, should have realized it also because he had planted spies deep within the atomic Manhattan Project.

Stage 2 of the cold war was immediately preceded by the atomic raids at Hiroshima and Nagasaki, which seemed to amplify immeasurably U.S. military power at the expense of the vast Red Army and led rapidly to diplomatic deadlock between Eastern and Western powers. This stage formally began with the breakdown of the London Conference of the Council of Foreign Ministers in September 1945. Byrnes and his British counterpart, Ernest Bevin, refused to conclude peace treaties with Hitler's former Eastern European allies, states now under Red Army occupation, because of flagrant Soviet violations of the Yalta accords. In the U.S. and British views, Stalin had agreed at Yalta, and in his talks with Hopkins, to encourage democratic governments in Rumania, Bulgaria, Poland, and elsewhere. But the Red Army occupation proved harsh and repressive; democratic elements were persecuted and suppressed.

Countering Western intransigence, Molotov suddenly refused to allow the foreign ministers of France and Nationalist China, staunch allies of Byrnes and Bevin, to participate in further discussions. Molotov also pressed, more firmly than at Potsdam, for Soviet UN trusteeships over former Italian colonies in North Africa, which Byrnes and especially Bevin opposed because of the prospect of Soviet power along the vital Mediterranean sea and air lanes between Europe and the Middle East. The result was mutually acknowledged deadlock and breakdown of the first postwar effort at East-West cooperation.

Although the London Conference collapse was certainly a fire bell in the night, it did not, of itself, bring on the cold war. But continuing pressures and unresolved matters drove Russia and the West farther apart. The atomic bomb was perhaps the chief but not the only divisive issue.

Molotov had chided Byrnes about Western monopoly of atomic power at London, and throughout the autumn of 1945 there was growing domestic and international pressure on the Truman administration to do something about "the bomb" within the context of the newly created United Nations. Although some in the administration, especially outgoing secretary of war Henry Stimson, halfheartedly suggested sharing the atomic secret with the Russians, Truman, Attlee, and Mackenzie King of Canada decided in mid-November to go alone to the United Nations and propose international controls on atomic energy. Stalin was thus completely excluded from the atomic club; Soviet influence over international nuclear policy was to be confined to whatever power it could muster in the UN context.

Western fears of sharing any major military secrets with Stalin were exacerbated by revelations of Soviet spying on the wartime atomic project. Igor Gouzenko, a code clerk in the Soviet embassy at Ottawa, defected in September 1945 and brought evidence of a Soviet spy ring, centered on Canadian scientist Allan Nunn May, within the wartime Manhattan Project. Eventually Gouzenko's evidence would convict British physicist

Klaus Fuchs and Americans David Greenglass and Ethel and Julius Rosenberg of treason. The notion of "Communist infiltration into the highest levels" of any enterprise or agency that attracted one's suspicions began to infuse U.S. attitudes and became a major factor in the emerging cold war mentality.

The atomic issue, the unresolved Eastern European peace treaties, evidence of growing Soviet support for dissident Communist elements in northern China and Manchuria, growing problems over two-power rule of Korea, and a climate of growing East-West mistrust induced Byrnes to call for another interim meeting of the Council of Foreign Ministers, which was held in Moscow in mid-December. In exchange for Soviet concessions on the Eastern European peace treaties, Byrnes agreed to a formula on the atomic issue. To mistrustful U.S. senators, led by Arthur Vandenberg and Tom Connally, this formula seemed to place data sharing before controls and inspection provisions. Truman was promptly persuaded that his secretary of state had blundered, and he in effect revoked the agreement by continuing to insist that the United Nations was the place to resolve the issue.

By the end of 1945, therefore, East-West relations were deadlocked, with no apparent formula or set of formulas to reverse the trend. Stage 3 of the developing cold war, which, in fact, marked the onset of complete mutual distrust, rapidly emerged in early 1946. By March the Soviets suddenly seemed to be probing and expanding their influence, if not their outright presence, around the periphery of the Eurasian land mass. Stalin still demanded trusteeships in North Africa, the Soviets were placing pressure on Turkey to modify or revoke the Montreux Convention and open up the Dardanelles to joint administration, and two-power occupation of Korea was breaking down into a Communist North Korea and an American-backed South Korea. Soviet support of rebel Communist forces in China, in violation of the Sino-Soviet Pact of the previous summer, seemed increasingly evident. And "election campaign" speeches by Communist party members, including Stalin himself, emphasized the dangers of "continued capitalist encirclement."

Moreover, the four-power occupation of Germany had increasingly become an issue in East-West relations. During the early months of peace, U.S., British, and Soviet officials got along rather well, and the major source of friction was the French, who were understandably determined to loot their former German masters and suppress any real signs of vigorous, independent political life or economic revival. But in early 1946 French revanchism declined and Soviet rapaciousness was viewed as a growing if not an entirely new threat. Finally, in May 1946, Gen. Lucius D. Clay, the U.S. commander in Germany, cut off all reparations shipments from the Western zones of occupation to the Soviet zone with the full support and cooperation of his British and French counterparts.

As the Kremlin was increasingly perceived as aggressively expansionist around the Eurasian rim and increasingly secretive and determined to impose its iron will throughout Russian-occupied Eastern Europe and Germany, the Truman administration, Congress, and, if the polls are correct, the American people reacted predictably. On 27 February 1946, Senator Vandenberg, in a memorable speech on Capitol Hill, asked rhetorically, "What are the Soviets up to?" and applied his question to Korea, Iran, Germany, and elsewhere. A week later Winston Churchill delivered his famous "iron curtain" speech at Fulton, Missouri, with Truman on the platform.

Following his world tour as President Truman's reparations ambassador, Edwin A. Pauley comments on activities in the Russian zone of North Korea and in neighboring Manchuria. Pauley reported that "Russian removals of machinery 'incapacitated' $2,000,000,000 worth of industry in Manchuria." 24 July 1946. (Associated Press/ Wide World Photos)

Even before these speeches, a hitherto obscure U.S. foreign service officer, George Kennan, transmitted a long telegram from the U.S. embassy in Moscow, assessing dispassionately and in scholarly detail the sources and thrust of Soviet conduct, which he claimed were grounded in a national history of violence, secrecy, and treachery and the Soviets' conviction that their country would always be menaced by hostile states. From this background, Kennan argued, stemmed a peculiar foreign and military policy of confrontation, careful expansion, and genuine, continued caution. Such a policy, Kennan argued, had to be confronted ("containment" as a policy was not yet clearly articulated) by U.S. strength in Europe if the entire exhausted Continent was not to fall under Soviet rule. Kennan was soon recalled to preach his ideas directly to his colleagues at the State Department.

Indeed, direct confrontation between Soviet and Western interests occurred within weeks of the Vandenberg, Churchill, and Kennan warnings. A crisis in Iran marked the transition to the fourth stage of the cold war between Russia and the West, a period of incessant confrontation. Since 1942 the Soviets and the Anglo-Americans had jointly occupied nominally independent Iran so that country could serve as a supply line for Lend-Lease supplies to the hard-pressed Red Army. At war's end British and U.S. forces gradually withdrew to allow Iran to resume full political independence. The Soviets, however, retained military units in the northern part of the country (Azerbaijan), ostensibly to support the Tudeh party, which Stalin claimed was being persecuted by the Tehran government. Rumors of an outright Soviet military coup against Tehran in March 1946 so alarmed and outraged the West that effective diplomatic pressure was mobilized against the Kremlin, which grudgingly carried out a gradual withdrawal from the country.

What had Truman himself contributed to the development of this new world crisis? In allegedly dressing down

Byrnes for allowing himself to be tricked by Stalin into agreeing to data exchange before atomic controls at Moscow, the president supposedly snapped that he was tired of "babying" the Russians. He certainly tacitly agreed with Churchill's iron curtain speech at Fulton. In the spring of 1946 he dispatched the battleship *Missouri* (for which he showed a special fondness because it symbolically represented his home state) to Constantinople, ostensibly to return the body of the Turkish ambassador, who had died suddenly in Washington. Actually, as everyone knew, this action was a show of force and support for the Turks, who were resisting Soviet pressures to share administration of the Dardanelles. The president certainly showed no desire to share the atomic secret with Stalin and indicated little sympathy with the Kremlin's problems with a U.S. atomic monopoly. There is no evidence that he initiated the recall of Kennan to the State Department as a tacit reward for proposing an attractive foreign policy in the long telegram, but he certainly did not oppose it. Nor did the president oppose or question the stiffening U.S. responses and reactions to Soviet behavior in China, Korea, and elsewhere. Truman seems to have acquiesced in a growing policy of Soviet containment that was imposed on him by events orchestrated from the Kremlin.

Whether, in fact, the Kremlin was orchestrating world events or was, along with the West, a victim of circumstance and uncontrollable developments is a compelling question deserving careful and exhaustive study. But, unfortunately, it cannot be answered without access to Soviet and Communist party archives. Without such documents, cold war historians, present and future, must be content with guesswork, cautious suggestion, and dispassionate reading and rereading of the slender Soviet public record of those years.

What is important about the rapid acceleration of the cold war from mid-1946 to the end of the Truman presidency is that it occurred in a world revolutionized by the destruction and promise of World War II. A great revolt against centuries of Western imperialism swept across much of Asia and lapped at the Mideast and Africa during the Truman years. Rather than viewing the cold war as only one element (arguably the most important) in this new world, Truman and his colleagues insisted on infusing cold war thought and assumptions into *all* aspects of national foreign policy. The result was a gradual escalation of Kennan's suggested containment policy to a global level that Kennan himself never envisioned, an eventual "pactomania" (not only creation of NATO but, during the Eisenhower years, SEATO, CENTO, ANZUS, and others), and a determination to confront and challenge any perceived "communist" expansion even if the extent of Kremlin support or involvement was unclear. As late as the Kennedy administration this predilection of U.S. foreign policy, which was developed and fostered by the Truman administration, often induced the United States to oppose legitimate anticolonial aspirations in much of the non-Western world.

Such developments were mostly in the future at the end of 1946. By February 1947, however, major new crises were brewing, caused partly by Kremlin expansion but primarily by the sudden appearance of fundamental weaknesses in the social and economic structures of Europe and the British Empire, which might tempt Stalin to new adventures. On 13 February the British informed the State Department that in their gravely weakened condition, brought on by the war and various persistent shortages, they could no longer maintain their commitments to support Greece (embroiled in a Communist–anti-Communist civil war) and Turkey. Truman promptly asked Congress for authority to begin direct U.S. aid to the two countries. The president phrased his request in broad terms, and it quickly came to be known as the Truman Doctrine. It should be the policy of the United States, Truman told Congress and the country, to support any free peoples who were resisting attempted subjugation by armed minorities or by outside pressures. In the somber atmosphere of early 1947 bipartisan foreign policy seemed to be the only realistic response to global crisis. The president got what he wanted, and in so doing he laid the foundations for a far broader international aid effort, the Marshall Plan.

It had become clear that, without help, Europe could not recover from the devastation of six years of total war. Too many resources, human and material, had been consumed. On 5 June, Secretary of State George C. Marshall offered U.S. aid to any European nations that would agree to coordinate their efforts for recovery and present the United States with a specification of needs and a coherent program. Marshall was careful not to exclude any European country on either side of Churchill's iron curtain, but the message was implicit that economic recovery was the best antidote to increased communist infiltration and subversion of the Western European sociopolitical order. For by this time communist elements had greatly increased their presence in both France and Italy, where outright street violence had broken out, reminiscent of the beginnings of the Nazi era. Thus, U.S. policymakers "held their breath" until Stalin did what it was fervently hoped he would do and denounced the Marshall Plan as an act of U.S. imperialism.

With the Truman Doctrine and the Marshall Plan, the cold war was firmly entrenched as the most important political reality of the postwar world. Three events in 1948 made the iron curtain impenetrable. In February the quasi-independent government of Czechoslovakia was overthrown by Communist elements from within, culminating in the suspicious death of Jan Masaryk. The Czechs were rapidly absorbed into the Soviet bloc. In April, responding to the repeated four-power failure to write a peace treaty with Germany and the resulting initiatives toward economic integration of the Western occupation zones, Stalin imposed a surface blockade of Berlin. The Western Allies quickly responded with an around-the-clock airlift that kept the West Berliners alive for the next thirteen months. Stalin finally lifted the blockade in May 1949 and agreed to another four-power conference. This too failed, and by that time the Western Allies were well on the way to creating an independent Federal Republic of Germany.

In May 1948, meanwhile, alarmed Western European governments met at Brussels to explore collective security against a perceived external and internal threat from the Communist East. The Brussels Pact among five Western European nations laid the foundations for the establishment of the North Atlantic Treaty Organization (NATO) in April 1949. Only a firm declaration of intent to provide for their own common defense allowed the Europeans to overcome historic U.S. reluctance to join "entangling alliances" such as NATO.

The creation of NATO in April 1949 and the formation of the Federal Republic of Germany the following October coincided with the so-called fall of Chiang Kai-shek's Nationalist China to the Communists and Soviet detonation of its own atomic weapon. Thus, 1949 seemed a culmination of the cold war, and it was fitting that Truman was inaugurated in his own right that year. For if Truman did not "start" the cold war, as New Left critics of the 1960s and early 1970s alleged, he undeniably embraced and politically used it as it developed. By 1949 he was a fervent "Cold Warrior."

But he was also a sincere Cold Warrior, one who firmly believed that collective New Deal and Fair Deal liberalism, as it had emerged over the past fifteen years, was the greatest antidote to totalitarian communism. Truman implied that the New Deal was not only the culmination of the U.S. political tradition but also the Western shield against the evil forces of global communism. In this context Truman as early as 1947 accepted a national security system that included a permanent Central Intelligence Agency and a government employee loyalty program that arguably reduced the rights and citizenship of the nation's civil servants.

To Truman there was no difference in totalitarian states. "I don't care what you call them," he told a special conference of radio news analysts in May 1947. "Nazi, Communist or Fascist or Franco, or anything else—they are all alike." By June 1948 the president had become more explicit: "The welfare of the world is wrapped up in the welfare of the United States. We now, whether we like it or not, are the leaders of the world." Truman also said that "communism succeeds only when there is weakness or misery or despair. It cannot succeed in a strong and healthy society. The nations of Western Europe, with our help, have checked the spread of communism by working together to help build up their economies, improve the welfare of their peoples, and so strengthen themselves."

Truman's cold war anticommunism was thus, at least through 1949, reactive and focused on Europe. By early 1950, however, such a geopolitically centered anticommunism no longer seemed to fit a rapidly changing international order. China had now "gone communist," and alarmed commentators pointed to Mao's January journey to Moscow without observing that its long duration suggested essential division rather than harmony between the two monoliths. The Soviets now had the bomb and probably were also working on a thermonuclear device. In Asia, the Soviets seemed to be supporting stubborn native resistance to reimposition of French rule in Indochina and the increasingly assertive and aggressive behavior of the Communist regime in Pyongyang. Chiang and his beaten forces huddled on Formosa, renamed Taiwan.

The West seemed on the defensive, and a bold new strategy was necessary. The fifth stage of the cold war (the final stage during the Truman presidency) had been reached. In April 1950 the National Security Council, in its memorandum NSC 68, proposed that the United States respond totally to the imagined global offensive by international communist forces directed by Stalin.

Two months later the basic premises of NSC 68 seemed borne out by the abrupt North Korean assault across the thirty-eighth parallel against the Western-backed Republic of Korea. Truman wasted no time when the dangers of the situation became obvious and sent in U.S. troops. Moreover, the United Nations was easily induced to follow in a spirit of collective security (the Soviet delegate, inexplicably called home for consultations, could not veto), and the Korean War rapidly took shape.

The war was originally supported in the United States because of the obvious Communist challenge to Western security. Also, by this time, deterioration of public hopes for a peace-

"Truman warns 'Good ol' Joe.'" Kasimierz J. Majewski, *Zgoda*, 8 January 1953.

ful and prosperous postwar world had been exploited by the junior senator from Wisconsin, Joseph R. McCarthy. The ostensible "decline" of the United States and the West in the face of the international Communist challenge was, according to McCarthy, the inevitable result of "red" infiltrators working within the State Department (and possibly other agencies of government) in close cooperation with "pinkos" and other forms of "fellow travelers."

It took three years of war to weaken support for the armed intervention in Korea and the McCarthy hysteria. Truman and his administration, meanwhile, were forced to echo the McCarthy line to some extent even as they expressed profound contempt for the man and his methods. Several historians have noted that the Truman administration itself may have laid the seeds for McCarthyism by sloppy counterespionage, which failed to protect the atomic project from long-term penetration, and by invoking employee loyalty oaths.

There were many casualties of both McCarthyism and the Korean War, and Truman can be considered one of them. His popularity at the time he left office was comparable to Richard Nixon's when he was forced out of the White House twenty-one years later. Only when passions cooled was it possible to see the president and his administration for what they had been: earnest, decent, loyal, hardworking men who fully reflected the strengths and weaknesses of the country they led. The United States under Truman came to world leadership with goodwill and arrogance, impatience and ignorance, determination and surprising generosity. And the cold war that Truman and his colleagues unwittingly helped to foster was waged in the same spirit. The United States in the Truman years both rescued and helped redivide a war-shattered world and, as a consequence, bequeathed forty years of turmoil and tension that may still be unspent.

A primary source for the period is Harry Truman's public papers, 1947–48, published by the U.S. Government Printing Office (from which Truman's quotations were taken for this essay). The first effort to define the nature and implications of the cold war was Walter Lippman's *The Cold War: A Study in U.S. Foreign Policy* (New York: Harper & Co., 1947). The current standard work on the subject is John Lewis Gaddis's *The United States and Origins of the Cold War, 1941–1947* (New York: Columbia University Press, 1972). A representative New Left revisionist account is Joyce and Gabriel Kolko's *The Limits of Power: The World and United States Foreign Policy, 1945–1954* (New York: Harper & Row, 1972), which categorically assigns all of the world's ills in these years to an aggressive U.S. foreign policy fueled by a rapacious capitalistic order. Such a perspective was the staple of a flood of academic writing about the cold war from around 1965 through the early 1970s. A more mature and restrained example of this genre is Daniel Yergin's *Shattered Peace: The Origins of the Cold War and the National Security State* (Boston: Houghton Mifflin, 1974). Thanks partly to the careful scholarship of Gaddis and others, the end of the Vietnam War, and the natural hunger of scholars to make a reputation not only by revisionism but by counterrevisionism, a more reasoned approach to explaining the cold war has appeared in recent years. See, for example, Lynn Etheride Davis, *The Cold War Begins: Soviet-American Conflict over Eastern Europe* (Princeton: Princeton University Press, 1974) and three regional studies of the cold war's impact: Akira Iriye, *The Cold War in Asia: A Historical Introduction* (Englewood Cliffs, N.J.: Prentice-Hall, 1974); Bruce R. Kuniholm, *The Origins of the Cold War in the Near East* (Princeton: Princeton University Press, 1980); and Geir Lundestad, *America, Scandinavia, and the Cold War, 1945–1949* (New York: Columbia University Press, 1980). An excellent current summary of the state of scholarship and inquiry is John Lewis Gaddis's *The Long Peace: Inquiries into the History of the Cold War* (New York: Oxford University Press, 1987).

LISLE A. ROSE

See also Berlin Airlift; China; Churchill, Winston S.; Containment; Czechoslovakia; Eastern Europe; Germany; "Get Tough" Policy; Greece; Kennan, George Frost; Korean War; Marshall Plan; North Atlantic Treaty Organization; NSC 68; Potsdam Conference; Red Scare; Soviet Union; Truman Doctrine; Turkey; World War II

Colonialism

See Africa; Imperialism; Indochina

Commander in Chief

In a broadcast to the armed forces just after Roosevelt's death on 12 April 1945, Truman said, "I have done as you would do in the field when the Commander falls. My duties and responsibilities are clear. . . . These duties will be carried on in keeping with our American tradition." Without preparation or warning Truman departed the comfortable obscurity of the vice presidency and became commander in chief of the greatest assemblage of military might the earth had ever seen.

By this time the war with Germany was in its final days, but the war with Japan was his to conclude. Armed Japanese strength in the home islands was placed at two million men; another two million were on Formosa and the Asian mainland. Within weeks of taking office the president approved a plan of assault against the Japanese strongholds involving a five-million-member attack force. The estimates of potential U.S. casualties varied widely, but about 450,000 men seemed likely to die or be disabled to compel Japanese surrender.

Shortly after his swearing-in, the new president was informed by War Secretary Stimson of a potential weapon that might shorten the war and preclude the necessity of an assault: the atomic bomb. Stimson explained to the president that because of its nature and unprecedented destructive potential, the weapon would affect future diplomacy and revolutionize military thinking. It would be necessary, he said, for the commander in chief to decide when, where, and—most important—*if* this device should be used. At his suggestion, Truman appointed a blue-ribbon panel, the Interim Committee, to advise the president as to whether the bomb should be used and the ramifications of using it. Reporting early in June 1945, the committee made recommendations that came down to three essential points: (1) there should be no test demonstration in uninhabited areas; the bomb should be used directly against Japan as soon as it was operational; (2) the target should be a city with war plants or other military installations; and (3) there should be no advance warning to the Japanese. On 23 July, Truman, who would later note, "to be President of the United States is to be lonely, very lonely at times of great decisions," ordered the atomic bombing of Japan.

On 6 August 1945 at 8:15 A.M., the city of Hiroshima, Japan, was destroyed by an atomic device, and seventy-five hours later, the seaport of Nagasaki was obliterated by a single bomb. The Japanese, who were trying to surrender prior to the first bomb, using the offices of the Soviets, were not given sufficient time to assess the impact of the cataclysm at Hiroshima before the second bomb was employed. Truman had accepted the "two-bomb strategy" of the Pentagon, which held that one bomb might be considered an experimental fluke; the second would serve notice of an unlimited capacity. There was no military reason for haste; Truman did not long deliberate the diplomatic advantages and disadvantages (the Russians were impressed; the European Allies were appalled).

Neither the invasion of Kyushu, scheduled for November, nor the atomic bombing of Japan was essential to the obtaining of a conditional surrender. This the president knew beforehand. He did not know that a substantial number of the scientists who developed the bomb had petitioned him not to use it. The "gentlemanly" distinction between military and civilian targets had vanished early in the war and precedents existed for using the

The bomb. (National Archives)

atomic devices. It is certain that he did not vigorously pursue any nonmilitary solution. In a sense, the project, ongoing for many years, had developed a momentum of its own.

On 10 August 1945, the Japanese accepted the Potsdam Declaration (unconditional surrender) with the condition that the reign of the emperor be preserved. In a move he would later regret, the president named Gen. Douglas MacArthur the virtual ruler of Japan and supreme commander of all U.S. military forces stationed in the Far East. Taking over in the final months of the war, Truman was not commander in chief so much as a steward carrying out a predetermined process: "I deserve no credit for the victory. . . . It was already won when I became President and all I had to do was carry out the program."

Truman defended his use of the bomb publicly for the rest of his life, but privately he had become convinced that nuclear devices had the potential for eliminating civilization on this planet. Postwar nuclear weapons policy during the Truman administration had three components. The first was an honest effort to prevent the spread of nuclear weapons by turning over control to the United Nations which failed, owing to Soviet distrust. Second, as the first commander in chief to possess the incredibly powerful device, Truman determined that the military should never have direct control over nuclear weaponry. This he achieved with the Atomic Energy Act (August 1946), which established a civilian body, the Atomic Energy Commission, with control over all uses of nuclear energy under direct mandate from another civilian, the commander in

chief. This act not only denied the military direct access to the bomb; it also expanded the power of the commander in chief at the expense of Congress. Lastly, having failed to achieve UN control over the bombs, Truman ordered the continuation of a research and development program, which was greatly accelerated by his directive following the first Russian atomic test (September 1949) and culminated in the development of the thermonuclear hydrogen bomb (November 1952), a device a thousand times more powerful than the bomb that had leveled Hiroshima.

In the years between World War II and the Korean War, the president attempted three major reforms in the American military and in the civil-military relationship: (1) creation of a universal military training system; (2) elimination of racism in the armed forces; and (3) unification of the services through a massive restructuring of institutional and command relationships.

U.S. military planners believed that postwar security considerations required that a ready reserve, made up of citizen-soldiers, be instantly available to augment the cadres of trained professionals. The military believed that the training of raw recruits after the outbreak of conflict was an extemporization the nation could no longer afford. What they proposed was mandatory military training of every young, able-bodied male citizen, a concept commonly called Universal Military Training (UMT). The military found a staunch ally in "Captain Harry." Despite major efforts by the president and the Pentagon, however, UMT legislation regularly failed of passage in a Congress chary of the political consequences of a concept burdened with well-founded fears of militarism and totalitarianism.

By 1948, partly because of the failure of the UMT proposals, Truman had ordered peacetime conscription to replenish the dwindling ranks in the army. Although not as undesirable as UMT, conscription resulted in a disproportionate military service obligation falling upon uneducated minorities, and in this period, the military services mirrored the prevailing racial attitudes in the United States. Blacks and other minorities were routinely assigned to the most menial tasks and were physically and socially segregated from white servicemen. Largely frustrated in his efforts to guarantee equal rights to all citizens by a reactionary bloc in Congress, the president now had much more success with the military. Invoking his authority as commander in chief in Executive Order 9981 (July 1948) Truman said: "It is hereby declared to be the policy of the President that there shall be equality of treatment and opportunity for all persons in the armed services without regard to race, color, religion or national origin." The services were slow to implement the order, with the exception of the air force under Secretary Stuart Symington's direction, but the commander in chief persisted. By the end of his term, the services had eliminated all de jure and much de facto racial bias.

Truman had become an early advocate of rationalizing the decision-making process in military affairs through unification of the services. "It was my opinion," he wrote, "that the Commander in Chief ought to have a co-ordinated and co-operative defense department that would work in peace and war." The president had to fight off considerable opposition, particularly from Navy Secretary Forrestal, but at last he obtained a compromise in the National Security Act (1947). The act created the National Military Establishment, within which the army, navy, and air force became separate, equal departments under civilian secretaries (who were not cabinet members). Heading this military monolith was a cabinet-level civilian, the secretary of defense. The commanding officers of each service formed a collective body, the Joint Chiefs of Staff. The legislation also established entities separate and distinct from the military establishment, the most significant of which were the National Security Council (NSC) and the Central Intelligence Agency (CIA).

In the period between World War II and Korea, the Truman administration faced several challenges, one of the most notable being Soviet pressures upon Berlin. Agreements reached in Big Three conferences had divided Germany into zones of occupation along a north-south axis, with the Soviet zone constituting the eastern half. Berlin, well within the Soviet zone, was divided into sectors much as the nation was. The Western powers' right of access to their respective sectors of Berlin was not formally defined, but initially the Russians granted ample access via highway, air corridor, canal, and railroad lines. In June 1948, however, Soviet officials cut off Allied land and water-borne access to Berlin. Some presidential advisers suggested that the United States should abandon Berlin as an indefensible enclave, whereas others argued for a major show of force. On 28 June, Truman ended discussion by telling his advisers the United States was staying in Berlin and ordering the air force to supply the immediate needs of the city (some eleven hundred tons of foodstuffs daily) entirely by air.

The actions of the commander in chief during the Berlin crisis were revealing. He bypassed the deliberative, institutionalized framework he had created with the National Security Act. The NSC policy recommendations were not ready when he decided, the CIA had failed to anticipate this eventuality and had little to contribute, and the Joint Chiefs were still debating alternatives. At no point in these days of decision did Truman seek congressional advice or approval for his actions. The Berlin crisis, then, was Truman's finest hour as commander in chief. He rejected suggestions to surrender (abandoning Berlin) or to begin a third world war (massing tanks on the autobahn). Instead he found the one peaceful path—the airlift—that would achieve a containment of Soviet expansionism without precipitating armed conflict.

During the Berlin crisis the president, upon the recommendation of the NSC, ordered B-29s, the primary delivery system for atomic bombs, to permanent station in Great Britain. The White House thus utilized the Berlin situation as a rationale for extending the atomic perimeter around the Soviet Union. Although the bombers could carry atomic weapons, the administration would neither confirm nor deny that they did. Walter Millis saw this action as marking a major divide in U.S. military policy: "The atomic arsenal had entered American thought as an appropriate instrument of policy for the future."

In a circumstance parallel to the division of Germany by the Allied forces, Korea was also divided for purposes of accepting the Japanese surrender. An arbitrary line (the thirty-eighth parallel) became the boundary between a Communist and a non-Communist nation. America had armed the South, and the Soviets the North; then both powers withdrew their own forces. Border clashes between the two Koreas culminated in a North Korean attack in June 1950. The North Korean People's Army (NKPA), spearheaded by powerful Russian-made T-34 tanks, began a drive down the Korean peninsula. The president approved the use of U.S. aircraft against targets south of the thirty-eighth parallel and ordered General MacArthur to provide the Republic of Korea (ROK) Army with whatever supplies were

Gen. Douglas MacArthur and his commander in chief, President Truman, during the Wake Island conference, October 1950. (Courtesy of the Harry S. Truman Library)

available. As the NKPA continued down the peninsula and status reports from MacArthur became increasingly gloomy, the president ordered ground combat forces into Korea on 30 June.

Although he had consulted with policy aides intensively over the previous hectic days, the president alone made this decision to commit U.S. forces to combat. Truman thereby bypassed the National Security Council he had created, which was just as well. The NSC had no contingency plans ready because the Korean peninsula was outside the designated American defensive perimeter. Moreover, the deliberative process of the council, wherein position papers are gradually coordinated and codified and percolate upward, was too time-consuming to be utilized in a crisis atmosphere.

The military actions in Korea, ordered by the president in his role as commander in chief, had placed America in a war without the consent of Congress. Although he initially considered asking Congress to sanction his actions, he settled for a White House meeting with the leadership where, on the advice of Secretary of State Dean Acheson, he told them of the actions he had taken. "I . . . recommended that the President should not ask for a resolution of approval," wrote Acheson, "but rest on his constitutional authority as Commander in Chief of the armed forces." He continued to rest on this authority for the remainder of his tenure.

The insertion of U.S. ground combat forces slowed but did not stop the surge of the NKPA. Soon the Korean and UN (largely U.S.) forces were reduced to maintaining a toehold on the extreme southeastern tip of the peninsula. In a brilliant amphibious maneuver, MacArthur struck at the port of Inchon deep behind enemy lines on 15 September. By the end of the month organized resistance ceased south of the thirty-eighth parallel. Having achieved the U.S. objective of driving the aggressors from South Korea, MacArthur now requested permission to pursue the fleeing NKPA into North Korea and crush all resistance. The Joint Chiefs and the NSC recommended that Truman accept this change of objective for which there appears to have been no imperative military need: containment had been achieved and South Korea was still nominally democratic. The commander in chief ordered his general to invade North Korea and conquer the NKPA, but, because of Red Chinese threats of intervention if U.S. forces touched the Yalu boundary with Manchuria, MacArthur was specifically instructed to employ only ROK forces in the provinces bordering the Yalu. On 24 October, disturbed by the slow progress of ROK forces, MacArthur told his field officers that he was lifting the restriction on the use of U.S. forces on the Chinese border, a manifest violation of specific orders from the commander in chief. Within days of his order, elements of the Chinese armies had entered the war and other units were being massed for attack along the Yalu River.

In the last two months of 1950, the Chinese/NKPA forces mounted a major offensive, driving the UN forces to a point just north of the thirty-eighth parallel boundary. On 29 December the Joint Chiefs transmitted a new directive to MacArthur, which told him he was to assume defensive positions that had the safety of his troops as the primary consideration. He would receive no additional U.S. forces. A major war was not to be fought in Korea and the possibility of general war was to be avoided. The directive represented a considerable change of policy. The objective of Korean unification had been abandoned. MacArthur, with no increase in forces, was told to wage a war of attrition against superior enemy numbers. If these goals were not obtainable, he was ordered to evacuate Korea entirely, his primary objective being changed to maintaining the security of Japan.

MacArthur, holding that there was no substitute for total victory, began to battle his military and civilian superiors in Washington. He used the press to attack his orders and belittle the president, rallying public and congressional opinion for his demand to be released from restrictions on the conduct of his military operations. In April 1951, the Joint Chiefs agreed unanimously that the president should fire MacArthur for his lack of sympathy with the policy of his government, his violation of specific directives of his commander in chief, and the threat he represented to the democratic principle of civilian supremacy.

MacArthur's actions had endangered America's civilian leadership. His arrogance was made clear in a speech he made in Massachusetts a few months after his dismissal: "I find in existence a new and heretofore unknown and dangerous concept that the members of the Armed Forces owe their primary allegiance and loyalty to those who temporarily exercise the authority of the executive branch of the government." Never as eloquent as MacArthur, but certainly more democratic, Truman said, "He was insubordinate and I fired him. . . . Sure I knew there would be a lot of stink about it, but I didn't give a damn. It was the right thing to do and I did it."

In defining the powers of the presidency the Constitution vests the holder of the office with only one specific title: commander in chief. The title and the obligations entailed cannot be separated from the political and bureaucratic functions of the position, but Truman, like many another president, treated the commander in chief as a distinct entity. He believed he should operate as the executor of all military policy. He did not personally determine these policies, but he did define the issues and objectives. Except in times of crisis, he relied upon the staff process, as channeled through the NSC, to present him with policy options which he modified, accepted, or rejected.

Thus, the president did not allow Congress, the defense secretary, or the Joint Chiefs to intrude upon his prerogatives as commander in chief. All but the most routine of military matters had to clear his desk prior to action. Theater commanders, however, were granted freedom from any tactical direction by this commander in chief: "I am not a desk strategist and don't intend to be one." Truman, much more than Franklin Roosevelt, institutionalized the military command function. With the National Security Act, he re-created the military institution, but bypassed the cumbersome structure when a need for command decision appeared urgent. He decided to remain in Berlin and left the staff mechanism free to determine how. He committed the United States to warfare in Korea solely on his own authority as commander in chief, ignoring constitutional checks against such action. He fired one of the most revered generals of the twentieth century and endured the subsequent political firestorm until he was vindicated by Gen. Matthew Ridgway's triumphs as MacArthur's successor and by the testimony compiled in the Far East hearings by Congress.

His most serious errors as commander in chief were the changing of the objective in the Korean War and the decision to employ the atomic bombs without fully exploring the diplomatic and political alternatives. On the other hand, both decisions were recommended to him by his military and diplomatic advisers.

In a sadly polarized postwar world, facing a rapid-fire series of changes and challenges that would have destroyed a lesser person, Truman did what he thought was right. He avoided the atomic maelstrom that threatened during his tenure of office, preserved the doctrine of civilian supremacy from a serious challenge, and maintained for his successors as commanders in chief ultimate authority over the ultimate weapon.

The most detailed exploration of the subject is Richard F. Haynes, *Awesome Power: Harry S Truman as Commander in Chief* (Baton Range: Louisiana State University Press, 1973). A brief analytical account is Wilber W. Hoare, Jr., "Truman," in *The Ultimate Decision: The President as Commander in Chief*, ed. Ernest R. May (New York: Braziller, 1960). A good, brief study, but with a broader base, is Robert H. Ferrell's *Harry S Truman and the Modern American Presidency* (Boston: Little, Brown, 1983). A highly detailed but useful survey is Clay Blair, *The Forgotten War: America in Korea, 1950–1953* (Garden City, N.Y.: Doubleday, 1987), although the work is flawed by a romanticized analysis of the function of field commanders. Many fine accounts of particular subjects or incidents are available, for example, Herbert Feis, *Japan Subdued: The Atomic Bomb and the End of the War in the Pacific* (Princeton: Princeton University Press, 1961); Richard M. Dálfiume, *Desegregation of the U.S. Armed Forces* (Columbia: University of Missouri Press, 1969); Paul Y. Hammond, *Organizing for Defense: The American Military Establishment in the Twentieth Century* (reprint, New York: Greenwood, 1977); Glenn D. Paige, *The Korean*

Decision, June 24–30, 1950 (New York: Free Press, 1968); and John W. Spanier, *The Truman-MacArthur Controversy and the Korean War* (Cambridge, Mass.: Belknap, 1965).

RICHARD F. HAYNES

See also Armed Forces, Racial Integration of the; Armed Forces, Unification of the; Atomic and Hydrogen Bombs; Berlin Airlift; Korean War; Selective Service/Universal Military Training

---

Commission on Organization of the Executive Branch of the Government

See Executive Branch, Reorganization of the

Committee for Economic Development

The Committee for Economic Development (CED) came into being in 1942 as a business organization concerned with the shape of the "postarmament" economy. The Department of Commerce assisted in the formation of the new group, whose aim was to formulate a brand of modern capitalism that would avoid the dangers of both statist dictation and laissez-faire drift. By 1947, the CED enjoyed a membership of 115 business leaders and university heads. After the war, the organization operated as a public policy research group; its business members, advised by outside scholars and the CED's own research staff, sought to devise policies that would provide high employment and cyclical stability in the economy. The group was particularly important in formulating innovative, conservatively Keynesian fiscal policies. It maintained a working relationship with Truman's Council of Economic Advisers and played a significant role in shaping and promoting the Marshall Plan. The CED influenced public policy by offering thoughtful ideas, by generating wide publicity for its suggestions, and by functioning as an informal personnel agency which helped channel business leaders into government service.

Karl Schriftgiesser, *Business Comes of Age: The Story of the Committee for Economic Development and Its Impact upon the Economic Policies of the United States, 1942–1960* (New York: Harper & Bro., 1960), and *Business and Public Policy: The Role of the Committee for Economic Development, 1942–1967* (Englewood Cliffs, N.J.: Prentice-Hall, 1967), are informed insider accounts. Robert M. Collins, *The Business Response to Keynes, 1929–1964* (New York: Columbia University Press, 1981), is a scholarly assessment.

ROBERT M. COLLINS

See also Business-Government Relations

Communism and Communists

Probably no single issue was to bedevil the Truman administration as much as that of communism. Concerned above all about containing the threat of what it perceived as aggressive Communist expansion throughout the world, the Truman administration found that it also had to deal with communism at home. Here, however, the danger was not so much to the nation's security as to the administration's public image, for Truman's right-wing opponents discovered that they could gain considerable mileage by attacking the Democratic regime as soft on communism. As a result, the Truman administration, though strongly anti-Communist anyhow, may well have been pressured into taking more repressive measures than it would otherwise have done.

At the time Harry S. Truman took over the presidency in the spring of 1945, the Communist party was experiencing a short-lived period of growth. Founded in 1919 in the aftermath of the Bolshevik Revolution in Russia, the American Communist party had been a small revolutionary sect that had had little impact on American political life. During the second half of the 1930s, when the Soviet Union's opposition to Nazi Germany impelled the international Communist movement to initiate the Popular Front and seek alliances with any individuals or groups who shared its distaste for Hitler, American Communists toned down their revolutionary rhetoric and built their party into the most important political organization on the Left. Individual party members participated in a variety of social and political movements, often in leadership positions. They were particularly active in organizing unions and antifascist groups, working during this brief Popular Front moment with thousands of non-Communist men and women who sympathized with the causes the party espoused. Even so, the party was never popular and never appealed to more than a small group of Americans.

The party's support for the Nazi-Soviet Pact of 1939 ushered in a two-year period of repression and decline, but the wartime alliance of the Soviet Union with the United States restored the Popular Front and enabled the party to grow to a peak of almost seventy-five thousand members. With the onset of the cold war, the government's limited toleration of domestic Communists came to an end; the party's identification with the United States' new Soviet enemy brought about a burst of anti-Communist repression. At the same time, the party's own response to the cold war, its abandonment of the Popular Front, its dogmatic support of Soviet policy, and its rigid and conspiratorial political style made an effective defense all but impossible. Never any kind of a threat to the American polity, the party, with its internal problems and governmental repression, was soon transformed into a tiny beleaguered sect.

Nonetheless, its existence and the supposed threat it posed to the welfare of the United States were to dominate domestic politics throughout the Truman years. It is important to realize that neither the Truman nor the Roosevelt administration had ever been sympathetic to communism. True, New Deal and Communist party programs overlapped in many areas; and during the 1930s and early 1940s some party members did hold government jobs. At the same time, however, there were conservatives within the government, especially within the Justice Department and the Federal Bureau of Investigation (FBI), who were highly suspicious of all political radicals and wanted the

MAMA!

OTHER PARTIES

10-23
MAULDIN

Drive begins to bar U.S. Communist party from
state ballots. (News Item)
Scientists still unable to explain elephants'
pathological dread of mice. (News Item)

By Bill Mauldin. Copyright 1946 by Bill Mauldin.

government to inaugurate a vigorous anti-Communist campaign. Although initially unwilling to mount such a campaign, leading members of the Roosevelt and Truman administrations had become concerned about suspected party members in the government's employ and, even before the Second World War was over, had been quietly trying to weed them out. Although no responsible official ever believed that the Communist party could overthrow the American government, there was considerable concern about the possibility that individual Communists in important or sensitive positions might inject the party line into American policy or spy for the Russians. As a result, even the most liberal members of the Truman administration agreed that—for both security and political reasons—Communists should not hold government jobs.

Despite the Truman administration's determination to eliminate possible subversives from the federal bureaucracy, the issue of Communists in government was too tempting for the administration's antagonists. Charges that the New Deal had been riddled with Communists whom the Truman administration permitted to remain continued to plague Truman throughout the rest of his presidency and even beyond. Outrageous as many of these charges were, they forced the administration to respond by increasing the severity of its own anti-Communist measures. In the summer of 1946, a subcommittee of the House Civil Service Committee threatened a major investigation. Truman immediately set up a special committee to look into the problem of loyalty among federal employees, and in March 1947, he implemented the committee's recommendations by

promulgating Executive Order 9835 establishing an elaborate loyalty-security program. The program, which reflected the political and bureaucratic concerns of the FBI, required security checks for every government employee and dismissed those who belonged to or even "associated" with any organization identified by the attorney general as communist, fascist, or totalitarian. Important in itself, the loyalty-security program soon became a model for similar programs in public and private institutions throughout the nation.

Despite criticism by civil libertarians that the program afforded insufficient protection to the accused employees, Executive Order 9835 did little to dispel the right-wing attacks. Congressional Republicans seemingly ignored the administration's anti-Communist activities and continued their campaign to prove that the Democrats had fostered Communist infiltration. Their main weapon in this campaign was the congressional investigating committee, a libel-proof arena for their attacks on the administration. The most influential congressional hearings took place in the summer of 1948 when the House Un-American Activities Committee (HUAC) heard ex-Communist witnesses Elizabeth Bentley and Whittaker Chambers sketch a scenario of Communist espionage within the executive branch. Despite Truman's dismissal of this testimony as a "red herring," the hearings produced enough evidence about such former officials as Alger Hiss and William Remington to legitimize the charges. Forced onto the defensive, the administration responded to HUAC's revelations by indicting both Hiss and Remington for perjury.

The Truman administration also initiated a broad-based attack on the Communist party itself. The centerpiece was the Justice Department's decision to prosecute the eleven top leaders of the American Communist party under the Smith Act, a little-used 1940 law that made it illegal for anyone "to teach and advocate the overthrow and destruction of the United States government by force and violence." Although many public figures, including Truman's own secretary of labor, Lewis Schwellenbach, advocated outlawing the party, J. Edgar Hoover and his allies within the Justice Department preferred invoking the Smith Act instead. Outlawing the party would, Hoover claimed, simply drive it underground. But prosecuting its top leaders would cripple it more effectively and would enable the government to use the forum of a highly publicized trial to expose the party's goals and activities and thus educate the American people about communism's supposed threat to the nation's security. Whether, in fact, Truman actually authorized the prosecution of the party's leaders personally or the Justice Department acted on its own is unclear. In any event, the fortuitous timing of the case, in July 1948, just as the presidential campaign was getting under way and HUAC was bringing the charges against Alger Hiss to public attention, certainly seemed politically advantageous.

The trial, which was in its time the longest such proceeding ever, turned into a battle of the books. The government and its witnesses put the party's ideology on trial and sought to show that communist theory, as contained in the writings of Marx, Engels, Lenin, and Stalin, committed the party to force and violence. Party general secretary Eugene Dennis and the other Communist defendants took an equally ideological position and tried to show that the party did not advocate force and violence. But even if the Communist leaders had taken a less "political" line and based their defense on the Smith Act's violation of the First Amendment right of free speech, it is unlikely that, given the highly charged atmosphere of the time, they would have been successful. Throughout the proceedings, the trial judge, Harold Medina, exhibited a strong bias against the defendants. And, at every stage of the appeals process, the federal judiciary asserted that national security concerns overrode the protection of individual Communists' political rights. With its 6–2 decision in the *Dennis* case in June 1951, the Supreme Court legitimized the federal government's campaign against the Communist party and, again in the name of national security, essentially exempted anti-Communist repression from constitutional restraints.

Once the Supreme Court rendered this decision, the Justice Department initiated action against the next level of party leadership and, in the so-called Second String cases, eventually rounded up 126 more party leaders in New York, Pittsburgh, Philadelphia, Baltimore, Cleveland, Hawaii, Los Angeles, New Haven, Detroit, St. Louis, Denver, Boston, Puerto Rico, and Seattle. In other actions, the Immigration and Naturalization Service, which had been harassing foreign-born Communists for years, rounded up dozens of left-wing aliens in a concerted drive to deport all foreign-born radicals from the United States.

These measures and similar ones at every level of society essentially destroyed the Communist party. On the defensive, its leaders in jail, and its members subject to all sorts of official and unofficial persecution, the party turned in on itself. To avert further damage, it sent many of its leading cadres underground, purged its ranks of all but its most pliant and dependable members, and devoted most of its energy to its own defense. By 1956, when Khruschev's revelations about Stalin's crimes led to massive defections from the already weakened party, American Communism had become little more than a memory.

Effective as the Truman administration's anti-Communist campaign obviously was, congressional conservatives continued to press for further action, insisting that the administration was still "soft on Communism." Senator Joseph McCarthy's charges simply amplified the earlier attacks. Until the Korean War, however, the administration and its congressional supporters had been able to keep Congress from passing any seriously repressive anti-Communist legislation. But in the summer of 1950, Congress finally passed the Internal Security Act (otherwise known as the McCarran Act), a law that, among other provisions, required the Communist party to register with the government as a subversive organization and established camps for the detention of suspected subversives during emergencies. Truman recognized the dangers of the measure, but Congress, most of whose members were either ideologically committed to the anti-Communist crusade or terrified of the electoral consequences of opposing it, easily overrode the presidential veto. By then, the campaign against American Communism had lurched out of control.

The last two years of Truman's presidency saw the increasingly embattled administration adopt steadily more repressive measures simply to preserve its own authority in the realm of internal security. In 1951, for example, it revised its loyalty-security program to make it easier to let suspect employees go. Yet, despite such actions, there was no way the administration could regain its control over the anti-Communist furor, and by attempting to outflank its right-wing critics, it actually contributed to the repression it deplored.

Despite the availability of FBI files and other documents released under the Freedom of Information Act, few scholars have attempted to incorporate those materials into their work on the Truman administration's treatment of domestic communism. As a result, even the most helpful studies are, at best, incomplete. The most useful single book about the Communist party during this period is Joseph Starobin, *American Communism in Crisis* (Cambridge: Harvard University Press, 1972). For the Smith Act cases, the definitive book is Micheal Belknap, *Cold War Political Justice* (Westport, Conn.: Greenwood Press, 1977); see also Peter L. Steinberg, *The Great "Red Menace"* (Westport, Conn.: Greenwood Press, 1984). The political pressures that shaped Truman's loyalty-security program are covered in Alan Harper, *The Politics of Loyalty* (Westport, Conn.: Greenwood Press, 1969). The best study of that program is Ralph S. Brown, Jr., *Loyalty and Security* (New Haven: Yale University Press, 1958). For an overall survey of every aspect of cold war anticommunism, see David Caute, *The Great Fear* (New York: Simon & Schuster, 1978).

ELLEN W. SCHRECKER

See also Civil Liberties; Federal Bureau of Investigation; Hiss-Chambers Case; House Committee on Un-American Activities; Loyalty Program; McCarran, Patrick Anthony; McCarthy, Joseph R.; Red Scare; Smith Act

Congress, United States

The years of Harry S. Truman's presidency were marked by frequent conflicts between Congress and the executive branch over both substantive policies and issues related to the constitutional separation of powers. Despite occasional setbacks for the White House, the period witnessed general expansion in the powers of the presidency.

Truman's tenure in the White House spanned four Congresses, the seventy-ninth through the eighty-second. The party breakdowns in these four Congresses, as shown in the accompanying table, illustrate the narrow majority the Democrats continued to enjoy in the immediate postwar era.

The lone Republican-controlled Congress in these years, elected in 1946, was the product of massive voter dissatisfaction with the Truman administration. The GOP campaign appeal in that year, which worked well, was simply: "Had Enough?" Among Republicans elected to Congress for the first time in 1946 were several who became nemeses of Truman, including John Bricker (Ohio), William Jenner (Indiana), Joseph McCarthy (Wisconsin), and Richard Nixon (California). In the wake of the elections, Truman confided to an old friend, "I don't expect this Congress to be any worse than the one I had to deal with for the last two years." He was wrong; in fact, the Eightieth Congress, while cooperating with him on foreign policy, gave him some of his greatest frustrations and legislative defeats. By 1948, the president had changed his mind. Labeling the Eightieth a "Do Nothing" Congress, he made it the foil for his successful presidential campaign that year.

Even when the Democrats were in the majority (1945–47, 1949–53), Truman faced powerful obstacles because actual control resided with the conservative coalition made up of Republicans and southern Democrats who opposed his domestic

GETTING TOUGHER ALL THE TIME.

JOHN Q TURNIP

Charles Werner, *Indianapolis Star*, 25 January 1952.

So, too, were key laws in the areas of taxation and immigration restriction.

This record of White House futility was reflected in a statistical analysis done by Congressional Quarterly (CQ), which found that, between 1947 and 1952, Congress completed action on only 199 of Truman's 464 legislative proposals (42.9 percent). Each year, in fact, congressional resistance seemed to increase. Annual rates of action completed on presidential requests, as computed by CQ, were: 1947, 47.7 percent; 1948, 45.7 percent; 1949, 44.1 percent; 1950, 44.1 percent; 1951, 40.4 percent; and 1952, 34.9 percent.

In the important area of foreign policy, the situation was different, as the developing cold war afforded the president greater latitude for action and elicited strong support from Congress. In vivid contrast to his problems with Congress in domestic policy matters, Truman secured passage for several far-reaching and innovative foreign policy measures, including Greek and Turkish aid, popularly known as the Truman Doctrine (1947); the European Recovery Program, or Marshall Plan (1947–48); participation in the Rio Pact (1947) and the North Atlantic Treaty Organization (NATO; 1949); and extension of the Trade Agreements Act (1948). Most of these measures were approved by the Republican-controlled Eightieth Congress, largely owing to the support and leadership of Senator Vandenberg, whom Truman courted assiduously.

Truman's successes in foreign policy might have canceled out his failures with Congress on domestic policy, except for two major factors: the emergence of anti-Communism as a potent political force that eventually escalated into McCarthyism; and the Korean War—or, more particularly, the conflicts generated by the way the president chose to conduct it. On the issue of internal security (anti-Communism), Truman attempted to preempt congressional action by establishing a vigorous federal loyalty and security program in 1947, but he soon found himself on the defensive anyway. Successful in averting passage of the Nixon-Mundt Communist registration bill in 1948 and 1949, the president could not make his veto stick against the repressive McCarran Internal Security Act of 1950, nor was he able to neutralize the vicious attacks of Senator Joseph McCarthy on the State Department, the Voice of America, and other executive agencies connected with foreign policy.

Party Alignment in Congress during Truman's Presidency

	SENATE	HOUSE
Seventy-ninth (1945–47)	56 Democrats 38 Republicans	242 Democrats 190 Republicans
Eightieth (1947–49)	51 Republicans 45 Democrats	246 Republicans 188 Democrats
Eighty-first (1949–51)	54 Democrats 42 Republicans	263 Democrats 171 Republicans
Eighty-second (1951–53)	49 Democrats 47 Republicans	235 Democrats 199 Republicans

programs. But partially offsetting the power of this coalition was an able Democratic congressional leadership team of Sam Rayburn in the House and Alben Barkley in the Senate. The skillful Rayburn continued as House Democratic leader throughout Truman's presidency, but Barkley left the Senate to become Truman's vice president in 1949, and his successors—Scott Lucas (1949–51) and Ernest McFarland (1951–53)—proved both less able than he and less committed to the Fair Deal program. Not coincidentally, the Senate, although nominally Democratic, was generally uncooperative with the president on domestic issues from 1949 on. It was fortunate for Truman that the formal Republican leadership during these years was also lackluster, although two of the party's leading spokesmen in the Senate, Robert A. Taft and Arthur Vandenberg, were powers to be reckoned with.

When Truman became president in April 1945, most observers anticipated a period of congressional-executive harmony, since he had been a well-liked and respected two-term senator. Within six months, however, his introduction of an ambitious twenty-one-point domestic program, later labeled the Fair Deal, created an impasse that was to last throughout his presidency. Truman administration proposals related to Social Security, national health insurance, aid to education, regional power development, full employment, and civil rights were all thwarted by conservative forces in Congress. Federal housing was one of the few administration measures to pass (in 1949). One of the most significant pieces of domestic legislation of the period, the Taft-Hartley Act (which proscribed certain labor union practices), was passed over Truman's veto.

Truman's decision to send American troops into war in Korea in June 1950 without seeking prior (or even retroactive) approval from Congress also helped erode his political position—especially after the "limited" war settled into a bloody stalemate in which American victory seemed unattainable. Resulting congressional frustrations fueled McCarthyism, revived conservative resistance to U.S. participation in NATO and the United Nations, and stimulated an assault, led by Senator Bricker, on presidential authority to negotiate executive agreements and treaties. Bricker's proposed constitutional amendment, which he introduced in 1951, was kept off the floor of Congress by the Democratic leadership, but it was favored by most congressional conservatives and a large part of the public.

Partisan antagonisms in Congress intensified during the Korean War. Republicans attempted to use the war as an issue in the 1950 elections, but with only limited success, and they pressed the president to dismiss Dean Acheson as secretary of state. The sharpest conflict came, however, in April 1951 when Truman ousted Gen. Douglas MacArthur from his command in Korea on ground of insubordination. After several months of Senate hearings on the conduct of the war, however, the MacArthur issue faded, and Truman's powers as commander in chief were left unchallenged. Another dramatic confrontation threatened in the spring of 1952, when Truman seized control of the steel industry to avert an industrywide strike; in this instance, congressional action was rendered unnecessary by the Supreme Court's decision that the seizure was unconstitutional. The preoccupation of Congress with these war-related issues and with the threat of Communist subversion made domestic reform a very low priority. Truman's Fair Deal program was thus effectively dead after 1950.

President Truman's overall record with Congress, then, was at best mixed. The foreign policy measures passed by the Eightieth Congress represented historic achievements produced by the president's avowedly bipartisan methods, but in no other area was he able even to approach such success. In part, of course, this situation reflected the political temper of the times. Although the Democratic victory in 1948 seemed to signal a revival of liberal pro–New Deal sentiment, the cold war and falling farm prices had as much to do with the electoral results as anything, and the resulting Democratic Eighty-first Congress proved not much more cooperative than its forerunner.

Truman's troubles with Congress were also due to systemic factors. Resentful of the powers that had accrued to Franklin D. Roosevelt during the depression and World War II, many in Congress—Democrats and Republicans alike—were resolved to reassert the prerogatives of the legislative branch in the postwar years. Moreover, even though Truman expanded and institutionalized the role of the president as initiator of legislation, he did not follow through very well. Like his predecessors, he allowed responsibility for White House relations with Congress to remain informal and dispersed; not until the Eisenhower administration was a distinct congressional liaison office established in the White House. As at least one student of the modern presidency has observed, Truman believed that his role was to articulate and propose an ambitious agenda, and that thereafter it was Congress's responsibility to enact it.

In the circumstances, the results were predictable. Truman and Congress clashed often and openly. Altogether, he vetoed eighty-three public bills, a figure very close to Eisenhower's eighty-one. But whereas Eisenhower was overridden twice, Truman was overridden eleven times. Only Andrew Johnson and Gerald Ford had more vetoes overturned by Congress. Perhaps such clashes were inevitable, as Congress sought to recapture powers it believed had been usurped and Truman—the first

president to face the challenges of governing a superpower in a truly global age—refused to give ground.

The years of Truman's presidency set the tone and balance in congressional-executive relations for at least a generation. Subsequent presidents played a prominent role in setting the legislative agenda and regularly relied on bipartisanship and cold war exigencies to ensure themselves a relatively free hand in foreign policy matters. In these ways, the postwar "imperial presidency" received substantial impetus from events during the Truman administration. On the other hand, Congress, revitalized by the Legislative Reorganization Act of 1946, significantly enlarged the scope of its investigative activities while Truman was president (most notable were the dramatic hearings conducted by the House Committee on Un-American Activities in the late 1940s, hearings on organized crime chaired by Senator Estes Kefauver in 1950–51, and the Senate hearings held after MacArthur's dismissal). This, too, was a trend that continued in the several administrations after Truman's.

Although Harry Truman believed he was ill-treated by Congress and regularly expressed his displeasure, he was a strong advocate of giving every former president a seat in the Senate. Undoubtedly, Congress would have become a more interesting place had that been done in his case.

Two of the most informative treatments of Congress during the years of Truman's presidency are Susan Hartmann, *Truman and the Eightieth Congress* (Columbia: University of Missouri Press, 1971), and Arthur M. Schlesinger, Jr., *The Imperial Presidency* (Boston: Houghton Mifflin, 1973). Truman's thoughts and reactions concerning the legislative branch are revealed in his two-volume memoirs, *Year of Decisions* (Garden City, N.Y.: Doubleday, 1955), and *Years of Trial and Hope, 1946–1952* (Garden City, N.Y.: Doubleday, 1956). The perspectives of the congressional opposition are well presented in Arthur H. Vandenberg, Jr., ed., *The Private Papers of Senator Vandenberg* (Boston: Houghton Mifflin, 1952), and James T. Patterson, *Mr. Republican: A Biography of Robert A. Taft* (Boston: Houghton Mifflin, 1972), which is the best of several biographies of leading political figures of the period. Robert Griffith, *The Politics of Fear: Joseph McCarthy and the Senate* (Lexington: University Press of Kentucky, 1970), stands out among the many solid studies of McCarthyism in its congressional setting. In addition, numerous monographs on particular policy issues focus on congressional politics during the period.

GARY W. REICHARD

See also Democratic Party; Eightieth Congress; Elections in the Truman Era; Employment Act of 1946; Fair Deal; House Committee on Un-American Activities; Republican Party; Senator; Smith Act; Taft-Hartley Act; Veto Power; entries for individual memebers of Congress

---

Congress of Industrial Organizations

See Labor

Connally, Thomas Terry

(19 August 1877–28 October 1963)
Democratic senator, 1929–53; chairman of Foreign Relations Committee, 1941–47, 1949–53. Born in the cotton country of central Texas in the wake of Reconstruction, educated at Baylor University and the University of Texas in the heyday of southern populism, elected to the Texas legislature in 1900 and Congress in 1917, and inspired by a vision of America's role in the world on a visit to Paris in 1919, Tom Connally brought to the Senate in 1929 a distinctive combination of states' rights conservatism and Wilsonian internationalism.

Although he considered himself a loyal Democrat, Connally opposed significant portions of Franklin Roosevelt's New Deal, and he rejected the Court-packing scheme of 1937. At the same time, however, he encouraged the president's halting efforts to stem the tide of fascism abroad and isolationism at home. He applauded recognition of the Soviet Union in 1933. He denounced what he called the "half-truths" of the Nye committee's allegations of collusion and profiteering during the First World War. He worked to weaken the neutrality legislation of the mid-1930s. And he supported Lend-Lease in 1941, comparing the fight against the Nazis to the defense of the Alamo.

By the time Truman—whom Connally, on the basis of their years together in the Senate, liked but did not especially admire—became president, Connally had been the ranking Democrat on the Foreign Relations Committee, and committee chairman, for nearly four years. Throughout Truman's tenure, Connally played a key role in forging the legislation that laid the foundation for America's cold war policy. In 1945 he returned from San Francisco, where he had served as vice-chairman of the American delegation to the first United Nations conference, to remind his colleagues in the Senate that "the League of Nations was slaughtered in this chamber" and to warn them that they would repeat the performance only at their country's peril. In 1947 he joined with his Republican replacement as Foreign Relations Committee chairman, Arthur Vandenberg, to hammer out the bill for aid to Greece and Turkey that became the basis for the Truman Doctrine. In 1948 he threw his considerable weight behind the legislation that made the Marshall Plan a reality. In 1949 Connally defended the Atlantic treaty as "the logical extension of the principle of the Monroe Doctrine," although he insisted on a revision guaranteeing the primacy of Congress in committing the United States to war. In 1950 the senator rallied to Truman's support in sending American forces to Korea. And he stood by the president when Truman fired Douglas MacArthur, agreeing to give the general a hearing in Congress but insisting on closing the sessions to the public and releasing transcripts only afterward.

On domestic matters, Connally broke with the administration on a number of occasions. He resisted the expansion of federal authority in the civil rights sphere, declaring this an unwarranted encroachment on the prerogatives of the states. He likewise opposed repeal of the Taft-Hartley Act.

Nonetheless, Connally's staunch support of the administration's foreign policy initiatives closely associated him in the public mind with the president. Facing a tough reelection battle in 1952, in a state where anti-Truman sentiment flourished, the four-term senator decided to call it a career. He retired to Washington, where he died in 1963 after a protracted period of failing health.

Connally appears in various studies of the origins of the cold war, especially those that pay attention to the legislative aspect of foreign policy. Beyond these, the best source is his own memoir, as told to Alfred Steinberg: *My Name Is Tom Connally* (New York: Crowell, 1954). The book, reflecting the man, is not long on introspection, but it does provide a sense of his forceful personality, and it is full of anecdotes.

H. W. BRANDS

Connelly, Matthew J.

(19 November 1907–10 July 1976)
Chief investigator for the Truman committee; executive assistant to Senator and Vice President Truman; appointments secretary to President Truman, 1945–53. Matthew J. Connelly was born in Clinton, Massachusetts, and graduated from Fordham College in 1930. A tall handsome man, Connelly gained Truman's confidence for his discretion, tact, and understanding of practical politics.

As appointments secretary, Connelly largely controlled personal and telephone access to the president in the Oval Office. As coordinator of Truman's schedule, he also helped shape the nature, timing, and place of the president's appearances outside the White House. Inclined politically toward conservatism, he sided with conservative members of the cabinet and staff against the president's liberal advisers. He counseled Truman on political appointments and patronage. His duties, however, did not permit him to contribute to the president's domestic and foreign policies except in a marginal way.

After Truman left office a federal grand jury indicted Connelly for conspiracy to defraud the government in a 1951 income tax evasion case involving a Saint Louis shoe broker. Additional charges of perjury and bribery for accepting a gift of clothing and oil royalties on discounted stock resulted in a conviction and a two-year prison sentence. After unsuccessful appeals, Connelly served six months of the sentence in 1960. Truman insisted that Connelly was a scapegoat for petty scandals in his administration, and he spoke at a fund-raising dinner to help pay for Connelly's legal defense. Privately, he wrote Attorney General Robert F. Kennedy to request a pardon for Connelly, and President John F. Kennedy granted a full and unconditional pardon in 1962.

Richard Neustadt has an astute analysis of Connelly's role as appointments secretary in Francis Heller, ed., *The Truman White House: The Administration of the Presidency, 1945-1953* (Lawrence: Regents Press of Kansas, 1980). A biographical sketch of Connelly appears in Eleanora W. Schoenebaum, ed., *Political Profiles: The Truman Years* (New York: Facts on File, 1978). Andrew J. Dunar has examined the conviction of Connelly and

Truman's efforts in his behalf in *The Truman Scandals and the Politics of Morality* (Columbia: University of Missouri Press, 1984). His papers and an oral history interview are in the Harry S. Truman Library.

FRANKLIN D. MITCHELL

Conservation

In 1945 before Harold Ickes resigned as secretary of the interior he helped formulate a proposal for a World Conservation Congress. What happened to this proposal suggests the fate of conservation during Truman's presidency. The State Department sought responsibility for the quickly renamed Scientific Conference on the Conservation and Utilization of Resources which would be held under United Nations auspices in 1949 at Lake Success, New York. Cast within the framework of foreign economic policy, the conference accomplished little. And the same can be said for the general theme of conservation during Truman's presidency; it had to give way to more pressing concerns affecting national security. Conservation measures and programs had no priority status and at times could be set aside in favor of enhanced resource development, stockpiling, foreign market considerations, and increased production. Security considerations predominated over environmental concerns, and there was little government pressure and at best ineffective private interest in promoting the cause of conservation.

In addition, the American public by and large in the postwar years was little interested in conserving or prudently managing natural resources or public lands. After years of deprivation, from the Great Depression through the war when supplies of everything but war materials were limited, the American public wanted to consume, develop to the point of exploitation, and partake of all the things that money could purchase. Deprived in the past, Americans wished to enjoy the products of an affluent society no matter what the cost and with little concern for the future. Energy development both for domestic consumption and national security became a matter of enhanced national interest. Aside from solar development, which attracted some attention, albeit limited, conservation practices were ignored as millions of dollars were pumped into developing oil shale, searching for and developing additional oil reserves, encouraging continued use of coal, generating further sources of hydroelectric power, developing peacetime uses for atomic energy, mining more strategic mineral resources, utilizing more forest products, and putting more land into production—all directed toward meeting domestic demands and ensuring adequate preparedness as international commitments expanded. Truman in his annual messages called for such developments while proclaiming that wise conservation and development efforts were all the more needed.

It was not that Truman opposed or was hostile to the cause of conservation. He was not. As a senator he had supported New Deal conservation measures. In numerous speeches as president he noted the marked depletion of natural resources with little thought of the future, and he called for long-range programs and funding to remedy the situation. If the cold war and the Korean War had not interfered, Truman no doubt would have devoted more time and attention to furthering and expanding the cause of wisely developing and prudently utilizing natural resources while preserving and carefully managing that portion of the land and seascape that fell within the purview of the federal government.

In October 1945 Truman spoke at the dedication of the Kentucky Dam at Gilbertsville, Kentucky. The sixteenth structure built by the Tennessee Valley Authority (TVA), it was the last on-river dam in the system. In his remarks Truman suggested that the agency had essentially completed its mission and "that same policy ought to be followed in other river valleys." But he never fought for other valley authorities. Although he favored a Columbia Valley Authority, he opposed the creation of one for the Missouri Valley. The point to be noted is that the concept of river valley authorities died during his presidency and that the TVA itself would face difficult times as it sought to further define its mission.

Replacing the concept of valley authorities in the West was the Pick-Sloan plan which became the major focus of water resource planning, particularly on the Great Plains. The Army Corps of Engineers and the Bureau of Reclamation, spurred by the drought and dust storms of the thirties and by floods during the war years, each formulated plans that were then merged, with each agency retaining its separate autonomy. The "abundant water" scheme of the corps called for flood control, navigation, and power, while the "scarce water" outlook of the bureau called for irrigation and power projects. Little effort was made to coordinate projects and respect the needs of Native Americans and others as the Pick-Sloan approach got underway, essentially dooming the valley-authority concept championed by Senator James E. Murray of Montana.

In one area, that of public lands, Truman in 1946 called for a new entity, the Bureau of Land Management, which would provide for the more effective administration of federally owned land, chiefly acreage unsuited for crop production in the arid or semiarid regions of the West and in Alaska. The bureau, a consolidation of the General Land Office (1812) and the Grazing Service (1934), dealt directly with issues pertaining to leasing, classifying, managing, and disposing of public lands. Grazing districts, land and survey offices, and some forestry areas came within its authority. With the functions of its two predecessors lumped together, the new agency during the Truman years began to formulate a concept of area development and multiple use management.

In his last years as president, Truman called attention to the role of the federal government in harnessing water resources and converting them to beneficial and productive use. In 1950 he created a Water Resources Policy Commission to review and evaluate programs and projects with the purpose of suggesting desirable legislation or changes in existing legislation pertaining to water resources. Although he did not establish a similar commission for land resources, he focused attention on this theme, indicating an awareness of the increased depletion of the nation's soil, forest, water, and mineral resources owing to rapid economic growth. In his annual budget message to Congress on 3 January 1950, Truman said, "If we are to continue to expand production and employment we must use our remaining resources with the greatest possible effectiveness, following sustained yield principles, developing resources as yet unused, and restoring where possible the resources we have depleted." These remarks reveal the thrust of his conservation concerns. He appealed to Congress and called for studies and further investigation, but little of significance occurred.

Unlike Franklin D. Roosevelt, Truman did not often visit the West, but when he did, conservation was often in the forefront of his remarks. In Casper, Wyoming, in May 1950 he proclaimed "that our natural resources are the cornerstone of a strong, free democracy" and "must be used to advance the well being and prosperity of all the people." To achieve this goal, government had to make sure that land, water, forest, and mineral resources were used wisely, "and not exploited for the benefit of just a few." Moreover, he explained "that soil and forest conservation, flood control, and the development of power, navigation, and irrigation must all be tackled and solved together," that a river valley could not be developed in a piecemeal fashion. He also in this address, which was a clear statement of his conservation views, spoke of conserving and improving rangelands, recognizing that "a well-grassed and a well-watered range was essential" to a "more productive and secure livestock industry." Good management of rangelands prevented erosion, helped in flood control, and protected "our investment in reservoirs." Truman also noted in speeches on this trip other conservation practices that needed tending: reseeding rangelands, reforesting cut-over and burned-over lands, expanding forest roads, developing tributary control and fishery protection, and conserving limited water supplies among others. In some of these speeches, Truman noted that foreign tensions, "a worldwide struggle to bring lasting peace to the world," commanded attention. It was this struggle, despite his interest in conservation, that in large part frustrated him in his battles for a dam at Hells Canyon on the Snake River, for a Columbia Valley Authority, for the Central Valley projects in California, and for the further development of the Colorado River Basin. The 1950 western trip represented the apogee of his concern for conservation during his presidency.

Just before he left office, Truman sent a special message to Congress regarding conservation policy. Citing the developments of his administration, noting the commissions he had established, and calling upon government to continue its efforts to further national programs of water and land development, he proposed an agenda for the Eisenhower administration in accord with his conservation philosophy. Truman could not cite a major victory in his conservation program, in part because in the immediate postwar years pressure groups, such as the Sierra Club, had yet to regain their membership and had not yet found a conservation issue upon which to focus national attention. And Truman himself had more immediate international concerns. Nevertheless, he considered conservation a pressing domestic concern. In his 1953 special message, almost his last official act, he noted the steady progress of his administration in continuing what the New Deal started. He sought to keep before the American public an awareness of the necessity to provide "a better basis for the development of our water and related land resources."

The best source for Truman's views on conservation is the *Public Papers of the Presidents, Harry S. Truman: 1945–53* (Washington, D.C.: U.S. Government Printing Office, 1961–66). In these eight volumes will be found all of Truman's significant speeches, messages, and papers touching on conservation. The comprehensive essays on the Truman administration's energy concerns in Craufurd D. Goodwin, ed., *Energy Policy in Perspective: Today's Problems, Yesterday's Solutions* (Washington, D.C.: Brookings Institution, 1981), relate closely to conservation. Although Elmo Richardson's

perceptive volume, *Dams, Parks and Politics: Resource Development and Preservation in the Truman-Eisenhower Era* (Lexington: University Press of Kentucky, 1973), discusses the Truman presidency, the main focus is on the Echo Park controversy and the Eisenhower administration. David Arlin Kathka, in "The Bureau of Reclamation in the Truman Administration: Personnel, Politics, and Policy" (Ph.D. diss., University of Missouri, 1976), examines an important aspect of conservation as practiced by an agency that would soon run amuck. For a critical view of conservation policy during the Truman years, see the comments in Clayton Koppes, "Environmental Policy and American Liberalism: The Department of the Interior, 1933–1953," *Environmental Review* 7, no. 1 (1953): 17–41.

RICHARD LOWITT

See also Army Corps of Engineers; Chapman, Oscar Littleton; Missouri River; Reclamation; Tennessee Valley Authority

Conservatism

In America, unlike Europe, conservatism has revolved around loyalty not to the state as such but to a Constitution that limits it. Hence, during the 1920s American conservatism as expressed by three presidents meant chiefly opposition to government and most of its functions, especially taxation, combined with a belief in maximum freedom for individual enterprise. In the 1930s, though deprived of power by the New Deal, conservatives retained these views, while adding to them an abhorrence of foreign alliances and involvements abroad regardless of merit or necessity. Isolationism, as it was called, became an integral part of conservatism even though many liberals believed in it also. After World War II conservatives took a leading part in demobilizing the military and struggled vainly to keep President Truman from establishing a new American foreign policy based on the containment of world communism.

They failed in this not merely because they were wrong but because postwar conservatism was inherently schizophrenic. On the one hand, conservatives were still isolationists, and on the other, extravagantly anti-Communist. The two could not be squared and the conflict between them led conservatives to take incompatible stands, beat humiliating retreats, and make indefensible attacks upon the loyalty and integrity of their opponents. The conservative dilemma was exemplified by Robert A. Taft (the son of former president William Howard Taft), who was elected to the U.S. Senate in 1938 and served there until his death in 1953, becoming the most respected leader of congressional Republicans.

An enemy of the New and Fair Deals, Taft was an isolationist before and after World II. Ardently anti-Communist, he was also opposed to any steps that might lead the country into war with Soviet Russia. Thus he tended to go in opposite directions upon being presented with concrete efforts to limit communism. When President Truman asked for aid to Greece and Turkey in 1947, on the grounds that otherwise they might become Communist, Taft opposed it because he didn't want to strengthen the iron curtain or risk war with the Soviets. He had other objections, too, none of which was met to his satisfaction, but in the end he voted for the aid bill anyway. When the

Marshall Plan for economic assistance to Western Europe was formulated, Taft responded similarly, calling it an "international WPA" and defective in many other ways as well. But having said this, he voted for it nevertheless.

Taft did draw the line when it came to the North Atlantic Treaty Organization (NATO), joining thirteen other senators in voting against ratification of the treaty in 1949. In his eyes NATO was "an offensive and defensive military alliance against Russia" and, as such, was "more likely to produce war than peace." On the other hand, he wanted the United States to defend the Nationalist Chinese remnant on Formosa after the mainland fell to the Communists in 1949, and a year later he supported the administration's decision to fight in Korea. When that war went badly, he condemned the administration for what he now called an illegal intervention. When Gen. Douglas MacArthur was relieved of his command, Taft reversed himself completely again, joining with MacArthur in urging that the war be won by broadening it.

Although many conservatives shared Taft's gyrations, others remained wedded to the old faith. In December 1950 former president Herbert Hoover spoke against overseas involvement as such, urging Americans to make the "Western Hemisphere the Gibraltar of Western Civilization." Former ambassador to Britain Joseph P. Kennedy called for an American withdrawal from both Europe and Korea. Isolationism was actually the only coherent and principled approach to foreign policy that squared with the conservative belief in limited government. Defending the Western Hemisphere would not cost much and would avoid the dangers of imperialism, the country's becoming a garrison state, and excessive powers accruing to the executive branch—all possibilities that worried thoughtful conservatives. The problem for a majority of conservatives, however, was that this opened up the real possibility of conceding both Europe and Asia to communism. For reasons that are far from clear not many seemed troubled about the fate of Europe, but China's fall alarmed them—so much so that many banded together in what became known as the China Lobby. It was not an organization but a movement dedicated to protecting Formosa and resisting all efforts at achieving a settlement with Communist China.

Their contradictory and untenable position on the cold war helps account for, though it does not fully explain, conservative support for McCarthyism. It is hard to believe that responsible conservatives supposed that Secretary of State Acheson was a "Red Dean" as Senator Joseph McCarthy called him, still less that George C. Marshall, former Army chief of staff, the "architect of victory" in World War II according to Winston Churchill, former secretary of state, and later secretary of defense, was a "living lie" and a "front man for traitors" as Senator William Jenner of Indiana charged.

Even by the rough-and-ready standards of American politics the abuse heaped upon the Truman administration was extreme. It remains a question why so many conservatives tolerated, and worse still, encouraged McCarthyism. How could they have regarded an administration that had created a tough loyalty program in 1947, proclaimed the Truman Doctrine of aid to anti-Communist governments, saved Berlin from the Soviets with an airlift, and gone to war against North Korea and Red China as tainted with the slightest degree of sympathy for communism? The usual explanation is that some conservatives did indeed believe the worst about Truman and liberalism, whereas others knew better but didn't care, thinking merely that McCarthyism would give them control of the government. Neither explanation does conservatism much credit.

Yet, though conservatives were able to block the Fair Deal and prevent the administration from achieving a Korean armistice, they were not very successful otherwise. Europe was not abandoned; China was not bombed; and the New Deal was not repealed, either under Truman or under his successor, for, though he was a Republican, President Eisenhower would not turn back the clock. Conservatives hobbled the Truman administration and victimized many individuals in the pursuit of treason, but failed otherwise. Not until Ronald Reagan became president would conservatism, greatly changed from what it had been in the Truman era, finally come to power.

An interesting history that began the revival of conservatism as a serious body of thought is Russell Kirk, *The Conservative Mind from Burke to Santayana* (Chicago: H. Regnery, 1953). A useful book that contains much material on postwar conservative ideas is Ronald Lora, *Conservative Minds in America* (Chicago: Rand McNally, 1971). There is a rewarding and suggestive essay on Senator Taft in Ronald Radosh, *Prophets on the Right* (New York: Simon & Schuster, 1975).

WILLIAM L. O'NEILL

See also Communism and Communists; Eightieth Congress; Elections in the Truman Era; Isolationism; Red Scare; Republican Party; Taft, Robert A.

Containment

Containment, a concept emphasizing prevention of further Soviet—and eventually Communist—advances while avoiding general war, and placing only a secondary stress on the rollback of Soviet power, became the cornerstone of U.S. foreign policy during the Truman administration.

By 1947 the United States had experienced two years of steadily worsening relations with the Soviet Union. In July George Kennan, head of the State Department's Policy Planning Staff, published (under the pseudonym "X") an article, "The Sources of Soviet Conduct," which set forth what was to be an influential strategy for dealing with the Soviet challenge. Kennan saw Soviet leaders as wedded to an inflexible ideology in order to justify their totalitarian power. Tenets of this ideology included a belief in the "innate antagonism between capitalism and Socialism" and therefore a presumption that conflict, rather than harmony of interests, would be the norm in international relations. On the other hand, Soviet faith in the infallibility of Marxist doctrine made Soviet policy, however aggressive and inimical, less adventurous than that of Nazi Germany, not geared to any specific timetable of conquest, and, indeed, not normally overtly warlike.

Given the nature of the Soviet threat, Kennan prescribed "long-term, patient but firm and vigilant containment of Russian expansive tendencies." Containment he defined as the "adroit and vigilant application of counterforce at a series of constantly shifting geographical and political points, corresponding to the shifts and manoeuvres of Soviet policy" and as

Edwin Marcus, 19 February 1945. (Library of Congress)

"unalterable counterforce at every point where [the Soviets] show signs of encroaching upon the interests of a peaceful and stable world." If the United States pursued this tactic consistently, it could have some hope in the long run of forcing "upon the Kremlin a far greater degree of moderation and circumspection" and even "promote tendencies which must eventually find their outlet in either the breakup or the gradual mellowing of Soviet power."

Elements of Kennan's analysis had apparent precursors and accompanists. In September 1946, a team chaired by the president's aide Clark Clifford had presented to Truman a secret report which emphasized the Soviet belief in irreconcilable conflict, the need to "confine Soviet influence to its present area," and the possibility that a resolute American stance might lead the Soviets over time to relent and accept a general settlement of differences. (Kennan had stated at the time that he had "no fault to find" with this report.) Truman's speech of March 1947 in support of military and economic aid to Greece and Turkey (the Truman Doctrine) went beyond the immediate subject at hand to proclaim American willingness to "assist free peoples" all over the world "in maintaining their freedoms," principally by the extension of economic aid. Kennan, however, was a recognized Soviet expert, wrote arresting prose, formulated a seemingly consistent overall strategy, and—perhaps unintentionally—employed a term that could be turned into a label. Many analysts, especially in the press, took "containment" to be official government policy, and Kennan, whose identity soon leaked, its formulator.

The concept was immediately controversial and, paradoxically, came to mean something different to both its supporters and its critics from Kennan's own interpretation. The influential commentator Walter Lippmann greeted the "X" article, which he assumed to be a more sophisticated version of the Truman

Doctrine, with a series of columns holding that containment, if implemented globally, would deplete American resources, leave all the initiatives to the Soviets, and signify U.S. abandonment of the United Nations. He also assumed that the term *counterforce* referred to local military actions.

Many years later Kennan in his memoirs claimed that Lippmann had misinterpreted his intentions. He stated that he had meant not the "military containment of a military threat, but the political containment of a political threat," and that the major defensive task of the West was the selective, geopolitical one of ensuring that four major industrial power centers—the United States, the United Kingdom, the Ruhr Valley, and Japan—did not fall under Russian control. He endorsed the essentials of Lippmann's critique, however, and for the misleading phraseology of the "X" article, he implicitly apologized.

Nonetheless there was an apparent harmony, so far as public elucidation was concerned, between the ideas in the Truman Doctrine and those in the "X" article. Truman used the abstract language of democracy and universal justice, whereas Kennan spoke in terms of power, but both appeared to signal a U.S. commitment to oppose communism everywhere. Nor is it certain that this harmony was only an apparent one, for it is not clear that Kennan had thought through either his strategy of applying containment selectively to the defense of major power centers or his preference for political and economic rather than military action, as of the time he wrote his article (December 1946). Plainly, however, he began to do so before it was published, for in internal policy discussions during the winter of 1947 on Greek-Turkish aid, he opposed military support of Turkey and the sweeping language of the Truman Doctrine.

Thus from the time containment was first publicly discussed there were already *two differing* concepts of containment: one based on the Truman Doctrine and what Kennan *appeared* to mean in the "X" article, and the other advocated by Kennan and some others in internal administration debates and not fully shared with the public. Was it the selective or the unlimited version of containment that had the most influence on leading policymakers? Which version became U.S. policy during the Truman administration? Was containment primarily a military or a diplomatic strategy in the eyes of its proponents?

Kennan doubted "whether Truman really read anything I ever wrote.... Certainly I don't think he grasped my position." As if to confirm this judgment, Truman wrote in retirement, after his foreign policy had been savagely attacked for timidity by the Republican Right: "Our foreign policy was mistakenly called by some a policy of containment. This is not true. Our purpose was much broader. We were working for a united, free and prosperous world." Obviously, Truman did not "grasp" containment's ultimate goal of modifying Soviet behavior. He saw it as a purely defensive concept, and he wanted to appear decisive, not defensive. His comment also reveals a lingering hope that eventually power politics could be supplanted by international harmony, a notion quite foreign to Kennan.

Truman's private papers and his *Memoirs* depict a man torn during his first term between a desire to be "firm" with the Russians anywhere they acted aggressively and doubts about whether the United States had the manpower or budgetary resources to do so. "Our friends the Russkies understand only one language—how many divisions have you—actual or potential," he wrote privately in 1948. Until 1950, however, he sought to keep the costs of "firmness" down by emphasizing economic over military aid wherever possible, and by substituting a huge reservoir of trained reservists (Universal Military Training) for a large standing military establishment. He was not by nature disposed, even privately, to write off any geographic area, unless U.S. resources in the vicinity were plainly inadequate, as in China. (Even there he was for a time receptive to Dean Acheson's strategy of gradually encouraging a Sino-Soviet split.) In one instance, the Iran crisis of 1946, he confronted Soviet encroachments *despite* a lack of appreciable U.S. power in the area. Although often prone to act upon geopolitical considerations, as in his support of Greek-Turkish aid, the Marshall Plan, and the North Atlantic Treaty Organization, he seldom analyzed them in advance of crises, and he could also disregard them, as in his prompt recognition of Israel in 1948.

The overall result of Truman's approach, despite his later disavowal of the term *containment*, was to forward the gradual implementation of its unlimited, popularly understood version. Truman from 1947 sought to contain Soviet expansion within limits dictated by his conception of the nation's military and his own political resources rather than by any grand strategic conception of which areas were, and which were not, vital to U.S. security.

Dean Acheson was far more directly influenced by Kennan, particularly the analysis of Soviet behavior, which helped mold Acheson's tendency to take Soviet hostility as a constant. Concerning the "long telegram" of February 1946, a precursor of the "X" article that Kennan sent from Moscow during his period as charge d'affaires, Acheson wrote later that Kennan's "historical analysis might or might not have been sound, but his predictions and warnings could not have been better. We responded to them slowly." Kennan's recommendations through the years on specific policies were another matter, for Acheson regarded him as a "contradictory" analyst capable of both "prophetic insight" and "suggestions of total impracticality."

In lawyerly fashion, Acheson in his memoirs described the "lines of policy" the administration gradually adopted as "not rules or doctrines" but precedents "which grew by the method of common law to aid the judgment of those who must make decisions." The precedents in turn constituted a *"corpus diplomaticum"* from which policymakers could draw. The second Truman administration—Acheson's period as secretary of state—put the "main lines of policy," which had been "set and begun" before 1949—Acheson's period as under secretary—into "full effect."

Were these merely the conclusions of hindsight? Although Acheson always saw Europe and the Middle East as the areas most vital to U.S. security, there are hints that he was more mindful of other regions while under secretary (1945–147) than is often supposed. During the Greek-Turkish aid hearings he stated: "There are other places where we can be effective. One of them is Korea, and I think that is another place where the line has been clearly drawn between the Russians and ourselves." He did not want to guarantee South Korea unconditionally and he did not consider it a very important place, but even in 1947 he thought it was important to keep the Soviets out of it. While the State Department was formulating the Truman Doctrine, Acheson told one aide: "If F.D.R. were alive I think I know what he would do. He would make a statement of global policy but would confine his request for money right now to Greece and Turkey." The qualifier "right now" suggests that the sweeping

nature of the Truman Doctrine was not just a device to sell Greek-Turkish aid to a hostile Congress.

Within the defense establishment, the military practice of ranking various areas by relative importance to U.S. security seemed, superficially, to be more in line with Kennan's own understanding of containment. For instance, SWNCC 360/1, a paper submitted by the Joint Chiefs of Staff to an interagency committee in 1946, ranked the usefulness to U.S. security of thirty-five countries in five geographic regions according to three different sets of criteria. Yet the criteria were far different from Kennan's. The Joint Chiefs were more disposed to take into account the economic hinterlands of the major noncommunist power centers. Thus they regarded certainly safe areas, such as Latin America and North Africa, as vital to U.S. security, whereas Kennan considered important only those portions of them adjacent to one of the major power centers. In addition, although the Joint Chiefs, like Kennan, ranked China and Korea far down the list, they were unwilling to abandon them altogether in situations short of general war and were more supportive of Chiang Kai-shek than was the administration.

With passage of the National Security Act in 1947, the U.S. government for the first time had machinery for the systematic adoption of approved governmentwide (classified) policy papers. An early paper treating the global response to Soviet policies was NSC 7, which spoke of organizing a "world-wide counter-offensive against Soviet-directed world Communism," and NSC 20/4, approved by the president in November 1948, saw "the domination of the world" as the ultimate objective of Soviet policy and behavior. Although the Soviets were not planning war to achieve this goal, military intimidation was an important Soviet technique. The United States should seek to reduce existing Soviet influence by promoting "the gradual retraction of undue Russian power and influence from the present perimeter areas around Russian boundaries and the emergence of the satellite countries as entities independent of the USSR." If taken literally, this language might seem to apply to North Korea as well as Eastern Europe. Although the context in which NSC 20/4 was prepared makes this unlikely, it is nonetheless noteworthy that geographical qualifications do not appear. But NSC 20/4 cautioned against overburdening military expenditures or permanently impairing the U.S. economy or fundamental U.S. institutions through excessive zeal.

The Korean War, of course, intensified the administration's commitment to resisting communism on a global basis. The United States increased its military budgets by a factor of three, prevented Chinese Communist conquest of Formosa by interdicting the Formosa Strait, and committed troops to NATO. Yet important steps sometimes associated with the Korean War actually antedated it, being instead most immediately stimulated by the collapse of Nationalist China and the Soviet test of an A-bomb in 1949.

With NSC 64 of February 1950, the United States initiated a policy of aid to the French in Indochina. An earlier paper, NSC 48/1 of December 1949, had stressed the importance of Southeast Asia's raw materials and its potential as a market for Japan. Perhaps most significantly, it stated that the "extension of Communist authority in China represents a grievous political defeat for us; if Southeast Asia is also swept by Communism we shall have suffered a major political rout the repercussions of which will be felt throughout the rest of the world." From April 1950,

U.S. efforts to negotiate a Japanese peace treaty, if necessary without the Soviets, intensified. Despite withdrawal of U.S. occupation troops from Korea in 1949, the administration vigorously supported military aid to Syngman Rhee's government. Although Acheson in his famous Press Club address of January 1950 left South Korea out of the U.S. "defense perimeter," he stressed U.S. "direct responsibility" to it as well.

Simultaneously, a joint State-Defense committee headed by Paul Nitze and Maj. Gen. Truman Landon worked from early 1950 to draft NSC 68, a new statement of overall policy. This landmark paper not only reiterated the doctrine of global resistance to communism contained in NSC 20/4; it also expanded a theme implicit in the quotation from NSC 48/1, thereby fashioning a new general rationale for the preservation of peripheral areas from communism: in a world power arena where perceptions were paramount and the perceptions of all the players might influence the outcome, the United States must not even *seem* to be losing the struggle anywhere. Unfavorable appearances might have a negative snowballing effect: "a defeat for free institutions anywhere is a defeat everywhere."

Obviously many of the drafters, and certainly Acheson, still believed that Western Europe was more important to U.S. security than most places in Asia, and U.S. military planning for the case of a general war was based on this premise. Yet a distinction between the desirability of stopping communism in all areas, and the necessity of stopping it in some areas, was difficult to make to the public and the Congress, as Acheson, who repeatedly tried, discovered; it was also hard to clear within the government. In addition, NSC 68 was partly a propaganda piece for internal administration consumption. Acheson regarded it as a vitally necessary but "ponderous collection of elementary ideas" whose purpose was "so to bludgeon the mass mind of 'top government' that not only could the President make a decision but the decision could be carried out." As a result of such considerations, general policy papers, even secret ones, were tending to become less sophisticated than their drafters.

At several points NSC 68 dwelt upon the new military situation created by Soviet atomic capability, which it assumed would develop rapidly. It plainly envisaged massively greater U.S. military expenditures, which some of its drafters hoped could be financed by a Keynesian policy of stimulating overall economic growth. The paper explicitly embraced a "policy of 'containment'" but bluntly stated that "without superior aggregate military strength" containment was "no more than a policy of bluff." It also introduced the notion of a period of maximum danger, in contrast to Kennan's depiction of the Soviets as infinitely patient. When NSC 68 was completed in April, Truman deferred action on it pending cost estimates. Late in the year he approved it "as a statement of policy over the next four or five years." It was the Korean War buildup that made possible the spending level spelled out by later papers in the NSC 68 series.

Critics of containment were of a great variety and grew more numerous with each year. The groups clustered around Henry Wallace in the Progressive party in 1948 ranged all the way from communist sympathizers to those who, like Wallace himself, believed that a "spheres of influence" settlement, which they hoped would permanently stabilize international relations, could be worked out with the Soviets. Opponents on the Right were more powerful, however. The Republican opposition to containment evolved over the years from isolationism to many new forms. Herbert Hoover's "Fortress America" strategy most resembled traditional isolationism, but called for heavy spending on naval and air forces. William Knowland and the so-called China Lobby believed that containment was a cloak-word for an excessively defensive Europe-first policy and that Chiang could have saved China if given more money and arms. In an address of December 1950, John Foster Dulles, identified with "Eastern internationalist" Republicans, sought to repudiate both the Fortress America policy and containment. He pointed out the difficulties of area defense and emphasized deterrence through the capacity for counterattack. This address foreshadowed the "massive retaliation" policy of the early Eisenhower years. By election time in 1952, containment, identified with the frustrations of Korea, neglect of China, and a general defensive passivity in the face of Soviet challenges, had acquired negative public connotations on which Richard Nixon capitalized in his famous identification of containment with appeasement, as in "Adlai [Stevenson] the appeaser . . . who got a Ph.D. from Dean Acheson's College of Cowardly Communist Containment."

Although the policy of containment was implemented more slowly than the Truman Doctrine and Kennan's "X" article appeared to call for, the importance of the sweeping language of 1947 should not be underestimated. In the words of Marvin Myers, "with talk begins responsibility," especially during a presidency whose public support was never broad or deep enough to enable it to modify or change course with impunity. Whatever the policy debates within the administration, no member of it had the public prestige that would allow him to set forth successfully a more selective version of containment, even if there had been an internal administration consensus on what it should be.

As codified in NSC 68 and the later, fundamentally similar NSC 135 and 141 series of papers, containment differed from Kennan's selective (and at the time publicly unexpressed) version in its heavy military emphasis, its refusal to differentiate between major and minor interests, and its specification of timetables of crucial danger. Containment nonetheless remained true to Kennan's vision in its rejection of general war as a solution to international competition and in its insistence that fundamental U.S. institutions not be subordinated to diplomatic, foreign policy, or military objectives. Toward the end of the Truman years, the term *containment* became almost a curse in public discourse, but variations on its theme were to have more staying power than was apparent at the time.

For George Kennan's original article, see "X," "The Sources of Soviet Conduct," *Foreign Affairs* 25 (July 1947): 566–82. For the "long telegram" of 22 February 1946, which includes a similar analysis of Soviet behavior and some anticipations of the containment concept, see Department of State, *Foreign Relations of the United States, 1946*, vol. 6, *Eastern Europe; the Soviet Union* (Washington, D.C.: U.S. Government Printing Office, 1969), 696–709. Written in December 1946, the "X" article was enthusiastically endorsed by Secretary of the Navy James Forrestal, cleared at middle levels in the State Department (Secretary Marshall did not see it before publication), and published anonymously. A leak via Forrestal soon revealed the author's name. These and other details of publication, as well as Kennan's later reflections on containment discussed above, are in his *Memoirs: 1925–1950* (Boston: Atlantic, 1969), 354–67, and in his "The Origins of Containment," in *Containment: Concept and*

Policy, edited by Terry F. Deibel and John Lewis Gaddis, 23–31 (Washington, D.C.: National Defense University Press, 1986). Clark Clifford's reminiscences of his group's September 1946 report are in the same volume, pp. 46–51, and the report itself, "American Relations with the Soviet Union," is printed in Arthur Krock, *Memoirs: Sixty Years on the Firing Line* (New York: Funk & Wagnalls, 1968), 419–82. Other than Kennan's, the single most important memoir bearing on containment is Dean Acheson, *Present at the Creation: My Years in the State Department* (New York: W. W. Norton, 1969). The most thorough scholar of containment is John Lewis Gaddis. In "Was the Truman Doctrine a Real Turning Point?" *Foreign Affairs* 52 (January 1974): 386–402, he argued that the Truman Doctrine was largely propaganda rhetoric and that real containment did not get underway until the Korean War. Amplification, and some modification, of this thesis followed in numerous articles, one of the best of which is "The Strategic Perspective: The Rise and Fall of the 'Defensive Perimeter' Concept," in *Uncertain Years: Chinese-American Relations, 1947–1950*, ed. Dorothy Borg and Waldo Heinrichs, 61–118 (New York: Columbia, 1980). The culmination of Gaddis's work is *Strategies of Containment: A Critical Appraisal of Postwar American National Security Policy* (New York: Oxford University Press, 1982). In it Gaddis gives an overview of Kennan's ideas and argues that Kennan was interpreting containment as early as 1947 (when Kennan opposed much of the Truman Doctrine). Eduard M. Mark in "The Question of Containment: A Reply to John Lewis Gaddis," *Foreign Affairs* 56 (January 1978): 430–40, contends that Kennan was inconsistent in his policy recommendations, and especially, that he advocated military means of containment more than he later acknowledged and did not always adhere to his supposed geopolitical priorities. (Gaddis's rejoinder is printed with Mark's article.) In *Architects of Illusion: Men and Ideas in American Foreign Policy, 1941–1949* (Chicago: Quadrangle, 1970), Lloyd C. Gardner emphasizes the tension between moralist and realist elements in Kennan's analyses and personality. Contemporary critiques of containment began with Walter Lippmann's *The Cold War: A Study in U.S. Foreign Policy* (New York: Harper, 1947), which draws on Lippmann's original newspaper pieces attacking "The Sources of Soviet Conduct." Thomas G. Paterson, ed., *Containment and the Cold War* (Reading, Mass.: Addison-Wesley, 1973), is a useful compendium of criticism of containment written from the Truman era through the early 1970s. Excellent studies of the regional application of containment ideas include Robert M. Blum, *Drawing the Line: The Origin of the American Containment Policy in East Asia* (New York: Norton, 1982), and Bruce R. Kuniholm, *The Origins of the Cold War in the Near East: Great Power Conflict and Diplomacy in Iran, Turkey and Greece* (Princeton: Princeton University Press, 1980). Thomas H. Etzold and John Lewis Gaddis, eds., *Containment: Documents on American Policy and Strategy, 1945–1950* (New York: Columbia University Press, 1978), is a collection of basic American policy papers on containment declassified as of the time of publication. Many additional materials on containment are available in pertinent volumes of the Department of State's official documentary series *Foreign Relations of the United States*, now virtually complete for the Truman years.

DAVID W. MABON

See also Acheson, Dean Gooderham; Clifford, Clark McAdams; Cold War; Kennan, George Frost; NSC 68; Truman Doctrine

Council of Economic Advisers

The Council of Economic Advisers was created by the Employment Act of 1946 to provide the president with first-rate economic advice on a regular basis. Prompted by memories of the Great Depression of the 1930s, the framers of the Employment Act shifted the question from *whether* the government would intervene to safeguard economic prosperity to *how* such intervention would be undertaken. They established the Council of Economic Advisers to aid the president in fulfilling the federal government's new formal commitment to maximum employment, production, and purchasing power. The new body was composed of three members, appointed by the president and confirmed by the Senate. The Employment Act specified that they be "exceptionally qualified" by virtue of "training, experience, and attainments" to interpret economic developments, appraise government programs, and recommend national economic policies. Behind the scenes, nine economists and one statistician constituted the council's initial professional staff. President Truman signed the Employment Act of 1946 into law in February, and the Council of Economic Advisers began operation in August 1946.

The original members of the council were Edwin G. Nourse, chairman; Leon H. Keyserling, vice-chairman; and John D. Clark. Nourse was a moderate conservative with excellent professional credentials; he had headed both the American Economic Association and the Social Science Research Council and was a vice president at the Brookings Institution when selected to lead the council. Keyserling had been in the vanguard of the New Deal; a graduate of Harvard Law School, he did not hold a doctorate in economics but had proven himself a brilliant student of political economy during his long government service, most notably as a trusted adviser to New York's Senator Robert F. Wagner. Clark had made a fortune in the oil business and then retired while in his early forties to study economics and undertake an academic career; he was serving as dean of the business school at the University of Nebraska when Truman tapped him to serve on the council. The mixture of professional and political backgrounds bespoke both Truman's sense of political balance and the fact that his own plans for the new agency were notably vague. He told his appointees, "Now you gentlemen just keep this national income up to 200 billion dollars and we'll be all right."

The Truman years were a time of both turmoil and achievement for the council. Internal discord was a problem at the outset. Nourse sought the appearance of scientific objectivity, and he opposed having council members testify before congressional committees for fear of being drawn into a political defense of administration policies. Keyserling and Clark thought otherwise, and Truman dawdled for two years before resolving the issue in their favor. Another less visible but more fundamental disagreement divided the council: Nourse viewed economic stability as the overriding concern, whereas Keyserling argued that only an emphasis on economic growth would enable the administration to achieve its social, economic, and national defense goals. Frustrated by such conflicts and irritated by the president's unwillingness to work closely with the council, Nourse resigned in October 1949. Keyserling subsequently succeeded him as chairman, and Roy Blough (and later Robert C. Turner) filled the council's third position. Under Keyserling's direction, the council enjoyed both a greater unity and a closer working relationship with the White House.

Among the council's achievements during the Truman years, three stand out as particularly notable. Not the least of these was the successful launching of the council itself, an institutional innovation that would significantly influence the making of national economic policy for a generation to come. At the same time, the council also left an intellectual mark by shifting the focus of discussion from a cyclical model of the economy to a growth model, thereby anticipating and preparing the way for what some have labeled the intellectual revolution in economic policy-making of the 1960s. Finally, the council could take some of the credit, although exactly how much remains uncertain, for the considerable success of national economic policy in the period 1945–53.

Stephen Bailey, *Congress Makes a Law: The Story behind the Employment Act of 1946* (New York: Columbia University Press, 1950), is a classic account of how the Council of Economic Advisers came into being. Edwin G. Nourse, *Economics in the Public Service* (New York: Harcourt Brace, 1953), and the Leon Keyserling interview in Erwin C. Hargrove and Samuel A. Morley, eds., *The President and the Council of Economic Advisers: Interviews with CEA Chairmen* (Boulder, Colo.: Westview Press, 1984), provide the perspectives of the two men who headed the council under Truman. Edward S. Flash, Jr., *Economic Advice and Presidential Leadership: The Council of Economic Advisers* (New York: Columbia University Press, 1965), remains the basic scholarly study of the council. Francis H. Heller, ed., *Economics and the Truman Administration* (Lawrence: Regents Press of Kansas, 1981), is a useful overview, and Walter Salant, "Some Intellectual Contributions of the Truman Council of Economic Advisers to Policy-making," *History of Political Economy* 5 (Spring 1973): 36–49, is an insightful specialized essay.

ROBERT M. COLLINS

See also Employment Act of 1946; Inflation; Keyserling, Leon; Nourse, Edwin Griswold

Council on Foreign Relations

The Council on Foreign Relations, a private, New York–based foreign policy research organization, helped define and publicize the Truman administration's new policy of containment of the Soviet Union. Council study groups and publications called for a reversal of wartime friendship with Moscow and a tough assertion of American military and economic power.

As the Second World War ended, leaders of the council became suspicious of Soviet intentions and insisted that the organization's recommendations note the dangers emanating from Moscow. To that end Isaiah Bowman, president of Johns Hopkins University and chairman of the council's Committee

on Publications, helped block publication of a report from a council study group on U.S.-Soviet relations which expressed sympathy for Moscow's "vital interests in having governments not unfriendly to her along her western frontier." Bowman's committee ruled against publication in July 1946 after the president of Johns Hopkins observed that recent worsening of U.S.-Soviet relations rendered the report's accommodating tone "out of date" and deplored any American effort to "appear in sackcloth and ashes before the Soviet leaders."

Having decided that the Soviet Union threatened U.S. interests, council leaders hoped to publicize their views. Hamilton Fish Armstrong, editor of *Foreign Affairs*, the council's quarterly journal, asked Soviet expert George F. Kennan, head of the State Department's newly formed Policy Planning Staff, to prepare an article explaining Soviet behavior. The result, "The Sources of Soviet Conduct," appeared in July 1947 under the pseudonym "X." In one of the most influential magazine articles ever written, Kennan called for "long-term, patient but firm and vigilant containment of the Russian expansionist tendencies."

In late 1950 the council directly encouraged President Truman to send Gen. Dwight D. Eisenhower to Europe as commander of the North Atlantic Treaty Organization (NATO) accompanied by a fresh contingent of 180,000 U.S. troops. Twelve members of a council study group on U.S.-European relations chaired by Eisenhower wrote the president that present NATO forces were "totally inadequate" and urged him to "tell the people the bleak facts. They will respond." Truman agreed, and when Ike took command of NATO early in 1951 he brought with him the reinforcements sought by the council's study group.

The standard scholarly work on the council is Robert D. Schulzinger, *The Wise Men of Foreign Affairs: The History of the Council of Foreign Relations* (New York: Columbia University Press, 1984). Fresh information on containment and the "X" article appears in Walter Issaacson and Evan Thomas, *The Wise Men: Six Friends and the World They Made* (New York: Simon & Schuster, 1986). The Council's archives are available to researchers at its headquarters: 58 E. 68th St., New York, NY 10021.

ROBERT D. SCHULZINGER

See also Containment; Eisenhower, Dwight David; Kennan, George Frost; North Atlantic Treaty Organization

Crime

The crime problem, especially the debate over organized crime, would serve as a significant embarrassment to the Truman administration. While the president and others sought to encourage local, state, and voluntary efforts against crime and delinquency, the administration itself would become embroiled in a distracting series of developments over the issue.

Law enforcement authorities had predicted that World War II would be followed by a sharp increase in juvenile delinquency, gang warfare, and organized crime. Postwar FBI statistics tended to confirm these predictions. At several national conferences sponsored by his attorneys general, Truman expressed his concern about the apparent increase in juvenile delinquency. He proclaimed April 1948 as a month for local groups to hold conventions and mobilize resources against youth crime. He especially tried to enlist the "gentler forces" of home and church in the campaign against juvenile delinquency.

Organized crime proved far less manageable. In response to growing publicity about the problem, the Justice Department in 1947 launched a "racket squad" to develop evidence for grand jury investigations in several large cities. Meanwhile, federal agents began to audit income tax returns of gambling entrepreneurs and well-known racketeers. At a Washington conference in February 1950, however, Truman and Attorney General J. Howard McGrath reminded local officials that they had to bear the chief burden of the fight against organized crime.

Frustrated at what they considered the passive attitude of the administration and its reluctance to share income tax and FBI records with municipal officials, several mayors and civic organizations began to lobby for a congressional investigation of gambling and syndicated crime. Tennessee senator Estes Kefauver, a liberal with presidential ambitions, sponsored a resolution for a broad-ranging probe. Administration suspicions about an investigation directed by the maverick Kefauver, as well as congressional intrigue, delayed Senate approval of the resolution until April 1950. Then the assassination of politician–gambling entrepreneur Charles Binaggio in a Kansas City Democratic clubhouse (beneath a large wall photograph of Truman) rendered further delay politically impossible.

Launched against the backdrop of the Binaggio killing in the president's home county, the Kefauver committee found itself engulfed in the politics of crime. Although Binaggio had cooperated with remnants of the Pendergast machine in Kansas City as late as 1946, he had become in fact a political rival. A full airing of the Kansas City situation would nonetheless touch upon Binaggio's ties to the Pendergast machine, which had sponsored Truman's early political career. Republicans were eager to embarrass the president and his party by focusing the committee's attention on big-city (mostly Democratic) machines which historically had tolerated, even protected, illegal gambling and other vice. For Kefauver to ignore these problems in Kansas City and other Democratic strongholds was to court the contempt of Republicans and the press. To explore them was to invite Truman's wrath and the charge of party disloyalty.

Kefauver attempted to finesse the problem. He initiated his investigation with a probe of gambling conditions in south Florida, and then, under considerable pressure, moved into Kansas City. There, however, he emphasized the monopoly aspect of the horse racing wire service in his hearings. Limiting political discussion to Binaggio's misdeeds, he tried to avoid open discussion of the Pendergast-Truman connection. After the 1950 elections, the committee did criticize former New York mayor William O'Dwyer, whom Truman had named ambassador to Mexico, and it clashed with lower-level officials in the Internal Revenue Service.

The president had little appreciation for Kefauver's efforts to contain the political fallout. Truman neither watched the televised hearings nor followed them closely through the newspapers. Briefed by his aides and senior congressional leaders, he developed a seriously distorted sense of the committee's work and an intense dislike for Kefauver, whom he contemptuously referred to as "Cowfever." Privately, he expressed considerable bitterness at the damage the committee and a hostile press did to his own reputation and to the Democratic party in Missouri,

Illinois, and New York. Nor did the difficulties end with the Kefauver committee. Linking the organized crime revelations to a series of exposés involving influence peddling by administration appointees in Washington, Republicans fashioned the "corruption" issue of the 1952 campaign.

Truman's sensitivity over the crime issue sprang from his own embarrassing past ties to the Pendergast machine and from his well-founded beliefs that the Democratic party itself could be damaged by a study of urban vice. His generally negative reaction to Kefauver, and his entrenched opposition to the senator's presidential ambitions, underscored both the president's peevish, unforgiving personality and his intense sense of party loyalty.

The fullest history of the crime issue is William Howard Moore, *The Kefauver Committee and the Politics of Crime, 1950-1952* (Columbia: University of Missouri Press, 1974). James Gilbert in *A Cycle of Outrage: America's Reaction to the Juvenile Delinquent in the 1950's* (New York: Oxford University Press, 1986), discusses the background of the delinquency problem in the war years and during the Truman administration. Andrew J. Dunar also finds Truman poorly informed and overly defensive in his useful *The Truman Scandals and the Politics of Morality* (Columbia: University of Missouri Press, 1984).

WILLIAM HOWARD MOORE

See also Election of 1952; Kefauver, Estes; Pendergast, Thomas J.; Scandals

Czechoslovakia

The "last" state in Eastern Europe to "fall" to the Communists was Czechoslovakia. From 1945 to 1948 it held a unique position in Eastern Europe. A democratic state during the interwar period, Czechoslovakia, unlike its neighbors, harbored no historic hatred of Russia and had a large native Communist party. Recognizing the international situation in 1945, President Edward Beneš, who had already been caught in one great power struggle at Munich in 1938, tried to maintain good relations with both Moscow and Washington. He hoped that his country would serve as a bridge between East and West.

Although Czechoslovakia seemed to be the one state in which American faith in the Yalta principles might be fulfilled, hopes proved to be illusory. In December 1945, under pressure from the American public to "bring the boys home," Washington withdrew the last U.S. troops stationed in Czechoslovakia (the only East European state which had an American contingent on its soil); henceforth, the United States could provide only moral support for the democracy. In 1946 free elections saw the Communist party win nearly 38 percent of the vote, enabling Klement Gottwald to form a coalition that included fellow Communists in such important posts as Interior (police) and Information. Soviet influence began to grow. In 1947, under pressure from Stalin, the Czechs reversed their initial decision to participate in the Marshall Plan. In world forums, Czech delegates, again constrained by Moscow, increasingly followed Soviet leads, an action that resulted in America withholding vital economic credits (thereby ironically strengthening the hold of pro-Soviet factions in the nation).

Despite the preponderance of Communists within the government and the demands of its Soviet neighbor, however, the Czech parliamentary system survived until February 1948. With elections scheduled for May and the likelihood that the Communist party would suffer a serious electoral defeat, Interior Minister Václav Nosek hurriedly began to purge the police of non-Communist elements. In protest, twelve members of the cabinet resigned in mid-February, hoping to force Beneš to call early elections before they could be rigged. Gottwald responded by demanding that Beneš name a Communist government (although Jan Masaryk, son of the first Czech president, could remain foreign minister). There is no direct evidence that the Soviet Union threatened to use force if Beneš refused (although the arrival in Prague of Deputy Foreign Minister Valerian Zorin has led many observers to believe that strong pressure was applied from Moscow); nevertheless, Beneš, elderly and in poor health, acceded to Gottwald's demands on 25 February. A week after the resignations, the "February Victory" was complete, and on 10 March authorities discovered the body of Masaryk beneath his apartment. Whether he committed suicide or was pushed by security agents (as was widely held), his death symbolized the death of Czech democracy.

In the words of President Truman, the fall of Czechoslovakia sent "shock waves" through the free world. War talk was common in the days following the takeover. Although Henry Wallace charged that the United States had precipitated the crisis (his seemingly callous attitude toward the death of Masaryk would prove politically costly), many believed that the Soviet Union would use Czechoslovakia as a springboard into Europe. As a result, Congress approved the administration's requests to fund the Marshall Plan, reinstated Selective Service, and increased military appropriations dramatically. Moreover, the events in Prague spurred Europeans not only to form a defensive alliance but also to initiate talks with the United States and Canada aimed at creating a transatlantic pact.

Many works on the Truman presidency contain references to Czechoslovakia. In, for example, *Shattered Peace: The Origins of the Cold War and the National Security State* (Boston: Houghton Mifflin, 1977), Daniel Yergin demonstrates how the Gottwald takeover helped cement the policy of containment. For events in Czechoslovakia itself, see Pavel Tigrid, "The Prague Coup of 1948: The Elegant Takeover," in *The Anatomy of Communist Takeovers*, ed. Thomas T. Hammond (New Haven: Yale University Press, 1975).

RICHARD FRUCHT

See also Cold War; Soviet Union

D

Daniels, Jonathan Worth

(26 April 1902–6 November 1981)
Temporary press secretary for and biographer of Truman. Jonathan Daniels was born in Raleigh, North Carolina, and educated at the University of North Carolina. A son of Josephus Daniels, he worked for the family's *Raleigh News and Observer* for most of his career and wrote more than a dozen books. A loyal Democrat, Daniels earned a reputation as a southern liberal in the 1930s for his support of labor unions, civil rights, and the New Deal. He edited the newspaper from 1933 until 1942, when he went to Washington, D.C., during the war. He worked as assistant director of the Office of Civilian Defense before becoming one of six presidential assistants in March 1943. Targets of his efforts for President Roosevelt ranged from wartime baseball to race relations. On 26 March 1945, he became Roosevelt's press secretary. After FDR's death, Daniels continued in the post until Truman named Charles Ross his permanent press secretary. Daniels returned to Raleigh to write and in early 1948 resumed the editorship of the family newspaper. Truman named Daniels to the Public Advisory Board of the Economic Cooperation Administration in June 1948.

During the 1948 presidential campaign, Daniels traveled widely with Truman and helped with speech writing, but in the spring of 1949, he refused Truman's offer to name him secretary of the navy. A few weeks later he decided to write a biography of the president, and *The Man of Independence* appeared early in the fall of 1950. Scholars have generally lauded its coverage of the prepresidential years: Daniels had Truman's cooperation in the project, he interviewed many of Truman's Missouri friends and acquaintances, and his journalistic skill effectively evoked the period.

Daniels continued to edit the *News and Observer* until the late 1960s when he retired to Hilton Head, South Carolina.

The only book-length treatment of Daniels is Charles W. Eagles, *Jonathan Daniels and Race Relations: The Evolution of a Southern Liberal* (Knoxville: University of Tennessee Press, 1982). For the 1948 campaign, see Irwin Ross, *The Loneliest Campaign: The Truman Victory of 1948* (New York: New American Library, 1968). For one scholar's evaluation of *The Man of Independence*, see Alonzo L. Hamby, "The Clash of Perspectives and the Need for New Syntheses," in *The Truman Period as a Research Field: A Reappraisal, 1972*, ed. Richard S. Kirkendall, 124 (Columbia: University of Missouri Press, 1974).

CHARLES W. EAGLES

See also Ross, Charles Griffith, for photograph

Demobilization

On 6 September 1944 the Department of War announced the demobilization program for personnel that would become effective upon the surrender of Germany. The program operated on a principle of discharging individuals rather than whole units. Although less flexible and less efficient than the unit system utilized after the Civil War and World War I, the individual system seemed more equitable and, therefore, would command the most widespread support. Under the program each service person accumulated points on the basis of parenthood, combat experience, overseas duty, and total service: twelve points for each child; five points for each military campaign or combat decoration; one point per month for overseas service; and one point per month for total service. On 8 May 1945—Victory in Europe, or V-E Day—the War Department announced that it would discharge personnel with eighty-five points. Although similar to the army plan, the navy's system calculated age as a factor, but not combat, and computed points differently for

The staggering challenge presented by demobilization is apparent in this view of U.S. forces in one Italian port, June 1945. (National Archives)

dependents. The Marine Corps adopted the army system and the Coast Guard used the navy's formula.

On 30 June 1945, six weeks before the war against Japan ended, the U.S. military forces stood at their all-time peak enrollments. The army comprised 8,267,958 soldiers; the navy reported 3,380,817 sailors and 1,166 major combat ships on duty; and the Marine Corps counted 474,680 men and women in uniform. At the time the air force served under the command of the army.

Despite the logic and clarity of the demobilization process, criticism arose. Most Americans failed to appreciate the time and logistics required to return to the United States the more than 7.5 million men and women stationed overseas in May 1945. Two other factors clouded public perception of demobilization. The drafting of young men continued, although at a monthly rate of 50,000 rather than 80,000, and the number of troops required for occupation in Japan and Germany remained uncertain.

Many in uniform and their family members judged the demobilization pace to be too slow. Across the country wives of servicemen organized about two hundred "Bring Back Daddy" clubs to attract attention and support for their cause. In December they flooded the congressional mail with baby shoes attached to notes that pleaded "Please bring back my daddy." On Christmas Day in Manila, 4,000 soldiers marched to the twenty-first replacement depot headquarters to protest the cancelation of a troopship sailing. On 6 January 1946, some 20,000 soldiers protested at command headquarters in Manila and booed the

general who attempted to explain demobilization policy. When Secretary of War Robert Patterson arrived in Yokohama, Japan, soldiers greeted him with boos, and other soldiers demonstrated in Paris and Frankfurt. Ten thousand enlisted men and officers in Batangas signed a telegram to President Truman. Soldiers held mass meetings in India, Korea, Austria, and the United States. But the army handled the agitation with restraint, and in mid-January the new chief of staff, Dwight D. Eisenhower, explained demobilization to Congress. The angry mood soon quieted.

At a news conference in April Truman reported that the army had discharged almost 7 million soldiers—"the most remarkable demobilization in the history of the world, or 'disintegration,' if you want to call it that." Indeed, on 30 June 1946, the nation's services were mere shells of their strength a year earlier. In terms of personnel on active duty, the army counted 1,891,011; the navy, 983,398; and the Marine Corps, 155,679. Sixty percent of these servicemen and women, moreover, had donned uniforms since V-E Day. A year later, with demobilization completed, corresponding figures were 991,285, 498,661, and 94,225.

Along with the sharp personnel reductions, the Pentagon closed hundreds of bases and camps around the nation and the world. The Navy Department scrapped some ships, transferred others to Allied nations, used obsolete ones for target practice, and placed some in mothballs. Between the summers of 1945 and 1947 the number of aircraft carriers on duty decreased from 28 to 14, battleships from 23 to 4, cruisers from 73 to 32, destroyers and destroyer escorts from 737 to 162, and submarines from 234 to 80. Despite the reductions, the United States still maintained the world's largest navy.

Before the nation decided to rearm in 1950, the reliance on atomic weapons, the budgetary austerity of politicians, and the absence of a major opposing surface navy pushed even lower the number of major combat ships on active duty and the numbers of men and women in uniform. Truman, meanwhile, starting in October 1945, tried in vain to win congressional support for the Universal Military Training program.

Because of the emphasis upon speed and volume, the massive demobilization experienced countless inevitable minor inefficiencies. Nevertheless, the inherently fair point system and the general prosperity of the country far outweighed the inefficiencies and helped produce a successful operation. At a press conference in May 1947, President Truman reminisced briefly about World War II. Its end, he summarized, "left us with a great many problems, particularly some 12,800,000 men under arms, whose mothers and fathers immediately wanted them discharged the next day—which couldn't be done." After describing the challenge of demobilization, he accurately concluded that "we got over that hump in very good shape."

R. Alton Lee, "The Army 'Mutiny' of 1946," *Journal of American History* 53 (December 1966): 555–71, describes discontent within the army over the demobilization schedule. Lee is critical of Truman. David R. B. Ross, *Preparing for Ulysses: Politics and Veterans during World War II* (New York: Columbia University Press, 1969), is a well-researched, detailed volume that focuses on the development of government policy for veterans from 1940 to 1946. Ross also is critical of Truman. For the president's public statements regarding demobilization, see the 1945, 1946, and 1947 volumes of *Public Papers of the President: Harry S. Truman* (Washington, D.C.: U.S. Government Printing Office, 1961, 1962, 1963).

KEITH W. OLSON

See also Veterans

Democratic Party

Fractious, bitterly divided geographically and ideologically, no longer bound by either Great Depression necessities or the power of Franklin Roosevelt's personal leadership, the Democratic party during the Truman years was, like the nation itself, in a state of transition. Only magic could have resolved the complex forces that almost inevitably led to the Republican succession, and Harry Truman was no miracle worker.

Traumatized by having "the moon, the stars and all the planets" fall on his shoulders, as he said when Roosevelt died, Truman had on his side only an unusually sympathetic honeymoon. Roosevelt's death came when Nazi Germany was on the verge of collapse and American military leaders still feared the high cost of subduing the Japanese. The new president also had to face the diplomacy of making peace and the politics of domestic economic reconversion. Whatever his course might ulti-

mately be, the "acceptable man" who had been chosen as FDR's running mate in 1944 had for the moment, at least, the best wishes of even those most disaffected by years of New Deal government. "Truman is honest and patriotic and has a head full of good horse sense," John Nance Garner, FDR's first vice president, wrote to Sam Rayburn. "All of this can be made into a good President."

Garner was close to those rural and largely southern Democrats who regarded the New Deal and its attendant federal bureaucracy as betrayers of the Jeffersonian heritage. He and his friends were soon disappointed. Before Truman's first year was over, they feared that the Man from Missouri was sounding very much like a New Dealer. But, at the same time, he fell short of satisfying the Far Left. Henry Wallace and his Progressive Citizens of America were even more openly hostile, which whittled down Truman's support to largely hard-core Democrats. Most of them either liked him for his enemies or were sufficiently bound by party loyalty and self-interest to have no other choice. By the time he was renominated in 1948, many longtime stress points within the Democratic party had cracked wide open.

Southern discontent was especially strong, a carryover from distaste for the New Deal. Steadily, since Wilson's day, the balance of power had shifted to the big cities. Nevertheless, in most southern states, the party, which was merely a "holding-company for a congeries of transient squabbling factions," held firm in the thirties. Such leaders as Ed Crump in Tennessee, Harry Byrd in Virginia, and the Longs of Louisiana retained their advantages as local potentates who were in a position to drive hard bargains. That reality was sufficient to stifle rumblings about party realignment in an era when Republicans were still the party of Yankees.

Whatever changes were foreseeable at that point were sped up by the conditions created when war came. With the possible exception of the Southwest, the Old South was affected more than any other region. The demands of war production siphoned labor off the farms and into industrial centers, altering the familiar agricultural dominance. Most important was the triggering of a movement that eventually led some one million blacks toward jobs in the North and West during the 1940s alone. Just as the pattern of farm labor was being changed, so was the institution of Jim Crow. War against Nazi champions of a "master race" exposed the paradox of rigid segregation and other abuses in a nation fighting for the four freedoms. The Supreme Court, in its 1944 decision in the case of *Smith* v. *Allwright* upheld the Fifteenth Amendment to the Constitution by outlawing so-called white primaries in Texas, thereby opening the door to gradual change. Before the war ended, poll taxes came under attack, especially when such money was extracted from blacks who were returning from combat. Even that, however, was not as serious as the infiltration of southern industry by labor organizers, especially those from the more militant, and often leftist, Congress of Industrial Organizations (CIO), which attempted to enroll both black and white workers. In a region that was traditionally more feudal than capitalist, such developments were seen as the ominous workings of radicals in Washington who were doing their best to deprive the South of the freedom to develop its own industrial base.

If they were not unhappy with the New Deal itself, other Democrats had different reasons for breaking old loyalties. In such northern cities as Boston and New York, voting patterns since 1936 demonstrated a trend among some Roman Catholics, especially Irish-Americans, away from Roosevelt and his

Reg Manning, 3 November 1952. Courtesy of the McNaught Syndicate.

Democrats and toward the Republican party. As the Democratic party had come to be the party of liberalism, it was also the party that condemned Gen. Francisco Franco and his Spanish Falangists as "fascists." Influenced by the escalating anti–New Deal rhetoric of Father Charles Coughlin, the "radio priest," some came to see Roosevelt himself as a symbol of softness toward communism. Thus conditioned, many voters found it easy to decide that the war had come to an end with the Soviet Union in firm control of Eastern Europe because Roosevelt had "sold out" American interests at Yalta.

Although they had presided over the liquidation of the Great Depression and the prosecution of a great war, Democrats were nevertheless on the defensive. Foreign policy rarely swings votes one way or another, except for the immediate question of peace or war, and the mid-term elections of 1946 were no exception. Most Americans still identified themselves with the Democratic party, but they largely agreed that Democrats were responsible for the problems of reconversion that touched off a simultaneous wave of inflation, strikes, and shortages of meat, housing, and gasoline. By November, two-thirds of those who responded to opinion surveys favored the passage of new laws to control labor unions. Not surprisingly, the party in power was given poor grades for being unable to do much about either shortages or inflation. A mid-September Gallup poll indicated that only 32 percent of the electorate was satisfied with the way President Truman was handling his job.

By late 1946, hopes for international cooperation were also fading. The deteriorating East-West climate contributed to perceptions of unease and incompetence, if not outright disloyalty.

Not since the early 1920s had the issue of "reds" been so intense. According to the Gallup survey, more than one-third of Americans of all social and economic classes agreed that Communists in the United States should be either killed or imprisoned. In the South, Democrats did not hesitate to fan fear of communism and racial hatreds in order to hold the line against labor organizers and political mavericks. Barriers to voting by poor whites were being modified to enable such "friends" to offset larger turnouts by blacks. Elsewhere, especially in areas with large numbers of Democrats of Eastern European ancestry, Yalta began to be used in condemnation of Roosevelt's dealings with the Russians.

If any single election can be said to have "sent a message" to Democrats, it was that of 1946. Republicans chosen that year were disproportionately influential in establishing the political agenda for the coming years. All in all, the GOP increased its number of seats in the House by fifty-seven and in the Senate by six, which gave the party majorities in the Eightieth Congress.

Almost immediately after the election, Truman acted on two fronts that seemed to have been influenced by the outcome. The first, Executive Order 9806 establishing a temporary Commission on Loyalty, was clearly affected by the voting. The second, Executive Order 9808, which created the President's Committee on Civil Rights to look into the entire question of race relations, had its origins before the elections. Each indicated where the president and the party were going. Within a year, they had led, in the first case, to scrutiny of government employees and, in the second, to a report containing recommendations that formed the basis for civil rights legislation in the coming years. Truman and the Democrats were clearly pursuing a twofold course—adjusting to changing political realities and moving ahead with an agenda for reforms.

Ironically, the Republican-controlled Eightieth Congress provided a handy opportunity. When Truman sought a greater international role for the United States in containing the Soviet Union, the opposition approved every substantive request. Domestic policies were another matter, especially the passage of the National Labor Relations Act of 1947 (Taft-Hartley) to check the power of unions. After the original bill that came out of the House was toned down and cleansed of its more strongly antilabor provisions, the entire package as modified by Republican Senate leader Robert A. Taft was passed by more than the two-thirds needed to protect it from a presidential veto. According to one of Truman's closest and most loyal economists, the President considered signing the bill into law but then, at the prompting of his secretary of labor, decided to veto it. He also appended a message that denounced the law with the "slave labor" rhetoric favored by the unions. Predictably, both houses overrode his veto. Just as predictably, the president had an issue. Finally, after meandering in and out of labor's favor during his first two years, Truman had become a champion of the working man.

In waging his celebrated 1948 campaign, that uphill fight against not only Thomas Dewey and the Republicans but also the defectors from the Democratic fringes, Henry Wallace and his Progressives and the States' Righters led by J. Strom Thurmond, Truman excoriated the Eightieth Congress by targeting the Taft-Hartley Act. Organized labor largely put aside earlier doubts and recognized that Truman was their only hope. In the farm belt, the newly appointed agriculture secretary, Charles Brannan, campaigned vigorously for his plan to subsidize growers, taking advantage of falling grain prices by recalling that Democrats had been the ones to come to the rescue in the past. Liberal intellectuals of the Americans for Democratic Action, which had been founded to counter the pro-Communist Wallaceites, had their peak moment of strength. "The 'right' may have the money, but the 'left' has always had the pen," wrote presidential assistant Clark Clifford. "He is the artist of propaganda. He is the 'idea man' for the people."

So convinced was the nation that Truman could not possibly win that the president's thirty-one-thousand-mile whistle-stop campaign took its place in lore as his solitary fight. Indeed, his efforts were in marked contrast to the cool complacency, even arrogance, of Dewey, his Republican rival. But without the New Deal base of Democrats to begin with, without the restoration of economic stability, and without consensual approval for his cold war initiatives, even that "loneliest campaign" would not have been enough. With Truman leading the battle, Democrats also regained control over both houses of Congress.

Still, in his second term, he was notably unable to do much with the legislature. Democratic majorities were not synonymous with votes for liberal bills, and Truman's Fair Deal program, enunciated at the start of 1949, was largely shelved by the continued congressional power of the so-called conservative coalition of Republicans and southern Democrats. His victories were relatively negligible compared with his losses. The most that can be said for his fight for such programs as national health insurance, repeal of Taft-Hartley, and Brannan's farm plan, and his efforts in behalf of a Missouri Valley Authority and a St. Lawrence Seaway Authority (which was enacted under Eisenhower) is that he kept alive the liberal agenda. During his last four years, the image of a liberal Truman remained intact, most dramatically in 1952 with his seizure of the Youngstown Sheet and Tube Company after management had raised prices in defiance of a wage settlement award that had been granted to its workers by the Wage Mediation Board. When the Supreme Court found his takeover unconstitutional, the president withdrew in defeat.

The dispute, a classic test of presidential power, only compounded Truman's troubles. His second term had hardly settled down, the Berlin blockade overcome, when Truman's most enduring area of strength, foreign policy, turned into a succession of setbacks. Communist advances abroad fed fear of subversion at home. A series of domestic spy cases convinced millions of Americans that Marxist successes in Europe and the Far East were aided by the laxity, if not outright treason, of Democrats in Washington. The Soviets' detonation of their first atomic bomb and Chiang Kai-shek's ouster from the Chinese mainland were regarded by many as confirmation of such suspicions. The unveiling of Joe McCarthy's personal anti-Communist crusade the following February, followed only a few months later by the invasion of South Korea and American intervention, intensified the hostility. When Truman later agreed with Gen. Douglas MacArthur on the need to drive the Communists out of their own territory, thereby expanding the original limits of the U.S. involvement, Chinese Communists then intervened. American soldiers suffered heavy losses, and the administration faced the need to engage in a more protracted conflict than anyone had imagined. Finally, when the president relieved General MacArthur of his command in April 1951 because of his open defiance of orders from Washington to keep the war limited, what little was left of Truman's popular standing began to unravel altogether.

The scenario thus played itself out. Although unaffected by the Twenty-second Amendment's two-term limitation, Truman announced that he would not be a candidate for another term. Earlier, along with some fellow Democrats, he had offered to support Eisenhower for the presidency. But the general's attitude toward organized labor helped rule that out. Eisenhower soon let it be known that he was a Republican and allowed himself to be convinced to relinquish his NATO command and return in order to campaign for his party's nomination. Truman, meanwhile, worked to convince Governor Adlai Stevenson of Illinois to become the Democratic candidate. On the third ballot, Stevenson beat out a maverick Tennessean, Senator Estes Kefauver, who had won a series of primary elections en route to the convention.

The war in Korea went on, and the Republicans nominated Eisenhower and Senator Richard M. Nixon. The Democrats began their "spell in the wilderness" in search of another consensus. Meanwhile, there was considerable movement in and out of their "big tent."

Books on the Truman era have been rolling forth in rapid succession. Coverage of his presidency and party politics is provided most comprehensively by Robert J. Donovan's two volumes, *Conflict and Crisis* and *Tumultuous Years* (New York: W. W. Norton, 1977, 1982). Two other works are essential for an understanding of his presidency: Donald R. McCoy, *The Presidency of Harry S. Truman* (Lawrence: University Press of Kansas, 1984), which makes some shrewd, hardheaded judgments, and, for an examination of the ideological continuities with the New Deal, Alonzo L. Hamby, *Beyond the New Deal: Harry S. Truman and American Liberalism* (New York: Columbia University Press, 1973). The fortunes of the Democratic party, including ethnic rivalries and an overview of the emerging southern rebellion, are discussed in Herbert S. Parmet, *The Democrats: The Years after FDR* (New York: Macmillan, 1976).

HERBERT S. PARMET

See also Americans for Democratic Action; Congress, United States; Dixiecrats; Elections in the Truman Era; Liberalism; Progressive Party

Dennis Case

See Civil Liberties; Communism and Communists; Loyalty Program

Dewey, Thomas Edmund

(24 March 1902–16 March 1971)

Governor of New York, 1943–55; Republican presidential candidate, 1944, 1948. Thomas E. Dewey was born in Owoso, Michigan, the son of a newspaper publisher. He graduated from the University of Michigan in 1923 and attended law school there for one year. He received his law degree in 1925 from

Republican presidential candidate, Thomas Dewey, and vice-presidential candidate, Earl Warren, with their families at the Dewey farm in Pawling, New York, 1948. (National Archives)

Columbia University and practiced law in New York City. In 1935 Governor Herbert Lehman, a Democrat, appointed Dewey a special prosecutor to investigate racketeering in New York City. He was elected New York district attorney in 1937 on the Republican and Fusion-Labor tickets and continued his rackets investigations, obtaining numerous indictments against racketeers and Tammany Hall leaders.

Dewey's well-publicized work as a prosecutor led to his nomination for governor of New York in 1938. Although he lost to Lehman by 64,000 votes, this close contest and his racket-busting reputation helped make him a presidential candidate in 1940. Dewey led on the first ballot at the GOP convention that year, but lost the nomination to Wendell Willkie on the third. In 1942, Dewey again ran for governor and was elected by a 600,000-vote margin. He was reelected in 1946 and 1950. As governor, Dewey promoted many state programs for health, highways, and education. He pioneered some of the first civil rights laws in America and created a state commission on discrimination. His record placed Dewey in the moderate wing of the Republican party. He once called himself a "New Deal Republican."

Dewey won the Republican presidential nomination twice. In 1944 he lost the general election to Franklin Roosevelt and Truman by 3.6 million votes out of 48 million cast. Although Dewey ran an aggressive campaign in which he harshly criticized the Roosevelt administration as being tired and mismanaging the government, the American voters were not disposed to change leaders in the middle of a war and FDR still displayed the political leadership that already had carried him to victory three times.

Dewey's best chance to win the presidency came in 1948. Public opinion polls showed him a likely winner over Truman. Once nominated, however, Dewey ran an uninspiring campaign. In contrast to his aggressive effort in 1944, he attacked Truman's programs mildly and ignored both the failure of the Democrats in Congress to support Truman and the success congressional Republicans had in promoting their program. Three factors dictated this strategy. First, he generally agreed with most of Truman's foreign and domestic policies. Second, the Republican party was divided on many issues and taking a firm stand would have hurt him with the opposing faction. Third, Dewey possessed great self-confidence, which bred complacency that led him to think an aggressive campaign was unnecessary. His virtually issueless campaign and his cold, aloof manner failed to inspire voters, and he received fewer votes than he had in 1944.

Dewey and Truman seldom spoke specifically of each other in the campaign. Each, however, did comment critically in private. Truman confided to his diary, "Dewey synthetically milks cows and pitches hay for the cameras just as that other faker, Teddy Roosevelt, did." Dewey wrote to a newspaper editor, Henry Wallace "would destroy—I think knowingly—everything that has made this country great. Harry Truman might but because of ignorance."

In 1952, Dewey led the moderate wing of the GOP in engineering the nomination of Gen. Dwight D. Eisenhower for president and selecting Senator Richard M. Nixon for vice president. Dewey did not seek public office after retiring from the governorship, but returned to the practice of law. He exercised almost no influence in politics for the remaining seventeen years of his life.

Dewey's major biographer is Richard Norton Smith, *Thomas E. Dewey and His Times* (New York: Simon & Schuster, 1982). Dewey wrote several volumes that outline his thinking and chronicle his work. The two most important are *Twenty against the Underworld* (Garden City, N.Y.: Doubleday, 1974) and *Thomas E. Dewey on the Two-Party System* (New York: Doubleday, 1966). Dewey's personal papers are housed at the University of Rochester.

THOMAS F. SOAPES

See also Election of 1944; Election of 1948; Republican Party.

Displaced Persons

Truman's displaced persons (DP) policy has often been overlooked because in many minds it was intrinsically associated with obtaining a homeland for the Jews in Palestine and also because he rarely spoke publicly on the issue. Ultimately, the president pursued the right goals and helped pave the way for the Displaced Persons Act of 1948, and its more humane version in 1950, but his efforts lacked the fervor associated with some of his more dynamic accomplishments.

Apparently the first Truman heard about the conditions of the DPs in Europe was in May 1945. Many American Jews were concerned about the treatment their brethren who survived the war in Europe were receiving from the military forces in Germany. At first Truman was not interested in the problem, but he nonetheless sanctioned a suggestion of his acting secretary of state, Joseph Grew, to send an investigating team, headed by Earl Harrison, dean of the University of Pennsylvania Law School, to check up on the European DPs.

Displaced persons included concentration camp survivors, civilians who fled the Axis forces or the Allies, those who had been bombed out, and returning soldiers whose homes had been destroyed or who refused repatriation to the Eastern zone. They numbered over half a million in the summer of 1945 and a million by December; the figure rose steadily during the next two years. Here German civilians quit their homes in the city of Rheindahlen as elements of the Ninth U.S. Infantry advance. (U.S. Army/National Archives)

Harrison and his entourage inspected about thirty DP centers in Europe in July 1945. What the group found—and subsequently reported to the president—was that perhaps 50,000 to 100,000 Jewish survivors along with maybe half a million other displaced Europeans (mostly Poles, Balts, and Ukrainians) were living a drab existence, with nothing to do and only a bleak future ahead. In one section of his report, "Needs of the Jews," Harrison outlined this group's special problems and detailed the indifferent care they were receiving. "As matters now stand," he concluded, "we appear to be treating the Jews as the Nazis treated them, except that we do not exterminate them."

The shocking revelations of the Harrison Report galvanized the president. He wrote to Gen. Dwight D. Eisenhower, commander in chief of the Allied forces in Europe, to improve the conditions of the DPs immediately, and he also approached Prime Minister Clement Attlee of Great Britain about opening the gates of Palestine for all European Jewish DPs who wanted to go there. (Then, and throughout the next five years, the DP problem would be viewed primarily as a Jewish one even though about 80 percent of the DPs were Christians.) The general did as he was told and ordered subordinates to make appropriate changes. Attlee, on the other hand, proposed an Anglo-American Commission of Inquiry (AACI) to investigate whether Palestine could absorb the DPs who wanted to go there. Truman agreed to the suggestion and the AACI was formed.

While the AACI prepared to embark upon its duties, Truman, after being persuaded to do so by several Jewish leaders, mandated on 22 December 1945 that all DPs be given preferred treatment within existing immigration laws. "This period of unspeakable human distress is not the time for us to close or narrow our gates," he said. Although known as the president's "Christmas present" to the DPs, Truman's efforts impressed few knowledgeable observers. The nation's quota system was such that a maximum of 14,000 places a year could be given to non-German DPs. When one considers that the number of DPs kept rising between 1945 and 1947 and that more than a million were in Germany in December 1945, the president's decision, known as the Truman Directive, amounted to little more than a gesture. Nonetheless, even this slight effort met with congressional opposition.

In April 1946, the AACI recommended the admission of 100,000 Jews to Palestine. But the British government then added the untenable stipulations that the Jewish army in Palestine had to be disbanded and the American government would have to supply military support before they would agree to this proposal. Attempts were made to renegotiate the recommendations of the AAIC during the summer of 1946, but provisions politically acceptable to both countries could not be worked out. Thus, in August 1946, fifteen months after the war had ended in Europe, the DPs remained in their assembly centers and their ranks were swollen by newcomers fleeing from the Communists in Eastern Europe. At that point, Truman announced that he would seek congressional legislation to bring an unspecified number of DPs to the United States.

In January 1947, the president urged Congress to turn its attention to the DP problem, but failed to specify a course of action. He did not utter another word publicly on the subject for the next six months. He neither endorsed the bill that Republican congressman William G. Stratton of Illinois introduced in April 1947 to bring 400,000 DPs to the United States nor sent a measure to Congress for its consideration.

Lack of publicly visible enthusiasm, however, did not indicate lack of concern or activity on the administration's part. Truman aides John R. Steelman and David K. Niles met with those people working vigorously to obtain DP legislation, and Niles also sent word to Stratton that, although Truman would not support his bill publicly, the president nonetheless approved of it.

There was also public pressure and congressional sentiment to get a DP act passed. The major reason for this was the establishment of a Citizens Committee on Displaced Persons (CCDP) in December 1946. The CCDP worked energetically to lobby citizens and Congress alike, and in less than a year and a half it had managed to swing the antiimmigration sentiments of the public and Congress to a commitment to aid some DPs. Therefore, the Republican-controlled Eighteenth Congress passed a DP act in 1948 that gave preference to Balts, Ukrainians, and the *Volksdeutsche* (people of German ancestry who had been living in East European countries before World War II, but who were expelled after the war), discriminated against the Jewish DPs who had reached Germany in 1946 and after, and favored agricultural workers. Truman, aware of the limitations of the act but not wanting to squelch the opportunities of those people helped by a bill calling for the admission of 205,000 DPs over a two-year period, signed it reluctantly but noted at the time that it was "flagrantly discriminatory" against Catholics and Jews. It indeed discriminated against the latter, but not the former.

One provision of the new DP act authorized the establishment of a DP commission to be appointed by the president. Truman chose three liberal commissioners to implement the new law, and they sought every loophole and stretched every ambiguity to help bring as many people as they could to the United States under the terms of the 1948 bill.

In 1949 and 1950, Truman successfully maneuvered behind the scenes with Congress to help get a more liberal and generous DP act passed. The act of 1950, which called for the admission of an additional 200,000 persons, eliminated all the discriminatory provisions of the 1948 measure.

In reassessing Truman's role in regard to the DPs, it is difficult to make a categorical assertion about his activities. It is questionable whether greater assertiveness on his part could have altered the British position about allowing more Jews into Palestine in 1945 and 1946 or could have changed congressional attitudes toward the DPs in 1947 and 1948. On the other hand, Truman's own endeavors reflected a desire to see the DP problem identified and solved in a humane fashion.

Leonard Dinnerstein's *America and the Survivors of the Holocaust* (New York: Columbia University Press, 1982) is the only work that covers the displaced persons issue from 1945 to 1950. Amy Zahl Gottlieb's "Refugee Immigration: The Truman Directive," *Prologue* 13 (Spring 1981): 5–18, is the most comprehensive analysis of that subject. Stephen K. Bailey and Howard D. Samuel, in *Congress at Work* (New York: Holt, 1952), have a first-rate chapter on the success of the CCDP in getting the DP act of 1948 passed.

LEONARD DINNERSTEIN

See also Niles, David K.; Palestine; United Nations Relief and Rehabilitation Administration; Zionism

Dixiecrats

The southern Democrats who broke with President Harry Truman on the issue of civil rights in 1948. As the post–World War II civil rights movement grew, President Truman began to speak and to take actions favorable to it. In February 1948 he asked Congress to pass legislation to assist the nation's minorities, especially blacks. Southern senators and representatives in Congress immediately denounced Truman, as did a number of influential southern newspaper editors. Twenty-one southern senators pledged to "stand guard" to prevent the enactment of any civil rights measure. Fifty-two southerners in the House of Representatives not only condemned Truman's message but also warned the president that the Democratic party would face "serious consequences" if it included a civil rights plank in its national platform for the 1948 election.

As plans were laid for the forthcoming Democratic National Convention, seven southern governors at a special meeting in Jackson, Mississippi, in March 1948 adopted a resolution specifically requesting that southern delegates be instructed to oppose Truman's nomination and recommending that all southern state Democratic conventions pledge their presidential electors to vote against any candidate who favored civil rights legislation. Although most southern Democrats were too deeply imbued with party loyalty to leave their organizations, even over such an emotional issue as black rights, others were willing to break with the party if it ignored their stand on the subject.

When Democrats gathered in July at their national convention in Philadelphia, the platform committee recommended to the convention a moderate statement on the civil rights issue. Die-hard southerners on the committee offered a states' rights minority resolution, but the convention members defeated it. When the convention then adopted a liberal civil rights plank, thirty-five delegates from Mississippi and Alabama walked out as a band played "Dixie." Most of the remaining southern delegates refused to support Truman's nomination.

The disgruntled southerners convened at Birmingham where they criticized the national Democratic party for being disinterested in the South's traditional stands on such matters as states' rights and the role of blacks in American society. They formed the States' Rights party, its members being called Dixiecrats. They recommended South Carolina governor Strom Thurmond and Mississippi governor Fielding Wright for president and vice president.

The Dixiecrats had no hopes of winning the election. Their strategy was to take enough votes away from Truman so that neither he nor his Republican opponent could win a majority in the electoral college. They hoped to have political bargaining power on civil rights issues if the election was thrown into the House of Representatives.

The emergence of the Dixiecrats forced southern Democrats to make a difficult choice, since the former appealed to southerners by arguing that they were "true Democrats." But the Dixiecrats did not convince those who were firmly committed to party regularity. Some southern Democrats whose priorities were states' rights and opposition to civil rights bolted to the Dixiecrats, but the majority did not. The Dixiecratic candidates won the electoral votes of only South Carolina, Alabama,

Mississippi, and Louisiana, where their party had captured the regular Democratic machinery.

The Dixiecrats did not leave the Democratic party. After the election, Dixiecratic governors remained powerful within their respective state Democratic organizations, and senators and representatives in the Congress retained their long-termed committee assignments as Democrats. Even so, Dixiecratic influence within the Democratic party began to disintegrate after the failure of the political apostasy. The Dixiecratic movement weakened the Democratic party in the South, assisting the growth of southern Republicanism.

The major primary sources are the States' Rights Democrats Papers, Department of Archives and History, Jackson, Mississippi. Two good unpublished works are R. C. Ethridge, "The Dixiecratic Movement" (Ph.D. diss., Mississippi State University, 1971), and G. C. Ness, "The States' Rights Movement" (Ph.D. diss., Duke University, 1972). Briefer but more readily available is Monroe Lee Billington, *The Political South in the Twentieth Century* (New York: Charles Scribner's Sons, 1975).

MONROE BILLINGTON

See also Civil Rights; Democratic Party; Election of 1948; South, The; Thurmond, James Strom

Douglas, Helen Gahagan

(25 November 1900–28 June 1980)

New Deal Democrat from Los Angeles; Congresswoman, 1945–50. Helen Gahagan Douglas, born in Boonton, New Jersey, was raised in the wealthy Park Slope district of Brooklyn, New York. From an early age, Douglas demonstrated a keen interest and talent in acting. She attended Berkeley Institute, a local private school, but graduated from the Capon School in Northampton, Massachusetts, in 1920. After two years at Barnard College, she moved to the Broadway stage where she became one of the top stars of the decade. In 1927, she began training as an opera singer. The famed producer David Belasco offered her in 1930 the starring role in *Tonight or Never* playing opposite the talented Melvyn Douglas. During the run of the production, the couple married and soon moved to Los Angeles so that Melvyn could begin a movie career.

In the 1930s, Helen continued some acting and singing engagements in the United States and Europe and had two children (Peter, 1934, and Mary, 1938). She had no success launching a film career. Her dissatisfaction with her flagging professional life and an awakening to Nazism in 1937 led her into the political ferment in Hollywood. The migrant issue attracted her principal attention. Her public stand urging state and national assistance for migrants resulted in her first exposure to red-baiting, a common experience of many liberals. This pattern continued throughout her political career.

Douglas's political activities attracted the attention of Aubrey Williams, director of the National Youth Administration. He introduced both Douglases to the Roosevelts late in 1939, and a fast friendship formed. Through Eleanor's influence and introduction to leading New Deal figures, Helen quickly became involved in Democratic politics.

Douglas made a striking figure in the political arena. Tall at five feet seven inches, of medium build, dark-haired, dignified, and uncommonly beautiful with a touch of Hollywood glamor, she immediately attracted attention. She complemented her physical attractiveness with a sharp mind, blunt observations, and an unusually powerful ability to generate energy from an audience. One New Dealer commented that when he first met Douglas, he found himself "subjected to an intense cross-examination—grilling might not be too strong a word."

In the early 1940s Douglas rose steadily to prominence in the ranks of California Democrats; in the fall of 1944, as an FDR-backed Democratic congressional candidate, she won the seat of retiring New Dealer Thomas Ford and entered Congress in January 1945 for the first of three consecutive terms. Her constituents represented a broad socioeconomic spread, with the majority lower middle class; many were returning veterans. The district included Chinatown and the largest black community west of Chicago. Housing conditions were among the worst in the nation.

Roosevelt's death in April 1945 devastated Douglas; she had lost her intellectual mentor and a special friend. She felt unconnected politically and personally to the new president. Yet over the next six years, she became a loyal Truman supporter both on the floor of Congress and through her appointment to the House Foreign Affairs Committee. Truman, in turn, accepted Douglas as an influential progressive liberal. She consulted with the president on various issues, especially those concerning California, such as the tidelands oil dispute. As a congressional neophyte and a woman, she had little chance to become a major figure sponsoring legislation through Congress, but often masterminded the signing of petitions to get bills out of committee and proposed successful amendments.

An uncompromising idealist, she impatiently lectured those of her colleagues whom she considered immoral and irresponsible, but also carefully cultivated relationships with leading members of Congress and the administration including Oscar Chapman, Charles F. Brannan, and Lyndon Johnson, her most faithful colleague and congressional adviser. Douglas also had close links to leading labor organizers, and by 1948, labor regarded her as their key supporter on the Hill, judging in part by its extensive financial support of her campaign.

Douglas spent considerable time crisscrossing the nation on behalf of the "average American." Utilizing her acting talent to engage an audience, she urged support for Truman and his Fair Deal measures, bluntly critiqued anti-Truman members of Congress, and urged voters to political action. She emphasized in particular the need for antiinflationary measures, civil rights legislation, and low-cost housing as well as the importance of building a strong free world.

Truman's recognition of Douglas's visibility, popularity, and competence, and particularly her key role as the House sponsor of the Atomic Energy Act of 1946, led him to name her as an alternate delegate to the United Nations for the 1946 session. Much to her disappointment, however, he did not reappoint her in 1947, presumably because she opposed his plan of aid to Greece and Turkey. She believed that this assistance should go through the United Nations. Douglas opposed Truman in other instances, too. Along with other anti-Communist liberals, for example, she protested the president's loyalty program for government employees. But such occasional opposition did not prevent mutual respect.

The support that Truman and many leading Democrats offered Douglas in her 1950 campaign against Richard M. Nixon clearly demonstrated the administration's recognition of Douglas's importance. Although Truman refused to play an active role in the 1950 elections, he criticized those who charged that Douglas was weak on Communism. Vice President Alben Barkley, House Speaker Sam Rayburn, Majority Leader John McCormack, several cabinet members, and leading Senate and House liberals came to California to speak enthusiastically for Douglas, pointing out the quality of her statesmanship and contribution to the Truman presidency.

Nixon defeated Douglas by a two-to-one margin in a campaign laced with innuendos that Douglas's liberalism linked her to Communism. The experience did not devastate her, but she never ran for political office again. The Douglas family moved to New York City, and Helen embarked on an active life of public speaking and serving on numerous boards of liberal groups. The women's movement and Watergate, each in its particular fashion, brought Douglas once again into the public eye. When she died after a long fight against cancer, liberals of the 1940s recalled her willingness to stand on her political principles, resisting pressure to compromise her position, and her "overriding purpose of trying to build a better world."

The Helen Gahagan Douglas papers, located at the Carl Albert Congressional Center at the University of Oklahoma, begin with Douglas's theater career and continue through her Senate defeat, although some materials cover the period 1950–80. Many other manuscript collections complement her papers including materials at the Harry S. Truman Library. The Regional Oral History Office at the Bancroft Library, University of California, Berkeley, conducted interviews with Douglas and twenty-six of her colleagues, friends, and family members, a very useful collection. Interviews by Ingrid Winther Scobie are part of the Oral History Research Center at Indiana University, Bloomington. Douglas's autobiography, A Full Life (Garden City, N.Y.: Doubleday, 1982), is disappointing as a reflective piece on her life and the historical context of the period. Other Scobie works include "Helen Gahagan Douglas: Broadway Star as California Politician," California History 66 (December 1987): 242–61, 310–14; "Helen Gahagan Douglas and the Roosevelt Connection," in Without Precedent: The Life and Career of Eleanor Roosevelt, ed. John Hoff Wilson and Marjorie Lightman, 153–75 (Bloomington: Indiana University Press, 1984); "Helen and Melvyn Douglas: Two Lives in Vermont," Vermont Life 36 (Summer 1982): 35–37; and "Helen Gahagan Douglas and Her 1950 Senate Race with Richard M. Nixon," Southern California Historical Quarterly 58 (Spring 1976): 113–26. A full-length biography by Scobie is to be published by Atheneum. Although little other secondary material has been published on Douglas, an interesting cover story by Lee Israel appeared in Ms. 2 (October 1973): 55–59, 112–19. The exceptions are the numerous books that treat the 1950 campaign. Most agree that Nixon conducted a vicious campaign. See in particular Frank Mankiewicz's Perfectly Clear: Nixon from Whittier to Watergate (New York: Quadrangle, 1973). Stephen E. Ambrose in Nixon: The Education of a Politician, 1913–1962 (New York: Simon & Schuster, 1987) is the first scholar to criticize Douglas's campaign, although his evidence is not entirely convincing. Few Truman scholars acknowledge Douglas's political contributions, in part because the inclusion of women does not fit within the normal definitions of political power. One exception is Alonzo L. Hamby, in Beyond the New Deal: Harry S. Truman and American Liberalism (New York: Columbia University Press, 1973). He calls

Douglas an "important independent liberal" and integrates her into postwar liberalism.

INGRID WINTHER SCOBIE

See also Liberalism; Nixon, Richard M.; Red Scare

Douglas, Lewis Williams

(2 July 1894–7 March 1974)

Ambassador to the Court of St. James. Born into a prominent copper mining family in Bisbee, Arizona, Lewis W. Douglas was educated at eastern preparatory schools and Amherst College and served as a first lieutenant in the Great War.

Soon after the war, Douglas began a life of public service. In 1923 he was elected to the state legislature and three years later won the first of four terms to the U.S. House of Representatives. In 1933 President Roosevelt named the young, fiscally conservative Arizonan to the Budget directorship. Unable to check New Deal spending programs, he resigned in August 1934, but was later recalled by FDR to head the War Shipping Administration.

In 1945 Douglas was appointed special economic adviser to Gen. Lucius Clay, the military governor of the American zone in Germany. After two months, he resigned that position because he disagreed with the directive governing American economic policy in occupied Germany that would strip the nation of its industrial might and thereby impoverish the Continent. Douglas took his concerns to Harry S. Truman. The new president was noncommittal about Germany but impressed Douglas with his intelligence, warmth, and character. Truman also had a high regard for Douglas and in April 1946 asked him to head the newly created World Bank. Douglas declined, but a year later he accepted Truman's invitation to become ambassador to Great Britain.

Enjoying a trusted relationship with Secretary of State George Marshall, Douglas helped influence the making of American foreign policy during the early cold war. His dispatches from London detailed the European economic crisis and warned that the Continent might be lost to communism unless the United States provided assistance. When the European Recovery Program, or Marshall Plan, was announced in the summer of 1947 Douglas became one of its most articulate and persuasive missionaries. In London and Paris he worked closely with Western European leaders to prepare a plan for European economic cooperation. Because of his firsthand knowledge of European economic conditions, congressional experience, and close ties on Capitol Hill, Douglas became a principal spokesman for the Marshall Plan in hearings before the House and Senate Foreign Relations Committees.

Douglas also participated in the military phase of containment. In the spring of 1948 he presided over secret Anglo-American-Canadian talks at the Pentagon which led to the formation of the North Atlantic alliance.

Throughout his ambassadorship, Douglas championed the economic revitalization of Western Germany as the key to European prosperity and the containment of communism. In 1948 he served as a delegate to the London Conference on Germany. At that meeting the Americans, British, and French reformed the currency and fused their zones of occupation into what became West Germany. In response, the Soviet Union established the Berlin blockade. Douglas supported the decision to remain in Berlin and to supply it by means of an airlift. His major role in London was to discuss the crisis with the Western powers and to coordinate a common response.

In the summer of 1948 Douglas also was actively involved in the Palestinian crisis. He opposed the creation of a Jewish state because it would anger the British, alienate Arabs, and perhaps allow Soviet penetration into the region.

Douglas's influence declined after 1948 for two reasons. First, Dean Acheson succeeded Marshall as secretary of state and relied less heavily upon the ambassador for advice. Second, in April 1949, Douglas suffered an eye injury that caused considerable pain and discomfort and the eventual loss of sight in his left eye, and forced his resignation in December 1950.

Affable, charming, and unpretentious, Douglas was an extremely popular diplomat. His service was praised in both England and America. Truman lauded his "wise counsel" and pointed out that the London mission rounded out "a career of singular versatility and usefulness."

After the London assignment, Douglas generally supported Republican presidential candidates, which angered Truman. When Douglas came out for Eisenhower in 1952 Truman exploded: "Some people take everything from the Party and give nothing." Eventually the two men patched up their differences, however. In 1969 Douglas wrote Truman that in the area of foreign policy "you will be rated by objective historians as the finest President we have ever had." Truman replied that he had "never given any thought to it. What is important to me is to have a judgment from one I hold in high esteem and whose opinion has a special meaning to me."

Lewis Douglas died in 1974 at the age of seventy-nine. His ashes were scattered over Jerome, the Arizona mining town where he had begun his public career fifty years before.

Robert P. Browder and Thomas G. Smith published a full-scale biography, *Independent: A Biography of Lewis W. Douglas* (New York: Alfred A. Knopf, 1986), based on the voluminous Douglas Papers at the University of Arizona, extensive interviews, including some with Douglas, and numerous archive collections in the United States, Canada, and Great Britain. For contemporary articles, see Bernice Cosulich, "Mr. Douglas of Arizona: Friend of Cowboys and Kings," *Arizona Highways* 29 (September 1953): 7–11, and feature stories in *Life*, 27 October 1947, 150–56; *Time*, 1 December 1947, 23–26, 29–30; *U.S. News and World Report*, 23 January 1948, 64–65; and *World Report*, 12 August 1947, 29–30.

THOMAS G. SMITH

See also United Nations (photograph)

Douglas, Paul H.

(26 March 1892–24 September 1976)

Democratic senator from Illinois, 1949–67. Paul Douglas was born in Salem, Massachusetts, graduated from Bowdoin College, and took his doctorate from Columbia University. While professor of economics at the University of Chicago, he published *The Theory of Wages* in 1935, served frequently as a labor arbitrator, and was president of the American Economic Association in 1947. He was a Chicago alderman, 1939–42 and served in the Marine Corps during World War II.

Usually liberal but independent, he described his relationship with Truman as "unfortunate" from the beginning. He had supported Eisenhower before the 1948 convention, investigated administrative corruption in the Reconstruction Finance Corporation, and opposed Truman's inflationary attempts to require the Federal Reserve to buy unlimited amounts of government bonds at low interest. But he supported the president strongly on attempts to break Senate filibustering, to repeal Taft-Hartley, and to promote public housing, civil rights legislation, and national health insurance. He defended NATO and the decision to fire MacArthur. Independently he fought for the Marine Corps, economy in government, tax reform, and controls on monopolies. He continued his career as liberal spokesman in the Senate through the Johnson administration. After 1967 he taught at the New School for Social Research.

The best source is still Paul H. Douglas, *In the Fullness of Time: The Memoirs of Paul H. Douglas* (New York: Harcourt Brace Jovanovich, 1972), which is unusually objective.

ALFRED B. ROLLINS, JR.

See also Housing (photograph)

Douglas, William O.

(16 October 1898–19 January 1980)

Associate justice, U.S. Supreme Court, 1939–75. William O. Douglas was born in Maine, Minnesota, and while still a young boy, moved with his family to California, ultimately settling in Cleveland, Washington, in 1904. After the father's death, the mother moved the family to Yakima, Washington, where they resided for the next twenty years. William was stricken with polio at the age of four and combated the subsequent weakness by hiking in the Washington mountains. As a result he became an avid outdoorsman and nature lover and a strong proponent of conservation throughout his entire career. He worked his way through Whitman College in Washington, graduating with honors in economics in 1920; taught school for two years in Yakima; and, because money was scarce, made his way east to the Columbia University Law School by hopping trains and eating with friendly hoboes.

Douglas worked his way through Columbia, graduating second in his class in 1925, and for two years worked for a Wall Street firm while teaching part time at Columbia. After moving to Yale a year later, Douglas became a leader in changing the way business law was taught. His specialty was corporate law, and by 1932 he was recognized as one of the foremost experts in financial law in the country. Appointed by President Roosevelt to investigate securities and exchange issues, Douglas produced an eight-volume study that became the basis for new legislation in that area. He was appointed to the Securities and Exchange Commission in 1934 and became its chairman in 1937. As a result of his pressure and the revelation of corruption in the New York Stock Exchange, a major reorganization of that body occurred in 1938.

Appointed to the Supreme Court in 1939 to replace Louis Brandeis, Douglas was, at forty-one, the youngest Supreme Court appointee since Joseph Story in 1811. Promptly becoming a member of the liberal wing of the Court, he developed an absolutist approach to civil liberties, especially with regard to the First Amendment.

When Roosevelt sought a new vice president in 1944, Douglas and Harry Truman were two of the candidates. Truman's champions had more political clout, and Douglas remained on the Court. Truman wanted Douglas to run for vice president with him in 1948, an opportunity he turned away, as he had the offer to become secretary of the interior in the Truman administration.

Douglas was usually at odds with the Truman appointees to the Court. His dissent in the *Dennis* case of 1951 was a notable statement deploring excessive curtailment of freedom of expression. In it, he maintained that the officers of the Communist party were charged not with advocating violent overthrow of the government themselves but with conspiring and teaching others revolution by promoting the works of Marx, Stalin, and Lenin. Douglas argued that the problem with the charge was that it was a conviction for speech alone, not speech accompanied by any violent or seditious acts, and that such speech should be protected under the First Amendment.

Douglas served on the Court until November 1975. He wrote numerous eloquent opinions in the speech/press area, and in areas involving fair procedure and civil rights. He particularly deplored the excesses of McCarthyism and strongly condemned the witch-hunts of the 1950s. Always impatient that the Supreme Court job could not keep him busy, he wrote over twenty books, mostly on environmental issues throughout the world, adding another dimension of public service to his long and distinguished career.

Douglas left two autobiographical volumes, *Go East, Young Man* (New York: Random House, 1974) and *The Court Years* (New York: Random House, 1980), the latter unfinished. Vern Countryman, *The Judicial Record of William O. Douglas* (Cambridge: Harvard University Press, 1974), is a topically arranged analysis of Douglas's Supreme Court record through 1971. James F. Simon, *Independent Journey: The Life of William O. Douglas* (New York: Harper & Row, 1980), is a complete biography of his personal and professional life. James C. Duram, *Justice William O. Douglas* (Boston: Twayne, 1981), examines Douglas's writings, focusing on themes, literary techniques, influences, and his place in American literature.

PAUL L. MURPHY

See also Supreme Court, United States (and photograph)

Draft

See Selective Service/Universal Military Training

Dubinsky, David

22 February 1892–17 September 1982)

Long-time president of the International Ladies Garment Workers' Union; leader of the Liberal party of New York; Liberal ally of Truman. David Dubinsky was born in Brest Litovsk, Russian Poland. His formal schooling ended in 1903 when at age eleven he was apprenticed to a baker in Lodz, Poland. While still a teenager, he became involved in labor activities and after being arrested as a labor agitator spent eighteen months in prison before being exiled to Siberia. Shortly after his father secured his release in 1910, he emigrated to the United States and found employment in the New York garment district, where he soon became a union activist.

Eventually rising to the presidency of the International Ladies Garment Workers' Union, Dubinsky was a proponent of industrial organization and an enthusiastic advocate of labor politics, but he was also uncompromisingly anti-Communist. After Communist elements gained control of the American Labor party, which he had helped organize in New York during the 1930s to channel labor support to Franklin Roosevelt, he and others founded the Liberal party of New York, which supported Truman's 1948 reelection campaign in that state.

The David Dubinsky Papers are located in the ILGWU Archives in New York. *David Dubinsky: A Life of Labor* (New York: Simon & Schuster, 1977) is a memoir on which A. H. Raskin, a long-time labor editor for the *New York Times*, collaborated with Dubinsky. Max D. Danish, *The World of David Dubinsky* (Cleveland: World Press, 1957), is a popular biography. For the best scholarly treatment of Dubinsky, see the special supplement of *Labor History* (Spring 1968) entitled "David Dubinsky, the I.L.G.W.U. and the American Labor Movement."

GARY M. FINK

See also Labor

Dulles, John Foster

(25 February 1888–24 May 1959)

Republican senator, 1949–51; ambassador to Japanese peace treaty conference, 1950–51. John Foster Dulles was born in Washington but spent his childhood in Watertown, New York, where his father ministered to the congregation of the First Presbyterian Church and taught at the Auburn Theological Seminary. A moral outlook on life therefore came naturally to young Dulles; so also did an interest in world affairs, for his grandfather, John Foster, served as Benjamin Harrison's secretary of state, and his uncle, Robert Lansing, would hold the same position under Woodrow Wilson.

Family tradition likewise figured in Dulles's decision to attend Princeton, where he enrolled in 1904 at the age of sixteen. Introverted and uncomfortable in crowds, he made little impression socially at the class-conscious university, but he excelled in academics and became valedictorian in his senior year. After graduate work at the Sorbonne, he returned to America to study law at George Washington University.

Dulles sped through a three-year curriculum in two, and in 1911 joined the Wall Street firm of Sullivan and Cromwell. The great war momentarily interrupted a climb to the top of the world of corporate and international law; he worked in army intelligence and with the War Trade Board, later joining the American peacemaking delegation in Paris under his old Princeton professor, Woodrow Wilson.

The American rejection of the League of Nations greatly disappointed Dulles. During the interwar decades, while building his fortune at Sullivan and Cromwell and his network of political contacts on the East Coast, he reflected on the reasons for the League's demise, and in 1939 he published *War, Peace and Change*, which made a forceful if unoriginal argument that the overly punitive Versailles settlement had contained the seeds of its own destruction.

A relative latecomer to the conviction that the United States must enter the fight against the fascists, Dulles nonetheless strongly advocated American participation in a successor to the League. As a result of this interest, and of Franklin Roosevelt's desire to create a bipartisan consensus for the United Nations, FDR selected Dulles, by then firmly associated with the Republican party, for a position on the American delegation to the San Francisco United Nations Conference in 1945.

Truman shared his predecessor's belief that Dulles made a better ally than foe, and the new president kept Dulles on after Roosevelt's death. But Dulles defied easy capture, and despite nearly eight years of yeoman service for the Truman administration, he retained his visibility as a spokesman for the internationalist wing of the Republicans. In 1948, after continued work at the United Nations and stints as adviser to James Byrnes and George Marshall, Dulles became in effect the Republican candidate for secretary of state on the ticket with Thomas Dewey, a Sullivan and Cromwell associate.

On the advice of Senator Arthur Vandenberg, Dewey and Dulles waged a cautious campaign, especially in matters of foreign policy, considering success all but certain and believing, as Vandenberg put it, that a race that destroyed the spirit of bipartisanship in foreign affairs would bring a Pyrrhic victory.

The Republicans guessed wrong, of course, about the outcome of the election, and following Truman's surprising win, the party went over into determined and vocal opposition. This shift created difficulties for Dulles, who agreed with most essentials of the Democrats' approach to foreign policy. While he was pondering his next move, Dulles was appointed by Governor Dewey to fill a vacant New York Senate seat. He initially intended to step down when the abbreviated term expired, but he changed his mind in 1950 and ran a spirited through ultimately losing race against Herbert Lehman. Generally refraining from attacks on the Democrats' handling of foreign affairs, Dulles otherwise took up the Republican war cry, lashing Lehman for being "soft" on Communism and declaring, "If I am defeated in this election, the greatest rejoicing will not be in New York or Washington but will be in Moscow."

Still hoping to make use of Dulles's diplomatic skills and to neutralize his opposition, Truman asked him to head the American team negotiating the Japanese peace and mutual security treaties. Again Dulles managed a skillful balancing act, achieving a signal success on behalf of the Truman administration without becoming identified with that administration.

Detecting the drift of the political winds in 1952, Dulles early attached himself to Dwight Eisenhower. As the author of the foreign policy plank of the Republican platform, Dulles demonstrated that he had no intention of repeating the performance of 1948. He blasted as defeatist the Democratic doctrine of containment and promised voters a self-confident and assertive alternative: the "liberation" of countries under Communist rule.

With Eisenhower's triumph, Dulles assumed the position he had long sought. Although he quickly retreated from liberation in favor of a policy that differed little from the Democrats', Dulles became one of the strongest secretaries of state of the twentieth century. He died in 1959 after a determined but losing battle against cancer.

Dulles was the subject of numerous studies written during and shortly after his tenure as secretary of state. None has stood the test of time particularly well. By far the best works on his life and career are Townsend Hoopes's critical but not entirely unsympathetic *The Devil and John Foster Dulles* (Boston: Little, Brown, 1973), and Ronald W. Pruessen's scholarly *John Foster Dulles: The Road to Power* (New York: Free Press, 1982). The latter carries the story through the Truman years; the rest is yet to come.

H. W. BRANDS, JR.

See also Election of 1948; Election of 1952

E

Eastern Europe

The question of Eastern Europe represented President Truman's baptism in foreign policy. Three global wars in the twentieth century originated in Eastern Europe. Two were armed conflicts. The third, a cold war, emerged in 1945 over the political future of the states making up a belt between the Baltic and Black seas: Poland, Czechoslovakia, East Germany, Hungary, Yugoslavia, Romania, Albania, and Bulgaria. The repercussions of the confrontation between the United States and Soviet Union in the region would, in turn, have an indelible effect upon American politics and diplomacy.

During World War II American officials sidestepped the issue of Eastern Europe. Although President Roosevelt privately expressed a belief that the Soviet Union had legitimate security interests in the area, publicly America stood behind the provisions of the Atlantic Charter—that is, territorial integrity and national self-determination. While Churchill and Stalin divided the Balkans into spheres of influence through an agreement establishing percentages for each nation, FDR sought to delay confronting such issues until the war's conclusion.

The naive nature of American policy, symbolized by the vague pronouncements issued at Yalta in 1945, meant that Truman, in effect, inherited a nonpolicy. Given the Soviet Union's desire to regain its 1941 boundaries and create a *cordon sanitaire* of friendly states along its frontier, Eastern Europe's fate was, in large measure, already determined by April 1945. With the territory occupied by the Red Army and the various Allied Control Commissions (chaired by Soviet representatives) serving as screens for Moscow's actions, Truman, who had been excluded from major policy decisions under his predecessor, was handed a virtual fait accompli. Yalta's Declaration on Liberated Europe spoke only of a commitment to free elections with the participation of all democratic forces. It contained no means of enforcement. Short of military posturing, a nonviable option given the American public's desire to demobilize, cut taxes, and leave the affairs of Europe behind, diplomatic avenues were limited at best. Moreover, until the defeat of Japan, Washington placed greater importance on securing Soviet aid in the Far East than the idealistic goals outlined at Yalta. This allowed Moscow even greater latitude in its activities.

Initially, Truman believed that although the United States could not force the Soviet Union to agree on all issues regarding Eastern Europe, it could prevail on most; by 1946 such optimism had disappeared. As long as Stalin steadfastly refused to allow political forces not subject to its dictates to control any of its neighbors to the west, neither tough talk by Truman to Soviet foreign minister Molotov in April 1945 nor forceful diplomacy at Potsdam nor Secretary of State Byrnes's attempts at more conciliatory negotiations in Moscow in December 1945 could alter the outcome. The Soviet grip on the region, detailed in reports such as that prepared by Mark Ethridge for Romania and Bulgaria in 1945, tightened as Moscow-trained officials dominated the most important posts in each government and opposition parties and politicians were systematically purged from positions of authority. Within three years, only Yugoslavia stood outside the iron curtain and that resulted not from U.S. actions but from a split between Stalin and Tito.

The impact of Soviet control of Eastern Europe upon the United States and the Truman administration was dramatic. As the wartime alliance dissolved (despite attempts at Potsdam to preserve at least a façade of unity), public opinion in the United States turned against the Soviet Union. Ironically, until 1946 most Americans considered the latter to be less imperialistic than Great Britain. In 1946 Republicans, appealing to a rising tide of anti-Communism, regained control of both houses of Congress. Anti-Communist sentiment, which eventually reached a fever pitch during the McCarthy era, grew in intensity after the Communist takeover in Czechoslovakia early in 1948. The determination to halt what came to be perceived as an ideological onslaught orchestrated in Moscow also led to strains within the Truman administration itself, including the split between the president and Byrnes, and the forced resignation (and eventual political opposition) of Secretary of Commerce Henry Wallace, who argued that the Soviet Union had as much right to construct a sphere of influence in Eastern Europe as the United States had to control Latin America with the Monroe Doctrine.

Finally, as the Soviet Union tightened its hold in Eastern Europe, Truman and his advisers moved rapidly toward the policy of containment, which included the Truman Doctrine, the Marshall Plan, and the creation of NATO. These were measures the United States could take while limiting the risks of war. As for Eastern Europe itself, the administration provided little more than moral support, perhaps encouraging anti-Communist forces to act in the belief that the United States would aid them in their struggle. If so, their hopes were without foundation; the United States had already conceded Eastern Europe as a Soviet sphere, choosing instead to halt the spread of communism elsewhere.

In retrospect, Truman had few, if any, options that might have transformed the ideals of the Declaration on Liberated Europe into reality. The United States probably could not have prevented what many saw as inevitable, given Soviet occupation of the region. Rather, the "fall" of Eastern Europe mobilized public opinion against the perceived Soviet threat. Eastern Europe thus became the litmus test to see whether the Grand Alliance could work, once the threat of Hitler's Reich was removed. The result was cold war.

Most general works on both the cold war and Truman deal with events in Eastern Europe from 1945 to 1948; few are devoted entirely to the matter of U.S. policy toward the Soviet bloc states. One of the few is that of Lynn Etheridge Davis, *The Cold War Begins: Soviet-American Conflict over Eastern Europe* (Princeton: Princeton University Press, 1974), a study exhaustive in its use of available sources and highly critical of American policy especially during the Roosevelt administration. John Lewis Gaddis, in *The United States and the Origins of the Cold War, 1941–1947* (New York: Columbia University Press, 1972), describes the lack of options open to increasingly frustrated American officials groping for some means of implementing the Yalta accords. Individual nations in Eastern Europe are examined in Thomas T. Hammond, ed., *The Anatomy of Communist Takeovers* (New Haven: Yale University Press, 1975), and Stephen D. Kersetz, *The Fate of East Central Europe: Hopes and Failures of American Foreign Policy* (South Bend, Ind.: University of Notre Dame Press, 1956), the latter a contemporary account which shows many of the passions felt by those who watched the events in Eastern Europe unfold after the war.

RICHARD FRUCHT

See also Cold War; Czechoslovakia; Germany; Poland; Potsdam Conference; Soviet Union; Yugoslavia

East Germany
See Germany

Eccles, Marriner Stoddard

(9 September 1890–18 December 1977)

Governor, Federal Reserve Board, 1934–36; member and chairman, board of governors, Federal Reserve System, 1936–51. Marriner S. Eccles was a Utah banker and businessman who by the time Truman became president had been chairman of the Federal Reserve Board (FRB) for nearly eleven years and was credited with transforming the Federal Reserve System from an instrument of big banking interests to an influential advocate of compensatory spending policy.

Between 1945 and 1951, initially as FRB chairman and then after 1948 as vice-chairman, Eccles was a strong advocate of antiinflation measures that the administration, especially Secretary of the Treasury John Snyder, refused to adopt or support. He also played a leading role in actions that in 1951 freed Federal Reserve policy from Treasury domination, a role that involved stringent criticism of administration policy and worsened his relations with the president.

After resigning from the Federal Reserve Board in 1951, he returned to the family business and in the 1960s became an outspoken champion of such causes as population control and withdrawal from Vietnam.

The three best accounts of Eccles during the Truman era are in Sidney Hyman, *Marriner S. Eccles* (Stanford: Stanford University Business School, 1976); Marriner Eccles, *Beckoning Frontiers* (New York: Knopf, 1951); and Herbert Stein, *The Fiscal Revolution in America* (Chicago: University of Chicago Press, 1969).

ELLIS W. HAWLEY

See also Economy; Fiscal and Monetary Policies

Economy, The

The Truman administration struggled with twin problems—stimulating economic growth and refinancing the World War II national debt—as the president and his economic policymakers faced the task of reconversion from a wartime to a peacetime economy. Millions of returning veterans needed jobs, and the nation was scaling back its war production machinery. Truman was determined to avoid a retreat to prewar unemployment or a repeat of the boom-bust cycle that had followed World War I, but the transition promised to be a difficult one.

The Treasury had the immediate burden of refunding the enormous war debt. Over the course of the war years, the national debt had grown fivefold, and the government held 60 percent of all outstanding public and private debt, compared with less than 25 percent before the war. The Treasury needed to convert its wartime borrowing, much of which was short term, to a more stable long-term footing, and it was eager to finance the debt at as low an interest rate as possible to keep the government's costs down. Low interest rates, however, might spur overly rapid economic growth and court inflation. That in turn might spark the very boom-bust cycle the administration was struggling to avoid.

Reconversion thus raised twin problems of generating jobs and financing the debt. Layered on top of these issues was a larger one: just what should the government's role in steering the economy be? In returning the economy to a peacetime footing, the Truman administration faced a crucial choice between Hoover's hands-off approach and Roosevelt's more activist role.

In dealing with these problems, Truman was a pragmatist, not an ideologue. His experience in small business and in government had produced moderate views and keen interest in economic affairs. "The federal budget was one of my more serious hobbies," Truman wrote in his *Memoirs*, "but it was also much more than that. In fact, I regarded it as one of the most important responsibilities of the President—a responsibility that never failed to prove thoroughly fascinating." Truman, in fact, claimed to have spent twice as much time in formulating the budget as any of his predecessors.

He was not wed to the rigid budget-balancing theories that had undone Hoover. Truman accepted a forceful government role in emergencies, and he acknowledged that such actions might produce deficits. But he was not converted to the economic philosophy of John Maynard Keynes, then growing in popularity with liberal economists, who preached the virtues of "compensatory economics": the conscious use of the federal budget to stimulate economic growth in sluggish times and to slow growth when the economy heated up. Truman had little patience with academic economists or their theories.

On the jobs front, the Employment Act of 1946 for the first time committed the federal government to promoting economic growth and employment for its citizens. The act created the Council of Economic Advisers, to be based in the Executive Office of the President, and required the president to set annual targets for economic growth. The bill also created the congressional Joint Committee on the Economic Report (later renamed the Joint Economic Committee) to review the president's plans.

The act was unquestionably a congressional, not a presidential initiative (although Truman in his *Memoirs* was not shy about taking credit for it). Nevertheless, it set the stage for postwar economic policy-making. For the first time, the president was required to *have* an economic policy and develop plans to promote it. It also created an institution to supply the president with economic advice. Most of all, it confirmed the affirmative role for government in promoting economic growth that Roosevelt and his administration had first articulated. The act was a triumph of the Keynesian economists' confidence in both government's ability to stimulate growth and their own ability to manage the mechanism rather than the traditional reliance on the free market.

Truman, however, was lukewarm about the Employment Act and delayed six months in naming his Council of Economic Advisers (CEA). Finally, in August 1946, he appointed Edwin G. Nourse as the first CEA chairman, along with Leon H. Keyserling and John D. Clark as council members. The new CEA represented a cross section of economic thought, a diversity that virtually guaranteed dissension on major issues. Nourse, in particular, was annoyed that he was unable to develop rapport with Truman, and he finally resigned in November 1949 after three years of service.

Keyserling eventually became chairman and built a staff consistent with his own liberal views. He developed satisfac-

Leon H. Keyserling (l.), vice-chairman of the president's Council of Economic Advisers, and Edwin G. Nourse, chairman, review their 7 April 1948 report to the president. The council advised the president that the need for standby rationing and wage-price controls was even greater than it had been at the time of his inauguration in January. (Associated Press/Wide World Photos)

tory—though certainly never close—relations with the president, who remained suspicious of economic advice in general and liberal views in particular. Unlike Nourse, the new CEA chairman also mingled economic analysis with publicly proclaimed policy positions. Under Keyserling, the CEA developed a coherent economic rationale for the president's Fair Deal program. The CEA also provided intellectual support for the administration's mobilization policies—promoting expanded military and civilian production instead of price controls—as the Korean War heated up. These modest successes scarcely overcame the CEA's problems, however. Keyserling's aggressive, liberal, public positions on economic matters eroded public—especially congressional—support for the council. When Truman left office, in fact, Congress allowed the CEA's appropriations to lapse, and only Arthur Burns's strong fight for the council within the Eisenhower administration saved it.

The economy gave Truman a series of tests:

1. *Reconversion and inflation*: From 1945 to 1948, the president faced the immediate task of switching the economy from war to peace. The gross national product (GNP) actually decreased 1.5 percent in fiscal year 1946, but it grew 10.5 percent the next year. Unemployment dropped in 1947 from 4 percent to 2.7 percent at year's end. These changes came at a large cost in inflation, however. After price controls were removed in July 1946, consumer prices rose 30 percent and wholesale prices an even more rapid 50 percent, the fastest increase in American history. By 1947, however, the growth in consumer prices slowed to a 9.1 percent increase, and prices rose only 3.0 percent in 1948. Treasury Secretary John Snyder contended that the price jump was unavoidable, and the administration pressed a multipoint price control program. Republicans in Congress

nevertheless pressed for a large tax cut. The administration believed that the proposal was unwise, with inflation threatening and a large federal debt to finance, but Congress nevertheless passed it in 1948 over Truman's veto.

2. *Recession and recovery*: The postwar boom led to a brief but serious recession in 1949–50. The GNP dipped 0.5 percent, and consumer prices actually dropped 2.4 percent in 1949. The Federal Reserve eased credit to help the economy out of its doldrums. The beginning of the Korean War in 1950, however, even more promptly brought the economy out of the recession.

3. *Korean War*: The conversion of the economy back to a wartime footing immediately drove consumer prices up, with a 5.3 percent increase in 1950. Unemployment dropped at the end of 1950 to 3.6 percent from 5.0 percent in 1949, and the GNP surged ahead 10.9 percent in fiscal year 1950 (compared with a 0.5 percent drop the year before). The Federal Reserve tightened credit, and Truman secured a tax increase from Congress and reestablished wage and price controls. The administration's strategy was different from the World War II approach. Truman aimed to pay a far higher share of the war's cost with taxes than with borrowing, and in this he largely succeeded.

4. *Reconversion, yet again*: The administration's last year was a far easier time. Tax increases helped reduce the federal deficit. The GNP grew 5.5 percent in fiscal year 1952, while unemployment shrank to only 2.7 percent. Consumer prices stabilized to a 1.6 percent annual rate of increase. After a turbulent six years, the administration's last months were a time of relative economic tranquility.

The smoother sailing was due in substantial part to a treaty of peace negotiated between the Treasury Department and the Federal Reserve. During World War II, the Fed had willingly agreed to support the Treasury's borrowing—by supporting an agreed-upon peg of 2.5 percent for the Treasury's longest-term bonds—to ensure that the government could market its wartime debt. When the war ended, the Treasury—led first by Secretary Morgenthau and then by Secretary Snyder—pressured the Fed to maintain its support. Their interest was transparent: interest rates threatened to rise with consumer demand, and the Fed's peg greatly reduced their costs in refinancing the debt.

Fed officials, however, fought against the peg because it tied their hands in battling inflation. To try to bring inflation under control, the Fed needed the flexibility to nudge interest rates higher. Federal Reserve Board Chairman Marriner Eccles's opposition to the peg cost him his job in 1948, when Truman refused to redesignate him chairman. Truman replaced Eccles with Thomas B. McCabe from the Philadelphia Federal Reserve Bank and hoped McCabe would be more pliant, but he was just as disappointed in the new chairman's struggle against the peg.

The continuing battles led to a showdown on 31 January 1951 at the White House between Truman and the Federal Reserve Board, the only time in the Fed's history that its members met as a group with the president. Truman lectured the board members on the nation's problems, and afterward he released a statement saying how pleased he was about the Fed's promise of cooperation. Federal Reserve Board members, however, remembered no such commitment, and Eccles, who for a time after McCabe became chairman remained on the board as a member, leaked copies of the meeting's minutes—which revealed no promise—to the newspapers. Backed by prominent members of the Congress, the Fed deftly forced Truman and the Treasury to

Clarence Batchelor, *New York Daily News* (1945–52). Copyright New York News Inc. Reprinted with permission.

back down. Treasury Assistant Secretary William McChesney Martin and Winfield Riefler, a top Fed economist, met privately a few weeks later and negotiated an "accord," which removed the peg and restored the Fed's flexibility in setting interest rates.

Thus, the Truman administration actively and, for the most part, successfully navigated its way through a mine field of reconversion, inflation, recession, another war, and another reconversion. Economic growth was, for the most part, energetic while inflation, despite bursts of price increases following the removal of World War II price controls and the outbreak of the Korean War, stayed mostly under control. By the end of the administration, unemployment had dropped to a level that most economists recognized as the lowest practicable. And perhaps most important, the administration had avoided the boom-bust cycle that paralyzed the nation after World War I.

The administration's most important legacies, however, were the Employment Act of 1946 and the accord. The act affirmed the government's active role in promoting economic growth and established an institutional presence in the White House for economic advisers. The accord reestablished the Fed's freedom of action after nine years of supporting the Treasury's debt. It marked the Fed's ascent into full maturity as an institution and set the stage for its growing power over the next generation. Ironically, these legacies developed largely despite—not because of—Truman, who had little use for the CEA and battled for years to keep the Fed at heel.

Several members of the Truman administration attended a conference convened by the Harry S. Truman Library Institute in May 1979. In *Economics and the Truman Administration* (Lawrence: Regents Press of Kansas, 1981), editor Francis H. Heller has assembled a collection of essays from this conference, with a mostly-favorable view of the administration's efforts. Truman's own *Memoirs*, especially volume 2, *Years of Trial and Hope* (Garden City, N.Y.: Doubleday, 1956), provides valuable insights about the president's views on economic affairs. Herbert Stein's *The Fiscal Revolution in America* (Chicago: University of Chicago Press, 1969) is the classic analysis of the government's growing role in economic management. Supplementing that are several useful studies of the Employment act of 1946 and the early workings of the Council of Economic Advisers: Edward S. Flash, Jr., *Economic Advice and Presidential Leadership* (New York: Columbia University Press, 1965); Hugh S. Norton, *The Employment Act and the Council of Economic Advisers, 1946–1976* (Columbia: University of South Carolina Press, 1977); and Stephen Kemp Bailey, *Congress Makes a Law* (New York: Vintage Books, 1950), which is an excellent case study of the law's passage. *Leadership at the Fed* (New Haven: Yale University Press, 1986), by Donald F. Kettl, contains extensive analysis of the struggle over the peg and the accord. Finally, the Harry S. Truman Library contains a remarkable collection of documents on economic affairs. Of special interest, in addition to the president's own papers, are the papers of leading economic policy officials, including Treasury Secretary John Snyder. The library's oral history interviews, notably with Snyder, are invaluable for researching the administration's economic policies.

DONALD F. KETTL

See also Committee for Economic Development; Council of Economic Advisers; Eccles, Marriner Stoddard; Employment Act of 1946; Fiscal and Monetary Policies; Inflation; Keyserling, Leon; Nourse, Edwin Griswold

The 1901 high school graduate would have been a college senior in 1905, the year of this picture, if he had pursued a higher education. Instead, he worked as a bank clerk from 1902 to 1906. (Courtesy of the Harry S. Truman Library)

Education

Harry Truman's mother and father, John and Martha Truman, felt a deep responsibility to provide their children with good education. His mother taught Harry to read before he was five, according to family memory, and his father read aloud with his son and helped him save money for books. His parents owned a library that Truman mastered so thoroughly that he drew on memories of it all his life for information, ideas, and images.

Truman entered school in 1892 at age eight. He graduated from high school in 1901, barely seventeen years old, after nine years of school. Most Independence school records were later destroyed in a fire, but Truman's surviving report cards indicate that he did well, making As and Bs.

School enriched Truman's life. His teachers offered him a solid grounding in composition and literature, history, Latin, and mathematics. He was dutiful and courteous, a favorite of the teachers. He may not have been as bright as classmate Charles Ross, a future Pulitzer Prize–winning journalist who became presidential press secretary when his friend made it to the White House, but historian Monte Poen, who had access to Truman's high school theme book, found his work equaled that of a present-day college honor student.

After he graduated in 1901, Truman intended to go on to college, but his father's finances became "entangled" and Harry had to go to work to help his brother and sister stay in school. He took practical courses at Spalding's Commercial College to prepare for a job. In the early 1920s, he attended night school for two years at the Kansas City School of Law, where he received a practical grounding in legal procedures that helped him in his later political career.

Truman was the only twentieth-century president not to attend college. He offset the inadequacies of his education, however, with a good mind, retentive memory, hard work and self-discipline, extensive reading, and solid public school instruction. Still, there were many gaps in his education. His knowledge of physical and social sciences, economics, and philosophy was limited. He prided himself on his mastery of history, but his was a fact-oriented, great-man kind of historical understanding. Truman's formal education did little to challenge his tendency to think in terms of nineteenth-century certitudes, to distrust ideas and intellectuals, and to see reality in black-and-white terms.

The Truman Library holds most of Truman's surviving school records and oral history transcripts from schoolmates and teachers. In later life Truman often referred to his school years in autobiographical notes, held by the library, and in his *Memoirs* and other published writings. For an examination of Truman's personality development during these years, see Richard S. Kirkendall, "Truman's Path to Power," *Social Science* 43 (April 1968): 67–73.

WILLIAM E. PEMBERTON

See also Reading

Edwards, India

(16 June 1895–)

Vice-chairman, Democratic National Committee; executive secretary, associate director, executive director of the Women's Division of the committee during the Truman administration. In her various roles in the Democratic National Committee (DNC), India Edwards always insisted that appeals to women voters not be treated as marginal and that President Truman make a significant effort to appoint women to represent his administration. Edwards herself became a visible and respected leader of the Democratic party. She delivered major addresses at the 1948 and 1952 Democratic National Conventions and was placed in nomination for the vice presidency at the 1952 convention.

Edwards also participated significantly in the effort to re-elect Truman in 1948. Amidst general pessimism, she was one of the few who was sure Truman was going to win, displaying a loyalty he appreciated. Traveling aboard his whistle-stop campaign train that autumn, Edwards once shared a breakfast alone with the president and his wife (whom Truman referred to as "the Boss"). Truman observed to Edwards, "India, sometimes I think there are only two people in the whole United States who really believe I am going to be elected and both of them are at this table. But the Boss is not one of them."

Edwards had begun her political career as a volunteer for the DNC in 1944. After two decades of work on the *Chicago Tribune*, where she served at one point as women's editor, she had left to be with her third husband in Washington, D.C. She then quickly became absorbed in speech writing and publicity for FDR's campaign that year. Edwards did not think that men in public life were ready to accept women in significant positions of leadership. For that reason, she declined President Truman's suggestion in 1951 that she become chairman of the DNC. Similarly, she recognized that her nomination as vice president the next year was no more than a symbolic gesture. Nonetheless, she was the most influential agent in encouraging Truman to advance women for a variety of appointments and nominations, including treasurer of the United States, ambassador to Denmark, Federal Communications Commission board member, and a number of judgeships. These appointments were not only important as symbolic "firsts" for women; they also brought many women into real involvement in government and opened the way for many who came later.

In 1953, when the Women's Division was integrated into the DNC, Edwards resigned as executive director because she believed that the merger would undermine the autonomy of women as a force within the party. Her devotion to the party nonetheless continued. She served as chairman of the volunteer committee for Kennedy's 1961 inauguration and was involved in the planning for the 1968 nominating convention. She worked for Adlai Stevenson's and Lyndon Johnson's campaigns and continued to serve in other public roles.

Edward's autobiography, *Pulling No Punches: Memoirs of a Woman in Politics* (New York: G. P. Putnam's Sons, 1977), recounts her career and involvement with the advancement of women within the Democratic party and includes much praise for Truman. Eleanor Roosevelt and Lorena A. Hickok, in *Ladies of Courage* (New York: G. P. Putnam's Sons, 1954), discuss on pp. 25–30 Edwards's role within the DNC and the Truman administration. See also Susan Ware, *Beyond Suffrage: Women in the New Deal* (Cambridge: Harvard University Press, 1981). In her epilogue to her discussion of the participation of women in the New Deal, Ware credits Edwards for advances under the Truman administration.

KARLA A. GOLDMAN

See also Women (and photograph)

Eightieth Congress

The Republican-controlled Eightieth Congress (1947–48) tested Truman's abilities to marshal legislative support for his containment policy, to defend and expand New Deal social and economic reform, and to position himself and the Democratic party for a successful comeback in the 1948 elections.

Although the diplomatic stance of the United States toward the Soviet Union had been toughening since the last year of World War II, it was during the Eightieth Congress that the nation articulated its commitment to contain the spread of communism and enacted the economic and military means to effect that policy. In the area of foreign affairs, Truman worked closely with the Republican leadership, cultivating the cooperation of Michigan senator Arthur H. Vandenberg, the leading spokesman for internationalism and bipartisanship in foreign policy.

In March 1947, the president announced before a joint session of Congress what came to be called the Truman Doctrine, a declaration that the United States must use its power everywhere to "support free peoples who are resisting attempted subjugation by armed minorities or by outside pressures." The immediate crisis, Truman said, was in the Mediterranean, and Congress responded within two months, authorizing by large margins economic and military aid to Greece and Turkey and effecting a major reorientation in foreign policy.

In 1948, legislators applied the Truman Doctrine to Western Europe, supporting the administration in even greater numbers. The Marshall Plan began with $5 billion of economic aid for the first year, and by 1951 the United States had contributed more than $13 billion for the economic rehabilitation of Europe. Congress also moved to strengthen Europe militarily, approving the Vandenberg Resolution which laid the groundwork for the North Atlantic Treaty Organization (NATO), the nation's first peacetime alliance. Finally, although Congress refused Truman's request for the Universal Military Training program, it increased military appropriations and enacted a temporary draft.

In contrast to his relations with the Eightieth Congress on foreign policy, Truman shunned consultation over domestic matters and suffered significant defeats in that area. Over his veto, Congress passed the Taft-Hartley Act which left government protection of collective bargaining intact but imposed significant restraints on the activities of organized labor. In 1947, Truman successfully vetoed two tax-reduction bills that favored higher income groups, but in 1948 the Republicans garnered enough Democratic votes to override his third veto. Although defeated on two major measures, the president's willingness to use his veto power forced Congress to modify some of the harsher aspects of the Taft-Hartley Act and to reduce the total revenue loss and provide greater relief for low-income groups in the tax-cut bill.

Although Truman adopted a conciliatory posture in the early months of the Eightieth Congress, by the end of the first session he had begun to take the offensive. Carefully separating foreign policy legislation from domestic measures, the president did not hesitate to attack the Republican leadership and to intensify his demands for a host of reform measures that he knew would not pass. In accordance with strategy proposed by a group of aides led by his special counsel Clark Clifford, Truman's primary aim was to reinvigorate liberal and labor elements of the Democratic party and accumulate political capital for the 1948 campaign.

Truman barraged Congress with demands for a national health insurance program, expansion of Social Security and increases in benefits, an increase in the minimum wage, a comprehensive housing program, measures to control inflation, federal aid to education, a farm program oriented toward increasing consumption, and civil rights legislation. As expected, Congress failed to enact any of these measures; but Truman had built his record, and he made sure that it did not escape public notice.

In his acceptance speech for the presidential nomination, Truman aroused a dispirited convention by lambasting the Eightieth Congress as the "worst" on record and calling it into a special session to make good on the promises in the Republican platform. The "Turnip Day session" (convened on 26 June, Turnip Day in Missouri) produced nothing but more ammunition for Truman. He called the record of the Eightieth Congress "my Exhibit A," warning voters that it represented a foretaste of what would come should they elect the Republican candidate, Thomas E. Dewey. Neither candidate rallied impressive numbers to the polls, but in the face of Democratic defections to the Progressive and the States' Rights candidates, Truman confounded every prediction by defeating Dewey with a two-million-vote margin.

Most remarkably Truman was able to use the Eightieth Congress for his own political purposes while retaining its support for major foreign policy initiatives. Congress did reject some administration requests for military expansion, it forced some compromises, and it encouraged him to exaggerate the Soviet threat to U.S. security and intensify cold war tensions. Nonetheless, Truman's careful cultivation of bipartisanship won approval for his highest foreign policy priorities. Moreover, although a chasm separated his domestic program from the legislative record, Truman had defended the substance of New Deal reform and mobilized a popular mandate for a number of liberal measures that were enacted in his second term. The Eightieth Congress had served him well.

Susan M. Hartmann, *Truman and the 80th Congress* (Columbia: University of Missouri Press, 1971), provides a full account. For the two most important measures passed by the Eightieth Congress, see Michael J. Hogan, *The Marshall Plan: The Launching of the Pax Americana* (Cambridge: Cambridge University Press, 1987), and R. Alton Lee, *Truman and Taft-Hartley: A Question of Mandate* (Lexington: University of Kentucky, 1966).

SUSAN M. HARTMANN

See also Congress, United States; Election of 1946

Eisenhower, Dwight David

(14 October 1890–28 March 1969)

Dwight D. Eisenhower, Truman's successor as president, grew up in Abilene, Kansas, only two-hundred or so miles from Independence, Missouri. Indeed, Dwight Eisenhower's older brother, Arthur, lived in a boarding house in Kansas City with Truman in 1905. Truman and Eisenhower had almost identical views on American foreign policy. But despite these similarities, their disagreements over domestic policy and partisan politics led them to become bitter personal enemies.

Ike first met Truman at Potsdam, in July of 1945, and at the time liked and admired the man. During Ike's tenure as army chief of staff (1946–48), he worked well with and for Truman. Truman in turn was impressed by Ike. In 1945 and again in 1948, Truman offered to support Eisenhower for the Democratic nomination for the presidency. Ike, had he accepted, would have been a sure winner. But he said no, and Truman ran himself, and won. Ike, who had also said no to the Republicans, resigned as chief of staff in February 1948 to assume the presidency of Columbia University, a post he held until the autumn of 1950 when Truman made him the first supreme commander of the North Atlantic Treaty Organization (NATO).

Through this period, Ike supported all of Truman's major decisions—the containment policy, the airlift to Berlin, the commitment to Korea, the Marshall Plan, the program to build a hydrogen warhead, the limitation of the war in Korea, and, most of all, NATO. Indeed, Ike had become Truman's principal and enthusiastic agent in making NATO a military reality. In the process, Ike worked closely with Truman's top advisers, including Dean Acheson, Averell Harriman, Robert Lovett, and George Marshall.

At the beginning of 1952, Ike left Paris to become a Republican candidate for the presidency. He accepted what he had rejected four years earlier because he was told that if he did not run, it would be Taft versus Truman. Ike objected to Taft because the senator had voted against NATO, and to Truman because of his liberal domestic policies. When Ike announced, Truman dropped out. Eisenhower won the Republican nomination, and Adlai Stevenson the Democratic.

The 1952 campaign destroyed the Ike-Truman relationship. Eisenhower began by blasting the foreign policy of the very men he had just been working with. Truman resented that, naturally enough, and grew furious when Ike began to associate himself more closely with the Republican right wing, most of all, Joe McCarthy. Ike's campaign was built around the theme of

James Roosevelt, leader of the southern California delegates to the 1948 Democratic National Convention in Philadelphia, waves to a crowd of supporters calling for a "winning ticket" of Eisenhower and Roosevelt. (Associated Press/Wide World Photos)

Fred Packer, 7 November 1952, *New York Mirror.*

"liberation," with an implied promise that an activist Republican president would somehow "liberate" the peoples of Eastern Europe. Truman's policy of containment was labeled "cowardly" by the Republicans, who also hinted that the cause was traitors in the State Department, traitors knowingly sheltered by Truman. The president's blood boiled when Eisenhower failed to defend George Marshall from McCarthy's accusation of treason. Truman thought—and said—that Ike's pledge to go to Korea if elected was the worst sort of political hucksterism. Truman declared his contempt for Ike: "The General doesn't know any more about politics than a pig knows about Sunday."

Eisenhower for his part thought Truman was guilty of extreme partisanship, poor judgment, inept leadership and management, bad taste, and undignified behavior. Worst of all, in Eisenhower's view, Truman had diminished the prestige of the office of the president.

Truman and Ike conferred only once after the election—for twenty minutes, most of it spent in cold silence. The transition on 20 January 1953 was the most hostile of the twentieth century. They never reconciled, never exchanged correspondence, never changed their minds.

The two men encountered each other two more times at funerals—the first, George Marshall's, the second, John Kennedy's. Before his own library was built, Eisenhower visited the Truman Library. He did not let Truman know he was coming, nor did he receive an invitation for coffee and a chat when guards informed Truman that he was there.

Just before Eisenhower was inaugurated, Truman reflected on the problems he would have and came up with a wonderfully accurate prediction: "He'll sit here," Truman said, "and he'll say, 'Do this! Do that!' *And nothing will happen.* Poor Ike—it won't be a bit like the army. He'll find it very frustrating." He was right about that.

Stephen E. Ambrose's two-volume *Eisenhower* (New York: Simon & Schuster, 1983, 1984) covers the Truman-Eisenhower relationship in some detail. Neither Truman nor Eisenhower expressed their real feelings toward the other in their memoirs. Merle Miller's *Plain Speaking: An Oral Biography of Harry S. Truman* (New York: G. P. Putnam's Sons, 1973, 1974) gives a better feel of Truman's attitude toward Ike, and William Bragg Ewald, *Eisenhower the President* (Englewood Cliffs, N.J.: Prentice-Hall, 1981), offers an insider's view of Ike's feelings toward Truman.

STEPHEN E. AMBROSE

See also Election of 1952; North Atlantic Treaty Organization (and photograph); Taft, Robert A. (photograph)

Election of 1934

In May 1934, Harry S. Truman turned fifty and real success seemed to have eluded him. The prevailing attitude of journalists on the 1934 Missouri political scene was that Tom Pendergast could make anyone the U.S. senator that year. Undoubtedly, Pendergast's backing was important, but the machine had developed certain outstanding limitations. That Pendergast saw a need for an exceptionally strong candidate to overcome these limitations is revealed by the fact that he rejected several lesser figures who sought his support.

In addition to the political liability of the machine's scandal-ridden reputation, Pendergast's candidate that year would face formidable opposition in the Democratic primary race. Jacob L. "Tuck" Milligan had announced his candidacy on 31 January 1934. He won the support of Missouri senator Bennett C. Clark, a campaigner known throughout the state who capitalized heavily upon the fame of his father, House Speaker "Champ" Clark. Furthermore, Milligan seemed to have the support of the national administration: Vice President John Nance Garner had urged him for some time to run for the U.S. Senate.

John J. Cochran from Saint Louis also entered the race. Both Cochran and Milligan had served intermittently in the House of Representatives from 1920, Cochran continuously since 1926. Washington correspondent Marquis Childs wrote glowingly of Cochran, describing him as by far the best candidate in the 1934 senatorial contest. A group of Washington reporters also attested to Cochran's ability by naming him as one of the five or six most useful members of the U.S. Congress.

The primary election strategies followed predictable patterns. The three Democratic hopefuls promised their full allegiance to Roosevelt's New Deal, and each asserted that he could make the greatest contribution to the fulfillment of this program. So frequently did John Cochran allude to this pledge that Republican opponents in Saint Louis referred to him as "rubber-stamp Jack." With such strong agreement about the New Deal, the campaign frequently degenerated into a heated battle of personalities in which Truman had the difficult task of defending his connections with the Kansas City machine.

One newspaper compared the division of Missouri to the tripartite division of Gaul. Milligan claimed the support of the rural areas because he resided in the small town of Richmond and had the backing of Senator Bennett C. Clark who had carried the rural areas against Pendergast in 1932. Cochran was assured of the support of his native Saint Louis, and Truman had Kansas City. Cochran and Truman believed that victory would go to the one who attracted more rural votes.

The August primary election returns gave Truman a narrow win over Cochran while Milligan ran a poor third. Truman had 276,850 votes; Cochran, 236,105; and Milligan, 147,614. The results clearly indicated Truman's success in the rural areas. If the Kansas City–Jackson County and Saint Louis City–Saint Louis County votes are disregarded, Truman would have won 134,707 to Cochran's 113,532 and Milligan's 128,401. Although Cochran won as many countries as Truman, Truman placed second in forty-nine and Cochran was runner-up in only twenty-six.

Although Truman's opponents charged that he was obscure and lacked political experience above the county level, his background was of such a nature as to give him strong grass-roots support. As president of the Missouri County Judge Association he maintained close contact with the 342 county judges throughout the state. The "courthouse gangs" spread the Truman name and accomplishments to the far corners of the state. Because the county judges often held top posts in the party's organization, their support could be crucially important in a tight primary contest. George Creel, a national writer on the Missouri scene, has called the Judges' Association one of the most potent political forces in the state. Being aware of its power, Truman had sent to every county in Missouri a copy of a book entitled *Jackson County—Results of County Planning*.

Truman's grass-roots support was pervasive. His active participation in veterans' organizations, in the Masons, and in the Baptist church broadened enormously his voter appeal. Having been a farmer himself, he appeared to understand the hardships they were suffering in those years. Finally, he had been a small businessman who had failed, and this unwittingly brought about a bond with those facing similar experiences as a result of the depression. Voters admired in particular the determination with which Truman was paying back his business debts.

Campaign emphasis on Kansas City vote frauds and criminal activities caused some to predict a heavy rural vote for Cochran and Milligan. But Richard Harkness, the United Press correspondent, pointed out that Truman defeated Cochran and Milligan in the "creek forks and grass roots," regardless of what people were saying. Some observers felt that Cochran ran as well as he did only because of the support he received from Republican voters: a study of the primary vote distribution showed that many of the countries carried by Cochran were normally Republican. Milligan lacked adequate support throughout the state, most of his county victories coming in the northwestern part of Missouri near his hometown.

Despite the fact that most of the metropolitan newspapers in Missouri and some of the rural press attributed his victory to Pendergast's influence, Truman obviously had appeal of his own. Two years earlier, in the 1932 primary, Pendergast's senatorial candidate did poorly in the rural areas and was soundly defeated. Truman needed Pendergast and the Kansas City vote to offset Cochran's Saint Louis support, but the balance of victory depended on the rural voters who could rebel against Pendergast if he offered unworthy candidates. Undoubtedly, Truman's record as county judge and his many friends throughout the state played a major role in overcoming the stigma of Pendergast's support outside of Kansas City.

After the tumult and excitement of the hard-fought primary contest, the general election campaign that fall was anticlimactic. Helped by the popular acceptance of the national administration, Truman won in November by over a quarter million votes and made large inroads into traditionally strong Republican areas in the state. Fate treated Truman kindly in providing him with a staunchly conservative Republican opponent, the incumbent Roscoe C. Patterson. Patterson had been elected to the U.S. Senate in 1928. By 1934, however, his support for Prohibition had lost him the support of many German Republicans in Saint Louis, and early in 1934, the Republicans of the Twenty-first Ward in Saint Louis had declared they would not support him if he were renominated for the Senate.

The election results amazed Patterson as Truman carried seventy-five counties in addition to Saint Louis City. Although the Kansas City machine turned in its usual heavy vote, so large a victory could not be attributed solely to the manipulations of a single organization. It belonged largely to Franklin Roosevelt's popularity, to national relief funds, and to the lack of leadership among the Republicans.

Although Truman's contribution was not nearly so critical as in the primary race, he deserved some credit for the wide margin of his victory. His honesty and sincerity gained the support of prominent Democrats such as Orlando V. Slaughter, a Grandview farm neighbor of Truman's, and William Southern, Jr., editor of the *Independence Examiner*, both fervent adversaries of the Pendergast organization. Some part of Truman's general election victory must also be charged to the lackluster image of his opponent. Even a normally Republican paper, the *Maryville Daily Forum*, rejoiced that Patterson had been retired to private life because of his ultraconservative posture and undistinguished record in the Senate.

The senatorial triumph brought Truman immense satisfaction, and he awaited his new responsibility with enthusiasm. At last he was gaining a sure foothold on the ladder of success.

The Truman Library contains records of his campaign strategies in 1934 as well as copies of speeches he made. Many of Patterson's speeches for the general election may be found among the Roscoe C. Patterson Papers in the Western Historical Manuscripts Collection, University of Missouri Library, Columbia, Missouri.

EUGENE F. SCHMIDTLEIN

See also Pendergast, Thomas J.

Election of 1940

Apprehension permeated Truman's feelings as the 1940 election approached. He had made a commendable record in his first term in the U.S. Senate, but the tide now seemed to be running against him. The conviction and imprisonment of Tom Pendergast in 1939 promised to weigh heavily against Truman's reelection. According to rumors in Washington, President Roosevelt offered Truman a way out by proffering an appointment to the Interstate Commerce Commission as a reward for his work on transportation legislation. Rumor also hinted that FDR would support Governor Lloyd C. Stark in the Missouri senatorial race. Maurice Milligan, the federal district attorney who had prosecuted Pendergast, promised to be a formidable obstacle to Truman's reelection if Stark should falter. Truman's hard-earned senatorial career appeared so much in jeopardy that he actually cried as he pondered his political future in early 1940.

Despite the bleak prospects and the advice of several close friends, however, Truman refused to withdraw. In his later years, Truman said there were two men whom he had hated and one was Stark; he was determined now to defeat him. In 1936 Stark had known that Pendergast's support was absolutely necessary to win the governorship and pleaded for Truman's help in persuading Boss Tom to give that support. After considerable hesitation, Truman finally asked Pendergast for the endorsement. Then, shortly after becoming governor, Stark turned on Pendergast and played a crucial role in sending him to prison. Truman would never forgive such political disloyalty.

Stark's unlimited ambition became Truman's asset in this election. During the course of the year, the Missouri governor attempted to run for president, vice president, secretary of the navy, governor-general of the Philippines, and senator from Missouri. His ego and superior airs were astounding and caused many Democrats to disavow him.

Other factors contributed to Truman's victory. Maurice Milligan's entry in the Democratic primary was critical in that Milligan split the anti-Pendergast vote with Stark. At the last minute, the Saint Louis machine under Robert Hannegan and Bernard Dickmann decided to support Truman because they wanted him and the Kansas City machine to support their gubernatorial candidate. Their backing helped him win St. Louis by 8,411 votes. Working in favor of Truman in the primary were his strong pro-Roosevelt voting record in the Senate, the support of organized labor (especially the railway unions) and of blacks in Kansas City and Saint Louis, and the many mistakes made by Stark. On the other hand, many Missouri newspapers opposed Truman because of their hostility to Pendergast. Truman won the primary by a scant 8,000 votes: Truman, 268,557; Stark, 260,581; and Milligan, 127,363. One can be sure that most of Milligan's votes would have gone to Stark had Milligan not been a contestant.

In the general election, Truman was opposed by Kansas City Republican Manvel Davis who ran against the "dictatorship" of FDR and the machine control of Missouri by Pendergast and Hannegan-Dickmann. Truman simply ignored Davis throughout the campaign and focused on Wendell Willkie and the national election. Despite the Missouri newspapers' attacks on FDR's leadership and his bid for a third term, Truman did not waver in his allegiance to the president. In September, a Gallup poll gave Roosevelt a comfortable lead in Missouri, but by the first of November the poll had conceded the state to Willkie. The *St. Louis Post-Dispatch* opposed a third term for Roosevelt and also the "destroyer deal." The editor called FDR our "first dictator" and asked the nation "to rise up and stop him." But later in the campaign, the *Post-Dispatch* abandoned Willkie because of his ineffective campaign and weakly endorsed Roosevelt.

Truman won the general election 930,775 to 886,876, a majority of only 44,399, while Roosevelt also won narrowly by 87,467. Truman carried the city of Saint Louis by 46,268, but lost St. Louis County by 24,632. He was victorious in only 48 of the 114 counties in the state. He derived considerable satisfaction when the *Post-Dispatch* summarized the election by writing "Senator Truman . . . has been, on the whole, a satisfactory senator. Now seasoned by experience, he should make an even better record in his second term. Mr. Truman in particular, with his progressive policies toward labor, may be expected to be useful in helping safeguard the administration's social gains."

Unquestionably, Truman felt better after the 1940 election. Maybe now the *Post-Dispatch* would stop calling him Pendergast's office boy. He felt much more self-assurance and looked forward to even greater effectiveness in the U.S. Senate.

Records on the 1940 election can be found in the Harry S. Truman Library in Independence. The Franklin D. Roosevelt Library in Hyde Park, N.Y., contains interesting correspondence between FDR and Stark, and Roosevelt's calendar shows a number of White House visits by Stark.

EUGENE F. SCHMIDTLEIN

See also Stark, Lloyd C.

Election of 1944

In 1944, for the first time in eighty years, the American people would be voting for a president in wartime. Every Democratic party leader knew that Franklin D. Roosevelt must and would be nominated for a fourth term. In hindsight, moreover, Roosevelt's victory in that election appears to have been inevitable. But that fact was not the certainty in 1944 it later seemed.

The backbone of the Democratic coalition was composed of persons who had come of age during the depression and New Deal years. But millions of these potential Roosevelt supporters now were in the armed forces, and Congress had made such limited provision for soldier voting that fewer than 100,000 GIs ultimately cast ballots. Millions of workers had migrated to centers of war production and were not registered to vote in their new homes. The election could be lost, therefore, not because the Republicans might prove more popular but because the Democrats might fail to mobilize effectively their diminished majority. The key to that mobilization was party unity, and the key to party unity lay in the selection of a vice-presidential candidate acceptable to the major factions.

The incumbent vice president, former agriculture secretary Henry A. Wallace, had alienated the white South and the party bosses by his flirtation with leftists and CIO unionists. He had handled his wartime assignments ineptly, and the party leadership was convinced that he must go. The leaders of the anti-Wallace forces included Democratic National Committee chairman Robert Hannegan of Missouri; DNC treasurer Edwin Pauley of California; Postmaster General Frank Walker; Ed Flynn, boss of the Bronx; and Mayors Frank Hague of Jersey City and Ed Kelly of Chicago.

During the spring of 1944 these men sifted alternatives to Wallace. They considered James F. Byrnes, former senator from South Carolina, Supreme Court justice, and now, as director of the Office of War Mobilization, the so-called assistant president. But he was disliked by labor and blacks, and his conversion from Roman Catholicism early in life could, it was feared, turn away big-city ethnic voters.

Attention soon focused on Senator Harry S. Truman. By 1944 he had won a solid reputation for probity as chairman of the Senate Special Committee to Investigate the National Defense Program. Although not a Senate leader, he had shed his image as Boss Pendergast's man and was, at sixty years of age, a well-liked, respected member of the club. Truman came from a border state with southern roots, but had retained ties with labor. The bosses were looking not for a candidate who would strengthen the ticket but for one who would not fatally weaken it. By that criterion, Truman seemed an eminently sensible choice.

At a White House dinner on 11 July, Roosevelt listened as the party leaders discussed each candidate. He finally agreed to support Truman and wrote Hannegan a note confirming his willingness to run either with the Missouri senator or with Justice William O. Douglas. Douglas's name apparently was added to avoid the impression that the president was dictating to the convention.

Roosevelt, however, left both Wallace and Byrnes with the impression that he was backing each of them. Scholars have struggled to explain the president's behavior. His ill-health, pre-

Campaign poster, 1944 (Courtesy of the Franklin D. Roosevelt Library)

occupation with the war, unwillingness to offend close associates, and instinctual guile have all been advanced as explanations. But whichever hypothesis is accurate, the result was a thoroughly muddled situation by the time the Democrats gathered in Chicago on 17 July to nominate a national ticket.

Truman was at the center of the confusion. He had denied any interest in the vice presidency since friends first had raised the possibility in 1942. He liked the Senate and feared the impact higher office would have on his family. Nor did he want to become president.

Truman thus arrived in Chicago prepared to nominate Byrnes for vice president. Furious back-room maneuvering meanwhile took place around the Missourian. Sidney Hillman, head of the CIO Political Action Committee, vetoed Byrnes and remained steadfast for Wallace. Truman fended off the bosses until the afternoon of 20 July, when Hannegan summoned him to a conference in the party chairman's hotel room. With the other bosses in attendance, Hannegan placed a call to Roosevelt, who was traveling west for a military conference. Roosevelt's voice rang out clearly asking, "Have you got that fellow lined up yet?" "No," Hannegan answered. "He's the contrariest Missouri mule I've ever dealt with." "Well, you tell him if he wants to break up the Democratic party in the middle of a war, that's his responsibility." The president hung up. "Oh, shit," Truman said. "Well, if that's the situation, I'll have to say yes. But why the hell didn't he tell me in the first place?"

The Wallace delegates forced the issue to a second ballot, but on the evening of 21 July Truman received the nomination.

He served as Roosevelt's surrogate in the fall campaign against the Republican ticket of Governor Thomas E. Dewey of New York and Governor John Bricker of Ohio. Whereas the president made only a few major addresses, Truman delivered fifty-four speeches across the nation.

Since the war was going well, it was not an issue. Instead, Dewey attacked Roosevelt for the president's alleged support of Communists in labor unions. The Republican nominee contrasted his youth and dynamism to that of an administration full of "tired old men." The latter tactic went hand in hand with a Republican whispering campaign about FDR's declining health.

Sadly, there was truth in the whispers. Truman met Roosevelt on 18 August for a strategy meeting and was appalled to find the president distracted and drained. Saying that "one of us has to stay alive," FDR refused to allow Truman to use an airplane in his travels.

On Tuesday evening, 7 November, Truman awaited the election returns in a suite at the Muehlebach Hotel in Kansas City. Roosevelt defeated Dewey decisively in the electoral college, winning 36 states and 432 electoral votes to 12 states and 99 electoral votes for the GOP ticket. The popular vote was closer, Roosevelt winning by 25,602,504 to 22,006,285 for Dewey. A united party had pulled off tight races in several states.

That night, Truman was restless and stayed up late talking to Harry Easley, an old friend. "He told me," Easley recalled, "that the last time he saw Mr. Roosevelt, he had the pallor of death on his face, and he knew he would be President before the term was out."

Knowledge of home-front America that year is vital to an understanding of the election of 1944. See John M. Blum, *V Was for Victory: American Society and Culture during World War II* (New York: Harcourt Brace Jovanovich, Vintage Books, 1976); Richard Polenberg, *War and Society: The United States, 1941–1945* (Philadelphia: J. B. Lippincott, 1972); and Alan Clive, *State of War: Michigan in World War II* (Ann Arbor: University of Michigan Press, 1979). The standard biographies and memoirs retell the story of Truman's nomination. The election is covered in detail by Leon M. Freidman in Arthur M. Schlesinger, Jr., and Fred Israel, eds., *A History of American Presidential Elections 1789–1968*, 4 vols. (New York: Chelsea House, 1971), 4:3009–57. The critical role of labor in the election is analyzed in James Foster, *The Union Politic: The CIO Political Action Committee* (Columbia: University of Missouri Press, 1975).

ALAN CLIVE

See also Democratic Party; Dewey, Thomas Edmund; Republican Party; Vice Presidency; Wallace, Henry Agard

Election of 1946

A sweeping, significant, yet temporary defeat for the Democratic party, the election of 1946 reflected the political impact of the transition from war to peace and the early troubles of Harry S. Truman's presidency. Although the developing cold war increasingly triggered discontent with Truman's conduct of foreign policy, domestic events provided the fundamental context and issues for the politics of 1946.

As inflation and labor unrest, not unemployment, dominated reconversion problems, Congress refused to grant Truman much of his liberal postwar program, and the relative wartime restraint and balance among interest groups disintegrated. Demanding higher wages, unions conducted an unprecedented wave of strikes, and walkouts in such crucial industries as steel, coal, automobiles, electricals, oil, and railroads threatened to paralyze the nation. Pressing with businessmen for an end to price controls, farmers withheld commodities—meat, most infuriatingly—from the market. Consumers coveted both low prices and abundant goods. Although only partly the fault of government, and often as much the result of congressional as of presidential action (or inaction), these strikes, shortages, black markets, inflation, and more were routinely blamed on Harry Truman.

Disarray and dissension within the administration, the displacement of New Dealers by conservatives and cronies, and the badly handled, much-publicized firing of Commerce Secretary Henry A. Wallace, moreover, dismayed liberals and further disturbed ordinary citizens. Too conservative for liberals, too liberal for conservatives, inconsistent and ineffective in his labor and price control policies, and at odds with labor, farmers, and business alike, Truman seemed too small for the job and certainly no substitute for Franklin D. Roosevelt. The gibe "to err is Truman" circulated widely, and the president's public approval rating, an astronomical 90 percent in August 1945 plunged to just 34 percent by September 1946. Exploiting the nation's problems, frustrations, and irritated impatience with Truman, and fiercely raising charges about domestic Communists as well, the 1946 GOP campaign was neatly summarized in its telling slogan: "Had Enough? Vote Republican."

Truman, normally a scrappy partisan barnstormer, announced in September that there would "be no tour" and took virtually no part in the campaign. He had in summer primaries intervened futilely in Montana and clumsily in Missouri, but those efforts, especially his apparent collaboration with the Pendergast machine and its unsavory tactics in Missouri, further tarnished his image. An unwelcome liability in the eyes of many Democratic politicians, Truman made not a single campaign speech during the autumn. Some of his actions—such as his humiliating mid-October removal of meat price controls, in order to bring meat back to the market and thus assuage angry consumers and rescue alarmed Democratic candidates—were, to be sure, politically motivated, but Truman displayed little inclination to go on the hustings. Preferring to broadcast recorded Roosevelt speeches, Democratic National Committee Chairman Robert Hannegan headed off a preelection radio address by Truman. The president merely waved silently from the back of the train on his way home to Missouri for the election.

The election results revealed that the nation had indeed had enough of its postwar troubles to vote Republican. Gaining nearly five dozen representatives and thirteen senators, the GOP swept to its first control of Congress (246–188 in the House, 51–45 in the Senate) since Hoover's presidency. Democratic losses were especially significant among the party's veteran urban-liberal-labor contingent. But though culminating the 1938–46 downward trend in Democratic and liberal strength, Republican gains were notable more for their breadth than for their depth and did not denote a rejection of the New Deal. Neither the aggregate division of the congressional vote nor the underlying voting patterns departed greatly from previous elections. Registering the general public discontent as well as specific regional, ethnic, and economic-group grievances, the Democratic vote (with the inevitable local variations and inconsistencies of any election) declined at much the same rate in most areas and constituencies. The striking GOP gains in Congress came because Republicans carried by relatively small margins many seats that the party had lost relatively narrowly in previous years. The returns thus demonstrated, on the one hand, that the Roosevelt coalition of voters forged in the depression remained substantially intact, and on the other, that the postwar politics of prosperity, inflation, cold war, and anti-Communism had diminished the salience of the Democrats' bread-and-butter reform issues and eroded the Democratic majority.

Indicative of the mixture of continuity and change that would characterize postwar politics and voting patterns, the election of 1946 also helped shape the politics of 1948. It sent to Washington the conservative Eightieth Congress that Truman so effectively pilloried in the 1948 campaign. Exacerbating the concerns of liberal Democrats about Truman and the prospects of their party and programs, it catalyzed both the formation late in 1946 of the Progressive Citizens of America, which played a crucial role in Henry Wallace's third-party candidacy in 1948, and the organization early in 1947 of the Americans for Democratic Action, which helped orchestrate the 1948 dump-Truman movement but then supported the president during the campaign. And the nature and results of the 1946 election informed presidential adviser Clark Clifford's trenchant late-1947 report on the "Politics of 1948" that helped structure Truman's combative and successful 1948 campaign and reverse the outcome of 1946.

Distinguished by a detailed, sophisticated examination of politics and voting patterns, the most comprehensive analysis of the election of 1946 is James Boylan, *The New Deal Coalition and the Election of 1946* (New York: Garland, 1981). See also chapter 5 of John W. Jeffries, *Testing the Roosevelt Coalition: Connecticut Society and Politics in the Era of World War II* (Knoxville: University of Tennessee Press, 1979).

JOHN W. JEFFRIES

See also Democratic Party; Eightieth Congress; Elections in the Truman Era; Republican Party

Election of 1948

Nineteen forty-eight stands as a most remarkable year in American electoral politics. The theatrics were all there: a salty, battling underdog, Harry Truman, relishing a "lonely" fight and defeating an arrogantly confident, barbed-witted and fastidious Thomas E. Dewey. Still, what can easily be lost is the reality that the significance of the election of 1948 was, in the long run, not so much the drama and excitement as what happened because the president was returned for another four years.

Had Truman been defeated, his record would have closed at that point. Such initiatives as aid to Greece and Turkey and

the Marshall Plan to prop up Western Europe would have stood virtually alone against a history that was otherwise unproductive, contentious, and sometimes confused. There would have been no Truman administration to provoke the sequence of events that governed national politics for at least the next two decades. Difficult as it may be to speculate what would have happened had Dewey won, it is nevertheless hard to imagine that the same breakdown of early cold war bipartisanship—especially the debates over the "loss" of China and the Korean War—could have happened with a Republican in the White House. Had the pollsters been right in 1948, neither Joe McCarthy nor Richard Nixon would have been given their opportunities, and one can only speculate how different would have been the conditions that, as we now know, ultimately favored the United States becoming involved in Vietnam. Rarely could one man have made that much difference, so Truman's success was even more important than it was intriguing.

From the standpoint of a comeback, it was remarkable. All in all, his standing had been moving downhill; in the spring of 1948, only 36 percent of respondents in a poll approved of his handling of the presidency. Few believed his chances warranted a good fight. Before and after the convention, he was the favored choice of few Democrats.

The delegates who renominated him could hardly have been more fatalistic nor their motions more desultory. Preconvention hunger for a winner encouraged the contemplation of such reluctant replacements as, among others, Gen.

"The Duet, or A Good Man Is Hard to Find," a satirical campaign poster by Ben Shahn. (Courtesy of the Progressive Labor party)

Dwight D. Eisenhower and Supreme Court Justice William O. Douglas. Anticipating defeat, many despairing Democrats even looked to the GOP for a candidate. One, Senator J. William Fulbright of Arkansas, suggested that Truman should step down in favor of Arthur Vandenberg, a Michigan Republican.

Republican frustrations over winning the White House seemed about over. The party's success in regaining the House and Senate two years earlier assuredly confirmed the exhaustion of depression era politics. Varied forces were splitting the New Deal coalition: rebellious southerners and angry anti-Communists on the Right; dissenting liberals and progressives on the Left, almost all dedicated to completing the economic and social agenda of the 1930s and to a considerable degree not convinced that Stalinist Russia was the sole ogre responsible for the iron curtain separating East from West. With rebels from the Left and Right coalescing around the Progressive Citizens of America and the States' Rights party, or Dixiecrats, large chunks were bound to be cut out of what remained of the normal Democratic vote.

Truman's weaknesses were clear. As party publicist Jack Redding explained to the Democratic national chairman, "The difficulty is that you're trying to picture the President as FDR. You're expecting the impossible. He isn't FDR. He isn't anything like that. Roosevelt was an Eastern aristocrat, educated at Groton and Harvard. Harry Truman is a Midwestern farmer." If the point was overstated, it was nevertheless apt, illustrating the dilimma of trying to win an election with an incumbent who seemed awkward (especially after FDR), inadequate to the great problems inherent in political and economic reconversion to peacetime, and of muddled ideology. Rescuing him from the White House seemed like the most humane thing one could do.

Differences over foreign policy were the least contentious parts of presidential politics in 1948. Only the Progressives behind Henry Wallace parted from the consensus. Neither Republicans nor Democrats, nor rebellious States' Righters, took much exception to Truman's early cold war initiatives. Only relatively small fringes at the right and left of the American mainstream raised many objections to the early military and financial aid programs, and fewer still had any qualms about trying to break the Soviet blockade of West Berlin; the around-the-clock airlift was still under way as the voters went to the polls.

Still, Truman's chances were written off by virtually all observers. Genuine enthusiasm for the administration was hard to find, confined for the moment largely to those with a stake in Democratic control over the national government. Among them were southerners who swallowed the departure from what they liked to call "Jeffersonian Democracy" and stood with traditional regional loyalties. One-party politics made for seniority, which, in turn, eased the way to influence on Capitol Hill, circumstances that conditioned acquiescence to such unpopular New Deal initiatives as the promotion of unions and legislation governing wages and hours. With the outstanding exception of attitudes toward unions, their interests were not far removed from northern big-city Democrats who rested their political base on a coalition of working-class ethnic groups. Having shown some signs of mutual cooperation even before the war, they came together even more closely in backing the president's resistance to Soviet expansionism.

On the left were followers of Henry Wallace, who was second only to Eleanor Roosevelt as a symbol of liberal continuity. Wallace's efforts to push Truman along New Deal lines came to an abrupt end in September 1946 when he was forced to resign as secretary of commerce after he had publicly criticized the administration for helping provoke East-West tensions. In short order, Wallace became the leader of the Progressive Citizens of America, which enthusiastically embraced, along with advocacy of friendship toward the Soviet Union, such causes as civil rights, higher wages and better working conditions, rent control, and aid for the creation of a Jewish state in Palestine. With Wallace as a third-party presidential candidate, they were optimistic about getting over 12 million votes.

Wallace as a potential candidate, however, provoked a rebellion among anti-Communist Democrats, many of them liberals. Widely suspected at the time but not confirmed was the close working relationship between Wallace and the American Communist party. Each had illusions about being able to use and control the other. Wallace accepted their support and resisted challenges to repudiate Soviet actions, even after the Czech coup that spring.

Shortly after the Progressives were organized, a band of liberal intellectuals and labor leaders came together to form the Americans for Democratic Action (ADA). Organized to oppose Wallace and to function as a liberal lobby within the party, the ADA became, along with organized labor, prominent among those resisting conservatism. Almost alone, they fought the battle in behalf of liberal anti-Communism. If they were unable to produce a winner, they at least wanted to come out of the Philadelphia convention with self-respect, and that meant making sure Democrats produced a forward-looking platform, one that recognized the importance of unionism and civil rights.

But, more than any other dissidents, the states' rights advocates seemed to seal Truman's defeat. Discontent in Dixie, which had been increasing since early New Deal days, was virtually suspended with the bombing of Pearl Harbor. The war, however, only accelerated social, economic, and cultural changes that caused southern unrest. Democratic administrations that were friendly to labor and critical of Jim Crow racial relations, unsympathetic to state claims to tidelands oil deposits, and insistent on continuing to advance the power of the federal government on a variety of fronts were straining party loyalties. Truman's open advocacy of civil rights legislation pushed matters to a head. The acceptance by the convention of a civil rights platform that was spearheaded by ADA liberals provoked a walkout by delegates from three southern states. At Birmingham, Alabama, their response was the formation of the States' Rights Democrats behind the presidential candidacy of Governor J. Strom Thurmond of South Carolina.

With the Republicans having nominated Dewey for a second time, Truman had his hands full. Undaunted by the pessimistic predictions, he waged a vigorous whistle-stop campaign, traveling some thirty-one thousand miles in appearances before an estimated 6 million people. His grass-roots speeches reached out to the common man. At every opportunity, he lashed out at the Republican party as the party of big business and denounced the GOP-controlled Eightieth Congress for trying to restrict organized labor by passing the Taft-Hartley Act. As he went along, the crowds increased in size and enthusiasm, but none of this made much of a difference to seasoned observers or to Dewey, who delivered lofty, ambiguous speeches about the evils of big government. Also insufficiently recognized was that droves of left-wing Democrats, increasingly put off by the Communist influence behind Wallace, were moving back to the president.

Nor were southern Democrats, especially those dependent on the national party organization, ready to defect en masse. At the same time, farmers, worried about falling grain prices and wooed hard by Truman, were siding with their economic interests and moving toward the party associated with price supports.

The outcome was not clear until the morning after Election Day, when Dewey conceded that Truman had won. The president's 303 electoral votes to 189 for Dewey and 39 for Thurmond were made possible by his two-million-vote margin over the Republican challenger. The States' Rights candidate fell far short of a majority even in the South, and Wallace wound up with no electors and only 1.5 million supporters, nearly half of them in New York, which at least enabled Dewey to win his home state. The Democrats, moreover, regained the majority in both houses of Congress.

Truman worked hard and fully deserved his triumph, but his success came from a number of circumstances beyond his control. His victory demonstrated the viability of the coalition brought together under FDR. Rather than delivering fatal blows, the Thurmond and Wallace candidacies enabled him to champion anti-Communism and racial equality. Utilizing the Taft-Hartley Act for all its political worth and taking advantage of the unstable agricultural conditions, he retained the loyalty of workers and farmers; the nation's breadbasket enabled him to put together the bloc of small states necessary to offset losses of the electoral votes of New York, Pennsylvania, and Michigan. His vigorous response to the Berlin blockade and leadership of what had, by 1948, become a cold war consensus also enhanced his stature. The leveling off of inflation and return to industrial stability provided additional reasons for voters' going along with the incumbent, who, along with everything else, had shown himself to be a far more appealing human being than his Republican opponent. His reelection *should* have been obvious all along. In the end, however, the triumph turned out to be ephemeral.

The 1948 campaign has been described from almost every angle imaginable. Allen Yarnell, *Democrats and Progressives: The 1948 Presidential Election as a Test of Postwar Liberalism* (Berkeley: University of California Press, 1974), finds that the Wallace candidacy toughened Truman's cold war rhetoric, a charge minimized by Alonzo L. Hamby in *Liberalism and Its Challengers: F.D.R. to Reagan* (New York: Oxford University Press, 1985) and *Beyond the New Deal: Harry S. Truman and American Liberalism* (New York: Columbia University Press, 1973). A comprehensive, readable, and dramatic account may be found in Irwin Ross, *The Loneliest Campaign: The Truman Victory of 1948* (New York: New American Library, 1968), but it should be read along with Richard S. Kirkendall's essay in Arthur Schlesinger, Jr., and Fred Israel, eds., *History of American Presidential Elections, 1789–1968*, vol.4 (New York: Chelsea House, 1971), which refutes the "lonely candidate" thesis.

HERBERT S. PARMET

See also Americans for Democratic Action; Democratic Party; Dixiecrats; Dewey, Thomas Edmund; Elections in the Truman Era; Progressive Party; Republican Party; Thurmond, James Strom; Wallace, Henry Agard

Election of 1950

The mid-term elections of President Truman's second administration occurred while the nation was facing many major issues. Their results lowered Truman's prestige, harmed his domestic and foreign programs, and set the stage for the Democratic party's loss in the following presidential election.

In May 1950 in Chicago, President Truman made a speech at the National Democratic Conference and Jefferson Jubilee, marking the opening of the 1950 congressional campaign. In his address Truman praised the Democratic party and its leaders in Congress and denounced the senators and representatives who had tried to defeat his Fair Deal and civil rights proposals. He said, "Now I hope by next January that some of the worst obstructionists will be removed." The Korean War began a few days later, preventing Truman from extensive campaigning. But three days before the election in a speech in Saint Louis he accused Republicans of being captives of the special interests, and he charged isolationist leaders with endangering the progress toward peace that had been made under a bipartisan foreign policy. On the farm issue, he declared, "Any farmer who votes for the Republican Party ought to have his head examined."

In the election campaigns Republicans charged that Democrats were soft on Communism, these charges set in the milieu of Senator Joseph McCarthy's claims that Communists were subverting the nation. Republicans also charged the Truman administration with corruption, some of it reaching to the White House staff. Truman's insistence on verbally supporting Alger Hiss, even though the latter had been convicted of perjury, gave Republicans election ammunition. Finally, Republicans played on the public's concern over growing inflation, rising taxes, labor unrest, and shortages of consumer goods.

The results of the elections were a setback for the Democrats. They suffered a loss of five seats in the Senate, retaining only nominal control of that chamber by two votes. In the House the Democrats lost twenty-eight seats, and their majority was reduced from ninety-two to thirty-five. Because some liberal Democrats had been defeated for reelection and since most of the southern Democrats were conservatives, Truman supporters were in a minority.

The results of the elections of 1950 strengthened congressional foes of Truman's Fair Deal, enabling them to prevent passage of his proposals. The Republican victories previewed Dwight D. Eisenhower's election to the presidency in 1952.

An excellent discussion of the 1950 elections is in Harold F. Gosnell, *Truman's Crises: A Political Biography of Harry S. Truman* (Westport, Conn.: Greenwood Press, 1980). For the impact of civil rights issues on the election and its results, see Donald R. McCoy and Richard T. Ruetten, *Quest and Response: Minority Rights and the Truman Administration* (Lawrence: University Press of Kansas, 1973).

MONROE BILLINGTON

See also Democratic Party; Elections in the Truman Era; Republican Party

Election of 1952

Even though Harry S. Truman was not a candidate in 1952, the election that year was a referendum on his presidency. The Democratic candidate, Governor Adlai Stevenson of Illinois, tried to distance himself from the administration, but found himself saddled with the liabilities that Truman himself would have faced as a candidate: the frustrating and bloody war in Korea, corruption in the administration, and allegations of "softness" toward domestic Communism. The fact that the GOP candidate, Gen. Dwight D. Eisenhower, was a bona fide military hero made Stevenson's task even greater.

Both parties underwent spirited internal battles to select their presidential nominees. In the Democratic party, Truman's announcement in late March 1952 that he would not run again left the field wide open. The party eventually settled on Stevenson (who had captivated the convention by his eloquent welcoming speech) over preconvention front-runners Estes Kefauver of Tennessee and Richard Russell of Georgia. Alabama senator John Sparkman was selected as Stevenson's running mate. The contest for the GOP nomination was between Senator Robert A. Taft, the favorite of party conservatives, and Gen. Dwight D. Eisenhower, backed by the moderate internationalist wing. After a bitter floor fight at the convention, Eisenhower was nominated. The strongly anti-Communist senator Richard Nixon of California was then nominated for the vice presidency.

The campaign was marked by considerable excitement. In September, Nixon's place on the Republican ticket was threatened by allegations that he controlled a large slush fund, but he saved himself by a masterful (if mawkish) televised speech, dubbed the "Checkers speech" because in it he insisted that the family's pet dog, Checkers, was the only possibly inappropriate gift he had ever accepted. In early October, Eisenhower made a flagrant miscue by seeming to endorse Senator Joseph McCarthy's vicious denunciation of Gen. George C. Marshall as a traitor. Any damage this gaffe might have done to Eisenhower's campaign, however, was countered by his dramatic pronouncement on 24 October that, to find a solution to the war, he would "go to Korea."

The election results were predictable. Eisenhower swamped Stevenson, taking 55 percent of the popular vote and winning the electoral college, 442–89. Meanwhile, the GOP won control of both houses of Congress for the first time since 1928 (48–47 in the Senate, with one independent; 221–214 in the House).

The outcome represented both a personal victory for Eisenhower and a repudiation of the Truman administration. The most important issues could be summarized as "K_1C_2" (Korea, corruption, and Communism). Analysis of the vote showed that the shift to Eisenhower and the Republicans had occurred in virtually all classes and groups, a phenomenon that marked 1952 as a classic "surge" election—one in which all short-term forces operated in favor of one party. The election has also been labeled a "deviating" election, since the normal majority remained intact while the minority won a temporary victory. This was apparent only later, of course; at the time, Eisenhower's victory appeared to be the harbinger of a new Republican era.

Charles Werner, *Indianapolis Star*, 19 September 1952.

The best concise treatment of the 1952 election is Barton J. Bernstein's essay, "The Election of 1952," in Arthur M. Schlesinger, Jr., and Fred Israel, eds., *History of American Presidential Elections, 1789–1968*, 4 vols. (New York: Chelsea House, 1971), 4:3215–3337. Preconvention activities in both parties are exhaustively covered in Paul T. David, Malcolm Moos, and Ralph Goldman, eds., *Presidential Nominating Politics in 1952*, 5 vols. (Baltimore: Johns Hopkins University Press, 1954). The best general study of political conditions that led to the Republican victory is Samuel Lubell, *The Future of American Politics*, rev. ed. (New York: Harper Colophon Books, 1965).

GARY W. REICHARD

See also Democratic Party; Eisenhower, Dwight David; Elections in the Truman Era; Republican Party; Stevenson, Adlai Ewing

Elections in the Truman Era

Elections in the Truman era (1946–52) demonstrated that the new Democratic majority that had emerged in the Roosevelt years constituted a long-term transformation of the American electorate. Before Harry S. Truman was elevated to the presidency in 1945, the Democratic party had amassed a series of

Lute Pease, 1952. (Library of Congress)

election victories. Franklin D. Roosevelt had won an unprecedented four presidential terms, and the Democratic party had controlled the House of Representatives with substantial majorities since 1930 and the Senate since 1932. It remained to be seen, however, if the Democratic majorities of the thirties and early forties would survive or disintegrate after Roosevelt was no longer a political factor. Indeed, the Republican party enjoyed increased strength in the U.S. Congress after 1938. In the House elected in 1942 the Republicans held only 10 seats fewer than the Democrats, and in 1944, with Roosevelt at the head of the ticket, Republicans still captured 190 House seats. A Republican resurgence in the postwar years seemed probable.

The election of the Eightieth Congress in 1946 provided an even more convincing indication that the Democrats might be losing control of the national government (see the accompanying table). Truman, suffering from inevitable comparisons with Roosevelt, was a disappointment to many northern liberal Democrats, and national politics was wracked by the tensions of postwar readjustment and the frustrations of the cold war. In the Eightieth Congress, for the first time since 1932, both Houses of Congress were controlled by the Republicans;

Truman seemed thoroughly discredited; and public opinion polls predicted that in 1948 the Republicans would win a presidential election for the first time since Hoover's victory in 1928.

The Republicans nominated Thomas E. Dewey of New York for president in 1948, and Truman was the choice of a glum, quarrelsome Democratic convention. Furious at the adoption of a strong civil rights platform, southern extremists formed the States' Rights Democrat (Dixiecrat) party and nominated Governor J. Strom Thurmond of South Carolina for president. To make Truman's prospects seem even more hopeless, Henry Wallace, one of Truman's outspoken Democratic critics, ran for president on a Progressive party ticket. Few gave Truman any chance to win, but he confidently launched a vigorous whistle-stop campaign in which he tailored his appeal to the ethnic and economic groups of the New Deal coalition. By a very slim margin Truman won perhaps the greatest upset victory in the history of presidential elections. Thurmond, the Dixiecrat candidate, did well in the Deep South where he carried four states, but he won only 2.4 percent of the national popular vote. Wallace, the Progressive, carried 8.3 percent of the vote in New York State, but his share of the national vote was also only 2.4 percent and he won no electoral votes. Democrats, furthermore, regained control of both the House of Representatives and the Senate.

Democrats retained control of both houses of Congress throughout Truman's second term by winning majorities again in the mid-term election of 1950, and Truman fought valiantly for the extension of New Deal reforms. His second term, however, was dominated by issues of the cold war—the McCarthy red scare, the collapse of Chiang Kai-shek's government in China, and the war in Korea. In 1952 the Republicans nominated the World War II hero Dwight D. Eisenhower for president, and Adlai Stevenson, governor of Illinois, became the Democratic standard-bearer. Stevenson distinguished himself as an eloquent and dignified campaigner, but he was no match in the public eye for General Eisenhower who won a landslide victory. Stevenson carried no states outside the South; several southern states voted for the general; and a Republican majority was elected in both houses of Congress.

Although the Truman era ended with a resounding victory for the Republican party, most analysts believed that a majority, or at least a plurality, of voters still identified with the Democratic party. Samuel Lubell, writing at the time in his classic *The*

Presidential Election Returns and Distribution of Seats in U.S. Congress, 1946–52

YEAR	VOTE FOR PRESIDENT		ELECTORAL VOTE FOR PRESIDENT	NUMBER OF SEATS, HOUSE		NUMBER OF SEATS, SENATE	
	Total	Percent					
1946				Dem	188	Dem	45
				Rep	245	Rep	51
1948	Truman 24,105,587	49.51	303	Dem	263	Dem	54
	Dewey 21,970,017	45.12	189	Rep	171	Rep	42
1950				Dem	234	Dem	49
				Rep	199	Rep	47
1952	Stevenson 27,314,649	44.38	442	Dem	211	Dem	48
	Eisenhower 33,936,137	55.13	89	Rep	221	Rep	47

Source: Congressional Quarterly, Inc., *Guide to U.S. Elections* (Washington, D.C.: Congressional Quarterly, 1975), 154–255, 293–94, 928.

Future of American Politics, concluded that the groups that made up the Democratic majority of the 1930s "were sufficiently divided to elect a Republican President, but . . . there still was no evidence that the Roosevelt coalition had disintegrated hopelessly and that a basic realignment of party strength was about to take place." The authors of *The American Voter* agreed. This group of social scientists argued that at least as late as 1956 a plurality of Americans identified themselves as Democrats. They concluded that the election of Truman in 1948 was a "maintaining" election—that is, an election in which "the pattern of partisan attachments prevailing in the preceding period persists and is the primary influence on forces governing the vote." The election of 1952, on the other hand, was a "deviating election," one in which "the basic division of partisan loyalties is not seriously disturbed, but the attitude forces on the vote are such as to bring about the defeat of the majority party." Thus in 1952, and in the election of 1956 as well, many Democrats voted for Eisenhower but continued to think of themselves as Democrats.

On the other hand, a considerable body of evidence exists to show that the Democratic majority was already in a process of disintegration and change by 1946. In 1951 Lubell reported evidence of an "economic and social revolution" in the South which he believed would bring fundamental alterations in the political system. Modernization of agriculture, urbanization, and industrialization, the development of a "new, politically insurgent middle class," and a new intensity in the demands of black southerners for equal rights suggested that many voters in the South would soon "bolt the Democratic ranks and make common cause with the Republicans in the North." Other scholars writing more recently reached similar conclusions. Everett C. Ladd and Charles D. Hadley in *Transformations of the American Party System* concluded that the sharp drop in the Democratic presidential vote in 1948 in the South was a decline "from which there has been no recovery." Truman won just over half (52 percent) of the vote in the South in 1948, and in 1952 and 1956 Stevenson could claim even a smaller portion. The percentage of southerners who identified themselves as Democrats slowly but steadily declined after the election of 1948 to the point that two decades later less than half of the southerners polled identified themselves as Democrats. In the Truman and Eisenhower years, however, the realignment of southern voters was confined largely to voting at the presidential level.

Other less dramatic but still significant changes in the Democratic coalition of the 1930s also began to take shape in the elections of the Truman era. James L. Sundquist in *Dynamics of the Party System* documented measurable, if at first small shifts to the Democrats in sixteen states outside the South. These shifts Sundquist observed amounted to "aftershocks of the earthquake that changed the shape of the party system in the New Deal era." Democratic strength increased in the late 1940s and 1950s as nonsouthern states developed more popular and effective Democratic political organizations. Ladd and Hadley noted that the Democratic percentage of the aggregate national vote for the House of Representatives declined after World War II and then slowly increased throughout the 1950s, and voters who identified themselves as Democrats consistently outnumbered Republican identifiers by a substantial margin throughout the Truman and Eisenhower years.

Ladd and Hadley attributed a substantial portion of this increased Democratic strength to gains in the northern middle class. An increase in the standard of living of most Americans after the end of the depression elevated many Democrats to middle-class status, and they and their children continued to vote Democratic in the postwar years. The nature of the middle class changed, moreover, as the proportion of the work force trained as managers and professionals increased. This "new" middle class had little reason to become Republican, and it found the Democratic commitment to a greater role for government compatible with its own interests and values. Although Americans of above average socioeconomic status remained substantially Republican, the shift to the Democrats in this high-status group was significant. Even so, the makeup of the coalition that gave the Democratic party majority status in the elections of the Truman era evolved only slightly after 1946. Except for the South, at least as late as 1960 the Democratic party claimed the loyalty of most urban industrial workers, Catholics, Jews, and blacks—the economic and ethnic groups that had constituted the core of the Democratic majority since the Great Depression.

Samuel Lubell's *The Future of American Politics*, 3d rev. ed. (New York: Harper & Row, Colophon Books, 1965), first published in 1951, is a perceptive study of the politics of the 1930s and 1940s. *The American Voter* (New York: John Wiley, 1960) by Angus Campbell, Philip E. Converse, Warren E. Miller, and Donald E. Stokes is mainly a study of voting behavior in the 1950s, but it provides very useful analyses of the 1930s and 1940s. Two indispensable studies that examine the evolution of the Democratic coalition in the 1940s and 1950s are James L. Sundquist, *Dynamics of the Party System: Alignment and Realignment of Political Parties in the United States* (Washington, D.C.: Brookings Institution, 1973), and Everett C. Ladd, Jr., and Charles D. Hadley, *Transformations of the American Party System: Political Coalitions from the New Deal to the 1970s*, 2d rev. ed. (New York: W. W. Norton, 1978). Jerome M. Clubb, William H. Flanigan, and Nancy H. Zingale, *Partisan Realignment: Voters, Parties, and Government in American History*, Sage Library of Social Research, vol. 108 (Beverly Hills: Sage Publications, 1980), is an excellent analysis of the New Deal realignment in the 1930s and the early stages of the deterioration of the new majority in the Truman years. The best published source of election statistics and other political data is Congressional Quarterly, Inc., *Guide to U.S. Elections* (Washington, D.C.: Congressional Quarterly, 1975). For studies that concentrate especially on the election of 1948, see Angus Campbell and Robert L. Kahn, *The People Elect a President* (Ann Arbor, Mich.: Survey Research Center, Institute for Social Research, 1952); Susan M. Hartmann, *Truman and the 80th Congress* (Columbia: University of Missouri Press, 1971); and Irwin Ross, *The Loneliest Campaign: The Truman Victory of 1948* (New York: New American Library, 1968).

HOWARD W. ALLEN

See also Congress, United States; Democratic Party; Dewey, Thomas Edmund; Dixiecrats; Eightieth Congress; Eisenhower, Dwight David; Election of 1946; Election of 1948; Election of 1950; Election of 1952; Progressive Party; Public Opinion Polling; Republican Party; South, The; Stevenson, Adlai Ewing; Thurmond, James Strom; Wallace, Henry Agard

Elsey, George McKee

(5 February 1918–)

George M. Elsey became one of Harry Truman's most valuable administrative aides through his contributions to the administration's foreign and defense policies and presidential leadership. Intelligence summaries written by Elsey while serving as an assistant naval aide in the White House intelligence and communications center during World War II facilitated Truman's preparations for the conduct of foreign affairs. The summaries also provided a model for the seminal report assembled in the summer of 1946 by Elsey and Clark Clifford on American-Soviet relations that provided undergirding for Truman's major cold war policies.

Elsey's writing skills and strong advocacy of presidential power drew him into domestic affairs beginning with the State of the Union message of 1947 and subsequent messages and speeches through 1951. He was the principal writer of Truman's 1948 whistle-stop campaign talks. Elsey was also responsible for reorienting Truman's inaugural speech from domestic to foreign affairs and for introducing a minor State Department official's idea for technical assistance to developing countries as Point Four of that message. He was heavily involved in managing the administration's public handling of its Korean War policies when he was transferred to the Mutual Defense Administration in December 1951. Elsey continued to assist the president's speech writers until Truman left office.

For the next several years Elsey worked as an official of several large organizations and corporations. In 1968 he reentered government service to serve as assistant secretary of defense in the administration of Lyndon B. Johnson. He assumed the presidency of the American Red Cross in 1970 and served in that capacity until 1983, when he became president emeritus.

For an analysis and description of Elsey's tasks, see Robert Underhill, *The Truman Persuasions* (Ames: Iowa State University Press, 1981). A biographical sketch of Elsey appears in Eleanora W. Schoenebaum, ed., *Political Profiles: The Truman Years* (New York: Facts on File, 1978). Elsey's papers and an oral history interview are housed in the Truman Library.

FRANKLIN D. MITCHELL

See also Clifford, Clark McAdams; Point Four Program; Speeches and Speech Writing

Employment Act of 1946

The Employment Act of 1946 established the Joint Economic Committee in Congress and the Council of Economic Advisers in the executive branch. It was the last manifestation of the New Deal commitment to full employment during the period of reconversion after World War II. The act, which mandated the federal government to develop policies aimed at the goal of full employment, was interventionist in intent. It sought to balance private marketplace decisions with federal policies on government spending so as to maintain employment and economic growth.

After the unexpectedly sudden end to the war in the Pacific in early August 1945, the economics of reconversion became Truman's major domestic political problem. Liberals and organized labor, fearing that postwar unemployment would reach levels comparable to those of the Great Depression, insisted that Truman prove himself the proper heir of Franklin Roosevelt by pushing for a revival of the New Deal, including its goal of full employment.

Truman's chances of retaining control of Congress in the 1946 elections hinged on holding the Left in the Democratic coalition. But the president's attempts in 1945 to work with conservative Democrats from rural districts had failed to win their support for his liberal program. Disillusioned with Truman's leadership, organized labor struck the auto and steel industries for substantially higher wages, thereby adding to the political disarray as well as to postwar inflation.

The Employment Act was the only piece of New Deal–style legislation to emerge from the hostile Seventy-ninth Congress, and many liberals considered it only a weak compromise. Truman's failures with Congress and the alienation of liberals and labor resulted in Democratic apathy and a Republican victory in the 1946 elections, their first since 1928.

On the politics of the reconversion period, see Mary H. Blewett, "Roosevelt, Truman, and the Attempt to Revive the New Deal," in *Harry S. Truman and the Fair Deal*, ed. Alonzo L. Hamby, 78–92 (Lexington, Mass: D. C. Heath, 1974). For an account of the passage of the legislation, see Stephen L. Bailey, *Congress Makes a Law* (New York: Random House, 1950). For information on the law and its use by the administration, see Hugh S. Norton, Mary A. Holman, and Saul Engelbourg, *The Employment Act and the Council of Economic Advisers, 1946–1976* (Columbia: University of South Carolina Press, 1977).

MARY H. BLEWETT

See also Council of Economic Advisers; Economy, The; Labor

England

See Great Britain

Evans, Thomas Lynn

(1 September 1896–1 September 1970)

Business executive and close friend of Harry S. Truman. Although born in Larned, Kansas, Evans spent most of his life in Kansas City, Missouri. There the enterprising Evans rose from a drugstore clerk to the wealthy owner of a chain of drugstores. In the early 1910s, Evans worked for the powerful Pendergast machine, which dominated Kansas City politics. During this time, Evans befriended Harry S. Truman, also a supporter of the machine. Evans and Truman remained lifelong friends.

In the 1920s, Evans was a fund-raiser and adviser during Truman's campaigns for the Jackson County judgeships. In later years, Truman repeatedly turned to Evans for similar assistance. Evans raised campaign money for Truman's election to the U.S. Senate in 1934 and for his Senate reelection in 1940.

He also helped guide Truman to the vice presidency in 1944. He was with Truman at critical strategy sessions during the 1944 Democratic National Convention in Chicago, when Truman reluctantly agreed to accept the vice-presidential nomination. Evans and other Truman associates then worked the convention to prevent a late surge by vice-presidential contender Henry Wallace. Truman's campaign manager for the 1944 race, the Kansas City businessman raised abundant funds and traveled on Truman's campaign train as it crisscrossed the country.

After Truman became president, Evans, now the owner of the Kansas City radio station KCMO, turned down an offer of a government post. He was, however, a frequent guest at the White House, the visitor whom the press often referred to as the president's "mystery man." When Truman returned to Missouri in 1953, he and Evans remained close. Evans visited Truman regularly and helped establish the Truman Library. Evans died in Kansas City in 1970.

Tom L. Evans's 787-page oral history interview is an indispensable source. This document, along with Evans's personal papers, is at the Truman Library. For a brief overview of Evan's career, see *The National Cyclopedia of American Biography* (Clifton, N.J.: James T. White, 1977), 57:448–49. Alfred Steinberg's *The Man from Missouri: The Life and Times of Harry S. Truman* (New York: G. P. Putnam's Sons, 1962) and Robert H. Ferrell's *Truman: A Centenary Remembrance* (New York: Viking Press, 1984) discuss Evans's role in Truman's career.

JAMES R. RALPH, JR.

See also Election of 1944

Executive Branch, Reorganization of the

Within days of Harry S. Truman's assumption of the presidency, he began to reorganize the executive branch of government. His first special message to Congress on 24 May 1945 was to request renewal of the president's authority to submit reorganization plans to Congress using the legislative veto procedure. After making extensive use of this authority for the next seven years, Truman boasted at the end of his presidency that he had accomplished more administrative reform than "all the other Presidents put together."

Truman turned quickly to administrative reform because such activity had often been a source of his success in the past. Truman's service in World War I gave him his first major administrative experience. He found that clear lines of command and orderly procedures provided a base from which he could exercise effective leadership. His experience as county court judge reaffirmed these lessons, winning him great approval for offering effective, businesslike administration in Jackson County, Missouri. Later his Senate committees gave him a good founda-

President Truman with former president Herbert Hoover, who was unanimously chosen chair of the twelve-member Commission on Organization of the Executive Branch of Government. 29 September 1947. (National Archives)

tion for understanding the operations of the executive branch of the federal government.

Conditions in 1945 also encouraged Truman to initiate reorganization. After years of extensive governmental change in response to the depression and war crises, the executive branch, Truman believed, had to prepare itself to enter a new era. Labor, welfare, and housing programs were a disorganized mess, he maintained; the State Department was poorly prepared to meet new global responsibilities; the military services needed unification in response to technological innovations and changing strategic goals. Poor organization led to such flawed performance by the bureaucracy that Truman believed it endangered the New Deal legacy. Although polls indicated that most people supported the New Deal reforms, one revealed that 53 percent of the respondents regarded the bureaucracy needed to carry out the programs as an "unmitigated evil." Truman, then, felt that he could protect the New Deal by reforming its administrative apparatus.

Despite opposition to reorganization from those who feared that change would adversely affect their interests, Truman won two grants of reorganization authority—the Reorganization Acts of 1945 and 1949—with the 1945 legislation the strongest such grant won by any president, before or since. Under these acts, Truman submitted forty-eight reorganization plans, thirty-three of which passed. He also cooperated with the Commission on Organization of the Executive Branch of the Government (the first Hoover Commission), a conservative body established by the Eightieth Congress in preparation for the anticipated Republican takeover of the White House after the election of 1948. Although the Hoover Commission set out to prepare a blueprint for dismantling the New Deal, Truman and his advisers converted the group into an effective body to advise on how to make the existing governmental structure work better.

Responding to Truman initiatives, Congress brought the military services together in the Department of Defense, rebuilt the Department of Labor, and gathered like programs into unified agencies to prepare the way for the later creation of the Departments of Health, Education and Welfare, Transportation, and Housing and Urban Development. As Washington built its global empire, Truman also helped construct the basic bureaucratic apparatus undergirding the national security state: the Central Intelligence Agency, the National Security Council, and the Joint Chiefs of Staff.

Reorganization strengthened the presidency, helped remedy some long-standing administrative problems, and reoriented a number of agencies in terms of policy by transferring favored programs to more receptive units than the ones they were in. It made, or gave the impression of making, the "big government" of modern America more efficient, economical, and controllable by the chief executive. Truman passed along to President Dwight D. Eisenhower a government probably as "inherently manageable" as it had ever been, according to Laurin L. Henry in his study of presidential transitions.

The Truman Library, Hoover Library, and National Archives contain most of the records generated by Truman's executive reorganization program. Peri E. Arnold traces the use of reorganization to create the modern managerial presidency in *Making the Managerial Presidency: Comprehensive Reorganization Planning, 1905–1980* (Princeton: Princeton University Press, 1986). William E. Pemberton analyzes the politics of administrative reform in *Bureaucratic Politics: Executive Reorganization during the Truman Administration* (Columbia: University of Missouri Press, 1979). Laurin L. Henry takes the measure of executive organization at the end of the Truman presidency in *Presidential Transitions* (Washington, D.C.: Brookings Institution, 1960).

WILLIAM E. PEMBERTON

See also Armed Forces, Unification of the; Central Intelligence Agency; Hoover, Herbert Clark; Joint Chiefs of Staff; National Security Council

Executive Order 9835

See Loyalty Program

F

Fair Deal

On 5 January 1949, President Truman delivered before Congress his State of the Union message, in which he pledged to "try to give every segment of our population a fair deal." With this passage, the president provided commentators with a label for his domestic programs, and not just those of his second term but those of his entire tenure as president.

Then and later, the Fair Deal served as a yardstick for measuring Truman's policies against the New Deal liberalism of his predecessor, Franklin D. Roosevelt. From 1933 through 1938, the heyday of the New Deal, Roosevelt had applied the full measure of his presidential powers in an attempt to lift the United States out of the Great Depression. With an occasional push from Congress, he had employed a variety of regulatory, fiscal, monetary, and welfare policies to discipline the capitalist system, elevate organized labor and agriculture to parity with big business, and make the federal government responsible for the economic stability of the country and the economic security of the individual. The New Deal permanently altered institutional relationships, but it failed to end the depression. After 1938, a coalition of Republicans and conservative Democrats in Congress stymied further reform efforts, and economic recovery had to await the industrial surge unleashed by World War II.

Liberals who envisaged a new era of reform at war's end were distraught when Truman entered the White House upon Roosevelt's death. To them, the new president's liberal credentials were highly questionable. As a senator, Truman had voted for New Deal legislation out of conviction when it reflected his midwestern progressivism, out of party loyalty when it violated his more cautious border-state instincts. Like FDR, he accepted the capitalist system (he dismissed liberal theorists who sought alternatives to capitalism as "crackpots"), and he believed it proper for the federal government to tackle economic and social problems. But he was less comfortable with Roosevelt's erratic experimentation and resort to deficit spending. Truman was, according to Robert Donovan, a pragmatic, middle-of-the-road senator, "a doer, not a dreamer." Compared to FDR, however, he seemed to many liberals a hick, a party hack, a man lacking sophistication, charisma, and vision—hardly the desirable heir to Roosevelt's legacy.

It is doubtful that Roosevelt himself could have fulfilled the hopes of ardent New Dealers. The conservative bloc still dominated Congress, but more important, the war had changed economic realities by ushering in what historian Barton Bernstein has called "the politics of inflation." Roosevelt had expanded Democratic rolls by dribbling out benefits to down-and-out groups grateful for anything they could get during the depression. Truman, on the other hand, confronted inflation as the major threat to postwar economic stability. To him, keeping inflation under control required withholding the higher wages and prices that many interest groups demanded with the passing of the depression. He tried to hold the line against pressures from business, farmers, workers, and consumers, but some appeals proved too strong to resist, especially when his closest supporters were offering conflicting advice over the wisdom of continuing wartime controls. Concessions, although inevitable, were made in an atmosphere of such confusion as to raise further doubts about his political acumen and leadership abilities. Until Truman could devise a more positive approach to the politics of inflation, his administration would continue to founder to the detriment of his personal popularity.

It took two years for that new approach to take shape. Meanwhile, after a hesitant beginning, Truman tried to keep his promise to expand and extend Roosevelt's programs. On 6 September, less than one month after the end of hostilities, he submitted to Congress, against the wishes of his more conservative advisers, a twenty-one-point plan for reconversion to peacetime. Among the proposals for economic development and social welfare contained in the message were a full-employment bill, unemployment compensation, an increase in the minimum wage and its extension to agricultural workers, a permanent Fair Employment Practices Committee (FEPC) to prevent discrimination in the hiring of minorities, a continuation of farm price supports, "public funds to clear slums and provide homes" for

Fred Packer, *New York Mirror*, 16 July 1952.

lower-income families, hospital construction, a limited tax reduction, and more public works projects to develop and conserve America's resources.

Liberals initially praised Truman for "outdealing" the New Deal, but congressional Republicans recoiled at the prospect of more "socialistic" legislation that would increase the power of the federal government to the detriment of the private sector. Besides echoing this view, conservative southern Democrats voiced their opposition to civil rights and to the proworker measures that could only increase the power of organized labor in a party traditionally dominated by its southern wing. Against the formidable power of the conservative coalition, Truman appeared ineffectual, even intimidated. His acceptance of an employment bill that omitted mandatory government spending to create jobs and his refusal to fight for the FEPC again brought into question his commitment to progressive programs. His frequent reversals on wartime controls and his feud with striking labor unions during the chaotic days of reconversion further alienated the liberal wing of the New Deal coalition (not to mention just about every other segment of the population). The 1946 elections, in which the GOP captured both houses of Congress for the first time in almost two decades, convinced many Democrats that they should no longer look to Truman as their standard-bearer.

The president, however, was not ready to abdicate his role as party leader. As the new Republican-dominated Eightieth Congress began hacking away at New Deal achievements, Truman and his advisers were devising a strategy to enhance his political appeal. As usual the inner circle split along conservative-liberal lines and as usual the president sided with the more liberal group. The strategy, which became the basis of the Fair Deal, combined the political savvy of Truman's special assistant Clark Clifford and the theories of economist Leon Keyserling. As described by historian Alonzo Hamby, what became known as the Fair Deal attempted "to adapt the New Deal tradition to postwar prosperity." Abundance, not scarcity, was the new economic reality, according to Keyserling. The war had demonstrated capitalism's capacity for unlimited growth, and that productive power provided the key to keeping inflation under control (by providing ample goods to meet demand) while ensuring all Americans a decent standard of living without having to redistribute the wealth. The federal government would continue to police the economy and provide services the private sector could not, but it no longer needed to restrict production (as the New Deal had done as a means of raising prices to foster recovery). To Keyserling, cooperation between government and the private sector was essential to ensure economic growth. On the political front, Truman would move *beyond* the New Deal by supporting programs designed to improve the quality of life in America.

In his 1948 State of the Union message, Truman asked Congress to legislate a "poor man's" tax cut, public housing, civil rights, a national health insurance program, federal aid to education, and the extension of New Deal benefits. These proposals were not new; they had just never received the priority the White House now accorded them. In succeeding weeks, Truman kept the pressure on Congress by submitting a series of messages demanding action on his legislative programs. The most controversial message concerned civil rights and endorsed legal (but not social) equality for blacks. Truman knew that Congress would reject his overtures, but that was part of the strategy. Having established his credentials as FDR's disciple and an innovative leader in his own right, he had built a platform that would carry him through the 1948 presidential campaign.

Hopes that Truman's "miracle" victory and the return of Democratic majorities to Congress would clear the way for Fair Deal reforms vanished inside of two years. The Republican–conservative Democrat coalition in Congress remained intact, while many liberals were skeptical of Keyserling's advocacy of consensus between the public and private sectors. The new Congress did extend certain New Deal programs and passed a public housing bill that, although catering to private interests, represented a significant legislative breakthrough. But the Taft-Hartley Act stayed on the books, a national health insurance program and Truman's proposals for farm legislation (the Brannan Plan) were dismissed as socialistic, and civil rights bills were filibustered to death (although Truman used his executive powers to desegregate the civil service and armed forces). War in Korea partially vindicated Keyserling's reliance on growth to check inflationary pressures, but the war, McCarthyism, and scandal directed public debate away from domestic reform, virtually foreclosing action on further Fair Deal legislation.

The historical verdict on the Fair Deal has yet to be rendered. Conservatives view it as another step toward big government and away from individual freedom, although many have made their peace with several of the programs Congress passed. Liberals tend to praise the Fair Deal for consolidating and extending New Deal legislation while adapting liberalism to the economic and social realities of the postwar world. New Left historians question Truman's commitment to civil rights and liberties and criticize the Fair Deal for ignoring too many of

America's disadvantaged and for accepting corporate capitalism and its inherent exploitative practices. These different views cannot be reconciled except to the extent that their proponents would agree that in providing the link between the New Deal and the Great Society of the 1960s, the Fair Deal set the agenda for domestic political debate for nearly two decades after Truman left the White House.

Sources of information on various aspects of the Fair Deal include *Public Papers of the Presidents of the United States: Harry S. Truman, 1945, 1948, 1949* (Washington, D.C.: U.S. Government Printing Office, 1961, 1964); Harry S. Truman, *Memoirs*, 2 vols. (Garden City, N.Y.: Doubleday, 1955, 1956); Robert J. Donovan, *Conflict and Crisis: The Presidency of Harry S Truman, 1945–1948* (New York: W. W. Norton, 1977) and *Tumultuous Years: The Presidency of Harry S Truman, 1949–1953* (New York: W. W. Norton, 1982); Alonzo L. Hamby, *Beyond the New Deal: Harry S. Truman and American Liberalism* (New York: Columbia University Press, 1973); Barton Bernstein, "The Politics of Inflation" (Ph.D. diss., Harvard University, 1963); and Alonzo L. Hamby, ed., *Harry S. Truman and the Fair Deal* (Lexington, Mass.: D. C. Heath, 1974).

LAWRENCE A. YATES

See also Brannan, Charles Franklin; Civil Rights; Employment Act of 1946; Fair Employment Practices Committee; Housing; Keyserling, Leon; National Health Insurance; Social Security; Urban Redevelopment

Fair Employment Practices Committee

Of all the committees concerned with civil rights, the Fair Employment Practices Committee (FEPC) may have had the longest and most tortuous history. It had its origins in Franklin D. Roosevelt's administration when, under pressure from A. Philip Randolph's march on Washington movement, the president issued an executive order in June 1941 creating a committee to oversee a policy of nondiscrimination in government employment and in private industries with defense contracts. Reorganized in 1943, Roosevelt's committee met its demise in June 1946 when Congress refused to authorize further appropriations.

From the onset of his presidency, Truman urged legislation to establish a permanent FEPC not only because he believed in its moral imperative but also because he was under pressure from black leaders who increasingly saw the significance of employment opportunity in their struggle for equal rights. By 1949, for example, the NAACP was giving the FEPC first priority.

Truman included appeals for a statutory FEPC in his State of the Union addresses and in his historic civil rights message of 2 February 1948. Over the years, opponents in and out of Congress labeled the FEPC un-American and even Communistic. In the campaign of 1948, form postcards mailed to southern workers contended that Truman was seeking to "force you to work with Negroes and other undesirables." Administration-sponsored bills came closest to enactment in 1950 when the House passed the McConnell bill. It lacked adequate enforcement provisions, however, and even it died in the Senate when its proponents failed to achieve cloture on debate.

Indeed, during the Truman presidency, the Senate never once voted directly on the FEPC, although in the ten-year period between 1942 and 1952, a total of seventy such bills were introduced in both houses. In the Senate, a coalition of midwestern Republicans and southern Democrats (with the occasional assistance of some western Democrats) successfully opposed cloture. The first president to champion a statutory FEPC, Truman had to wait until 1964 to see its enactment in the Civil Rights Act of that year, which finally gave legislative legitimacy to the seven presidentially appointed employment committees and boards that existed between 1941 and 1964.

Faced with congressional intransigence during his administration, Truman emulated his predecessor and created two such committees by executive order, the first—the Fair Employment Board in the Civil Service Commission—on 26 July 1948. Then on 3 December 1951—in a belated response to mounting pressure from black leaders and after a series of executive orders that banned discrimination in private industries with government contracts—Truman created the President's Committee on Government Contract Compliance (CGCC). By investing the committee with an inelegant and awkward title, Truman sought to avoid the political onus of the letters "FEPC" and also any connection with Roosevelt's committee because of the restrictions of the Russell amendment of 1944, which subjected FEPC appropriations to congressional approval; the CGCC was funded from existing government agencies. Short-lived and without adequate enforcement powers, the CGCC could not hope for major accomplishment, but its existence made it impossible for subsequent administrations to ignore the political necessity of similar committees.

On the early history of the FEPC, see Louis Ruchames, *Race, Jobs, & Politics: The Story of FEPC* (New York: Columbia University Press, 1953). For Truman's frustrations with Congress over the FEPC, see Donald R. McCoy and Richard T. Ruetten, *Quest and Response: Minority Rights and the Truman Administration* (Lawrence: University Press of Kansas, 1973). For presidential action on the FEPC from Roosevelt to Lyndon Johnson, see Ruth P. Morgan, *The President and Civil Rights: Policy-Making by Executive Order* (New York: St. Martin's Press, 1970).

RICHARD T. RUETTEN

See also Civil Rights

Family

See Ancestry; individual family members

Farm Experience

After Harry S. Truman graduated from high school in 1901, he worked for several years in Kansas City banks. Although he believed that finance was one of the paths, along with farming and the military, that men usually followed to success, even greatness, he found that banking did not fulfill him. By 1906, he was ready to try farming. His grandmother Harriet Louisa Young and his uncle Harrison Young persuaded his parents, John and Martha Truman, to move to the family farm near Grandview, Missouri, and take over management of that large operation. In 1906 Harry joined his family and stayed on the farm eleven years. He regarded his move to the farm as an opportunity to change the direction of his life: "I thought of Cincinnatus and a lot of other farm boys who had made good and I thought maybe by cussing mules and plowing corn I could perhaps overcome my shyness and amount to something."

He found these years satisfying in many ways. He established himself as a man of worth in his father's eyes and proved to himself that he could do the physical labor and mental work involved in running a large, diverse operation of 600 acres (the average Missouri farm was 125 acres) with an additional several hundred acres of rented land. After his father died in 1914, he had to run the whole operation himself, with the help of farmhands. His self-confidence grew, and he toughened physically, learning to handle animals and machinery and farmhands and to make complicated decisions based on the weather, commodity markets, interest rates, and the other imponderables that farmers confronted.

Most observers agreed that the Trumans were good farmers, perhaps above average, and the farm was in an excellent location to tap the nearby Kansas City market. Truman later recalled that it brought in about fifteen thousand dollars a year. Yet, he wrote, as thousands of farmers had before and have since: "We never did catch up with our debts. We always owed the bank something—sometimes more, sometimes less—but we always owed the bank." After Louisa Young died in 1909, a lawsuit over the estate burdened the farm with a huge mortgage. Poor crops, low prices, weather disasters, John's death, and Harry's leaving the farm for war service compounded the difficulties.

But despite the hardships, these were not bleak years for Truman. He improved farm operations and output and won the respect of most of his neighbors. He served as president of a local Farm Bureau chapter, worked with the 4-H Club, joined

the Baptist church, and became active in Freemasonry. He attended the parties, box suppers, and picnics of rural society and enjoyed the cultural life of nearby Kansas City. Historian Richard Kirkendall believes that it was during these years that Truman underwent an important personality change that prepared him for politics: he became more gregarious, sociable, and self-confident than in his earlier years.

Truman got over his shyness enough to take quick advantage of an opportunity to reestablish contact with Bess Wallace. Bess brought a new focus to Harry's life, and his struggle for financial success on the farm assumed added intensity. He wrote her: "I am so crazy to make things go I can hardly stand it." In 1916, when the high farm prices brought on by World War I still did not provide the financial breakthrough that Truman wanted, he tried to make a quick return by investing in and helping manage a mining firm and an oil company, but both failed.

When the war started in Europe, it did not seem to make an impact on Truman at first. But banking and farming had not fulfilled him; his dreams of wealth in mining and oil had not paid off; and the farm seemed now to offer only a life of drudgery. When Woodrow Wilson took the United States into the war, Truman seized the opportunity to leave the farm, never to return.

Nevertheless, he did not regard his farm years as wasted. He had learned to manage an organization, to free the gregarious and sociable aspects of his personality, and to take risks to achieve his goals. He saw clearly that his time on the farm had given him the maturity and confidence he needed to move on to other careers.

In his *Memoirs* and other writings, Truman often referred briefly to his life on the farm. The best record of those years is found in the many letters he wrote to Bess Wallace, in which he discussed his daily work, social activities, and dreams for the future. These letters are at the Truman Library. The library also holds several oral history interviews with people who remembered Truman as a farmer, including one by Gaylon Babcock whose views of Truman as a farmer were less than flattering. The Grandview farm has been restored and is open to the public. Richard S. Kirkendall provides the best examination of the Truman farm operations and a convincing analysis of the meaning of these years for Truman's personality development in "Harry S. Truman: A Missouri Farmer in the Golden Age," *Agricultural History* 48 (October 1974): 467–83.

WILLIAM E. PEMBERTON

See also Truman, John Vivian

The junior partner of J. A. Truman & Son, Farmers, with his mother and maternal grandmother in front of the Grandview farmhouse. (Courtesy of the Harry S. Truman Library)

Farms

See Agriculture

Fascism

Political conceptions of fascism and/or sudden political amnesia about it during the Truman era were shaped by the developing cold war conflicts over defascistization and denazification in

Germany and Europe, and internal political struggles over civil liberties in the United States. Earlier, widely held views of fascism as right-wing dictatorship—dictatorship coming to power with upper- and middle-class support to thwart social revolution and using militarization and war as the solution to internal economic problems—were eclipsed by conceptions of fascism as either mass hysteria or totalitarian politics closer to communism than to traditional authoritarian forms of conservatism.

In the 1920s and 1930s in the United States, the right-wing-dictatorship view (held most actively by Progressives, New Deal liberals, and leftists) was shaped by concrete events such as the enthusiastic welcome that Italian elites and conservatives throughout the world generally gave to Mussolini's fascist regime for defeating the Italian Left and establishing order. Later, the Nazi party's use of anticommunism along with anti-Semitism to mobilize support, its endorsement by prominent German aristocrats and businessmen, and its use of the Reichstag fire to whip up an anticommunist hysteria and establish an open terroristic dictatorship provided further evidence to support the view of fascism as a product of the existing economic and social system—a dictatorship of the Right supported by those who usually supported and profited from right-wing regimes.

In the 1930s, the social-economic definition of fascism stood behind a politics of uniting the Center and the Left against big business interests and organizations like the Liberty League, which were seen as comparable to the German elites who had used anticommunism to win support for fascist movements.

Nazi Germany's promulgation of an anti–Comintern Pact to mobilize allies and divide opponents in 1936, fascist Italy's and Germany's use of anticommunism as a rationale for their intervention on the side of General Franco and the fascist Falange in the Spanish civil war (1936–39), and Conservative British prime minister Neville Chamberlain's policy of noncooperation with the Soviet Union and "appeasement" of the fascist powers, capped by the Munich agreement (1938), provided a continuing chain of evidence for those who defined fascism in social-economic terms as right-wing dictatorship supported internationally by the same conservative elites who had endorsed it internally.

For others, however, the German-Soviet Nonaggression Treaty of August 1939, called by the U.S. press the Hitler-Stalin Pact, helped spread the view that Nazi Germany and the Soviet Union were comparable totalitarian dictatorships. World War II, an economic boon to U.S. business, strengthened conservative forces at home by eliminating the depression that had energized liberalism and the Left and eroded the base of support in the United States for the social-economic interpretation of fascism. The anticommunist political atmosphere of the cold war period further made social-economic definitions of fascism difficult to sustain. Such definitions now seemed communist-inspired, as the amorphous, essentially conservative, and idealist totalitarian theory of mass politics became a rationale for transforming wartime antifascism into cold war anticommunism.

The totalitarian concept had been born as an ideal of first German and then Italian fascism; it was applied in the 1930s to the Soviet Union and the communist movement by diverse opponents of Popular Front politics.

The Truman administration, seeking to defend free enterprise and free markets, abandoned any application of the social-economic explanation of fascism and used its influence in occupied Germany and its economic power over Western Europe and England to resist popular movements to nationalize industry. These movements focused most strongly on those industries that were notorious for their support of fascism and collaboration with the Nazis. Whereas the Munich Agreement was used during World War II as evidence of the disasters of a policy aimed at isolating the Soviet Union, the Truman administration, from 1947 on, freely equated postwar Soviet policies with those of prewar Nazi Germany, contending that U.S. foreign policy had as its purpose the defense of a "free world" against "communist totalitarianism." The Munich Agreement was used as a reproach to all critics of its cold war policies: the critics were "neoisolationists" or "appeasers of Soviet totalitarianism."

Furthermore, the Americans for Democratic Action (ADA) was established in 1947 as an organizational center for cold warriors of liberal orientation, uniting intellectuals, professionals, and trade unionists on a policy of equating fascism and communism under the "totalitarian." rubric, which divorced social-economic content and interest from its analysis of politics. In 1948, President Truman's reelection and the disastrous showing of Henry Wallace and the Progressive party greatly strengthened those in labor and intellectual circles who made the totalitarian theory the basis for conflating fascism with communism and Nazi Germany with the Soviet Union and carrying out organizational purges of those who opposed them.

Arthur Schlesinger, Jr., a prominent political intellectual and leading ADA member, popularized the totalitarian theory, in *The Vital Center* (1949), an influential work among liberals which stressed the continuity between the New Deal and Truman's Fair Deal, and between totalitarian fascism and communism. Hannah Arendt, an émigré German social theorist, did much the same thing for a narrower academic audience in *The Origins of Totalitarianism* (1949), equating the rise of fascism and its policies with Soviet policy under Stalin. In the McCarran Internal Security Act of 1950 and the McCarran-Walter Immigration Act of 1952, the totalitarian concept and its equating of fascism with communism (without concretely defining totalitarianism, fascism, or communism) were written into laws aimed at restricting political activity on the Left in the United States and restricting foreigners with left-wing beliefs and/or associations from visiting the country.

By the end of the Truman administration, eight years after the victory of the Allies over the fascist Axis, fascism in mainstream media and intellectual circles was defined both as a form of totalitarianism (an evil ideology producing an evil system) and as a thing of the past, supplanted by the greater totalitarian evil, communism. Social-economic definitions of fascism were now incompatible with cold war policies, since so many cold war allies of the United States in Asia and Latin America could easily fall under such definitions.

For those interested in the social-economic interpretation of fascism, Robert Brady's late 1930s classic *Spirit and Structure of German Fascism* (reprint, New York: Lyle Stuart, 1971) is perhaps the best introduction. Arthur Schlesinger, Jr., *The Vital Center* (1949; reprint, New York: Da Capo, 1986), contains, in its analysis of U.S. and world politics, the most influential and accessible expression of the totalitarian definition of fascism in the Truman period.

NORMAN MARKOWITZ

See also Americans for Democratic Action; Arendt, Hannah; Cold War; Communism and Communists; McCarran, Patrick Anthony; Schlesinger, Arthur Meier, Jr.

Federal Bureau of Investigation

Until the 1930s a minor federal agency of limited powers, the Federal Bureau of Investigation exploded in size and influence during the war years—demonstrated by the growth in the number of FBI agents from 326 in 1932, 609 in 1936, and 898 in 1940 to 4,886 in 1945 (with the bureau's budget increasing sixfold—from $6.3 million to $35.9 million—between 1939 and 1946). With the postwar dissolution of the bureau's wartime intelligence service in South America, FBI personnel were pared back by 1946 to 3,559. By 1952, however, bureau employment had more than rebounded to 7,029. If the immediate catalyst to the bureau's growth had been World War II, the war's end did not bring about retrenchment. The onset of the cold war and President Truman's executive decisions instead permanently altered the course of bureau history.

This development was not inevitable. For one, Truman brought to the presidency deep suspicions about FBI director J. Edgar Hoover's objectives and priorities. Fearful that the FBI could become a "gestapo" and convinced that the bureau improperly monitored the sexual activities of prominent Americans, Truman as a senator also worried that the FBI might act to advance conservative interests. Indeed, in the early 1940s Truman had opposed the legalization of wiretapping because he feared that the FBI might target labor unions. But when he was abruptly elevated to the presidency upon Roosevelt's death in April 1945 and confronted what he soon viewed as an interrelated foreign and domestic problem of Soviet expansion and Communist subversion, Truman abandoned his earlier reservations. His resulting actions, and, as important, inactions, ensured the bureau's evolution into a powerful, autonomous agency.

On the one hand, Truman's concerns over the personal loyalty of Roosevelt holdovers in the executive branch and over leaks to the press led him to turn to Hoover's FBI to perform a series of extremely sensitive and potentially risky intelligence operations. The most sensitive involved the FBI's initiation of a so-called White House Survey to weed out those employees who were not personally loyal to the recently elevated president. Truman's aides Edwin McKim and James Vardaman in particular solicited Hoover's assistance to identify the sources of leaks, notably to syndicated columnist Drew Pearson. As part of this project, the FBI director agreed to wiretap Treasury Department official Edward Prichard and Washington lobbyist Thomas Corcoran (but rejected as too risky a request to tap Pearson) on the understanding that "if it became known that we [the FBI] were investigating these people, it would be incumbent upon both the president and him [Vardaman] to deny that any such investigation had been ordered." White House military aide Harry Vaughan in time assumed this liaison responsibility and thereafter worked "closely with the Director of the FBI." Hoover continued to assist the Truman White House after 1945, both by forewarning the president of potential scandals and regularly forwarding reports on the plans of the president's radical and liberal critics, having acquired this information through the FBI's extensive wiretaps and surveillance activities.

Hoover's FBI, however, was not the unquestioning servant of the White House. Having his own political agenda and seeking presidential authorization to expand the FBI's role, the ambitious Hoover fully exploited the Truman administration's concerns about Communist activities. He succeeded in convincing the president to issue a series of secret directives authorizing an expansion of FBI wiretapping, investigations of "subversive activities," a liaison program with the Senate Internal Security Subcommittee, and establishment of a preventive detention program. Hoover's recommendations implied that Truman's approval merely reaffirmed directives issued by President Roosevelt or would safeguard individual liberties from vigilantes or would limit FBI investigations to ascertaining foreign direction of the activities of individuals and groups in the United States. In fact, Hoover radically expanded the FBI's powers without having to secure controversial legislation.

Concurrently, and without the president's or his attorney general's knowledge and authorization, Hoover expanded the FBI's role to that of "educating" public opinion. Under this ambitious political program instituted in February 1946 and refined thereafter, Hoover leaked derogatory information to prominent conservatives in Congress and the media. In February 1951, he started a formal "Responsibilities Program" under which he leaked information to state governors and carefully selected public personalities (for example, former Republican president Herbert Hoover). The FBI director even assisted, but discreetly to avoid discovery, those conservatives seeking to convince the public that the Truman administration had knowingly permitted "Communists in government." These carefully camouflaged leaks included assistance to the House Committee on Un-American Activities in its 1947 investigations of Hollywood, Congressman Richard Nixon in the highly publicized Hiss-Chambers confrontation in 1948, and, most notably, Wisconsin senator Joseph McCarthy following his emergence into national prominence in February 1950. Truman by that time had lost control over the FBI; it had in effect become an autonomous agency able to circumvent both presidential and congressional oversight. This was graphically illustrated by Hoover's unilateral decision of July 1950 to reestablish the bureau's American Legion Contact Program, having concluded that "it was not necessary to contact the [Justice] Department prior to starting this program." Hoover's 1950 decision contrasted with one in 1940 to seek Attorney General Robert Jackson's consent prior to establishing such a program.

The contradictory nature of Truman's relationship with the FBI—whether tacit approval or ignorance of its activities—constituted his administration's legacy, one of continued bureau growth and independence.

Because FBI records had been totally closed to any independent research until recently, most monographs on the Truman presidency shed little light on the agency's role. As historians have begun to research FBI records (some declassified at the Truman Library and others available through the Freedom of Information Act), the relationship between the Truman administration and the FBI can now be understood. The best studies, although they do not focus on Truman's presidency, are Athan Theoharis, *Spying on Americans: Political Surveillance from Hoover to the Huston Plan*

(Philadelphia: Temple University Press, 1978); Athan Theoharis and John Stuart Cox, *The Boss: J. Edgar Hoover and the Great American Inquisition* (Philadelphia: Temple University Press, 1988); Kenneth O'Reilly, *Hoover and the Un-Americans: The FBI, HUAC, and the Red Menace* (Philadelphia: Temple University Press, 1983); and Frank Donner, *The Age of Surveillance* (New York: Knopf, 1980). Useful earlier accounts of the Truman administration's internal security policies are Alonzo Hamby, *Beyond the New Deal: Harry S. Truman and American Liberalism* (New York: Columbia University Press, 1973), and Robert Donovan, *Conflict and Crisis: The Presidency of Harry S Truman, 1945–1948* (New York: W. W. Norton, 1977) and *Tumultuous Years: The Presidency of Harry S Truman, 1949–1953* (New York: W. W. Norton, 1982).

ATHAN THEOHARIS

See also Civil Liberties; Hoover, J. Edgar; Red Scare

Federal Republic of Germany
See Germany

Federal Reserve Board
See Eccles, Marriner Stoddard; Economy, The

Finances, Personal

Harry S. Truman's father, John Anderson Truman, prospered in the years from Harry's birth in 1884 until 1901 when the elder Truman lost heavily in grain-futures trading in Kansas City. Later, as a partner with his father in their Grandview farm, young Harry probably assumed at least part of his father's debts upon the elder Truman's death in 1914.

Neither his work as a bank clerk and bookkeeper nor that as a farmer allowed Harry Truman to erase the family's debts. Hoping to gain a nest egg for marriage, he invested and worked in a lead and zinc mine in Oklahoma, but he lost $7,500 before giving up on this venture in September 1916. Still searching for elusive fortune, Harry then invested $5,000 in an oil land-lease and exploration business, Morgan and Company, and served as an officer in the organization. Most of the company's leases expired while Truman was serving in the army, and several attempts to find oil had resulted in dry holes. He probably did little better than break even on this enterprise. Upon his return from the army in 1919, Harry sold his interest in the Grandview farm, netting around $15,000.

Truman, now married, used some of his savings to establish a haberdashery, in partnership with army pal Eddie Jacobson. The partners closed shop in 1922, still owing $35,000 to creditors. Truman was not able to satisfy his last creditor until 1935.

Entering politics in 1922, Truman served several terms as a county judge at a salary of $6,000 per year, which was aug-

mented modestly by fees from other duties. While out of office in 1925–26, Truman earned about $5,000 from selling memberships in the Kansas City Auto Club and a small additional income from part ownership of a savings and loan business.

As a U.S. senator, Truman earned $10,000 per year, a substantial sum during the depression. Yet, the expenses of campaigning for office, of living in Washington, D.C., and of maintaining a second household in Independence consumed most of his income. When Truman became vice president and then president in April 1945, the family's finances improved significantly. The president earned $75,000 per year, plus $25,000 in travel expenses, until January 1949 when the chief executive's pay was increased to $100,000, to which was added $50,000 for official expenses. Information is not available on how much the Trumans were able to save from his presidential salary.

Between early 1953 and November 1956 Truman spent $153,000 of his own money on maintaining an office in Kansas City. He said that only by selling some of the farmland he had inherited from his mother did he avoid "financial embarrassment." Concerning income from the sale of his *Memoirs*, he claimed that after paying a tax rate of 67.5 percent, he would net only $37,000 over a five-year period.

In 1958 Congress passed a bill to provide pensions for former presidents. Truman received $25,000 annually, plus office space and equipment and an additional $50,000 for office expenses. Unquestionably, any money worries for the former president were now over. Between 1959 and 1969 the president's bank balances fluctuated at levels from $84,000 to $208,000. He appears to have kept about $2,000 available in ready cash.

Upon his death in December 1972, Harry S. Truman's estate amounted to approximately $600,000. He left the bulk of his property to his widow, Bess, and daughter, Margaret.

Although sketchy on the subject, the most useful documentation on Truman family finances may be found in the Truman Library's papers of Harry S. Truman pertaining to family, business, and personal affairs, the papers of Eben Ayers, and the desk file in Truman's postpresidential files. The most revealing published accounts are in Margaret Truman Daniel, *Bess W. Truman* (New York: Macmillan, 1986), and in Richard Miller, *Truman: The Rise to Power* (New York: McGraw-Hill, 1986).

NIEL M. JOHNSON

See also Business Ventures; Farm Experience

Fiscal and Monetary Policies

Fiscal and monetary policies constitute the federal government's chief weapons in the struggle for economic stability and optimal economic growth. Fiscal policy comprises the government's taxing and spending practices. It is the product of executive and congressional interaction and is usually embodied in legislation such as revenue acts and appropriations measures. Monetary policy regulates the supply of money and credit in the economy and is carried out primarily by the nation's largely autonomous central bank, the Federal Reserve.

In the Truman years, fiscal and monetary policies were applied to an economy that had been transformed by World War II. The explosion of government spending for military purposes had finally brought about a recovery from the Great Depression of the 1930s. The enforced saving and the deferral of consumption that accompanied the war effort created significant backlogs of demand, and these subsequently eased the reconversion to a peacetime economy. Population growth (the beginning of the fabled baby boom), technological change, a dramatic expansion of the middle class, and increased federal activity (especially in the defense sector)—all contributed to the maintenance of prosperity during the Truman period.

World War II had also produced an intellectual and political climate hospitable to the idea that fiscal policy in particular should be used to cushion deflationary declines and dampen inflationary excesses. The notion that the government should act as the balance wheel of the economy lay at the heart of Keynesian economic theory, and the ideas of the British economist gained many converts among American intellectuals. More concerned with the practical than the theoretical, leaders in business, labor, and government searched for ways to ensure that the wartime prosperity would be continued. Many came to view fiscal policy not merely as a way to pay the government's bills but also as an important instrument for the achievement of the nation's larger economic goals. President Harry Truman viewed the budget as "one of my more serious hobbies" and took great pride in his grasp of its details. He also recognized, however, that the budget had broad ramifications: "Government programs," he said in his first budget message, "are of such importance in the development of production and employment opportunities . . . that it has become essential to formulate and consider the federal budget in light of the nation's budget as a whole."

Truman's ideas on the role of macroeconomic policy derived more from his own business and governmental experience than from a commitment to any doctrine. His views on fiscal policy were, by the standards of the day, thoroughly moderate. Leery of both abstract ideas and intellectuals, he was no wild-eyed Keynesian. He believed in balancing the budget. "There is nothing sacred about the pay-as-you-go idea so far as I am concerned," he wrote, "except that it represents the soundest principle of financing that I know." But he would not attempt to press his preference for a balanced budget to the point of raising taxes in the midst of an economic downturn in order to avoid a deficit. In the same fashion, Truman believed it important to achieve a budget surplus in boom periods not simply for book-keeping purposes but, more important, in order to moderate the boom's inflationary tendencies.

Truman saw much less overall usefulness in monetary policy. The president was philosophically committed to low interest rates. He also believed strongly in the need to uphold the value of the government's own securities; as a young man, he had seen government bond prices plunge after World War I, and he was determined not to preside over a repetition of that experience. His emphasis on low interest rates and stable bond prices precluded the active use of monetary policy as a weapon against inflation. Thus armed with a preference for a tight fiscal policy and an easy-money monetary policy, Truman faced a wide variety of economic problems from 1945 to 1953.

The end of World War II presented the administration with its first great economic challenge—the immediate transition to

Clarence D. Batchelor, *New York Daily News* (1952). Copyright New York News Inc. Reprinted with permission.

a peacetime footing. War orders dropped off rapidly after the defeat of Germany, and precipitously after Japan's surrender. In September 1945, Truman called for a limited tax reduction to help bolster consumer demand and foster business expansion. The Revenue Act of 1945 became law less than two months later. In the event, the transition to peace went more smoothly than many observers had anticipated; by the end of 1946 the gross national product had virtually regained its wartime peak. The tax cut undoubtedly helped support disposable income, but the real key was a consumer buying spree of unprecedented proportions. The result was a new phase of economic activity, the postwar boom of 1946–48, and with it came the problem of sustained inflation.

Prices rose rapidly in 1946, and the inflationary surge continued into 1948. The administration sought to counteract the inflationary pressures by holding down expenditures—a difficult task in the postwar political and diplomatic environment—and maintaining existing tax rates. The federal budget yielded a slight surplus in 1946 and a considerably larger one in 1947. Macroeconomic policy became a divisive political issue when the Republicans in Congress sought to reduce taxes yet again. Truman insisted that a tax cut would be "unsound fiscal policy," and Secretary of the Treasury John W. Snyder observed, "So long as inflationary pressures persist, there is good reason for maintaining high taxes." The battle raged over several years. Twice in 1947 Truman successfully vetoed tax-cut bills on the grounds that they were inequitable and untimely—"the wrong tax reduction at the wrong time." In the face of unrelenting political pressure, the president recommended a small, redistributive tax reduction in January 1948. In the end, however, the Republican drive for a major tax cut triumphed; on 2 April 1948, the Revenue Act of 1948 was enacted into law over yet another presidential veto. The resultant $5 billion tax cut was, in the words of the economist and historian Herbert Stein, "politically astute . . . but economically irresponsible." Its timing was also terribly lucky, for it took effect just in time to give the economy a needed expansionary boost as the economic situation shifted from inflation to recession.

The nation's first postwar recession ran from November 1948, to October 1949, and was, by all standards, both mild and brief. The administration was slow in recognizing the change in circumstances. As late as January 1949, Truman called for a $4 billion tax increase, a proposal that, if implemented, would have had a deflationary impact on an already sagging economy. Once the onset of the recession was recognized, the administration adopted a cautious, passive countercyclical approach. The president warned, "We cannot expect to achieve a budget surplus in a declining national economy." The economy's "automatic stabilizers"—the tendency of consumption to be sustained in a downturn by decreases in the taxes generated at existing progressive rates and by increases in unemployment compensation, farm aid payments, and other welfare transfers—provided a cushioning effect and yielded a budget deficit. The speedy recovery from the recession reflected good fortune—the fact that the economically perverse tax cut of 1948 was now suddenly very helpful—and the fundamental strength of the economy as much as the sagacity of federal macroeconomic policy. The toleration of the deficit was, however, significant proof of the administration's acceptance of at least the passive side of the so-called Keynesian revolution. By the middle of 1950, the economic recovery was almost complete.

The final phase of economic activity during the Truman years was dominated by the Korean War. The outbreak of fighting in June 1950 brought the problem of inflation back to center stage. Consumers rushed to stock up on items traditionally in short supply during wartime. Fueled by increased military spending, federal expenditures for new goods and services more than doubled between the fourth quarters of 1950 and 1951 and continued to rise, albeit more slowly, for the remainder of Truman's tenure. The administration reacted to the hostilities by recommending a tax hike, and the resulting Revenue Act of 1950 took effect on 1 October. An excess-profits tax was added in January 1951, and in October 1951 there followed still another major tax increase, set to yield an additional $5.7 billion. Truman urged further increases to meet the deficits that arose as expenditures outraced receipts, but congressional opposition doomed strict adherence to a pay-as-you-go philosophy; the fiscal years ending on 30 June 1952 and 1953 saw deficits of $4 billion and $9.4 billion, respectively. On the whole, however, federal fiscal policy, in conjunction with the general wage and price controls applied in January 1951 and an autonomous lessening of consumer demand, proved successful in stabilizing the economy during the Korean War years.

The Korean War phase also witnessed the liberation of monetary policy from the straitjacket that had constrained it throughout the Truman years. The administration had enforced an agreement struck by the Federal Reserve and the Treasury Department in 1941, which committed the Fed to the support of the market for government securities rather than to the pursuit of overall economic stabilization. As a result, in both inflation and downturn the Fed found itself following a policy that ran directly counter to the stabilization needs of the economy as a whole; in inflationary times, it created new money and in declines it withdrew money from the system in order always to maintain the price of government bonds. Thus stripped of its most formidable weapon—the selling or buying of government securities in the open market—the Federal Reserve was reduced to using less effective measures to combat the inflation of the postwar boom: the regulation of consumer credit, a change in reserve requirements, and hikes in the discount rate. When the Fed chafed under the arrangement, Truman supported the Treasury position, pointedly telling the central bankers, "Now gentlemen, you represent the greatest financial institution in the history of the world, except the Treasury of the United States." Finally, after a bitter struggle, the president and the Treasury Department acquiesced in the famous "monetary accord" of March 1951, which reestablished both a flexible monetary policy in the service of economic stabilization and the institutional independence of the Federal Reserve. The reemergence of a flexible monetary policy and the relative success of the administration's fiscal approach stand as the major developments in macroeconomic policy in the Truman era.

A. E. Holmans, *United States Fiscal Policy, 1945–1959: Its Contribution to Economic Stability* (London: Oxford University Press, 1961), and Herbert Stein, *The Fiscal Revolution in America* (Chicago: University of Chicago Press, 1969), are solid, clearly written studies. Lewis H. Kimmel, *Federal Budget and Fiscal Policy, 1789–1958* (Washington, D.C.: Brookings Institution, 1959), places the policies of the Truman administration in a broad historical context, as does Milton Friedman and Anna J. Schwartz, *A Monetary History of the United States, 1867–1960* (Princeton: Princeton University Press, 1963). A narrower but still useful examination of monetary policy is James Knipe, *The Federal Reserve and the American Dollar: Problems and Policies, 1946–1964* (Chapel Hill: University of North Carolina Press, 1964).

ROBERT M. COLLINS

See also Economy, The; Inflation

Formosa

American policy toward Formosa (now Taiwan) during the Truman administration is the story of the evolution of a major interest. Such interests, lying between the vital and the peripheral, are characterized by concern for U.S. credibility in areas that may have some strategic value, as well as by the expenditure of considerable power and resources in their defense. The belief that Communist China would become a client state of the Soviet Union and the availability of greater military resources gradually led American policymakers to the conclusion that the United States should prevent the Chinese Communists from completing their revolution and taking Formosa. Having made that decision, the United States began a commitment that would guarantee Kuomintang control of Formosa for the indeterminate future.

Questions about Formosa first surfaced in the fall of 1948 as the Chinese Revolution neared its conclusion. Responding to a State Department request for an assessment of the island's strategic value, the Joint Chiefs of Staff opined that it would be "most valuable" if Formosa could be denied to the Communists; but given the state of U.S. military preparedness, the Joint Chiefs counseled the use of only "economic and diplomatic" steps to achieve that end. This assessment and a similar one by Gen. Douglas MacArthur led to a decision by the National Security Council and the president in early 1949 to foster an autonomous local government, using vigorous economic aid to support its existence.

Although the United States remained reluctant in early 1949 to move beyond diplomatic and economic steps, the use of force always remained an option, especially as events of that year seemed to demonstrate greater Chinese Communist–Soviet closeness. Accordingly in February 1949 civilian policymakers once again asked the Joint Chiefs for an appraisal of Formosa's strategic worth. Communist control of the island, they responded now, would constitute "a major contribution to enemy capabilities" because "Formosa's strategic importance is . . . great." But because of global obligations in areas of greater strategic value, the military leaders advocated only a minor escalation of American power, specifically the stationing of fleet units at Formosan ports to back the diplomatic and military moves.

Unable to develop any other alternative toward the problem on the Chinese mainland, Secretary of State Dean Acheson and his State Department colleagues hoped to promote eventual Soviet–Chinese Communist discord. Consequently they feared that any military action would prove disadvantageous and might create "an irredentist issue"; for the time being at least, they decided against placing U.S. fleet units in Formosan waters. In 1949 Acheson indicated that he was temporarily subordinating Formosa to the larger China question but was nonetheless willing to see it as a major American concern.

The influx of mainland Chinese coupled with Chiang Kai-shek's apparent determination to hold power on Formosa precluded the promotion of an autonomous regime there and soon demonstrated the futility of the economic and diplomatic approach. Among the options the State Department then considered was taking the issue to the United Nations and creating a UN-sponsored independent Formosa. George Kennan, director of the State Department's Policy Planning Staff, contemplated a still bolder approach in the summer of 1949, one in which the United States would unilaterally abrogate the Cairo Declaration and out of strategic concerns assert authority over the island. Although Kennan's idea never gained acceptance, it is significant as an indication of the direction in which American policy was moving by late 1949.

A close examination of the policy process in 1949–50 reveals that civilian officials of the Truman administration kept returning to the Joint Chiefs of Staff for evaluations of Formosa's value and that military advisers continued to make their recommendations according to the condition of U.S. power. In December of 1949, with the availability of funds under the Military Assistance Act and with their continuing belief in the great strategic value of Formosa, the Joint Chiefs finally took the step of recommending the granting of military aid to support the Nationalists on the island. To write off Formosa, the Joint Chiefs believed, not only would allow for the loss of a strategic asset but would produce disastrously negative effects among those people in the rest of Asia on whom the United States would ultimately have to rely in containing communism.

Neither Secretary of State Acheson nor the director of the Office of Far Eastern Affairs, Walton Butterworth, was ready to accept this analysis. They did not want to undermine the new policy of portraying the Soviet Union as the main imperialistic menace to China unless strategic need required it; and they remained impressed by the Joint Chiefs' earlier assessment that the use of military power was not warranted by Formosa's value. It also seemed apparent that in the likely event that the island fell to the Communists, any military aid given to the Nationalists would become Communist property, a matter about which British officials repeatedly warned in the fall of 1949. Despite an abundance of contrary advice, President Truman supported his secretary of state, and he and Acheson defended it in comments to the press in January 1950. This meant that Formosa would remain outside the U.S. defense perimeter—for a while.

That did not end discussion of the matter. Dean Rusk, who on 28 March 1950 became assistant secretary of state for Far Eastern affairs, worked assiduously for a change in policy to accord with the Joint Chiefs' advice. "A strong stand at Formosa," he told Acheson, "would involve a slightly increased risk of early war. But sometimes such a risk has to be taken to preserve peace in the world." The secretary of state himself worried about the threat of a Soviet-exploited Formosa, and the State Department deliberations of the previous eighteen months certainly demonstrate a grave concern. That Acheson had not yet recommended a commitment to Formosa when the Korean War broke out resulted in part from bureaucratic inertia which only some sort of shock could change. Korea was as much the occasion for U.S. intervention as the reason for it.

War in Korea on 25 June 1950 led not only to U.S. intervention there but to the defense of the Nationalist government on Formosa through the placing of the Seventh Fleet in the Formosa Strait. Afterward the United States wrote a security pact with the Nationalists and through the fifties and sixties made a substantial contribution to Chiang Kai-shek's regime. The commitment of these decades aside, historians have portrayed the decision of June 1950 as an unwise reversal of previous policy, a change in direction made necessary in large measure by the climate of opinion in the United States which was influenced by the China Lobby and particularly assertive members of the Republican party.

The commitment of June 1950 represented neither a true reversal of policy nor the effect of political pressure. The Joint Chiefs had always maintained that action "extending to war itself" might necessitate military intervention, and the island had become quite important to American officials, if not vital. The State Department indicated on several occasions that it would be guided by the Joint Chiefs' estimate of Formosa's strategic value; their estimate was understated only because of the condition of U.S. military power. Policymakers, including Secretary Acheson and President Truman, in any event ultimately based their decisions mainly on strategic rather than political assessments. Secretary of State Acheson, who made the recommendation to send the Seventh Fleet to Formosan waters, had never foreclosed the option of military force. It seems doubtful that his determination to avoid further entanglement in China's civil conflict could have withstood a Communist attack on Formosa even without war in Korea. In sum, the decision to defend Formosa flowed directly from the complicated deliberations of the previous eighteen months, during which time Formosa underwent transformation from a peripheral to a major interest.

For further reading on the Formosa issue during the Truman administration, one should consult the corpus of scholarship dealing with Sino-American relations in the late 1940s. Particularly important are books by Nancy Tucker, *Patterns in the Dust* (New York: Columbia University Press, 1983), which emphasizes Secretary of State Dean Acheson's disaffection for the Nationalists and desire to normalize relations with the new government of China; Dorothy Borg and Waldo Heinricks, eds., *Uncertain Years: Chinese-American Relations, 1947–1950* (New York: Columbia University Press, 1980), which includes a chapter by Warren Cohen on "Dean Acheson and China," stressing Acheson's desire to recognize Communist China and the political pressures on the administration to back the Nationalists on Formosa, and one by John L. Gaddis, "The Strategic Perspective," in which the author argues that the United States even before the Korean War worried about control of Formosa by hostile forces. Other valuable works are William Stueck, *The Road to Confrontation: American Policy toward China and Korea, 1947–1950* (Chapel Hill: University of North Carolina Press, 1981), which focuses on the strategic assessment of Formosa and the policy deliberations within the executive branch of the U.S. government, and Russell D. Buhite, *Soviet-American Relations in Asia, 1945–1954* (Norman: University of Oklahoma Press, 1981), which treats Formosa within the framework of a new categorization of U.S. interests.

RUSSELL D. BUHITE

See also Chiang Kai-shek; China

James V. Forrestal. (National Archives)

Forrestal, James Vincent

(15 February 1892–22 May 1949)

Secretary of the navy, 1944–47; first secretary of defense, 1947–49. James Forrestal was born in what is now Beacon, New York, to James and Mary (Toohey) Forrestal. He attended Dartmouth College before transferring to Princeton University as a sophomore. There he edited the *Daily Princetonian*, was a member of the prestigious Cottage Club, and was active in sports. Although of average height and weight, he was aggressive, and once while boxing had his nose broken. In 1915, after failing a course in English six weeks before graduating, he suddenly left the university.

Except for serving as a naval aviator during World War I, Forrestal until 1940 sold bonds for the Wall Street firm of William A. Read and Co. (later Dillon, Read, & Co.), then became a partner (1923), and finally was made president (1928). A compulsive worker, he obtained wealth, power, and social position, yet he was shy, introspective, and emotionally insecure. On 12 December 1926, he married Josephine Ogden of Huntington, West Virginia, and had two sons, Michael and Peter.

President Franklin D. Roosevelt chose Forrestal, of his own political party, to help him during his naval buildup. Forrestal, however, served as a special administrative assistant for only two months before he became the first under secretary of the navy on 22 August 1940. As such he successfully coordinated the navy's procurement program. After Secretary of the Navy Frank Knox died in May 1944, he became the naval secretary.

Three major goals occupied Forrestal in his new position: to continue the war to its end, keep procurement in civilian hands, and defend the navy from decimation if the services were unified. In pursuit of the second goal, he had already, as under secretary and with Knox's support, convinced Roosevelt to deny procurement power to the fleet commander, Adm. Ernest J. King. His third concern was influenced by his visits to the Southwest Pacific in 1942, Kwajelein in 1944, and Iwo Jima in 1945, where he saw the great value of naval aviation and of amphibious operations.

Army air forces leaders hoped to gain independent status if the services were unified. If they succeeded, problems to be solved would include the roles, missions, and organization of the postwar services. The army wished to take over the Marine Corps, "the navy's second army"; the air force concentrated on strategic bombing and wished to take over naval aviation; the navy stuck to its task force organization, in which surface, subsurface, air, and amphibious forces could be tailored to perform any function.

On the army's side was the new president, Harry S. Truman, who as a senator during the war had characterized the services as inefficient, sloppy in managing wartime contracts, and unconcerned about "what the cost was." Truman wished to curtail military leaders' input into economic and political matters. Further, while a vice-presidential candidate, Truman had called for a single military department comprising the military, naval, and air branches. As president, however, he gave up his demand for a single chief of staff and agreed to the navy's retaining its carrier- and water-based aviation as well as the Marine Corps.

After Forrestal suggested that economic and political matters, intelligence, research, and procurement all be included in a new organization, a compromise was reached in the National Security Act, which Truman signed on 26 July 1947. To head the new National Military Establishment, which Forrestal had originally opposed, Truman named him as the first secretary of defense on 17 September.

With only three special civilian assistants, Forrestal tackled the reorganization of the three services and sought to obtain a unified defense budget and win agreement from the services on their roles and missions. Meanwhile he was almost the only cabinet member to disagree with many of Truman's key policies. Among these were low defense budgets, priority for the air force rather than balanced forces, civilian rather than military control over atomic weapons, the strengthening of the National Security Council, and the partitioning of Palestine. Doubting his loyalty (Forrestal probably contributed to Thomas E. Dewey's campaign in 1948), Truman on 1 March 1949 asked Forrestal for his immediate resignation in favor of Louis A. Johnson.

Overworked at the office and with an ailing wife at home, Forrestal showed signs of mental and physical exhaustion that pointed to extreme depression and paranoia. While resting in Florida, he attempted suicide. He was admitted on 2 April 1949 to the Bethesda Naval Hospital, and on 22 May, he plunged to his death from an unguarded window. He was buried with military honors at Arlington National Cemetery on 25 May.

A large collection of Forrestal papers is at the Firestone Library, Princeton University. His career as secretary of defense is covered in Paolo E. Coletta, *The United States Navy and Defense Unification, 1947–1953* (Newark: University of Delaware Press, 1981), and in Walter Millis, ed., *The Forrestal Diaries* (New York: Viking Press, 1951). See also *Dictionary of American Biography*, suppl. vol. 4, s.v. Forrestal, James Vincent.

PAOLO E. COLETTA

See also Armed Forces, Unification of the

France

American relations with France during the Truman era stand in marked contrast to relations under Franklin Roosevelt. Roosevelt's contempt for French imperial pretensions and his deep dislike of Gen. Charles de Gaulle strained the wartime partnership. Although some tensions persisted under Truman, American policy generally reflected the State Department's view that "the best interests of the United States" required the reestablishment of a strong France as a "bulwark of democracy on the continent of Europe."

President Truman himself embodied both the sentimental attachment and the lingering prejudices Americans had about the land of Lafayette. He was proud of his service in the American Expeditionary Force to France in 1918, although he did not remember fondly a French captain who carelessly fired an artillery battery over his troops, causing him some permanent hearing damage. While in France Truman was also deeply homesick and thought such Parisian tourist attractions as the Folies-Bergère were "disgusting." In his first days as president, Truman faced some difficult moments in dealing with de Gaulle, whose forces seized the Aosta Valley in Italy and would not withdraw until the United States threatened to cut off their supplies. This and other related problems with the proud general led Truman to share Roosevelt's distaste for one of the "little Caesars" the war produced.

Yet Truman, like most Americans, had a high regard for France and the French people, a strong sympathy going back, as he told the French foreign minister in 1945, "to the founding of this nation." In Truman's eyes France had been the victim of German aggression three times within a century, and the president endorsed the strong pro-French attitudes of his State Department advisers. American diplomats valued France not only for historical and cultural reasons; they believed a strong France would help maintain the balance of power in Europe. In more immediate terms a stable and democratic France guaranteed both the security of the communications and supply lines of American troops occupying Germany and the enforcement of any new peace treaty with the defeated foe. The State Department argued in April 1945 that it was important to treat France "in all respects on the basis of her potential power and influence rather than on the basis of her present strength."

Indeed the France of 1945 was only a shell of its former imperial self, humiliated and weakened by military defeat and occupation, and deeply divided along class and social lines. After the liberation, French leaders set out to modernize their country's economy, provide leadership to the rest of Europe, and restore the empire. They also hoped they could remain neutral should any clash occur between capitalist America and communist Russia, a stance dictated in part by domestic politics. The French Communist party (PCF) was one of the most loyal allies of Moscow outside of Eastern Europe. It had played an active role in the resistance after Hitler's attack on Russia and in 1945 garnered almost 30 percent of the electorate's support. The PCF became a part of the governing coalition after de Gaulle's resignation in January 1946.

The problem of reconciling these ambitious national goals with the reality of the nation's weakness and social divisions, however, led moderate and even socialist French leaders to turn increasingly to the United States. The Fourth Republic's fragile governing coalitions faced the daunting task of apportioning the high costs of wartime occupation and postwar modernization among a deeply divided citizenry. The Monnet Plan alone—a modernization effort led by the French internationalist Jean Monnet—called for some $11 billion in imports between 1946 and 1949. France also hoped to finance this program through the exploitation of German resources, particularly coal, and its policy aimed at the separation from Germany of the Rhineland, the Ruhr industrial region, and the rich mining area of the Saar. In Berlin French representatives obstructed the creation of central German agencies as provided under the Potsdam agreements, a stance that elicited continual protests from Gen. Lucius Clay, the American commander in Germany. Although the United States resisted the French-proposed separation of Germany's industrial heartland, the State Department nevertheless was reluctant to press the French too hard to end their obstruction. It worried about France's internal stability and was increasingly concerned about possible Soviet expansionism in Western Europe. The department also tried to ease France's economic plight with a loan of $550 million through the Export-Import Bank in December 1945. Through the Byrnes-Blum arrangements of May 1946, the United States provided a further $650 million loan and the promise of a $500 million World Bank credit.

The crucial turning point in American-French relations arrived in 1947, with the coming together of America's cold war concerns about the future of Western Europe and a domestic political crisis in France. Secretary of State George Marshall's belief after the Moscow Foreign Ministers Conference in April 1947 that the Soviet Union was blocking European economic recovery, hoping to exploit these conditions for its expansionist goals, led him to the proclamation of the Marshall Plan in June 1947. In France, the continuing inflation and the costs of modernization created additional strains on the governing coalition, as the Communists refused to go along with the government's wage policy. Non-Communist French leaders began to fear the intentions of their coalition partners. In January 1947 the French foreign minister Georges Bidault told the State Department that the Communists "proposed to eradicate Western civilization." The Soviet refusal to endorse French control of the Saar, the one aspect of France's German policy that the United States had supported, further soured the French on the desire to remain neutral between the two superpowers. In May 1947 the Communists were expelled from the French government, and a "Third Force" of moderates and socialists consolidated their control, helped along by interim American economic assistance of $312 million provided before the Marshall Plan went into effect in April 1948. This assistance allowed the French to avoid severe food rationing and hardship during the winter. The American aid represented some two-thirds of the French bread ration, and 60 percent of its oil and 20 percent of its coal requirements.

Over the years 1948–52, the United States supplied France with some $2.7 billion in Marshall Plan assistance, helping the nation feed its people, stabilize its democratic government, and advance its modernization program. But Marshall Plan assistance to Europe also brought, at American insistence, the economic recovery of West Germany. French worries about Germany had led the country to sign the Dunkirk Treaty with Great Britain in March 1947, and it unsuccessfully opposed American efforts to include Germany in the Marshall Plan. With the Czech coup of February 1948, France began to see both Germany and the Soviet Union as posing potential threats to its security. In March 1948 France joined with Britain and other West European nations in the Brussels Pact and after its ratification sought to attach the United States to Western Europe's defense. As the premier, Henri Queuille said in February 1949, "The United States must never permit France and Western Europe to be invaded by Russia as they were by Germany. [But] France, in her position as Europe's advance guard, cannot hold the fort alone." With the signing of the North Atlantic Treaty on 4 April 1949, the United States pledged itself to defend Western Europe. At the same time, however, the United States insisted that the occupying powers agree to give the West Germans limited independence, and the Federal Republic of Germany, under the leadership of Chancellor Konrad Adenauer, officially came into existence in September 1949.

The development of a separate West German state presented the French with both a dilemma and an opportunity. The Americans, led by Secretary of State Dean Acheson, were encouraging them to take the lead in "integrating" their former enemy into Western Europe. Only through such integration could Germany become a stable and peaceful democracy and resist the lure of neutralism and reunification under Soviet domination. In the leadership of Adenauer the French also had a man dedicated to achieving a lasting rapprochement. At the same time the Americans were insisting on ending the controls on the German economy that were the last remnants of the Potsdam policy. The French response came in a bold and creative initiative proposed in May 1950 by Foreign Minister Robert Schuman, himself a man of the Lorraine border region. The Schuman Plan, actually formulated by Jean Monnet, involved the creation of a joint authority over Europe's coal and steel industry and a pooling of French and German resources that promised to be a major step in the peaceful reconciliation of the two countries and perhaps in the creation of a united Europe. The Americans supported it enthusiastically, and the American high commissioner in Germany, John J. McCloy, even used the powers of his office to pressure German industrialists to accede to the agreement.

When the outbreak of the Korean War in June 1950 brought the additional American demand for German rearmament, the French again countered with an integrationist scheme. But the Pleven Plan, involving the creation of mixed divisions of French and German soldiers, was as much designed to hinder German rearmament as it was to promote European integration. Redesigned and renamed by the Americans as the European Defense Community (EDC), it became part of the Bonn-Paris accords of May 1952, which restored Germany's sovereignty. Although the EDC would be rejected by the French Assembly in August 1954, by the end of the Truman era the French found themselves increasingly linked in political, economic, and military terms with their former enemy.

The rapid change in policy toward Germany, and the perception that the Americans seemed to favor the Germans more and more, tended to increase anti-American sentiment in France. The growing American role in France's war against the Communist insurgency in Indochina also contributed to this sentiment. Before 1950 Washington had tended to discourage French efforts to reassert control over its former colony, although it also distrusted the Vietnamese leader, Ho Chi Minh, seeing him as a dedicated Communist and a tool of Soviet imperialism. With the fall of China and the outbreak of the Korean War, the United States began a major program of economic and military assistance to support the French effort in Indochina. Although the United States wanted the French to grant greater autonomy to the Vietnamese, Acheson was reluctant to pressure them, fearful that they might say, "All right, take over the damned country. We don't want it." But the war dragged on without any sign of victory. By the end of 1952 the United States was paying almost 40 percent of the cost of the war, and non-Communist voices in France were beginning to demand withdrawal. The "real" problem, Acheson warned the Eisenhower administration, was the "French will to carry on the . . . war."

Although Indochina would prove a tragic legacy of American-French relations during the Truman presidency, the overall verdict is not nearly as grim. With American assistance France was able to modernize its economy and stave off the Communist challenge to its political democracy. With American prodding the country also began the long road toward reconciliation with Germany, one of the lasting success stories of postwar diplomacy. Although France under de Gaulle would leave NATO in 1967, it remains a part of the Western alliance and has moved closer to the United States in recent years. Although not all the evidence supports his conclusion, one is tempted to agree with the French historian Jean-Baptiste Duroselle that "Franco-American relations have never lost the mysterious charm that assures them a place apart in the history of mankind."

The documentary record of American relations with France can be followed in the Department of State's *Foreign Relations of the United States*, Annual volumes (Europe, Western Europe, European Security and the German Question, and Indochina) 1945–54 (Washington, D.C., 1970–85). There is no single monographic study of those relations, although Alfred Grosser, *The Western Alliance*, trans. Michael Shaw (New York: Vintage, 1982), provides insight into the French perspective. Along the same lines is Jean-Baptiste Duroselle, *France and the United States*, trans. Derek Coltman (Chicago: University of Chicago Press, 1976). State Department sympathies for France are detailed in John Gimbel, *The Origins of the Marshall Plan* (Stanford: Stanford University Press, 1976). The social and economic conflicts of postwar France and the role of American aid are explained incisively in John S. Hill, "Inflation and the Clash of Interests in France, 1944–1948" (Ph.D. diss., Brandeis University, 1987). For the relationship between France's policy of European integration and America's view of European security, see Thomas A. Schwartz, "The Skeleton Key: American Foreign Policy, European Unity, and German Rearmament, 1949–1954," *Central European History* 19 (December 1986): 369–85, and the forthcoming *America's Germany: John J. McCloy and the Federal Republic of Germany*. On America's growing involvement in Vietnam, the best book remains George C. Herring, *America's Longest War: The United States and Vietnam, 1950–1975*, 2d ed. (New York: Alfred A. Knopf, 1986).

THOMAS SCHWARTZ

See also Imperialism; Indochina; Marshall Plan; North Atlantic Treaty Organization

Frankfurter, Felix

(15 November 1882–22 February 1965)

Associate justice, U.S. Supreme Court, 1939–62; former professor, Harvard Law School. During the 1930s Felix Frankfurter helped staff a number of New Deal agencies and was an influential although informal adviser to Franklin Roosevelt, who named him to the Supreme Court in 1938.

Frankfurter's judicial philosophy stemmed directly from his two mentors, Oliver Wendell Holmes, Jr., and Louis D. Brandeis, who had argued that courts should defer to legislative judgment and refrain from voiding statutes merely because judges disagreed with particular economic or social policies. At a time when conservative judges were blocking a variety of reform measures, this was considered the liberal view, and it was a policy that Frankfurter had strongly espoused in his writings as a law professor.

But by the time Frankfurter took his seat on the Supreme Court, the judicial agenda had begun to move away from a concern with economic matters to questions of civil liberties. Many people had expected Frankfurter to take a lead in this area, since he had so often fought for unpopular causes in the 1920s. One can, in fact, find a libertarian strain in Frankfurter's decisions, especially in his repugnance to governmental efforts to ferret out Communists by limiting their rights. "The heart of the matter," he wrote in *Joint Anti-Fascist Refugee Committee v. McGrath* (1951), "is that democracy implies respect for the elementary rights of man, however suspect or unworthy; a democratic government must therefore practice fairness, and fairness can scarcely be obtained by secret, one-sided determination of facts decisive of rights." He also proved a strong defender of the search and seizure provisions of the Fourth Amendment.

But his belief in judicial restraint led him to support some state and federal limitations on speech and other First Amendment rights, and he parted company from many former admirers when he supported the Smith Act, which made it unlawful to organize a party that taught or advocated violent rebellion (*Dennis v. United States* [1951]), and when he protested against the liberal wing of the Court, led by Hugo Black, taking an activist role in expanding Bill of Rights protections.

Frankfurter never enjoyed a close relation with Truman, and although he tried to send advice periodically through some of his former pupils, he had relatively little influence outside the Court. There, however, he did establish a doctrine of judicial restraint which, even if it had limited influence in his own time, would have significant consequences in later years as the pendulum swung away from judicial activism.

Frankfurter was married to the former Marion Denman on 20 December 1919; they had no children. He suffered a stroke in April 1962, which led to his retirement from the Court the following August.

Frankfurter's legal papers are at the Harvard Law School; the balance are in the Library of Congress. A good introduction to his legal philosophy is Mark Silverstein, *Constitutional Faiths* (Ithaca: Cornell University Press, 1984). There is no good full biography comparable to Michael Parrish's *Felix Frankfurter and His Times* (New York: Free Press, 1982), which covers only the pre-Court years. See also the sympathetic portrait by Paul Freund in *Dictionary of American Biography*, suppl. 10, 260–65.

MELVIN I. UROFSKY

See also Supreme Court, United States (and photograph)

Fulton, Hugh Alfred

(24 May 1908–23 October 1962)

First chief counsel of the Truman committee. On 1 March 1941 the Senate approved a proposal by Senator Harry S. Truman to create a Senate Special Committee to Investigate the National Defense Program and named Truman as chairman. Knowing that the chief counsel would be critical to the committee's success, Truman asked Attorney General Robert H. Jackson for "the best investigator you've got." Jackson recommended

Fulton, an experienced U.S. attorney, who had gained a reputation for his investigations and prosecutions of, among others, an investment banker, a utility company executive, and a federal judge. A 1931 graduate of the University of Michigan Law School, Fulton had practiced with a prominent Wall Street law firm for seven years before becoming a federal attorney in 1938.

When he first met Fulton, Truman was not impressed: "He came in wearing a derby hat, a big fat fellow with a squeaky voice. I said to myself, 'Oh, shucks.'" Nevertheless, Truman hired Fulton, paying him more than half of the committee's initial budget and assuring him that he would not be subjected to political pressure. As it turned out, Fulton and the Missouri senator worked extremely well together, usually conferring daily. While the committee, especially Truman, set broad policies and strategies, Fulton hired and trained an excellent staff and supervised detail work. His efforts were instrumental in helping the Truman committee earn its reputation as a model congressional investigative body.

Fulton resigned as chief counsel in September 1944, shortly after Truman became the Democratic party's vice-presidential nominee, and resumed his law practice. The following April, the morning after Truman was sworn in as president, Fulton met with his former boss, apparently believing that he was in line for a key appointment in the new administration. Fulton was destined to be disappointed. The chief executive, angered by reports that the lawyer was bragging that he was going to be a virtual "acting president," never offered Fulton a position. Truman later told an interviewer that Fulton had "gotten too big for his britches." Actually, Fulton had lost some of the president's respect months earlier by sending out announcements advertising that he was going into private law practice, an action Truman felt was unethical. The break between the two men was never healed. Fulton practiced law successfully in Washington and New York City and served as an officer and director for several businesses until his death in 1962.

For Fulton's work as chief counsel, see the sources listed for entry on the Truman committee. The break between Fulton and Truman is discussed in Merle Miller, *Plain Speaking: An Oral Biography of Harry S. Truman* (New York: Berkley Publishing, 1973), and Margaret Truman, *Harry S. Truman* (New York: William Morrow, 1973).

JIM F. HEATH

See also Truman Committee

G

Gates-Wallace-Truman House

The two-and-a-half-story, white-frame house at 219 North Delaware Street in Independence, Jackson County, Missouri, was the home of Harry and Bess Truman from the time of their marriage on 28 June 1919 until their deaths. The home became known as the Summer White House during the Truman presidency and is now a national historic site operated by the National Park Service.

Bess Truman's maternal grandfather, George Porterfield Gates, a partner in a thriving Independence milling company, purchased the property in 1867 and expanded the original house in 1885. In 1904, Bess, her three brothers, and her mother, Madge Gates Wallace, moved into the Gates house in the aftermath of her father's suicide. Bess became head of the household, caring not only for her younger brothers and elderly grandparents but also for the emotionally devastated Madge Wallace as well. It was to this close-knit family's compound that Harry Truman first came courting Bess Wallace in 1910. Upon their marriage, Bess's strong sense of family responsibility compelled her new husband to move into his in-laws' home. It was in their second-floor bedroom that their only child, Mary Margaret, was born on 17 February 1924.

Following Truman's 1934 election to the U.S. Senate, the Trumans moved to Washington, D.C. Every June, however, mother and daughter returned to 219 North Delaware Street to spend the remainder of the year. Senator Truman returned frequently, but he divided his time between home and political trips across Missouri.

With Truman's succession to the presidency, the home underwent a frenzied renovation. Neighbors helped supervise the painting of the Summer White House a brilliant white. The city of Independence installed a flagpole on the northwest lawn in time to welcome the new president home for his first visit on 27 June 1945. Later that year, the Secret Service built a small guard booth adjacent to the carriage house for the two permanent agents. It was not until 1949 that former president Herbert Hoover convinced the Trumans to put up a fence to keep souvenir hunters out. On 24 June 1950, when Secretary of State Dean Acheson called about the invasion of South Korea, President Truman was at home reading in his library.

Although the public referred to it as the Summer White House, the family did its best to keep their Independence home out of the limelight, mostly to shield the fragile Madge Wallace. Although the Trumans tolerated their public life in the White House, their lives in Independence remained intensely private. They enjoyed visiting with friends and relatives on the home's many porches, an activity that inspired the construction of the "Truman balcony" when the executive mansion was renovated.

In January 1953, Harry and Bess Truman retired from national politics and returned to Independence. They purchased the other interests in the house from Madge Wallace's estate and undertook many interior changes. His home served as the base from which Truman concentrated fund-raising efforts to build his presidential library. The 1955 groundbreaking and 1957 dedication receptions were held at the house; in between the Trumans also hosted the wedding reception for their daughter, Margaret, and E. Clifton Daniel.

An October 1964 fall in the upstairs bathroom triggered Harry Truman's decline from good health. Work at the Truman Library and his usual neighborhood walks became rare as he spent most of his time reading in the home's book-lined library. President Lyndon Johnson visited frequently and signed two proclamations in the Trumans' living room, one of which designated 24 October an annual UN Day. Following Truman's death on 26 December 1972, his widow remained in the house where she and her husband had found such happiness and comfort. Furniture and personal items were left as if the home had been frozen in time. Upon Bess Truman's death on 18 October 1982, her estate and daughter deeded 219 North Delaware Street to the people of the United States.

Prior to 1982, almost nothing was known about the Truman home because the family permitted only a few inside their private domain; journalists and photographers were banned. A body of historical research has since been performed by the National Park Service. Ron Cockrell's *Historic Structures Report, History and Significance, Harry S Truman National Historic Site* (Omaha: National Park Service, 1984) was the first detailed history of the home. Cockrell's *The Trumans of Independence: Historic Resource Study, Harry S Truman National Historic Site* (Omaha: National Park Service, 1985) presents an overview of the Truman family in Independence. These U.S. government publications are available through the National Technical Information Service.

RON COCKRELL

See also Independence, Missouri

Genealogy

See Ancestry

George, Walter Franklin

(29 January 1878–4 August 1957)

Judge and Democratic senator from Georgia. Walter F. George's career constituted a rapid rise from humble beginnings. Born the son of a Georgia tenant farmer, he graduated from Mercer University with a bachelor's degree in science in 1900, and with a law degree a year later. After practicing law for a few years in Vienna, Georgia, he rose to become solicitor general, superior court judge, judge of the state court of appeals, and associate justice of the state supreme court, before he entered politics in 1922. Elected to the U.S. Senate to fill the vacancy left by the death of populist Thomas E. Watson, he served in that body until his retirement in 1956. During his Senate tenure, he was president pro tempore for a time, and he chaired several important committees, including Finance, Foreign Relations, and Postwar Economic Policy and Planning during World War II. Before the 1935 session of Congress, George supported most New Deal measures, but when the program veered to the left, he resisted bills that favored labor at the expense of his business supporters.

George's conservatism became nationally known during his alignment with Republican senator Robert A. Taft and others in the conservative coalition. After opposing FDR's Court-packing attempt, George won reelection in 1938 in spite of the president's personal campaign against him in the state primary. During the Truman years, George took the traditional Democratic stand on the Taft-Hartley Act, but he opposed the administration's defense of Alger Hiss because of what George called "the state of the public mind." He supported the United Nations and other international measures, albeit with reservations. When the president called for a Jewish state, George considered it a "serious error for the United States to assume the responsibility of England in Palestine." George supported the Truman Doctrine as a means for halting Soviet expansion, although he feared that it would intensify the cold war while protecting British interests.

He opposed certain features of the Marshall Plan (the inclusion of conditions for acceptance of aid constituted interference in other countries' domestic affairs) and NATO (only Congress could authorize troops to Europe), and he considered the Mutual Defense Assistance Act of 1949 too expensive.

As his stands highlighted the breakdown in the bipartisan foreign policy sought by the Truman administration, his later support for Eisenhower revived that approach. During the 1950s George worked for the Geneva summit conference and for the administration's China policy, although he broke with the White House on the Middle East because he thought the issues were too complex to permit an American policy. Until his death, he was the president's special ambassador to NATO.

There are no biographical studies of George nor any monographs on him. For sketches, see the *Dictionary of American Biography* Supp. 6 (1980), and Allan A. Michie and Frank Rhylick, *Dixie Demagogues* (New York: Vanguard, 1939), 187–201. Useful references appear in James T. Patterson, *Congressional Conservatism and the New Deal* (Lexington: University Press of Kentucky, 1967), and Robert J. Donovan's two studies: *Conflict and Crisis: The Presidency of Harry S Truman, 1945–1948* (New York: Norton, 1977), and *Tumultuous Years: The Presidency of Harry S Truman, 1949–1953* (New York: Norton, 1982). Some of George's memoirs are in the Columbia University Oral History Collection.

HOWARD JONES

Germany

Truman's outlook on Germany's international role was molded during World War I. He recalled in the 1930s, "The World War made a tremendous impression on me." In part, Truman's enthusiasm for the crusade against the "Hun" grew out of his Wilsonian belief that "we fought for the highest ideals that have ever been the cause of any conflict in the history of the world," but his idealism was also undergirded by a more hardheaded strategic assessment of what a German victory would mean for American security. Writing home from France, where he saw service as an artillery captain, he stated, "I wouldn't be left out of the greatest history-making epoch the world has seen for all there is to live for because there'd be nothing to live for under German control."

As a local politician in Jackson County, Missouri, after the war, Truman left few traces of any continuing interest in foreign affairs, but his dormant internationalism revived following his election to the U.S. Senate in 1934. After a brief flirtation with isolationism, he came to see the Second World War as "a continuation of the one we fought in 1917 and 1918." His belief that it would be "a most difficult world in which to live by our democratic way if Britain is conquered" recalled his earlier strategic views. Germany's misdeeds were further magnified in Truman's mind by the "systematic slaughter" of the Jews by "Nazi beasts."

Where President Roosevelt saw German culture at the roots of Nazi aggression, Truman saw only defective leadership,

Many German civilians refused to believe first reports of the Holocaust. Here, U.S. soldiers require the people of a nearby town to walk past Nazi victims, Jewish women who starved during a three-hundred-mile forced march. (U.S. Army/National Archives)

"a bunch of thugs" engaged in little more than "political gangsterism." Because Truman tended to view history as the struggle for freedom against ambitious world conquerors, he felt that aggressive ideologies merely expressed the will-to-power of unscrupulous leaders. According to Truman's democratic faith, all people, including the German people, were innately good. As he put it, "The combined thought and action of the whole people of any race, creed or nationality will always point in the Right Direction." Thus the war was "Hitler's folly," foisted on a "deluded Hitlerian populace."

German aggression was also symptomatic of larger structural problems in Europe. In a prewar Armistice Day address, he noted that "France and the old Austro-Hungarian empire were the only two really self-contained nations on the continent." As president, he realized when it came time to discuss Germany's fate in 1945 that "our only hope for good from the European War is restored prosperity to Europe and future trade with them." Although this would require a moderate peace and an economically revived Germany, at first neither Truman's liberal internationalist faith nor his strategic sensibility provided him with clear-cut policies for Germany's future.

He was, like almost everyone else, clear on the need to demilitarize and denazify the country and anxious to avoid a repetition of the sorry history of the Versailles settlement in which Germany made good on high reparations demands by infusions of capital from the United States. Beyond that, however, Truman's hands were tied by wartime agreements which envisioned a joint Allied occupation of Germany. The need to find a German settlement agreeable to America's Soviet partner resulted in a provisional agreement at Potsdam in August 1945, one based on the hope that a solution to the German problem would grow out of an amicable four-power administration of the country.

After an initial phase of enthusiasm for Allied cooperation, relations with the Soviets deteriorated. From the first, economic chaos in occupied Germany made necessary large infusions of American aid which made Soviet demands for large reparations seem unrealistic. Equally distressing was the failure to agree on a common economic program. Most important, by the middle of 1946 American policymakers began to suspect that the Soviets were positioning themselves for a power grab in Germany. By this time, the Soviet problem had replaced the German problem in Truman's mind. One aide recalled him saying in 1947 that "there isn't any difference in the totalitarian states, I don't care what you call them. You call them Nazis, Communists, Fascists, Franco, or anything else, they are all alike."

The failure of Allied cooperation in Germany, coupled with economic distress in Western Europe which threatened to bring Communist governments into power, led gradually to the formulation of a German policy more in line with Truman's liberal beliefs. With a view to ending the debilitating economic paralysis within the country, the British and American occupation zones were merged early in 1947. The logic of recovery led inexorably to the inclusion of these zones in the dramatic plan for European recovery proposed in June 1947 by Secretary of State George Marshall. As one State Department official summed it up: "To talk about the recovery of Europe and to oppose the recovery of Germany is nonsense. People can have both or they can have neither." Pursuing this logic to the end, the Western powers in 1948 agreed to create a government for the Western zones to replace military rule.

These moves had serious strategic implications, as the Russians chose to respond in June 1948 with a blockade of Berlin. Although the former German capital lay 110 miles deep within the Soviet zone of occupation, wartime agreements had provided that Berlin be run jointly by the Allies. As a sign of displeasure at the West's independent course in Germany, Stalin closed off all land and water access routes. In the administration debate over the U.S. response, Gen. Lucius D. Clay, who ran the American occupation, argued that a cave-in would mean the end of the American position in Europe. "If we move out of Berlin, we have lost everything we are fighting for," he insisted. Although Truman indicated that "this was his opinion also," he rejected Clay's recommendation for military moves against the Russians, choosing instead to resupply the city of two million by air.

With the success of the Berlin airlift the Soviets lifted the blockade in 1949 in return for a resumption of four-power talks on Germany. By that time, however, the administration's view was that there was nothing to talk about. Truman's influential secretary of state, Dean Acheson, believed that any parleys on Germany were doomed to sterility. In contrast to those in the government who continued to favor a comprehensive German settlement, Acheson was convinced that "there would be fewer and less painful difficulties by going ahead with the West German government than by attempting to unite Germany first." In other words, to reunite Germany it would first be necessary to divide it.

Acheson argued that since 1945 Germany had been "only a geographical expression, a word." Assuming that talks with the Soviets would not improve this state of affairs, he thought that the creation of a prosperous German rump state tied to the West was far more desirable than the prospect of continued great-power dissension. Despite the qualms of many Germans that the tough American position would mean the permanent division of their country, the Truman administration pressed forward with the creation in 1949 of the Federal Republic of Germany. The birth of the *Bundesrepublik* did not end four-power control, however, nor did it restore German sovereignty. Those steps would come during the Eisenhower administration a few years later.

Galvanized by the war scare that swept through Europe at the outset of the Korean conflict in June 1950, American strategists realized that the military vulnerability of Western Europe could be remedied only by the rearmament of West Germany. Speaking for the Joint Chiefs of Staff, Gen. Omar Bradley informed Truman that "unless we re-arm Germany soon we will lose it." An unhappy Truman informed Acheson, "This is a most difficult subject about which to talk." His gut reaction was that the Joints Chiefs proposal was "decidedly militaristic." He recalled that the 100,000-man army that had been permitted to the Germans in the 1920s "was used for the basis of training the greatest war machine that ever came forth in European history."

Truman's reluctant recognition of strategic logic, coupled with his opposition "to anything which would permit a revival of German militarism," resulted in his willingness to go along with a French proposal known as the Pleven Plan. Although it contained some utopian supranational features, the practical aim of Pleven's proposal was to forestall the danger of a renascent Reich by merging German soldiers into a common European army. By 1952, the structure of the European Defense Community (EDC) and the scope of the German military and financial contribution had been worked out. In return, the occupation would be ended and sovereignty granted to the West German state. The EDC scheme eventually failed, but the idea of German rearmament did not, as the next administration saw to it that the Federal Republic and its new army became a sovereign member of the North Atlantic Treaty Organization in 1955.

Hoping to prevent a remilitarized Germany, the Soviets in 1952 made a final offer of a comprehensive peace settlement, holding out the prospect of a united and neutral Germany. Acheson saw the Soviet proposal as one with "the usual apparent hooks in it," but given its appeal to Germans interested in unification, he advised the president that turning it down out of hand would be "ill-advised." This public relations approach to negotiations ensured in advance that subsequent diplomatic parrying on the proposal would come to nothing.

Although Truman rarely involved himself in the details, the German policy collectively hammered out by his administration bore the unmistakable signature of his long-held ideological and strategic views. His liberal internationalism sanctioned the rapid economic recovery of West Germany, and his view of history as a struggle against aggressive despotisms justified West Germany's integration into an alliance system that sought to prevent the domination of Europe by the USSR. In retrospect, Truman's approach to Germany made possible long-term European stability, but by setting aside any immediate prospects for German reunification it also ensured a tense future for subsequent diplomacy on German issues.

Cloyd J. Sweigert, *San Francisco Chronicle* (1945–52).

Truman's views on Germany are scattered. The evolution of his early thinking may be gleaned from two useful collections edited by Robert H. Ferrell: *Dear Bess: The Letters from Harry to Bess Truman 1910–1959* (New York: W. W. Norton, 1983) and *Off the Record: The Private Papers of Harry S. Truman* (New York: Harper & Row, 1980). A recent biography of Truman's prepresidential years by Richard Lawrence Miller, *Truman: The Rise to Power* (New York: McGraw-Hill, 1986), contains information on Truman's views on Germany and foreign policy in general during the 1930s and World War II. A few items of interest can be found in Truman's unpublished papers in the Harry S. Truman Presidential Library, Independence Missouri. No single volume specifically addresses the broad contours of Truman's German policies, although a few deal with important facets like the Berlin crisis or rearmament. The list of primary and secondary works dealing with his administration's German policy as part of its larger cold war strategy is too lengthy to enumerate. But Truman's personal views on the issue, which are rather meager and lacking in nuance given its importance and complexity, are directly accessible from the documentary collection, *Foreign Relations of the United States* (Washington, D.C.: Department of State, annual volumes). Truman's two-volume autobiography, *Year of Decision* and *Years of Trial and Hope* (Garden City, N.Y.: Doubleday, 1955, 1956), also furnishes some revealing insights.

FRANK A. NINKOVICH

See also Berlin Airlift; Fascism; Potsdam Conference; War Crimes Trials; World War II

"Get Tough" Policy

President Harry Truman's "get tough" policy toward the Russians had its inception in his conversation with Soviet foreign minister V. M. Molotov in Washington on 23 April 1945. For Truman's critics his strong language merely fulfilled the predictions of those who had feared that the new president would abandon Roosevelt's easy, conciliatory manner in his relations with the Soviets. Still Roosevelt had approached Stalin as the leader of a wartime military coalition that limited the areas of decision to military strategy and placed a heavy premium on agreement. At Yalta in February 1945 the exchanges among Roosevelt, Churchill, and Stalin produced apparently satisfactory arrangements only because the three wartime leaders refused to pursue issues to the point of disagreement, at least in principle.

During succeeding weeks, however, U.S. relations with Russia became strained. Russia's efforts to transform military into political control of Romania and Poland created consternation in the American diplomatic corps. From Moscow, Ambassador Averell Harriman warned Washington that Soviet behavior, unless countered effectively, would nullify the Declaration on Liberated Europe signed at Yalta. On 6 April, Harriman repeated his warning: "It now seems evident that . . . they intend to go forward with unilateral action in their domination of their bordering states." Harriman advised Washington to assert its purposes in Europe with the same determination displayed by Moscow and make the Russians "realize that they cannot continue their present attitude except at great cost to themselves."

Throughout March and early April Roosevelt acknowledged his burgeoning doubts concerning the future of U.S.-Soviet cooperation. The more the war receded into history, the more Russian policy seemed to depart from the wartime principles that were to guide the political and territorial reconstruction of Europe. On 31 March, Roosevelt reminded Stalin that the creation of the new provisional government of Poland did not conform to the procedures agreed to at Yalta. To the end, however, Roosevelt refused to face the consequences of a total breakdown of U.S.-Russian relations. Shortly before his death on 12 April the president recommended to Churchill that the Western Allies minimize their problems with the Kremlin.

After mid-April 1945 President Truman faced the challenge of confronting the Soviets effectively on the issues posed by their policy in the areas occupied by Russian armies. Soviet behavior in Eastern Europe presented the Western powers with two genuine policy choices in their defense of the principle of self-determination. They could either compel the Russian forces to withdraw to Russia's prewar frontiers or persuade the Kremlin to withdraw. The first alternative was militarily unacceptable. The West was not prepared, physically or emotionally, to engage the Russians in a war over Eastern Europe; no Western interest demanded such a decision. The second alternative was equally unpromising because the West had nothing to offer the Kremlin to encourage its compliance with the Yalta accords.

Unable to compel Russia to cooperate in the reconstruction of Europe in accordance with Western principles, yet unable to ignore Russia's defiant and repressive behavior, the Truman administration adopted the only course remaining—a rhetorical get tough response to Soviet behavior. After receiving a series of adverse reports on Eastern Europe during his first days in office, Truman learned on 17 April that the Kremlin planned to sign a mutual assistance agreement with the provisional government of Poland. The president informed his advisers that he would lay it on the line when Molotov visited Washington a few days later. Adm. William D. Leahy, the president's chief of staff, predicted that "Molotov would be in for some blunt talking from the American side." Harriman, in Washington because of Roosevelt's death, urged Truman to adopt a firm stand on the Polish question and insist on the inclusion of pro-Western Poles in the new Polish government. The president replied that he was not afraid of the Russians; nor did he intend to compromise any American principles to win their favor.

Truman's meeting with Molotov on 22 April was cordial. The president reminded the Russian minister that "in its larger aspects the Polish question had become for our people the symbol of the future development of our international relations." Molotov reassured the president that the two countries could reach the desired agreements on the Polish issue. At the White House meeting on 23 April Secretary of State Edward R. Stettinius informed Truman that the subsequent conversations with Molotov had gone badly. "In fact," said Stettinius, "a complete deadlock had been reached on the subject of carrying out the Yalta agreement on Poland." The Kremlin, the secretary complained, seemed intent on imposing a Communist regime on the Polish people. Truman replied that "our agreements with the Soviet Union had so far been a one-way street and that this could not continue." Others present at the meeting urged caution. Secretary of War Henry L. Stimson preferred that the United States move slowly on the Polish issue. The Russians, he reminded the president, had carried out all their military engagements faithfully. Gen. George C. Marshall, like Stimson, hoped that the administration would avoid an open break with the Kremlin over Poland. Truman pledged to issue no ultimatum; he would merely clarify the U.S. position.

Later that afternoon Truman informed Molotov that the American and British proposals on Poland were reasonable and embodied the maximum Western concessions. The U.S. government, the president declared flatly, would not be a party to any Polish political arrangements that did not represent all Polish elements. "The Soviet Government must realize," he said, "that the failure to go forward at this time with the implementation of the Crimean decision on Poland would seriously shake confidence in the unity of the three governments and their determination to continue the collaboration in the future as they have in the past." Molotov insisted that the Soviets intended to honor the Yalta decisions, but he continued to skirt the question of Soviet compliance with the Western proposals on Poland. Truman then informed Molotov that American friendship with Russia could continue "only on a basis of mutual observation of agreements and not on the basis of a one-way street." To Molotov's complaint, "I have never been talked to like that in my life," the president replied, "Carry out your agreements and you won't get talked to like that." A week later Truman boasted to an astonished Joseph E. Davies, former U.S. ambassador to the Soviet Union, that he let Molotov have it straight.

Historically, strong language had effected little change in the policies of antagonists. Still, Washington insiders reacted favorably to Truman's toughness. Arthur H. Vandenberg, Republican leader in the Senate, found enough solace in Truman's words to confide to his diary, "FDR's appeasement of Russia is over." The United States and Russia could live together in the postwar world, wrote Vandenberg, "if Russia is made to understand that we can't be pushed around." Admiral Leahy rejoiced at the president's new mood. "Truman's attitude in dealing with Molotov," he noted in his memoirs, "was more than pleasing to me. I believed it would have a beneficial effect on the Soviet outlook." Secretary of the Navy James V. Forrestal asserted at the White House meeting on 23 April that Russia had established a pattern of unilateral action throughout Eastern Europe. Therefore, he advised, "we might as well meet the issue now as later on." Some top officials in the State Department agreed with that judgment.

Truman's verbal confrontation with Molotov on 23 April established the get tough policy toward the Soviet Union. Unable to coerce the Kremlin with credible military or economic pressure, the Truman administration had recourse only to words, whether soft and conciliatory, or tough and threatening. Throughout the remainder of 1945 the president refrained from verbal abuse in his public and private discourse on Soviet matters. His new secretary of state, James F. Byrnes, attempted to use his well-known diplomatic skills on Molotov and Stalin, largely in an effort to convince them that Russian security did not require regimes in Eastern Europe dominated by the Kremlin. Byrnes's concessions on Romania and Bulgaria at Moscow in December 1945 troubled the president, largely because he could discover no satisfactory quid pro quo. "We gained only an empty promise of further talks," he complained. On 5 January 1946, the president advocated a tougher line. "Unless Russia is faced with an iron fist and strong language," he told Byrnes, "another war is in the making. . . . I do not think we should play compromise any longer." Recalling his blunt language to Molotov in April 1945, the president observed: "I was sure that Russia would understand firm, decisive language and action much better than diplomatic pleasantries."

By 1946 tough language had become a defense against Republican charges of weakness and failure. Republican editors and politicians demanded success in U.S. foreign policy where there had been none. Facing partisan pressure at home as well as diplomatic intransigence abroad, Byrnes assumed a firmer, more demanding posture toward the Russians at the succession of Paris meetings held during 1946. At one period of stalemate in the Paris Peace Conference of September Truman wired Byrnes to "do everything you can to continue but in the final analysis do whatever you think is right and tell [the Russians] to go to hell if you have to." In the end Byrnes achieved a series of treaties for Germany's wartime satellites in Eastern Europe. Whether Byrnes's adoption of a get tough stance, rather than Soviet interest in obtaining the treaties, produced the necessary Russian compliance is doubtful. In lieu of diplomatic agreement tough language often comprises the only evidence that the U.S. government is pursuing desired ends. Such rhetorical toughness may be effective in sustaining support for established goals; without added inducements it seldom, if ever, renders such goals achievable.

The following works supply more information and a range of opinion on this policy: Thomas G. Paterson, *On Every Front: The Making of the Cold War* (New York: W. W. Norton, 1979); John Lewis Gaddis, *The United States and the Origins of the Cold War* (New York: Columbia University Press, 1972); and Daniel Yergin, *Shattered Peace: The Origins of the Cold War and the National Security State* (Boston: Houghton Mifflin, 1977).

NORMAN A. GRAEBNER

See also Cold War; Containment; Eastern Europe; Poland; Soviet Union

G.I. Bill

See Veterans

Great Britain

Before the Second World War a British Foreign Office official wrote a memorandum about a play in which a character acting as a prime minister was asked to state the most important thing in the world. The prime minister answered, "Love—and Anglo-American relations." That answer was even more appropriate during and after the war, especially during the presidency of Harry S. Truman.

When the Man from Missouri became president in April 1945 Britain was diving into economic crisis. Bombing had destroyed millions of homes and thousands of factories. Torpedoes had cut merchant shipping in half, and exports after the war were less than a third of the late depression years. National income was plummeting and external debt soaring, and the government estimated that the war had cost a fourth of the nation's wealth. Furthermore, a year after Germany's defeat Britons still were on wartime rationing while they faced the awesome job of reconstruction.

This crisis had an impact on British foreign affairs: the U.K. was forced to cut back on its world responsibilities, eventually give its colonies independence, and form a new relationship with its stronger wartime Allies, the Soviet Union and the United States. A British diplomat stated his nation's new position vis-à-vis Russia and America: Britain was "Lepidus in the triumvirate with Mark Antony and Augustus."

The Churchill and Attlee governments understood their position and conducted similar policies toward the Allies. They opposed Soviet expansion throughout the world and especially in Europe; yet without the necessary power to prevent it, they realized they had to rely on the United States. Thus, British officials continually attempted to stimulate their American counterparts to assume more world responsibilities and to stand up and prevent possible Russian expansion. Those officials realized, however, that for the future there would be no pretense of an equal Anglo-American partnership, and that after a century of world leadership they would have to swallow their pride and become America's "junior partner," provoking the "lumbering giant" to confront the Russian Bear.

Churchill adopted this aim with Franklin Roosevelt and then with Harry Truman. Like his predecessor, Truman held some suspicions of British intentions and initially hoped to cooperate with both Allies to establish a just peace in Europe. Roosevelt had not briefed his vice president on foreign affairs, so Truman admitted being "plenty scared" as a new leader facing a myriad of international problems. During the summer of 1945 and at his only conference with Stalin and Churchill, the American liberal attempted to play the role of honest broker between the Russian Communist and English Conservative.

The policy was naive, for as Truman realized during the remainder of 1945 and early 1946 the Western democracies had similar postwar aims which the Soviets opposed. This was espe-

The bombed-out remains of Coventry Cathedral. This aerial view shows U.S. soldiers gathered for services in May 1945. (National Archives)

cially true concerning free elections and trade in areas liberated by Allied armies; the Russians prohibited elections and established communism while the democracies protested.

By 1946, then, British influence and especially Soviet behavior convinced Truman to adopt a tougher stance toward Moscow while increasing cooperation with London. The president launched a trial balloon in March 1946; he invited former prime minister Churchill to give an address at Fulton, Missouri. Truman had discussed the contents of the speech and introduced the Englishman by stating that he would have "something constructive to say." Churchill delivered his famous iron curtain speech which condemned Soviet rule in Eastern Europe and called for an Anglo-American military pact. The administration supported, and Congress passed, a postwar reconstruction loan for Britain—but not one that had been promised during the war for the Soviet Union. The two democracies agreed to merge their zones in Germany, and by autumn British and Canadian military officials visited Washington and began secret talks on arms standardization, joint weapons research, and common tactical doctrines. Britain and the United States decided not to disband the Combined Chiefs of Staff, which had been so effective during the war, and the British maintained offices at the Pentagon. By 1947 the democracies had initiated an officer-exchange program and the U.S. Air Force had begun testing bombs made in the United Kingdom.

The British continued their attempts to induce the United States to become more involved in Europe; the result was the Truman Doctrine. Early in 1947 a freak winter storm crippled the United Kingdom. The Labour government of Clement Attlee and Foreign Secretary Ernest Bevin decided to cut international responsibilities, especially those in Greece, Palestine, and India. But while they were planning to quit the Middle East and give independence to their largest colony, they still maintained a military force in Greece, an impoverished nation engulfed in civil war. Britain supported conservative and moderate Greeks against a coalition of leftists which included Communists. In February, however, London informed Washington that His Majesty's government no longer could spend the millions necessary to maintain democracy in Greece and that aid would terminate at the end of March. This forced a decision from the Truman administration, and the result was the Truman Doctrine.

The doctrine demonstrated that in relation to the Soviet Union and communism the Americans and British had adopted a common policy that eventually would be called containment; yet other issues during Truman's first years in office divided the two democracies. Americans advocated independence for colonial peoples and the demise of the empire, a somber thought to many Britons. Whereas the United States supported liberal trade policies throughout the world, the British complained that they would not be able to compete since their factories had been targets of the Luftwaffe; American ideas of free trade sounded too much like economic imperialism. Britain also resented the Truman administration's policies monopolizing atomic secrets and the occupation of Japan. After all, Britain had participated in developing the bomb and in the Pacific war and wanted to share those responsibilities. The complex problem of Palestine raised animosity. While the United Kingdom was attempting to control an impossible situation and prevent war in the Middle East, Americans were demanding the immediate establishment of a Jewish homeland.

These issues raised tensions, but the threat of communist expansion continually prompted the democracies to cooperate closely. The British welcomed the American proposal to rebuild Europe, the Marshall Plan, and both Truman and Attlee supported the unification of the three Western zones of Germany which created West Germany. In 1948 Communists in Czechoslovakia staged a successful coup and the Soviets began the Berlin blockade. In response, Bevin advocated "some form of union in Western Europe . . . backed by the Americans and the Dominions," a plan that was received warmly by Truman. The result was the creation of the Western European Union; the next year America joined, whereupon it became the North Atlantic Treaty Organization.

The democracies naturally agreed that communism had to be challenged in Asia, but occasionally they disagreed on tactics. After the Communist victory in China the British often attempted to influence the new government of Mao Tse-tung by offering the carrot, whereas the Americans used the stick; thus, although both thought that China's serious economic problems could be used to the West's benefit, Britain offered as much trade as possible and the United States restricted it in an attempt to force concessions from the Chinese. On the matters of recognition and admittance of the People's Republic into the United Nations, London felt that supporting China would provide an opportunity for its leadership to become more independent of the Soviet Union; Washington took the position that withholding recognition would force the People's Republic to improve its behavior. Neither policy worked, as the new nation became closely allied with Moscow and entered the Korean War, actions that again elicited closer Anglo-American relations. Truman and Attlee responded by sending troops under the auspices of the United Nations.

Thus, in the last years of the Truman administration the British again were performing the same role they had when the Missourian became president—they were America's foremost ally, the valuable junior partner.

American official postwar documents were opened for inspection in the first half of the 1970s; later in the decade British records were released, and since then many valuable books have been published. The first was Terry H. Anderson's *The United States, Great Britain, and the Cold War, 1944–1947* (Columbia and London: University of Missouri Press, 1981), which concentrates on Anglo-American relations toward the Soviet Union. Robert M. Hathaway expanded the topic to include economic and colonial issues in *Ambiguous Partnership: Britain and America, 1944–1947* (New York: Columbia University Press, 1981). More recent surveys include Richie Ovendale, *The English-Speaking Alliance: Britain, the United States, the Dominions, and the Cold War, 1945–1951* (Boston: George Allen & Unwin, 1985), and Richard A. Best, Jr., *"Co-operation with Like-Minded Peoples": British Influences on American Security Policy, 1945–1949* (Westport, Conn.: Greenwood Press, 1986). Other useful books include William Roger Louis, *The British Empire in the Middle East, 1945–1951: Arab Nationalism, the United States, and Postwar Imperialism* (Oxford: Clarendon Press, 1984); Edwin W. Martin, *Divided Counsel: The Anglo-American Response to Communist Victory in China* (Lexington: University Press of Kentucky, 1986); and Alan Bullock, *Ernest Bevin: Foreign Secretary, 1945–1951* (London: Heinemann, 1983).

TERRY H. ANDERSON

See also Attlee, Clement Richard; Churchill, Winston S.; Imperialism; India; North Atlantic Treaty Organization; Palestine; Potsdam Conference; World War II

Greece

Developments in American relations with Greece during the Truman administration reflected the major reorientation in U.S. foreign policy during the immediate postwar years. Indeed, Greece was a focal point in this process.

Prior to President Roosevelt's death, the United States displayed limited interest and involvement in Greek affairs. Great Britain had for decades considered Greece as its bailiwick, and Winston Churchill bargained for continued British influence there in October 1944 when he drew up the controversial "Percentages Agreement" with Joseph Stalin in Moscow. Following Greece's liberation that same month, the Roosevelt administration expressed concern over Britain's heavy involvement in Greece's internal affairs and its aggressive methods in responding to the civil uprising in December–January by the Communist-dominated forces of EAM/ELAS, the wartime resistance organization.

American criticism of the British role in Greece became less sharp in the months after the war ended, primarily in response to growing concerns over East-West differences and Soviet policy in Eastern Europe. In the fall of 1945 Truman seriously considered a British request for financial help to Greece. The State Department drafted a note calling for the Greek government to place its finances on a sounder footing before American assistance could be considered. Reflecting on the heavy sacrifices of the Greek people in the wartime struggle against the common enemy, Truman believed the wording too harsh and asked for some changes. He added, "I can't help but feel extremely friendly to the Greeks," but conceded, "I am not an expert in the matter." In January 1946 Secretary of State James F. Byrnes announced a $25 million Export-Import Bank loan with an accompanying note that Athens should take "energetic steps to put its internal house in order."

America encouraged the holding of national elections for the forming of a government responsive to the will of the people. Although the leftist parties abstained from the elections held on 31 March 1946 under foreign supervision, Washington labeled them reasonably fair. A similar judgment followed the 1 September 1946 plebiscite approving the return of King George II. American policymakers through diplomatic channels aired criticism of the corruption, inefficiency, and ruthless antileftism employed by the rightist parties but publicly refrained from outright criticism of Greek governments.

The repressive tactics of rightist governments contributed to the outbreak of renewed civil war in 1946. The Communists resumed hostilities in the spring and during the fall proclaimed the formation of the Democratic Army. Receiving some support from Greece's northern Communist neighbors, the rebel forces challenged the Greek government's ability to control sections of the countryside. In turn, the British government on 21 February 1947 formally announced to the Truman administration that it would be unable to continue assistance to Greece and Turkey after 31 March and requested immediate consultations for the purpose of shifting to the United States the burden of such assistance.

After lengthy consultations with his advisers, Truman responded forcefully before a joint session of Congress on 12 March with his momentous Truman Doctrine which was to be "America's answer to the surge of expansion of communist tyranny." The president requested emergency aid of $300 million for Greece and $100 million for Turkey. The broader implications for a dramatically augmented world role for America came in the president's judgment that "it must be the policy of the United States to support free peoples who are resisting attempted armed subjugation by armed minorities or by outside pressures." With congressional approval the United States provided aid to the two eastern Mediterranean countries, while also committing itself to contain Soviet and Communist expansion. The cold war had begun.

American military and economic aid played a decisive role in bringing an end to the Greek civil war by the early fall of 1949. With the continuation of assistance under the Marshall Plan and Mutual Security Act, Greece's financial, military, and political problems were brought under control during the 1950s. Rescued from threatened Communist domination, Greece, now closely linked with the Western camp, would experience stability, recovery, and considerable economic growth. These ties were further solidified when the Truman administration supported Greece's entry into NATO in 1952.

Many Greeks thus have good reason to be grateful to Truman. To express these sentiments, the Greek-American organization AHEPA (American Hellenic Educational Progressive Association) donated a statue of Truman to Greece in 1963, and it was positioned prominently in central Athens. This statue, however, came to symbolize the controversial political legacy of the Truman administration for Greece. Concurrent with the commitment to support Greece in 1947 came a growing, at times heavy-handed, American involvement in Greek affairs. Many liberals and virtually all leftists have come to attribute the more than three decades of rightist domination in Greek politics and the armed forces to the domineering policies of the United States—which, in their opinion, also sacrificed Greek national interests on a number of occasions. Two explosions rocked Truman's statue during the military dictatorship (perceived by Greeks as American-supported) in 1970 and 1971, and in March 1986 a revolutionary group, to protest the visit of Secretary of State George Shultz, planted a bomb that produced significant damage. Largely responding to pressure from Greek-American organizations, Andreas Papandreou's socialist government quietly restored the statue to its original spot after more than a year's absence, but only after loud political debate that evoked painful references to long-standing divisions in Greek society.

Lawrence S. Wittner in *American Intervention in Greece, 1943–1949* (New York: Columbia University, 1982) provides a revisionist analysis, concluding that the Truman Doctrine became a model for U.S. intervention in other countries. John Iatrides offers more balanced treatment in several articles, including "Greece and the Origins of the Cold War," in *Greece in Transition*, ed. John T. A. Kouwoulider, 236–51 (London: Zeno, 1977), and "Greece and the United States: The Strained Partnership," in *Greece in the 1980s*, ed. Richard Clogg, 150–72 (London: Macmillan, 1983).

S. VICTOR PAPACOSMA

See also Cold War; Great Britain; Marshall Plan; Truman Doctrine

Green, William

(3 March 1873–21 November 1952)

Coal miner, AFL president, Truman ally. Born into a coal-mining family in Coshocton, Ohio, William Green began working in the mines at age sixteen after eight years of formal education. He joined and became an active member of the United Mine Workers union, eventually rising to the position of international secretary-treasurer and a vice president of the American Federation of Labor (AFL).

Green, who was elected AFL president after Samuel Gompers's death in 1924, became involved in Harry Truman's political life in a significant way as early as 1940 when, following the lead of several other labor leaders, he wrote a letter to the head of the Missouri State Federation of Labor urging the state's organized labor movement to return its junior senator to Washington. With even greater enthusiasm four years later, Green once again endorsed Truman, this time for the office of vice president, an action taken at least in part to discourage the nomination of South Carolina senator James Byrnes, who was unacceptable to the labor movement.

Nevertheless, shortly after Truman became president, his relationship with the labor chief dissolved into acrimony as a series of postwar industrial disputes threatened the administration's postwar economic planning. Truman's vigorous opposition to and eventual veto of the Taft-Hartley Act, however, led to a reconciliation between the two men prior to the 1948 general elections.

The William Green Papers are located in the AFL-CIO Archives at the George Meany Center for Labor Studies. There is also a small collection of papers in the Green Letterbooks in the Library of Congress. A book by Max D. Danish, *William Green* (New York: Inter-allied Publications, 1952), was written for a popular audience.

GARY M. FINK

See also Labor

H

Hannegan, Robert Emmet

(30 June 1903–6 October 1949)

Robert Hannegan figured significantly in Harry Truman's career at two crucial points: 1940 and 1944. Born in St. Louis, Hannegan practiced law there after graduation from St. Louis University, became an active Democrat, and served as chief aide to Mayor Bernard F. Dickmann during the 1930s. By 1940, he had become a person of some power in the city as chair of the Democratic committee and boss of the Twenty-first Ward. His chief political interest at the moment was the nomination of his fellow townsman Lawrence McDaniel for the governorship. Fearing that Hannegan would support Governor Lloyd Stark's challenge to Truman's renomination to the Senate, several of Truman's political allies warned Hannegan that if he did back Stark, they would retaliate against McDaniel. Subsequently, on the eve of the election, Hannegan came out for Truman; many other ward bosses followed his lead, and Truman, who had received less than four thousand votes in that city six years before, now picked up more than seventy thousand, an important factor in his victory in a close election.

Four years later, Hannegan played a major role in the movement to make Truman the Democratic nominee for vice president. With Truman's help, Hannegan had obtained appointment as collector of revenue for the Eastern District of Missouri in 1942, had moved up to commissioner of internal revenue the next year, and was appointed chair of the Democratic National Committee in January 1944. His rise meant that a representative of the urban machine faction of the Democratic party and a Truman ally was in a key position in the politics of 1944. The chairman and his lieutenants quickly pushed Truman to the forefront of party affairs in hopes of strengthening the party and developing a replacement for Vice President Henry A. Wallace, who seemed to Hannegan and his associates to be unsafe and radical and likely to drive voters away from the party. Truman appeared to be more sensible and attractive.

Hannegan worked against Wallace and for Truman both in the White House and at the Democratic party's national convention in Chicago. He helped persuade Roosevelt not to insist that the convention renominate Wallace and to announce that Truman was acceptable to him. At the convention, Hannegan drew upon his status as national chairman and his ability to pose as the representative of the absent president to argue that Roosevelt preferred Truman, an argument Hannegan supported with a letter he had obtained from FDR stating that he would be "very glad" to run with either Truman or William O. Douglas and that either "would bring real strength" to the ticket. Hannegan hoped to persuade delegates to switch to Truman on the second ballot. Enough did to obtain the nomination for him.

Soon after Truman became president, he appointed Hannegan postmaster general. In that capacity, he improved the postal service, and as a presidential adviser, he recommended steps that would strengthen the president with organized labor and the liberals. Forced by health problems to retire in 1947, he soon died of heart failure in his native city.

There is neither a collection of Hannegan papers nor a biography, but aspects of his career are documented in the Truman Papers (among others), in memoirs of the period, including oral histories in the Truman Library, and in the *St. Louis Post-Dispatch* and other newspapers. Richard L. Miller's *Truman: The Rise to Power* (New York: McGraw-Hill, 1986) is a recent work that pays some attention to Hannegan and offers some guidance to the sources on him. Harold F. Gosnell in *Truman Crises: A Political Biography of Harry S. Truman* (Westport, Conn.: Greenwood Press, 1980) writes even more about the man. There is a sketch of his life in Eleanora W. Schoenbaum, ed., *Political Profiles: The Truman Years* (New York: Facts on File, 1978).

RICHARD S. KIRKENDALL

See also Election of 1940; Election of 1944

Harriman, W. Averell

(15 November 1891–25 July 1986)

Businessman, diplomat, presidential adviser. W. Averell Harriman, the son of railroad magnate and financier Edward H. Harriman, was educated at prestigious Groton Academy and Yale University. He began a highly successful business career with his father's Union Pacific Railroad. On the eve of American entry into World War I, he went into the shipping business and later founded a major New York banking house. One of Harry Hopkins's "tame millionaires," Harriman worked closely with the New Deal during the depression years, demonstrating a marked ability to get things done while serving with the National Recovery Administration and the Business Advisory Council of the Department of Commerce.

During World War II, Harriman emerged as one of Roosevelt's closest advisers. In early 1941, he went to London as the president's personal Lend-Lease expediter, responsible for facilitating the delivery of U.S. supplies to England. In that capacity, he also undertook several important missions to the Soviet Union and, on 1 October 1943, was appointed ambassador to Russia. He attended all the major wartime conferences and established close personal relationships with both Winston Churchill and Joseph Stalin.

W. Averell Harriman. (OWI/National Archives)

The ambassador played a crucial role in the shaping of U.S. policy toward the Soviet Union in the first weeks of the Truman presidency. Long concerned about Soviet expansionism and fearful that the United States was being too accommodating toward Stalin, he had advocated a "firm but friendly quid pro quo" policy on such things as Lend-Lease and postwar economic assistance. When Roosevelt died, Harriman immediately returned to Washington and sought to commit the new president to a tougher line. The result—not always what Harriman intended—was a firmer stand on the Polish issue, Truman's famous dressing-down of Soviet foreign minister Molotov on 23 April, and the termination of Lend-Lease to the Soviet Union after V-E Day. When James F. Byrnes became secretary of state, Harriman's influence waned, and he resigned in February 1946.

Harriman subsequently served the Truman administration in various capacities. Shortly after he returned from Moscow, he accepted an appointment as ambassador to the Court of St. James. He worked effectively with the Labour government of Clement Attlee and in his spare time negotiated with the Russians a peace treaty for Romania. In September 1946, he was called back to Washington to replace the controversial Henry A. Wallace as secretary of commerce.

Harriman played a key role in the Marshall Plan. As secretary of commerce, he headed a nonpartisan committee that drafted proposals that became the basis for the Economic Cooperation Act. In the spring of 1948, he was given the title of U.S. special representative in Europe for the Economic Cooperation Administration. In that capacity, he served as a veritable theater commander in peacetime, coordinating the efforts of business and government in the various member countries and traveling throughout Europe to oversee the distribution of vast quantities of American money and supplies. He went about his work with his customary single-mindedness and attention to detail. Journalist Theodore White compared him to a "tank crushing all opposition."

Upon the outbreak of the Korean War, Harriman returned home to serve as the president's special assistant for national security affairs, becoming a major adviser and troubleshooter on Korea and other foreign policy matters. He helped sell NSC 68 to Truman and helped persuade the Joint Chiefs of Staff to approve Gen. Douglas MacArthur's scheme for a counteroffensive at Inchon. He defended Dean Acheson against the attacks of right-wing Republicans, and played a crucial role in the firing of his old duck-hunting companion, MacArthur. Harriman's role in the Korean War anticipated that of later national security advisers. From 1951 to 1953, he served as head of the Mutual Security Agency, once again directing the nation's foreign aid program.

During their eight years of working together, Harriman and Truman developed a deep mutual admiration. Harriman especially appreciated Truman's loyalty, and Truman respected Harriman's reliability, his honesty in assessing complex situations, and his knack for getting things done.

After the Truman administration, Harriman continued to play an important role in the nation's politics and diplomacy. He made a brief unsuccessful attempt to secure the Democratic nomination for the presidency in 1952, but in 1954 he won election as governor of New York. He was defeated for reelection by Nelson A. Rockefeller in 1958. When the Democrats returned to power in 1961, Harriman returned to Washington, serving in the Kennedy administration as a roving ambassador and then as assistant secretary of state for Far Eastern affairs and under secretary of state for political affairs. He negotiated the 1962 Geneva agreement on Laos and the nuclear test ban treaty and helped engineer the coup that overthrew Ngo Dinh Diem. Among the New Frontiersmen, he was known as "the Crocodile" for the snappish way in which he dealt with ill-considered proposals. Uncomfortable with Lyndon B. Johnson's escalation of the Vietnam War, Harriman nevertheless took responsibility for handling the various Vietnam peace initiatives. When formal negotiations opened in Paris in April 1968, Harriman was appointed chief U.S. negotiator. Forced to leave government with the election of Richard Nixon, he remained an esteemed elder statesman until his death in 1986.

Harriman's early career is ably summarized in W. Averell Harriman and Elie Abel, *Special Envoy to Churchill and Stalin 1941–1946* (New York: Random House, 1975). Reflections on his career are also contained in his *America and Russia in a Changing World* (Garden City, N.Y.: Doubleday, 1971). The careers of Harriman and five of his fellow establishment figures are covered in Walter Isaacson and Evan Thomas, *The Wise Men: Six Friends and the World They Made* (New York: Simon & Schuster, 1986).

GEORGE C. HERRING

See also "Get Tough" Policy; Korean War; Marshall Plan; NSC 68

Harry S. Truman Library

The Harry S. Truman Library is a manuscript repository, museum, and library which is operated by the Office of Presidential Libraries of the U.S. National Archives and Records Administration. The library houses the personal and official papers of Harry S. Truman, the papers and oral history transcripts of his associates and family, and other unpublished and published material pertaining to Truman's personal life, career, and presidency. The museum displays relevant documents, cartoons, photographs, artifacts, and other memorabilia as well as a replica of the Oval Office during his time as president. The graves of Truman and his wife, Bess Wallace Truman, are located in the courtyard of the library.

As an avid student of history, Truman was concerned lest his files be lost to posterity. He deposited, in 1949, records of his speeches and some films in the National Archives. In 1950 he successfully recommended legislation authorizing the National Archives to receive papers of high government officials including the president. Truman, however, decided that year to follow Franklin D. Roosevelt's precedent in establishing a presidential library under the jurisdiction of the National Archives. Thus in July the Harry S. Truman Library, Inc., was created to solicit funds for constructing an appropriate building. By 1957 the organization had raised $1.8 million for that purpose. Emphasizing that the library would be basically a research institution, Truman also formed an advisory committee of scholars to help plan the library and its programs.

Truman hoped that the federal government would accept ownership of and operate his library. His successor as president,

Dwight D. Eisenhower, also grew interested in establishing a similar institution to house his presidential records. The National Archives and Records Service (NARS) proposed regularizing the acquisition of contemporary presidential papers and the administration of presidential libraries. This received enthusiastic bipartisan support, and in 1955 Congress passed the Presidential Libraries Act. This legislation authorized NARS to accept documentary and other historical materials pertaining to living ex-presidents as well as land and buildings for their libraries.

The city of Independence, Missouri, had already donated to the Truman Library, Inc., 13.2 acres of land located on a knoll only five blocks from the Truman residence. Construction of the spacious one-story Indiana limestone building—described by one scholar as resembling Queen Hatshepsut's temple on the Nile—was begun in 1955. Completed in 1957, the building along with the site and Truman's papers then became federal property. Additions to the building in 1968 and 1980 made it a roughly circular structure.

A veteran archivist, Philip C. Brooks, served as director of the Truman Library until 1971 when he was succeeded by his assistant, Benedict K. Zobrist. Truman and Brooks intended that the library would become more than a copy of the Franklin D. Roosevelt Library. It would, of course, become a significant research center and a popular museum. The library also served as Truman's office for the rest of his life, and it was the site of many film showings, lectures, and other public meetings. More important, the Harry S. Truman Library Institute for National and International Affairs was created in 1957. It became very active, helping to develop the library's collections, sponsoring conferences of scholars and public figures, printing conference proceedings, financing research grants, awarding a major book prize, and publishing a newsletter, later named *Whistle Stop*, containing research articles and news of the library.

As of 1987, the library's holdings consisted of some 14 million pages of Truman's papers and four hundred of his associates', 4,600 microforms, 85,000 photographs, 325,000 feet of motion picture film, 40,000 books, 400 oral history transcripts, 24,000 museum objects, and significant quantities of other printed items, dissertations, and audiovisual materials. The library's holdings are available for research, although some items are restricted because of security requirements or donor stipulations. The library opened its doors for research in May 1959, and 4,550 people had used the collections by 1987, many of them for extended periods of time. The museum has been open to the public since 1957; 6 million people had visited it by 1987. Tens of thousands of people have attended conferences or other meetings, seen films, or heard lectures at the library since 1957.

For a history of the Truman Library and the federal presidential library system, see Donald R. McCoy, *The National Archives: America's Ministry of Documents, 1934–1968* (Chapel Hill: University of North Carolina Press, 1978). Among the several informative articles dealing with the library is Philip C. Brooks, "The Harry S. Truman Library—Plans and Reality," *American Archivist* 25 (January 1962): 25–37. See also *Historical Materials in the Harry S. Truman Library* (Independence, Mo.: Harry S. Truman Library, 1984) with addendum available from the library.

DONALD R. McCOY

Hassett, William D.

(28 August 1880–29 August 1965)

Correspondence secretary to Harry S. Truman. Born in Northfield, Vermont, Hassett attended Clark University for two years before embarking upon a career as a reporter for various newspapers and wire services. He entered government service in 1933 as a publicist for the National Recovery Administration; in 1935 he joined the White House staff as an assistant to the press secretary and assumed primary responsibility as Roosevelt's correspondence secretary in 1944. President Truman retained Hassett in this post until ill-health forced Hassett's retirement in July 1952.

Hassett oversaw the handling of mail from private persons and wrote appropriate replies for either his or the president's signature. He drafted Truman's proclamations for special occasions and letters of congratulation and condolence. Politically sensitive letters or routine greetings to organizations of major importance were handled by either policy or operations members of the White House staff. Hassett's letters of polite refusal to people making a personal request of the president were known as "Hassett Valentines." When Truman's letter writing got him into difficulty with the public, Hassett quipped to him that the president wasn't keeping him busy enough.

Truman enjoyed discussing history and literature with Hassett and publicly referred to him as "Doctor" after Norwich University conferred an honorary degree upon Hassett in 1946. When Hassett retired, Truman wrote a generous letter of appreciation with the postscript: "Mr. Hassett didn't get this one up. The 'Old Man' himself wrote it."

Richard Neustadt has a brief account of Hassett's duties as Truman's correspondence secretary in *The Truman White House: The Administration of the Presidency, 1945–1953,* ed. Francis Weller (Lawrence: Regents Press of Kansas, 1980). Hassett wrote about his experiences with Truman in "President Was His Boss," *Saturday Evening Post,* 10 October 1953, 19–21; and 28 November 1953, 38–39. Hassett's papers are in the Franklin D. Roosevelt and Harry S. Truman libraries.

FRANKLIN D. MITCHELL

Hastie, William Henry

(17 November 1904–14 April 1976)

William Hastie was born in Knoxville, Tennessee, the only child of William Henry and Roberta Child Hastie. He graduated from Dunbar High School in Washington, D.C. (1921), Amherst College (1925), and Harvard Law School (1930), which he entered after having taught at Bordentown (N.J.) Manual Training School (1925–27). Valedictorian at Dunbar and Amherst, he was a *Law Review* editor at Harvard where he later obtained an S.J.D. (1933).

Before he and Harry Truman entered each other's life,

The Honorable William H. Hastie, governor of the U.S. Virgin Islands, 17 May 1946. (National Archives)

Hastie was a private practitioner in Washington, a faculty member at Howard University Law School (1930–37), an assistant solicitor in the Department of the Interior (1933–37), a U.S. district judge in the Virgin Islands (1937–39), a civilian aide to Secretary of War Henry L. Stimson (1940–43), and a dean of the law school at Howard (1939–46).

By 1946, a description once in vogue among blacks fitted Hastie perfectly: he was "tall, tan, and terrific." A hero to many, he was particularly hailed for his opposition to racism in the armed forces and for his work as a lawyer with the National Association for the Advancement of Colored People (NAACP) whose coveted Spingarn Medal he received in 1943. He was a national figure but not a Truman favorite, and yet Truman appointed him governor of the Virgin Islands in 1946.

The appointment was made after Truman, who had heard that Hastie had opposed President Franklin D. Roosevelt in 1944, was told by Secretary of the Interior Harold L. Ickes that Roosevelt had intended to name Hastie to the post as successor to Governor Charles Harwood. Noteworthy in the history of "firsts" for Afro-Americans, the appointment was also important in world history: it enhanced Hastie's ability to harvest black votes indispensable to Truman's victory over Governor Thomas E. Dewey in 1948.

No one asked Hastie to "give 'em hell for Harry." No one had to. At political risk, Truman had joined the battle against racism, destined (in Hastie's words) to take the federal government "to new and higher ground" from which no successor could ever fully retreat. The president was not flawless, but Hastie saw him as "a person who probably made a great number of small mistakes, but rarely a big one."

At the beginning, Truman was to Hastie "just another midwestern Senator"; in the end, however, he was "one of the great Presidents." And Hastie? Appointed by Truman to the U.S. Court of Appeals for the Third Circuit in 1949 (again, a "first"), he proved to be the consummate jurist. He became chief judge in 1968 and was a senior judge from 1971 until his death in 1976.

Perspective on Hastie's era is provided by various works, notably Richard Kluger's *Simple Justice: The History of Brown v. Board of Education and Black America's Struggle for Equality* (New York: Knopf, 1976), and Hastie's "Toward an Equalitarian Legal Order, 1930–1950," *Annals of the American Academy of Political and Social Science* 407 (May 1973): 18–31. But regarding the crossing of Hastie's and Truman's paths, the best sources are black newspapers and Hastie's papers at Harvard Law School Library, especially the transcript of his interview by Jerry N. Hess, oral historian for the Harry S. Truman Library, on 5 January 1972. The Hastie-Truman relationship is also treated in Gilbert Ware, *William Hastie: Grace under Pressure* (New York: Oxford University Press, 1984).

GILBERT WARE

See also Black Americans; Civil Rights

Health

For most of his life, Truman was a man of robust health, subject more to the ravages of stress than to ordinary physical illnesses. Although born with eyesight so myopic that at least one recorded examination found him "blind" (20/400) in both eyes without corrective lenses, he appears to have been physically sturdy until his final years. His only serious childhood disease was diphtheria, which struck him at the age of nine; he was partially paralyzed for several months before making a complete recovery.

As a man in his twenties and thirties he displayed high energy levels, doing hard farm work with minimal rest and handling grueling military training and combat activity with little difficulty. In his forties he had some relatively extensive dental problems that required some bridgework; they do not appear to have been extraordinary by the standards of those days, however. In 1929, he was hospitalized for minor rectal surgery to correct an anal fistula.

His physical problems, however, appear insignificant in comparison to the stresses of officeholding. While presiding judge of the Jackson County Court (1927–34), he reacted with increasing frustration to lack of recognition (real or imagined), the difficulties of balancing machine associations with a dedication to honest government, and the necessity of cutting the county payroll during the depression. From time to time, he sought refuge from the pressures upon him with solitary stays as an unregistered guest at one or two downtown Kansas City hotels. (At one of them, the Pickwick, he made liberal use of the establishment's stationery to commit his anger to paper.) He also sought refuge in travel. It appears to have been at this stage of his life that headaches became a relatively frequent problem.

His terms in the U.S. Senate called forth similar symptoms, which were intensified by his habits of hard, detailed work, sometimes to the point of exhaustion, and by loneliness for his family during the periods his wife and daughter were away in Missouri. In 1937, 1941, and 1943, he checked into the Army-Navy Hospital at Hot Springs, Arkansas, suffering from what seems to have been bouts of nervous exhaustion. They were characterized by headaches, nausea, vomiting, and a sense of continual weariness. On each occasion, military physicians could find little wrong with him physically. Various doctors recommended increased exercise for "flabby heart muscles," new eyeglasses, a thyroid supplement, and moderate doses of phenobarbitol (apparently meant as a tranquilizer). In each case Truman left considerably refreshed after a week or two of rest.

There are some indications that the strain had begun to take a physical toll on Truman by the time he became president. His blood pressure, usually very low, had become just a bit above normal, and he had developed what must have been a very mild pulmonary edema. (A pulmonary edema—a buildup of fluid in the lung tissues—is an early warning that the heart is not pumping adequately and may be the first sign of congestive heart failure.) The physical debility yielded to treatment by his White House physician, Dr. Wallace Graham, who prescribed primarily a regimen of exercise and regular periods of relaxation. Throughout his presidency, Truman handled a heavy work load and displayed abundant energy. He was hospitalized for a few days because of an intestinal infection in late 1952.

In retirement Truman yielded slowly to the debilitating inroads of old age. Laid low for a time by critical gall bladder surgery in 1954, he bounced back to lead an active life until he underwent surgery once again in 1963, this time for an intestinal hernia. The following year he slipped and fell in his bathtub at home, breaking two ribs. Although the injuries were minor, they effectively marked an end to Truman's busy public life. The fall may have been caused by increasing episodes of vertigo, which forced him to give up his customary morning walks. Arthritis in the knees and hips further limited his mobility. Late in 1972, Truman was hospitalized with lung congestion; he died of kidney failure and heart disease at Research Hospital, Kansas City, Missouri, 26 December 1972.

The best published source for information on Truman's health is Margaret Truman, *Bess W. Truman* (New York: Macmillan, 1986). Alfred Steinberg, *The Man from Missouri* (New York: G. P. Putnam's Sons, 1962), is also useful and appears accurate. A major unpublished source, rich in its detail for the prepresidential period, is Medical File, Army Personnel Records of Harry S. Truman, Truman Library. Truman's death certificate is in Miscellaneous Historical Documents File, No. 621, Truman Library.

ALONZO L. HAMBY

See also Personal Writings; Walking

Health Insurance, National

See National Health Insurance

Henderson, Loy Wesley

(28 June 1892–25 March 1986)

Diplomat Loy Henderson was born in Rogers, Arkansas, and graduated from Northwestern University in 1915. He joined the State Department in 1921 and served at posts in Europe and the Near East. He worked with George Kennan and Charles ("Chip") Bohlen at the American embassy in Moscow and witnessed the purge trials of the late 1930s.

In March 1945 Henderson became head of the Division of Near East and African Affairs, where he encouraged close Anglo-American cooperation. "There is one fact facing both the United States and Great Britain," he stated. "That is the Soviet Union." He advised Truman and Acting Secretary Dean Acheson to take a strong anti-Soviet stand during the Iran crisis of 1946, and helped formulate the Truman Doctrine after the announcement of British withdrawal from Greece and Turkey in early 1947. His support for Britain's Palestine policy, however, drew accusations of his being "pro-Arab" from Zionist groups and demands for his resignation.

Truman chose Henderson as America's first ambassador to India in 1948 and appointed him ambassador to Iran in 1951. Henderson concentrated on resolving the crisis over Prime Minister Mohammad Mossadegh's nationalization of the Anglo-Iranian Oil Company. An American-supported coup d'etat overthrew Mossadegh in 1953 and resulted in a division of oil royalties between the new regime and a consortium of American and British oil companies.

Henderson was appointed a deputy under secretary of state in 1955 and participated in negotiations concerning the Suez Canal in 1956–57. He retired from the Foreign Service in 1961.

There is no biography of Loy Henderson, but his early career is discussed in Martin Weil, *A Pretty Good Club: The Founding Fathers of the U.S. Foreign Service* (New York: W. W. Norton, 1978), and George F. Kennan, *Memoirs, 1925–1950* (Boston: Little, Brown, 1967). Henderson's role in the formulation of the Truman Doctrine and other cold war programs is described in Dean Acheson, *Present at the Creation: My Years in the State Department* (New York: W. W. Norton, 1969).

STEPHEN G. MARSHALL

See also Iran; Truman Doctrine

Hennings, Thomas Carey, Jr.

(25 June 1903–13 September 1960)

Democratic senator from Missouri, 1951–60. Son of a well-known Saint Louis judge and lawyer, Thomas C. Hennings, Jr.,

enjoyed a comfortable childhood. He graduated from Cornell University, where he ran track, and then received a law degree from Washington University at Saint Louis in 1926. After serving as an assistant circuit attorney in Saint Louis for six years, he gained election to the U.S. House of Representatives in 1934. In his three terms as a congressman, Hennings supported Franklin Delano Roosevelt and the New Deal. Shortly after leaving Congress, Hennings joined the navy. He served in Puerto Rico and Hawaii as a lieutenant commander until 1943, when severe illness forced him to return to Saint Louis.

In 1950 Hennings ran for a U.S. Senate seat from Missouri. Although President Harry S. Truman backed another Democratic contender, Hennings won the Democratic primary. He then beat incumbent Republican senator Forrest C. Donnell in the general election.

Appointed to the Subcommittee on Privileges and Elections, Hennings played a leading role in the Senate's first investigations into the conduct of Senator Joseph McCarthy of Wisconsin. In 1951, Hennings coauthored a report that criticized McCarthy's role in the successful 1950 back-street campaign against Democratic senator Millard Tydings of Maryland. The next year the Missouri senator was the driving force behind a report critical of Senator McCarthy for obstruction of the Senate's investigations and for financial improprieties. This report became an important document in the Senate's subsequent censure of McCarthy, which Hennings heartily endorsed.

Handsome and eloquent, Hennings was welcomed by powerful conservatives into the inner Senate circle known as "the club." He remained, however, an ardent liberal. He supported Truman's legislative program and continued to champion liberal causes, especially in the field of civil liberties, during the Eisenhower presidency. Hennings opposed measures designed to curb the powers of the Supreme Court, criticized government secrecy, fought for the Civil Rights Act of 1957, and successfully challenged the Bricker Amendment in 1954, which would have limited the president's treaty-making powers. Truman thought that Hennings and his fellow Democratic senator during the 1950s, Stuart Symington, gave Missouri the best Senate representation it had ever had. Plagued by poor health shortly after his reelection in 1956, Hennings died in Washington, D.C., at the age of fifty-seven in 1960.

The fullest account of Hennings's career is Donald J. Kemper, *Decade of Fear: Senator Hennings and Civil Liberties* (Columbia: University of Missouri Press, 1965). For a broader discussion of Hennings's opposition to McCarthy, see Robert Griffith, *The Politics of Fear: Joseph R. McCarthy and the Senate* (Lexington: University Press of Kentucky, 1970), and Richard Fried, *Men against McCarthy* (New York: Columbia University Press, 1976). Hennings's papers are at the University of Missouri, Columbia.

JAMES R. RALPH, JR.

See also Joseph R. McCarthy

Highway Policy

In April 1945, President Harry S. Truman inherited legislation, passed in 1944, that had committed the federal government to a vastly expanded program of highway building. Truman endorsed the idea of unlimited mobility and economic development associated with road building, especially the construction of the Interstate Highway System with its immense capacity and safety design features. But during the Truman presidency, road building was only one of several projects on the public works and national agendas. In particular, rapid construction of housing for returning veterans took precedence. After June 1950, moreover, Truman continued to limit the expenditures of funds and materials for road building; the Korean War took precedence. The net result was that Truman celebrated the developmental aspects of highway building in his public announcements and in the councils of his administration, but in subsequent years agreed only to a modest increase in federal road expenditures beyond those approved in 1944.

In November of that year, President Franklin D. Roosevelt had signed the Federal Aid Highway Act, allocating $500 million for each of the next four years to construct highways, a fourfold increase over 1940. In addition, the act committed the federal government to financing a portion of the expenses of constructing the Interstate Highway System, a network of highways approximately forty thousand miles in length intended to carry about 20 percent of the nation's traffic. These programs started slowly, however, owing to inflation, shortages of materials, and division among members of the road-building and user communities regarding highway priorities. In particular, political leaders in rural and urban areas sought increased highway appropriations to promote growth and relieve congestion. In 1949, in fact, rural representatives introduced legislation to create an agency dedicated solely to farm road construction, threatening a further diminution of the ability of road engineers to service increasing traffic volumes in urban areas. By 1950, then, even the vast program authorized in 1944 seemed inadequate.

President Truman was often at the center of negotiations, consistently attempting to contain highway expenditures as part of his effort to reduce inflation. In August 1946, he froze highway spending to give priority to housing. In 1948, he asked Congress to reduce highway allocations to $300 million annually, but Congress nevertheless provided $450 million. After June 1950, because of the Korean War, Truman requested that Congress lower spending outlined in pending legislation. By 1952, however, the demand for highway building was overwhelming. Between 1945 and 1952, motor vehicle registrations had increased from 31 million to 53 million, including more than 9 million trucks. Congress rejected Truman's request and increased annual appropriations to $575 million, including for the first time $25 million designated for construction of the Interstate Highway System. Road engineers and organized highway users, however, had proposed spending more than $800 million, including a substantial increase for the Interstate System.

President Truman presided over the initial stages of a remarkable increase in federal highway spending and construction activities; mileage for farm and city increased rapidly. Truman endorsed these developments. Yet he also maintained Roosevelt's approach to highway policy, viewing federal road spending as one of many tools for economic development. Between 1944 and 1952, federal highway allocations had increased only $75 million. Despite strong pressures from Congress, road builders, and highway users, the Truman administration subordinated highway policy to housing, inflation, and war.

Jean Labatut and Wheaton J. Lane, eds., in *Highways in Our National Life: A Symposium* (Princeton: Princeton University Press, 1950), offer contemporary discussions of both the problems facing highway builders and the importance of roads to American society during the early postwar period. Mark H. Rose, in *Interstate: Express Highway Politics, 1941-1956* (Lawrence: University Press of Kansas, 1979), analyzes the social bases of American highway politics, focusing in particular on efforts to fund construction of the Interstate Highway System. Bruce E. Seely, *Building the American Highway System: Engineers as Policy Makers* (Philadelphia: Temple University Press, 1987), focuses on the role of engineers in the Bureau of Public Roads from the late 1890s through the 1950s. For another overview of highway-building efforts in this country, see U.S. Department of Transportation, Federal Highway Administration, *America's Highways, 1776-1976: A History of the Federal-Aid Program* (Washington, D.C.: U.S. Government Printing Office, 1977). This volume, published at the time of the nation's bicentennial, is the official history of the federal aid program.

MARK H. ROSE
BRUCE E. SEELY

Hiroshima

See Atomic and Hydrogen Bombs; Japan

Hillman, Sidney

(23 March 1887–10 July 1946)

Sidney Hillman was born in the Lithuanian village of Zagare. His rabbinical education was interrupted by the 1905 Russian revolution and he was forced to flee to the West as a political refugee in 1906. In 1914, he became the first president of a newly formed union of men's clothing workers, the Amalgamated Clothing Workers of America. In the 1930s, he was a founder and vice president of the Congress of Industrial Organizations (CIO).

During the 1944 presidential campaign, the Republican party tried to discredit its opponent by suggesting that the Democratic party had become the political hostage of the CIO. The evidence amounted to a widely circulated rumor, first appearing in a story by Arthur Krock in the *New York Times*, that President Roosevelt had given Sidney Hillman, vice president of the CIO and chairman of its Political Action Committee (PAC), veto power over the choice of Roosevelt's vice-presidential running mate. Allegedly Roosevelt had instructed Democratic chieftains regarding the vice-presidential selection to "Clear it with Sidney." That slogan soon became a lightning rod for anti–New Deal anxieties about the radical inclinations of the new industrial union movement. Republican presidential candidate Thomas Dewey, for example, proclaimed, "I do not propose to be silent when the New Deal through Mr. Roosevelt's political lieutenant, Hillman, strikes up a cynical alliance with Browder's communists."

Actually, Dewey and the Republican high command greatly

exaggerated Hillman's power. The CIO's PAC, founded a year earlier, was officially committed to the renomination of Vice President Henry Wallace. It was a mark of its embattled defensive political position, however, that for some months prior to the Democratic party convention, Hillman was frankly advised by the party chiefs of Wallace's dwindling chances. By July of 1944, PAC could do no more than checkmate the candidacy of James Brynes, a foe of the CIO since the days of the sit-down strikes of the late thirties. Truman's nomination, though vetoed by Hillman, was not subject to his formal approval. The Missouri senator visited Hillman during the Chicago convention to seek his endorsement. The PAC chairman made it clear that should Wallace falter, he and, presumably, the rest of the CIO leadership were prepared to throw their weight behind Truman. Rather than symbolizing the labor movement's capture of the Democratic party, Truman's candidacy thus represented the CIO's failure to prevail with its preferred choice.

Hillman was probably more favorably disposed than the rest of the CIO top brass, but even he had reservations about Truman. During the early years of the war, when Hillman served as associate director general of the Office of Production Management, he had been rather severely interrogated by Truman's Special Senate Committee to Investigate the National Defense Program about alleged improprieties in the letting of contracts. Truman went so far as to say, "If Mr. Hillman cannot, or will not, protect the interests of the U.S., I am in favor of replacing him with someone who can and will." Although he worked unreservedly on behalf of the national ticket in 1944, Hillman remained privately skeptical and by June of 1945 was expressing his reservations about the new president.

Shortly before his death in 1946, Hillman, who had concealed his anger over President Truman's increasingly hostile attitude toward the labor movement longer than the rest of his CIO colleagues, finally attacked Truman publicly as an "autocrat" on the occasion of the president's dramatic threat to Congress to draft the striking railroad workers. This breach between Truman and the liberal-labor alliance would not be truly repaired until the presidential campaign of 1948.

Matthew Josephson's *Sidney Hillman: Statesman of American Labor* (Garden City, N.Y.: Doubleday, 1952) is the only thorough, but largely uncritical biography of Hillman. Len DeCaux's autobiography, *Labor Radical: From the Wobblies to the CIO* (Boston: Beacon Press, 1970), although critical of Hillman's "class collaborationism," contains substantial material on his political activities in the 1940s. Steven Fraser, "Sidney Hillman: Labor's Machiavelli," in *Labor Leaders in America*, ed. Melvyn Dubofsky and Warren Van Tine (Urbana: University of Illinois Press, 1987), presents a synoptic account and interpretation of Hillman's career.

STEVEN FRASER

See also Labor

Hiss-Chambers Case

Everything about Alger Hiss seemed to be in its proper place. Educated at Johns Hopkins and Harvard Law, he clerked for

Supreme Court justice Oliver Wendell Holmes at the recommendation of Felix Frankfurter, went into private practice in New York and Boston, and then came to Washington to help make the New Deal work. After two years with the Agricultural Adjustment Administration (AAA), he moved over to the Senate to work on the Nye committee investigation of the munitions industry and then returned to the executive branch briefly as a special counsel for the Department of Justice before finally settling in with the State Department. Rising rapidly, Hiss served as executive secretary of the Dumbarton Oaks Conference, accompanied Franklin D. Roosevelt to the principal World War II summit at Yalta in the Crimea, and presided in San Francisco as secretary-general at the United Nations Conference on International Organization. He left State in 1947 to become president of the Carnegie Endowment for International Peace, with his impeccable patrician-as-reformer credentials intact. A year later, his world fell apart, and the very New Deal–Fair Deal lineage he had been so proud of made his story a cause célèbre.

In August 1948 testimony before the House Committee on Un-American Activities (HUAC), a senior editor at *Time* magazine accused the Carnegie Endowment president of having once been a member of a Communist party cell with a mission to influence the foreign and domestic policies of the Roosevelt administration. When Whittaker Chambers accepted Hiss's dare to repeat his charge without the benefit of congressional immunity, he was greeted with a slander suit. The action, Chambers claimed, led him to retrieve a dusty package of documents that had sat for years in a dumbwaiter in the Brooklyn home of his nephew's mother. These documents, sixty-five pages of retyped State Department dispatches and four handwritten notes, were supplemented by three undeveloped rolls and two developed strips of microfilmed documents which Chambers had hidden in a hollowed-out pumpkin on his Westminster, Maryland, farm. All the documents, dated from fall 1937 to spring 1938, Chambers said, had been smuggled out of the State Department by Hiss for transmittal in one form or another to the Soviet Union.

Hiss was tried twice for perjury—the ten-year statute of limitations having run out on any possible espionage charge. Ultimately, the trials hinged on the relative credibility of the two protagonists, Hiss with his background and impressive bearing and the fat, droopy, brooding Chambers, an admitted betrayer of friends and country alike and now self-proclaimed champion of the Christian West. Chambers's most recent perjury concerned the dating of the pumpkin paper documents, as he had previously testified under oath on numerous occasions that he had left the Communist party in late 1937 (or very early 1938). Yet the pumpkin papers were dated as late as 1 April 1938. Not surprisingly, the first trial ended in a hung jury. By January 1950, however, the political climate had changed considerably. Although the troubling discrepancy regarding the break date was never resolved, the jury in the second trial sided with Chambers, finding Alger Hiss guilty on two counts of perjury.

Alistair Cooke has said the Hiss case symbolized a generation on trial; but the case really represented a symbolic trial of the Democratic party. One month after the perjury conviction, Senator Joseph R. McCarthy (R.-Wis.) waved in the air what he said was a list of 205 (or whatever; he was not clear on the exact number) Communists in the State Department. He would go on

Clarence D. Batchelor, *New York Daily News* (1952). Copyright New York News Inc. Reprinted with permission.

to accuse the Harry S. Truman administration of being soft on Communism, to refer to Democratic presidential candidate Adlai E. Stevenson as "Alger—I mean Adlai," and to describe the Roosevelt and Truman incumbency as "twenty years of treason." Richard M. Nixon (R.-Calif.), the HUAC member who rode the Hiss case into a Senate seat and then the vice presidency, repeated these charges in a softer, more effective tone. Although conceding "the loyalty of Democrats," he criticized the party's "misguided officials" who were "blind . . . to the danger" of Communist infiltration and only interested in "covering up" the Truman administration's shameful record of "clearing and hiring" Alger Hiss and "six thousand" other "security risks."

This sort of rhetoric had been part and parcel of domestic politics since 1946, with Republican members of Congress and a few conservative Democrats increasingly challenging the loyalty of New Deal and Fair Deal personnel. President Truman responded in March 1947 by establishing a federal employee loyalty program, in the hope that he might somehow "take the ball away from Parnell Thomas," the New Jersey Republican and HUAC chairman who would, ironically, be indicted on a payroll scam and go on to the federal penitentiary in Danbury, Connecticut. But in establishing the program Truman announced that "the presence within the Government service of any disloyal or subversive person constitutes a threat to our democratic processes." Earlier, Attorney General Tom Clark emphasized "the serious threat which even one disloyal person

constitutes to the security of the Government of the United States." Clearly, the administration was promising something (absolute security) that it could not deliver. Hiss's conviction made that clear, and at the same time discredited the president's attempt to dismiss the case as a "red herring." In fact, Truman had ignored an FBI report about Hiss back in December 1945. One of the other persons named in that report, Harry Dexter White, was actually promoted in the aftermath to head the International Monetary Fund (IMF). White was a bigger fish than Hiss, but the IMF chief died of a heart attack in the midst of the HUAC hearings in August 1948.

The Hiss case provided the Republican party with the ammunition needed to launch a credible attack on the integrity of Roosevelt and Truman administration personnel. In the simplest of terms, Republicans argued that Hiss was what he appeared to be—namely, a typical liberal, the type of person New Dealers and Fair Dealers cherished. And this liberal "prototype," to use his prosecutor's word, was a Soviet agent. Beyond that, Hiss had attended the Yalta Conference, and Yalta was at the very heart of McCarthyite symbolism. The United States emerged from World War II an economic and military giant with a nuclear monopoly to boot, and yet had experienced a string of foreign policy reversals in the immediate postwar years, notably the lowering of the iron curtain across Eastern Europe and the "loss" of China to Mao Tse-tung's Communists. The search for scapegoats led from FDR and the Democratic party to Yalta, where the president had discussed Eastern Europe and China with Joseph Stalin, and from Yalta to the State Department and Alger Hiss, and from Hiss to Chambers and all the way around again to Comrade Stalin. Adlai Stevenson dismissed the notion that "a few sinister men in the State Department caused the Chinese revolution" and "gave Eastern Europe to the Communists at Yalta" as a "myth," nothing more than a "Republican formula for political success." But Hiss's conviction gave the McCarthyites enough credibility to plunge the nation into a protracted and wasteful search for subversives. "Without the Alger Hiss case," one student of that era noted, "the six-year controversy that followed might have been a tamer affair, and the Communist issue somewhat more tractable."

The Hiss-Chambers confrontation reverberated throughout the Truman years and into the next three decades. Chambers lived quietly on his farm, published an 808-page memoir, and died in 1961 at the age of sixty. Hiss served forty-four months on the perjury charges, wrote his own book, and continued to press his innocence on every front. In the more recent past he filed a coram nobis action in U.S. District Court asking that his conviction be expunged from the record because of wholesale invasions of privacy and intrusions into the defense camp by federal prosecutors and FBI agents. Based largely on files only recently declassified under the Freedom of Information Act of 1966 (as amended in 1974), the petition demonstrates the abysmal nature of cold war political justice. Regardless of the question of Hiss's guilt or innocence, the internal security bureaucracy had invested heavily in Chambers's credibility and proved willing to do almost anything to vindicate the witness and support the broader soft-on-Communism critique of the Truman administration. In October 1983, nonetheless, the Supreme Court refused to consider the coram nobis petition. Six months later, Chambers received a posthumous Presidential Medal of Freedom, the country's highest civilian honor—a gesture to a man who symbolized "a generation's disenchantment with statism," Ronald Reagan said, and a sign that the passions and partisanship of that earlier time remained, like Hiss himself, alive and well.

Allen Weinstein, who concluded that Chambers told the truth and Hiss lied, has written the most important recent book on the case, *Perjury* (New York: Knopf, 1978). Chambers's account of his life and times, *Witness* (New York: Random House, 1952), is fascinating, though not always credible, whereas Hiss's book, *In the Court of Public Opinion* (New York: Alfred A. Knopf, 1957), reads like a lawyer's brief. Hiss has also recently published his memoirs, *Recollections of a Life* (New York: Seaver Books/Holt, 1988). The coram nobis action and accompanying appendixes (mostly photocopies of FBI documents) are readily available in Edith Tiger, ed., *In Re Alger Hiss*, 2 vols. (New York: Hill & Wang, 1979, 1980). Finally, specific aspects of the Hiss case are explored in Athan Theoharis, ed., *Beyond the Hiss Case* (Philadelphia: Temple University Press, 1982), particularly in essays by Theoharis, "Unanswered Questions: Chambers, Nixon, the FBI, and the Hiss Case," pp. 246–308; Victor Navasky, "Weinstein, Hiss, and the Transformation of Historical Ambiguity into Cold War Verity," pp. 215–45; and Kenneth O'Reilly, "Liberal Values, the Cold War, and American Intellectuals: The Trauma of the Alger Hiss Case, 1950–1978," pp. 309–40.

KENNETH O'REILLY

See also House Committee on Un-American Activities; McCarthy, Joseph R.; Nixon, Richard M.; Red Scare

Hoffman, Paul Gray

(26 April 1891–8 October 1974)

A Republican businessman in a Democratic administration, Paul G. Hoffman served Harry S. Truman as the first administrator of the Marshall Plan. Born in Chicago, Hoffman spent his childhood in a nearby suburb. After one year at the University of Chicago he started to work for a local car dealer. Intelligent and hardworking, he possessed an easy sociability and self-confidence that made him an immediate success as a car salesman. By the age of thirty-four, he had become a millionaire owner of a Studebaker dealership in southern California when Studebaker's president persuaded him to move to South Bend, Indiana, as vice president in charge of sales and member of the board.

It was as president of Studebaker after 1935 that Hoffman began to attract wide public attention. While helping to lead the company back from bankruptcy, he became active in public affairs. Most important, in 1942 he helped establish the Committee for Economic Development (CED). Experience as the CED's first chairman convinced Hoffman that peace and prosperity depended upon the expansion of international trade. By 1946 he was also convinced that the Soviet Union represented the major threat to that goal.

A lifelong Republican identified in the press as a progressive business leader, Hoffman fully supported the Truman administration's foreign policy while the cold war emerged. In 1946 President Truman appointed him to a committee of businessmen to give advice about financing international recon-

struction. The next year, Hoffman played a leading role on the President's Committee on Foreign Aid. After helping to mobilize public support for the Marshall Plan, Hoffman visited East Asia on a high-level fact-finding mission early in 1948. It was no surprise, therefore, when President Truman nominated a reluctant Paul G. Hoffman in April 1948 to serve as the first administrator of the Marshall Plan. For political reasons, the president needed a Republican businessman to head the new program. Hoffman enjoyed strong congressional support.

As head of the Marshall Plan, Hoffman confronted three major tasks. He had to select effective administrators to operate the Economic Cooperation Administration (ECA); he had to persuade the taxpayers and Congress to give away several billion dollars; and he had to persuade European aid recipients to cooperate with one another and with the agency. He succeeded in all those tasks in part because of his own abilities and in part because he received the full support of the president. The lone Republican in a Democratic administration, he was wary of Truman's partisanship, but the president did not interfere or impose patronage appointments. For his courageous leadership and constructive help, Truman earned Hoffman's high regard and deep affection.

By appointing him to the Marshall Plan post, Truman did Hoffman an enormous favor. Experience running the ECA began Hoffman's "real education" by opening his eyes to matters about which he had been unaware. In 1950, he resigned from the ECA not to return to Studebaker but to head the Ford Foundation. Thereafter, he worked to promote peace and international prosperity. During the 1950s, he urged President Eisenhower, a personal friend, to use trade and foreign aid for that goal. From 1959 until 1971, when he retired, Hoffman headed the United Nations Development Programs.

Alan R. Raucher's *Paul G. Hoffman: Architect of Foreign Aid* (Lexington: University Press of Kentucky, 1985) is a comprehensive biography of Hoffman's entire career. With *The Marshall Plan and Its Meaning* (Ithaca, N.Y.: Cornell University Press, 1955), Harry B. Price came close to writing the official history of the Marshall Plan and its role in Truman's containment policy. In *Bureaucracy, the Marshall Plan, and the National Interest* (Princeton: Princeton University Press, 1972), Hadley Arkes critically assessed the administration of that foreign aid program.

ALAN R. RAUCHER

See also Committee for Economic Development; Marshall Plan

Holland, Louis Edward

(20 June 1878–25 May 1960)

Kansas City business leader, close friend of Harry Truman, and first head of the Smaller War Plants Corporation during World War II. Born in Parma, New York, Lou Holland started to work at age thirteen in a box factory and, like Truman, did not go to college. In 1902 he moved to Kansas City, Missouri, and took a job in the engraving business. A few years later he founded the Holland Engraving Company and subsequently established two related companies.

Holland's business ventures prospered, and he soon became a leader in a variety of civic and professional activities. Gregarious and enthusiastic by nature, he was one of the organizers of the National Better Business Bureau, was a three-term president of the Associated Advertising Clubs of the World, served as president of the Kansas City Chamber of Commerce between 1925 and 1927, and cooperated closely with judge Truman on road-building and other projects.

After World War II broke out in 1939, the United States launched serious efforts to strengthen the nation's military power. A longtime champion of small business, Holland used his abundant energy to help organize the Mid-Central War Resources Board with the purpose of assisting small industrial plants and shops in Kansas and Missouri obtain defense contracts. As president of the Mid-Central Board, Holland played a major role in putting together a thirty-two-company pool which garnered a sizable navy contract.

Such efforts were not enough to silence growing criticism that small companies were largely being ignored while big business received the overwhelming bulk of lucrative government contracts. By 1942 dissatisfaction was strong enough that in early summer Congress passed the Small Business Act creating both a Smaller War Plants Division (SWPD) within the War Production Board (the principle mobilization agency) and an independent Smaller War Plants Corporation (SWPC) with a capital stock of $150 million to use for making loans to small manufacturers.

Donald M. Nelson, the chairman of the War Production Board (WPB), sensibly decided to name the same person to direct both the SWPD and the SWPC. He chose Holland who had two important credentials for the position: his record as president of the Mid-Central Board and his close friendship with Senator Truman, chair of the powerful Senate committee charged with investigating industrial mobilization.

Holland's career in wartime Washington was both frustrating and short. Appointed on 11 July 1942, he failed to increase the share of government contracts awarded to small firms fast enough to satisfy some key members of Congress, especially Wright Patman, the aggressive chairman of the House Committee on Small Business. Despite efforts by Nelson late in 1942 to strengthen Holland's organizations and testimonials of support by officials of the War and Navy Departments, political pressure on the White House to change the leadership of the small-business programs continued to build. On 19 January 1943, Nelson abruptly told Holland that he was being replaced. The WPB chief asked him to stay on as an assistant to his successor, Col. Robert Johnson, and Holland initially agreed to do so. An angry Truman assured his fellow Missourian that he was not going "to sit idly by and let my friend's throat be cut," giving him some hope of repairing the damage to his reputation. Holland quickly realized, however, that he was in an impossible situation, and in mid-February he wrote a bitter letter to Nelson resigning from federal service.

Holland deserved some but not all of the blame for failing to make the SWPD and SWPC function more effectively. Neither petulant nor hot-tempered, he was perhaps too patient with the hostile, or at least indifferent, treatment small business concerns received from many WPB and military officials. Significantly, no broadly based small-business organization existed to support Holland's efforts with vigorous political pressure. One of his problems was that he moved too slowly to build an efficient organization. But in part that was because other federal agencies had already absorbed most experienced personnel by the time the Small Business Act became law. His unfamiliarity with the way the government worked was a serious handicap, and though Nelson ultimately provided some needed assistance to Holland, the help came too late.

In an effort to get to the bottom of why his friend had been fired, Truman led a lengthy Senate debate in February about the government's small-business program. While absolving Nelson of blame, the senator concluded that there was a conspiracy on the part of the WPB to break up the SWPC. Many of Truman's fellow senators agreed that Holland had done a commendable job, but in the House Patman's criticism of Holland won support.

After leaving Washington, Holland returned to his business enterprises in Kansas City. President of the American Automobile Association from 1949 to 1951, he continued until his death in 1960 to play an active role in business and civic affairs.

The Holland papers at the Truman Library are extensive and informative, but little has been published about his long and active career. See Jim F. Heath, "Frustrations of a Missouri Small Businessman: Lou E. Holland in Wartime Washington," *Missouri Historical Review* 68 (April 1974): 299–316.

JIM F. HEATH

"Hollywood Ten"

See Civil Liberties; Movies and the Movie Industry; Red Scare

Homes

See Farm Experience; Gates-Wallace-Truman House; Lamar, Missouri

Honors

See Awards; Portraits and Memorials

Hoover, Herbert Clark

10 August 1874–20 October 1964)
When Truman succeeded Roosevelt in the presidency in 1945, Herbert Hoover had been a former president for a dozen years. Ignored by Truman's predecessor, Hoover now found the doors to the White House and to public service opened to him once again. Their relationship during Truman's presidency was not warm, however, as the two men were of different political parties and decidedly partisan in their attitudes.

Truman and Hoover shared midwestern small town–rural origins, but there the similarity in their backgrounds ended. Whereas Hoover had escaped from West Branch, Iowa, at the age of eleven—first to Oregon, then California, and then the world—Truman's first five decades were spent in his native Missouri, except for his service in World War I. Hoover accumulated a sizable fortune in mining and mining promotion before he was forty, whereas Truman worked as a bank clerk, bookkeeper, farmer, and haberdasher. Born a decade before Truman, Hoover seemed much more than one decade ahead of the Missourian. During World War I, while Truman served as an army captain, Hoover was in Woodrow Wilson's war cabinet, first as U.S. food administrator and then as director of the American Relief Administration in armistice Europe. When Truman became a county judge in 1922, Hoover was in his second year as secretary of commerce in Warren G. Harding's cabinet. Six years later, in 1928, Hoover was elected to the presidency.

But their fortunes changed. The onset of the Great Depression deprived Hoover of a possible second term, and he faded from the Washington scene only a short time before Truman appeared on it. Hoover turned the White House over to Franklin Delano Roosevelt in March 1933, and Truman entered the Senate two years later. For the next decade it was Truman who was at the center of action, first as senator and then as vice president, while Hoover was shunned by the Roosevelt administration. And when Hoover did reappear, at last, on the Washington scene, it was Truman who cast him in the roles.

When Truman became president on 12 April 1945, Hoover was certain it would be a change for the better. He approved of the new president's initial speech to Congress and set to work learning more about him. Truman's background encouraged Hoover to believe that he would be more conservative than his predecessor. Hopeful that the new president would discard Roosevelt's vindictiveness and make use of his talents, Hoover wrote to his sister, "Now that there has been a change in Washington, I may be on the move often." Little could the seventy-one-year-old former president have anticipated how much "on the move" he would be during the Truman presidency!

Within days after Truman became president, his administration began to tap Hoover's expertise for dealing with the critical food shortages in occupied and liberated Europe. On 28 May 1945, Hoover entered the White House for the first time since he had left it over a dozen years earlier, summoned by Truman for a discussion of the European food problem. Thereafter, Hoover continued to advise the Truman administration. Reviewing the first three months of Truman's presidency, Hoover wrote to a fellow Republican: "Never has this country felt so relieved as during the last 90 days. The new President is rapidly altering the 'party line' and there is a much more hopeful feeling that we will pull through the postwar troubles."

The food situation in Europe continued to deteriorate through the winter of 1945–46. Late in February 1946, Truman flew Hoover to Washington from a fishing trip in Florida and named him honorary chairman of the new Famine Emergency

Homeless children in Warsaw surround Herbert Hoover, chairman of the Famine Emergency Committee and coordinator of food supplies for thirty-eight countries. April 1946. (National Archives)

Committee. At Truman's request, Hoover traveled the world investigating conditions and searching for sources of food with which to meet the crisis. This problem had scarcely been solved when Truman entrusted him with new responsibilities. In the summer of 1947, the president appointed Hoover chairman of the new Commission on Organization of the Executive Branch of the Government, soon known popularly as the Hoover Commission. Far from being merely a titular head, despite his advanced age, Hoover dominated the commission through his expertise and capacity for hard work. The commission's agenda, and the effort to get its recommendations adopted, occupied much of the next two years of his life.

Although entrusted by Truman with such responsibilities, Hoover would not remain silent in his opposition to many of the president's policies, particularly in foreign affairs. He was a vocal opponent of the strain on American resources which he foresaw in the Truman Doctrine, the Marshall Plan, and the stationing of U.S. ground forces in Europe under NATO. Late in 1950, amidst the dramatic charges of Communist infiltration of the federal government trumpeted by Senator Joseph McCarthy and others, Truman offered Hoover the chairmanship of a proposed bipartisan commission to investigate the charges. Hoover declined, suggesting instead that Congress should create such a commission or launch an inquiry itself. Clearly, partisanship intruded between the two men during Truman's presidency, and Hoover could not avoid feeling a certain amount of pleasure at the Democratic president's discomfiture concerning these and other circumstances.

The partisan feelings on both sides did not end immediately after Truman left the White House. A year after Truman returned to private life, Hoover declined an invitation to attend a dinner honoring the Missourian's seventieth birthday, complaining of Truman's "many personal attacks upon me." But Hoover added that he "had a higher opinion both of Mr. Truman personally and of many of his policies than many of my political colleagues," and he expressed optimism that "the time will yet come when he and I can join to forward matters of public interest." In mid-October 1955, Truman paid a courtesy call on Hoover in New York City and their friendship was launched. Hoover helped raised money for the Truman Presidential Library and was on hand for its dedication, and Truman repaid the compliment with an appearance at the dedication of the Hoover Presidential Library in 1962.

Late in 1962, Hoover expressed his debt to Truman in a letter he wrote to him:

> Yours has been a friendship which has reached deeper into my life than you know. I gave up a successful profession in 1914 to enter public service. I served through the first World War and after, for a total of about 18 years. When the attack on Pearl Harbor came, I at once supported the President, and offered to serve in any useful capacity. Because of my varied experiences during the first World War, I thought my services might again be useful; however, there was no response. . . . When you came to the White House, within a month you opened the door to me to the only profession I knew, public service, and you undid some disgraceful action that had been taken in the prior years. For all of this and your friendship I am deeply grateful.

Two years later Hoover was dead, at the age of ninety.

The relations between Hoover and Truman are dealt with in two books that concentrate on Hoover's career after he left the White House: Gary Dean Best, *Herbert Hoover: The Postpresidential Years, 1933–1964*, 2 vols. (Stanford: Hoover Institution Press, 1983), and Richard N. Smith, *An Uncommon Man: The Triumph of Herbert Hoover* (New York: Simon & Schuster, 1984). For a full biography the best choice is David Burner, *Herbert Hoover: The Public Life* (New York: Knopf, 1979).

GARY DEAN BEST

See also Executive Branch, Reorganization of the (and photograph)

Hoover, John Edgar

(1 January 1895–2 May 1972)

Director, Federal Bureau of Investigation. Born in Washington, D.C., J. Edgar Hoover (as he preferred to be called) was the son and grandson of minor civil servants employed in the print shop of the Coast and Geodetic Survey. Hoover attended public schools in the District of Columbia, where he excelled as student and debater more because of his dogged determination and ambition than intellectual curiosity or superior intelligence. For financial reasons, Hoover had to work full time at the Library of Congress while attending George Washington University Law School at night.

Three months after U.S. involvement in World War I, the recent law graduate secured employment in the Alien Enemy Bureau of the Department of Justice. Although inexperienced, he fully exploited the opportunity the department's expanded internal security responsibilities proferred to win promotion in August 1918 to head the Radical (later renamed General Intelligence) Division. In this position, the ambitious bureaucrat and conservative ideologue played a key role in planning the mass dragnet raids to deport (under provisions of the Immigration Act of 1918) first members of the Union of Russian Workers in November 1919 and then members of the Communist and Communist Labor parties in the more infamous Palmer Raids of January 1920.

With Harding's election to the presidency, and the reorganization of the leadership of the Bureau of Investigation (formally named the Federal Bureau of Investigation in 1935), Hoover won promotion to the assistant directorship of the bureau owing to his experience and commitment to antiradical investigations. An ensuing series of scandals eventually led Harding's successor, Calvin Coolidge, to fire Attorney General Harry Daugherty on 28 March 1924, replacing him with the respected dean of Columbia Law School Harlan Fiske Stone. Dismissing William Burns as bureau director on 9 May Stone initiated a perfunctory search for a successor, appointing Hoover the next day as acting director. He was at the time only twenty-nine years old. Hoover's administrative reforms to ensure the professionalism of the bureau impressed Stone, who in December 1924 ended Hoover's probationary status.

Although the attorney general had banned bureau investigations of political activities, Hoover did not abandon his antiradical crusade. Unknown to Stone, the bureau—discreetly, to avoid discovery—continued to monitor dissident organizations and activists like the American Civil Liberties Union and

J. Edgar Hoover. (The Constant Collection; courtesy of the Franklin D. Roosevelt Library)

the Workers party, the temporarily renamed Communist party. Sensitive to the changed political winds and to the budgetary constraints that pared back the bureau's personnel, Hoover instituted a series of changes to ensure a more professional and efficient bureau. But given prevailing states' rights convictions, strengthened during the 1920s by revived opposition to the federal regulatory role instituted during the Progressive Era, the bureau Hoover headed remained a relatively minor agency, with only limited investigative responsibilities.

This all changed during the 1930s and 1940s. For one, President Roosevelt, consistent with his call for a more intrusive federal presence to promote economic recovery and regulate business abuses, pressed for an expanded federal law enforcement role to curb the crime wave of bank robberies, kidnapping, and hoodlum activities that local and state police seemed incapable of handling. In 1934, Roosevelt actively lobbied for enactment of a federal anticrime program to extend federal jurisdiction to bank robbing, kidnapping, extortion, and racketeering. He complemented this legislative effort with a well-orchestrated media campaign to alter the public's conception of the bureau to that of a highly professional, indispensable organization—represented by the omnipresent incorruptible G-man. By the end of the decade, Hoover had emerged as a popular folk hero.

World War II and the cold war, not the Great Depression, permanently altered public policy, however, and elevated Hoover to the position of equality with the president. A fear of spies—whether German between 1940 and 1945 or Soviet after 1945—ultimately enabled the ambitious director to transform

the bureau into an all-powerful, autonomous agency. By relying for authority on secret presidential directives and crafting procedures to avert discovery of his unilateral authorization of "clearly illegal" investigative activities, Hoover effectively neutralized any challenge to his administration of the bureau.

This transformation was wrought during Truman's administration. Hoover succeeded in expanding the bureau's powers, first, by servicing the intelligence interests of the White House and, second, by developing a covert alliance with conservatives in the Congress and the media. On the one hand, he volunteered information to advance the president's political and policy interests; on the other hand, he selectively leaked information to conservative politicians like Joseph McCarthy and Richard Nixon and conservative reporters like Fulton Lewis, Jr., and Don Whitehead. Underscoring Hoover's political conservatism, these leaks were intended to "educate" the public that a serious internal security threat existed and that the Truman administration was indifferent to this threat.

By 1950, Hoover had consolidated his position, which he sustained and refined during the succeeding Eisenhower and Kennedy administrations. This tendency toward increased autonomy was reversed in the late 1960s owing to the combination of a revived, more skeptical liberalism and Hoover's personal vulnerability. Although he reached the mandatory retirement age of seventy in January 1965, Hoover was able to continue as director because of President Johnson's waiving the requirement for "an indefinite period of time." Ironically, this dependence on continued presidential support occurred at a time when an aroused press, Congress, and public began to question Hoover's leadership and were less vulnerable to his ploy of questioning his critics' loyalty.

Anxious to sustain his threatened tenure, Hoover had the FBI fulfill the blatantly political requests of the Johnson and Nixon White Houses. At the same time, fearful of congressional and press disclosure, Hoover in 1965–67 prohibited the continued use of the "clearly illegal" techniques he had authorized since the 1940s.

Hoover's fears proved warranted. His directorship became an issue in the 1968 presidential primaries, and influential members of Congress and reporters began to monitor more closely the actions of the bureau. By the fall of 1971, Nixon's key advisers urged him to demand Hoover's resignation, having concluded that he had outlived his usefulness and was becoming a political albatross. Nixon, however, deferred acting on this recommendation until after the 1972 presidential election. But, on 2 May 1972, Hoover died in his sleep of a heart attack, ending an unprecedented forty-eight-year tenure as head of a federal agency. Although eulogized by official Washington, Hoover's reputation soon fell victim to a more critical reassessment. Released FBI records (publicized during congressional investigations of 1975–76 or in response to Freedom of Information Act requests) documented the scope of Hoover's abuses of power and his undercutting of constitutional proscriptions for oversight and accountability.

Until the 1980s, Hoover's success in preventing research into FBI files foreclosed any serious biography. Published accounts either were based on carefully orchestrated releases or were written by former FBI agents and officials. Independent research into Hoover's life and career became possible only with the passage in 1974 of amendments to the Freedom of Information Act. To date the best studies are those of Athan G. Theoharis and John Stuart Cox, *The Boss: J. Edgar Hoover and the Great American Inquisition* (Philadelphia: Temple University Press, 1988), Richard Powers, *Secrecy and Power: The Life of J. Edgar Hoover* (New York: Free Press, 1987), Frank Donner, *The Age of Surveillance* (New York: Knopf, 1980), and Sanford Ungar, *FBI* (Boston: Atlantic–Little, Brown, 1975).

ATHAN THEOHARIS

See also Federal Bureau of Investigation

Hoover Commission

See Executive Branch, Reorganization of the; Hoover, Herbert Clark

Hope, Clifford Ragsdale

(9 June 1893–16 May 1970)

Attorney, business executive, and Republican member of the House of Representatives. Clifford Hope, who was born in Birmingham, Iowa, and received a degree from Washburn Law School, represented the vast wheat-growing Fifth District of Kansas in Congress. He was the ranking Republican on the House Agriculture Committee during the Truman administration and chaired the committee during the Republican-controlled Eightieth Congress. Because Hope believed that marketing research would prevent post–World War II surpluses, he was instrumental in the passage of the Research and Marketing Act of 1946.

During the Eightieth Congress, Hope opposed the Truman administration on several agricultural issues, especially during the debate over the wool bill in 1947 and the Agricultural Act of 1948. Hope successfully amended the 1947 wool bill to impose import fees, but President Truman vetoed the bill as a step toward economic isolation.

In 1948, Hope fought the Truman administration proposal to restore flexible price supports and gained House backing to continue supports at 90 percent of parity. The Senate approved flexible price supports, but Hope prevailed in the Conference Committee and the Agricultural Act of 1948. The congressman supported the Brannan Plan in 1949 and a continuation of rigid supports for two more years in the Agricultural Act of 1949. He took a similar position toward rigid price supports during the Korean War when the Defense Production Act was amended in 1952.

For more information on Hope's policies, see Douglas E. Bowers, "The Research and Marketing Act of 1946 and Its Effects on Agricultural Marketing Research," *Agricultural History* 56 (January 1982): 249–63; and James L. Forsythe, "Postmortem on the Election of 1948: An Evaluation of Cong. Clifford R. Hope's Views," *Kansas Historical Quarterly* 38 (Autumn 1972): 338–59.

JAMES L. FORSYTHE

See also Agriculture

Hopkins, Harry Lloyd

(17 August 1890–30 January 1946)

Adviser to and envoy for President Truman. Harry Hopkins was born in Sioux City, Iowa, and grew up in Grinnell. After graduating from Grinnell College, he moved to New York City, where he became a successful social work administrator. During the Great Depression he managed federal relief for the unemployed in President Franklin D. Roosevelt's New Deal. The energetic Hopkins possessed a keen analytical mind and the courage to accept responsibility, traits that made him a supremely qualified crisis manager. During World War II, as special assistant to President Roosevelt, he coordinated wartime production, supply, and grand strategy, advised Roosevelt on Allied relations, and attended the major summit conferences.

Upon assuming office, President Truman immediately conferred with Hopkins, who encouraged him to carry on Roosevelt's policies. When difficulties arose shortly with the Soviet Union, which was balking at organizing the United Nations and seemed to be violating previous agreements about forming a government in Poland, Truman approached the Russians with sharp and uncompromising complaints. When they became even more intransigent, he sent Hopkins to Moscow to negotiate directly with Marshal Joseph Stalin.

Truman hoped that Hopkins would persuade Stalin to accept his interpretation of wartime agreements, but Hopkins preferred to compromise with the Soviets in order to maintain Allied unity. At his meetings with Stalin between 25 May and 6 June 1945, he conceded that Communists should dominate the new Polish government. In return Stalin accepted the American interpretation of UN voting procedures and agreed to cooperate in other areas.

Although pleased by Hopkins's accomplishment, which helped establish the United Nations and cleared the way for the later Potsdam Conference, Truman rejected his request to discuss his negotiations with British prime minister Winston Churchill. Truman hoped this would show the Soviets that the United States was not "ganging up" against them and would allow America to mediate between its two allies. This approach, however, differed from the Roosevelt-Hopkins strategy of promoting Soviet-British agreement, as at the Yalta Conference. Thus, Hopkins's mission foreshadowed Truman's departure from Roosevelt's diplomacy.

After reporting on his mission, Hopkins retired from government service. In September, Truman awarded him a Distinguished Service Medal. Shortly thereafter, Hopkins's health failed, and in January 1946, he died.

The fullest account of Hopkins's life is George McJimsey, *Harry Hopkins: Ally of the Poor and Defender of Democracy* (Cambridge: Harvard University Press, 1987). Robert E. Sherwood, *Roosevelt and Hopkins: An Intimate History* (New York: Harper & Brothers, 1948), has much useful source material and emphasizes Hopkins's relationship with Roosevelt. Dwight William Tuttle, *Harry L. Hopkins and Anglo-American-Soviet Relations, 1941–1945* (New York and London: Garland Publishing, 1983), carefully describes Hopkins's diplomatic activities, including his mission for President Truman.

GEORGE T. McJIMSEY

House Committee on Un-American Activities

Beginning in 1948, and for the rest of his presidency, the House Committee on Un-American Activities (HUAC) was a thorn in Truman's side. It had started out in 1938 as a special committee, but became a standing committee of the House with guaranteed annual appropriations in 1945 as the result of a parliamentary maneuver by John E. Rankin of Mississippi. Although a Democrat, Rankin was, like most of HUAC's members, an ardent enemy of the New and Fair Deals. He was also a racist and an anti-Semite. In 1947, when Republicans took control of Congress, J. Parnell Thomas of New Jersey, as ranking majority member, became the committee's chairman.

Thomas muzzled Rankin to a certain degree, but with the aid of newly elected Richard M. Nixon, he made HUAC more effectively antiadministration than it had ever been. On 1 March 1948, from his hospital bed, Thomas issued a preliminary report to the committee charging that Dr. Edward U. Condon, director of the National Bureau of Standards and a distinguished scientist, was "one of the weakest links in our atomic security." Although short on evidence Thomas maintained that in Condon's file at the Department of Commerce was a letter from J. Edgar Hoover, FBI director, justifying his accusation. Thomas's investigator had seen the letter but was prevented from copying it in full by administration directives meant to secure the confidentiality of loyalty reports. If any loophole remained, it was closed on 14 March 1948 by another executive order specifically denying Congress access to loyalty reports except with the president's approval. On 22 April, by a vote of 300 to 29, the House ordered the secretary of commerce to surrender Hoover's letter, which Truman contemptuously refused to allow. A subsequent House bill designed to force executive departments to produce information on demand was equally ineffective as the Senate failed to address it.

Although Truman was able to safeguard government files, he could not protect his administration from suffering politically as a result of the committee's investigations, nor could he keep himself from playing into its hands as the Hiss case demonstrated. On 3 August 1948 Whittaker Chambers, an editor of *Time* magazine but formerly a Soviet espionage agent, testified before HUAC that in his capacity as a spy in the 1930s he had dealt with, among others, Alger Hiss, later an assistant secretary of state and, at the time Chambers testified, president of the Carnegie Endowment for International Peace. Two days later Truman characterized HUAC's activities as "a red herring"—a way of diverting public attention from its own shortcomings. A week later, when asked if he still thought so, Truman said, "Yes, I do. . . . the strongest type you can smell." More incautiously still, Truman again endorsed the red herring characterization on 9 December, months after it was apparent that Hiss was, if not guilty, at least not so obviously innocent as he had seemed at first.

This was bad enough, since the evidence against Hiss continued to mount, but worse was to come. Dean Acheson, who became Truman's secretary of state in 1949, knew Alger Hiss, his subordinate in the State Department at one time, although not as well as he knew Alger's brother Donald, also a former underground Communist, who was one of his law partners. It was

as a private lawyer that Acheson helped Alger draw up the statement he read to HUAC on 5 August.

Acheson was a conservative anti-Communist, but he also believed deeply in friendship which would lead him to make, as Robert J. Donovan put it, "a comment that was to be a political calamity for President Truman." On 22 January 1950 Hiss was convicted of perjury for falsely denying his past participation in espionage. Three days later at a press conference Acheson, whose professional and personal ties with Hiss were well known, was asked about the conviction. In response Acheson said, "I do not intend to turn my back on Alger Hiss." His explanation that he was motivated by Christian charity did little to protect the administration from devastating criticism. The president could have shielded himself from it to a degree by dismissing Acheson, but he valued his secretary of state too much and, in any case, hated HUAC and would not give its members the satisfaction.

Truman's own piscatorial definition came back to haunt him. A member of HUAC, Herold Velde, told the press that Hiss's conviction had cooked Truman's red herring, and "I hope he enjoys eating it." Richard Nixon, whom Truman especially detested, could not help gloating, too: "Rather than the herring on the hook, I think that Mr. Truman is on the hook."

Truman remarked more than once, and as late as April of 1959, that HUAC was "the most un-American thing in the country today." That may well have been true but, so far as his own fortunes were concerned, was quite irrelevant. In his struggles with the committee Truman could not win. Except for Nixon (whom Martin Dies, its first chairman, wistfully described as "the only Congressman ever to profit by anti-Communist activity"), HUAC's members were obscure politicians with nothing to lose. Defying the committee by denying it access to loyalty reports gained Truman little, for HUAC could then charge him with protecting traitors or security risks, even when, as in Condon's case, there was little if anything to hide. On the other hand, if Truman had given way, that would have damaged him too and further demoralized government officials. Acheson erred politically in standing by Alger Hiss, Truman by allowing red herrings to be put into his mouth. But his basic problem with HUAC, while the red scare lasted, was that on loyalty issues he had few choices available to him, all of them bad.

The standard history of HUAC is Walter Goodman, *The Committee* (New York: Farrar, Straus & Giroux. 1968). Allen Weinstein, *Perjury: The Hiss-Chambers Case* (New York: Alfred A. Knopf, 1978), is an outstanding example of historical detective work that convincingly refutes the many books that have sought to establish Hiss's innocence. Robert J. Donovan, *Tumultuous Years: The Presidency of Harry S Truman 1949–1953* (New York: W. W. Norton, 1982) is very good on Truman's handling of the red scare generally and of HUAC in particular. Another sensible account is Alan D. Harper, *The Politics of Loyalty: The White House and the Communist Issue, 1946–1952* (Westport, Conn.: Greenwood, 1969).

WILLIAM L. O'NEILL

See also Hiss-Chambers Case; Nixon, Richard M.; Red Scare

House of Representatives, United States

See Congress, United States

Housing

Housing issues played an important role in the politics of the Truman administration. In addition to having to deal with a serious nationwide housing shortage at the end of World War II, the administration sought to establish programs that would ensure decent housing for all American citizens. This commitment led to the enactment of the Housing Act of 1949 which was one of the few legislative victories of the Fair Deal. In 1947 several housing programs were consolidated into the new Housing and Home Finance Agency, the forerunner to the cabinet-level Department of Housing and Urban Development established in 1965.

The postwar housing shortage presented the Truman administration with one of its greatest challenges of the postwar reconversion period. President Truman appointed Wilson Wyatt to the post of housing expediter in December of 1945 to head a Veterans' Emergency Housing program. Wyatt pursued an ambitious program but encountered severe difficulties created by a series of crippling strikes and other problems. During the 1946 congressional elections Republicans used the housing shortage as one of several issues with which to criticize administration policies. The substantial Republican victory in the November elections led Truman to scuttle the program. Wyatt angrily resigned, his program having reached 70 percent of its 1946 goal of 1.2 million housing starts.

The passage of the Housing Act of 1949 marked the legislative high point of the Fair Deal. This omnibus housing bill brought to a conclusion a four-year political struggle between real estate interests and advocates of public housing. The central issue was a proposal to construct 810,000 units of low-cost public housing. Other major but relatively noncontroversial provisions established a new approach to slum clearance and urban redevelopment, and authorized substantial increases in Federal Housing Administration mortgage insurance. Opposition was located primarily in the House of Representatives where it was led by Jesse Wolcott (R.-Mich.) and a rural-oriented coalition. Truman used that opposition effectively in his criticism of the Eightieth Congress and the Republican party during his campaign in 1948. The Housing Act established a national housing policy goal of "a decent home for every family in

Paul Douglas and a group of senators visit an impoverished neighborhood four blocks from the Capitol during the debate in 1949 on the federal long-range housing bill. L. to r., Thomas Green (D.-R.I.), Paul Douglas (D.-Ill.), Wayne Morse (R.-Oreg.), Raymond Baldwin (D.-Conn.), and Homer Ferguson (R.-Mich.). (Associated Press/Wide World Photos)

a suitable environment," but it has not been achieved even now. Many scholars and urban leaders have viewed public housing as a major policy failure.

A less controversial provision of the 1949 act, slum clearance and urban renewal, proved to have a much greater impact upon urban America than public housing. The act removed the requirement of the Wagner Housing Act (1937) that an equivalent number of new housing units be built to replace those razed during a renewal project. Consequently, most cities across the nation sponsored "renewal" programs which "cleared" existing older inexpensive housing and replaced it with such developments as high-cost apartment complexes, government buildings, shopping centers, and public plazas—but seldom housing for the displaced poor.

Although the Fair Deal public housing and slum clearance programs failed to achieve the new-housing goal, the Truman administration's expansion of existing FHA mortgage insurance programs had a major long-term impact upon the structure of American housing markets, for FHA policies stimulated home ownership in the new suburbs while simultaneously discouraging the rejuvenation of older housing in the central cities. Policy manuals explicitly required residential racial segregation, the result being that all-white suburbs grew rapidly at the expense of the older central cities, thereby intensifying residential segregation patterns.

President Truman often spoke convincingly about the importance of decent housing as a fundamental right of Americans, regardless of income. He undoubtedly believed that the Housing Act moved the nation a long way toward that goal. But the legacy of the Truman record in housing was an aborted emergency program for veterans, the disappointment of public housing, the destruction of substantial amounts of existing low-cost urban housing under the new urban redevelopment concept, the mandating of residential segregation through FHA policies, and the encouragement of massive expansion of the suburbs to the serious detriment of the older central cities.

The literature on housing issues of the Truman administration is substantial. Mark Gelfand, *A Nation of Cities: The Federal Government and Urban America, 1933–1965* (New York: Oxford University Press, 1975), provides a useful overview of the growth of federal programs that affected urban areas, including housing and urban renewal. Davis R.B. Ross, *Preparing for Ulysses: Politics and Veterans during World War II* (New York: Columbia University Press, 1969), provides an excellent summary of veterans' housing issues, Richard O. Davies, *Housing Reform during the Truman Administration* (Columbia: University of Missouri Press, 1966), discusses the Truman administration's treatment of housing issues, with primary emphasis upon public housing. See also Paul F. Wendt, *Housing Policy: The Search for Solutions* (Berkeley and Los Angeles: University of California Press, 1963), Lawrence M. Friedman, *Government and Slum Housing* (Chicago: Rand-McNally, 1968), and William L.C. Wheaton, et al., eds., *Urban Housing* (New York: Free Press, 1966), for representative perspectives from several of the social sciences. Barton J. Bernstein, "Reluctance and Resistance: Wilson Wyatt and Veterans' Housing in the Truman Administration," *Register of the Kentucky Historical Society* 65 (January 1967), is important, as is Kenneth T. Jackson, "Race, Ethnicity, and Real Estate Appraisal: The Home Owners Loan Corporation and the Federal Housing Administration," *Journal of Urban History* 6 (August 1980). Jackson's *The Crabgrass*

Frontier: The Suburbanization of the United States (New York: Oxford University Press, 1985), is a major contribution not only to the process of urban decentralization but also to the structure of American housing markets.

RICHARD O. DAVIES

See also Suburbanization; Urban Redevelopment; Veterans

HUAC

See House Committee on Un-American Activities

Humphrey, Hubert Horatio, Jr.

(27 May 1911–13 January 1978)

Democratic senator from Minnesota and liberal rebel in the second Truman administration. Hubert Humphrey was born in Wallace, South Dakota. After graduation from the University of Minnesota, he joined his father's drugstore business as a pharmacist. In 1940 he took his M.A. in political science from Louisiana State University, and then taught at Minnesota and Macalester College. He was head of the Works Progress Administration in the state from 1941 to 1943, and became active in Democratic politics. He was Minnesota manager for the Roosevelt-Truman campaign of 1944, although he personally admired Henry A. Wallace.

Physically disqualified from military service, he became mayor of Minneapolis in 1945 and was a founder of the merged Democratic–Farm Labor parties in 1946. He became disenchanted with the group, however, when it was torn by rivalries between traditional liberal Democrats and Communists over leadership of the organization. Wallace's attacks on Truman's foreign policy also alienated him. He developed a strong anti-Communist position and became national chairman of the liberal Americans for Democratic Action at its founding meeting in January 1947. Taking control of the Democratic Farm Labor party at its annual meeting in 1948, he was nominated to run against Senator Joseph Ball. Two of his allies also gained important positions: Orville Freeman, who became chair of the party in the state, and Eugenie Anderson, who became Democratic national committeewoman.

Humphrey jumped aboard the Democratic draft-Eisenhower movement of 1948 early on. He personally hoped to emerge as vice-presidential candidate, even if Truman could not be unseated. But Eisenhower's refusal to run left the rebels without a candidate or a bargaining position. Nevertheless, Humphrey acquired at the Philadelphia convention both a reputation for fiery liberal leadership and the firm enmity of many conservatives. He made a powerful speech demanding a much stronger civil rights plank than the Truman leadership favored. "The time has arrived for the Democratic party to get out of the shadow of states' rights," he said, "and walk forthrightly into the bright sunshine of human rights." The plank was adopted and some southern delegates walked out to run their own third-party candidate. Humphrey got much credit and blame for both.

Back home, Humphrey overwhelmed Senator Ball, who had supported the Taft-Hartley Act and opposed the formation of NATO. Although Senate leaders looked askance at the brash, talkative newcomer, he vigorously supported Truman's policies for public housing, education, and Social Security; favored public ownership of atomic energy facilities; and introduced fifty-seven bills and resolutions in his first year. He shared with Senator Paul Douglas aggressive fights for tax reform, particularly for the elimination of special benefits for the oil and gas industries. He was politically clever, persuading Truman to appoint Republican governor Luther Youngdahl to the bench to upset Republican plans in Minnesota. He was courageous, integrating the Senate dining room and challenging the southern leadership at every turn. But he remained throughout the Truman administration the frustrated leader of a liberal minority.

Defeated by John F. Kennedy for the 1960 presidential nomination, Humphrey finally hit his stride as the leader of the new liberal agenda in the Kennedy and Johnson administrations. In 1964, he was elected vice president on the Lyndon Johnson ticket, but in 1968 was defeated for the presidency by Richard Nixon. He returned to the Senate in 1971, where he served until his death. He had been a paramount liberal spokesman of his generation.

Carl Solberg, *Hubert Humphrey: A Biography* (New York: W. W. Norton, 1984), makes full and careful use of the manuscript resources. Michael Amrine, *This Is Humphrey: The Story of the Senator* (Garden City, N.Y.: Doubleday, 1960), is also objective and well balanced, but covers the early period more thoroughly. Hubert Humphrey, *The Education of a Public Man: My Life and Politics* (Garden City, N.Y.: Doubleday, 1976) is a frank autobiography.

ALFRED B. ROLLINS, JR

See also Americans for Democratic Action; Election of 1948; Liberalism

Hydrogen Bomb

See Atomic and Hydrogen Bombs

I

Ickes, Harold Leclair

(15 March 1874–3 February 1952)

Secretary of interior, 1933–46. The "old man," as Harry Truman sometimes called Harold Ickes, had been czar of the Interior Department, party war-horse, and a terrible-tempered but unswerving liberal for twelve years when Truman assumed office. Born in Altoona, Pennsylvania, Ickes had been active on the fringes of Chicago progressive politics as an urban reformer before Roosevelt put him into his cabinet at age fifty-nine. There Ickes set about rehabilitating Albert Fall's former lair with a ferocious energy and fearless confidence in his own righteousness. Operating from a single desk in a large public room, meeting friend and foe alike in full view of everyone, he shouldered staggering responsibilities as oil administrator under the National Recovery Administration (NRA) code and as public works administrator. In the latter job he spent billions with unquestionable integrity, but at a pace many criticized. Most adamant about protecting the nation's public lands from exploitation and preserving nonrenewable natural resources, Ickes sought to make the Interior Department into a true department of conservation through political aggrandizement and superior administration.

During World War II Ickes controlled most energy sources as solid fuels administrator, directed the Petroleum Administration for War (PAW), and headed negotiations for an Anglo-American pipeline in the Middle East. Convinced that postwar stability would depend in large measure on the availability and control of petroleum resources, Ickes sought to protect American reserves and to lay the basis for a national policy on foreign oil. Concerned above all with the nation's present and future demand for oil, Ickes supported Henry Wallace for the vice presidency in 1944 and greeted Truman's rise to the presidency in April 1945 with skepticism as to his leadership and vision, particularly regarding conservation matters.

Truman was acquainted with Ickes's volatility and his tenaciousness as a political infighter. The two men were uncomfortable with each other from the start. Ickes often sent his under secretary to cabinet meetings, and Truman, familiar with Ickes's penchant for resigning, waited him out. Although the Senate had rejected the Anglo-American oil treaty in 1944, Ickes continued negotiations for Middle Eastern oil rights while Truman placated him with occasional references to a Department of Conservation.

The inevitable collision came over a series of Truman appointments which Ickes regarded as inferior. He was particularly upset by the nomination of California oilman Edwin Pauley for under secretary of the navy. Truman refused to move oil reserves from the Navy to the Interior Department or to solicit Ickes's opinion of his nominee, although Ickes's reservations were well known.

Ickes had known Pauley since NRA days and had been impressed with his work on oil tanker exchange and on the PAW staff. But he became suspicious of the California fund-raiser's motives after a May 1944 conversation in which Pauley inferred that he could raise $300,000 for party coffers if the government dropped its claims to offshore oil lands. Eventually Ickes was subpoenaed to testify before the Naval Affairs Committee, which was holding hearings on the Pauley nomination, and during his second appearance on 5 February 1946 read parts of his diary and other memoranda detailing serious conflicts of interest between the naval appointment and Pauley's petroleum business. Two days later Truman drew the issue by suggesting that Ickes "could very well be mistaken the same as the rest of us." So after thirteen years in office, but only ten months under Truman, Ickes resigned on 13 February 1946 rather than "commit perjury for the sake of the party." Although Ickes had hoped to delay his departure, Truman gave him three days to clear out. Ickes responded with a dramatic press conference which kept him in the news for weeks after.

Truman later suggested that Ickes's fatal flaw was in thinking himself more important than he was. But by 1948, the Pauley affair had dimmed, and Ickes, who busied himself with a thrice-weekly column in the *New York Post* and regular contributions to the *New Republic*, campaigned for Truman's reelection with particular zest, adding a characterization of Thomas E. Dewey as "the candidate in sneakers" to political literature.

Ickes died in February 1952, almost six years to the day after leaving the cabinet. Correspondence between Truman and Ickes reveals that the two men mellowed, recognizing and respecting each other's patriotic earnestness. Perhaps both men acknowledged, albeit privately, that at root, their relationship had been doomed because they were so very much alike.

The best information on the relationship between Ickes and Truman is found in manuscript collections, especially Ickes's unpublished diary in the Library of Congress, Washington, D.C. Early impressions of Truman are found in *The Secret Diary of Harold L. Ickes*, vol. 3 (New York: Simon & Schuster, 1954). Oil matters are explored in Linda J. Lear, "Harold L. Ickes and the Oil Crisis of the First Hundred Days," *Mid-America*. January 1981, 3–17, and Stephen J. Randall, "Harold L. Ickes and U.S. Foreign Petroleum Policy Planning," *Business History Review* 57 (Autumn 1983): 367–87. The best book on federal energy policy for this period is John G. Clark, *Energy and the Federal Government: Fossil Fuel Policy, 1900–1946* (Urbana: University of Illinois Press, 1987). Ickes spoke eloquently on the future of nations dependent on oil in "An Oil Policy: An Open Letter by Harold L. Ickes to the Members of Congress, May 30, 1947," Papers of Thomas Connally, Manuscript Division, Library of Congress. Robert J. Donovan gives an account of Ickes's resignation from Truman's perspective in *Conflict and Crisis* (Garden City, N.Y.: Doubleday, 1955). Insight into the problems of old New Dealers in the Truman administration is found in William E. Leuchtenburg, *In the Shadow of FDR* (Ithaca: Cornell University Press, 1983). Clayton Koppes suggests a new interpretation of Ickes's conservation policies and how they were changed under Truman in "Efficiency/Equity/Esthetics: Towards a Reinterpretation of American Conservation," *Environmental Review* 11 (Summer 1987): 127–46, and "Environmental Policy and American Liberalism: The Department of Interior, 1933–1953," *Environmental Review* 7 (Spring 1983): 17–41. For Ickes's early life, see Linda J. Lear, *Harold L. Ickes: The Aggressive Progressive, 1874–1933* (New York: Garland Publishing, 1981), and for a controversial psychological portrait of Ickes, see Graham White and John Maze, *Harold Ickes of the New Deal* (Cambridge: Harvard University Press, 1985).

LINDA J. LEAR

See also Conservation; Oil Policy

Imperialism

In the late twentieth century few terms have become as value-laden as *imperialism*. As it is regularly used as an epithet to be hurled indiscriminately at one's political opponents, any meaningful use of *imperialism* as an analytical tool first requires definitional precision. Yet such precision is extremely difficult to attain; even leading scholars disagree profoundly about the meaning of the term. "Imperialism, in its most precise traditional usage," according to historian David Healy, "means the forcible extension of governmental control over foreign areas not designated for incorporation as integral parts of the nation."

By Bill Mauldin. Copyright 1946 by Bill Mauldin.

Other scholars have insisted upon a far broader application of the concept. "When an advanced, industrial nation plays, or tries to play, a controlling and one-sided role in the development of a weaker economy," argues William A. Williams, "then the policy of the more powerful country can with accuracy and candor only be described as imperial."

Under the first usage, a discussion of imperialism during the Truman presidency could be restricted almost exclusively to the European imperial empires. When Truman entered the White House those empires still spanned the globe, posing some fundamental dilemmas for the new president and his chief foreign policy advisers. Under the broader usage urged by Williams, any discussion of imperialism during the Truman years would also have to consider the extent to which the United States itself became imperialistic, perhaps even the globe's preeminent imperial state, during that period. This essay will address each of those issues in turn.

The determination of the European imperial powers to maintain—or restore—control over their colonial possessions presented the Truman administration with a host of complex diplomatic problems. The United States viewed continued imperial rule not only as anachronistic but as dangerously destabilizing. In the view of top American officials, only a more liberal colonial policy, one aimed at preparing native elites for ultimate self-rule, could establish the necessary basis for long-term order, stability, and economic prosperity throughout the developing world. Yet the European powers resisted adamantly U.S. efforts to promote change in their colonial territories. As British prime minister Winston Churchill declared angrily during the Second World War, he had not become the King's first minister "in order to preside over the liquidation of the British Empire."

Given the importance that the Truman administration attached to working with its European allies on a broad range of postwar diplomatic initiatives, it should not be surprising that policymakers in Washington consciously sought to avoid friction over divisive—and highly emotional—colonial issues. The deepening cold war reinforced that inclination. When European priorities came into conflict with American policy objectives for the colonial world, the Truman administration thus often found it necessary to moderate its antiimperialism.

Such was the case in Southeast Asia. Truman, like Franklin D. Roosevelt, believed that order and stability in the area could best be achieved by the peaceful, evolutionary movement toward native self-government under Western tutelage. Expecting that the reassertion of European authority in that region would be relatively smooth and orderly, American policymakers were almost completely unprepared for the depth and intensity of the nationalist rebellions that erupted there in the wake of the Japanese surrender. Within days of the atomic bomb blasts over Hiroshima and Nagasaki, nationalists in the Dutch East Indies and French Indochina boldly proclaimed independent republics. Those startling developments undermined the bedrock assumptions upon which American policy had been based. In response, the Truman administration promulgated a policy of strict neutrality and noninvolvement. Intent on maintaining warm relations with its European allies, and yet unwilling to alienate colonial nationalists who looked to the United States for support, the administration saw no viable alternative. Studied noninvolvement remained the keynote of American policy toward the colonial upheavals in Southeast Asia until 1947.

The Truman administration would periodically assert that it favored any movement toward eventual self-government in both Indochina and the Indies while conceding the legal right of France and Holland as "territorial sovereigns" to restore their prewar rule. In practice, that stance worked to the distinct advantage of the imperial powers. As Stanley K. Hornbeck, the Asian expert who served as U.S. ambassador to Holland during the early postwar years, later recalled: The United States "in effect attempted to support neither side and yet favored one and hoped not unduly to offend the other." Broader global concerns help explain the Truman administration's manifest tilt toward the colonial powers. At a time of rising U.S.-Soviet tensions, it judged the maintenance of close ties with the French and Dutch to be a major national interest. During the early years of the cold war era Europe was the critical battleground; Southeast Asia rated as a distinctly secondary priority.

The Truman administration hoped that its own record in the Philippines could serve as a useful model for other colonial powers to follow. Moving quickly to honor Roosevelt's wartime pledge, the United States with great fanfare granted independence to its Asian colony on the Fourth of July, 1946. Referring to "this great experiment in Pacific democracy," Truman boasted that the United States and the Philippines had "already charted a pattern of relationships for all the world to study." Yet the United States retained enormous influence in the Philippines after independence, perhaps best symbolized by the massive American military bases at Clark Field and Subic Bay and the dependent economic relationship enshrined in the Bell Trade Act. Indeed, the postindependence relationship between Washington and Manila suggests that the United States neither expected nor desired a precipitous removal of European influence from the colonial areas.

While the intransigence of the French and the Dutch in the face of nationalist challenges frustrated U.S. policymakers, they applauded the evolution of a more enlightened British colonial policy. Prime Minister Clement Attlee's Labour government committed itself firmly to early independence for India and other Asian possessions and proved true to its word. American officials publicly congratulated Great Britain for its wisdom and statesmanship at the creation of independent regimes in India, Pakistan, Burma, and Ceylon. Those decisions conformed perfectly with the American vision of a peaceful and gradual evolution of the developing world from colonialism to self-rule.

By 1949 cold war priorities led to sharply differentiated American responses to the continuing colonial conflicts in Southeast Asia. In that year the United States pressured the Dutch to grant independence to their rebellious colony, paving the way for the establishment of an independent Indonesian Republic. At about the same time, the Truman administration drew up plans for direct American military and economic assistance to the French in Indochina. Thus while the United States speeded the move toward decolonization in one territory, it became a silent partner in a war of colonial reconquest in the other.

Several interrelated factors contributed to the American policy reversal in Indonesia: the nationalist movement there had unmistakably demonstrated its anti-Communist character by suppressing a revolt by the Indonesian Community party; the Netherlands not only violated unilaterally a United Nations–backed agreement, but its second major military offensive, launched in December 1948, proved largely ineffective and counterproductive; the Dutch offensive, moreover, which had generated strong congressional opposition, threatened to hold up passage of the Atlantic Pact and jeopardize funding for the European Recovery Program, two major administration priorities.

To American policymakers Indochina presented a starkly different picture. The Vietnamese independence movement had been controlled, from its inception, by Communists. As the cold war heated up in 1948 and 1949 the protracted hostilities there took on new significance. Increasingly, leading American officials saw the French effort to crush Ho Chi Minh's guerrilla forces as part of the West's worldwide struggle to contain an inexorably expanding Communist movement, a movement directed from behind the Kremlin's walls. The establishment in October 1949 of a Communist regime in China reinforced that view. On 7 February 1950, the United States formally recognized the establishment by France of nominally independent governments in Vietnam, Laos, and Cambodia. American officials privately derided those regimes as puppet states lacking genuine independence or cohesion. Nonetheless, in the absence of acceptable alternatives the Truman administration lent its support to the experiment. The State Department, perhaps in an act of wishful thinking, called U.S. recognition "consistent with our fundamental policy of giving support to the peaceful and democratic evolution of dependent peoples toward self-government and independence." On 8 May the United States quietly announced the extension of military assistance to the French, beginning an ultimately tragic involvement in Indochina. The next month, after the outbreak of war in Korea, the Truman administration deepened that commitment.

Although Asia certainly provided the most dramatic—and

bloodiest—colonial confrontations of the Truman years, the conflict between intransigent imperial powers and assertive nationalist movements was a global phenomenon during the early postwar years. In the Middle East antiimperial struggles, although less violent, were perhaps equally far-reaching in their consequences. They presented American leaders once again with the problem of choosing among competing, even contradictory, diplomatic objectives.

The Truman administration believed that American policy goals in the Middle East, as in Asia, would be well served by the progressive evolution of formerly dependent peoples into responsible, orderly, self-governing nation-states. Yet, as in Asia, the administration's antiimperial inclinations had to be balanced against its perceived defense needs in the cold war. The oil-rich Middle East, according to senior American officials, was economically and strategically indispensable to the West. Following the Korean War of June 1950, administration planners feared the possibility of outright Soviet aggression in the region. That defense priority led American officials to judge remaining European colonial outposts, such as the mammoth British base at Suez, to be especially valuable. Truman's vigorous support for the creation of Israel despite determined Arab resistance—a move explained more by personal and political than by foreign policy considerations—further complicated America's position in the region.

Nearly all of Truman's major policies toward the postwar Middle East, then, can be seen as the product of conflicting policy goals. On the one hand, his administration sought to bolster the newly independent nations in the area; on the other, it backed Israel and supported the continued European presence in various Arab states, actions deeply resented by Arab nationalists. When Truman left office the region's daunting internal and security problems appeared no closer to resolution. The bitter Arab-Israeli dispute, various intra-Arab tensions, lingering resentment over Western colonialism, and the area's vulnerability to Soviet military power—all had defied easy solutions.

Viewed broadly, the eruption of nationalist movements throughout the third world following World War II and their consequent challenge to imperial rule must rank as one of the most profound and far-reaching developments in modern world history. Certainly those nationalist stirrings created numerous new problems—and opportunities—for the Truman administration. How effectively did the administration respond to those challenges? At best, the record is a mixed one. Certainly one can argue that the administration deserves credit for helping to bring about the relatively peaceful transition from colonialism to independence in many areas. That so many nations could achieve independence within so short a period of time and with so little bloodshed is at least in part a tribute to the constructive role played by the United States. American support for Indonesia's independence is perhaps its most striking accomplishment in this regard, although the Truman administration's quiet role in helping speed independence for India, Pakistan, Burma, and Ceylon should not be overlooked. That accomplishment was limited, however, by the administration's failure to understand the depth of nationalist sentiments in Asia, the Middle East, and throughout the developing world. It tended to overlook the historical roots of local and regional developments in the rush to strengthen America's global defense posture vis-à-vis the Soviet Union. Revolutionary nationalist demands were thus seen through the invariably distorting lens of East-West conflict. The results of the approach—in Indochina and the Middle East especially—often proved counterproductive, fostering instability rather than stability.

Can Truman's foreign policy itself fairly be labeled imperialistic? According to the broad definition of imperialism employed by Williams and other scholars, it is the exercise of *control* over the affairs of weaker states rather than the possession of outright sovereignty that best defines an imperial relationship. There can be little doubt that the United States exerted a profound influence over numerous other countries in the economic, political, military, and cultural spheres during the Truman years. At the close of the war the United States was producing an astonishing 50 percent of the world's goods. It had established the dollar, through the Bretton Woods agreements, as the keystone of international currency exchanges. It was the world's leading investor, its chief source of credit, the principal extractor of raw materials, and the foremost supplier of new technologies. American Marshall Plan aid helped reconstruct a war-ravaged Europe. Moreover, the United States possessed the strongest naval and air forces in the history of the world; maintained a monopoly on humanity's most destructive weapon, the atomic bomb; sent occupying forces to Japan, Korea, Germany, and Austria; signed security agreements with dozens of allies; and established an impressive string of military bases around the globe. Everywhere, it seemed, American styles of food, clothing, consumer products, and mass culture were being emulated. "The United States was the locomotive at the head of mankind," bragged Secretary of State Dean Acheson, "and the rest of the world was the caboose." Without exaggeration, the United States stood astride the postwar world as a modern-day Colossus.

Do those undeniable facts warrant the term *imperial* as a description of Truman's foreign policy? That the United States played a dominant role in its relations with many weaker states during the Truman era cannot be questioned. If one accepts Williams's definition of *imperialism*, then clearly the United States must rank as an imperial power by that criterion alone. But such an evocative term as *imperialism* usually connotes much more than mere influence; for many it also connotes exploitation and manipulation. Can the available evidence sustain those more sinister implications of the label? Not without serious distortion of the historical record. Many European and Asian nations feared Soviet intentions as much, if not more, than the United States and actively courted an economic and military relationship with Washington. To call the resulting relationships one-sided would be grossly inaccurate. Even at the time American planners realized that by rebuilding Japan and Western Europe they would help create economic power centers that could ultimately rival the United States. If the concept is to retain any real meaning, we must employ it fairly and consistently, remaining sensitive to the negative connotations inherent in such an emotionally laden term. Given those considerations, the more narrow, traditional definition of *imperialism* may remain the most useful one.

The historical literature on imperialism is voluminous. Two provocative studies that consider the United States an imperial power and offer a comparative perspective are Tony Smith, *The Pattern of Imperialism: The United States, Great Britain, and the*

Late-Industrializing World since 1815 (New York: Cambridge University Press, 1981), and Phillip Darby, *Three Faces of Imperialism: British and American Approaches to Asia and Africa, 1870–1970* (New Haven: Yale University Press, 1987). William A. Williams's critical assessment of American imperialism can be found in his controversial study, *The Tragedy of American Diplomacy*, 2d rev. ed. (New York: Dell, 1972). For a more cautious use of imperialism as a description of American foreign policy, see David Healy, "Imperialism," in *Encyclopedia of American Foreign Policy: Studies of the Principal Movements and Ideas*, ed. Alexander DeConde, 2:409–16 (New York: Scribner's, 1978). Solid monographs on the Truman administration's response to imperialism in Asia include Gary R. Hess, Jr., *America Encounters India, 1941–1947* (Baltimore: Johns Hopkins Press, 1971); Robert J. McMahon, *Colonialism and Cold War: The United States and the Struggle for Indonesian Independence, 1945–49* (Ithaca: Cornell University Press, 1981); and Gary R. Hess, *The United States' Emergence as a Southeast Asian Power, 1940–1950* (New York: Columbia University Press, 1987). On the Middle East an indispensable work is W. Roger Louis, *The British Empire in the Middle East, 1945–1951: Arab Nationalism, the United States and Postwar Imperialism* (New York: Oxford University Press, 1984).

ROBERT J. McMAHON

See also Africa; France; Great Britain; India; Indochina; Iran; Philippine Islands; Revolution

Inauguration

Inauguration Day, Thursday, 20 January 1949, found the weather in Washington chilly but clear. President Truman enjoyed an early breakfast with members of Battery D, his World War I outfit, and then attended a brief prayer service. The inauguration ceremony, scheduled for noon at the Capitol, began twenty minutes late. After the vice president was sworn in, Truman placed his left hand on two Bibles provided for the occasion and repeated the oath of office. Because he had delivered the State of the Union message just two weeks before, his inaugural address emphasized foreign policy and is best remembered for its appeal to combat communism by making Western technology available for the development of backward countries (the Point Four program). After lunch at the Capitol, Truman and Vice President Alben Barkley reviewed the three-hour inaugural parade. The traditional White House reception that followed had to be held at the National Art Gallery because of work being done on the Executive Mansion. Closing a long day, the president and his family attended the Inauguration Ball at the National Armory.

Details concerning Truman's inauguration can be found in the Eben Ayers Diary and the Inauguration File at the Harry S. Truman Library, Independence, Missouri. Robert J. Donovan, in *Tumultuous Years: The Presidency of Harry S. Truman, 1949–1953* (New York: W. W. Norton, 1982), offers an interesting account of the day.

LAWRENCE A. YATES

Independence, Missouri

City and county seat of Jackson County, located ten miles east of downtown Kansas City, Independence was the home of Harry S. Truman for most of his life. Platted in 1827, Independence until the late 1840s was the major outfitting and departure point for the Oregon and Santa Fe trails. In 1849 the California gold rush brought new life to the town, and in that year it was incorporated as a city.

In 1831, the Mormons had settled in Independence when the city was designated as Zion by their founder, Joseph Smith. In 1833 they were forced to leave because of their religious tenets, but Independence has continued to hold an important place in Mormon belief. A schismatic group, the Reorganized Church of Jesus Christ of Latter-day Saints returned to Independence after 1865 and made the city their world headquarters.

During the Civil War, Independence, most of whose inhabitants were southern sympathizers, was the scene of several hard-fought skirmishes. After the war the town became the commercial and trading center for a prosperous agricultural area in eastern Jackson County. Despite its proximity to Kansas City, which had become the major city in the area, Independence retained, until well into the twentieth century, many of the attributes of a typical small midwestern town characterized by thrift, hard work, and a sense of community, combined with the traditional Puritan virtues. This was the environment in which Harry Truman grew to manhood. Although later tempered by his experience in the army and the rough-and-tumble of politics, this upbringing inevitably affected his thoughts and attitudes in later years both in and out of office.

Harry S. Truman moved to Independence in 1890 at the age of five with his parents, John Anderson and Martha Ellen Truman, and his brother and sister, J. Vivian and Mary Jane. The Trumans' first home in Independence was located on Crysler Street in the southeast part of the city; in 1896 they moved to 909 West Waldo Avenue nearer the downtown area. Truman attended the Independence public schools, graduating from high school in 1901. During his first year in high school he held a part-time job at Clinton's Drugstore on the courthouse square, sweeping floors, emptying trash, and acting as general factotum. For most of the next eighteen years, after his graduation from high school, Truman, though a frequent visitor, lived away from Independence. After service in World War I, he returned and married his childhood sweetheart, Bess Wallace, in the Trinity Episcopal Church on North Liberty Street. After marriage the couple made their home in the Wallace family mansion, which remained Truman's residence for the remainder of his life.

The courthouse square in the heart of Independence long served as the focal point of the community's social and economic life. When Truman held office as eastern judge of the Jackson County Court from 1923 to 1924 and later as presiding judge from 1927 to 1934, he had an office in the courthouse. This building, which was rebuilt in 1932–33 while Truman was presiding judge, incorporated portions of six earlier courthouse buildings and additions.

After his election to the Senate and later as president, Truman returned to Independence frequently to visit old friends and touch political base. Notable among his visits to his hometown during the White House years were the 27 June 1945 homecoming celebration held in the RLDS Auditorium to honor

Truman on his ascendancy to the presidency; the victory celebration held in Independence on 3 November 1948 after Truman's unexpected victory in the 1948 presidential election; and the welcome-home reception on 23 January 1953 at the Independence railroad station attended by nearly ten thousand persons, when the Trumans returned to Independence after retirement from the White House. During these years, he also regularly returned to Independence on election days to vote at his longtime balloting place at the Memorial Building, a civic structure a few blocks from his home. As president he spent every Christmas in Independence with the exception of 1947 and 1952.

There was never any doubt in Truman's mind as to where he would live after leaving the White House. When asked at a press conference whether he planned to return to Independence, he replied, "Certainly. That's my home." In 1957 the Harry S. Truman Library was completed to house Truman's presidential papers and memorabilia. Located six blocks from Truman's home, the library building included an office suite for his personal use, and until 1966, when illness forced him to curtail his activities, Truman visited this office daily. Both President Truman and Mrs. Truman are buried in the library's courtyard.

When President Truman first entered the White House, Independence still had the same boundaries it had had when he was a schoolboy. In 1948, however, the city was enlarged from 3.4 to 10.3 square miles. Seven additional annexations between 1956 and 1975 increased the city's total land area to 78 square miles. Its population, which in 1900 numbered less than 7,000, had grown by 1950 to nearly 37,000; at the time of Truman's death it exceeded 110,000, making it one of the largest cities in the state. Although a number of small industries had been established in the city after World War I, Independence remained primarily a bedroom community. With the shifting of retail trade to the many shopping malls and strips that sprang up in all parts of the city in the 1960s and 1970s, the courthouse square ceased to be the hub of the city's commercial activities as it had been for over a hundred years. Many of the stores on the square now became specialty and gift shops catering to the thousands of tourists who come to Independence to tour the Truman Library's Museum and the Truman home. As President Truman noted in a letter to a friend written in 1950: "The Independence that I knew in 1890 long since disappeared in every particular; the Independence I knew in 1928 . . . has also disappeared, and I suppose the one of the present day will be a thing of the past in another twenty years and that is as it should be."

There is no adequate history of Independence. Detailed information about President Truman's early years in the city can be found in Jonathan Daniels, *Man of Independence* (Philadelphia: J. B. Lippincott, 1950), and Richard L. Miller, *Truman: The Rise to Power* (New York: McGraw-Hill, 1986). Bernd Foerster, *Independence, Missouri* (Independence: Independence, Missouri, 1978) is a survey of architecturally and historically important buildings in the area and includes photographs and maps. "Harry S. Truman's Missouri," *Life* 18 (1945): 75–83, offers photographs and text about Independence and Truman's friends and associates.

BENEDICT K. ZOBRIST

See also Gates-Wallace-Truman House; Missouri

India

Franklin Roosevelt created great expectations in India about the future of Indo-American relations. During World War II, he made no secret of his opposition to colonialism and sent two envoys to India whose visits were interpreted by Indian nationalists as a discreet endorsement of their demand for independence from Great Britain. Thus when the war was over, America enjoyed a great deal of goodwill among Indian nationalists. President Truman was not long in office before it began to evaporate.

There were several reasons for this. Probably the most important was the fanatical anti-Communism that had begun to permeate American domestic politics by the time India gained its independence on 15 August 1947. Fear of appearing pro-Communist forced the Truman administration to demand anti-Soviet foreign policies from its allies, and it was difficult for Americans to sympathize with the leftist politics and socialist economics that had formed the ideological core of the Indian freedom struggle.

Jawaharlal Nehru, India's first prime minister, was a social democrat and had been a founding member of the Soviet-sponsored League against Imperialism based in Brussels. He was also an intellectual who seemed arrogant to many, and who selected as UN delegate V. K. Krishna Menon, a brilliant, outspoken, and abrasive leftist who believed India to be more endangered by predatory capitalists than by international communism. Given the anti-Communist hysteria in America, it is remarkable that relations between India and the United States were not worse than they were. For while Nehru was very tough on Communists at home, he was also determined to have a modified socialist economy and a nonaligned foreign policy, both of which were anathema in the United States.

Truman's first two ambassadors to India, Henry F. Grady and Loy W. Henderson, did not conceal their intense disapproval of these tendencies. Grady frequently chided Indian journalists for their socialist views. Henderson and Nehru did not like each other, and Henderson's dispatches were full of contemptuous comments about the arguments Nehru had made to him in explanation of his foreign policy. Nehru's first visit to the United States in 1949 tended more to reinforce negative attitudes on both sides than to clear the air. Dean Acheson later wrote that Nehru arrived "in a prickly mood" and "was one of the most difficult men with whom I have ever had to deal."

Then Truman appointed Chester Bowles, the liberal New Dealer, as ambassador in the fall of 1951. Bowles admired Nehru and received a good press in India for his frankness and genuine concern for India's problems. Relations improved considerably.

But for the most part, the years of the Truman administration were marked by the emergence of numerous disagreements between the two countries. Almost immediately came the Kashmir dispute. The U.S. tilt toward Pakistan on this issue was bitterly resented in India. Then the independence movements in Indonesia and Indochina caused friction. Remembering its own independence struggle, India saw the United States as siding with the colonial Netherlands and France.

In the prevailing atmosphere, even President Truman's effort to help alleviate India's desperate food shortage with a loan for wheat purchases did not help relations much; the amount granted was far short of what India needed, and the lengthy debate about it in Congress greatly offended Indian politicians.

But the issues that created the most tension between the two countries were the Chinese Revolution and the Korean War. Nehru believed that Communist rule in China was irreversible, and the new Chinese government should be integrated into the international community. He consequently extended diplomatic recognition to Peking and argued that Mao's government should be allowed to occupy China's permanent seat on the Security Council. The United States, on the other hand, was determined to ostracize China and keep alive hopes that Chiang Kai-shek on Formosa would one day reconquer the mainland.

These differences greatly influenced India's view of the Korean War. Although India joined the United States in condemning North Korea's aggression, Nehru annoyed the Americans by refusing to send even a token military contingent. Indian diplomacy was aimed at ending the conflict and lessening the tensions of the cold war, but the Truman administration, under pressure from the China Lobby and the McCarthyites, was afraid of appearing soft on communism.

After Gen. Douglas MacArthur had pushed the North Koreans back across the thirty-eighth parallel and was marching north toward the Chinese border, the Indians warned that China would enter the war. The Americans, thinking it unlikely and sensing an opportunity to unify all of Korea under a pro-American government, allowed MacArthur to charge ahead.

But the Indians had been correct. China entered the war, and MacArthur, taking heavy casualties, was pushed back across the thirty-eighth parallel. Having been right about both China and Korea did not make the Indians more popular in Washington.

As Indo-American relations have never been a major element in the literature on U.S. foreign policy, one finds the best coverage of the subject in books about Indian foreign policy. The Truman years are the focus of R. P. Kaushik's *The Crucial Years of Non-Alignment* (Delhi: Kumar Brothers, 1972) and the still useful *India and the United States* by Lawrence K. Rosinger (New York: Macmillan, 1950). Truman's policies are placed in a broader historical context in Charles H. Heimsath and Surjit Mansingh, *A Diplomatic History of Modern India* (Bombay: Allied Publishers, 1971).

MARSHALL WINDMILLER

See also Bowles, Chester Bliss; Henderson, Loy Wesley; Imperialism

Indian Policy

The Truman years were a time of transition in Indian affairs. Federal officials repudiated separate tribal self-rule, the policy of the Indian Reorganization Act (IRA; 1934), in favor of a public policy designed to terminate federal control over Indian life and property. President Harry S. Truman supported termination because he had little interest in New Deal community programs. Truman was determined to encourage racial integration, uphold the civil rights of Indians and other minorities, and pro-

vide them with employment opportunities in an expanding postwar capitalist economy.

After 1945, Secretary of the Interior Oscar L. Chapman, Indian commissioners William A. Brophy, John R. Nichols, and Dillon S. Myer, and other members of the Truman administration followed an assimilationist Indian policy mandated by Congress. There was bipartisan support in Congress for equal Indian citizenship, the abolition of the federal trust over Indian property, increased state responsibility for Indians to replace New Deal statism under the IRA, and the rapid economic development of western United States. President Truman encouraged the reorientation of Indian-white relations by signing the 1946 Indian Claims Commission Act. This legislation set the stage for termination by permitting Indians to sue the government to settle claims for past injustices. Truman also signed the Navajo-Hopi Rehabilitation Act (1950), which authorized the expenditure of $88 million over a ten-year period to help these two tribes combat poverty, illiteracy, and poor health.

The drive to abrogate federal jurisdiction over Indians gained momentum when Truman in May 1950 appointed Dillon S. Myer as Indian commissioner. Myer worked closely with members of Congress who favored termination. Furthermore, he allowed Indians more control over their real estate, made changes in Indian education to promote assimilation, and created a Voluntary Relocation Program at the Indian Bureau to help Indians find employment off their reservations. Myer also established a program to formulate long-range tribal termination planning and drafted unsuccessful legislation to end federal authority over Indians residing in California and Oregon.

Myer failed to gain widespread Indian support for his termination programs. The National Congress of American Indians adamantly rejected the abolition of the federal trust relationship without tribal consent. Myer's ability to manage the Indian Bureau diminished further when he became involved in a bitter controversy over the right of Indians to hire independent attorneys to prepare their claims cases and challenge termination. In November 1950, Myer issued a Indian Bureau memo that regulated both claims and general counsel contracts. The commissioner believed that the bureau was obligated under existing law to prevent questionable legal activities by tribal attorneys. Most Indians disagreed with Myer's position. His regulations appeared to violate their legal and constitutional right to private counsel. Consequently, Myer and the Truman administration lost a historic opportunity to advance the cause of Indian self-determination.

Valuable sources of information are Richard Drinnon, *Keeper of Concentration Camps: Dillon S. Myer and American Racism* (Berkeley: University of California Press, 1987); Clayton Koppes, "From New Deal to Termination: Liberalism and Indian Policy, 1933–1953," *Pacific Historical Review* 46 (November 1977): 543–66; and Francis Paul Prucha, *The Great Father*, vol. 2 (Lincoln: University of Nebraska Press, 1984).

KENNETH R. PHILP

See also Chapman, Oscar Littleton

Indochina

The Truman administration had a heavy impact on Indochina. Without its support France could never have mounted any substantial effort at reconquest, and Ho Chi Minh's Vietminh would probably have come to control all of Vietnam within a year of the departure of the British and Nationalist Chinese postwar occupation forces in mid-1946. (The Allies had assigned responsibility for disarming and repatriating Japanese troops in the southern half of Indochina to Britain and in the northern half to Chiang Kai-shek's government.)

Although outraged by the collaboration of the Vichy French regime in Indochina with the Japanese, Franklin Roosevelt shortly before he died had drawn back from his earlier insistence that France be denied reestablishment of its rule there. He had decided that such a policy was untenable because of more important U.S. objectives in Europe and North Africa whose attainment required French support. Truman and his advisers came to the same conclusion. Although they politely urged the French—unsuccessfully—to make concessions to the demands of the Vietnamese in order to blunt Ho Chi Minh's appeal, never did they question French sovereignty over Vietnam. The Truman administration's approach to Indochina was crucially affected by the fact that its top priorities lay in Western Europe, especially in plans for its economic reconstruction and the building of a military shield against Soviet power. Those U.S. interests decisively overshadowed a still-significant anticolonial sentiment among many Americans.

With French patriotism smarting from the ignominy of defeat and occupation by the Nazis, American officials had reason to believe that application of pressure to induce France to give up control over any of its colonies risked the loss of its cooperation in Europe. Truman's advisers believed that such pressure could shake the precarious balance of French domestic politics to the benefit of the then powerful French Communist party, which itself initially in the postwar years supported France's military campaign in Indochina out of fear that opposition would cost votes.

Thus, the Truman administration did not contest the measures whereby the British and Nationalist Chinese, before departing Vietnam, shoe-horned in some sixty-five thousand French troops; nor did it protest the British commander's use of large numbers of Japanese troops in much of the fighting against the Vietminh. For most of the incoming French forces the United States provided the transport—either directly in American ships or by supplying Paris with credits for purchase of seventy-five U.S. troop transports. French troops whom the United States had armed for an expected assault on Japan were permitted to keep these weapons and use them in Indochina. Of greater importance, the Truman administration privately allowed France to transfer to Indochina a large part of the modern weaponry officially supplied for defense of Western Europe. As the head of the American economic mission to Vietnam later put it, the United States provided France with the military equipment "for a colonial reestablishment [in Indochina] indirectly by way of Paris."

For the first Truman administration no reliable tally of the large amount of U.S. military equipment funneled to the French in Indochina is available; but the Joint Chiefs of Staff's estimate for the three years 1950–52 include 302 naval vessels, 304 aircraft, 1,224 tanks and other combat vehicles, 20,274 transport vehicles, 2,847 pieces of artillery, and 120,792 small arms. In addition, the United States "lent" the French for service in Indochina an aircraft carrier and 54 large transport planes (as well as a team of American mechanics to service them).

Most crucial of all to France's military campaign in Indochina was the Truman administration's consistent financial backing—covert before 1950 and only partly public after that. Until then large American credits to France were not specifically designated for this purpose; but just as senior U.S. officials understood that many of the arms provided to France for the defense of Western Europe were being siphoned off for use in Vietnam, so they acquiesced in a substantial part of U.S. funds earmarked for the restoration of France's devastated economy being utilized to pay most of the costs of its military effort in Indochina.

Despite the magnitude of U.S. assistance, the French army could not prevail in Vietnam and had begun to lose ground more than two years before the Chinese Communists reached the Vietnam border and were able to augment the Vietminh's supply of weapons. The deteriorating position of the French brought the Truman administration to endorse France's "Bao Dai solution," wherein the ex-emperor of Vietnam, who had worked with the Japanese as well as prewar France, was drafted back into service. Aimed at providing an alternative channel for Vietnamese nationalism to compete with that dominated by the Vietminh, this plan in fact never drew significant support away from the standard of Ho Chi Minh. American officials understood that Bao Dai stood little chance even if the French were prepared to hand over significant authority to him, which, despite persistent U.S. urging, they steadfastly refused. Nevertheless, seeing no other alternative to the Vietminh, the Truman administration made clear its support of Bao Dai even before the French Chamber of Deputies formally endorsed him in February 1950 (and before Moscow or Peking finally recognized the government of Ho Chi Minh that same month).

Although in retrospect it might appear unrealistic for Truman not to have come to terms with a leadership which U.S. intelligence acknowledged was much more popular than Bao Dai's, it must be remembered that the president and his senior advisers saw communism as a global monolith controlled by Moscow, with Ho Chi Minh as its minion, and were unable to appreciate that in Vietnam (as they did perceive in Yugoslavia) nationalism and communism could fuse. Strongly reinforcing their unwillingness to accommodate to the fact that the main thrust of Vietnamese self-determination favored the Communist-led Vietminh was the sharp political cutting edge of the "loss-of-China" charge that was used against the administration so effectively in the 1950 congressional election. For the Democratic party to be seen as acquiescing in additional Asian territory passing under Communist control was believed to risk grave political damage. These perceptions help explain why, in the face of the Communists' victory in China, the Truman administration steeled itself to back Bao Dai, and then quickly commenced a program of overt aid to the French military effort in Vietnam, greatly expanding this with the outbreak of the Korean War.

The Truman administration's indirect intervention in Vietnam was clearly not influenced by any U.S. economic stake there—existing or potential, for the French had always rigorously excluded American investment and commercial relations with their colony and gave no indications they would permit any significant change in that policy in the postwar period. Of most critical importance to American involvement was the role of France in the attainment of U.S. objectives in Europe, and later the belief that a continuing French military presence in Vietnam could help contain Chinese Communist power. And once the United States had taken an active anti-Communist posture in Indochina, the exigencies of American domestic politics, especially after they came under the influence of Senators McCarthy and McCarran, ensured that this posture would be maintained.

Dean W. Acheson, *Present at the Creation* (New York: W. W. Norton, 1969), makes clear how little understanding Truman's principal foreign policy adviser had of the situation in Indochina and the extent to which his Eurocentric policies militated against support of Vietnamese self-determination. Philippe Devillers, *Histoire du Viet-Nam de 1940 à 1952* (Paris: Editions du Seuil, 1952), is a classic that remains unchallenged as the best account of French Indochina policy and Franco-Vietnamese relations during the Truman period. George C. Herring, "The Truman Administration and the Restoration of French Sovereignty in Indochina," *Diplomatic History* 1 (1977): 97–177, is by far the best treatment of the diplomatic dimension; it is also sensitive to pertinent aspects of American domestic politics. George McT. Kahin, *Intervention: How America Became Involved in Vietnam* (New York: Knopf, 1986; paperback, Doubleday Anchor Books, 1987), draws on recently declassified relevant American and British documents.

GEORGE McT. KAHIN

See also France; Imperialism; Revolution

Inflation

President Harry S. Truman dealt with a multitude of economic problems and fears from a traditional concern about inflation, which seems always to occur after war, to the fear of a future economy of underconsumption and underemployment, an ideological legacy from the New Deal. Truman's solutions were worked out in a particular political context. For example, both New Dealers and Keynesian economists such as Alvin Hansen believed that a deficit fiscal policy would move the economy to the politically desirable goal of full employment. But classical economists such as Edwin Nourse, first chairman of the Council of Economic Advisers, worried that such a fiscal policy would contribute to future inflation because the economy could not meet all the public demands for national security and domestic welfare reforms. Inflation, therefore, was just one on a list of theoretical economic concerns.

On a more immediate and practical level, many Americans wanted a rapid return to a peacetime economy. The political pressures to end price controls were considerable. The Truman administration rapidly solved problems of physical conversion to a peacetime economy, but strong consumer demands added to potential inflation. With neither depression nor inflation being politically desirable, the Truman administration sought economic growth and full employment as alternatives to any potential inflation.

Events and new advisers guided the Truman presidency to-

ward a change in attitude toward inflation. From 1945 to the election of 1948, Harry S. Truman followed conventional economic wisdom. Although claiming his heritage from New Deal liberalism, Truman, after the end of World War II, wanted a balanced budget with tax surpluses reducing the national debt and curbing inflation. Even after the disastrous congressional election of 1946, James Webb, director of the budget, and John Snyder, secretary of the treasury, advised Truman to seek budget surpluses.

With the approach of the 1948 election, Clark Clifford and a group of liberals argued for a bolder economic policy, since conservatives, in and out of the Republican party, rejected Truman, balanced budget or not. The Employment Act of 1946 ironically came to Truman's political rescue. Although politically cool to the law, Truman appointed Edwin G. Nourse (chairman), Leon Keyserling, and John D. Clark to the first Council of Economic Advisers.

As a classical economist, Nourse's major concern was inflation. In the historical context of New Deal liberalism and potential growth via deficit fiscal policy, Nourse, until his resignation, maintained a tempestuous relationship with Leon H. Keyserling whose economic sentiments fit the political necessities facing the Truman administration. In the majority of policy decisions Clark supported Keyserling's suggestions. By personal desire and political experience Truman wanted congressional cooperation in achieving balanced budgets and surpluses if possible. But his electoral victory in 1948 ended Truman's fiscal "conservatism." If leaders pick their advisers and thereby choose their advice, the outcome of the Nourse-Keyserling dispute meant Truman's acceptance of cold war liberalism—guns and butter for all.

Finally resigning on 9 September 1949, Nourse did not support peacetime price and rationing controls for the president. Prior to his resignation Nourse and conservatives like John Snyder and John Steelman urged a ceiling on defense spending and cuts in domestic expenditures. A group led by Keyserling and Clark urged increased domestic spending and additional taxes and controls while restricting military expenditures. Keyserling and Clark won. Leon Keyserling became the second chairman of the Council of Economic Advisers. In the remaining years of his long life, Nourse rejected postwar liberalism at every opportunity.

In the meantime, the Truman presidency successfully controlled inflation by beginning a postwar expansion that lasted over twenty years. It was Truman's political fortune that inflation was not a major concern during his presidency. The American economy on balance performed in fine fashion. European economic recovery and the Korean War created minimal distractions from inflation while domestic reforms continued as America became an economic and political world power. In retrospect, having experienced the inflationary fire storms and foreign policy reversals from 1968 to 1980, many Americans would look upon the Truman administration as the golden age of postwar liberal economic optimism.

Harry S. Truman: The Man From Indenpendence, ed. William F. Levantrosser (New York: Greenwood Press, 1986), contains four articles dealing with economic policy. Of particular importance are Geoffrey T. Mills, "Harry S. Truman and Price Control: Two Episodes of Inflation Control, 1945–1952" and Donald K. Pickens, "Truman's Council of Economic Advisors and the Legacy of New

Deal Liberalism." Alonzo L. Hamby, *Beyond the New Deal: Harry S. Truman and American Liberalism* (New York: Columbia University Press, 1973), is an excellent account of the ideologies and the advice proffered to Truman during his presidency.

DONALD K. PICKENS

See also Council of Economic Advisers; Economy, The; Fiscal and Monetary Policies; Keyserling, Leon; Nourse, Edwin Griswold

---

Influence Peddling

See Scandals

Interests

See Masonic Order; Music; Personal Writings; Reading; Walking

---

Internal Security Act

See Communism and Communists; Loyalty Program; McCarran, Patrick Anthony

---

Internationalism

The *first* decision that President Truman made, after the death of Franklin D. Roosevelt, was to continue the United Nations Conference on International Organization, as planned, at San Francisco. Affirmed in Truman's answer to a reporter's question immediately after he took the oath of office in the White House on 12 April 1945, the decision reflected the basic priorities, the haste, and the immense responsibility of the new president.

Truman did not have a grand vision of the postwar world order. He was not a world statesman, although he soon proved the equal of Roosevelt, Churchill, or Stalin. He tended to think first of military preparedness as the bulwark of peace and then of a continued grand alliance, the latter perhaps as the political foundation of the new United Nations.

The Truman administration pursued policies of international cooperation with the Soviet Union until March 1947. Thereafter, with the Truman Doctrine, the Marshall Plan, and the North Atlantic treaty, it pursued the more nationalist policy of containment, which continues to the present day.

John Churchill Chase, *New Orleans States*, 6 October 1950. Courtesy of the *New Orleans Times-Picayune*.

Nevertheless, the Truman administration produced some major and lasting achievements in internationalism. The president, by carefully adhering to the Yalta agreements—especially regarding the veto power in the UN Security Council—and to wartime planning for an international security organization, saw the San Francisco conference to a successful conclusion. "The Constitution of my own country," he said in his address to the final plenary session, "came from a Convention which—like this one—was made up of delegates with many different views. ... When it was adopted, no one regarded it as a perfect document. But it grew and developed and expanded. And upon it was built a bigger, a better, a more perfect union."

The charter of the United Nations preserved the principle of the absolute national sovereignty of states only for the Big Five: the United States, Soviet Union, United Kingdom, China, and France. All other founding (and subsequently admitted) states accepted various forms of majority rule in the several groups that made up the organization. Any inadequacies of the charter, it was thought, would be met by an amendment procedure (Article 109) that called for a review conference in 1955.

Two days after signing the charter on 26 June 1945, President Truman said at the University of Kansas City: "It will be just as easy for nations to get along in a republic of the world as it is for us to get along in the Republic of the United States." Such statements are now looked upon as cases of overselling the United Nations, but they indicate the sincere hopes of the time, at the highest levels of government, for an international security organization that could be relied upon by all nations for their defense and harmonization of interests. At the Potsdam Conference soon after, an enterprising United Press reporter enquired about the meaning of his Kansas City statement, and the president rather shyly drew from his wallet the famous verses of Tennyson's "Locksley Hall" (see below), which Truman said he had carried there since 1910.

Truman won Senate ratification of the UN charter, achieving a goal that had eluded Woodrow Wilson and Franklin D. Roosevelt. Judging by the vote (89–2), isolationism was dead in the United States, although Senator Vandenberg's speeches asserting that the United Nations did not limit U.S. sovereignty or have any binding effects indicated how modest was the step. His speeches were a warning that isolationist sentiment still existed, a point that Senator Connally confirmed with his well-known reservation to U.S. adherence to the World Court.

Truman within the United Nation's first year launched the historic U.S. plan for the international control of atomic energy (the Baruch plan), which called for abolition of the veto in atomic energy matters and hence for significant limits on all nations' sovereignty. But constitutionally the Baruch plan was not well thought out and was pressed in an atmosphere of atomic diplomacy which led to its failure—with serious consequences for the subsequent nuclear arms race.

The Truman administration must be credited with its Point Four proposal (1949), which began U.S. commitment to international development aid, and with its general blessing on projects of European union, which was a vital political source for the European Defense Community and the more successful European Economic Community. Truman responded instantly to the North Korean invasion of the South in June 1950 by mobilizing the United Nations. Security Council collective security measures (in the absence of the Soviet Union, which was then boycotting the United Nations for its refusal to seat Red China). But the Korean police action did not set a lasting pattern, although the Uniting for Peace resolution in the General Assembly of November 1950 led to repeated special sessions whenever the Security Council, because of the veto, has been unable to act.

The Truman administration, on the other hand, must be debited for almost abandoning the United Nations and for setting the direction of great-power politics to the present. And in contrast to Truman's occasional ringing statements on the United Nations must be set such a basic statement on U.S. national foreign policy as his Navy Day address of 27 October 1945, which laid out a program for East-West disputes on Poland, Germany, the satellites (formerly of Germany, now of the Soviet Union), the Dardanelles, and other international waterways.

The Truman Doctrine and the Marshall Plan were conceived and largely justified outside the United Nations. The North Atlantic Treaty, with its very loose construction of Article 51 (permitting collective self-defense but not independent regional security organizations), was all but a repudiation of the United Nations. West German rearmament—the ultimate counterthreat to the Soviet Union—became possible in 1949 and a reality in 1955. Although the North Koreans, if not the Russians, clearly committed an act of armed aggression in June 1950, the administration's decision in September to carry the counterattack north of the thirty-eighth parallel, implying the unification of Korea by force, was contrary to the charter and surely unwise.

The containment policy, using primarily political and economic means, easily glided over into deterrence policies relying on overwhelming military means and ending in the doctrine of "mutually assured destruction." And NSC 68, which put the country of Washington and Jefferson on a permanent cold war footing, received its stamp in 1950 during the Truman administration.

It is not enough to say that the United Nations failed because the cold war destroyed the unanimity of the Big Five. One must ask, *why* did the cold war develop? From an internationalist perspective, the reason seems to be that the United Nations was neither structured nor empowered to restrain the leaders of the great powers that they might resolve their disputes without recourse to threats and use of force. One wonders what the result would have been in 1946, say, before fears had driven out hopes, if the General Assembly had been made representative of peoples and had been given the power to enact law.

It appears now that Stalin was motivated by Russia's historic need for secure borders—not by dreams from Bolshevik days of world revolution. With his country in ruins, he had no ambition for world conquest. Certainly Truman did not. Something like what was needed at the time is represented historically by the brave if doomed later career of Henry Wallace, whose reputation has lately enjoyed a restoration. Wallace saw clearly that U.S. demands for overseas bases, the monopoly of atomic weapons, and the B-36 bomber were just as surely threats of "encirclement" to the Soviets as subversion and coups in Eastern Europe were threats of "expansion" to Americans. A strong United Nations then, as now, would have required the same wrenching national self-criticism and restraint that Wallace demanded. Only in a spirit of mutual respect and of willingness to give way on some point affecting national pride can international organization become the new basis of the search for freedom and justice—that is, for peace.

The Truman administration, though it set back through lack of vision the cause of internationalism for at least one generation, did not destroy the United Nations. The UN Atomic Energy Commission and the Commission for Conventional Armaments were united in 1952, and the United Nations has continued to be a multilateral forum for the debate on disarmament. The Universal Declaration of Human Rights, announced by Eleanor Roosevelt and her colleagues in 1948, was followed by two covenants—on political and civil rights and on economic, social, and cultural rights—in 1966. One of the great triumphs of the United Nations, encouraged by the Truman administration, has been decolonization, bringing independence and self-government to peoples long under the domination of European imperial powers. Over the years, as global problems have been recognized as needing global solutions, the United Nations has been the locus for the establishment of new organizations devoted to such purposes as peacekeeping, the law of the sea, disaster relief, economic development and assistance to developing countries, and problems concerning world health, the environment, population growth, and food and agriculture.

If the passions rooted in the Second World War and revived in the cold war are now spent, there may come a reasonable opportunity for what Truman admired in those Tennyson verses he carried:

For I dipt into the future, as far as human eye could see,
Saw the Vision of the world, and all the wonder that would be;

Saw the heavens fill with commerce, argosies of magic sails,

Pilots of the purple twilight, dropping down with costly bales;

Heard the heavens fill with shouting, and there rain'd a ghastly dew
From the nations' airy navies grapling in the central blue;

Far along the world-wide whisper of the south wind rushing warm,
With the standards of the peoples plunging thro' the thunder storm;

Till the war-drum throbb'd no longer, and the battle-flags
    were furl'd
In the Parliament of man, the Federation of the world.

The following works are recommended for further reading: Joseph Preston Baratta, "Was the Baruch Plan a Proposal of World Government?" *International History Review* 7 (November 1985): 592–621; Thomas M. Campbell, "Nationalism in America's U.N. Policy, 1944–1945," *International Organization* 27 (1973): 25–44; J. Garry Clifford, "President Truman and Peter the Great's Will," *Diplomatic History* 4 (Fall 1980): 371–85; Richard N. Current, "United States and 'Collective Security': Notes on the History of an Idea," in *Isolation and Security*, ed. Alexander DeConde, 33–55 (Durham, N.C.: Duke University Press, 1957); Thomas L. Hughes, "The Twilight of Internationalism," *Foreign Policy* 61 (Winter 1985–86): 25–48; Wilson Miscamble, "The Evolution of an Internationalist: Harry S. Truman and American Foreign Policy," *Australian Journal of Politics and History* 23 (August 1977): 268–33; Lawrence S. Kaplan, "Isolationism, the United Nations, and the Cold War," in *Culture and Diplomacy: The American Experience*, ed. Morrell Heald and Lawrence S. Kaplan, 215–41 (Westport, Conn.: Greenwood Press, 1977); Warren G. Kuehl, "Internationalism," in *The Encyclopedia of American Foreign Policy*, ed. Alexander DeConde, 443–54 (New York: Scribner, 1978); Warren F. Kuehl, "Concepts of Internationalism in History," *Peace and Change* 11, no. 2 (1986): 1–10; Roland N. Stromberg, *Collective Security and American Foreign Policy: From the League to NATO* (New York: Praeger, 1963); J. Samuel Walker, *Henry A. Wallace and American Foreign Policy* (Westport, Conn.: Greenwood Press, 1976); Richard J. Walton, *Henry Wallace, Harry Truman and the Cold War* (New York: Viking Press, 1976); and Lawrence D. Weiler and Anne P. Simons, *The United States and the United Nations: The Search for International Peace and Security* (New York: Manhattan Publishing Co., 1967).

JOSEPH PRESTON BARATTA

See also Point Four Program; United Nations; United Nations Relief and Rehabilitation Administration

International Trade

To restore a peaceful and prosperous world order after World War II, President Truman assigned high priority to establishing the conditions for expanding international trade. His administration provided economic assistance to help rehabilitate the war-torn economies of Western Europe and Japan, initiated multilateral negotiations to reduce trade barriers and establish a world trade organization, and took important steps to open the U.S. market to imports.

In charting this internationalist course, Truman sought to avoid the mistakes of the interwar period. As he knew, global commerce had expanded briskly in the century before World War I, but two world wars and a global depression left serious distortions and imbalances. To shelter their domestic economies from these disruptions, many nations had turned to protective trade barriers and other "beggar-thy-neighbor" trade and currency practices. But to President Truman and his aides, such expedients were self-defeating: they had strangled commerce and plunged the world into economic warfare in the 1930s. As he said in a speech at Baylor University in 1947, "Nobody won the last economic war. . . . We must not go through the thirties again. . . . The choice is ours. We can lead the nations to economic peace or we can plunge them into economic war."

Despite the president's own determination to promote international economic cooperation, it was unclear at the close of World War II whether other nations had the resources and the resolve to abandon protectionist expedients and create, instead, an open international economy in which market forces, not governments, directed the flow of resources. A basic problem was the dollar shortage, a problem with several dimensions. As a short-run financial problem, Western Europe and Japan lacked the production to earn dollars required to pay for imports of raw materials and capital equipment essential to restoring their domestic economies. These countries also seemed to have a persistent long-term dollar problem: their industries apparently were unable to compete successfully for export markets with American firms.

In the late 1940s American industry set the global standard for product quality and technological leadership, and American products were in global demand. Unlike the Europeans and Japanese who had to import raw materials and then add value to make export sales of finished products, the United States was a diversified exporter with a relatively self-sufficient resource base. During these years it was not uncommon for the United States to export 10 percent of its automobile production, 25 percent of its trucks, 21 percent of metal-working machine tools, 10 percent of steel, and substantial quantities of footwear and consumer electrical products, such as radios and toasters. Along with manufactures, the United States sold abroad significant quantities of farm products and raw materials—wheat, cotton and petroleum.

To steer Western Europe and Japan away from protectionism and toward full participation in an open trading community, the Truman administration provided generous reconstruction aid. Indeed from 1946 to 1952 the United States financed the dollar shortage, providing approximately $24 billion in grants and credits to Western Europe and Japan, an amount equal to their cumulative trade deficits with the United States.

Meanwhile, Truman's aides took the lead in multilateral negotiations to roll back trade barriers and write a charter for an international agency to regulate trade. This initiative reflected the vision of former secretary of state Cordell Hull, who during World War II encouraged his assistants to develop plans for a commercial counterpart of the United Nations. At Geneva, Switzerland, in 1947, representatives of twenty-two nations simultaneously engaged in bilateral product-by-product negotiations to reduce tariffs and trade barriers and deliberated plans for an International Trade Organization. Although accurate measurement of tariff concessions is extremely difficult, three rounds of multilateral trade negotiations (Geneva, 1947; Annecy, France, 1948; Torquay, England, 1950) during the Truman years brought a 27 percent reduction in the average rate of duty on all U.S. dutiable imports. Many of the foreign concessions obtained by the United States, however, were merely bindings of existing duty rates, not actual tariff reductions. Such a result was acceptable to U.S. negotiators apparently because they feared other countries might impose even steeper duties and restrictions on U.S. exports to conserve scarce dollars.

Out of the many individual bargains at Geneva emerged a single multilateral pact, known as the General Agreement on Tariffs and Trade (GATT). It contained a schedule with thousands of trade concessions and provisional clauses covering a range of trade policy issues. Central to GATT was the unconditional most-favored-nation principle in which contracting parties pledged to apply no higher tariffs or internal taxes on imports from any party to the agreement than to imports of the same products from any other country.

Efforts to establish a permanent trade agency continued at Havana, Cuba, in 1948. This conference completed the draft charter for the International Trade Organization (ITO), a grandiose proposal providing rules not only on tariffs and quotas but also on commodity, antitrust, and employment issues. When Congress refused to approve U.S. membership in the ITO, the GATT became by default the international vehicle for coordinating national trade policies and for conducting multilateral trade negotiations.

Overall, it is important to note that international political and security concerns shaped President Truman's approach to international trade. Convinced, as he was, that trade restrictions fostered economic warfare and that the dollar shortage was the greatest international economic problem impeding recovery and threatening stability in Japan and Western Europe, President Truman and his aides took bold action to open U.S. markets to imports. In trade negotiations the United States tolerated foreign discrimination against American exports for balance of payments reasons, while agreeing to pare down U.S. barriers, especially on manufactured products. Undoubtedly, this altruistic approach, which successor administrations continued, contributed importantly to a gradual but persistent increase in the share of manufactured imports from 18 percent of imports in 1946 to 23 percent in 1955 and 56 percent in 1970. Opening the American market to foreign producers also facilitated the recovery of Western European nations and Japan—countries that were to become both America's strong partners in defense and vigorous competitors in trade.

Perhaps the best up-to-date introduction to the complex web of legal, economic, and historical issues is a legal text, John H. Jackson and William J. Davey, *Legal Problems of International Economic Relations*, 2d ed. (St. Paul, Minn: West Publishing, 1986). Robert A. Pastor addresses trade issues in his *Congress and the Politics of U.S. Foreign Economic Policy, 1929–1976* (Berkeley: University of California, 1980). Among the classics, consult Gerald Curzon, *Multilateral Commercial Diplomacy* (New York: Frederick A. Praeger, 1965), for a solid analysis of GATT; Richard N. Gardner, *Sterling-Dollar Diplomacy*, rev. ed. (New York: McGraw-Hill, 1969), on postwar planning; and Clair Wilcox, *A Charter for World Trade* (New York: Macmillan, 1949), on the ill-fated ITO.

ALFRED E. ECKES

See also Bretton Woods System; Reciprocal Trade Agreements

Iran

American policy toward Iran in the early years of the Truman administration focused on the question of Soviet withdrawal from Azerbaijan in northwest Iran. Under the Tripartite Treaty of Alliance signed by Britain, the Soviet Union, and Iran on 29 January 1942, the three countries agreed that Allied forces would withdraw from Iran within six months of an armistice or peace between the Allied and Axis powers. On 2 March 1946, however, six months after the surrender of Japan, the Soviets had not withdrawn their troops.

Following World War II, the Soviets violated understandings reached during the war as to the sovereignty and territorial integrity of Iran, and supported separatist movements in Azerbaijan and Kurdistan in northwestern Iran. Although Stalin assured Secretary of State James Byrnes in December 1945 that he had no designs, territorial or otherwise, on Iran, and no intention of infringing upon its sovereignty, Soviet actions suggested otherwise. Following extremely difficult discussions with the Iranian prime minister in Moscow and after the date set for evacuation, Stalin moved a heavy Soviet armored force of at least two hundred tanks into northern Iran in an apparent attempt to intimidate and ultimately control the government in Tehran.

The crisis that ensued was protracted and complicated. Referral of Soviet-Iranian differences to bilateral discussions subjected the Iranians to heavy-handed Soviet intimidation, suggesting to U.S. officials the value of anticipating rather than reacting to Soviet initiatives and the desirability of airing differences in a public forum. The Iranian case occasioned Andrei Gromyko's walk-out from the newly formed UN Security Council and was central to the hardening of American attitudes toward the Soviet Union in the early years of the cold war. It crystallized the administration's understanding of Soviet tactics, conditioned its reaction to Soviet policies toward Turkey, and schooled U.S. officials in traditional balance-of-power politics.

The Soviets withdrew from Iran in May 1946. The separatist movements they supported, however, collapsed only in December 1946. Both developments were due to skillful Iranian diplomacy, firm U.S. policies, and the possibility that Stalin saw further confrontation in Iran as detrimental to his designs on Turkey. In October 1947, the Iranian Majlis rejected a controversial oil agreement into which Iran had been pressured the previous year as a condition for Soviet withdrawal. Meanwhile, although Iran's independence clearly was central to the balance of power between East and West that was undergirded by the Truman Doctrine, Iran was not included in the public discussion of aid to Greece and Turkey primarily because Britain—which had important oil interests in Iran—had not requested that the United States include Iran in its new responsibilities. As a result, in the aftermath of the Azerbaijan crisis, U.S. officials were unsympathetic with Iran's obsessive desires for parity with Turkey and saw little basis for new commitments.

It is important to note that the United States saw collaboration with Britain as central to the policy of containment in the Near East, where the cornerstone of Secretary of State George Marshall's policies was the maintenance of Britain's declining position to the greatest extent possible. Such collaboration, however, impeded better relations with Iran's emerging nationalist forces, whose differences with Britain threatened to undermine the very policy Anglo-American ties were designed to effect. The problem became even more acute under Secretary of State Dean Acheson when Mohammad Mossadegh, leader of the National Front, became prime minister in April 1951. Mossadegh sought to terminate the Anglo-Iranian Oil Company's (AIOC) exploitation of Iran's resources—under a 1933 agreement Iran received 16.5 percent of the royalties paid by AIOC, which in 1950 produced 6 percent of the world's oil—and in May nationalized the oil industry. By October strikes had forced the British to close down and withdraw from the largest refinery in the world at Abadan. Britain would accept nationalization only under conditions that would have nullified the concept, since "just compensation," as they interpreted it, included compensation for the concession itself and future profits from it. Their concern was not only AIOC properties, but the precedent that the seizure of AIOC would set for British interests in the Persian Gulf and throughout the world.

Britain's strategy for dealing with Mossadegh was predicated on the assumption that economic pressure would bring him to his knees and that, if the United States refused to assist him, he would come around. U.S. policy, on the other hand, was increasingly governed by a sense of urgency. One of President Truman's initial responses to the Korean War had been a concern that if the United States did not act, the Soviets would move into Iran and take over the Middle East. In 1951, the Soviets had begun to pursue a more moderate course of action toward Iran, and the administration was concerned that Iran might drift toward neutrality.

Acheson believed British policies were "stupid" and U.S. officials, who were concerned with preventing the Soviets from gaining influence in Iran, believed that the AIOC was subordinating broader political considerations to commercial interests. They sought greater flexibility on the part of Britain, whom they deterred from intervening militarily in Iran, and they attempted to find formulas that would help mediate differences. Following the election of a Conservative government in Britain in October 1951, however, the United States was reluctant to oppose Prime Minister Winston Churchill's tough line toward Iran. The United States made up for Britain's diminished refinery capacity and foreign exchange losses and made financial assistance to Iran contingent on Iran's reaching an agreement with Great Britain. This limited Mossadegh's options and forced him into a corner.

Nevertheless, at the end of 1952, the United States would not consider a British proposal backed by Churchill and Anthony Eden to overthrow Mossadegh. The State Department explored a solution in collaboration with the major oil companies, while the Joint Chiefs of Staff advocated a break with the British, arguing that animosity would be greater if the United States failed to act than if it did. Efforts to resolve the problem, however, failed, and the problem was passed to the Eisenhower administration.

Bruce R. Kuniholm, *The Origins of the Cold War in the Near East: Great Power Conflict and Diplomacy in Iran, Turkey and Greece* (Princeton: Princeton University Press, 1980), is the most important source for understanding the Iranian crisis of 1945–46 from the U.S. point of view. William Roger Louis, *The British Empire in the Middle East: Arab Nationalism, the United States, and Postwar Imperialism* (Oxford: Clarendon Press, 1984), is the most important

source to date for understanding British policy in Iran from 1945 to 1951. Ruhollah Ramazani, *Iran's Foreign Policy, 1941–1973: A Study of Foreign Policy in Modernizing Nations* (Charlottesville: University of Virginia Press, 1975), is the best book on Iran's postwar foreign policy. Mark Hamilton Lytle, *The Origins of the Iranian-American Alliance, 1941–1953* (New York: Holmes & Meier, 1987), a "neorevisionist" interpretation, provides another perspective on U.S. policy in Iran. Kuniholm, "U.S. Policy in the Near East: The Triumphs and Tribulations of the Truman Administration," in a volume on the Truman administration to be published by Cambridge University Press, is a useful overview of the Truman administration's policies.

BRUCE R. KUNIHOLM

See also Cold War; Great Britain; Oil Policy

Isolationism

Harry Truman was never an isolationist, either during his years in the Senate or during his presidency. The Japanese attack on Pearl Harbor had struck isolationism a blow from which it never recovered. By the time Truman took over the reins of government in April 1945, isolationism commanded little political strength and even less respectability. The vilification of isolationism made it easier to build bipartisan consensus, but it also inhibited free discussion of foreign policy alternatives.

Traditionally isolationists had opposed intervention in European wars and involvement in "entangling alliances." They guarded American sovereignty and freedom of action. But they did not want to cut America off from the rest of the world, and they recognized the necessity for foreign trade. After World War II they wanted the United States to reduce its role in Europe; some wanted a larger role in Asia. They urged expanded powers for Congress and restrictions on presidential authority.

After Roosevelt's death, President Truman pressed ahead with plans for the United Nations Conference in San Francisco. He kept the same bipartisan delegation that Roosevelt had named earlier—including Senator Arthur Vandenberg of Michigan, a former isolationist. When the Senate, on 28 July 1945, voted adherence to the UN charter, the opposition could muster only two negative votes with one other paired against. Those were provided by three Republicans: William Langer of North Dakota, Henrik Shipstead of Minnesota, and (on his death bed) Hiram Johnson of California. Of the three, Johnson died the day the United States dropped its first atom bomb on Japan, Shipstead was turned out of office the next time he faced voters in 1946, and crusty old Langer continued his lonely role in the Senate until death took him in 1959.

Each election removed more old isolationists from the political scene. In 1946 voters turned out, besides Shipstead, Wisconsin's Robert M. La Follette, Jr., Massachusetts's David I. Walsh, and Montana's Burton K. Wheeler. All had been noninterventionists before Pearl Harbor. In 1948 the elderly Arthur Capper of Kansas decided not to run for another term, and Illinois voters ousted C. Wayland Brooks. Vandenberg and Henry Cabot Lodge, Jr., turned so far from their earlier isolationism that they became Republican leaders of bipartisanship and containment. In the Senate, Kenneth S. Wherry, who represented small businessmen and farmers from the Great Plains state of Nebraska, emerged to advance later versions of isolationism. But like others, Wherry rejected the isolationist label. To be identified as an isolationist during the Truman era was to invite political defeat and popular disdain.

Remnants of isolationism also survived in the press and historical writing. The *Chicago Tribune* and Hearst newspapers never repudiated their prewar attitudes. Felix Morely and John T. Flynn were among writers who attacked internationalists and their ideas. Charles A. Beard, Charles C. Tansill, and Harry Elmer Barnes (all noninterventionists before Pearl Harbor) wrote revisionist histories indicating America's course to war under FDR. They failed, however, to win acceptance in dominant professional circles. They and their interpretations were as discredited as isolationism itself.

Each of the Truman initiatives to preserve peace and contain the Soviet Union encountered opposition, some of it reflecting isolationist values. Among those who wrote, spoke, or voted against Truman's Marshall Plan, Truman Doctrine aid to Greece and Turkey, and the North Atlantic Treaty were Senators Robert A. Taft and John W. Bricker of Ohio, Edwin C. Johnson of Colorado, William Jenner of Indiana, Wherry, and Langer. But that opposition could marshal only twenty-three votes in the Senate against aid to Greece and Turkey, seventeen against the Marshall Plan, and thirteen against the North Atlantic Pact. Comparable patterns prevailed in the House of Representatives.

In 1949 the triumph of the Communists in China sparked a search in America for scapegoats to blame for "what went wrong." Early in 1950, Republican senator Joseph R. McCarthy of Wisconsin initiated his attacks on the administration with charges of Communist influences. In 1950–51 the bipartisan consensus on foreign affairs was shaken when major addresses by former ambassador Joseph P. Kennedy, former president Herbert Hoover, and Senator Taft set off a "Great Debate" on foreign affairs. All had been prewar noninterventionists. Kennedy would have withdrawn American forces from both Europe and Asia. He urged building hemispheric defenses. Hoover called for a "Fortress America" with emphasis on American strategic air and naval power. Taft wanted to limit involvement in Europe while focusing greater attention on Asia.

The casualties, costs, and frustrations of fighting the limited war in Korea from 1950 to 1953 provoked growing criticism. Some of that came from isolationists. When Gen. Douglas MacArthur's calls for stronger actions against China led Truman to dismiss him in 1951, MacArthur became a hero and political hope for critics of Truman's foreign policies.

Old isolationists, neoisolationists, McCarthyites, Asia-firsters, conservative Republican nationalists, and devotees of General MacArthur did not agree on what the United States ought to do in foreign affairs. But they seized on those unsettling developments to strike back at the internationalist foreign policy establishment that had downed and humiliated them during the 1940s. The elections of 1952 might provide their opportunity to win vindication at the polls and to set America once more on traditional paths. But that was not to be. The Republican nomination of the charismatic military hero Dwight D. Eisenhower successfully blocked the paths to the presidency for both Taft and MacArthur.

The challenges to peace and security from the Axis states and then from Communist Russia, the development of nuclear weapons and effective delivery systems, the growth of cities and their accompanying industrial and financial capacities, the fur-

ther erosion of rural and small-town America, talented leadership by the foreign policy establishment, and the power of the presidency under Truman—all combined to weaken and discredit isolationism. Neither America nor the world could ever go back to what had been in international affairs.

The best scholarly studies on this subject are Justus D. Doenecke, *Not to the Swift: The Old Isolationists in the Cold War Era* (Lewisburg, Pa.: Bucknell University Press, 1979), David R. Kepley, *The Collapse of the Middle Way: Senate Republicans and the Bipartisan Foreign Policy, 1948–1952* (Westport, Conn.: Greenwood Press, 1988), and Joan Lee Bryniarski, "Against the Tide: Senate Opposition to the Internationalist Foreign Policy of Presidents Franklin D. Roosevelt and Harry S. Truman, 1943–1949" (Ph.D. diss., University of Maryland, 1972). Doenecke traces the roles of prewar isolationists during the cold war. Bryniarski underscores the erosion of rural–small business bases for isolationism. On revisionist historians, see Wayne S. Cole, "American Entry into World War II: A Historiographical Appraisal," *Mississippi Valley Historical Review* 43 (March 1957): 595–617.

WAYNE S. COLE

Israel

Harry S. Truman is renowned among Israelis as the American president who granted the world's first official recognition of the Jewish state within minutes of the state's proclamation on 14 May 1948. In announcing de facto recognition, Truman stole a march on the Soviet Union which followed shortly thereafter with a more formal de jure recognition, a legal subtlety that nevertheless gave Moscow little credit in Zionist history.

Immensely popular with the idealistic American public at the time, Truman's act of recognition was nevertheless controversial within the foreign policy establishment for decades to come. He had taken the decision against the virtually unanimous advice of his diplomatic advisers, who immediately charged him with making a cheap bid for the so-called Jewish vote in the 1948 presidential election.

Modern scholarship on the Truman era reflects the contemporary disagreements over the president's motives. Diplomatic historians emphasize the undoubted domestic political interests pressing a relatively inexperienced and unpopular chief executive into a gesture toward the articulate Jewish-American constituency. Armed with the extensive documentation of the State Department, they argue the overwhelming strategic interests of the United States in the Arab world and thus the danger to the national interest of identifying with the problematic cause of Zionism.

Broader-based analysis, however, muddies this depiction of a president playing politics with foreign policy. In the first place, diplomatic recognition, although dramatic, was a symbolic gesture far short of what Zionist pressure groups were demanding of the United States. Jewish activists were quick to recognize that the gesture was half-hearted; the full de jure recognition which the Soviet Union had granted did not come from the United States until January 1949, after the election was won.

"See It Now" producer and host Edward R. Murrow interviews Israeli prime minister David Ben-Gurion at Kibbutz Sde Boker, his home in the Negev Desert. (Boston Public Library)

Second, Truman vehemently withheld more tangible acts of support for the new Jewish state, besieged as it was by Arab armies all around. He refused to lift an official embargo on arms shipments to Israel, despite loud demands from American Zionist organizations throughout the 1948 election campaign. This embargo was hardly water-tight, as supporters of Israel found numerous ways to flout the sanctions and provide essential war matériel to the Jewish forces, but as a matter of official policy Truman rebuffed the angry demands of Jewish constituencies.

The United States firmly supported UN mediation and compromise efforts through the summer and fall of 1948, efforts that Israelis felt undermined their position against the Arab armies. Truman refused to use his support for Israel as a campaign issue until the last weeks, when his Republican opponent, Thomas E. Dewey, took the initiative in accusing him of betraying the new state.

The final flaw in the diplomats' portrayal of a president leading only from domestic political calculations is that the Jewish vote did not, in fact, elect Truman president. Although financial support from wealthy Jewish interests was crucial early in his candidacy and inclined his sympathies toward the interests of constituents who had helped him when he needed them, Truman was able to balance his policy in full knowledge that the Jewish vote would not be decisive for him. Some 65 percent of American Jews lived in the three large states of New York, Pennsylvania, and Illinois, with 110 electoral votes among them. Truman lost all three states—and won the election.

Why, then, did the Baptist from Missouri come down so hard on the Israeli side, in opposition to what his foreign policy experts were advising? In many ways, his recognition was an impulsive act. Truman was a man who had no patience for the complexities of diplomacy and political science, who instead felt a personal bond of sympathy with a kindly (and crafty) old man who had called upon him, Dr. Chaim Weizmann, longtime leader of world Zionism. In the absence of pressing arguments to the contrary, Truman always chose to lead from humanitarian considerations—in this case, the miserable plight of a hundred thousand homeless Jews in Europe who had survived the Nazi Holocaust but had no place to go. Israel was the only country in the world willing to take them in.

Not that cynicism is totally missing from the Truman record. "My only interest is to find some proper way to take care of these displaced persons," he had written an old Senate crony. "It is to our own financial interest to have them taken care of because we are feeding most of them."

Evidence abounds that Truman had not considered very deeply, and did not really understand, his impulsive act in Israel's first hour. "I think the report of the British American Commission of Palestine [sic] was the correct solution," he wrote the day after he granted recognition, "and I think, eventually, we are going to get it worked out just that way." What apparently escaped him was that the 1946 Anglo-American Committee of Inquiry (to use its correct name) had recommended the precise opposite of the course Truman took in 1948.

From his first weeks in the presidency, Truman's mind-set was on guard against the "striped-pants boys" in the State Department. "In those days nobody seemed to think I was aware of anything," he wrote in his *Memoirs*. He bristled at a memorandum "in effect telling me to watch my step, that I didn't really understand what was going on over there and that I ought to leave it to the 'experts.'"

More influential to his thinking was an eyewitness account of the European refugee camps by Earl Harrison, dean of the University of Pennsylvania Law School. "The misery it depicted could not be allowed to continue," he wrote, without bothering to consult the State Department about the foreign policy implications of his concern.

Truman was elated at the vote of the UN General Assembly in November 1947 to partition Palestine into separate Jewish and Arab states, and he turned a statesmanlike blind eye to all the American pressures on wavering delegates to get the necessary majority. In the diplomatic maneuvering that followed, he received Dr. Weizmann at the White House, again without the State Department's knowledge, and blandly gave him assurances of support that the diplomatic machinery undercut the very next day. Truman's dismay at having misled "the little doctor" stayed with him to the end.

Truman's ardor for Jewish statehood, for the realization of age-old Zionist yearnings, clearly does not bear close examination. Happy to accept whatever political benefits came to him, and delighted at being able to shoot down his "striped-pants boys," Truman nevertheless looked back in some wonder and sheepishness at the standing his impulses had brought him. "Those Israelites have placed me on a pedestal alongside of Moses," he wrote.

The classic work remains J. C. Hurewitz, *The Struggle for Palestine* (1950; reprint, New York: Schocken Books, 1976). Arguing the diplomatic perspective against Truman's policy are John Snetsinger, *Truman, the Jewish Vote and the Creation of Israel* (Stanford: Hoover Institution, 1974), and Evan M. Wilson, *Decision on*

Palestine (Stanford: Hoover Institution, 1979). See also Zvi Ganin, *Truman, American Jewry and Israel, 1945–1948* (New York: Holmes & Meier, 1979), and Peter Grose, *Israel in the Mind of America* (New York: Knopf, 1983). A fresh British perspective comes in Nicholas Bethell, *The Palestine Triangle* (New York: Putnam's, 1979). Bringing the conflicts in American policy up to date is Steven L. Spiegel, *The Other Arab-Israeli Conflict* (Chicago: University of Chicago Press, 1985).

PETER GROSE

See also Jacobson, Eddie; Jewish-Americans; Palestine; Roosevelt, Anna Eleanor; Zionism

Italy

When Harry Truman assumed office in April 1945, the United States faced four major interrelated problems in Italy: rebuilding the economy, dismantling the military occupation authority, negotiating an equitable peace treaty, and assisting moderates in their efforts to create a democratic, pro-Western regime on the ruins of fascism.

The Truman administration successfully dealt with these problems, establishing an enduring link between the United States and the new Italian state. The United States put its immense political, military and economic power at the service of a moderate-conservative coalition dominated by Italy's Christian Democratic party. With U.S. aid, the Christian Democrats defeated the political challenge of the Italian Left and established their control over the Italian state. Truman reaped major domestic political benefits from the anti-Communist crusade in Italy as Italian-Americans rallied to the president's support during his successful 1948 reelection campaign.

During the first Truman administration, the United States and its Italian allies succeeded in integrating Italy into an emerging U.S. sphere of influence. The United States used its influence to encourage the writing of an Italian constitution that established a democratic republic. It negotiated an Italian peace treaty with the Soviet Union that permitted economic recovery but required Italy to surrender its fleet and colonies and some territory. Massive U.S. assistance, capped by the Marshall Plan, fueled Italy's economic recovery.

During the second Truman administration, the emphasis of U.S. policy shifted from democratic state building to security assistance, support for Italian involvement in the economic integration of Europe, and efforts to weaken the Italian Communist party. The United States supported Italian membership in NATO primarily to ensure Italy's internal security against the Communists. After the outbreak of the Korean War in June 1950, the United States assisted Italian efforts to nullify the military clauses of the 1947 peace treaty and make a contribution to Europe's defense against the Soviet Union. U.S. "offshore procurement programs" rebuilt the Italian defense industry while challenging Communist control of the Italian labor movement. The United States encouraged efforts to break up Communist-dominated labor unions and the fellow-traveling Italian Socialist party. It supported changes in the election laws designed to ensure a permanent majority for anti-Communist forces. To strengthen Italy's recovery and its ability to resist communism and to reinforce democracy in Western Europe, the United States favored Italian participation in the European Coal and Steel Community.

Norman Kogan, *Italy and the Allies* (Cambridge: Harvard University Press, 1956), explores the wartime and early postwar evolution of the U.S.-Italian relationship. John Harper, *America and the Reconstruction of Italy* (New York: Cambridge University Press, 1986), deals with postwar economics. E. Timothy Smith, "The United States, Italy and NATO" (Ph.D. diss., Kent State University, 1981), covers security issues. James Edward Miller, *The United States and Italy, 1940–1950* (Chapel Hill: University of North Carolina Press, 1986), is the most complete treatment of Truman administration policies.

JAMES EDWARD MILLER

See also Fascism

J

Jackson, Robert H.

(13 February 1892–9 October 1954)

"The real complaining party at your bar is Civilization," Robert H. Jackson, the U.S. chief of counsel proclaimed to the International Military Tribunal in Nuremberg, Germany, in 1945. Jackson appreciated President Truman's charge to prosecute the leading German war criminals. It was, Jackson believed, "perhaps, the greatest opportunity ever presented to an American lawyer." Scarcely six months later, however, Truman and Jackson were estranged.

A country lawyer from New York, Jackson became a "Roosevelt lawyer" in 1935. By 1938, he had become solicitor general and, by 1940, attorney general. Jackson, Franklin Roosevelt believed, "would some day make a great liberal President." When Senator Truman established his national defense inquiry he told Jackson: "I want the best investigator that you have on your payroll." Jackson complied, recommending Hugh Fulton for the job. Later that year, Roosevelt appointed Jackson to the Supreme Court.

President Truman asked Jackson to head the Nuremberg prosecution on 29 April 1945. A month later, Jackson thanked the president for his "encouragement" in the immense task. Jackson's day-long opening salvo on 21 November 1945 against "aggressive war-making" and the Germans' crimes was a widely hailed masterpiece. As the trial stretched into the spring, however, Jackson clashed with the presiding judges and neglected administrative routines. When he cross-examined Hermann Goering, many criticized Jackson for allowing the wily chief defendant too much latitude in his responses. The German general, they claimed, had outflanked the American judge. Eventually, Goering and eleven others were executed, seven were imprisoned, and three were acquitted.

While still in Europe, Jackson's attention returned to the Court. He expected to succeed Chief Justice Harlan Fiske Stone, who died in April 1946. Instead, Truman appointed Fred Vinson. Jackson blamed Justice Hugo Black and blasted him publicly in June. Jackson's statement violated the Court's traditions. "It surely is a lucky thing I did not make Jackson Chief Justice," Truman confided to his wife in a letter in June. "He has surely gone haywire. . . . It is terrible for public confidence in the courts."

Jackson's remaining years on the Court, until his death in 1954, were quieter. He joined Felix Frankfurter against Black's libertarian faction and championed property rights. In various cold war free speech cases he respected governmental prerogatives. "The Constitution does not make conspiracy a civil right," he concurred in *United States* v. *Dennis et al.*, a 1951 case upholding the Smith Act. But in the 1952 steel seizure case Jackson opposed Truman's order to seize the nation's steel mills. By defying the president during a crisis—a nationwide steel strike during the Korean War—Jackson sought to limit executive authority. Some whispered that this decision marked Justice Jackson's revenge on President Truman.

Eugene C. Gerhart, *America's Advocate: Robert H. Jackson* (Indianapolis: Bobbs-Merrill, 1958), is a competent and sympathetic biography that focuses on Jackson's political career. A fine collection of selections from Jackson's best opinions, featuring a good analytic introduction, can be found in Glendon Schubert, *Dispassionate Justice: A Synthesis of the Judicial Opinions of Robert H. Jackson* (Indianapolis: Bobbs-Merrill, 1969). The literature on the Nuremberg trials is considerable. *The Nuremberg Trial*, by Ann Tusa and John Tusa (New York: Atheneum, 1984), provides a thorough account of the trial and balances Gerhart's less critical portrayal of Jackson at Nuremberg. Two books by Jackson worth exploring are *The Nürnberg Case, As Presented by Robert H. Jackson, Chief of Counsel for the United States, Together with Other Documents* (New York: Alfred A. Knopf, 1947) and *The Strategy of Judicial Supremacy: A Study of a Crisis in American Power Politics* (New York: Alfred A. Knopf, 1941), which places the Roosevelt Court-packing scheme in historical and legal perspective. Only scattered references to Jackson appear in most Truman biographies.

GIL TROY

See also Supreme Court, United States (and photograph); War Crimes Trials

Jackson County Court

After Truman received his army discharge in May 1919, he returned home determined to make changes in his life. He sold his share of the Grandview farm to his family, married Bess Wallace, and opened a men's clothing store in Kansas City. The store did well at first, but in 1922 it went under during the postwar depression.

As his store was failing, friends active within the Democratic party urged Truman to run for judge of the eastern district of Jackson County. The Trumans had long been involved in a minor way in Jackson County politics, loyal to that faction of the Democratic party controlled by Kansas City political boss Thomas J. Pendergast. Harry Truman had strengths to offer the Pendergast Democrats in 1922. He was a popular veteran at a time when that voting bloc was powerful, and he was a Baptist and Mason, which was important to a Catholic-dominated machine under attack from the Ku Klux Klan. Harry and Bess Truman had relatives and friends all over the county whom they could turn to for help during the campaign. Truman drew on all those strengths to win.

During Truman's 1923–24 term he teamed with Henry F. McElroy to dominate the three-member court, which was an executive body that administered county affairs. The two Pendergast men improved government operations while eliminating some nonessential jobs. The "unnecessary" jobs that disappeared, however, were usually held by loyalists of Joseph Shannon and Miles Bulger, who were challenging Pendergast for control of the Democratic party. The 1924 election turned into a brawl with the Shannonites and other Pendergast enemies joining the Republicans to defeat Truman and McElroy.

After the Democratic chiefs in Kansas City made peace, Truman returned to politics and won election in 1926 as presiding judge. He was now prepared for that phase of his career that marked him as a public servant with special qualities. As Truman took up his new responsibilities, he found Jackson County roads, buildings, and finances strained to the limit. The county was growing rapidly and had a population of 470,000 at the end of his first term in 1930. He quickly moved first to bring order to public affairs and then to develop new programs.

He did not lose sight of political reality. Whatever he accomplished would have to be achieved through the Pendergast organization. While Truman benefited from machine support, it fed off of his victories and successes. He bragged that he could deliver eleven thousand honest votes on Election Day; he controlled over nine hundred patronage jobs and millions of dollars in county purchasing.

In 1928 the county had passed a $7.5 million bond issue. Truman had publicly pledged to voters to spend the money honestly, and he told the story many times in his life of how Pendergast allowed Truman to honor his commitment. But that was not the whole story. In the privacy of his hideaway office in the Pickwick Hotel in downtown Kansas City, Truman poured out his despair in a series of handwritten documents that revealed the corruption and squalor of the machine he helped build. Pendergast did let him spend the bond money honestly—but with strings attached. Truman estimated that he had to let his associates steal a million dollars from the general reserve; otherwise they would have stolen half the bond money: "I wonder if I did right to put a lot of no-account sons of bitches on the payroll and pay other sons of bitches more money for supplies than they were worth in order to satisfy the political powers and save $3,500,000.00."

Nevertheless, Truman's popularity stemmed not from machine shenanigans but from real and solid achievements that benefited the people of Jackson County. He was a progressive in the tradition of those who fought for planning, efficiency, and economy in government. He organized the Regional Plan Association of Kansas City, presided over the Missouri Planning Association, served on the board of directors of the National Conference of City Planning, belonged to the American Civic Association, and published a book, *Results of County Planning*.

Truman's popularity and reputation for fairness largely stemmed from his massive road program. He built one of the nation's first and most successful metropolitan road systems. Before Truman's program, the automobile craze caused mounting traffic that pounded Jackson County "pie-crust" roads to pieces. Truman's completed system left everyone in the county within two and one-half miles of a concrete road and connected the county and city roadways. A farm spokesman estimated that the system would save farmers $275,000 a year in transportation costs. The program also paid off politically by adding to Truman's reputation for effective and honest administration and by putting good Pendergast Democrats to work.

Truman also gained respect from municipal reformers by promoting tax reform; county, regional, and state planning; and government reorganization. Truman could not deliver machine support to achieve most of his plans, but his work shaped his administrative ideas. Structural unity and clear lines of responsibility and authority were goals he later fought for as president.

Truman's achievements, his governmental reform, and his reputation for effectiveness and honesty won him wide support. In 1930 he won reelection by a huge majority. He extended his building and reform programs during the next four years. His work within the urban machine continued to shape his political understanding. For example, he gained a fresh understanding of black Americans. Truman was a product of traditional southern racial values and views, but Pendergast, more interested in political power than in honoring outmoded racist mores, moved the Democratic party toward recognition of the twenty thousand blacks in Jackson County. Truman and other local leaders helped by building or improving black institutions, ending police brutality against blacks, and rewarding black political allies. By the time Franklin D. Roosevelt took power, Kansas City blacks were already solidly Democratic.

Truman later claimed to be a New Dealer from the start. His views, however, seemed to fit those of a progressive-minded small businessman. The depression ushered in an agonizing time for Truman as he struggled to maintain solvency by paring away government services and employees. Economic collapse did not provoke an innovative response from him as it did some government leaders at the time. Rather, he responded as most politicians did: by applying business-minded values to achieve retrenchment.

In 1934, Truman left the court to enter the U.S. Senate. The satisfaction he received from his effective work during the county court years and his enhanced self-image empowered Truman to reach for new achievements as he entered politics at the state and national level. His work in Jackson County had taught him new political skills and gave him an understanding of metropolitan problems and needs that he drew on as president when he formulated housing, health, civil rights, and reorganization programs.

In his autobiographical notes, Truman often referred to the county court and Pendergast years. In those written in his Pickwick Hotel room he discussed his work without adding gloss. The "Pickwick Notes" are held by the Truman Library. Lyle W. Dorsett traces the rise and fall of the Pendergast machine in *The Pendergast Years* (New York: Oxford University Press, 1968). Richard L. Miller explains Truman's central role in building the power of the machine in *Truman: The Rise to Power* (New York: McGraw-Hill, 1986).

WILLIAM E. PEMBERTON

See also Pendergast, Thomas J.

Jacobson, Eddie

(17 June 1891–25 October 1955)

Eddie Jacobson was born in New York City of Russian parents who had emigrated to the United States in the early 1880s. In mid-1905 the family moved to Kansas City where Eddie lived for the rest of his life.

His friendship with Harry S. Truman became the central dimension of Jacobson's life. It began casually enough as the two young men in Kansas City sought to find direction in their lives. It is not entirely clear when the two first met. On leaving school, Eddie worked in the clothing industry and probably met Truman in 1905 or 1906 when the latter was a bank clerk at the Union National Bank. The relationship was renewed and strengthened by the bonds of army experience and a short-lived postwar business venture. As the career paths of the two men diverged over the next twenty-five years, it continued on an informal but close level until, in the final decade of his life, a formal and public dimension was added to Jacobson's friendship with Truman.

Jacobson was significant in Truman's life for several reasons. He was, first, instrumental in getting Truman off on the right foot in the army in World War 1. Following his enlistment in 1917, Eddie was mustered into the same unit as Truman (129th Field Artillery, or Second Missouri Field Artillery attached to the Thirty-fifth Division). At boot camp, First Lieutenant Truman was appointed regimental canteen officer. He and Sergeant Jacobson organized and ran the canteen at Camp Doniphan, Oklahoma, considered one of the best run in the service. Truman later said that the reputation he acquired at Camp Doniphan was instrumental in his ending up as commander (captain) of Battery D. Eddie also ran a little "blind pig" (a bootleg bar) at the front in France at one time, selling wine and cognac he had traded from the French for tomatoes. Truman's participation in this venture is not recorded!

Following the war, in 1919, Jacobson and Truman went into partnership and opened a haberdashery across the street

Eddie Jacobson. (National Archives)

from the Hotel Muehlebach. It was a short-lived venture, as the depression of 1921–22 forced the business into liquidation in 1922. Both men, however, took great pride in the fact that all creditors were fully paid. The relationship between Truman and Jacobson at this time was a happy-go-lucky one and remained so. In December 1919, Jacobson married his childhood sweetheart, Bluma Rosenbaum, and Truman (who married in June of that year) helped "kidnap" Bluma and take her to Jacobson's father's house for the wedding. Throughout the twenties and early thirties Jacobson was a congenial host at poker parties Truman attended, along with Hermann Rosenberg, another army buddy, and Charles Hipole, a Jewish Kansas City friend.

For twenty-three years after the store closed, Jacobson worked as a traveling salesman in Missouri and Kansas, selling shirts and earning "a modest but comfortable living." In February 1945 he opened his own haberdashery in Kansas City. Characteristically, on his first visit home after he became president, Truman made a personal call on his old friend at his new shop, causing something of a riot with his retinue of aides, Secret Service men, and reporters.

The relationship was not all one-sided, however. Jacobson helped raise money from Kansas City Jews for Truman's 1948 campaign. He placed full-page advertisements in the *Kansas City Jewish Chronicle* urging his fellow Jews to vote for Truman, and in one instance, when it looked as if Truman might be stranded in Omaha for lack of funds, Jacobson was able to raise the six thousand dollars owed Union Pacific to enable "the Chief" to continue his whistle-stop tour through the Midwest.

The highlight of Eddie Jacobson's life was, without doubt, the role he played in the events surrounding Truman's recognition of Israel. Although he was an observant Reform Jew (he belonged to Congregation B'nai Jehudah) and paying member of B'nai B'rith, Jacobson was a typical midwestern Jew in that he had little or no interest in Zionism, Jewish history, or communal affairs until 1945–46. According to his Kansas City lawyer friend A. J. Granoff, Maurice Bisgyer, national executive vice president of B'nai B'rith, met with Jacobson and Granoff in June 1947 at the Hotel Muehlebach to ask Eddie to intercede with Truman to persuade the British government to admit Jewish refugees into Palestine. Granoff says that this meeting "ignited a deeply spiritual cause of truly historic proportions which raised Eddie from obscurity and absorbed the last eight years of his life." The meeting probably took place two years earlier, however, for Jacobson had visited Truman with his B'nai B'rith friend and Truman's poker-playing war buddy Hermann Rosenberg as early as June 1945 to seek the president's assistance for Jewish displaced persons in Central Europe. Jacobson saw Truman about the Palestine issue many times over the next five to seven years as the future of Palestine and Israel unfolded. These meetings covered a wide range of matters—American support for partition, the boundaries of the Jewish state, Truman's reluctance to see Zionist leader Chaim Weizmann, de jure recognition of the new state, the status of Jerusalem, and the level of American economic assistance to Israel.

Jacobson's role in the events is controversial. Some have argued that because of his intervention with Truman, Jacobson will be "immortal in Jewish history"; and indeed he was feted by Weizmann and honored by B'nai B'rith and Israel. Others have pointed out that Jacobson's position was well known to Truman and had little special influence on him, for the president had to take a much broader look at the issue "and not just listen to somebody whom he had known for thirty or more years." What can be said with certainty is that Jacobson was instrumental in convincing Truman that the United States should support the partition plan proposed by the United Nations, that he was the reason Truman met finally with Chaim Weizmann at a critical time in the history of the Palestine-Israel issue, and that he helped pursuade Truman to increase economic aid to the new state in early 1952.

Significant differences of opinion emerged between the White House and the State Department over the best policy to pursue in relation to Palestine in the period 1945–49, and Truman was subjected to considerable pressure by groups ranging from emotional Zionist spokesmen to vehement anti-Zionist members of the State Department. Not surprisingly, the president vacillated—depending on the direction advice came from and its intensity. He personally identified with the plight of the surviving Jewish refugees, but he resented the attacks of organized Zionist pressure groups. Despite strong pressure from the State Department to withdraw U.S. support for partition in the months preceding Israel's establishment, Truman reused—he had given his word to Weizmann and Jacobson. Truman frequently made decisions independently of departmental advice, especially when he felt strongly on an issue. In these instances he was far more likely to depend on the opinions of his friends. In the case of Israel, Eddie Jacobson was one such friend, and Truman listened.

The most detailed accounts of the relationship between Jacobson and Truman are to be found in Frank J. Adler, *Roots in a Moving Stream: The Centennial History of Congregation B'nai Jehudah of Kansas City, 1870–1970* (1972), and Peter Grose, *Israel in the Mind of America* (New York: Knopf, 1983). Zvi Ganin, *Truman, American Jewry and Israel, 1945–1948* (New York: Holmes & Meier, 1979), and Steven L. Spiegel, *The Other Arab-Israeli Conflict: Making America's Middle East Policy from Truman to Reagan* (Chicago: University of Chicago Press, 1985), analyze the impact on Truman of American Jewish activity. References to Jacobson are to be found in Truman's *Memoirs* (Garden City, N.Y.: Doubleday, 1955), and his *Autobiography*, ed. Robert Ferrell (Boulder: Colorado Associated University Press, 1980), as well as in Margaret Truman, *Harry S. Truman* (New York: Morrow, 1973), and Jonathan Daniels, *The Man of Independence* (Philadelphia: J.B. Lippincott, 1950). Material on Jacobson is also contained in the following oral histories at the Truman Library in Independence: A. J. Granoff, George M. Elsey, Edward D. McKim, Ted Marks, A. J. Steven, and Harry H. Vaughan.

IAN J. BICKERTON

See also Business Ventures; Jewish-Americans; Zionism

Japan

The "Japs," President Harry S. Truman noted during the July 1945 Potsdam Conference, were "savages, ruthless, merciless and fanatic." Still, as the "leader of the world for the common welfare," America should use its new atomic bomb against military targets and "not women and children." Truman's views shone as a beacon of moderation compared to the vengeful views articulated by ordinary citizens and national leaders. Prominent Americans spoke of "gutting the heart of Japan with fire," and turning its cities and people to "ashes" in revenge for the attack upon Pearl Harbor. Senator Theodore Bilbo (D.-Miss.) called on American occupation troops in Japan to "sterilize every damn one of them so in one generation there would be no more Japs." Even President Franklin D. Roosevelt toyed with a proposal to "cross breed" Japanese with docile Pacific Islanders in order to eliminate the "primitive brains" and "barbarism" of the "enemy race."

Beneath this racist rhetoric, however, policy planners in the State, War, and Navy departments developed a comprehensive, moderate, and humane reform program before the first American soldier reached Tokyo. Rejecting calls to exterminate the Japanese or to join them in an anti-Soviet alliance, the high-level State-War-Navy Coordinating Committee (SWNCC) adopted a plan to demilitarize and democratize the defeated Axis partner through an exclusively American occupation. When General MacArthur, the supreme commander for the Allied powers, landed in Japan at the end of August, he carried a blueprint to disarm and demobilize the armed forces, establish a democratic political process, protect civil liberties, give land to the tillers, and dissolve the giant industrial monopolies (the *Zaibatsu*) that dominated the economy and supported aggression.

A combination of military pressure (blockade by the U.S. Navy, conventional bombing by the air force, the entry of the Soviet Union into the Pacific war, and the dropping of two

A Japanese farmer watches the landing of U.S. troops on the beach at Wakayama, 1945. (U.S. Army/National Archives)

atomic bombs) and political bargaining had brought the war in the Pacific to an end in mid-August. Eager to save lives and keep the Soviets from claiming an occupation zone, Truman modified demands for an "unconditional surrender." He encouraged the "peace faction" in Tokyo by agreeing that the emperor could remain, provisionally, on the throne. Although this probably did speed surrender, it also gave the discredited imperial system a new lease on life.

Despite Truman's description of Douglas MacArthur as "Mr. Prima Donna, Brass Hat, Five Star MacArthur," he bowed to political pressure in appointing the general Allied (really American) occupation commander. MacArthur's heroic status and influence within the Republican party (he was a likely presidential candidate for 1948), the president lamented, meant that "politically he couldn't do anything else." Truman expressed relief that Tokyo was far away and hoped that MacArthur would not stray far from the reform agenda given him.

Most Japanese, it turned out, were disillusioned with the militarists and nationalist fanatics who had brought on the war. They cooperated enthusiastically with the political reforms introduced by the Americans. A small number of senior leaders were tried and executed for war crimes, and a modest political purge barred exponents of aggression from participating in government. Under the guidelines established by the conquerers, moderate conservatives quickly secured control of the Japanese government and have dominated it ever since.

The occupation imposed a new constitution which banned war and armed forces, established civil liberties and representa-

tive government, and gave women legal (though not actual) equality. A daring agrarian reform program ended tenancy, immunizing Japan from the peasant rebellions then sweeping China and Southeast Asia. Labor unions were granted legal status, and plans were discussed to reorganize Japanese industry.

In spite of impressive political and social reforms, Japan's loss of empire and Asian markets after 1945 plunged the economy into a steep decline. Washington provided emergency relief, but neither the administration nor MacArthur took responsibility for assisting recovery. Until 1947, the Truman administration focused its Asia policy on efforts to avert civil war in China. Also, residual wartime hatred inclined few Americans to favor rebuilding Japan.

But American interests changed dramatically during 1947. The continued economic slide of Western Europe and divided Germany raised the specter that the Soviets, even without the use of force, might take advantage of growing chaos. Mediation efforts in China collapsed and the civil war appeared to favor the Communists, making a stable, pro-American Japan a new priority in Asia. The Truman administration considered it vital to rebuild the economies of both Western Europe and Japan in order to "contain" Soviet power and ensure the stability of a global noncommunist economy. At the same time as Truman proposed the Marshall Plan for Europe, his administration endorsed the Economic Recovery in Occupied Areas (EROA) program to fund Japanese reconstruction.

Unfortunately, Occupation Commander MacArthur had a different agenda. In mid-1947 he decided to seek the Republican presidential nomination the next year. Any Washington-controlled aid program in Japan, he feared, would diminish his own stature and call into question his accomplishments. Accordingly, he denounced the administration's aid proposal, insisting that Japan was already rehabilitated and ready for a peace treaty. In an effort to woo American liberal support, he promoted a radical plan to break up Japanese industrial monopolies, even though he had opposed the program for two years. Ironically, by now the Truman administration had turned around completely and favored assisting, not dissolving, centralized heavy industry.

Truman felt politically constrained from acting against MacArthur. Any effort to fire or reprimand him, the president believed, would only make him a martyr and boost his political fortunes. Truman decided to await the results of the April 1948 Wisconsin primary before acting. MacArthur, whom many Americans admired as a general but feared as a politician, lost the election badly. With the general's political aura in tatters, Truman approved a plan to change basic policy.

The president now backed the State and Defense departments which called for a reversal of many occupation reforms. Even though he left MacArthur in place, Truman authorized sending new personnel to Tokyo. With direct backing from the White House, these officials implemented the so-called Reverse Course, imposing tough restrictions on labor unions, providing economic aid to large, export-oriented industry, and recentralizing the police force. MacArthur's influence in Japan waned quickly. Only his appointment as commander in Korea, in the summer of 1950, restored his prominence.

During the later years of the occupation, the United States abandoned its initial plan to diminish Japanese economic and political influence. Washington now favored Japan's reemergence as a major regional power bolstering the noncommunist states surrounding China. Recovery, however, still lagged behind that of Europe until the Korean War brought a flood of military orders which accelerated Japan's transformation into first a regional and then a world economic power.

In September 1951, the Truman administration finally decided the time had come to restore Japanese sovereignty. At a conference in San Francisco, the United States and its Allies signed a peace treaty ending the occupation effective in April 1952. The Soviet Union refused to endorse the settlement since it permitted the United States to retain major military bases in Japan. Tokyo's other large neighbor, the People's Republic of China, was barred by Washington from attending the conference.

In contrast to the failures of American foreign policy elsewhere in postwar Asia (especially in China and Vietnam), the Truman administration accomplished most of its goals in Japan. The former enemy emerged from six years of American tutelage as a stable, democratic nation, linked to the Western military alliance. Ironically, an important (if misguided) motive for growing U.S. military involvement in Southeast Asia after 1950 was to keep communism out of areas deemed vital for Japanese economic security. Before the Pearl Harbor attack, Japan's leaders had justified their conquest of China and Southeast Asia on similar grounds. As one prominent American diplomat admitted ruefully, near the end of the occupation, "we have got to get Japan back into, I am afraid, the old Co-Prosperity Sphere."

John W. Dower, *War without Mercy: Race and Power in the Pacific War* (New York: Pantheon, 1986), examines the racial dimensions of Japanese-American conflict. Christopher Thorne, *Allies of a Kind: The United States, Britain and the War against Japan* (New York: Oxford University Press, 1978), is a masterful account of Allied diplomacy in the Pacific during World War II. Michael Schaller, in *The American Occupation of Japan: The Origins of the Cold War in Asia* (New York: Oxford University Press, 1985), gives an account of Japan's role in American foreign policy in Asia from 1945 to 1950. Dower, in *Empire and Aftermath: Yoshida Shigeru and the Japanese Experience, 1879–1954* (Cambridge: Harvard University, Council on East Asian Studies, 1979), analyzes the life and times of Japan's major postwar political figure. See also D. Clayton James, *The Years of MacArthur*, vol. 3, *Triumph and Disaster, 1945–64* (Boston: Houghton Mifflin, 1985). The final volume of this definitive biography centers on the general's role in occupied Japan and the Korean War.

MICHAEL SHALLER

See also Atomic and Hydrogen Bombs; MacArthur, Douglas; Stimson, Henry L.

Japanese-Americans

Although Senator Truman did not participate in any of several senatorial debates about the incarceration and fate of the Japanese-Americans, as president he greatly facilitated the process of their rehabilitation and redress. In a 15 July 1946 ceremony on the Ellipse south of the White House he awarded the Nisei 442d Regimental Combat Team its seventh presidential unit citation. In congratulating the men, Truman, probably without intended irony, noted that his "predecessor" had called

Americanism "not a matter of race or creed [but] of the heart." The president went on to point out that the Nisei had "fought not only the enemy, but [also] prejudice—and you have won."

On 2 February 1948, he devoted the last three points of his special ten-point message on civil rights to issues of special concern to Japanese-Americans. Point eight called for Hawaiian (and Alaskan) statehood, point nine for dropping racial bars to naturalization, and point ten for settling the evacuation claims of Japanese-Americans.

Only the last goal was quickly attained. The president had pointed out that "more than one hundred thousand Japanese-Americans were evacuated from their homes in the Pacific states solely because of their racial origin" and successfully urged the Congress to pass legislation already before it. On 2 July 1948, Truman signed the Japanese-American Claims Act which appropriated $38 million to settle all property loss claims, not nearly enough, most commentators now agree.

The president had urged what he called "equality in naturalization." Under American law all foreign-born Asians had been "aliens ineligible to citizenship." Between 1943 and 1946 Congress passed separate statutes dropping the bars for Chinese, Filipinos, and natives of (then) India. Equality in naturalization was achieved in the 1952 McCarran-Walter Act passed over Truman's veto. The veto message praised the equalization but found "this most desirable provision ... embedded in a mass of legislation which would perpetuate injustice."

Statehood for Hawaii, important because the high proportion of Asian-Americans there would surely result in Asian-American senators and representatives, was delayed even longer, coming only in 1959.

Although much has been written "explaining" the practical benefits Truman sought to reap from his civil rights proposals, it is difficult to imagine what domestic political gain can have been expected from measures benefiting Japanese and other Asian-Americans. The president himself called for these measures both as a matter of justice and as a weapon to use in the cold war: "If we wish to inspire the peoples of the world whose freedom is in jeopardy, if we wish to restore hope to those who have already lost their civil liberties, if we wish to fulfill the promise that is ours, we must correct the remaining imperfections in our practice of democracy."

For a discussion of the postwar evolution of civil rights for Japanese-Americans, see Roger Daniels, *Asian America: Chinese and Japanese in the United States since 1850* (Seattle: University of Washington Press, 1988). On Truman and civil rights generally, see Donald R. McCoy and Richard T. Ruetten, *Quest and Response: Minority Rights and the Truman Administration* (Lawrence: University of Kansas Press, 1973), and William C. Berman, *The Politics of Civil Rights in the Truman Administration* (Columbus: Ohio State University Press, 1970).

ROGER DANIELS

Jewish-Americans

Numbering close to five million, American Jews were strongly but not invariably in President Truman's camp throughout his years in office. Newly arrived in the political and social elites, members of the Jewish community were gaining in wealth and public impact during the 1940s, first in the nation's cultural life, then in political influence. Although their votes were but a small fraction of the electorate, Jewish intellectual energies and organizational cohesion on issues of particular interest gave Jewish-Americans a voice in politics far stronger than their numbers would suggest.

Predominantly liberal, on the left wing of the political spectrum, Jews had been among the beneficiaries of the New Deal and consequently remained solid in their loyalty to President Franklin D. Roosevelt. During his lifetime, doubts about his insensitivity to Nazi persecution of Jews and to the growing Zionist aspirations for a Jewish state in Palestine were muffled. The Jewish vote mounted steadily for Roosevelt during his four campaigns and was virtually unanimous in 1944.

Truman inherited most, though not all, of the Jewish support enjoyed by his predecessor. Statistics cannot be precise, but between 60 percent and 75 percent of the Jewish vote went Democratic in 1948—not that this was decisive, for Truman lost the three states of New York, Pennsylvania, and Illinois where the Jewish population was largest. A significant minority, perhaps 15 percent to 20 percent, of Jews voted for the far left challenger, Henry A. Wallace; a smaller percentage went to Thomas E. Dewey, the Republican candidate.

Neither socially nor politically, however, was the Jewish community a monolithic bloc. Even the cause of Zionism, the dominant issue for the Jews of the late 1940s, had been a source of deep contention before and during World War II. The campaign for Jewish statehood was spearheaded by a populist minority; the upper crust of the status-conscious Jewish community had been suspicious and even contemptuous of a new nationalism that they feared could endanger their status as loyal Americans. Only the shock of the Holocaust, and the vivid evidence of a Jewish population destroyed, converted the Jewish leadership of the United States to the once-radical ideology of Zionism.

Among Zionists themselves, moreover, were deep splits which prevented a concerted Jewish effort during Truman's first term. Largely it was a matter of tactics, of how best to exercise political influence toward the realization of Jewish statehood. The long dominant Zionist faction, led by Rabbi Stephen Wise, favored "quiet diplomacy," gentle persuasion within the political elites, an approach that Wise believed to have worked well under his friend President Roosevelt. But Wise's posture of "respectability" came under increasing challenge from advocates of more vehement pressure tactics, a growing faction led by the bombastic Rabbi Abba Hillel Silver.

Truman, buffeted between partisans of the two factions, made no secret of his annoyance at what he regarded as publicity-seeking Jews pushing themselves into his counsels. Wise was near the end of his life when Truman became president, but his partisans were sympathetically received at the White House by presidential aide David Niles. Silver, by contrast, was at the height of his rhetorical effectiveness, but he made the fatal mistake of pounding on the presidential desk during a meeting with Truman, who refused ever to see him again.

In his personal attitudes, Truman evidenced some of the superficial social anti-Semitism of the times; his letters and off-hand statements expressed occasional and lighthearted ethnic slurs. But from early in public life, Truman railed against anti-Semitic bigotry. In one of his Missouri campaigns, opponents from the Ku Klux Klan spread dark innuendos built on the fact that Truman's grandfather was named Solomon. "I am not Jewish," Truman snapped back, "but if I were I would not be ashamed of it."

Much has been made of Truman's lifelong friendship with Eddie Jacobson, his Jewish partner in the haberdashery business. On the evidence, Jacobson's role in inclining his old friend toward support for the state of Israel seems overdrawn. Jacobson was no Zionist, although like most American Jews he got caught up in the drive for Jewish statehood after the horrors of the Holocaust became known. The two cronies often met after hours in the White House but almost never to talk politics. Jacobson was a simple man, and Truman valued the friendship for moments of mellow nostalgia, not political insight.

But at one critical juncture in 1947, Jacobson successfully played upon Truman's loyalty to get his old friend to receive Dr. Chaim Weizmann, the aged Zionist leader. The meeting was perfunctory, insignificant in itself, yet it has often been cited for guiding Truman's personal sympathies toward the decision to recognize the Jewish state when it was finally proclaimed a year later.

The Jewish-American community and its role in the Truman years is fully explored in Peter Grose, *Israel in the Mind of America* (New York: Knopf, 1983), which also contains further references. See also Zvi Ganin, *Truman, American Jewry and Israel, 1945-1948* (New York: Holmes & Meier, 1979). For the broader context, see Robert J. Donovan, *Conflict and Crisis* (New York: W. W. Norton, 1977), a masterful account of the first Truman administration, and Nathaniel Weyl, *The Jew in American Politics* (New Rochelle, N.Y.: Arlington House, 1968). The annual *American Jewish Yearbook*, published by the American Jewish Committee, New York, and the Jewish Publication Society of America, Philadelphia, is valuable for reference and analytical discussions.

PETER GROSE

See also Israel; Jacobson, Eddie; Zionism

Johnson, Louis Arthur

(10 January 1891–24 April 1956)

Secretary of defense. The son of Marcellus A. and Katherine Arthur Johnson, Louis A. Johnson was born in Roanoke, Virginia, and attended its schools before graduating from the University of Virginia in 1912 with an LL.B. degree. Admitted to the bar, he began practice in Clarksville, West Virginia. More than six feet tall and weighing more than 250 pounds, the articulate Johnson was a stump spellbinder. He served in the West Virginia House of Representatives from 1916 to 1924. Meanwhile he also served with the American Expeditionary Force, from which he was discharged as a major. He then resumed his law practice, and was a delegate to the Democratic National Convention of 1924.

Johnson married Ruth Frances Maxwell on 7 February 1920 and had two daughters. He helped organize the American Legion, of which he was national commander in 1932. His four-year tour, 1936–40, as assistant to Secretary of War Harry H.

Louis Johnson is sworn in as secretary of national defense by Chief Justice Vinson, 28 March 1949. (National Archives)

Woodring, it was said, hastened industrial preparedness and shortened World War II by eighteen months. He also served as chairman of the Finance Committee of the Democratic National Committee from 1936 to 1940 and again in 1948. By raising funds that enabled President Harry S. Truman to make a belated "swing about the circle" that helped him win reelection, Johnson was in a position to demand and obtain the post of secretary of defense on 23 March 1949.

Johnson heavily favored the air force and wished to merge the Marine Corps with the army and naval aviation with the air force. To support his own attempt to win the presidency in 1952, he would try to save $1.5 billion from the small defense budgets President Truman allowed.

He was disliked by military men because he refused to listen to advice and won his way by "cracking heads together." Moreover, he was so rude that Secretary of State Dean Acheson thought him mad. When Johnson abruptly canceled the construction of a supercarrier the navy needed to test new technologies, he was investigated by Congress. The Representative Carl Vinson report on unification ("Revolt of the Admirals") indicated that the secretary of defense had erred in seeking to merge the services and superseded his authority by canceling the carrier; Vinson promised that when funds were available the navy would get its carrier.

While Johnson persisted in "economizing," National Security Council Paper No. 68 of March 1950 recommended increasing annual defense spending from $18 billion to $50 billion

by 1954. Moreover, Truman depended more for policy direction during the Korean War on Acheson than on Johnson, unification in the field proved farcical, and the Marine Corps and naval aviation Johnson had denigrated proved their worth. In addition Johnson urged a preventive war against the Soviet Union while Truman hoped to avert World War III. Johnson therefore lost the confidence of the people, embarrassed Truman, and became expendable. Truman told him to write out his own resignation effective 20 September 1950, and to mention George C. Marshall as his successor. Clearly, Johnson had failed as secretary of defense.

Johnson served as a director of two savings and loan associations in Clarksville until his death from a brain malady in 1956.

Silhouettes of major Pentagon personnel are found in Carl W. Borklund, *Men of the Pentagon: From Forrestal to McNamara* (New York: Praeger, 1966). Johnson's tenure as secretary of defense is traced in Paolo E. Coletta, *The U.S. Navy and Defense Unification, 1947–1953* (Newark: University of Delaware Press, 1981). Truman's version of his relations with Johnson is in his *Memoirs* 2 vols. (Garden City, N.Y.: Doubleday, 1955–56).

PAOLO E. COLETTA

See also Cabinets (photograph)

Johnson, Lyndon Baines

(27 August 1908–22 January 1973)

Born near Stonewall, Texas, and educated at Southwest State Teachers College in San Marcos, Texas, Lyndon B. Johnson arrived in Washington as a congressional secretary in 1932. By 1937, he was in the House of Representatives, where he became known as a New Deal "yes-man." When Franklin Roosevelt died, Johnson cried: "He was just like a daddy to me." The ambitious Texan's relations with President Truman proved more turbulent. Planning a Senate run, Congressman Johnson opposed parts of Truman's Fair Deal. He voted for the antiunion Taft-Hartley Act in 1947, and during his successful 1948 senatorial campaign, he called Truman's civil rights program "an effort to set up a police state in the guise of liberty."

In the Senate, Johnson continued to support Truman's domestic policy only intermittently, but he embraced Truman's foreign policy. Johnson was a Cold Warrior. As a congressman he had approved the Truman Doctrine and the Marshall Plan to stop "Stalin from overrunning the world." When the United States entered the Korean War, Johnson hailed Truman's "inspired act of leadership."

Truman preferred Johnson, now the Senate majority leader, to John F. Kennedy for president in 1960—although Truman's first choice was the Missouri senator Stuart Symington. Truman then warned Johnson not to accept the vice presidency under the "immature" Kennedy. Johnson ignored the advice.

When President Kennedy was assassinated and Johnson became president in 1963, Truman's health was waning, limiting their contacts. They did, however, discuss the parallels between

Korea and Vietnam. According to an aide, George Reedy, Johnson "was hoping to be regarded as a man who had emulated Harry S. Truman and stood up against communism when it was critical."

On 30 July 1965, President Johnson flew to Independence to sign the Medicare bill. In honoring Harry Truman, who had first suggested a comprehensive national health insurance program in 1945, Johnson said, "We have come back here to his home, to complete what he began." This tribute symbolized how much the country—and Johnson himself—had changed.

Scattered throughout Ronnie Dugger's tendentious but thorough *The Politician: The Life and Times of Lyndon Johnson, The Drive for Power, from the Frontier to Master of the Senate* (New York: W. W. Norton, 1982), is a full account of Johnson's relations with Truman during the 1940s and 1950s. Robert J. Donovan occasionally refers to Johnson in his two volumes on the Truman presidency, *Conflict and Crisis: The Presidency of Harry S Truman, 1945-1948* and *Tumultuous Years: The Presidency of Harry S Truman, 1949-1953* (New York: W. W. Norton, 1977, 1982). Robert J. Donovan's *Nemesis: Truman and Johnson in the Coils of War in Asia* (New York: St. Martin's/Marek, 1984) parallels Johnson's foreign policy with Truman's rather convincingly. Robert A. Caro's biography, *The Years of Lyndon Johnson: The Path to Power* (New York: Alfred A. Knopf, 1982) chronicles Johnson's life through the Roosevelt administration. Caro's next volume will begin with Johnson's congressional career during Truman's presidency and should offer an authoritative account.

GIL TROY

Joint Chiefs of Staff

The body of high-ranking officers that functioned as the principal military advisory group to the president and, after July 1947, to the National Security Council and the secretary of defense as well. Consisting of the chiefs of the army, navy, and air force, and a chairman, it was assisted by the Joint Staff and miscellaneous committees whose number varied from year to year. President Roosevelt had created the Joint Chiefs system in early 1942 as the American counterpart to the British Chiefs of Staff Committee. The two groups served during the rest of the Second World War as the Anglo-American Combined Chiefs of Staff, advising Presidents Roosevelt and Truman and Prime Ministers Churchill and Attlee on matters of strategy, high command, logistics, and overall direction of the global war against the Axis. Neither Roosevelt nor Truman issued a specific directive or executive decree formally chartering the Joint Chiefs, but the body and its supplementary organization continued to serve President Truman significantly, if without legal validation, for nearly two years after the end of World War II.

The Joint Chiefs system received its statutory authority under the National Security Act of July 1947—a landmark measure that also established the National Security Council, the Office of the Secretary of Defense, the Department of the Air Force, and the Central Intelligence Agency, among other provisions. Operating under the authority and direction of the president and the secretary of defense, the Joint Chiefs of Staff was charged with formulating joint strategic and logistical plans, setting up unified commands as needed, developing policies for joint military training, coordinating programs in military education, and working with the Military Staff Committee of the United Nations, as well as other tasks the president or the secretary of defense might assign it.

An amendment to the National Security Act in August 1949 formally established the position of chairman of the Joint Chiefs of Staff. Fleet Adm. William D. Leahy had served informally in this role since July 1942 when Roosevelt had appointed him as chief of staff to the president, a post he continued to hold under President Truman until March 1949. The acting chairman for the next five months was General of the Army Dwight D. Eisenhower, who functioned on a part-time basis since he was also holding the presidency of Columbia University. General of the Army Omar N. Bradley held the chairmanship in a full-time capacity from August 1949 to August 1953, retiring shortly after the Korean War ended. Bradley outranked the rest of the Joint Chiefs, but under the terms of the 1949 amendment he did not vote and did not exercise actual command over the other Joint Chiefs or any of the armed services, although he was given more control over the Joint Staff and the committee structure than his predecessors.

Truman and Leahy became fast friends, working well together on matters concerning the Joint Chiefs and thinking along similar lines on cold war policies. Although he appeared to like and respect Bradley, surely far more than Eisenhower, President Truman often turned for advice on strategy and policy in the Korean War to Secretary of Defense George C. Marshall, Secretary of State Dean G. Acheson, and Presidential Assistant W. Averell Harriman before seeking the input of Bradley and his colleagues on the Joint Chiefs of Staff.

During the Korean conflict of 1950–53, the American military establishment began to revive from its post-1945 demobilization doldrums and niggardly budgets, reaching a fairly balanced and potent level of combat readiness by the end of the Truman presidency, but ironically, the influence of the Joint Chiefs diminished somewhat over the period after World War II. In part, this was due to inadequate defense funding to 1950, administrative flaws in the organization of the Joint Chiefs system, and strategic confusion in adjusting to both cold war and limited war situations. Also, agencies such as the Office of the Secretary of Defense, the National Security Council, the Department of State's Policy Planning Staff, and the Central Intelligence Agency began to assume increasing responsibilities in the formulation of strategy and national security policies.

The relative decline of the influence of the Joint Chiefs, however, was not for want of gifted, experienced leaders serving on that body during the Truman administration. Besides the chairman already mentioned, they included Generals Marshall (1945), Eisenhower (1945–48), Bradley (1948–49), and J. Lawton Collins (1949–53) as army chiefs of staff; Admirals Ernest J. King (1945), Chester W. Nimitz (1945–47), Louis E. Denfield (1947–49), Forrest P. Sherman (1949–51), and William M. Fechteler (1951–53) as chiefs of naval operations; and Henry H. Arnold (1945–46), Carl A. Spaatz (1946–48), and Hoyt S. Vandenberg (1948–53) as army air force (to 1947) and air force chiefs of staff. All these men had distinguished records in high command during World War II, but most of them did not demonstrate exceptional leadership in their later roles on the Joint Chiefs of Staff. The ebb for the Joint Chiefs as a body was the command crisis precipitated by General of the Army Douglas MacArthur that culminated in Truman's reliance chiefly upon other advisers in curbing MacArthur's defiant course in Korea and in relieving him of his commands in April 1951.

The documents of the Joint Chiefs of Staff are in Record Group 218 of the National Archives, Washington, D.C. A judiciously selected portion of these materials has been published in microfilm in *Records of the Joint Chiefs of Staff, 1945–1953*, 70 reels (Frederick, Md.: University Publications of America, 1978). Of fundamental importance to this topic is the official series prepared by the Historical Division of the Joint Chiefs of Staff, *The History of the Joint Chiefs of Staff: The Joint Chiefs of Staff and National Policy, 1945–1953*, 4 vols. in 5 (Wilmington, Del.: Michael Glazier, 1979), the individual volumes being as follows: vol. 1, *1945–1947*, by James F. Schnabel; vol. 2, *1947–1949*, by Kenneth W. Condit; vol. 3 (in 2 pts.), *The Korean War*, by Schnabel and Robert J. Watson; and vol. 4, *1950–1952*, by Walter S. Poole. The principal collections of papers of the individual chiefs of 1945–53 are located in the Library of Congress, the Naval Historical Center, and the Marine Corps Historical Center, all in Washington, D.C.; the Dwight D. Eisenhower Library, Abilene, Kans.; the U.S. Army Military History Institute, Carlisle, Pa.; the U.S. Military Academy Library, West Point, N.Y.; the Air Force Historical Research Center, Maxwell Air Force Base, Ala.; and the Hoover Institution on War, Revolution, and Peace, Stanford University, Calif. Of the thirteen officers who served on the Joint Chiefs of Staff during this period, six published notable memoirs: Leahy, Eisenhower, Bradley, Collins, King, and Arnold. Biographies, ranging from adequate to excellent, have been written on these men, as well as on Marshall and King. Most of these primary and secondary works, however, deal mainly with their World War II roles rather than their post-1945 careers.

D. CLAYTON JAMES

See also Armed Forces, Unification of the; Bradley, Omar Nelson; Eisenhower, Dwight David; Leahy, William Daniel; Marshall, George C., Jr.

Judgeships
See Jackson County Court

K

Kansas City, Missouri

Although Harry Truman grew up in the small town of Independence, he was drawn from an early age to the nearby metropolis of Kansas City, located at the confluence of the Kansas and Missouri rivers. Possessing a population of about 164,000 when Truman graduated from high school in 1901, the city grew rapidly through his adult years; by the time he became president in 1945 it had well in excess of 400,000 residents. (Missouri's first city, Saint Louis, 250 miles across the state, was twice as large, older, more settled, more refined, and prone to regard its cross-state rival as a crude, disorderly upstart.)

A regional grain and livestock marketing center, Kansas City was also a major rail hub with a growing manufacturing economy. It was already well established as one of the most wide open cities of the trans-Mississippi West with a traditionally tolerant attitude toward liquor, gambling, and prostitution. An urban outpost of the border South, the city did not have large and varied immigrant enclaves, although it did possess a sizable black population. By the 1920s, it was one of the nation's jazz capitals. During Truman's years in Independence (1890–1903) and on the farm in Grandview (1906–19), Kansas City was easily accessible to him by interurban transit, passenger train, and automobile.

Young Harry's first regular contacts with the city came at the age of fourteen, when he began serious piano lessons. He was a pupil of Mrs. E. C. White, who had studied in Europe with some of the masters of the art and who introduced her young student to the great Ignace Paderewski when the Polish maestro performed in Kansas City. Later it became the scene of Truman's early jobs as a clerk at Commerce Bank and Union National Bank. From 1903 to 1906, he lived in a boarding house on the fringe of the downtown business district, ushered at a vaudeville theater on weekends, and thoroughly enjoyed a wide range of available entertainment from light comedy and soft-shoe dance acts to Shakespeare and grand opera.

A quest for male comradeship seems to have motivated the young bank clerk's decision to enroll in a new National Guard artillery battery formed by Capt. George Collins in 1905. The officers appear to have been successful business and professional men; among them was Lt. Fred Boxley, an attorney who became the Truman family lawyer and later served as a key adviser when Truman was presiding judge of the Jackson County court. A good many of the enlistees were aspiring younger individuals like Harry in search of friendship, useful contacts, and older mentors. Truman served as battery clerk in its early years. He remained a member of the unit after moving to the farm in 1906 and reenlisted for a second three-year term in 1908. Because of the pressures of farm work, he decided against a third hitch, but he retained a social membership in the battery.

During this period, Truman also frequently came into the city for Masonic gatherings. Moreover, along with his future brother-in-law, Frank Wallace, he attended political meetings of Mike Pendergast's Tenth Ward Democratic Club, thereby establishing his first formal relationship with the Pendergast machine.

In 1917, after deciding to rejoin the Guard, he continued his affiliation with the Kansas Citians rather than with Independence Guardsmen, right down to participating vocally in the successful campaign of Kansas Citian Karl D. Klemm for regimental commander. Among the important Kansas City friendships Truman acquired in his World War I military service were those with James Pendergast, Mike's son, and Marvin Gates, a wealthy Republican real estate developer who later provided valuable contacts with the city's business establishment.

Kansas City also served as the base of most of Truman's early business ventures. The oil exploration and brokerage concerns in which he was a partner with David Morgan were headquartered downtown. Although the enterprise came close to a couple of big strikes, he closed out his association with Morgan on little more than a break-even basis. In return for Truman's share in the business, Morgan gave him a house on Karnes Boulevard in the upscale Penn Valley district of the city. Truman soon traded it for a partial interest in a midtown apartment building at Thirty-ninth and Bell streets. Although heavily encumbered with mortgages, both properties strike one as good investments that probably would have been profitable had Truman stayed with them. Instead, he swapped his Bell Street interest for a farm in Johnson County, Kansas, in the hope of a price resurgence in rapidly depreciating farmland. Unable to maintain mortgage payments, he lost the property to foreclosure.

The city, of course, provided the setting for Truman's most famous business enterprise, the Truman-Jacobson haberdashery, an outgrowth of his army friendship with Eddie Jacobson. Truman appears to have hoped that it would provide him entrée into the local business elite and apparently expected Jacobson to do most of the active managing. Located in the heart of downtown across the street from the fashionable Muehlebach Hotel, the haberdashery was in retrospect an ill-conceived attempt to compete with much larger and better capitalized providers of men's furnishings. Truman provided all the equity capital for it and borrowed heavily in addition. A bet on continued easy credit and unbroken postwar prosperity, the business failed in the sharp recession of 1920–22, which hit the agricultural foundation of the Kansas City economy with special severity.

After 1926, when he was elected presiding judge, Kansas City served as Truman's political base, providing most of his votes in countywide elections and giving him the overwhelming margin needed to win the Democratic senatorial nomination in 1934. His support was derived mostly (although not exclusively) from his occasionally uneasy alliance with the political coalition headed by Boss Tom Pendergast. As chief county administrative officer, Truman built a valuable reputation for honesty which won him some backing and considerable respect from two primarily Republican organizations, the reformist Civic Research Institute and the Kansas City Chamber of Commerce. As a senator, he worked hard to represent the interests of local entrepreneurs and civic boosters. In the late 1920s and early 1930s, he also enjoyed generally favorable coverage and frequent editorial support from the regionally influential *Kansas City Star*. Toward the end of the thirties, however, the *Star* became increasingly critical of his defense of the Pendergast organization.

Pendergast in truth had become a liability as the city developed a national reputation for corruption and lawlessness. With the collapse of the machine in 1939, Truman experienced a substantial erosion of his Kansas City vote, although he still could poll a plurality there in the three-way senatorial primary of 1940. His continued success as a statewide politician was underwritten by his establishment of new support in the city of Saint Louis, where he also was the leading vote-getter in 1940. After 1940, he spurned opportunities to become more deeply involved in local politics and began to establish a reputation as a valuable national legislator. Significantly, the work that gave him that reputation, the Special Committee to Investigate the National Defense Program, was initiated partly in response to complaints from Kansas City area businessmen.

During his presidency, some of Truman's critics identified him with Kansas City and it with corruption; his admirers were more inclined to portray him as the Man of Independence. For several years after his presidency, Truman maintained an office in downtown Kansas City and was a daily fixture on the scene there. With the completion of the Truman Library, which included personal office facilities for him, he ended his close relationship with the city, spending the last dozen or so years of his life largely in Independence.

Among the best sources of Kansas City life and politics during the period of Truman's activity there are Richard Lawrence Miller, *Truman: The Rise to Power* (New York: McGraw-Hill, 1986); William Reddig, *Tom's Town* (Philadelphia: J. B. Lippincott, 1947); and *The WPA Guide to 1930s Missouri* (reprint, Lawrence: University Press of Kansas, 1986).

ALONZO L. HAMBY

See also Business Ventures; *Kansas City Star*; Military Career; Pendergast, Thomas J.

Kansas City Star

Boasting a circulation of upwards of 400,000 by 1950, the *Kansas City Star* (combined with its morning edition, the *Times*) was a powerful force in western Missouri—and, indeed, in the entire region at the great bend of the Missouri River. Founded in 1880 by William Rockhill Nelson as a product of the new age of "independent" journalism, it eschewed the role of the old party journals and delivered news unalloyed by partisanship. Seeking appeal among rank-and-file Kansas Citians, it built a following by offering entertaining human interest stories and, above all, by crusading in the community interest, all for the price of two cents. The *Star* conducted campaigns to control grasping private utilities, improve streets and highways, foster rapid transit, construct cultural facilities, and establish the city's famous park system. Above all, in nonpartisan fashion, the *Star* attacked political corruption and called for reform at all levels of government. It sought to cleanse Kansas City of the excesses of bossism as practiced by the developing Jim Pendergast machine and demanded a commission-type local administration. In state politics it endorsed progressive reformers of both parties, and in 1912 it crusaded all-out for Progressive Theodore Roosevelt for the presidency. These attributes of modern independent journalism were presented to the public, curiously enough, in the old-fashioned format of small headlines and type, and no illustrations, cartoons, or comics.

In 1925, ten years after, "Baron" Nelson's death, the *Star* was sold to the paper's employees, soon to be dominated by Roy A. Roberts, general manager, who editorially moved the *Star* in a conservative political direction, so that it came to be known chiefly as a Republican paper. In national politics it supported all GOP candidates for president beginning with Harding in 1920, and it was especially opposed to the League of Nations.

The *Star*'s chief interest was in local affairs, however, particularly in its increasingly persistent and determined campaign to smash the Pendergast machine, which after 1911 was captained by Jim's brother Tom. The paper finally succeeded in its long struggle in the late thirties, it helped to uncover the vast vote frauds and personal corruption involving insurance company payoffs that were responsible for sending Pendergast to prison.

As for Truman, the *Star* respected him as a person and praised him as "a faithful and economical public servant" when he was a judge in Jackson County. By 1932 Judge Truman had compiled such a record, principally in road building, that the *Star* remarked, "Jackson County has found him a capable and honest public official." In the 1934 senatorial campaign for the Democratic nomination Truman ran as an unabashed candidate of the Pendergast machine and won in a hot three-way race. As a Republican journal the *Star* took little part in the primary, and futilely supported the GOP candidate in the general election. When the senator ran for reelection, in 1940, he was again involved, fortunately for him, in a three-way race for renomination, in which his opposition again was split. On this occasion the *Star* took to referring to Truman as the "machine candidate," although by now the Pendergast organization was in a shambles, in no small part because of the efforts of the *Star* itself. In 1940 the paper actually saw eye-to-eye with the senator in the necessity for a military buildup because of the Hitler menace, but because Truman was a loyal New Dealer in domestic matters and considered dangerously prolabor, the *Star*, as usual, favored the Republican candidate in the November election, again without success but also without rancor.

In 1944, when Truman was hand-picked by Franklin Roosevelt as his vice-presidential running mate, the *Star* predictably was firmly for Dewey on the ground it was time for a change, but the rumor around Kansas City was that Roy Roberts privately would have liked to have spoken favorably of Truman. In any event, the paper was simply silent on the vice presidency. But it was of some significance that on 13 April 1945, the day after Truman acceded to the White House, the only newspaperman granted a private interview was Republican Roberts. Nevertheless, in 1948 when Truman was running for the presidency on his own, the paper sharply criticized him for being bitterly partisan toward the GOP-dominated Eightieth Congress, while praising Dewey, once again the GOP candidate, for seeking "with deliberation, confidence and composure" to bind the nation together in a program of "moderation." In brief, while the *Kansas City Star* after 1934 normally opposed Truman, it was chiefly from the viewpoint of a Republican paper with conservative principles and a paper that had campaigned in season and out against the Pendergast machine. But never did it impugn Truman's personal integrity. It knew him too well.

For the early history of the *Kansas City Star*, see Icie F. Johnson, *William Rockhill Nelson and the Kansas City Star* (Kansas City: Burton Publishing Co., 1935); Charles E. Rogers, "William Rockhill Nelson and His Editors of the Star," *Journalism Quarterly* 26 (March 1949); Rogers's Ph.D. dissertation, "William Rockhill Nelson: Independent Editor and Crusading Liberal" (University of Minnesota, 1948); and Will Irwin, "The Power of the Press," *Collier's* 21 January 1911, 15. For a study of the *Star* in its later years, see William Jackson Bell, "A Historical Study of *The Kansas City Star* Since the Death of William Rockhill Nelson, 1915–1949" (Ph.D. diss., University of Missouri, 1949).

JULIAN S. RAMMELKAMP

See also Jackson County Court; Pendergast, Thomas J.; Press, The

Kefauver, Estes

(26 July 1903–10 August 1963)

U.S. senator from Tennessee whom Truman sought to deny the Democratic presidential nomination in 1952 and 1956. Born

near Madisonville, Tennessee, the son of a local politician–hardware merchant, Carey Estes Kefauver attended public schools and the University of Tennessee before earning a law degree from Yale University in 1927. Kefauver then practiced in Chattanooga and dabbled in local civic and political activities. In 1939, he won election to the U.S. House of Representatives where he generally supported liberal positions and took special interests in antimonopoly studies and congressional reform.

A committed Brandeisan, Kefauver perceived economic and political problems in terms of monopoly power or bossism. His proposals for congressional reform involved limitations on the powers of committee chairs and the curbing of the filibuster. These proposals, in addition to his unwillingness to defer to Tennessee's powerful senator Kenneth McKellar, frequently placed Kefauver at odds with senior members of the Congress who sought to frustrate his ambitions and isolate him from President Truman. In 1948, Kefauver, donning a coonskin cap and attacking the statewide political influence of McKellar and Memphis boss E. H. Crump, won election to the U.S. Senate.

Frustrated by congressional leaders and the seniority system, the tall, bespectacled Kefauver sought to win a national following (and perhaps a place on the national ticket) by an assiduous courtship of the press. With that in mind, he chaired a series of sensational televised hearings on gambling and organized crime in 1950–51. The Kefauver committee toured fourteen major cities, making contact with local civic groups and newspapermen and exploring the "cartel" of organized crime. Because most of the urban centers were under Democratic control, Kefauver somewhat unwittingly embarrassed party incumbents with his revelations. While outwardly cooperative with the committee, President Truman harbored deep reservations about the senator from Tennessee. By instinct a loyal party and organization man, Truman had become convinced by congressional leaders and the White House staff that Kefauver was a political lightweight, careless about Democratic party interests and excessively ambitious.

The committee had transformed Kefauver into a presidential possibility by 1952. When the president delayed any final announcement of his own intentions, Kefauver plunged into a series of primaries. Even though he tried to avoid direct criticism of Truman, he did benefit from a general frustration with the president. He defeated a pro-Truman slate in New Hampshire in March, shortly before the embarrassed president announced his decision not to seek reelection. Although he entered the convention with the single largest block of delegates and led in public opinion polls, Kefauver was unacceptable to many party leaders. A combination of southern, big-city, and liberal forces (later joined by the president) blocked Kefauver and threw the nomination to Illinois governor Adlai Stevenson. Although Truman exaggerated his own role in the selection process, he had assisted in denying both the presidential and vice-presidential honors to Kefauver.

In 1956, Kefauver again sought his party's presidential nomination. With Truman soured on Stevenson, the Tennessee senator briefly hoped for the former president's support, but Truman instead endorsed New York governor Averell Harriman. After losing in the primaries, Kefauver threw his support to Stevenson, who won the nomination and accepted Kefauver as his vice-presidential running mate. A disappointed Truman then announced his support for the Democratic ticket.

Defeated in the second Eisenhower landslide, Kefauver gave up his presidential ambitions and returned to the Senate, where the seniority system now began to work in his favor. He chaired hearings on administered pricing in the drug, automobile, and steel industries. Although Truman never overcame his suspicions of the Tennessee senator, he would sometimes share Kefauver's antimonopoly positions (as in the 1962 debate over the Kennedy communications satellite bill). Kefauver died of a heart attack in 1963 while in the midst of several antitrust campaigns.

Charles L. Fontenay, *Estes Kefauver: A Biography* (Knoxville: University of Tennessee Press, 1980), is a full and persuasive study, touching on the senator's personal as well as public life. Joseph Bruce Gorman, *Kefauver: A Political Biography* (New York: Oxford University Press, 1971) is useful, especially for the 1952 campaign. William Howard Moore, *The Kefauver Committee and the Politics of Crime, 1950–1952* (Columbia: University of Missouri Press, 1974), explores the conflicting pressures on the Tennessee senator during the organized crime investigations. Truman's jaundiced views on Kefauver are available in Robert H. Ferrell, ed., *Off the Record: The Private Papers of Harry S. Truman* (New York: Harper & Row, 1980), and Monte M. Poen, ed., *Strictly Personal and Confidential: The Letters Harry Truman Never Mailed* (Boston: Little, Brown, 1982).

WILLIAM HOWARD MOORE

See also Crime; Elections in the Truman Era

Kelly, Edward Joseph

(1 May 1876–20 October 1950)

Mayor of Chicago, 1933–47; boss of the powerful Chicago Democratic machine. Edward J. Kelly was born and raised in the predominantly Irish neighborhood of Bridgeport in Chicago. He came to public attention as chief engineer of the Sanitary District and president of the South Park Board. In 1933 the city council chose Kelly to succeed martyred mayor Anton Cermak, the victim of an abortive assassination attempt on President-elect Franklin D. Roosevelt. As the chief executive of America's second city and the most powerful politician in Illinois, Kelly wielded considerable influence within national Democratic circles and frequently advised President Roosevelt on political matters.

In 1944 Kelly was one of the many big-city bosses opposed to the retention of Vice President Henry A. Wallace, whom the party leaders disdained as an uncooperative visionary. Although Kelly originally posed William O. Douglas as an alternative, he quickly fell in line behind the consensus choice of the bosses, Harry S. Truman. Because Chicago hosted the Democratic National Convention that year, Kelly was in an excellent position to deflect popular support from Wallace to Truman. Kelly kept the Illinois delegation committed to favorite-son Scott Lucas through the first convention ballot for vice president and then engineered the switch to Truman during the second ballot, which stampeded the delegates to the Missouri senator. Kelly's shameless manipulations led the *New York Times* to call Truman's selection the "second Missouri Compromise" and journalist James A. Hagerty to term the outcome "a triumph of the bosses." Kelly called it simply "good politics."

No longer mayor at the time of the 1948 Democratic National Convention, Kelly attended as Illinois national committeeman and avidly supported Truman's reelection. After the 1948 campaign the former mayor settled into a life of semiretirement, occasionally going to the downtown office of his engineering consulting firm and generally avoiding politics. He died suddenly of a massive heart attack in 1950 and was buried in Calvary Cemetery, Chicago.

The lone biography of Kelly is Roger Biles, *Big City Boss in Depression and War: Mayor Edward J. Kelly of Chicago* (DeKalb: Northern Illinois University Press, 1984). See also Biles's chapter on Kelly in *The Mayors: The Chicago Political Tradition*, ed. Paul M. Green and Melvin G. Holli (Carbondale: Southern Illinois University Press, 1987). Lyle W. Dorsett includes a chapter on Kelly in his *Franklin D. Roosevelt and the City Bosses* (Port Washington, N.Y.: Kennikat Press, 1977).

ROGER BILES

See also Elections in the Truman Era

Kennan, George Frost

(16 February 1904–)

Diplomat and writer. George Kennan was born in Milwaukee, Wisconsin, and attended Princeton University. After graduating in 1925, he joined the State Department and was selected to become a specialist in Soviet affairs. He studied Russian history, language, and culture at Riga and other posts in Central Europe. While assigned to the Berlin embassy in 1931, he married Annelise Sorenson, a Norwegian citizen.

Kennan put his specialized training to use in 1933, when he accompanied Ambassador William Bullitt to the Soviet Union. While secretary at the Moscow embassy, Kennan worked with other Soviet experts, including Charles ("Chip") Bohlen, Loy Henderson, and Elbridge Durbrow. Kennan also witnessed the purge trials of the late 1930s, which he later described as "a sort of liberal education in the horrors of Stalinism."

Kennan's work in Moscow was punctuated by assignments to other posts: Vienna, Prague, and Berlin in the late 1930s; Lisbon and London in the early 1940s. He returned to Moscow as minister-counselor in 1945–46 and analyzed Soviet behavior in the new postwar environment. His famous "long telegram" of 22 February 1946 warned that the Stalin regime was still "a political force committed fanatically to the belief that . . . there can be no permanent modus vivendi [with the United States]." He urged that "our public be educated to realities of Russian situation."

Navy secretary James Forrestal and other advisers of President Truman shared these views, so Kennan was brought back to Washington to lecture at the National War College. He published his ideas as "The Sources of Soviet Conduct" (*Foreign Affairs* 25 [July 1947]: 566–82). He described Soviet aggression as a different force than traditional Russian expansionism. It was also the product of a communist ideology which was incompatible with the existence of any other independent governments. The proper American response was "a policy of firm containment, designed to confront the Russians with unalterable counter-force at every point where they show signs of encroaching upon the interests of a peaceful and stable world." Kennan published his article under the pseudonym "X," but many readers regarded it as an unofficial statement of the Truman administration.

In April 1947, Secretary of State George Marshall offered Kennan the opportunity to implement the new policy of "containment." He was to organize a Policy Planning Staff, which would develop long-range policy, anticipate future problems, and coordinate planning activities. Within weeks Kennan had assembled a top-level team of thinkers, whose initial papers covered the problem of European recovery, the implementation of the Marshall Plan, and the future of Germany. The Planning Staff went on to address virtually every aspect of American foreign policy, particularly as it concerned Soviet behavior. Marshall also used the Planning Staff to prepare his department's papers for the National Security Council (NSC), and he designated Kennan a consultant to the NSC. Newspaper columnists (who had discovered Kennan's authorship of the "X" article) were soon describing Kennan as the "diplomatic chief of staff" and "America's global planner."

Kennan's influence during 1947–49 was symbolized by the location of his Planning Staff office—immediately adjacent to that of the secretary of state. Kennan and his nine to twelve Planning Staff members would receive copies of action reports, incoming telegrams, and all other forms of departmental intelligence. Many of the members specialized along geographical or functional lines: Kennan was the Soviet expert; Jacques Reinstein concentrated on Germany; John Paton Davies on China; Robert Tufts on economics; Robert Joyce on political operations; and Charles ("Tick") Bonesteel on politicomilitary matters. Members would draft initial papers on their subjects, which were read and debated at length by the entire staff. Kennan would then retire with his notes to a private room at the Library of Congress and compose the final version presented to the secretary of state.

Kennan was at the height of his career in 1949, but was also having grave doubts about American foreign policy. He believed that the policy of containment actually implemented by Truman and Dean Acheson was far too rigidly anti-Communist, that it tried to impose military solutions upon what were essentially political problems, and that it would result in the permanent division of Germany and the European continent. But like the Sorcerer's Apprentice, Kennan discovered he was unable to halt the process he had initiated. Throughout 1949, Kennan had a series of disagreements with Acheson, who later stated, "Kennan has never, in my judgment, grasped the realities of power relationships, but takes a rather mystical attitude toward them." Kennan finally turned the Planning Staff over to his deputy director, Paul Nitze, at the end of 1949. Nitze was already involved in preparing NSC 68, and his views of Soviet intentions and the proper American policies were much closer to those of Truman and Acheson.

Kennan took an extended leave of absence during 1950–51 and wrote *American Diplomacy, 1900–1950* (Chicago: University of Chicago Press, 1951). He returned to Washington and served as American ambassador to the Soviet Union during May–October 1952. His Foreign Service career ended abruptly in early 1953, after President Eisenhower appointed John Foster Dulles the new secretary of state. Both Kennan's name and the expression he had coined, "containment," were anathema to conservative Republicans, so Dulles forced Kennan—along with Nitze and several other prominent Foreign Service officers—out of the State Department.

During the following years, Kennan divided his time between writing and working his 235-acre farm in southern Pennsylvania. His tall and slender figure became a familiar sight in Princeton, where he was appointed a permanent professor at the Institute for Advanced Studies in 1956. He wrote more than a dozen books on diplomatic history and contemporary international relations, frequently focusing upon the formation of mass psychology and its impact on foreign policy. *Soviet-American Relations, 1917–1920: Russia Leaves the War* (Princeton: Princeton University Press, 1956) won the 1957 Pulitzer Prize for history, and *Memoirs, 1925–1950* (Boston: Little, Brown, 1967) won the 1968 Pulitzer Prize for biography. President Kennedy appointed him ambassador to Yugoslavia in 1961–63.

George Kennan has written two volumes of *Memoirs, 1925–1950*, and *1950–1963* (Boston: Little, Brown, 1967, 1972). Both contain excerpts from his private diaries, which are not open to the public; but portions of his correspondence have been accessioned by Princeton University. His early career is discussed in Martin Weil, *A Pretty Good Club: The Founding Fathers of the U.S. Foreign Service* (New York: W. W. Norton, 1978), and his activities during the cold war years are mentioned in Dean Acheson, *Present at the Creation: My Years in the State Department* (New York: W. W. Norton, 1969). Kennan's intellectual influence on Forrestal and others in the Truman administration is analyzed in Lloyd C. Gardner, *Architects of Illusion: Men and Ideas in American Foreign Policy, 1941–1949* (Chicago: Quadrangle Books, 1970).

STEPHEN G. MARSHALL

See also Cold War; Containment

Kennedy, John F.

(29 May 1917–22 November 1963)

Elected to the Eightieth Congress from the Eleventh District of Massachusetts (Boston-Cambridge-Charlestown), John F. Kennedy began his political career as a new-generation Democrat, one influenced only minimally by the social and economic thinking that was behind much of the New Deal. Although his father had been a Roosevelt appointee to the Securities and Exchange Commission and ambassador to Great Britain, Joseph Kennedy and FDR differed on key issues. They had, in fact, become estranged before the president was reelected in 1940.

Young Jack Kennedy, in effect, inherited the hostility that existed toward Ambassador Kennedy. He forever remained the son of the man Truman called "as big a crook as we've got anywhere in this country." Kennedys, according to Truman, cared only for money and power. "Don't drink Scotch, drink bourbon," he told his friends. "Every time you do you put money in Joe Kennedy's pocket."

To Truman, young JFK was nothing more than a rich upstart who would have been nothing without his "daddy." It was his daddy, Truman and everyone else was certain, who engineered and helped "buy" his first election to Congress. Of course, it was true that the ambassador's wealth enabled him to develop an efficient network of support. But it was also true that Jack's own recent reputation as a wartime hero in the South Pacific, exploited to the hilt by the older Kennedy, made it easier to mobilize the district's war veterans. As an early representative of that new postwar electorate, Jack Kennedy quickly became identified as a supporter of government-assisted housing, which was much in demand during that period.

His district called for bread-and-butter liberalism, so he voted against the Taft-Hartley Act (which he privately supported), but he stood with critics of Truman's foreign policy in denouncing the administration for the "loss" of China to the Communists. He also parted with the White House over the adequacy of civil defense and voted to override the president's veto of the McCarran Act. In 1952, the same year the president stepped down and the Democrats nominated Adlai Stevenson, Kennedy defeated Senator Henry Cabot Lodge and took his place in the Eighty-third Congress as a Democratic senator from Massachusetts.

The Truman-Kennedy relationship never really warmed up. There was, at times, some begrudging respect from the ex-president, but he never thought Kennedy should have reached the top in the first place, often citing his youth and inexperience and the problem of having a Roman Catholic on the national Democratic ticket. Their conflict became most public when, just days before Kennedy was nominated, Truman called him an impatient, immature, and inexperienced young man whose only gift was in controlling a prearranged convention. Truman nevertheless joined the applause for Kennedy's inaugural address and, good Democrat that he was, kept his criticism out of the press. "I hope he learns to be a little more outspoken about issues," he told Merle Miller in a private interview, "but I have yet to see it."

For the most complete examination of John F. Kennedy's early career, see Herbert S. Parmet, *Jack: The Struggles of John F. Kennedy* (New York: Dial, 1980). Doris Kearns Goodwin, *The Fitzgeralds and the Kennedys* (New York: Simon & Schuster, 1987) contains the fullest and best-informed account of the backgrounds of those two political families.

HERBERT S. PARMET

Kerr, Robert Samuel

(11 September 1896–1 January 1963)

Governor of Oklahoma, U.S. senator. Robert Samuel Kerr, the son of a tenant farmer, was born in the Chickasaw Nation in Indian Territory. After high school, Kerr taught in a country school to finance a two-year correspondence course from East Central Normal School. At the University of Oklahoma he studied law, but a legal career was not his goal. Early in life he had told his father he wanted three things: a family, a million dollars, and the governorship of Oklahoma. He achieved all three—in that order.

As the founder of Kerr-McGee Oil Industries, Kerr amassed a fortune which enabled him to contribute generously to Democratic candidates at both state and national levels. In 1940 he was elected to the Democratic National Committee, and until his death in 1963, he was the party's most successful and energetic fund-raiser. As governor of Oklahoma (1943–47), he used wartime prosperity to stabilize the state's troubled finances and to develop a diversified industrial base. But his chief contribution was to bring a sense of dignity and maturity that ended Oklahoma's turbulent but colorful era of "Wild West" politics.

Kerr achieved national prominence as the Democratic National Convention's keynote speaker in 1944 where he also helped implement the strategy that resulted in Truman's nomination for the vice presidency. As president, Truman acknowledged his debt by intervening with the Army Corps of Engineers to facilitate Kerr's bold plan to develop the Arkansas River Basin as a navigable inland waterway system.

At six feet three inches tall, the over-two-hundred-pound nonsmoking, teetotalist Kerr had the self-assurance characteristic of men of strong religious beliefs and great wealth. Elected to the Senate in 1948, Kerr allied with the powerful southern leadership. Realizing that effective committee work was the path to influence, he selected the Public Works Committee as his first power base. Before the end of his freshman term, he had vaulted over Democratic colleagues with greater seniority to secure seats on the coveted Senate Finance and Democratic Policy committees. Although he twice refused the position of majority leader in the 1950s, at his death he was acknowledged with respect, if not affection, as "the uncrowned King of the Senate."

Kerr's freshman term in the Senate coincided with Truman's single full term as an elected chief executive. In 1950 Kerr led the congressional forces trying to exempt oil and gas producers from Federal Power Commission regulation. In spite of Truman's assurances to Kerr, Lyndon Johnson, and Sam Rayburn "that he approved the bill and would accept it if passed by Congress," he firmly vetoed the legislation. In 1951, for several days Kerr was the only Democrat to defend the commander in chief against the outrage over MacArthur's firing. It was a gracious gesture from a proud senator whose pet legislative project had been unexpectedly jettisoned a year earlier. Later when Kerr tried for and lost the Democratic presidential nomination in 1952, he defended his failed strategy by saying he had been "assured that Truman would leave the convention alone." Although Kerr felt betrayed in both instances, he privately admitted that a president's constituency and therefore his viewpoint were markedly different from a senator's.

Kerr's power in the Senate developed in the late 1950s and matured only in the two years before his death. As an individual rather than an institutional power, his greatest asset was his undoctrinaire approach to politics. At the end of an exhausting legislative session as John F. Kennedy's "shadow leader," Kerr suffered a heart attack and died in Washington, D.C., in January 1963.

The Robert Samuel Kerr Papers in the Western History Collections, Bizzell Memorial Library at the University of Oklahoma, Norman, consist of public and private papers from 1943 to 1963. The collection is rich in material relating to Kerr's political career as governor and senator, but there is little material on his personal life or business career. There is no comprehensive biography of Kerr. Anne Hodges Morgan's *Robert S. Kerr: The Senate Years* (Norman: University of Oklahoma Press, 1977) analyzes how Kerr acquired and used power through the legislative process. His business activities are examined in John S. Ezell's *Innovations in Energy: The Story of Kerr-McGee* (Norman: University of Oklahoma, 1979). Kerr's obituary appeared in the *New York Times*, 2 January 1963.

ANN HODGES MORGAN

Keyserling, Leon

(22 January 1908–9 August 1987)

Economic adviser to President Truman. Born in Beaufort, South Carolina, Leon Keyserling spent his adult life in New York City and Washington, D.C. The climax of his career was his appointment as chairman of the Council of Economic Advisers through which he contributed significantly to the success of Truman's economic policies. Keyserling's career illustrated an interesting relationship between governmental bureaucracy and the changing tactics of liberalism from the New Deal to the Fair Deal and beyond. In short, Keyserling was a dedicated New Deal liberal who knew how to function in governmental service by shaping his ideas and language to meet the political demands of the time.

In 1928, Keyserling graduated from Columbia University with a major in economics, later pursuing part-time graduate studies in economics at the same school. (Because he lacked a Ph.D. in the field, his later critics rejected his advice, saying he was not a "professional" economist.) He completed a law degree from Harvard in 1931.

His mentor, Rexford Tugwell, brought Keyserling to Washington, D.C., where he served on Jerome Frank's staff at the Agricultural Adjustment Administration and then rather quickly became legislative assistant to Senator Robert F. Wagner. Keyserling was invaluable: he participated in drafting several important acts for the New Deal, particularly the famous 7A section of the National Industrial Recovery Act. After four years with Wagner's office, he was for two years on the staff of the Senate Committee on Banking and Currency. From 1937 to 1946 he was general counsel to the U.S. Housing Authority, later the National Housing Authority.

In 1944 he won second prize in a Pabst Beer essay contest on the postwar economy; his essay "The American Economic Goal" was published in volume fifty-nine of the *American City* (Herbert Stein won first place). Keyserling's themes were the political desirability of economic growth and full employment, ideas that were the ideological foundations of his thought and public service.

Through his relationship to Senator Wagner, Keyserling played a key but hidden role in the writing of the Employment Act of 1946. He was appointed to the first Council of Economic Advisers (CEA). From the beginning Keyserling quarreled with Edwin G. Nourse, the chairman, over a variety of issues. By the end of 1949, Nourse had resigned and liberals lobbied for Keyserling's appointment to the chairmanship. For reasons never made clear in the historical records his appointment came over a year later; meanwhile he served as temporary chairman of the CEA.

Although he had a reputation as an Ivy League liberal ideologue with a large ego and haughty manners, Keyserling worked at keeping in touch with a wide range of politicians, including Robert A. Taft who once provided a letter of commendation. In fact, Keyserling accepted the social objectives of the New Deal, but he often criticized New Deal tactics, particularly any connection with or influence of Keynesian thought. He always kept his audience in mind. Economic growth with government-business cooperation in some type of national planning was his ideal. Truman too had an ambivalent relationship with the New Deal legacy until events pushed him toward his Fair Deal in the election of 1948. And Keyserling's greatest achievement was his articulation of Truman's aspirations and style into the Fair Deal program.

Keyserling's first significant contribution was his work in the Clark Clifford group that mapped Truman's strategy for the election of 1948. As a member of the CEA Keyserling was not shy about his public support of the Chief's politics and policies. In fact Truman and Keyserling's relationship on economic policy was similar to the president's connection with Dean Acheson in foreign policy.

During his tenure on the CEA, Keyserling became closer to President Truman. For example, in a Kansas City speech in 1949, the president, citing Keyserling's figures of a $4,000 minimum family income and $300 million national income as goals, employed the rhetoric of liberal optimism, saying economic growth should be realized through government–private enterprise cooperation and planning. The two men worked closely together in dealing with the fiscal aspects and economic consequences of the Korean conflict, particularly the issues of inflation and price controls. In July 1950, for example, Keyserling, believing the nation was not ready for a mobilization policy, successfully argued against it, and Truman agreed with him.

In line with President Truman's administrative style, he never interfered with Keyserling's public activities—speeches, interviews, and so on. Keyserling's idea of a "National Prosperity Budget" with stated economic goals, government-business cooperation, and an aggressive antitrust policy drew criticism from both liberals and conservatives. But though the president personally was cool to the idea, he stood by his chairman.

In the years of retirement after 1952, Keyserling, a tireless worker, founded and guided the Conference on Economic Progress, a nonprofit, nonpolitical organization concerned with contemporary issues of public policy. He often appeared before congressional hearings dealing with wage contracts and public employees. With other economists, Keyserling helped draft the Full Employment and Balanced Growth Act of 1978 (the Hawkins-Humphrey Act), a fitting expression of his economic philosophy.

His career was long and distinguished—he took part in or commented on American politics from the New Deal to the "Reagan Revolution." But the centerpiece of his career was his participation in the Truman administration. As Alonzo Hamby observed, Keyserling "had defined important goals for the Administration—there were many ways of promoting economic growth—and had captured the friendship and admiration of the president." Indeed, it was a real achievement for a man of ideas in a world of governmental bureaucracy.

Harry S Truman: The Man from Independence, ed. William F. Levantrosser (New York: Greenwood Press, 1986) is essential reading; the essays cover a wide range of topics: Leon H. Keyserling, "Harry S Truman: The Man and the President," pp. 235–44, is a firsthand evaluation; Donald K. Pickens, "Truman's Council of

Economic Advisers and the Legacy of New Deal Liberalism," pp. 245–64, provides a broad historical context. Despite his underestimation of Keyserling's contributions, Robert J. Donovan's two volumes, *Conflict and Crisis: The Presidency of Harry S Truman, 1945–1948* and *Tumultuous Years: The Presidency of Harry S Truman, 1949–1953* (New York: Norton, 1977, 1982) are good, solid narratives.

DONALD K. PICKENS

See also Council of Economic Advisers; Economy, The (and photograph); Inflation

Key West, Florida

In November 1946, President Truman took the first of eleven working vacations in Key West, Florida. The trips, scheduled once or twice a year, usually during Washington's colder months, afforded Truman the opportunity to escape the frenetic activity of the capital, provided him with a hideaway for uninterrupted meetings with his staff and other officials, and, most important, allowed him time to relax. Fishing, sunbathing, card games, and touring reinvigorated the president, even if he was not able to escape completely from the demands of his office. From the Little White House, as his quarters at a naval submarine station were called, Truman monitored domestic and international events, met frequently with the press, drafted speeches, and devised political strategy.

Even when Truman was not in Key West, the Little White House was used for government business, as in March 1948, when the secretary of defense and Joint Chiefs of Staff met there to work out an agreement on the respective roles of the military services. After the president left office in 1953, he made four visits to the Key West retreat as a private citizen.

Files on the Key West retreat are located in the Harry S. Truman Library, Independence. The house is mentioned in Truman's *Memoirs*, vol. 2, *Years of Trial and Hope* (Garden City, N.Y.: Doubleday, 1956).

LAWRENCE A. YATES

Kline, Allan Blair

(10 November 1895–14 June 1968)
President, American Farm Bureau Federation, 1947–54. Born in Waterbury, Nebraska, Allan Kline received a B.A. from Morningside College in Sioux City, Iowa, and thereafter farmed in the state. His election as president of the American Farm Bureau Federation in 1947 represented a shift from a cotton to a corn orientation for the bureau. Under his leadership, the bureau supported flexible price supports and accepted the possibility of quotas as a part of national agricultural policy.

Kline supported the concept of full food production and, if necessary, subsidization of food consumption. Although he op-

posed controls on production, he felt that if they were established, there should be a central authority over them.

Kline kept the Farm Bureau behind flexible price supports at its 1948 convention, further moving the organization away from southerners who supported rigid price supports. After the election of 1948, he believed that Truman received the farm vote that year because of the flexible support features of the 1948 agricultural bill.

Kline vigorously opposed the plan proposed by Secretary of Agriculture Charles F. Brannan in 1949. He objected to the governmental controls required for farmers to receive price guarantees, thought that the government would intrude on all aspects of farming as a result of the plan, and was concerned about the extensive costs of administration the plan would entail. He also opposed the restriction on the cut-off formula in the Brannan Plan, which would have had an adverse impact on those with large farms, a group heavily represented in the bureau. Flexible price supports were adequate to adjust production, he believed.

During the Korean War, Kline attacked the Office of Price Stabilization and its effort in early 1951 to control inflationary prices and wages. His position was that any controls tended to destroy American freedom.

He also led Farm Bureau criticism of Secretary Brannan's effort in 1951 to evaluate the contribution of the Department of Agriculture to family farms. Kline and the bureau argued that it was a political ploy and an effort to build support for Brannan's farmer production controls and payments.

Kline, who served as president of the bureau until 1954, also continued on the Board of Directors of the Federal Reserve Bank of Chicago in the years after the Truman administration. He became during this period active in trade negotiations.

Allen J. Matusow, *Farm Policies and Politics in the Truman Years* (Cambridge: Harvard University Press, 1967), and Leo M. Christenson, *The Brannan Plan: Farm Politics and Policies* (Ann Arbor: University of Michigan Press, 1959), are good sources of information on agricultural issues during the Truman years.

JAMES L. FORSYTHE

See also Agriculture; Brannan, Charles Franklin

Korean War

Harry Truman was at his home in Independence when the Korean War broke out on a quiet Saturday evening (24 June 1950, Washington time), and his secretary of state advised that he remain there. Remain there he did, for one fateful day in which the secretary and his close advisers acted to propel American involvement in war on the Asian mainland. We may take this sequence as symbolic of the president's relationship to Korea policy throughout his administration: he was often as distant from critical decisions as Korea was distant from his preoccupations. Yet events in Korea paralleled critical policy shifts in the Truman years and ultimately "destroyed" his administration, in the words of the man who made most of the decisions—Dean Acheson.

The president had no hand in the original American policy toward Korea, a multilateral postwar trusteeship, because it was "Roosevelt's baby" (in Averell Harriman's words). Franklin Roosevelt thought Korea, like Indochina, would need some years of tutelage after release from colonial bondage to prepare Koreans for independence, to give the Soviets some say in a country on their border, and to stave off radical nationalist movements. The State Department clung to this vintage example of internationalism through early 1947, in spite of widespread opposition to the policy both from Koreans and from Americans in the U.S. military government that ran southern Korea from 1945 until 1948.

Harry Truman was temperamentally little inclined toward Roosevelt's penchant for ambiguous artifice, preferring the certainties of troops on the ground and, later, containment of communism. On 25 August 1945, the daily journal of the American occupation army (then on Okinawa) had Truman "anxious to have Korea occupied promptly," this coming two weeks after the American decision to divide Korea into Soviet and American occupation zones. When Jimmie Byrnes returned four months later from a foreign ministers' conference with Soviet agreement to a modified version of Roosevelt's trusteeship program, he found the president dissatisfied with him and tired of "babying the Soviets."

Truman was more influenced at this time by the views of George Kennan and Ambassador Harriman, both of whom refracted events in Korea through the prism of Soviet behavior in Eastern Europe, and by his friend Edwin Pauley, who told him in mid-1946, after his survey of Korea, that Communists were threatening to take over the industrial facilities left in Korea by the Japanese, and therefore that the United States ought to hold on in Korea "until a democratic (capitalistic) form of government is assured." It is, however, unlikely that the president paid much attention to Korea. Yet it is from early 1946 that Korean policy begins to move in tandem with the broader shifts in American global policy that define the origins of the cold war.

When the president enunciated his Truman Doctrine, Korea was right behind Greece and Turkey as a key containment country. The prime mover here was Acheson, then an under secretary who often functioned as acting secretary of state during the famed "fifteen weeks" in the spring of 1947. The State Department developed a $600 million package of economic and military aid for southern Korea, and Acheson testified secretly in Congress that Korea was a place where the United States had drawn the line against communism. Congress and the Pentagon balked at this kind of expenditure for Korea, however, and so Acheson sought collective security through the United Nations. There John Foster Dulles guided various resolutions through to the conclusion that the government of Syngman Rhee, inaugurated as the Republic of Korea (ROK) in August 1948, could claim to be recognized by the United Nations. Thus Dulles became recognized as "the father of the ROK," to Koreans if not

U.S. Marines catch up on lost sleep after five days and nights of fighting along the southern tip of the Choisin Reservoir, Korea. (U.S. Marine Corps photo by Sergeant F. C. Kerr)

to a distant president who perhaps wondered what this quintessential Republican was doing in acting on behalf of his administration.

The State Department wanted containment in Korea not because the peninsula was intrinsically important but because it symbolized the prestige of American commitments around the globe. The Pentagon thought Korea the wrong place to make a stand in time of general war and wanted American troops to come home. That they did at the end of June 1949, but left behind was a larger American military advisory group and a bigger aid mission than that in Greece and Turkey. The line was still drawn in Korea, in spite of the absence of American ground forces (there were none in Greece or Turkey, either). Perhaps the president understood this, because when the war broke out he remarked that Korea was another Greece, only later inflating his rhetoric to call it another Munich.

Acheson sought to define the ambiguities of indirect containment in his famous Press Club speech on 12 January 1950, where he seemed to leave the ROK outside a "defense perimeter" that he drew all by himself, with no consultation with the president. In fact this speech was to be the public version of NSC 48, a document that Truman signed at the end of 1949 and that represented a thorough reappraisal of Asia policy inaugurated six months earlier as Mao's forces consolidated their victory in China. Essentially the new policy brought containment to Asia, including Indochina, months before the Korean War, with a commitment to "check" and "where possible to reduce" the spread of communism. Containment had already come to Korea, de facto, but Acheson didn't want Syngman Rhee to know this, lest he take off north across the thirty-eighth parallel. Thus the ambiguity at the Press Club.

Although Korea policy in 1945–50 has a retrospective coherence, given what we know now, it was based on a bad misreading of the forces contending for dominance on the peninsula. The Americans thought they could quickly disestablish the widespread leftist movement they found in the South in the fall of 1945, if the occupation were allowed to do "the few things" deemed necessary "on the spot" (in John J. McCloy's words). But this led to a major rebellion in several provinces in the fall of 1946 and then to a guerrilla insurgency that occupied much of the Korean army's attentions in 1948–50.

The North Korean Communists under Kim Il Sung (who established his leadership under Soviet auspices in 1946 and who was thought to be masquerading as a resistance leader against the Japanese) were always perceived to be incapable of action independent of Soviet desires. Yet Kim had fought in Manchuria from 1932 onward, as had many others in the top leadership, and by 1950 at least half their army had also fought in the Chinese civil war—a little known fact that accounts both for the North's initial battle successes in the summer of 1950, and in part for the Chinese decision to come to North Korea's aid toward the end of the year.

The assumption of Soviet wire-pulling dictated U.S. involvement when the People's Army leaped across the parallel in June 1950. Once again the critical decisions were pushed forward by Acheson and ratified by Truman. On 27 June the president ordered American air and naval forces into the fray and three days later committed ground troops. By terming this a "police action," Truman was able through his executive powers to bypass Congress's responsibility for declaring war—immediately outraging conservative senator Robert Taft of Ohio. The United Nations resolved that the North Koreans had committed "a breach of the peace and an action of aggression," and approved the creation of a United Nations Command under Gen. Douglas MacArthur. Although fifteen nations later sent some form of support for the war effort, the United States provided the great bulk of ground troops, air and naval forces, supplies, and money—often bearing the costs for allied contingents. The first American soldiers entered the fighting on 4 July south of Seoul, where they were cut to pieces by North Korean units.

Acheson later called this set of decisions "the finest hour" of Truman's administration. For him Korea was not important in itself; rather, these events would galvanize the resolve of America and its allies, especially in Europe, and help push through a reluctant Congress the enormous new defense commitments entailed in NSC 68. It was the latter consideration that led him to remark in 1954, "Korea came along and saved us." But the Korean War also induced schizophrenia in Acheson: by late 1950 the Truman policies had led to "the worst American defeat since Bull Run" and a crisis that, he said later, destroyed the administration. The ostensible causes of this were China's intervention in the war and the provocative behavior of MacArthur, but they actually ran to the deep splits within the administration itself.

Throughout much of the summer, Americans watched as a peasant army, with no air cover and limited capacity for resupply, and supposedly doing Russian bidding, outfought American and South Korean forces. North Korean units kept rolling southward in three waves in July: main force units pressed down from Seoul, capturing the city of Taejon and an American general, William F. Dean; the Sixth Division swept through the Southwest and turned abruptly for an eastward march toward Pusan; and units on the east coast pressed southward also toward Pusan. Although by early August they had gobbled up seven-eights of the peninsula, MacArthur, with the introduction of the American First Marine Division, was able to hold a line in the Southeast known as the Pusan Perimeter. Fighting was still intense and precarious along the perimeter on 15 September when MacArthur launched a tactically brilliant invasion at the port of Inchon. Within ten days Seoul was recaptured, and the North Korean army seemed to have been destroyed. The status quo ante June 1950 was restored.

Truman and Acheson had entered this war with the intention of implementing containment and punishing aggression; it was a war for the defense. But other members of the administration—the defense secretary, Louis Johnson, State's top Asia man, Dean Rusk, the new roving ambassador, John Foster Dulles—embodied a policy that went beyond containment, to a taking of the initiative colloquially known as "rollback." This emphasis was reflected in NSC 48's commitment not just to check communist advance but to "reduce" it where feasible.

By mid-July, Johnson, Rusk, Dulles, and others were pushing for a policy that would unite Korea, not just restore the thirty-eighth parallel. What little opposition there was to this policy (mainly from George Kennan and elements in the CIA) melted away in the wake of MacArthur's victory at Inchon. Thus the president approved NSC 81 in late September, officially authorizing a rollback into North Korea. Rollback was MacArthur's policy as well, but it cannot be blamed on him: a broad coalition backed the march to the Yalu. South Korean patrols crossed the parallel on 30 September, and the fateful race was on. A week later, and after much misgiving, the United Nations also resolved to back the entry into the North. Thus began the one serious attempt in postwar history to demolish an established Communist regime.

Chinese and North Korean materials now available make several interesting things clear: first, that Inchon was no surprise to the North Koreans—they just could not do anything about an amphibious landing involving a flotilla of 270 ships and phalanxes of air cover; second, that People's Army officers were ordered to pull back rapidly ahead of onrushing allied troops, except for a temporary defense of Seoul and Pyongyang, to regroup in northern mountains; third, that by doing so they meant to suck the UN forces into the North (thus to stretch their supply lines), and suck the Chinese into entering the battle.

By early August the Chinese were beginning to send signals that they would not tolerate an occupation of North Korea, and by late September, coterminous with the NSC 81 decision, they resolved to enter the fighting—both to safeguard their important political/industrial frontier in the Northeast and to pay the Koreans back for their participation in the civil war. The first Chinese "volunteer" units crossed the Yalu around 15 October, just as Truman flew out for an odd and much-debated meeting with MacArthur at Wake Island—their first ever. The president was worried about Chinese involvement and about a field general whom he did not trust, but he also wanted to bask in MacArthur's popularity with congressional elections around the corner.

On 24 October MacArthur, utilizing the wide latitude given him by the Joint Chiefs of Staff, ordered UN forces to advance all the way to the border with China; they reached the Yalu at Chosan two days later. Just then a combined Sino-Korean army came roaring out of the mountains to decimate American and South Korean units, only to fade away after a few days of intense fighting. This thrust was combined with Chou En-lai's active diplomacy to get the UN forces to withdraw. On 4 November Chou stated that the main American objective was not Korea but China itself, something that was probably true of MacArthur if not Truman. But for three weeks after 6 November, Chinese forces stayed out of the battle; it was the last chance to avert a Sino-American showdown.

Truman and Acheson thought the Chinese were bluffing and continued to back MacArthur, although the CIA became increasingly worried about the large numbers of Chinese entering Korea. At a press conference on 16 November, Truman said that he had no interest in a conflict with China. But by now the rollback momentum was being carried by events in the field, as MacArthur prepared for an ill-concealed final offensive—his armies divided in two (the Eighth Army and the Tenth Corps) for reasons that still vex military historians, his armies facing a combined Sino-Korean force of at least 300,000 soldiers, now registering frequently in intelligence surveys. The offensive jumped off on 24 November, and again American forces made it to the Yalu River. But then the Chinese and North Koreans struck en masse, sending MacArthur's forces reeling back in perhaps the worst defeat ever suffered by an American army. Within two weeks Pyongyang was again under North Korean control, and by New Year's Day, 1951, the enemy unleashed an offensive that retook Seoul.

In Washington the worst crisis of the postwar period—in many ways graver than the Cuban missile crisis, with widespread belief in the imminence of World War III—led to moments of near panic in the cabinet, a declaration of national emergency by the president, and increases in defense spending to $50 billion—three times its level when the war began. Important voices in the Defense Department wanted to evacuate Korea, fearing for the American position in Japan and Europe. The State Department urged continued fighting in Korea, as always on the argument that withdrawal would deal a stiff blow to American prestige and commitments around the world.

The crisis eased with Gen. Matthew Ridgway's success in restoring vigor and morale to UN forces, culminating in the recapture of Seoul for the last and final time in February, combined with fairly clear indications that China's goal was to restore North Korea, not march again on Pusan. By now the administration had given up the rollback policy in favor of a cease-fire that would maintain a divided Korea; it was concerned with a rising neoisolationism in the United States and with restoring confidence in American policy among the allies, especially the British. Senator Taft on 5 January had accused Truman of usurping authority "in violation of the laws and the Constitution" to fight "an undeclared war," and Herbert Hoover had called for a neoisolationist "Gibraltar of the West."

It was at this time, therefore, that Korea became "the limited war," and it was the Chinese who limited it. MacArthur, of course, refused to countenance a stalemate that had resulted from an American defeat; limited war was an oxymoron to a man who believed in no "substitute for victory." The problem was that his victories had called forth new wars, and Truman had no stomach for war on the China mainland. On 7 March MacArthur complained that he could not strike at China's warmaking potential, a week later he defied Truman by saying the American goal should be "the unification of Korea," and on 24 March he destroyed Truman's cease-fire initiative by openly calling for attacks on China. The last straw came when MacArthur sent a telegram lambasting Truman's policy to Republican critic Joe Martin, the House minority leader.

On 11 April the president relieved the general in what many took to be the finest and most courageous decision of his administration. MacArthur got a hero's welcome without precedent in American history when he landed in San Francisco on 17 April, and Truman's popularity plummeted—all the way to an approval rating of only 24 percent in June 1951. But slowly a reversal of judgment began, as prolonged Senate hearings convinced even Republicans that MacArthur had violated his mandate; eventually the justice of Truman's decision was recognized, and MacArthur faded into retirement—as he himself had predicted in a masterful speech before a joint session of Congress.

By this time Ridgway's generalship and Chinese restraint had brought the battle lines just about to the demarcation line that still exists today between the two Koreas. Thus peace talks began in July 1951, but they did not conclude until two years later, and after a terrible bloodletting—mostly on the Chinese and Korean side. Meanwhile Harry Truman had determined that he would not run for another term, and so the Korean War came to an end only after Dwight Eisenhower became president.

The Korean War exacted a fearful toll in lives, mainly among the Koreans themselves. It was, after all, a *Korean* war, fought over Korean issues—something ill-understood at the time and still missed in most American treatments of the war. Some 33,000 Americans died in the Korean fighting, compared to the total casualty figure of about 4 million, of whom half were Korean civilians. The Chinese lost about 900,000, and both Korean armies about 800,000. Most of the civilian casualties came from American bombing, which left North Korea looking like a moonscape by 1953. Today only the armistice signed on 27 July 1953 holds the peace; there was no peace treaty.

For Americans, the Korean War had far greater significance than is generally recognized. Now frequently termed "the forgotten war," it contributed mightily to the huge defense budgets and global commitments that still define American strategy. While globalizing containment, the results of the war ended serious attempts at rollback, despite Dulles's 1950s rollback rhetoric. National security bureaucracies proliferated apace in the early 1950s, a transformation of the American state matched only by the domestic bureaucracies of the New Deal. The Korean War years fashioned a cold war consensus that still circumscribes political debate, helped on by McCarthyism and in lesser measure by the internal security programs of the Truman administration. The war hastened the partial remilitarization of Japan and West Germany and hardened East-West lines for a generation. A mutually beneficial Sino-American relationship was postponed for two decades, and the "lessons" of Korea deeply shaped American strategy in Vietnam—primarily in defining a victory as a permanently divided Vietnam rather than an invasion of North Vietnam which always raised the specter of another legion of Chinese "volunteers." Thus China limited both the Korean and Vietnam wars and drew the line on American expansion in East Asia.

The literature on the Korean War has taken a quantum leap forward in recent years; those interested in further reading could start with two recent introductory overviews, both of which embody scholarly findings from more demanding monographs: Peter Lowe's *The Origins of the Korean War* (New York: Longman, 1986), which dwells on the 1945–50 prelude, but takes the account up to the Chinese intervention, and Burton Kaufman's *The Korean War* (Philadelphia: Temple University Press, 1986), which covers the years 1950–53 and emphasizes the broad range of American domestic reaction to the war. Glenn Paige's *The Korean Decision* (Glencoe, Ill.: Free Press, 1968) has the best narrative account of the Truman administration's decision to intervene in Korea. Bruce Cumings has sought to balance the Korean side of the war with the American in *The Origins of the Korean War*, the first volume of which appeared in 1981 (Princeton: Princeton University Press), with the second volume due out from the same publisher in 1989, carrying the story to early 1951. Recent scholarly accounts by diplomatic historians include William Stueck's *The Road to Confrontation* (Chapel Hill: University of North Carolina Press, 1981), James Matray's *The Reluctant Crusade* (Charlottesville: University of Virginia Press, 1986), and Rosemary Foot's *The Wrong War* (Ithaca, N.Y.: Cornell University Press, 1986). I. F. Stone's *The Hidden History of the Korean War* (1952; reprint, Boston: Little, Brown, 1988) still makes for fascinating reading, and he got most things right in a critical account based on close reading of newspapers. The best military history is Roy Appleman, *South to the Naktong, North to the Yalu* (Washington, D.C.: U.S. Government Printing Office, 1961), although it covers only the first six months of the war. Ronald Caridi's *The Korean War and American Politics* (Philadelphia: University of Pennsylvania Press, 1968) is a good study of the impact of the war on domestic politics. The best study of China's involvement is still Allen Whiting, *China Crosses the Yalu* (Stanford, Calif.: Stanford University Press, 1960).

BRUCE CUMINGS

See also China; Cold War; MacArthur, Douglas; Military Spending; United Nations

L

Labor

Labor, organized and unorganized, pledged its cooperation with government and industry in mobilizing the American economy for World War II and thereafter supported the war effort. Although differences of opinion and occasional breakdowns in labor-management relations occurred, labor generally maintained its pledge during the wartime emergency. After V-J Day, however, worker anger and frustration that had been building steadily during the war burst forth into an unprecedented period of industrial conflict that brought the American economy dangerously close to collapse, thus providing Harry Truman with one of the most serious challenges of his presidency.

During the years immediately preceding the war, labor unrest had revolved around problems of unemployment and union organization. Such was not the case during the war. Indeed, jobs were plentiful, overtime was available to almost all employees, and union recognition was urged in most war labor programs. The primary problems, then, related to wage rates and the effort of many employers to use the wartime emergency either to maintain or to reestablish their hegemony over the workplace. The wage problem grew from the administration's effort to control inflation through the use of price and wage controls. Demands by workers in "Little Steel" precipitated the latter. Workers in the nation's smaller steel companies (those other than United States Steel) were demanding a dollar-a-day wage increase to compensate for increased prices and adjust prevailing inequities.

In response the War Labor Board announced the "Little Steel Formula," which became the administration's wage control policy. The formula limited wage increases during the war to the 15 percent rise in the cost of living that had occurred between 1 January 1941 and 1 May 1942. While labor generally supported the effort to control inflation, including the use of wage controls, it did so only on condition that prices also be controlled and that existing inequities be adjusted. The administration's failure to hold the line on prices and its frequent insensitivity to existing inequalities created considerable unrest.

During 1943 alone 13 million man days of labor were lost to strikes, most of them short term and unauthorized. A few, such as the strikes in the coal fields, were called and led by union leaders, creating intense public antipathy toward the union movement.

Industrial unrest during and after World War II created a political dilemma for Democratic administrations. Working-class political influence had grown along with the organized labor movement during the 1930s, and by the early 1940s, labor had become a critically important element in the Democratic coalition upon which the party's electoral fortunes rested. Moreover, organized labor's sophistication in the exercise of its political power had grown apace. After the liberal electoral setback in the 1942 elections, the Congress of Industrial Organizations replaced its Non-Partisan League with a Political Action Committee headed by Sidney Hillman, which took a very active role in the 1944 general elections. Meanwhile, public attitudes toward organized labor had grown increasingly hostile because of sit-down strikes during the thirties and wartime strikes, particularly those led by John L. Lewis of the United Mine Workers.

Thus, when Harry Truman took the oath of office as the nation's thirty-second president on 12 April 1945, he confronted a difficult and confusing political and industrial relations environment that required great wisdom and tact. At times, especially in the early months of his administration, he seemed to be exercising very little of either.

As a visible member of Tom Pendergast's Democratic organization in Kansas City and Jackson County, Harry Truman's labor support had come naturally in his early campaigns. Kansas City's political boss had developed a good working relationship with the city's labor movement, many leaders of which were themselves integral members of the Pendergast machine. To be sure, Truman occasionally offended labor while serving as presiding judge of the Jackson County Court. Nevertheless, local labor leaders staunchly supported him in all his campaigns, including his two contests for the U.S. Senate. The importance of the Pendergast connection was especially evident in those Senate races, as organized labor in the eastern areas of the state exhibited less enthusiasm for Truman's candidacy and worried about his close connections with the Pendergast organization. In the general elections, however, labor rallied around Truman as the Democratic party candidate.

Truman's Senate voting record established him as a loyal New Deal Democrat and a good friend of organized labor. Although he voted for a resolution condemning the sit-down strike, he also voted against the antilabor Smith-Connally bill, and supported such important labor legislation as the National Labor Relations Act (Wagner Act), the Fair Labor Standards Act, and a bill prohibiting the use of strikebreakers and spies in labor disputes. Truman, however, earned his most enthusiastic accolades from organized labor for his work as chairman of the Special Committee to Investigate the National Defense Program (the Truman committee). Although he condemned wartime strikes and urged labor leaders "to act responsibly" during the emergency, the Truman committee's reports on defense contracting were considered honest and fair and earned the Missouri senator the confidence of labor leaders representing both the American Federation of Labor (AFL) and the Congress of Industrial Organizations (CIO). That goodwill became especially important in 1944 as Franklin Roosevelt and the national Democratic party leadership made decisions concerning the vice-presidential nominee that year. Ultimately, Truman was the only one of four potential candidates who was totally acceptable to labor. The CIO supported the incumbent, Henry Wallace, but Wallace was unacceptable to the AFL; the leadership of both federations opposed James Byrnes, and neither felt entirely comfortable with William O. Douglas. Consequently, Truman quickly became the compromise choice of the labor movement as well as the party as a whole.

Although a strong advocate of the organized labor movement, Truman did feel that labor leaders had a responsibility to use their power and influence to protect and defend the public welfare even on those occasions when doing so threatened labor's short-term interests. Obviously, Truman and labor leaders did not always view labor's responsibility and the public welfare in precisely the same way; during the immediate postwar years, this was to inspire a bitter conflict between Truman and his oldest labor allies, the railroad brotherhoods.

Truman's relationship with the labor movement began to disintegrate almost immediately after he took the presidential oath of office. The problems of reconversion to peacetime production without a crippling recession, runaway inflation, or massive unemployment weighed heavily on the new president's mind, and he often dealt summarily with those who appeared to threaten his postwar economic design. This certainly appeared to be the case when a postwar strike wave threatened to overwhelm the nation in the days immediately following V-J Day. A series of strikes signaled by a walkout in the petroleum industry in September 1945 was precipitated by a number of circumstances: the termination of the Little Steel Formula, the relaxation of federal wage controls and the return to collective bargaining, problems associated with reconversion that resulted in a reduction in the hours of labor, an associated decline in take-home pay, and a determination by management to reestablish its authority and control over the workplace.

The administration's response to this unprecedented outbreak of industrial conflict took a number of forms. A National Labor-Management Conference was convened in Washington

Philip Murray, president of the CIO, calls for repeal of the Taft-Hartley Act at the opening session of the Oil Workers International Convention, 1 September 1952. (Associated Press/Wide World Photos)

in November 1945 to promote harmony between the two. Although the results were disappointing and the conference itself was generally regarded as a failure, it did focus national attention on the difficult problems of economic reconversion and the need for a national policy to govern conflict resolution in critical industries.

The perceived desirability of such machinery was enhanced by an automobile workers' strike against the General Motors Corporation that occurred shortly before the conference adjourned. Many in the administration, including Secretary of Labor Lewis Schwellenbach and President Truman, had become increasingly committed to the type of fact-finding boards and cooling-off periods that had been written into the Railway Labor Act of 1926, and in early December 1945, Truman appointed such a board to investigate the issues involved in the General Motors strike. Meanwhile, he called upon automobile workers to go back to work while waiting for the board to report its findings. He then further shocked his labor allies by calling for legislation that would have mandated such a fact-finding procedure in certain instances. Philip Murray of the CIO characterized the Truman proposal as a "union-busting" measure that would ultimately destroy labor organizations, and Walter Reuther of the United Automobile Workers quickly rejected Truman's back-to-work request. Whereas some liberals viewed the Truman proposals as an effective ploy to undercut the advocates in Congress of even more repressive legislation, labor leaders generally regarded the Truman proposals as a break with the prolabor policies of the Roosevelt administration. Thereafter, the relationship between the administration and the labor movement grew steadily more antagonistic.

By February 1946 over 2 million workers had gone on strike. The single largest group belonged to the United Steelworkers of America, which was demanding a wage increase of two dollars a day. Meanwhile, strikes also hit the mining and railroad industries. The strikers demanded more than the 18.5 cents an hour Truman had recommended in the steel industry dispute as well as the resolution of a number of nonwage issues.

Efforts to end the strike failed, however, and the administration seized the mines and railroads and resumed their operation under government supervision. Two of the railroad brotherhoods (the Brotherhood of Locomotive Engineers and the Brotherhood of Railway Trainmen) rejected a settlement that had been accepted by eighteen other railway unions, and struck on 23 May 1946, paralyzing the nation's railroad transportation network. An angry president addressed the Congress asking, among other things, for authority to draft striking workers into the armed forces.

Chastising his former allies in the labor movement and challenging the unpopular John L. Lewis perhaps salved the president's wounded ego and soothed public opinion, but ultimately it proved beneficial primarily to his political adversaries. As the president increasingly focused his anger on labor while ignoring the intransigence of industry leaders who often were responsible for precipitating industrial disputes, he helped create a climate of public opinion fostering the promotion of the antireform, antilabor legislation he would then have to spend much of the remainder of his administration trying to fend off. Meanwhile, his relationship with the labor movement, a crucial element of the coalition Roosevelt had so effectively put together, reached its nadir.

The postwar strike wave plus fears of Communist-inspired labor radicalism fed a growing anti-Communist frenzy and everything associated in the public mind with the "red menace." The combination proved disastrous for the Democratic party and its labor allies in the mid-term elections of 1946. Smarting from its conflicts with the Truman administration, the labor movement devoted little time or energy to the congressional elections, especially in terms of getting out the prolabor Democratic vote. In the end, a very low voter turnout redounded much to the advantage of the Republican party. Only 73 of 318 House and 5 of 21 Senate candidates endorsed by labor's Political Action Committee were elected. For the first time since 1928, the Republicans secured majorities in both houses of the Congress, and they then used that control to launch a full-scale attack on organized labor and the New Deal.

In fact, even before the convening of the Eightieth Congress in January 1947, the labor movement had already witnessed a deluge of hostile legislative initiatives on both the state and the federal levels, including the Smith Act, the Case Act, and the Hobbs Act. With public sentiment now clearly favoring amendments to the National Labor Relations Act to "equalize" bargaining power between labor and management, labor leaders were forced to make their peace with Truman. He clearly represented the last bastion of defense against a hostile Congress.

For labor, however, the rapprochement came too late. Hostile legislation, titled the Labor-Management Relations Act, easily passed both houses of Congress, severely restricting certain industrial and political practices in which labor had engaged. Truman vetoed the measure, firmly recementing his relationship with the labor movement, but Congress quickly overrode the veto, and the bill became law. The Taft-Hartley Act, as it came to be widely known, closely followed the provisions favored by the National Association of Manufacturers. It defined certain labor practices as "unfair," forbade unions to engage in them, and contained a hodgepodge of other restrictions that significantly altered the national labor policy developed under the New Deal.

Charles Werner, *Indianapolis Star*, 12 August 1952.

Reversing the lethargy that had characterized its approach to the 1946 mid-term elections, the labor movement sought to make the 1948 general elections a referendum on the Taft-Hartley Act and the other antireform measures passed by the Republican Eightieth Congress. In the face of the Dixiecrat challenge from the right and the Wallace candidacy on the left, organized labor rallied around Truman for the Democratic presidential nomination and in the general elections. It also took a very active role in congressional elections, supporting the candidacies of those who promised to vote for the repeal of Taft-Hartley and campaigning against those who had voted for the offensive legislation. The result was a stunning reversal of the Republican victory two years earlier. Although voter turnout remained low, labor obviously got its vote out, and it claimed a great victory. Truman, whom virtually every prognosticator had consigned to defeat, was reelected, and labor claimed credit for the election of 16 prolabor senators and 172 congressmen. Despite the election victories, however, the conservative coalition in Congress remained strong enough to turn back labor's efforts to alter substantially the Taft-Hartley Act. Again in the 1950 congressional elections, the labor movement sought to elect senators and representatives sympathetic to its cause, but a symbolic effort to defeat Ohio senator Robert A. Taft, cosponsor of the offensive legislation, failed as did several other efforts to unseat hostile legislators.

While the legislative front commanded much labor attention during Truman's second term, other issues with both economic and political implications continued to plague both the administration and the labor movement. The undermining of price controls following the wage settlements of 1946 created an inflationary surge that soon wiped out the increased purchasing power workers had secured in earlier negotiations. Although labor achieved important wage concessions in the second round of postwar wage negotiations, union leaders worried that another price increase would simply create another wage-price spiral that would again erode labor's hard-fought gains.

Among other proposals, labor's program for confronting this difficult economic dilemma included price and rent controls and an increased minimum wage as well as a variety of fringe benefits, such as pension funds, health and welfare programs, and vacation and holiday pay. The economic recession of 1949 led to demands for greater unemployment compensation coverage and eventually to another round of wage negotiations. After American intervention in the Korean War, labor again sought an effective price control program. The Economic Stabilization Agency the Truman administration created under the provisions of the Defense Production Act of 1950 failed to control inflation, and labor charged that Defense Mobilization director Charles E. Wilson, whom Truman had appointed to administer the program, was insensitive to labor concerns. Consequently the labor representatives on the Economic Stabilization Agency resigned, demanding creation of a more effective price control policy and more stringent rent controls. Although this action once again strained the relationship between Truman and his labor allies, eventually it resulted in the creation of a more effective price stabilization agency and in tighter rent control provisions in the Defense Production Act of 1951.

Despite all the acrimony that periodically disrupted Truman's relationship with organized labor, the Roosevelt-Truman years marked a significant watershed in the power and influence of the labor movement in American politics. Although labor leaders were once again welcomed to the White House during the Kennedy and Johnson administrations, they came more as suppliants than as power brokers in their own right.

Several good scholarly studies examining labor policies during the Truman years are now in print. Among the better are R. Alton Lee, *Truman and Taft-Hartley: a Question of Mandate* (Lexington: University of Kentucky Press, 1966); Arthur F. McClure, *The Truman Administration and the Problems of Postwar Labor, 1945–1948* (Cranbury, N.J.: Associated University Presses, 1969); and Maeva Marcus, *Truman and the Steel Seizure Case: The Limits of Presidential Power* (New York: Columbia University Press, 1977).

GARY M. FINK

See also Dubinsky, David; Employment Act of 1946; Green, William; Hillman, Sidney; Lewis, John L.; Murray, Philip; National Labor Relations Board; Railroad Unions; Reuther, Walter P.; Schwellenbach, Lewis B.; Taft-Hartley Act; Truman Committee

Labor-Management Relations Act of 1947

See Taft-Hartley Act

Lamar, Missouri

Harry Truman's birthplace. Platted in 1857, Lamar, Missouri, began rapid growth in 1880–81 when the Kansas City, Ft. Scott, and Gulf Railroad and the Missouri Pacific reached the town. In 1889 it had a population of 3,500. Harry S. Truman was born in a twenty-by-twenty-eight-foot cottage there in 1884. His father, John Anderson Truman, traded in horses and mules in a lot across the street from the home. Young Harry was only ten months old when the family moved away to Harrisonville, Missouri.

He did not return to Lamar until 1934 when he was running for the Senate. Ten years later, on 31 August 1944, he opened his vice-presidential campaign in Lamar, drawing the largest crowd in Barton County's history. Of that event, Truman wrote, "The man who introduced me took up a great deal of time that I was supposed to have so my speech didn't get over very well." Nevertheless, Truman added, "I have always enjoyed visiting in that part of the State." Truman visited his birthplace for the last time on 19 April 1959, the day the home was dedicated and opened to the public.

Another claim to fame for Lamar is the fact that frontier marshall Wyatt Earp began his lawman's career in the town in 1870. One of his cousins, Walter Earp, owned and lived in the Truman birthplace for many years before the United Auto Workers of America purchased it in 1957 and presented it as a gift to the State of Missouri.

A brief but worthy account of Truman's birthplace is available in a pamphlet by N. R. Johnston, *The Harry S. Truman Birthplace* (1973). A few scattered references to Lamar may be found in the President's Personal Files of the White House Central Files in the Truman Library.

NIEL M. JOHNSON

Landis, James McCauley

(25 September 1899–30 July 1964)

Chairman of the Civil Aeronautics Board. James M. Landis was born to missionary parents in Tokyo, Japan, where he spent his first thirteen years. After achieving a brilliant record as a student at Princeton and Harvard Law School, he served as law clerk to Supreme Court justice Louis Brandeis. In 1926 he joined the Harvard Law School faculty, rising to full professor by age twenty-eight, and dean by thirty-seven.

During the New Deal's "first hundred days," Felix Frankfurter invited Landis to Washington to draft the Federal Securities Act. This led to Landis's appointments to the Federal Trade Commission and the Securities and Exchange Commission, which he chaired from 1935 to 1937. During World War II, he served as director of the Office of Civilian Defense, and U.S. economic minister to the Middle East.

After the war, the dissolution of Landis's marriage made life at Harvard unbearable for him. In 1946 he resigned both as

James M. Landis. (National Archives)

dean and as professor to accept President Truman's offer to chair the Civil Aeronautics Board (CAB). Truman considered it a "ten strike" to add to his administration such a prominent New Dealer and recognized authority on federal regulation. Landis leaped at the chance to reenter federal service, but never felt the same admiration or affection for Truman that he had for Franklin Roosevelt.

Landis found the CAB an inefficient agency that had fallen years behind in its case load and had grown susceptible to political influence. He pressed to accelerate procedures and cut work loads to give board members time to plan a coherent national air route system. Yet, as chairman, he had little authority to lead and often voted with the minority. By supporting efforts to open the industry to new competition, Landis frequently battled with the larger, established airlines. He especially opposed Pan American Airways' plan to merge all American overseas flights into a single flag carrier. In response, the airlines lobbied to remove Landis as CAB chairman.

President Truman assured congressional Democrats that he intended to give Landis another term. But on 26 December 1947, Truman called Landis to the White House to say that he had decided against his reappointment. "When I became President, Ed Flynn told me that I'd have to be a son of a bitch half the time," Truman remarked apologetically. "This is one of the times." Congressional leaders retaliated by blocking confirmation of Landis's replacement, and for months the post remained embarrassingly vacant.

When he left the CAB, Landis joined the staff of Joseph P. Kennedy, Sr., an association that also made him an adviser to Senator John F. Kennedy. After Kennedy was elected president, he directed Landis to prepare a study on regulatory reform. The "Landis Report" criticized the Truman and Eisenhower administrations for poor appointments to the commissions. "Jim ought to know something about it," quipped Truman. "He was one of

the appointees." Landis's triumphant return to Washington was cut short by the discovery that he had failed to file income tax returns for several years. He was convicted, sentenced to thirty days imprisonment, and suspended from law practice. Shortly after his release, he drowned accidentally in the swimming pool at his home.

See Donald A. Ritchie, *James M. Landis: Dean of the Regulators* (Cambridge: Harvard University Press, 1980), a full biography, and Thomas K. McCraw, *Prophets of Regulation: Charles Francis Adams, Louis D. Brandeis, James M. Landis, Alfred E. Kahn* (Cambridge: Harvard University Press, 1984), an evaluation of Landis's impact on the evolution of federal regulation.

DONALD A. RITCHIE

See also Aviation, Commercial

Latin America

The Truman administration developed its policies toward Latin America within the context of the cold war, and from a global perspective, the region did not rank as a foreign policy priority. As Soviet-American tensions escalated after World War II, United States policymakers increasingly focused on Europe, the Middle East, and Asia—the initial points of major contention between the two superpowers. Indeed, whereas Europe received about $25 billion in military and economic assistance during the Truman years, the South and Central American nations received less than $1 billion. Yet it would be inappropriate to conclude that the Truman administration ignored Latin America. Indeed, the region was so important to the United States that it could not be neglected.

By 1950 private U.S. investment in the region reached a value of $6 billion, more than any other region of the world except Canada. Latin America in 1950 also purchased approximately $2.7 billion worth of U.S. goods, which amounted to 50 percent of the region's total imports. In addition to these economic interests, nearby Latin America also provided sites for a number of crucial U.S. military bases and contained the strategic Panama Canal. Although the region did not face direct Soviet aggression, the Truman administration feared that it might become a prime target for Communist subversion simply because it was so vital to the United States. Given America's enormous influence in the area, Washington did not deem expensive foreign aid programs to be an essential diplomatic tool in Latin America. Still, the Truman administration worked vigorously to maintain U.S. predominance in the Western Hemisphere and to minimize Soviet influence there.

U.S. officials believed that Communism might make inroads in Latin America, in part, by exploiting long-standing tensions in inter-American relations. During the first third of the twentieth century, frequent U.S. military interventions, especially in the Caribbean region and Central America, had embittered much of Latin American opinion against the "Colossus of the North." Franklin D. Roosevelt proclaimed his Good Neighbor policy in 1933 and pledged nonintervention in the internal affairs of neighboring republics. But Roosevelt preserved much of the United States' influence by cultivating warm relations with unpopular military strongmen such as Anastasio Somoza in Nicaragua and Rafael Trujillo in the Dominican Republic. World War II further demonstrated the limits of Good Neighbor diplomacy, for many of the Latin American nations viewed Washington's elaborate system of mutual defense pacts as another manifestation of Yankee domination.

Economic issues also strained relations. Extensive trade with the United States and other industrial nations had relegated most Latin American economies to a disadvantaged status as suppliers of raw materials and foodstuffs. This mode of development, critics charged, retarded industrial growth and enriched only foreign investors and a small domestic elite. As part of the Good Neighbor dictum, President Roosevelt established the Export-Import Bank and promised financial assistance to spur industrialization. But Ex-Im loans involved only small amounts of capital and were usually directed toward Latin America's traditional export sectors. During the war years the South and Central American nations benefited somewhat from a steady demand for their exports, but at war's end most Latin American economies still centered around the export of one or two primary products.

Harry S. Truman possessed only a superficial knowledge of this history. As a U.S. senator, he had devoted little time to foreign affairs. He did make a brief visit to Mexico and several Central American states in 1939, but it does not appear that he examined conditions in these countries very closely. In one letter to his wife, Bess, Truman referred to President Somoza of Nicaragua, whose acquaintance he had just made, as a "regular fellow." In the same letter, he lavished praise on Guatemala's repressive dictator, Jorge Ubico. Truman showed no indication of understanding that U.S. policies in these countries had nurtured discord as well as friendly authoritarian governments.

By the time Truman became president in 1945, Latin America's discontent had intensified. Long years of resentment had given rise to a number of popularly based nationalist movements such as the Auténticos in Cuba, Acción Democrática in Venezuela, Apra in Peru, the MNR in Bolivia, the Arévelo/Arbenz regime in Guatemala, and the Peronists in Argentina. All espoused a variety of nationalistic political and economic policies, including protective tariffs, restrictions on foreign investment, and in some cases expropriation of private property. The government of Col. Juan D. Perón in Argentina even adopted a neutralist stance in the cold war. Informed observers noted that Latin America's weak Communist parties played no significant part in these movements. But President Truman and his closest advisers believed that Latin American nationalism might easily give way to Soviet intrigue. As George Kennan explained, Latin America was a place from which the Communists could "broadcast their seeds of provocation of hatred and busily tend the plants which sprout in such vigor and profusion."

Downplaying the indigenous roots of Latin American discontent, the Truman administration developed a number of policies designed primarily to protect U.S. interests from Soviet advances in the area. In military affairs, the administration moved to consolidate the regional defense system that had evolved during the war. Most South and Central American nations agreed on the desirability of regional defense, but advocated arrangements that would place restraints on unilateral actions by any member, including the United States. U.S. military planners, however, did not intend to abdicate hemispheric leadership. They were especially eager to maintain access to

wartime bases and to sustain Latin America's dependence on U.S. military supplies. As Assistant Secretary of War John McCloy concluded, regional defense should "protect our concept of preclusive rights in the hemisphere." In the spring of 1945, President Truman followed the Pentagon's advice and gave his approval for an inter-American conference on military organization to be held in Rio de Janeiro the following October.

The proposed Rio Conference faced strong opposition from State Department officials who argued that the region did not face a direct Soviet threat, that the Latin American states could ill-afford a defense buildup, and that militarization would strengthen antidemocratic forces in the region. Some noted the contradiction between the administration's condemnation of a growing Soviet sphere of influence in Eastern Europe and its own pursuit of preclusive rights in the Western Hemisphere. The State Department managed to delay the Rio Conference until March 1947, when President Truman, increasingly alarmed by cold war events in Europe, broke the logjam. "In my opinion," Truman fumed, "the striped pants are trying to run South America. They won't be allowed to do that."

The American states finally gathered at Rio de Janeiro in September 1947 and accepted the Inter-American Treaty of Reciprocal Assistance. The Rio Pact provided that the United States would coordinate the region's defense policy, control the supply of arms and equipment to its allies, and assist in the training of Latin American military officials.

The Truman administration further extended U.S. political and military influence in Latin America the following year at another inter-American conference in Bogotá, Colombia. One of the most important outcomes of the Bogotá Conference was the establishment of the Organization of American States (OAS). The OAS charter expressly forbade intervention, direct or indirect, in the internal and external affairs of any member nation. The United States nonetheless preserved substantial freedom of action by insisting that the organization allow for the adoption of measures "for the maintenance of peace and security in accordance with existing treaties." This loophole facilitated later U.S. interventions in Guatemala (1954) and the Dominican Republic (1965), cases in which the United States argued that Soviet influence in these countries posed a threat to the region.

Under Truman's leadership, the United States worked to protect its economic as well as its political and military interests in Latin America. While the Communist threat was a real concern, Latin American nationalism posed a more immediate danger to U.S. business interests. The Truman administration reacted sharply to state-imposed restrictions on free enterprise and defended the United States' "open door" principles on trade and investments. In Argentina, where the pro-Axis sympathies of the wartime government had already alienated the United States, Ambassador Spruille Braden undertook the most active campaign. In addition to condemning "excessive nationalism" in economic affairs, Braden interfered directly in Argentina's 1946 presidential election by publishing an exposé that alleged Nazi ties to nationalist leader Juan D. Perón. After the Peronists easily won the election, the Truman White House soothed relations with Argentina by recalling Braden and inviting that nation to participate in the Rio Pact. But the problem of economic nationalism in Latin America persisted.

These issues resurfaced in 1948 at the Bogotá Conference. The Latin American representatives demanded that Washington accept commodity agreements that set higher prices for their exports, allow restrictions on foreign investment, and increase the level of U.S. economic assistance. The U.S. delegation, nonetheless, refused to go along with any significant departure in hemispheric economic relations and once again condemned economic nationalism. It did grudgingly offer to increase Export-Import credits by $500 million, but warned that commitments elsewhere limited the United States' ability to help its southern neighbors. Secretary of State George C. Marshall summarized the United States' position when he declared that "private capital, whether domestic or foreign, would have to be counted upon to do the main part of the job."

The unwillingness to extend substantial amounts of economic aid continued throughout the remainder of the Truman presidency. Most administration officials agreed that the region's economic malaise provided the major impetus for political unrest. The president even addressed this problem in his January 1949 inaugural address which called for the establishment of his famous Point Four economic assistance program for lesser developed nations. But the administration failed to rally the Congress behind the program as it had done for the Marshall Plan aid to Europe. As a result, Point Four never involved more than a trickle of funds to Latin America.

After the outbreak of the Korean War in June 1950, the Truman White House did undertake new aid programs in Latin America, but the initiative involved military rather than economic aid. Convinced that Communist North Korean aggression constituted only part of a larger global threat, Truman sought to bolster non-Communist defenses throughout the world, including Latin America. The Mutual Security Program of 1951 complemented the Rio Pact treaty by appropriating $38,150,000 in Latin American military aid for fiscal year 1952. The Truman administration promised that additional military assistance would be forthcoming the next year. These policies helped to align the United States ever more closely with South and Central American military establishments.

By the end of the Truman years, a foundation for postwar inter-American relations had been established. The Truman administration worked out its Latin American policies within the framework of its global, anti-Communist objectives. Underemphasizing regional realities, it often confused Latin American nationalism with communism and at times simply viewed nationalism as a threat to U.S. interests. To maintain its predominant position in the area, the United States used a variety of economic, political, and military resources. The administration relied most heavily, however, on military programs. In the long run, this approach failed to address the region's mounting social and economic problems and often served to heighten Latin American criticisms of U.S. policies. These trends did not augur well for the future of inter-American relations.

The Truman years are covered in a number of works that survey the history of inter-American relations. Donald M. Dozer's *Are We Good Neighbors? Three Decades of Inter-American Relations, 1930–1960* (Gainesville: University of Florida Press, 1961) provides a general overview of U.S. relations with Latin America during the Truman period, highlighting the breakdown of FDR's Good Neighbor policy and wartime cooperation. Bryce Wood's *The Dismantling of the Good Neighbor Policy* (Austin: University of Texas Press, 1985) provides a similar but updated interpretation. In *Inevitable Revolutions: The United States and Central America* (New York: W. W. Norton, 1984), Walter LaFeber focuses on the

Central American nations and emphasizes the continuity from the Roosevelt to the Truman years. Under both administrations, LaFeber observes, the United States worked to maintain a long-established system of "neo-dependency" in the region. In *The United States and South America's Economic Development, 1945–1975* (New York: New Viewpoints, 1976), Samuel Baily examines the Truman administration's emphasis on military rather than economic aid in South America and provides an excellent account of U.S. opposition to economic nationalism. Cole Blasier's *The Hovering Giant: U.S. Responses to Revolutionary Change in Latin America, 1910–1985* (Pittsburgh: University of Pittsburgh Press, 1985) includes an analysis of the Truman administration's difficulties in relations with radical nationalists in Guatemala and Bolivia. For a concise treatment of Truman and Latin America, written from a cold war revisionist perspective, see David Green, "The Cold War Comes to Latin America," in *Politics and Policies of the Truman Administration*, ed. Barton J. Bernstein (New York: New Viewpoints, 1974).

DENNIS MERRILL

Lattimore, Owen

(29 July 1900–31 May 1989)

Owen Lattimore, the author of dozens of books and articles about Asian affairs, is best known as the first public victim of McCarthyism. Born in Washington, D.C., Lattimore spent his childhood in China, his school years in Europe, and his early adult life in central Asia, studying its politics and culture. In 1934 he became the editor of *Pacific Affairs*, published by the Institute of Pacific Relations. Four years later he joined the faculty of Johns Hopkins University as director of the Walter Hines Page School of International Relations. During World War II, Lattimore served as the head of Pacific operations for the Office of War Information. Though never an employee of the State Department, he worked closely with its personnel in the 1940s, and his opinions were respected by those who helped formulate Far Eastern policy.

By 1950 Lattimore had become a major target of the so-called China Lobby, a group of well-placed American journalists, politicians, and business persons who strongly supported the Nationalist government of Chiang Kai-shek. The China Lobbyists claimed, quite correctly, that Lattimore had praised some of the worst abuses of Stalinism, from the Moscow show trials of the late 1930s to the brutal labor camp at Kolyma. What really angered them, however, was Lattimore's belief that Chiang's corrupt and unpopular regime would surely fall to Mao Tse-tung's Communist armies and that America must adjust its policies accordingly. When this happened in 1949, Lattimore was neither surprised nor disappointed. He called for a "flexible policy" in Asia, claiming it was wrong to portray the Chinese Communists as Russian puppets, wrong to deny them diplomatic recognition, and wrong to support junior versions of Chiang in South Korea, Indochina, and elsewhere.

Today, these views on Asia seem remarkably prophetic. At the time, however, the China Lobby (and much of the American Right) equated them with treason. In the spring of 1950, Senator Joseph McCarthy called Lattimore the "top Russian spy" in

America, adding "I believe you can ask almost any school child who the architect of our far eastern policy is, and he will say, 'Owen Lattimore.'" Both statements were preposterous; a special Senate committee described them as "a distortion of the facts on such a magnitude as to be truly alarming." But the damage had been done. In this highly charged atmosphere, people were more willing to believe the accusers than the accused. China had fallen to the Communists, and *someone* had to take the blame. In 1950 that someone was Owen Lattimore.

A few months later, the professor published a book about his troubles, *Ordeal by Slander*. In fact, his ordeal was just beginning. In 1951 the Senate Internal Security Subcommittee decided to investigate the Institute of Pacific Relations, which, it believed, had engineered the "conspiracy" to discredit Chiang Kai-shek. Chaired by Pat McCarran of Nevada, a notorious redbaiter, the committee summoned Owen Lattimore as its primary witness. Lattimore spent twelve days on the stand; his angry interrogation filled almost eight hundred pages. To no one's surprise the committee's final report described him as "a conscious articulate instrument of the Soviet conspiracy."

This was not the end of it. At McCarran's insistence, Lattimore was indicted on seven counts of perjury. The case dragged on for three years before the charges were dismissed. Although Johns Hopkins honorably restored Lattimore's faculty status—he had been suspended during his indictment with full pay—the professor left the United States in 1963 to take a teaching position at Leeds University in England. His ordeal was finally over.

For a first-hand account of Lattimore's battle with the red hunters, see his *Ordeal by Slander* (Boston: Little, Brown, 1950). For other accounts of Lattimore, his political views, and his various struggles, see David Caute, *The Great Fear* (New York: Simon & Schuster, 1978); Stanley Kutler, *The American Inquisition* (New York: Hill & Wang, 1982); and William O'Neill, *A Better World* (New York: Simon & Schuster, 1982).

DAVID M. OSHINSKY

See also McCarran, Patrick Anthony; McCarthy, Joseph R. (and photograph); Red Scare

William D. Leahy. Artist: Bernard Godwin. (Courtesy of the Franklin D. Roosevelt Library)

Leahy, William Daniel

(6 May 1877–20 July 1959)

President's military chief of staff and chairman of the Joint Chiefs of Staff. Born in Hampton, Iowa, the son of a prosperous lawyer, William Leahy moved with his family to Wisconsin when he was still a boy. Leahy wanted to attend West Point but settled instead for an appointment to the Naval Academy. He was a good student, ranking fourteenth among forty-seven members of the Class of 1897 upon graduation. His career as a junior officer was varied and especially exciting. He served on the battleship *Oregon* during her race around Cape Horn in the Spanish-American War and during the Asiatic fleet's bombardment of the Taku Forts in the intervention in China's Boxer Rebellion. Happenstance also placed him on the scene during several interventions by American naval forces in the Caribbean and Central America in the Progressive Era. In 1915 this record brought him to Washington where he became an aide to Navy Secretary Josephus Daniels and formed a lifelong friendship with the young assistant secretary Franklin D. Roosevelt.

When America entered World War I, Leahy took command of the ex-German liner *Matoika*, a troop transport, although he made only one cruise to Brest and back to Norfolk as her skipper before being assigned to Europe to investigate British and French naval gunnery. After the Armistice, he served as senior naval officer afloat in Turkish waters during the Chanak War and the Russian Civil War when, not for the first time, his considerable diplomatic skills were put to the test. After a noteworthy command of the battleship *New Mexico*, he returned to Washington in 1933 when Roosevelt, now president, named his friend to be chief of the powerful Bureau of Navigation. Four years later, FDR picked Leahy to be his second chief of naval operations, a post in which the admiral worked assiduously for fleet expansion until 1939. He retired that year from the navy and was named to the governorship of Puerto Rico.

After the fall of France in World War II, Leahy became ambassador to Vichy, where he established a personal relationship with Marshal Petain that enabled him to persuade Petain not to turn the French fleet over to the Germans. Leahy, however, failed to prevent Vichy from falling completely under German influence in 1942. In July of that year, after the unexpected death of his wife, Leahy was recalled to wartime Washington to become Roosevelt's military chief of staff and the first chairman of the Joint Chiefs of Staff.

As the highest ranking and most influential officer of the armed forces, Leahy performed his greatest service for his country during and after World War II. Articulate and cosmopolitan, Leahy was an enormously talented bureaucrat who shrewdly stayed above the strident interservice disputes over strategy and command that divided the army's General Marshall and the navy's Admiral King. Instead, Leahy provided a conduit between the Joint Chiefs and the White House and became increasingly involved in the conduct of foreign policy. He supported an early second front in France, backed King's plan for the fleet to conduct a Central Pacific offensive against Japan, but sided with MacArthur's proposal to return to the Philippines in 1944. Although Leahy after the war claimed to have opposed on moral grounds the use of the atomic bomb to force Japan to surrender, no written record supports this assertion and considerable evidence exists to refute it.

Leahy disagreed with Roosevelt's wartime policy of appeasing Russia, and when Harry Truman became president in April 1945 and asked Leahy to stay on in the White House, the admiral urged him to take a stiffer line with the Soviets. Leahy was responsible for the premature cancelation of Lend-Lease to Russia in July 1945 and partly responsible for Truman's strong stance in defense of Iran, Turkey, and Greece the following year. Leahy stayed above the fray of the unification fiasco and thereby preserved his unique authority, but he failed to convince Truman to maintain a strong defense after 1946. A persistent backer of the Nationalist Chinese, he also had little impact on Truman's hostile approach to Chiang Kai-shek's crumbling regime.

Illness forced Leahy, now a five-star fleet admiral, to retire at the start of Truman's second term in 1949, but his name appeared atop the navy's active list until his death ten years later. A crafty manipulator, Leahy retained the absolute trust of two presidents who themselves appreciated the shrewd use of power. Nonetheless, few who knew Leahy would have quarreled with Truman's assessment that "there never was a finer man or an abler public servant." Known for his honesty, direct manner, and political pragmatism, Leahy concealed a devout Christianity, humanitarianism, and concern for the moral fate of mankind. In a characteristic passage in his memoirs, he mourned the passing of the chivalrous warfare of the professionals of 1898 and its replacement by the devastation of total war and nuclear weapons which he and his contemporaries had brought about.

Leahy's book of memoirs, *I Was There* (New York: McGraw-Hill, 1950), was based mostly on his multivolume diaries, now located in the Library of Congress. Henry H. Adams's biography, *Witness to Power* (Annapolis: Naval Institute Press, 1985), is poorly researched and does not do justice to its subject. Leahy's personal and official papers, upon which this essay is based, can be found in the Library of Congress, the Naval History Division in the Washington Navy Yard, and the State Archives Building in Madison, Wisconsin.

ROBERT W. LOVE, JR.

See also Joint Chiefs of Staff

Lend-Lease

The means of inter-Allied supply in World War II, Lend-Lease was originally devised to get aid to Britain in 1941. The Neutrality Acts required other nations to pay cash for U.S. supplies. With Britain in dire peril and running out of dollars, Franklin Roosevelt in December 1940 came up with Lend-Lease, a simple but ingenious means of getting desperately needed supplies to a friendly nation. The United States would lend or lease items or services to nations whose defense was deemed vital to the defense of the United States. After a long and bitter debate in Congress, the Lend-Lease Act passed with partisan majorities and was signed into law on 11 March 1941. It signified the end of American neutrality and the beginning of a period of nonbelligerency. Up to Pearl Harbor, Britain was the major beneficiary of Lend-Lease, but aid was extended to other nations fighting Germany, including the Soviet Union.

After the United States entered the war, Lend-Lease became the mechanism through which nearly $50 billion of aid was rendered to some forty nations. The major Allies received the lion's share, Britain getting $31 billion, the Soviet Union $11 billion, and China $1 billion. But Lend-Lease funds sent American machinery and technical know-how to many other places across the world, including areas such as the Middle East, India, and North Africa where American influence had previously been slight. Shortages of supplies and shipping limited its effectiveness in the early days of the war, but shipments later expanded enormously and Lend-Lease contributed significantly to the fighting capabilities of the Grand Alliance.

The termination of Lend-Lease brought much controversy to the early days of the Truman presidency. When the war in Europe ended, Truman, without warning, terminated Lend-Lease to the Soviet Union, even turning around some ships at sea. The Soviets complained bitterly, and Truman modified the order, permitting some shipments to proceed. The president insisted that he was merely following the letter and spirit of the law. Critics at the time and later accused him and his advisers of trying to bludgeon the Soviet Union into accepting U.S. foreign policy goals. Apparently learning nothing from this incident, Truman, at V-J Day, abruptly terminated Lend-Lease to all nations. This time the British protested loudest. Truman was probably right in claiming that congressional restrictions left him little freedom in the handling of Lend-Lease, but the V-E Day and V-J Day terminations were poorly handled and did much damage to relations with the major Allies.

After the war, Lend-Lease settlements were negotiated with recipient nations. Some Allies insisted that Lend-Lease should be written off as a contribution to the common cause, but the United States kept careful accounts and presented "bills." Still, payment was required only for civilian goods that would have postwar value and represented only a small portion of the total aid rendered. The United States asked for $650 million from Great Britain, for example, and $1.3 billion from the Soviet Union. In all, Lend-Lease represented a vast improvement over earlier methods of inter-Allied supply, and it helped avoid the sort of war debts tangle that had developed after World War I.

For the origins of Lend-Lease, see Warren F. Kimball, *The Most Unsordid Act: Lend-Lease, 1939–1941* (Baltimore: Johns Hopkins

Press, 1969). There is no good overall history of Lend-Lease operations, but the Russian program is covered in George C. Herring, Jr., *Aid to Russia, 1941–1946: Strategy, Diplomacy, the Origins of the Cold War* (New York: Columbia University Press, 1973).

GEORGE C. HERRING

Lewis, John L.

(12 February 1880–11 June 1969)

Conflict between Harry S. Truman and John L. Lewis ran through the Truman presidency like a red thread. From 1946 through 1952, strikes in the soft coal fields erupted almost every year. With the federal government playing a major role in efforts to end these walkouts, there were ample opportunities for confrontation between these two acerbic and combative men. Key public issues, however, lay behind the personal clashes. The United Mine Workers (UMW) achieved innovative health and pension benefits through the strikes. At the same time, however, the Truman administration's resort to punitive action through injunctive and court proceedings raised critical questions about the relationship of labor unions to the national security state. For Truman personally, widely heralded victories over Lewis in the courts provided a badly needed fillip for the harassed president.

By the mid-1940s, Lewis had given up on earlier efforts to attempt to reshape American politics or to recast the Democratic party. Legislative representatives of the UMW played little role in the domestic legislation of the Truman years, apart from controversy over the June 1947 Taft-Hartley Act and the shaping of the 1952 Federal Mine Safety Act. Nor did Lewis join in the debate over Truman's critical foreign policy initiatives, in contrast to his vigorous dissent from Roosevelt's pre–World War II measures.

In the bituminous strikes, however, Lewis suffered bitter defeats and won famous victories, with the federal government playing a leading part in both. The 1946 strike, for example, gained for the UMW the establishment of pathbreaking welfare, retirement, and medical provisions, reflecting Lewis's deepening concern with the health and pension needs of an aging labor force in an industry notorious for its unsafe and unhealthy working conditions. Indeed, the breakthrough for the UMW occurred in May, after Truman had ordered Secretary of the Interior Julius A. Krug to seize and operate the mines under federal authority. The Lewis-Krug agreement established the principle of a welfare and retirement fund, financed by employer contributions based on the amount of coal mined. This was a seminal contract, meeting a profound human need in the coal communities and in one stroke legitimating a whole new agenda for postwar collective bargaining throughout American industry.

But federal operation also brought one of Lewis's most galling defeats. Determined to reopen the contract negotiated with Krug, Lewis precipitated a renewal of the strike on 20 November. Krug, acting in Truman's behalf, secured an injunction, and on 4 December, Federal District Judge T. Alan Goldsborough found Lewis and the UMW guilty of contempt, assessing huge fines on both.

Sharp clashes occurred again in 1948, 1949–50, and 1952. In each case, Lewis's UMW sought expansion of pension and medical benefits, and in each case the administration ultimately assumed an adversarial role vis-à-vis the union. In 1948, Lewis's defiance of a Truman back-to-work order under the new Taft-Hartley Act resulted again in heavy fines and bitter acquiescence on the part of UMW members. The 1949–50 dispute smoldered for ten months, as defiant miners remained out of the pits despite injunction threats. In the 1952 dispute, miners struck in effect against the Korean War Wage Stabilization Board's refusal to approve a contract negotiated with the Bituminous Coal Operators' Association.

For Lewis, Truman and his agents served as convenient examples of illegitimate use of governmental power. In similar clashes with Roosevelt during World War II, Lewis had carefully refrained from personal attacks on the president, but now he pulled out the rhetorical stops. Truman was "totally unfitted for the presidency" and was "a malignant, scheming sort of an individual . . . [who was] dangerous to the United States." Polemics aside, however, the specter of the federal government compelling men to work through punitive court orders did highlight the powerful weapons available to the modern American state.

For his part, Truman found Lewis vexing as an adversary and convenient as a whipping boy. Unlike most other laborites, Lewis refused to amend his own agenda. He bridled when government officials slighted the protocols of collective bargaining. So widely detested was Lewis, however, that Truman made political capital out of his court victories over the UMW chief. Union strikes during the war, however understandable in view of the poverty of the mining communities and the carnage in the wartime pits, had left a legacy of public hostility toward Lewis that Truman exploited. Politically dependent on the unions and accused by conservatives of favoritism toward organized labor, Truman could exhibit Lewis's scalp as a means of establishing his independence and forcefulness of action. Thus, after Goldsborough's 1946 contempt conviction, declared presidential aide Clark Clifford, "there was a big difference in the Old Man from then on. He was his own man at last."

Melvyn Dubofsky and Warren Van Tine, *John L. Lewis: A Biography* (New York: Quadrangle/New York Times Co., 1977), the standard biography of Lewis, covers the Truman-Lewis conflict in some detail. See also Joanna Healey Shurbet, "John L. Lewis: The Truman Years" (Ph.D. diss., Texas Technological University, 1975). Philip A. Taft, *Organized Labor in American History* (New York: Harper, 1964), provides context. Waldo E. Fisher, *Collective Bargaining in the Bituminous Coal Industry* (Philadelphia: University of Pennsylvania Press, 1948), and Colston E. Warne, "Industrial Relations in Coal," in *Labor in Postwar America*, ed. Colston E. Warne (Brooklyn: Remsen Press, 1949), are specialized studies. U.S. Department of the Interior, Coal Mines Administration, *A Medical Survey of the Bituminous-Coal Industry* (Washington, D.C.: U.S. Government Printing Office, 1947), reveals the bases for Lewis's bargaining agenda.

ROBERT H. ZIEGER

See also Labor

Liberalism

As the United States emerged from the Second World War, liberals were united in their commitment not only to defend but also to expand the New Deal. After more than a dozen years of strong presidential leadership through depression and war, American liberalism defined itself in terms of Franklin D. Roosevelt's policies, promises, and practices. Roosevelt's dominance obscured disagreements among his supporters, as liberalism was neither an organized political movement nor an explicit body of ideas, but rather a broad reformist position within the American political spectrum. His towering presence hid both weaknesses within the reform coalition and the strength of opposing forces. Postwar liberals thus faced the enormous challenge of replacing an irreplaceable leader and maintaining unity and momentum behind reform in an increasingly hostile political climate.

Liberalism had long since discarded its nineteenth-century commitment to limited government in favor of an activist state dedicated to safeguarding and promoting the welfare of its citizens. This fundamental shift in liberal thought was rooted in the early twentieth century when Progressive reformers perceived that the social, political, and economic dislocations wrought by large-scale industrialization, urbanization, and immigration could not be solved on an individual or community level. These reformers began to build the modern American state, but it was the near-total collapse of the economy in the 1930s that mandated a greatly expanded role for government. Responding to the manifest misery caused by the depression, New Deal liberals deepened their commitment to the efficacy of government action as they broadened its role in American society. The demands of total warfare in order to defeat the fascist challenge served only to reinforce the importance of government in their thoughts and plans.

The liberal agenda for the postwar world was built upon the experience of fighting both the depression and the war. In his final State of the Union address in 1944, Roosevelt eloquently reaffirmed the liberal dream calling for "a second Bill of Rights under which a new basis of security and prosperity can be established for all." Included in this expansive vision was the right to useful employment, adequate earnings for food, clothing, and recreation, decent housing, good education, improved health care, aid for the elderly, and an end to racial discrimination. Indeed, many liberals hoped to use the war effort itself to advance the cause of social justice in America and spoke of postwar reconstruction in New Deal terms. Henry Wallace, the leading spokesman for this vision, had declared that "the century that we are entering—the century that will come of this war—can be and must be the century of the common man." From the war would emerge a "worldwide new democracy" dedicated to achieving freedom from want.

To most liberals, Roosevelt's victory in 1944 promised a reinvigoration of social reform after the war. Although Wallace had been denied renomination for the vice presidency, he had been replaced by a loyal supporter of the New Deal, Harry S. Truman. Liberals paid scant attention to the fact that for all its rhetorical support of continued reform, the Roosevelt administration subordinated its domestic goals to maintain a foreign policy consensus. The armed forces, for example, remained segregated as the president chose not to take advantage of wartime powers to challenge America's racial caste system. Nor did the administration use military contracts to advance liberal plans for restructuring the American economy, choosing instead to work with big business on a basis that guaranteed corporate giants substantial profit and the nation continued economic concentration. As the president saw it, "Dr. Win the War" superseded "Dr. New Deal."

During the war, the return of prosperity largely obscured the relative absence of social reform. A booming economy provided full employment, rapidly banishing the hunger and homelessness of the depression despite shortages in consumer goods. Abundant overtime pay filled savings accounts even as wage controls frustrated organized labor. The benefits of a dynamic war economy even reached down to those on the bottom of the American economic ladder—blacks, migrant workers, working women, and other poor people—who had the most to gain.

Wartime prosperity intensified the fear that postwar demobilization would plunge the nation back into economic stagnation and thus led most liberals to structure their plans for the future around the maintenance of federal economic controls. Nonetheless, as they recognized the enormous social benefits of economic expansion, an enlarged vision of a liberal commonwealth blossomed. Liberal writers envisioned a massive rebuilding of American cities with slum clearance and extensive public housing, an expanded public health system, a modernized national transportation network, a greatly improved educational system, a plethora of rural development projects, an expansion and improvement of Social Security, and a concerted attack on inequality throughout American society.

The indisputable value of economic growth, however, also encouraged Americans to believe that the nation's remaining social problems would largely evaporate in a healthy economy. When postwar reconversion was accomplished with little government control and was followed not by a recession but by a boom built upon consumer spending, it was clear that the nation had entered a new economic era. Prosperity, rather than depression, was the central fact of postwar life. The necessity for government action to secure minimum living standards—which had been at the heart of New Deal liberalism—thus seemed less pressing. Instead, postwar liberals imagined an ever-expanding economy inexorably improving the quality of American life. The temptation to place faith in economic expansion rather than in social reform grew as liberals found opportunities for the passage of reform legislation increasingly limited. By the early fifties, this was reinforced by a cold war consensus that made many liberals wary of social movements.

Indeed, fundamental changes in the postwar world situation affected liberalism every bit as much as the economic boom. During the war, most liberals were little troubled by the alliance with the Soviet Union. Recognizing the enormous burden that Russia bore in the war effort, they had been pleased with the resurrection of a popular front against fascism despite serious misgivings about Joseph Stalin. Continued cooperation between the United States and the Soviet Union was central to the liberal hopes for peace and prosperity in the postwar world. When the wartime alliance crumbled even before the guns fell silent on 15 August 1945 and tension hardened into a bitter ideological struggle, liberalism became wracked by confusion and bitter division.

At first, Truman's hard-line stance with the Russians shocked most liberals. They viewed his moralistic pronouncements on the Soviet Union as intemperate and counterproductive. Recognition of the inevitably tragic consequences of the growing rift led to unfavorable comparisons between Truman and his predecessor. Roosevelt, liberals believed, rightly or wrongly, would have found common ground to maintain the alliance and build a strong United Nations. Truman in contrast seemed to exacerbate the conflict. The failure to submit atomic weapons to United Nations' control angered many. It was the proclamation of the Truman Doctrine in March 1947, however, that gave urgency and intensity to their disaffection. The president had declared a policy that liberals had resisted since the end of the war, a policy in which the United States cast itself as a global policeman to resist Communist expansion worldwide, even where this allied the United States with repressive authoritarian regimes. In response, liberal opponents to the cold war organized the Progressive Citizens of America (PCA) in December 1946. Its spiritual head was Henry Wallace whom Truman had fired as secretary of commerce when he publicly dissented from the administration's foreign policy.

By this time, however, substantial numbers of American liberals had converted to anti-Communism in response to Soviet actions in Eastern Europe. These liberals created their own organization, Americans for Democratic Action (ADA). The domestic vision of these two branches of liberalism remained remarkably similar. What divided them was the issue of communism, not just in foreign policy but in domestic life as well. Whereas the PCA remained open to all progressives, including domestic Communists, the ADA statement of principles read that we "reject any association with Communists or sympathizers with communism in the United States as completely as we reject any association with Fascists or their sympathizers." The ADA stand was both principled, as many liberals now saw communism as a form of totalitarianism, and tactical, as these liberals also recognized their domestic vulnerability on the communist issue. Crushing Democratic party losses in the 1946 mid-term elections convinced many that a tough anti-Communist position was the only politically viable one for liberals.

Indeed, an emerging cold war consensus rapidly swamped the opposition and brought most liberals into the anti-Communist camp. The Marshall Plan had much to do with this. Although designed as a complement to the Truman Doctrine, liberals saw it as an affirmative departure that held the promise of rebuilding a war-torn Europe—just the type of New Deal redevelopment program that they had always envisioned. At the same time, events in Europe seemed to prove that Russia posed a threat to democratic institutions throughout the world. For many, the turning point came in the winter and spring of 1948 with the Communist takeover of Czechoslovakia and the Berlin blockade. When liberals came to see the Soviet Union as an expansionist totalitarian power, they invariably enlisted in the cold war. Anti-Communism thus became a central tenet, indeed often the principle tenet, of postwar liberalism as the Soviet Union was understood to threaten everything in which liberals believed.

Conversion to a cold war perspective expedited a rapprochement between most liberals and the Truman administration. Truman's early days in office had seemed to hold great promise for liberal reform. In his first major postwar address, he moved quickly to propose a twenty-one-point reform program crowned by a full employment bill, national health insurance, federal housing legislation, and increases in the minimum wage and Social Security benefits. His program, however, quickly bogged down in Congress. The Employment Act of 1946 ended up as a vague statement of principles rather than a plan for action, and other proposals fared far worse. In the face of Truman's growing preoccupation with foreign affairs and appointment of many conservative Democrats to important administrative positions, liberals became his sharpest critics. Comparing him unfavorably to Roosevelt, they blamed the failure of reform programs on his lack of leadership. For a time, the disastrous 1946 elections left most liberals estranged from the White House.

All this changed rapidly in 1947–48. As liberals accepted Truman's foreign policy, the president strongly reaffirmed his commitment to domestic reform. After repeatedly wavering on labor issues, his stinging veto of the Taft-Hartley bill and support for strong civil rights legislation marked a clear policy convergence between the administration and ADA liberals. Equally important, Truman's combative conduct of the presidential election campaign finally assuaged long and deeply held liberal doubts about his ability to offer the type of inspirational leadership necessary to reinvigorate the reform coalition. Campaigning on domestic issues, he aggressively championed the full range of liberal positions, including a sweeping civil rights plank that liberals had inserted in the Democratic party platform. On foreign policy, Truman used anti-Communism to great effect, both to diffuse the challenge to his leadership from Henry Wallace and the Progressive party and to minimize foreign policy differences between himself and his Republican opponent, Thomas Dewey. In the process, Truman turned the election into a referendum on the New Deal and won an election that most liberals had believed lost.

Astounded by Truman's improbable victory, liberals embraced the president and his administration as the rightful heir of the Roosevelt legacy. Gaining confidence from his election, Truman sought to defend and extend that legacy by promising "every segment of our population and every individual . . . a fair deal." Truman's Fair Deal included virtually the entire liberal agenda: a labor program based on repealing Taft-Hartley and raising the minimum wage, an agricultural program to increase production and prosperity on the farm, expanded Social Security, federal aid to education and housing, national medical insurance, regional development programs, tax reform, and civil rights. With Truman exercising bold leadership, liberals united behind him and envisioned a new era of social reform.

This was not to be. The impassioned mix of uncompromising anti-Communism with liberal reform that Truman used to resurrect the Roosevelt coalition proved an unstable base for the Fair Deal. After having made ample use of anti-Communism to isolate Henry Wallace and the Progressive party, Truman and his liberal supporters found themselves subjected to withering attacks from anti-Communist conservatives. Reform programs floundered in Congress as relentless red-baiting undermined their credibility. Ironically, since early 1947 Truman had attempted to preclude the use of anti-Communism against his administration by developing his own internal security program. Yet, the Federal Employee Loyalty Program served only to legitimize a crusade against internal subversion. Indeed, characterized by reckless disregard for civil liberties, Truman's program pioneered the techniques of political inquisition that disfigured American public life. Although many liberals deplored the compromise of civil liberties, almost all accepted the logic of the anti-Communist crusade that put domestic radicals beyond the pale of American politics. In the end, they too were victims of that crusade that cast suspicion upon all social criticism and plans for reform.

By 1950, the liberal vision that had seemed so expansive in 1945 no longer occupied an important place on the nation's political agenda. As the cold war intensified and the nation plunged into the Korean conflict, Truman concentrated his limited political capital on foreign affairs. Fair Deal programs continued to receive verbal support, but the president's overriding concern was the maintenance of a foreign policy consensus. With defense expenditures mounting, less money was available for social programs. In the tense years that followed, those willing to speak out for liberal reform certainly were fewer, quieter, and less hopeful.

During the Truman years, the president and his liberal supporters did succeed to some degree in defending and amplifying the New Deal. The Eighty-first Congress passed legislation to expand Social Security, raise the minimum wage, and build some low-income housing. The Fair Deal, however, fell far short of promise as no action was forthcoming on civil rights, health care, education, or regional development. In large part this was due to the strength of the opposition. Liberalism, however, also changed during these years. Conversion to anti-Communism led many to celebrate the virtues of the United States in contrast to the vices of its totalitarian enemies. The step from celebration to social complacency was a short one, made more attractive by the virulent opposition to reform. In these prosperous times, many liberals lost sight of the poverty and injustice that persisted. They believed that the nation's basic social problems had been solved and those that remained required administrative action rather than mass social reform.

From the early twentieth century, liberalism had placed its hopes for social change in the federal government, particularly in national administrative agencies and presidential leadership. Progressive Era reformers looked to Theodore Roosevelt and Woodrow Wilson for inspiration and to independent regulatory boards to administer the American economy. Although acting in the name of "the people," these reformers distrusted mass-based party politics. Likewise, the New Deal solution, which was reinforced by the experience of the Second World War, was predicated upon beneficent presidential leadership and an expansion of administrative agencies. It was not until the postwar period, however, that liberals explicitly celebrated the virtues of administration as an alternative to popular politics.

Underlying this position was a deep distrust of the masses in general and mass political participation in particular which was blamed for the totalitarianism of both the Nazis and the Communists. Many liberal thinkers saw a similar danger in America in the popular support accorded a demagogue like Joseph McCarthy. In response, postwar liberalism took on a decided antiparticipatory quality that severely limited its appeal and ability to garner popular support. In the process, the liberal commitment to established rules, procedures, and institutions deepened, often overshadowing concerns about social justice.

In retrospect, it can be seen that postwar liberals clearly succeeded in maintaining and in some ways expanding the reform tradition in arduous times. The New Deal was preserved and institutionalized. At the same time, postwar liberals served as a bridge between the reforms of the thirties and the broader dreams of the sixties. Nonetheless, the reliance on presidential leadership and incremental administrative reform left liberalism with an elitist heritage that has handicapped it ever since. Equally important, the marriage of liberalism to the cold war in which Truman played a central role had particularly disastrous effects. During the fifties, the crusade against Communism at home cast a red tint on liberal dreams for reform and stalled social progress for the decade. When this dark cloud lifted in the sixties, liberal reform reached its zenith, but continued liberal commitment to a cold war foreign policy brought the dream for a more just America down in the flames of the war in Vietnam.

An excellent introduction to liberal thought is provided by Richard H. Pells's fascinating synthesis of postwar intellectual development, *The Liberal Mind in the Conservative Era: American Intellectuals in the 1940s and 1950s* (New York: Harper & Row, 1985). Arthur M. Schlesinger, Jr.'s influential essay, *The Vital Center: Our Purposes and Perils on the Tightrope of American Liberalism* (Boston: Houghton Mifflin, 1949), remains the best example of the recycling of liberalism after the war. The often strained, but ultimately symbiotic relationship between Truman and liberal reformers is covered with sympathy and thoroughness in Alonzo Hamby's *Beyond the New Deal: Harry S. Truman and American Liberalism* (New York: Columbia University Press, 1973). Sharing with his subjects the central cold war premise that equated communism on the left with totalitarianism on the right, Hamby rejects the notion that Truman's anti-Communism crippled liberal reform, arguing instead that liberals accomplished about all they could in the conservative climate of the postwar years. A far more critical view is offered in a series of essays edited by Barton Bernstein, *Politics and Policies of the Truman Administration* (Chicago: Quadrangle Books, 1972). Anti-Communism, the liberal response to it, and responsibility for it are covered in exhaustive detail by David Caute's *The Great Fear: The Anti-Communist Purge under Truman and Eisenhower* (New York; Simon & Schuster, 1978). William Chafe's *The Unfinished Journey: America since World War II* (New York: Oxford University Press, 1986) does an excellent job of locating the evolution of postwar liberalism within a broad overview of recent American history.

MARK KORNBLUH

See also Americans for Democratic Action; Democratic Party; Elections in the Truman Era; Fair Deal; New Deal; Progressive Party; Wallace, Henry A.

Lilienthal, David Eli

(8 July 1899–14 January 1981)

A key figure in the development of the Tennessee Valley Authority and the Atomic Energy Commission. Lilienthal was born in Morton, Illinois, the son of immigrants from Austria-Hungary. He attended schools in Indiana and was graduated from DePauw University and the Harvard Law School. He practiced law with Donald R. Richberg in Chicago, served in the early 1930s as a member of the Wisconsin Public Service Commission, and was appointed in 1933 as one of the first three directors of the Tennessee Valley Authority (TVA). He became chairman of the authority in 1941. Lilienthal conducted the legal defense of the new agency against the challenges of the private utilities, was largely responsible for developing TVA's electric power program, and successfully opposed Secretary Harold

L. Ickes's efforts to bring the authority within the jurisdiction of the Department of Interior. He created political support for TVA by popularizing its freedom from politics, "grass-roots democracy," and decentralization.

In 1946 President Truman called on Lilienthal to head the new Atomic Energy Commission (AEC), which his administration had worked hard to establish. Lilienthal seemed to be a natural choice for this important position. A man of great drive and personal ambition, he was a creative administrator with impressive rhetorical and public relations skills and a capacity for uniting technology and politics. He had earlier served as chairman of a board of consultants to advise a committee headed by Under Secretary of State Dean G. Acheson in developing an American plan for the international control of atomic energy. The result was the so-called Acheson-Lilienthal Report, which recommended the concept of an international agency with positive developmental functions. Now, when his appointment went before the Senate, Truman stuck by him in a long and bitter confirmation fight conducted by Lilienthal's conservative opponents. Lilienthal, an ardent admirer of Franklin D. Roosevelt, had expressed consternation "at the thought of that Throttlebottom, Truman" taking over the presidency. But he soon developed respect and esteem for the thirty-third president and later dedicated the second volume of his *Journals* to him.

Lilienthal and his fellow commissioners faced the challenging task of rebuilding the nation's atomic energy program. Under Lilienthal's leadership, the AEC began to develop a nuclear arsenal. Like Truman, the AEC chairman was a firm believer in civilian control of atomic energy, and he emphasized the importance of public knowledge of and education in this new field.

Despite its progress, the AEC encountered a series of crises in 1949: a debate over the question of reviving Anglo-American atomic cooperation, fear that Communist espionage would destroy the commission's fellowship program, a lengthy investigation of the commission's alleged lax security standards, and a difficult decision over construction of the hydrogen bomb. Lilienthal, with Truman's sturdy support, survived Senator Bourke B. Hickenlooper's charges that the AEC chairman was guilty of "incredible mismanagement." Although the commission was divided over the question of building a new superweapon and Lilienthal wanted to delay work on it, he reluctantly decided to support the undertaking. But exhausted and dispirited, he resigned on 15 February 1950. His tenure was troubled and in some respects unsuccessful, but he played a major role in transforming the AEC into an effective, modern agency.

After leaving the AEC, Lilienthal organized a private overseas development company and acted as a consultant on atomic energy projects. He died in 1981.

There is as yet no good biography of Lilienthal, but his activities and ideas during the 1940s are chronicled in *The Journals of David E. Lilienthal*, vols. 1 and 2 (New York: Harper & Row, 1964). For Lilienthal and atomic energy, see the indispensable *A History of the Atomic Energy Commission*, vol. 1, *The New World, 1939/1946* (University Park: Pennsylvania State University Press, 1962), by Richard G. Hewlett and Oscar E. Anderson, Jr., and vol. 2, *Atomic Shield, 1947/1952* (University Park: Pennsylvania State University Press, 1969), by Hewlett and Francis Duncan.

DEWEY W. GRANTHAM

See also Atomic Energy Commission; Nuclear Energy

Lippmann, Walter

(23 September 1889–14 December 1974)

Walter Lippmann, the Harvard-educated (B.A., 1910) syndicated columnist and author, had a low regard for Harry S. Truman and was often a harsh critic of his leadership. He believed Truman to be a "weak President and at heart a jingo," an inept and insecure leader who was prone to rash decisions and false bravado. Lippmann supported Thomas Dewey in the 1948 presidential election, and like most other journalists, he assumed the New York governor would be an easy winner. In 1952, he backed Dwight D. Eisenhower thinking that the World War II hero would provide Americans with the qualities Truman lacked.

Lippmann was frequently at odds with Truman administration policy. Although he supported the stipulation that Japan surrender unconditionally, he regretted that the United States had been the first nation to use atomic weapons, and he believed that Truman should have made a greater attempt to negotiate with the Japanese. Americans, he warned, should not overestimate the new weapons. They were poor military and diplomatic instruments because they aimed at "the extermination of civilians" and were so powerful that they could not be used "moderately." Much depended on how well Americans understood the possibilities of their power "*within* its limitations."

Lippmann did advise massive American support for the economic recovery of Europe, an idea that lay behind the Marshall Plan. He also supported internationalism, and he helped convince Republican senator Arthur Vandenberg to approve the administration's plans for the United Nations. Yet Lippmann remained pessimistic about establishing a world government strong enough to abolish war because the Soviet Union would never enter such a federation and the process of establishing it would "be a long and bloody business of subduing and pacifying separatists and rebels all over the globe."

Truman, Lippmann believed, also misread the Soviet threat. The columnist took issue with the containment policy set forth in *Foreign Affairs* in the summer of 1947 by George Kennan. Where Kennan saw the Soviets driven by irrational—even paranoid—concerns about security and by a messianic ideology, Lippmann, in a series of articles in the *New York Herald-Tribune*, argued that the Soviet desire for security was deeply rooted in Russian history and predated the Bolshevik Revolution. He worried that containment would spread American resources too thin.

Although Lippmann approved of the president's aid to Greece in 1947, he considered the Greek government too authoritarian, and he feared the Truman Doctrine's sweeping rhetoric endorsed unlimited intervention. Lippmann was the son of New York German-Jewish parents, but he was not enthusiastic about the creation of Israel. He opposed the partition of Palestine and favored an Arab-Jewish confederation protected by American and British power. He disagreed with Pentagon and State Department strategists who urged a military alliance with Western Europe and he felt NATO to be unnecessary. The threat of American nuclear retaliation, not an alliance, would deter a Soviet invasion of Western Europe.

Truman's handling of Asian affairs often upset Lippmann. He attacked the administration's China policy for its inconsistency (by spring 1950 he felt Secretary of State Dean Acheson had lost public support and should resign), and he also blamed Truman and Acheson for developments in Korea. Initially surprised by the North Korean invasion, he cautiously supported Truman's decision to supply the South Koreans and pursue a United Nations' resolution. But he warned about committing American troops, charged that Truman and Acheson had failed to offer a clear definition of Korea's importance to American security, and considered the decision to send UN troops north of the thirty-eighth parallel to be "one of the greatest mistakes in our history."

Often insensitive to government abuses of civil liberties, Lippmann made little objection to the loyalty program launched in 1947 and Truman's and Eisenhower's subsequent efforts to broaden it. He disliked McCarthyism, was sympathetic to its victims, and believed the Wisconsin senator had shattered the "mystic chords of memory, which make it possible for men to be free, and to differ, and yet to be one people." But he wrote comparatively little about this issue nor did he write much about the Hiss case or the espionage trial of Julius and Ethel Rosenberg. Although sympathetic to J. Robert Oppenheimer, Lippmann did not believe that the government was obligated to retain his security clearance.

As biographer Ronald Steel argues, Lippmann seems to have shared many of Truman's policy goals, and although he often criticized the administration's tactics, he failed to provide a penetrating critique of its cold war assumptions. Lippmann did not so much stand outside the system as he "felt an insider's responsibility for making the system work." Yet, "having only a guidepost of national interest, lacking a philosophical approach or ideological commitment, reluctant to accept the part that economic demands or imperial ambitions might play in explaining American foreign policy, Lippmann was unable to take a consistent approach to the issues he wrote about" during the Truman years.

The best overall treatment of Walter Lippmann's life is Ronald Steel, *Walter Lippmann and the American Century* (New York: Vintage Books, 1980). For a penetrating critique of Lippmann's political philosophy, see Morton S. White's epilogue in *Social Thought in America: The Revolt against Formalism* (Boston: Beacon Press, 1949, 1957, 1959). For a more recent treatment of Lippmann's ideas, see D. Steven Blum, *Walter Lippmann: Cosmopolitanism in the Century of Total War* (Ithaca: Cornell University Press, 1984). Lippmann published more than three dozen books during his career. The following works appeared during the Truman years: *The Cold War: A Study in U.S. Foreign Policy* (New York: Harper, 1947); *Commentaries on Far Eastern Policy* (New York: American Institute of Pacific Relations, 1950); *Isolation and Alliances: An American Speaks to the British* (Boston: Little, Brown, 1952); and *Public Opinion and Foreign Policy in the United States* (London: Allen & Unwin, 1952). The Walter Lippmann Papers are at Yale University.

STEPHEN L. VAUGHAN

See also Press, The

Lloyd, David D.

(6 June 1911–11 December 1962)

Administrative assistant, 1948–56. Born in New York City, Lloyd was educated at Harvard and graduated from Harvard Law School in 1935. His affinity for New Deal liberalism took him to Washington for a career in government service. He was research director of Americans for Democratic Action when he was recruited by the White House to write speeches for the Truman presidential campaign of 1948.

Lloyd exerted a liberal influence as a key contributor to Truman's messages, speeches, legislative proposals, and political strategy. His loyalty was questioned indirectly by Senator Joseph R. McCarthy in 1950, but Truman refuted the unfounded allegation. Lloyd continued to serve Truman after the White House years as fund-raiser for the president's library and as an occasional speech writer.

Brief sketches of Lloyd appear in Ken Heckler, *Working with Truman: A Personal Memoir of the White House Years* (New York: G. P. Putnam's Sons, 1982), and *Who Was Who in America*, vol. 4 (Chicago: Marquis Who's Who, 1968). The Lloyd papers are housed in the Harry S. Truman Library.

FRANKLIN D. MITCHELL

See also Speeches and Speech Writing

Lovett, Robert Abercrombie

(14 September 1895–7 May 1986)

Assistant secretary of war for air, 1941–45; under secretary of state, 1947–49; deputy secretary of defense, 1950–51; secretary of defense, 1951–53. Born in Huntsville, Texas, Robert Lovett accompanied his family to New York when he was fifteen. He graduated from Yale University in 1918 where he was elected to Phi Beta Kappa and then spent a year each at Harvard Law School and Harvard Business School. At Yale he first became interested in airplanes and during World War I helped form a unit of Yale pilots who served in that war.

After the war he went to work for the banking firm of Brown Brothers, married the senior partner's youngest daughter, became a partner in 1926, and was instrumental in effecting the merger of Brown Brothers firm with Harriman Brothers. Work assignments took him to Europe and London during the 1930s, where he became convinced that a new world conflict would soon ensue. Retaining his interest in aviation, he realized the airplane would play a significant role in the upcoming war and wrote a report on aircraft production in 1940. It so impressed Secretary of War Henry L. Stimson, he asked Lovett to become his special assistant and later assistant secretary of war for air. Stimson gave Lovett an almost free hand in developing the aircraft for the army air forces. Through his close association with the chief of the army air forces, Gen. Henry H.

Arnold, Lovett came to know and advise Gen. George C. Marshall, the army chief of staff.

Lovett also impressed Marshall, and when President Truman asked the general to become secretary of state following the war, Marshall recruited Lovett as his under secretary. The two worked very closely, and Lovett later claimed he had been Marshall's alter ego. Although Lovett never developed the easy relationship with the president that he had with Arnold and Marshall, the under secretary did work very closely with Truman throughout the Berlin crisis and during Marshall's frequent absences. He also helped the president and Senator Arthur Vandenberg persuade Congress to adopt the Marshall Plan for European recovery.

When Marshall agreed to become secretary of defense in 1950 following the outbreak of war in Korea, he indicated that he would stay for only six months and that he wanted Lovett as his deputy and successor. After helping to oversee the buildup of U.S. forces during the Korean War, Lovett became secretary of defense when Marshall retired in 1951.

After the Truman administration, Lovett returned to Brown Brothers Harriman, served as a director of the Columbia Broadcasting System, and continued to be active in government but in an advisory capacity. He refused a cabinet post under President John F. Kennedy because of ill-health but lived on for another twenty-five years.

The best single source on Lovett during his early life and tenure as assistant secretary of war for air is Jonathan A. Fanton, "Robert A. Lovett: The War Years" (Ph.D. diss., Yale University, 1978). Forrest Pogue mentions Lovett in his early volumes on Marshall, but the relationship between the pair is vividly portrayed in Pogue's final volume, *George C. Marshall: Statesman 1945–1959* (New York: Viking Press, 1987). Truman's *Memoirs*, vol. 2, *Years of Trial and Hope* (New York: Doubleday, 1956), and Margaret Truman, *Harry S. Truman* (New York: William Morrow, 1973), present Lovett in a favorable light.

GEORGE M. WATSON, JR.

Loyalty Program

Spurred on by the revelation of a Soviet spy ring operating in Canada and news that classified State Department papers had been pilfered, a number of congressmen, in mid-1946, pushed hard for legislation that would tighten loyalty and security procedures inside the federal civil service. And although Attorney General Tom C. Clark shared their concern, President Truman initially saw no need to move in the direction Clark and others had recommended. The resounding Republican victory in the congressional election of 1946 forced Truman to act. Knowing that many Republicans were eager to exploit his now perceived weakness, he sought to protect his political flank by creating a temporary commission to examine the question of employee loyalty and to propose a course of action for him to follow.

On 1 February 1947 the commission brought in its report, which recommended to the president that a loyalty program be established with sufficient safeguards to protect individual rights and procedural due process. Truman, needing a buffer be-

tween himself and Congress, issued Executive Order 9835 on 22 March 1947, which established, formally and officially, the first loyalty program ever created by a president of the United States.

In specific terms, Executive Order 9835 spelled out the workings of a program that sanctioned the administrative firing of an employee if "reasonable grounds" existed for believing that that employee was either disloyal in belief or, worse, subversive in practice. In addition, the order provided the attorney general with the authority he needed to list particular organizations or groups as ideologically unfit for membership by those on the federal payroll.

Consistent with the recommendations of the temporary commission, Truman's order also sought to shield accused individuals from a possible abuse of administrative power, by providing them with a right to counsel and the opportunity to offer evidence. Because those guarantees for individual rights were built into the program, Truman, probably with a good conscience, could write Philip Murray, president of the Congress of Industrial Organizations, that civil liberties were not threatened by Executive Order 9835.

Truman's belief notwithstanding, he gave away in practice what he denied in theory. By letting the FBI assume a far greater responsibility for investigating charges and presenting evidence to the Loyalty Review Board, Truman dealt the procedural protections provided by his order a body blow. Since that evidence was protected by the principle of confidentiality, the accused would find it nearly impossible to challenge the reliability of the sources and the evidence used against them.

By 1948, neither the fear of Norman Thomas, the country's leading social democrat, or the concern of Walter White, executive secretary of the National Association for the Advancement of Colored People, that the loyalty program was a threat to civil liberties carried much weight with this president. He was now too busy protecting himself from persistent attacks by powerful conservative elements in Congress whose support he might desire for his foreign policy initiatives.

The rise of McCarthyism and the outbreak of the Korean War accentuated the administration's move toward an even harder and more inflexible position with regard to loyalty and security procedures. Although Truman created the Nimitz Commission on 28 January 1951 to investigate past practices of the Loyalty Review Board, he capitulated once again to political pressures coming from inside his administration and from Congress. On 28 April 1951, even before the Nimitz Commission could prepare its report, Truman issued Executive Order 10241 that changed the rules by which the Loyalty Review Board operated. The board was now instructed to remove individuals from the federal payroll if there was "a reasonable doubt as to the loyalty of the persons involved." No longer would "reasonable grounds" be necessary as a cause for dismissal. Later, the Loyalty Review Board, operating on its own initiative, instituted procedures that allowed it to review the records of those persons who had been originally cleared on the basis of the 1947 order.

Although Truman was not happy with these new procedures, it was now too late for him to rectify the damage to civil liberties caused by his administration's obsession with the politics of loyalty and his pandering to the red scare. By the time he left office, his loyalty program had produced no evidence of espionage; nevertheless several hundred people were either cashiered or denied job opportunities—all in the name of national security.

A domestic by-product of the cold war in its most virulent phase, the loyalty program emerged from the welter of fear and hysteria that enveloped national politics during the Truman years. The fact that it was created by a president who probably knew better is evidence that the threat to civil liberties and political dissent in the post–World War II era did not come solely from the Republican right but also from the center of the political spectrum as well.

Among the more significant works that focus on the Truman loyalty program are Eleanor Bontecou, *The Federal Loyalty-Security Program* (Ithaca: Cornell University Press, 1953); Alan Harper, *The Politics of Loyalty: The White House and the Communist Issue, 1946-1952* (Westport, Conn.: Greenwood Press, 1969); and Athan Theoharis, *Seeds of Repression: Harry S. Truman and the Origins of McCarthyism* (Chicago: Quadrangle, 1971). Bontecou's study is a good administrative history of the subject. Harper's work does not excuse Truman but sees him as victimized by exigencies of domestic politics and the ineptitude and caution of the federal bureaucracy. Theoharis's monograph pictures Truman as a political crusader who used the issue of loyalty and security to establish his anti-Communist credentials at home and abroad.

WILLIAM C. BERMAN

See also Civil Liberties; Red Scare

Lucas, Scott Wike

(19 February 1892–22 February 1968)

Democratic U.S. representative, 1935–39; U.S. senator from Illinois, 1939–51. Born near New Claudlersville, Illinois, to farmers William D. and Sarah Underbrink Lucas, Scott Lucas graduated from Illinois Wesleyan University Law School in 1914 and opened a law office at Havana, Illinois. A successful criminal lawyer, he was state's attorney of Mason County from 1920 to 1925 and chaired the State Tax Commission from 1933 to 1935. He married Edith Biggs in 1923 and had one son, Scott, Jr. In the U.S. House of Representatives from 1935 to 1939, Lucas specialized in agricultural issues and supported most New Deal farm, welfare, and labor legislation and the isolationist Neutrality Act of 1935. In 1937 he broke with President Franklin D. Roosevelt on the U.S. Supreme Court reorganization plan.

Lucas served two terms as a U.S. senator from 1939 to 1951. Although from an isolationist region, he favored aid to the Allies short of war, and preparedness measures from 1939 through 1941. During World War II, the moderate liberal backed Roosevelt's internationalist policies and authored soldier-vote legislation. He backed the United Nations as a means of preserving world peace and security and initially believed that the United States could continue collaboration with the Soviet Union following World War II. His moderate liberal voting record, decisive reelection victory in November 1944, and subsequent appointment to the Foreign Relations Committee enhanced his political prestige among Democratic senators. In 1946 he chaired the Democratic Senatorial Campaign Committee and was selected minority whip, making him second in command to Alben Barkley of Kentucky.

Lucas subsequently became less independent and usually defended President Harry S. Truman's domestic and foreign policy programs whether or not he personally agreed with them. During the Eightieth Congress (1947–48), he voted to sustain Truman's veto of the antilabor Taft-Hartley Act. Since Lucas personally favored the act, however, he was pleased when the Senate overrode the president's veto. Lucas backed universal military training, but the Senate did not include that idea in the Selective Service Act of 1948. Truman's cold war policies, designed to contain Soviet expansion, won Lucas's endorsement. He supported the Truman Doctrine authorizing $400 million in economic and military assistance to Greece and Turkey in 1947 and the Marshall Plan promoting economic recovery for Western Europe in 1948. Some Democrats favored removing Truman from the Democratic party ticket in 1948, but Lucas loyally campaigned for him in Illinois.

After Truman's upset presidential victory in November 1948, Barkley became vice president. The Democrats regained control of the Senate and selected Lucas as majority leader. He worked closely with Barkley, House Speaker Sam Rayburn, and House Majority Leader John McCormack to plan legislative strategy for the Eighty-first Congress (1949–50). As chair of the Democratic Party Policy Committee and Party Caucus, Lucas often became embroiled in Senate floor debate and spent much time working behind the scenes. He defined his legislative role as "harmonizing the different views of the different groups" within the Democratic party and obtaining legislation satisfying "the greatest number of people in the nation."

The affable Lucas encountered mixed results as majority leader. Only forty of the fifty-four Democratic senators consistently defended Truman's Fair Deal domestic legislation, making Lucas's task difficult. A civil rights advocate, he supported a permanent Fair Employment Practices Commission, abolition of the poll tax, and an antilynching law, but the conservative coalition blocked those measures. He was hospitalized three weeks for a stomach ulcer in 1949 following a lengthy Senate filibuster by Republicans and southern Democrats against civil rights legislation. The same year, he helped steer the National Housing Act and federal aid to education bill through the Senate. His other important legislative successes included securing an extension of the Reciprocal Trade Agreements Act, an expansion of the Rural Electrification Administration, an increase in the minimum wage from forty to seventy-five cents an hour, an enlargement of Social Security coverage and benefits, and an increase in federal economic assistance to small businessmen and farmers.

On the other hand, Lucas split with Truman by opposing the agricultural Brannan Plan and national health insurance in 1949 and by voting to override the president's veto of the Internal Security Act of 1950. Nevertheless, the Senate battle for ratification in 1949 of the North Atlantic Treaty Organization pact to defend Western Europe, along with financing of both the Marshall Plan and Truman's Point Four program for third-world nations, saw Lucas at the forefront of the debates. And in June 1950, he defended Truman's controversial decision to intervene in the Korean War with American troops.

Prior to the 1950 elections, the president had campaigned for Lucas at a Chicago rally that May, and had written him, "I need you—our country needs you." At the polls in November, however, former Republican congressman Everett Dirksen unseated Lucas, reflecting voter protest against some Truman Fair Deal programs, the Korean War, and Senator Kefauver's Crime

Committee investigations in Illinois. Some moderate, internationalist Republicans, who had liked Lucas's earlier independence, defected to Dirksen this time because Majority Leader Lucas had aligned too closely with Truman's policies.

Lucas resumed his private law practice in Washington, D.C., with branch offices in Chicago and Springfield, Illinois. In 1968 he died of a massive cerebral hemorrhage en route to Florida by train. The independent, self-made man had become a figure of national prominence largely through his own merits and political skill. As majority leader, he had played a key role in securing Senate acceptance of several of Truman's domestic and foreign policy programs. The president lost an effective ally when Lucas left the Senate.

The Scott W. Lucas Papers are located at the Illinois State Historical Library, Springfield, Illinois. For Lucas's congressional role, see Edward L. Schapsmeier and Frederick H. Schapsmeier, "Scott W. Lucas of Havana: His Rise and Fall as Majority Leader in the United States Senate," *Journal of the Illinois State Historical Society* 70 (November 1977): 302–20. See also Susan M. Hartmann, *Truman and the 80th Congress* (Columbia; University of Missouri Press, 1971); Robert J. Donovan, *Tumultuous Years: The Presidency of Harry S Truman, 1949–1953* (New York: W.W. Norton, 1982); Alonzo Hamby, *Beyond the New Deal: Harry S. Truman and American Liberalism* (New York: Columbia University Press, 1973); and Donald R. McCoy, *The Presidency of Harry S. Truman* (Lawrence: University Press of Kansas, 1984). For biographical background, see *National Cyclopaedia of American Biography*, vol. G, pp. 136–37; *Current Biography*, 1947, pp. 399–401; and Lucas's obituary in the *New York Times*, 23 February 1968.

DAVID L. PORTER

M

MacArthur, Douglas

(26 January 1880–5 April 1964)

Commander of Allied forces in the Southwest Pacific theater of World War II, in the occupation of Japan, and during the first nine months of the Korean War. Brilliant but flawed and controversial throughout his fifty-two years of army service, Douglas MacArthur won distinction in World War I as an aggressive, combat-experienced general and later as a reform-minded West Point superintendent and an able but appropriations-limited army chief of staff. After retiring from the U.S. Army in 1935, he spent six years as Philippine military adviser. Recalled to active duty in mid-1941 as head of American army forces in the Far East, he led the defense of the Philippines until, on President Roosevelt's orders, he went to Australia in March 1942 where he became Allied commander in chief of the Southwest Pacific Area. In April 1945 President Truman gave him the additional title of commander in chief of U.S. Army forces in the Pacific and, four months hence, the post of supreme commander for the Allied powers for the Japanese surrender and subsequent occupation.

MacArthur's authority in Japan extended to commanding the Allied (largely American) occupation forces and to heading the American army–dominated administration that executed or implemented occupation policies in nonmilitary as well as military affairs. Policies for occupied Japan were supposed to be formulated by the U.S. State-War-Navy Coordinating Committee and the thirteen-nation Far Eastern Commission, with a four-power Allied Council for Japan advising him in Tokyo. In reality, MacArthur often ignored the Allies and sometimes informed his Washington superiors *after* he had undertaken occupation reforms or changes. Under his effective, if autocratic, leadership the large bureaucracy of the occupation administration oversaw the repatriation and demobilization of Japan's military and naval forces, the purge of large numbers of militarists and supranationalists from public positions in Japan, the partial dissolution of that nation's powerful business combines, the growth of trade unionism, the promotion of women's rights, the restructuring of Japanese educational and police systems (mainly along American lines), and the development of large-scale public health programs that helped stem epidemics in the war-ravaged country.

Among the occupation achievements of which he was most proud was the Japanese constitution of 1947, which incorporated some of the best liberal, democratic features in various Western constitutions. The boldest and perhaps most successful of the occupation economic initiatives was a sweeping land reform program that produced a large, independent class of landholding peasants and nearly wiped out absentee landlordism. Although early Allied policy for occupied Japan did not provide for relief and rehabilitation, MacArthur's concern and persistence led to massive American aid shipments to relieve the Japanese people during food and fuel shortages.

In 1948 the Truman administration, now envisioning Japan as a future ally in the cold war, reversed its formerly punitive policies toward the Japanese economy and started working toward its rehabilitation. The economy did not begin to surge, however, until the Korean War when Japan became the base of operations for American and other UN forces, with enormous profits going to all sorts of Japanese enterprises ranging from producing and repairing vehicles to entertaining soldiers on leave.

Beginning in January 1947, MacArthur served not only as head of the occupation in Japan but also as commander in chief of the Far East Command, which was made up of all U.S. ground, air, and sea forces in Japan, the Ryukyus, Korea (to 1948), the Marianas, the Bonins, and the Philippines. Since December 1944 he had held the five-star rank of general of the army.

Two weeks after the Korean War began in late June 1950, Truman chose him to be the commander in chief of the newly established United Nations Command, which would assist the South Koreans in repelling the North Korean invasion south of the thirty-eighth parallel. MacArthur's forces, centered around the American Eighth Army, finally halted the North Korean ad-

Charles Werner, *Indianapolis Star*, 4 April 1949.

vance along the Naktong River, or Pusan perimeter, in the southeast corner of South Korea. In mid-September, after a considerable buildup of men and matériel from America and about sixteen Allied nations, MacArthur launched a daring amphibious assault at Inchon, a port near Seoul. Caught by surprise, the North Koreans were driven out of Seoul and most of South Korea in short order, the Communist units' withdrawal turning into a rout. UN forces entered North Korea in early October, the Eighth Army capturing Pyongyang, the North Korean capital, and the American Tenth Corps advancing separately up the east side of North Korea. Students of tactics have been arguing ever since about the wisdom of MacArthur's division of his forces for the push toward the Manchurian border, with most concluding that it was a mistake, even if more apparent in retrospect than at the time.

The tactical implications of the divided advance became important in late November when, after some earlier limited probes against UN units, huge numbers of Communist Chinese troops hit MacArthur's divided forces as they neared the Yalu River, the border between North Korea and Manchuria. For the next six weeks the Chinese offensive continued, forcing the UN divisions south of the thirty-eighth parallel again. In mid-January 1951, after MacArthur's repeated predictions to Washington of impending disaster in Korea, Lt. Gen. Matthew B. Ridgway, the new leader of the Eighth Army, revitalized that outfit and launched a counteroffensive that by mid-spring had forced the Chinese and North Korean units north of the thirty-

eighth parallel along the central and eastern parts of the front line across the peninsula.

Although President Truman had selected MacArthur to head the occupation of Japan, the Far East Command, and the UN forces in the Korean conflict, tensions had been gradually mounting between the president and his top general in the West Pacific since the end of World War II. A number of high-handed actions by MacArthur had rankled Truman, including the general's rejection of invitations to visit the White House and his occasional obstructionist tactics when Washington directives on the occupation did not suit him. MacArthur, in turn, underestimated Truman's abilities as president and believed he was too much influenced by officials who favored a Europe-first priority in American global military commitments. As the years passed without the two men personally conferring at length—they met only once, for several hours on Wake Island in mid-October 1950—each increasingly perceived the other in the stereotyped image his own confidants had long nourished. Thus Truman's picture of MacArthur became that of the imperious, egotistical, vain, and uncooperative proconsul in Tokyo who had presidential ambitions. At MacArthur's headquarters in Tokyo his closest advisers encouraged him in the notion that Truman was impetuous, tainted with liberal and pro-British sympathies, and lacking in professional competence to make the high-level decisions on strategy and overall direction of the Korean War.

By the spring of 1951, Truman and MacArthur were at loggerheads chiefly over strategic plans for the unprecedented limited war in Korea, over civil-military relations, and over the chain of command in the American military establishment. The president became convinced that their differences were fundamental and irreconcilable and that the Far East commander was guilty of insubordination for disobeying several of his orders and directives. The last episodes that precipitated Truman's final decision on the general included MacArthur's brazen thwarting of the president's effort to negotiate a cease-fire in late March and a letter of the general's that was read on the floor of the U.S. House in early April wherein MacArthur sharply criticized administration policies on the Korean conflict.

Truman summarily relieved him of his several commands on 11 April 1951, after consulting with a number of his key advisers, especially Secretary of State Dean G. Acheson, Secretary of Defense George C. Marshall, Chairman Omar N. Bradley of the Joint Chiefs of Staff, and Ambassador-at-large W. Averell Harriman. MacArthur was accorded enthusiastic public welcomes by huge crowds across the nation later that spring, highlighted by his emotional address to a joint session of Congress. The pro-MacArthur, anti-Truman public excitement quickly waned, however, during the Senate's hearings in May and June on his dismissal, particularly after the Joint Chiefs testified that his strategic proposals on Korea were unsound and might lead to World War III.

Small but influential right-wing Republican groups tried in vain in 1944, 1948, and 1952 to obtain MacArthur's nomination as the party's presidential candidate, and he delivered the keynote address at the Republican National Convention in 1952. MacArthur served thereafter as chairman of the board of Remington Rand, Inc., 1952–55, and of Sperry Rand Corporation, 1955–64.

General MacArthur's personality and character were extremely complex, and the combination of his contradictory personal traits, his extreme range of political beliefs from reactionary to liberal, and his forte at role playing has made it virtually impossible for most of his colleagues, much less biographers, to probe fully his real nature. President Truman surely was by no means alone in not being able to understand this richly gifted but tragically flawed commander.

The bulk of MacArthur's personal papers are in the archives of the MacArthur Memorial, Norfolk, Va.; the official records of his commands are mainly located in the National Archives, Washington D.C., and the Washington National Records Center, Suitland, Md. Douglas MacArthur, *Reminiscences* (New York: McGraw-Hill, 1964), unhappily, is replete with significant omissions and errors. Charles A. Willoughby, ed., *Reports of General MacArthur*, vol. 1 supplement, *MacArthur in Japan: The Occupation—Military Phase* (Washington, D.C.: Department of the Army, 1966), is his headquarters chronicle to 1948. William J. Sebald, with Russell Brines, *With MacArthur in Japan: A Personal History of the Occupation* (New York: W. W. Norton, 1965), is the most perceptive account of the occupation commander by an insider, Sebald, who headed his headquarters' diplomatic section. The authoritative study of his leadership in the Korean War is part of the army's official history of the conflict: James F. Schnabel, *Policy and Direction: The First Year, U.S. Army in the Korean War* (Washington, D.C.: U.S. Army Center of Military History, 1972). The most extensive account of MacArthur's career, from 1945 to 1953 is D. Clayton James, *The Years of MacArthur*, vol. 3, *Triumph and Disaster, 1945-1964* (Boston: Houghton Mifflin, 1985).

D. CLAYTON JAMES

See also Commander in Chief (and photograph); Japan; Korean War

---

McCarran, Patrick Anthony

(8 August 1876–28 September 1954)

U.S. senator from Nevada, 1933–54. McCarran was born in Reno, Nevada, and raised on a sheep ranch east of that town. He attended the University of Nevada, 1897–1901, read in the law, and after 1905 became a leading attorney, specializing in criminal defense and divorce cases. He represented Mary Pickford in a famous divorce in 1920. Although he served a term on the Nevada Supreme Court, 1913–18, he was otherwise excluded from office by the statewide political machine of George Wingfield. With the closure of the Wingfield banks in 1932, however, he managed to win election to the U.S. Senate as a Democrat and, having built a powerful personal political organization, secured reelection in 1938, 1944, and 1950. His local position in Nevada politics was buttressed by meticulous attention to the needs and desires of constituents and close ties to the gambling industry.

As a freshman senator, McCarran obtained choice committee assignments. He eventually chaired the District of Columbia Committee from 1941 to 1944, but it was his positions on the Appropriations and Judiciary committees that gave him his influence. From 1944 to 1946 and 1949 to 1952 he was chairman of the Judiciary Committee. Although not popular with fellow senators, he had a commanding personality, a willingness to work hard and attend to details, and a ruthless knowledge of precisely how to use his position on committees to bolster his power. Columnist Robert Allen called him a "political hog," and he was obsessed by the most mundane aspects of patronage. A vindictive man, he knew who his enemies were, and he did not forgive them their sins. By July 1952, the *Washington Post*, which detested him, called him the most powerful figure in Congress.

McCarran believed deeply in legislative (particularly senatorial) prerogatives and was naturally antagonistic to any strong executive. He was a lone wolf, both personally and ideologically, within the Senate and his vote was often unpredictable. He was a skilled practitioner of the legislative process and was responsible for such important acts as the Civil Aeronautics Act of 1938, the Airport Act of 1946, the McCarran Internal Security Act of 1950, and the McCarran-Walter Immigration Act of 1952, the latter two of which passed over President Truman's veto. He first obtained national prominence as an articulate critic of President Roosevelt's plan to reorganize the Supreme Court in 1937. He did his best to stop the influx of postwar refugees from Europe after World War II.

McCarran remains best known for his internal security investigations in the early 1950s. Up to the time of President Truman's reelection in 1948, he had basically hewed to the prevailing bipartisan foreign policy including support for aid to Greece and Turkey and the Marshall Plan in 1947–48. But his positions changed in 1949, and he vociferously argued for more aid to the Chinese Nationalist government and some aid to Franco's Spain. He was friendly to Senator Joseph McCarthy, and far more influential than the Wisconsin senator in obtaining his way in the Senate and bullying his ideas onto the federal bureaucracy. He chaired the Senate Internal Security Subcommittee in well-publicized investigations of the Institute of Pacific Relations which led to its demise and the ruin of the State Department careers of John Carter Vincent, John Paton Davies, Jr., and John Stewart Service. McCarran also forced the Justice Department to prosecute Owen Lattimore. The senator sincerely believed that China had "fallen" because of conspiracy and betrayal within the State Department. He also believed there was one individual, unnamed, unknown, directing the operations of the Communist party in America, but he never found precisely who that man was, although many were suspected. Toward the end of his life, as he descended into gloom, he predicted the inevitability, if not the desirability, of war with the Soviet Union.

Truman and McCarran loathed each other. Their emnity dated from the legislative battles of 1938 to create a Civil Aeronautics Authority. Although the final act was mainly McCarran's handiwork, Truman took credit for it, and the two battled bitterly for months over the final provisions. McCarran thought that Truman was not fitted by background or ability to be president and deluded himself that the chief executive was soft on communism. McCarran's hatred was reciprocated in full measure by Truman, who believed the senator was a provincial from the smallest state in the union—that "awful, sinful place . . . which should never have been made a state," as the president put it. Truman would have agreed with Senator Paul Douglas of Illinois who called McCarran as evil a man as he had ever met in the Senate. Dean Acheson dismissed him as "not a person who in the eighteenth century would have been termed a man of sensibility." Senator McCarran was, withal, a man of great natural abilities who never surmounted the limitations of his background, character, and worldview.

There is no full-scale biography of Patrick A. McCarran. Jerome E. Edwards, *Pat McCarran, Political Boss of Nevada* focuses on the senator's political career in Nevada. McCarran's papers are housed at the Nevada Historical Society in Reno. A small, but valuable, assortment of McCarran material is also available in the Eva Adams papers in the Special Collections Department of the University of Nevada–Reno Library.

JEROME E. EDWARDS

See also Lattimore, Owen; Red Scare

McCarthy, Joseph R.

(14 November 1908–2 May 1957)

Joseph Raymond McCarthy was born on a 143-acre farm near Appleton, Wisconsin. His main trademarks—boundless energy and wild risk-taking—were apparent from the beginning. The fifth of seven children, he quit school at fourteen, began a poultry business, went bankrupt, returned to high school, crammed four years of course work into two semesters, and entered Marquette College, a Jesuit school, in the fall of 1930. At Marquette, McCarthy was known as a hustler—a brash, reckless fellow who would do anything to achieve his ends. He earned big money playing high-stakes poker in the taverns around Milwaukee. He became the president of his senior class after a rugged—some said dishonest—election campaign. And he made headlines as a boxer, nicknamed "Smiling Joe," for his ability to take enormous punishment in stride.

After getting his law degree in 1935, McCarthy moved back to the Appleton area. Joining the Democratic party, he campaigned unsuccessfully for district attorney as both "a militant New Dealer" and "an authority on poultry raising." The loss taught him a lesson: Democrats were unpopular in northern Wisconsin. Running his next race for circuit judge unattached, he pulled off a stunning upset. At twenty-nine the youngest state jurist in decades, McCarthy attracted all sorts of attention. Newspapers criticized him for giving "quickie" divorces to political friends. The State Supreme Court censured him for destroying evidence. Still, McCarthy was a popular judge. His energy was boundless, and his personal style, free of pomp and solemnity, was tailor-made for his small-town constituents.

McCarthy soon tired of his judicial duties. His real love was politics. He hoped to run for the U.S. Senate, but his plans were sidetracked when the Japanese bombed Pearl Harbor in 1941. Although exempt from military service, McCarthy joined the Marines and served for three years as an intelligence officer at Bougainville, debriefing combat pilots after their bombing runs over Japanese-held islands. Before long, however, news reached Wisconsin that McCarthy had become a tail-gunner, flying dangerous missions and spraying more bullets than any Marine in history. He even claimed to have suffered a "war wound" when his plane crash-landed on an airstrip.

Communists in the Institute of Pacific Relations shape U.S. State Department policy, charges Senator Joseph McCarthy. According to the senator, proof of his allegation lies in the 200,000 documents his investigators discovered hidden in a barn near Lee, Massachusetts. 29 October 1952 (Associated Press/Wide World Photos)

Almost none of this was true. McCarthy did fly a few "safe" missions in the tail-gunner's seat, strafing targets that the Japanese had already abandoned. His "war wound" was a broken foot. It occurred during a hazing incident on a troop ship, when he fell down a stairwell. Nevertheless, McCarthy requested—and received—an Air Medal, four stars, and the Distinguished Flying Cross, awarded for twenty-five missions in combat. Such were the exploits of "Tail-Gunner Joe."

In 1946, McCarthy entered Wisconsin's Republican senatorial primary. His opponent was Robert M. La Follette, Jr., a three-term senator who belonged to the state's leading political family. La Follette did not bother to campaign; McCarthy never stopped. Having no record to stand on, the thirty-eight-year-old challenger bragged about his war exploits and berated La Follette, then fifty-one, for failing to enlist. His campaign flyers read: "TODAY JOE MCCARTHY IS HOME. He wants to SERVE America in the SENATE. Yes, folks, CONGRESS NEEDS A TAIL-GUNNER."

McCarthy edged La Follette by five thousand votes. A few months later, he was part of the GOP landslide that gave Republicans control of Congress for the first time in eighteen years. As a freshman senator, McCarthy was known for his raucous behavior. Angry colleagues accused him of lying, of manipulating figures, of disregarding the Senate's most cherished traditions.

He lobbied so aggressively for the soft-drink companies that reporters dubbed him the "Pepsi-Cola Kid." By 1950, his political future was in jeopardy. Senate leaders had stripped him of his one major committee assignment (Banking), and his reelection chances looked grim. What he needed was a big issue, a major theme, to energize his faltering career.

The issue he chose, Communists in government, was not exactly new. On 9 February 1950—one month after Alger Hiss went to prison and one week after Klaus Fuchs confessed to atomic espionage—Senator McCarthy delivered a speech on "Communist subversion" to the Ohio County Women's Republican Club in Wheeling, West Virginia. America was losing the cold war, he said, "because of the traitorous actions of those . . . who have had all the benefits that the wealthiest nation on earth has had to offer—the finest homes, the finest college educations, and the finest jobs in Government we can give." Then came the bombshell, the words that would make McCarthy an instant celebrity. "While I cannot take the time to name all of the men in the State Department who have been named as members of the Communist Party and members of a spy ring," he added, "I have here in my hand a list of 205 . . . a list of names that were known to the Secretary of State and who nonetheless are still working and shaping policy of the State Department."

The senator had no list. He knew of no Communists in the State Department—or anywhere else. But the newspapers printed his charges, and the public was intrigued. McCarthy, after all, was not talking about socialist tendencies or left-wing bias; he was claiming to have the *names* of 205 traitors like Alger Hiss. Even better, his charges offered a simple and compelling explanation for America's demise in the world. The Communists were "winning" the cold war because traitors in our own government were aiding their cause. The real enemy was in Washington, D.C.

President Truman was furious. He viewed McCarthy as both an opportunist and a point man for the Republican party, which was using the "Communist issue" for political gain. The president vented his anger in a personal letter to McCarthy that went unsent. Spotted, perhaps, by a horrified assistant, it read: "You are not even fit to have a hand in the operation of the Government of the United States. I am very sure that the people of Wisconsin are extremely sorry that they are represented by a person who has as little sense of responsibility as you have." In a calmer moment, Truman wrote Vice President Barkley that McCarthy's behavior reminded him of an old fable about a mad dog who went around biting people. To deter him, the dog's master had placed a clog around the dog's neck. Even though the clog was a badge of dishonor, the dog foolishly viewed it as a positive symbol. The moral, Truman concluded, was that some men "often mistake notoriety for fame, and would rather be remarked for their vices and follies than not to be noticed at all."

As Truman expected, prominent Republicans rallied to McCarthy's side. Senator Robert A. Taft of Ohio, known as Mr. Republican, privately dismissed McCarthy's charges as "nonsense." Yet he told McCarthy himself to keep plugging—"if one case doesn't work out, bring up another." Taft shrewdly viewed McCarthy as the party's new alchemist, the man who could turn fear and distrust into Republican votes.

In the spring of 1950, the Senate formed a special committee to investigate McCarthy's charges. Chaired by Democrat Millard Tydings of Maryland, the committee called dozens of witnesses, including Joe McCarthy. By this time, the Wisconsin senator had rearranged both his numbers and his charges: 205 had become 57 and then 81. His "Communists" had become "dupes," "fellow travelers," and "security risks." McCarthy did claim, however, that one of his cases, Professor Owen Lattimore of Johns Hopkins University, was "the top Russian spy" in America. The charge was pure fiction, but the headlines were real. In the end, the Tydings committee split along partisan lines. The Democrats' majority report claimed that McCarthy had perpetrated a "fraud and a hoax . . . on the Senate." But the Republican members refused to sign it.

The report was overshadowed by news of the North Korean invasion of South Korea. With American troops now battling Communist forces in Asia, McCarthy's message seemed more popular than ever. In the 1950 elections, the Republicans picked up five seats in the Senate and twenty-eight more in the House. McCarthy personally campaigned against Millard Tydings, who went down to a stunning defeat. By year's end, McCarthy was a towering national figure. His face adorned the covers of *Newsweek* and *Time*. A new word had been coined to describe his antics, "McCarthyism." Several people—Owen Lattimore, columnist Max Lerner, and cartoonist Herbert Block—took credit for it, although McCarthy told everyone that the Communists were responsible.

As the 1952 campaign approached, his attacks grew even bolder. He called Secretary of Defense George C. Marshall a traitor, mocked Secretary of State Acheson as the "Red Dean of fashion," and described President Truman as a drunkard, adding, "The son of a bitch should be impeached." During the campaign itself, McCarthy claimed, falsely, that the *Daily Worker* had endorsed Democrat Adlai Stevenson for president. At several points, he made the ugly slip "Alger . . . I mean Adlai." And so it went.

Some Republicans were disturbed by McCarthy's behavior. Among them was Gen. Dwight D. Eisenhower, the party's presidential nominee. Eisenhower loathed McCarthy, yet he refused to criticize the senator in any meaningful way. He feared that a battle with the senator would split the Republican vote and cost him the election. As it turned out, however, the general's silence about McCarthyism would continue well into his presidential term.

McCarthy was easily reelected in 1952. With Republicans now in control of Congress, he expected to receive a committee chairmanship—a possibility that frightened the Senate's GOP leaders. McCarthy was a poor team player. If he kept hammering at Communists in government, he would now be attacking a *Republican* administration. To guard against this, GOP leaders offered him the chairmanship of a minor committee known as Government Operations. McCarthy gladly accepted. He knew that Government Operations had a Permanent Subcommittee on Investigations with the stated though little used authority to scrutinize "government activities at all levels." It lacked only an aggressive chairman, willing to lay claim to what was rightfully his.

McCarthy filled the committee's staff positions with former prosecutors, FBI agents, and professional anti-Communists. For the job of chief counsel he chose Roy Marcus Cohn, a brilliant, abrasive young attorney from New York. In short order, Chairman McCarthy began investigating "Communist influence" in government. His early targets included the Voice of America, the Government Printing Office, the Central Intelligence Agency, and the Foreign Service. At the same time, other bodies like the House Committee on Un-American Activ-

Owen Lattimore (l.), professor at Johns Hopkins University and author of *Ordeal by Slander,* with Boston clergyman Donald G. Lothrop, who invited the professor to lecture about his experience as a target of "McCarthyism." (Arthur Hansen/Boston Public Library)

ities searched for Communists in America's schools, churches, and labor unions.

McCarthy got much of his information from the FBI, which secretly opened its files to his investigators. Other material came from "patriotic" or disgruntled federal workers, who kept the senator well stocked with rumors, classified documents, and ideas for new investigations. McCarthy's hearings did not uncover any Communists. They did ruin a number of careers, however, and undermine the morale of countless government workers. The worst damage was done to the U.S. Army. In the fall of 1953, Cohn and McCarthy literally paralyzed the Army Signal Corps at Fort Monmouth, New Jersey, by charging that a spy ring was in operation there. Then the senator berated an army general for mishandling the case of a "subversive" dentist under his command. President Eisenhower had heard enough. He could not bear the thought of continued attacks upon his favorite institution. At long last, McCarthy had attacked the one target guaranteed to pit the Republican White House against him.

Early in 1954, the Senate decided to investigate the running feud between the army and McCarthy. At Eisenhower's insistence, Republican leaders agreed to televise the daily hearings. The president wanted the American people to see McCarthy in action. It proved to be a wise strategy. The cumulative impression of McCarthy's day-to-day performance—his windy speeches, his endless interruptions, his frightening outbursts, his crude personal attacks—was truly devastating. The highlight of the hearings came on 9 June 1954, when Army Counsel Joseph N. Welch asked the senator, "Have you no decency, sir? . . .

Have you left no sense of decency, sir? . . ." The audience burst into applause.

A few months later, the Senate censured McCarthy for "conduct . . . contrary to Senatorial traditions." The vote was 67–22, with only Republican conservatives opposed. Many believed that McCarthy's censure was linked to the easing of cold war tensions at home. The Korean War was over, Stalin was dead, the radical right was in disarray. For McCarthy himself, things came apart at a wicked rate of speed. The press now ignored him and his influence disappeared. When he rose to speak in the Senate, his colleagues drifted from the floor. Shunned and humiliated, unable to get his message across, he spent his final days drinking in private, railing bitterly against those who had deserted his cause. Joe McCarthy died of acute alcoholism in 1957 virtually alone. He was forty-eight years old.

The most recent biography of Senator McCarthy is David M. Oshinsky's *A Conspiracy So Immense: The World of Joe McCarthy* (New York: Free Press, 1983). Other biographies include Thomas Reeves, *The Life and Times of Joe McCarthy* (New York: Stein & Day, 1982), and Richard Rovere, *Senator Joe McCarthy* (New York: World, 1959). For McCarthy's influence on our political institutions, see Robert Griffith, *The Politics of Fear* (Lexington: University of Kentucky Press, 1970), and Richard Fried, *Men against McCarthy* (New York: Columbia University Press, 1976). For differing interpretations of McCarthyism, see William F. Buckley, Jr., and L. Brent Bozell, *McCarthy and His Enemies* (New York: Regnery, 1954); Daniel Bell, ed., *The Radical Right* (Garden City, N.Y.: Doubleday, 1963); Earl Latham, *The Communist Controversy in Washington from the New Deal to McCarthy* (Cambridge: Harvard University Press, 1966); and Michael Rogin, *The Intellectuals and McCarthy* (Cambridge: MIT Press, 1967).

DAVID M. OSHINSKY

See also Red Scare (and photograph)

McGrath, J. Howard

(28 November 1903–2 September 1966)

U.S. senator, 1947–49; chairman, Democratic National Committee, 1947–49; attorney general, 1949–52. Born in Woonsocket, Rhode Island, J. Howard McGrath became active in Democratic politics as a student at Providence College in the 1920s. He held several offices in state politics and was serving as governor of Rhode Island when he seconded Truman's vice-presidential nomination at the 1944 Democratic National Convention. He accepted Truman's nomination as U.S. solicitor general in September 1945 and served until October 1946, when he resigned to mount a successful campaign for a Senate seat from Rhode Island. Truman selected him to be chairman of the Democratic National Committee in September 1947. McGrath supported Truman's reelection bid, fought to maintain party cohesion, and helped chart the successful campaign strategy in 1948. He served concurrently in the Senate, where he compiled a 99 percent proadministration voting record.

Truman rewarded McGrath's loyalty by nominating him in August 1949 to replace Attorney General Tom Clark, who had accepted a seat on the Supreme Court. As attorney general, McGrath supported administration policies in controversial areas such as civil rights and loyalty investigations. But McGrath was more politician than administrator, and critics considered him ineffective.

Scandals in the Bureau of Internal Revenue (BIR) engulfed the Justice Department in 1951 and dominated McGrath's last months as attorney general. The failure of the Justice Department to pursue its investigation of corruption by collectors of internal revenue, compounded by Truman's dismissal of Assistant Attorney General T. Lamar Caudle for his involvement in the BIR scandals, led Truman to consider asking for McGrath's resignation late in 1951. McGrath fought to hold his job, and Truman, instead of firing him, gave McGrath responsibility to continue the BIR investigation. McGrath appointed a prominent New York Republican, Newbold Morris, to head the probe. Understaffed, underfunded, and unsupported by the Justice Department, Morris's inept investigation foundered, and McGrath fired him. The attorney general had failed a second time to clear up the scandal, so Truman asked for his resignation in April 1952.

Relations nonetheless remained warm between McGrath and Truman. When the former unsuccessfully sought the Rhode Island Democratic Senate nomination in 1960, Truman supported him. McGrath died of a heart attack in 1966.

McGrath's performance as attorney general is assessed in Robert J. Donovan's *Tumultuous Years* (New York: W. W. Norton, 1982) and Andrew J. Dunar's *The Truman Scandals and the Politics of Morality* (Columbia: University of Missouri Press, 1984).

ANDREW J. DUNAR

See also Scandals

Mao Tse-tung

(26 December 1893–9 September 1976)

Leader of the Chinese Communist revolution. Mao Tse-tung was born in the Hunan village of Shaoshan to a middle peasant family. At age sixteen he left home seeking a modern education. At Peking University while serving as a library assistant in 1918 he discovered Marxism and in 1921 participated in the First Congress of the Chinese Communist party (CCP), motivated less by doctrine than nationalism. In 1927 he found the key to ultimate success by basing the CCP movement on the peasantry.

Mao forced Harry Truman, who knew little about foreign affairs and less about American relations with Asia, to grapple with civil war and then Communist ascendancy in China. The reluctance with which Truman approached these issues reflected his sense of China as distant and inscrutable, having minimal significance in the global balance of power. China's instability, arising out of the Japanese war and Mao's determination to take control, meant, however, that the Chinese could not be ignored.

In 1945, his first year in office, Truman dispatched George Marshall to mediate the conflict between America's wartime ally Chiang Kai-shek and the Communists who, under Mao's leadership, emerged from their anti-Japanese struggle as serious challengers to Kuomintang (KMT) rule. Marshall's willingness to accept the mission, given his reputation as a war hero, rescued the White House from the embarrassment of Patrick Hurley's resignation as ambassador in which Hurley accused traitors in the Department of State of undermining his efforts to bring peace to China. Initially Mao cooperated in Marshall's attempts to negotiate an agreement with Chiang, trying to use the talks to prevent substantial American aid to the KMT and to arrange CCP participation in a coalition government. Mao's expectations diminished, however, as it became clear that despite Chiang's intransigence the Americans would not abandon his cause. Fighting soon erupted again, leading Truman at the end of 1946 to withdraw Marshall.

Truman's disillusionment extended as well to his evaluation of the Nationalist government. He felt contempt for Chiang as an ineffective administrator, surrounded by corrupt sycophants who embezzled American aid and depleted scarce internal resources. Nevertheless Truman's determined anti-Communism led him to believe that he could not abandon the KMT and support Mao. After a brief attempt to compel Chiang's cooperation through an arms embargo in 1946 and 1947, Truman resigned himself to an ongoing, if minimal, assistance program. Truman probably also vetoed Ambassador John Leighton Stuart's proposed trip to Peking in June 1949 to meet with Mao and explore future relations. During 1949 the American president was infuriated by the detention of American consul general Angus Ward in Mukden and contemplated blockading the China coast. Mao's July 1949 "lean-to-one-side" declaration of pro-Soviet policy further alienated Truman.

But the president did recognize that the KMT's days were numbered. He authorized the August 1949 China White Paper to explain the regime's impending fall and why the United States was not responsible. It enraged American China Lobbyists and Chiang's supporters in Formosa. Mao saw it as confirmation of his deepest suspicions regarding American involvement in the civil war. He issued a bitter rejoinder in his *Renmin Ribao* editorial "Farewell Leighton Stuart."

The rapid disintegration of KMT fortunes confronted Truman with painful choices in China. Should the United States flee with Chiang partisans to Formosa, or should it try to come to terms with Mao's new Communist regime on the mainland? Truman did not want to encourage Communism by recognizing Mao, but he did consider it important to retain contacts with the Chinese people. Accordingly, on 5 January 1950 Truman declared that the United States would not intervene to preserve the generalissimo's fortunes should Mao launch an invasion across the Formosa Straits. Intelligence estimates indicated that Formosa would fall in the summer of 1950 through a combination of Communist assault and internal collapse.

Truman's effort to disengage failed when war broke out in Korea. The president immediately interposed the U.S. Seventh Fleet in the Formosa Straits. With attention focused on Korea, Truman sought to prevent Mao or Chiang from initiating a distracting confrontation.

The North Korean attack also prompted renewal of the debate over Mao's degree of independence from Stalin's control. Truman had accepted the idea that the communist world was not a monolith and had responded with aid to Tito's expulsion from the bloc in 1948. Mao, like Tito, had come to power on his own, and analysts argued that he had scorned bad advice in order to bring his revolution to victory. Perhaps a pragmatic

Mao would recognize that the United States could meet China's enormous material and technical requirements, whereas a war-ravaged Soviet Union could not. Developments in Korea, however, dampened American hopes for a Sino-Soviet split.

Truman originally intended the Seventh Fleet intervention to be temporary, but he was never able to extricate his administration. Mao, outraged, had to give up plans to take Formosa. He gave little credence to Truman's assertions that the United States meant China no harm, particularly as American troops in Korea approached the Chinese border. The Nationalists adeptly turned the marriage of necessity into a long-term commitment. After PRC forces intervened in the Korean conflict in October 1950, bonds between Washington and Taipei grew stronger through extensive economic and military aid as well as collaboration in intelligence matters. Truman froze all Chinese assets in the United States, imposed a total embargo on trade with the mainland, and became a staunch opponent of Chinese entry into the United Nations.

By the end of his administration, Truman's flexibility in foreign policy had been seriously diminished and his domestic standing irreparably damaged by the American political repercussions of Mao's success in China. The Republican party, through the excesses of Senator Joseph McCarthy, used the fall of China to discredit Truman and ensure a GOP presidential victory in 1952.

Among the abundant reviews of Mao Tse-tung's life and times the best include Stuart Schram's *Mao Tse-tung* (New York: Simon & Schuster, 1966) and a broader study by Maurice Meisner, *Mao's China—and After* (New York: Free Press, 1986). Efforts by Truman and his administration to come to grips with Mao's rise to power are explored in Dorothy Borg and Waldo Heinrichs, eds., *Uncertain Years: Chinese American Relations 1945–1950* (New York: Columbia University Press, 1980); Tang Tsou's comprehensive but somewhat out-of-date *America's Failure in China, 1941–1950* (Chicago: University of Chicago Press, 1963); Akira Iriye, *The Cold War in Asia* (Englewood Cliffs, N.J.: Prentice-Hall, 1974); and Nancy Bernkopf Tucker, *Patterns in the Dust: Chinese-American Relations and the Recognition Controversy, 1949–1950* (New York: Columbia University Press, 1983). Excellent specialized studies on aspects of the period include Steven I. Levine's study of the Marshall mission, *Anvil of Victory* (New York: Columbia University Press, 1987), and Edwin W. Martin's *Divided Counsel: The Anglo-American Response to Communist Victory in China* (Lexington: University of Kentucky Press, 1986).

NANCY BERNKOPF TUCKER

See also Chiang Kai-shek; China (and photograph); Korean War

Marshall, George C., Jr.

(31 December 1880–16 October 1959)

Born in Uniontown, Pennsylvania, George C. Marshall was educated at the Virginia Military Institute (1897–1901). He was commissioned a second lieutenant in the U.S. Army in February 1902. In World War I, he became widely known as a superb staff officer as a result of his work as chief of operations, First Division, planner at General Headquarters, and chief of operations, First Army, in France. He became chief of staff of the army (including the army air corps) on 1 September 1939, the day the war began in Europe, and completed his tour of duty 20 November 1945. He was to serve almost as long under President Truman as he had under President Roosevelt.

Marshall and Truman began working together when the Missouri senator became chairman of the Senate Select Committee to Investigate the National Defense Program. Often referring to the general as "America's greatest soldier" or the "greatest living American," Truman called on him during his eight years in office to undertake four important tasks. After Marshall had supposedly retired, the president asked him first to head a mission to China, December 1945–January 1947, and then to be secretary of state, January 1947–January 1949, president of the American Red Cross, September 1949–September 1950, and secretary of defense, September 1950–September 1951. In the case of at least three of the appointments, it was believed that Marshall's prestige would allay some criticism of the administration. Marshall's insistence on a nonpartisan policy in the State Department and his firm refusal to consider any elective political office was a source of strength to the administration in the years 1947–49 when both houses of Congress were controlled by Republicans. The general's only disagreement with the president came when Marshall raised objections at a White House briefing, saying that Truman's staff was urging immediate recognition of Israel for purely domestic political reasons.

In his final report as chief of staff in the fall of 1945, Marshall made clear that the United States could not return to prewar isolation, for the war had brought the country new responsibilities of world leadership. He returned to this theme in an award ceremony at the Pentagon on his retirement of chief of staff in November 1945. He insisted that "along with the great problem of maintaining the peace we must solve the problem of food, of clothing and coal and homes."

On the day that Marshall returned to his retirement home, President Truman asked him to go to China as his representative to seek a cease-fire between the Chinese Communists and Nationalists, to integrate their fighting forces, and to support an effort to bring all Chinese political elements into one government. After a year of frustrated efforts, Marshall announced that his mission had failed, and President Truman then named him to succeed James F. Byrnes as secretary of state. The general took office on 21 January 1947. In his first important speech as secretary, Marshall told an audience at Princeton University on 22 February, "If the world is to get on its feet, if the productive facilities of the world are to be restored, if democratic processes in many countries are to resume their functioning, a strong lead and definite assistance from the United States will be necessary."

Even as Marshall spoke, the British government was asking the United States to assume its commitment to support the governments of Greece and Turkey against Communist aggression. Returning to Washington, Marshall conferred with Dean Acheson and then with representatives of the armed forces and recommended that the president assume this burden. In his Truman Doctrine speech to Congress the president asked for aid

George Catlett Marshall, 1949. Artist: Thomas Edgar Stephens. (National Portrait Gallery, Smithsonian Institution; gift of Ailsa Mellon Bruce)

Truman and submitted to Congress before the end of the year. In hearings before congressional committees and in later public appeals to rally support, Marshall campaigned as though he were running for office. He made effective use of his nonpartisan approach by working closely with Republican senator Vandenberg to advance the legislation. The European Recovery Program was enacted in the late spring of 1948. The president christened it the "Marshall Plan."

German problems dominated Marshall's last year at the State Department. The growing appeal of the Marshall Plan, development of a new currency for Germany, and British and U.S. moves toward giving the Germans a measure of self-government stirred the Soviet government in June to blockade all rail and highway communications from the West into Berlin. Gen. Lucius Clay led the Western Allies to institute a successful airlift of supplies for their zones in Berlin. Marshall was in favor of firmness, insisting that the United States should stay in Berlin, but advocating continued negotiations to end the blockade. These efforts consumed many hours of the meeting of the UN General Assembly in Paris during November and December 1948. The crisis had not yet ended when Marshall left office, but the continuing success of the airlift eased the way to an end of the blockade under Acheson.

On other fronts, Marshall was active in two Latin American conferences in 1947 and 1948. The first, at Rio de Janeiro, saw him trying to improve cooperation with countries to the south. The second, at Bogotá, was accompanied by rioting which threatened to disrupt the conference, but Marshall helped get a strong pact against outside aggression and backed the establishment of a new Latin American organization.

In 1948 Marshall was advised to have an operation for removal of a cyst on his right kidney, but he postponed any treatment until after the UN Assembly meeting. After Truman's stunning election victory that year, Marshall returned to Washington for removal of the diseased kidney. He resigned from office on 21 January 1949, the day after the inauguration.

When the presidency of the American Red Cross became vacant in the fall of 1949, Truman asked Marshall to take this position. Marshall helped effect changes recently recommended by a special panel, traveled widely to strengthen the organization, and after the Korean War started, worked to place the Red Cross in a position to deal with the demands of the new conflict.

Within a few days after the beginning of the Korean War, the president decided that he must have a new secretary of defense. Reverses in the Far East and strained relations between Secretary of Defense Louis Johnson and many of his colleagues led the president to ask Marshall to accept one more key assignment. Marshall agreed to serve for six months if Robert Lovett would become under secretary and succeed him when he left. Congress had to change the Unification Act to permit Marshall, who had served actively in the armed forces less than ten years earlier, to hold the office. He became secretary of defense in late September 1951 and served for almost a year, bringing his wartime expertise and prestige to the task of increasing appropriations and manpower for the armed forces. He emphatically supported Truman's effort to limit extension of the conflict in the Far East and agreed with the decision to relieve Gen. Douglas MacArthur of his Far East command in the spring of 1951. In the congressional hearings that followed MacArthur's dismissal, Marshall stood firm on the principle of civilian control of the armed forces. Particularly useful was Marshall's

to Greece and Turkey and added the suggestion that the United States should offer support to free peoples attempting to avoid subjugation by armed minorities or outside aggressors.

After weeks of negotiations at meetings of the Council of Foreign Ministers in Moscow to conclude treaties of peace with Germany and Austria, Marshall was convinced that Stalin sought to benefit from economic chaos in Europe. The secretary returned to the States to stress the possibility of European economic collapse. He had proposed a State Department Policy Planning Staff in January, and it was now activated under George Kennan. Marshall asked it for suggestions within a few weeks on a way to help Europe.

Drawing on studies already being made, Kennan on 23 May proposed that Europe take the initiative, select a committee to make an inventory of European needs and assets, and then ask the United States for aid. Four days later, Under Secretary of State for Economic Affairs Will L. Clayton, back from an international conference in Geneva on world economic problems, warned that the needs of Europe were desperate and critical. Marshall asked that a speech be drafted for him to give at Harvard University on 5 June, forwarding the Kennan and Clayton outlines and a short summary of his own.

Marshall's call for European action was answered by a European plan drawn up by sixteen countries. This plan, including an emergency aid provision and a larger four-year program costing approximately $17 billion, was accepted by President handling of the strains between the Pentagon and the State Department.

Not long before Marshall's final retirement, he was violently attacked in statements by Senator Joseph McCarthy. The matter became an issue in the 1952 presidential election when Gen. Dwight Eisenhower, the Republican candidate, removed from a speech he made in Wisconsin a statement defending Marshall from McCarthy's charges. Truman ever afterward accused Marshall's former protégé of base ingratitude.

In 1953, the Nobel Committee in Oslo awarded the Peace Prize to General Marshall. The chairman of the committee explained that this first presentation to a professional soldier was not for his outstanding military service but for his leadership in rehabilitating the European economy.

After nearly half a century of service as a soldier-statesman frequently compared with George Washington, Marshall died in 1959 and was buried in Arlington National Cemetery. Truman and Eisenhower, among the many who attended the final rites at the Fort Myer chapel, sat next to each other.

The authoritative work on General Marshall is the four-volume biography by Forrest C. Pogue. (New York: Viking Press, 1963–87). Volume 4 concerns Marshall and the Truman administration. Many of Marshall's official and personal papers and transcripts of several hundred interviews by Pogue in the United States and abroad are in the George C. Marshall Library, Lexington, Virginia. Two volumes of a projected six-volume collection of Marshall's papers have been published under the editorship of Dr. Larry Bland (Baltimore: John Hopkins Press, 1982). A third is in progress. The U.S. State Department Foreign Relations volumes for the years 1946–51 are essential to any study of Marshall. The Historical Office of the Department of Defense has issued a volume by Steven L. Rearden, *The Formative Years*, and another by Doris Condit is soon to be published on Marshall and Lovett as secretaries of defense.

FORREST C. POGUE

See also Armed Forces, Unification of the; China; Johnson, Louis Arthur; Marshall Plan; Truman Doctrine; United Nations (photograph)

Reg Manning, 12 October 1951. Courtesy of the McNaught Syndicate.

Marshall Plan

The European Recovery Program, which was proposed in 1947 and in operation from 1948 to 1952, is generally considered to be one of the major achievements of the Truman administration.

The issue of systematic American aid to promote the economic recovery of Europe came to the fore within the administration in early 1947, when the European economies were struggling, with little success, to overcome the destruction and dislocation produced by World War II and the likelihood of agreement with the Soviet Union on a postwar settlement was rapidly receding.

After the British announced in February that they would no longer be able to provide economic and military support to Greece, and after the United States had decided to include Tur-

key in any proposal to fill the vacuum thus created, Under Secretary of State Dean Acheson, with the cooperation of Secretary of War Robert Patterson and Navy Secretary James Forrestal, set the State-War-Navy Coordinating Committee (SWNCC) to studying "situations elsewhere in the world which may require analogous financial, technical and military aid on our part." On the same day, 5 March 1947, Under Secretary of State Will Clayton penned the first of several memoranda proposing that the United States extend financial and technical aid to what he referred to as "gravely threatened nations." Gen. Dwight D. Eisenhower, the army chief of staff, suggested a study along these lines a few weeks later.

President Truman gave public support to such a policy in a speech at Baylor University shortly before his Truman Doctrine address of 12 March in which he urged Congress to authorize aid, at least to Greece and Turkey, in order "to assist free peoples to work out their own destiny in their own way . . . primarily through economic and financial aid which is essential to economic stability and orderly political processes."

On 7 April, Truman asked Acheson to replace him, four weeks hence, as speaker at Delta State Teachers College in Cleveland, Mississippi, where he had promised to deliver an "important" address. Acheson proposed as his subject the urgent need for economic assistance to European countries and readily won the president's approval both for the topic and, later, for the prepared text. The result was a speech on 8 May, which Truman was later to call "the prologue to the Marshall Plan."

Secretary of State George C. Marshall, whose name, at Truman's insistence, the ultimate plan would bear, had joined in this ongoing process on his return from a futile meeting of the Council of Foreign Ministers in Moscow. "The recovery of Europe has been far slower than had been expected," he had told a radio audience on 28 April. "The patient is sinking while the doctors deliberate." On the following day, he had instructed the State Department's new Policy Planning Staff (PPS), headed by George Kennan, to look into the matter of European recovery and to propose a possible course of action. On 5 June, having studied a SWNCC report of 21 April, a PPS report of 23 May, a new Clayton memorandum of 27 May, and the text of Acheson's remarks in Mississippi, he delivered his celebrated commencement speech at Harvard, which offered American funding for a cooperative European economic recovery program.

At the time Marshall made his speech, there was no plan per se, but there was the idea, widely shared in the State and War departments and strongly supported by Truman, that an aid program was urgently required, would have to involve a high degree of inter-European cooperation, would in some fashion come to include Germany, and would have to be developed soon, preferably by the prospective recipients. Further ad hoc assistance, of the sort that had been dispensed almost since the war's end, was already being discussed as "interim aid," in anticipation of a more formal "permanent" arrangement. It was the alacrity of the European response, however, that led to speedy work on what would become the Marshall Plan. British foreign secretary Ernest Bevin did not even wait for the full text of the Harvard speech before contacting his French counterpart, George Bidault. "I grabbed the offer with both hands," he later told the National Press Club in Washington.

Truman publicly endorsed the as yet nonexistent Marshall Plan in a speech before the Canadian Parliament on 11 June and appointed three committees on 22 June to give guidance on an international assistance program. Bevin and Bidault, in the meanwhile, had invited Soviet foreign commissar Vyacheslav Molotov to meet with them in Paris to formulate a joint response to the American initiative. That meeting, which took place from 27 June to 1 July, brought Russian refusal to subscribe to what *Ukrainskaya Pravda* had already referred to disparagingly as the "Marshall Doctrine," with the result that the states of Eastern Europe under Soviet domination also could not participate. Invitations sent on 3 July to twenty-two European countries, including Turkey but excluding Spain, eventually brought sixteen favorable responses, all of them from Western Europe.

The immediate effects of Marshall's proposal were thus to harden the division of Europe and to convert American economic assistance into an instrument for winning the developing cold war. That this was its primary purpose was maintained not only by the Soviet Union but also by later critics who, noting the clear relationship to the Truman Doctrine, took literally the president's sometime comment that it and the Marshall Plan were "two halves of the same [containment] walnut." The truth, however, is more complex.

The Marshall Plan, from the outset, contained requirements for the disclosure of assets and needs that the Soviet Union was likely to reject, as well as for a degree of economic cooperation among the aid recipients that was not readily compatible with the Soviet economic system. Nor was there ever any question but that, as Clayton put it, "the United States must run this show." Concern was expressed throughout the discussion stage that the Russians could make implementation of an aid program extremely difficult, that their participation might make it hard to win congressional approval for both financial and ideological reasons, and that Soviet refusal to participate might, in practical terms, well prove a godsend.

Marshall's Harvard speech nevertheless made the point that the proposal was "directed not against any country or doctrine but against hunger ... and chaos," though the intended "revival of a working economy in the world" was also "to permit the emergence of political and social conditions in which free institutions can exist"—a formulation that prompted Bevin and Bidault to contact Molotov.

Truman, from the beginning, saw the proposed American aid as serving two major purposes: (1) it would lead to "the recovery of production abroad [which] is essential both to a vigorous democracy and to a peace founded on democracy and freedom," that is, to precisely what, in U.S. eyes, the Soviet Union had thus far prevented, and (2) "it is essential to a world trade in which our businessmen, farmers and workers may benefit," that is, to the maintenance of prosperity in the United States. He also laid stress on its humanitarian intent—the rehabilitation of Europe by those who had helped destroy it—later citing Missouri and Kansas after the Civil War as historical models. In theory at least, the active participation of the Soviet Union would have to be welcomed in all of these enterprises, even if it might be easier to do without it. To "play it straight," as George Kennan advised, therefore meant to include the Soviet Union, and invitations were in fact sent to nations on both sides of what Winston Churchill had, a year earlier, dubbed the iron curtain. The division of Europe, though not unforeseen and not unacceptable, was thus a fallback position, not the primary aim.

In July, the Committee of European Economic Cooperation (CEEC) was established, and, on 12 September, its members—Austria, Belgium, Denmark, France, Greece, Iceland, Ireland, Italy, Luxembourg, the Netherlands, Norway, Portugal, Switzerland, Turkey, and the United Kingdom—outlined the first actual plan. It was to be a four-year program to promote economic recovery in the participating countries and, at the insistence of the United States, West Germany as well, through (1) the restoration of agricultural production to prewar levels and of industrial production to somewhat higher ones, (2) the creation and maintenance of stable internal conditions, (3) the establishment of an organization to promote and expand economic cooperation among the participating countries, and (4) the elimination of the dollar deficit in each country through the increase of exports. American capital needed to achieve these aims had been estimated at $22 billion but was scaled down, on American advice, to $17 billion before the proposal was formally presented.

Representatives of the CEEC came to Washington in October and, in discussions with State Department officials, worked out more specific and detailed plans which could be submitted for congressional approval. The formal proposal to set up a European Recovery Program (ERP) along those lines was submitted by the president to Congress on 19 December as the Economic Cooperation Act. "Can you imagine its chances for passage in an election year in a Republican Congress," he later asked rhetorically, "if it is named for Truman and not Marshall?"

Although the debates in both the House and the Senate were prolonged and sometimes bitter, the yeoman efforts of

Senator Arthur Vandenberg of Michigan as well as of Marshall and others, in and out of the administration, were instrumental in producing approval by margins of better than four to one on 3 April 1948—in time to affect the Italian elections of 18 April in which a Communist victory had been feared. Truman had wanted to name Acheson, then temporarily out of the State Department, to administer the Marshall Plan as head of the Economic Cooperation Administration (ECA), but was persuaded to name the Republican president of the Studebaker Corporation, Paul Hoffman, instead. Secretary of Commerce Averell Harriman was named as special representative to the participating countries. The launching of the Marshall Plan thus became, on all counts, a prime example of America's bipartisan foreign policy, which was in itself a major achievement of the Truman administration and a source of pride for the president.

Between 1948 and 1951, Congress authorized $13,348,800,000 for the ERP and actually appropriated over $13 billion, of which $12 billion were distributed by the ECA for the purposes specified in its original mandate. Some 70 percent of that went to Great Britain, France, Italy, and West Germany. During 1951–52, the last year of the Marshall Plan, funds were increasingly channeled into military assistance, and subsequent aid to "Marshall Plan countries" was provided largely under the Mutual Security Program.

In economic terms, the Marshall Plan was a considerable success. Production levels in Europe rose even more rapidly and more steeply than had been proposed in 1947, as factories, and indeed whole cities, were rebuilt with the help of ERP funds. By 1950, prewar production levels had been exceeded by 25 percent overall. Dollar deficits shrank, though not as consistently as had been anticipated, and inflation was largely brought under control. Levels of employment rose sharply, as did the level of intergovernmental cooperation. The European Payments Union of 1950 and the European Coal and Steel Community of 1952 paved the way for the later European Common Market.

By 1952, the European economies, aided immensely by the influx of American capital, had indeed essentially recovered and were heading into a period of widespread prosperity. Marshall Plan payments, moreover, rather than draining American resources as opponents had charged, in various ways supported production at home and thus bolstered the American economy as well. Far from sliding into a postwar depression, as many, including Truman, had feared, the United States, too, entered a period of sustained prosperity.

Politically, the Marshall Plan helped stabilize some of the more shaky European governments, undercut the Communist parties in France and Italy, was a major factor in bringing a democratic Federal Republic of Germany into being, welded much of Western Europe into an effective anti-Soviet bloc, and thus promoted both the division of Europe and the free world–communist world confrontation of the cold war. It did not provide the means for winning that war, but it did lay the foundation for the uneasy stalemate that kept the peace in the ensuing decades.

Truman always regarded the Marshall Plan as one of his greatest achievements, and entertained few doubts concerning either its appropriateness or the value of its long-term results. Just after the adoption of the Economic Cooperation Act in 1948, the president melodramatically told the Gridiron Club: "God Almighty, on two different occasions, has appointed us to do a job. This time we must do it." He remained convinced that this time we had. "The Marshall Plan saved Europe," he told

Merle Miller in 1962, "and that's something I am glad I had some part in helping to accomplish."

Although the Marshall Plan is discussed in all of the works dealing with Truman and his presidency, and indeed in most of those on postwar Europe or the United States, the literature on the plan itself is remarkably slight. The fullest description remains Harry B. Price's now otherwise somewhat dated *The Marshall Plan and Its Meaning* (Ithaca, N.Y.: Cornell University Press, 1955). Joseph M. Jones's insider account of the bureaucratic origins of both the Truman Doctrine and the Marshall Plan, *The Fifteen Weeks (February 21–June 5, 1947)* (New York: Viking Press, 1955), remains both enlightening and suggestive. Another explanation for the thinking behind the plan, which, though not wholly persuasive, provides a useful perspective, is found in John Gimbel's *The Origins of the Marshall Plan* (Stanford, Calif.: Stanford University Press, 1973). Michael J. Hogan's *The Marshall Plan: America, Britain and the Reconstruction of Western Europe* (Cambridge: Cambridge University Press, 1987) details the labyrinthine discussions and negotiations in Washington and Europe which shaped and reshaped the Marshall Plan, and attempts to place the enterprise within the framework of a larger American economic foreign policy. The origins and enactment of the plan also receive much attention in the fourth and final volume of Forrest C. Pogue's biography *George C. Marshall: Statesman, 1945–1949* (New York: Viking Press, 1987).

MANFRED JONAS

See also Cold War; Harriman, W. Averell; Hoffman, Paul Gray; Marshall, George C., Jr.; Truman Doctrine

Masonic Order

One facet in the life of Harry S. Truman that has been overlooked consistently by his biographers is the profound effect that his membership in Masonic organizations had upon him. To ignore the Masonic influence on Truman is to overlook the expression of some of his most eminent qualities.

Of the many ideas and principles important to the concept of Masonry, universal brotherhood is probably the most widely known. Tolerance of diverse religious "denominations and persuasions" was the first principle adopted in the eighteenth-century constitutions. Mutual assistance and the promotion of secular education are also important concepts. The modern public school movement in the United States has had no more consistent group of supporters than the Masons. Of fundamental importance are the beliefs in a Supreme Being and in the immortality of the soul, the use of the Bible or other holy scriptures in every lodge, the imposition of secrecy concerning the group's rites, the acceptance of an allegory or legend relating to the building of King Solomon's Temple, and the use of symbolism based on the stonemason's craft. The chief allegories and symbols are contained in the three degrees or admissions ceremonies of the lodge: Entered Apprentice, Fellow Craft, and Master Mason. A petitioner, or candidate, who is accepted by ballot is "brought to light" in these three degrees and becomes a Master Mason. No man may become a candidate except at his own unsolicited request.

Former president Harry S. Truman dons a borrowed fez at the Shriners' annual convention, 11 July 1955. (Associated Press/Wide World Photos)

While working on the family farm near Grandview, Missouri, Truman petitioned the Belton Lodge and received his third degree on 9 March 1909. He was elected Junior Warden of the lodge in 1910. A year later he was instrumental in the organization of the Grandview Lodge and was elected its first Master when it become a chartered lodge. In 1925 he was appointed a District Deputy Grand Master and Lecturer, and in 1930 he was appointed Grand Pursuivant. He served as Grand Master of Missouri in 1940–41. Truman's personal life and his public programs were permeated with Masonic ideals. The thirteenth Mason to occupy the presidency, Truman was only the second to have served as a Grand Master. More than one hundred years earlier, his idol, Andrew Jackson, had served as Grand Master of Tennessee.

Although Truman's primary Masonic interest was the Blue Lodge, he did belong to most of the appendant bodies: the Scottish Rite Lodge, the York Rite, the Ancient Arabic Order of Nobles of the Mystic Shrine, the Order of DeMolay, and the Order of the Eastern Star. As a result of his military service, Truman was a member of the National Sojourners, an organization of Masons who had been officers in one of the armed forces.

He was furthermore the recipient of many honorary memberships in Masonic bodies throughout the world. Particularly noteworthy were his appointments as Honorary Deputy First Grand Principal of the Supreme Grand Lodge of Royal Arch Freemasons of Scotland and as Honorary Past Grand Master of the Grand Lodge of Israel.

Truman wholeheartedly accepted a tenet that has remained largely unchanged through the years of one of the world's largest and oldest fraternal organizations: to make good men better. He practiced both personally and professionally the basic mission of Masonry which was to help build a better world through its unique process of building better men to live in it, "by urging the practice of brotherly love for all, charitable relief for those who may be in need, and morality and good citizenship in every community." Truman once wrote, "Freemasonry is a system of morals which make it easier to live with your fellow man, whether he understands it or not."

Masonic influence in community life and politics has clearly diminished in this country since World War II. Some historians see the rise of the modern corporation and the development among employees of a corporate sense of identity and fraternity as being partly to blame for Masonry's decline. An unkind assessment is that the Masons are just old men clinging to the past. But this was not so in Harry Truman's world of the 1940s when Masons were at the core of power and money in America.

Truman was the only president to attain the thirty-third and last degree of the Supreme Council of the Scottish Rite for the southern jurisdiction, which honor was accorded to him on 19 October 1945 at the House of the Temple, Washington, D.C. President Harding had been nominated, but he died before the degree was conferred.

At Truman's request, the cornerstone of the Truman Library was laid with Masonic ceremonies on 6 July 1957 by the Grand Lodge of Missouri, and he was buried in December 1972 with Masonic honors. As Truman had stipulated, the service was conducted by W. Hugh McLaughlin, Grand Master of Missouri.

The most complete account of Truman's Masonic affiliations is *Brother Truman: The Masonic Life and Philosophy of Harry S. Truman* by Allen E. Roberts (Highland Springs, Va.: Anchor Communications, 1985). See also *The Freemason*, spring 1973, published by the Grand Lodge of Missouri. The Harry S. Truman Library has files on Truman's Masonic life; see especially "Information on Harry S. Truman's Masonic Career," C. Warren Ohrvall, editor.

ARTHUR F. MCCLURE II

Memorials

See Portraits and Memorials

Military Career

As a boy, Harry S. Truman developed an interest in the military by reading biographies of great military leaders of the past. He considered a military career and planned to seek appointment to West Point until he learned that his poor eyesight would disqualify him. In 1905 he joined a newly formed Kansas City National Guard artillery battery and participated in drills and

Captain Truman, France, 1918. (Courtesy of the Harry S. Truman Library)

summer encampments for several years. He let his enlistment expire in 1911, however, because of the demands of work on the family farm.

After the United States entered World War I in April 1917, Truman joined a Missouri National Guard field artillery regiment in Kansas City and won election as an officer. Federalized as the 129th Field Artillery Regiment of the Thirty-fifth Division, the regiment went to Fort Sill, Oklahoma, for training in September. Truman learned to compute barrages and fire the French 75mm artillery guns that he would use in combat. He ran a regimental canteen that outperformed all others on the base.

His success at Fort Sill won Truman a promotion and appointment to an advance party that preceded the regiment to Europe. From his arrival in France in April 1918 until he rejoined his regiment, he underwent rigorous training at the School of Fire in Montigny-sur-Aube, following a schedule so intense that he compared it to West Point.

Shortly after he rejoined his regiment in Angers, Truman took command of Battery D, a predominantly Irish-Catholic contingent with a reputation for rowdiness and intransigence. Truman took control and began to demonstrate his capacity to lead. The battery had its first test under fire late in August 1918 in the Vosges Forest in an area designated as a "quiet sector." In an encounter remembered in battery lore as the "Battle of Who Run," several men, including the leading sergeant, panicked and fled when their positions came under fire. Truman's display of courage in rallying the "stayers" won him

the respect and loyalty of his men. In early September, the regiment rejoined the Thirty-fifth Division as a reserve unit for the St. Mihiel offensive.

The last five days of September 1918 were the height of Truman's combat experience. Battery D's artillery joined in the opening barrages of the Meuse-Argonne offensive on the morning of 26 September. After firing its assigned barrages, the 129th FA regiment followed the Thirty-fifth Division's infantry regiments across hilly shell-pocked terrain that had been a no-man's-land. Mud and enemy fire inhibited progress. Truman alternated between directing barrages from forward observation posts and advancing with his battery. He described the action at the time as "the most terrific experience of my life."

Truman's regiment spent the last weeks before Armistice near Verdun, firing barrages when required, even in the early morning hours of 11 November, the day the war ended. The regiment remained in France until spring and returned home in May 1919.

Truman's ties to the military did not end with his return to civilian life. He joined the Officers Reserve Corps and rose to the rank of colonel. He attended summer encampments, usually at Fort Riley, Kansas, in the 1920s and 1930s, returning even during his first term in the Senate. He was one of the founders of the Reserve Officers Association in Kansas City, and remained active in the American Legion and other veterans' organizations for years.

Truman's military experience had a profound influence on his political career. It gave him self-confidence and the conviction that he had the capacity to lead. "My whole political career is based on my war service and war associates," he later claimed. Veterans formed the core of his support in his Jackson County campaigns, and his work with veterans' organizations helped provide statewide contacts for his 1934 Senate campaign. During his first term, he adopted American Legion positions on defense as his own. He served on Senate committees responsible for military appropriations and policy. His knowledge of the military contributed to the success of the Truman committee, which investigated defense expenditures during World War II and gave him the national reputation that made possible his nomination as vice president in 1944.

In the presidency, Truman relied on military principles of organization and proposed legislation that reflected his own military background. He called for expanded National Guard and reserve units, universal military training, and military reorganization. His ideas on national health insurance and civil rights drew on army experiences. Several advisers and one cabinet member—Secretary of the Treasury John W. Snyder—were military associates.

From rear-ranks private to colonel, and from Senate military committee membership to commander in chief, Truman saw the military from more perspectives than perhaps any other American president.

Richard Miller's *Truman: The Rise to Power* (New York: McGraw-Hill, 1986) is the most detailed study of Truman's military career. Many of Truman's letters home from Fort Sill and France were included in Robert H. Ferrell, ed., *Dear Bess* (New York: W. W. Norton, 1983).

ANDREW J. DUNAR

See also Battery D

Military Spending

Following the Second World War, Harry S. Truman was determined to hold military spending to the minimum necessary to meet the nation's defense commitments. A strong American economy, which Truman viewed as a national defense priority, required controlling excessive military outlays. Nevertheless, the need to maintain a significant standing peacetime military force, increased tensions with the Soviet Union, and the onset of the cold war put pressure on Truman to expand the defense budget. Although Truman resisted massive increases in military spending, the Korean War forced a threefold increase in the defense budget.

When Truman became president in 1945, U.S. military spending was the greatest in the nation's history. The military requirements of the Second World War peaked at $81.6 billion in FY 1945 (1 July 1944–30 June 1945). With the unexpected end of the war with Japan in August, however, rapid demobilization could not be restrained. Truman would have preferred a slower pace of demobilization, but the public clamor to bring the troops home was such that he did not believe that he could offer active resistance. Demobilization, in any event, served his policy of curbing spending to combat inflation. Defense expenditures thus fell to $44.7 billion in FY 1946 and all the way to $13.1 billion in FY 1947.

Despite these enormous reductions, the United States retained a significant peacetime military force. Even following demobilization, the armed forces in 1946 were four times larger than in 1940 when the military budget was only $1.8 billion. During the war, Franklin D. Roosevelt had decided to maintain a comparatively large peacetime military force, and this policy was willingly carried through by Truman when he became president. The unprecedented American support of a large standing army was sustained by the need for occupation troops in Germany and Japan, the fear of further chaos on the international scene, and the guilt over abandoning Europe after the First World War.

Truman knew that U.S. resources were not unlimited. The specter of depression and the reality of postwar inflation required a strong economy. Truman and his advisers believed that unrestrained military spending would result in persistent budget deficits, bringing about rampant inflation or confiscatory taxes and economic controls. Neither was palatable, and until the Korean War, the Truman administration sought to maintain a balanced budget intended to promote a healthy economy and reduce the public debt. Defense considerations were by and large subordinate to the broader requirements of fiscal policy and the national interest.

Truman was not oblivious to the deterioration of relations with the Soviet Union or to the fear of Soviet expansionism. Nonetheless, he believed that America's most appropriate response to the Russian threat was economic rather than military. Indeed, the administration seriously entertained the idea that the Soviets wanted the United States to drive itself into bankruptcy through military spending. Adequate U.S. military strength was an undoubted requirement, but Truman preferred foreign economic aid and military assistance programs rather than military action to discourage Soviet aggression. Thus, the immediate fruits of the 1947 Truman Doctrine were economic aid and military assistance to Greece and Turkey totaling $400 million. In the same manner, the Marshall Plan was a multibillion-dollar economic assistance plan designed to forestall the economic and political collapse of Europe. Because of Truman's emphasis on budget restraint, foreign aid funds were taken mostly out of military spending.

Until confronted with military disaster in Korea, Truman held fast to the belief that the United States should maintain only the minimum defense required to meet evident security needs. He wanted to be ready to defend the United States, but he did not want to support a large military establishment prepared to fight a war he did not expect to come. Thus, he argued for a balanced and sensible defense the nation could afford. The president's policy was endorsed by Secretary of State George Marshall who feared that a massive U.S. military buildup could bring about the very military confrontation that the administration wanted to prevent.

The Truman administration, therefore, attempted to maintain a stable military capability in the face of growing cold war tensions which increased American commitments abroad. Consequently, American responsibilities under the North Atlantic

Miliary Spending, 1945–54

FISCAL YEAR	TOTAL GOVERNMENT SPENDING (BILLIONS OF $)	MILITARY SPENDING (BILLIONS OF $)	DEFENSE AS % OF TOTAL GOVERMENT SPENDING	GROSS NATIONAL PRODUCT (BILLIONS OF $)	DEFENSE AS % OF GROSS NATIONAL PRODUCT
1945	95.2	81.6	85.7	211.9	38.5
1946	61.7	44.7	72.4	208.5	21.4
1947	36.9	13.1	35.5	231.3	5.7
1948	36.5	13.0	35.6	257.6	5.0
1949	40.6	13.1	32.2	256.5	5.1
1950	43.1	13.1	30.4	284.8	4.6
1951	45.8	22.5	49.1	328.4	6.9
1952	68.0	44.0	64.7	345.5	12.7
1953	76.8	50.4	65.6	364.6	13.8
1954	70.9	46.6	65.7	364.8	12.8

Source: John Lewis Gaddis, *Strategies of Containment: A Critical Appraisal of Postwar American National Security Policy* (New York: Oxford University Press, 1982), 359.

Treaty Organization (NATO) threatened to outstrip the United States' conventional military power. In Truman's mind the American monopoly of the atomic bomb, to a large extent, compensated for the discrepancy between America's commitment to defend Europe and conventional capability. Truman told David E. Lilienthal, chairman of the Atomic Energy Commission, that the atomic bomb was the "mainstay" against Soviet expansionism in Europe. Thus the bomb not only provided an atomic shield for Europe but also enabled Truman to maintain a tighter rein on military spending than otherwise might have been prudently possible.

Truman enthusiastically suppressed military spending. In 1946, as part of a governmentwide effort to balance the budget, he ordered that the defense allocation not exceed one-third of total national revenues. He also adopted the "remainder method" of calculating military spending: the military budget would be determined by first subtracting civilian requirements from the overall budget and then providing defense the "remainder." The president optimistically envisioned a time when defense spending would level off at $6 to $7 billion annually.

Not everyone within the government agreed with Truman's approach to military spending. Republican conservatives in Congress frequently scrutinized the budget more closely than Truman. When the Republicans won control of both houses in the 1946 election they mounted significant opposition to Truman's fiscal policies. In January 1947, he submitted a FY 1948 defense budget request of $11.2 billion, a decrease of almost 15 percent over FY 1947. The Joint Congressional Committee on the Legislative Budget, however, recommended trimming $1.75 billion off the administration figure. The House of Representatives agreed with the committee, but the Senate, largely through the influence of Arthur H. Vandenberg, Republican senator from Michigan, voted to hold budget cuts to a minimum. In the resulting conference committee, the Senate budget figures prevailed.

Pressure on Truman to increase defense spending, both from the military and to a lesser extent from Truman's civilian defense advisers, was as intense as the pressure to decrease defense spending. The military services collectively believed that Truman's requests for defense appropriations were insufficient, and the army, navy, and air force individually were convinced that they were also being slighted in favor of the other branches. In the midst of the 1946 demobilization, Truman was angered to discover that the navy was lobbying on Capitol Hill for an FY 1947 budget of $6.5 billion when he had recommended $4.5 billion. He indicated to Harold D. Smith, his budget director, that not only was he offended by the navy's behavior but he also believed the navy had breached discipline. Truman considered firing the chief of naval operations and threatened to veto any bill that appropriated the sums the navy wanted.

As his budget problems with the military intensified, Truman came to suspect that interservice rivalry was a major cause of the Pentagon's heavy spending and blatant lobbying for larger appropriations. Part of the problem had been the autonomy of the armed forces, which the National Security Act of 1947 had sought to unify by placing the services under the nominal suzerainty of the secretary of defense. Endowed with only weak authority and unable to control the military establishment, James V. Forrestal, the first secretary of defense, was nonetheless responsible for submitting combined coordinated military budgets. From 1947 through 1949, Forrestal was caught between recalcitrant service secretaries demanding sharply increased appropriations and the president insisting upon austere defense budgets. Truman remained steadfast in the face of service demands and unshaken by Forrestal's dilemma. Commenting on the president's tightfisted hold on military spending, Forrestal observed, "In Harry Truman I have seen the most rocklike example of civilian control that the world has ever witnessed."

Truman's first concession toward increasing military spending came in the spring of 1948 when the international situation appeared so threatening that even he thought it prudent to expand the nation's military capability. In early March, the United States, Great Britain, and France agreed to the economic and political integration of West Germany, a move that was bitterly opposed by the Soviet Union. Simultaneously, Czechoslovakia erupted in political crisis. The Communists staged a coup, and on 10 March, Jan Masaryk, Czech foreign minister, either committed suicide or, as Truman suspected, was the victim of foul play. Truman responded to the heightened tensions by appearing before a special joint session of Congress, condemning the "ruthless course" of Soviet policy, and asking for enactment of Universal Military Training, full funding of the Marshall Plan, and the buildup of U.S. ground capabilities. "What Truman wanted to do," recalled James E. Webb, the new budget director, "was to give the Soviets a signal that although we had cut down on military spending, we were ready to go back up again."

Truman, at the same time, was not going to release his tight hold on the budgetary reins. He proposed a supplemental appropriation to the FY 1949 budget of $1.5 billion. The three services, however, submitted requests for an additional $8.8 billion, an amount that Truman, influenced by the fact that the Republican-controlled Congress had cut taxes over his veto, would not even consider. Ultimately, Forrestal convinced Truman that $1.5 billion was insufficient, and the president agreed to submit a request to Congress for $3.2 billion. Nonetheless, Truman told the Joint Chiefs of Staff and the service secretaries that the $3.2 billion request was excessive in terms of what its impact on the economy would be. Despite his reservations, he expected their public and private support, both to the FY 1949 supplemental request and to the FY 1950 defense budget request which would have a ceiling of $14.4 billion.

The Pentagon, nevertheless, submitted FY 1950 requests to Forrestal totaling almost $29 billion. Forrestal told the services to submit a reduced figure, and the secretaries pared back their budget requests to $23.6 billion. Finally, a distraught Forrestal submitted a budget of $16.9 billion. Believing that his November 1948 election victory confirmed public backing for his fiscal policies, Truman insisted on the $14.4 billion budget. Moreover, the National Security Council in NSC 20/4, adopted in the fall of 1948, supported the president's contention that a $14.4 billion budget would not endanger national security. At the beginning of his second term in 1949, Truman had no intention of sponsoring a policy of major rearmament.

Events requiring drastic revaluation of military spending overwhelmed the Truman administration in 1949. The takeover of China by the Communists and the explosion of a Soviet atomic bomb in the fall of 1949 forced Truman into a reappraisal of basic national security policy. Under the direction of Secretary of State Dean Acheson and Paul Nitze, director of the State Department Policy Planning Staff, the National Security Council produced NSC 68, the most significant assessment of national security policy since World War II. Delivered to

Truman in April 1950, NSC 68 focused on the threat posed by an aggressive international communism centered in the Kremlin and by the military capability of the Soviet Union. Acheson and Nitze recommended the reordering of U.S. priorities that would require a significant increase in national defense. The United States, NSC 68 noted, held clear superiority only in the field of atomic weapons, but even this lead was in jeopardy with the advent of Soviet atomic capability. The maintenance of a credible deterrent, Acheson and Nitze argued, required not only accelerated development in the nuclear field but also a greatly expanded conventional military capability. Although NSC 68 did not mention the costs that such a buildup would entail, preliminary estimates by Truman's advisers suggested annual appropriations of $35 billion to $40 billion.

Truman's immediate questions about NSC 68 focused on the cost of a military buildup and its impact on the American economy. He postponed action on the report until his chief economic advisers had had a chance to determine its budgetary and economic implications. Historian Steven Rearden suggests that Truman's willingness even to discuss NSC 68 reflected the president's deep concern over the Soviet military threat. Yet even the Soviet threat did not appear to loosen Truman's hold on the nation's purse strings. His apparent worry was the promise of substantial increases in military spending. He could support the thrust of NSC 68 because it avoided recommending specific cost and force levels requiring commitment to large-scale outlays. His delay, Rearden speculates, was a tactical move to give the Bureau of Budget time to reduce the military increases to palatable levels. The president would have had to increase military spending to reassure Congress and the public, but it is doubtful that he would have supported in peacetime the full-blown military buildup recommended in NSC 68.

The onset of the Korean War in June of 1950 smashed Truman's resistance to increased military spending and swept away his reservations about implementing NSC 68. The war itself required increases in manpower, equipment, supplies, and consequently military spending. At the same time, the administration was gripped by fear that the Korean action presaged Soviet aggression elsewhere in the world, most probably in Germany. The attack on South Korea, for Truman and his advisers, seemed to justify the warnings of NSC 68 about Soviet intentions. The administration, in a complete reversal of policy, thus instituted a military buildup far beyond the necessities of the Korean War.

At a cabinet meeting on 14 July 1950, Secretary of State Acheson stated that the most important thing that the United States could do to counter North Korean aggression was to step up military production and expand military capabilities. Acheson wanted to strike fear into the United States' enemies and deter further aggression. Truman agreed and on 19 July sent a message to Congress requesting a supplemental military appropriation of $10 billion to increase forces in Korea, augment U.S. forces above and beyond that needed for Korea, and provide for military assistance to U.S. allies. On 30 September 1950, the National Security Council adopted NSC 68 as the nation's security policy. Following the Chinese intervention in Korea in November 1950, Truman requested an additional military appropriation from Congress of $18 billion.

All pretense of defense budget austerity was thus obliterated by the Korean War. For the remainder of Truman's second term, the military budget, and with it military spending, continued to expand largely unabated. Ironically, it was this legacy of

military spending that Dwight D. Eisenhower inherited in 1953 and to which Eisenhower responded with his own attempts to keep military spending in line.

A comprehensive monographic history of Truman's military spending policies has not been written. The essential outline of that policy can be traced in Robert J. Donovan's two-volume history, *Conflict and Crisis: The Presidency of Harry S Truman, 1945–1948* and *Tumultuous Years: The Presidency of Harry S Truman, 1949–1953* (New York: W. W. Norton, 1977, 1982). Chapter-length analyses of the development of the FY 1949, 1950, and 1951 military budgets, as well as of NSC 68, can be found in Steven L. Rearden's history of the Office of the Secretary of Defense, *The Formative Years, 1947–1950* (Washington, D.C.: U.S. Government Printing Office, 1984). Warren R. Schilling's "The Politics of National Defense: Fiscal 1950" provides a detailed look at legislative-executive interaction on the military budget, and Paul Y. Hammond's "NSC-68: Prologue to Rearmament" discusses Truman's outlook toward the policy study before the outbreak of the Korean War. Both are found in Schilling, Hammond, and Glenn H. Snyder, *Strategy, Politics, and Defense Budgets* (New York: Columbia University Press, 1962). Richard F. Haynes, *The Awesome Power: Harry S. Truman as Commander in Chief* (Baton Rouge: Louisiana State University Press, 1973), offers a brief appraisal of Truman's role in the budget battles with the military.

JACK M. HOLL
TERRENCE R. FEHNER

See also Korean War; Mobilization; NSC 68

Minton, Sherman

(20 October 1890–9 April 1965)

Associate justice, U.S. Supreme Court, 1949–56. Sherman Minton was born in Georgetown, Indiana. He graduated with an LL.B. from Indiana University in 1915 and an LL.M. from Yale in 1916. Admitted to the Indiana bar, he practiced law in that state and in Florida before being appointed public counselor for the Indiana Public Service Commission in 1933. Elected to the U.S. Senate in 1934, he quickly became a close friend of his Senate colleague Harry Truman, whom Minton, when he was subsequently a presidential assistant, recommended to Franklin Roosevelt to head a committee investigating wartime profiteering. Minton was appointed by Roosevelt to the U.S. Circuit Court of Appeals for the Seventh Circuit in Chicago at about the same time Harry Truman became vice president. The two men remained close friends and confidants through the years.

When Justice Wiley Rutledge died in 1949, Truman promptly appointed Minton to replace him, feeling that his Senate record had demonstrated his liberal tendencies and that he would strengthen the liberal bloc on the Court. Minton, like Truman, had a narrow view of a justice's role. Both had supported Roosevelt's Court-packing plan, feeling the pre-1937 Court should have respected judicial restraint.

Minton's Court career was generally undistinguished. He turned out to be one of the most conservative members of the

Court. Besides his strong belief in judicial restraint, he thought government should have a wide latitude of power. Voting for individual claims less than 15 percent of the time, he helped destroy the liberal bloc's influence upon civil liberties decisions, and the Court ceased to defend civil liberties as it had prior to his appointment. In *United States* v. *Rabinowitz* (1950), Minton upheld a search without a warrant after a valid arrest by arguing that the Fourth Amendment prohibited only "unreasonable searches" and that the test for reasonableness depended only on whether the search itself was reasonable, not whether it was reasonable to obtain a warrant. In *United States ex rel, Knauff* v. *Shaughnessy* (1950), he upheld the exclusion from the country, without a hearing, of a war-bride, maintaining that a hearing would have harmed the national interest by disclosing information of a confidential nature. He joined with the majority in the *Dennis* case and subsequently voted to uphold a New York law providing for the removal of teachers on disloyalty grounds.

After 1950, Minton found himself generally in the conservative minority on the Court. Although he participated in the unanimous decision in *Brown* v. *Board of Education* (1954), his personal commitment to civil rights was generally thin and cautious. In the case of *Terry* v. *Adams* (1953), in which the Court held that a pre-primary election in Texas could not exclude blacks, Minton in a lone dissent argued that he could find no state action, since it was an unofficial pre-primary, thereby defending the exclusion.

Minton retired from the Court in October 1956 because of ill-health and died nine years later. Constitutional scholars have regarded him as a "failure" among Supreme Court justices; it was his senatorial career that was a more positive monument to his political acumen and his obvious skills as a political tactician.

Henry L. Wallace wrote a thorough and sympathetic account of Minton's work: "Mr. Justice Minton: Hoosier Justice on the Supreme Court," *Indiana Law Journal* 34 (1959): 145. See also George D. Braden, "Mr. Justice Minton and the Truman Bloc," *Indiana Law Journal* 26 (1951): 153. Minton's work is also discussed in C. Herman Prichett, *Civil Liberties and the Vinson Court* (Chicago: University of Chicago Press, 1954), and Walter Murphy, *Congress and the Court* (Chicago: University of Chicago Press, 1962). Richard S. Kirkendall, "Sherman Minton," in *The Justices of the United States Supreme Court*, ed. Leon Friedman and Fred Israel, 4:2639–61 (New York: Chelsea House, 1969), is a useful brief biography, with representative cases.

PAUL L. MURPHY

See also Supreme Court, United States (and photograph)

Missouri

Missouri was *home* to Harry Truman. He wrote in November 1956: "I've been to many countries in Europe, South and Central America. I've been to Mexico and Canada. And while I had great receptions in all of them—I still favor Missouri as the best place to live. I've had every political office, nearly, from precinct to President of the United States, and I came back home to live at the end of it all."

Jonathan Daniels in *The Man of Independence* quoted Mark Twain as having once remarked during a visit to India, "All that goes to make the *me* in me was in a Missourian village on the other side of the globe." Daniels notes that the same could be said for Harry Truman. Truman's roots went deep into the Missouri past. Both sets of grandparents had migrated from Kentucky to the western Missouri frontier in the 1840s. Although both grandfathers died when he was quite young, Harry had strong memories of them and their farms, where he spent many pleasant times as a preschooler. He later recalled: "I had just the happiest childhood that could ever be imagined. My brother, Vivian, and I and two or three of the neighborhood boys used to have a great time playing in the pasture south of the house out at Grandview."

The family moved to Independence when Harry was six, and he literally grew up with the town. When the family moved there in 1890, it had a population of 6,380. By the time he retired from public office sixty years later it had grown to 36,963. And Edgar Hinde, longtime Independence postmaster and Harry's friend from Battery D days, could observe: "I think when Harry came back to Independence from Washington, he sort of hoped he could live like everybody else. He'd been used to going up around our old country square here, and he always knew everyone there. . . . Of course, Independence is no longer a small town; it's a small city. . . . And there are all the visitors, all wanting to take a look at Harry Truman."

Truman never forgot his roots. Although he got his start in politics through the Pendergast machine, he quickly established a network of friendships across Missouri through participation in the state's association of county judges, the American Legion, Masonic bodies, the National Old Trails Association, and the Reserve Officers Association. He strengthened these further by serving in a number of state posts following the Democratic triumph of 1932. Consequently he had his own statewide reputation, aside from the Pendergast connection, when he ran successfully for the U.S. Senate in 1934.

Whether as senator or president, Harry Truman was always concerned to promote the interests and image of his home state. It was his fear that Missouri industries were not getting their fair share of defense contracts that led him, in part, to propose his World War II Senate investigating committee, which propelled him into the national limelight. As president, he made certain that the Japanese surrender document was signed on the USS *Missouri*. He loved to show off his piano-playing talents by performing "The Missouri Waltz." When he endorsed Westminster College's invitation to Winston Churchill, he added, "This is a wonderful school in my home state."

Harry Truman referred frequently to his Missouri background and experiences. Wherever he went, he tied Missouri into his conversation, usually through some association, often contrived, with the place of the moment. At the end of the 1948 campaign, he proclaimed that he had been "born and raised in the 'show me' state," had "learned how 'show me' works," and had been "showing them."

When Harry Truman assumed the presidency, journalists and others sought to try to understand him in relation to his Missouri roots. Hence the state received a great deal of attention and analysis. Observers were particularly concerned to make the contrast between Truman, the small-town Missourian, and Roosevelt, the country gentleman of Hyde Park. But

Missouri characteristics, though they appeared to be many, failed to produce an overall composite. Harry Truman was a son of Missouri, but he remained distinctively himself.

The best treatment of Truman's relationship to Missouri throughout his political career is to be found in Richard S. Kirkendall, *A History of Missouri*, vol. 5, *1919-1953* (Columbia: University of Missouri Press, 1986). The most comprehensive appraisal of his ancestral development, although Truman criticized an occasional detail, is Jonathan Daniels, *The Man of Independence* (Philadelphia and New York: J. B. Lippincott, 1950). Truman's boyhood remembrance and the observation by Edgar Hinde may be found in Merle Miller, *Plain Speaking: An Oral Biography of Harry S. Truman* (New York: Berkley Publishing, 1973). Truman's 1956 statement is in Monte M. Poen, ed., *Strictly Personal and Confidential: The Letters Harry Truman Never Mailed* (Boston: Little, Brown, 1982).

WILLIAM E. PARRISH

See also Independence, Missouri; Kansas City, Missouri; Lamar, Missouri; Missouri River; Outstate Missouri

Missouri River

Harry Truman believed the Missouri River was the key to his home state's prosperity if it could only be controlled. Throughout his career, from presiding judge in Jackson County to president of the United States, Truman expressed a keen interest in plans that might treat the river as a comprehensive whole and develop it for the betterment of the Missouri Valley's residents. His interest in the river led him to support first Gen. Lewis Pick's plan for development and ultimately the Missouri Valley Authority. But whatever the plan, Truman's primary concern was to halt the almost annual floods that hampered Missouri's growth and development.

The Missouri overflowed its banks in 1943 in an incredible demonstration of destructive power. Flood waters reached their highest levels in eighty years, 2.5 million acres disappeared under swirling, muddy water, nine people died, and the cost of the damage exceeded $50 million. Control of the Missouri River became an urgent priority.

Both the Army Corps of Engineers and the Bureau of Reclamation had responsibilities on the Missouri River and both introduced comprehensive plans for flood control in the Missouri Basin. Senator Truman applauded the corps' plan developed by Pick, but Congress, faced with two development plans for the Missouri River, deadlocked. The deadlock was broken after a Montana Democrat, Senator James Murray, introduced a Missouri Valley Authority (MVA) bill that proposed to reorganize water resource development along the lines of a Tennessee Valley Authority (TVA). The Army Corps of Engineers and the Bureau of Reclamation reacted quickly with a compromise known as the Pick-Sloan Plan. The agreement, designed to show interagency cooperation, included $150 million worth of projects that only a few days earlier were considered worthless by one agency or the other and contained no justification of costs and numerous duplications. The agreement's architects did not

know whether sufficient water existed to provide for both upstream irrigation and downstream navigation. Despite these problems, the 1944 Pick-Sloan Plan effectively sidetracked efforts to authorize a Missouri Valley Authority.

Senator Truman's support for the Pick-Sloan Plan was pragmatic. Truman wanted a comprehensive plan and Pick-Sloan provided one that would build earthen levees, concrete floodwalls, and 105 dams, all of which promised relief for flood-ravaged Missouri. During Truman's campaign for the vice presidency he called for the creation of an independent valley authority in the Missouri Valley, but after his election he did nothing to further the cause. In fact, Truman referred Murray's reintroduced MVA bill to a hostile committee. Truman's action may have been appropriate (he thought so), or a mistake, or part of maneuverings against the bill. In any case, his action helped kill the MVA in 1945.

Truman's early support for an independent valley authority may have been mixed, but he began his presidency by strongly advocating a regional authority in the Missouri Valley. His "Twenty-One-Point Message" called for an MVA based on the TVA model and he sent Congress several messages of support for the concept. Opposition, though, developed at several levels. The Bureau of Reclamation and the Army Corps of Engineers launched a public relations campaign to demonstrate their newfound harmony, and the influential senator John Overton, a Louisiana Democrat, backed by the governors of ten Missouri Basin states, told Truman no new organization was necessary since the bureau and the corps had settled their differences and developed a comprehensive plan for the valley. Overton noted that since both the House and the Senate had approved the Pick-Sloan Plan the legislature must have been satisfied with it.

When Harold Ickes left the Department of the Interior in 1946 Truman was presented with the opportunity to appoint a secretary who would support the MVA concept. Julius "Cap" Krug was Truman's choice. Krug, a former chief power engineer for the TVA, became an outspoken proponent for developing the Missouri River on the TVA model. In the fall of 1946 Krug went on the offensive against the Pick-Sloan Plan, telling people it would not effectively develop the Missouri River and that the administration favored valley authorities.

Truman's appointment of Krug and his messages to the Congress appeared to be strong indications of his support for an MVA. But he also told the press that he would let the Congress act on the authority issue and not intervene. The Seventy-ninth Congress ignored the MVA.

In the spring of 1947 the Missouri River again overflowed its banks and Senator Murray again called on President Truman to push for a Missouri Valley Authority. Truman declined. Instead he approached Gen. Raymond Wheeler of the Army Corps of Engineers to get together with Secretary of the Interior Krug and Commissioner of Reclamation Michael Straus and come up with a joint comprehensive plan to control the waters not just of the Missouri River but of the entire Mississippi Basin. Truman apparently believed that given the climate established by the Eightieth Congress executive action might be more productive than efforts to get legislative approval. It was not. Despite Truman's directive the Bureau of Reclamation refused to work with the corps and no new plan emerged.

The Missouri Valley Authority was not an issue in the campaign of 1948. Instead Truman emphasized his support for development of the Missouri River—water for irrigation and cheap hydropower—rather than administrative reform. Truman carried all but Oregon in the West because his campaign promised to spend money on dams, not because he promised independent valley authorities.

After Truman's reelection he continued to support a Missouri Valley Authority in his speeches while MVA proponents in the Congress reintroduced bills again and again. But the legislation never came close to passing or even aroused significant interest during the remainder of Truman's presidency.

Although Truman became an advocate of the Missouri Valley Authority, he did not abandon the Pick-Sloan Plan completely. He continued to support appropriations for the flood control projects included in the plan, and he blamed its critics for the Missouri River floods of 1951 and 1952. If more dams and levees had been built, he believed, the devastation on the Missouri's flood plain would not have occurred.

Truman's fascination and frustration with the Missouri River and its potential continued throughout his life. He thought much had been accomplished toward the goal of controlling the river, but he knew there was even more to do. Ironically, his own lack of effective support for the MVA was a contributing factor in its failure and, ultimately, in plans to develop and control the river.

Several books have been written about the politics of developing the Missouri River. One of the more objective early studies is Marion E. Ridgeway, *The Missouri Basin's Pick-Sloan Plan: A Case Study in Congressional Policy Determination* (Urbana: University of Illinois Press, 1955). An interesting critical study is Michael Lawson, *Damned Indians: The Pick-Sloan Plan and the Missouri River Sioux, 1944–1980* (Norman: University of Oklahoma Press, 1982).

DAVID A. KATHKA

See also Army Corps of Engineers; Reclamation

Charles Werner. *Indianapolis Star,* 2 March 1951.

Mobilization

Military disaster in Korea in the fall of 1950 forced the Truman administration to declare limited mobilization, including price and wage stabilization measures which precipitated union unrest, government seizure of the steel industry, and the steel strike of 1952.

American hopes of reunifying Korea by defeating the North Korean army were dashed when Chinese troops poured across the Yalu River in October 1950 to reinforce the beleaguered and weary North Korean forces. Chinese intervention not only ended Gen. Douglas MacArthur's hope of a quick, decisive victory, but also created several political crises for the Truman administration, among them the need to mobilize the United States for what would become a protracted conflict with Communist troops on the Korean peninsula.

On 15 December 1950, in a televised national address, Truman declared a national emergency which included limited mobilization. As Robert Donovan has observed, the proclamation was psychologically as well as legally useful. Truman, determined not to overreact to the Chinese intervention, nonetheless

believed he needed to demonstrate firm leadership for the sake of both the American people and the United States' allies. The proclamation signaled that the United States would not abandon Korea despite grave military setbacks. On the other hand, limited mobilization indicated that the United States was not preparing to fight an all-out war either. Truman wanted especially to reassure European allies that the United States would not retreat into "Fortress America." The country would not surrender in Korea, Truman assured British prime minister Clement Attlee. For Americans to leave Korea, they would have to be pushed out, he said.

Truman's limited mobilization included beefing up the U.S. armed forces, speeding up production and procurement of war matériel, and seeking to stabilize prices and wages. The army, navy, and air force were strengthened through intensified recruiting, stepping up the draft, and calling up elements of the National Guard. Total strength of the armed forces increased from 2,213,410 in December 1950 to 4,973,007 in December 1952, an increase of 125 percent.

Legally, mobilization also helped speed the procurement process as the United States built up its fighting capability. Truman's proclamation of national emergency enabled the Defense Department to obtain priority for military contracts over certain civilian contracts, hastening the conversion of selected industries from civilian to military production. In effect, according to Truman, limited mobilization enabled the United States to reach 1954 military procurement goals by the end of 1952. Dramatically, military spending increased from $13.1 billion in FY 1950 to $44 billion in FY 1952, mushrooming from almost a third of the federal budget in 1950 to almost two-thirds in 1952.

The Defense Production Act, signed by the president on 8 September 1950, provided Truman with the authority to impose price and wage controls. Initially, the president encouraged industry and labor to curb spiraling prices and wages voluntarily. When this proved unsuccessful, Truman first imposed controls in the automobile industry, followed by a general wage and price freeze (except for farm prices) on 25 January 1951.

Truman's policy of economic stabilization was administered by the Office of Defense Mobilization headed by Charles E. Wilson, former president of General Electric. Under Wilson was located the Economic Stabilization Agency whose Office of Price Stabilization and Wage Stabilization Board regulated prices and wages, respectively. Despite apparent success in checking inflation, however, Truman's economic controls remained among the administration's most unpopular programs.

Truman's economic stabilization program was most severely tested by the steel strike of 1952. Before it was over, the president had plunged the country into a constitutional crisis by seizing the steel industry only to be overruled by the Supreme Court which declared his action unconstitutional.

In November 1951 the steel union had announced that it would strike when its contract expired. With increased war production, steel industry profits were up and Truman sympathized with the steelworkers' determination not only to increase wages to meet the rising cost of living but also to improve working conditions within the industry. When management refused to negotiate, the union announced it would go out on strike 31 December.

The administration's price and wage stabilization program now appeared to hang in the balance. Although Truman's sentiments were with the workers, he believed he could neither allow a long steel strike, which would disrupt crucial supplies for troops in the field, nor condone wage increases in the steel industry, which management would offset with a raise in prices. Truman's dilemma was compounded by his reluctance to invoke the Taft-Hartley Act, considered to be antiunion by labor. Truman believed the Defense Production Act had provided him another alternative for settling the labor dispute. He referred the matter to the Wage Stabilization Board (WSB) for fact-finding and a recommendation. In the meantime, the union agreed to hold off its strike until the WSB made its report.

On 20 March 1952, the board recommended a wage increase for steelworkers that was less than the union demanded but more than industry was willing to grant without a substantial increase in steel prices. Truman believed the WSB's recommendation was fair and workable, but Wilson reported that industry would flatly reject the recommendation without a price increase. Truman was willing to grant the industry a small increase, but not one sufficient to placate management. Ultimately, a frustrated Wilson resigned, feeling the president had insulted him during their dispute over industry's need for compensation.

Wilson's departure marked the collapse of the government's efforts to negotiate a settlement. The union announced it would go on strike 9 April. Truman now believed he had few options to avert a national crisis. He did not believe he could allow a long steel strike. Although he had exhausted his WSB option, he was still unwilling to invoke the Taft-Hartley Act. But he had no other explicit authority to intervene in labor disputes in the interest of national security. Truman might have asked Congress for such legislation, but that request would no doubt have exacerbated the political controversy. Secretary of Defense Robert Lovett and Atomic Energy Commission chairman Gordon Dean both advised that a long steel strike would seriously damage U.S. mobilization efforts. Finally, acting under the counsel of Chief Justice Fred Vinson, Truman decided that seizure of the steel mills in the interest of national security was among the inherent powers of the presidency.

On 8 April under Executive Order 10340 Truman seized the steel mills. He justified his action over national radio and television. "Our national security and our chances for peace," he declared, "depend on our defense production. Our defense production depends on steel." Federal seizure of the steel mills, which meant government operation of the plants through the industry's managers and workers, created political pandemonium.

The steel industry immediately challenged Truman in court where they won a victory in the U.S. District Court for the District of Columbia. Despite the fact that the court might have found precedents set by Woodrow Wilson and Franklin Roosevelt for industry seizure, Judge David A. Pine, a strict constructionist, enjoined Truman's seizure, ruling that the president derived no such inherent powers from the Constitution.

The administration appealed Judge Pine's ruling to the Supreme Court where the president was confident of victory from judges appointed by two successive Democratic administrations. But on 2 June 1952, the president was stunned by the Court's 6–3 decision upholding Judge Pine's ruling: the president had acted unconstitutionally by seizing the steel industry.

Truman had now exhausted his options. He still refused to invoke the Taft-Hartley Act despite the urging of some White House advisers. On 10 June, after the union had shut down steel production, Truman appealed to Congress for legislation giving him power to deal with the crisis. His appeal was futile, and the steel strike dragged on for fifty-three days. Negotiations ended almost where they had started with industry allowed to increase the price of steel to offset the workers' raise in pay. The constitutional crisis was over, without, apparently, grave damage being done to the nation's defense effort or its economic stability.

Robert Donovan's *Tumultuous Years: the Presidency of Harry S Truman, 1949–1953* (New York: W. W. Norton, 1982) contains a chapter each on mobilization and the steel strike and seizure. Truman's *Memoirs*, vol. 2, *Years of Trial and Hope* (New York: Signet Books, 1956), also provides insightful chapters on these issues. John Edward Wiltz's "The Korean War and American Society," in *The Korean War: A 25-Year Perspective,* ed. Francis H. Heller (Lawrence: Regents Press of Kansas, 1977), describes the impact of mobilization on the home front. Maeva Marcus, in *Truman and the Steel Seizure: The Limits of Presidential Power* (New York: Columbia University Press, 1977), has written the definitive history of the controversy. Also useful are *Public Papers of the Presidents, Harry S. Truman, 1950–1952* (Washington, D.C.: U.S. Government Printing Office, 1965).

JACK M. HOLL
TERRENCE R. FEHNER

See also Inflation; Korean War; Labor; Military Spending

Monetary Policy

See Fiscal and Monetary Policies

Morse, Wayne Lyman

(20 October 1900–22 July 1974)

Senator from Oregon, 1944–68. Wayne Morse was raised on a Wisconsin farm, attended public schools in Madison, and imbibed the politics of progressivism at the University of Wisconsin from which he graduated in 1922. Morse earned a law degree at the University of Minnesota and a doctorate of jurisprudence at Columbia University, where Raymond Moley served as his dissertation adviser.

In 1929, Morse moved to Eugene to become assistant professor and subsequently dean of the law school at the University of Oregon. He served the Roosevelt administration as labor arbitrator for the Pacific Coast area and as a public member of the National War Labor Board. In 1944 he was elected Republican senator from Oregon. In these posts, Morse displayed the fierce independence which was the hallmark of his entire public life.

Morse called Truman's request for authority to draft striking railroad workers in 1946 "one of the cheapest exhibitions of ham acting I have ever seen." The senator subsequently apologized, and the two developed a friendly relationship based largely on Morse's willingness to defy Republican leaders and support the president. He took Truman's side, for example, on the Taft-Hartley Act, the firing of MacArthur, and the seizure of the nation's steel mills in 1952, and he launched an early and vigorous attack on Senator Joseph McCarthy. So great was Truman's respect that when scandals rocked the administration in 1951, the president asked Morse to become attorney general "to clean up the mess," an offer Morse appreciated but declined.

During the 1952 elections, Morse resigned from the Republican party, declaring, "The Republican party left me," and in 1960 he waged an unsuccessful campaign for the Democratic presidential nomination. No less a maverick as a Democrat, Morse began in 1964 an unrelenting opposition to U.S. involvement in the war in Vietnam. Morse lost his Senate seat to Robert Packwood in 1968, and he died in 1974 in the course of his second effort to regain it.

Robert A. Smith, *The Tiger in the Senate: The Biography of Wayne Morse* (Garden City, N.Y.: Doubleday, 1962), is the only book-length biography. Written by a journalist while Morse was still in the Senate, it was judged by Morse to be full of inaccuracies. Lee Wilkins, *Wayne Morse: A Bio-Bibliography* (Westport, Conn.: Greenwood Press, 1985), contains a long biographical essay and a detailed, annotated bibliography. The Wayne Morse Papers are at the University of Oregon in Eugene.

SUSAN M. HARTMANN

See also Housing (photograph)

Movies and the Movie Industry

The first post–World War II year, 1946, marked the high point of motion picture popularity in the United States in terms of total attendance figures. Over the remaining years of the Truman era, however, the movie industry suffered a series of ruptures that irrevocably altered its relations to American popular culture. These included the purge of Communists and radicals from the movie field, begun in 1947 at hearings of the House Committee on Un-American Activities (HUAC) and intensifying throughout the period; the 1948 Supreme Court decision declaring the movie industry a monopoly in violation of the Sherman Anti-Trust Act, leading to divorcement of theater ownership from production/distribution companies, and ending the era of the studio system; and the introduction of commercial television broadcasting, which, with other social, leisure, and entertainment factors, inaugurated a steady decline in motion picture attendance. In film production, the period was marked especially by the emergence of the film noir genre of dark, pessimistic urban crime melodramas, as well as the resurgence of such other genres as the musical and the western.

The 1947 HUAC hearings into "Communist Infiltration of the Motion Picture Industry" remain perhaps the most vivid aspect of American movie history during the Truman period. The attack on radical influence in entertainment and media was part of the conservative postwar agenda, abetted by Republican con-

By Bill Mauldin. Copyright 1947 by Bill Mauldin.

trol of the Eightieth Congress following the 1946 elections and also, in the view of radicals, by President Truman's loyalty and security program inaugurated in March 1947. Several divisive jurisdictional strikes in the movie industry during 1945 and 1946 hardened ideological battle lines between Hollywood's left- and right-wing adherents, the latter organized during the war as the Motion Picture Alliance for the Preservation of American Values.

When public hearings began in October 1947, HUAC's interest quickly shifted from the issue of Communist propaganda in movie content to the purging of "subversives" from motion picture work. Some ten "unfriendly" witnesses were called, primarily left-wing writers active in the Screen Writers Guild, and they refused on First Amendment grounds to answer questions about their political beliefs and affiliations. They were cited for contempt of Congress, and after their constitutional arguments were rejected on appeal through the federal courts, all the "Hollywood Ten" served terms of up to a year in prison. In November 1947, meanwhile, the movie producers' association declared that its companies would no longer employ Communists or other subversives, and the Hollywood blacklist was born. Scores of persons lost their jobs, while others went through a process of "clearance," which usually involved recanting past liberal convictions in order to keep working. A second round of hearings began in 1951 in which, in order to avoid the blacklist, witnesses were required to name names of other persons involved in past radical activities.

Although the long-term impact of the HUAC hearings and the blacklist is open to debate, it seems clear that their immediate effect was to stifle the postwar impulse toward socially conscious films, represented by such award-winning works as *The Best Years of Our Lives* (1946), *Gentleman's Agreement* and *Crossfire* (both 1947), and *Treasure of the Sierra Madre* (1948).

Difficulties erupted on another front in 1948 when the Supreme Court decided the decade-old Paramount antitrust case against the motion picture industry (*United States v. Paramount Pictures, Inc., et al.*, 334 U.S. 131). It was during the Truman administration, in October 1945, that the suit, originally begun in 1938, was brought to trial. Truman's Justice Department then appealed what it considered to be a too-lenient decision of the district court declaring the movie industry in violation of the Sherman Act but proposing remedies short of divorcement. The Supreme Court sent the case back to the lower court, which in 1949 decreed the necessity of ending the industry's vertical integration.

Over the following five years each of the industry majors—Paramount, MGM-Loew's, Warner Brothers, RKO, and Twentieth Century-Fox—under consent decrees sold off its theater holdings. The studio system that had led Hollywood film to global domination between the world wars was gradually dismantled. Without the guaranteed playdates that theater ownership provided, film production decreased, and the studios let go their stock companies of performers and directors on long-term contract. By the early 1950s a new system began to emerge whereby the studios served as financiers and distributors of independently produced films. (In the 1980s the Reagan Justice Department, professing a different antitrust philosophy, vacated the movie industry consent decrees, and production/distribution companies ventured again into theater ownership.)

The *Paramount* case and its aftermath left the movie industry in a disadvantageous position to respond effectively to television's challenge. Movie attendance, in any case, began to decline in the late 1940s even before many homes had television receivers. Among factors cited were population shifts to suburbia and the focus of returning veterans on establishing families, as well as an emphasis on participatory recreational activities in leisuretime. After 1949 the growing availability of television greatly accelerated the impact of these trends.

The movie industry did not ignore television or underestimate the new medium's potential as much as has sometimes been claimed, but its responses were curtailed in the wake of the *Paramount* case. With the government supervising the breakup of the movie monopoly after 1949, it was hardly tolerant of any perceived efforts by movie companies to gain dominance in television, either through station ownership or programming production. During the Truman years these brakes on movie company involvement allowed new television industry structures to solidify before the movie industry began to participate actively in television in the mid-1950s.

The relation of movie styles and themes to these changes in politics, industry, and popular taste is a subject that has not received sufficient study. Postwar film noir is a significant case in point. This is perhaps the only film movement or genre in American movie history that was identified and named in critical discourse rather than as part of common industry usage. Numerous urban crime films were seen to have important visual and narrative similarities: a harsh urban setting, darkly lit and photographed at disturbing odd angles; a male protagonist, involved with an alluring, dangerous woman, lured into lawlessness or falsely accused and often telling his story in flashback, seeking a lost selfhood through retrospection. Many of these films were drawn from novels and stories written during the Great Depression and carried into the postwar period themes of despair and rebellion more common to the 1930s.

Interpretations of film noir stress these films' possible ties to post-nuclear anxiety or to dilemmas of veterans' peacetime adjustment. One could also point out the number of noir films created by movie industry radicals, inscribing their critique of American society in genre guise. The major wave of film noir ran from 1945 to 1951, coinciding closely with the Truman years but also with the period of apogee and decline in American film popularity, as well as the growing imposition of the blacklist. Could these works intended as popular art have nevertheless gone against the grain of public taste and contributed to the movie industry's difficulties? In any case, by the end of the Truman era, such traditional genres as musicals, westerns, costume epics, and spectacle films again dominated American movie production.

For an overview of the movies, see Robert Sklar, *Movie-Made America: A Cultural History of American Movies* (New York: Random House, 1975). The most comprehensive work on Communism in the movie industry is Larry Ceplair and Steven Englund, *The Inquisition in Hollywood: Politics in the Film Community, 1930–1960* (Garden City, N.Y.: Anchor Press/Doubleday, 1980). A provocative study of the period combining film theory and history is Dana Polan, *Power and Paranoia: History, Narrative, and the American Cinema, 1940–1950* (New York: Columbia University Press, 1986).

ROBERT SKLAR

See also House Un-American Activities Committee

Murphy, Charles S.

(20 August 1909–28 August 1983)

Presidential aide, 1947–50; special counsel to the president, 1950–53. Charles Murphy, a native of North Carolina, was educated at Duke University. After completing a law degree at Duke in 1934, he went to Washington, D.C., and began a twelve-year stint in the Office of the Legislative Counsel of the U.S. Senate. While there, he assisted Senator Truman in drafting legislation, the most important piece being the resolution establishing the committee to investigate the national defense program, chaired by the Missouri senator during World War II.

In January 1947 Murphy joined the White House staff with orders from Truman to report directly to him. On a practical level, he worked closely with Special Counsel Clark Clifford, specializing in the preparation of White House legislation and in the analysis of pending legislation cleared by the Budget Bureau. His first assignment from Truman involved the preparation of the bill merging the armed forces.

Murphy enhanced his participation in Democratic politics by joining Clifford in the Monday night meetings at the Wardman Park Hotel arranged by Oscar "Jack" Ewing shortly after the Republican victories in the congressional election of 1946. The Ewing group, composed of a few key liberals in the federal government, was formed partly to counteract the influence of conservative friends and advisers of Truman such as Secretary of the Treasury John W. Snyder and Assistant to the President John Steelman. Murphy later discounted the efforts by liberal and conservative advisers to influence the president, arguing that Truman had come to the White House with liberal views built on practical experience.

As administrative aide, Murphy became fully immersed in the drafting of messages, addresses, speeches, and legislation for the administration. Drafts of reports that originated elsewhere, such as the president's economic reports written by the Council of Economic Advisers, also came under the review of the White House staff to the displeasure of the council's first chairman, Dr. Edwin A. Nourse. The "young whippersnappers," as Nourse called Murphy and the other aides, deliberately scheduled redrafting sessions for late afternoons on the last day before submission of the report. By midnight Nourse, much older than the staff and tired by the process, would readily agree to changes in wording.

During the presidential election year of 1948 Murphy made major contributions to the strategy, speeches, and speaking effectiveness of President Truman. Despite the importance some scholars have placed on the James H. Rowe, Jr.–Clark Clifford memorandum on the grand strategy for the election of President Truman in his own right, Murphy later recalled that he had never seen the document during the campaign; moreover, he believed that the memo's call for an appeal to the liberal Democratic coalition with a sharp attack on the Republican Eightieth Congress echoed rather than established the president's philosophy and approach. He conceived the idea of preparing an outline rather than a formally written speech, thus allowing Truman to speak extemporaneously or to read from the outline. When Truman successfully employed the new approach in the spring of 1948, he was well on his way to a greater speaking effectiveness that contributed significantly to his upset victory that year.

Truman promoted Murphy to the position of special counsel to the president when Clark Clifford retired from government service on 1 February 1950. Thereafter, Murphy's agenda reflected the priorities of the administration brought on by the cold war and the Korean War and involved him heavily in defense and foreign policy problems. Although he did not have a mandate to operate in either of these two important areas, as chief speech writer Murphy helped determine policy by virtue of determining what the president would say, how he would say it, and when he would say it. Murphy also dealt with the political fallout from congressional investigations and public charges of corruption in the Truman administration. He prepared the agenda for the president's meetings with congressional leaders and handled calls from members of Congress concerned about specific legislation.

Murphy increased his effectiveness as special counsel by adding a few talented and knowledgeable aides to the White House staff, including David Bell and Richard Neustadt from the Budget Bureau. The team that he headed thus served Truman with greater ease and efficiency than the staff that operated during the tenure of Murphy's two precedessors. At no time, however, did Murphy or the other special counsels serve as a chief of staff. Truman wanted his cabinet officers and heads of agencies and executive units to have direct access to him, although he permitted the special counsel and aides to supplement the work that came from other offices.

In retrospect, Murphy reflected that Truman had organized his staff "just about right in terms of achieving a balance between definite, continuing responsibilities and the flexibility to meet special problems, having enough institutionalization but not too much, distributing responsibility among staff members so that they did not build their own empires, and keeping the number of staff members who reported directly to him both manageable and diverse." Murphy worked well within that context.

Murphy joined a private law firm when the Truman administration ended in January 1953. President John F. Kennedy appointed him under secretary of agriculture and he served in that capacity until 1965, when President Lyndon B. Johnson appointed his chairman of the Civil Aeronautics Board. He completed his career in government service as counselor to President Johnson in 1968.

Two valuable sources of information on Murphy's role as aide and special counsel are Francis Heller, ed., *The Truman White House: The Administration of the Presidency, 1945–1953* (Lawrence: Regents Press of Kansas, 1980), and Ken Heckler, *Working with Truman: A Personal Memoir of the White House Years* (New York: G. P. Putnam's Sons, 1982). The former contains Murphy's own essay on the Truman White House and his experiences there. A biographical sketch appears in Eleanora W. Schoenebaum, ed., *Political Profiles: The Truman Years* (New York: Facts on File, 1978). The Charles Murphy Papers are in the Harry S. Truman Library.

FRANKLIN D. MITCHELL

See also Speeches and Speech Writing

Murphy, Frank

(13 April 1890–19 July 1949)

In a notable public career that spanned three decades, Frank Murphy was closely associated with Franklin Delano Roosevelt but had a distant relationship with Harry S. Truman. Born in Sand Beach (later Harbor Beach), Michigan, and baptized Francis William, Murphy received the LL.B. in 1914 from the University of Michigan. He served in the army in World War I before being sworn in on 9 August 1919, as first assistant U.S. attorney for the Eastern District of Michigan. Except for a brief period as a private attorney (1922–23), he devoted his life to public service. He was successively judge of the Detroit Recorder's Court (1924–30), mayor of Detroit (1930–33), last governor-general of the Philippines and first high commissioner to the islands (1933–36), governor of Michigan (1937–38), attorney general of the United States (1939–40), and justice of the U.S. Supreme Court (1940–49).

As a public official, Murphy was steadily associated with great events. As mayor of depression-ridden Detroit, he anticipated the New Deal. He contributed importantly to the transition of the Philippines from colony to commonwealth and ultimate independence. As governor, he played the key role in the resolution of the great General Motors sit-down strike and fashioned one of the few state New Deals. During a remarkable year as attorney general, he founded the present Civil Liberties Division of the department, negotiated peace terms in Harlan County, directed a spectacular war against crime that resulted in the successful prosecution of important political figures, and initiated major antitrust suits. As a Supreme Court justice, he wrote notable opinions and dissents in labor and civil liberties cases and anticipated some of the major decisions of the Warren Court of the 1950s and 1960s.

When Thomas Pendergast, whom Murphy as attorney general, had successfully prosecuted, arrived in Leavenworth to begin his prison term, Murphy instructed that a photograph of the Kansas City boss in prison garb be made available to a *Kansas City Star* reporter. An irate Senator Truman phoned the director of the Bureau of Prisons to demand that Pendergast be treated no differently from other federal prisoners. Truman's regard for Murphy declined further when the attorney general sought to assist the U.S. attorney in Kansas City, Maurice A. Milligan, in pursuing his investigation of crime and corruption by arranging for the appointment of two assistants to whom Truman objected.

While Murphy was on the Supreme Court, President Truman designated the justice to represent the United States in returning the body of Manuel Quezon to the Philippines. The president, who reportedly thought Murphy to be a "nut," was, however, unresponsive to occasional signals from the unhappy justice that he wished to be appointed to some other federal position. Murphy's repeated absences from the Court because of illness in the 1948 term led to an unconfirmed magazine report that the president had sought to induce the justice to resign. Murphy died of a coronary thrombosis in Ford Hospital in Detroit in 1949.

Murphy's career is most fully treated in the three-volume study by Sidney Fine, *Frank Murphy: The Detroit Years* (Ann Arbor:

University of Michigan Press, 1975); *Frank Murphy: The New Deal Years* (Chicago: University of Chicago Press, 1979); and *Frank Murphy: The Washington Years* (Ann Arbor: University of Michigan Press, 1984). Richard D. Lunt, *The High Ministry of Government: The Political Career of Frank Murphy* (Detroit: Wayne State University Press, 1965), deals with Murphy's pre–Supreme Court years. Murphy's service on the Court is the principal concern of J. Woodford Howard, *Mr. Justice Murphy* (Princeton: Princeton University Press, 1968).

SIDNEY FINE

See also Supreme Court, United States

Murray, Philip

(25 May 1886–9 November 1952)

President of the United Steelworkers of America and the Congress of Industrial Organizations (CIO), Philip Murray by all accounts was the most important union official during the Truman era, a time of sharp industrial conflict.

Born in Scotland of Irish-Catholic working-class parents—his father, a miner; his mother, a weaver—Murray came to the United States with his father at the age of sixteen. The two immediately went to work in a coal mine in western Pennsylvania. A tall, well-built, self-educated young man, whose family had taught him the value of the union cause, Murray caught the eye of higher union officials. He was "quite a soft-soaper," as one put it, willing to use his fists, but friendly and usually able to win his way with words instead. Murray climbed the United Mine Workers hierarchy and in 1920 the union's new president, John L. Lewis, chose him as the union's international vice president.

In 1936 Lewis selected "Phil"—as he was called by almost everyone—to head the Steel Workers Organizing Committee, a newly formed group of union officials established to win contracts from U.S. Steel and the other huge, historically antiunion steel firms. But in 1940 Murray and Lewis split over whether to support Franklin Roosevelt for a third term as president—Murray being the FDR backer. Failing to receive working-class support, Lewis resigned. Thus Phil Murray became president of the CIO at the very time Harry Truman entered the national political scene.

Although Murray had virtually idolized Roosevelt, his view of Truman was originally unfavorable. At the Democratic convention in 1944 Murray privately objected to Roosevelt's decision to replace left-of-center Henry Wallace with the comparatively more conservative Truman as nominee for vice president. Two years later he made a splash by joining the new Progressive Citizens of America, a committee of liberals and left-wingers, some of them Communist-allied, created to dump Truman as the Democratic nominee for president in 1948 or even form a new party altogether.

But despite his serious initial reservations, Murray brought the industrial unions into a tight alliance with the Truman administration after 1947. A devout Roman Catholic, Murray was concerned about Soviet suppression of the church in Eastern Europe. Priests associated with the labor movement, like Father

Charles Owen Rice of Pittsburgh with whom Murray was personally close, pressured him in this regard.

Even more important, however, in explaining Murray's decision was congressional passage of the antiunion Taft-Hartley Act, a revision of the 1935 National Labor Relations Act, in June 1947 over President Truman's veto. With the majority in Congress lined up against the unions, with the steel corporations' newspaper *Iron Age* urging management to fight "socialism in America" in the political realm, with audiences failing to respond when he toured the country denouncing Taft-Hartley—what defense do I have, Murray reasoned, except to make amends with the White House?

Having committed himself, Murray moved decisively. He quit the Progressive Citizens of America, joining instead the domestically liberal but firmly anti-Communist Americans for Democratic Action. Murray fired Lee Pressman, the CIO's attorney and a close adviser to him for declining to follow suit. He had the CIO pass uncompromising anti-Communist resolutions and seize dissenting local councils. Further, he devoted all the resources of the CIO and the Steelworkers to registering new union voters for the 1948 election and raising money for Truman's presidential campaign. "Men of steel, you mighty legions of labor, . . . of one of the mightiest labor organizations in the entire world," he implored the Steelworkers' convention delegates, "devote your time and your energies on this political and legislative front. . . . give it your dollars. . . . fight them out on the political battlefield."

Under Murray's direction the 1949 CIO convention expelled those of its constituent unions whose leaders had failed to support Truman's campaign or were in one way or another associated with the Communist party. There were ten such unions, composing roughly a third of the CIO's membership. There was irony in this historic move, for Murray personally still preferred Progressive candidate Henry Wallace, but Truman was president and Wallace, the Communists' choice.

Murray's decision to form an unqualified alliance with Harry Truman had positive benefits for the Steelworkers and the CIO at first. Truman was elected. The president's appointment of a public fact-finding board in the steel dispute of 1949 enabled the Steelworkers to obtain company-paid pensions for its members, an achievement otherwise probably impossible, given the advent of a recession. In dealing with the more adversarial John L. Lewis of the United Mine Workers, President Truman acted quite differently, invoking the cooling-off provision of the Taft-Hartley Act. More generally, Murray's adoption of a super-patriotic stance deflected (at least temporarily) intense public antilabor sentiment (built up in the aftermath of the massive 1946 strikes) away from the CIO (and AFL) and toward the smaller, expelled, left-wing unions.

Despite the close Murray–White House bond, however, the unions did not meet their most highly proclaimed goal—repeal of the Taft-Hartley Act. And Murray suffered major defeats in 1952, first losing a mammoth strike in steel in the spring and summer, even though Truman had temporarily seized the mills, and then losing future help from Washington, when the Republicans captured control of the White House and Congress in November. Having been in poor health for several years and under great stress during those months, Murray died several days after the November election.

Despite his significance in labor and political and economic history generally, the only published biography of Philip Murray is an essay by Ronald W. Schatz, "Philip Murray and the Subordination of the Industrial Unions to the United States Government," in *Labor Leaders in America*, ed. Melvyn Dubofsky and Warren Van Tine, 234–57 (Urbana: University of Illinois Press, 1987). A symposium of scholars, union founders, and early labor leaders was held at Pennsylvania State University in November 1986 to mark the centennial of Murray's birth and the fiftieth anniversary of the founding of the Steelworkers' union. The proceedings were published in *Forging a Union of Steel*, ed. Paul Clark, Peter Gottlieb, and Don Kennedy (Ithaca: Cornell University ILR Press, 1987). For more general interpretations of the relationship between the Truman administration and organized labor, see Mike Davis, *Prisoners of the American Dream* (London: Verso, 1986), especially chaps. 2–3; Christopher L. Tomlins, *The State and the Unions* (Cambridge: Cambridge University Press, 1985); and Robert H. Zieger, *American Workers, American Unions, 1920–1985* (Baltimore: Johns Hopkins University Press, 1986), chaps. 3–5. Zieger is sympathetic to the labor-government alliance; Davis and Tomlins, extremely critical.

RONALD SCHATZ

See also Labor (and photograph); Taft-Hartley Act

Music

To Harry S. Truman, the art of music was more than a relaxing diversion: it was a lifelong avocation that formed an integral part of his personality and inner spirit. Only one other U.S. president, Thomas Jefferson, shared Truman's intense love of music. Like Jefferson, Truman performed, attended concerts, and recognized his family's musical talents.

Encouraged by his musical mother, Truman studied piano from age eight to sixteen, primarily with Grace Matthews White, a pupil of the renowned Theodor Leschetizky. He never had to be coerced to practice which he claimed was "pleasure and not work," adding that the only reason he missed being a musician was because he "was not good enough." He especially loved classical music—the works of J. S. Bach, Beethoven, Mozart, Chopin, Liszt, Mendelssohn, MacDowell, Debussy, and Gershwin. Located in the Truman Library at Independence are many of the pieces he studied, such as Chopin's Valse op. 42, in A-flat Major, and Paderewski's Minuet op. 14, no. 1, both bearing his signature. Another favorite, which he memorized from beginning to end shortly before becoming a senator, was Mozart's Sonata no. 9 in A Major, K. 331. Contrary to the legend, Truman disliked the ubiquitous "Missouri Waltz," but he enjoyed other American vernacular music, such as the songs of Stephen Foster and tunes from early musical theater.

While he was president, Truman enjoyed playing the piano both for himself and for others. During his administration five pianos graced the presidential homes: the East Room Steinway concert grand presented to Franklin Roosevelt in 1938; a Baldwin concert grand donated in 1952; Margaret Truman's Steinway grand and a Gulbranson spinet on the second floor of the White House; and another Steinway grand used in Blair House. Although the president admitted that his "fingers wouldn't always work" on the pieces he knew, he would play them anyway. On various occasions he unabashedly performed for Joseph Stalin, Winston Churchill, John F. Kennedy, Eugene List, Lauren Bacall, and Grandma Moses, as well as some 30 million Americans during his televised tour of the newly renovated White House in 1952.

Continuing a century-old tradition, Truman invited several distinguished guest entertainers to perform at the White House. But because the family lived at Blair House for several years during the renovations, only one season of concerts was held at the White House. Unlike other administrations that often included both classical and popular programs, the Truman concerts were only classical and were held after white-tie state dinners with the assistance of Steinway & Sons. The series comprised fifteen-year-old pianist Sylvia Zaremba (26 Nov. 1946), baritone Lawrence Tibbett (3 Dec. 1946), soprano Helen Traubel (17 Dec. 1946), pianist Oscar Levant (14 Jan. 1947), tenor Frederick Jagel (28 Jan. 1947), and Carroll Glenn and Eugene List, violinist and pianist (11 Feb. 1947). List, a young army sergeant and friend of Truman's, had played for Truman, Churchill, and Stalin at Potsdam before the close of World War II, with the president himself turning the pianist's pages.

Harry Truman always supported and encouraged his daughter, Margaret, throughout her career as a singer. He gave Margaret her first music lessons, followed her debut with the Detroit Symphony Orchestra on 16 March 1947, but lovingly and judiciously advised her not to fool herself. "You know what it takes," he said. After Margaret's Constitution Hall concert in December 1950, critic Paul Hume of the *Washington Post* wrote a harsh review of her singing that has become the most talked-about critique in the annals of music criticism. Bristling, the president dashed off his vitriolic reply to Hume that was later reprinted in the *New York Times*. But Truman's run-in with Hume was not limited to his daughter: when pianist Gina Bachauer received less than a rave review after her concert, Truman once again voiced his vehement disapproval.

Truman's knowledge and love of music is symbolized by the numerous musical gifts he received from great performing artists and world leaders. No other president of the United States has been presented with so many autographed musical manuscripts, rare first editions, and fine facsimile scores, and these are housed in the Truman Library. But perhaps more than any other musical encomium, Truman treasured the elegant gold medal he received from the city of Salzburg, Austria—Mozart's home—on 4 October 1951. Inscribed on the medal were the words "It is with deepest gratitude, Mr. President, that we remember the good deeds of the citizens of the United States of America. Without this help the cultural life of our country would not have grown again so soon."

For more on Harry S. Truman and music, see Elise K. Kirk, *Music at the White House: A History of the American Spirit* (Champaign: University of Illinois Press, 1986), and Brian Lingham. ed., *Harry Truman: The Man . . . His Music* (Kansas City: Lowell Press, 1985). For personal reminiscences of her father's musical attitudes, see Margaret Truman, *Harry S. Truman* (New York: William Morrow, 1973). Other important materials relating to Truman and music are primary sources—letters, memoranda, clippings, diaries—among the presidential papers in the Truman Library, Independence.

ELISE K. KIRK

N

National Association for the Advancement of Colored People

The National Association for the Advancement of Colored People (NAACP), founded in 1909, was the nation's premier civil rights organization when Truman entered the White House in 1945. Its effectiveness derived mainly from lobbying, litigation, and high-level negotiations, and its executive secretary, Walter F. White (1893–1955), had assembled a civil rights coalition that included industrial unionists, civil libertarians, progressive clergy, and the leaders of several reform-minded ethnic and women's groups. The NAACP enjoyed easy entreé in governmental circles during the New Deal years, and with wartime prosperity and the international crusade against fascism, the group's membership swelled to 351,000 in 1945 and 395,000 in 1946. From the late 1930s onward, legal counsel Thurgood Marshall attacked discrimination in housing, transportation, voting, and education, a campaign capped in 1954 by the unanimous Supreme Court decision in *Brown* v. *Board of Education of Topeka* (347 U.S. 483).

Putting aside their initial suspicions, the NAACP and the Truman administration found a ready ally in each other. The NAACP favored the socioeconomic policies of the Fair Deal and leaned noticeably to Truman in 1948 because of his civil rights advocacy. The cold war gave him and the NAACP ample opportunity to express their mistrust of communism and to encourage liberal reforms at home that would improve America's image abroad, especially among emerging third world nations. Furthermore, the NAACP and the president shared an enthusiasm for the United Nations; on two occasions (1945 at San Francisco and 1948 in Paris) Walter White served as a civilian adviser to the American delegation at a UN meeting.

The Truman administration recognized the NAACP's importance and that of the urban-based, black constituency it represented. On 29 June 1947, the president addressed the asso-ciation's annual conference; White House adviser Clark Clifford referred specifically to Walter White and the black vote in the famous 1947 blueprint for a Truman reelection; and the Justice Department entered an amicus curiae brief in the 1948 *Shelley* v. *Kraemer* housing case (334 U.S. 1). After meeting with a Walter White delegation on 19 September 1946, Truman appointed the President's Committee on Civil Rights (PCCR). Its report (*To Secure These Rights*, submitted in October 1947) contained numerous recommendations already on the NAACP's agenda: for example, enactment of a federal Fair Employment Practices Committee and an end to poll taxes. The PCCR proposals formed the core of Truman's civil rights package, which was defeated by conservatives in the Eighty-first Congress (1949–50) but was largely achieved in the 1960s.

In its last two years, the Truman administration faced a reactionary climate inhospitable to civil rights, as public attention and government priorities shifted from domestic reforms to charges of subversion and international crises like the Korean War. Nonetheless, the NAACP retained its civil rights primacy, until the rise of Martin Luther King, Jr., and a new generation of activists in the late 1950s.

Donald R. McCoy and Richard T. Ruetten, *Quest and Response: Minority Rights and the Truman Administration* (Lawrence: University Press of Kansas, 1973), is an overview. Richard Kluger's *Simple Justice: The History of "Brown v. Board of Education" and Black America's Struggle for Equality* (New York: Alfred A. Knopf, 1976) contains a review of litigation for the Truman years, and Robert L. Zangrando, *The NAACP Crusade against Lynching, 1909–1950* (Philadelphia: Temple University Press, 1980), includes a discussion of politics and civil rights in the same era.

ROBERT L. ZANGRANDO

See also Armed Forces, Racial Integration of the; Black Americans; Civil Rights; Civil Rights, President's Commission on; Fair Employment Practices Committee

National Health Insurance

When on 30 July 1965 President Lyndon B. Johnson signed Medicare into law at the Harry S. Truman Library, he told the nation that it had "all started really with the man from Independence." Harry Truman, Johnson said, had "planted the seeds of compassion and duty" that led to enactment of Medicare—national health insurance for the aged through an expanded Social Security system.

Truman was the first president to endorse publicly a national health insurance program. His predecessor, Franklin D. Roosevelt, had intended to do so, but death intervened. Like Roosevelt, Truman had become alarmed that during the war one-third of the nation's Selective Service draftees had failed their induction physicals. Valuing his own military experience, Truman considered these draft rejection figures "a crime," a tragic waste. They meant, he believed, that the average citizen could not afford a physician's services to stay healthy. "That is all wrong in my book," he said. "I am trying to fix it so the people in the middle-income bracket can live as long as the very rich and the very poor."

Initially, Truman's national health insurance proposal was far more sweeping than the Medicare program enacted twenty years later under Lyndon Johnson. A Social Security expansion bill cosponsored in Congress by Democratic senators Robert Wagner (N.Y.) and James Murray (Mont.), along with Representative John Dingell (D.-Mich.), incorporated Truman's blueprint for health care. Known popularly as the W-M-D bill, it provided (in contrast to Medicare) physician and hospital insurance for *working-aged* Americans *and* members of the worker's family. A federal health board headed by the U.S. surgeon general would administer the program with the government retaining the right to fix fees for service. Doctors could choose whether or not to participate.

A combination of factors prevented congressional passage of the W-M-D bill. After the war public interest in social reform waned: a much-feared postwar depression did not materialize, and organized labor, chief lobby behind the president's program, alienated millions when it conducted crippling nationwide strikes. Then, too, Congress, dominated since before the war by a conservative voting bloc of Republicans and rural Democrats, turned even more conservative after the Republican party swept the 1946 congressional elections, and the American Medical Association (AMA) launched the most intensive lobbying campaign in American history to defeat the W-M-D bill.

The AMA (representing a majority of the nation's physicians) took advantage of growing public concern over Russia's intentions abroad and Soviet espionage in the United States. It labeled the president's national health insurance plan "socialized medicine," and, using rhetoric that anticipated the McCarthy era (Truman White House staffers were called "followers of the Moscow party line"), the AMA and its allies sought to link in the public's mind advocacy of national health insurance with the alleged Communist menace.

Despite organized medicine's vociferous attack, Harry Truman doggedly advocated national health insurance. Although he lacked Roosevelt's artistry at public persuasion, he repeatedly asked Congress to legislate his plan, and he carried the issue to the American people in his successful 1948 presidential election campaign. Not until after the Korean War had begun would Truman bow before insurmountable political opposition. In 1951 he appointed a Commission on the Health Needs of the Nation, which marshaled additional facts concerning shortcomings in health care. At the same time, Truman endorsed a compromise plan to provide federal hospital insurance for the aged, the precursor to Medicare.

Even though he was defeated, President Truman's advocacy of national health insurance produced major changes in American medical economics. It drew public attention to the country's health needs, and by the time Truman had left office Congress had legislated funds to construct hospitals, expand medical aid to the needy, and provide for medical research. Also, because the AMA in its fervent battle to defeat Truman's government health insurance idea, had as an alternative promoted private, nonprofit health insurance, more Americans than ever came to enjoy protection from financial ruin owing to sickness. Whereas citizens held only 28 million Blue Shield–Blue Cross insurance policies when Harry Truman became president, they had over 61 million policies when he retired to Independence, Missouri.

For Truman's promotion of national health insurance and the organized opposition it evoked, see Monte M. Poen, *Harry S. Truman versus the Medical Lobby: The Genesis of Medicare* (Columbia: University of Missouri Press, 1979). The AMA's campaign against Truman is well described in "Medical Economics and Doctor Politics," in Stanley Kelley, Jr., *Professional Public Relations and Political Power* (Baltimore: Johns Hopkins Press, 1956), chap. 3. Daniel S. Hirshfield's *The Lost Reform: The Campaign for Compulsory Health Insurance in the United States from 1932 to 1943* (Cambridge: Harvard University Press, 1970) traces developments under President Roosevelt, and Theodore R. Marmor examines the later campaign in *The Politics of Medicare* (Chicago: Aldine, 1973). Especially helpful for an overall examination of the issue is Ronald L. Numbers, ed., *Compulsory Health Insurance: The Continuing American Debate* (Westport, Conn.: Greenwood Press, 1982).

MONTE M. POEN

National Labor Relations Board

Created under the provisions of the National Labor Relations Act passed by Congress in 1935, the National Labor Relations Board (NLRB) was empowered to supervise enforcement of the provisions of the act, including the right of employees "to self-organization, to form, join, or assist labor organizations to bargain collectively through representatives of their own choosing, and to engage in concerted activities for the purpose of collective bargaining."

Originally conceived as a three-member board, the NLRB aroused controversy almost from the beginning. The original Roosevelt appointments to the board were distinctly prolabor in their thinking, and their decisions aroused the ire of conservatives and business leaders. Ironically, controversy also existed within the labor movement; leaders of the American Federation of Labor considered the board to be too sympathetic to the views of the rival Congress of Industrial Organizations, and they supported amendments to the act that would have qualified the board's authority to act in certain situations.

Much of the NLRB's early activities revolved around investigating complaints of unfair labor practices and supervising elections to determine collective bargaining units. By the time Harry Truman took the oath of office as the nation's thirty-second president, the board had already investigated over thirty-six thousand cases involving unfair labor practices and had held twenty-four thousand representational elections. For his part, Truman had a supportive view of the activities of the NLRB and essentially continued the New Deal labor policies of his predecessor.

The situation changed, however, with the passage of Taft-Hartley—the Labor-Management Relations Act. The Taft-Hartley Act increased the NLRB membership from three to five and created an independent counsel which was to assume jurisdiction over the prosecutorial functions of the board; such prosecution was to be conducted only when findings of fact were grounded on substantial evidence. In an effort to demonstrate his good faith in enforcing the provisions of Taft-Hartley and despite his vocal opposition to and veto of the law, Truman appointed a Republican, Robert N. Denham, as the first general counsel. A strong advocate of the law, Denham then used the position to which Truman had appointed him to campaign against the president's efforts to modify or repeal Taft-Hartley.

The standard treatment of labor legislation during the period is contained in Harry A. Millis and Emily Clark Brown, *From the Wagner Act to Taft-Hartley* (Chicago: University of Chicago Press, 1950). In a less substantial book, R. Alton Lee, *Truman and Taft-Hartley: A Question of Mandate* (Lexington: University Press of Kentucky, 1966), concentrates specifically on Truman's involvement with Taft-Hartley.

GARY M. FINK

See also Labor; Taft-Hartley Act

National Science Foundation

At 6:00 A.M., 10 May 1950, President Truman announced from the rear platform of his train in Pocatello, Idaho, that he had just signed an act creating the National Science Foundation (NSF), an independent federal agency to formulate national science policy and support basic scientific research and education. He recalled that the act originated in Vannevar Bush's report, *Science: The Endless Frontier*, submitted to him on 5 July 1945.

In fact, the legislation had earlier origins. Beginning in 1942 Truman's Senate colleague Harley M. Kilgore (D.-W.V.) sought to mobilize science and technology for the country's war effort. His bill provided for a permanent National Science Foundation by the war's end. Bush's report, requested by President Roosevelt in November 1944, aimed to ensure that postwar academic science would receive public support, but allocated by scientists, not public officials.

On 6 September 1945, Truman asked Congress for science legislation, which had already been proposed in Kilgore's bill and in another favored by Bush and conservative scientists

which Senator Warren G. Magnuson (D.-Wash.) had introduced. Hearings on the bills began in October 1945 and opened a five-year debate.

Congress debated control over the agency, ownership of patents resulting from government-sponsored research, geographic distribution of research funds, and support of social as well as natural sciences. The act of 1950 compromised on these issues. Thus, instead of parceling out some funds by formula, the agency was to avoid "undue concentration"; and the term "other sciences" left a loophole for support of the social sciences in addition to that mandated for mathematical, physical, biological, medical, and engineering sciences. The control issue was more difficult. In 1947 Truman, insisting on presidential appointment of the agency's director, pocket-vetoed a bill vesting control in an independent board. The compromise of 1950 provided for a part-time policy-making National Science Board of twenty-four members and a director, all to be appointed by the president and confirmed by the Senate.

In November 1950 Truman nominated the twenty-four board members, and in March 1951 appointed Alan T. Waterman, a physicist and chief scientist of the Office of Naval Research, as director. Reappointed by President Eisenhower, Waterman continued as director until 30 June 1963, cautiously avoiding science policy formulation and conflict with other federal science agencies.

The NSF's small early budgets—still under $5 million at the end of Truman's presidency—were spent for graduate fellowships and basic research projects in colleges and universities. Not until after the Soviet Union launched Sputnik I in October 1957 did the agency become an important force in U.S. science.

The origins and early years of the NSF are related in J. Merton England, *A Patron for Pure Science: The National Science Foundation's Formative Years, 1945–57* (Washington, D.C.: National Science Foundation, 1982); Milton Lomask, *A Minor Miracle: An Informal History of the National Science Foundation* (Washington, D.C.: National Science Foundation, 1976); and C. Milton Rowan, "Politics and Pure Research: The Origins of the National Science Foundation, 1942–1954" (Ph.D. diss., Miami University, Oxford, Ohio, 1985; available through University Microfilms). All three studies are based on primary source materials and are well documented.

J. MERTON ENGLAND

National Security Council

The often controversial history of the National Security Council found President Harry Truman playing a major role only after its creation by the National Security Act of 1947.

The idea for such a council emerged out of complicated concerns at the close of World War II. A jerry-built apparatus of national security had functioned tolerably well under Franklin Roosevelt's subtle leadership. But that apparatus lacked statutory authority and effective coordination in key areas. If it were unchanged, it seemed certain to perpetuate the rivalries and confusion among the armed services which, ever since Pearl Harbor, had been the stuff of headlines. And it seemed ill suited to the lesser talents (as judged, at least, by some of Truman's subordinates) of an accidental president. The National Security Council was above all the brainchild of Navy Secretary James Forrestal, who saw it as a mechanism for coordinating a complex governmental apparatus and a way to head off the more thorough unification of the armed services he deeply feared. It also responded to the intellectual and political fashions of the times: "national security" was replacing "national defense" and "foreign policy" as a favored category, reflecting broadened concepts of mobilizing national resources in an age of world war and cold war.

Before 1947, Truman gave the council little thought other than to accept it as part of the political compromise that produced partial unification of the services. After 1947, he and his staff seized the initiative from Forrestal and began fashioning it into an instrument of the presidency. Several factors gave them room to maneuver and define. The enabling legislation was itself invitingly vague. Confusion and bickering within the new National Military Establishment (superseded in 1949 by the Department of Defense) hampered Forrestal's effort to shape the new agency. And the State Department, led by George C. Marshall and attentive to both its interests and the president's, dominated the minimal substantive work done in the council's first two years. Above all, perhaps, Truman's intuitive grasp of the politics and prerogatives of the council was decisive. That Forrestal's conception of the council "represented a unique attempt to force an advisory council on an inexperienced 'accidental' president was not lost on this self-educated student of American history," Anna Kasten Nelson has observed. Aided by talented individuals on his staff, the president made the council his own instrument of policy.

In its first years, while the struggle to capture and define it unfolded, the council was at best a minor instrument for formulating and implementing policy. Even its most famous statement in these years, NSC 68—that "deeply flawed document" (John Lewis Gaddis) justifying vastly increased military forces—was drafted outside the council's system and got Truman's blessing before the council reviewed it formally. And 1950's critical decision to intervene in the Korean conflict received no formal review by the council. Only after the war's outbreak did Truman make regular use of the council for high-level review and implementation of policy, and at that point he began to attend its meetings frequently. By then he knew he could control it and—besieged at home and abroad—perhaps knew better now that he needed it.

Playing a vital role after 1950, the council was not yet the powerful, troublesome agency it would become. No strong national security adviser as yet served it; its staffing and substantive work still drew heavily on departments and other agencies; its challenge to the State Department was not yet fully realized; its plunge into back-channel diplomacy and rogue intelligence operations was still years away. Truman did not foresee what the council would become, but by fashioning it so effectively as a tool of the presidency, he unwittingly helped prepare the way.

A fine source on the competition to define and control the council is Anna Kasten Nelson, "President Truman and the Evolution of the National Security Council," *Journal of American History* 72 (September 1985): 360–78. John Lewis Gaddis, *Strategies of Containment* (New York: Oxford University Press, 1982), illuminates the substance of the council's work during the Truman

years. Steven L. Rearden, *History of the Office of the Secretary of Defense*, vol. 1, *The Formative Years* (Washington, D.C.: Office of the Secretary of Defense, 1984), contains a wealth of information about politics, procedures, and individual papers.

MICHAEL S. SHERRY

See also Forrestal, James Vincent; NSC 68

Native Americans

See Indian Policy

NATO

See North Atlantic Treaty Organization

Neustadt, Richard E.

(27 June 1919–)

Special assistant in the Bureau of the Budget, 1946–50; White House assistant and presidential aide, 1950–53. Born in Philadelphia, Neustadt was educated at the University of California, Berkeley, and earned advanced degrees from Harvard University. His work in the Budget Bureau on clearance of legislation by federal agencies and bureaus brought him in close contact with the White House staff, which he formally joined in 1950. Neustadt wrote the White House version of the 1952 Democratic platform and the president's farewell address of 1953.

A biographical sketch of Neustadt is in Nelson Lichtenstein, ed., *Political Profiles: The Kennedy Years* (New York: Facts on File, 1976). Neustadt's incisive account of the White House staff during the last years of the Truman administration is in Francis E. Heller, ed., *The Truman White House: The Administration of the Presidency, 1945–1953* (Lawrence: Regents Press of Kansas, 1980). Among the many works that draw in part upon his experience in the executive branch are Neustadt's "Presidency and Legislation: The Growth of Central Clearance," *American Political Science Review* 48 (September 1954): 641–71, and *Presidential Power: The Politics of Leadership* (New York: John Wiley, 1960). His White House files are housed at the Truman Library.

FRANKLIN D. MITCHELL

New Deal

Harry Truman considered himself a New Dealer before entering the U.S. Senate in 1935. He had gained an insider's view of the New Deal as national reemployment director for Missouri and as a member of the state planning board responsible for coordinating state and national planning programs, and he had publicly supported New Deal relief programs.

Truman entered the Senate toward the end of the New Deal's creative phase (1933–36), when the administration and congressional insurgent liberals controlled the legislative agenda. Untested on matters of national politics and with few well-developed convictions regarding the New Deal, Truman at first loyally supported administration measures and assumed a moderate position on liberal proposals. Over the next ten years, he carefully and selectively supported New Deal initiatives, sensibly responded to the interest groups upon which the fortunes of the Democratic party rested, and patiently and adroitly maneuvered into a position of influence within the Senate.

During the New Deal's defensive phase (1937–40), a coalition of conservative Democrats and Republicans thwarted most attempts to extend the New Deal. Conservatives gained new strength in those years, as insurgent liberals lost numbers and momentum and the Republican party began its recovery after 1938. Truman and other moderates increasingly aligned with the remaining liberals to support the few new initiatives of those years.

The war years (1941–45) brought a consolidation phase, when many original New Deal programs were discontinued or limited through conservative compromise. During this period, Truman often joined with liberals attempting to save threatened programs, such as the National Youth Administration.

Truman remained a moderate liberal on most issues, but his relative position on the New Deal had changed, because the ideological spectrum shifted. He was not an integral part of the liberal reform wing of the New Deal. His voting record was attributable more to party and presidential loyalty than to ideological commitment to liberal reform.

A brief overview of Truman's voting record on the most prominent New Deal issues helps define the limits beyond which he believed the New Deal should not extend.

Truman voted for the major New Deal relief and welfare measures, such as the Social Security Act, the Wagner-Steagall Housing Act, and the establishment of the Public Works Administration. He withheld support for liberal amendments to these programs, but, once they were on the books, Truman labored to preserve them. Except for public housing, he regarded the financing and management of relief and welfare as essentially a local responsibility.

On revenue and taxation matters, Truman favored a balanced budget and increased taxes to pay for the costs of the New Deal and the wartime buildup. He supported Roosevelt on the so-called Wealth Tax Act of 1935, but usually opposed the efforts of Robert La Follette of Wisconsin and other liberal insurgents to expand graduated income taxes.

Business regulation concerned Truman more than any other issue area. Visible and effective as a member of the Interstate Commerce Committee, Truman directly participated in the preliminary investigations and writing of the Civil Aeronautics Act of 1938 and the Transportation Act of 1940. His legisla-

tive leadership and close association with Burton K. Wheeler of Montana earned respect from old-guard progressives, such as Louis D. Brandeis and George Norris. Not a trustbuster in the midwestern populist-progressive sense, Truman favored a competitive, but government-regulated economic system. He publicly assailed the "Wall Street interests," especially investment bankers and railroad holding companies, but his overall voting record reflected an independent, flexible attitude toward business.

Coalition politics in Tom Pendergast's Kansas City had sensitized Truman to the importance of interest groups. He was particularly attuned to the importance of black voters, regarding their support as pivotal to his narrow reelection in 1940. He had one of the most pro–civil rights voting records in the Senate, straying only once on thirty-five roll calls. He supported antilynching legislation, favored the elimination of poll taxes, opposed southern efforts to increase state control over absentee voting by members of the armed forces, and objected to attempts to weaken or dismantle the Fair Employment Practices Committee.

Deference to electoral realities also influenced Truman's position on labor. In 1935, he voted for the National Labor Relations Act, but wavered on the Guffey Coal Stabilization bill drafted by the United Mine Workers. Later, he helped strengthen the Fair Labor Standards Act, but risked the wrath of liberals and union leaders by supporting James F. Byrnes's resolution condemning sit-down strikes. During the war years, he failed to vote on some measures dealing with arbitration and wage controls, but was still considered prolabor.

From 1935 to 1940, Truman voted for New Deal agriculture measures more consistently than most Democrats, border state senators, and many farm state senators. During the war years, he broke with the farm bloc, opposing their attempts to disrupt Roosevelt's price stabilization program through recomputation of parity and opposition to consumer subsidies.

Truman's relations with the New Deal contributed to his selection as FDR's running mate in 1944. The Missouri senator had voted for the administration's major domestic programs and compiled a voting record acceptable to the Democratic coalition.

For Truman's assessment of his record on the New Deal, see his *Memoirs, 1945: Year of Decisions* (Garden City, N.Y.: Doubleday, 1955). He wrote there, "I was a New Dealer from the start. In fact, I had been a New Dealer back in Jackson County, and there was no need for me to change." See also *Dear Bess: The Letters from Harry to Bess Truman 1910–1959*, ed., Robert H. Ferrell (Boulder: Colorado University Press, 1980) for occasional candid assessments of Roosevelt, his Senate colleagues, and his own political fortunes. Gary M. Fink and James W. Hilty, "Prologue: The Senate Voting Record of Harry S. Truman," *Journal of Interdisciplinary History* 4 (Autumn 1973): 207–35, summarizes Truman's voting patterns on major issues and compares them to those of his colleagues. For an earlier view based on available records, see Eugene F. Schmidtlein, "Truman the Senator" (Ph.D. diss., University of Missouri, 1962). Analyses of the ebb and flow of the New Deal can be found in James T. Patterson, *Congressional Conservatism and the New Deal: The Growth of the Conservative Coalition in Congress, 1933–1939* (Lexington: University of Kentucky Press, 1967); Arthur Schlesinger, Jr., *The Politics of Upheaval, 1935–36* (Boston: Houghton Mifflin,

1960); and James W. Hilty, "Voting Alignments in the U.S. Senate, 1933–1945" (Ph.D. diss., University of Missouri, 1973). The latter analyzed voting alignments on fourteen domestic and foreign policy issue areas and ranked each senator on scales approximating the liberal-conservative continuum, thus permitting the evaluation and comparison of individual voting records, such as Truman's. Alonzo Hamby, *Beyond the New Deal: Harry S. Truman and American Liberalism* (New York: Columbia University Press, 1973), provides a clear picture of the ideological and practical limits of Truman's liberalism.

JAMES W. HILTY

See also Senator

News Media
See Press, The

Niebuhr, Reinhold

(21 June 1892–1 June 1971)

Theologian, social philosopher, educator, journalist. Born in Wright City, Missouri, Reinhold Niebuhr grew up in the parsonage of a German immigrant pastor, graduated from what is now Elmhurst College, Illinois (1910), and Eden Theological Seminary, St. Louis (1913), and completed B.D. and M.A. degrees at Yale (1915). After thirteen years as a pastor in Detroit during Henry Ford's heyday, he taught Christian ethics at Union Theological Seminary in New York from 1928 to 1960. Renowned for his Gifford Lectures, *The Nature and Destiny of Man* (2 vols., 1941, 1943), Niebuhr led a recovery in American Protestantism of its biblical and theological heritage in creative relationship with modern culture. Founding Christianity and Crisis to counter pacifism in face of the Nazi menace, he wrote for secular as well as religious journals. Once a socialist, he came to support the New Deal alternative to Marxist ideology and laissez-faire capitalism. In *The Children of Light and the Children of Darkness* (1944), he held that democracy flourishes best when human nature is understood in both its self-centered tendencies and its capacity for goodwill.

During Truman's presidency Niebuhr occasionally advised the State Department's Policy Planning Staff, but it was chiefly as a publicist that he influenced opinion and affairs. As the postwar rift between Russia and the West began, he wrote that "we will have to be prepared to be outraged by many things which Russia does in eastern Europe," an area "regarded by Russia as its strategic security belt." But, traveling through impoverished Germany in 1946, he saw that Stalin hoped for an ideological victory there and deplored Henry Wallace's attack on Secretary Byrnes's policy of assurance that U.S. forces would stay to resist any Russian moves. Early in 1947 he joined in organizing Americans for Democratic Action as an instrument of New Deal liberals who, eschewing fellow-traveler illu-

sions, "agree with the Administration policy of patience and firmness toward Russia."

Meanwhile, warning that "the whole of western Europe is sinking in an economic morass," Niebuhr urged U.S. aid and supported the Marshall Plan as an act in which "motives of national self-interest converge with motives of generosity." Viewing the Berlin blockade as Stalin's effort to show Europe, recovering with Marshall aid, that the United States would yield to pressure, he backed the airlift. Also in 1948, he stood for the establishment of Israel, since "it is right that a homeless people should have a homeland," urging terms that would "finally appeal to the Arab world as just." Pleased by Truman's election victory, he noted "a sense of direction" in his Fair Deal message calling for civil rights and a housing program. He supported the NATO treaty "primarily because the European nations desire it."

As Mao's forces conquered China, Niebuhr held that aid to Chiang was futile, since his regime, corrupt and failing to carry out land reform, was "unable to win the moral allegiance of its people." Furthermore, communism there posed "no foreseeable strategic threat as in Europe." After news of the Russian A-bomb, he approved American development of the H-bomb as a deterrent, on the assumption that Russia would develop it. As anti-Communist hysteria grew in 1950, he lamented "the tumult and distraction occasioned by Senator McCarthy's irresponsible charges against the State Department" and denounced the "silly provisions" of the Internal Security Act. He backed defensive action in South Korea, but opposed General MacArthur's readiness "to venture into vast and problematic operations in Asia which might end in disaster in both Europe and Asia," and approved his dismissal by Truman. He stressed the limits of U.S. military power in Asia.

In 1951 Niebuhr wrote that "a President who is not a political genius has managed to achieve a fairly consistent foreign policy that does some justice to the vast responsibilities which our power implies and is cognizant of the hazards of our age." In 1966 he said, "In retrospect, I would say that Truman was one of the great Presidents."

Niebuhr's later books include *Faith and History* (1949), *The Irony of American History* (1952), *The Self and the Dramas of History* (1955), and *The Structure of Nations and Empires* (1959). During the 1950s and 1960s he opposed self-righteous anti-Sovietism while supporting the Western cause, emphasized U.S.-Soviet partnership in avoiding nuclear war, supported the civil rights movement, and opposed U.S. military involvement in Indochina. Among his notable themes was the pursuit of proximate solutions in politics without sentimentality or despair. Despite a stroke in 1952, Niebuhr lost none of his brilliance as teacher and writer; after retiring, he lived much of the time in Stockbridge, Massachusetts, until his death in 1971.

June Bingham, *Courage to Change* (New York: Scribner, 1972), is a rich and accurate portrait of Niebuhr. D. B. Robertson, *Reinhold Niebuhr's Works: A Bibliography*, rev. ed. (Lanham, Md.: University Press of America, 1983), is indispensable for research. For a critique of Richard W. Fox, *Reinhold Niebuhr: A Biography* (New York: Pantheon, 1985), see Charles C. Brown, "Niebuhr Still Shapes the Conscience of a Nation," *Books & Religion* 14 (October 1986): 5, 12–13. The Reinhold Niebuhr Papers are at the Library of Congress.

CHARLES C. BROWN

Niles, David K.

(23 November 1892?–28 September 1952)

David Niles was one of the few presidential advisers who successfully made the transition from the Roosevelt to the Truman administrations. The son of immigrant Jews, Niles grew up in Boston and was for many years head of the Ford Hall Forum. In the 1930s he came to the attention of Harry Hopkins, who brought him to Washington in 1935. Eventually he became a presidential assistant, specializing as a political liaison with minority groups. Considering how well known most presidential aides are, relatively little is known about Niles; Roosevelt once described him as having a "passion for anonymity."

Niles remained with Truman specializing in minority affairs, and played a key role in relations between the president and Jewish groups. Many credit him with convincing Truman to support plans for a Jewish homeland in Palestine, and then recognizing the state of Israel shortly after its creation. He also fostered the president's civil rights policy, serving as a bridge to the NAACP.

Stomach cancer forced his retirement in 1951, and he died the following year. He never married.

The David Niles Papers are in Brandeis University. Perceptive portraits are George Q. Flynn's account in *Dictionary of American Biography*, supp. 5, ed. John A. Garraty (New York: Charles Scribner's Sons, 1977), and that by Leonard Dinnerstein in *Franklin D. Roosevelt: His Life and Times*, ed. Otis L. Graham, Jr., and Meghan Robinson Wander, 294–95 (Boston: G. K. Hall, 1985). See also the obituary in the *New York Times*, 29 September 1952. Sources differ on whether he was born in 1890 or 1892.

MELVIN I. UROFSKY

See also Jewish-Americans

Senator Richard M. Nixon, 9 October 1951. (Boston Public Library)

Nixon, Richard M.

(9 January 1913–)

Harry S. Truman did not like Richard M. Nixon—*at all.*

Actually, the policies of the two men had much in common. Separated by over twenty years, the presidencies of the two men can be considered bookends to two phases of the cold war—Truman's at the beginning of that peculiar semiwar between the United States and the Soviet Union, Nixon's when the bipolar conflict was becoming obsolete in a multipolar world. Both men distinguished themselves in foreign policy and advocated what are now considered liberal domestic policies. Nixon's achievement in civil rights and social service even outstripped Truman's.

Curiously, their backgrounds and personalities also made them more alike than any other two U.S. presidents in this century. Both battled their way up in American politics from poor, obscure families; both were outside the Eastern Establishment. According to Stephen E. Ambrose, "Both thrived on crises [and]

spoke in exaggerated terms, hurling threats and predicting disasters." Their campaigning style made them suspect to American intellectuals, and with the rank and file of their parties neither could measure up to the popularity of such presidents as Franklin D. Roosevelt, Dwight D. Eisenhower, and John F. Kennedy. Moreover, while showing little affection in public, both Truman and Nixon tried to protect the privacy of their wives and children. Partly because of this refusal to exploit their families and partly because of policies and personalities, neither enjoyed a good press.

Similarities notwithstanding, Truman saw little he recognized in himself when he thought about Nixon. The reason is easy to trace. Nixon in the 1952 (and to a lesser degree in the 1956) presidential campaign charged that the Democratic party in general and the Truman administrations in particular had shielded members of the Communist party working for the federal government. Truman insisted that Nixon was pinning a label of treason on the Democratic party and had personally called him a traitor. In particular he cited a speech of 27 October 1952 in Texarkana, Arkansas, when the Republican candidate said that Truman, Adlai Stevenson, and Dean Acheson were "traitors to the high principles in which many of the nation's Democrats believe." Nixon stopped short of using the word *traitor* in the way Truman said he did. But he came close when he made such statements as "I charge that the buried record will show that Mr. Truman and his associates, either through stupidity or political expediency, were primarily responsible for the unimpeded growth of the Communist conspiracy in the United States. I further charge that Mr. Truman, Dean Acheson, and other administrative officials for political reasons covered up this Communist conspiracy and attempted to halt its exposure."

And so Truman was as hostile as anyone could be. Throughout the 1950s he insisted that Nixon had committed "criminal libel" and "lied" about the Democratic party. In 1958, when commenting on the role of the vice president as presiding officer of the Senate, he referred to Nixon as "squirrel-head." The former president actively campaigned against Nixon in 1960, belittling dramatic incidents of his vice presidency—incidents Nixon would glorify in his 1962 best-seller, *Six Crises*: "Mr. Nixon lacks the moral sensitivity which the occupant of the White House should possess. . . . he is impetuous, quick to act, rash, and on occasions his conduct is irresponsible." Most revealing, however, were the private comments Truman made about Nixon. Writing to Acheson in the fall of 1960, he described Nixon as "a dangerous man. Never has there been one like him so close to the Presidency."

When Nixon ran for the governorship of California in 1962, Truman flew out to California to save the Democratic party and the country from the former vice president, even though this was only a state campaign. In a San Francisco hotel room he wrote some notes on the back of envelopes for what must have been an incendiary speech on 11 September 1962: "choice between [Governor] Brown, a kindly man and the opposite . . . a mean, nasty fellow. That fellow couldn't get into the front door of the White House. Now he's trying to sneak in over the transom."

Truman supporters shared his dislike for Nixon. When the ex-president visited the Senate in June 1953 and the Associated Press carried a photograph of them together, a rank-and-file Democrat wrote the former president: "Is this a trick picture or did they catch you off guard when snapped?" Another wrote: "Harry you better be fumigated after this one. This skunk on your left has not lost his aroma. . . . even dandruff off this bird stinks." Years later, in 1969, when visiting in Independence, the then President Nixon presented Truman with the piano he had played twenty years earlier in the White House. One observer expressed pleasure that Truman would again have his presidential piano in the library but warned that Nixon was making the gesture "not for you but for himself."

For a while Nixon seems to have attempted to return Truman's dislike of him. In *Six Crises* and the first volume of his *Memoirs* he was quite critical of his predecessor for trying to obstruct the House Un-American Activities Committee investigation of the Hiss case by refusing the cooperation of the Justice Department and FBI. Ironically, some of Nixon's criticisms could have applied to himself during the Watergate scandal. Four times in *Six Crises* he referred to Truman's remark in 1948 about the Hiss case's being a "red herring," concluding that the former president's error was a "sheer stubbornness in refusing to admit a mistake." He noted that not even "the immense power of a President who had just won re-election could stop the march of truth."

Later, as Nixon's Watergate problems mounted, he tried to build a case out of Truman by comparing their actions. For example, he noted that Truman had pardoned "dozens of his fellow Democratic workers . . . convicted of vote fraud in the 1936 elections" in Boss Tom Pendergast's Missouri and that he had "put up a stone wall" and refused to cooperate with the investigation of the Hiss case.

Ultimately nostalgia took over, as Nixon tried to draw sol-ace from the same actions taken by Truman that he had earlier criticized—both before and after Watergate. He insisted that Truman would not have tolerated the leak of the Pentagon Papers and noted that "the old bastard" had remained loyal to people "who were guilty as hell." He consoled himself with the thought that when Truman had been under attack during the Korean War he did everything to prevent the impression that the administration was "coming apart at the seams," and vowed to do the same thing with Watergate. When it looked as though the Ervin committee was going to subpoena Nixon, he reminded its members that Truman had refused to appear before Congress in 1953. Finally, Nixon grasped at straws and compared one demand by Senator J. William Fulbright for Truman's resignation in 1946 with demands for his own in 1974.

Since resigning as president in 1974, Nixon has mentioned Truman in every one of his books. The emphasis has been on foreign policy. Now he seems to like Truman.

In 1982 in *Leaders*, he admitted what he had omitted from his *Memoirs*, namely, that he had supported General MacArthur when Truman had dismissed him during the Korean War. "I am not among those who think that he [MacArthur] has not made decisions which are subject to criticism," Nixon had said in his first major speech as a new Republican senator. "But I do say that in this particular instance he offers an alternative policy which the American people can and will support. He offers a change from the policies which have led us almost to the brink of disaster in Asia—and that means the world."

Nixon has praised Truman's European policies, but has been critical of his "myopia" regarding the Far East. He has noted how unprepared Truman was for the presidency because Roosevelt "had kept him in the dark on major issues." In contrast, according to Nixon, "Eisenhower was determined not to make the same mistake with me."

The relationship between Nixon and Truman will remain alive for the American public through the former Republican president's books. But years ago it was not that way. Truman, understandably, did not deign to mention Nixon in his own *Memoirs*.

The best sources of information about Truman's attitudes toward Richard Nixon are materials in the Harry S. Truman Presidential Library because there is no one work that deals with them both. The only book to stress the similarities between Nixon and Truman (but not the relationship or attitudes they shared about each other) is Stephen E. Ambrose, *Nixon: The Education of a Politician, 1913–1962* (New York: Simon & Schuster, 1987). It also contains interesting information on Nixon's attacks on the Truman administration during the Hiss affair. All of Nixon's books, but particularly his two-volume *Memoirs* (New York: Grosset & Dunlap, 1978), make numerous positive and negative comments about Truman. Truman's two-volume *Memoirs* (New York: Doubleday, 1955) do not mention Nixon at all. Valuable tidbits about Truman's lingering dislike of Nixon can be found in Robert H. Ferrell, ed., *Off the Record: The Private Papers of Harry S. Truman* (New York: Harper & Row, 1980).

JOAN HOFF-WILSON

See also Douglas, Helen Gahagan; Hiss-Chambers Case; House Committee on Un-American Activities

Norris, George W.

(11 July 1861–2 September 1944)
U.S. senator from Nebraska, 1913–43. Although George W. Norris and Harry S. Truman knew and respected one another as fellow U.S. senators, they were not particularly close as colleagues, rarely working together on Senate business or meeting in political gatherings. Both men, however, were devoted and dedicated New Dealers. And just prior to his death in 1944, Norris, in a limited but nevertheless significant way, furthered Truman's career.

Truman had expressed his admiration for Norris in a personal note following the Nebraska senator's defeat in the 1942 mid-term election. Truman wrote, "I have always considered you a shining light in a sea of legislative darkness. You are one of the ideals which I had when I came here who did not turn out to have clay feet. I have always considered you intellectually honest—and I still do."

Norris in turn helped make Truman's nomination as vice president in 1944 more palatable to New Dealers who wanted Henry A. Wallace on the ticket again and were disturbed about the Missouri senator's connections with the Pendergast machine in Kansas City. Norris, who had favored Wallace prior to the Democratic convention, argued that in Truman the party had a man who could not "in any degree" be controlled by any special interest. He called Truman "a very conscientious progressive" and believed that in some quarters his candidacy would strengthen the ticket. Although he was concerned that Truman's nomination might alienate black voters and to that extent was a mistake, he never wavered in his high regard for the Man from Missouri.

See Richard Lowitt, *George W. Norris: The Triumph of a Progressive, 1933–1944* (Urbana: University of Illinois Press, 1978), wherein Norris's contacts with Truman, and particularly his role in the 1944 campaign, are discussed. In the Truman literature on his earlier career, Norris is barely mentioned. Occasionally an author, such as Alonzo Hamby in *Beyond the New Deal* (New York: Columbia University Press, 1973), mentions that Truman at the outset of his career in the Senate thought that Norris and other progressives scorned him because of his background. And Jonathan Daniels in *The Man of Independence* (1950; reprint, Port Washington, N.Y.: Kennikat Press, 1971) quotes Norris in his discussion of the 1944 campaign.

RICHARD LOWITT

North Atlantic Treaty Organization

President Truman, always sensitive to historical continuities, observed in his *Memoirs* that the North Atlantic Treaty was a simple straightforward document. On the occasion of the signing of the treaty on 4 April 1949, he claimed that "if it had existed in 1914 and 1939, supported by the nations who are represented here today, I believe it would have prevented the acts of aggression which led to two world wars." At a state dinner that night he announced, "We have really passed a milestone in history today." Forty years later, Truman's judgment needs no revision.

Unlike the League of Nations after a generation, the North Atlantic Treaty Organization (NATO) still survives; and, unlike the United Nations, it survives as a meaningful alliance and organization more than a generation after its creation. The Atlantic alliance began as a response to a European perception that the world destroyed by the ravages of World War II could not be rebuilt without American involvement. It was not simply a question of a promissory statement of American concern for the fate of Western Europe or even of a massive economic aid program and a modest military support system, all of which were either in process or in prospect by the end of 1947. What was needed was a sense of confidence in Europe that the pull of a communist system would not undermine whatever aid or promises the United States had been willing to make hitherto. This could be provided by a complete abandonment of the cherished American tradition of nonentanglement with Europe that had begun with the revolution and was enshrined in mythic American concepts associated with Washington's farewell address, Jefferson's first inaugural address, and the Monroe Doctrine.

The decision of the United States to join Europe in a military alliance, no matter how carefully the treaty was disguised, was an anguished one. In retrospect, however, it appears to have been relatively easy. The treaty was one of a succession of actions taken by the Truman administration in which Congress and the nation played passive and compliant roles. The Senate votes certainly indicated the administration's success, but they masked the evasions, hesitations, and fears of all kinds that plagued American planners as they embarked on a new adventure. For the military, an alliance could drain an already weak establishment; for Congress, it could arouse the isolationism that had been so virulent in the past; for supporters of the United Nations, it could undercut the growth of a new world order and lead to the very war it was designed to prevent; and for the administration, it could victimize American wealth and resources as Europeans utilized an alliance to bleed the superior power.

Hostility from the new converts to the United Nations, more than from the discredited isolationists of the 1930s, accounted for many of the twists and turns followed by the Truman administration in moving from the Truman Doctrine to the North Atlantic Treaty. It helped explain why over eight months of negotiations were required before the treaty could be signed. But when the document was completed, it offered a pledge to the Europeans that an attack upon one of the member states would be considered an attack against all. The primary role of the alliance in 1949 was to deter the Soviet Union both from promoting internal subversion and from embarking on external aggression against the European powers. It was expected that the promise of entanglement that the United States had failed to give in 1914 and 1939 would perform these functions.

Next to the achievement of collective security, the resolution of the German problem inherited from World War II was a vital concern. It took a number of forms. First, the existence of NATO rationalized a defense of Western Germany and served as an umbrella for its evolution into a Western-oriented ally. It

The first supreme commander of the armed forces of NATO, Dwight D. Eisenhower, in a 1947 photo. (National Archives)

was no coincidence that the Bizonia and Trizonia, the monetarized Anglo-American and Anglo-American-French zones of Germany, were the site of a Federal Republic. The abandonment of expectations for a Western-Soviet rapprochement was rendered permanent by the merging of the zones. It was even less a coincidence that the Federal Republic was created a month after the treaty was signed, or that the West would press for admission of the new republic into other European organizations before the summer of 1949 was over. Although it is too much to assert, as some scholars have, that American postwar policy centered on the reconstruction of Germany, it was obvious that an appropriate reconstruction of Europe itself, economically as well as militarily, required the exploitation of German resources and their incorporation into the West. Germany was the unstated major issue in every meeting of the allies and in most of the planning sessions within the United States, even as it was excluded from a membership role in the alliance.

More obvious, because it was always on the surface, was the French aspect of the German problem. All Europeans, but the French in particular, had suffered too recently from bestiality at the hands of Germans to exorcise the experience from their memory. For the French the threat of communism and of Soviet expansionism always had to be weighed against the German menace. The latter was in fact the substance of the Anglo-French treaty of Dunkirk in 1947 and the nominal object of the Brussels treaty of 1948. The French demanded an active British presence on the Continent as much as an American presence to

guarantee against the resurgence of a dangerous Germany. French rehabilitation was a vital element in the American association with Europe, all the more so because of the powerful Communist party minority which seemed poised to bring down the Fourth Republic. But France throughout this period was a difficult partner, at one and the same time wanting American military support and guarantee against Soviet expansionism and yet resenting what its statesmen perceived to be an Anglo-American condominium dedicated to the control of Europe.

Although the military component of an alliance ordinarily is the predominant one, this does not seem to have been the case in the creation of NATO. the Benelux countries, prime movers in its earliest stages, always held aloft aspirations of a united Europe as a goal of the alliance. In this they were joined by Canada, the most articulate champion of nonmilitary collaboration and, through a speech of Prime Minister Louis St. Laurent in 1947, the first member to propose a security pact within the United Nations free from a Soviet veto. If there was a long-run purpose in the North Atlantic Treaty, it was neither the half-hearted claim of strengthening the United Nations nor the expectation of creating a powerful military establishment. Rather, it was the hope of breaking down the barriers of national sovereignty that had plagued the West since the advent of the nation-state and that were held responsible for most of the disasters of the twentieth century.

For an Atlantic association to succeed, the United States had to be engaged as a deus ex machina to do what Europeans could not do for themselves. Although compromises among themselves were necessary, the primary concessions in the negotiations for an alliance were made to break down American resistance to membership. Thus Portugal was important for its vital strategic assets in the Azores. Iceland and Canada were not only part of the northern Atlantic communication links between the continents but also served to show latent American isolationists that NATO was more than an entangling European alliance in disguise. Scandinavia and Italy in 1949 were less significant for northern and southern flanks of a potential defense organization than for the weaknesses that made membership in the alliance a psychological prop to their national morale.

The foregoing rationalizations suggest makeshift elements in the creation of the alliance, political trade-offs that explain membership in the alliance of a nation without a border on the Atlantic and a nation with little claim to a common democratic tradition. The charges are justifiable; diplomacy had to address the realities of the time, and the primary reality for Europeans was the necessity to enlist the United States in an alliance. Economic recovery hung on a sense of political and military security that only American involvement could provide.

Many of these issues were deferred by an event that transformed the alliance into an organization in June 1950. The invasion of the Republic of Korea by North Korean forces on 25 June 1950 was a turning point in the history of the alliance, and perhaps in the history of American foreign relations as well. The impact on NATO of an action on the eastern extremity of Eurasia was immediate and dramatic. The conclusion reached by the National Security Council, led by the State Department and supported by the Joint Chiefs of Staff, was that the Korean War was a Soviet test of the West's steadfastness and that a divided Germany could be the next site of Soviet aggression if steps were not taken to deter it. The result was a reassessment of the Atlantic alliance with a view to providing a defense of Europe that would thwart a Korean-style invasion from Eastern Germany.

The first consequence of this understanding was a massive increase in military assistance, followed, after two NATO Council meetings, by a commitment of American troops to European territory in the winter of 1951. The recommendations of NSC 68 for a major increase in the military budget, which had remained as vague and theoretical as most movements in NATO until then, were well on the way to being fulfilled.

The second major consequence was the restructuring of NATO's organization. Regional planning groups disappeared, production and finance committees were revitalized, and a sophisticated military headquarters was created in Paris, led by a distinguished U.S. general, Dwight D. Eisenhower. Under his leadership a series of command decisions was made that embraced the defense of all of Western Europe. A similar command appeared in maritime form in the Atlantic, each under the Standing Group, all accomplished within six months after the beginning of the Korean War. Political reorganization followed in the course of 1951, as the NATO Council assumed new functions for the second time in two years. Initially it was designed as a coordinating body, a periodic meeting place for foreign ministers. At the New York meeting of the Council in 1950 a Deputies Council was established to provide continuity for the foreign ministers. This in turn yielded to an office of secretary-general and permanent representatives to advise him, which emerged from the Lisbon meetings in February 1952.

A third change was the new geographic shape of NATO. Greece and Turkey entered in 1952, and the Federal Republic of Germany in 1955. The former was the easier to negotiate. Greece and Turkey, original sites of cold war confrontation, had held associate status since the beginning. The need to offer a southern flank of Europe's defense overcame objections to their membership, even though it challenged the Atlantic character of the alliance.

And last, the German question was revived and acquired and urgency that had been lacking before the Korean War. Against strenuous French objections American pressures brought Germany closer to the alliance and within the frame of the military organization. Through an elaborate device first broached by the French, the Federal Republic would provide troops for the defense of Europe within a supranational community under the auspices of NATO. The alternative might have been the abandonment of Europe by the United States, or a German-American military alliance which would have isolated France and destroyed the Atlantic pact. Although French concerns ultimately forced the shelving of the European Defense Community, a climate of accommodation was reached between 1950 and 1954 which permitted all Europeans, including the French, to accept the Federal Republic into NATO through a special relationship.

Inevitably, the dramatic changes in NATO were accompanied by severe strains. The allies failed to fulfill their part of the bargain. For example, they were unable to meet the timetables for building up their ground forces, as promised at the Lisbon meeting of the North Atlantic Council in February 1952. France stubbornly refused to accept the European Defense Community, with its German component. The United Kingdom's demand for a Mediterranean command under British leadership delayed settlement of command responsibilities in that theater until the beginning of the Eisenhower administration. And in all

these conflicts, the United States was not above attempting coercion on a number of levels and at various times.

If the smaller allies were able to hold their own in the contest with the superpower, it was through a process in which decisions would be made by consensus. The result was that many decisions could not be made at all or, if made, would be attenuated to the point of nullity.

Still, Europe's defense was enhanced enormously in the years following the Korean War. There was a defense position from north to south of which the earlier forces could scarcely have even dreamed. And as the organization developed, the bastions of national sovereignty eroded or crumbled. The status-of-forces agreements that followed the stationing of American troops in Europe accorded to the host countries the right to try American citizens charged with crimes against their citizens in their own courts under their own laws. This was a necessary concession mutually accepted, but one that deprived American citizens of their constitutional rights. Similarly, the infrastructure agreements begun earlier and taken over by NATO not only encouraged interdependence of national military forces but broke sovereign jurisdictions by allowing pipelines, aircraft, and a communications system to cross national borders freely in the service of a common defense. The result was the interdependence of national armies, a mixture that seemed to make the internecine European wars of the first half of the twentieth century an anachronism in the second half. Four years later, the community of interests that Truman identified on the treaty's signing remained in place. The new president—former supreme commander Eisenhower—was able to continue building on an infrastructure established by his predecessor.

From 1949 onward, there has been a steady outpouring of publications on NATO in its many dimensions. Most of them were ephemeral, the products of a particular crisis, military or political. In contrast, only a few books have concentrated on the history of the United States and NATO, as opposed to the flood on worldwide American foreign policy since World War II. A thorough review of the literature on the early years of NATO may be found in Lawrence S. Kaplan, "NATO and Its Commentators: The First Five Years," *International Organizations* 8 (November 1954): 447–67. An updating of this bibliographical essay was made thirty years later in "NATO and Its Commentators: The First Five Years Revisited," in *The United States and NATO: The Formative Years*, by Laurence S. Kaplan, 204–21 (Lexington: University Press of Kentucky, 1984); portions of this essay appeared in this book. The major monographs on the establishment of NATO are Escott Reid, *Time of Fear and Hope: The Making of the North Atlantic Treaty, 1947–1949* (Toronto: McClelland & Stewart, 1977), and Nicholas Henderson, *The Birth of NATO* (Boulder, Colo.: Westview, Press, 1983), the commentaries of a Canadian and a British diplomatist, respectively. Other noteworthy studies of the formative years include Alan K. Henrikson, "The Creation of the North Atlantic Alliance, 1948–1952," *Naval War College Review* 32 (May–June 1980): 4–39, and Timothy P. Ireland, *Creating the Entangling Alliance: The Origins of the North Atlantic Treaty Organization* (Westport, Conn.: Greenwood Press, 1981). Lawrence S. Kaplan, *A Community of Interests: NATO and the Military Assistance Program, 1948–1951* (Washington, D.C.: U.S. Government Printing Office, 1980), deals with one of the most significant aspects of the alliance.

LAWRENCE S. KAPLAN

See also Cold War; Eisenhower, Dwight David; France; Germany; Great Britain; Greece; Isolationism; Italy; NSC 68; Soviet Union; Turkey

Nourse, Edwin Griswold

(20 May 1883–7 April 1974)
Chairman, Council of Economic Advisers, 1946–49.

Born in Lockport, New York, Edwin Nourse grew up in suburban Chicago where his father supervised music activities for a public school system. He graduated from Cornell University in 1906, majoring in economics, and then taught public school for two years. He began graduate studies at the Wharton School and completed a Ph.D. at the University of Chicago in 1915. In a pioneering 1917 essay, he defined the content of agricultural economics, which he taught at the universities of South Dakota, Arkansas, and Iowa State. In 1922 he joined the newly formed Institute of Economics at the Brookings Institution, where for the next two decades he published numerous articles and books on agricultural policy. In 1942 he was elected president of the American Economic Association.

Nourse brought estimable professional credentials to the newly authorized Council of Economic Advisers (CEA) when President Truman named him chairman in July 1946. A creature of the Employment Act of that year, the CEA was to report periodically to the president on economic trends to assist the White House in developing its policies. Nourse's selection fitted comfortably with the conservative economic thinking then shared by the president, Budget Director James Webb, and Treasury Secretary John Snyder that fiscal policy should be directed toward budget surpluses to reduce the national debt and counter postwar inflation.

Nourse's affinity with administration leaders did not preclude a conflict within the administration over economic policy. In contrast to liberals, who would increasingly advocate programs to promote overall economic growth to fund cold war initiatives, conservatives embraced a minimum of governmental economic interventions and an economy more influenced by vigorous competition among labor, industry, and capital. Nourse strongly espoused limiting federal spending, financing national security programs at the expense of promoting domestic consumption, and capping defense spending, He opposed, just as energetically, market controls to fight inflation in 1948 or spending programs to counter recession in 1949. His opposition to CEA members' testifying before Congress in 1948 to defend administrative programs exposed a deep conflict within the council and symbolized administrative discord over economic policy.

Although Nourse shared with Truman a conservative view of the role of the federal government within the economy, their differences precluded them from working together effectively. Nourse's academic background inclined him toward an appreciation of abstract theories and ambivalence about policy implications. He was suspicious of partisan politics and expected the president to draw directly on the CEA for analysis of economic trends. Truman, however, was bored by professional expertise in any form, particularly economists. Following one particularly

exasperating encounter with Nourse, who had presented his report in an "on the one hand–on the other hand" manner, the president is reported to have cried out, "Why can't someone bring me a one-handed economist?"

Rather than participate in Nourse's seminar, Truman assigned John Steelman the responsibility of dealing with the CEA. In the one instance where Nourse attempted to insert his expertise into the administration's farm program, the Brannan Plan, Truman rejected his overture out of hand, lecturing Nourse on the politics of the issue. Nourse would later express dismay that Truman had refused to be tutored on economic verities as Eisenhower would be by Arthur Burns.

Conflicts within the CEA between Nourse and Leon Keyserling and the isolation of the council from the Oval Office led Nourse to submit his resignation in December 1948, when a second Truman term was determined. Truman, however, discouraged his resigning for almost a year. The delay deluded Nourse into thinking his views would prevail over Keyserling's. The chairman's position became increasingly untenable when Keyserling proved an effective advocate for administration policies before public bodies, his economic growth policies gained ascendancy within the administration, and his capacity for working successfully with various ad hoc task forces made him a key administration player. When Nourse resubmitted his resignation in October 1949, the president accepted it.

After retirement, Nourse maintained an office at the Brookings Institution and devoted much time and energy to justifying his resignation. His departure from public life symbolized a turning point in Truman economic policies and represented the last of the faceless expert. The future of the CEA would be one of advocacy and serving as a policy agent for the president.

The Nourse papers are deposited with Cornell University and the Truman Library. His memoir is *Economics in the Public Service* (New York: Harcourt, Brace, 1953). For a laudatory biography, see Joseph G. Knapp, *Edwin G. Nourse: Economist for the People* (Danville, Ill.: Interstate Printers Publishers, 1979).

WILLIAM O. WAGNON, JR.

See also Council of Economic Advisers; Economy, The (and photograph); Fiscal and Monetary Policies; Inflation; Keyserling, Leon

NSC 68

The noted National Security Council paper of April 1950, NSC 68, was the last in a series of NSC documents, spanning two years, that sought to define an adequate national strategy to meet the Soviet challenge. In early 1950 when President Harry Truman ordered both the development of the hydrogen bomb and a review of American security policy, by the State and Defense departments, the Soviet challenge appeared especially acute. In September 1949 the Russians detonated an atomic device, thereby breaking the American atomic monopoly. Shortly thereafter the Chinese Nationalists withdrew their remaining forces to Formosa, leaving Mao Tse-tung, allegedly a puppet of

Moscow, in control of the Chinese mainland. In February 1950 Mao signed a treaty of friendship with the Soviet Union. Already the Communist-led forces of Ho Chi Minh threatened to eliminate French power from Indochina. The Kremlin, it seemed, was about to leap from Eurasia to Africa and South America.

While acknowledging these dangers, President Truman, backed by his key advisers, opposed increases in the defense budget for fiscal years 1950 and 1951. Indeed, the president denied that Russia's apparent gains were a cause for alarm or required any change in U.S. defense policy. Truman believed in a balanced budget. The report of the Committee on the National Security Organization of January 1949 asked the armed services to recognize the fact "that the strength of the Nation's economy is directly related to the Nation's defense strength." The projected military budget of some $15 billion for FY 1950, the committee argued, was "already imposing strains on the civilian economy and on the underlying human, material, and financial resources on which effective military strength depends." Military experts agreed that a budget of such magnitude would in time be fatal to the national economy. Planners projected a military budget for FY 1951 of $13.5 billion.

Those who took the Soviet threat more seriously—journalists and members of Congress—charged that the administration's defense economies endangered the country's security. Those economies, believed members of the House Armed Services Committee, carved away sinew and muscle from the nation's defense structure. Despite the preferences of the Truman leadership, the defense budget, by 1950, had become an issue of public concern. The president responded to the burgeoning criticism when, on 31 January 1950, he called upon the departments of State and Defense to "undertake a re-examination of our objectives in peace and war, and of the effects of these objectives on our strategic plans, in light of the probable fission bomb capability . . . of the Soviet Union." For over two months the State-Defense Policy Review Group debated the Soviet threat and a proper U.S. response to it. Eventually the group produced the document known by its NSC serial number, NSC 68. Secretary of State Dean Acheson called it "one of the most important documents in American history." Its chief author was defense expert Paul Nitze. The document, consisting of sixty-six pages, was classified top secret, but its proponents intended that its conclusions reach the public and Congress, as well as the administration itself. In advocating a greatly expanded defense establishment, NSC 68 acknowledged the role of government in creating "the national will and a solid, resolute expression of that will."

The report embodied notions of danger designed to attract attention. Like its predecessors, the document described Soviet expansionism in global, limitless terms. It concluded that the USSR, "unlike previous aspirants to hegemony, is animated by a new fanatic faith, antithetical to our own, and seeks to impose its absolute authority over the rest of the world. Conflict has, therefore, become endemic and is waged, on the part of the Soviet Union, by violent and nonviolent methods in accordance with the dictates of expediency." Only by recognizing that threat could the United States frame an adequate response. "The issues that face us," NSC 68 warned, "are momentous, involving the fulfillment or destruction not only of this Republic but of civilization itself." Thus defeat at the hands of the Soviet Union would be total defeat. "These risks," the document continued, "crowd in on us, in a shrinking world of polarized power, so as to give us no choice, ultimately, between meeting them effectively or being overcome by them."

The report demanded massive increases in defense spending, supported by higher taxes and federal deficits. Half measures were dangerous and invited war. Budgetary considerations, the document concluded, "will need to be subordinated to the stark fact that our very independence as a nation may be at stake." Such language did not impress the president. Upon reading and endorsing the document, he announced that the defense budget for 1951, would be smaller than that of 1950; Defense Secretary Louis Johnson anticipated a defense budget of $10 billion for 1952. Acheson took the issue to the country, but to no avail. What Acheson could not achieve the North Koreans did when they invaded South Korea in late June 1950. An Acheson aide recalled, "We were sweating over it, and then . . . thank God, Korea came along." Immediately the administration requested and received a $10 billion increase in the defense budget for FY 1951. By December, three additional appropriations raised the initial $13.5 billion to $48.2 billion. The document had reflected an insider's view of the danger of Soviet and Soviet-inspired aggression; for Congress and the American people generally, the Korean War made that danger a reality.

The following books contain accounts of the issuing of NSC 68 and the battle over the defense budget: John Lewis Gaddis, *Strategies of Containment* (New York: Oxford University Press, 1982); Dean Acheson, *Present at the Creation: My Years in the State Department* (New York: W. W. Norton, 1969); and Warner R. Schilling et al., *Strategy, Politics, and Defense Budgets* (New York: Columbia University Press, 1962).

NORMAN A. GRAEBNER

See also Cold War; Military Spending; Mobilization; National Security Council

Nuclear Energy

On 20 July 1945, after learning details about the astonishing power of the first atomic bomb test in the New Mexico desert, President Truman wrote in his diary: "It seems to be the most terrible thing ever discovered, but it can be made the most useful." His view of both the dreadful and the potentially beneficial capacities of nuclear energy anticipated a similar popular reaction after atomic bombs devastated Hiroshima and Nagasaki. The beginning of the atomic era triggered a pervasive fear of nuclear war and unthinkable destruction. At the same time, it spawned images of a technology that could perform a breathtaking array of tasks to improve living standards and provide new vistas of comfort and convenience. A plethora of books and articles projected a future served by atomic airplanes and automobiles, power plants and weather control devices, vitamin tablets and cancer cures. *Newsweek* reported that "even the most conservative scientists and industrialists [are] willing to outline a civilization which would make the comic-strip prophecies of Buck Rogers look obsolete." Despite the cautionary rejoinders of scientists, economists, and other experts who

Clarence D. Batchelor, *New York Daily News* (1950–53). Copyright New York News Inc. Reprinted with permission.

warned that such visions were at best premature and at worst fanciful, high hopes for the peaceful atom, at least in the immediate aftermath of the war, prevailed.

But military applications of atomic energy, not civilian ones, were the focus of concern and activity throughout the Truman administration. This was apparent in the Atomic Energy Act of 1946, which created the Atomic Energy Commission (AEC) and broadly defined its functions. The act established civilian control of the AEC and cited the need to develop the peaceful atom, but it gave the government exclusive authority over nuclear technology and emphasized the military uses of atomic energy. In the increasingly tense atmosphere of the cold war, the promise of civilian nuclear power seemed much less urgent than the quest for advances in nuclear weapon technology. Truman played only a peripheral role in the lengthy debate over the provisions of the act, but without his support, those who favored civilian dominance of the AEC might have lost their battle with advocates of an agency run by the military.

Despite the preeminence of its military activities, the AEC did not entirely neglect civilian applications of atomic energy. Truman's choice for first chairman of the agency was David E. Lilienthal, who was particularly outspoken in hailing the untapped potential of the peaceful atom. The AEC sponsored programs intended to inform the public about "the bright side of the atomic energy picture." It expanded the production and dis-

tribution of radioisotopes used in medicine and industry, which was the most immediate and apparent nonmilitary achievement of nuclear science.

The AEC also took steps to investigate the possibilities of producing electric power from atomic fission. Lilienthal and his colleagues were dismayed in July 1947 when a panel of nuclear experts advised them that technical difficulties and uranium fuel shortages would impede the growth of civilian nuclear power for decades. Even if those obstacles were overcome, the government monopoly of nuclear data imposed by the 1946 act prevented private industry from working on the peaceful uses of the atom. The AEC attempted to deal with those problems in two ways. One was to grant security clearances to representatives of companies interested in nuclear development and allow them to examine technical information relevant to building power reactors. In turn, the companies participating in the program submitted proposals for designing and constructing nuclear plants. This process took too long to show clear results during the Truman administration, although it did indicate that at least some industrial leaders wanted to move ahead on nuclear power if the restrictive terms of the 1946 act were eased.

The other way the AEC sought to encourage peaceful atomic development was to build several test reactors designed to provide information for civilian as well as military purposes. On 21 December 1951, an experimental breeder reactor, operated at the AEC's National Reactor Testing Station in Idaho, generated electricity from atomic fission for the first time. At its peak output on the following day, the amount of power the test produced was enough only to run the reactor's electrical equipment and light the building in which it was housed. But in symbolic terms it was a landmark achievement. If atomic energy had not come close to fulfilling the inflated claims for its capabilities, at least it had proven to be a potential source of energy in the future.

The faltering pace of progress in investigating and obtaining civilian benefits from nuclear energy inevitably drew criticism and caused disillusionment. As early as 1947, John W. Campbell, Jr., author of a book entitled *The Atomic Story*, asserted, "For the general public the much advertised atomic age is about to open with a dull thud of disappointment and a growing conviction that it has been badly oversold." The hopes for the peaceful uses of the atom, even the realistic ones, were subverted by the priority the Truman administration assigned to military applications, which culminated in the crash effort to develop the hydrogen bomb. By the end of his presidency, it was clear that in his 1945 diary notes Truman had underestimated the destructive force of nuclear energy, which the hydrogen bomb dramatically increased, and overstated the potential benefits of atomic power, which had yet to be realized.

Richard G. Hewlett and Francis Duncan provide a richly detailed account of the policy aspects of peaceful nuclear development in *Atomic Shield, 1947/1952: A History of the United States Atomic Energy Commission*, vol. 2 (University Park: Pennsylvania State University Press, 1969). George T. Mazuzan and J. Samuel Walker, *Controlling the Atom: The Beginnings of Nuclear Regulation, 1946-1962* (Berkeley and Los Angeles: University of California Press, 1984), briefly discuss civilian nuclear energy during the Truman years as a prelude to the growth of the industry after 1954. In a probing analysis of the cultural dimensions of atomic energy,

Paul Boyer suggests that the government tried to soothe public fears about nuclear war by emphasizing the potential benefits of atomic technology. See *By the Bomb's Early Light: American Thought and Culture at the Dawn of the Atomic Age* (New York: Pantheon Books, 1985).

J. SAMUEL WALKER

See also Atomic and Hydrogen Bombs; Atomic Energy Commission; Lilienthal, David Eli; Science and Technology

Nuremberg Trials
See War Crimes Trials

O

Office of Price Administration

The Office of Price Administration (OPA) implemented price controls, rent controls, and rationing from 1941 through 1946. With the end of the war and the loss of much of the agency's support, the vigorous efforts of OPA administrator Chester Bowles to continue necessary controls were largely out of step with the rest of the Truman administration. By 1946, the rationing program had been terminated, and throughout that year OPA and price controls provoked fierce controversy in Washington and across the nation. In late June President Truman vetoed as too weak a bill to continue price controls, but a month later he reluctantly signed another inadequate extension bill because of huge price increases in July. After the 1946 elections—when the Republican victory came partly because of shortages and other problems identified with the OPA—Truman lifted the remaining price controls. In 1947 rent control was transferred to the National Housing Agency.

The best account of the OPA remains Henry C. Mansfield, *A Short History of OPA* (Washington, D.C.: U.S. Government Printing Office, 1947).

JOHN W. JEFFRIES

See also Bowles, Chester Bliss

Office of the Presidency

See Presidency

Oil Policy

Oil policy in the Truman years was strongly influenced by the previous history of business-government relations in the oil industry, significantly shaped by questions of supply, demand, and security, and deeply affected by Harry S. Truman's personal and political views about big business.

Domestically, the Truman years saw the consolidation of the public-private partnership in oil that had taken shape during the New Deal. State prorationing laws, in particular in Texas, where the Texas Railroad Commission kept a lid on almost half of U.S. productive capacity, limited production to the amount that could be sold at prevailing prices. The federal role was confined largely to issuing estimates of demand and prohibiting interstate shipments of oil produced in excess of state prorationing orders. Internationally, Truman presided over the reemergence of corporatist strategies for managing the world oil economy. Attempts during World War II to secure the U.S. stake in foreign oil through such initiatives as government ownership of foreign oil properties and an agreement with Great Britain to manage the world's oil had failed because of strong political and ideological opposition to state involvement in corporate affairs and divisions within the oil industry.

By the end of World War II, leading U.S. public and private policymakers had become concerned that the oil industry would no longer be able to find oil from domestic sources at the rate necessary to meet future needs. During the war, the voracious appetite of modern warfare for oil, coupled with shortages of steel and labor, had threatened to overtake the nation's ability to supply its needs from domestic sources. After the war, continued materials shortages and increased civilian demand strained productive capacity as the United States intensified its embrace of patterns of social and economic organization premised on high levels of oil use. Although shortage soon gave way to glut, postwar increases in production and reserves were achieved largely through greatly expanded drilling and development efforts, an indication that new oil reserves were becoming harder to find.

Truman's desire to assert a larger federal role in domestic oil affairs led to a bitter clash with the oil industry, coastal oil-producing states, and states' rights advocates over the issue of offshore or tidelands oil. In September 1945, Truman, on the advice of Secretary of the Interior Harold L. Ickes, issued a proclamation asserting federal jurisdiction over "the natural resources of the subsoil and sea bed of the continental shelf." Soon thereafter, he instructed the Justice Department to institute legal action to secure explicit recognition of national control. The nomination of California oilman and Democratic party fund-raiser Edwin W. Pauley as under secretary of the navy brought the issue to public attention when Ickes publicly charged that Pauley had offered to arrange large contributions to the Democratic party if efforts to assert federal jurisdiction were dropped. Despite the shattering impact of the issue on Democratic party unity, Truman, in August 1946 and again in May 1952, vetoed joint resolutions passing title to the states. Meanwhile, the Supreme Court in cases involving California, Texas, and Louisiana ruled in favor of federal jurisdiction. Although Truman, four days before leaving office, signed an executive order setting aside offshore oil lands as a naval reserve, his successor soon signed legislation turning over title to submerged lands within historic boundaries to the coastal states.

Truman also clashed with the oil industry over federal support for synthetic liquid fuel development, which he viewed as necessary for national security, but which the industry saw as creating unwelcome competition. Rising oil imports threatened to become a source of conflict in 1949 and early 1950 as state prorationing agencies cut back production in order to maintain prices, but increased demand owing to the Korean War dampened the issue for the rest of Truman's term. Truman also tried unsuccessfully to reduce the oil depletion allowance and to eliminate the tax deduction for intangible drilling expenses, and in June 1952, he authorized a grand jury investigation of an alleged international petroleum cartel involving the leading U.S. oil companies.

Truman's relations with the oil industry were not wholly adversarial. In the spring of 1946, he authorized the establishment of an Oil and Gas Division in the Department of the Interior to oversee federal oil policy and, shortly thereafter, supported creation of an industry advisory group, the National Petroleum Council, to promote cooperation between the oil industry and the federal government. Cooperation was also the hallmark of the Petroleum Administration for Defense, established during the Korean War to manage the nation's oil supplies.

During Truman's presidency, a renewed public-private partnership in foreign oil policy took shape as the United States increasingly looked, as it had before the war, to private oil companies to secure the national interest in foreign oil. Although private corporations rather than government agencies were the chief instruments of U.S. foreign oil policy, the government's role of maintaining an international environment in which private companies could operate with security and profit deeply involved the United States in ensuring the security and stability of the Middle East and containing economic nationalism in Latin America.

The problem of integrating Saudi Arabia and Kuwait into the world oil economy without disrupting markets and prices was solved through private rearrangement of ownership shares in Middle East reserves. Although this solution tightened private control of the world oil economy and limited competition, the U.S. government raised no objections because it also served larger public policy goals of securing U.S. concession rights in the Middle East and facilitating the development of Middle East oil, thus reducing the drain on Western Hemisphere oil reserves.

U.S. assumption of responsibility for European recovery increased the strategic and economic significance of the Middle East. With the Truman Doctrine and support of Iran, the United States took major steps toward assuming Britain's traditional role as the guardian of Western interests in the region. Truman's support of a Jewish homeland in Palestine complicated, but did not nullify, U.S. efforts in this regard. In addition, Marshall Plan aid not only provided dollars for Western Europe to buy U.S.-owned oil from the Middle East; it also preserved markets for U.S. oil companies with holdings in the region. U.S. tax regulations granting credits for foreign taxes also contributed to the stability and Western orientation of the Middle East by shifting the burden of increased payments to the producing countries from the oil companies to the U.S. Treasury.

The problem of economic nationalism, best exemplified by Mexico's nationalization of foreign firms in 1938, complicated U.S. efforts to promote Latin American oil development. The United States opposed nationalization not only because of the threat to U.S. oil companies but also because of concerns that nationalist policies would restrict U.S. access to the region's resources. Flexible policies maintained the U.S. position in Venezuela, the world's leading oil exporter. State Department efforts to pressure Mexico into reversing nationalization were neutralized by Truman and Congress, however, and Mexico's oil industry remained nationalized.

Although a corporatist foreign oil policy achieved U.S. strategic and economic goals, conformed to U.S. ideological precepts, and accommodated U.S. private interests, its limits became evident following Iran's nationalization of the British-owned Anglo-Iranian Oil Company in the spring of 1951. The United States opposed the Iranian action because of concerns that other countries might follow its example, but it also feared that the use of force to reverse nationalization could drive Iranian nationalists into the waiting arms of the Soviet Union. U.S. efforts to mediate the dispute failed because of British intransigence and U.S. reluctance to countenance a settlement that gave Iran real control over its oil industry. The result was a stalemate. Efforts to involve the major oil companies in a solution of the Iranian situation also led Truman, in January 1953, to end the Justice Department's criminal antitrust investigation of the major oil companies in favor of a civil suit. Final disposition of both the cartel case and the Iranian dilemma fell to the Eisenhower administration.

Robert Engler's classic study, *The Politics of Oil: Private Power and Democratic Directions* (Chicago: University of Chicago Press, 1961), remains an indispensable guide to the people, policies, and issues of oil policy in the 1940s and 1950s. The early chapters of Richard H. K. Vietor, *Energy Policy in America since 1945: A Study of Business-Government Relations* (New York: Cambridge University Press, 1984), examine Truman's domestic oil policies. David S. Painter, *Oil and the American Century: The Political Economy of U.S. Foreign Oil Policy, 1941–1954* (Baltimore: Johns Hopkins

University Press, 1986), provides an in-depth analysis of foreign oil policy in the Truman years.

DAVID S. PAINTER

See also Conservation; Ickes, Harold LeClair; Iran; Pauley, Edwin Wendell, Sr.; Saudi Arabia

Outstate Missouri

Outstate Missouri is that part of the state outside the metropolitan areas of Kansas City and Saint Louis. The farming region in the north and northwest was settled in the nineteenth century by migrants, many of them farmers, from Indiana, Ohio, and Illinois. German Protestants and Catholics settled in the northeast part of the Ozarks and along the Missouri River just west of Saint Louis. Farmers from the hill country of eastern Kentucky and Tennessee settled in the hills of the Ozarks in the south central part of the state and parts of the agricultural southwest. All these areas supported the Union in the Civil War and Republican candidates in local and national elections in the twentieth century. Migrants from the upper South dominated the region known as "Little Dixie" in northeast and central Missouri, the eastern Ozarks, and the Bootheel in the southeast. In the early to mid-nineteenth century these farmers maintained substantial slave populations, traded with the South, and backed the South in the Civil War. Voters in these areas usually supported Democrats. Harry Truman's mother was one of those outstate Missourians who held strong southern sympathies.

The economy of outstate Missouri has always been dominated by agriculture and related businesses, and the family farm has been the dominant form of farming. Outstate Missouri was not especially prosperous during Truman's time. The standard of living in various rural areas differed greatly and resembled southern more than northern and western farm states. It was highest in the northwest, where corn and livestock were the major crops, and lowest in the Ozarks, where many farmers produced crops solely for their own use, and the Bootheel, where cotton-producing tenant farms were numerous. Most Missouri farms were small (45 percent had fewer than one hundred acres in 1950), and many were not highly mechanized, still relying on mules and horses in the middle of the twentieth century. Many farms in the Ozarks and Bootheel lacked running water and electricity. One-room schoolhouses were still numerous in the state's rural areas into the 1950s. Missouri's farm population declined approximately 25 percent in the 1940s, as ninety rural countries lost population.

Not all of outstate Missouri was rural. It included such small cities and large towns as St. Joseph, Springfield, Columbia, Jefferson City, and Cape Girardeau. People in these places relied on agricultural industries, transportation, education, and government for their livelihoods. Some of these towns, such as Columbia and Cape Girardeau, grew rapidly in the 1930s and 1940s, whereas others, like St. Joseph, stagnated or declined.

Outstate Missouri was important to Harry Truman. He was born in the village of Lamar, southeast of Kansas City, and operated a farm in Grandview from 1906 to 1917. Truman identified strongly with Missouri, especially with its rural areas. He often emphasized his origins on a Missouri farm and presented himself to America as a man from a small rural town rather than a big-city machine politician. He developed many friends outstate through his work in Masonry, the Reserve Officers Association, the American Legion, and the state's association of county judges.

The area was important to his political career. In the closely contested 1934 senatorial primary, he received more votes here than he did in Jackson County (Kansas City) and would not have been nominated without them. Outstate votes were also important to him in the 1940 primary. With the decline of the Pendergast machine, Truman received only 20 percent of his votes from Jackson County, much less than in 1934. He made up part of this loss outstate. As senator, Truman worked hard to obtain military contracts and bases for this area during World War II. He even argued for putting plants in the state's smaller cities, especially St. Joseph. He had little success in this effort because the military preferred to deal with large companies and outstate Missouri had few large firms.

In 1944 Truman received official notification of his nomination for vice president at his Lamar birthplace. Roosevelt and Truman lost outstate Missouri in November but carried the state with votes from the two large cities. But in 1948 Truman led the ticket in the state and carried outstate Missouri, recreating the Roosevelt coalition of 1936. Key to this change of fortunes was Truman's exploitation of farmers' concerns that Republicans would destroy federal farm programs. This argument had powerful appeal in outstate Missouri because of its precarious economy. After the election, Truman said he was especially pleased because "my home state stood by me so well."

For a detailed review of Missouri's history during Truman's political career, including many economic facts about the outstate region and a thorough bibliography, see Richard S. Kirkendall, *A History of Missouri, 1919 to 1953* (Columbia: University of Missouri Press, 1986). For a review of trends in Missouri politics, see Thomas F. Soapes, "The Fragility of the Roosevelt Coalition: The Case of Missouri," *Missouri Historical Review* 72 (October 1977): 38–58.

THOMAS F. SOAPES

See also Farm Experience; Lamar, Missouri; Missouri

P

Pacifism

Pacifism—the conviction that violence and killing are unequivocally wrong—is the most absolute and constant element within the several peace, antiwar, and nonviolent movements that have ebbed and flowed throughout American history. At the outset of the Truman era, religious pacifism centered around the historic peace churches, the American Friends Service Committee, the Fellowship of Reconciliation (FOR), led by A. J. Muste, and the Catholic Worker movement, headed by Dorothy Day. For secular pacifists, the War Resisters League served as a focal point. The issues that most occupied pacifists during Truman's presidency were conscription, the cold war, the proliferation of atomic and nuclear weapons, and the conflict in Korea.

At the end of the Second World War, pacifist appeals to Truman on behalf of conscientious objectors, whose release from public service camps and prison lagged behind the demobilization of military personnel, fell on deaf ears. The board Truman appointed in 1946 to review war resisters' appeals for amnesty also produced disheartening results. As one resister recalled in 1969: "President Truman did not declare an amnesty in the usual sense—he simply pardoned a few people, about 10 percent of the cases. The other 90 percent are still criminals today."

Denouncing Universal Military Training (UMT) as a system that would make young men unfit for responsible citizenship by imposing on them "mechanical, unquestioning obedience," and as a devious way to avoid unemployment, pacifists formed a coalition with labor and other liberal groups (the National Council against Conscription) to defeat the UMT law requested by Truman. Draft-card burnings were part of this campaign. Those among the four hundred to five hundred refusers who did not destroy their cards mailed them directly to the president.

The extension of Selective Service, which Congress ratified after the defeat of UMT, prompted opponents of the draft to establish a permanent center of support and counseling for draft resisters, the Central Committee for Conscientious Objectors.

Black civil rights activists, under the leadership of A. Philip Randolph, threatened civil disobedience against the Selective Service law until Truman issued Executive Order 9981, directing that racial discrimination in the armed forces be ended as soon as possible.

Meanwhile, Gandhian nonviolence against racism became the primary technique of the Congress of Racial Equality (CORE), which James Farmer guided to an independent existence from its start as a committee of the FOR. Despite the enlightened recommendations put forward in the most significant civil rights document of the Truman administration, *To Secure These Rights*, the goals and tactics of CORE activists were more far-reaching than any civil rights action taken by the president.

Truman's decision to end World War II by dropping atomic bombs on the civilian populations of two Japanese cities had horrified pacifists. Dorothy Day expressed particular outrage at the confidence and satisfaction with which the president announced the results of that decision: "Truman is a true man of his time in that he was jubilant. He was not a son of God, brother of Christ, brother of the Japanese, jubilating as he did."

In 1946, when atomic scientists, led by Albert Einstein, formed an Emergency Committee to raise public awareness about the dangers of atomic weapons, pacifists hoped for an alliance that would work against the continued manufacture of these weapons. Most concerned scientists, however, found the pacifist goal to be either unrealistic or politically unwise. A minority of scientists who did adopt the pacifist viewpoint established the Society for Social Responsibility in Science in 1949. They were joined eventually by seven Nobel Prize winners, including Einstein, shortly before his death. These scientists were among those who opposed Truman's decision to develop the hydrogen bomb. Pacifists organized nationwide protests against the new weapon, to no avail.

Viewing the cold war as "mutual entrapment" of people living on both sides of the U.S.-Soviet rivalry, pacifists decried loyalty investigations and other anti-Communist initiatives of the Truman era. They harbored strong skepticism toward the Truman Doctrine and the Marshall Plan, questioning whether

"The Girl:" Don't wonder that hope deferred maketh the heart sad."

WORLD PEACE

COLUMBIA

VERSAILLES TREATY
CORDON SANITAIRE
THE WAR TO END WAR
UNITED NATIONS
MARSHALL PLAN
ECA
NATO

THE GOLD BRICK

Clarence D. Batchelor, *New York Daily News* (1949). Copyright New York News Inc. Reprinted with permission.

the emergency in Greece that occasioned the former was serious enough to warrant unilateral action by the United States and viewing the latter more as an extension of the anti-Communist offensive than genuine humanitarian aid. A network of pacifist cells developed in the Midwest. Calling themselves Peacemakers, the members of this network sought alternatives to the habits and life-styles of cold war America. These alternatives included refusing to support military expansion and the stockpiling of nuclear weapons by withholding income taxes.

Pacifist opinion was divided when Henry Wallace campaigned against Truman in 1948. For some, Wallace's critique of the cold war was a compelling advance toward peace. Others distrusted Wallace's ties with the Communist Left and questioned the sincerity of his internationalist rhetoric. Truman's victory over both Wallace and the Socialist candidate, Norman Thomas, ratified the president's foreign policy and left him free to pursue the cold war. During his second term the ranks of organized pacifism thinned. When war erupted in Korea in 1950, a small core of pacifist resisters was unable to rally support from even their traditional allies when they disputed the terminology of a "UN police action," charging that "a truncated UN has been conscripted as an ally of the U.S.," and warned that the conflict could be a "spark to set the world afire."

The political climate of the Truman presidency was a harsh environment for pacifists. Nonetheless, they endured, planting seeds for both the nonviolent civil rights revolution and the massive movement against the war in Vietnam which trans-

formed American society in the post-Truman years—and for the antinuclear and related environmental protection struggles that continue into the present day.

Peter Brock, *Twentieth Century Pacifism* (New York: Van Nostrand Reinhold, 1970), provides definition and historical perspective. Because the history of pacifism is intertwined with the history of internationalist and antiwar movements, it figures in most general surveys of such movements, such as Lawrence Wittner, *Rebels against War: The American Peace Movement 1933–1983* (Philadelphia: Temple University Press, 1984). As both leaders and symbols of pacifist commitment Dorothy Day and A. J. Muste are prime exemplars. See Nancy L. Roberts, *Dorothy Day and the Catholic Worker* (Albany: State University of New York Press, 1984), and Jo Ann Ooiman Robinson, *Abraham Went Out: A Biography of A. J. Muste* (Philadelphia: Temple University Press, 1982).

JO ANN ROBINSON

Palestine

Truman's views on Palestine and its Arab population have remained largely obscured by his administration's policies toward the Zionist movement and the state of Israel. The president seems to have concurred with the firm recommendation of the Joint Chiefs of Staff "that no U.S. armed forces be involved" in carrying out the proposals of the 1946 Anglo-American Committee of Inquiry on Palestine. The reasons given were, first, that the country's military establishment had already been stretched to its limits by existing postwar commitments and, second, "that the political shock attending the reappearance of U.S. armed forces in the Middle East would unnecessarily risk such serious disturbances throughout the area as to dwarf any local Palestine difficulties," pushing the region "into anarchy" and turning it into "a breeding ground for world war." In addition, Truman expressed on several occasions his belief that any escalation of the conflict between Arab and Jewish residents of Palestine would provide the Soviet Union with opportunities to expand its influence over regional affairs.

Despite repreated British admonitions to the contrary, the president perceived little contradiction between his advocacy of greater Jewish immigration to Palestine and his general sympathy for the political and economic aspirations of the indigenous population. As he wrote to the king of Saudi Arabia in July 1946, "I am sincere in my belief that the admission to Palestine of 100,000 Jewish refugees this year would neither prejudice the rights and privileges of the Arabs now in Palestine, nor constitute a change in the basic situation." Six months later, Truman advised the king that "in supporting the establishment of the Jewish National Home in Palestine the United States had no thought of embarking upon a policy which would be prejudicial to the interests of the indigenous population of Palestine, and it has no such thought at the present time." The primary objective of American policy was to ensure that "the fundamental rights of both the Arab and Jewish population of Palestine shall be fully safeguarded and that in Palestine Arabs and Jews alike shall prosper and shall lead lives free of any kind of political or economic oppression." To that end, Truman announced in September 1946 that the United States was considering a $300 million loan to improve the living conditions of the local Arab community.

In the wake of the 1948 war, Truman urged the Israeli authorities to reassure Arab villagers in areas occupied by Jewish forces that their lives and property would be protected by the new regime. When it became clear that the Israeli government had no intention of repatriating Palestinians displaced during the fighting, the president attempted to persuade Tel Aviv to allow one-fourth of the Arab refugees to return as a token gesture that would "make it possible for [him] to continue his strong and warm support for Israel and efforts being made by its government to establish its new political and economic structure on a firm basis." As winter approached, Truman authorized the State Department to solicit donations from private American relief organizations to provide Palestinian refugees with food and shelter and to make a concerted effort to "urge upon the Provisional Government of Israel and other governments concerned the need for repatriating Arab and Jewish refugees under conditions which will not imperil the internal security of the receiving states." That October he ordered the American armed forces to assemble blankets, vaccines, winter clothing, and foodstuffs for delivery to these refugees; and when the United Nations voted to allocate some $32 million to assist displaced Palestinians at the end of the year, the president announced that Washington would fund half of the costs involved in the program. But despite Truman's best efforts, Israeli officials consistently rejected the administration's entreaties to repatriate Arab refugees. By the summer of 1947 the president was left with no choice but to express his approval of a short-lived proposal by the Provisional Government's Transfer Committee to allow 100,000 Arabs to return to their homes as a way out of the "deadlock" surrounding the refugee issue.

On the other hand, Truman took little interest in the tug-of-war for jurisdiction over Jerusalem among Israeli, Jordanian, and UN officials that followed the 1948 war. He indicated in a letter to Francis Cardinal Spellman in mid-May that unrestricted access to the holy places located in and around the city would probably not require the creation of an internationalized enclave under UN auspices. The administration's unwillingness to play a leading role in the deliberations of the UN Trusteeship Council regarding the final disposition of Jerusalem contributed greatly to the collapse of formal negotiations among the parties concerned and the eventual division of the city into Israeli- and Jordanian-governed sectors.

Michael J. Cohen's *Palestine and the Great Powers 1945–1948* (Princeton: Princeton University Press, 1982) is arguably the most authoritative work on Truman's policies toward Palestinian affairs, although Robert J. Donovan's *Conflict and Crisis* (New York: W. W. Norton, 1977) covers most of the same ground in a more readable and somewhat less polemical fashion. For Truman's views regarding the Palestinian refugees and Jerusalem, respectively, see Benny Morris, *The Birth of the Palestinian Refugee Problem, 1947–1949* (Cambridge: Cambridge University Press, 1987), and Yossi Feintuch, *U.S. Policy on Jerusalem* (New York: Greenwood Press, 1987).

FRED H. LAWSON

See also Displaced Persons; Israel; Zionism

Patterson, Robert Porter

(12 February 1891–22 January 1952)

Attorney; secretary of war, 1945–47. Born in Glen Falls, N.Y., Robert P. Patterson was educated at Union College (Schenectady) and Harvard Law School. Upon graduation, he joined a prestigious law firm led by a former secretary of war, Elihu Root. The lure of adventure soon overcame the promise of a comfortable practice, and Patterson enlisted as a private in the New York National Guard (Seventh Regiment) stationed on the Mexican border. He served with distinction as an army captain in World War I and was awarded the Distinguished Service Cross, a Purple Heart, a Silver Star, and advancement to the rank of major prior to discharge.

Patterson returned to the practice of law, establishing his own firm in 1920. In that same year he married Margaret T. Winchester, with whom he had four children. President Hoover named Patterson to a U.S. district court judgeship, and later Franklin Roosevelt elevated him to a seat on the Second Circuit Court of Appeals. Throughout this period Patterson remained an army reserve officer.

In July 1940, Henry L. Stimson, accepted Roosevelt's nomination as secretary of war on condition that another Harvard Law School graduate, Judge Patterson, be named as his aide. Patterson's principal functions as assistant secretary of war were military procurement and general administrative tasks. Patterson soon displayed an exceptional talent for leadership and administration. He demonstrated "absolute concentration on the job. ... He tolerated no compromises, no frills," in Bernard Baruch's estimation. In December 1940, Congress amended the National Defense Act, creating a new chief deputy, under secretary of war. Stimson named Patterson to the post, granting him broad authority to function in matters involved with industrial mobilization and military procurement.

In the sense that World War II would be won by the side that could best mobilize the economic resources available, Patterson played a pivotal role in the war years. As the matériel demands escalated at a mind-boggling rate, he transferred most of the thousand or so members of his staff to the authority of the Commanding General, Army Service Forces, Lt. Gen. Brehon Somervell. This transfer of the production, procurement, and related activities of the under secretary's office to a military officer could have damaged the principle of civilian control severely had it not been for the character of the leaders involved.

As national productivity reached its limits during the war, a clash developed between the War Production Board and the army as to what constituted "essential" civilian requirements. In many cases, military needs could be met only by reducing civilian allocations. Increasingly, Patterson emerged as spokesman for military procurement imperatives, frequently testifying before the Truman committee. In fact, six days after Pearl Harbor, Patterson wrote to President Roosevelt: "It is in the public interest that the Committee should suspend for the time being. It will impair our activities if we have to take time out to supply the Truman Committee all the information it desires."

The Truman committee did not suspend activity, however, and in December 1942 Patterson testified against proposals to remove the military procurement function from the War De-

Robert P. Patterson. (National Archives)

partment. He argued successfully that effective military operations were inseparable from military control over procurement. A year later he testified to the Truman committee that it had erred in reporting that defective aircraft engines had been received from Curtiss-Wright. Apprised to the contrary, the under secretary personally called upon Senator Truman and admitted he had been mistaken. In subsequent meetings, the two formed a strong bond of mutual respect.

During the war, Patterson also oversaw the penal system of the army and served as the War Department representative on the War Manpower Commission and the War Production Board. He was honored for his labors with the Distinguished Service Medal at the conclusion of the war.

On 18 September 1945, a few days after the war ended, Henry Stimson, as planned, resigned as secretary. President Truman announced he had selected Patterson as successor. Prior to the announcement, the president had given Patterson the choice of a Supreme Court justiceship. Typically, Patterson, who would have dearly loved to join the High Court, told the president he would serve where Truman determined he was most needed.

In October 1945, Patterson and Navy Secretary Forrestal warned the president that the continuous acceleration of demobilization in response to domestic pressures was endangering the U.S. strategic military posture. Truman agreed with them but continued the pace of demobilization. By mid-1947, because of demobilization politics, White House budget cuts, and further cuts by Congress, the U.S. Army ranked sixth in size among the nations of the world. Partly to offset this manpower deficit, Truman urged upon Congress the passage of a universal military training bill. The president found Patterson to be a staunch ally. The secretary endorsed the "Plattsburg Idea" (military training camps for all male civilians). Despite the best efforts of the president and the secretary, the proposal failed of passage, largely because this Spartan concept was considered antithetical to democratic principles.

In May 1947, because of severe budgetary cutbacks, the secretary recommended to Truman that U.S. peacekeeping forces stationed in Korea be withdrawn. The president ordered the Joint Chiefs of Staff to consider the advisability of Patterson's suggestion. In September, the Joint Chiefs told the president that removing U.S. forces was acceptable because Korea, from the standpoint of U.S. military security, was of limited strategic value. In the presidential campaign of 1952, Eisenhower blamed the Department of State (and Truman, by implication) for removing forces from South Korea, thus precipitating the North Korean attack. Truman bitterly denounced the charge; pointing out that Eisenhower was one of the Joint Chiefs when the policy was approved, he added, "The withdrawal of American forces from Korea was proposed . . . by Secretary of War Robert Patterson, a Republican."

Soon after World War II, Truman ordered Patterson and Navy Secretary Forrestal to develop a plan of military unification. The resulting interservice bickering, labeled by reporters "the Battle of the Potomac," underscored the need for legislation. Patterson's views were much closer to the president's than Forrestal's. Among many other things, the navy secretary was opposed to creation of the office of defense secretary. Under White House pressure, Forrestal worked out a compromise with Patterson which became the National Security Act of 1947. The act established the army, navy, and air force as equal departments under supervision of a cabinet-rank "secretary of defense." Truman asked Patterson to accept appointment to the new post, but he declined, explaining that his strained financial condition would not permit his remaining in government service. He resigned as secretary of war (army) in 1947, and Forrestal became secretary of defense.

Returning to the firm he had founded (Patterson, Belknap and Webb), he prospered as an attorney, served as President of the Council of Foreign Relations, and of the New York City Bar. In 1952 he died in an airplane crash while returning from legal business in Buffalo.

A brief biographical sketch appears in *Who's Who in America*, vol. 25, *1948–1949* (Chicago: A. N. Marquis, 1948), 1914. An accurate and objective biographical sketch of Patterson by A. Russell Buchanan is in the *Dictionary of American Biography*, supp. 5 *1951–1955* (New York: Charles Scribner's Sons, 1977), 538–39. His activities as under secretary of war are described at length throughout two volumes of the *United States Army in World War II* series: see R. Elberton Smith, *The War Department: The Army and Economic Mobilization* (Washington, D.C.: Office of the Chief of Military History, Department of the Army, 1959), and John D. Millett, *The Army Service Forces: The Organization and Role of the Army Service Forces* (Washington, D.C.: Office of the Chief of Military History, Department of the Army, 1954). Patterson receives favorable treatment in Forrest C. Pogue, *George C. Marshall*, vols, 2–3 (New York: Viking Press, 1965, 1973). Succinct portraits of Patterson and his rival James Forrestal may be found in Charles

Hurd, "No. 2 Men with No. 1 Jobs," *New York Times Sunday Magazine*, 7 December 1941, 9, 36. The Patterson Papers are housed in the Mss. Division, Library of Congress.

RICHARD F. HAYNES

See also Armed Forces, Unification of the

Patton, James George

(8 November 1902–17 February 1985)

President, National Farmers Union, 1940–66; political ally of Truman. Born in Bazar, Kansas, and educated at Western State College in Gunnison, Colorado, Jim Patton worked for the Colorado Farmers Union and rose to the top of the National Education and Cooperative Union of America (also known as the National Farmers Union, or NFU), becoming president in 1940 and serving until 1966.

Throughout the Truman presidency, farm interest group politics intensified the decidedly partisan split of World War II. The NFU, under Patton, became rigidly supportive of the Democratic party in an attempt to continue the high level of fixed price supports after the war. The American Farm Bureau Federation (AFBF) and its president, Allan Kline, found the Republican party more favorable to AFBF's flexible market-directed price support plan. Patton, who was an avowed farm populist as well as a man of shrewd intelligence, believed that large-scale farmers would benefit and flourish to the detriment of small-scale producers under flexible and thus less stable supports.

Despite his strong beliefs and his service on several commissions during both the Roosevelt and Truman administrations, Patton found the NFU on the losing side of major farm price policy battles during Truman's tenure. The passage of the flexible price support plan in the Agricultural Act of 1948 and the defeat of the full income support levels of the Brannan Plan in 1949 were decried by Patton as major blows against family farming in America. The most significant of Patton's successes with Truman, albeit a compromised one, was the Employment Act of 1946. Aware that full employment would do much to promote the sale and expansion of farm products, Patton was one of the act's key proponents. Patton's plan, although it did not carry, would have vested far more economic authority with the chief executive through the Employment Act.

Although Patton did little to shape the specific direction of farm price support policy, he remained an articulate and vigorous spokesperson for family farming throughout his years with the NFU. Even in the face of policy disagreement from most state Farmers Unions, Patton provided an ongoing critique of federal policies that promoted large-scale concentrated agricultural production. In doing so, he helped maintain the spirit of both farm populism and Jeffersonian democracy as these enhanced demands for higher levels of commodity price support and farm income stabilization policy.

Patton, as a consequence of the force of his arguments, played a role in agricultural policy debates through the 1960s. In many ways, despite changing agricultural conditions, he personally kept alive a rhetoric that was important to farm income policy conflicts of the 1970s and 1980s. After retiring and until just before his death, Patton kept an active public life as both a consultant and as a social activist organizing retired union members.

Three writings are especially useful. For the greatest information on Patton, see Charles Henry Livermore, "James G. Patton: Nineteenth-Century Populist, Twentieth-Century Organizer, Twenty-First-Century Visionary" (Ph. D. diss., University of Denver, 1976). For Patton's role in the NFU, see John A. Crampton, *The National Farmers Union: Ideology of a Pressure Group* (Lincoln: University of Nebraska Press, 1965). The National Farmers Union put together a posthumous publication in tribute: see *In Fond Remembrance: National Farmers Union Award for Meritorious Service to Humanity* (Denver: NFU, 4 March 1986). Patton's papers are in the Western Museum of History, University of Colorado, Boulder.

WILLIAM P. BROWNE

See also Agriculture; Brannan, Charles Franklin; Employment Act of 1946; Kline, Allan Blair

Pauley, Edwin Wendell, Sr.

(7 January 1903–28 July 1981)

Oil magnate; presidential adviser; U.S. representative, Allied Reparations Commission, 1945–46. Ed Pauley was a tough, talkative, self-made California oil tycoon with an impressive record of fund-raising for the Democratic party and powerful connections within his state's industrial and financial community. Standing over six feet tall, Pauley was brawny and athletic and looked as though he should be cast as a detective in a Dashiell Hammett movie. Instead he speculated in commodities and real estate, sailed yachts (winning the Trans-Pacific Race in 1939), and managed oil companies, including his own diversified and independent Petrol Corporation.

Pauley's successful fund-raising as treasurer of the Democratic National Committee eliminated party deficits by 1944 and made him the spokesman for right-wing California Democrats. He also served as Roosevelt's special representative to Britain and the Soviet Union on Lend-Lease tanker exchange and as a dollar-a-year man on the staff of the Petroleum Administration for War. In the latter capacity, ironically, he won high marks from Interior Secretary Harold Ickes and brought such talented oil men as Ralph Davies onto the staff. Although President Roosevelt had considered Pauley for a high naval appointment, his oil connections were questioned by Eleanor Roosevelt, and at the time of FDR's death, Pauley's appointment languished.

The new president and the California oilman and politician had already established good relations. Pauley had first come to Truman's attention in 1941 while serving as secretary of the Democratic National Committee. Three years later, he took over as director of the Democratic National Convention in Chicago and worked aggressively for Truman's nomination for the vice presidency, telling the *New York Times*, "We're not nominating the vice president; we're nominating the next president."

Truman liked and admired Pauley's toughness and acumen.

He first appointed him U.S. representative to the Allied Reparations Commission (1945–46) with the rank of ambassador. When the Soviets refused to allow Pauley into Manchuria and North Korea to estimate Japanese industrial holdings, he returned to Washington with a reputation as a strong negotiator. Truman had him in mind for secretary of defense in a reorganized military system but made a strategic miscalculation by nominating him on 18 January 1946 for under secretary of navy. The president was probably correct in thinking that Pauley would be effective in the Pentagon, but underestimated his political vulnerability as a California oil executive with well-known interests in offshore oil leases.

Pauley's nomination to the sensitive navy post particularly irritated Harold Ickes, who never entirely trusted Pauley. He had been especially suspicious of his lobbying and fund-raising activities since the two had had a conversation about the government's pending tidelands suit on the way home from Roosevelt's funeral. Ickes's opposition to Pauley's nomination, well known in government circles and among important journalists, resulted in his being called as a witness before the Senate Naval Affairs Committee in February 1946. The secretary read portions from his diary citing instances in which Pauley appeared to suggest that oilmen would make campaign contributions if the federal government would drop its claim to offshore holdings. Although Pauley denied any wrongdoing and Truman persisted in backing him, the nomination was dead when Ickes used the occasion to resign on 13 February 1946.

Pauley remained an unofficial member of Truman's "kitchen cabinet," and the president named him special assistant to the secretary of the army in 1947 only to be embarrassed once again when the Commodity Exchange Authority was forced to reveal in January 1948 that Pauley was a leading speculator. He denied that any of his earnings had come as a result of inside information, but resigned before Truman had the opportunity to question him.

Pauley returned to his expanding California oil business, incorporating Pauley Petroleum which acquired important Mexican offshore oil leases, and to his activities as regent of the University of California, Los Angeles, where he had earned two degrees in the College of Commerce and Business Administration. He continued to be a kingmaker in Democratic party politics and an unofficial adviser to John F. Kennedy and particularly to Lyndon B. Johnson. Edwin Pauley made major contributions to the University of California, where a sports arena bears his name, and to the Los Angeles Art Museum. He died at age seventy-eight in Beverly Hills.

There is no biography of Edwin Pauley nor disposition of his papers. His role in postwar oil affairs is described in Michael B. Stoff, *Oil, War and American Security* (New Haven: Yale University Press, 1980), and Robert Engler, *The Politics of Oil: A Study of Private Power and Democratic Directions* (Chicago: University of Chicago Press, 1961). Pauley's friendship with Truman is detailed best in Robert J. Donovan, *Conflict and Crisis* (New York: W. W. Norton, 1977), in Truman's *Memoirs: Year of Decision* (Garden City, N.Y.: Doubleday, 1955), and in Merle Miller's oral history *Plain Speaking* (New York: Berkeley Publishing, 1973). Pauley's successful dealings with the Soviet Union are covered in the President's Secretary's File, Harry S. Truman Library, Independence. Pauley's relationship with Ickes dates from the 1933 NRA codes and can be followed in *The Secret Diary of Harold L. Ickes* (New York: Simon & Schuster, 1953, 1954) and the unpublished diary in the Library of Congress, Washington, D.C. The diary is the best source for the quarrel over Pauley's nomination as under secretary of navy. Pauley's obituary appeared in the *New York Times*, 29 July 1981.

LINDA J. LEAR

See also Cold War (photograph); Ickes, Harold LeClair

Pendergast, Thomas J.

(27 July 1870–26 January 1945)

One of the burdens Harry S. Truman had to bear was his early affiliation with the Democratic political machine in Kansas City, Missouri, dominated by Thomas J. Pendergast. Raw-boned, thick-necked, fond of wearing spats, and, by middle age, large of girth, Tom Pendergast very much fit the stereotype of the corrupt city boss popularized by the cartoonist-illustrator Thomas Nast. Tom Pendergast's undisputed influence over local and state politics led pundits to label Kansas City "Tom's Town" and Harry S. Truman, arriving on Capital Hill after his election in 1934, "the Senator from Pendergast."

Legend has it that the economic and political rise of the Pendergast family began in 1881 with a horse race. Twenty-five-year-old James Pendergast, an iron puddler by trade, bet his savings on a long shot named Climax and won. The lucky, second-generation Irishman used his winnings to open an inn and the Climax Saloon near the railway station in Kansas City's booming industrial district. Starting there, he built a base in the local Democratic party. After Jim was elected alderman in 1892, he called on three brothers, John, Mike, and Tom, to help consolidate the gain. John looked after the saloon interests. Mike liked rough-and-tumble organizing. Tom—sixteen years younger than Jim—seemed to excel at everything.

As the Pendergast organization grew, the minority Republicans sometimes put up a respectable challenge, but the main difficulties came from another faction of the Democratic party, one led by Joseph B. Shannon. Divided over patronage far more than policy, the Pendergast-Shannon split colored Kansas City politics until the end of the 1930s. Early on, according to a reputable observer, one of Shannon's men belittled Pendergast's supporters by calling them "Goats," an equation of "Shanty Irish" with the animals many of them kept in their dooryards. Girding for political battle, Jim Pendergast was reminded that Shannon and many of his supporters made their homes in a nearby valley replete with small wildlife. "When we come over the hill like goats, they'll run like rabbits," he roared. The labels stuck—Democrats all, but the distinction between the Pendergast Goats and the Shannon Rabbits was all-important.

Jim Pendergast died in 1911. His little brother, by then known as "Big Tom," proceeded to transform the Jackson Democratic Club from a Pendergast organization into a Pendergast machine. Like bosses in other cities, Pendergast offered supporters services, favors, and assistance they could obtain in no other quarter. In return, he profited from gambling, prostitu-

Thomas J. Pendergast, 2 July 1938. (Associated Press/Wide World Photos)

tion, protection, and favors to his legitimate interests in saloons, liquor distribution, real estate, and the Ready Mixed Concrete Company. The latter enjoyed a brisk business with contractors who did work for the city and county governments—someone estimated Ready Mixed profits at a quarter million dollars in a bad year, twice that in a good one.

Tom Pendergast lived very well in a fortresslike mansion on Ward Parkway, the city's most prestigious address. He treated his family to the things money could buy, and he indulged himself in an orgy of betting on the ponies that some said was costing him at least a million a year by 1933. Still, he ran his political empire from three upstairs rooms in a modest building at 1908 Main Street on the fringe of the downtown business district.

Pendergast's power largely depended upon his ability to control patronage in Kansas City and in surrounding Jackson County. He virtually locked up control of Kansas City in 1926 when he joined with reformers to set up a council–city manager government. The small council, easier for Pendergast to control, compliantly installed his hand-picked manager, Henry F. McElroy. In 1931, after voters approved bonds for over $40 million worth of new buildings, roads, parks, water systems, and other improvements, Pendergast, through McElroy, could always find a job for a deserving man. Pendergast controlled even more jobs after 1935 when Roosevelt appointed organization man Matthew Murray head of the Works Progress Administration (WPA) in Missouri. Construction financed by the bond

issue and the concentration of WPA jobs meant that the depression hit Kansas City later and less viciously than other cities.

The business of Jackson County was the responsibility of three administrative "judges." Elected by district, the judges comprised the county court, in reality an administrative committee. The Pendergast family asked Harry S. Truman to stand for judge of the county's eastern district in 1922. Apparently they understood that Truman's credentials as a veteran, Baptist, Mason, and county road overseer, and his southern heritage were valuable in offsetting meaner images of other Goats in the minds of the eastern district's many country folk. Truman won in 1922, but campaign errors caused him to lose in 1924—the only election he ever lost. The Goats regrouped in 1926; Truman became presiding judge of the three-man county court, a position he retained until he became U.S. senator.

Truman never challenged Pendergast's first claim on dispensing approximately nine hundred jobs under the county court's jurisdiction. And he accepted as reality the fact that contracts sometimes had to go to unscrupulous friends of "the Boss." It was not that Truman was callous. "I wonder if I did right," he wrote in a moment of candor, "to put a lot of no account sons of bitches on the payroll and pay other sons of bitches more money for supplies than they were worth" in order to appease the machine and be left alone to spend the bulk of the county budget efficiently. Unlike many Kansas City Goats, Truman never used public office as a means of personal enrichment, although he was acutely aware of the possibilities. "Am I a fool or an ethical giant?" he asked himself. "I don't know."

Truman acquired a reputation for integrity and efficiency that helped the Pendergast machine, and Pendergast paid off with the chance to run for the U.S. Senate in 1934. Henry McElroy's reputation in City Hall was less impressive. But it was not until he quit his post in 1939 that auditors discovered his "country bookkeeping" methods covered a deficit of over $20 million in city accounts.

Although Pendergast had made possible Harry Truman's election to the U.S. Senate, the Kansas City boss appears to have had no control in matters that Truman considered "Senate business." Truman later said that Pendergast "only talked to me once about my work in the Senate." (And that was when Roosevelt asked Pendergast to prod Truman into supporting his candidate for Senate majority leader.) Truman defined "Senate business" narrowly. Patronage was not Senate business, nor was Missouri and Jackson County politics. And on those matters Pendergast and Truman were in close communication. Historian Richard Miller considers Pendergast and Truman "co-equals" in plotting out the course of local politics; indeed, he assigns equal responsibility for the corruption that was involved in implementing their plans.

Tom Pendergast's health began to fail in 1936—first he had a heart attack and then three abdominal operations. During this time of weakness, U.S. District Attorney Maurice Milligan, Missouri's governor Lloyd Stark, a local reform group headed by Rabbi Samuel S. Mayerberg, and agents of the Treasury Department and FBI all began to probe irregularities in Kansas City ranging from vote fraud to failure to pay income tax.

On 22 May 1939 Tom Pendergast was convicted of tax evasion and sentenced to fifteen months in Leavenworth Penitentiary. After serving a year and a day he was free, but only on condition that he not gamble and not participate in political activity of any kind for five years. He did not live out his parole.

Thomas J. Pendergast died in 1945. In assessing his practice of politics, the imprecise art of the possible, some, probably most, observers were struck by the magnitude of his sins and weaknesses. But stalwarts spoke of honesty, loyalty, and good intentions. Vice President Harry S. Truman, for one, was saddened. He flew to Kansas City from Washington for the funeral. "I'm as sorry as I can be," said Truman. "He was my friend and I have always been his."

Lyle W. Dorsett, *The Pendergast Machine* (New York: Oxford University Press, 1968), is the standard work. William M. Reddig, *Tom's Town: Kansas City and the Pendergast Legend* (Philadelphia: Lippincott, 1947), has stood the tests of time and scholars exceptionally well and has been reprinted (University of Missouri Press, 1986). The most satisfying analysis of the relationship between Pendergast and Truman is in Richard Lawrence Miller, *Truman: The Rise to Power* (New York: McGraw-Hill, 1986).

RICHARD D. MCKINZIE

See also Election of 1934; Jackson County Court; Kansas City, Missouri; *Kansas City Star*

Perkins, Frances

(10 April 1880–14 May 1965)

Frances Perkins is best known as Franklin D. Roosevelt's secretary of labor (1933–45), the first woman cabinet member in American history. She was born in Boston, Massachusetts, and graduated from Mount Holyoke College in 1902. As a social reformer during the Progressive Era she served on the New York State Factory Commission which was set up to investigate the Triangle Shirtwaist Factory fire of 1911. Her work on the commission put her in contact with Alfred E. Smith, who became governor of New York in 1918. Smith appointed her to the New York State Industrial Board, and in 1928 Governor-elect Franklin D. Roosevelt appointed her the Industrial Commissioner for New York State. Perkins had a long and effective working relationship with Roosevelt. As secretary of labor during the New Deal era, she was able to influence a great deal of the social policy and labor legislation, in particular, the Social Security Act of 1935 and the Fair Labor Standards Act of 1938.

Perkins did not attain a similar influence in the Truman administration. When President Roosevelt died, she resigned her position as secretary of labor and was replaced by Lewis B. Schwellenbach. When Truman asked what post would interest her, she suggested the Social Security Board because of her longtime commitment to the program. Instead, on 12 September 1945, he appointed her to the Civil Service Commission, a position she held until Truman left office in 1953. Although Perkins found her years with the Civil Service Commission less stimulating than the years in the Labor Department, she nonetheless tackled her new job in her usual high-principled and energetic style. She was determined to see that the commission did not become a government tool for invading the privacy of job applicants and employees. Her long years in government service had strengthened her belief in the right to privacy as the basis of human liberty. This was a value that carried over into her personal life as well.

When Eisenhower became president in 1953, Perkins resigned from the Civil Service Commission and became a lecturer on labor policy. In 1955 she was affiliated with Cornell's School of Industrial and Labor Relations as a highly respected visiting professor. She remained intellectually active until her death in 1965.

George Martin's *Madam Secretary: Frances Perkins* (Boston: Houghton Mifflin, 1976), is a nearly exhaustive treatment of Perkins's life and career. Aside from Martin's work, which contains a chapter on the Truman administration, little else has been published on those years. Perkins's papers are deposited at the Schlesinger Library, Radcliffe College, the Franklin D. Roosevelt Library at Hyde Park, and in the Department of Labor Records at the National Archives. Columbia University's Rare Book and Manuscript Library contains the largest collection of Perkins's papers outside the National Archives and includes a collection reflecting her work with the U.S. Civil Service Commission. It is described in *Fifty United States Civil Service Commissioners*, published by the commission's library in 1971. In addition, Perkins's Oral History at the Columbia University Oral History Research Office consists of over five thousand transcript pages recounting both her private life and her public career.

WINIFRED D. WANDERSEE

See also Women

Personality

When Harry Truman became the thirty-third president of the United States on 12 April 1945, very little was known about him as a person. In his eleven years as a senator he had rarely spoken in public and made few efforts to become known outside his home state of Missouri. How he was seen there depended on who judged him: his opponents saw him mainly as an associate of Kansas City's boss Tom Pendergast and charged him with the corruption they alleged pervaded the Pendergast machine; his admirers rated him as a dedicated, hard-working public servant.

A full-length scholarly biography of Harry Truman still remains to be published; when it is, one may assume it will go a long way toward answering the question: what manner of man was Harry S. Truman? In the meantime, various increments of his personality picture allow a preliminary assessment.

1. *Family influences*: Truman's father, John, was reported to have been easily aroused to anger which, however, always quickly subsided. There are numerous instances in his oldest son's public career that show a similar pattern of behavior. He also appears to have inherited his liking for music from his father. A few authors have pointed to his mother's influence (and his relations with her) as much more important. But in view of the fact that Harry Truman was thirty years old when his father died, the analogy to, say, Franklin Roosevelt breaks down. What is known is that Truman's mother took a strong interest in Harry's schooling (including his musical education) and that his childhood illnesses made him perhaps more dependent on her than might otherwise have been the case. It is certain (as his let-

Young Harry, about 1896. (Courtesy of the Harry S. Truman Library)

they could and would do and differences in ancestry, religion, or wealth were of secondary importance.

This emphasis upon personal worth permeates the record of Truman's relationships in public life. His steadfast support of those he considered his friends (be they Dean Acheson or Tom Pendergast) was only one manifestation. Those who worked closely with him, from the men in his World War I artillery unit to the members of his staff in the White House, were assured of his support, sometimes to Truman's disadvantage.

3. *The wartime experience*: There can be little doubt that World War I marked a watershed in the life of Harry Truman. Most biographical sketches of him contain next to nothing of the first thirty-three years of his life; the first event noted usually is "Commanded Battery D, 129th Field Artillery in the First World War." Truman himself never failed to highlight the importance he attached to this experience and gave it visible expression when he brought the surviving members of the unit to Washington to take a place of honor in the ceremonies of Inauguration Day, 1949.

Truman did not aspire to be an officer. He hoped that his fellow citizen-soldiers in the National Guard unit (in which he had attained the rank of corporal) would consider him worthy to be a sergeant. His election to a first lieutenancy came as a surprise to him, but, characteristically, he applied himself to his new duties with diligence and intensity. By the time his unit reached the front lines in France on July 1918, he was a captain and in command of Battery D. By the time he returned to civilian life in 1919, his ability to provide leadership had stood the test.

It is striking how the war experience changed the man. Before the military service period, Harry Truman had been a bank clerk, had tended the family farm, and had engaged in a few (mostly unsuccessful) business ventures. He had been as faithful a member of the Masons as he had been of the National Guard.

ters to "Dear Mama" reveal) that he revered her throughout her life.

But it is also evident that, from an early time in young adulthood, Harry Truman made his own decisions and that, whomever he was working for, whether his family or a Kansas City bank, he was conscientious and gave the job his best. The Protestant work ethic was clearly part of his inheritance.

2. *The early environment*: Independence, Missouri, was (and still is) a southern town. But it is also close to "where the West begins." It is not without significance that Thomas Hart Benton's floor-to-ceiling mural painting that greets the visitor to the Truman Library depicts "The Opening of the West"—the theme had been the former president's personal choice. The scenes painted by the artist reflect the frontier spirit that had been a reality in the days when Truman grew up in Grandview and Independence. At that time much of what lay west of his hometown was still underpopulated or even unpopulated. Oklahoma—the northeast corner of which touches the southwest corner of Missouri—was still legally Indian Territory. Kansas, a mere ten miles west of the town of Independence, was actively recruiting settlers for its "wide-open spaces" in England and on the European continent. This was country where status counted little and achievement received ready recognition. It was also a setting in which the harshness of conditions imposed a premium on cooperation. People were judged here on what

Senator Truman and his wife, Bess, 19 July 1944. (United Press International/Bettman Archives)

But he had been a follower rather than a leader. After the war he not only accepted but to a degree sought the opportunity to serve the public and readily assumed proffered responsibilities. He retained his reserve commission in the army and was one of the organizers of the Reserve Officers Association. He moved quickly through the advanced degrees of Masonry and, by 1924, was Deputy Grand Master of Missouri. He ran, successfully, for public office. His rise in the political arena was at least partly due to the fact that the veterans of Battery D were a ready nucleus of a personal following.

Survivors of that World War I organization were, understandably, queried about the roots of this loyalty. Their responses, of course, varied considerably, but what they had in common might be summarized thus: we came to know Harry Truman as a man of common touch and uncommon dependability; if he told us something would be done, we knew that it would be done. As one of them put it, "He always gave more than he asked."

Much later, a more sophisticated observer, the novelist John Hersey, offered this analysis:

> President Truman seemed to think of himself sometimes in the first person and sometimes in the third—the latter when he had in mind a personage he still seemed to regard, after nearly four years in office, as an astonishing tenant in his body: the President of the United States. Toward himself, first-personally, he was at times mischievous and disrespectful, but he revered this other man, his tenant, as a noble, history-defined figure. Here was a separation of powers within a single psyche, and a most attractive phenomenon it was, because Harry Truman moved about in constant wonder and delight at this awesome stranger beneath his skin. And to some extent this wonder and delight must have elevated and purged the mere man.

Roy Jenkins, the former British labor leader, saw what he called the "paradox of Truman" in a somewhat different dichotomy:

> He was an intellectual amongst political "pros" and a political "pro" amongst intellectuals. He absorbed many facts, and he thought about them a good deal, but his conversation involved no spinning of general theories. He neither possessed nor aspired to intellectual or social sophistication. His speech and his writing . . . were generally splendidly direct, but the choice of words was rarely distinguished, and the sentiments sometimes narrow and intolerant: "Sissy" was one word which he employed a good deal. . . . When once asked at a school question and answer session, after he had been President, whether he had been popular as a boy, he replied: "Why no, I was never popular. The popular boys were the ones who were good at games and had big, tight fists. I was never like that. Without my glasses I was blind as a bat, and to tell the truth, I was kind of a sissy."
>
> This interplay provided part of the formation of his personality and character. He was an "anti-sissy" sissy, a puritan from the poker rooms, a backwood politician who became a world statesman not just because he was President of the United States in the plenitude of its power but because he had an exceptional sense of duty and power of decision, and because he could distinguish big issues from little ones, and was as generally right on the big ones as he was frequently wrong on the small ones.

The quotation from John Hersey is from *Aspects of the Presidency* (New York: Ticknor & Fields, 1980) which, in part, builds on a two-part article originally published in 1950 in the *New Yorker*. The passage by Roy Jenkins is from his *Truman* (New York: Harper & Row, 1986). Other books that provide glimpses of Truman's personality are Margaret Truman (Daniel), *Harry S. Truman* (New

York: William Morrow, 1973); Harold F. Gosnell, *Truman's Crises* (Westport, Conn.: Greenwood Press, 1980); Ken Hechler, *Working with Truman* (New York: G. P. Putnam's Sons, 1982); David E. Lilienthal, *The Journals of David E. Lilienthal*, vol. 2, *The Atomic Energy Years* (New York: Harper & Row, 1964); and Alfred Steinberg, *The Man from Missouri: The Life and Times of Harry S. Truman* (New York: G. P. Putnam's Sons, 1962). Several of the contributions to Francis H. Heller, ed., *The Truman White House: The Administration of the Presidency 1945–1953* (Lawrence: Regents Press of Kansas, 1980), and William F. Levenstrasser, ed., *Harry S. Truman: The Man from Independence* (Westport, Conn.: Greenwood Press, 1986), provide suggestive anecdotal material. Richard Lawrence Miller's *Truman: The Rise to Power* (New York: McGraw-Hill, 1986), while full of detail about Truman, especially his formative years, falls short on analysis. James David Barber's chapter on Truman in *The Presidential Character*, 2d ed. (Englewood Cliffs, N.J.: Prentice-Hall, 1977) collects a good deal of the anecdotal material available at the time of writing, concluding that, in Barber's taxonomy of the presidents, Truman should be considered an "active/positive." Portions of this entry have been adapted from Francis H. Heller, "Truman," in Lord Longford and Sir John Wheeler-Bennett, eds., *The History Makers* (London: Sidgwick & Jackson, 1973); reprinted in Kenneth W. Thompson, ed., *Portraits of American Presidents*, vol. 2, *The Truman Presidency: Intimate Perspectives* (Lanham, Md.: University Press of America, 1984).

FRANCIS H. HELLER

See also Business Ventures; Farm Experience; Health; Jackson County Court; entries for family members

Personal Writings

Truman's personal writings fall into three relatively distinct categories: correspondence to family and friends, diaries and personal memoranda (some of which are long and autobiographical), and published works.

Truman's career often took him far from his family and friends, and he wrote to them diligently. Many of his letters have been collected and published. Taken together, they constitute the best source for understanding his personal frame of mind from his mid-twenties into his late seventies.

Truman did not keep a regular diary but did from time to time jot down comments on events and individuals of importance to him. He also wrote five surviving autobiographical memoranda at varying times in his life; they are a remarkable record of significant reminiscences, salient events, and the meaning of things as he saw them.

In World War I, he maintained a tiny pocket diary that contains terse highlights of his year in France; he also kept a slightly larger "black book" in which he made blunt comments on the performance of his men. After the war, he began, but did not finish, an autobiographical account entitled "Two Years in the Army"; it covers his childhood, his years as a young adult, and his early National Guard service. He also prepared accounts of his battlefield experiences, apparently for the use of his regiment's historian, Jay M. Lee. Sometime during his first term in the U.S. Senate, he wrote a long account entitled "The Military

Career of a Missourian," which breaks off midway through the Meuse-Argonne campaign.

The only surviving contemporary personal comments from Truman's years as a county officeholder are an irregular series of memoranda written on Pickwick Hotel stationery between 1930 and 1934. Frequently angry in tone, they express Truman's frustrations with many of his political associates and with the problems of having to work with the Pendergast machine. The most important, dated 14 May 1934, is Truman's first successful attempt at a complete account of his life.

There are three other relatively complete handwritten autobiographies. The first, on U.S. Senate stationery, was probably done in 1935 and is entitled "My Impressions of the Senate, the House, Washington, etc." It surveys Truman's life from his childhood through his early Senate years. Another was written in early 1945, probably to help Frank McNaughton and Walter Hehmeyer in their preparation of the biography *This Man Truman*. The third was written in late 1951 or early 1952 for William Hillman's *Mr. President*.

All the autobiographies appear to have been written strictly from memory and are more useful for their demonstrations of the way in which Truman interpreted his own life than for detailed factual material. His intermittent diary entries, some angry, some reflective, some simply documenting his activities, similarly are probably best used for understanding his state of mind rather than his firm intentions at various points of his presidency.

Truman sold his *Memoirs* to Time Inc. for the then enormous sum of $600,000 shortly after leaving the presidency. The undertaking consumed more than two years, producing a huge manuscript that required considerable editing before publication. Truman's primary helpers were William Hillman and David Noyes, two longtime friends and supporters from the communications media, and Francis Heller, a young professor from the University of Kansas who did much of the necessary editing and rewriting. Truman called on many members of his administration for assistance.

Many of Truman's letters may be found in two collections by Robert H. Ferrell: *Off the Record* (New York: Harper & Row, 1980), and *Dear Bess: The Letters from Harry to Bess Truman, 1910–1959* (New York: W. W. Norton, 1983). Monte M. Poen, *Strictly Personal and Confidential: The Letters Harry Truman Never Mailed* (Boston: Little, Brown, 1982), is an offbeat and often revealing collection of usually angry letters that Truman wrote but did not mail. Of the handwritten autobiographies, most of the one written in 1945, along with excerpts of the 1952 work and some other Truman material, can be found in Robert H. Ferrell, *The Autobiography of Harry S. Truman* (Boulder: Colorado Associated University Press, 1980). Much of the same material is also contained in Charles Robbins, *Last of His Kind* (New York: William Morrow, 1979). William Hillman's *Mr. President* (New York: Farrar, Straus & Young, 1952) is a slightly sanitized collection of interview material, snippets from correspondence, and various personal writings. Truman's *Memoirs* (Garden City, N.Y.: Doubleday, 1955, 1956) are almost entirely an account of his presidency. Only a few chapters, written primarily from memory, discuss Truman's prepresidential life. The first volume, *Year of Decisions* (1955), ranges over its author's first year in office. The second, *Years of Trial and Hope* (1956), covers the rest of the Truman presidency on a much less detailed but brisker fashion. Written in the restrained, dignified style

that has come to be deemed appropriate for presidential memoirs, the two volumes display little of Truman's saltiness. They are not factually definitive, but they faithfully express his conception of his presidency. The original, unedited manuscript is available at the Truman Library. Truman's other book, *Mr. Citizen* (New York: Bernard Geis, 1960), is a less substantial but considerably more readable account of his thoughts and activities during his first seven years out of office. It also contains a few of the syndicated newspaper columns he wrote on an irregular basis in the late 1950s and early 1960s for the North American Newspaper Alliance. All unpublished documents mentioned above are at the Truman Library.

ALONZO L. HAMBY

Petroleum

See Oil Policy

Philippine Islands

The themes that surface in any examination of Philippine-American relations during the Truman period reveal the fact that a high degree of paternalism and ethnocentrism suffused U.S. policy toward the new island nation. Although Philippine independence finally became a reality in 1946, the United States' desire to guarantee political and economic stability as well as a pro-American orientation of Philippine foreign policy often called the country's sovereignty into question.

Under the Bell Trade Act of 30 April 1946, a host of provisions gave the United States extraordinary influence in the Philippine economy. The act set mutually advantageous trade quotas and tariff duties on a long list of products over a twenty-eight-year period. But more important, the trade agreement specified that the free convertibility of the peso with the dollar, the value of the peso in terms of the dollar, and the free transfer of funds to the United States would continue until the president of the United States ruled otherwise. The measure further stipulated that Americans would have free and equal access to Philippine natural resources and mineral lands if they became accessible "to any person."

Having "given" the Filipinos the two-party system with elections and all the trappings of American democracy, U.S. officials became impatient when the Philippine political system did not work as expected. Their frustration grew with the inability of the government to deal with the radical insurgency known as the Huk rebellion, which Washington (and Manila) soon identified with the international Communist movement. During the regime of Manuel Roxas, 1946–48, the United States gave aid to the Philippines as part of its early implementation of the containment policy.

The rise of Elpidio Quirino to power in the period 1948–53 brought out the contempt for Filipino political leadership that historically lay just beneath the surface among American policymakers. Throughout the Quirino presidency State Department officials worked either to remove him from power or, after the beginning of the Korean War, to portray him as a great embarrassment and an obstacle not only to stability in the Philippines but to American goals in the region.

The Communist victory in China and the Korean War brought an even greater signal of American contempt: the U.S. commitment to rebuild Japan as the central non-Communist country in Asia. This decision hurt the Philippine leadership for two reasons: it suggested that the United States had now become insensitive to Japanese wartime atrocities, and it gave the Filipino government much less leverage in dealing with Washington. In American policy major questions of Philippine sovereignty clearly became secondary to U.S. strategic considerations.

Because of the multiple problems of the Philippine economy, President Truman in 1951 sent Daniel Bell, former under secretary of the treasury, to make a thorough study of conditions there. Bell's report recommended sweeping reform in almost every area of Philippine life with accompanying American military and economic aid; and it boldly reminded Filipinos of their satellite status with the United States. The Mutual Defense Treaty of 1951 between the United States and the Philippines stipulated that an attack on the Philippines would result in U.S. action in accord with its constitutional processes, certainly not an automatic guarantee nor the kind of firm and unambiguous commitment desired by many Philippine leaders.

Especially useful works covering U.S. policy toward the Philippines are Richard E. Welch, Jr., "America's Philippine Policy in the Quirino Years (1948–1953): A Study in Patron-Client Diplomacy," in *Reappraising an Empire: New Perspectives on Philippine-American History*, ed. Peter Stanley (Cambridge: Harvard University Press, 1984), in which the author stresses the ethnocentric insensitivity of American policymakers; Claude A. Buss, *The United States and the Philippines: Background for Policy* (Washington, D.C.: American Enterprise Institute for Public Policy Research–Hoover Institution, 1977), a book of synthesis that surveys the entire period of American involvement; Sung Yong Kim, *United States–Philippine Relations, 1946–1956* (Washington, D.C.: Public Affairs Press, 1968), which depicts the conflict between Philippine nationalism and American paternalism in the Truman-Eisenhower era; George E. Taylor, *The Philippines and the United States: Problems of Partnership* (New York: Frederick Praeger, 1964), which reflects the strategic perspective of the United States regarding Southeast Asia in 1964; and Stephen Rosshamm Shalom, *The United States and the Philippines: A Study of Neocolonialism* (Philadelphia: Institute for the Study of Human Issues, 1981), the subtitle of which indicates the main theme.

RUSSELL D. BUHITE

See also Imperialism

Point Four Program

In his inaugural address of 20 January 1949, President Truman explained the major components of his foreign policy. The first three points sounded familiar: support for the United Nations, the Marshall Plan, and the North Atlantic Treaty Organization. But the fourth point surprised some listeners. Truman an-

nounced that the United States would "embark on a bold new program" to provide technical assistance to peoples in the "underdeveloped areas" whose "economic life is primitive and stagnant." He extolled self-help, private foreign investment, and greater production as necessary to "prosperity and peace." Using common postwar language—that economic stability could check political extremism (in other words, communism) and war—the president intended to harness traditional American humanitarianism, the exportation of American know-how, and overseas investment to the cold war goal of winning friends in the Middle East, Africa, Asia, and Latin America.

By 1949 the cold war in Europe had stalemated. But in what we now call the third world, decolonization was sending many new states into the international system. American leaders sought to attract the former colonies to the side of the United States in the cold war. Some of these new nations, like India and Indonesia, had chosen nonalignment or neutrality in the Soviet-American contest. In the U.S. sphere of influence in Latin America, the new program seemed to promise a better investment climate. Point Four also seemed to serve strategic interests by ensuring the flow of vital raw materials.

"I think the first problem that the State Department had to solve was what in the hell the man was talking about," recalled an official. Indeed, Truman and his advisers had not consulted chief diplomatic officers before his address. Point Four actually derived from an opportune merger of Truman political needs and foreign policy goals. The president's aides were looking for a "dramatic topic" to follow his stunning 1948 victory, and a low-level State Department official, Benjamin H. Hardy, supplied it. In mid-December 1948 Hardy met with White House assistant George Elsey and made the case for a new technical assistance program especially for rural areas. Although Hardy cautioned him that his State Department superiors did not want technical assistance mentioned in the address because no plan had been formulated, Elsey seized upon the suggestion. Thus, as Elsey put it, "a speech in search of an idea, and an idea in search of a speech" became the fourth point in the inaugural address.

Point Four soon became victimized by State Department lethargy, pressing cold war crises, and Capitol Hill politics. "We weren't able to get the people into it that could have given it life and color and drama," Clark Clifford remembered. "It just became another State Department program, and finally, I think, pretty well died on the vine." Not until 24 June did the president ask Congress for Point Four legislation and a first-year appropriation of $45 million. With Republicans voting overwhelmingly against it, Point Four nevertheless passed in May 1950 as the Act for International Development. The president signed the legislation on 5 June, less than three weeks before the outbreak of the Korean War. The act authorized only $35 million for technical assistance. Congress caused further delay by waiting until September to appropriate only $26.9 million, and not until December of 1950 did the new Technical Cooperation Administration (TCA) within the State Department get a director.

Truman officials increasingly emphasized private American investment as the best means to ensure third world economic development. But business leaders found the foreign investment climate uninviting, with its political instability, nationalist stirrings, and inadequate dollar exchange procedures. American private capital preferred Canada and Western Europe or quick-profit areas rich in raw materials like oil. The administration's offering of "investment guarantees" did little to induce investors to shift their capital; by 1957 American investments in Asia and the Middle East totaled $2 billion, but $1.5 billion of that was invested in petroleum, bypassing the critical agricultural sector.

If the private investment component of Point Four proved inadequate, so did the technical assistance program. Appropriations increased to $155.6 million in 1953, but in that year the TCA was merged into the military-minded Mutual Security Agency and lost its identity. Point Four soon had the special function of increasing imports of strategic raw materials.

Point Four technicians numbered fifteen hundred in 1953 and visited thirty-five countries. They dug compost pits in India, combated locusts in Iran, and instructed teachers in Peru. As well, one thousand foreign nationals came to the United States in 1953 to study. But these laudable individual efforts fell far short of meeting profound third world problems. Critics complained that Point Four had been oversold and that it had raised false expectations in developing nations. Egypt's Gamal Abdel Nasser denounced Point Four as a new imperialist instrument. Others grumbled that Point Four simply contributed to the further entrenchment of local elites and that many projects, such as airfields, seemed more designed to benefit the United States than the recipients.

Hastily announced, originally neglected by the State Department, shoved aside by dramatic cold war events, hampered by limited appropriations, resisted in parts of the third world, spurned by American business, and diverted to military purposes, Point Four faltered early. It thus failed to satisfy Truman's cold war goal of aligning third world nations with the United States or of erasing the conditions that produced economic inequality, social disorder, and political turmoil. But technical assistance remained within American foreign aid programs, and Point Four's lofty appeals for economic growth and human uplift echoed later in the speeches and policies of Dwight D. Eisenhower and John F. Kennedy and stirred in the memories of those Americans and foreigners who, however minimally, improved health, education, and food supplies through their projects.

The basics of Point Four can be found in William Adams Brown, Jr., and Redvers Opie, *American Foreign Assistance* (Washington, D.C.: Brookings Institution, 1953). Jonathan B. Bingham, a Point Four administrator, gives an inside view in *Shirt-Sleeve Diplomacy* (New York: John Day, 1954). For critical studies, see Robert A. Packenham, *Liberal America and the Third World* (Princeton: Princeton University Press, 1973), and Thomas G. Paterson, *Meeting the Communist Threat* (New York: Oxford University Press, 1988). For a case study, see Philip Glick, *The Administration of Technical Assistance: Growth in the Americas* (Chicago: University of Chicago Press, 1957). Other works include Jahangir Amuzegar, "Point Four," *Political Science Quarterly* 73 (December 1958), and Robert Daniel, "Pioneering Point Four," *Agricultural History* 29 (July 1955).

THOMAS G. PATERSON

Poland

Prominent among the diplomatic problems that Franklin D. Roosevelt bequeathed to his successor was the future of Poland.

Immediately at issue were Poland's border with Germany and the composition of the interim government that was to rule the country until elections were held. The overarching question, however, was whether the Poles would enjoy the "free and unfettered" elections the Big Three had promised them at the Yalta Conference of February 1945.

The American interest in Poland was both principled and pragmatic. The traditional support of the United States for democracy is familiar. Less well understood, however, has been the practical importance of Poland's fate to America. From a point early in World War II Washington had understood that postwar Poland would be a client of the Soviet Union. Although desirable in themselves, free elections were especially important because they promised to dilute Soviet control. American officials believed (correctly, as subsequent history showed) that complete Soviet domination of Poland, the most important country of Eastern Europe, would alarm Western Europe into organizing itself into a military bloc, perhaps to put the Continent on the path to another war. "Poland's geographic position is such," the State Department had warned Roosevelt in 1944, "that she will inevitably be under strong Russian influence," but that influence should not be "so dominant as to affect international political stability."

President Truman, anxious to follow his predecessor's policy of winning the Soviets to cooperation with the United States, was initially accommodating in dealing with them over Poland. This has been somewhat obscured by the fact that on 12 April 1945 he upbraided the Soviet foreign minister, V. M. Molotov, for his government's interpretation of the Yalta accord on Poland. (The Russian reportedly said, "I have never been talked to like that in my life"—an improbable statement, considering that his master was Joseph Stalin.) Truman's approach to Molotov had been influenced by the ambassador to the Soviet Union, W. Averell Harriman, who had hurried back from Moscow to impress his views on the fledgling chief executive. Harriman's difficult years in the USSR had persuaded him that the Soviets respected only those who dealt with them firmly. Stalin, however, reacted to Truman's toughness with an artful show of defiance tempered by hurt feelings that caused Truman to doubt the wisdom of Harriman's counsel. He turned increasingly for advice to his friend Joseph E. Davies, for whom the Soviets could do no wrong. Davies, who had been the ambassador to the USSR in the late 1930s, enjoyed a huge if undeserved reputation as an expert on that country because of his correct prediction in 1941 that Moscow would not fall to Hitler.

By May Truman had turned toward conciliation. This is clearly shown by his approach to the question of Poland's interim government. Two bodies claimed to be the provisional government. One, composed of Poland's prewar political parties, had operated in London since 1941. The other, dominated by Communists, had been organized by the Soviets at Lublin in eastern Poland late in 1944. It was agreed at Yalta that "the Provisional Government which is now functioning in Poland should be reorganized on a broader democratic basis with the inclusion of democratic leaders from Poland itself and from Poles abroad." These were to be selected by a commission of representatives of the Big Three. The Lublin regime was clearly to be the nucleus of a new provisional government, but how large a nucleus? The Lublinites, supported by the Soviets, claimed that they should have a veto over the "democratic leaders" selected by the commission. Roosevelt swore that he would not accept the "thinly disguised continuance" of the Lublin regime sure to result. There matters stood at his death. In late May Truman sent Harry L. Hopkins to Moscow to break the impasse. Hopkins negotiated, and Truman accepted, an agreement with Stalin that was just the "thinly disguised continuance" of the Lublin regime that FDR had disdained, for it gave the Lublinites three-quarters of the portfolios in the new government.

Truman and his new secretary of state, James F. Byrnes, also effectively accepted the Soviet position on Poland's western border, albeit for a price. The conferees at Yalta had ruled that the eastern third of prewar Poland should go to Russia, with Poland to receive an undefined compensation from Germany. The Anglo-American position was that the River Oder should be the new border; Stalin argued for the westernmost of the two rivers called Neisse. At the Potsdam Conference (16–26 July 1945) Truman and Byrnes, meeting for the first time with Stalin, agreed to Polish administration of the disputed territory, pending a peace conference, in exchange for Soviet acceptance of the American formula for extracting reparations from Germany.

Truman found at Potsdam that he liked and respected Stalin, whom he compared to his political mentor, Tom Pendergast. He accepted a reiteration of the pledge made at Yalta that there would be free elections in Poland. In this he was mistaken. The United States pressed for Polish elections throughout 1946 using its only inducement: credits for the purchase of American goods. Progress toward elections was slow and marked by the increasingly severe repression of non-Communists. Poland received few credits—and those only to produce coal sorely needed in Western Europe. The Polish government, to be sure, was interested in American money; late in 1946 it requested credits totaling $600 million. But this counted for little beside the reality that the Polish Communist party could not win an honest election. When the elections were finally held in January 1946 the Communists found it necessary, as one of their leaders later delicately explained, "to adjust the results."

The fraud apparently did not cause Truman to change his opinion of Stalin personally. "I like old Joe," the president declared in 1948. "He is a decent fellow." The trouble, it seemed, was that his colleagues in Moscow would not let him keep his promises. Many Americans, of course, took a different view of Stalin's responsibility for Soviet policies. But for nearly all in the United States the fate of Poland was proof that Soviet pledges were valueless and that the relationship with the USSR was to be competitive rather than cooperative.

The most reliable account of Polish-American relations is to be found in Richard C. Lukas's two books, *The Strange Allies: The United States and Poland, 1941–1945* (Knoxville: University of Tennessee Press, 1978) and *Bitter Legacy: Polish-American Relations in the Wake of World War II* (Lexington: University Press of Kentucky, 1982). For the American role in Eastern Europe generally, see Eduard Mark, "American Policy toward Eastern Europe and the Origins of the Cold War, 1941–1946: An Alternative Interpretation," *Journal of American History* 68 (September 1981): 313–36.

EDUARD MARK

See also Eastern Europe; Potsdam Conference; Soviet Union; Stalin, Joseph

Portraits and Memorials

In a 1967 letter, former President Truman wrote, "It has been, and is, my personal preference not to encourage the building of any memorials or monuments to me. I consider that whatever useful acts may have been performed during my administration were in fact the acts of the American people." His advice notwithstanding, hospitals, schools, roads, sports complexes, and other public facilities bear his name, including more than a dozen in the Kansas City metropolitan area alone. Other memorials worldwide include a twelve-foot statue in Athens, Greece, sculpted by Felix de Weldon and erected by the American Helenic Educational Progressive Association in 1963 to commemorate the Truman Doctrine; and the Harry S. Truman International Center for the Advancement of Peace, constructed on the campus of Hebrew University in Jerusalem in 1968. Of a less structural nature is the Harry S. Truman Scholarship Foundation, established in 1974 by act of Congress (Public Law 93–642) to award college scholarships annually to promising students from all parts of the country who plan to pursue careers in public service.

Truman was the subject of numerous portraits, most of which were painted after he had become president. Earlier portraits painted from life included one oil of Truman as Jackson County judge by Mitchell Henderson (late 1920s or early 1930s), an oil of Truman as U.S. senator by Edgar Faris (1935, Harry S. Truman Library), and a pastel of Truman as vice president by Larry Pendleton (1945, Harry S. Truman Library).

Austrian-born Greta Kempton was the most prolific painter of Truman pictures. She painted the president's official portrait for the White House in 1947. In addition, the president sat for her for three other portraits (1949, Masonic Grand Lodge of Missouri; 1949, School District of University City, Missouri; begun 1948, completed 1970, National Portrait Gallery), as well as a portrait of the Truman family (1952, State Historical Society of Missouri).

Other prominent portraits of the president painted from life included those by Jay Wesley Jacobs (1945, Harry S. Truman National Historic Site), English artist Frank O. Salisbury (1947, Harry S. Truman Library), Augustus Vincent Tack (1947, National Portrait Gallery), and John Slavin (1948, Harry S. Truman Library). Lesser paintings included those by Tade Styka (1948, Harry S. Truman Library), Seymour Stone (1946, Harry S. Truman Library), Onestus Uzzell (1948, Dallas County, Texas, Women's Democratic Club), and George Schultz (1949, Harry S. Truman Library).

In what became his final portrait from life, the eighty-six-year-old former president was painted by his friend Thomas Hart Benton as he sat at home in his favorite chair reading (1971, Benton Trust).

No comprehensive study has been made of the Truman portraits. Greta Kempton's portraits of the Truman family and his cabinet were the subject of a 1987 exhibition at the Harry S. Truman Library. A catalog of the exhibition is available from the library.

CLAY R. BAUSKE

See also Awards; Benton, Thomas Hart

Potsdam Conference

Harry Truman, who had closely followed President Roosevelt's diplomatic moves over the years, was not an admirer of summit diplomacy, and he was not pleased by Winston Churchill's repeated efforts to persuade him to agree to an early conference with Joseph Stalin. The new chief executive wanted first of all to get his administration in order and to see the war through to a successful conclusion. Churchill's overriding focus, on the other hand, was already on the postwar world, and he was convinced that another summit with the Soviet leader was an urgent necessity.

The Germans having surrendered unconditionally on 7 May 1945, Truman finally agreed to meet with Churchill and Stalin, and he set off from Norfolk on the heavy cruiser USS *Augusta* on 7 July, accompanied by Secretary of State James F. Byrnes and Adm. William D. Leahy, chief of staff to the commander in chief. The president was not, however, looking forward to the meeting. As he wrote his mother and sister before leaving, "I have a brief case all filled up with information on past conferences and suggestions on what I'm to do and say. Wish I didn't have to go, but I do and it can't be stopped now."

Truman's hopes and objectives for the Potsdam Conference were disarmingly simple. As he recorded his first night at sea: "I am making this trip determined to work for and win the peace. I am giving nothing away except I will do everything I can to save starving and war-battered people but I hope we will be able to help people to help themselves. This is the only sound policy."

The president landed at Antwerp on the morning of 13 July and, after driving to Brussels, arrived in Berlin by plane in mid-afternoon. The city was a picture of desolation and destruction. "Never," Truman wrote, "did I see a more sorrowful sight."

When the State Department Historical Division was preparing its important two-volume documentary collection on the Potsdam Conference in the late 1950s, the former president declined to share some of his illuminating personal records, including extended diary notes he made at the time, which were discovered at the Truman Library only in 1979. These records allow us to follow Truman's impressions and actions better than does any comparable presidential record presently available.

The president's attitude had not fundamentally changed since he succeeded Roosevelt. He was determined to avoid even the appearance of prior arrangements with Churchill, whom he met for the first time at Potsdam on the morning of 16 July; on the other hand, he looked forward to his first session with Stalin, which took place the following day.

On both meetings Truman recorded his views. About his initial session with Churchill, he wrote: "We had a most pleasant conversation. He is a most charming and a very clever person—meaning clever in the English not the Kentucky sense. He gave me a lot of hooey about how great my country is and how he loved Roosevelt and how he intended to love me etc., etc. Well, I gave him as cordial a reception as I could—being naturally (I hope) a polite and agreeable person. I am sure we can get along if he doesn't try to give me too much soft soap."

About his first meeting with Stalin on 17 July, Truman recorded: "Just spent a couple of hours with Stalin. . . . Promptly a few minutes before twelve I looked up from the desk and there

Truman in the foreground, left of center, at the Potsdam Conference. (National Archives)

stood Stalin in the doorway. I got to my feet and advanced to meet him. He put out his hand and smiled. I did the same, we shook, I greeted [Soviet Foreign Minister V. M.] Molotov and the interpreter, and we sat down. After the usual polite remarks we got down to business. I told Stalin that I am no diplomat but usually said yes and no to questions after hearing all the argument. It pleased him.

"I asked him," Truman continued, "if he had the agenda for the meeting. He said he had and that he had some more questions to present. I told him to fire away. He did and it is dynamite—but I have some dynamite too which I'm not exploding now . . . [a reference to the atomic bomb, just successfully tested]. Most of the big points are settled. He'll be in the Jap War on August 15th. Fini Japs when that comes about. We had lunch, talked socially, put on a real show drinking toasts to everyone, then had pictures made in the back yard. I can deal with Stalin. He is honest—but smart as hell."

The following day Truman lunched alone with Churchill and informed him about the successful A-bomb test at Alamogordo, New Mexico, on 16 July. The prime minister was ecstatic. He told his physician, Lord Moran: "It is the Second Coming. The secret has been wrested from nature. The Americans spent £400 million on it. They built two cities. Not a soul knew what they were working at. It gives the Americans the power to mould the world. It may displace fuel; a fragment gives 800 horse-power. If the Russians had got it, it would have been the end of civilization. Dropped on London, it would remove the City. It is to be used in Japan, on cities, not on armies. We thought it would be indecent to use it in Japan without telling the Russians, so they are to be told today. It had just come in time to save the world."

In mid-afternoon, the president and Byrnes met with Stalin and Foreign Minister Molotov at Stalin's villa. The Soviet leader informed Truman about a Japanese message concerning possible peace terms, and the two lost no time agreeing on the terms of a formal reply. As Lisle A. Rose has noted, "Stalin was certainly not about to facilitate Japanese diplomacy. Any threat to an early Soviet intervention in the Pacific war was a threat to Soviet expansionist designs in northeast Asia as legitimized by Roosevelt at Yalta."

The president came away highly pleased. It was, he noted in his diary, "a most satisfactory meeting. I invited him to come to the U.S. Told him I'd send the Battleship Missouri for him if he'd come. He said he wanted to cooperate with U.S. in peace as we had cooperated in War but it would be harder. Said he was grossly misunderstood in U.S. and I was misunderstood in Russia. I told him that we each could help to remedy that situation in our home countries and that I intended to try with all I had to do my part at home. He gave me a most cordial smile and said he would do as much in Russia."

The Potsdam Conference, which lasted until 2 August, was held in strictest wartime secrecy. The Big Three, Truman well knew, faced a long list of difficult and complex issues. They ranged from establishing an occupation system for defeated Germany, agreeing on postwar reparations, changing boundaries in Central and Eastern Europe, and providing for free elections in recently liberated areas. Some of these or related problems had fruitlessly occupied lower-echelon negotiators for months.

In addition, there remained the murky Japanese situation. No one could be certain how close Hirohito's battered empire was to final defeat and surrender. At the moment, the Soviet Union was not at war with Tokyo and declined, for that reason, to participate in formal summit actions concerning the Pacific war. That refusal further complicated Big Three discussions of postwar East Asian affairs.

Truman's overriding military objective was to bring about Soviet entry into the war against Japan, which Stalin had already agreed to at Yalta, and this was arranged in short order, since the Soviets were not anxious to be left out of the last phase of the hostilities. "A start has been made and I've gotten what I came for," the president wrote his wife on 18 July. "Stalin goes to war August 15 with no strings on it. . . . I'll say that we'll end the war a year sooner now, and think of the kids who won't be killed. That is the important thing."

On the other hand, much as Truman may have wanted to avoid political issues, they could not indefinitely be ignored. On 24 July, the Big Three got around to growing differences in the liberated Balkan countries, where Churchill was deeply concerned about the conduct of Soviet forces and local Soviet-appointed or controlled officials.

Using language he had first employed in his famous telegram to Truman on 15 May (see Churchill, Winston), the prime minister told Stalin: "about Rumania, and still more Bulgaria, we know almost nothing. Our missions in Bucharest were hemmed in so closely as almost to amount to internment."

A bitter exchange, as recorded in the official British minutes (not published until 1984), ensued:

"Premier Stalin asked whether it was necessary to make these statements without their being verified.

"Mr. Churchill said that he knew his facts, which had been reported officially by our military mission and diplomatic representative. Premier Stalin would be astonished to read the catalogue of incidents to our missions in Bucharest and Sofia. They were not free to go abroad. An iron curtain had been rung down.

"Premier Stalin said that these were fairy tales.

"Mr. Churchill said that they were not fairy tales. . . . The conditions of our mission [at Bucharest] had been most painful and had caused great distress."

Privately, the president may have agreed with Churchill's assessment. But he remained aloof and sought to move the discussion onto the next point, a posture the prime minister understandably resented.

In subsequent years, Truman became distinctly more sympathetic with Churchill's position. As he wrote Eleanor Roosevelt on 16 March 1948: "When I arrived at Potsdam . . . I found that the Poles, at the suggestion of Russia, had moved into eastern Germany and that Russia had taken over a section of eastern Poland. The agreement at Yalta provided for free and untrammeled elections in Rumania, Bulgaria, . . . and Poland. I found a totalitarian Soviet Government set up in Poland, in Rumania . . . and in Bulgaria. Members of our commissions in Bulgaria and Rumania were treated as if they were stableboys by the Russians in control in those two countries. Russia has not kept faith with us."

When it came to German occupation policies, on the other hand, it was Truman who found himself in the middle. The Soviets demanded huge reparation payments, and Churchill seemed agreeable to letting them have what they could get, a position to which Truman was vigorously opposed.

As time went on, the president became increasingly perturbed over specific Soviet demands. On 25 July, he recorded: "At the Conference Poland and the Bolsheviki land grab came up. Russia helped herself to a slice of Poland and gave Poland a nice slice of Germany, taking also a good slice of East Prussia for herself. . . . For the fourth time I restated my position and explained that territorial cessions had to be made by treaty and ratified by the Senate."

Remembering the protracted bitter arguments over reparations following the First World War, Truman was determined not to repeat the experience. He noted that Roosevelt had allowed the Soviets to "mention twenty billions of reparations—half for Russia and half for everybody else. Experts say no such figure is available.

"I've made it plain," Truman continued, "that the United States of America does not intend to pay reparations this time. I want the German war industry machine completely dismantled and [as] far as U.S. is concerned the other allies can divide it up on any basis they choose. Food and other necessities we send into the restored countries and Germany must be first lien on exports before reparations. If Russians strip country and carry off population of course there'll be no reparations."

Not long before the end of the conference, the president returned to the reparations issue in a letter to his wife. "The whole difficulty," he wrote, "is reparations. Of course the Russians are naturally looters and they have been thoroughly looted by the Germans over and over again and you can hardly blame them for their attitude. The thing I have to watch is to keep our skirts clean and make no commitments.

"The Poles," he continued, "are the other headache. They have moved into East Prussia and to the Oder in Prussia, and unless we are willing to go to war again they can stay and will stay with Bolsheviki backing—so you see in comes old man reparations again and a completely German-looted Poland."

On reparations as on boundary changes, Truman wanted to avoid final binding commitments. They should be made only at a future peace conference, with treaty agreements having to be ratified by the U.S. Senate. The president couldn't have dreamed that no such German peace conference would ever be held and that the de facto arrangements made at Potsdam would become de jure agreements in the Nixon-Ford seventies.

The president, in turn, had a favorite scheme of his own—namely, the internationalization of the leading waterways, including the Panama and Suez canals, the Rhine, the Danube, and the Dardanelles, a proposal he formally introduced on 23 July. It was, the late Herbert Feis has written, "the boldest paper submitted at Potsdam, . . . and could have been the most transforming." But Stalin raised objections and Truman's proposal got nowhere.

There were still other occasions when the president had an opportunity to learn, or at least to sense, what the essential Stalin was like. "At one of [their state] dinners," Margaret Truman has written, "Dad's already sinking opinion of Marshal Stalin slipped even lower. They began discussing Poland, and Dad asked him what happened to the thousands of Polish officers who the Germans said were slaughtered by the Russians in Katyn Forest after they had surrendered to the Russian army in 1940. Marshal Stalin shrugged. 'They just went away,' he said, and dropped the subject."

Despite such incidents, other differences, and, occasionally, irreconcilable deadlocks, Truman maintained a measure of confidence in the Soviet dictator. "I like Stalin," he wrote his wife on 29 July. "He is straightforward, knows what he wants and will compromise when he can't get it. His Foreign Minister [Molotov] isn't so forth-right."

The president was concerned, too, about who might succeed Stalin. "I am wondering," he wrote on 30 July, "what would happen to Russia and Central Europe if Joe suddenly passed out. If some demagogue on horseback gained control of the efficient Russian military machine he could play havoc with European peace for a while. I also wonder if there is a man with the necessary strength and following to step into Stalin's place and maintain peace and solidarity at home. It isn't customary for dictators to train leaders to follow them in power. . . . Uncle Joe's pretty tough mentally and physically but there is an end to every man and we can't help but speculate."

It might be added that Truman's opinion of Stalin did not change significantly in the months following Potsdam. Former secretary of state Edward R. Stettinius, Jr., quoted him in late October 1945: "The President said . . . it would be a real catastrophe if Stalin should die at the present time. If this happened, there would be no telling what might happen inside Russia. There was a possibility that the army might get control. . . . He said he thought that Stalin was a moderating influence in the present Russian government."

Much has been written since the 1960s—most of it uninformed or ideological speculation—about "atomic diplomacy," the alleged role of the atomic bomb at Potsdam. That some of Truman's top advisers, including Byrnes and Leahy, pressed him to reconsider U.S. policy toward the Soviet Union, there can be little doubt. In view of the president's agreeable relations with Stalin at that time—"I liked the son-of-a-bitch," Truman recalled later about those days—the contemporary political importance of the new superweapon should not be exaggerated.

As already noted, Truman had been informed about the successful Alamagordo test on 21 July and, at the end of his meeting with Churchill and Stalin on July 24, had told the Soviet leader that "we have perfected a very powerful explosive which we are going to use against the Japanese and we think it will end the war."

Stalin seemed unsurprised, which—considering the Soviet spy network operating in the United States—was entirely understandable. Indeed in his war memoirs, published in English translation in 1971, Marshal Gregory Zhukov wrote pointedly that "Stalin . . . *pretended* he saw nothing special in what Truman had imparted to him" (emphasis added). In any case, the bomb was not further discussed by the Big Three. There is no persuasive evidence that it was a major factor in Anglo-American calculations at the conference, and certainly not—the available record seems clear—in the president's mind.

The Potsdam Conference was not, of course, without its lighter moments and more pleasant diversions. Truman, for instance, invited some promising young U.S. musicians to perform for the Big Three. He summarized the occasion on July 20: "It was my turn to feed 'em at a formal dinner last night. Had Churchill on my right, Stalin on my left. We toasted the British King, the Soviet President, the U.S. President, the two honor guests, the foreign ministers, one at a time, etc., etc., ad lib. Stalin felt so friendly that he toasted the pianist when he played a Tskowsky (you spell it) piece especially for him. The old man loves music. He told me he'd import the greatest Russian pianist for me tomorrow. Our boy was good. His name is [Eugene] List and he played Chopin, Von Weber, Schubert, and all of them."

On the other hand, some of the other conference pomp and formalities struck the president as bordering on the absurd. As he wrote his daughter on 25 July: "Churchill . . . phoned

General Harry Vaughan, my *chief* of protocol, that he would greatly, very greatly appreciate it if I would arrive a few minutes late as I happened to be the senior guest and Uncle Joe should realize it."

At 10:40 P.M. on 1 August, the Big Three, accompanied by their top advisers, met for their final session. There was a last-minute squabble between Truman and Stalin about whether to mention the president's proposal for the internationalization of waterways in the final communiqué. Stalin repeatedly demurred, leading Truman to exclaim: "I cannot understand that man." To his mother, the president wrote on 30 July: "You never saw such pig-headed people as are the Russians. I hope I never have to hold another conference with them—but, of course, I will."

Outwardly, however, the prevailing atmosphere remained agreeable. The president said he hoped the next Big Three meeting would be in Washington. "May God grant this," Stalin reportedly said. In fact, the three men never met again.

Early the following morning, Truman flew to England, where he lunched at Plymouth with King George VI. Later that afternoon, the president, again accompanied by Byrnes and Leahy, boarded the *Augusta* for the voyage home. At lunch with the crew on 6 August, Truman was informed that the Hiroshima bomb had been successfully delivered.

On the afternoon of 7 August, the president landed at Newport News, Virginia. Two evenings later, he addressed the nation from the White House, summarizing the work and significance of the Potsdam Conference. "There was," Truman declared, "a fundamental accord and agreement upon the objectives ahead of us.

"The three Great Powers," he concluded, "are now more closely than ever bound together in determination to achieve that kind of peace. From Teheran, and the Crimea, from San Francisco and Berlin—we shall continue to march together to a lasting peace and a happy world!"

But privately Truman sensed that approaching victory did not mean approaching peace.

The places to begin reading are Truman's *Memoirs*, vol. 1, *Year of Decisions* (Garden City, N.Y.: Doubleday, 1955), Margaret Truman's admirable biography, *Harry S. Truman* (New York: Morrow, 1972), Robert H. Ferrell's *Off the Record: The Private Papers of Harry S. Truman* (New York: Harper & Row, 1980), which contains the President's long-unknown diary entries, and Ferrell, ed., *Dear Bess: The Letters from Harry to Bess Truman, 1910–1959* (Boston: Little, Brown, 1982), which contains additionally revealing comments to Mrs. Truman. The two-volume *The Conference of Berlin (The Potsdam Conference)* (Washington, D.C.: U.S. Government Printing Office, 1960), in the series *Foreign Relations of the United States*, edited by G. M. Richardson Dougall, is one of the great achievements of its kind. The official *Documents on British Policy Overseas*, ser. I, vol. I (London, 1984) confirm the lack of effective Anglo-American communications in the Potsdam era. There are some important details (and omissions) in Winston Churchill's *Triumph and Tragedy* (Boston: Houghton Mifflin, 1953), Lord Alan Bullock, *Ernest Bevin: Foreign Secretary, 1945–1951* (New York: Norton, 1983), and Kenneth Harris, *Attlee* (New York: Weiderfield and Nicholson, 1982). No account of the subject is more important and thoughtful than Henry L. Stimson and McGeorge Bundy, *On Active Service in Peace and War* (New York: Harper, 1948). James F. Byrnes told his version in *Speaking Frankly* (New York: Harper

& Row, 1947), based on his contemporary notes. William D. Leahy, *I Was There* (New York: McGraw-Hill, 1950), is a revealing account by the chief of staff to the president. More recent scholarship—Herbert Feis, *Between War and Peace: The Potsdam Conference* (Princeton: Princeton University Press, 1960) and *The Atomic Bomb and the End of World War II* (Princeton: Princeton University Press, 1966), Robert J. Donovan, *Conflict and Crisis: The Presidency of Harry S Truman, 1945–1948* (New York: W. W. Norton, 1977), and Gregg Herken, *The Winning Weapon: The Atomic Bomb in the Cold War, 1945–1950* (New York: Knopf, 1980)—is generally critical of Truman policy.

FRANCIS L. LOEWENHEIM

See also Byrnes, James Francis; Churchill, Winston S.; Eastern Europe; Poland; Stalin, Joseph; Stimson, Henry L.

Presidency

When Harry S. Truman succeeded Franklin D. Roosevelt as president in April 1945, the office was a powerful one because of the vast expansion of its authority during the Great Depression of the 1930s and World War II. Suddenly thrust into the presidency, Truman was uneasy about his new responsibilities. "I'm not big enough for this job," he told Senator George Aiken. Truman only gradually became comfortable in the office, being reluctant even in 1947 to run for election as president the next year. That he did run reflected his growing success in controlling the executive branch as well as his desire to vindicate himself and his policies. He had developed a remarkable degree of self-assurance by 1948, which he repeatedly demonstrated throughout the rest of his presidency in the face of many problems.

Truman had numerous things to complain about as president: the glare of publicity; constant criticism; security restrictions; information leaks; long work days, often in a crisis environment; occasional scandals in his administration; and the stubbornness of some of his associates. As he wrote in 1947, his job entailed an "impossible administrative burden" and taking "all sorts of abuse from liars and demagogues." This underlay his fulminations, usually private, against various political figures, publishers, commentators, businessmen, and labor leaders. Truman often bemoaned his office, referring to the executive mansion, for example, as the "Great White Prison" and saying, "It's hell to be President." The lesson was, he wrote in 1952, "Don't raise your boy to be President of the United States." These outbursts must have had a therapeutic effect, however, for Truman usually demonstrated great pride in being president, and he left office in 1953 with his ego strengthened.

If the presidency had buoyed his self-confidence, Truman in turn had a great impact on the institution. He had tremendous respect for the office. As he said in October 1945, it was "the greatest responsibility that ever has fallen to a human being." He had long shared Woodrow Wilson's and Franklin D. Roosevelt's view that the presidency was crucial to the achieving of high ideals at home and abroad. Thanks to the phenomenal growth of presidential powers after 1933, Truman had the means as well as the motive to pursue that end. He would struggle ceaselessly to maintain and expand those executive powers he believed necessary to gaining economic security and world peace and enhancing freedom and democracy.

Truman constantly sought public support for his policies. He was unusually accessible to the press, holding 324 news conferences. He talked and corresponded with a huge number of officials and citizens. Moreover, he often traveled the land to see and be seen by the public, doing "everything," as one reporter wrote, "except have himself shot from the mouth of a cannon." Truman had his secrets, but he strove to be forthright in his public statements on his basic thought and policies. He was sometimes disappointed with the public's response, but in the most important way Americans did not fail him. His fear that they would roll back executive powers after World War II was largely unrealized. Not only did most Americans enjoy the bounties they received as a result of Roosevelt's New Deal, but they also looked to the government for further economic security. Truman was thus able to preserve and even extend social welfare programs and occasionally to use executive powers in forwarding American prosperity.

Furthermore, if Truman could not achieve genuine world peace, he was able to expand presidential authority as commander in chief and chief diplomat in order to maintain a powerful American presence internationally. The emergence of the cold war between the United States and the Soviet Union and later the Korean War ensured the public's support for this aim. Truman had qualms about the costs of mounting military power, but, as he saw it, at stake were the nation's survival and its way of life. Thus he was seldom timid about using his pow-

ers. Truman, for example, held that the president could determine when there was a national emergency endowing him with inherent extra powers (unless Congress deemed otherwise); was not required to give Congress confidential information ("it's pretty hard to serve a subpoena on the President.... Who's going to enforce it?"); had "discretionary power" in spending appropriations ("I don't think he can be forced to spend"); and could engage in military action when necessary ("because wars are no longer declared in advance"). He also used the veto power liberally, 250 times, a number exceeded only by Grover Cleveland and Franklin Roosevelt. In justifying his broad interpretation of his powers, Truman said that the president "has to act for whatever is for the best of the country."

Then there was the administrative side of his job. He assiduously recruited people for service in the executive agencies and White House offices who were reliable, practical, and forthright, men in his own mold. He required them to give him advice and information and to carry out his decisions effectively and faithfully. If his subordinates did their jobs loyally, he backed them fully; if they did not, they had to answer to him. Truman might suffer fools occasionally, as in the case of Harry Vaughan, his military aide, but he rarely put up long with those who did not work by his rules. Thus there were the forced resignations or firings of those who acted contrarily, for example, Interior Secretary Harold Ickes, Commerce Secretary Henry Wallace, Defense Secretary Louis Johnson, and Gen. Douglas MacArthur.

Truman sought to keep the number of executive agencies and their personnel to a minimum of what was needed for effec-

President Truman's inaugural medal by Julio Kilenyi. (Courtesy of the Harry S. Truman Library)

tiveness, but he wanted considerably more help close at hand. The number of presidential aides increased from 30 in 1945 to 85 by 1952 and the total White House staff more than doubled to 285. Truman was the first president to rely significantly on, in effect, a chief of staff, his special counsels, first Clark Clifford and then Charles Murphy. Although these men, other presidential assistants, and the director of the Bureau of the Budget had important responsibilities, Truman kept the reins of power firmly in his own hands. He also effectively used recently developed governmental machinery such as the Joint Chiefs of Staff, the Council of Economic Advisers, and the National Security Council as well as the Budget Bureau and the cabinet. Other tools included ad hoc advisory committees such as the President's Committee on Civil Rights. These were not new to federal administration, but there were many more of them now.

It all added up to an unprecedented emphasis on organization and hierarchy, so that the president became less a formulator of policy than the foreman of policy formulators. Everything of importance came to him, and he made the final decisions. The sign on his desk, THE BUCK STOPS HERE, had great significance. One senior administration official, Frank Pace, Jr., concluded that Truman had "created the institution of the Presidency" by refining the structure of government and demanding more accountability than ever before. The presidency was now less a personal office than an institutional one that organized the powers that had accrued to the executive branch since 1933. As such Truman played Augustus to Roosevelt's Caesar by institutionalizing the vastly more powerful presidency at home, making permanent its great international role, and constantly pressing for new executive programs.

Truman built on the bases laid by his predecessors to structure what Arthur M. Schlesinger, Jr., would later call "the Imperial Presidency." This often got him into trouble—for example, the severe criticism of "Mr. Truman's War" in Korea and the Supreme Court's stinging rebuff for the government's seizure of the steel mills in 1952. The development of the presidency under Truman had its worrisome aspects. Saying, as he did, "If I think it is right, I am going to do it" sounded a bit like Louis XIV's "L'etat c'est moi." Yet Truman, as "a democrat," often limited his use of power in favor of "flattering, kissing and kicking people to get them to do what they are supposed to do anyway." After all, it was up to the president, the Congress, the judiciary, and the public to decide how far each could go. Truman generally played this bruising game by the rules, however often he was disappointed and abused.

And Truman was abused. Partly because of this he was rarely a popular president in his time, falling to a low Gallup poll approval rating of 23 percent in November 1951 and leaving office in 1953 with only a 31 percent rating. He thought he had done "his level best" as president, but, he wrote his daughter, Margaret, "Your dad will never be reckoned among the great." Yet time can change perceptions. In an Arthur M. Schlesinger, Jr., 1962 poll of scholars on presidential greatness, Truman tied James K. Polk for eighth place in the near-great category. He scored sixth in Gary Maranell's 1970 poll of presidential accomplishment and ranked eighth in polls conducted by the United States Historical Society in 1977, the *Chicago Tribune* in 1982, and Robert K. Murray and Tim H. Blessing in 1983. Whatever the reason—his decisiveness, courage, forthrightness, folksiness, concern for the people, or impact on the presidency—Harry S. Truman had come to be seen as a near-great president.

The literature on Truman and the presidency is voluminous. Highly pertinent are Robert J. Donovan, *The Presidency of Harry S Truman: Conflict and Crisis, 1945–1948* and *Tumultuous Years, 1949–1953*, 2 vols. (New York: W. W. Norton, 1977, 1982); Donald R. McCoy, *The Presidency of Harry S. Truman* (Lawrence: University Press of Kansas, 1984); and Bert Cochran, *Harry Truman and the Crisis Presidency* (New York: Funk & Wagnalls, 1973). For an interesting symposium on the Truman presidency by administration officials, see Francis H. Heller, ed., *The Truman White House: The Administration of the Presidency, 1945–1953* (Lawrence: Regents Press of Kansas, 1980). For Truman's comments on the presidency, see *Public Papers of the Presidents of the United States: Harry S. Truman, 1945–1953*, 8 vols. (Washington, D.C.: U.S. Government Printing Office, 1961–66); Robert H. Ferrell, ed., *Off the Record: The Private Papers of Harry S. Truman* (New York: Harper & Row, 1980); and relevant manuscript material in the Harry S. Truman Library, Independence.

DONALD R. McCOY

See also Biographers and Public Reputation; Commander in Chief; Executive Branch, Reorganization of; Veto Power

Presidential Papers

See Harry S. Truman Library; Personal Writings

Press, The

All his life, Harry S. Truman was a voracious reader of books, magazines, and especially of newspapers. But from his early political years in Kansas City during the twenties to his last months in the White House in 1951–52, his relations with the press were, to say the least, mixed.

Newspapers played an important role in Missouri politics in the 1920s and 1930s, and much of the time they were critical of Truman's friends and political associates, especially the powerful Pendergast machine. As Raymond P. Brandt, Washington bureau chief of the *St. Louis Post-Dispatch*, recalled later, its "editorial policy was against Truman, at *all* times, because of his connection with the Pendergast machine."

Such criticism left Truman unmoved. "Truman never repudiated his origins," Marquis Childs, a veteran Washington reporter and critical Truman watcher, wrote in his memoirs. "He never turned his back on Pendergast, nor did he forgive those, of whom I was one, who had helped bring about the boss's downfall and prison sentence." On the contrary, Truman regarded many newspaper investigations as politically inspired or grossly one-sided and frequently designed to serve the newspapers' interests, which were usually Republican or conservative Democratic.

From his first race for the U.S. Senate in 1934 to the 1948 presidential campaign, Truman was rarely the beneficiary of many major newspaper endorsements. For example, on the eve of the 1940 Missouri Democratic primary, the *St. Louis Post-Dispatch* declared that "the nomination of Harry Truman . . . would be . . . a sad defeat for the people of Missouri." Not to be outdone, the conservative *St. Louis Globe-Democrat* throughout its news columns inserted the admonition: "Save Missouri—Vote against Truman."

As Truman wrote his sister, Mary Jane, on 12 May 1948: "It seems that every man in the White House was tortured and bedeviled by the so-called free press. They were lied about, misrepresented and actually libeled and they had to take it and do nothing. The old S.O.B. [Joseph Pulitzer] who owned and edited the St. Louis Post Dispatch and the New York World was in my opinion the meanest character assassin in the whole history of liars who have controlled newspapers—and that includes old man Hearst and Bertie McCormick! Some day, I hope a mucker will come along and dig up the facts on the distorters of news and facts. I had thought that pictures and the radio would cure the news liars—but they—the liars—have taken over both."

Truman nevertheless remained an unfailing reader of what he called the "sabotage press," unlike John F. Kennedy who, although he usually enjoyed a favorable press, on one occasion in 1962 ostentatiously canceled the White House subscription to the Republican *New York Herald Tribune* because of the paper's repeated criticism of his administration.

Irving Perlmeter, assistant White House press secretary from 1950 to 1953, recounted later, "The President customarily awoke between 5 and 6 o'clock in the morning and before breakfast would go through four or five of the principal papers in quite considerable detail." Truman, moreover, didn't hold newspapers' editorial opposition to him against their White House reporters. As Raymond Brandt recalled, "Truman always said, 'that damn paper of yours, but I like you.'" In fact, Truman once remarked, "When the press stops abusing me, I'll know I am in the wrong pew."

There were, on the other hand, periods in Truman's career when he received a favorable press. From its first days in early 1941, Truman's Senate Committee to Investigate the National Defense Program had the benefit of a strongly admiring and supportive press. As the senator traveled around the country, his inspection trips frequently turned into triumphal visits. Indeed, that highly favorable press coverage probably had much to do with catapulting Truman onto the Democratic ticket at the Chicago convention in July 1944.

Truman was affronted by partisan attacks not only on himself but on the Democratic party and President Roosevelt, of whom he was a not uncritical admirer. As he wrote Mrs. Truman in 1942: "The Washington papers are still giving the Congress the dickens and without justification. That psychological sabotage sheet the *Herald* had a nasty editorial . . . and so did the Washington *Post*. . . . They'd rather lose the war if that would discredit the President. . . . How they all hate the New Deal."

During his first months in the White House, Truman's relations with the press seemed friendly. On 15 April, the new president recorded in his diary: "Told newspapermen if they ever prayed, which I much doubted, that they had better pray for me now." The press had reason to be pleased with some of the new chief executive's first actions. For example, whereas Roosevelt—whose relations with the press were, on the whole, less cordial than is now remembered—had prohibited verbatim quotation or publication of his press conferences (the full texts of which were not published until 1972), Truman changed the rules to permit their publication in their entirety.

But the character of his press conferences soon underwent a subtle change. Robert G. Nixon of International News Serv-ice, who attended them all, recalled in 1970: "Roosevelt ran his own press conferences. Truman did so to a lesser degree. He was often on the receiving end, instead of the delivering end. Many times . . . he was in real hot water." His press conference responses were usually less ruminative than those of his predecessor, and occasionally his terse comments led to unforeseen consequences. For example, Truman's unfortunate suggestion on 30 November 1950 that the United States might use nuclear weapons in Korea brought British prime minister Clement Attlee flying across the Atlantic to assure himself that this was not the president's intention. Dean Acheson, Truman's secretary of state from 1949 to 1953, reportedly said he used to keep a "boxful of clarifications" for use after presidential news conferences.

Truman's early honeymoon with the press did not last long. As he encountered increasing domestic and international problems in 1946–47, press criticism of his performance steadily mounted. Following the 1946 congressional elections which produced the Republican-controlled Eightieth Congress, Walter Lippmann, the columnist, suggested that Truman resign, and in 1948 proposed that Truman step aside and allow the party to nominate its Senate leader, Alben W. Barkley of Kentucky, as a kind of caretaker candidate.

The press's condescending treatment of the president carried over into the 1948 campaign. The overwhelming majority of the country's newspapers—leading and otherwise—endorsed his Republican opponent, Governor Thomas E. Dewey of New York. "There was not much left to the presidential campaign," *Time*, the Luce-owned weekly, reported on 25 October 1948, "except counting the votes. Harry Truman might get a good share of the popular vote, but few people, outside of Harry Truman, gave him even an outside chance of getting the electoral votes necessary for election." For the most part, Truman bore this dismissive treatment with equanimity. And he savored few moments more than when, after having won, he held up a copy of the *Chicago Tribune*'s early election-night edition with its famous headline, DEWEY DEFEATS TRUMAN. It was "a classic blunder," wrote Walter Trohan, its Washington correspondent, "which will live to embarrass it in all political history."

The outbreak of the Korean War in June 1950 brought the president a new wave of journalistic criticism. In August 1950, while U.S. forces were desperately trying to push back North Korean forces, the usually sober *New York Herald Tribune* ran an extended series on U.S. vulnerability to Soviet attack, concluding that the Truman administration was soft and neglectful of "Communism's steady advance."

Truman, in turn, became increasingly angry at what he called "all the lying slander you see in public life in this country today, and in the newspapers." Indeed, by late 1951, Senator Joseph R. McCarthy's reckless and unfounded charges of Communist infiltration of the government increasingly dominated the press, which seemed also to delight in the discovery of a series of minor scandals, one of which led to the president's dismissal of Attorney General J. Howard McGrath in 1952.

Few things angered Truman more than the press's mindlessly publishing what he regarded as vital national security information. In 1951, he wrote, but didn't send, a letter to Arthur Krock: "We are faced with the most terrible responsibility that any nation ever faced. . . . If we could spend one year's military appropriation to develop the Euphrates Valley, the plateau of Ethiopia, the table land of South America—if we could

TRUMAN PRESS CONFERENCE

THERE'S ONE
CONSOLATION—
AFTER JAN 20
MAYBE WE CAN
RELAX A BIT!

WASHINGTON D.C.
FIRE DEPT.

Daniel Blair Dowling, *New York Herald Tribune*, 12 December 1952. I.H.T. Corporation. Reprinted by permission.

open the Rhine-Danube waterway, the Kiel Canal, the Black Sea Straits to free trade, if Russia would be a good neighbor and use her military expenditures for her own economic development, I would not have to scold the publishers for giving away our military secrets. Wish you'd do a little soul searching and see if at *great* intervals the President may be right."

Although not covered by the terms of the Twenty-second Amendment, Truman had long decided not to seek another term in 1952, and his surprise announcement of that decision at the annual Jefferson-Jackson dinner on 29 March 1952 was greeted with widespread approval in the press. When he left office in January 1953, few press commentaries suggested that, within a decade or so, his reputation and stature would attain heights reached by few other presidents. As *Fortune* magazine summed up prevailing opinion in February 1952: "The precise shading of mediocrity to be assigned to him may well occupy the historians for many years." And some journalists, like some historians, never significantly altered that early critical stance.

But Arthur Krock was one who did. In 1968, the former Washington correspondent of the *New York Times*, who had written critically about Truman on many occasions, wrote that the president's "personality is that of a very charming man whose determination sticks out all over him. Nearly invariably he showed complete courage in making momentous decisions and an iron backbone that kept him from ever going back on such a decision once made. In these respects alone he would, in my judgment, rate as a 'strong President.' And in these instances of paramount policy-making he seldom sought to shift to others

the initiative for the policy or the blame for adverse consequences. Truman was the one President who, though I wrote as critically about him as I have about any other, never held it against me personally. We became friends, on his motion, and he never reproached me for any criticism or changed his friendly attitude toward me."

The passing of time did little to alter the retired president's mixed view of the press. As he put it in a letter in 1967 to President Lyndon B. Johnson, who was having his own problems with the media: "The attitude and behavior of the press from our earliest beginning has been vexing and irritating to all administrations. I did not let the press worry me, and I never let them divert me from what I knew I had to do. The press is conditioned by its movements in the day-to-day news and issues— and has not managed to develop a sense of the future."

Truman read and reacted to the press virtually all his life. His voluminous—invariably outspoken, highly critical—comments may be found in two collections by Robert H. Ferrell, *Off the Record* (New York: Harper & Row, 1980), and *Dear Bess: The Letters from Harry to Bess Truman, 1910–1959* (Boston: Little, Brown, 1982). Some of his most pithy comments are in Monte Poen, ed., *Strictly Personal and Confidential: The Letters Harry Truman Never Mailed* (Boston: Little, Brown, 1982), to which add Margaret Truman's invaluable biography, *Harry S. Truman* (New York: Morrow, 1972). Herbert Lee Williams, *The Newspaperman's President: Harry S. Truman* (Chicago: Nelson-Hall, 1984), by a man who helped the former president with his *Memoirs*, is an indispensable introduction, based on Williams's University of Missouri Ph.D. dissertation available at the Truman Library. A number of leading Washington correspondents have left detailed impressions. See, for instance, Arthur Krock, *Memoris: Sixty Years on the Firing Line* (New York: Funk & Wagnalls, 1968) and Marquis Childs, *Witness to Power* (New York: McGraw-Hill, 1975). Robert J. Donovan's increasing strictures are incorporated in his two-volume Truman biography, *Conflict and Crisis* and *Tumultuous Years* (New York: W. W. Norton, 1977, 1982). Walter Lippmann's doubts and hostility are represented in Ronald Steel, *Walter Lippmann and the American Century* (New York: Vintage Books, 1980), and John Morton Blum, ed., *Public Philosopher: Selected Letters of Walter Lippmann* (New York: Ticknor & Fields, 1985). See also the invaluable contemporary views of James E. Pollard in *Journalism Quarterly* 28 (Fall 1951) and 30 (Summer 1953), none of which matches Truman's contemporary and subsequent responses.

FRANCIS L. LOEWENHEIM

See also *Kansas City Star*; Lippmann, Walter; *St. Louis Post-Dispatch*; Short, Joseph Hudson; Ross, Charles Griffith

Progressive Party

The Progressive party was created during 1947 and early 1948 in response to three forces: Henry A. Wallace's vision and ambitions, liberal disenchantment with Truman's policies, and the support of the Communist party for a "popular front" third party. Wallace treated the party as a personal vehicle for his campaign for peace and justice.

In July 1948, the Progressives nominated Wallace for president and Senator Glen Taylor of Idaho for vice president. They adopted a platform repudiating the Marshall Plan and interventions in Greece, Turkey, and China, and demanding the abolition of atomic weapons, of monopoly, and of racial segregation. Democrats and Republicans in their campaigns focused on the influence of Communists in the third party. The Soviet Union weakened Wallace's claims that the United States and the USSR could and must cooperate, with its Czech coup in February and the Berlin blockade in June 1948. Wallace lost ground during the campaign and polled only 1,157,172 popular votes and no electoral votes. He may have increased the president's conservative support by drawing the fire of anti-Communists.

Various points of view about the Progressive party are expressed in Curtis Daniel MacDougall, *Gideon's Army* (New York: Marzani & Munsell, 1965); Allan Yarnell, *Democrats and Progressives: The 1948 Election as a Test of Post-War Liberalism* (Berkeley: University of California Press, 1974); and Karl Schmidt, *Henry A. Wallace: Quixotic Crusade, 1948* (Syracuse, N.Y.: Syracuse University Press, 1960). The most thorough and objective source is Norman D. Markowitz, *The Rise and Fall of the People's Century: Henry A. Wallace and American Liberalism, 1941–1948* (New York: Free Press, 1973).

ALFRED B. ROLLINS, JR.

See also Election of 1948; Wallace, Henry Agard

Public Opinion Polling

Public opinion polling has been a significant factor in elections in the United States since the 1920s, but the roll played by the polls in the election of 1948 was especially significant. In that year the public opinion organizations of Archibald Crossley, George Gallup, and Elmo Roper predicted that the Republican presidential candidate, Thomas E. Dewey, would easily defeat Harry S. Truman. When it became clear that Truman had won the election and their predictions had been far off the mark, the polls came under severe public criticism. It was recalled that only a few years before, in 1936, the *Literary Digest* poll had incorrectly forecast that the Republican Alfred M. Landon would defeat President Franklin D. Roosevelt, and many began to question the reliability of all public opinion polls.

Before 1948 the Crossley, Gallup, and Roper polls had established a solid record. They had predicted a Roosevelt victory in 1936; and with the demise of the *Literary Digest* poll, they had become the national leaders in public opinion polling. They utilized sample sizes significantly smaller than the enormous number of responses collected by the *Literary Digest* poll, but these samples were thought to be statistically representative of the national electorate and hence much more reliable. Yet now in 1948, only twelve years after the *Literary Digest* debacle, all three organizations were wrong. (See the accompanying table for the actual votes cast and the pollsters' predictions.)

The reaction to the failure of the polls to predict Truman's victory was instantaneous. Journalists, who perhaps had been too uncritical of the polls, were embarrassed, and the polling organizations devastated. Social scientists also felt threatened by the public attack on the general reliability of public opinion sampling since much social science research depended upon the accuracy of this measuring device. Eight days after the election the Social Science Research Council appointed a committee to conduct an inquiry into the methods and data used by the polling organizations and to report on the cause of their failure. Their report was completed in December 1948 and published in 1949.

The committee found that the pollsters had presented their results to the public in a manner that implied more scientific certainty than the precision of polling justified. Thus the polling organizations contributed to their difficulties by promoting an unjustified confidence in the accuracy of polling before the election which helped create the negative reaction after the election. "The failure of the polls," said the report, "was due to neglecting the possibility of a close election and the necessity of measuring preferences very accurately just before the election." The pollsters also had failed to take into account errors known to have existed in the preelection polls in previous elections, and they had not used the newest techniques in sampling and interviewing.

The report also found that all three polls had interviewed a disproportionately small number of respondents with little education, a problem reminiscent of the difficulties of the *Literary Digest* poll. This had been done to compensate for the tendency of voters of lesser education to vote infrequently. In 1948 the "undecided voters," who were mainly those with little education, were allocated in the pollsters' predictions in proportion to the distribution found among the decided voters. The size of the undecided group in the preelection samples in 1948 was about 15 percent of those polled, much larger than in 1944. Examination of postelection surveys indicated that many in this group decided very late and voted for Truman. In short, a late, undetected shift to Truman among the "undecided" contributed much to the polling error in the election of 1948.

This combination of mistakes seemed to explain much of the inaccuracy of the 1948 forecasts, and the experience probably served to improve polling methods. The failures of polling that year did not discourage the long-term use of public opinion

Presidental Election of 1948, Total Votes and Pollsters' Predictions

	PERCENTAGE OF TOTAL VOTE				
	TRUMAN	DEWEY	WALLACE	THURMOND	TOTAL
National vote	49.5	45.1	2.4	2.4	99.4
Crossley prediction	44.8	49.9	3.3	1.6	99.6
Gallup prediction	44.5	49.5	4.0	2.0	100.0
Roper prediction	37.1	52.2	4.3	5.2	98.8

sampling, and in the years since, political candidates, news organizations, and social scientists have found public opinion polling increasingly useful.

The most helpful study of the use of polling in the election of 1948 is the report of the committee appointed by the Social Science Research Council: Frederick Mosteller, Herbert Hyman, Philip J. McCarthy, Eli S. Marks, and David Truman, *The Pre-Election Polls of 1948: Report to the Committee on Analysis of Pre-election Polls and Forecasts* (New York: Social Science Research Council, 1949). See also Leo Bogart, *Silent Politics: Polls and the Awareness of Public Opinion* (New York: Wiley Interscience, 1972), and Irwin Ross, *The Loneliest Campaign: The Truman Victory of 1948* (New York: New American Library, 1968).

HOWARD W. ALLEN

R

Racial Integration

See Armed Forces, Integration of the; Black Americans; Civil Rights

Radicalism

See Communism and Communists

Radio and Television

During the years of Harry Truman's presidency, radio began yielding to television its position as the nation's preferred medium of in-home entertainment and information. In this transition era, Truman was the last of the radio, but also the first of the television, presidents.

As a "radio-orator" President Truman, whether reporting to the nation or campaigning for its votes, spoke to millions familiar with Franklin D. Roosevelt's masterful radio technique and enviable voice. Aware that here, as in other matters, he performed in FDR's shadow, Truman worked to improve his skills and develop a unique broadcast style. Utilizing professionals like J. Leonard Reinsch as early as the 1944 campaign, the Missourian matured as a radio speaker. Truman later admitted that no one "had as rotten a delivery as I did to begin with." But *Time*, after Truman's first two presidential broadcasts, judged that he had "made a virtue out of making himself plain—and that made it easy to believe what he said."

This "plain-speaking" president used the electronic media as Roosevelt had and as his successors would: to attempt to shape public opinion in such crises as the Korean War. Although Dwight Eisenhower became the first president skillfully to exploit television's unique visual qualities, Harry Truman was the pioneer. On 5 October 1947, for example, he made the first speech ever televised from the White House. Political scientist Elmer Cornwell concludes that Truman, in his role as leader of public opinion, employed the electronic media as a fire brigade responds to emergencies—giving reflexive treatment to diverse problems as they arose, an approach different from Roosevelt's.

Candidate Truman in 1948 made effective use of broadcast communications, as his party spent more than the complacent Republicans on media. It was the last of the radio campaigns and the last in which presidential nominees, instead of employing spot announcements to tout their virtues, relied upon direct broadcast appeals to voters. As Truman embarked on what many considered a doomed campaign, his running mate Alben Barkley advised: "Go out there and mow 'em down." The president's response set the tone of the radio campaign: "I'll mow 'em down, Alben . . . and I'll give 'em hell." Truman's blunt, aggressive, concise sentences transmitted well over the airwaves, better than opponent Thomas Dewey's polished addresses. One authority has determined that radio broadcast 74 of Truman's 337 campaign speeches, 20 of them to national audiences. Reinsch believed it "absolutely vital" to Truman's success that many local stations carried his remarks at whistle-stops in September. This coverage allowed the president to project his message and personality to voters on their home ground.

Given television's unknown potential as a campaign tool and its small audience in 1948, Democratic radio director Kenneth Fry advised its use only "on a limited basis. Shows should be short and visual." Truman made four video campaign appearances, two of them on network television. His Jersey City speech on 5 October was the first paid political appearance on television by any presidential candidate. The decision of both parties to locate their nominating conventions in Philadelphia was an early sign of television's power to reshape American politics. That city was on the coaxial cable which fed programs to the northeastern television audience, which owned most of the nation's sets.

The postwar television boom brought unprecedented growth and profits to the broadcasting industry. Responding to the end of wartime restrictions and shortages, manufacturers resumed production of radio and television sets. The Federal Communications Commission (FCC) authorized a significant expansion of FM broadcasting and issued licenses to new television stations, although it froze the latter's total number at 108 from 1948 to 1952. Truman appointee Frieda B. Hennock spearheaded the commission's decision to reserve some television channels for educational purposes. And in 1949, the commission established the "fairness doctrine," requiring broadcasters to present conflicting viewpoints on "controversial issues of public importance." But other FCC actions weakened broadcast regulation in the public interest. Although its report, *Public Service Responsibilities of Broadcast Licensees*, dubbed the "blue book" (1946), asserted a renewed commitment to base license renewals on past program performance, in practice the commission wilted before industry criticism of its plan to require of all stations cultural and public affairs programs. *Broadcast* magazine, for example, called FCC members "stooges for the communists" for trying to implement the 1934 Communications Act. During the Truman administration the commission also rescinded its policy (the AVCO rule) of calling for competitive bidding when lucrative licenses were transferred to the new owners of stations, a policy that broadcasters had strongly opposed. In effect, broadcast licenses became private property.

The cold war had an impact on American broadcasting. Rooted in wartime precedents, the federal government's role as broadcaster grew, as the Armed Forces Radio Service provided programming to military personnel and the Voice of America beamed propaganda to Soviet-dominated areas. At home, the unfounded fear of Communist subversion in broadcasting resulted in ruined careers. The privately published *Red Channels: The Report of Communist Influence in Radio and Television* (1950), listed 151 writers, directors, and actors who had supposedly advanced the Soviet cause in their professional work. Many experienced blacklisting, as network executives, station owners, and sponsors preferred to abandon controversial talent rather than endanger profits. Historian Erik Barnouw called the list "a roll of honor."

Television's ability to fix the nation's attention on a single, extended event, first demonstrated within fifteen months of Truman's departure from Washington in the Army-McCarthy hearings of 1954, was reaffirmed by the networks' subdued but tasteful coverage of the former president's funeral in 1972.

Erik Barnouw, *The Golden Web: A History of Broadcasting in the United States, 1933–1953* (New York: Oxford University Press, 1968), provides the most comprehensive account of the subject. On Truman's use of the media, see Elmer E. Cornwell, Jr., *Presidential Leadership of Public Opinion* (Bloomington: Indiana University Press, 1965). On the 1948 presidential campaign, see Harrison B. Summers, "Radio in the 1948 Campaign," *Quarterly Journal of Speech* 34 (December 1948): 432–38; Raymond L. Carroll, "The 1948 Truman Campaign: The Threshold of the Modern Era," *Journal of Broadcasting* 24 (Spring 1980): 173–88; and Carroll, "Harry S. Truman's 1948 Election: The Inadvertent Broadcast Campaign," *Journal of Broadcasting and Electronic Media* 31 (Spring 1987): 119–32.

ALAN HAVIG

Railroad Unions

Although their support did not become politically significant to Harry Truman until the elections of 1940, the Missouri railroad brotherhoods first supported him in his campaign for the U.S. Senate in 1934. Considerable division existed within the Missouri labor movement at that time concerning candidates for the Democratic nomination for the vacant Senate seat. Union leaders in the western half of the state generally supported Truman, whereas eastern labor leaders endorsed the popular St. Louis congressman John Cochran. Meanwhile, the Brotherhood of Railroad Trainmen, which had recently broken its alliance with the Pendergast organization in Kansas City, supported a third candidate. Once Truman had received the nomination, however, organized labor (including the railroad brotherhoods) rallied to his support, and he swept easily to an election victory.

During his first term in the Senate, Truman strengthened his ties to organized labor by compiling a solid New Deal voting record, including positive votes on such labor measures as the National Labor Relations Act and the Fair Labor Standards Act. Moreover, railroad labor was especially indebted to him for his supportive activities on the Senate Interstate Commerce Committee and for his opposition to a proposed 15 percent wage reduction, designed to relieve the railroad industry during one of its periodic financial crises.

Truman needed all the support he could muster in the 1940 Democratic primary when he was challenged by the popular Democratic incumbent governor, Lloyd C. Stark. Stark had established a progressive reform record during his term in the statehouse and had played an important role in bringing down the increasingly corrupt Pendergast machine in Kansas City. With Tom Pendergast, his most influential political benefactor, in jail, Truman turned to the labor movement for support. Labor, particularly railroad labor, responded positively and aggressively, even though Truman's principal opponent, Governor Stark, also had created a favorable labor record. The railroad brotherhoods provided much of the financing for the primary campaign. They created and distributed substantial quantities of campaign literature and sponsored large rallies in the state's principal cities. Moreover, *Labor*, the national organ of the brotherhoods published in Washington, D.C., and circulated to all brotherhood members, printed 500,000 copies of a special edition dedicated to Truman's reelection. With such assistance, Truman won a close, hard-fought primary election victory and then rather easily was returned to the U.S. Senate as organized labor once again united behind his reelection campaign.

During World War II, Truman's fairness to labor as chairman of the Special Committee to Investigate the National Defense Program and his vote against the hostile Smith-Connally Act of 1943 seemed to warrant organized labor's confidence in him. Not surprisingly, therefore, the railroad brotherhoods supported his nomination as the Democratic party's vice-presidential nominee in 1944. That friendship and alliance, however, was severely strained in the weeks and months immediately following Truman's ascension to the presidency.

Reflecting a release of frustration with wartime restrictions and fears about the postwar economy, an unprecedented wave of strikes hit the nation shortly after V-J Day. Growing unemployment, the loss of overtime resulting in reduced take-home pay, and rapidly increasing prices had all produced great pressures for wage adjustments during the reconversion period. Responding to a strike in the steel industry in the fall of 1945, the administration proposed an 18.5-cent wage increase that became the pattern for settlement during the first round of wage adjustments in the postwar period. (Price concessions to business, however, undermined the significance of the increased wage.)

Shortly after the war's end, the railroad brotherhoods had demanded a wage increase and changes in work rules. After protracted negotiations eighteen of the twenty brotherhoods agreed to limit their wage demands and to permit the Railroad Labor Board to arbitrate the disputes. The Brotherhood of Railroad Engineers and the Brotherhood of Railroad Trainmen, however, refused to drop their demands for work rules changes and rejected arbitration. Consequently, their dispute was referred to an emergency board. In what appeared to be a joint decision, both boards proposed only minor changes in work rules and awarded the brotherhoods a 16-cent wage increase which failed to match the 18.5 cents that had become standard in other industries.

A national railroad strike followed the brotherhoods' rejection of the award. The government then seized the railroads, and Truman threatened to operate them under federal protection if the strikers did not return to work. Even though a settlement had been reached a few minutes earlier, Truman then appeared before Congress and, among other things, asked for the authority to conscript striking railroad workers. The president's excessive response to the situation shocked labor, particularly railroad labor, which assumed it had a special relationship with the president. Nevertheless, like others in the labor movement, most railroad brotherhoods made their peace with the president when confronted by the legislative assault on labor launched by the Eightieth Congress. One of Truman's oldest allies, however, Alvanley Johnston of the Brotherhood of Locomotive Engineers, along with several other prominent labor leaders, refused to support Truman's renomination in 1948. Yet, after the Democrats chose Truman, Johnston joined other labor leaders in endorsing his candidacy against Republican challenger Thomas E. Dewey.

Arthur F. McClure, *The Truman Administration and the Problems of Postwar Labor, 1945-1948* (Cranbury, N.J.: Associated University Presses, 1969), is a thoughtful, well-researched, but narrowly focused study. Less well researched but still valuable in many ways is Joel Seidman, *American Labor from Defense to Reconversion* (Chicago: University of Chicago Press, 1953). Joseph G. Rayback, *A History of American Labor* (New York: Free Press, 1966), still the most reliable survey of American labor history, provides the larger historical context in which Truman's labor policies were developed and executed.

GARY M. FINK

See also Election of 1940; Labor; Senator; Steelman, John Roy

Rayburn, Sam

(6 January 1882–16 November 1961)

Speaker or Democratic minority leader of U.S. House of Representatives during the Truman administration. Sam Rayburn represented a rural northeast Texas congressional district from 4 March 1913 until his death on 16 November 1961. The eighth of eleven children, Rayburn was born in Roane County, Tennessee, and with his family moved near Bonham, Texas, at the age of five. His father, a former Confederate soldier, was a small cotton farmer. Rayburn attended Mayo College in Commerce, Texas, and briefly taught school. In 1906 he was elected to the Texas House of Representatives where he served for six years, the last two years as its Speaker. While in the Texas House of Representatives, he studied law at the University of Texas and was admitted to the bar.

In 1912 he ran for a vacant seat in the U.S. House of Representatives and was elected. In his early years in Congress, he was regarded as a populist Democrat who was closely aligned with Congressman John Nance Garner.

Rayburn's only legislative committee assignment in his lengthy congressional career was the powerful Interstate and Foreign Commerce Committee which had jurisdiction over much regulatory legislation. In 1931 he became chairman of the committee, and in 1932 he was partly responsible for engineering the Roosevelt-Garner ticket. With the inauguration of Roosevelt in 1933, Rayburn, through his committee chairmanship, became one of the workhorses of the New Deal. Through his committee flowed such legislation as the Emergency Railroad Transportation Act of 1933, the Securities Act of 1933, the Securities Exchange Act of 1934, the Communications Act of 1934, the Utility Holding Act of 1935, and the Rural Electrification Act of 1936. In part because of his strong loyalty to Franklin Roosevelt, Rayburn was elected floor leader of the House of Representatives on 4 January 1937. After the death of Speaker William Bankhead, he was elected Speaker on 16 September 1940.

Rayburn was known for his legislative skill, his integrity, his temper, and his formidable physical presence. Short, with a broad chest, he had a short neck, a large head which was almost completely bald, and a granitelike face into which were set smoldering eyes. Although he relaxed and laughed when he was among friends, his public appearance was extremely stern, severe, and intimidating.

By the time Harry Truman was first elected to the U.S. Senate in 1934, Sam Rayburn was already one of the most influential figures in the House of Representatives. Perhaps because of their common origins and their strong Democratic party loyalties, they formed a friendship while Truman was still in the Senate. Truman, for example, supported Rayburn for the vice presidency in 1944. And it was from Rayburn's hideaway room in the Capitol that he was summoned to be told of Roosevelt's death and his own ascension to the presidency.

Rayburn was a regular confidant of Truman's during his years in the White House. Truman recalled, "We'd get together on what had to be done, then try to do it. When we made an agreement he would stand pat on it and so would I. We never tried to put each other in the hole. When we had a meeting neither of us would give out statements that might put the other on the spot. We both had the same thing in mind—to make the government proceed."

Truman's faith in Rayburn was such that he invited Rayburn to cabinet meetings—an honor Rayburn declined—and urged that the Speaker be placed behind the vice presidency in the line of presidential succession. Rayburn, who lacked expertise in foreign Affairs, primarily advised Truman on domestic policy. But he was a strong supporter of the Marshall Plan and other Truman administration foreign policy initiatives. Like Truman, Rayburn opposed the Taft-Hartley Act even though this legislation was strongly supported in Texas. He did bow to political pressure from his district and oppose Truman's civil rights initiatives, although he remained staunchly loyal to Truman and the Democratic party when the Dixiecrat revolt occurred in 1948.

Convinced at first that Truman would be defeated in 1948, he was impressed with the president's whistle-stop speeches, one of which was delivered in Rayburn's hometown of Bonham. With the Truman victory in 1948, Rayburn again became Speaker, a position he had lost when the Republicans gained control of the House after the 1946 elections. He served as Speaker for the remainder of the Truman presidency. With the 1952 Republican election victory, Rayburn once again lost the Speakership, but regained it after the 1954 elections when the Democrats won control of the House. He held that position for the rest of his life.

After Truman's retirement, he and Rayburn remained friends. Rayburn helped Truman get a presidential pension, and Truman visited Bonham for the 1957 dedication of the Sam Rayburn Library and for Rayburn's funeral in 1961. Shortly thereafter, Harry Truman wrote in a review of the biography *Mr. Sam*, "Sam Rayburn and the junior senator from Missouri were close personal friends. Time and time again we sat in my office 240 Senate Office Building, and in his private office, known as his hideaway in the Capitol Building and discussed the affairs of the nation." Truman continued, "As a member of the so-called Big Four Sam Rayburn was a tower of strength to the President of the United States. I can hear him say time after time when I made a tough statement on foreign affairs or on legislation pending, 'Now, Mr. President, let's consider that.' Well, we always did and the program was improved by his views."

One of the best descriptions of Rayburn's appearance and his personality is found in chapter 18 of Robert A. Caro, *The Years of Lyndon Johnson: The Path to Power* (New York: Alfred A. Knopf, 1982). Johnson was Rayburn's protégé. Anthony Champagne, *Congressman Sam Rayburn* (New Brunswick, N.J.: Rutgers University Press, 1984), examines Rayburn from the perspective of his congressional district, showing how he was able to be elected and reelected for almost half a century. The earliest book-length biography of Rayburn, C. Dwight Dorough, *Mr. Sam* (New York: Random House, 1962), is packed with details on Rayburn's life both in his district and in Washington. Its weakness is in placing him in clear political context; its strength is in being the most detailed analysis of his life. The best examination of Rayburn as a congressional actor is D. B. Hardeman and Donald C. Bacon, *Rayburn: A Biography* (Austin: Texas Monthly Press, 1987), which includes a superb treatment of Rayburn's role in the New Deal. Alfred Steinberg, *Sam Rayburn: A Biography* (New York:

Hawthorn Books, 1975), is well written and less cluttered with detail than Dorough's biography, but it contributes little new material on Rayburn's life and career.

ANTHONY CHAMPAGNE

See also Congress, United States

Reading

Truman was an avid reader. His greatest interests were history and biography, but his reading was both extensive and diversified.

A lengthy bout in 1894 with diphtheria and its aftereffects, a temporary paralysis of arms, legs, and throat, combined with a reluctance from the age of eight to participate in sports and roughhousing for fear of breaking his eyeglasses, encouraged Truman to spend much of his boyhood reading. By the time "I was thirteen or fourteen years old," he said, "I had read all the books in the Independence Public Library and our big old Bible three times through." In part Truman's reading was influenced by his mother who taught him to read before he was five and selected many of his earliest books. His high school English teacher, Matilda ("Tillie") Brown, may also have contributed significantly, for according to Truman she "was a genius at making us appreciate good literature. She also made us want to read it."

His love of reading did not abate after he graduated from Independence High School in 1901, at least not during the years 1906–17 when he worked his family's farm in Grandview, Missouri. Truman's letters to his future wife, Bess Wallace, during that period often contained comments about his latest readings, both serious and light, popular and classical. Service as an army officer during World War I and in the postwar reserves, course work in the Kansas City School of Law (1923–25), and a prepresidential political career that began in 1922 undoubtedly afforded Truman opportunities to diversify and expand his reading, although this is not documented.

During his presidency and after, Truman read voraciously. On vacations he was known to take books with him for both relaxation and learning. The news media reported in 1946 that the president read about thirty thousand words a day, including newspapers and official reports. Visitors often remarked that they found Truman surrounded by books and deeply engrossed in reading. How appropriate it was, therefore, that the last portrait for which he posed depicted him in his eighty-sixth year reading in his study with a stack of books under his left arm.

When asked during his second term of office by reporter William Hillman what books influenced him most, he indicated that they were the Holy Bible and the works of William Shakespeare. But Truman repeatedly stated in interviews and in his *Memoirs* that books on history and biography were his favorites. "The lives of great men and famous women intrigued me, and I read all I could find about them." The four-volume set of biographies *Great Men and Famous Women*, by Charles Francis Horne, which his mother had given him as a boy, had made a lasting impression. Truman later contended that these volumes and other early readings in history and biography inspired him as a youth, "nourished and sustained" his interest in government and public service, and served as invaluable tools of instruction. "These lessons [of history] were to stand me in good stead years later, when I was to be confronted with similar problems."

There is little evidence, however, that during his formative years he read books dealing with current issues and ideas. His early reading tended, rather, to focus on historical figures and societies of ancient times. As to the history of his own country, he appeared far more interested in the early years of the Republic and the Civil War. Consequently, in response to inquiries as to his favorite books on U.S. history, Truman would recommend primarily the memoirs of politicians and generals of the Civil War and Reconstruction period, as well as books on Jefferson, Jackson, and Lincoln by such authors as Claude Bowers, Marquis James, and Carl Sandburg.

Truman himself readily admitted the limitations of his boyhood reading. "The library was not too good where we lived. . . . I know I read the wrong books, but I read a lot, and I suppose I got some good ones now and then." His habit as a youngster of taking home and poring carefully over volumes of the *Encyclopaedia Britannica* he later regarded as "silly."

But Truman's extensive reading was not lost upon him. As a boy he became an authority and arbiter on biblical and historical questions among family and friends; as president and senior statesman he would surprise and impress his associates with his knowledge of people, nations, events, and good books.

The best published sources on Truman's reading are the first volume of Truman's *Memoirs: Year of Decision* (Garden City, N.Y.: Doubleday, 1955), Margaret Truman's *Harry S. Truman* (New York: William Morrow, 1973), and Robert H. Ferrell's *Dear Bess: The Letters from Harry to Bess Truman, 1910–1959* (New York: W. W. Norton, 1983). Interesting insights and anecdotes may also be found in William Hillman's *Mr. President* (New York: Farrar, Straus & Young, 1952), Truman's *Mr. Citizen* (New York: Bernard Geis, 1953), and Charles Robbins's *Last of His Kind* (New York: William Morrow, 1979). Truman's papers at the Harry S. Truman Library, Independence, contain a number of letters that reveal Truman's reading interests and tastes. Also, the Truman Library's Oral History Collection includes interviews with Truman's sister, Mary Jane, cousin Mary Ethel Noland, and teacher Mrs. W. L. C. (Adelia Hardin) Palmer which offer brief but enlightening comments on Truman's boyhood reading. Information about Truman's personal collection of books can be found in the following two articles by Elizabeth H. Safly in the Harry S. Truman Library Institute newsletter: "Truman's Books: The Post-Presidential Years," *Whistle Stop* 7, no. 1 (Winter 1979): 1–3, and "Truman's Books: Part II," *Whistle Stop* 7, no. 2 (Spring 1979): 1–3.

GEORGE H. CURTIS

Recession of 1949

See Economy, The; Fiscal and Monetary Policies

Reciprocal Trade Agreements

The Reciprocal Trade Agreements (RTA) were a creative failure. Although the trade mechanism established under RTA in the 1930s reversed the upward trend in U.S. tariffs, it proved incapable of significantly reviving world commerce. Yet in demonstrating the shortcomings of bilateralism, RTA laid the groundwork for Bretton Woods and the General Agreement on Tariffs and Trade (GATT).

The RTA act of 1934 was a depression-era measure to expand foreign markets for American goods and reduce national unemployment. For a period of three years, the president had the authority to enter into executive pacts to reduce tariff agreements by up to 50 percent with countries that had been granted "most-favored nation" status. The aim of Secretary of State Cordell Hull, the main impetus behind RTA, was clear: to bypass the protectionist Congress, which had recently passed the notorious Smoot-Hawley Tariff, and to maximize the volume of world trade, which in Hull's view was a prerequisite to international peace.

The Roosevelt administration reached agreements with only twenty-eight countries, most of them, like Haiti and Finland, small and insignificant to U.S. trade. The RTA legislation, renewed by Congress in 1937, 1940, and 1943, helped roll back U.S. tariffs from an average of 59 percent in 1932 to 28 percent in 1945. Yet worldwide tariff levels remained prohibitively high until after the war, sharply curtailing commerce.

In 1945, the Truman administration was able to win extension of the RTA. As a creditor nation, the White House argued, the United States should cut existing tariffs in half. President Truman worked closely with House Speaker Sam Rayburn and other congressional leaders to defeat several Republican-sponsored amendments that would have given Congress veto power over the agreements.

Yet even with this success, American policymakers soon realized that the bilateral, country-by-country approach that RTA embodied was hopelessly complex and burdensome. Europe might collapse before Washington had time to negotiate new agreements with each and every one of its war-wracked allies. What were needed, Truman and his aides realized, were multilateral organizations that could sweep aside trade barriers, regulate currencies, and provide fresh capital for European reconstruction. By 1947, the Bretton Woods institutions, the Marshall Plan, and the GATT had supplanted RTA as the key elements of U.S. foreign economic policy. (RTA remained on the books as a means by which the executive could negotiate trade agreements with countries that lay outside the other institutions.)

The RTA was a failed experiment, but one that had served its purpose. During a time when protectionism was ascendant, it had kept alive the principle that freer trade was in the U.S. national interest.

On the origins of RTA, see Robert M. Hathaway, "1933–1945: Economic Diplomacy in a Time of Crisis," in *Economics and World Power*, ed. William H. Becker and Samuel F. Wells, Jr., 277–331 (New York: Columbia University Press, 1984), and Robert A. Pastor, *Congress and the Politics of U.S. Foreign Economic Policy* (Berkeley: University of California Press, 1982). On Truman's trade policy, see Robert A. Pollard, *Economic Security and the Origins of the Cold War, 1945–1950* (New York: Columbia University Press, 1985).

ROBERT A. POLLARD

See also Bretton Woods System; International Trade

Reclamation

The federal reclamation program, providing irrigation water and hydroelectric power to seventeen western states, contributed to the growth and development of the postwar American West. The program, however, became embroiled in a number of political controversies involving public power, acreage limitation, interagency fighting, and the preservation of spectacular western canyons in their pristine state.

President Harry Truman's support for federal expenditures on western dam projects continued efforts begun by the New Deal but interrupted by World War II. That support, coupled with the Republican-controlled Eightieth Congress's opposition to such expenditures, enlarged Truman's electoral base in the West. Under Secretary of the Interior Oscar Chapman, Truman's campaign manager there, used the president's record of support for irrigation and public power to advantage in forging a decisive victory in the region, a victory that was key to his reelection. Though Truman successfully parlayed federal expenditures into votes, he less successfully dealt with a number of other reclamation issues.

Truman had appointed Michael W. Straus commissioner of reclamation in 1945, and Straus held the post through 1952. A chain-smoking bear of a man, Mike Straus, unlike his predecessors, was not a trained engineer. He had joined the New Deal in 1933 as a public relations specialist and through the 1930s worked closely with Harold Ickes. Straus thought of himself as a liberal in the Ickes mold, but he was more politically pragmatic than his mentor.

Having discovered in the 1930s that hydroelectric power could provide the income to pay the reimbursable expenses of dam and reservoir construction that irrigation farms had for years been unable to pay, the Bureau of Reclamation under Truman and Straus attempted to promote and expand public power in the West, and especially in California, by building its own transmission lines. The lines would carry electric power from bureau dams to public preference customers such as municipalities. Backed by Truman, the bureau attempted from 1946 to 1952 to secure funding for the transmission lines, but Congress would not go along with this approach. While Congress balked, the bureau and the Department of the Interior negotiated "wheeling" agreements that allowed private companies to transmit and sell federal power. This policy undercut the public power program. As the budget for 1952 was being worked out, the administration dropped its request for money to build its own lines.

The public power issue in California was closely tied to the land limitation controversy. To prevent land monopolies in the West, the Reclamation Act of 1902 had included a provision limiting the water from federal reclamation projects to the amount needed to irrigate 160 acres, or 320 acres if the farm was owned by a husband and wife. The issue came to a head during the 1940s. The Bureau of Reclamation tried to enforce the 160-acre limit on the Central Valley Project, an irrigation project that involved vast amounts of private land owned by large corporations. Powerful opponents emerged when Straus, backed by Truman, announced that the bureau would require that farmers in the valley sign a contract to sell all their excess lands before they could get water. Furthermore, he hired a regional director, Richard Boke, committed to enforcing the law. Senator Sheridan Downey, a California Democrat, led attempts to rid the law of the limitation or to fire those responsible for enforcing it. Downey questioned their loyalty, called the law socialistic, and tacked a rider to Interior's appropriation bill that denied funds for paying the salaries of the commissioner and regional director because they were not engineers. Truman was forced to sign the bill, but maintained his support for the two embattled officials.

The law was not repealed and Straus and Boke kept their jobs, but a new program of "technical compliance" undermined the original intent of the law to prevent large corporations from obtaining federal subsidies. Under Straus's technical compliance program, the large landowners could avoid the restriction by paying construction costs charged to their land or selling their excess land over a period of ten years while in the meantime using subsidized water for all of it. The law would not actually be changed until the early 1980s.

Bureaucratic infighting between the Army Corps of Engineers and the Bureau of Reclamation hampered Truman's efforts on behalf of resources. In California, the bureau and the corps wrestled over water development in the Central Valley where the corps was favored by farmers wanting to escape the acreage limitation law. Truman consistently supported the bureau in the dispute, but he was unable to solve the problem.

The infighting also stymied development in the Missouri and Columbia basins for years. Attempts to coordinate water resource development in the two valleys met with frustration as the two agencies entered into collusion and undermined attempts to create valley authorities. The bureau and the corps entered into the Pick-Sloan Plan in the Missouri Valley in 1944 and the Newell-Weaver Plan in the Columbia Valley in 1948. Although Truman went on record several times in favor of a TVA model for the Columbia and Missouri valleys and created both the Hoover Commission and the President's Water Resources Policy Commission to review water resource development, bureaucratic opposition was too strong and no significant changes were made.

During most of reclamation's first half century the values behind federal water development went unquestioned. Dams and reservoirs were built because they were necessary to the economic health of the arid West. But when the Bureau of Reclamation proposed flooding Dinosaur National Monument, cries of opposition reverberated across the country. A new group of conservationists for the first time in the postwar era challenged the idea that economic growth should be given the highest priority. Truman disagreed, insisting that development of western lands was more important than preserving old dinosaur bones. The preservationists succeeded in delaying the project until the mid-1950s when it was killed.

Harry Truman continued and finished a number of New Deal reclamation projects, but reclamation suffered several setbacks during his administration. Wheeling contracts undercut the expansion of public power, and technical compliance avoided the intent of the acreage limit in reclamation law. Both infighting and collusion helped defeat attempts to create new valley authorities. And finally, preservationists emphasizing aesthetic conservation instead of economic development halted or complicated the building of new dams.

A good survey of reclamation under Truman may be found in Michael C. Robinson, *Water for the West: The Bureau of Reclamation, 1902–1977* (Chicago: Public Works Historical Society, 1979). Clayton R. Koppes provides an excellent and controversial discussion of the lack of continuity between the reclamation policies of the Roosevelt administration and those of Truman in "Environmental Policy and American Liberalism: The Department of the Interior, 1933–1953," *Environmental Review* (Spring 1983): 17–41.

DAVID A. KATHKA

See also Army Corps of Engineers; Chapman, Oscar Littleton; Conservation; Missouri River; Rural Electrification Administration; Tennessee Valley Authority

Reconstruction Finance Corporation

President Hoover had founded the Reconstruction Finance Corporation (RFC) in 1932 to extend low-interest loans to financial institutions and railroads suffering from the depression. It was the forerunner of New Deal agencies, and proved so versatile that it outlived many of them. Jesse Jones, RFC administrator under President Roosevelt, expanded the RFC's role by broadening its loan authority and creating subsidiary agencies. By the end of World War II, the RFC had dispersed more than $35 billion in loans, expenditures, and investments.

The flexibility that made the RFC so valuable in depression and war proved to be its undoing during the Truman presidency. Conceived as a temporary agency during a national emergency that had now passed, the RFC was plagued by weak leadership after the resignation of Jesse Jones. Even former president Hoover called for its abolishment. The economic uncertainties of reconversion clouded the picture: some economists expected inflation, others recession; some members of Congress wanted to make the RFC permanent, others sought to abolish it. Although the Truman administration limited credit in many areas, total RFC loans increased, often with little attention paid to sound business practices or statutory limitations.

Congressional committees began investigating the RFC as early as 1945, evaluating whether to extend its charter. Although the early hearings exposed questionable loans, the most damaging revelations came during an investigation by a subcommittee of the Senate Banking and Currency Committee begun in February 1950 under the chairmanship of Senator J. William Fulbright, a Democrat from Arkansas. A committee report entitled "Favoritism and Influence" not only criticized loans and loan procedures but alleged that the RFC directors had been subject to outside influence. The committee singled out Donald S. Dawson, a Truman administrative assistant in charge of personnel recruitment, as the center of an influence ring that shaped RFC policy. The most colorful allegation charged that former RFC examiner E. Merl Young, a friend of Dawson, had

given his wife, who was a White House stenographer, a $9,540 mink coat that had been charged to the account of an attorney for a firm that received an RFC loan. Truman called the report "asinine" and claimed it was an attempt to embarrass him. The RFC investigation soon became part of Republican charges of corruption in the Truman administration.

Dawson's subsequent appearance before the committee exposed its most serious shortcoming—the inability to distinguish illegalities and improprieties from justifiable actions by public officials whose jobs required frequent contact at many levels of the bureaucracy. The committee proved nothing against Dawson. Antagonism between Truman and Fulbright hindered the inquiry, but when Truman submitted an RFC reorganization plan it included the committee's recommendation to replace the directors with a single administrator.

Jules Abels's *The Truman Scandals* (Chicago: Henry Regnery, 1956) and Andrew J. Dunar's *The Truman Scandals and the Politics of Morality* (Columbia: University of Missouri Press, 1984) both examine the RFC scandals at length.

ANDREW J. DUNAR

See also Scandals

Reconversion

See Economy, The

Red Scare

The Truman (and early Eisenhower) years were marked by overwrought fears of Communist sway in American life and by excessive government-led efforts to crush that influence. That the nation experienced a red scare following the Second World War, as it had after the first, is not surprising. Vast dislocations triggered by both wars prompted many Americans to yearn for surcease from rapid change. Conservatives sought to return to customary patterns of behavior and to curtail the reach of government which had expanded in wartime and in the two prewar reform periods. And finally, in both wars, the labor movement had attained an influence that management resented.

But in other ways the two scares differed. The first followed the Bolshevik Revolution which could barely sustain itself, let alone bolshevize the world. The second arose as Soviet power stretched well into Europe. Both outbreaks targeted alien "subversives," but more so in 1919–20, when over seven hundred people were deported, than in the forties and fifties, when some two hundred were sent away. The first scare lasted less than two years; the second, roughly a decade.

Reg Manning, 9 March 1953. Courtesy of the McNaught Syndicate.

foreign policy with disloyalty, and some argued that Thomas E. Dewey was Hitler's preferred candidate in 1944.

Yet the second red scare was mostly propelled by a partisan dynamic within the Republican party. Conservatives had long red-baited New Dealers, especially in the 1944 campaign. The Communist issue dappled the 1946 campaign; after their victory, Republicans claimed a mandate to clean house. The frustration of their electoral hopes yet again in 1948 greatly emboldened the GOP's right wing (already attuned to the Communist issue) and lowered resistance to red-baiting among moderate Republicans.

Amenable public opinion also sustained the second red scare. In postwar polls, large majorities endorsed outlawing membership in the Communist party or making Communists register with the government. Most Americans were not overcome by fear of communism, but their broad disdain for that doctrine ensured a permissive consensus for punitive steps. Vigilantism was extant but limited, reaching its peak in a riot following Paul Robeson's 1949 concert in Peekskill, New York. The most telling anti-Communism originated with potent institutions, especially those of government, rather than at the grass roots.

After the war, several powerful entities mobilized against the red menace. J. Edgar Hoover, director of the FBI, was staunchly anti-Communist. In 1946 the FBI launched an "educational" program to implant his views among politicians, journalists, and other opinion leaders. The U.S. Chamber of Commerce also crusaded actively, issuing pamphlets warning of red sway in government, labor, and other sectors. Potent segments of the press beat the drums, as did Catholic leaders, both lay and clerical, and veterans' groups.

Divided over the emerging hard line toward the USSR and on whether or not to tolerate Communist involvement in its activities, the political Left chose sides on the issue of communism. The CIO's 1946 convention passed a resolution critical of the Communists, and in 1949–50 the CIO expelled twelve Communist-dominated unions from its ranks. In January 1947 liberal anti-Communists founded Americans for Democratic Action.

The communism issue was ripening. In 1946 a House subcommittee had urged Truman to appoint a commission to weigh the loyalty problem and to create a new government loyalty program. He temporized, but soon after the November election he acceded to political reality by naming a President's Temporary Commission on Employee Loyalty (PTCEL). Most members of that body assumed that a loyalty problem existed, albeit on scanty evidence. A report to that effect was submitted on 20 February 1947.

Truman's Executive Order 9835 of 22 March created the Federal Employee Loyalty Program. (Some have suggested that the proximity between issuance of the order and the Truman Doctrine speech eight days earlier was tactical, not just coincidental, but the 1946 election and Truman's and the PTCEL's work loads, not strategy, account for the timing.) The loyalty of applicants for federal jobs was now scrutinized. Incumbent employees' names were checked against FBI files and vetted more fully if need be. If charges were made, an employee could have a hearing, but the identity of accusers was kept secret. A dismissal ruling could be appealed to the head of an agency and then to a Loyalty Review Board. The catch-all basis for dismissal was a finding of "reasonable grounds . . . for belief" that the employee was disloyal. Membership in a group on the attorney general's

The cold war gave birth to the second red scare, but much of the apparatus of anti-Communism predated that conflict. The rise of conservative opposition to the New Deal and concern over foreign-inspired fifth-column threats had quickened fears in the late 1930s. Communism and fascism became intertwined in the public mind—particularly after the Nazi-Soviet Pact. In 1938 the Special Committee on Un-American Activities led by Texas congressman Martin Dies launched the first sustained congressional investigation of Communism. The Dies committee pioneered many techniques later associated with McCarthyism.

Antisubversive gestures multiplied. The 1939 Hatch Act denied federal employment to members of groups advocating overthrow of the government. The Smith Act of 1940, reflecting the era's xenophobia, required that aliens be fingerprinted and register with the federal government. It also criminalized teaching or advocating the "duty, necessity, desirability or propriety of overthrowing or destroying any government in the United States by force or violence" or organizing or joining a group with that goal.

Franklin Roosevelt loathed the Dies committee but shared with other liberals its concern with the fifth column. In 1936 he had renewed the FBI's mandate for political surveillance (of which it had been stripped in the 1920s). Prodded by Congress, he set up a rudimentary loyalty program in 1942. New Dealers also helped sharpen political rhetoric. In the 1939–41 "battle against isolation," some of them equated opposition to FDR's list of totalitarian, fascist, communist, or subversive organizations often led to dismissal.

A security program, first applied to the War and Navy departments and extended to the State Department in 1946, also operated. The program empowered an agency's head to dismiss anyone whose continued employment endangered national security. Grounds for ouster included disloyalty, but also such categories as loose talk, excessive drinking, or being at risk because one had relatives behind the iron curtain. Many loyal employees were let go as "security risks," yet the assumption persisted that they were disloyal as well because the two programs were commonly confused.

Truman expressed solicitude for civil liberties, but his loyalty program let a malign genie out of the bottle. As FBI probes proliferated and a heavy-handed loyalty-security bureaucracy grew, the program became oppressive. Some critics considered its flaws inherent. What else could one expect of a system meant to ferret out "potential subversives"? Horror stories multiplied. Neighbors or coworkers turned in employees for such heresies as entertaining blacks or stating unorthodox views. One employee was quizzed on his opinion of chastity; many, on their taste in reading. Brief or innocent or unknowing ties with groups named on the attorney general's list could end careers. One loyalty board member half-seriously advised limiting one's memberships to the Methodist church.

Employment tests proliferated. A port security program launched during the 1950 Korean crisis swept twenty-five hundred suspect longshoremen and sailors off the waterfront. Recipients of Atomic Energy Commission fellowships were tested for loyalty. Employees of defense contractors had to undergo security checks. Some companies enforced loyalty programs of their own.

Responding to political pressure, the Truman administration in 1948 indicted the top leaders of the Communist party under the Smith Act. (It also hustled to deport Communists who were aliens.) During a long trial in 1949, the prosecution argued that the revival of the American Communist party in 1945 constituted unlawful seditious conspiracy. In *Dennis* v. *United States* (1951), the Supreme Court affirmed the convictions of the eleven party leaders. This ruling prompted similar indictments of over a hundred second-string party leaders in the next several years. Finally, the Supreme Court's 1957 *Yates* decision terminated such prosecutions.

These exertions may have abated pressures to legislate against Communism, but they did not cool the issue. The Eightieth Congress mounted twenty-two probes of Communism. State legislatures also acted. Before 1950, anti-Communism inquests took place in California, New York, Oklahoma, Illinois, Michigan, Washington, Maryland, and Illinois. Thanks to its 1947 probe of Communism in Hollywood and the 1948 hearings at which Whittaker Chambers and Alger Hiss confronted each other, the House Un-American Activities Committee (HUAC) held supremacy in this field.

In 1947 the "Hollywood Ten," citing the First Amendment, declined to divulge their party connections to HUAC. They went to jail when their conviction on contempt of Congress was upheld in 1950. (Only the Fifth Amendment protected a witness's refusal to testify.) Soon a blacklist cast a pall over fearful Hollywood. Leftist actors, writers, and directors were denied work in the film industry unless they testified freely about their associations—named names—before committees. The blacklist also extended to radio and television. It was enforced

jointly by politicians who hunted purported reds, patrioteers who hounded them, a small group of ex-FBI men who made a business of listing them, and advertisers and entertainment industry officials who feared to employ them. Several hundred persons lost their jobs in show business.

Employment sanctions sprouted elsewhere. Teachers in some states had faced loyalty oaths since the 1920s. As early as 1941, New York City teachers charged as Communists were fired; in 1949 a new purge began. By one estimate, some three hundred New York City teachers were fired; perhaps another three hundred lost jobs elsewhere in the nation. In 1949 three University of Washington professors were fired after a legislative committee's loyalty probe; this episode raised the issue of the place of Communists in higher education. The consensus was that they forfeited any right to teach. Loyalty programs often covered state and local government workers, and lawyers too faced sanctions, notably disbarment. At its most absurd, the mania for loyalty programs and oaths encompassed wrestlers in Indiana, washroom attendants in New York City, and public housing tenants in various cities.

In 1949–50, several dire happenings heightened fears of the red menace. China "fell" to the Communists and the Soviets exploded an A-bomb in late 1949. In January 1950, after two long trials, Alger Hiss was convicted of perjury. Hiss's guilt appeared to many to indict the whole New Deal tradition, spurred Republican red-baiting, and dispirited liberals. In this context, on 9 February 1950, Senator Joseph R. McCarthy made his notorious charges of Communist infestation of government. An inquiry headed by Democratic senator Millard Tydings failed to subdue the slippery McCarthy, and the outbreak of war in Korea and such events as the arrest of Julius and Ethel Rosenberg for atomic espionage kept fears of subversion alive.

The Korean War touched off the high red scare. In September, Congress passed the Internal Security Act sponsored by Senator Pat McCarran. A potpourri of draconian proposals, some offered by liberals as (debatably) lesser evils, the law required that Communist action and front groups register with a newly created Subversive Activities Control Board and provided for detention of subversives in the event of a presidentially declared national security emergency. The McCarran Act was a frightening but generally empty gesture. Detention camps were readied, but never used. (This part of the law was repealed in 1971.) Efforts to force the Communist party to register dragged on fruitlessly into the 1960s.

The 1950 elections witnessed new levels of red-baiting and dirty politics. McCarthy campaigned against several Democrats (including Tydings) who lost. Although less potent than vaunted, his seeming political muscle deepened his colleagues' fear of him. Given wide berth by timid Democrats, encouraged or tolerated by Republicans who foresaw political gains, he continued to assail the Truman administration and to seize headlines. But HUAC and the new Senate Internal Security Subcommittee (SISS) led by McCarran did more actual investigating of Communism in the Eighty-second Congress. Although McCarthy stamped his name on the era, other political leaders and institutions played roles at least as important in bringing repression to American life.

After 1950, victims of the purge multiplied. Battered by McCarthy, HUAC, SISS and the loyalty-security program, most of the "China hands" (Foreign Service officers who had differed with the pro–Chiang Kai-shek orthodoxy imposed by conservatives) left government—some by firing as security risks, some by expedient resignation. Under right-wing pressure Truman tightened the loyalty standard in 1951: "reasonable doubt" of an employee's loyalty now provided grounds for dismissal. When HUAC returned to Hollywood in 1951, the blacklist lengthened. Rising numbers of teachers lost jobs. The McCarran-Walter Act, passed over Truman's veto in 1952, stiffened sanctions against aliens and even naturalized citizens whose loyalty was questioned.

Some observers hoped Dwight D. Eisenhower's election as president would bring improvement. The burdens of empowerment, along with McCarthy's persisting unruliness, did lead to his censure and the end of his influence in late 1954. Both HUAC and SISS, however, continued to practice the politics of exposure, albeit somewhat less flamboyantly.

Yet Ike too demanded a loyal bureaucracy. His 1953 executive order revamped the loyalty-security system, scrapping the loyalty program but extending the security program to all departments. Employees now had fewer avenues of appeal, and dismissal still bore a heavy stigma. Republicans soon boasted of how many dismissals they had wrought. Angered by this numbers game, the Democrats, on recapturing Congress, mounted three investigations of the program in 1955. These plus the publicity surrounding several noted security cases (especially J. Robert Oppenheimer's) and journalistic exposés of injustices helped discredit security programs.

Chief Justice Earl Warren's Supreme Court also moderated the red scare. Beginning in 1955, decisions curbed the security program, mildly restrained HUAC, ruled that federal antisedition laws preempted state laws, halted use of the Smith Act against second-string Communists, gutted the registration provision of the McCarran Act, and ended denials of passports to radicals. The underside of this period came with the launching in 1956 of the FBI's COINTELPRO program, which entailed stepped-up surveillance and sabotage of the feeble Communist party. Soon FBI agents were unwittingly snitching on fellow agents. Political snooping by the FBI (and other intelligence agencies) against other groups, including the civil rights movement, proliferated until it was exposed by congressional probes of the 1970s.

The red scare's impact defies exact measurement. Since loyalty-security proceedings were shrouded in secrecy, and many sanctions were informal and covert, the human damage remains hard to assess. By one estimate, over 13 million employees—about one in every five—were affected by some loyalty or security program. Truman's loyalty program denied jobs to or dismissed 560 people, and many more were investigated. Roughly twice as many were dismissed under the security program up to 1953. By mid-1955, Ike's security program picked off 343 employees. Many more resigned before loyalty or security proceedings were completed. By one estimate, the total number of government and nongovernment dismissals was over 11,000. This figure may be low, and it does not encompass those subject to less formal economic pressures.

There were broader effects on American life. The civil rights and peace movements were retarded; labor's left wing was crushed. Some see the students of the fifties' "silent generation" as products of the political climate. Radicalism—and even tamer varieties of critical thought—took a holiday. The age of investigations refined a breed of timid government officials. One result was the nation's ossified policy toward China. The fear of another inquest like that on "who lost China" may have

had some adverse effect on decision making during the Vietnam War.

David Caute, *The Great Fear: The Anti-Communist Purge under Truman and Eisenhower* (New York: Simon & Schuster, 1978), ranges widely but not always accurately. Old but useful in Ralph S. Brown, Jr., *Loyalty and Security: Employment Tests in the United States* (New Haven: Yale University Press, 1958). Robert Justin Goldstein's *Political Repression in Modern America* (Cambridge: Schenkman, 1978) argues that the impact of this phenomenon on American life has been underestimated. Richard M. Freeland, *The Truman Doctrine and the Origins of McCarthyism: Foreign Policy, Domestic Politics, and Internal Security, 1946-1948* (New York: Alfred A. Knopf, 1972), scores the Truman administration for helping incite the red scare, as do many recent scholars. Some work by Athan Theoharis is in this vein, but his *Spying on Americans* (Philadelphia: Temple University Press, 1978) stresses the FBI's role, as does Kenneth O'Reilly, *Hoover and the Un-Americans: The FBI, HUAC, and the Red Menace* (Philadelphia: Temple University Press, 1983). Earl Latham, *The Communist Controversy in Washington from the New Deal to McCarthy* (Cambridge: Harvard University Press, 1966), sees the political frustration of the GOP, especially its conservative wing, as a key to the rise of McCarthyism. See also Larry Ceplair and Steven Englund, *The Inquisition in Hollywood: Politics in the Film Industry, 1930-1960* (Garden City, N.Y.: Anchor/Doubleday, 1980); Ellen W. Schrecker, *No Ivory Tower: McCarthyism and the Universities* (New York: Oxford University Press, 1986); and Robert Griffith and Athan Theoharis, eds., *The Specter: Original Essays on the Cold War and the Origins of McCarthyism* (New York: Franklin Watts, 1974).

RICHARD M. FRIED

See also Americans for Democratic Action; Civil Liberties; Communism and Communists; Federal Bureau of Investigation; Hiss-Chambers Case; Hoover, John Edgar; House Committee on Un-American Activities; Loyalty Program; McCarran, Patrick Anthony; McCarthy, Joseph R.; Nixon, Richard M.; Rosenberg Case; Smith Act

Regulatory Agencies

The legacies of New Deal and wartime business-government relations prompted President Truman to extend reforms to the regulatory commissions. Yet congressional fears of increasing executive power and specific controversies of the era forestalled reform of the nation's regulatory apparatus between 1945 and 1953. Those reforms that did take place were tied to specific cases and did little to enhance the government's ability to regulate the economy.

Since the first federal regulatory agency was established in 1887 (the Interstate Commerce Commission), questions of authority and politics have shaped the evolution of the so-called independent commissions. Who should control the fourth branch, the president or Congress? Progressive goals of efficiency suggested the former; democratic ideals suggested the latter. How much should politics intervene? Again, progressive ideals had no room for politics, whereas the very nature of the regulatory task—managing private business—assumed political activity. Truman's reforms fell victim to such historical continuities, as well as to a general American weariness with government experimentation in the economy.

As senator in the 1930s, Truman had witnessed the flowering of progressive ideals in which experts efficiently and pragmatically regulated business. He had supported extension of federal authority into banking, securities, holding companies, airlines, power, and management-labor relations. When he became president, and following the pragmatic method, Truman realized there was room for improvement. Focused as they were on specific industries (except for the Federal Trade Commission), the regulatory agencies acted independently of an overall national economic policy. Each agency, moreover, was bogged down in administrative detail, producing conflicting policies and excessive delays that were the antithesis of progressive goals. These problems President Truman attempted to solve by coordinating economic policy in the executive branch, establishing more efficient bureaucracies, and strengthening the powers of the commission chairpersons. The conservative coalition of Republicans and southern Democrats, however, frustrated Truman's approach to pragmatic reform. Although none of the independent agencies was involved in the scandals that plagued the Truman administration, at least one, the Federal Power Commission, became embroiled in the anti-Communist crusade that Truman had helped bring about.

Franklin Roosevelt had left Truman one agency from which he could mount an effort to rationalize national economic policy-making, the Bureau of the Budget (BOB), which had been moved to the Executive Office in 1939. In 1946 Congress authorized another potentially helpful agency, the Council of Economic Advisers (CEA). Still, the CEA was only advisory in capacity; and the BOB tended to emphasize cost reduction as the method of improving regulatory performance. Consequently, the commissioners found themselves with less money or fewer personnel with which they were supposed to do more. The BOB eventually admitted that its approach was partly responsible for the agencies working against one another rather than as a coordinated whole. Truman believed in the ongoing nature of pragmatic reform, and gaining support from the Hoover Commission's task force on the regulatory agencies, he requested from Congress in 1949 the authority to reorganize the commissions under the executive branch. But Congress, jealous of growing executive power, allowed only piecemeal reform within each agency.

In addition to efficiency reforms, Truman tried to appoint better personnel and to strengthen the powers of the individual agencies by consolidating authority in the chairpersons of each one. Gale E. Peterson, the leading student of regulation under Truman, has suggested that these appointments represented a powerful tool, for the commissions accounted for about 10 percent of all presidential appointments. Indeed, Truman inaugurated a new approach when he ordered background checks on candidates and met with them before confirmation. Once appointed, the chairs were expected to keep Truman informed and to keep problems off his desk, but the president did not intervene on specific issues. Truman balanced experience, place of residence, and party affiliation (the latter sometimes based in statute requirements) when choosing commissioners. In 1948, this process led him to appoint the first female federal regulatory commissioner, Frieda B. Hennock, to the Federal Communications Commission. Nonetheless, frequent vacancies and less-than-inspiring appointees stymied Truman's continuous efforts at reform.

The Leland Olds affair was central to the regulatory tale of the Truman presidency, for it not only indicated Truman's views on what regulation should do but also reflected how politics interfered in regulatory matters. In 1949 Truman nominated Olds as chair of the Federal Power Commission (FPC) because Olds had proven during two previous terms to be an expert on electrical power controls. Operating in the progressive-populist vein Truman preferred, Olds was concerned, first, that the consumer pay the lowest rates possible and, second, that the power companies receive an adequate but not extortionate return on their investments. Despite having been confirmed twice before, Olds faced intense opposition from senators of three leading natural gas–producing states—Oklahoma, Colorado, and Texas. These senators dredged up essays in which a young Olds had praised communist ideals. Truman fought the charges because they were irrelevant given Olds's record as FPC commissioner and because Truman perceived the issue as the "interests" against the "little guy." Truman and Olds lost the fight, despite help from Eleanor Roosevelt and other progressive forces. Ironically, then, the anti-Communist crusade Truman had helped promote came back to haunt his attempt to bolster the effectiveness of the regulatory agencies.

Truman's attempts to coordinate and to improve the performance of the federal regulatory agencies met a fate similar to that of most New Deal and Fair Deal programs to reform the less desirable consequences of capitalism. Only modest efforts were attempted and the result was that no regulatory agencies were abolished or seriously curtailed in their routine activities; but, then, no new coordinated actions were implemented either. No national policy on petroleum or transportation emerged from Truman's efforts, but here the president faced the inherent structural strife within two major industrial groups. The Securities and Exchange Commission was the most successful in controlling its designated industry, but success in the 1940s and 1950s is attributable more to a strong beginning in the 1930s and to the peculiar structure of that business than to Truman's influence. The Federal Trade Commission, as always, was caught up in the country's (and Truman's) ambivalent attitudes toward monopoly and antitrust policies.

The regulatory apparatus would limp along into the 1960s without overall coordination. In that decade, for the first time, economists convinced the lawmakers that the New Deal–Fair Deal approach to regulation was at best inefficient and at worst antithetical to a capitalist economy. As the Truman administration's record suggested, however, the demise of progressive regulation had its roots in bureaucratic lethargy, political intervention, and struggles between the president and Congress.

The best factual account of the regulatory agencies under Truman is Gale E. Peterson's *President Harry S. Truman and the Independent Regulatory Commissions, 1945–1952* (New York: Garland Publishing, 1985), which is the published version of Peterson's dissertation of 1973. It supplies the basic information on each of the regulatory commissions and highlights the importance of the Bureau of the Budget. A broader view of regulation during the period is found in Thomas K. McCraw, *Prophets of Regulation* (Cambridge: Harvard University Press, Belkmap Press, 1984), especially chapter 6. The Leland Olds affair can be followed in PPF

5124 and OF 235 at the Harry S. Truman Library. Alonzo Hamby, *Beyond the New Deal: Harry S. Truman and American Liberalism* (New York: Columbia University Press, 1973), furnishes an incisive context in which Truman's attitudes toward reform are analyzed.

WILLIAM R. CHILDS

See also Budget, Bureau of the; Executive Branch, Reorganization of the

Religion

John and Martha Ellen Truman provided well for their son's spiritual education. Both parents were Baptists, but after moving to Independence near the turn of the century, they took Harry to a Presbyterian Sunday school because of its convenient location. By age twelve, the young Truman had purportedly read the Bible twice, cover to cover. At eighteen, he joined the Baptist church because, he said later, it gave "the common man the shortest and most direct approach to God."

The role religion played in the Truman presidency cannot be precisely documented. Truman did not consider himself an extremely religious man or a strong Baptist. The contempt he held for political ideologues extended equally to religious zealots. ("My grandfather used to say that when he heard his neighbor pray too loudly in public he always went home and locked his smokehouse.") President Truman attended church regularly, sprinkled his conversation with references to biblical parables and Christian principles, and, at one point, implored the world's religious leaders to mount an anti-Communist crusade. When some Protestant groups criticized his swearing, poker playing, and "slight libations" and expressed outrage when he appointed an ambassador to the Vatican, their protests changed neither his habits nor his decision.

In general, the religious teachings he had embraced as a youth formed a critical part—but only a part—of the belief and value system through which, as president, he filtered and evaluated external events and individual behavior. The sense of morality, justice, and fair play he derived from religion was often violated, but his responses to these offenses were usually tempered by more secular considerations.

For more information on Truman's attitude toward religion, see Robert H. Ferrell, ed., *Dear Bess: The Letters of Harry to Bess Truman, 1910-1959* (New York: W. W. Norton, 1983); Robert H. Ferrell, ed., *The Autobiography of Harry S. Truman* (Boulder: Colorado Associated University Press, 1980); and Harry S. Truman, *Memoirs*, vol. 1, *Year of Decisions* (Garden City, N.Y.: Doubleday, 1955). There is a Truman and Religion file in the Truman Library in Independence.

LAWRENCE A. YATES

Reorganization Acts of 1945, 1949

See Executive Branch, Reorganization of the

Republican Party

The Republican party had fallen to second place in American politics in the 1930s when Franklin D. Roosevelt's New Deal initiated political realignment. The Republican party's rank and file were primarily business people, white-collar managers, and others who opposed the growth of the federal bureaucracy and its regulation of the economy, some farmers who still held a belief in the individualism of the farm, and a few social groups who had supported the GOP since the Civil War. Gone was support from most blacks and many workers who thought their interests were better served by the New Deal. By 1945, the party's image was one of firm opposition to the New Deal, even though this image was not entirely accurate.

During the Truman administration, Republicans were divided in their response to the New Deal. Some Republicans from the midwestern farm states and congressional leaders Robert A. Taft and Joseph Martin tried to limit or repeal these programs while they also opposed Truman's plans to expand the New Deal through national health insurance and a Fair Employment Practices Commission. Most Republicans in Congress agreed with Taft and Martin and pursued tax reduction, termination of wartime controls, and reduction in the power of organized labor. Despite their stated opposition to the New Deal, however, some Republicans, including Taft, supported housing, education, and income maintenance programs. Other Republicans went even further. Thomas E. Dewey, who called himself a "New Deal Republican," and others in the eastern states and urban areas wanted to adopt some New Deal programs as their own.

Neither did Republicans develop a monolithic front on foreign policy questions. Many, such as Senator William Knowland and Congressman Walter Judd, emphasized the importance of Asia to American interests and criticized Truman for failing to provide adequate military assistance to American allies there, blaming the president for the Communist takeover in China and the invasion of Korea. These Republicans opposed European aid programs, believing that such assistance was too costly and less effective than military action. Other Republicans, led by Senator Arthur Vandenberg, supported Truman's European aid programs. Despite this division, the Republican party supported the developing consensus promoted by Truman that Communism was a threat to America and that the United States had a major role to play in containing Communist influence.

This consensus was important to the Republicans, for the issue of Communist subversion of American institutions was significant in defining the party's political personality. Republicans used the Communist issue extensively in attacking the Democrats. They charged that organized labor was infested with Communists and that labor's coalition with that party would lead to the Democrats' domination by Communists. Republicans attacked Truman's domestic policies as bringing the communist economic system to America. They also charged that Communist gains in Europe and Asia and Soviet development of an atomic bomb were aided by Communist influence in the State Department. This issue provided a source of uncommon unity for Republicans. All across the party's spectrum, from conservatives Joseph McCarthy and William Jenner to moderates Richard Nixon and Harold Stassen, Republicans hammered at the issue. For its 1952 campaign the GOP coined the alliterative slogan: "Korea, Corruption, and Communism." This issue did not advance the party's long-term fortunes, however, for few American voters transferred their allegiance to the GOP because of it.

Republicans failed during the Truman administration to improve substantially their standing with the voters. In 1946 they were successful in using public dissatisfaction with inflation, labor disputes, continued shortage of consumer goods, and the Communist issue to gain control of both houses of Congress for the first time since 1928. They failed to build on these gains in 1948 and lost Congress and the presidential race when Truman and the Democrats reunited the Roosevelt coalition of the 1930s. Republicans modestly increased their congressional forces in 1950 and regained control of both houses by narrow margins in 1952. In that year, with the support of the moderate wing of the party, Gen. Dwight D. Eisenhower won the presidential nomination and recaptured the presidency for the Republicans. As later events showed, however, this success in 1952 was not the beginning of a long-term Republican resurgence.

George H. Mayer's essay, "The Republican Party, 1932–1952," in *The History of American Political Parties*, vol. 3: *1910–1945: From Square Deal to New Deal*, ed. Arthur M. Schlesinger, Jr., 2259–92 (New York: Chelsea House, 1973), emphasizes the party's failure to grow but offers limited analysis of why it failed. Mayer has also written a chronologically broader study, *The Republican Party, 1854–1964* (New York: Oxford University Press, 1964). Susan M. Hartmann analyzes the relationship between congressional Republicans and Truman in *Truman and the 80th Congress* (Columbia: University of Missouri Press, 1971). The party's story is also told in biographies of its leaders. Among the best of these are James T. Patterson, *Mr. Republican: A Biography of Robert A. Taft* (Boston: Houghton Mifflin, 1972); Richard Norton Smith, *Thomas E. Dewey and His Times* (New York: Simon & Schuster, 1982); and Herbert S. Parmet, *Eisenhower and the American Crusades* (New York: Macmillan, 1972). The latter is encyclopedic on the 1952 campaign. This topic is updated by Stephen E. Ambrose, *Eisenhower: Soldier, General of the Army, President-Elect* (New York: Simon & Schuster, 1983). Ambrose has also written *Nixon: The Education of a Politician, 1913–1962* (New York: Simon & Schuster, 1987). On the limited electoral impact of the Communist issue, see Michael Paul Rogin, *The Intellectuals and McCarthy* (Cambridge: MIT Press, 1967).

THOMAS F. SOAPES

See also Congress, United States; Conservatism; Eightieth Congress; Elections in the Truman Era

Reputation

See Biographers and Public Reputation

Retirement

Harry Truman's retirement spanned the period from 20 January 1953 to his death on 26 December 1972. He and Bess spent virtually that entire time in the modest Victorian home at 219 North Delaware, Independence, Missouri. The slow-paced, private, and neighborly existence of a small midwestern community proved a welcome relief from the tumultuous life of Washington, D.C. Yet Truman never completely retired from public life. Party leaders and government officials still sought his assistance, and Truman himself ambitiously pursued his own goals.

Few twentieth-century ex-presidents were more active than Truman who strengthened the ex-presidency, an institution in its own right. He spent his early retirement writing his well-received presidential *Memoirs*. When the final volume was published in 1956, Truman had already regained much of the popularity he had lost late in his presidency. The following year he officially dedicated the Harry S. Truman Presidential Library after having raised private funds to construct the contemporary building about half a mile from his home. For the next seven years, Truman regularly went to his office in the library. He especially relished talking with schoolchildren in the library auditorium, edifying them with sprightly accounts of the American past. He also enjoyed taking invited guests on his patented tours.

Former president Truman in front of the new Jackson County voting machines, 2 November 1954. (Associated Press/Wide World Photos)

During the 1950s Truman responded to the invitations and challenges of Congress. He testified, for example, on the issue of presidential disability and on behalf of the repeal of the Twenty-second Amendment limiting a president to two terms. He successfully lobbied against Republican attempts to transfer immigration and passport control from the House Judiciary Committee to the House Un-American Activities Committee. He worked with congressional Democrats for public housing and farm legislation and against a tax bill beneficial to large insurance companies. Most important, Truman also used his influence with the Democratic congressional leadership to institutionalize the ex-presidency: the Former Presidents Act of 1958 provided ex-presidents with franking privileges, a $25,000 annual allowance, a staff stipend, and office space and furnishings. Through Truman's encouragement, the Senate passed the Pell Act in 1963 which allowed former presidents to address that body. Truman became the first to do so the following year.

The postpresidential years also represented a time of political frustration. Truman had hoped to provide useful bipartisan service to President Dwight D. Eisenhower, but Ike ignored him, causing Truman privately to speak of the "White House Bonehead." Throughout the 1950s, newswriters frequently alluded to a Truman-Eisenhower feud. Moreover, Truman failed to impose his presidential candidates upon Democratic national conventions despite his success on behalf of Democratic aspirants in congressional campaigns from 1954 through 1962. At the Chicago convention in 1956, he dramatically endorsed the liberal governor of New York, Averell Harriman, even though Adlai Stevenson clearly remained the delegates' overwhelming choice. In 1960 Truman again unsuccessfully challenged the Democratic front-runner, John F. Kennedy, by backing his fellow Missourian, Senator Stuart Symington. In both instances, Truman confused popularity and power; ex-presidents have far less of the latter. Nevertheless, in both 1956 and 1960, he actively supported the Democratic presidential tickets. In time he came to respect President Kennedy, but his relationship with Kennedy's successor, Lyndon Baines Johnson, was much closer. They had worked together politically in the 1950s when Johnson became Democratic leader in the Senate. Truman soon expressed strong empathy for Johnson's travail in Vietnam partly as a consequence of his own frustration in Korea and his staunch anti-Communism.

On domestic issues, especially civil rights, Truman had become out of touch with liberal sentiment. His once progressive views on civil rights seemed dated as he lambasted sit-in participants as "bad citizens" and freedom riders as "northern busybodies." He publicly called Martin Luther King, Jr., a troublemaker. To civil rights advocates, Truman's gradualism, which he hoped would preserve Democratic unity and prevent southern violence, represented nothing more than a defense of the status quo.

Truman's health began to fail by the mid-1960s. As late as 1959, the *New York Times* had found him "pink and fit, with the crisp smile and sparkling eyes and the same handshake." But in a 1964 bathroom fall, he cracked a couple of ribs and injured his head. He never completely recovered and became increasingly frail and much less responsive to public issues. He died the day after Christmas in the year 1972 at the age of eighty-eight and was buried in the courtyard of the Truman Library.

The only scholarly study on Truman's ex-presidency is James N. Giglio, "Harry S. Truman and the Multifarious Ex-Presidency," *Presidential Studies Quarterly* 12 (Spring 1982): 239–55. Truman also wrote about his retirement years in *Mr. Citizen* (New York: Geis Associates, 1960).

JAMES N. GIGLIO

Reuther, Walter Philip

(1 September 1907–9 May 1970)

Walter Reuther was born in Wheeling, West Virginia. His father, a German immigrant workman, was a trade unionist and socialist who reared his sons in the beliefs that all workers needed unions and that the capitalist system needed reconstruction. Reuther, trained as a diemaker, worked for the Ford Motor Company from 1927 to 1932. Accompanied by his younger brother Victor, he then spent more than two years (1933–35) in Europe including a period of employment in a Soviet automobile factory. Returning to the United States in 1935, he threw himself into the early organizing campaigns of the United Automobile Workers (UAW). In 1936 he became president of Local 174 in Detroit and was elected to the UAW's general executive board. Proving himself in all dimensions of union leadership, he advanced to director of the General Motors Department (1939–46), vice president of the UAW (1942–46), and president (1946–70). In addition, he was president of the Congress of Industrial Organizations (CIO), 1952–55, and vice president of the American Federation of Labor–Congress of Industrial Organizations (AFL-CIO), 1955–67.

Reuther's political perspective was shaped by his lifelong involvement in the labor movement. Union leaders and the rank and file, he believed, must participate in politics to achieve their goals. A member of the Socialist party until 1938, he moved toward the Democratic party as President Franklin D. Roosevelt and the New Deal edged toward the left. During World War II he established a friendly working and personal relationship with both President and Mrs. Roosevelt, whose political liberalism he warmly admired.

Reuther's relationship with Truman centered on two events. The first was Truman's role in the strike of General Motors workers in 1945–46, the longest and most bitterly contested strike of the postwar period. When the war ended Truman had issued an executive order permitting pay increases if there was no resulting price increase. Reuther immediately proposed that General Motors grant its workers a 30 percent wage increase, an amount sufficient to maintain wartime take-home pay despite the loss of overtime and other premiums, and that the corporation pledge not to increase the prices of its cars. Negotiations failed and the strike began in November 1945. Truman, concerned about the strike's impact on the economy, appointed a fact-finding board to determine General Motors' ability to pay the wage increase. The corporation denounced the government's intervention and refused to cooperate.

To this point, Reuther's and Truman's views were complementary. As the economic costs of the strike mounted, however, Truman, in Reuther's view, began to waver. The government approved a settlement of the steelworkers' strike that granted the steel companies a substantial price increase. Under pressure to settle, Reuther tried to enlist Truman directly in the cause by sending the president a well-publicized telegram arguing that the union was upholding the administration's price stabilization program. "The fight of the General Motors workers is your fight and the fight of every American. It demands your immediate and militant support." Truman, persuaded by Secretary of Labor Lewis Schwellenbach that Reuther was desperately trying to stave off defeat in order to rescue his bid for the UAW presidency, "got . . . up on his high horse," as Robert Donovan wrote in *Conflict and Crisis*, and refused to do anything. The strike was finally ended on terms that Reuther had previously denounced.

The second event was Truman's bid for reelection in 1948. Although Reuther generally supported the Truman administration's foreign policy positions and, of course, the veto of the Taft-Hartley Act, he was suspicious of the president's liberal commitment, his competence, and, at least until 1948, his political effectiveness. Surrounded by cronies and conservative businessmen, Truman, Reuther believed, had floundered in handling reconversion, fighting inflation, and dealing with some other issues. He had shown neither the liberal vision nor the political skills needed to keep the Democratic party on course.

In June 1948 Reuther bluntly told a *Detroit News* reporter that Truman was a man "with his heart in the right place but a man not adequate for the job he inherited." As an influential member of Americans for Democratic Action (ADA), Reuther became involved in an effort to dump Truman from the Democratic ticket and replace him with a more liberal and more politically promising candidate. Reuther preferred Associate Justice William O. Douglas of the U.S. Supreme Court. Other ADA leaders, however, wanted Gen. Dwight D. Eisenhower, whose politics were unknown but whose popularity was enormous. The ADA board approved a resolution endorsing Eisenhower "and/or" Douglas, but the movement collapsed when Eisenhower announced that he was unavailable. Reuther agreed to a UAW endorsement of Truman but, like many observers, believed the president was headed for defeat. The UAW's efforts in the campaign were directed toward helping liberal congressional candidates, and Reuther welcomed an expected realignment of the parties, following Truman's defeat, that would unite liberals against the conservative opposition. With Truman's victory, Reuther offered his congratulations and dropped all plans for political realignment and a new liberal political party.

Truman apparently viewed Reuther as a liberal dogmatist with boundless ambition and self-confidence. His view, perhaps, was shaped by CIO president Philip Murray. Following a meeting Reuther attended, President Truman told Murray, "Phil, that young man is after your job." "No, Mr. President," Murray replied, "he really is after your job."

Although he never became president of the United States, Reuther established close and supportive relationships with Democratic presidential candidate Adlai E. Stevenson, and with Presidents John F. Kennedy and Lyndon B. Johnson. He remained president of the UAW until his death in 1970 in an airplane crash.

Accounts of the Reuther-Truman relationship may be found in John Barnard, *Walter Reuther and the Rise of the Auto Workers* (Boston: Little, Brown, 1983), Frank Cormier and William J. Eaton, *Reuther*

(Englewood Cliffs, N.J.: Prentice-Hall, 1970), and Irving Howe and B. J. Widick, *The UAW and Walter Reuther* (1949; reprint, New York: Da Capo Press, 1973).

JOHN BARNARD

See also Labor

Revolution

When Harry S. Truman assumed the presidency in 1945 he confronted a revolutionary world. The destruction wrought by World War II and the removal of Germany and Japan from positions of political authority left much of the globe in a state of political, social, and economic disarray. In formerly occupied areas various groups competed to replace Nazi and Japanese regimes, a context that often gave rise to revolutionary movements. In Asia and the Middle East, European empires had begun to crumble and nationalist movements for self-determination took shape. Although *revolution* is in many ways a relative term, it implies an internally induced process in which a society undergoes an abrupt and fundamental change in the status quo. In the postwar setting, some revolutions produced sudden and substantive changes in political organization. Some involved radical efforts to alter social and economic systems. Many revolutions took place within a relatively peaceful context; others spurred violent upheaval. Taken together, these revolutionary conditions posed a major challenge to the United States which had recently assumed the mantle of world leadership.

As heirs to a revolutionary heritage, President Truman and many other Americans seemed instinctively to sympathize with the revolutionary aspirations of others. But Americans' attitude toward revolution was actually ambivalent, in part, because the American Revolution itself had featured only limited social and economic change. Americans grew uneasy when uprisings evolved toward more radical stages rather than resulting in United States–style constitutional government. Moreover, in the twentieth century, the United States had emerged as a world power with burgeoning economic and political interests that tended to further inhibit support for revolutions.

Although U.S. interests dictated support for Cuba's rebellion against Spain in the 1890s, the McKinley administration soon after suppressed an indigenous, anti-American uprising in the Philippines. Defining the Caribbean region as an American sphere of influence in 1904, President Theodore Roosevelt proclaimed that the United States would police that revolution-prone area. During the next three decades Washington frequently employed military force against uprisings in countries such as the Dominican Republic, Haiti, Mexico, and Nicaragua. American antipathy toward revolution reached new heights after the Bolshevik seizure of power in Russia in 1917. Soviet confiscation of private property and advocacy of worldwide, class-based revolution ran counter to Wilsonian hopes for the evolution of a stable, capitalistic, and democratic world order.

Such was the historical legacy inherited by the Truman administration. In keeping with tradition, the Truman White House did not oppose all revolution, but tended to embrace only those that showed promise of conforming to America's limited revolutionary experience. As the leader of the capitalistic free world, and with extensive economic and political interests to protect, the United States usually condemned upheavals that threatened to undermine the international equilibrium. In the emotional atmosphere of the cold war, moreover, the United States often perceived the hand of the Soviet Union behind revolutionary movements. More often than not, the containment of Soviet power and the containment of revolution became mutually reinforcing policy goals.

The Truman administration's first encounter with foreign revolution occurred in Europe, where American economic and security interests were paramount and the Soviet threat seemed most ominous. In much of Eastern Europe, Soviet occupation during and immediately following World War II helped bring to power a number of revolutionary Communist regimes. The pattern and extent of Soviet influence varied—Poland and Romania witnessed Soviet-backed takeovers during the war, Soviet-supported governments came to power in Hungary and Czechoslavakia in 1947 and 1948 respectively, and Joseph Tito in Yugoslavia carried out a Communist revolution independent of the Soviet Union. Although the Truman administration protested these fundamental changes in the political makeup of the region, it ultimately conceded that Eastern Europe constituted a Soviet sphere of influence and undertook no direct intervention against these revolutions.

The administration soon came to believe, however, that the Soviets might take advantage of postwar political and economic distress by supporting locally inspired revolutions outside of Eastern Europe. The most dramatic revolutionary event took place in Greece where Communist-led rebels backed by Yugoslavia battled the British-backed conservative government in Athens. A turning point came in early 1947 when the British government informed Washington that it could no longer provide the Greek government with badly needed economic and military support. Because the Greek leftists received aid and sanctuary from Communist Yugoslavia, and Yugoslavia was viewed as a mere client of Moscow, American policymakers concluded that the Kremlin directed the rebellion.

President Truman addressed Congress on 12 March 1947 on the need to extend aid to Greece and its neighbor Turkey. Enunciating the now-famous Truman Doctrine, the president declared that the world had been divided between two ways of life and urged Americans to commit themselves to helping "free peoples" and to oppose "totalitarian regimes." Setting down principles that would help guide U.S. policy toward revolutions throughout the post–World War II era, Truman further proclaimed that "it must be the policy of the United States to support free peoples who are resisting attempted subjugation by armed minorities or by outside pressures." The president omitted important details—such as the lack of evidence directly linking the Greek Communists to the Soviet Union, and the corrupt and undemocratic nature of the Greek government. Truman also overlooked the fact that throughout history most violent revolutions, including the American Revolution of 1776, had been carried out by minority factions often with support from an external power. In short, the open-ended Truman Doctrine committed the United States to an extremely counterrevolutionary policy.

The Truman Doctrine contained an additional line of reasoning that helped fashion America's response to revolutions in the postwar era. Invoking what would later become known as the "domino theory," the president warned Congress that failure to halt the revolutionary tide in Greece might lead to catastrophe elsewhere. "If Greece should fall under the control of an armed minority," he explained, "the effect upon its neighbor Turkey would be immediate and serious." According to Truman, "confusion and disorder" might spread throughout the Middle East and on to Western Europe. The president's sweeping statements indicated that the administration's counterrevolutionary goals would have to be pursued beyond Greece.

The administration soon focused its attention on Western Europe. Unlike Greece, the Western European nations did not experience armed insurgencies. Instead, they faced the prospect of Communist electoral success. By 1947, Communist party power in France and Italy in particular had risen dramatically, and the Truman administration feared the peaceful extension of Soviet influence. From France, Ambassador Jefferson Caffrey employed alarmist language to describe the growing popularity of communism as "the advance of the 'Soviet Trojan Horse.'" The administration based its foreign policy in Western Europe on support not for conservative protectors of the status quo but for reformist Christian Democrats who might guide their nations along the path of progressive, capitalistic, postwar reconstruction. Economic aid, made available through the Marshall Plan, became the chief tool of American diplomacy. The $12 billion plan, announced in June 1947, provided aid to help rebuild Europe's shattered economy, reduce hunger, and reestablish a vigorous trade with the United States. But it was also designed to help combat political instability and revolution.

The Truman administration's counterrevolutionary policies proved effective in Europe. By 1949 the Greek Communists had been beaten back, and Christian Democrats reigned securely in France and Italy. But beyond Europe, in the non-Western or third world, American policymakers confronted a more complex and ambiguous revolutionary setting. World War II and the weakening of European colonial rule in much of Asia and the Middle East unleashed intense nationalism across the southern half of the globe. Even in independent nations, widespread poverty and breakdowns in governmental authority often spawned political radicalism and revolution. These unstable conditions threatened U.S. economic and security interests, but they also defied easy management by outsiders.

The Truman administration did not always oppose revolutionary change in the third world. When revolutions occurred peacefully, or when Soviet influence seemed to be absent, the administration accommodated fundamental changes in the status quo. The United States granted independence to the Philippines in 1946, confident that pro-American elements would dominate the new government. Washington also looked favorably upon Britain's peaceful transfer of power to moderate nationalists in India and Pakistan in 1947 and Burma and Ceylon in 1948. Even in cases such as Israel in 1948 and Indonesia in 1949, where considerable bloodshed accompanied movements for self-determination, the United States lent its support to non-Communist nationalists. During the early 1950s, when populist governments in Iran, Guatemala, and Bolivia either expropriated or regulated the holdings of foreign-based corporations, the Truman White House grudgingly tolerated such measures, owing in part to the lack of evidence pointing to direct Soviet involvement.

FANNING THE FLAMES OF NATIONALISM

Charles Werner, *Indianapolis Star,* 30 January 1952.

Yet the third world also produced revolutions that the Truman administration refused to condone. In China and Indochina, armed rebels adopted Marxist ideology and advocated sweeping social reforms on behalf of impoverished peasants. In each instance, the administration mistakenly viewed the uprisings as primarily Soviet-inspired and applied the counterrevolutionary principles set forth in the Truman Doctrine. Washington, however, did not succeed in establishing control over the two Communist revolutions in Asia.

In China, the administration attempted to defeat Mao Tsetung's Communist movement after 1945 by providing over $2 billion in military and economic aid to the corrupt authoritarian regime of Chiang Kai-shek. Some U.S. officials drew attention to long-standing disputes between Chinese and Russian Communists, and the limited nature of Soviet support for the former. Still, when Chiang's government approached collapse in late 1949, the Truman administration spurned Mao's secret overtures for negotiations and refused to grant diplomatic recognition to the new revolutionary regime. Having suffered a major foreign policy defeat, Washington simply refused to acknowledge new realities in China. In Indochina, where the Communist leader Ho Chi Minh organized a postwar, anticolonial rebellion against French rule, the United States acquiesced in France's effort to crush the uprising. In early 1950, following the China debacle, Washington began to provide direct military assistance to French forces. Fearing the spread of communism to Southeast Asia, the United States had deepened its military involvement in what would prove to be an intractable Asian revolution.

The administration's difficulties with China and Indochina demonstrated that some third world revolutions remained

largely immune to U.S. influence and suggested that the Truman Doctrine might be ill suited to non-Western regions. Indeed, President Truman seemed to speak to the problem in his inaugural address of 20 January 1949. In outlining the famous fourth point to his foreign policy, Truman called for a "bold new program" of economic and technical assistance for emerging areas. White House officials subsequently argued that the Point Four program would serve as an antidote to Communist revolution and help create a base for capitalist development in the third world. Although they certainly underestimated the difficulties inherent to the development process, the Point Four approach showed promise. It was clearly a more flexible policy than the Truman Doctrine and was better designed to deal with the root causes of political unrest. The administration and Congress, however, never made economic aid to non-Western nations a policy priority. Congress did not even act on Point Four in 1949, and when it was passed in May 1950, allocated a mere $35 million for the entire third world.

Revolutions have constituted a major element in global politics throughout the post–World War II era. As the first administration to confront these conditions, the Truman administration failed to come to terms with some of the major revolutions of its time and established important precedents that have since hindered America's ability to form an effective response. America's resistance to radical change has persisted well beyond the Truman years.

There is no single monograph that examines America's response to revolution during the Truman years. The topic has been touched upon, however, in a number of studies analyzing American attitudes toward revolution in the post–World War II era. One of the seminal works dealing with the subject is Senator J. William Fulbright's *The Arrogance of Power* (New York: Vintage Books, 1966). As is the case with much of the literature, Fulbright's study was influenced by the Vietnam War experience, and emphasizes America's limited revolutionary heritage and its difficulties in accommodating radical change in the third world. Gabriel Kolko also examines U.S. opposition to third world revolutions in *The Roots of American Foreign Policy: An Analysis of Power and Purpose* (Boston: Beacon Press, 1969), but argues that America's capitalist economy, especially its need for markets and raw materials, explains American efforts to suppress leftist revolutions. Richard Barnet's *Intervention and Revolution: The United States in the Third World* (New York: World Publishing, 1968) focuses on U.S. opposition to Communist insurgencies, and includes a thoughtful account of Truman's policies toward the Greek civil war. In *Liberal America and the Third World: Political Development Ideas and Foreign Aid and Social Science* (Princeton: Princeton University Press, 1973), Robert A. Packenham provides a starting point for understanding American economic development theory since 1945 and the use of foreign aid in both Europe and the third world as an antidote to revolution. Walter LaFeber discusses American antipathy for revolution and covers the Truman administration's policies toward volatile Central America in his book, *Inevitable Revolutions: The United States in Central America* (New York: W. W. Norton, 1984). Taking a broader approach, William Appleman Williams's *America Confronts a Revolutionary World: 1776–1976* (New York: William Morrow, 1976) is a collection of essays, written from the author's well-known revisionist perspective, that provides a sweeping account of the history of American attitudes and policies toward revolution. In dealing with the Truman years, Williams emphasizes the long-term ramifications of America's counterrevolutionary goals in Greece and China. In *Ideology and U.S. Foreign Policy* (New Haven: Yale University Press, 1987), Michael Hunt has written what is probably the most penetrating analysis of the subject. As part of his overall study of foreign policy ideology, Hunt highlights America's historical ambivalence toward foreign revolutions and gives a concise overview of the Truman years.

DENNIS MERRILL

Roosevelt, Anna Eleanor

(11 October 1886–7 November 1962)

Harry Truman learned he was president of the United States when Eleanor Roosevelt summoned him to the White House to inform him of her husband's death. They offered each other help. Although Truman graciously delayed his move into the executive mansion, Mrs. Roosevelt was packed and on her way to Hyde Park within days. The personal and political relationship that ensued combined grudging respect and persistent confrontation.

If Eleanor Roosevelt had been able to name the vice-presidential candidate in 1944, Henry Wallace would have been renominated. She believed he best shared her ideals for a secure and peaceful postwar world. Truman, she feared, represented the expediency of "boss-supported" politicians. But with FDR's blessing, Truman and his party backers had prevailed. Now he was president, unable to ignore the influence of FDR's widow.

In December 1945, Truman phoned Mrs. Roosevelt to ask her to join the U.S. delegation to the General Assembly of the United Nations. After some self-deprecating hesitation, she accepted, for the post offered a welcome focus for her public activism. Truman, for his part, hoped it would tie the respected guardian of New Deal liberalism to his administration. Her UN responsibilities, especially her chairing of the commission that wrote the Universal Declaration of Human Rights, brought her worldwide recognition. But the political gains for Truman proved elusive. The UN appointment stemmed neither her constant stream of advice nor her public criticism of policies with which she disagreed.

By 1947, her misgivings covered both domestic and foreign affairs. After Republican victories in the congressional elections the previous year, she shared the concern of many liberals that Truman was surrendering to the conservative, business-oriented wing of the Democratic party. She attended the all-day founding session of the Americans for Democratic Action (ADA), supporting the assembly of "New Deal exiles" with both words and money. The ADA came to be viewed as the bastion of the non-Communist left when Henry Wallace and his growing legion of radical supporters lay claim to FDR's mantle, but its original targets were Truman, his appointments, and his policies.

Eleanor Roosevelt was also wary of American foreign policy and growing militarism. Although she decried deceptive and hostile Soviet practices, she disliked the aggressive implications of the Truman Doctrine. His assurance that aid to Greece and Turkey was neither an assumption of traditional British

Eleanor Roosevelt, of the U.S. delegation, and U.S. Secretary of State Dean Acheson listen intently during a session of the UN General Assembly as Sweden denounces the Soviet Union for refusing to arbitrate a dispute concerning the shooting down of Swedish planes over the Baltic. 16 October 1952 (Associated Press/Wide World Photos)

roles nor a military solution to political problems failed to convince her. She wrote to tell him so. And when policy assumed the form of a naval show of force in the eastern Mediterranean, she shared her displeasure with all readers of her newspaper column.

At the same time, her support for the creation of a Jewish state became unflagging. Any sign of administration hesitation on behalf of the UN plan for partitioning Palestine brought letters of insistence from Eleanor Roosevelt. When the new state of Israel was invaded by its Arab neighbors, the barrage of correspondence continued. To her, American support for UN peacekeeping forces would ensure both the security of Israel and the integrity of UN decisions. Her reminders to Truman on both counts were incessant.

But an absence, not a torrent, of words marked their relationship during the 1948 campaign. The Roosevelt sons had tried to draft Dwight Eisenhower for the nomination. Their mother did not endorse their activities but neither did she dissociate herself from efforts to deprive Truman of renomination. Using her work at the United Nations as an excuse, she wrote the anxious president that "I have not and I do not intend to have a part in pre-convention activities."

Eleanor Roosevelt used the same dodge to avoid an endorsement after he was renominated. She stated her loyalty as a Democrat from which support for Truman had to be assumed. To her friends she confided her lack of enthusiasm for "such a weak and vacillating person [who] made such poor appointments in his Cabinet." She did respond to a last-minute plea for a radio address from Paris on Truman's behalf, recognition of the political clout seasoned campaigners believed she carried. Truman's victory surprised and pleased her, but she insisted he would still have to be closely monitored and constantly pressured to toe the progressive line.

UN activities consumed her attention after the election. She approved Truman's Point Four program which emphasized economic aid to developing nations. But as red-baiting increased at home, so did attacks on the United Nations and the principles of international cooperation. At the time of the 1952 national convention, Truman pleaded with her to defend the United Nations. She did so eloquently, but more out of personal conviction than out of any sense of loyalty to the president. He had pointedly failed to back her son James in his bid for governor of California two years before. Eleanor Roosevelt never forgot or forgave political slights to her family.

Confrontation occurred when the two aging Democrats tangled at the 1956 convention. Truman held a news conference advancing the candidacy of New York governor, Averell Harriman. Eleanor Roosevelt, who supported Adlai Stevenson, then met the press and countered the former president's remarks that Stevenson lacked knowledge of foreign policy. He was far more familiar with world affairs than Truman had been when he became president, she said quietly.

They also fenced on a personal level. Every Memorial Day, Eleanor invited a prominent speaker and guests to the Rose Garden at Hyde Park where FDR was buried. Bess and Harry Truman received annual invitations. Each year they accepted and each year, as the date neared, something prevented their attendance. In 1957, with more than a hint of sarcasm, Eleanor wrote her daughter, "I think Harry Truman *may* come this year." She had attended the dedication of the Truman Library earlier that year and wrote friends that "Mr. T beamed all day & we were *most* friendly." Truman did reciprocate and this time delivered the formal address at the Rose Garden ceremony.

Still they clashed. Eleanor Roosevelt permitted Democrats to use the occasion of her seventy-fifth birthday to hold a fundraising dinner. Eight presidential contenders sat on the dais and toasted the former First Lady. Truman presided. In concluding remarks, he castigated the "certain kind of liberals" who harmed the party. When the guest of honor rose to acknowledge the tributes, she turned directly to Truman and berated him for not welcoming all liberals into the Democratic fold. It was merely "a little difference," she wrote her daughter, but the *New York Times* devoted a full page to the confrontation.

Less than three years later, Harry Truman stood with John F. Kennedy and Dwight D. Eisenhower at the Rose Garden funeral of Eleanor Roosevelt as the three American presidents pondered the impact of this singular political figure.

The Eleanor Roosevelt–Harry S. Truman correspondence and copies of her columns, "My Day," can be found in the Eleanor Roosevelt collection at the Franklin D. Roosevelt Library, Hyde Park. Joseph Lash describes their relationship in *Eleanor: The Years Alone* (New York: W. W. Norton, 1972). Personal comments to family and friends can be found in letters collected and annotated by Lash in *A*

World of Love: Eleanor Roosevelt and Her Friends, 1943–62 (Garden City, N.Y.: Doubleday, 1984) and by Bernard Asbell in *Mother and Daughter: The Letters of Eleanor and Anna Roosevelt* (New York: Coward, McCann, & Geoghegan, 1982). William E. Leuchtenburg stresses the role of the former first lady as guardian of the FDR legacy in *In the Shadow of FDR: From Harry Truman to Ronald Reagan* (Ithaca, N.Y.: Cornell University Press, 1983).

LOIS SCHARF

See also Liberalism

Roosevelt, Franklin Delano

(30 January 1882–12 April 1945)

President of the United States, whose death elevated Truman from the vice presidency. Franklin D. Roosevelt cannot have been much impressed with Senator Harry Truman when they first talked in February 1935. Truman in his old age recalled, "I was practically tongue-tied," and attributed this to his awe of the presidency. Still Roosevelt himself, with his grand gestures, his easy camaraderie, his command of factual detail, his long, varied, distinguished career, and his great popularity with the people, must have seemed pretty awesome to the Missouri farm boy–businessman–county judge.

Roosevelt was concerned about Truman's association with Tom Pendergast, the notorious boss of Kansas City, but since Truman himself seemed unprepossessing, remaining silent in the Senate and seeking no legislation of his own, Roosevelt saw no need to pay much attention to him. His was a reliable, even a rubber-stamp vote for New Deal measures throughout his first

President Franklin D. Roosevelt with Vice President-elect Harry S. Truman and Vice President Henry A. Wallace, Washington, D.C., 10 November 1944. (United Press International/Bettmann Archives)

term; he even endorsed the Supreme Court–packing plan in 1937. He went off the reservation only twice, voting to override Roosevelt's veto of the veterans' bonus payment bills (1935–36) and refusing to desert Senator Pat Harrison when the White House (working through Pendergast) sought his support for Senator Alben Barkley for majority leader (1937). Truman was a firm party man, a politician who kept his promises and remembered his friends, a New Deal senator who found the company of anti–New Deal colleagues congenial, a supporter of Roosevelt's foreign policy who got on well with many isolationists. Still, his chances of renomination in 1940 looked dim in view of the conviction of Tom Pendergast for income tax evasion and the crumbling of his machine.

Roosevelt had become fond of Governor Lloyd Stark of Missouri, one of the earliest and most vociferous callers for a third term. Stark, claiming to be the man who destroyed Pendergast, announced against Truman and seemed to be the administration's candidate. But Roosevelt remained neutral in the primary, perhaps because he believed Truman's contention that Stark was disrupting the party, perhaps because he knew that Truman was one of his reliable foreign policy supporters, and perhaps because he knew how popular Truman was in the Senate. In the 1940 primary Truman put together a winning combination for survival: a vigorous personal campaign; a strong civil rights appeal to black voters (especially strong in St. Louis); full support from unions, especially railroad labor; endorsements by many senators, including his Missouri colleague Bennett Champ Clark, isolationist anti–New Deal Democrat; and late support from one of the St. Louis bosses, Robert E. Hannegan. He won a narrow primary victory, followed by a bigger one over his Republican opponent in November.

By this time Franklin Roosevelt was mainly concerned with building up the country's defenses while helping Britain to survive. On all the critical fights, from the repeal of the arms embargo ("cash and carry") in the fall of 1939 through the passage of the Lend-Lease Act in March 1941, Truman was a firm administration man. Already an experienced senatorial investigator—a skill he learned on the Interstate Commerce Committee from its redoubtable chairman Burton K. Wheeler of Montana—he secured passage of a resolution to set up a special committee to investigate the national defense program (February 1941). On a postelection trip he had found evidence of mismanagement in the hasty construction of army camps and profiteering on defense contracts. The committee had minuscule funding to begin with, but it had the backing of the Senate leadership and it included some of the ablest senators of both parties. Over the next three and a half years the Truman committee made headlines as a watchdog, often embarrassing military procurement officers as well as contractors and manufacturers, but essentially acting as a constructive, supportive force which Roosevelt soon came to appreciate.

Truman himself was a staunch supporter of the war effort, chiefly concerned to see that government funds were properly spent. He had now established a national reputation, thanks to his ability to find and retain good staff, his congenial relations with his committee colleagues, and his generally positive relations with the Roosevelt administration. He was also a strong advocate of American membership in a postwar collective security system. He supported the resolution developed by members of his committee calling upon the president and Congress to start planning such a body. This resolution (popularly known as B2 H2) was seen as premature by Roosevelt. But Truman and his Republican committee colleague, Joseph Ball of Minnesota, toured the Great Plains states in mid-summer 1943 under auspices of the United Nations Association, speaking in nineteen cities in what had been the heartland of isolationism.

By early 1944 Democratic leaders had begun to worry about the problem of presidential succession. The precariousness of Roosevelt's health was not widely known but his increasing irritability and testiness were. As the country was by now convinced that victory was near, the home front seemed to relax, to Roosevelt's displeasure. In February, infuriated by the refusal of Congress to grant a large increase in taxation, he vetoed a revenue act, calling it "a tax relief bill providing relief not for the needy but for the greedy." Majority Leader Barkley responded with a hot refutation, called for an override, and announced his resignation. The Democrats promptly reelected him unanimously and both houses overrode the veto, a unique action. Although Roosevelt was persuaded to make his peace with Barkley, it was now clear that the president was beginning to lose some of his political skills, as well as much of his famous amiability.

Roosevelt himself decided to run for a fourth time and no serious effort was made to block his renomination, in spite of what was known or questionable about his health. He was determined to lead his country to victory over Germany and Japan and to take part in establishing a lasting peace. He wrote Democratic National Chairman Robert E. Hannegan that if the convention nominated him, "I would accept and serve, but I would not run in the usual partisan, political sense." Roosevelt, never content to be a mere Democrat, now could take an above-politics stance as commander in chief.

Although he said in public that he preferred to have Vice President Henry A. Wallace as his running mate again, he did not seriously resist the efforts of Democratic leaders to dump Wallace. Wallace, whose recently developed passion for civil rights had antagonized many southerners, whose enthusiasm for continued friendship with the Soviet Union had alarmed many, and whose ardent advocacy of a government-directed economy upset many businessmen and farmers who had tired of wartime restrictions and controls, would have been even harder to put over than he had been in 1940. Now Roosevelt left Wallace to sink or swim. He sank—and was held down by city bosses and southerners in control of the convention who were determined to have a less controversial man on the ticket.

The man they settled on was Senator Truman. Edward J. Flynn, boss of the Bronx, summed up their reasoning in his memoirs: Truman had an excellent record with his investigating committee; he was a friend of labor; "he seemed to represent to some degree the conservatives in the party"; he came from a border state; and he had not made "racial remarks." Flynn concluded, "He just dropped into the slot." Much has been written by participants as well as historians about how Truman came to be nominated, but it can be boiled down to the triumph of practical politicians over the prophets of a new social order. The *New York Times* said of Truman: "If his selection does not add perceptible strength to the Democratic ticket, it certainly seems less likely to weaken it than most of the alternative choices that have been discussed."

Roosevelt's fourth-term campaign was launched with his rousing, hilarious speech to a Teamsters Union dinner in Washington on 23 September 1944. It overcame the effects of a photo taken in San Diego in July which showed him to be gaunt

Within four hours of Roosevelt's death, stable accession had been ensured. His wife and daughter at his side, Harry S. Truman is sworn in as thirty-third president of the United States by Chief Justice Harlan Fiske Stone. 12 April 1945. (Abbie Rowe, National Park Service/Courtesy of the Harry S. Truman Library)

though he could scarcely have been ready emotionally for his great responsibilities.

Truman entered office "in the shadow of FDR." He saw the war to an end without making a significant change in policy. Amicable relations with the USSR were already on the decline before 12 April because of Soviet occupation policies in Eastern Europe. Truman, in his abrupt way, halted Lend-Lease shipments to Europe, but he also sent Harry Hopkins, Roosevelt's wartime troubleshooter, to see Stalin in an attempt to show continuity of the wartime alliance. Out of Hopkins's mission came the summit conference at Potsdam in July, the last of the great wartime meetings.

On domestic issues, Truman could do little until after V-J Day. On 6 September he presented Congress with a twenty-one-point domestic program, essentially calling for the implementation of FDR's "Economic Bill of Rights," first proposed in his State of the Union address on 11 January 1944. Truman's program included some things he had already asked for (authority to continue economic controls, expanded unemployment compensation, and a permanent Fair Employment Practices Committee) as well as a long list of new measures to meet new problems (including full employment, farm supports, and public works). It was a shopping list, a declaration of intent, an affirmation of liberalism. But the twenty-one-point program fell on deaf ears in the midst of mounting problems of postwar readjustment and reconversion. Soon many New Deal liberals lost their faith in Truman and his new crew, many of them Missouri cronies with conservative views.

The Roosevelt coalition had come undone in the early postwar reaction. It is likely that it had already run out of steam. Truman had inherited the office from Roosevelt, but he would have to find his own way to develop programs, winning support in Congress and the country amidst international crises, rapid social change, and political uncertainties. The Roosevelt era was truly over.

and worn, and of a poorly delivered address he had made on 11 August at Bremerton Navy Yard, upon his return from his mid-summer trip to Hawaii and the Aleutians. Roosevelt did not make any other political speeches until late in the campaign, when he delivered major addresses in New York, Philadelphia, Chicago, Washington, and Boston. Truman crossed the continent on a strenuous speaking tour, designed in part to show himself to the American people while stressing the need to keep the experienced leadership of Roosevelt. Truman was never much of an orator, but he had learned how to punch over his message. He had at least a small share in FDR's fourth-term victory.

Between Election Day and the death of Roosevelt, Truman did not attract much public attention. After his inauguration he presided over the Senate but had no other major role to play. Roosevelt went off to Yalta for his last summit conference, returning to report to Congress in a rambling, listless speech. Truman helped secure the confirmation of Wallace as secretary of commerce in a bitter battle, but, as Margaret Truman has said, "The President continued to make no effort to bring Dad into the inner circle of the administration." On 12 April 1945 Franklin Roosevelt died at Warm Springs, Georgia, following a massive cerebral hemorrhage. Truman was now president,

Roosevelt's associates have left many autobiographies and diaries. Three of the most interesting for the Roosevelt-Truman connection are Edward J. Flynn, *You're the Boss* (New York: Viking, 1947); Samuel I. Rosenman, *Working with Roosevelt* (New York: Harper, 1952); and *The Price of Vision: The Diary of Henry A. Wallace, 1942–1946*, ed. John Morton Blum (Boston: Houghton Mifflin, 1973). Margaret Truman, *Harry S. Truman* (New York: Morrow, 1973) is informative about her father's reactions to Roosevelt. Basic for an understanding of FDR's health in his last year is Howard G. Bruenn, "Clinical Notes on the Illness and Death of President Franklin D. Roosevelt," *Annals of Internal Medicine* 72 (April 1970): 579–91. Vivid, if undocumented, is Jim Bishop, *FDR's Last Year* (New York, Morrow, 1974); his attempt to show Roosevelt's increasing decrepitude is marred by his efforts to read the mind of his characters. Basic for an understanding of the Roosevelt legacy are two major studies: Alonzo L. Hamby, *Beyond the New Deal: Harry S. Truman and American Liberalism* (New York: Columbia University Press, 1973), and William E. Leuchtenburg, *In the Shadow of FDR: From Harry Truman to Ronald Reagan* (Ithaca, N.Y.: Cornell University Press, 1983).

ROBERT E. BURKE

See also Election of 1944

Roosevelt, James

(23 December 1907–)

California Democratic National Committeeman (1948–52); a leader of the movement to draft Dwight D. Eisenhower for the Democratic presidential nomination in 1948. James Roosevelt, the eldest son of President Franklin D. Roosevelt, was born in Hyde Park, N.Y., and graduated from Harvard College. A partner in a Boston insurance firm from 1935 to 1937 and again briefly after World War II, from which he returned as a colonel in the U.S. Marine Corps, he had been prominent on a number of occasions as an aide to his father. He was chairman of the California State Democratic Committee in 1946 and an unsuccessful candidate for governor in 1950.

Early in Truman's presidency, Roosevelt became disenchanted with the president's failure to follow up on New Deal measures and with his conservative appointments. An organizer of the Independent Citizens Council of the Arts, Sciences and Professions, he moved back to mainstream Democratic politics during 1947 and worked behind the scenes to promote General Eisenhower's candidacy. Meanwhile, his brothers Elliott and Franklin, Jr., issued a public call for the general to accept the nomination, and the Americans for Democratic Action began to build an organization. Truman was incensed and angrily confronted Roosevelt during a California speaking trip. Eisenhower, who had already refused Truman's offer to deliver the nomination to him and who had discouraged the draft talk, finally took himself out of the race on the eve of the national convention. Left without a candidate, the movement to dump Truman collapsed, and the president went on to victory feeling that he owed nothing to the liberal group which had tried to deny him a second term.

Roosevelt later served as Democratic representative from California in Congress from 1955 through 1967, when he retired to private life.

A judicious summary of James Roosevelt's activities during the Truman period is to be found in Richard S. Kirkendall, "1948," in *History of Presidential Elections, 1789–1968*, ed. Arthur M. Schlesinger, Jr., 4:3099–3214 (New York: Chelsea House, 1971). Curtis Daniel MacDougall, *Gideon's Army* (New York: Marzani & Munsell, 1965), details much of Roosevelt's political activity from 1946 to 1948.

ALFRED B. ROLLINS, JR.

See also Eisenhower, Dwight David (photograph); Election of 1948

Rosenberg Case

On 16 June 1950, an obscure New York City electrical engineer Julius Rosenberg was picked up for questioning by the FBI. His apprehension marked the beginning of the "Rosenberg Case," which was only one element in the U.S. government's long-term investigation into Soviet espionage in the wartime atomic bomb

Hy Rosen, *Albany Times Union.*

project. Earlier revelations from the defection of Soviet code clerk Igor Gouzenko in Canada had led to the conviction of British scientist Alan Nunn May in 1946. Gouzenko's disclosures, as well as some material deciphered by means of a captured Soviet code book, led U.S. investigators to assume that there were also other Soviet agents in the Manhattan Project.

By the beginning of 1950, these various clues had led to the apprehension first of Klaus Fuchs, an important British physicist, and then of Harry Gold, Fuchs's American courier. Gold's confession implicated David Greenglass, a former machinist at Los Alamos. Greenglass named his brother-in-law, Julius Rosenberg.

At that point, the confessions stopped and the "case" began, for Rosenberg denied his guilt. Ultimately, both he and his wife, Ethel, Greenglass's sister, were tried, convicted, and sentenced to die. The cold war atmosphere of 1951 and the Rosenbergs' obvious Communist sympathies enabled the government to get the verdict it sought. Recently released FBI documents, however, make it clear that the main reason Ethel was put on trial was to force her husband to confess. President Truman for once "passed the buck" and left his successor to decide whether or not to grant clemency to the couple.

Although the Rosenbergs died on 19 June 1953, their case did not. The problem is that, even with the release of thousands of pages of FBI documents, the case still rests on the perhaps questionable testimony of one man, David Greenglass. The deaths of the Rosenbergs may have made it impossible for historians ever to find out the whole truth.

The recent study by Ronald Radosh and Joyce Milton, *The Rosenberg File* (New York: Holt, Rinehart & Winston, 1983), concludes that the Rosenbergs were guilty. The books by Walter and Miriam Schneir, *Invitation to an Inquest* (New York: Pantheon, 1983), and by the Rosenbergs' sons, Robert and Michael Meeropol, *We Are Your Sons*, 2d ed. (Urbana: University of Illinois Press, 1986), take the other side.

ELLEN W. SCHRECKER

See also Red Scare

Rosenman, Samuel Irving

(13 February 1896–24 June 1973)

New York politico, jurist, presidential adviser. Samuel Rosenman was special counsel to Franklin Roosevelt at the time of the president's death. Asked to stay on in office by President Truman, he continued to serve until February 1946, when he returned to private law practice in New York City. Despite the brief tenure, he and Truman developed an intimate political and personal association that ended only at Truman's death.

Rosenman was born in San Antonio, Texas, of Russian-Jewish immigrants who subsequently migrated to New York City. An honor graduate of Columbia College, he received a law degree, also from Columbia, after service as a lieutenant in World War I. During 1928, Rosenman, by then a veteran state legislator, was "loaned" by Tammany Hall to Franklin Roosevelt for his gubernatorial campaign and remained to serve in a variety of capacities in Roosevelt's gubernatorial and presidential administrations. Rosenman's most celebrated efforts were his contributions as speech writer, initiator of Roosevelt's brains trust, and editor of the thirteen-volume *Public Papers and Addresses of Franklin D. Roosevelt*.

During the earliest days of the Truman administration, Rosenman was arguably the White House staff member most useful in helping the president retain continuity with his predecessor. Furthermore, drawing upon his resources as a Roosevelt confidant, he served as publicist for Truman's domestic program as "New Deal thinking." After leaving Washington for financial reasons, Rosenman continued to perform as a Truman adviser (Israeli and labor issues in particular), but he declined Truman's offers of appointment as attorney general and as a court of appeals judge.

Rosenman remained professionally and politically active until the end of his life. He died in his sleep on 24 June 1973 after being hospitalized for lung congestion and a heart ailment.

Rosenman's ultimate assessment of Truman is provided in *Presidential Style: Some Giants and a Pygmy in the White House* (New York: Harper & Row, 1976), which he, with his wife, Dorothy Rosenman, was preparing at the time of his death and which she completed. His memoir *Working with Roosevelt* (New York: Harper & Bros., 1952), does not detail the Truman years, although there are references to him. For a more systematic effort to chronicle the Truman-Rosenman relationship, see Samuel B. Hand, *Advise and Counsel: A Political Biography of Samuel I. Rosenman* (New York: Garland Publishing, 1979).

SAMUEL B. HAND

Ross, Charles Griffith

(9 November 1885–5 December 1950)

Press secretary, 1945–50. A boyhood friend and classmate of Harry S. Truman, Charles G. Ross had gained considerable acclaim as a professor, Pulitzer Prize–winning reporter, editor, and Washington correspondent before being summoned to the White House after Truman's ascendancy in 1945. For five years he served as Truman's press secretary, although in fact, he filled a larger role. He was a close friend, trusted adviser, and confidant, a man who quietly helped frame policy—in tone and content—as well as announce it.

The son of a mining prospector father and a mother who supplemented the family income by giving piano lessons, Ross was born at Independence, Missouri. Encouraged by his grandmother who had been a schoolteacher, Ross began to read at an early age and at five, wrote short compositions to submit to her for her approval. He entered the Noland Grade School in 1891. A classmate was young Harry Truman, with whom he became fast friends. Both were avid readers (Ross's interests were in literature, while Truman preferred history and biography) and enthusiastic students. A favorite teacher of both was Matilda Brown—"Miss Tillie," as she was known—who taught English. When the class was graduated in 1901, Miss Tillie astonished

Charles Ross (l.) and Jonathan Daniels. (National Archives)

the spectators after the ceremony by throwing her arms around an embarrassed Ross and kissing him on the cheek. "When the rest of you do something worthwhile," she announced, "you'll get your reward, too." It was a lighthearted gesture, which Ross and Truman never forgot. More than forty years later, when Truman found himself in the White House, he sent for Charlie Ross, talked him into becoming his press secretary, and then suggested they call Miss Tillie to report the news to her—and to remind her that he too was now entitled to his reward.

After Ross graduated, Phi Beta Kappa, from the University of Missouri in 1905, he took a reporting job on the *St. Louis Post-Dispatch*, a crusading paper that had attained national prominence under its founder, Joseph Pulitzer. After three years there, Ross left to become part of the original three-man faculty at the University of Missouri's School of Journalism, the first such school in the world. Ross, an able teacher, became a full professor in 1918. During this period he wrote extensively, including one of the first textbooks on reporting. It was during these years, too, that he met Florence Griffin, whom he married on 20 August 1913; they would have two sons. In 1917 he took a sabbatical leave in Australia, where he worked as a subeditor on the *Melbourne Herald*.

Following his return to the United States in 1918, he rejoined the staff of the *Post-Dispatch* to set up its Washington bureau. Ross covered virtually every major national political story during the twenties and early thirties, and one of his investigative reports won the Pulitzer Prize for 1931. Shortly after, Pulitzer recalled Ross to St. Louis and put him in charge of the *Post-Dispatch*'s famed editorial page, which he directed from 1934 to 1938, after which he returned to Washington as a columnist and contributing editor. His work for the *Post-Dispatch* ended finally in April 1945, when Roosevelt's death put Harry Truman in the White House. Among the first persons Truman sent for was his old classmate, who reluctantly agreed to serve as press secretary.

Truman was to face some difficult moments in his dealings with the press. Massively distrustful of editors and columnists, he felt at ease only with the handful of reporters who covered the White House on a regular basis. Having received some early favorable comment on his snappy responses to reporters' questions (and understandably determined to appear confident and on top of the presidency), Truman often shot from the hip at news conferences, creating problems for himself and his undermanned, overworked press office. Given the amount of time Truman devoted to preparing for his weekly news conferences, however, the wonder is that he made no more mistakes than he did. Normally he would spend only the last thirty minutes before each conference cramming for it; in that frantic half-hour, Truman would meet with his press secretary and other advisers who would suggest the kinds of questions that might come up and help him formulate appropriate responses. More often than not, Ross and the staff anticipated the questions accurately. Nevertheless, the weekly news conference could be a wrenching experience for those in the press office. A successful conference was one where nothing awful happened.

"Truman gives out more news at one press conference than Roosevelt customarily gave out at ten," Ross wrote in September 1945. "Often a Roosevelt conference was nothing more than a sparring match between reporters and the president. . . . I think there is a greater flow of information under this administration than ever before. As far as possible, we are operating in a goldfish bowl." Despite this defense, however, there were repeated problems with leaks, and with hostile columnists and editorial writers. Ross, who was not an especially efficient administrator, brought some of the problems on himself. Official trips and other matters for which he had to arrange press coverage were apt to be disorganized. Nor was Ross overly concerned with spot news, for most of his own career had been devoted to news analysis. He knew little about the cut-throat competition that exists between reporters, especially wire service and broadcast journalists.

Ross rarely attempted to sell the president, to promote him for maximum effectiveness with the media. Ross released news as it happened, with little concern for optimal timing. One example of this occurred in June 1947 when Ross released several first-rate news stories on the same day that Secretary of State George C. Marshall was announcing his monumental European relief project in a major address at Harvard. As a result, Marshall was nearly knocked off the front pages by, of all people, the White House press secretary. "Ross never tried to gild a fact," the *New York Times* White House correspondent wrote his editor the night Ross died. Of all the tributes Ross received, this perhaps would have meant the most to him.

After five years in the White House—during which time he had had only five vacation days—Ross began to deteriorate physically, his Lincolnesque face reflecting the strain. A press conference fiasco of 30 November 1950 left reporters and their worldwide audiences with the erroneous impression that Truman was actively considering use of the atomic bomb against the North Korean and Chinese forces in Korea. Clarifications were issued and some sense of perspective was restored, but the headline damage had been done. Five days later, on 5 December 1950, Prime Minister Clement Attlee of Great Britain was in Washington for talks with Truman. Ross briefed the reporters afterward and then agreed to conduct an additional briefing for the NBC television cameras. While the crew was setting up for the interview, Ross slumped over at his desk, dead of a heart attack.

In the obituary tributes that followed, Ross was given highest marks for personal and professional integrity as a journalist and as a public official. Evaluations of his performance as a presidential image maker were less generous. The public image of Truman—often that of a cocky, profane man—was seriously misleading. In private, those in his inner circle said, Truman was quiet, soft-spoken, modest to the point of humility, and intensely respectful of his subordinates. This reversed the usual practice of many public personalities who behave impeccably in public but less so in private. Thus it was ironic that Truman's press secretary, the man who was supposed to cultivate his public image, was in fact far more effective with the Truman the public never saw. In private, Ross was an enormous restraining influence, arguably the most effective one Truman ever had. Time after time Ross would intercept some letter Truman had written in anger; Truman would follow the advice of "the old philosopher," as he called Ross, and throw the offending letter into the fire. Similarly, statements and speeches were often softened at Ross's behest.

It may be significant that on the evening Ross died—the night of Margaret Truman's Washington debut as a concert singer—Truman unloosed his famous profane letter to the *Washington Post*'s music critic who reviewed the performance unfavorably. Had Ross been alive, that letter would probably never have been mailed. Ross had helped create an atmosphere of moderation throughout the White House, a contribution whose importance would not be fully appreciated until after his death.

For a biography of Ross, see Ronald T. Farrar, *Reluctant Servant: The Story of Charles G. Ross* (Columbia: University of Missouri Press, 1968). Ross is also mentioned in Farrar, "Harry Truman and the Press: A View from Inside," *Journalism History* 8, no.2 (1981): 56.

RONALD T. FARRAR

See also Press, The; *St. Louis Post-Dispatch*

Rural Electrification Administration

When Harry Truman became president in April 1945, the task of electrifying farms and rural homes had already recovered from the delays imposed by World War II. Created in 1935 by executive order and given statute authority in 1936, the Rural Electrification Administration (REA) had managed to equip about one-third of America's farms with electricity by 1941. The REA was popular and Congress had passed the Pace Act in 1944 which set the interest rate of REA loans to the electric cooperatives at 2 percent. During the postwar years congressional supporters of the agency, such as John Rankin of Mississippi, managed to obtain generous appropriations for it, in some cases providing more funding than the REA officers requested. Strong lobbying by the National Rural Electric Cooperative Association (NRECA) partly accounted for the congressional funding. That development, plus farm prosperity and the wartime savings of families, which enabled them to wire their homes and purchase appliances, meant that electrification proceeded rapidly. Truman supported the REA, and when he left the White House, about 90 percent of America's farms had electric service.

Some minor controversy occurred over the construction of hydroelectric dams whose power was sold to REA cooperatives. The electrical industry opposed the generation of power for public bodies, but Truman strongly supported it. Hydroelectric dams, however, accounted for only a small portion of REA electricity—less than 20 percent—and their construction caused no significant debate over public power.

For a thorough history of the development of rural electrification, 1920–55, see D. Clayton Brown, *Electricity for Rural America: The Fight for the REA* (Westport, Conn.: Greenwood Press, 1980). One of the first histories of rural electrification (and written from a journalistic point of view) is Marquis Childs, *The Farmer Takes a Hand* (Garden City, N.Y.: Doubleday, 1953).

D CLAYTON BROWN

See also Army Corps of Engineers; Conservation; Reclamation

Russell, Richard Brevard, Jr.

(2 November 1897–21 January 1971)

U.S. senator from Georgia, 1935–71; critic of Truman's liberalism, especially his civil rights program. Richard B. Russell, Jr., was the first son and fourth child of thirteen children raised by Judge Richard B. and Ina Russell. Born in Winder, Georgia, Russell was educated at Gordon Military Institute at Barnesville and at the University of Georgia Law School. Upon graduation in 1918, he served seventy-nine days in the navy and then settled down in Winder to practice law with his father.

Very intelligent and highly ambitious, this scion of one of Georgia's leading families found a small-town law practice dull and unrewarding. In 1920 he ran successfully for a seat in the state House of Representatives and subsequently served five terms, including two, 1927 and 1929, as Speaker. In 1930 he was elected governor on a reform platform that called on the people to overthrow what he labeled the special interests. He concentrated on building additional highways and maintaining support for the state's public schools, calling them "the twin highways to progress." His main achievement as governor, however, was the reorganization of Georgia's state government. One important aspect of this reform was provision for a Board of Regents which established unified governance for all the institutions of higher education in the state.

When Senator William J. Harris suddenly died in 1932, Russell decided to run for the unexpired term. In another vigorous statewide campaign, he defeated Congressman Charles Crisp by a healthy margin and was sworn in as the nation's youngest senator on 12 January 1933. Until his death thirty-eight years later, no one challenged him for his Senate seat except Eugene Talmadge whom Russell soundly defeated in 1936.

In the early New Deal years, Russell supported most of the Roosevelt programs and was an especially strong backer of farm relief legislation. He was also the principal sponsor of the school lunch program. Russell cooled to the Roosevelt administration, however, when the president attempted to meddle in Georgia politics in 1938 and some New Dealers began to press for greater rights for blacks.

By the early 1940s, Russell had emerged as one of the country's leading senators. His growing seniority, his strong committee assignments, including Appropriations and Naval Affairs, his hard work, and his understanding of Senate rules combined to invest him with increasing power.

Two years after Russell arrived in Washington, he found Harry S. Truman, the new senator from Missouri, sitting two rows back of him in the Senate Chamber. Russell liked his new colleague, but considered him average. He remarked years later that no poll of senators or of the general public would have placed Truman among the top twenty senators. Nevertheless, when Truman became president, Russell wanted to support the new administration. He strongly backed Truman's efforts to block Russian expansionism, but believed that the president's initial responses were too timid. After passage of the Marshall Plan, which Russell supported, he opposed most foreign economic aid. Russell believed that such assistance was wasteful and a drain on taxpayers without sufficient or commensurate benefits to the United States. He supported Truman's efforts to help farmers, federal aid to education, and several other of the president's domestic policies.

Russell broke with Truman over two major issues—labor legislation and civil rights. He voted for the Taft-Hartley law and to override Truman's veto. But it was Truman's stand on civil rights that most alienated Russell. Raised in a strictly segregated state, Russell was thoroughly imbued with the rightness of racial segregation. He did not dislike blacks and was not a Negro baiter like some other southern politicians. But racial mixing in schools and elsewhere, especially interracial marriage, was abhorrent to him. He feared that civil rights laws would be only an entering wedge to what he called "mongrelization" of the white race and the destruction of his beloved Anglo-Saxon culture. Indeed, Russell had become head of the southern bloc in the Senate which had successfully turned back most major civil rights bills during the previous decade. He called Truman's 2 February 1948 speech on civil rights "the most outrageous affront to the people of our section that we have had to face since Reconstruction."

Russell and most southerners strongly opposed Truman's renomination in 1948, mainly because of the president's stand on civil rights. After considerable pressure from southerners, Russell permitted his name to be placed in nomination at the Democratic convention as token opposition to Truman and the party platform. Despite Truman's renomination, Russell did not join the Dixiecrats. He voted for Truman, but refused to work for his reelection.

Nevertheless, in his second administration Truman found Russell an important backer on his defense policies and the Korean War. His greatest help to the president, however, came in 1951 after Truman fired Gen. Douglas MacArthur. Russell chaired the Senate committee that investigated this highly emotional controversy and quietly defused the issue. But Russell continued to fight Truman's civil rights proposals. By 1952 Russell had become so unhappy over the Democratic party's stand on civil rights that he finally agreed to make a serious bid for the presidential nomination. At the Democratic convention he received a high of 294 votes, mainly from southerners, before losing to Adlai Stevenson.

Russell served in the Senate until January 1971, the equivalent of three terms after Truman left the White House. As chairman of the Armed Services Committee during most of that period, he worked hard to build up the nation's military strength. He opposed American involvement in Vietnam, but once U.S. forces were committed, he favored blockading and bombing North Vietnam into submission. He also was always a strong friend of American farmers and worked hard to enact helpful farm relief laws.

But much of his effort in the post-Truman years was directed at resisting civil rights laws. Nevertheless, Congress passed important acts in 1964 and 1965. By that time Russell headed a weak and ineffective southern bloc in opposing most of the aspects of President Lyndon Johnson's Great Society program. Suffering from deteriorating health in the 1950s and 1960s, and increasingly out of tune with the major directions of national life, he was greatly discouraged about the nation's future. Nevertheless, during his thirty-eight years in the Senate, Russell had made his mark.

Russell was a man of wide interests, including sports, and he was a voracious reader. He never married and led a rather restricted social life. In many respects he was a good example of the southern elite—talented, reserved, polite, deferential to women, and politically wise. Many people admired him, but few could be called intimate friends. He died of respiratory difficulties at Walter Reed Army Medical Center on 21 January 1971 and a few days later was buried in the family cemetery at Russell just outside Winder, Georgia, his birthplace.

Two useful studies of Russell's career are Karen Kalmar Kelly, "Richard B. Russell: Democrat from Georgia" (Ph.D. diss., University of North Carolina, 1979), and David D. Potenziani, "Look to the Past: Richard B. Russell and the Defense of Southern White Supremacy" (Ph.D. diss., University of Georgia, 1981). Gilbert C. Fite is currently writing a full-scale biography of Russell.

GILBERT C. FITE

See also South, The

Russia

See Soviet Union

S

St. Louis Post-Dispatch

On a hot August day in 1934 a "scream," according to an observer, was heard around the country. In a tone of outrage the *St. Louis Post-Dispatch* declared that an "obscure" county judge named Harry S. Truman who was "scarcely known outside the confines of Jackson County" had been foisted on the Democratic party of Missouri as its candidate for the U.S. Senate by an unsavory "city boss," Tom Pendergast of Kansas City. Ironically, the author of the paper's editorial was Charles G. Ross, a schoolmate of Truman's back in Independence and one day to be President Truman's press secretary. The scream was heard countrywide because the *Post-Dispatch* had become one of a handful of nationally known liberal journals, and its protest placed a stigma upon Truman that he never quite lived down.

The *Post-Dispatch* was founded in 1878 by Joseph Pulitzer, a Hungarian immigrant who utilized the paper to fashion a style of mass circulation journalism which, when taken to the *New York World* four years later, revolutionized American newspaper publishing. As it developed, the style stressed sensational, gossipy news and entertainment features such as sports and comics to attract a mass readership. As part of this style Pulitzer invented a technique known as "multiple crusading," again often couched in sensational terms but also motivated by a genuine dedication to the public's welfare. As such Pulitzer joined—indeed, helped inaugurate—what would evolve after 1900 into the Progressive movement of reform which sought to adjust American democracy to the new age of industrialism and urbanism. Because Pulitzer looked upon the *World* as his national pulpit, he confined his St. Louis paper to local and regional issues. But even here the paper acquired wide notice when Claude Wetmore, *Post-Dispatch* city editor, and Lincoln Steffens coauthored the famous piece "Tweed Days in St. Louis" for *McClure's* magazine. The paper crusaded for years to destroy St. Louis's brand of bossism, the corrupt Ed Butler machine, which reformer Joseph Folk finally accomplished. Aided by the *Post-Dispatch*, Folk discovered that some public utility magnates belonged to a group of powerful financial and industrial interests. The paper dubbed the group the "Big Cinch," contributing to Butler's downfall. In state politics, the *Post-Dispatch* backed Folk for the governorship and supported him in reforms at the state level, including establishment of state regulation of business and industry and, even, the beginnings of protection for the laboring classes.

The *Post-Dispatch* gradually shed its confinement to local and regional affairs after 1911 when a second Joseph Pulitzer, upon his father's death, became the paper's publisher. A key figure in this change was Oliver K. Bovard, who acquired a towering reputation nationally as the *Post-Dispatch*'s managing editor. Bovard established a Washington bureau for his paper and appointed Charles Ross its chief. Ross directed a group of correspondents among whom was Paul Y. Anderson, a key reporter in helping Senator Thomas Walsh uncover the Teapot Dome scandal. The paper launched into numerous crusades including one on behalf of Anna Lerner whom the State Department refused to let enter the United States, suspecting her of communist sympathies. This crusade illustrates another facet of the *Post-Dispatch*'s policy for which the paper was to become famous—its concern for civil rights. In accomplishing these purposes the paper's editors and reporters developed a close relationship with a coterie of radical senators, Republican and Democrat, who stood for the same principles and issues the paper fought for. One of them, George W. Norris of Nebraska, called the *Post-Dispatch* the "*Manchester Guardian* of America."

From the first the *Post-Dispatch* tended to support Democrats in presidential elections, on the grounds that they favored internationalist policies abroad and opposed Republican policies of business privilege at home. In 1936, however, Joseph Pulitzer II, coming into his own as active director of his paper's policies and influenced—so it was said—by wealthy friends, opposed what he believed to be the excesses of New Deal policies which were choking the "competitive system," and he directed the paper to endorse Alfred Landon against Franklin Roosevelt. In so doing, he dropped ardent New Dealer Clark McAdams as editorial editor and installed Charles Ross in his place; soon after, Oliver Bovard, whose outlook was even left of Mc-Adams's, resigned as managing editor. This was not the last time Pulitzer exerted his authority.

Given its history of consistent and vigorous opposition to corruption in politics together with Pulitzer's distaste for New Deal centralization, it was scarcely surprising that the *Post-Dispatch* became a militant opponent of Harry Truman when he entered statewide politics in 1934 under the tutelage of the notorious Boss Pendergast. The paper dismissed as irrelevant Truman's personal qualifications, saying, in Ross's words, "He may have been, for all we know, a capable Judge; he may become a capable Senator." What mattered was that a corrupt machine, utilizing fifty thousand "ghost" votes, had imposed this man upon the people of Missouri. Moreover, the paper said, "Judge Truman . . . has declared himself unqualifiedly for the New Deal and all its works." In 1940, when Truman ran for re-election, the *Post-Dispatch* was even more vehement, saying that his election would be "a sad defeat for the people of Missouri," and between news items ran the line BEAT TRUMAN. The paper never cooled in its dislike of the senator; in 1944, when the paper supported FDR for a fourth term, it simply ignored the presence of Truman on the ticket as candidate for vice president. In 1948 when he ran for election as president, Joseph Pulitzer was still so hostile to Truman that, once more, this time riding roughshod over his entire editorial staff save one, he had the *Post-Dispatch* endorse Thomas E. Dewey, accusing Truman for "demagogy" for his attacks on the Republican "no-good, do-nothing" Congress. The paper condemned Truman for a "supine surrender to pressure groups" which "may end the economic flexibility necessary to a competitive democratic economy."

Yet, as a liberal paper, the *Post-Dispatch* more often than not supported the president's policies. Although it sharply criticized Truman for cronyism in making mediocre appointments to such offices as Supreme Court justice and castigated him for his loyalty program's encroachment on civil liberties, the *Post-Dispatch*, led by Editorial Editor Irving Dilliard, strongly supported Truman's struggle against McCarthyism as well as, generally, his Fair Deal continuation of the New Deal. In foreign affairs the *Post-Dispatch* applauded Truman's path-breaking Greek-Turkish aid bill, establishment of the North Atlantic Treaty Alliance, and, above all, the Marshall Plan. Most spectacular was the paper's support of the president's firing of Douglas MacArthur as Far East commander during the Korean War. Indeed, the *Post-Dispatch* was one of few journals in the United States to fearlessly come to the aid of this often-beleaguered president.

The material bearing on the *Post-Dispatch* is voluminous. Most important are primary sources, particularly the complete file of the newspaper itself from 1878 to the present, the Joseph Pulitzer I collections at Columbia University and the Library of Congress, and the Joseph Pulitzer II collection in the Library of Congress. Most of these are available in microfilm. Among general histories of the *Post-Dispatch* are Charles G. Ross and Carlos F. Hurd, *The Story of the Post-Dispatch* (published by the paper, 1950), and Roger Butterfield, "The St. Louis Post-Dispatch—Pulitzer's Prize," *Collier's*, 16 December–23 December 1950. For material involving Harry S. Truman and the *Post-Dispatch*, see Jonathan Daniels, *The Man of Independence* (Philadelphia: J. B. Lippincott, 1950); Richard Lawrence Miller, *Truman: The Rise to Power* (New York:

McGraw-Hill, 1986); Alonzo L. Hamby, *Beyond the New Deal: Harry S. Truman and American Liberalism* (New York: Columbia University Press, 1973); and, for Truman's private observations, Robert H. Ferrell, ed., *Dear Bess: The Letters from Harry to Bess Truman, 1910–1959* (New York: W. W. Norton, 1983).

JULIAN S. RAMMELKAMP

See also Press, The

Saudi Arabia

Although Harry Truman lacked Roosevelt's personal fascination with Saudi Arabia, he took an active interest in promoting American interests there. The driving force behind the Truman administration's interest was securing the vast potential of Arabian oil. The administration left most of this to private American oil companies; yet between 1945 and 1953, Truman approved a wide variety of initiatives designed to enhance American-Saudi ties and to support the companies' efforts. In many respects, the origins of the special relationship between the United States and Saudi Arabia had its roots in the Truman years. Indeed, despite the strains that developed over American support for the establishment of Israel, the Truman administration by 1953 could justly claim that it had left U.S.-Saudi relations in better shape than it had found them.

Like his predecessor, Harry Truman had little exposure to the Middle East or its oil when he entered the White House, although, through his chairmanship of a Senate committee investigating the national defense program, he had been exposed to the problems of the wartime oil shortage and supply. Like many in the foreign policy community, the new president was struck by the growing importance of petroleum to waging war and to securing the peace.

It was his advisers at State and Defense as well as the indomitable Harold Ickes who began to familiarize Truman with the particulars of Middle East oil and draw his attention to the specifics of the situation in Saudi Arabia. In fact, within months of his assuming office, State Department officials sought the president's formal approval for economic aid to the Saudi king Abdul Aziz Ibn Sa'ud and permission to construct an airfield for U.S. military use at Dhahran in eastern Saudi Arabia. In spite of the diminished importance of the airfield from a military perspective and the doubts of many State Department economists about the wisdom of subsidizing the Saudis, Truman approved both initiatives.

Both of these issues—subsidizing the Saudis until oil revenues increased and military assistance—were to become the focus of the Truman administration efforts to support Saudi Arabia. In an effort to enhance U.S.-Saudi ties and thus preserve the American stake in Saudi oil, U.S. officials, led by the Department of State, lobbied for Export-Import Bank loans in 1946 and again in 1950. Later under Point Four, the United States dispatched a technical team to help streamline the Saudi budgetary and administrative system. Similarly, despite later difficulties over U.S. access to the Dhahran airfield, American interest in the facility and the establishment of a military training mission reflected the importance the United States attached to making good on its commitments to Saudi Arabia.

What drove this interest was the significance of Saudi oil in the eyes of the foreign policy and defense establishments. The government's oil experts saw Saudi oil not so much as a source for the United States but as a way to support European recovery without draining Western Hemisphere reserves—deemed vital in the event of another war. Although the United States left the development of oil to the private companies, administration officials seemed determined to do what they could to facilitate American companies' interests, thereby boosting those of the American government. One of the projects that had almost unanimous official support was the Trans-Arabian Pipeline (TAPLINE)—a pipeline officials believed would make Middle East oil more available for European recovery. Toward this end, the government approved the companies' requests for special licenses for the export of steel.

The end of the war seemed to ease the anxieties of those in government interested in securing the American stake in Saudi oil, but the postwar period created new challenges. Those State Department officials who had resented and feared Great Britain's traditional influence in Saudi Arabia now saw new threats from the Soviet Union and from increasing American involvement in the Palestine question. If American interests in the Middle East were to be protected, they argued, the United States would have to deny the Soviets opportunities and enhance relationships with key Arab governments. Soviet ambitions in the Middle East combined with a Palestine policy that alienated the Arabs, State Department officers repeatedly warned their superiors, were a deadly combination that could threaten American access to oil and open up avenues for Soviet advances. While the government's Middle Eastern experts argued that Ibn Sa'ud was perhaps the least likely ruler to want to deal with the Soviets, they were concerned that he would also seek to distance himself from the United States. Indeed, as guardian of the holy cities of Mecca and Medina, Ibn Sa'ud was acutely sensitive to anything affecting Jerusalem, Islam's third holiest site.

Nonetheless, Truman, who was clearly irritated by the intense lobbying of both the Zionists and his own State Department on the Palestine issue, seemed to give little weight to either Saudi Arabia or its oil as he made his decision to support the November 1947 UN partition plan or to recognize the new state of Israel in May 1948. A number of calculations influenced Truman's thinking. First, he seemed determined to support American commitments to a Jewish homeland, particularly after the Nazi genocide against European Jewry; second, there were important electoral considerations; third, by the spring of 1948, it appeared that the Zionists were prepared to establish a state regardless of what the United States did; and finally, his political advisers said that Ibn Sa'ud needed the United States more than America needed him and thus that he was unlikely to strike out against American oil interests. In the end, this prediction proved correct. Ibn Sa'ud was willing and able to separate his own economic and political stake in maintaining a U.S. connection from his opposition to American policy toward Palestine. Although it would be more difficult for Ibn Sa'ud's successors to follow his example, the Palestine issue continued to be a manageable factor in U.S.-Saudi relations until Ibn Sa'ud's death in 1953.

The Truman administration's policies toward Saudi Arabia invariably overlapped with the U.S. approach to Middle East oil. Among the best treatments of Truman and Arabian oil are Irvine H. Anderson, *Aramco, The United States, and Saudi Arabia: A Study in the Dynamics of Foreign Oil Policy* (Princeton: Princeton University Press, 1981), and David S. Painter, *Oil and the American Century: The Political Economy of U.S. Foreign Oil* (Baltimore: Johns Hopkins University Press, 1986). For a broader look at U.S.-Saudi relations between 1945 and 1953, see Malcolm Peck, "Saudi Arabia in United States Foreign Policy to 1958: A Case Study in the Sources and Determinants of American Policy" (Ph.D. diss., Fletcher School of Law and Diplomacy, 1970). The best treatment of Truman, Saudi oil, and the Palestine issue can be found in Aaron David Miller, *Search for Security: Saudi Arabian Oil and American Foreign Policy, 1939-1949* (Chapel Hill: University of North Carolina Press, 1980).

AARON D. MILLER

See also Israel; Oil Policy

Sawyer, Charles

(10 February 1887–7 April 1979)

Secretary of commerce, 1948–53. Charles Sawyer, born near Cincinnati of schoolteacher parents, graduated from Oberlin College and the University of Cincinnati. He practiced law, engaged in state and local Democratic politics, served as lieutenant governor of Ohio, and owned a string of newspapers. Following a brief stint on Truman's Loyalty Review Board, Sawyer accepted the president's invitation in May 1948 to replace Harriman as head of the Commerce Department.

As a cabinet member, Sawyer attempted to reverse antibusiness attitudes within the administration. He emphasized cooperation between business and government and reinvigorated the Business Council as a network for channeling business ideas into the Fair Deal. During the 1949 recession, Sawyer undertook a nationwide tour, soliciting suggestions from businessmen about federal economic policy. In April 1952, he was at the center of the constitutional crisis over the administration's seizure of the steel industry, although his role was administrative rather than policy-making.

Throughout his tenure, the secretary's relations with Truman were cordial, and although the president appreciated that Sawyer alone among cabinet members had practical election experience, his contribution to the Fair Deal was managerial. Sawyer returned to Cincinnati at the conclusion of the Truman administration to resume his legal, business, community service, and philanthropic activities.

Sawyer's personal papers are on deposit at the Truman Library. His memoir, *Concerns of a Conservative Democrat* (Carbondale: Southern Illinois University Press, 1968), provides details on his life.

WILLIAM O. WAGNON, JR.

See also Cabinets (photograph)

Scandals

Charges linking Truman administration officials to corruption in federal agencies emerged during Truman's second term as president. By 1952, the Republicans could exploit the "mess in Washington" as a campaign issue. None of the allegations charged that Truman himself was involved in illicit activities, although critics often raised the specter of his earlier associations with the Democratic machine in Kansas City, charging that Pendergast politics had come to Washington.

Slow to recognize corruption as a threat to his administration, Truman discounted charges against his subordinates as attempts by political opponents, the opposition press, or publicity-seeking congressional committee chairs to embarrass the president. Convinced of the loyalty of close subordinates, he refused to acknowledge corruption, real or alleged, as a significant problem. His intransigence often fostered adversarial relationships with critics that had political costs.

A pattern of presidential reaction emerged in response to relatively minor incidents during Truman's first term. Secretary of the Interior Harold Ickes, warning of the danger of another Teapot Dome, resigned in 1946 in opposition to the nomination of California oilman Edwin Pauley to be under secretary of the navy. Pauley withdrew his name from consideration, but the following year he became the center of another controversy. He and Brig. Gen. Wallace H. Graham, the president's personal physician, were among those charged with speculation in grain futures after the president condemned the practice. Truman backed both men and retained Graham as his doctor.

The major scandals of Truman's presidency erupted during his second term. Influence peddling uncovered by congressional investigations, abuse of the lending authority of the Reconstruction Finance Corporation (RFC), and corruption within the Bureau of Internal Revenue (BIR) composed the bill of particulars for the corruption issue exploited by Republicans in 1952.

In the summer of 1949, the president's military aide, Maj. Gen. Harry H. Vaughan, became enmeshed in controversy. The Senate's Investigations Subcommittee charged that influence peddlers known as "five-percenters" gained favors through their access to Vaughan. The investigation did not prove that Vaughan had done anything illegal, but his receipt of a deep freezer became a symbol of corruption. Truman refused to admit any wrongdoing, failed to deal with Vaughan's indiscretions, and fostered a mutually uncompromising relationship with the congressional committee investigating the role of the five-percenters. Similarly, Truman and Senator J. William Fulbright battled over corruption in the RFC for months, provoking revelations that embarrassed the administration before Truman accepted reforms similar to those proposed by the committee.

During 1951, an investigation of the BIR revealed that tax officials had accepted bribes, used their offices to generate other business, embezzled federal funds, and tolerated corruption by subordinates. The scandal prompted the dismissal of several collectors of internal revenue, an assistant attorney general, and the chief counsel of the BIR. An investigation under the Department of Justice collapsed, precipitating the dismissal of Attorney General J. Howard McGrath, the highest ranking victim of the scandals.

The president and his staff tried to develop a positive response to the corruption issue late in 1951. Yet, little that was original or effective emerged. The administration relied principally on plans originated by others, which sought to reorganize executive agencies and place their employees under civil service. A limited response that met with only partial success, the administration's effort failed to remove the corruption issue from 1952 presidential politics. As a major Republican issue, it influenced the Democratic presidential nomination and the fall campaign. The issue fostered division between Democratic candidate Adlai E. Stevenson and the president. Although Truman campaigned vigorously, his effort was directed as much toward salvaging the reputation of his administration as electing Stevenson.

Truman maintained his reputation for personal integrity in spite of the scandals, but his faith in the integrity of his subordinates and his loyalty to them were often counterproductive.

Jules Abels's *The Truman Scandals* (Chicago: Henry Regnery Co., 1956) is based on the transcripts of congressional hearings. Andrew J. Dunar's *The Truman Scandals and the Politics of Morality* (Columbia: University of Missouri Press, 1984) examines the reactions of the Truman administration to charges of scandal.

ANDREW J. DUNAR

See also Election of 1952; Ickes, Harold LeClair; Pauley, Edwin Wendell, Sr.; Reconstruction Finance Corporation; Vaughan, Harry H.

Lute Pease, 1952. (Library of Congress)

Schlesinger, Arthur Meier, Jr.

(15 October 1917–)

The Truman years were great years for Arthur Schlesinger, Jr. The son and namesake of a prominent historian, Schlesinger graduated from Harvard College in 1938 and spent one year at Cambridge University. He avoided the "Ph.D. mill" with a three-year stint at Harvard's prestigious Society of Fellows and wartime intelligence work. In 1945 he published *The Age of Jackson*, which portrayed Andrew Jackson as an activist liberal president in the tradition Franklin Roosevelt exemplified. An impressed Harry Truman read the book on his vacation cruise. The book resulted in a 1946 Pulitzer Prize and a tenured position in Harvard's history department.

In 1947 Harvard's "boy wonder" helped found the Americans for Democratic Action (ADA), an organization combining the liberal social idealism of the 1930s with the anti-Communism of the 1940s. Characteristically, Schlesinger and his allies supported Truman's loyalty program—with reservations. Although not quite wild about all of Harry's domestic policies, they preferred Truman to Henry Wallace's Communist-tainted Progressive campaign in 1948.

In his 1949 book, *The Vital Center: The Politics of Freedom*, Schlesinger positioned liberalism between the extremist perfectionism of both the Left and the Right. "The spirit of the new radicalism is the spirit of the center," Schlesinger argued, "the spirit of human decency opposing the extremes of tyranny." Jonathan Daniels praised the Niebuhrian essay as "one of those books which may suddenly and clearly announce the spirit of an age to itself."

Although increasingly disappointed with Truman on the domestic front (fearing liberals were being taken for granted, Schlesinger supported the floor revolt at the 1950 ADA convention critical of the Democratic party), Schlesinger defended Truman's foreign policies. He advised the Economic Cooperation Administration in 1948 and the Mutual Security Administration in 1951–52. Schlesinger's qualified admiration of President Truman was most apparent in the book he coauthored in 1951 with Richard H. Rovere, *The General and the President and the Future of American Foreign Policy*. The authors applauded Truman's "great and simple courage" in Korea and debunked the "MacArthur myth." But they criticized the president's failure to sell the policy to the American people. "President Truman has the great virtue of rising to occasions," the authors wrote. "He lacks the greater virtue of transcending them." Truman, in short, was "a Polk rather than a Jackson or a Roosevelt."

In his subsequent work as the memoirist of John F. Kennedy's thousand days, the biographer of Robert F. Kennedy, and a leading twentieth-century historian, Schlesinger continued to give Truman qualified praise. In a twist reflecting the slowed advance of reform and the traumas of Vietnam, Schlesinger the historian preferred Truman's domestic policy to his foreign policy. In *The Cycles of American History* (1986), Schlesinger hailed Truman's Fair Deal as years "of action and passion, of idealism and reform." In his historical polemic against Richard Nixon and the Vietnam War, *The Imperial Presidency* (1974), Schlesinger blamed Truman's Korea policy for "dramatically and dangerously enlarg[ing] the power of future President to take the nation into major war." Schlesinger has repeatedly characterized Truman as "doughty"—a doer, not a leader.

Schlesinger's biography has yet to be written. His entry in *Current Biography* (1979), pp. 329–32, surveys his career. In *Beyond the New Deal: Harry S. Truman and American Liberalism* (New York: Columbia University Press, 1973) Alonzo L. Hamby places Schlesinger and the ADA in a broader context. Steven M. Gillon, *Politics and Vision: The ADA and American Liberalism, 1947–1985* (New York: Oxford University Press, 1987) illuminates Schlesinger's relationship with the ADA.

GIL TROY

See also Americans for Democratic Action; Liberalism

Schwellenbach, Lewis Baxter

(20 September 1874–10 June 1948)

Secretary of labor, 1945–48. Lewis Schwellenbach was born in Superior, Wisconsin, one of four children of German-American parents. When he was eight, his family moved to Spokane, Washington, where his father died six years later, forcing the teenager to work to help support his family. Schwellenbach worked his way through the University of Washington and received his law degree in 1917; shortly thereafter he entered the U.S. Army as a private. Following his discharge in 1919 he practiced law, specializing in labor law. During the 1920s he became interested in politics and ran unsuccessfully for governor in 1932. With strong labor support he was elected to the U.S. Senate in 1934, as a part of a group of freshman Democrats known as the "Young Turks." This group included Carl Hatch, Sherman Minton, and Harry S. Truman.

After he took his seat in the Senate in January 1935, Schwellenbach soon began to make his presence felt as an acknowledged leader of the "Young Turks." In 1935, he and Truman won national attention by curbing one of Huey Long's oratorical sprees. The episode was an early indication of the developing friendship between the two men. During Truman's 1940 reelection campaign, Schwellenbach traveled to Sedalia, Missouri, to make a speech in support of his candidacy.

In the Senate Schwellenbach established a record as a spokesman for labor. In 1939 he announced his candidacy for reelection, but later decided not to run when President Roosevelt announced he would appoint him to the district judgeship for the eastern district of Washington after he had completed his Senate term. Some observers considered the judgeship a reward for the outspoken New Deal senator.

In 1945, six weeks after Truman became president, he appointed Judge Schwellenbach to succeed Frances Perkins as the nation's fifth secretary of labor. He took over the post on 1 July 1945. The appointment was applauded by William Green, president of the American Federation of Labor.

By the end of 1945, Schwellenbach's duties became arduous as strike after strike swept the country, seriously interfering with Truman's postwar reconversion plans. For months the auto industry in Detroit was tied up. Later the steelworkers and electrical workers went on strike. The trainmen and locomotive engineers' brotherhoods tied up the nation's transportation system for forty-eight hours until President Truman took drastic actions. Nevertheless, Schwellenbach's close friendship with Philip Murray, president of the CIO, withstood political differences during this period, and in May 1946, when the CIO was making strong attacks on the Truman administration, he was invited to appear as a speaker at the United Steelworkers convention.

Congressional opposition to labor power grew rapidly throughout 1946 and many measures were proposed to curb labor's excesses. Schwellenbach persuaded Truman to veto the Case bill which provided for a thirty -day cooling-off period before calling a strike. Schwellenbach also opposed the Taft-Hartley Act which passed over Truman's veto in 1947. In March of that year Schwellenbach lost much of his liberal support when he openly advocated that legislation be passed to outlaw the Communist party on the grounds that its purpose was to destroy the government.

Schwellenbach, suffering from poor health, limited his activities during his last days in office. He died in 1948.

For further information on Truman and Schwellenbach, see *Congressional Directory, 1945; Who's Who in America, 1944–45;* and *Current Biography*, 1945. See also Arthur F. McClure, *The Truman Administration and the Problems of Postwar Labor, 1945–1948* (Rutherford, N.J.: Fairleigh Dickinson University Press, 1969), and R. Alton Lee, *Truman and Taft-Hartley: A Question of Mandate* (Lexington: University of Kentucky Press, 1966).

ARTHUR F. McCLURE II

See also Labor

Science and Technology

During World War II the structure of American scientific research and development underwent a fundamental shift. Before the war American science, relatively small in scale, had been funded primarily from regular university budgets and eleemosynary sources. The federal government's role was limited to mission-oriented research in specific fields, chiefly agriculture and the military (the army and navy research agencies and the National Advisory Committee for Aeronautics). In the late 1930s no military service spent more than $7 million on research annually, and the average annual federal contribution represented 18 percent of total national investment in scientific research and development.

This pattern of scientific activity changed markedly in World War II, which was sometimes called "the physicists' war." Much of the country's best scientific talent spent the war working on military research, organized by the Office of Scientific Research and Development (OSRD), headed by Vannevar Bush and James B. Conant. The best-known ventures were the atomic bomb, developed by the Manhattan Project, and radar, a product of the Radiation Laboratory at the Massachusetts Institute of Technology. Scientists, industrialists, and government officials came out of the war convinced that the advancement of science, economic growth, and national security dictated continuation of the close ties forged during the war.

But organizing national research in peacetime raised two divisive issues—control of atomic energy and establishment of a national science foundation. The military implications of atomic energy in the emerging cold war made this issue urgent.

The May-Johnson bill of 1945, inspired by the War Department, would have placed atomic energy almost entirely under military control. Many scientists mobilized against the bill, arguing that so valuable and dangerous a resource should not be dedicated solely to military use. They supported a measure proposed by the liberal senator Brien McMahon (D.-Conn.), for a civilian Atomic Energy Commission (AEC). Supported by the Truman administration, the McMahon bill became law and the AEC began operation in 1947. Its first head was David E. Lilienthal, former chief of the Tennessee Valley Authority. The subsequent history of nuclear energy, however, belied the hopes expressed by many early supporters of civilian control of atomic energy. Weapons applications dominated AEC research. As to nonmilitary uses, the agency, playing the contradictory roles of promoter of peaceful nuclear energy and watchdog of nuclear safety, gave priority to the development of a nuclear power industry but neglected to require adequate safeguards.

The effort to create the National Science Foundation (NSF) took five years, from the end of the war to 1950. Liberal senator Harley Kilgore (D.-W.Va.) proposed the establishment of such a federal agency in 1945. His NSF would support basic research in both natural and social sciences; it would distribute some of its funds on a geographical basis, be directly responsible to the president, and control patents derived from work it supported. The patent provision aroused strong opposition from industry, but the most formidable counterattack came from Bush as head of the OSRD. In 1945 he sketched his version of an NSF in a highly influential report, *Science—The Endless Frontier*. Bush also supported civilian-controlled basic research, but he wanted to reduce the foundation's direct accountability to the president, omitted any geographical apportionment of funds (money would go to the "best" researchers wherever located), opposed funding for social science, and skirted the patent issue. A bill reflecting Bush's views was passed by the Eightieth Congress in 1947 but vetoed by Truman because the foundation would have been too independent of the president. The political stalemate ended in 1950 when a bill close to Bush's desires, but headed by a presidential appointee, was passed by Congress and received Truman's assent. Limited by its organic act to expenditures of $15 million per year, the NSF began operation with a tiny appropriation of $350,000. Funding climbed slowly in the 1950s and grants were about evenly divided between the physical and biological sciences; 2 percent was devoted to historical, philosophical, and sociological studies of science.

Both the delay in the NSF's establishment and its low level of funding enabled the Department of Defense and the AEC to assume the lion's share of federal funding for scientific research and development, particularly in the physical sciences. The Defense Department and the AEC together accounted for more than 90 percent of federal support for the physical sciences from 1949 to 1960 and a lesser amount in other specialties. In fiscal year 1952 national security agencies spent $3.1 million for basic research in physics, and the NSF, $10,000. Though national security funding did not dominate other fields, these statistics suggest the marked shift to federal funding in all branches of science.

After World War II the United States boasted by far the largest scientific establishment in the world. No longer overshadowed by Europeans in theoretical studies, American scientists came into their own, as was indicated by their growing dominance in Nobel Prize awards. Scientific progress had become closely tied to the state's national security apparatus.

Basic sources on the structure of postwar science are Paul Forman, "Behind Quantum Electronics: National Security as Basis for Physical Research in the United States, 1940–1960," *Historical Studies in the Physical and Biological Sciences* 18, no. 1 (1987): 149–229, and Daniel J. Kevles, *The Physicists: The History of a Scientific Community in Modern America* (New York: Knopf, 1977). On specialized topics, see Paul Boyer, *By the Bomb's Early Light: American Thought and Culture at the Dawn of the Atomic Age* (New York: Pantheon Books, 1985); J. Merton England, *A Patron for Pure Science: The Formative Years of the National Science Foundation* (Washington, D.C.: National Science Foundation, 1982); Clayton R. Koppes, *JPL and the American Space Program: A History of the Jet Propulsion Laboratory* (New Haven: Yale University Press, 1982); Walter McDougall, ... *The Heavens and the Earth: A Political History of the Space Age* (New York: Basic Books, 1985); Alice Kimball Smith, *A Peril and a Hope: The Scientists' Movement in America, 1945–1947*, rev. ed. (Cambridge: MIT Press, 1971); Alex Roland, *Model Research: The National Advisory Committee for Aeronautics, 1915–1958* (Washington, D.C.: U.S. Government Printing Office, 1985); Gregg Herken, *The Winning Weapon: The Atomic Bomb in the Cold War, 1945–1950* (New York: Knopf, 1980); Richard G. Hewlett and Oscar G. Anderson, *The New World: A History of the United States Atomic Energy Commission*, vol. 1, *The New World, 1939/1946* (University Park: Pennsylvania State University Press, 1962), and Hewlett and Francis Duncan, vol. 2, *Atomic Shield, 1947/1952* (University Park: Pennsylvania State University Press, 1969).

CLAYTON R. KOPPES

See also Atomic Energy Commission; Lilienthal, David Eli; National Science Foundation; Nuclear Energy

Security Program

See Loyalty Program

Selective Service/Universal Military Training

Truman, a veteran of World War I and a reserve officer in the 1920s and 1930s, had long considered the problem of how to provide an adequate military force to the nation. By 1940 he was convinced that a purely volunteer system was inadequate and voted in the Senate for peacetime conscription. As president in April 1945, he inherited a Selective Service System that had produced 10 million men through the draft. This World War II draft experience, especially the high rejection rate for illiteracy and physical defects, convinced Truman that a postwar system was needed to help rehabilitate American youth. Demobilization in 1945, however, pushed the idea into the background.

With the end of the war the nation demanded elimination of the draft and the demobilization of all draftees. The need for garrison troops delayed action, but by 1947 Secretary of War Robert Patterson argued that a raise in pay and other benefits would make possible an all-volunteer army. Although Truman had doubts about the prospects for volunteers, he agreed to allow the draft to expire in March 1947.

The president also felt that Universal Military Training (UMT) might be substituted for the draft. Rather than simply seeking active-duty soldiers, UMT would focus on the rehabilitation of youth. In December 1946 Truman appointed an Advisory Commission on Universal Training, headed by Joseph E. Davies. Noting that the 30 percent rejection rate of draftees was "a terrible reflection on a free country," the president drew upon his eclectic reading of history to warn that great republics perish when their people become fat and lazy. Compulsory training would promote the "moral and spiritual welfare of our young people."

The mere creation of the commission generated considerable political opposition. Organized labor, educational institutions, and church groups all objected to UMT. Critics argued that moral training should be left to private and family responsibility. Only veterans' groups and army leaders supported the idea.

Despite the favorable report of the commission, issued in May 1947, prospects for UMT remained slim. But in early 1948 Russian moves in Czechoslovakia gave concreteness to warnings about a Communist menace. Truman began a revision of military manpower policy. A renewal of the draft was the first order of business because, as the president anticipated, volunteers had failed to appear and Gen. Alfred M. Gruenther admitted that the nation now had less than three divisions available for an emergency. Although willing to accept a temporary draft, the Republican leaders of the Eightieth Congress, Senator Robert Taft and Representative Joseph W. Martin, opposed UMT. Even the draft extension was limited to two years. Budgetary concerns and the rhetoric surrounding the atomic bomb and air power made Congress unreceptive to the need for trained reserves.

Truman's reelection in 1948 hardly represented a mandate for rearmament or mobilization. The draft continued to function but acted only as an incentive to promote volunteering. In three months of operation Selective Service drafted only thirty-five thousand men, and by February 1949, all inductions were ended. The secretary of the army announced that enough volunteers were available for current strength levels.

The draft itself verged on expiration, but in June 1950 North Korea invaded South Korea. Faced with the new challenge to the peace and Joseph McCarthy's anti-Communism crusade, Congress followed Truman's lead and extended the draft for twelve months. The president also hoped that the Korean crisis might inject life into the nearly moribund UMT plan. Under instructions from the White House in 1951, the Department of Defense, now headed by George Marshall, tried to combine an extension of the draft with the UMT proposal. The chaos of Korean mobilization demonstrated the need for such a reserve force. In the emergency, veterans of World War II were called back to fight because younger men were untrained. This recall caused a political fallout that rocked Congress and the White House.

But when the draft-UMT bill was submitted to congressional committees the same old opponents appeared. More important, the situation in Korea stabilized. The Department of Defense cut draft calls in half for March and April amid rumors of peace. In this new climate, Congress decided to give the president only half a loaf. The Universal Military Training and Selective Service Act, which passed in June 1951, extended the draft for four years and provided a verbal formula for UMT. But Congress refused to allow the implementation of UMT until after a newly created National Security Training Commission studied the issue.

When Truman left office in early 1953 UMT remained a mere plan without implementation. Draft calls began dropping and the stalemate in Korea turned public opinion against involvement in limited wars. Soon the new Republican leadership shifted mobilization strategy to air power and atomic weapons.

Secondary literature of importance includes the general overview by Joe P. Dunn, "UMT: A Historical Perspective," *Military Review* 61 (1981): 11–18. Frank D. Cunningham, "Harry S. Truman and Universal Military Training," *Historian* 46 (May 1984): 397–415, offers a recent scholarly analysis. For a broad view of conscription since 1940, see George Q. Flynn, *Lewis B. Hershey: Mr. Selective Service* (Chapel Hill: University of North Carolina Press, 1985).

GEORGE Q. FLYNN

See also Mobilization

Senate, United States

See Congress, United States

Senator

The third of January, 1935, marked a significant day in the life of Harry S. Truman. After fifty years of varied undertakings, he finally experienced a sense of accomplishment on a scale he had dreamed of—he had become a U.S. senator. Suspicion and contempt followed him because of the Pendergast connection, but the role of senator spurred him to more intensive action to prove his independence and ability and to disprove the idea that he was completely subservient to Pendergast.

Success did not come easily or quickly. In 1935 the Democratic side of the Senate was so crowded that a new tier of seats along the back wall had to be constructed to accommodate thirteen new Democratic senators. With such a numerical superiority, some Democratic leaders refused to recognize the new "senator from Pendergast." Almost daily some editorial or cartoon in the Missouri newspapers lampooned the Kansas City leader.

When Truman arrived in the Senate, Carl Hayden of Arizona advised him to be a "work horse" rather than a "show horse." Said Truman, "I soon found that the real business of the Senate was carried on by unassuming and conscientious men, not by those who managed to get the most publicity." Truman

devised a few simple rules to govern his actions: work hard; pick only a few areas in which to become expert; observe senatorial courtesy and tradition; endorse faithfully the Roosevelt program; and concentrate on committee work rather than floor speeches in the Senate. Very few people would consider Truman a political philosopher; his genius was essentially practical with a tendency to simplify complex issues, as is indicated by his rules. Such formulae revealed his notable simplicity and directness of approach which could easily become qualities of mediocrity in others, but which would become qualities of success for Truman.

In view of his Jackson Country experience, Truman's two major committee appointments, Appropriations and Interstate Commerce, were indeed fortunate. One of his chief assignments as country presiding judge had been budget making. The federal budget involved much larger funds, but the "principles were the same." In his first term, his chief work centered on transportation and interstate commerce. Not by accident did he concentrate his efforts here. He knew that in Missouri the manufacture of transportation equipment constituted a major industry which ranked fourth in the number of industrial employees. In addition, the state had eleven thousand miles of railroad track. From history, Truman recognized the need for a highly developed transportation system within an industrialized economy. He helped conduct a railroad investigation to eliminate certain financial malpractices in the important rail centers of St. Louis and Kansas City. Furthermore, foreseeing the continually increasing importance of air transportation, he played a significant part in the foundation of the Civil Aeronautics Authority. His first senatorial term culminated in the writing and passage of the Transportation Act of 1940 which coordinated the regulation of all modes of transportation except aviation which remained under the Civil Aeronautics Authority.

Truman's endeavors in transportation contributed significantly to his political strength with the Railroad Brotherhoods throughout the state and nation. The Missouri Railway locals included fifty thousand members, many of whom enthusiastically backed Truman after his strong opposition to railway wage cuts in 1938 and 1939. Truman voted for the Wagner Act, the Social Security Act, the 1937 Wage-Hour Act, the Fair Labor Standards Act, and other prolabor legislation.

At the same time Truman had many friends in business, especially small business. The bankers praised Truman's work on the railroads because many of them held large amounts of railroad securities. The Merchants Association of Kansas City and many large department stores around the state appreciated his work in their behalf on the Freight Forwarded Bill in 1940. In southwest Missouri, Truman supported the Table Rock power project which promised to advance business development in that area.

Unquestionably Truman enjoyed and derived the most benefit from his work on the Interstate Commerce Committee with its chair, Burton K. Wheeler, a Montana Democrat. The committee's investigation of one type of holding company had just culminated in the Public Utility Holding Company Act of 1935. Now Wheeler undertook the unraveling of the financial wizardry of the railroad industry. The magnitude of the investments aroused great interest among businessmen and government officials. Some observers referred to the hearings as the most interesting since the Teapot Dome and Daugherty inquiries. The railroad investigations revealed essential elements of Truman's economic philosophy: a strong distrust of Wall Street, a plea for small business operations whenever possible, a defense of labor, opposition to government ownership, and the acceptance of government regulation of business. It appears that Truman was influenced greatly by the thought of Justice Louis Brandeis. The Missouri senator can clearly be identified as a neo-Brandeisian New Dealer.

Assuredly, Truman had been a work horse throughout his first term. Roosevelt could identify no one in the Senate with a more loyal voting record on the administration's proposals. Nevertheless, Roosevelt seemed to back Lloyd Stark in the Missouri senatorial primary of 1940 and Truman became angry. The president had kept Truman at a distance throughout the first term because of Pendergast. Interestingly, in 1937, Roosevelt had called Pendergast in order to put pressure on Truman to support Alben Barkley for Senate majority leader. Truman had committed his vote to Pat Harrison and would not switch.

Another interesting part of the first term was Truman's friendship with Vice President Garner. Garner liked Truman from the start and taught Truman the ways of the Senate and how to get along. Even though many differences developed over Roosevelt's proposals, the two men remained close and Truman profited from the association in wisdom and shrewdness.

During his reelection campaign in 1940, Truman saw and heard about waste in military contracts as the country prepared for war. The investigation of these rumors led to the creation of a Special Committee to Investigate the National Defense Program which came to be known as the Truman committee. When the death of Roosevelt catapulted Truman to the presidency and reporters attempted to catch the nation up on the career of the Missouri senator, the accounts ignored the first term almost completely and concentrated on the activities of the Truman committee. The railroad investigations had dealt in receiverships, bankruptcies, overextended funded debt—terms the average American neither comprehended nor cared to comprehend. On the other hand, the thousands of new soldiers and sailors and their families could easily understand badly constructed barracks and the lack of planes, guns, and equipment.

The success of the Truman committee resulted from its clarity of purpose and Truman's adroit investigatory skills which he had honed in the railroad inquiries. To help win the war constituted the primary purpose, and for the Truman committee this meant achieving the maximum and quickest production of war supplies at the least cost to the taxpayer. In the process, Truman could have alienated himself from the Roosevelt administration since so much of the confusion and waste sprang from lack of leadership. Truman, however, looked upon his committee as a protective device for Roosevelt and hoped to shield him from the abuse Wilson had suffered after World War I. In past wars, hostility usually developed between Congress and the executive and impeded the war effort, but Truman worked hard to maintain close rapport. Moreover, the senator wanted to safeguard the private enterprise system. Most of the investigations indicated that businessmen expected to make exorbitant profits during the war. By frustrating some of these expectations, Truman received the sobriquet of "Billion-Dollar Watchdog."

Textbooks have frequently cited the Truman committee when they describe the ideal way for Congress to investigate wrongdoing. Truman, for the first time, enjoyed good press coverage. The committee worked hard to develop and maintain this positive relationship by providing frequent and extensive briefings so that reporters could follow the work intelligently. The whole operation was planned and controlled with meticulous care. Other factors contributed significantly to the committee's success. Good personnel and high morale characterized the Truman staff throughout the investigations. Six of the ten senators were freshmen and Truman wanted it so because he knew they would be youthful, energetic, ambitious, and free "from the illusions that they were great statesmen." Their close rapport and objectivity became apparent in that there were no minority reports to the committee's findings and conclusions.

How good was Truman as a senator? The best testimony has to be that his senatorial accomplishments made him a vice-presidential possibility in 1944 and only a small number of people could claim such distinction. The vice presidency took on great significance in 1944 because of Roosevelt's health. Some observers have said that Truman was no one's first choice, but everyone's second choice. Also, Truman consistently denied that he wanted the job. He always proclaimed that he was perfectly content with his work in the Senate. There is some evidence, however, that Truman wanted the vice presidency and worked very adroitly to push aside his opposition while making it appear publicly that the power brokers came to him to seek his acceptance of the nomination. Truman certainly exhibited great political skill throughout the preconvention maneuverings.

Some critics have suggested that Roosevelt picked Truman in 1944 because he would hurt the ticket less than any of the alternative candidates. This judgment could be turned around: Truman was selected because he added the most to the ticket. The other candidates failed because this or that important group would not accept their candidacy. Truman's record had more and wider appeal. One of the strongest groups that rallied to his side was labor, and some prominent businessmen supported him because of the sound economic philosophy that came through in the railroad and national defense investigations. Farmers and blacks also liked Truman, and so did many southerners. As Harry Hopkins said, "Truman wasn't somebody pulled out of a hat." Roosevelt had had his eye on him for some time, Hopkins went on, and had noticed how popular Truman was around the nation.

Surely, the ambition that Truman so strongly felt throughout his life was being satisfied in a way that he had never thought possible. Through his hard work and perseverance, he had developed far beyond his own expectations and those of some people who had underestimated him.

The U.S. Senate records are the best source for information on the Truman committee, the railroad hearings of the 1930s, the founding of the Civil Aeronautics Authority, and other matters in which Truman was involved in the Senate. The Truman Library contains materials on his senatorial career. See also Donald H. Riddle, *The Truman Committee* (New Brunswick, N.J.: Rutgers University Press, 1964), and Truman's *Memoirs*, vol. 1, *Year of Decisions* (Garden City, N.Y.: Doubleday, 1955). For his personal reactions to these years, see Robert H. Ferrell, ed. *Dear Bess: The Letters from Harry to Bess Truman, 1910–1959* (New York: W. W. Norton, 1983).

EUGENE F. SCHMIDTLEIN

See also Election of 1934; Election of 1940; Election of 1944; New Deal; Transportation Act of 1940; Truman Committee

Short, Joseph Hudson

(11 February 1904–18 September 1952)

Presidential press secretary. Joseph H. ("Joe") Short was born in Vicksburg, Mississippi, and educated in the local public schools. He graduated from Virginia Military Institute in 1925 and first aspired to a military career. He turned to journalism, however, after editing the VMI newspaper. He worked on newspapers in Vicksburg, Jackson, and New Orleans before joining the Richmond bureau of the Associated Press in 1929. Transferred to Washington in 1931, he worked successively for AP (1931–41), the *Chicago Sun* (1941–43), and finally the *Baltimore Sun*. He first became acquainted with Harry Truman when he covered the special Senate committee investigating wartime defense contractors, and their friendship developed when Short joined the vice-presidential campaign train in 1944. After Truman became president, Short traveled more than 125,000 miles on presidential trips, including the chief executive's visits to Mexico City in 1946, Brazil in 1947, and Bermuda and Key West, as well as the whistle-stop campaign in 1948. Short also served as president of the National Press Club in 1948.

In December 1950 the president's press secretary, Charles G. Ross, died suddenly, and on 8 December Truman announced the appointment of Joseph Short to the post. Short at the time was vice president of the White House Correspondents' Association, and his appointment to the office was unprecedented: no press secretary had ever come from the corps of regular White House reporters. "For most newsmen," *Newsweek* said, "it was a happy choice," portending better relations between the working press and the president.

Short added two assistants to the Office of the Press Secretary, Irving Perlmeter, a former information officer with the Department of Treasury, and Roger Tubby, a former press officer in the Department of State. Short's office was responsible for responding to around-the-clock telephone inquiries, handling the details of the president's speaking schedule and newsreel takes, and supervising print media releases. In addition, Short himself conducted 337 press conferences during his tenure of which the most momentous was the conference convened at 1:00 A.M. on 11 April 1951 to announce the dismissal of Gen. Douglas MacArthur. Short's office also helped the president prepare for his press conferences, and it was Short who developed the practice of taping the proceedings.

Devoted to the president, Short was one of a group of presidential senior staff personnel which included Special Counsel Charles Murphy and Assistant to the President John Steelman, all of whom met with the president six mornings a week. Trusting in Short's judgment, Truman turned to him for advice on sensitive matters such as the removal of Newbold Morris in 1952 as special investigator within the Justice Department, the forced resignation of Attorney General J. Howard McGrath, and the hearings of irregularities within the Reconstruction Finance Corporation. Some disaffected newspapermen observed that Short was too protective of the president and tended "to act less like a press relations expert than a confidential policy adviser." Most members of the press, however, appreciated Short's integrity and abilities, respected his loyalty to the president, and understood the precautions he took to protect the president during times of national emergency.

Like his predecessor, Short died in office, succumbing to a heart attack in September 1952, just as he was recuperating from a viral infection. Marquis Childs wrote in his column, "I saw two men killed in that job, Charles Ross and Joe Short." Truman eulogized him as "a trusted and valued assistant." Short was survived by two sons and a daughter, all under the age of thirteen, and his wife, Beth Campbell Short, whom Truman named five days later to the office of correspondence secretary that had been recently vacated by William D. Hassett.

The most useful manuscript sources on Short are in the Truman Library and include his own press conferences and files and oral history interviews with Irving Perlmeter, Eben Ayers, George Elsey, Beth Short, Robert G. Nixon, and others. Useful books are Francis Heller, ed., *The Truman White House: The Administration of the President, 1945–1953* (Lawrence: Regents Press of Kansas, 1980); Robert J. Donovan, *Tumultous Years: The Presidency of Harry S Truman* (New York: W. W. Norton, 1982); and Ken Hechler, *Working with Truman: A Personal Memoir of the White House Years* (New York: G. P. Putnam's, 1982). The fullest biographical sketches on Short are in the *Current Biography Yearbook* (1951), the *Dictionary of American Biography: Supplement V*, and his obituaries in the *Washington Post* and *New York Times*.

MARTHA H. SWAIN

See also Press, The; Ross, Charles Griffith

Smith Act

The Alien Registration Act of 1940, popularly known as the Smith Act, is a federal criminal statute that forbids teaching or advocating the violent overthrow of any government within the United States, organizing a group to engage in such teaching or advocacy, and being a member of such an organization. Its enactment climaxed a five-year campaign in the late 1930s by members of Congress determined to obtain legislation proscribing the Communist Party of the United States (CPUSA). Because of the World War II alliance between the United States and the Soviet Union, however, federal prosecutors used the new law first against Trotskyists and domestic fascists.

After the development of the cold war, the Truman administration came under attack by Republicans for doing too little to combat Communism. To counter this charge, it obtained Smith Act indictments against all twelve members of the national board of the CPUSA in July 1948. A tumultuous trial in the New York courtroom of Federal District Judge Harold Medina the next year ended with the conviction of all the indicted radicals except one whose case was severed because of ill health. The convicted Communists appealed, arguing that the Smith Act violated the First Amendment's guarantees of freedom of expression. In *Dennis v. United States*, 341 U.S. 494 (1951), the Supreme Court ruled against them, holding that the law was constitutional.

Following the *Dennis* decision, federal prosecutors moved against dozens of second-string Communist leaders in cities across the country. The government charged most of them with conspiracy to violate the Smith Act, but seven were indicted for membership in the CPUSA. Although these prosecutions began during Truman's presidency, the Eisenhower administration carried forward cases commenced by its predecessor and also initiated new ones. Eventually, the government secured Smith Act indictments against 133 Communists. Of those whose fate was decided by a trial court, just under 89 percent were convicted. So intense was popular hostility toward Communists that only one jury acquitted any defendants.

The Supreme Court's decision in *Yates* v. *United States*, 354 U.S. 298 (1957), brought a halt to the Smith Act prosecutions. In that case the Court ruled that because of the statute of limitations, no one else could be tried for organizing the CPUSA and that in order to convict a Communist of teaching or advocating the violent overthrow of a government, the Justice Department would have to prove the person had urged listeners to take some action toward that end rather than merely believe in such action. Federal prosecutors lacked the type of evidence the Court demanded, so they dropped some of the cases they had initiated. Courts of appeal threw out the rest. The Smith Act remains on the Statute books, but, given the way the Supreme Court has interpreted the First Amendment since the late 1960s, a prosecution of a Communist or anyone else under that law would probably be held unconstitutional today.

The most complete study of the Smith Act and prosecutions under it is Michal R. Belknap, *Cold War Political Justice: The Smith Act, the Communist Party and American Civil Liberties* (Westport, Conn.: Greenwood Press, 1977). Also good on the *Dennis* case are Peter L. Steinberg, *The Great 'Red Menace': United States Prosecution of American Communists, 1947-1952* (Westport, Conn.: Greenwood Press, 1984), and Michal R. Belknap, "Cold War in the Courtroom," in *American Political Trials*, ed. Michal R. Belknap (Westport, Conn.: Greenwood Press, 1981), pp. 232-62. Much less valuable is Kevin J. O'Brien, "*Dennis v. United States*: The Cold War, the Communist Conspiracy and the F.B.I." (Ph.D. diss., Cornell University, 1979). Although now rather dated, Robert Mollan, "Smith Act Prosecutions: The Effect of the Dennis and Yates Decisions," *University of Pittsburg Law Review* 26 (1965): 705-48, remains after *Cold War Political Justice* the best secondary source on the post-*Dennis* Smith Act cases.

MICHAL R. BELKNAP

See also Communism and Communists; Red Scare; Supreme Court, United States

Snyder, John Wesley

(21 June 1895–8 October 1985)

Banker, public official, businessman, adviser to President Truman. Serving successively as federal loan administrator (April–July 1945), reconversion director (July 1945–June 1946), and secretary of the treasury (June 1946–January 1953), John W. Snyder exerted a strongly conservative influence on the making of economic and fiscal policy and was regarded by Truman as a "tower of strength and common sense." But he was also a frequent target of liberal critics, who regarded him as the epitome of the "Missouri influence" and of "government by crony." He was seen to represent a regrettable relapse into "business as usual."

Snyder was born in Jonesboro, Arkansas, the son of the local druggist. He attended Vanderbilt University for one year and was employed in his uncle's business operations prior to entering the army during World War I. He served in France as a captain in the field artillery and remained active in the military reserve after the war. Between 1919 and 1930 he held positions in a series of banks in Arkansas and Missouri. In 1931 he began a governmental career, first as a federal bank receiver and conservator in St. Louis, then as regional director of the Reconstruction Finance Corporation (RFC) in the same city, and finally as head of the RFC subsidiary that financed the building of defense plants. In 1943 he became a vice president of the First National Bank in St. Louis, and it was from this position that he returned to Washington as one of Truman's first administrative appointees. His acquaintance with Truman had begun in France in 1918, and subsequently they had trained together in the military reserve, worked together on political projects, and developed a close and lasting personal friendship.

As an official, Snyder built a reputation for cutting red tape and getting things done. He also held the hinterland's views concerning the evils of tight money and Wall Street domination, and he took an active role in shaping and helping to implement the administration's foreign aid, international trade, and executive reorganization programs. But in other respects, he tended to be cautious, orthodox, and conservative. He wanted to consolidate rather than expand the New Deal's social programs. He had little use for the "new economics" that the Council of Economic Advisers was trying to apply. He came down on the side of the decontrollers and deregulators in the reconversion debates, one result being concessions to the construction and steel industries that were strongly opposed by Price Administrator Chester Bowles. And in fiscal management, he stressed the orthodox principles of maintaining confidence in the credit of the United States, retiring the debt in periods of prosperity, reducing the commercial bank holdings of federal securities, and keeping the Treasury's operating costs as low as possible. These, as he saw them, were the essentials of "good financing," and his progress in implementing them was in his mind and in that of President Truman evidence of administrative success.

One major policy battle in which Snyder had Truman's support yet still lost was that over maintaining the World War II arrangement under which the Federal Reserve Board assisted government financing by pegging interest rates at low levels. Snyder viewed this as essential to expanded production, government economy, and the maintenance of moral commitments to the purchasers of war bonds, and with this assessment Truman was in general agreement. But in the view of Marriner Eccles, the chairman of the Federal Reserve Board (FRB), the arrangement was contributing to inflationary pressures. He wanted to free monetary policy as an antiinflation tool, and eventually, in 1951, the Federal Reserve Board would succeed in scrapping the arrangement and reestablishing its independence from the Treasury. This did not come, however, without a good deal of friction between Snyder and Eccles, and it was widely believed that Snyder was behind Truman's 1948 decision not to redesignate Eccles as FRB chairman.

Following the change of government in 1953, Snyder became president of the Overland Corporation, by that time an investment firm, and continued in that capacity until his retirement in 1966. He was also active in a variety of philanthropic endeavors and continued to serve as a member of the Business Advisory Council and a Treasury advisory board. In recalling his service during the Truman era, he took greatest pride in having three years of budgetary surpluses, in having retired $15 billion of the national debt, in having cut the bank holdings of U.S. debt by $25 billion, and in having increased the holdings of savings bonds by $8 billion.

There is no biography of Snyder. Helpful biographical sketches can be found in *Current Biography* (1945), *Political Profiles: The Truman Years* New York: Facts on File, 1978), *National Cyclopedia of American Biography* (1952, 1967), and Robert I. Vexler, *The Vice-Presidents and Cabinet Members* (Dobbs Ferry, N.Y.: Oceana Publications, 1975). See also the discussion in Cabell Phillips, *The Truman Presidency* (New York: Macmillan, 1966), and in Herbert Stein, *The Fiscal Revolution in America* (Chicago: University of Chicago Press, 1969).

ELLIS W. HAWLEY

See also Cabinets (photograph); Economy, The; Fiscal and Monetary Policies

Socialist Party

See Thomas, Norman Mattoon

Social Security

Social Security has evolved into the nation's biggest domestic program. Nearly every wage earner now pays taxes into the system, and virtually every senior citizen is eligible for benefits. More than a quarter of all American households currently receive monthly Old Age and Survivors Insurance (OASI) benefits under Title II of the act. This single Social Security benefit is the most important source of income for older Americans.

In contrast, when Harry Truman became president, only 58 percent of the civilian labor force was contributing to the program. Many of these employees had not yet paid enough FICA taxes to meet eligibility requirements when they retired. Only a quarter of the senior-citizen population qualified for Title II benefits. Although the original act made 65 the official retirement age, the average man began to collect at 69.4 years of age in 1945; female employees entitled to Social Security benefits were on the average a year younger when retiring. The average male worker received a monthly check worth $24.50 from Social Security. Since OASI benefits were pegged to a participating employee's prior earnings, the average female retiree received $19.50 a month. Additional benefits were authorized for a retired worker's spouse and/or survivors, and an average couple received $38.50 a month. Widows of eligible pensioners got $20.20, but a widower could not collect on his wife's prior contributions.

Thus after ten years of operation, Social Security provided minimal support for retired workers. President Truman, however, shared Roosevelt's opinion that Social Security was "a development toward a goal rather than a finished product." Accordingly, he gave the program's architects room to maneuver and time to sort out priorities.

Under Title I, Old Age Assistance was granted to applicants who met age, residency, and needs requirements established by the various states and approved by a federal Social Security Board. Other provisions earmarked limited funds for a state-level unemployment compensation scheme, aid to dependent children, relief to the blind, grants for maternal and child welfare, rural public health services, and professional training. The logic was to channel funds to people vulnerable to various social risks at specific junctures over the life course in ways that would complement existing public and private programs and strengthen traditional values.

Nonetheless Truman's incremental approach faced stiff opposition, particularly when he tried to expand retirement provisions. The Republican-dominated Eightieth Congress excluded newspaper vendors from Social Security coverage and narrowed the definition of "employee" in Title II. Angry, Truman made these "reforms" a campaign issue in the 1948 election. "Time and again I have recommended improvements in the Social Security law," the president told delegates to the Democratic convention on 15 July. "Congress studied the matter for two years, but couldn't find the time to extend or increase the benefits. But they did find time to take Social Security benefits away from 750,000 people, and they passed that over my veto."

Social Security Administration officials worried that if Congress remained disinclined to expand the OASI program, it would languish. Twice as many people in 1949 were receiving Old Age Assistance (OAA) under Title I as were drawing OASI benefits. The average OAA benefit was $42 a month, 68 percent larger than the average Title II check. Convinced that the goals of a progressive social insurance policy should be to reduce the need for assistance to the smallest extent possible, the future of Social Security, in their view, was at stake. Truman agreed.

On 5 January 1949, the president recommended expanding Social Security in his State of the Union message. After much congressional deliberation, Truman signed thirty major changes in the act into law on 28 August 1950. Mandatory coverage was extended to approximately 8 million people, notably domestic and farm workers whose low earnings made them among the country's most economically vulnerable groups in retirement. The nonfarm self-employed (except professionals), federal civilian employees not under a federal retirement system, U.S. citizens employed outside the United States by American employers, and workers in Puerto Rico and the Virgin Islands were also required to participate. Voluntary coverage was extended to another 2.5 million workers, principally state and local government employees not covered by a public retirement system and about 600,000 employees of nonprofit organizations.

Reduced eligibility requirements and a revision in the benefit-calculation formula, moreover, afforded more people a higher level of basic protection than ever before. Average benefits for current recipients were increased 77.5 percent, the largest proportional increase in the program's history. Truman did not get everything he wanted, however. Congress rejected his idea to include benefits for permanently and totally disabled persons under Title II. This recommendation was viewed as a Trojan horse in the president's campaign for a national health insurance plan.

On balance, the 1950 amendments had the immediate effect Truman desired. In February 1951, the number of persons receiving OASI benefits for the first time surpassed the number receiving Title I benefits. Six months later, more money was distributed to older Americans through Title II than through Old Age Assistance. As more and more people had a stake in OASI, the pressures for programmatic expansion increasingly outweighed the forces of containment.

During his presidency, Truman made several administrative changes that compartmentalized Social Security's function. On 16 July 1946, he abolished the Social Security Board (replacing it with a single commissioner) and placed the Children's Bureau within the Social Security Administration. Under his Reorganization Plan No. 2 (20 June 1949), employment service and unemployment service activities were transferred to the Department of Labor. Social Security was being positioned to fit under the aegis of the Federal Security Agency, the forerunner of the Department of Health, Education and Welfare.

In making these bureaucratic changes, Truman relied heavily on the advice of his Social Security commissioner, Arthur Altmeyer, who had been with the program from its formative years. Altmeyer, in turn, nurtured the careers of public servants such as Robert Ball, Wilbur Cohen, and Robert Myers, who gave the fledgling system credibility in Congress and developed esprit de corps deep within the ranks. This generation of leaders was to guide the program's development with remarkable success for the next two decades and influence key features of the 1977 and 1983 amendments. For this reason, the successes and disappointments that occurred during Truman's presidency had an importance beyond 1953. Memories recalled and skills refined then shaped subsequent policy-making strategies.

W. Andrew Achenbaum, *Social Security: Visions and Revisions* (New York: Cambridge University Press, 1986), is a comprehensive overview of the evolution of policy-making from the 1930s through the 1983 amendments. Arthur J. Altmeyer, *The Formative Years of Social Security* (Madison: University of Wisconsin Press, 1968), is a judicious insider's chronicle of legislative and administrative developments between 1934 and 1954. A revisionist study by Jerry R. Cates, *Insuring Inequality* (Ann Arbor: University of Michigan Press, 1983), claims that Social Security's leaders viewed assistance plans as a prime competitor to their programmatic agenda. Wilbur J. Cohen and Robert J. Myers, in "Social Security Act Amendments of 1950," *Social Security Bulletin* 13 (October 1950): 3–14, offer a comprehensive summary of the passage and provisions of the measure.

W. ANDREW ACHENBAUM

See also Fair Deal

South, The

Harry Truman's accession to the presidency was at least in part the result of southern support, and the fate of his policies was heavily dependent upon the support of southerners in Congress.

Keith Temple, *New Orleans Times-Picayune*, 22 July 1952.

But Truman's domestic proposals precipitated the disruption of the Democratic South and confronted the Truman administration with bitter sectional opposition. Truman's liberal course was not anticipated by southern leaders, since he came from the border state of Missouri, had been friendly with southerners in the U.S. Senate, and was descended from forebears who owned slaves and sympathized with the Confederacy. Truman had been raised, as he later wrote, "amidst some violently prejudiced Southerners." In 1944 southern delegates to the Democratic National Convention lent their support to the Missourian rather than to the reform-minded Henry A. Wallace in the selection of the party's vice-presidential nominee. When Truman became president on 12 April 1945, many southerners hoped that he would turn away from the New Deal and reverse the liberal direction of his predecessor.

Southern conservatives were soon disappointed in these hopes. With the end of the war the new president made it clear that he intended to continue the New Deal. In early September 1945, he sent Congress a set of guidelines for action in dealing with pressing social and economic questions, including endorsement of a permanent Fair Employment Practices Committee (FEPC). Many white southerners identified the FEPC proposal with militant labor organizations, viewed it as unwarranted federal interference with the region's labor practices, and feared that it might be the entering wedge in an assault on white supremacy. Southern members of Congress were divided in their response to other administration recommendations, but a significant number of them opposed Truman's economic controls and reconversion policies as well as his position on such matters as the full employment bill, new labor legislation, and jurisdiction over offshore oil deposits. Southern senators and representatives, who exerted great influence in committee and parliamentary proceedings, frequently entered into informal voting arrangements with Republicans. This conservative coalition often defeated the president's reform proposals.

It was Truman's decision to sponsor a civil rights program that most disturbed southern congressmen and a substantial part of the region's white population. An outburst of murders, lynchings, and violence directed at southern blacks brought pressure on the White House for federal intervention, and in December 1946 Truman established the President's Committee on Civil Rights, a panel made up of fifteen distinguished leaders, including two prominent southerners. The committee's report, *To Secure These Rights*, was a comprehensive set of recommendations for congressional and administrative action to overcome racial discrimination in the United States. Although these recommendations no doubt went further than Truman had expected, he sent a special message to Congress in February 1948 urging passage of a broad civil rights law.

Southern politicians were sharply critical of Truman's civil rights program. "If it were not for Southern Democrats," Representative John Bell Williams of Mississippi asserted, "Henry Wallace would be in the White House today instead of Harry Truman. Southern Democrats have always been the best friends that President Truman or the Democratic Party ever had." Truman no longer had any real concern for the South, men like Williams complained; he had become the spokesman of an urban coalition composed of labor unions, ethnic groups, blacks, and intellectuals. Although the outpouring of southern criticism may have exaggerated the likelihood of early enactment of civil rights legislation, it reflected the white South's continued commitment to its long-established system of racial segregation and its hypersensitivity in the midst of rapid economic and social change. Some southern leaders spoke darkly of withholding their support from the Democratic ticket in the presidential election of 1948.

Although Truman was committed to civil rights and was anxious to blunt Henry Wallace's appeal to black voters, he hoped to retain the support of the South. He did not push hard for his equal rights recommendations and sought in other ways to mollify the white South. The president and his advisers assumed that, however exasperated southerners might be with the administration, they would not break their long tradition of Democratic loyalty. Truman seemed to be willing to accept a mild civil rights plank in the party platform of 1948, but during the convention a bitter struggle developed over the wording of that section. When liberals won in a close vote, the Mississippi delegation and half of the delegates from Alabama walked out of the convention. Although the other Dixie delegates remained, only a handful of them voted for Truman's nomination. Most of the southerners cast their votes for Senator Richard B. Russell of Georgia in a symbolic protest against Truman and the leadership of the national party.

A revolt of the southern Democrats had been brewing for months, and it now culminated in the organization of the States' Rights party and the nomination of Governor J. Strom Thurmond of South Carolina for president and Governor Fielding L. Wright of Mississippi as his running mate. The Dixiecrats, as they were soon dubbed, conducted a vigorous campaign during the following months in an effort to unite the South against the regular Democratic ticket. But their success was limited. They won only four Deep South states, while Truman, profiting from traditional Democratic support and the reluctance of southern politicians to forsake federal benefits and political ties with the national party, carried all the rest. Although some southerners supported the States' Rights Democrats because of shared hostility toward New Deal economic policies, the Dixiecrat movement gathered most of its strength from the racism and sectionalism that had always frustrated political realignment within the region and perpetuated the Solid South. Most southerners remained loyal to the national Democratic party. Still, the Dixiecrats provided a means of channeling the South's growing sense of political isolation, and it led to a real political division in the region.

Truman's unexpected victory in 1948 and the Fair Deal he unveiled in 1949 enjoyed few triumphs. His civil rights program, national health plan, federal aid to education proposals, and labor reform recommendations were all defeated, often with the aid of conservative Democrats from the South. On the other hand, Congress acted favorably on the administration's recommendations for the extension of the New Deal in such areas as Social Security, the minimum wage, public housing, and natural resource development, measures that appealed to many southerners. Black southerners applauded Truman's desegregation of the armed forces, appointment of Afro-Americans to federal positions, and efforts to guarantee fair employment practices in civilian jobs. Some white southerners also approved of these actions. "I never did believe that the great mass of Southerners had the same viewpoint as the minority Dixiecrat contingent," Truman wrote in his *Memoirs*. "I believe the vast majority of good Southerners understand that the blind prejudices of past generations cannot continue in a free republic."

The relationship between Truman and the South was complex and shifting—sometimes harmonious but often strained. Southerners and their representatives in Congress, though divided and frequently opposed to Truman's domestic reforms, provided indispensable support for his national defense and foreign policies. A large number, perhaps a majority, of the region's inhabitants appreciated Truman's efforts to use federal power to facilitate regional development. They liked his support of the Tennessee Valley Authority, agricultural subsidies, federal aid for public health facilities, and assistance to higher education. Southern liberals, a disparate band of Democratic loyalists, organized labor members, blacks, social reformers, and intellectuals, found much to admire in Harry Truman's presidency and looked to him for help in modernizing and humanizing southern institutions and accelerating the South's long-awaited economic rehabilitation. Southern conservatives, on the other hand, strongly disliked Truman's broad conception of presidential power, his taxing and spending policies, and his civil rights program, which challenged the jurisdiction of Jim Crow.

Truman's political priorities disrupted the Solid South and set in motion a process of partisan realignment that eventually transformed southern politics. Thus the South entered a period of great economic, social, and political change during the Truman years, and the thirty-third president, however unwittingly, became an important factor in promoting that change.

Truman's relationship with the South has not been systematically explored by scholars. His own thinking is revealed in his *Memoirs*, 2 vols. (Garden City, N.Y.: Doubleday, 1956), and the politics and policies of his administration are treated in Donald R. McCoy, *The Presidency of Harry S. Truman* (Lawrence: University Press of Kansas, 1984), and Robert J. Donovan, *The Presidency of Harry S. Truman*, 2 vols. (New York: Norton, 1977, 1982). William C. Berman's *The Politics of Civil Rights in the Truman Administration* (Columbus: Ohio State University Press, 1970) is a lucid analysis of that subject, but see also Donald R. McCoy and Richard T. Ruetten, *Quest and Response: Minority Rights and the Truman Administration* (Lawrence: University Press of Kansas, 1973). Conflict and dissension in the Democratic party are thoughtfully examined in Robert A. Garson, *The Democratic Party and the Politics of Sectionalism, 1941–1948* (Baton Rouge: Louisiana State University Press, 1974). Emile B. Ader's *The Dixiecrat Movement: Its Role in Third Party Politics* (Washington, D.C.: Public Affairs Press, 1955) is also useful. For broader developments in the South during the Truman period, see Charles P. Roland, *The Improbable Era: The South since World War II* (Lexington: University Press of Kentucky, 1975).

DEWEY W. GRANTHAM

See also Civil Rights; Dixiecrats; Election of 1948; Elections in the Truman Era; George, Walter Franklin; Russell, Richard Brevard, Jr.; Thurmond, James Strom

South Africa

See Africa

Soviet Union

Harry S. Truman brought to the presidency no strong views regarding the Soviet Union. On those few occasions prior to 1945 when he did express himself on the nation and its system of government, his words revealed, if anything, indifference. In January 1919, while a member of the American Expeditionary Force in France, the thirty-four-year-old Truman wrote to his future wife that he "didn't give a whoop (to put it mildly) whether there's a League of nations or whether Russia has a Red government or a Purple one." Like other American doughboys, he just wanted to go home. During the twenties and into the thirties, as a county judge, he immersed himself in local politics and paid little attention to foreign affairs, apparently writing or saying nothing publicly about the Soviet Union.

When Germany invaded the Soviet Union in June 1941, Truman, now senator from Missouri, declared that the United States should support whichever side seemed to be losing. Although some have interpreted this remark as indicative of an unsympathetic or even hostile attitude toward the Soviet Union, it is more reflective of Truman's isolationist tendencies and his belief that the key to American security was the absence of a dominant European power. During World War II, he voiced none of the admiration for the Red Army and all things Soviet, as did

Churchill, Truman, and Stalin at the Potsdam Conference, July 1945. (U.S. Army/Courtesy of the Harry S. Truman Library)

some Americans, nor did he, on the other hand, share the uneasiness in some quarters about possible Soviet postwar expansionism. For much of the war he served as chairman of the Special Committee to Investigate the National Defense Program. Even with his election as vice president in November 1944, Truman remained detached from foreign affairs. He was not briefed by President Roosevelt or his advisers on foreign policy matters.

With his succession to the presidency in April 1945, Truman made it one of his highest priorities to learn what had transpired at Roosevelt's wartime conferences with Churchill and Stalin, particularly the increasingly controversial accords reached at Yalta. Recognizing the need for a crash course on the Soviet Union, he eagerly sought the views of others. Some scholars have claimed that the new president was unduly influenced by anti-Soviet advisers and, as a result, reversed FDR's essentially cooperative policy toward the Soviet Union. In fact, in those first few months, Truman turned both to those who favored a hard policy and to those who preferred a soft one toward the Soviets. He later recalled how he had listened to Joseph Davies, "a Russophile as most of us were." The only staunch anti-Soviets he numbered among his advisers were Adm. William Leahy and Edward Pauley. This was a time of rapid learning, and the president, buffeted by events and frequently conflicting advice, vacillated in his attitudes toward the Soviet Union. Truman did maintain FDR's essentially cooperative policy through the summer of 1945, however, despite certain anxieties about Soviet behavior, especially with regard to

Poland, and a few of his own actions, such as the abrupt termination of Lend-Lease shipments to the Soviet Union that seemed to signal a harder line. It should be pointed out that Truman, perhaps influenced by a strain of Anglophobia among some of his advisers, was nearly as upset with British policy as he was with the Soviets.

During the trying transition from war to peace, Truman noted blemishes on the faces of each member of the Anglo-Soviet-U.S. alliance. The new president went so far as to equate some features of Soviet communism with the operations of American capitalism: "A common everyday citizen [in the Soviet Union] has about as much say in his government as a stockholder in the Standard Oil of New Jersey has about his Company." Truman had a live-and-let-live attitude toward the Soviets: "They evidently like their government or they wouldn't die for it. I like ours so let's get along."

Truman also saw great similarities in the propagandizing of the three major powers: "Russians distribute lies about us. Our papers lie about and misrepresent the motives of the Russians—and the British outlie and outpropagandize us both." Americans, he felt, were always sending missionaries and political propagandists to foreign countries. "But when Russia puts out propaganda to help our parlor pinks—well, that's bad—so we think. There is not any difference between the two approaches except one is 'my' approach and the other is 'yours.'"

In addition to the British, Truman's irritation in these early months was as much with the "Crazy American Communist" as it was with the Soviet Union. Although only a minuscule number of Americans were Communists, Truman felt they owed their loyalty to Stalin, not to the American president. Knowing full well that he did not have the authority, Truman half in jest said he would like to send all the American Communists to Russia, where he was sure that Stalin would ship them to Siberia or to concentration camps.

It is clear that at first Truman had a relatively open mind about the Soviet Union. His major worry was that the Soviet Government might not carry out agreements it had made. As a person who prided himself on candor and trustworthiness, Truman made these the most important criteria by which to judge Soviet behavior. When Soviet foreign minister Molotov visited Washington in April 1945, Truman spoke sharply, to the consternation of some of the other Americans present, about the seeming lack of Soviet adherence to the Yalta accords. Molotov replied that he had never been spoken to that way before. Truman responded that if he carried out his agreements, he would not be spoken to that way. He reassured Eleanor Roosevelt that he had "been trying very carefully to keep up all my engagements with the Russians because they are touchy and suspicious of us."

Truman asked FDR's close adviser Harry Hopkins to journey to Moscow in May 1945 to ease the strained relations with the Soviet Union. Hopkins was instructed to tell Stalin "exactly what we intended to have in the way of carrying out agreements, purported to have been made at Yalta." He was also to emphasize Truman's desire "to have a fair understanding with the Russian Government—that we never made commitments which we did not expect to carry out to the letter" and that "we intended him to carry his agreement out to the letter and we intended to see that he did." Truman told Hopkins "he could use diplomatic language, or he could use a baseball bat if he thought that was the proper approach to Mr. Stalin."

The Potsdam Conference in July 1945—Truman's only face-to-face meeting with the Soviet leader—was the turning point in his view of the Soviet Union. He had resisted Churchill's suggestion that the two of them meet separately prior to the conference because Stalin already felt "we're ganging up on him." He went into the conference hopeful of further progress on some of the outstanding issues and anxious to secure quick Soviet entry into the Pacific war. Truman came away with a favorable impression of Stalin, commenting how much he liked "the little son of a bitch." Noting that the Soviet leader was at least six inches shorter than he and that even Churchill was taller than Stalin, Truman complained that the press had portrayed him "the little man in stature and intellect."

The aftermath of the Potsdam Conference confirmed his doubts about Soviet trustworthiness. In later years he wrote that he was "an innocent idealist" who had been misled by Stalin at the conference table. Although several agreements were reached at Potsdam, they were broken "as soon as the unconscionable Russian dictator returned to Moscow." Truman felt that at the conference the Western powers had "been faced with an accomplished fact and were, by circumstances, almost forced to agree" to Soviet occupation of Eastern Poland and Polish incorporation of Eastern Germany. "It was a high-handed outrage." He was especially piqued by the fact that concessions had been made to the Soviet Union in return for its entry into the war against Japan, something that turned out not to be needed.

Daniel Blair Dowling, *New York Herald Tribune*, March 1949. I.H.T. Corporation. Reprinted by permission.

Truman quickly abandoned the diplomatic approach. He became convinced that the way to achieve results with the Soviets was to talk toughly. In 1946, Soviet pressures against Iran, which he likened to tactics that had resulted in the Soviet Union's incorporation of the Baltic states and its growing influence in Poland, led Truman to adopt a tougher stance. "I'm tired of babying the Soviets," he complained. Softness toward the Soviets was the underlying cause of the dismissal of both Secretary of State James Byrnes and Secretary of Commerce Henry Wallace. During the spring 1948 crisis that began with the Communist takeover of Czechoslovakia, Truman gave major addresses appealing for the reinstitution of the draft, establishment of Universal Military Training, and increased defense expenditures. "Our friends, the Russkies," he observed in a draft speech, "understand only one language—how many divisions have you—actual or potential."

During the Korean armistice negotiations, Truman was deeply angered by Communist charges that the United States mistreated its prisoners of war. Recalling the fate of German and Japanese prisoners taken by the Soviets during World War II, as well as the Polish officers murdered at Katyn, he noted in his diary that an agreement with the Soviet Union "wouldn't be worth the paper it is written on." Asserting that the Soviet Union had broken every agreement made at the wartime conferences, he railed that the Soviets have "no morals, no honor." He also hurled a rhetorical threat at Stalin: "Now do you want an end to hostilities in Korea or do you want China and Siberia destroyed? You may have one or the other, whichever you want. ... You either accept our fair and just proposal or you will be completely destroyed."

Certainly there was a growing element of an ideological crusade in Truman's conception of the cold war. His abortive 1952 effort to appoint a diplomatic representative to the Vatican, the president explained to a Protestant clergyman, was based on a desire "to organize the moral forces against the immoral forces. ... Stalin and his crowd had no intellectual honesty and no moral code" and had broken thirty or forty treaties with the West. By establishing diplomatic relations with the Holy See, Truman merely wanted to "organize Exodus XX, Matthew V, VI & VII to save morals in the world."

But throughout his administration he viewed the Soviet Union more as a continuation of Russian despotism—a nation ruled by a gang of crooked politicians—than as the carrier of a revolutionary contagion. Commenting on how the "dictatorship of the proletariat is no different from the Czar or Hitler," Truman observed in the spring of 1945 that there was "no socialism in Russia," since it was "the hotbed of special privilege." He seems to have clung to this view. Some years after leaving the White House, in 1956, he noted that Soviet harsh treatment of the satellite countries had been based on the "teachings of Jenghis Khan and Tamerlane." He admired the sturdiness of the Soviet people, but believed they had been "oppressed and downtrodden by dictatorships from the time of Ivan the Terrible and Peter the Great to this very day."

Despite the centrality of the subject to the Truman presidency, no satisfactory analysis has been done of Truman's views toward the Soviet Union. The only effort is a superficial monograph by Herbert Druks, *Harry S. Truman and the Russians, 1945–1953* (New York: Robert Speller & Sons, 1966). Snippets of Truman's thoughts on the Soviet Union, however, can be gleaned from Robert Ferrell's edited

collections, *Dear Bess: The Letters from Harry to Bess Truman, 1910–1959* (New York: W. W. Norton, 1983) and *Off the Record: The Private Papers of Harry S. Truman* (New York: Harper & Row, 1980).

RONALD D. LANDA

See also Cold War; Containment; Potsdam Conference; Revolution; Stalin, Joseph

Spain

During the years 1945–48 the Truman administration wholeheartedly endorsed the international ostracism of the Spanish government of Gen. Francisco Franco. This policy was premised on (1) the fact that Franco had received German and Italian assistance during the Spanish civil war and in turn had granted some material and "volunteer" military support to the Axis during Wor!d War II, and (2) the widely held, if not entirely accurate, contention that Franco was one of two surviving "fascist" dictators (Salazar of Portugal being the other) in postwar Europe. This antipathy was manifested in a number of concrete diplomatic actions, including Spain's official exclusion from UN membership in 1945; two UN resolutions in February and December 1946 which called on member nations to break diplomatic relations with Franco and barred Spain from applying for membership in any UN agency; and the United States' decision to exclude Spain from the Marshall Plan.

With an increase in East-West tensions in late 1948, however, a number of high-ranking military and State Department officials in the Truman administration started to reevaluate this anti-Spanish animus. Ignoring powerful liberal/leftist opposition both in the United States and in Western Europe, these officials pointed to the fact that Spain could be a potentially useful component in the alliance systems the United States was building against Soviet expansionism. Despite his continued personal dislike for the Franco government, President Truman gradually acquiesced to a move to reestablish links with Spain. In December 1950 he appointed Stanton Griffis American ambassador to the country, ending a four-year diplomatic interregnum, and in the spring of 1951 he allowed the U.S. Export-Import Bank to grant $62.5 million in tightly controlled loans to Spain. In April 1952 this policy change became even more pronounced as the Truman administration initiated negotiations with the Franco government to establish a military accord outside the NATO alliance. The result of this initiative was a bilateral U.S.-Spanish military pact concluded by the Eisenhower administration in September 1953.

More detailed information concerning the Truman administration's policy toward Spain can be found in two recent and useful works: R. Richard Rubottom and J. Carter Murphy, *Spain and the United States since World War II* (New York: Prager Publishers, 1984), and James W. Cortada, *Two Nations over Time: Spain and the United States, 1776–1977* (Westport, Conn.: Greenwood Press, 1978).

SHANNON E. FLEMING

Special Committee to Investigate the National Defense Program

See Truman Committee

Speeches and Speech Writing

The American president, by virtue of his office, is the nation's persuader-in-chief, and his performance in that role is vital to his administration's success. Scholars from all disciplines recognize that presidential utterances, no matter in what format they are presented, carry the potential for momentous consequences. Over the years oratory has come to suggest grandiloquence, and in that sense no one could properly call Harry Truman an orator. But his great respect for knowledge and his reliance upon facts combined to make him a stimulating speaker even if not an eloquent one.

During Truman's presidency, the White House filing system arbitrarily classified his speeches as "addresses," "remarks," "messages," and "toasts." Addresses were speeches of major importance delivered before recognized bodies or the public at large. They were usually broadcast and received the widest publicity. Remarks, generally shorter and less formal, ranged from an impromptu talk before a group of visiting teachers in the Rose Garden to a rear-platform spiel during a cross-country campaign. Messages included the annual State of the Union report and other speeches made to Congress and were devoted almost exclusively to discussion of requested legislation. Toasts were routine tributes paid by the president, usually at social functions.

Aristotle divided public speeches into three categories: deliberative (advice), forensic (an attack or defense), and demonstrative (praise or blame). Traditionally, American presidents have linked their public speeches to what classicists called demonstrative discourse wherein the speaker could proclaim broad doctrines of human conduct such as that found in Lincoln's Gettysburg Address or Theodore Roosevelt's Man with the Muckrake. Ceremonial occasions offered proper forums in which the chief executive could remind the public of the nation's basic principles. When Harry Truman took to the bully pulpit, though, it usually was to debate specific political issues. His speeches were mainly deliberative inasmuch as he was endeavoring to persuade people to support some course of action.

Truman's basic outlook and attitudes were formed by circumstances of his training and experience. The strong influence of his family had implanted in him an orientation showing usually two paths, one of which he had to choose. No matter whether it was a question of paving or not paving a road in Jackson County or halting or continuing Lend-Lease shipments to Russia, there had to be a decision. Another predilection was his faith in established institutions. His decisions often grew from his recognition of civic and political establishments, his sense of loyalty to family and friends, his faith in the supremacy of his country, and his reverence for the Constitution. His military service in World War I was a third experience that left an indelible imprint on his approach to problems. That experience reinforced his preference for discipline and orderliness, and for following established lines of authority. Furthermore, his army training as a young man helped etch his image of military commanders, with one notable exception, in heroic proportions. Each of these attitudes and predilections appeared in Harry Truman's speeches.

Among legacies that President Truman inherited was a public expectation that following a major international conference the president would report to the American people. Accordingly, he delivered a radio address on 9 August 1945, almost immediately upon his return from the Potsdam Conference. In recounting plans the Big Three had agreed upon there for dealing with defeated Germany, he asserted that all Nazism would be eradicated and that the centralized armament industry, which had made the Wehrmacht possible, would be broken up. He directed his remarks toward the immediate future of Europe by insisting that people must be fed, not just in Germany but in countries overrun by the Nazis. The paramount military matter discussed at Potsdam, he said, was winning the war against Japan, and he justified use of the atomic bomb because it had been dropped on Hiroshima, "a military target." At the time it was delivered there was relatively little public response to the Potsdam address, not only because Truman as yet lacked personal persuasive stature but because the dramatic news of the dropping of the bomb captured most headlines. His address was not in the pattern of Roosevelt or Churchill; no one argued that it was a great speech.

Truman and his staff chose Navy Day, 27 October 1945, as the occasion for his first comprehensive address on foreign policy. This speech was delivered in Central Park, New York City, and was broadcast by all major radio networks. The event helped usher in a new era of reporting public affairs because it was the first time a presidential speech was televised. Viewers in New York, Philadelphia, and Schenectady were able to see and hear their president. The most important paragraph in the speech was one containing the seed of the Truman Doctrine: "We shall refuse to recognize any government imposed upon any nation by the force of any foreign power. In some cases it may be impossible to prevent forceful imposition of such a government. But the United States will not recognize any such government."

Probably the most important single speech President Truman gave during his seven and a half years in office was his Greek-Turkish aid message of 12 March 1947. It is hard to overestimate the significance of this speech, for it marked the end of American isolationism and set a pattern in the cold war from which retreat would be difficult. By late 1946, the tottering Greek government, which had relied heavily on British military and economic aid, found itself unable to deal with guerrilla forces then receiving increased support from their Balkan neighbors—Yugoslavia, Bulgaria, and Romania. Faced with military weakness and a collapsed economy at home, Britain announced it would withdraw from its traditional role as guarantor of Western interests in the Mediterranean. Truman's address contained no hyperboles, alliterative slogans, or striking contexts that might add vividness; instead it was a straightforward argument that was convincing to Congress and the American people. Within the address were three plainly stated points that became the heart of the Truman Doctrine:

- I believe that it must be the policy of the United States

to support free peoples who are resisting attempted subjugation by armed minorities or by outside pressures.

- I believe that we must assist free peoples to work out their own destinies in their own way.
- I believe that our help should be primarily through economic and financial aid which is essential to economic stability and orderly political processes.

The Truman Doctrine was slightly more than three years old when another international crisis arose which tested even more severely Truman's foreign policies. The event was the Korean War. Again, it fell upon him to advance the case. On 1 September 1950—barely three months after smoldering hostilities in the disputed peninsula of Korea flared into open warfare—Truman in a speech broadcast from the White House tried to clarify America's role in the conflict. Clarification was necessary because of remarks by Gen. Douglas MacArthur, UN commander, remarks that many persons interpreted as a changed policy that would expand the fighting. Truman's speech emphasized the "limited war" aspect of American action, and he hoped that his statements would make it plain that he and not MacArthur announced policy for the United States. This speech by the president, however, was not enough to settle the confusion about U.S. aims in the Far East, and the Korean policy became the subject of acrimonious, often partisan debate. There arose the so-called Great Debate of 1950.

One point of view was advanced by such men as former ambassador to Great Britain Joseph P. Kennedy, former president Herbert Hoover, and Senator Robert A. Taft (R.-Ohio). Their thesis was that the policy of containment had failed and a major revision of foreign policy was necessary. Against this view was arrayed the official policy of the administration led by Truman and supported by Secretary of State Dean Acheson. A few Republican leaders lined up behind Truman, and among those who agreed with him was his rival in 1948, Governor Thomas E. Dewey of New York. Gen. Dwight Eisenhower, who was not yet identified publicly with either major political party, also endorsed the administration's basic position. Truman led his supporters by insisting that policies advocated by the Kennedy-Hoover-Taft school would be a "retreat" which could only ensure eventual world victory for the Communists.

The brouhaha over the firing of General MacArthur fueled the controversy even further. President Truman had flown to Wake Island in October of 1950 for the purpose of conferring with the general, but that conference did not prevent the latter from continuing to make public statements that were not consonant with those coming from official Washington. Consequently, Truman in the following April relieved the famous general of his duties. On the issue of dismissal, Truman felt his logic was so solid that once the step had been taken he could remain aloof from public outcry. As months passed, it became apparent that the core of the controversy was whether the president's or the field commander's strategy should prevail.

The skilled whistle-stop campaigner in a comfortable setting. With the president on the train platform are his wife and daughter. Independence, Missouri, 1946. (Courtesy of Bert Landfried, John Knox Village, Lees Summit, Missouri)

Time proved to be on Truman's side, and when the initial uproar aroused by the drama of dismissal had spent itself, Truman's arguments stood even stronger.

It cannot be said that Truman or members of his administration were persuasive enough to make the war in Korea a popular one but when the fires of domestic politics had burnt out, there was little doubt that he had been able to rally public support for his decision to act instantly in that crisis. His case for containment remained intact.

Nearly every observer of the American presidency regards Truman's upset of the pollsters in 1948 one of the most remarkable episodes in his entire career. At his party's convention in Philadelphia, Truman captured the nomination despite a walkout of Dixiecrats and defection from supporters of Progressive candidate Henry Wallace. Truman's acceptance speech was delivered extemporaneously although it was in no way impromptu, for it had gone through several carefully drawn drafts before being put in outline form. The undeniable high point came when he revealed he would call Congress back into a special session: "On the 26th day of July—which out in Missouri they call Turnip Day—I am going to call that Congress back and I am going to ask them to pass laws halting rising prices and to meet the housing crisis which they say they are for in their platform."

In the period between Labor Day and Election Day that fall, President Truman made seven campaign trips extending over 19,928 miles. He spoke in twenty-nine states, usually giving his major address at night in order to take advantage of extensive radio coverage. In addition to 26 major addresses, he gave approximately 244 extempore talks of the whistle-stop variety; although extemporaneous, the talks were based on remarks planned and scheduled by shrewd and meticulous staff members.

From the beginning of the United States, American presidents have relied upon aides, consultants, and writers. The business of being president is too great to permit any one person to have all details readily available in mind, and the increasing tasks of office allow little respite when he can retire to his study and go through the labor of preparing a speech. When Truman came into office he had no time to assemble his own group of speech writers. Therefore, he asked Samuel Rosenman, veteran speech writer for Roosevelt, to help prepare several important early speeches. Rosenman did not have the authority he had enjoyed as writer for Truman's predecessor, but he did stave off efforts from a host of lesser writers and political allies of the new president.

Shortly after completing his first year in the presidency, Truman chose Clark Clifford as his special counsel and chief speech writer. Clifford had helped draft Truman's address on Universal Military Training and arguments for unifying the armed forces and combining the intelligence activities of the State, Navy, and War departments—a combination that became the forerunner of the Central Intelligence Agency. In May 1946, there were threatened strikes from both coal miners and railroad workers. Angered by the union leaders' refusals to accept his administration's directives, Truman scribbled out an intemperate speech he wanted to make about the impasse. His original draft was so vehement, however, that Clifford rewrote the entire manuscript, taking out much of the sting and giving the address force but presidential dignity.

Although he started mainly as a speech writer, Clifford's contribution to Truman's administration went far beyond that.

After the coal crisis in November 1946, Clifford was in on all the major decisions and many minor ones taken in the years between 1946 and 1950. For most of that period, however, he functioned more as planner and organizer of arguments than actual writer of messages.

Clifford's administrative talents helped him secure able assistants. His most dependable and by far most prolific aide was George McKee Elsey. Perhaps because he was thirty-four years junior to Truman and often overshadowed by the charismatic Clifford, Elsey could easily be the forgotten man in the Truman administration. He had a part in helping prepare Truman for the Potsdam Conference, and in the summer of 1946 he wrote an important and consequential one-hundred-thousand-word report for the president entitled "American Relations with the Soviet Union." *New York Times* columnist Arthur Krock later asserted that not only did this "Russian Report" supply Truman with details of changed American-Soviet relations, but it charted the course that led to such programs as the Truman Doctrine, the Marshall Plan, and the North Atlantic Treaty Organization.

During the campaign of 1948, Elsey wrote outlines for the president to use in most of his rear-platform talks. Elsey prepared more than three hundred outlines, by far the largest literary contribution of the tour. Unfortunately, these outlines were not kept because they were deemed too primitive to be of lasting value.

After the November election, Elsey started writing two important speeches: the inaugural and the State of the Union. At first, Truman wanted the inaugural message to be devoted to domestic issues—the ones that had helped him win. Elsey believed that the occasion warranted remarks aimed beyond Congress and America; the speech, he argued, should focus on world problems. He seized upon an idea offered first by Benjamin Hardy of the State Department. The idea was to offer American scientific and technical assistance to underdeveloped areas of the world. Such an offer would contrast with cold war rhetoric and would be a humanitarian gesture in keeping with America's superpower role. In the several drafts of this address, Elsey reduced five main topics to four. Thus the new program of technical assistance to underdeveloped countries became known simply as Point Four. When enacted into law, Truman's Point Four set up the Technical Cooperation Administration; the United Nations built upon the concept and created a Technical Assistance Administration; the British Commonwealth nations invited others to join in a single but similar program for South and Southeast Asia. A decade later, John F. Kennedy, as a senator, called for a Peace Corps to be built upon agencies that owed their genesis to Truman's Point Four.

There were other writers who helped prepare speeches for President Truman. Charles S. Murphy succeeded Clifford as special counsel in 1950 and for the next two years served as a major speech writer. Before the Truman administration ended, several other persons were called in at one time or another. One was David D. Lloyd, a particularly versatile writer. David E. Bell was one of several economists from the Bureau of the Budget drawn into the White House staff for message preparation. Other writers included James L. Sundquist, David H. Stowe, and Richard S. Neustadt. None of these, however, could match the contributions that Rosenman, Clifford, or Elsey had made to Truman's rhetoric. The writers agreed that it was their job to match words and style to President Truman's basic ideas and personality. Elsey summarized it best:

We [the writers] were seekers of information, clarifiers of position, and simplifiers of documents. In all this, we were adherents to the Truman philosophy that the best way to persuade is to present the facts and let the facts speak for themselves. Truman had an appetite for facts, plain and unvarnished, and lots of them. . . . his persuasions were as effective as they were because they were a reflection of his personal convictions. No ghostwriter ever put words into his mouth that did not reflect deepseated convictions.

Truman never became a strong platform interpreter of prepared manuscripts. In the summer of 1947 after giving a speech he knew he had delivered poorly, he told an aide, "This is quite a job for a farmer." At the outset of his White House years he realized that extempore delivery suited him best. His voice, although nasal and not rich in resonance, projected reasonably well. Pacing was a constant problem. Even after aides urged him to slow down, his usual rate was about 150 words per minute, far faster than that of most experienced speakers. Nor were Truman's gestures very expressive. Critics referred to the way he placed his hands about a foot apart squarely in front of his body as a "chopping-wood gesture." Many delivery traits had become ingrained since his early years in Missouri politics, but even critics agreed that as he gained poise and confidence in the presidency his platform speaking improved. Actually, aides were never very successful in altering his manner of presentation, and as he immersed himself in the role of chief executive he became too busy to be bothered with what he considered trivia.

Truman never aspired to oratorical eloquence. He looked upon his speeches as practical steps necessary in winning support for momentous decisions taken during his crisis presidency. He wanted his talks to be serious, clear, and convincing. Although as a speaker Truman always suffered by comparison with his predecessor, the charismatic Franklin Roosevelt, his public persuasions nevertheless helped buttress far-reaching political accomplishments of his administrations: the Fair Deal, aid to Greece and Turkey, the Marshall Plan, the Berlin airlift, and the Korean War.

The most detailed study of Truman as a speaker, including his methods of preparation, delivery, and relations with speech writers, will be found in Robert Underhill, *The Truman Persuasions* (Ames: Iowa State University Press, 1981). Several excellent biographies of Truman also present relevant material about his most important public addresses. Among these are Robert J. Donovan's *Conflict and Crisis: The Presidency of Harry S Truman, 1945–1948* (New York: W. W. Norton, 1977) and *Tumultous Years: The Presidency of Harry S Truman, 1949–1953* (New York: W. W. Norton, 1982). Other biographies that mention Truman's speech making include Cabell Phillips, *The Truman Presidency* (New York: Macmillan, 1966), and Bert Cochran, *Harry Truman and the Crisis Presidency* (New York: Funk & Wagnalls, 1973).

ROBERT UNDERHILL

See also Clifford, Clark McAdams; Elsey, George McKee; Lloyd, David D.; Murphy, Charles S.; Neustadt, Richard E.; Rosenman, Samuel Irving

Stalin, Joseph

(21 December 1879–5 March 1953)

Head of state in the Soviet Union during Truman's presidency; Truman's antagonist at Potsdam and during the cold war. Born in the village of Gori, Georgia, as Iosif Vissarianovich Dzhugashvili, but known to history under the pseudonym "Stalin" which he assumed as a radical student, Joseph Stalin was sixty-five years old and a veteran diplomat when Harry Truman became president on 12 April 1945. As head of the Communist Party of the Soviet Union (CPSU) since 1924, he had exiled or executed all rivals in the 1930s. Having formed an alliance with Hitler in 1939, he refused to believe British intelligence's warning of an imminent invasion by Germany in 1941. When the attack came at 4:15 A.M. Moscow time, 22 June, he suffered a nervous breakdown that rendered him immobile for the first eight days of the war. On 30 June, he created the State Defense Committee, became its chairman, and cloistered himself inside the Kremlin with a private secretariat for the rest of his life, the last Soviet leader to live permanently inside the Kremlin. Only on 3 July, nearly two weeks after the German invasion, did he address the nation by radio.

From mid-July 1941 onward Stalin requested massive aid from the West. He wanted Britain (1) to open a "second" front in France (ignoring the "first" front the British had maintained in France while he was allied with Germany) and/or the Arctic or Balkans, and (2) to send troops to the Soviet Union via Archangel or Iran to fight the Germans on Soviet soil. He also asked for considerable quantities of aluminum and steel and a *minimum monthly* shipment of four hundred planes and five hundred tanks. As the Germans approached Moscow, Stalin apparently lost another battle with his nerves on the night of 16–17 October and abandoned Moscow until the eighteenth.

German troops streamed across the Soviet Union's western borderlands in autumn 1941 and were welcomed in many areas as liberators from Stalin's collectivized farms and man-made famine. With the survival of the Soviet state in doubt, Stalin nevertheless found time to bargain long and hard for a clause in an Anglo-Soviet treaty of alliance that would have had Britain recognize the 1939–40 Soviet territorial annexations in Eastern Europe made under the Hitler-Stalin treaty. Despite British rejection of the clause, Stalin approved the treaty in May 1942. When Churchill told Stalin, at a meeting in Moscow in August of that year, that an Anglo-American force would invade northern Africa rather than France, Stalin fumed, "Perhaps British soldiers are afraid to fight the Germans!" This statement typified Stalin's selective use of history, but it was apparently the only time he lost his composure in the presence of a Western leader.

As the Soviet Union became more successful in the war, particularly in 1943 after Lend-Lease had put the Red Army's supplies and artillery pieces onto Studebaker trucks to speed its advance toward Germany, "Uncle Joe" became a darling of the West. By 1945 when Roosevelt died and Truman became president Stalin had greater name recognition in the United States than Truman did.

In July of that year, when he was ready to meet Truman at Potsdam, Stalin was at the height of his power. As the Red Army

Joseph Stalin in 1944. Artist: B. Karpov. (Courtesy of the Franklin D. Roosevelt Library)

had become successful, he had become more assertive in negotiations with the West in pursuit of postwar Soviet advantages. At home, he became increasingly exalted as the "cult of the personality" grew. By the time he met Truman, Stalin had added to his positions as head of the CPSU and chairman of the State Committee of Defense, the posts of minister of defense, chairman of the Council of Ministers (premier), and supreme commander of the Soviet armed forces. He had already met Churchill three times and Roosevelt twice. Soviet troops occupied all of Eastern Europe, and the Soviet flag flew atop the Reichstag in Berlin. In June he was exalted as "Generalissimo," a title imported for the occasion. Matching such experience and skill at the negotiating table, after only three months in office, was Truman's first major challenge in the diplomatic arena.

By April 1945, Truman knew Stalin's biography and Soviet history (including the Katyn Forest massacre) well enough to find both morally repugnant, and he considered the Russians perfidious in the commitments they had made in the Yalta agreement. But he thought that by appealing directly to Stalin, he could extend the fragile, but pragmatic wartime alliance into peacetime for the purposes of restoring the war-ravaged nations of Europe and Asia and implementing Roosevelt's idea of a United Nations organization. Before Potsdam, he informed Foreign Minister Molotov personally of his irritation over Russian noncompliance with the Yalta commitments and sent Harry Hopkins to Moscow to communicate these feelings directly to Stalin. Success of the Hopkins mission reassured Truman of the efficacy of appealing personally to Stalin. But meeting him in person at Potsdam would seriously diminish, though not totally destroy, Truman's hopes for personal diplomacy with him.

Although Truman admired Stalin's negotiating style at Potsdam, he came away convinced that Stalin was an unmitigated expansionist. Committed to getting the Soviet Union into the war against Japan, Truman resolved at the same time to exclude the Soviet Union from all possible opportunities for expanding their influence. Letters from Potsdam to his wife and sister reveal this mixture of attitudes: "Stalin goes to war August 15. . . . We'll end the war a year sooner now, and think of the kids who won't be killed!" (18 July). "Uncle Joe gave his dinner last night. . . . He talked to me confidentially at the dinner and I believe things will be all right in most instances" (22 July). "I like Stalin. He is straightforward. Knows what he wants and will compromise when he can't get it. . . . He seems to like it when I hit him with a hammer. . . . Russia and Poland have gobbled up a big hunk of Germany" (25 July). "The Russians are naturally looters" (31 July). "You never saw such a pig-headed people as these Russians." Stalin accepted in principle Truman's invitation at Potsdam to visit the United States, and Truman repeated the invitation soon after Churchill's iron curtain speech in Missouri. But Khrushchev in 1959, not Stalin, was the first Soviet secretary-premier to visit the United States.

Having decided on the ship coming home from Potsdam to deny the Soviet Union any occupation zone in Japan, Truman was on a course that led in 1947 to a policy to deny the country any zone anywhere in the world into which its influence could expand. Competition between Stalin and Truman to expand their respective nations' influence characterized their relationship during the remainder of their political lives. Less than two months after the Truman presidency ended, Stalin suffered a stroke and died in 1953.

The major biographies of Stalin are Isaac Deutscher, *Stalin: A Political Biography*, 2d ed. (New York: Oxford University Press, 1967); Adam B. Ulam, *Stalin: The Man and His Era* (New York: Viking Press, 1973); and Robert C. Tucker, *Stalin as Revolutionary, 1879–1929: A Study in History and Personality* (New York: W. W. Norton, 1973). Truman's impressions of Stalin are best seen in two collections edited by Robert H. Ferrell: *Dear Bess: The Letters from Harry to Bess Truman, 1910–1959* (New York: W. W. Norton, 1983), and *Off the Record: The Private Papers of Harry S. Truman* (New York: Harper & Row, 1980).

CHARLES E. TIMBERLAKE

See also Cold War; Containment; Potsdam Conference; Revolution; Soviet Union (and photograph)

Stark, Lloyd C.

(23 November 1886–17 September 1972)

In a strange way, Lloyd C. Stark played a crucial role in Truman's political career. Truman's dislike for Stark provided the extra incentive that drove Truman to a tremendous victory in the 1940 senatorial primary election just when his political career seemed dead. This victory becomes even more interesting and important when one studies his upset victory over Dewey in 1948 for the presidency. Observers could see Truman's combative nature and his adeptness in the role of underdog. Opponents consistently underestimated his ability and political acumen.

Stark was born in Louisiana, Missouri, the son of a family that had achieved national prominence in the nursery business, especially from the development of the Stark Golden Delicious apple. After graduating from the U.S. Naval Academy in 1908 and serving in the U.S. Army during World War I, he returned to the family nursery business and worked closely with his father. In 1935, he became board chairman of Stark Brothers Nurseries.

Stark made a bid for governor in 1932 but lost, and in 1936, he begged Truman to convince Pendergast to support a second try. Reluctantly, Truman agreed to talk to Boss Tom. After considerable argument, Pendergast finally conceded and supported Stark's candidacy. Stark was elected, but after his inauguration, he turned on Pendergast and played an important role in the conviction and imprisonment of the Kansas City boss. Truman was furious and his hatred for Stark never diminished over the years.

Despite an ability to charm FDR, Stark's limitless egotism and insensitivity antagonized most of the Missouri Democratic leaders. Truman was greatly pleased when U.S. Federal District Attorney Maurice Milligan entered the Democratic senatorial primary race and split the anti-Pendergast vote with Stark. Clearly the split helped Truman defeat Stark by 8,000 votes out of 656,501 cast for the top three Democratic candidates.

As governor, Stark ended the "Boss Rule" era in Missouri politics. He was also able to bring the Kansas City police under state control and to balance the state budget. He had promised to conduct the affairs of state like a good business, to give a full dollar of service for every dollar of state money and make the state government efficient and economical. His crusade for good government and the downfall of Boss Pendergast remain the cornerstone of his reputation in Missouri.

After World War II, Stark returned to his family business and had little impact on the political scene.

The Lloyd C. Stark Papers are located in the Western Historical Manuscripts Collection, University of Missouri–Columbia. There is also material on Stark in the Roosevelt Library, Hyde Park, New York, and the Truman Library, Independence.

EUGENE F. SCHMIDTLEIN

See also Election of 1940

States' Rights Party
See Dixiecrats

State Strike
See Mobilization

Steelman, John Roy

(23 June 1900–)

Assistant to the president 1946–53. Born on his father's small cotton farm near Thornton, Arkansas, John Steelman managed to acquire an education while working to help support his family. World War I opened the doors of college, and he took advantage by enlisting in the Student Army Training Corp at Henderson Brown College in nearby Arkadelphia. Following his discharge in 1918, Steelman remained in school, supporting himself by a variety of means and, in the process, acquiring five degrees, the last a Ph.D. in sociology and economics from the University of North Carolina in 1928. He met Frances Perkins, Roosevelt's secretary of labor, in 1934 when she delivered a commencement address at Alabama College where Steelman was a young professor. They discussed his work arbitrating local labor disputes, and by the year's end he had moved to Washington to become her roving labor conciliator.

Steelman's shift from academe to government led to a prominent career in industrial relations at a time when government's involvement in labor-management problems was expanding. In 1937 he became chief of the U.S. Conciliation Service and managed that agency's effort to reduce strikes and keep industrial peace as the nation's economy moved first into preparedness and then mobilization after Pearl Harbor. Steelman's work came to Truman's attention in the course of the senator's work on the special committee investigating mobilization contracts. The conciliator's reputation in Washington was sufficient that political gossip named him a probable successor to Perkins, who wanted to retire. But when she acceded to FDR's appeal to remain in the cabinet after the 1944 election, Steelman resigned from government service and opened a public relations office in New York. Following the change in administration subsequent to FDR's death, Steelman consulted with the Labor Department on reorganization plans, but refused an invitation to serve as under secretary to Truman's replacement for Perkins.

When Truman asked Steelman to join the White House staff in October 1945 to advise him on reconversion industrial relations, Steelman agreed. Following V-J Day, industrial unrest jeopardized a smooth economic transition from war to peace. Since wartime economic controls had given the executive branch enormous power over prices and wages and since union leaders and their management counterparts wanted to deal directly with the White House, the president was at the center of the controversy. In this context, Truman turned to Steelman for assistance in finding an acceptable balance between wage demands and higher prices without depression or runaway inflation.

Typical of this task was Steelman's handling of negotiations in early 1946 between the railroad brotherhoods and the carriers over accepting a presidential emergency fact-finding report to resolve a dispute about wages and work-rule changes. Truman insisted the contestants accept the report, but leaders for the trainmen and engineers balked, precipitating a crisis. The resolute union leaders refused Steelman's efforts at mediating, and Truman, manifesting his early combative approach to issues, asked Congress for authorization to conscript recalcitrant union members and keep the economy running. Steelman's conciliating skills proved insufficient to prevent this confrontation, but he did succeed in getting the trainmen and engineers to concede at the very time Truman was addressing Congress, thus averting a strike.

In June 1946, Truman made Steelman director of the Office of War Mobilization and Reconversion (OWMR). Its head, John Snyder, had moved to the Treasury, and the agency's role in administering economic controls was under heavy assault, particularly from a Congress interested in severely paring executive power. Following Truman's lead, Steelman advocated maintaining controls as the best hedge against inflation until production levels could catch up with consumer demand. When Republicans won control of Congress in November, however, the president recognized the bleak prospects for continuing controls and abolished OWMR by executive order on 17 December 1946. Steelman dutifully decontrolled as speedily as possible.

In dissolving Steelman's job, Truman created another for him as assistant to the president. In this position, Truman said, Steelman would "continue to aid me in coordinating federal agency programs and policies." The title prompted criticism about delegating presidential powers, but the job's responsibilities and Steelman's performance in carrying them out indicated that Truman was implementing a compatible and functional staffing arrangement at the White House for the balance of his administration. Charles Murphy as counsel would handle policy initiatives and partisan matters, James Webb would coordinate all budget considerations, and Steelman would oversee existing programs and policies. His own staff size would vary, but included as many as forty assistants and clerks. The president included Steelman frequently in Key West excursions and Potomac cruises, where White House staff combined recreation with the business of state.

The scope of Steelman's responsibilities included a diversity of domestic federal activities, but he was particularly useful as a troubleshooter. For instance, when the head of the newly authorized National Security Resources Board proved troublesome after the 1948 election, Truman assigned Steelman the job of reorganizing the board until a new head could be found. The president often referred bickering cabinet members to the assistant to work out their disagreements. Steelman also continued his role as the White House's chief labor mediator, taking part in the negotiations in the coal and rail strikes of 1948 and the steel seizure and strike of 1952.

Truman designated Steelman to manage the White House transition following Eisenhower's victory in 1952. He worked with Sherman Adams in preparing the Republicans to take over the executive offices and remained on the federal payroll for several months into the new administration. In returning to private life, Steelman resumed his consulting business before retiring to Naples, Florida, in the 1960s.

Steelman has informed the Truman Library he has no private papers, although he consented to an oral history interview which is closed to researchers at the library in Independence. The record of his activities is found in the White House Official File available at the library. For his views on the White House, see John R. Steelman and H. Dewayne Kreager, "The Executive Office as Administrative Coordinator," *Law and Contemporary Problems* 21 (Autumn 1956): 688–709. See also William O. Wagnon, Jr., "John Roy Steelman: Native Son to Presidential Advisor," *Arkansas Historical Quarterly*

27 (Autumn 1968): 205–25. A sculptured bust of Steelman is on exhibit in the Rotunda of the Capitol in Little Rock.

WILLIAM O. WAGNON, JR.

Stettinius, Edward Riley, Jr.

(22 October 1900–31 October 1949)

Businessman, diplomat. Edward R. Stettinius, Jr., was born in Chicago and educated at the University of Virginia. The son of a prominent businessman, the younger Stettinius himself achieved a meteoric rise in business circles in the 1920s and 1930s. He rose to be assistant to the president of General Motors with responsibility for public and labor relations. In 1934, he joined U.S. Steel and in 1938 became chairman of the board. During these same years, Stettinius cooperated closely with the New Deal. Along with Averell Harriman and Nelson Rockefeller, he was known as one of New Dealer Harry Hopkins's "tame millionaires."

During World War II, Stettinius served in the government. Between 1938 and 1941, he participated in the drive for industrial mobilization, heading the War Resources Board and serving in the Office of Production Management. In August 1941, Roosevelt appointed him to head the fledgling Lend-Lease program, through which the United States was sending military assistance to other nations. Stettinius remained in that position until late 1943, earning a reputation as one of Washington's ablest administrators. This success brought him appointment as under secretary of state in 1943. He subsequently served as secretary of state from October 1944 to July 1945. He took a special interest in the founding of the United Nations, chairing the Dumbarton Oaks Conference in 1944 and heading the American delegation to the San Francisco Conference in 1945.

Stettinius's association with Truman was brief and notably unpleasant. One of Truman's first decisions as president was to replace Stettinius as quickly as possible with James F. Byrnes. The new president had little confidence in the secretary of state he had inherited from Roosevelt. Inexperienced in foreign policy, Truman recognized his special need for skilled advice in this area, and he turned to Byrnes whom he respected for his political savvy. Truman permitted Stettinius to complete his work with the San Francisco Conference and then replaced him. Stettinius was appointed the first U.S. representative to the United Nations, but he found himself isolated and without influence and he resigned in June 1946.

After retirement from government, Stettinius involved himself in several private business ventures and served as rector of the University of Virginia before his death in 1949.

The best overall account of Stettinius's career is Thomas M. Campbell and George C. Herring, eds., *The Diaries of Edward R. Stettinius, Jr., 1943–1946* (New York: New Viewpoints, 1975). Stettinius recounts his own role in diplomacy in *Roosevelt and the Russians* (Garden City, N.Y.: Doubleday, 1949). For the Truman-Byrnes-Stettinius "triangle," see Robert Messer, *The End of an Alliance: James F. Byrnes, Roosevelt, Truman, and the Origins of the Cold War* (Chapel Hill: University of North Carolina Press, 1982).

GEORGE C. HERRING

Stevenson, Adlai Ewing

(5 February 1900–14 July 1965)

Although there was very little difference in their stands on substantive issues, it is hard to imagine two more different Democratic party leaders than Adlai Stevenson and the man who preceded him. Born into the midwestern patriciate, Stevenson, a graduate of Princeton, served briefly as a lawyer in the Agricultural Adjustment Administration early in the New Deal and then practiced corporate law in Chicago until he returned to Washington to serve as special assistant to Secretary of the Navy Frank Knox during World War II. Stevenson's later federal service included a significant second-echelon role with the American delegation in establishing and organizing the United Nations. He was catapulted into national prominence by winning election in 1948 as governor of Illinois by a margin of more than 570,000 votes while Truman was carrying the state by fewer than 34,000 votes. It was Stevenson's first campaign for any office and his only successful one. He soon was much discussed as a possible Democratic presidential candidate. Early in 1952 Truman twice offered Stevenson his unqualified endorsement for the nomination, and twice Stevenson refused it saying that he wished only to run for reelection as governor.

Finally, during the Democratic National Convention in Chicago—which he addressed as host governor—Stevenson allowed his name to be placed in nomination and, as he was in the process of winning the nomination on the fourth ballot, received the support of the president. Truman then flew to Chicago to back the party's new standard-bearer. Stevenson's campaign was probably doomed from the start. Truman himself wrote privately in December 1952 that he doubted "if anyone could have won on the Democratic ticket in 1952." In campaigning, however, Stevenson revamped the Democratic National Committee, distanced himself from the administration in power, and even, at one point in the campaign, seemed to agree with the Republican theme that there was "a mess in Washington" to be cleaned up. All these actions created permanent bad feeling between Truman and Stevenson. The president's supporters, then and later, have dismissed Stevenson as indecisive, with one partisan historian even sneering at his "appallingly coy manner." There is also a debate as to whether Truman's late support was significant to Stevenson's nomination. Stevenson supporters saw Truman and his unpopular administration as albatrosses around the candidate's neck. Stevenson admirers today see the Illinoisan's brilliant campaign speeches as candles lighting a dark decade, whereas Truman supporters are more prone to look at the "bottom line" and argue, as did Truman, that Stevenson did not get the Democrats all the votes to which they were "entitled."

Unlike other modern defeated presidential candidates, Stevenson assumed and held the titular leadership of the party and secured the presidential nomination again in 1956 without the help of Truman, who backed the candidacy of W. Averell Harriman. Truman did support Stevenson again during the campaign itself. After failing to get a third presidential nomination in 1960, Stevenson accepted an appointment from John F. Kennedy as ambassador to the United Nations. While serving in that position under Lyndon Johnson he fell dead from a heart attack in a street in London.

From the time of his first presidential campaign Stevenson captured and held the admiration of liberal intellectuals. He did so not by deed but by word: his speeches, which are often better read than listened to, helped educate and civilize a generation. He seemed, more than any other figure of his time, to stand for conscience in politics.

The best possible introduction to Stevenson is the superb edition of his letters and papers: Walter Johnson, ed., *The Papers of Adlai Stevenson*, 8 vols. (Boston: Little, Brown, 1972–79). The most thorough biography is John Bartlow Martin, *Adlai Stevenson of Illinois* (Garden City, N.Y.: Doubleday, 1976) and *Adlai Stevenson and the World* (Garden City, N.Y.: Doubleday, 1977). The most important of the many collections of Stevenson's speeches and writings are Michael J. Maher, ed., *An Illinois Legacy: Gubernatorial Addresses of Adlai Stevenson, 1949–1954*, (Bloomington, Ill.: Greystone Press, 1985); *Major Campaign Speeches, 1952* (New York: Random House, 1953); *Call to Greatness* (New York: Harper, 1954); *What I Think* (New York: Harper, 1956); *The New America*, ed. Seymour F. Harris, John Bartlow, and Arthur Schlesinger (New York: Harper, 1957); and *Looking Outward: Years of Crisis at the United Nations*, ed. Robert L. Schiffer and Selma Schiffer (New York: Harper, 1963).

ROGER DANIELS

See also Election of 1952

Stimson, Henry L.

(21 September 1867–20 October 1950)

In the evening of 12 April 1945, after Harry S. Truman had been sworn in as president of the United States and had met briefly with members of the cabinet, Secretary of War Henry L. Stimson remained behind to speak with him alone on a matter of grave national urgency.

What Stimson had to say doubtless shook the new chief executive, if it did not come entirely as a surprise. The secretary of war informed Truman for the first time about the country's most carefully guarded military secret. Since 1941, a team of scientists, working under the direction of Maj. Gen. Leslie R. Groves, had been engaged in the development of a new weapon of unimaginable power, code-named S-1. No one was certain when the device would be ready for testing, but it was hoped it would be within a few months. Once available, the bomb could be used, if necessary, against Nazi Germany or Imperial Japan if the war in the Pacific continued as expected for another year or more.

Mr. and Mrs. Henry L. Stimson and President Truman. (National Archives)

President Truman had come to know Henry Stimson during the Second World War when Stimson, in 1941, was the first witness to appear before the Truman committee. Appointed by President Roosevelt as secretary of war in 1940, Stimson had served in various governmental capacities over a span of thirty years. He had not been much pleased with FDR as an administrator and had made no secret of his dissatisfaction. Now he was happy to find that the new president was everything Roosevelt had not been.

Under Truman, cabinet meetings were not long, rambling sessions dominated by presidential anecdotes. Truman was systematic and orderly. He wanted to hear what cabinet members had to say, even if he did not always follow their advice. Unlike Roosevelt, too, Truman invariably came prepared to meetings. As Stimson wrote on 18 April: "It was a wonderful relief to preceding conferences with our former Chief to see the promptness and snappiness with which Truman took up each matter and decided it. There were no long drawn out 'soliloquies' from the President, and the whole conference was thoroughly businesslike."

For his part, the president found the secretary of war a no less admirable associate, and he was pleased when, unlike some other members of FDR's cabinet, Stimson stayed on. The two men rapidly developed a close collaboration. For one thing, although they both fully supported the Grand Alliance of World War II, they shared certain doubts about the troubling direction of East-West relations in the early months of 1945. Truman had long questioned Stalin's good faith and long-term intentions, and, in the weeks following the Yalta Conference, Stimson became increasingly concerned over accumulating evidence that the Soviet Union was systematically violating agreements made with President Roosevelt before his death.

On 25 April, Truman and Stimson, joined by General Groves, sat down to discuss the atom bomb project. Stimson handed the president a long memorandum beginning "Within four months we shall in all probability have completed the most terrible weapon ever known in human history, one bomb of which could destroy a whole city." Stimson concluded by recommending the appointment of an Interim Committee to consider the postwar atomic policy of the United States, as well as to study the possible employment of the bomb against Japan (although such use had been taken for granted by Roosevelt earlier in the war). The president agreed with the secretary's recommendation and appointed Stimson chairman of the new body. Its members included James F. Byrnes, incoming secretary of state; Vannevar Bush, president of the Carnegie Institution of Washington and director of the Office of Scientific Research and Development; Karl T. Compton, president of the Massachusetts Institute of Technology; James B. Conant, president of Harvard University; Ralph A. Baird, under secretary of the navy; William L. Clayton, assistant secretary of state; and George L. Harrison, one of Stimson's close advisers.

At a meeting on 6 June, Stimson brought Truman up-to-date on the group's work. On one crucial point, to be discussed repeatedly in coming months, Stimson told the president the committee agreed "there should be no revelation to Russia or anyone else of our work on S-1 until the first bomb had been successfully laid on Japan." If at the forthcoming summit conference, "the Russians should bring up the subject and ask us to take them in as partners, I thought that our attitude was to do just what the Russians had done to us, namely to make the simple statement that as yet we were not quite ready to do it.

"We then also discussed," Stimson recorded in his diary, "further quid pro quos which should be established in consideration for our taking them into partnership. He said he had been thinking of that and mentioned the same things that I was thinking of, namely of settlement of the Polish, Rumanian, Yugoslavian, and Manchurian problems."

At the same meeting, Stimson and Truman also discussed political aspects of the steadily intensifying air war against Japan. "I told [the President]," Stimson wrote, "how I was trying to hold the Air Force down to precision bombing but that with the Japanese method of scattering its manufacture it was rather difficult to prevent area bombing." He added, "I did not want to have the United States get the reputation of outdoing Hitler in atrocities."

On 30 April, Hitler had committed suicide; on 8 May, the Third Reich surrendered unconditionally; and by late June the president was preparing to travel to Potsdam to meet with Winston Churchill and Joseph Stalin.

Unlike Roosevelt's trips to Tehran and Yalta, Truman's journey to Potsdam was carefully prepared, and Stimson played an important role in those preparations. For instance, at a meeting of the President's top military advisers at the White House on 18 June—a meeting that included Admirals Leahy and King, General Marshall, and Navy Secretary Forrestal—there was this exchange about the necessity, but also the serious danger, of invading the Japanese homeland: "The President said that as he understood it the Joint Chiefs of Staff, after weighing all the possibilities of the situation and considering all possible alternative plans were still of the unanimous opinion that the Kyushu operation [the invasion plan] was the best solution under the circumstances. . . .

"Mr. Stimson agreed with the Chiefs of Staff that there was no other choice. . . . It was his opinion that there was a large submerged class in Japan who [did] not favor the present war and whose full opinion and influence had never yet been felt. He felt sure that this submerged class would fight and fight tenaciously if attacked on their own ground. He was concerned that something should be done to arouse them and to develop any possible influence they might have before it became necessary to come to grips with them.

"The President stated that this possibility was being worked on all the time. He asked if the invasion of Japan by white men would not have the effect of more closely uniting the Japanese.

"Mr. Stimson thought there was every prospect of this. He agreed with the plan proposed by the Joint Chiefs of Staff as being the best thing to do, but he still hoped for some fruitful accomplishment through other means."

As time went on, Stimson and Truman continued to talk about highly sensitive aspects of war and occupation. On 2 July, the secretary told the president: "I regard these two subjects, viz: the effort to shorten the Japanese war by a surrender and the proper handling of Germany so as not to create such harshness in seeking vengeance as to make it impossible to lay the foundations of a new Germany which will be a proper member of the family of nations, as two of the largest and most important problems that I have had since I have been here. . . . In both cases I have to meet the feeling of war passion and hysteria which seizes hold of a nation like ours in the prosecution of such a bitter war."

In a memorandum for the president dated 2 July, the secretary of war laid out his views about the surrender and postwar treatment of Japan at some length: "I believe Japan *is* susceptible to reason in such a crisis to a much greater extent than is indicated by our current press and other current comment. Japan is not a nation composed wholly of mad fanatics of an entirely different mentality from ours. On the contrary, she has within the past century shown herself to possess extremely intelligent people, capable in an unprecedentedly short time of adopting not only the complicated technique of Occidental civilization but to a substantial extent their culture and their political and social ideas. Her advance in all these respects during the short period of sixty or seventy years has been one of the most astounding feats of national progress in history—a leap from the isolated feudalism of centuries into the position of one of the six or seven great powers of the world.

"I think," he concluded: "the Japanese nation has the mental intelligence and versatile capacity in such a crisis to recognize the folly of a fight to the finish and to accept the proffer of what will amount to an unconditional surrender."

As plans moved forward for the Potsdam Conference, Truman did not initially invite Stimson to accompany the delegation, for he wished to spare the older man the strain of a demanding journey to Europe. But when Stimson indicated his interest in going, the president concurred.

Although not a member of the official party, the secretary played an important advisory role during his ten days at Potsdam. As Stimson recorded in his diary: The president "was very cordial about my usefulness. . . . I called on him almost every day in the morning before they went to the Conference and he told me what had happened the preceding day and discussed with me certain things which came within my jurisdiction. These were, first, the treatment of Germany both in itself and in its effect on the rehabilitation of Europe; and second, the Far Eastern war and S-1."

At 7:30 P.M. on 16 July, word of the successful bomb test at Alamagordo, N.M., arrived from the United States, and Stimson took the message to Truman and Byrnes. On the morning of 21 July, General Groves's own report arrived by special courier. "It gave," Stimson recorded in his diary, "a pretty full and eloquent report of the tremendous success of the test and revealed far greater destructive power than we expected." Stimson, the president, and Secretary Byrnes, "read the report in its entirety and we then discussed it. . . . [The President] said it gave him an entirely new feeling of confidence."

In view of some recent literature about "The Winning Weapon"—that is to say, the political uses of the bomb—it should be added that there is no evidence that Stimson ever considered it to be a political matter, nor did the president, then or later.

Stimson's labors at Potsdam dealt largely with the atomic bomb and the conclusion of the war against Japan. In a 16 July memorandum to the president, Stimson repeated his earlier recommendation "that warnings be delivered to Japan, designed to bring about her capitulation as quickly as possible." On the other hand, Stimson was prepared to allow the Japanese to retain their imperial dynasty if they insisted, and on 24 July he added in his diary: "I spoke [to Truman] of the importance which I attributed to the reassurance of the Japanese on the continuance of their dynasty, and I had felt that the insertion of that in the formal warning was important and might be just the thing that would make or mar their acceptance. . . . I hoped that the President would watch carefully so that the Japanese might be reassured verbally through diplomatic channels if it was found that they were hanging fire on that one point. He said that he had that in mind, and that he would take care of it."

Another topic weighed heavily on Stimson's mind. On what targets should the new atomic bomb be dropped? Stimson had been deeply angered by Tokyo's long record of unspeakable crimes and cruelty against civilians, dating back to Japan's initial attack on Manchuria in September 1931, when he was secretary of state. Nevertheless, as secretary of war, he was strongly opposed to the dropping of the bomb on certain civilian Japanese targets. They included the city of Kyoto, which, as Stimson wrote later, "had been the capital of ancient Japan and was a shrine of Japanese art and culture." The president concurred that Kyoto should be spared.

At the same time, Stimson—who well remembered the crises of the 1920s and 1930s that produced Hitler and the Second World War—was no less concerned about the destruction of Central Europe, and on 22 July he sent to the president another memorandum on "The Rehabilitation of Europe as a Whole." "I am impressed," he wrote, "with the great loss in economic values on the Continent, but even more with the loss in widespread moral values which destruction and war conditions have caused in Europe.

"We have immediate interests in a return to stable conditions—the elimination of distress conditions to ease our problems to administration and the speed and success of our redeployment. But our long-range interests are far greater and much more significant.

"One hope for the future is the restoration of stable conditions in Europe. . . . Under famine, disease and distress conditions, no territory or people will be concerned about concepts of free speech, individual liberty, and free political action. All the opposite concepts flourish in such an atmosphere. If democratic interests are not given an opportunity to grow in western and middle Europe, there is little possibility they will ever be planted in Russian minds."

At noon on 25 July, Stimson met briefly with Stalin and then returned to the United States, followed by Truman, on 2 August. The Japanese ignored the ultimatum issued by the United States, Great Britain, and China, and the first atomic bomb was dropped on Hiroshima on 6 August; when the Tokyo authorities still refused to accept the Allies demand, a second bomb was dropped on Nagasaki three days later. Almost immediately, the government indicated its readiness to accept peace terms, and discussions began looking toward Japan's formal surrender.

The issue of Japan's retaining the imperial dynasty went unresolved almost to the last. The subject was discussed at length at a White House conference on 10 August. In his diary, Stimson recorded: "The President . . . asked me what my opinion was and I told him that I thought that even if the question hadn't been raised by the Japanese we would have to continue the Emperor ourselves under our command and supervision in order to get into surrender the many scattered armies of the Japanese who would own no other authority and that something like this use of the Emperor must be made in order to save us from a score of bloody Iwo Jimas and Okinawas all over China and the New Netherlands."

In the event, Stimson's position prevailed, and Japan's formal surrender took place on board the battleship USS *Missouri* anchored in Tokyo Bay on 2 September 1945.

Stimson's own career was rapidly drawing to a close. On 4 September he wrote his formal letter of resignation and the following day presented it to the president, who recorded on his appointment sheet: Stimson "told me he is quitting on account of physical condition. Hate to see him go."

Before he retired, another important question confronted Stimson, Truman and the cabinet. How, if at all, was the new weapon to be shared with the Soviet Union, and what arrangements should be made for its international control? It was a subject Stimson had been thinking about for many months, and, in a memorandum of 11 September, the secretary set forth his views for the president.

The critical passages read: "I consider the problem of our satisfactory relations with Russia as not merely connected with but as virtually dominated by the problem of the atomic bomb. Except for the problem of the control of that bomb, those relations, while vitally important, might not be immediately pressing. The establishment of relations of mutual confidence between her and us could afford to await the slow progress of time. But with the discovery of the bomb, they became immediately emergent. Those relations may be perhaps irretrievably embittered by the way in which we approach the solution of the bomb with Russia. For if we fail to approach them now and merely continue to negotiate with them, having this weapon rather ostentatiously on our hip, their suspicions and their distrust of our purpose and motives will increase."

The following day, Stimson met with Truman and recorded in his diary: "Our talk about the bomb was the most important. He read over our memorandum on that subject and my letter explaining that my present views were not at variance with the warning I gave him last summer at Potsdam about freedom of speech in Russia. . . . His view on the whole thing was in accord with me. He thought that we must take Russia into our confidence." In the accompanying letter, Stimson said, "When in Potsdam, I talked with you about the question whether we could be safe in sharing the atomic bomb with Russia while she was still a police state and before she put into effect provisions assuring personal rights of liberty to the individual citizen.

"I still recognize the difficulty and am still convinced of the ultimate importance of a change in Russian attitude toward individual liberty but I have come to the conclusion that it would not be possible to use our possession of the atomic bomb as a direct lever to produce the change. I have become convinced that any demand by us for an internal change in Russia as a condition of sharing in the atomic weapon would be so resented that it would make the objective we have in view less probable.

"I believe that the change in attitude toward the individual in Russia will come slowly and gradually and I am satisfied that we should not delay our approach to Russia in the matter of the atomic bomb until that process has been completed."

On 21 September, an entire cabinet meeting was devoted to the future of the bomb and atomic science. As it happened, it was also the last cabinet meeting Stimson attended before his retirement, and his views were listened to with special attention. As he recalled later in his memoirs, he favored sharing the secret of the atom—but not the bomb itself—with Great Britain and the Soviet Union. The scientific secret of the bomb could not be retained, and so there should be free exchange of scientific information among members of the United Nations. During the discussion a number of cabinet members supported Stimson, including Under Secretary of State Dean Acheson (sitting in for Secretary of States James F. Byrnes), Commerce Secretary Henry A. Wallace, Postmaster General Bob Hannegan, and Abe Fortas, substituting for Interior Secretary Harold L. Ickes.

Navy Secretary Forrestal proposed further study of the question, although in his diary he reported himself strongly opposed to the Stimson proposal, as were Treasury Secretary Fred M. Vinson, Attorney General Tom Clark, and Agriculture Secretary Clinton P. Anderson. No final decision was reached at the time, although the president appeared to favor Stimson's position, as he wrote Mrs. Truman the following day.

The cabinet meeting followed a ceremony in the Rose Garden of the White House, at which the president conferred the Distinguished Service Medal on Stimson. "If anyone in the government was entitled to [the medal]," Truman wrote his wife, "it is that good man."

The former secretary spent the next five years in active retirement at his estate on Long Island, closely watching the unfolding international scene. His hopeful expectations were not to be realized. In late 1945–1946, relations between Moscow and Washington and London steadily deteriorated, and the president rejected the kind of sharing of atomic information Stimson had recommended in September 1945.

In September 1946 Stimson told Navy Secretary Forrestal, who visited him, that "the way things had now developed he thought we should not delay in going forward with the manufacture of all the atomic missiles we could make." According to Forrestal's diary, at a White House lunch on 23 December 1946, Secretary of State Byrnes reported to the president on a visit from Stimson and declared "that in view of the conduct and general attitude of the Russians since the cessation of hostilities [Stimson] saw no reason to be in any particular hurry to give them any information about atomic energy or the atomic bomb."

The United States gradually developed its tougher policy toward the Soviet Union, a course of action Stimson publicly supported from time to time. He backed the establishment of the North Atlantic Treaty Organization and favored the proposed program of Universal Military Training.

In the first years after Hiroshima and Nagasaki, there were no signs of the "atomic revisionist" view that developed in the later 1950s and 1960s. Nevertheless, as if anticipating the arguments, Stimson wrote several widely read articles in 1946–47, explaining and defending American nuclear strategy at the end of the war. In *Harper's magazine* in February 1947, he discussed "The Decision to Use the Bomb." Would "a different diplomatic or military course . . . have led to an earlier surrender?" he asked. He did not believe so: "The only road to early victory," he wrote, "was to exert maximum force with maximum speed." Should "American policy . . . have been controlled or at least influenced by a desire to avoid the use of the atomic bomb?" He had felt, he said, that "if victory could be speeded by using the bomb, it should be used; if victory must be delayed in order to use the bomb, it should *not* be used." So far as he knew, "this view was fully shared by the President and all his associates."

The former's secretary's health had been declining for some time, and the president was deeply saddened to learn of his death in October 1950. No tribute could surpass what Truman wrote Stimson on his retirement in 1945:

"It is difficult to estimate the value of the long public service in which you have attained high eminence in such diverse fields of activity. You have held three Cabinet posts under four Presidents. To the discharge of the duties of each of these posts you have brought wisdom, vision and true statesmanship. No one saw more clearly that you how the shape of things to come was fore-shadowed in the Japanese aggression in Manchuria. Historians will speculate whether the holocaust which spread over the whole world within a decade could not have been prevented had your advice as Secretary of State been followed. The Nation and the world are familiar with the inadequacy of our Army when you went back to the Department of War, a little more than five years ago. Under your administration it reached the greatest strength in our history and became the best trained and best equipped army in the world."

In his oral biography, *Plain Speaking*, Merle Miller quoted Truman as saying: "Stimson was a man you could trust. One hundred percent." That trust and confidence was undoubtedly mutual.

The president's warm tribute to his secretary of war is contained in his *Memoirs*, vol. 1, *Year of Decisions* (Garden City, N.Y.: Doubleday, 1955). Stimson included his own appreciation of the new president in Stimson and McGeorge Bundy, *On Active Service in Peace and War* (New York: Harper & Row, 1948), to which may be added Bundy's invaluable *Danger and Survival: Choices about the Bomb in the First Fifty Years* (New York: Random House, 1988). Stimson's full record is in his voluminous papers available at the Yale University Library. He recorded much of what he saw and heard in his personal diary, edited by Francis L. Loewenheim and Harold D. Langley, *The Politics of Integrity: The Diaries of Henry L. Stimson, 1929–1945* (in press). Gregg Herken, *The Winning Weapon: The Atomic Bomb in the Cold War, 1945–1950* (New York: Knopf, 1980), contains more liberal criticism of Truman and Stimson. Walter Isaacson, *The Wise Men: Six Friends and the World They Made* (London and Boston: Faber and Faber, 1986), is an attempt, not invariably successful, to strike a new balance.

FRANCIS L. LOEWENHEIM

See also Atomic and Hydrogen Bombs; Japan; Potsdam Conference; Soviet Union; World War II

Strikes
See Labor

Suburbanization

Truman's presidential years witnessed one of the great land rushes in American history. Perhaps 10 million people moved to the suburbs to live mostly in single-family, free-standing houses on lots of modest size. This massive migration absorbed about half the country's 1945–53 population growth of 19,637,000. Many more people settled in "infill" areas of the central cities, some as small as one or a few houses, others indistinguishable from large suburban tracts.

Altogether Americans put up 10,153,000 units of private, nonfarm housing during Truman's presidency. Yearly starts were 325,000 in 1945, but soared to 1,908,000 in 1950, an all-time record. In 1953 they settled back to 1,402,000 and thereafter remained on a rough plateau.

This phenomenon shared some characteristics with prewar suburbanization, including a quasi-rural environment, almost complete exclusion of nonwhites, and (from 1935) the assistance of the Federal Housing Administration (FHA). In other ways, it departed from the past. The unprecedented 1,908,000 starts of 1950 compared with only 530,000 in 1940. The new homes arose from a housing shortage, soaring family formations, prosperity, the rise of merchant builders capable of constructing hundreds or thousands of houses per year, and private and public policies channeling consumers into suburban housing.

Early in the postwar period, housing shortage horror stories abounded. An Omaha newspaper advertisement boasted a "Big Ice Box, 7 by 17 feet. Could be fixed up to live in." Elsewhere old trolley cars and surplus grain bins were converted to living quarters. The problem lay not in the numbers of nonfarm living units, for they rose from 23,300,000 in 1930 to 31,281,000 in 1945. Rather, the numbers disguised reality. They took no account of makeshift conversions from single- to multiple-family housing, aging, inadequate maintenance, and the distribution of housing. Cities and areas of war-spawned industrial and military facilities suffered grievous shortages.

Family formation surged during and after the war. The number of husband-wife families, 26,971,000 in 1940, rocketed to 34,400,000 in 1950. Not surprisingly, 6,000,000 families lived doubled up in 1947, and two years later, despite booming house construction, more than 2,500,000 did. Indexes of prosperity make concrete the statement of William Levitt, the big-time house builder, that the banks were "busting with money." Bank assets, $67,804,000 in 1940, burgeoned to $181,427,000 in 1953. Total savings and other time deposits climbed from $31,855,000 to $90,895,000 in the same years.

The merchant builder was a phenomenon new to the postwar scene. The Levitt firm captured a large share of the attention, for it was both pioneering and successful. Abraham Levitt, an established builder involved in wartime housing, saw the possibilities of an inexpensive postwar suburbia. Together with sons William and Alfred, Levitt integrated his business by setting up his own suppliers and contractors, thereby throwing out many middleman markups and union rules. The firm used mechanization, preassembly, and an elaborate division of labor into spray painters, window installers, and other specialists who moved from house to house, repeating their team functions. It began in 1947 on Long Island, New York, where, on 1,400 acres, it built 17,000 identical homes of 800 square feet, to house some 70,000 people at about $8,000 per house. The firm refined its techniques in two later "Levittowns" but its message was clear early on: the builder who adopted some features of assembly-line manufacture would dominate the industry.

Neither the merchant builder nor mass suburbanization would have been possible without federal intervention, however. Truman's sympathy for housing showed in his refusal to divert heavy funding from housing assistance to highway construction. The FHA was the most influential federal presence, for it guaranteed loans on home mortgages. The house involved had to meet the FHA's inspection requirements and its neighborhood had to pass muster also. Lenders could loan at low rates for extended periods because they were protected from default by insurance policies purchased by home owners who received FHA-insured mortgages.

Postwar home buyers could qualify for FHA-guaranteed loans at 10 percent down and twenty years to pay. The FHA made an important commitment to big builders like Levitt. It promised in advance to guarantee loans on houses built to its specifications. With the FHA commitment in hand, the builder went to his lenders and secured abundant financing at low interest rates. All this happened before a bulldozer had disturbed so much as a leaf or twig; thus the builder risked little of his own capital. The Veterans Administration (VA) operated an even more generous program for home-buying veterans of World War II.

The bright side of suburbanization obscured some less palatable realities. The suburbs were beyond the financial reach of many urban dwellers. They were virtually closed to racial minorities. The FHA usually would not guarantee loans to blacks, and it was more reluctant to loan on older houses than newer. The upshot was that blacks had to pay high prices and interest rates for central city houses and that affluent whites had an incentive to suburbanize rather than buy or improve an aging house in the central city.

Truman acted against racial discrimination in 1949 when he forced the FHA to guarantee loans in the suburban interracial Rolling Plain development near Chicago. That same year he acted again. In line with the Supreme Court's 1948 decision nullifying racial exclusion clauses in deed covenants, the administration announced that after 15 February 1950 the FHA would no longer insure mortgages on land subject to such clauses. Truman's actions did not strike at the heart of FHA policy, but they did reflect his civil rights concerns.

By the end of the Truman presidency it was clear that most Americans in the childbearing and child-raising years wanted suburbia. Some social thinkers argued that Americans should want something else or that they were not presented with real choices. But there was no evidence that many fled suburbia for row houses in the central city.

Richard O. Davies, *Housing Reform during the Truman Administration* (Columbia: University of Missouri Press, 1966), is excellent. Kenneth T. Jackson, *Crabgrass Frontier: The Suburbanization of the United States* (New York: Oxford University Press, 1985), is standard and skeptical of suburbia's cost, values, and future.

WILLIAM H. WILSON

See also Housing

Supreme Court, United States

The U.S. Supreme Court during the Truman presidency may properly be designated the Vinson Court, both because Fred M. Vinson's tenure as chief justice of the United States (1946–53) coincided almost exactly with Harry S. Truman's occupancy of the White House and because the Court in those years displayed a coherence of personnel and outlook. Truman made four appointments to the Court: Harold Burton, a conservative Ohio Republican senator; Vinson, a conservative Kentucky Democrat; Tom Clark, another conservative Democrat who was Truman's attorney general; and Sherman Minton, an Indiana Democratic senator and federal judge. Because the last three replaced prominent liberal members of the New Deal Court (Harlan Fiske Stone, Frank Murphy, and Wiley B. Rutledge, respectively), the Truman Court veered away from liberal activism. Paul L. Murphy aptly characterized the Court's approach to issues in the late forties and early fifties in a description of Vinson's outlook: "He now sought in every way possible to accommodate the Court to the tensions of the times, to avoid public controversy, and to minimize the Court's role as a policy-making and power body." Justice Robert H. Jackson, disturbed by his experiences as chief prosecutor at the Nuremberg war crimes trials, and Justice Felix Frankfurter, converted to a policy of judicial restraint that did not quite comport with his earlier reputation as a New Dealer and civil libertarian, lent their weight to converting a Court that might have been merely quiescent to one that was overtly conservative in outlook. This left only Justices Hugo F. Black and William O. Douglas to expound the views of a liberal and activist judiciary, while Stanley F. Reed occupied a moderate, centrist position.

Given this ideological orientation, it is ironic, first, that almost all the significant constitutional issues coming before the Vinson Court involved questions of civil liberties and civil rights and, second, that the Court's legacy on these issues was mixed rather than consistently doctrinaire. In these areas, the Court operated within a framework established in the famous footnote 4 of *United States* v. *Carolene Products Co.* (1938), whereby it squinted suspiciously at legislation infringing the Bill of Rights, inhibiting democratic political processes, or oppressing minorities. Combined with the Court's irreversible retreat from its previous policy of substituting judges' policy preference for that of the Congress and the state legislatures on questions of economic regulation, this new orientation was popularly known as the "preferred freedoms" doctrine or, more invidiously, as the judicial double standard.

The Vinson Court was divided between two approaches to Bill of Rights issues. The one embraced by Justices Black and

Douglas was known as judicial absolutism, because of Black's insistence on a literalist reading of the First Amendment and because he maintained that all the inhibitions of the first eight amendments to the Constitution were wholly binding on the states. Justice Frankfurter was the foremost exponent of polar opposite positions. He believed that the Court must balance the competing values of the individual's interest in, say, free expression against the state's interest in some other goal of public policy, such as national security. Drawing on a tradition established by Justices Oliver Wendell Holmes, Jr., and Benjamin N. Cardozo, most recently in *Palko* v. *Connecticut* (1937), Frankfurter insisted that the Court's judgment on incorporating the Bill of Rights as a restraint on the states had to be guided by "fundamental principles of liberty and justice which lie at the base of all our civil and political institutions," a position derided by Black as a neo–natural law view. This debate flared between the two in *Adamson* v. *California* (1947), with Black in dissent insisting that total incorporation of the Bill of Rights was mandated by the framers' intent and Frankfurter rejecting that position in a scholarly concurring opinion.

The Vinson Court was faced with important First Amendment freedom-of-speech issues, some growing out of the McCarthyite response to the cold war and others reflecting different sources of social tension. In *Dennis* v. *United States* (1951), the most important of its First Amendment decisions, the Court reworked the clear-and-present-danger test originated by Justice Holmes in *Schenck* v. *United States* (1919) into a conservative doctrine suggested by Judge Learned Hand in the Court of Appeals below: "courts must ask whether the gravity of the 'evil,' discounted by its improbability, justifies such invasion of free speech as is necessary to avoid the danger." Chief Justice Vinson's opinion thus adopted a balancing and bad-tendency approach to freedom-of-speech questions.

The Court did little to impede the witch-hunting of the second red scare. It upheld the constitutionality of the non-Communist affidavit provisions of the 1947 Taft-Hartley Act in *American Communication Association* v. *Douds* (1950). Vinson relied on a balancing approach and seemed to relegate political association to an inferior position relative to speech, where it enjoyed a lesser measure of First Amendment protection. Yet in *Joint Anti-Fascist Refugee Committee* v. *McGrath* (1951), the Court upheld appellant's effort to remove its name from a list of subversive organizations compiled by the attorney general under President Truman's 1947 Executive Order 9835, which had created a federal employee loyalty program. This decision suggested that the Court might provide some constitutional security for political association. But that promise proved chimerical in *Adler* v. *Board of Education* (1951), when the Court upheld the power of the states to require public employees—in this case, schoolteachers—to take an oath that they did not belong to subversive organizations or support the overthrow of government by force and violence.

The Vinson Court in 1950. Front row, l. to r.: Associate Justices Felix Frankfurter and Hugo L. Black, Chief Justice Fred M. Vinson, and Associate Justices Stanley F. Reed and William O. Douglas. Rear, l. to r.: Associate Justices Tom C. Clark, Robert H. Jackson, Harold H. Burton, and Sherman Minton. 8 June 1950. (Associated Press/Wide World Photos).

In the area of church-state relations, the Vinson Court began constitutional adjudication of establishment clause questions. In *Everson* v. *Board of Education* (1947), Justice Black for a five-judge majority explicitly elevated Thomas Jefferson's wall-of-separation metaphor to the status of constitutional doctrine to guide the Court in deciding establishment clause issues—here, state reimbursement to parents of parochial school children for transportation expenses. *McCollum* v. *Board of Education* (1948) struck down a state released-time program in which children attended religious education classes in public schools, but four years later the Court accepted a comparable program where the children were released early to attend such classes in private facilities (*Zorach* v. *Clauson*, 1952). All these decisions were controversial and divisive both on and off the Court. No matter which way doctrine and dicta led, whether toward strict separation or toward accommodation of church and secular interests, the Court's efforts to fashion workable establishment clause precedents seemed only to provoke heated critique and to lead it ever deeper into an impenetrable thicket of policy-making on religious questions.

Two wars presented problems that the Court had to resolve in the Truman years. It vigorously condemned establishment of military courts in Hawaii, accompanied by closure and disruption of regular civilian courts (*Duncan* v. *Kahanamoku*, 1946). But the Court upheld military authority when the question was one of the court-martial jurisdiction to try a notorious Japanese general as a war criminal (In re *Yamashita*, 1946). The justices reached inconsistent results in treason trials of German-Americans who had aided saboteurs. In *Cramer* v. *United States* (1945), a 5–4 Court adopted an extremely narrow definition of the constitutional phrase "overt act," requiring actions to be treasonous on their face, but in *Haupt* v. *United States* (1947) it substantially relaxed this requirement. Nevertheless, the very high threshold for treason in the United States, originally established by John Marshall in Aaron Burr's treason trial, remained intact.

The Korean War raised different questions. The major constitutional confrontation of that conflict came when President Truman ordered military seizure of the nation's steel mills to prevent a strike that might interrupt war matériel production. A divided Court (6–3) held his action unauthorized by the Constitution or laws in *Youngstown Sheet and Tube Co.* v. *Sawyer* (1952) and a violation of the separation of powers doctrine.

The Court's relationship with the executive branch was much more harmonious in civil rights cases. President Truman's vigorous and courageous actions combating discrimination, such as his orders desegregating the armed forces and all federal civilian employment, and the Truman-appointed Committee on Civil Rights' 1947 report, *To Secure These Rights*, were complemented by the Court's energetic action against racial discrimination. The justices delegitimated segregation in interstate transportation in *Morgan* v. *Virginia* (1946, holding that state-mandated segregation of interstate commerce facilities was unconstitutional) and *Bob-Lo Excursion Co.* v. *Michigan* (1948, inconsistently upholding state power to mandate equal access on international transportation facilities). In the landmark residential segregation case, *Shelley* v. *Kraemer* (1948), the Court gravely weakened the sixty-five-year-old state action doctrine by holding that state court enforcement of a racially restrictive real estate covenant was action by the state and thus a violation of the Fourteenth Amendment.

Art Bimrose, *Oregonian*, 4 June 1952.

The Vinson Court's principal contribution to the accelerating civil rights movement of the postwar years was its steady erosion of segregation in higher education. In a series of cases—*Sipuel* v. *Board of Regents* (1948), *Sweatt* v. *Painter* (1950), *McLaurin* v. *Oklahoma State Regents* (1950)—a unanimous Court persistently voided state refusals to admit blacks to state graduate and professional schools or, in the last case, a state attempt to segregate a black graduate student after he was admitted. The culmination of this trend, of course, was the decision in *Brown* v. *Board of Education* (1954). In this case, the Vinson Court heard the first set of arguments.

The record of the Supreme Court in the Truman years appears in retrospect variegated. In cases involving national and state security, the majority displayed great respect for legislative judgment, state police power, and the societal goals of stability and order. Yet in the equally controversial civil rights cases, the Court disparaged these values in favor of a judicial intervention that overrode state sovereignty and legislative judgment. Accommodationist in its approach to some First Amendment problems, the Court proved activist in others. Although a majority of its members was predisposed to conservative approaches to constitutional issues, the Vinson Court's record nevertheless appears pragmatic in a long view. It created little new doctrine, but it served as a bridge between an era that resolved the issues of the constitutional revolution of 1937 and the later activism of the Warren Court.

Two good surveys of the Supreme Court during the Vinson years are contained in Paul L. Murphy, *The Constitution in Crisis Times, 1918–1969* (New York: Harper & Row, 1972), and William F. Swindler, *Court and Constitution in the Twentieth Century: The New Legality, 1932–1968* (Indianapolis: Bobbs-Merrill, 1970). Biographies of the individual members of the Court can be found in Leon Friedman and Fred L. Israel, eds., *The Justices of the United States Supreme Court, 1789–1969*, 4 vols. (New York: Chelsea House, 1969). Issues of civil liberties are considered in Stanley I. Kutler, *The American Inquisition: Justice and Injustice in the Cold War* (New York: Hill & Wang, 1982); C. Herman Pritchett, *Civil Liberties and the Vinson Court* (Chicago: University of Chicago Press, 1954); and Harold W. Chase, *Security and Liberty: The Problem of Native Communists, 1947–1955* (Garden City, N.Y.: Doubleday, 1955). Edward S. Corwin provided a thoughtful consideration of freedom-of-speech issues as they appeared after *Dennis* in "Bowing Out Clear and Present Danger," *Notre Dame Lawyer* 27 (1952): 325–59. Studies of civil rights issues in the Vinson years include Clement E. Vose, *Caucasians Only: The Supreme Court, the NAACP and the Restrictive Covenant Cases* (Berkeley: University of California Press, 1959); Irving F. Lefberg, "Chief Justice Vinson and the Politics of Desegregation," *Emory Law Journal* 24 (1975): 243–312; and Dennis Hutchinson, "Unanimity and Desegregation: Decision-Making in the Supreme Court, 1948–1958," *Georgetown Law Journal* 68 (1979): 1–96. The authoritative study of the *Youngstown* case is Maeva Marcus, *Truman and the Steel Seizure Case: The Limits of Presidential Power* (New York: Columbia University Press, 1977).

WILLIAM C. WIECEK

See also Burton, Harold Hitz; Civil Liberties; Civil Rights; Clark, Tom Campbell; Douglas, William O.; Frankfurter, Felix; Jackson, Robert H.; Minton, Sherman; Murphy, Frank; Vinson, Fred M.

Symington, Stuart

(26 June 1901–14 December 1988)

Stuart Symington served the Truman administration from 1945 to 1951, occupying five positions. Born in Amherst, Massachusetts, he graduated from Yale University in 1923 after serving as a lieutenant in the American Expeditionary Force, 1918–19, during World War I. He became a successful businessman, saving the Emerson Electric Company of Saint Louis, Missouri, from bankruptcy and becoming president of the firm and chairman of the board. During World War II he made Emerson Electric the world's largest manufacturer of power-operated gun turrets for aircraft. While engaged in the war effort, his style of management caught the attention of Harry S. Truman, then a senator from Missouri who was investigating war production.

Since peace came with dramatic swiftness, the United States found itself with a mountain of war matériel and military installations that it no longer needed. Truman called upon Symington to help get rid of the surplus. Symington heeded the advice of his father-in-law, James W. Wadsworth, a Republican congressman, and in July 1945 became administrator of the Surplus Property Administration.

Symington had planned to stay in government for only six months, but President Truman wanted him to stay longer and offered him his choice of three positions: assistant secretary of the navy for air, assistant secretary of state, or assistant secretary of war for air. Symington felt that his business background would be of greater service to the army air forces than to the navy or the Department of State. He had, after all, dealt with the air arm during the war and was somewhat familiar with its problems and methods of operating. Moreover, military aviation stood at the threshold of independence from the army and was therefore facing the kind of reorganization in which Symington could make effective use of his background in management.

The National Security Act of 26 July 1947 established the Department of the Air Force, as one of three departments within the national military establishment. On 18 September 1947, the Office of the Secretary of the Air Force was officially activated, and Stuart Symington took the oath of office. As he had done when he was assistant secretary of war for air, Symington continued to represent the air force before Congress, and the role of advocate took an increasing proportion of his time.

During 1949 he became involved in a congressional investigation, the so-called B-36 controversy, that called into question his integrity and the reputation of the uniformed leadership of the new air force. Under investigation were charges that the air force had yielded to outside pressure in selecting the B-36 bomber, but in January 1950, a House investigative committee exonerated the service. The committee reported that there was not a "scintilla" of evidence to support the charges of collusion, fraud, corruption, influence, or favoritism.

With the B-36 investigation completed, Symington soon became disgruntled with the lack of funding for the air force. Under the financial restraints imposed by President Truman, the secretary doubted that the air force could perform in peacetime, let alone in time of war. After a three-year struggle to gain increased funds, Symington resigned, telling the president that he was willing to accept another position within the administration. The president concurred, and Symington stayed on as chairman of the National Security Resources Board and then administrator of the Reconstruction Finance Corporation. In 1952, he won election as Democratic senator from Missouri—though without Truman's support in the primary—and subsequently served four terms. In 1959, he emerged as a strong contender for his party's presidential nomination, this time with Truman's backing.

Paul I. Wellman, *Stuart Symington: Portrait of a Man with a Mission* (New York: Doubleday, 1960), is the only book about Symington. It is a political biography written at the time when the senator was a serious candidate for the 1960 presidential nomination. A good article about Symington as senator is Flora Lewis, "The Education of a Senator," *Atlantic* December 1971, 55–64. For an account of his tenure as secretary of the air force, see George M. Watson, Jr., "Stuart Symington: The First Secretary of the Air Force," *Aerospace Historian* 34, no. 3 (Fall 1987): 185–90.

GEORGE M. WATSON, JR.

See also Armed Forces, Unification of the; Military Spending

T

Taft, Robert A.

(8 September 1889–31 July 1953)

Republican senator from Ohio. Born in Cincinnati, the son of President William Howard Taft, Robert A. Taft graduated from Yale University in 1910 and from Harvard Law School in 1913, both times at the head of his class. Admitted to the Ohio bar in 1913, he began practicing in Cincinnati. Poor eyesight kept him out of World War I, but he served as assistant counsel for the U.S. Food Administration from 1917 to 1919, and counsel to the American Relief Administration in Europe in 1919 and 1920. In 1921, he was elected to the first of three terms in the Ohio House of Representatives and was speaker in his last year, 1926. He then returned to private law practice with the Cincinnati firm of Taft, Stettinius and Hollister. In 1931–32, he served a term in the Ohio Senate. In 1938 he was elected to the U.S. Senate, where he served until his death. Although he never achieved his hope of becoming the Republican nominee for the presidency, he was one of the Senate's most influential members.

In the Senate, no conservative was held in more respect. An intellectual who wore rimless glasses and spoke with a metallic voice, Taft lacked broad popular appeal but was worshiped by his followers. As with many of his fellow midwesterners, he frequently voiced suspicion of eastern monopolists, mass circulation magazines, and Wall Street speculators. The small businessman, the senator genuinely believed, was the key to the nation's progress. Yet in many ways, Taft lacked the narrowness and crude gregariousness that the popular mind so often associates with the heartland. More than is commonly supposed, Taft drew his ideas from both the East and the Middle West, while remaining somewhat aloof from the cultural milieu of either section. He endorsed U.S. membership in the League of Nations and the United Nations, and fervently believed that international law could resolve major disputes among nations. His voting record was more liberal than that of most congressional conservatives, but for all of Taft's own moderation, his views often reinforced rather than converted those of a more dogmatic persuasion.

When Truman assumed the presidency, Taft offered him the assistance of the Republican party. He also made a personal plea for a peace with Japan that would have nullified the unconditional surrender policy and left Japan with Formosa. In the spring of 1945, Truman deemed Taft intelligent, ethical, and trustworthy; Taft claimed that Truman was frank and decisive, and had strong conservative leanings. Yet, like almost everyone else, he was concerned that the new president lacked the education and background necessary to analyze major problems. Taft was soon disillusioned with Truman, finding him "as much a New Dealer as Roosevelt." Taft strongly opposed the Bretton Woods agreement, the provisions of the Potsdam agreement ceding part of East Germany to Poland, proposals for Universal Military Training, and Truman's tariff-making authority.

By 1946, Taft was one of the president's leading foes. In April, he claimed that Truman's request to draft strikers "violated every principle of American jurisprudence," and it was his parliamentary maneuvering that defeated Truman's proposal. In June Taft submitted an amendment to a price control bill that would have left producers with large profits, and when Truman vetoed the bill, he singled out the Taft amendment for particularly sharp criticism. In the 1946 congressional campaign, Taft accused Truman of coveting Communist support and of seeking a Congress "dominated by a policy of appeasing the Russians abroad and of fostering Communism at home."

In June 1947, Taft, as chairman of the Senate Labor and Public Welfare Committee, and Fred A. Hartley (R.-N.J.), chairman of the House Education and Labor Committee, drafted a labor-management relations bill that outlawed the closed shop, secondary boycotts, and jurisdictional strikes; it called for cooling-off periods and authorized the president to use the injunction in strikes involving national health or safety. Once it passed the Congress, it met with Truman's veto. The president claimed that the bill contained "seeds of discord which would plague the nation for years to come," and the measure gave Truman a chance to brand Taft, who was not an enemy of un-

Robert A. Taft, 12 December 1951. (Arthur Hansen/Boston Public Library)

ions, as labor's foe. On 23 June, Congress overrode Truman's veto.

On 12 March 1947, Truman called for a $400 million appropriation to aid Greece and Turkey in resisting revolutionary pressure. He also pronounced his famous Truman Doctrine of resisting "attempted subjection by armed minorities or by outside pressures." In his critique, Taft claimed that the proposal divided Europe into spheres of influence and might impel the Soviets to fight. Taft also raised probing questions concerning the reality of any Soviet threat to American security, the dependence of Greek guerrillas upon the Soviet Union, the tie between Greece and the security of the Near East, the absence of any role for the United Nations, the autocratic nature of the Greek regime, and the role of Congress in administering the program. Yet, not wanting to handicap the president, Taft voted for the proposal.

Taft was equally suspicious of the Marshall Plan. Although he endorsed the administration's goals of preventing both starvation and communism, he asserted that the European Recovery Program would "give the Russians a basis for the charge that we are trying to dominate the countries of Western Europe." He also claimed that Europe's hardship was exaggerated; that the Soviets sought no war; that America's priority must be a solvent, healthy domestic economy; and that excessive lending overseas, by creating an artificial demand, would lead to inflation and then to depression at home. Taft ultimately supported such aid,

but always after attempting to reduce drastically the sums involved.

Truman, neglecting to acknowledge Taft's proposals of federal aid to education and housing, attacked the Eightieth Congress in general and Taft in particular for apathy toward public needs. Yet when Taft failed to get the Republican nomination for the presidency in 1948, Truman said, "He was deserving of it, and he is an honorable man. . . . He would be a much tougher candidate than Governor Dewey."

Taft, in July 1949, was one of thirteen senators to vote against the Atlantic Pact, the major administration proposal that established the North Atlantic Treaty Organization. Claiming that the pact violated the Constitution and was hardly a credible military deterrent, he proposed replacing the treaty with a unilateral extension of the Monroe Doctrine. When, in January 1951, Truman sought to send four divisions to Europe, Taft denied that the president had such power. He further claimed that such a move would provoke the Soviets unnecessarily. He also accused the administration of deceiving the Senate when, in 1949, it had given assurances that no American troops would be sent, and he denied that U.S. ground forces could ever contend with the millions of Russian troops massed in Germany.

In December 1949, however, the prominent antiinterventionist left himself open to charges of inconsistency by supporting Herbert Hoover's proposal to extend naval protection to Formosa and the Pescadores Islands. Moreover, in a major speech delivered on 5 January 1951, the Ohio senator endorsed a "reasonable alliance" with England, France, Canada, and Australia, one that would protect such strategic areas as North Africa, Spain, the Suez Canal, Singapore, and the Malaya peninsula.

When the Korean War broke out, Taft claimed that Truman had little choice but to draw the line. In a major speech on 28 June 1950, he called upon his fellow citizens to support the American commitment "wholeheartedly and with every available resource." He said, however, that the United States should have left fighting troops in South Korea, demanded the resignation of Secretary of State Dean Acheson, accused Roosevelt and Truman of softness in dividing Korea at the thirty-eighth parallel, and alleged "a complete usurpation by the president of authority to use the armed forces of the country." Furthermore, in July, he attacked Truman's efforts to establish price and wage controls, claiming that the president sought "abitrary and dictatorial control over the entire economy." By January 1951, when the Chinese Communist forces had radically changed the nature of the Korean War and were threatening to rout American forces, Taft said that Truman should have stayed out of Korea. The United States, he continued, should consider falling back to a defensible position in Japan and Formosa and "unshackle" Chiang Kai-shek's forces on Formosa.

When, on 10 April 1951, Truman relieved Gen. Douglas MacArthur of command, Taft suggested that the president be impeached, a suggestion he repeated when Truman seized the steel mills in 1952. He backed many of MacArthur's proposals, including the bombing of Manchuria and aiding guerrillas on the Chinese mainland. "This Korean War is a Truman war," he said. In January 1952, he attacked the president for initiating truce talks.

Truman hoped that Taft would win the Republican presidential nomination in 1952, for he thought that any Democrat

Reg Manning, 27 September 1952. (Courtesy of the McNaught Syndicate).

Pa.: Bucknell University Press, 1979). For Taft's own cold war views, which involve an extensive critique of the Truman leadership, see his *A Foreign Policy for Americans* (Garden City, N.Y.: Doubleday, 1951).

JUSTUS D. DOENECKE

See also Conservatism; Isolationism; Labor; Republican Party; Taft-Hartley Act

Taft-Hartley Act

The Labor-Management Relations Act of 1947, popularly known as the Taft-Hartley Act, made major revisions in national labor policy. In response to labor unrest caused by the Great Depression, public opinion had supported the enactment of the Wagner Act in 1935. That law established a new national labor relations policy which encouraged workers to join unions. It made illegal certain practices management had used to discourage unionization, including interference with freedom of speech, discrimination against union workers, refusal to bargain collectively, and management domination of company unions. An independent regulatory commission of three, called the National Labor Relations Board (NLRB) was established to administer the law, hear complaints, issue cease-and-desist orders on unfair labor practices, supervise elections, and certify bargaining agents.

Members of the early NLRB viewed their primary function as assisting labor organizers in their efforts to encourage workers to join a union. This governmental support stimulated certain labor leaders to organize workers in mass industries and resulted in a major split in the American Federation of Labor (AFL). Most AFL leaders insisted on limiting membership to craft workers, so the mass industries unions broke away and formed the Congress of Industrial Organization (CIO) in 1937. The AFL, believing the NLRB was interpreting the Wagner Act to benefit the rival CIO, soon joined management in efforts to amend the labor policy. But at the same time the AFL also got in the race to organize mass industries workers.

As a result of these organizational drives, and the creation of maintenance-of-membership clauses during World War II (union members had to remain members during the life of the contract), union membership jumped from less than 3 million at the beginning of the Great Depression to about 15 million by the end of World War II. The reconversion process following the war brought widespread labor unrest. Based on the experience of previous postwar periods, workers expected significant unemployment, and an inflation that would wipe away their wartime gains. As a result of being caught in a wage-price squeeze, several million workers struck in late 1945 and 1946. A frustrated public, wanting consumer goods denied them by striking workers, turned against labor and their leaders. The news media helped inflame this attitude by headlining the strikes and emphasizing the tremendous power union leaders had acquired through NLRB actions. Republicans, campaigning in the off-year elections of 1946, emphasized the "uncontrollable power" of "irresponsible labor leaders" and promised voters they would revise the national labor policy, if elected. As a re-

could defeat him. By this time, Truman was furious with Taft, writing in July, "Look what he's done to himself. When a fellow is not honest intellectually, what can we expect." During the presidential campaign, when Truman toured the country, Taft followed him, taking issue with the president's claims.

When Eisenhower became president, Taft strongly backed the new administration until his death in 1953 of cancer. After Taft had died, Truman mellowed toward his long-time rival. In his *Memoirs*, while conceding they differed strongly on "what the role of government was in relation to the people," Truman called the senator "a highly ethical, straightforward and honorable man," one "who spoke for his side vigorously and ably" and whom he held in the highest respect.

Taft's papers are located in the Library of Congress. James T. Patterson, *Mr. Republican: A Biography of Robert A. Taft* (Boston: Houghton Mifflin, 1972), is the definitive biography of the Ohio senator. Superior treatments of Taft's foreign policy can be found in Henry W. Berger, "Bipartisanship, Senator Taft, and the Truman Administration," *Political Science Quarterly* 90 (Summer 1975): 221–37; Geoffrey Matthews, "Robert A. Taft, the Constitution, and American Foreign Policy, 1939–53," *Journal of Contemporary History* 17 (July 1982): 507–22; and Ronald Radosh, *Prophets on the Right: Profiles of Conservative Critics of American Globalism* (New York: Simon & Schuster, 1975). To understand how Taft fits into a much wider isolationist context, see Justus D. Doenecke, *Not to the Swift: The Old Isolationists in the Cold War Era* (Lewisburg, sult, the Republicans captured control of both houses of Congress for the first time since 1931.

Representatives in the new Eightieth Congress introduced seventeen bills to change national labor policy on the first day the House met. The House Committee on Labor and Education produced a bill, sponsored by Fred Hartley, Jr. (R.-N.J.), that was a collection of most of the antiunion legislation that had been introduced in the previous decade. In the Senate, Robert A. Taft (R.-Ohio) authorized a more moderate bill. The resulting conference committee produced what would become the Taft-Hartley Act, which contained most of Taft's ideas. Caught up in the antiunion fervor that swept the country in the postwar era, southern Democrats joined Republicans in June 1947 to pass the act by a vote of 320–79 in the House and 57–17 in the Senate.

The philosophy behind the Taft-Hartley Act was that, under the Wagner Act, the NLRB had favored unions, which had resulted in labor leaders achieving uncontrollable power; now the national government would act as an impartial referee in labor-management conflicts. The Taft-Hartley Act amended the Wagner Act by listing a series of unfair labor practices unions could no longer pursue. The measure outlawed the closed shop and permitted a union shop only through petition and election. Section 14(b) went even further by permitting states to enact "right to work" laws that banned compulsory union membership. Unions could not refuse to bargain collectively, use secondary boycotts, engage in jurisdictional strikes, or curtail an employer's right to free speech. National government employees were forbidden to strike, union officials had to sign a non-Communist affidavit, the check-off for union dues was prohibited unless voluntary, and unions could not use their funds for political contributions or expenditures.

The national emergency strike provisions were the most important aspect of the law. If a threatened strike would present a national emergency in the president's opinion, he could obtain an injunction against the strike and appoint a fact-finding board to determine the issues. Meanwhile, the Federal Mediation and Conciliation Service would attempt to help the two sides reach an agreement. Sixty days later, if the conflict had not been resolved, the fact-finding board would report to the president. Fifteen days later, the employees would vote on the employer's latest offer. If it was rejected, five days later, the injunction would be dissolved and the right to strike revived, thus establishing an eighty-day cooling-off period.

Union officials immediately and vociferously denounced the Taft-Hartley Act as a "slave labor law," and demanded that President Truman veto it. Truman, looking toward the election of 1948 and realizing that the Democrats needed labor support to win, found himself in a dilemma. As he described the situation to a sympathetic NLRB member, he was prolabor but believed that certain union practices should be curtailed. He thought that the Taft-Hartley Act was a good law and that a veto would be overridden. "So we're going to have a pretty good law on the books in spite of my veto," he reasoned, "and if I veto it, I'm going to hold labor support in the election next year." Truman thus vetoed the Taft-Hartley Act, and Congress promptly overrode his veto by four-to-one majorities, the most severe congressional rebuff to a president since the Supreme Court fight a decade earlier.

Harry Truman campaigned for the presidency in 1948, using the Taft-Hartley Act as a major issue. He warned workers that he had tried to protect them with a veto; if they did not turn out and vote for Democrats, the Republicans would win both Congress and the White House and thus leave unions exposed to even more severe attacks. When Truman won in the greatest upset in the history of presidential elections, he concluded that the labor vote had been the decisive factor; labor leaders agreed. When the new Democratic-controlled Congress assembled, the Truman administration led an all-out fight to repeal Taft-Hartley. Senator Taft countered with an offer to change the act's most undesirable provisions, but union leaders and Truman insisted that the entire act be scrapped. Although the Democrats controlled Congress, a combination of southern Democrats and Republicans held a majority and refused to repeal their handiwork of the previous Congress. In 1951 the legislators made the only change that would occur in this law by removing the restrictions on the union shop. Costly elections had shown that over 85 percent of the voting workers favored a union shop, so the members of Congress were willing to concede this point.

The Taft-Hartley Act is the only major alteration Congress has made in any New Deal policy. Application of the act has proven it is not a "slave labor law," and unions have learned to live with it. Harry Truman's opinion that it was good legislation was correct, and he and successive presidents have invoked its injunctive provisions on many occasions. He was also right in believing that it was a handy political weapon to keep on hand, and perhaps he was not too disappointed in his failure to achieve its repeal in 1949.

R. Alton Lee, *Truman and Taft-Hartley: A Question of Mandate* (Lexington: University of Kentucky Press, 1966), is the standard political history of the enactment of the law. Harry A. Millis and Emily Clark Brown, *From the Wagner Act to Taft-Hartley* (Chicago: University of Chicago Press, 1950), is an indispensable contemporary account by a former NLRB member. Arthur F. McClure, *The Truman Administration and the Problems of Postwar Labor, 1945–1948* (Rutherford, N.J.: Fairleigh Dickinson University Press, 1969), traces labor unrest in the postwar era. See also "The Taft-Hartley Act after Ten Years: A Symposium," *Industrial and Labor Relations Review* 11 (1958), and Erwin S. Mayer, "Union Attitudes toward the Taft-Hartley Act, 1947–1954" (Ph.D. diss., University of Washington, 1956).

R. ALTON LEE

See also Labor; Taft, Robert A.

Taiwan

See Formosa

Television

See Radio and Television

Tennessee Valley Authority

A federal agency created by Congress in 1933 to develop the Tennessee River and its tributaries, the Tennessee Valley Authority (TVA) was one of the most imaginative and successful of all New Deal projects. It applied the concept of multipurpose river development to an area comprising forty thousand square miles and covering parts of seven states. Navigation, flood control, and maximum production of hydroelectric power, centering in the great dams on the Tennessee, not only necessitated the coordination of three vital functions but also encompassed many related activities that touched the lives of the people in the valley. After surviving a series of threats to its independence in the 1930s and making a notable contribution to national defense in World War II, the TVA was emerging from its formative stage when Harry S. Truman became president.

Truman had been a consistent supporter of the TVA in the Senate, and as president he proved to be a committed advocate of its work. In 1945 he reappointed David E. Lilienthal as chairman of the agency, despite considerable opposition to him derived from his identification in the public mind with public power and New Deal liberalism. In a comprehensive message to Congress devoted to reconversion in September 1945, the new president paid his respects to "the example of the Tennessee Valley Authority, which has inspired regional resource development throughout the entire world." A few weeks later he described the TVA as no longer an experiment but "a great American accomplishment."

Following the war, the hydroelectric turbines in TVA dams were unable to meet the growing demands for electricity in the valley. This led the authority to ask Congress for funds to supplement its existing power system with steam plant generation. Truman endorsed the TVA's request, but the Republican-controlled Eightieth Congress, reflecting the strong opposition of private utilities, prevented such an appropriation in 1948. Approval came the next year, however, and during Truman's second term Congress appropriated money for the construction of two new dams, seven steam plants, and additional transmission lines. Truman endorsed the extension of the valley authority idea to other regions, but his recommendation for establishment of a Columbia Valley Administration died in Congress. His enthusiastic advocacy of TVA and other water resource projects was an important feature of his domestic reform program.

See Erwin C. Hargrove and Paul K. Conkin, eds., *TVA: Fifty Years of Grass-Roots Bureaucracy* (Urbana: University of Illinois Press, 1983), an authoritative overall assessment; Gordon R. Clapp, *The TVA: An Approach to the Development of a Region* (Chicago: University of Chicago Press, 1955), an illuminating discussion; and North Callahan, *TVA: Bridge over Troubled Waters* (New York: A. S. Barnes, 1980), a popular account.

DEWEY W. GRANTHAM

See also Army Corps of Engineers; Conservation; Lilienthal, David E.; Missouri River; Reclamation

Thomas, Norman Mattoon

(20 November 1884–20 December 1968)

As Socialist party standard-bearer, Norman Thomas ran in every presidential election from 1928 to 1948. Born in Marion, Ohio, Thomas was valedictorian of his Princeton University class of 1905 and a graduate of Union Theological Seminary in 1911. His studies for ordination as a Presbyterian minister infused his turn toward socialism with a middle-class moralism and elements of Christian pacifism.

At the height of his popularity during the presidential election of 1932, Thomas received 884,781 votes. He subsequently watched his support dwindle, owing in part to Roosevelt's appeal among left-liberals and the working class and in part to his increasing association with isolationism. In his race against Truman in 1948, Thomas polled 139,572 votes, up from the nadir of 80,518 in 1944.

Thomas explained his opposition to Truman in the immediate aftermath of the 1948 election in a letter: "One of the worst features of the re-election of Mr. Truman is that it gives free play to the militarists who have controlled him so far." He warned that if the United States attempted to undertake "the insane policy of trying to conquer the victorious Chinese Communists we shall be in war over our necks and the military influence will permeate every phase of American life."

Nevertheless, Thomas's own fierce anti-Communism led him during the Truman years to embrace the thesis of "Red Fascism," equating Soviet and Nazi totalitarianism. The CIA, eager to subsidize reformist socialists in hopes of crushing the remnants of the left and the Communist party, helped fund the Socialist party during the 1950s and Thomas's Institute for International Labor Research in the early 1960s. As Sidney Hook in a July 1982 essay for *Commentary* recalled: "When it was unable to pay its rent ... Thomas ... telephoned Allen Dulles of the CIA and requested a contribution.... he said that he and Dulles had been friends and classmates at Princeton ... and that he solicited the contribution purely on the basis of his personal friendship."

A prolific author and prominent critic of both the Republican and the Democratic parties for over five decades, Thomas remained the chief spokesman for the American Socialist party until shortly before his death in 1968.

For a general overview of the American left, see Milton Cantor, *The Divided Left: American Radicalism 1900–1975* (New York: Hill & Wang, 1978). Particularly perceptive about socialist politics in the early postwar decades is Maurice Issermann, *If I Had a Hammer ...: The Death of the Old Left and the Birth of the New Left* (New York: Basic Books, 1987). Bernard Johnpoll, *Pacifist's Progress: Norman Thomas and the Decline of American Socialism* (Chicago: Quadrangle Books, 1970), is perhaps overly harsh in blaming Thomas for the decline of the Socialist party, but is excellent in showing how Thomas's middle-class moralism was at odds with the earlier working-class socialism of his predecessor Eugene Debs.

JOHN TRUMPBOUR

Thurmond, James Strom

(5 December 1902–)

Senator from South Carolina; presidential candidate, 1948. Strom Thurmond was born in Edgefield, South Carolina, and in 1923 he received a B.S. degree from Clemson College. In the 1930s he served in the South Carolina Senate and as a circuit judge. After serving in the army during World War II, he was South Carolina's governor from 1946 to 1950.

In 1947 he criticized the recommendations of President Harry Truman's Committee on Civil Rights. A few months later he approved Mississippi governor Fielding Wright's suggestions that southern Democrats break with the president and the national Democratic party if they continued to press for civil rights for blacks. In May 1948 when a group of southern Democrats gathered at Jackson, Mississippi, to lay plans to oppose Truman and the national party's commitment to civil rights at the forthcoming Democratic National Convention, Thurmond delivered a keynote address filled with anti–civil rights emotion. He declared that "all the laws of Washington, and all the bayonets of the Army cannot force the Negroes into Southerners' homes, schools, churches . . . and places of amusement." When the national convention adopted a civil rights statement unacceptable to many southerners, delegates from Mississippi and Alabama walked out. At a subsequent southern caucus, Thurmond shouted, "We have been betrayed and the guilty shall not go unpunished!"

The southern dissidents organized the States' Rights party (popularly known as the Dixiecrats) and nominated Thurmond and Wright for president and vice president, respectively. Thurmond denounced Truman's civil rights statements and proposals and endorsed racial segregation. The Dixiecrat candidates were on the November ballot in thirteen states and polled 1.2 million votes, although the Thurmond-Wright ticket ultimately carried only four southern states where it had officially replaced the regular Democratic party nominees.

In 1950 Thurmond lost a Democratic primary battle for governor when his opponent criticized him for lacking party loyalty. When South Carolina's Democratic party kept Thurmond's name off the U.S. Senate primary ballot in 1954, he defied tradition by winning election as a write-in candidate. In 1964 Thurmond joined the Republican party, and in 1988 he was still serving in the U.S. Senate.

The major primary sources for Thurmond's interaction with Truman are the States' Rights Democrats Papers, Department of Archives and History, Jackson, Mississippi. Two good unpublished works are R. C. Ethridge, "The Dixiecratic Movement" (Ph.D. diss., Mississippi State University, 1971), and G. C. Ness, "The States' Rights Movement" (Ph.D. diss., Duke University, 1972). Helpful but too laudatory is Alberta Lachicotte, *Rebel Senator: Strom Thurmond of South Carolina* (Greenwich, Conn.: Devin-Adair, 1966).

MONROE BILLINGTON

See also Civil Rights; Dixiecrats; Election of 1948; South, The

Tobin, Maurice Joseph

(22 May 1901–19 July 1953)

Secretary of labor, 1948–53. Described as a tall, handsome man with "boyish frankness," an engaging smile, and great speaking ability, Maurice Tobin was a New Deal Democrat who defeated James M. Curley for mayor of Boston in 1936 and won the governorship of Massachusetts in 1944. Because of an open break with Curley and a nationwide Republican landslide in 1946, he lost his campaign for reelection.

In the summer of 1948, when Secretary of Labor Lewis Schwellenbach died, Harry Truman searched for a replacement. His assistant for labor affairs, John Steelman, Teamsters president Dan Tobin, and former New York senator James Mead all declined the position because they believed the tenure would last only five months until Thomas Dewey moved into the White House. Truman then persuaded Tobin to serve. The choice was good for both men: Tobin faced a tough primary battle in Massachusetts, and if victorious, a difficult campaign against the governor who had defeated him in 1946; Truman needed this Irish Catholic New Englander who was supported by unions in order to help win their endorsement in 1948. In the next few months, Tobin delivered some 150 speeches in twenty states, and the labor vote helped Truman win the presidency.

Tobin set out to rebuild his disorganized department over the next four years and successfully fought for a number of changes beneficial to workers. He urged an increase in the minimum wage to seventy-five cents, which Congress approved in 1949, and he improved the wages and working conditions for seamen and railroad and government employees. He persuaded Truman to move the United States Employment Service (created by the Wagner-Peyser Act of 6 June 1933) and the Employment Insurance Service from the Federal Security Agency to the Labor Department. He also established the Federal Safety Council in the Bureau of Labor Statistics and extended the Wagner-Peyser Act to Puerto Rico and the Virgin Islands. During the Korean War, Tobin supported the steelworkers in their strike of 1952, and opposed the administration's wage controls because he thought they placed workers in an unfair wage-price squeeze.

Tobin died of a heart attack just six months after he left public service.

There is no full-length biography of Tobin. See the *Biographical Directory of the United States Executive Branch, 1774–1977; Dictionary of American Biography*, Supp. 5; and his obituary in the *New York Times*, 20 July 1953.

R. ALTON LEE

See also Cabinets (photograph); Labor

Transportation Act of 1940

The Transportation Act of 1940 brought rail, motor, and water carriers under uniform, centralized control and placed inland water carriers under federal jurisdiction for the first time. It authorized the Interstate Commerce Commission (ICC) to establish maximum and minimum rates for rail, motor, and water carriers and created a board to study the effectiveness of the three transportation systems.

Railroad companies had urged Congress to place inland water carriers under ICC jurisdiction. Trains handled around two-thirds of the nation's traffic, but suffered inadequate earnings and extensive bankruptcies. Railroad companies protested that the ICC required railroads, but not inland water carriers, to adopt minimum rate levels for carrying goods. The water carriers consequently had charged much lower rates than railroads for transporting agricultural and industrial products.

President Franklin D. Roosevelt in 1938 established two committees to investigate the national transportation system. The first committee, consisting of three ICC members, recommended immediate federal assistance be given to railroads and that a government agency regulate all forms of transportation including water carriers. The other committee, comprising six railroad officials, urged the ICC to establish uniform guidelines and transportation rates and proposed the establishment of a board to examine the financial and physical conditions of all railroad, water, and motor carriers.

Inland water carriers, however, opposed changing existing national transportation policy because they could compete with railroads only by charging lower rates for carrying products. Government regulation of inland water carriers, they warned, would drive them out of business and give railroads a monopoly of traffic.

In April-May 1939, Democrats Burton Wheeler of Montana and Harry Truman of Missouri drafted a transportation bill in the Senate Interstate Commerce Committee. Their measure recodified the entire Interstate Commerce Act, placed inland water carriers under federal regulation, and proposed a transportation board to investigate railroad, water, and motor carriers. Wheeler and Truman, who argued that "everybody ought to be treated alike," led the Senate floor battle for the measure in May 1939. The Senate rejected an amendment to prevent federal regulation of inland water carriers and overwhelmingly approved the Truman-Wheeler bill.

The House Interstate Commerce Committee, headed by Democrat Clarence Lea of California, changed the Senate version considerably. The committee retained the existing Interstate Commerce Act, added a new section covering inland water carriers, rejected the transportation board idea, and retained the provision authorizing the ICC to regulate inland water carriers. In July 1939, the House approved the Lea version and added three amendments. Members of the Rivers and Harbors and Merchant Marine and Fisheries committees inserted the Wadsworth amendment allowing inland shippers to charge lower rates, the Jones amendment giving agricultural carriers the same freight rate advantages enjoyed by industrial carriers, and the Harrington amendment preventing any railroad mergers from displacing workers.

In April 1940, the conference committee largely accepted the Senate version, dropping the Wadsworth and Jones amendments but retaining the Harrington amendment. Protests by shipping and farm organizations, however, influenced the House to recommit the bill in May 1940. The conference committee then accepted the Jones amendment, but still rejected the Wadsworth amendment. The House and Senate accepted the conference report in August 1940 and September 1940, respectively.

Under the Transportation Act, inland water carriers were subjected to the same ICC regulations as rail and motor companies. Senator Truman lauded the act as "the most excellent piece of transportation legislation that has been offered to the country" and predicted it "would do more for transportation than any bill which has been passed since the Interstate Commerce Commission was set up." The Transportation Act proved effective, although American entry into World War II delayed the progress of the transportation board.

For the background and congressional role in passing the act, see David L. Porter, *Congress and the Waning of the New Deal* (Port Washington, N.Y.: Kennikat Press, 1980); Porter, "Representative Lindsay Warren, the Water Bloc, and the Transportation Act of 1940," *North Carolina Historical Review* 50 (Summer 1973): 273–88; and Eugene F. Schmidtlein, "Truman the Senator" (Ph.D. diss., University of Missouri, 1962). For the provisions and impact of the act, see Ralph L. Dewey, "Transportation Act of 1940," *American Economic Review* 31 (March 1941): 15–26; Truman C. Bigham, "The Transportation Act of 1940," *Southern Economic Journal* 8 (July 1941): 1–21; Robert W. Harbeson, "The Transportation Act of 1940," *Journal of Land and Public Utility Economics* 17 (August 1941): 291–302; William J. and Robert W. Hull, *The Origin and Development of the Waterways Policy of the United States* (Washington, D.C.: National Waterways Conference, 1967); and Ari and Olive Hoogenboom, *A History of the ICC* (New York: W. W. Norton, 1975).

DAVID L. PORTER

See also Senator

Truman, Elizabeth Virginia Wallace ("Bess")

(13 February 1885–18 October 1982)

Wife of the president. Born in Independence, Missouri, Bess Wallace Truman was the only daughter (and eldest child) of David and Madge Gates Wallace. Her maternal grandfather, George Porterfield Gates, owned a profitable milling business and her paternal grandfather had served as one of the town's early mayors. Bess attended local public schools, but at age eighteen, her life abruptly changed when her father committed suicide. Madge Wallace, with four children to raise, returned to live with her parents, and Bess altered any plans she may have had to go away to school; she enrolled instead in a finishing school, Barstow, in Kansas City. According to the Trumans' only child, their daughter Margaret, it was David Wallace's death, more than any other single event, that shaped Bess's adamant insistence on privacy. Madge Wallace, always self-centered and critical of others, became even more so, and Bess humored her by staying nearby and concentrating on improving her tennis and her housekeeping skills.

Bess Truman. (Hessler Studio of Washington, D.C./Courtesy of the Harry S. Truman Library)

Harry Truman met his future bride when both were youngsters and attended the same schools. For his part, at least, it was love at first sight, and almost sixty years later, as president, he wrote, "You are still on the pedestal where I placed you that day in Sunday School in 1890." The courtship was prolonged, however, and his letters to Bess during those years suggest his strong determination to succeed at something—farming, mining, drilling for oil—in order to win not only Bess's approval but also that of her mother. In the latter endeavor, it is not clear that he succeeded. After their marriage in 1919, Bess and her husband made their Independence home with Madge Wallace (and even during the years in Washington, Madge resided with them much of the time), but evidence compiled by Margaret Truman suggests a rather tense truce between the courteous, attentive Harry and his mother-in-law.

Bess's participation in her husband's career was, by his own evaluation, considerable. When he opened a haberdashery, she kept the books. Later, in Washington, she worked for a salary in his Senate office. In the prepresidential years, she added to his "plain folks" reputation by dressing simply, entertaining rarely, and doing the housework in their rented Washington apartment. A very private person, she received little attention in the capital, and when Harry was suddenly elevated to the presidency in 1945, few reporters—or even Democratic party headquarters—could supply accurate information about her.

Harry's epitaph for Bess was simply "First Lady, the United States of America, April 12, 1945–January 20, 1953," but all evidence indicates that this was the part of her long life that she liked the least. Even casual observers noted her distaste for performing as White House hostess. The capital press corps, accustomed to a communicative Eleanor Roosevelt, expected Bess to continue holding regular press conferences, and at first, she agreed to do so. But then, when Frances Perkins pointed out that no First Lady before Roosevelt had faced the press, Bess canceled her meeting and never agreed to another one. Minimal information on White House social events and the First Lady's schedule came from her secretaries. When Bess finally agreed to answer reporters' written questions, she did so on paper and responded "No Comment" to nearly a third of the queries. On Harry's choice of career, she was both adamant and clear, answering "Definitely did not" to the question of whether she had wanted him to be president. By refusing to talk with reporters, she gained the reputation of being enigmatic. A *New York Times* reporter called her "a riddle" after three years in the White House, and Margaret Truman judged her the "least understood" member of the family.

For Harry, Bess's role was clear. He introduced her to the public as "the Boss" and he explained to a reporter that he had conferred with her on many important issues, including the use of the atomic bomb, the Marshall Plan, postwar rebuilding, and the Korean military action. Margaret Truman gave her mother credit for helping obtain increased funding for the National Institutes of Health and for arranging for theater groups to tour abroad under the auspices of the State Department.

The inevitability of a public role for the president's wife was never quite understood by either Bess or Harry. He insisted that he, as the elected official, was open to any criticism but that his wife and daughter were not fair targets. Bess acted as though her actions—except for the requisite ceremonial appearances which she made—were her own business. Her attendance at a reception of the Daughters of the American Revolution, after that group had refused permission for a black pianist (who happened to be married to a congressman) to perform in its Constitution Hall, earned her the nickname from the congressman of "Last Lady of the Land." She took long summer vacations with her mother in Independence in spite of her husband's complaints of loneliness in the capital.

Against all criticism, Harry Truman defended his wife. When Washington reporters described her as "dull, dumpy and distant," he responded that she looked the way a woman of her age ought to look. When a friend noted a billboard slogan that said "Gentlemen Prefer Blonds," Harry countered, "Real gentlemen prefer gray."

One of the last First Ladies to be born in the nineteenth century, Bess remained very much a person of a premodern age. Until after the White House years, she rarely traveled by plane, and unlike a later generation of political wives, she never took speech lessons or appeared to cultivate the contacts and skills that render a politician's wife a public asset to her husband's career. Harry's closest political associates were rarely her guests.

After the White House, the Trumans lived quietly in Independence in the same house where they had resided as newlyweds. Bess survived her husband by nearly ten years, and she is buried beside him in the courtyard of the presidential library in Independence.

For an evaluation of Bess Truman's record as First Lady, see Betty Boyd Caroli, *First Ladies* (New York: Oxford University Press,

1987), especially pages 201–10. Margaret Truman included considerable material on her mother in her autobiography, *Souvenir: Margaret Truman's Own Story* (New York: McGraw-Hill, 1956), and in her book about her father, *Harry S. Truman* (New York: William Morrow, 1973). In a later book, which she described as "the most difficult I have ever written," Margaret focused on her mother: *Bess W. Truman* (New York: Macmillan, 1986). In this last volume, Margaret exaggerates her mother's feminism and tempers her influence, citing instances of Bess's feeling shut out of presidential decisions in the White House. In spite of its rather misleading title, Jhan Robbins's *Bess and Harry: An American Love Story* (New York: G. Putnam's Sons, 1980) offers many examples of the wife's influencing the husband from the beginning of their marriage. Harry's letters to Bess make up a large volume: Robert H. Ferrell, ed., *Dear Bess: The Letters from Harry to Bess Truman, 1910–1959* (New York: W. W. Norton, 1983). These letters indicate the closeness of the relationship and Harry's trust in Bess. Maurine Beasley's insightful article, "Bess Truman and the Press: A Case Study of a First Lady as Political Communicator," in *Harry S. Truman: The Man from Independence*, ed. William F. Levantrosser (New York: Greenwood Press, 1986), 207–16, concludes that, in spite of her distaste for dealing with reporters, Bess Truman, like all First Ladies after Eleanor Roosevelt, could not ignore the press.

BETTY BOYD CAROLI

See also Gates-Wallace-Truman House; Personality (photograph); Roosevelt, Franklin D. (photograph); Speeches and Speech Writing (photograph)

The president's parents, John Anderson and Martha Ellen Truman, on their wedding day, 28 December 1881. (Courtesy of the Harry S. Truman Library)

Truman, John Anderson

(5 December 1851–2 November 1914)

Father of Harry S. Truman. John Truman was one of five children of Anderson Shippe (or Shipp—it is not clear when the final "e" was added to the family name) Truman and Mary Jane Holmes (1821–78). His parents had moved from Shelby County, Kentucky, to Westport Landing (later Kansas City), Missouri, in either 1841 or 1842 and it was there that he was born. Little is known of his childhood, although he apparently showed little interest in school and did not stay with it long. He married Martha Ellen Young on 28 December 1881. They had three children: Harry, born in 1884, Vivian, born in 1886, and Mary Jane, born in 1889.

John Truman grew up on a farm and, until he was thirty years old, worked as a farmer. Family history has it that, even as a child, he had always been interested in livestock trading, and it was to this occupation he turned following his marriage—when he also left the farm and moved to Lamar. This was followed by further moves, first to Harrisonville and then to a farm ("Dye's") outside that Cass County community, but in 1887 he returned to farming when the family moved in with John's father-in-law, Solomon Young, in Grandview. Then, in 1890, the family moved again, this time to Independence, mainly to enable the oldest boy, who had just reached school age, to attend a city school but also to allow John to have another try at the cattle and mule trading business. Eventually he also tried his hand at real estate deals and speculated in the grain futures market, both

with some success. By 1901, however, he had suffered severe reverses, and in 1904 (after a brief period of residence in Kansas City) he returned to farming, this time near the town of Clinton. The following year a flood wiped out his corn crop, and he found it necessary to move to the Grandview farm of his widowed mother. He worked there until his death nine years later. Off and on throughout the years he also dabbled with the development of useful household and farm utensils but failed to attain any commercial successes with his inventions.

Politics began to interest him in the late 1880s. He never ran for office but was active in Democratic party affairs throughout his life. His sons recalled that "Cleveland was his idol." He served as a delegate to the state convention in 1908, was elections judge in Grandview in 1910, and was named road supervisor in 1912—all of which suggests that he was regarded as a loyal party worker.

Physically John Truman was a small man, standing five feet six inches tall and weighing 140 pounds. He had rather fine features and is said to have carried himself "very erect." Speaking to Merle Miller, President Truman said that his father had been "a small, feisty man, fastidious in dress and manner. . . . if he did not like what you did, he'd fight you." Others described him as quick of temper but reliable in all his dealings. If these characterizations suggests that Harry Truman owed much of his personal makeup to his father, this also appears to apply to the love of music the son shared with his father (and which his mother early encouraged). John Truman is reported to have been fond of singing. Although he was unschooled in music, he enjoyed singing with others and, according to his sons, would often sing by himself while attending to the farm chores.

There is little documentary evidence concerning Harry Truman's relationship with his father, but occasional references—for instance, in the *Autobiography* and in anecdotal material related by Alfred Steinberg in *The Man from Missouri*—suggest that the two apparently were always cordial. John Truman evidently was neither stern and forbidding nor particularly demonstrative with his son. It is reported that he never laid a hand on Harry but would often scold him severely. It is certain that Harry Truman rarely disobeyed his father.

Although John Truman was certainly not a successful man in his business ventures, he evidently enjoyed the respect of his neighbors. When he died in 1914, in the aftermath of surgery to repair an intestinal block he had incurred as a result of overexertion while working on one of the roads under his supervision, the *Independence Examiner* eulogized him as "an upright citizen whose death will be a blow to his community."

John Truman is the subject of the opening chapter of Bela Kornitzer's *American Fathers and Sons* (N.p.: Hermitage Press, 1952). The brief narrative is based on interviews with John Truman's children and other members and friends of the family. A photograph of John Truman is included. Anecdotal information about him may also be found in *The Autobiography of Harry S. Truman*, ed. Robert Ferrell (Boulder: Colorado Associated University Press, 1980); in the president's *Memoirs* (Garden City, N.Y.: Doubleday, 1955); in Merle Miller, *Plain Speaking: An Oral Autobiography of Harry S. Truman* (New York: G. P. Putnam's Sons, 1973); in Richard Lawrence Miller, *Truman: The Rise to Power* (New York: McGraw-Hill, 1986); in Alfred Steinberg, *The Man from Missouri: The Life and Times of Harry S. Truman* (New York: G. P. Putnam's Sons, 1962): and in Margaret Truman, *Harry S. Truman* (New York: Morrow, 1973).

FRANCIS H. HELLER

Truman, John Vivian

(25 April 1886–8 July 1965)

Brother of the president. The relationship between Harry Truman and his only brother, Vivian, was apparently always friendly and caring, and it remained so throughout their lives. Vivian was a staunch Democrat who never became active in politics, although in his retirement he served as an election commissioner for Jackson County. In 1935 the Farm Housing Administration appointed Vivian Truman as a field representative, and by 1948 he had advanced to district director of the agency. Understandably, it was widely rumored that he had owed his initial appointment and his subsequent advancement to the political influence of his older brother. Vivian, however, insisted always that he had seen an announcement of the opening, had applied for the position, and had been accepted on his merits. His advancement, it has been noted, was no faster than was customary in the agency.

The future president (r.) and his younger brother, Vivian, in 1888. (National Archives)

Vivian was married to Luella Campbell (1888–1978), and they had five children: J. C., Fred, Harry, Gilbert, and Martha Ann (Swoyer).

Harry Truman and Vivian, along with their sister, Mary Jane, shared ownership of the family farm in Grandview after their mother's death in 1947. In the early 1950s, when President Truman wished to locate his presidential library on a section of the farm, Vivian adamantly opposed giving up the site the architects considered the best location, for he regarded it as the most fertile portion of the farm. The president deferred to his brother and eventually accepted the city of Independence's offer of a site in Slover Park, where the Truman Library now stands. The three Trumans then sold the major part of the farm which became the site of Truman Corners shopping center. Vivian and his family continued to live on the remaining farm property until his death there in 1965.

True to the modest life he chose to lead, Vivian Truman has received very little attention from scholars and journalists. The Truman Library has a file containing personal data and some newspaper clippings. Other library files, such as those relating to the planning of the library and the sale of the family farm, include limited material on Vivian.

FRANCIS H. HELLER

Truman, Martha Ellen Young

(25 November 1852–26 July 1947)

Mother of the president. Martha Ellen Young was born in Jackson County, Missouri, the daughter of Solomon and Harriet Louisa Gregg Young. The couple had married in Shelby County, Kentucky, in 1838 and in 1841 moved to Missouri. Here Solomon Young drove cattle along the Santa Fe Trail while Harriet ran their farm and cared for their growing family which eventually included seven children. The border raids of the early Civil War years disrupted the Youngs' life and destroyed the farm on two occasions. The family eventually relocated near Grandview, establishing what would become known as the Truman farm.

As a young woman, Martha Young absorbed the discipline and work habits associated with farm life, lessons she later passed on to her son Harry. It has been said that Harry Truman's habit of rising at 5:30 A.M. derived from his mother's farm girlhood. Martha also learned the skills expected of a young woman of her day, including stitching samplers, playing the piano, studying Scripture, and reading. Her education was furthered by her attendance at the Ladies' Baptist College in Lexington, Missouri. In her leisure time, she became an adept horsewoman and social dancer. In later years, she was known to joke that as a girl she was "what you might call a lightfoot Baptist," but added that she always rode sidesaddle and never wore trousers.

A believer in late marriage, another view her son Harry would later act upon, Martha Young married when she was twenty-nine. On 28 December 1881, she wed John Anderson Truman, thirty years of age, who had grown up on a neighboring farm and was a longtime friend. The couple soon relocated in Lamar, Missouri, where John became a farmer and horse and mule trader. It was in Lamar that the couple suffered the stillbirth of their first child. Then on 8 May 1884, Harry S. Truman was born and was followed by John Vivian in 1886 and Mary Jane in 1889.

As full-time wife and mother, Martha Truman lived the philosophy that "if you get married, you ought to stay home and take care of your babies and the home." She maintained that she raised her children "to do the right thing. . . . they may make mistakes but they'll be honest mistakes and that's only human." Martha indulged Harry's dream of becoming a soldier by allowing him to camp out on the prairie and read endlessly about the great military figures in history. She also encouraged his love of reading in general and hired a piano teacher for him, thus supporting two interests she herself had long cherished.

Martha's life changed considerably in 1914 when her husband died and again in 1917 when Harry joined the army to serve in World War I, leaving his mother, and particularly his sister, Mary Jane, to run the family farm. When he returned, Harry soon married, but the strong mother-son bond that had been forged during the years did not dissolve.

Martha Truman remained a strong force in her son's life until her death at age ninety-four in 1947. Frequent telephone calls and letters from son to mother, even during his years as president, maintained the ties between them. An astute political observer and devoted Democrat, she frequently acted as a sounding board or adviser for him. In 1934, at age eighty-two,

The president's mother, Martha Ellen Truman. (National Archives)

Martha Truman campaigned for her son in his bid for a Senate seat and ten years later chaired the first meeting of Democratic women workers in his campaign for the vice presidency. Although she was widely quoted during the campaign as saying that Harry "plowed the straightest furrow in Jackson County," her family later denied it.

When her son became president, Martha received great and not always welcome attention. She resisted the many precautions taken by the Secret Service on her behalf. When she came to the notice of the nation through a Mother's Day visit to the White House in 1945, she deplored the "fuss and feathers" that surrounded her arrival. "Fiddlesticks," she supposedly exclaimed. "I wouldn't have come if I'd known all these people were going to be here." That same year the Order of the DeMolay presented President Truman with a portrait of his ninety-two-year-old mother. And in 1946, the Golden Rule Foundation of Missouri proclaimed her the Missouri Mother of the Year. At the time of her death in 1947, the national media not only reported her death but also speculated upon her great and lasting influence upon the president.

Harry S. Truman's letters to "Dear Mamma" are perhaps one of the best demonstration of his continuing attachment to and respect for Martha Truman. The frequent notes that flowed from his pen, despite the heavy demands of the presidency, not only expressed his innermost thoughts and political doings in pithy terms but also reflected homely philosophies much like her own.

A standard biographical account is found in Doris Faber, "Martha Young Truman: Lightfoot Baptist," in *The Mothers of American Presidents* (New York: New American Library, 1968), 48–62. Other information is contained in articles and her obituaries held by the Truman Library. The "Dear Mamma" letters that reveal so much of the mother-son tie are also in the Truman Library.

GLENDA RILEY

See also Farm Experience (photograph); Truman, John Anderson (photograph)

Truman, Mary Jane

(12 August 1889–3 November 1978)

Sister of the president. Mary Jane Truman, born near Grandview, Missouri, was the only daughter of John Anderson and Martha Young Truman. She grew up on the Truman farm established by her maternal grandfather, Solomon Young. She recalled that her older brother, Harry, often rocked her to sleep and played the piano with her.

The president's sister, Mary Jane Truman. (National Archives)

When Harry joined the Army in 1917, Mary Jane ran the family farm. She remarked that she had to "hire the help, buy supplies, and arrange for the sale of products." Proudly, she added that Harry said she "had done as good a job as he would have done."

Mary Jane, who never married, lived with her mother until Martha died in 1947. Mary Jane suffered many medical problems before her own death in 1978 at age eighty-nine.

The president's sister was active in the Order of the Eastern Star and became Worthy Grand Matron of the Eastern Star of Missouri in 1950. She regularly corresponded with Harry, visited him in the White House, and reportedly imparted some of her own wry philosophy to him.

In a rare interview in 1976, she assessed her brother's presidency: "I think that Harry did what he believed was right. . . . I know that he was conscientious and wanted to do the right thing, not especially for himself but for the country." Of her own life, she most remembered her work with the Eastern Star and the First Baptist Church of Grandview.

Articles and obituaries, letters to Mary Jane from Harry, and an oral history interview conducted by Jerald L. Hill and William D. Stilley on 2 January 1976 are held by the Harry S. Truman Library. Although they do little to reveal Mary Jane's personality, they do demonstrate her close ties with her brother.

GLENDA RILEY

Truman, Mary Margaret (Daniel)

(17 February 1924–)

Only child of the president; singer; writer. Margaret Truman, who was christened Mary Margaret, spent her childhood years in the Truman home on North Delaware Street in Independence, Missouri. As an only child and the sole grandchild in the Wallace family, she lived, in her words, "largely in a world of adults, well disposed toward me."

Despite his frequent absences from home, Harry Truman encouraged his daughter to further herself in a number of ways. He purchased a baby grand piano for her and became her first piano teacher. He urged her to pay serious attention to school studies. And in a series of letters that began when she was three, Margaret's father assured her that she was capable of achieving whatever she wanted.

In 1934, when her father was elected to the U.S. Senate, Margaret began spending the first half of each year in Washington, D.C., and the second half in Independence. In Washington, she attended Gunston Hall, a private school for young women. When she graduated in 1942, Margaret sang at the exercises and her father delivered the commencement address.

She then entered George Washington University, majoring in history and international relations. When her father succeeded to the presidency in April 1945, Margaret's life became more complex as a result of social obligations and ever-present Secret Service guards. When she graduated from college in 1946, she received her diploma from the hands of her father, the president.

After graduation, Margaret Truman pursued her long inter-

On the occasion of her concert debut with the National Symphony Orchestra, Margaret Truman shares her happiness with Metropolitan Opera soprano Helen Traubel, 27 November 1949. (Associated Press/Wide World Photos)

est in becoming an opera singer. Although her father had once hoped she would become a concert pianist and both he and Margaret realized that many people would charge her with trading on his position, he encouraged her. In May 1947, Margaret made her radio debut and in August appeared for the first time on the concert stage. Reviews ranged from the very positive to recommendations for further training.

After several particularly harsh reviews of her singing appeared in the Pittsburgh papers in October 1947, Truman wrote his daughter that if he ever met one of the critics he would "bust" him in the nose. Then he added that she should "take stock and do whatever is necessary for the next step. You'll have my backing whatever you do, but I want you to do what will be most likely to take you to the top of the ladder."

Margaret Truman also fulfilled her many responsibilities as the president's daughter, occasionally acting as hostess at White House events. And in 1948, she and her mother accompanied Harry Truman on his whistle-stop campaign, when he was seeking a term as president in his own right.

Margaret later wrote that during these years, despite his continuing support of her activities, she was aware that her father was very anxious to become a grandparent. Thus, it was with great pleasure that he announced her engagement to Clifton Daniel, Jr., a New York newspaper editor, early in 1956.

The wedding took place in April of that year, creating a union that eventually produced four sons, much to Truman's delight.

Shortly before her marriage, Margaret Truman turned from her singing career to develop a growing interest in writing. Her first work, *Souvenir: Margaret Truman's Own Story*, was followed by numerous other books, including a series of murder mysteries set in Washington, D.C., locales. Among her best-known works are *Harry S. Truman, Letters from Father*, and *Bess W. Truman*. In a 1986 television appearance, Margaret said that the last book, showing her mother's great influence on her father, was the most difficult she had written. With her sons now grown, Margaret Truman Daniel continues to write and participates in community affairs and the activities of the Truman Library.

Margaret's relationship with her father was close throughout his life. Addressing her as Marg, Margie, Sistie, and Baby, he frequently apologized for his absences at critical moments in her life and wrote of his loneliness for her and Bess. In 1945, he remarked, "That old barn [the White House] is terribly lonely for me alone" and confided his unhappiness that his becoming president had caused personal difficulties for her. In a particularly poignant, undated birthday telegram, he said "Happy Birthday I Hope You Can Persuade Your Mother To Be For The President." The father-daughter bond was often based on an exchange of aid and support.

Besides Margaret Truman Daniel's autobiography, *Souvenir*, written with Margaret Cousins (New York: McGraw-Hill, 1956), other sources of information about her are numerous articles, the many letters between her and her father, and the Papers of Clifton and

Radio show co-hosts Margaret Truman and Mike Wallace, the "Weekday" team, 19 October 1955. (Boston Public Library)

Margaret Truman Daniel, all held by the Truman Library. Other books she has written include *White House Pets* (New York: D. McKay, 1969); *Harry S. Truman* (New York: Morrow, 1972); *Women of Courage* (New York: Morrow, 1976); *Murder in the White House* (New York: Arbor House, 1980); *Letters from Father: The Truman Family's Personal Correspondence* (New York: Arbor House, 1980); *Murder on Capitol Hill* (New York: Arbor House, 1981); *Murder in the Supreme Court* (New York: Arbor House, 1982); *Murder in the Smithsonian* (New York: Arbor House, 1983); *Murder on Embassy Row* (New York: Arbor House, 1985); and *Bess Truman* (New York: Macmillan, 1986).

GLENDA RILEY

See also Roosevelt, Franklin D. (photograph); Speeches and Speech Writing (photograph)

Truman Committee

Although the official name of the Truman committee was the Senate Special Committee to Investigate the National Defense Program, it quickly and permanently became identified with its first and most prominent chairman, Senator Harry S. Truman. Established on 1 March 1941, the committee functioned until mid-1948. It was, however, the committee's work between 1941 and 1944, the period when American industry was converting from the production of civilian to military goods, that earned it a reputation as an exceptionally responsible and effective congressional investigative body. The conversion period coincided with the time Truman headed the committee. His leadership brought him a measure of fame and contributed significantly to his selection as the Democratic party's vice-presidential nominee in 1944. By then, the Truman committee had issued thirty-two of the fifty-one reports it would ultimately produce and had developed clear procedures and operating policies.

In his *Memoirs* Truman explained that by early 1941 he had become convinced that the huge arms contracts generated by the country's burgeoning military expansion were being awarded on the basis of favoritism, primarily to big companies. Small firms, lacking political influence and lobbying clout, were being ignored and in many cases forced out of business. To remedy this situation Truman proposed a special committee to investigate the defense program. Although the Roosevelt administration's initial reaction was something less than enthusiastic, Truman's colleagues approved his proposal and named him as chair. The Senate resolution creating the committee, which included four other Democrats and two Republicans, gave it broad powers to make a full and complete study of the defense program with special emphasis on the types, terms, costs, and geographic distribution of contracts; how contracts were awarded and how well contractors performed; the utilization of small businesses; and the effect of the defense program on labor. The committee was charged with reporting its findings and recommendations to the Senate but was not authorized to consider legislation or report out bills.

In proposing the committee Truman had asked for a beginning budget of twenty-five thousand dollars. He got only fifteen thousand dollars and spent over half to hire Hugh Fulton as the committee's chief counsel. Recommended highly by Attorney

General Robert H. Jackson, Fulton proved to be a superb choice. The full committee met once or twice a week, usually in a small room—known as "Harry's Doghouse"—behind the senator's office. Since the members had many other duties besides the investigative committee, the work done by its small staff was crucial. Fortunately, the investigators and clerical employees hired by Truman and Fulton were both energetic and efficient.

The Truman committee quickly gained respect for its efforts, to a large extent because its members—in noticeable contrast to most other wartime congressional investigative committees—did not try to use its activities to create self-serving publicity. The committee devoted much of its time to examining the actions of the War Production Board (WPB), the federal agency primarily concerned with industrial mobilization after Pearl Harbor. Donald M. Nelson, the head of the WPB, met frequently with the committee, usually to defend his agency's actions. After the war, Nelson wrote that he always "enjoyed tremendously the little brushes which we had with Harry Truman's investigators, who were invariably able men." They were, Nelson noted, "honest, impartial, and objective."

Although Nelson's views represented the majority opinion about the Truman committee, not everyone was so flattering. In particular the committee and the military services were often at odds. The armed services believed that nothing should interfere with military objectives. Consequently, the army and navy objected when the Truman committee raised questions about the costs of weapons contracts, insisted on protecting opportunities for small businesses, or wanted to allocate scarce raw materials to the production of essential civilian goods. The committee got along fairly well with James V. Forrestal, the navy official most concerned with industrial mobilization. But the committee's relations with his army counterparts, Under Secretary of War Robert P. Patterson and Gen. Brehon B. Somervell, were far less pleasant.

The contributions of the Truman committee were significant. Estimates of money saved by the committee's efforts range as high as $15 billion. As the watchdog of industrial mobilization, the committee was a key source of information about the domestic side of the war. Even more important, as a sympathetic critic of the War Production Board, the committee helped raise public confidence in the way the war effort was being managed. Truman deserves much of the credit for the committee's success. Determined not to use it for personal political glory or to allow other members to use it for theirs, he insisted that the committee exercise restraint. Hardworking and disciplined, the Truman committee became a model for subsequent congressional investigative bodies.

Donald H. Riddle, *The Truman Committee* (New Brunswick, N.J.: Rutgers University Press, 1964), is a perceptive case study although not a definitive historical account of the committee. Also useful are Truman's *Memoirs*, vol. 1, *Year of Decisions* (Garden City, N.Y.: Doubleday, 1955), and Stephen K. Bailey and Howard D. Samuel, *Congress at Work* (New York: Henry Holt, 1952).

JIM F. HEATH

See also Fulton, Hugh Alfred; Senator

Truman Doctrine

For nearly two years after he became president, Harry Truman followed a wavering course in foreign affairs. Determined to emphasize domestic policy and to complete the unfinished business of the New Deal, he favored rapid withdrawal of U.S. forces from Europe and the early conclusion of peace treaties with Communist-controlled countries in Eastern Europe, although he also supported Britain's request for a huge $3.75 billion reconstruction loan and briefly considered a similar loan to the Soviet Union.

It took the president some time to face the global economic consequences of the war. Leaving for the Potsdam Conference in early July 1945, Truman seemed unaware of the enormity of the losses the war had produced in Europe. Just before departing, the president had conferred with four senators recently back from the Continent and came away unpersuaded. Their song, he recorded, was "that France would go Communistic, so would Germany, Italy, and the Scandinavians; and there was grave doubt about England staying sane. The Pope, they said, was blue as indigo about the situation. All of them except Senator——assured me that the European world is at an end. . . . Europe has passed out so often in the last 2,000 years—and has come back, better or worse than ever, whichever pleases the fancy, that I am not impressed with cursory glances of oratorical members of the famous 'Cave of the Winds' on Capitol Hill."

The president's senatorial visitors, however, were not as mistaken as he first believed. The economic and social conditions of Central and Western Europe continued steadily to deteriorate, especially during the catastrophic winter of 1946–47, the harshest since 1881, bringing most of the area to a virtually complete standstill. The British government, in particular, saw its remaining foreign exchange dwindling rapidly and, with it, the country's ability to sustain its existing international commitments, including those to Greece and Turkey. Facing an "economic Dunkirk," the Attlee government in early 1947 decided to inform Washington of the perilous straits in which it now found itself.

Accordingly, on Friday afternoon, 21 February 1947, Lord Inverchapel, the British ambassador to the United States, telephoned the State Department seeking an immediate appointment with Secretary of State George C. Marshall to deliver an urgent communication from his government. The call was to change the course of American history and international affairs for the remainder of the twentieth century.

The point of the British notes—there were, in fact, two of them—was short and simple. The most severe winter in modern memory, coming on top of the devastating economic losses of World War II, had paralyzed the British economy and left the country virtually broke. As the first installment of a major contraction of its international obligations, Britain would have to cease its support of the governments of Greece and Turkey, which were threatened by Communist-supported civil war or direct Soviet aggression. Indeed Britain would have to pull out in a matter of weeks. If the United States chose not to pick up the British burden, there was serious danger that one or both countries would quickly fall under Communist domination or control.

Although there had been some informal discussion about the United States assuming part of Britain's responsibilities in the region, the British notes arrived as a distinctly unwelcome and untimely surprise. At the mid-term elections in November 1946, the Republicans had captured control of both houses of Congress, and economy in government—including foreign aid—was a Republican watchword. Truman faced one of the bleakest and most dangerous periods of his young administration.

The voluminous records of the State Department, published in 1971, confirm how well the U.S. government was informed about steadily deteriorating economic conditions in Central and Western Europe. The records also suggest how remarkably unprepared the country and the administration were to respond to the rapidly changing situation in which the United States found itself. Once the British notes arrived, the luxury of a considered response vanished virtually overnight.

Almost instantly, President Truman, Marshall, and Under Secretary of State Dean Acheson put the Department of State and other agencies to work, drawing up papers and plans on what might be done to help. Never before in peacetime—not even in December 1940, when Franklin D. Roosevelt had hastily devised the Lend-Lease program to keep Britain from going under—had the U.S. government responded so expeditiously to a foreign crisis.

On 27 February 1947, Truman called congressional leaders, Democrats and Republicans, to the White House. They knew nothing of the British notes, but the president told them of his desire to aid Greece and Turkey and asked their help in getting a program passed. Truman turned over the meeting to Marshall, who left no doubt of the seriousness of the situation. "A crisis of the utmost importance and urgency has arisen in Greece and to some extent in Turkey," the secretary of state declared. "This crisis has a direct and intimate relation to the security of the United States."

In the event the United States failed to aid Greece, Marshall continued, "Soviet domination might . . . extend over the entire Middle East to the borders of India. The effect of this upon Hungary, Austria, Italy and France cannot be overestimated. It is not alarmist to say that we are faced with the first crisis of a series which might extend Soviet domination to Europe, the Middle East and Asia." At his cabinet meeting on 7 March, Truman discussed the Greek situation at great length. According to Navy Secretary James V. Forrestal, Truman said that "he was faced with a decision more serious than had ever confronted any President." Three days later, Forrestal wrote, "It is my opinion that world events may move within the next six months at almost the same speed as they did in 1940."

In the days and weeks that followed, it was the often maligned bureaucracy that busily prepared the necessary paperwork, but it was Truman who provided the driving force. He had fought in Europe in World War I. He had followed World War II from a leadership position in the Senate and as vice president and president. Whatever his earlier inclination, the president sensed the time had come for the United States to go beyond the pronouncements of Woodrow Wilson and Franklin Roosevelt. Declarations of principle like the Fourteen Points and the Four Freedoms no longer sufficed. Unlike leaders in Great Britain at the height of its power in the nineteenth century, Truman recognized the United States could not remain oblivious to the far-reaching changes going on around it in the world.

The president planned to set forth his views and recommendations in an address to a joint session of Congress, but he didn't much care for some early State Department drafts, one of which, as he wrote in his *Memoirs*, "made the whole thing sound like an investment proposition." Truman especially zeroed in on one passage. Where the State Department drafters called for him to say "I believe it should be the policy of the United States," Truman recalled, "I took my pencil, scratched out 'should' and wrote in 'must.'"

Not surprisingly, the president's proposed address went through numerous drafts and revisions. About the specific objectives of the new U.S. policy there was never any question. One of those who believed the time had come for the country to enunciate a new and broader foreign policy was Clark M. Clifford, by early 1947 the president's counsel and one of his principal speech writers. As Forrest C. Pogue wrote later, Clifford "saw early . . . [that] the time seemed ready for a strong stand in favor of countries menaced by the U.S.S.R."

At 1:00 P.M. on 12 March 1947, Truman went before Congress to deliver what has rightly become one of the legendary addresses of modern American foreign policy, as he asked for $400 million in economic and military assistance. Over forty years later the president's words still retain their dramatic ring. He was recommending not merely a specific new aid program but an entirely new international policy, the like of which the United States had never known before.

"At the present moment in history," Truman declared, "nearly every nation must choose between alternative ways of life. The choice is too often not a free one. One way of life is based upon the will of the majority, and is distinguished by free institutions, representative government, free elections, guarantees of individual liberty, freedom of speech and religion, and freedom from political oppression. The second way of life is based upon the will of the minority forcibly imposed upon the majority. It relies upon terror and oppression, a controlled press and radio, fixed elections, and the suppression of personal freedom."

Moreover, Truman's new policy went far beyond military aid and security. "I believe," the president continued, "that it must be the policy of the United States to support free peoples who are resisting attempted subjugation by armed minorities or by outside pressures. I believe we must assist free peoples to work out their destinies in their own way. . . . The seeds of totalitarian regimes are nurtured by misery and want. They spread and grow in the evil soil of poverty and strife. They reach their full growth where the hope of a people for a better life has died. We must keep that hope alive. The free peoples of the world look to us for support in maintaining their freedom. If we falter in this leadership, we may endanger the peace of the world— and we shall surely endanger the welfare of this nation."

The immediate response to Truman's address—"probably the most enduringly controversial speech . . . made by a President in the twentieth century," Robert J. Donovan wrote later— was largely, but not universally, favorable. The 1946 elections had strengthened the extreme Right and Left in both major parties. Max Lerner, the noted political scientist and editor (by the 1980s of a very different persuasion), accused Truman of a demagogic appeal to the anti-Communist Right. Demonstrating the political insight that was to make him a New Left favorite a generation later, Senator Robert A. Taft (R.-Ohio) declared, "If we assume a special position in Greece and Turkey, we can hardly reasonably object to the Russians continuing their domination in Poland, Yugoslavia, and Bulgaria."

Eleanor Roosevelt, for whom the president's admiration was not unlimited, wrote asking if it was not more important to pursue progressive policies at home, as a way of combating Communism abroad. Truman agreed that "there must be social progress at home." But, he added, we cannot "overlook the fact that as much as the world needs a progressive America, the American way of life cannot survive unless other peoples who want to adopt that pattern of life throughout the world can do so without fear and in the hope of success."

Although faced with the hostile Eightieth Congress he was later to denounce effectively, the president nevertheless was able to achieve an extraordinary degree of bipartisanship. Truman could hardly have succeeded without the support of men like Senator Arthur H. Vandenberg (R.-Mich.). But his administration displayed an adaptability and flexibility that, for the moment at least, effectively isolated his opponents in both parties, Right and Left. By 22 May 1947, the Greek-Turkish aid program was law.

It has been said that the Truman Doctrine, as the president's new policy soon became known, ushered in a new era of globalism designed to make the United States the "policeman of the world," that it thrust the country into endless and dangerous confrontations with communism all over the world—confrontations for which the United States was politically and militarily unprepared. Indeed, according to some critics of the Truman Doctrine, it was that policy which landed the country in Vietnam twenty years later.

Almost certainly, that interpretation of the Truman Doctrine assigns far too much responsibility to the new policy. It is very much like saying, for instance, that the Open Door policy in China—first enunciated by Secretary of State John Hay in the McKinley administration in 1899—was responsible for the outbreak of war between the United States and Japan in 1941.

The possible long-range implications of the president's address were not ignored during the extended congressional debate on the Greek-Turkish aid programs, but the differences between principle and policy were never conclusively resolved. There was, however, before the Senate Foreign Relations Committee, this illuminating exchange between Under Secretary Dean Acheson and Senator Tom Connally (D.-Texas), ranking minority member of the committee:

Connally: This is not a pattern out of a tailor's shop to fit everybody in the world and every nation in the world, because the conditions in no two nations are identical. Is that not true?
Acheson: Yes, sir; that is true, and whether there are requests, of course, will be left to the future, but whatever they are, they have to be judged, as you say, according to the circumstances of each specific case.

For all the attention the Truman Doctrine was to receive in the years that followed, it was never elaborated into a fully developed U.S. global strategy. It never achieved, that is to say, anything like the standing of the Monroe Doctrine, the Open Door policy, or, for that matter, even the Kellogg-Briand Pact.

However that may be, Truman's immediate considerations seemed both simpler and less far-reaching. He summed up his reasoning in a letter to his daughter from Key West on 13 March 1947, the day following his historic address to Congress. "This terrible decision I had to make," the president wrote, "had been over my head for about six weeks. Although I knew at Potsdam that there is no difference in totalitarian or police states, call them what you will, Nazi, Fascist, Communist or Argentine Republics. You know there was but one idealistic example of Communism. That is described in the Acts of the Apostles.

"The attempt of Lenin, Trotsky, Stalin, et al., to fool the world and the American Crackpots Association, represented by Jos. Davies, Henry Wallace, Claude Pepper and the actors and artists in immoral Greenwich Village, is just like Hitler's and Mussolini's so-called socialist states.

"Your Pop had to tell the world just that in polite language."

For what the president and the State Department knew and when they knew it about the mounting problems in Greece and Turkey, see G. M. Richardson Dougall, ed., *Foreign Relations of the United States*, vol. 5 (Washington, D.C.: U.S. Government Printing Office, 1971). Truman's own version of events is contained in his *Memoirs*, vol. 2, *Years of Trial and Hope* (Garden City, N.Y.: Doubleday, 1956). Joseph M. Jones, *The Fifteen Weeks* (New York: Viking Press, 1965), remains indispensable (Jones was a ranking official in the State Department's Bureau of Public Affairs). There are important details in Dean Acheson, *Present at the Creation: My Years in the State Department* (New York: W. W. Norton, 1969), and some in Forrest C. Pogue, *George C. Marshall: Statesman, 1945–1959* (New York: Viking Press, 1987). George F. Kennan, *Memoirs, 1925–1950* (Boston: Little, Brown, 1967), contains a critical dissent and Charles E. Bohlen, *Witness to History, 1929–1969* (New York: Norton, 1973), gives another inside perspective. *The Forrestal Diaries*, ed. Walter Millis (New York: Viking Press, 1951), and *The Private Papers of Senator Vandenberg*, ed. Arthur H. Vandenberg, Jr., and Joe A. Morris (Boston: Houghton Mifflin, 1952), are useful for background. Robert J. Donovan, *Conflict and Crisis: The Presidency of Harry S. Truman, 1945–1948* (New York: W. W. Norton, 1977), gives rise to some doubts. New Left interpretations, beginning with Lloyd C. Gardner, *Architects of Illusion: Men and Ideas in American Foreign Policy, 1941–1949* (Chicago: Quadrangle Books, 1970), contain the expected. The recent monograph of Howard Jones, *"A New Kind of War": American Strategy and the Truman Doctrine in Greece* (New York: Oxford University Press, 1989), adds important new details from official U.S. records. Francis L. Loewenheim, ed., *The Historian and the Diplomat: The Role of History and Historians in American Foreign Policy* (New York: Harper & Row, 1967), attempts to place the subject in the intellectual development of U.S. diplomacy.

FRANCIS L. LOEWENHEIM

See also Acheson, Dean Gooderham; Clifford, Clark McAdams; Containment; Great Britain; Greece; Kennan, George F.; Marshall, George C., Jr.; Turkey

Truman Library

See Harry S. Truman Library

Turkey

U.S. policy concerning Turkey during the early years of the Truman administration was influenced primarily by the Soviet Union's dealings with the countries on its southern flank. Stalin himself had negotiated the frontier between Turkey and the Soviet Union in 1921. As a Georgian, moreover, he had little love for the Turks. According to Premier Khrushchev, Stalin was teased and goaded by the head of his huge police network, Lavrenti Beria (like Stalin, a Georgian), into demanding territory from Turkey, which was thought to be vulnerable because of its neutral role in World War II. Kars and Ardahan in eastern Turkey had briefly (between 1878 and 1921) been part of Russia, and the Soviets, through irredentist claims on the part of the Georgian and Armenian Soviet Socialist Republics, sought to legitimate their claims to the region. Stalin also sought, through diplomatic pressures and a war of nerves, to gain control of the Bosporus Straits.

The development that crystallized U.S. policy in the region was a Soviet request in August 1946 for Turkey to agree to the joint defense of the straits. Although seemingly innocuous, the request was more ominous in view of Stalin's previous maneuvering on the straits and recent Soviet behavior toward Iran. The Turks, whose continued mobilization of a 500,000-man army required expenditures totaling 38 percent of their budget, were hard pressed to continue standing up to the Soviets without some kind of support. The result was President Truman's decision on 15 August 1946 to resist Soviet aggression with all means at his disposal, including, if necessary, the force of arms. As a result of this decision, which he regarded as his most important since the bombing of Hiroshima, the United States reformulated its policies on Iran, Turkey, and Greece, established what became the Sixth Fleet in the Mediterranean, and began to implement what became the policy of containment—even before that policy was consciously articulated.

Public pronouncement of U.S. policy came in the spring of 1947 after the British, previously advised of the president's decision, in February informed the United States that Britain would have to withdraw its forces from Greece and Turkey. The U.S. reaction, which followed logically from the president's decision in August 1946, was articulated on 12 March 1947 in the Truman Doctrine, which called for a $400 million appropriation to aid Turkey and Greece. The Truman Doctrine's rhetorical excesses, perceived as necessary to gain public support, signaled a departure from President Roosevelt's policies of noninvolvement in the region and in effect committed the United States to maintaining the balance of power in the Near East.

The extent of the U.S. commitment, however, though substantial in terms of economic and military assistance, was nonetheless subject to extended debate within the Joint Chiefs of Staff and between the United States and Britain. Although Turkey's strategic role was seen as vital, the Joint Chiefs expected that in a war the Western Allies would be able to conduct only a delaying action in Turkey (along the so-called outer ring of Allied defenses) and would be forced to retreat to a more tenable position along Britain's line of communications centered in Suez (the inner ring). Competing priorities in Europe and the Far East, moreover, called into question the U.S. contribution to Turkey's defense in the event of war.

The Korean War resolved the difficulty over priorities. While Turkey pressed for inclusion in the North Atlantic Treaty Organization (NATO), enormous increases in the defense budget appeared to obviate the need for distinguishing between vital and peripheral concerns and made it possible for the Joint Chiefs to underscore Turkey's crucial role to the West. The U.S. need for foreign support of its policies, meanwhile, coupled with the performance in Korea of Turkey's 4,500-man brigade, which Gen. Douglas MacArthur called "the bravest of the brave," created further opportunity for Turkey to urge early implementation of NATO's military planning on defense of the Mediterranean and to press even harder for admission.

What the Turks desired was a security guarantee that would give them a credible deterrent against the Soviet Union. What they could provide in return was a strategic role in the defense of Europe: if Turkey were a cobelligerent, its bases would threaten the Soviet southern flank; its large army would deter a Soviet threat to either the Balkans or Iran; its land mass would serve as a buffer between the Soviet Union and the Middle East, whose oil supplied 75–80 percent of all European oil requirements and was central to the recovery of Europe; it also would control the straits, thus preventing Soviet egress into the Mediterranean.

By May 1951 President Truman had decided that the United States should press for Turkey's membership in NATO. In September the NATO Council voted unanimously to extend an invitation to Turkey to join the alliance, and in February 1952 the country was admitted to full membership.

Bruce R. Kuniholm, *The Origins of the Cold War in the Near East: Great Power Conflict and Diplomacy in Iran, Turkey and Greece* (Princeton: Princeton University Press, 1980), is the most useful source for understanding U.S. policy toward the "northern tier" states in the early cold war. Harry N. Howard, *Turkey, the Straits and U.S. Policy* (Baltimore: Johns Hopkins University Press, 1974), is the best book for understanding the complicated straits problem. Kuniholm, *The Near East Connection: Greece and Turkey in the Reconstruction and Security of Europe, 1946–1952* (Brookline, Mass.: Hellenic College Press, 1984), provides a useful overview of U.S. policy toward Greece and Turkey during the Truman administration.

BRUCE R. KUNIHOLM

See also Containment; Great Britain; North Atlantic Treaty Organization; Soviet Union; Truman Doctrine

U

Unions

See Labor

United Automobile Workers

See Labor

United Mine Workers

See Labor

United Nations

The creation of an international organization to settle disputes peacefully between nations had been an objective of American foreign policy during World War II. When Harry S. Truman assumed the presidency, that goal had almost been achieved. Fifty nations at an international conference in San Francisco in April and May 1945 launched the United Nations. In the United States, bipartisan political groundwork during the years of the Roosevelt administration ensured that the nation would participate in the new organization without repeating the post–World War I debacle that defeated American adherence to the League of Nations covenant. U.S. Senate approval was anticlimactic.

In 1945, Americans viewed the United Nations as the world's leading peacekeeping organization. Public leaders actually oversold the world body. Under the UN charter, five major powers—China, France, Great Britain, the Soviet Union, and the United States—were designated permanent members of a supreme Security Council and each was vested with veto power. Unanimity, then, would determine the success of the organization. The charter also provided for a weaker General Assembly, in which all member nations would have an equal vote and each nation could voice its concerns on issues. Other organizational elements were set up to carry out mostly nonpolitical administrative tasks.

As the cold war developed in the early Truman presidential years, meetings at the United Nations, particularly in the Security Council, amounted to a verbal battlefield on which the two intransigent power blocs voiced their positions. Outvoted on most issues, the Soviet Union relied on its veto to maintain some semblance of equality. During 1946, when the major nations attempted to resolve the veto question through procedural means, its use by the Soviet Union came to symbolize for Americans not only the deepening cold war but also the inability of the world body to achieve much when the two sides were in contest. By the time of the opening of the annual fall General Assembly meeting in October 1946, the Soviets had cast eleven vetos in the Security Council. In instances when there was no major power confrontation, however, the United Nations scored some successes. The council, for example, managed to arrange a truce in the conflict between the Dutch and the Indonesians in 1946 and made recommendations for a truce and plebiscite to settle the conflict over Kashmir between India and Pakistan.

The early confrontation with the Soviets on the UN world stage merely confirmed to the Truman administration that most elements of American foreign policy could never be carried out through the new organization. Officials nonetheless recognized that the president had taken a strong public position in support of the world body as a cornerstone of American foreign policy. To disregard the United Nations would create serious credibility problems for the administration. So the United States had to balance whatever unilateral policy it might set with a show of continued support for the United Nations.

IF IT TOOK 8 WEEKS, *SAN FRANCISCO TIME*, TO DRAW IT UP, WHAT IS YOUR ESTIMATE, *IN WASHINGTON TIME*, OF HOW LONG IT WILL TAKE THE SENATE TO RATIFY IT?

VANDENBERG

CONNALLY

TRUMAN

UNITED NATIONS CHARTER

James T. Berryman, *Washington Star* (1945). Copyright *Washington Post*. Reprinted by permission of the D.C. Public Library.

Truman fortunately had a zealous spokesman at the American Mission to the United Nations whose belief in the organization was so fervent that he could genuinely voice support for both American policy and the United Nations even when one seemed to contradict the other. Truman appointed Warren R. Austin as the nation's first ambassador to the United Nations in June 1946. Although an anti–New Deal Republican senator from Vermont since 1931, Austin had bucked the Republican isolationist party line throughout his congressional years with an internationalist view of foreign policy that ultimately called for the United States to assume leadership in the postwar world. The senator's bipartisan foreign policy views made him one of Truman's better appointments. Austin's reputation both as a Republican and as a UN man throughout his six-year ambassadorial tenure made the UN aspect of foreign policy a little easier to handle for American policymakers.

Four episodes during the Truman presidency provide a sample of the relationship of the United Nations to Truman's leadership of American foreign policy. American aid to Greece and Turkey that resulted in the proclamation of the Truman Doctrine, American membership in the North Atlantic Treaty Organization (NATO), the controversy over Palestine, and the outbreak of the Korean War showed in several ways how U.S. foreign policy used the United Nations when it was convenient, but just as easily dismissed the world body if it was too troublesome to involve it substantively.

When Great Britain notified the United States in February 1947 that it could no longer support its client states Greece and Turkey, it brought a crisis to the American foreign policy establishment. The government's response was not just to fill the void created by Britain's departure but to set a policy that had been evolving since the war's end. Based largely on an emerging view of the Soviet Union as a worldwide menace, Truman went to Congress to ask for assistance to Greece and Turkey and to declare that it was time to help other states wherever they were "resisting . . . armed minorities or . . . outside pressures." Nowhere in his speech did the president mention the United Nations. Only later did his advisers realize that the omission was a blunder even though they knew that the world body could not help in the situation. Consequently, officials mounted a substantial effort to convince members of Congress and the American people that the United States had not forsaken the United Nations. The administration used Austin in several forums to argue that the unilateral action of the United States was, in effect, support of the world organization. The argument stated that the United Nations was an evolving organization and therefore was not in a position to help; nonetheless, America's action and the objectives of the organization juxtaposed. It really meant that the Truman administration had no intention of placing such a crucial issue before the United Nations where Soviet actions could stymie it.

Truman's decision in 1948 for the United States to join NATO also had implications for support of the United Nations. When the cold war shattered the model of the United Nations as a peacekeeper, American supporters of NATO effectively used the regional and self-defense articles of the UN charter to justify not only the creation of NATO but also American participation. Thus American spokesmen in 1949 argued publicly that the decision to defend Europe through the collective security of NATO amounted to support of the United Nations. Since its members were bound not to use force except in self-defense, administration officials argued that self-defense treaties like NATO increased the merit of the nonaggressive ideal of the charter. The United States also supported that ideal by joining NATO. That rationale, however, again showed the necessity of compromise between the idealism of the United Nations and the realities presented by the emerging cold war.

Palestine became a UN issue in 1947 when Great Britain turned the problem over to the world body after spending many troublesome years as the mandatory for the area. In bringing the matter to the General Assembly, the issue underscored a relatively new American presence in the Middle East as well as the influence of the Jewish bloc in the United States which had long supported a homeland in Palestine. Subsequently, the administration followed a flexible policy designed not to antagonize either the domestic Jewish community or the oil-rich Arab states. Throughout tortured debates over Palestine partition before the General Assembly in 1947 and 1948, the frustrating American policy is best characterized by the comment of an exasperated Warren Austin urging Arabs and Jews to come together and "settle this problem in a true Christian spirit." After the United States supported the UN decision for partition in the fall of 1947, then reversed itself at the eleventh hour, and then again reversed itself by immediately recognizing Israel's proclamation of the new Jewish state in May 1948, the flexible U.S. policy again showed disdain for support of UN decisions when they interfered with the perceived national interest of the United States.

Korea, superficially divided at the thirty-eighth parallel at

Secretary of State George C. Marshall and U.S. Ambassador to the United Nations Lewis Douglas at a session of the UN General Assembly in Paris, 30 September 1948. (Associated Press/ Wide World Photos)

the end of World War II between Soviet and American occupying forces, had been turned over to the United Nations for resolution in 1947. There the General Assembly decided that the country should be unified under one government, but implementation languished because of the cold war impasse. Meanwhile, separate antagonistic governments were established in the North and the South.

When North Korean forces attacked across the thirty-eighth parallel on 25 June 1950, American response turned to the Security Council in part because the Korean question was a continuing UN matter. But American national interest was directly involved since the United States included South Korea in its Far Eastern defense perimeter, notwithstanding Secretary of State Dean Acheson's January 1950 statement to the contrary. So President Truman might have ordered defensive military action without going to the United Nations. That he chose to use the Security Council turned out to be a notable achievement for the world body. The Soviet Union fortunately had not attended meetings of the council since the preceding January. Its representative, Jacob Malik, had staged the latest of several dramatic walkouts in support of the seating of Mao Tse-tung's People's Republic of China to replace Chiang Kai-shek's Nationalist Chinese government as the permanent Chinese Security Council representative. So when the United States brought the North Korean aggression issue to the Security Council and requested support of the United Nations to repulse the invasion, agreement prevailed among those permanent representatives present. By the time Malik returned to the council to assume his term as chairman for the month of August, the necessary resolutions had been passed that allowed a military response to the North Korean aggression.

The Truman administration capitalized on the situation to score both a propaganda victory and to advance American policy in Korea. By leading UN forces against the aggressors, the United States could legitimately voice support for the collective security measures taken under the blue and white banner of the world organization. Without the Soviet veto, the United Nations worked just as its founders had hoped it would. Many called the situation the finest hour of the world body.

By the early fall of 1950 the UN forces, under the military command of Gen. Douglas MacArthur, had pushed the North Koreans back to the thirty-eighth parallel. Flush with success, the United States then used the 1948 General Assembly resolution calling for a unified Korea to justify crossing the parallel to "liberate" the whole peninsula. The widening of the conflict ultimately brought the military forces of Red China into the war. The People's Republic had no intention of allowing a unified pro-American Korean government to be located along its Manchurian border. After massive Chinese intervention in November of 1950, the tide of battle turned against the UN forces until 1951 when the two sides reached a bloody deadlock roughly along the thirty-eighth parallel. The stalemate lasted through the remainder of the Truman years and considerably lessened both the popularity of the president and the credibility of the United Nations in comparison to their days of glory in the summer of 1950.

Truman's foreign policy decisions helped diminish the international optimism that had been expressed for the United Nations in 1945. Although Truman and Austin continued publicly to support the ideal of collective security represented by the world group, reality showed the organization to be only a place to debate and marshal support for American policy. In other words, the United Nations afforded the American ambassador and his foreign counterparts a world stage, but the words of the actors often seemed to have little substance.

The flavor of the relationship of the Truman administration with the United Nations can be gleaned from many sources. Candid snatches from different vantage points are found in Dean Acheson, *Present at the Creation: My Years in the State Department* (New York: W. W. Norton, 1969), and in Trygve Lie, *In the Cause of Peace: Seven Years with the United Nations* (New York: Macmillan, 1954). George T. Mazuzan looks at the relationship through the career of Truman's only ambassador to the world body: *Warren R. Austin at the U.N., 1946–1953* (Kent: Kent State University Press, 1977). Thoughtful analysis of the United Nations and both the Greek-Turkish crisis and NATO has been written by Lawrence S. Kaplan, *The United States and NATO: The Formative Years* (Lexington: University of Kentucky Press, 1985), and by Thomas M. Campbell, Jr., "NATO and the United Nations in American Foreign Policy: Building a Framework for Power," in *NATO after Thirty Years*, ed. Lawrence S. Kaplan and Robert W. Clawson (Wilmington, Del.: Scholarly Resources, 1981), 131–48. The emotional Palestine situation is nicely evaluated by John Snetsinger, *Truman, the Jewish Vote, and the Creation of Israel* (Stanford: Hoover Institution Press, 1974). The best recent scholarship on Korea is in Bruce Cumings, ed., *Child of Conflict: The Korean-American Relationship* (Seattle: University of Washington Press, 1983).

GEORGE T. MAZUZAN

See also Internationalism; Korean War; Palestine; United Nations Relief and Rehabilitation Administration

United Nations Relief and Rehabilitation Administration

On 9 November 1943 at the White House, representatives from forty-four nations signed an agreement that established the United Nations Relief and Rehabilitation Administration (UNRRA). Its immediate goals included the planning and administration of "measures for the relief of victims of war ... through the provisioning of food, fuel, clothing, shelter, and other basic necessities, medical and other essential services." During its three and a half years of operation, the international agency distributed 9 million tons of food, built hundreds of hospitals, dispensed medicine to prevent epidemics, provided shelter for 1 million displaced persons, and assisted in the reconstruction of transportation systems. Expenditures came to approximately $4 billion, with half of the total allocated to China ($518 million), Italy ($418 million), Greece ($347 million), and Austria ($135 million); and half to various Eastern European nations and Soviet republics.

Despite its impressive accomplishments, UNRRA incurred a barrage of criticism. Members of Congress and the press criticized its haphazard accounting procedures and delays in the distribution of aid—problems that were probably unavoidable given logistical difficulties in war-torn areas. The major source of controversy, however, centered on the agency's potential political impact in certain nations. Although Americans headed UNRRA's central organization and the United States provided three-fourths of its funds, critics decried the fact that recipient countries administered the local distribution of aid. Charges arose that various East European governments, at Soviet urging, used UNRRA for political purposes and siphoned off supplies to the Red Army and other local military establishments. Although UNRRA aid indirectly bolstered some Communist regimes, the international agency actually tried to avoid politics and distributed the assistance on the basis of need. Most of the accusations of corruption, moreover, went unsubstantiated.

Reluctant to defend the unpopular program, however, the Truman administration refrained from countering its critics. In mid-1947 Washington effectively killed operations by cutting off American funds. Thus, an experiment in international cooperation ended. In the future, the United States would favor bilateral foreign aid programs that guaranteed greater administrative control and more substantial political returns.

Thomas G. Paterson devotes a chapter to UNRRA in his *Soviet-American Confrontation: Postwar Reconstruction and the Origins of the Cold War* (Baltimore: John Hopkins University Press, 1973). See also Robert A. Pollard, *Economic Security and the Origins of the Cold War, 1945–1950* (New York: Columbia University Press, 1985). For an official history, consult George Woodbridge et al., *The History of the United Nations Relief and Rehabilitation Administration*, 3 vols. (New York: Columbia University Press, 1950).

DENNIS MERRILL

See also Displaced Persons; United Nations

By Bill Mauldin. Copyright 1946 by Bill Mauldin.

Universal Military Training

See Selective Service/Universal Military Training

Urban Redevelopment

Urban redevelopment was an innovation of the Truman administration intended to clear urban slums and blighted areas and replace them with improved housing under private auspices.

The new extension of federal responsibility appeared in Title I of the Housing Act of 1949, which divorced slum clearance from the construction of low-income public housing. It did so in two ways. First, although the act required "predominantly residential" construction on the cleared area, it could be middle-income or even luxury housing. Second, the act permitted the clearing of blighted areas also for predominantly residential use. A slum was a degraded dwelling district, whereas blight often was associated with the mixed-use gray areas surrounding downtowns. Blighted districts contained substandard and obsolete buildings, the speculative value of which was too high to permit a developer to assemble them for renovation or razing.

Title I authorized the Housing and Home Finance Administration (HHFA) to finance a local public agency (LPA) to cover most of the expenses of assembling, clearing, preparing, and selling or leasing slum and blighted land. Each project would lose money because the fair market value of the land, once assembled, cleared, and prepared for its new use, would be less than the value of the parcels that had been purchased individually. The difference between the purchase price and the sale price was the "net project cost." Federal grants covered up to two-thirds of this cost. Usually the grants were used to repay the federal loans advanced to buy the land in the first place.

The other third of the net project cost had to be funded from local or state government grants-in-aid, which could be in cash or in the costs associated with clearing and preparing the land for sale. Other provisions were intended to save the urban citizen from the potential tyranny of the LPA. Among many safeguards, the act directed the LPA to hold a public hearing before purchasing any land and to provide for the equitable rehousing of those displaced.

Why did this precedent-shattering arrangement become law? Truman pressed hard for it. The component organizations of the real estate lobby either favored urban redevelopment or only mildly opposed it, for it promised advantages for private enterprise. Not the least of these was the net project cost, often called the "writedown." The writedown was no giveaway to a developer, for he had to pay fair market value for cleared land, but it enabled him to buy the land at a price he could not have managed himself.

Public housing experts also favored urban redevelopment. By 1949 some of them recognized that slums were diverse communities in which not every resident was poor or suffered horrible conditions. Merely leveling slums and replacing them with public housing created two undesirable situations. Public housing imposed income limits on its tenants, replacing slum diversity with a one-class residential area. Second, the public housing did not rehouse all the former slum dwellers. Why not try, instead, a program permitting cities to introduce middle-class housing on a sizable scale in lower-class residential areas near downtown? This view dovetailed with the real estate lobby's enthusiasm for federally assisted private housing and for reviving the cities' central business districts.

Finally, urban redevelopment broke precedent only at the federal level. As with many other programs, the states anticipated federal action. By 1949 some twenty-five state legislatures had passed enabling acts allowing their cities to create slum clearance and redevelopment authorities. Soon after the Housing Act passed, most of the others permitted cities to expand their already existing public housing authorities or to set up separate redevelopment authorities or to create whatever LPA they desired.

Very little actual redevelopment occurred during Truman's presidency. When the eminent housing expert Catherine Bauer surveyed the redevelopment scene in September 1951 she found grants reserved for more than two hundred projects but work begun on only one. The delay occurred because even the best-organized local agencies needed time to absorb the requirements of federal legislation and to select project sites acceptable both to the Division of Slum Clearance and Urban Redevelopment of the HHFA and to developers. Elsewhere, politicians, bureaucrats, and business people had to be convinced of Title I's advantages. It was a lengthy process in either event. In a few instances, such as the "Pittsburgh Renaissance" orchestrated by Richard King Mellon and others of the city's elite, redevelopment was already well under way, using a variety of nonfederal funds. Whether those projects, or any others, could revitalize the centers of America's cities remained an open question.

Jewel Bellush and Murray Hausknecht, eds., *Urban Renewal: People, Politics, and Planning* (New York: Anchor Books, 1967), is a useful compilation. Harold Kaplan, *Urban Renewal Politics: Slum Clearance in Newark* (New York: Columbia University Press, 1963), reveals how it was done under one ambitious, tough redevelopment administrator.

WILLIAM H. WILSON

See also Housing

USSR

See Soviet Union

V

Vandenberg, Arthur Hendrick

(22 March 1884–18 April 1951)

Republican U.S. senator from Michigan, 1928–51. Arthur Vandenberg was born in Grand Rapids, Michigan, the son of harness manufacturer Aaron and Alpha Hendrick Vandenberg. He attended the University of Michigan Law School in the 1900–1901 academic year. He married Elizabeth Watson of Grand Rapids in May 1906 and had three children. After his wife died of a brain tumor in May 1917, he married schoolteacher-journalist Hazel H. Whittaker on 14 June 1918.

Vandenberg had gone to work for the *Grand Rapids Herald* in 1902 and served as its editor and publisher from 1906 to 1928, gaining considerable influence in State Republican politics. He belonged to the Republican state central committee from 1912 to 1918 and chaired the Michigan Republican state conventions in 1916 and 1928.

Upon the death of Senator Woodbridge N. Ferris, Vandenberg was appointed to the U.S. Senate on 1 March 1928. Michigan voters elected him to full terms in 1928, 1934, 1940, and 1946. From 1929 to 1933, Vandenberg usually supported Republican president Herbert Hoover on domestic legislative measures. After Democrat Franklin D. Roosevelt was elected president in 1932, Vandenberg approved of most early New Deal measures except the National Industrial Recovery Act and the Agricultural Adjustment Act of 1933. He became Senate minority leader in 1935 and then rejected most New Deal measures except the Banking Act and the Social Security Act of 1935. An advocate of a balanced federal budget and reduced taxation, Vandenberg contended that President Roosevelt had increasingly infringed on congressional power. Vandenberg opposed the National Labor Relations Act of 1935, Roosevelt's U.S. Supreme Court reorganization plan of 1937, and the Fair Labor Standards Act of 1938. As a Foreign Relations Committee member, he led Republican resistance to Roosevelt's foreign policies in the 1930s. Besides backing the Nye committee hearings, the "insulationist" favored the Neutrality Acts of 1935–37

and protested both the Selective Service Act of 1940 and the Lend-Lease Act of 1941.

Vandenberg gradually shifted from an "insulationist" to internationalist position after American entry into World War II. He helped develop bipartisan foreign policy cooperation between the president and Congress. In 1943 the Michigan Republican helped author the Connally Resolution for U.S. membership in the United Nations, subject to U.S. Senate ratification as a treaty. Vandenberg insisted, however, that Republicans be consulted in postwar planning. The Senate on 10 January 1945 heard Vandenberg contend that no nation could exist safely as an isolationist. The eloquent senator urged the United States to take bold leadership in improving world affairs and helping establish the United Nations. His widely applauded speech influenced the conversion of several Republican isolationists to internationalism. Roosevelt appointed him as a delegate to the San Francisco Conference, where the Michigan Republican helped draft Articles 51–54 of the UN charter in April 1945. These articles encouraged regional collective defense pacts to help maintain international peace and security. In July 1945, he played a major role in securing overwhelming U.S. Senate ratification of the UN charter.

After World War II, Vandenberg supported Democratic president Harry S. Truman's containment policies. Vandenberg believed that the Soviet Union threatened American security by armed aggression and urged the United States to contain the spread of communism through a bipartisan foreign policy. In February 1946, Vandenberg stated, "We can live together in reasonable harmony if the United States speaks as plainly upon all occasions as Russia does." Truman appointed Vandenberg as a delegate to the first and second UN General Assemblies 1946 and as adviser to Secretary of State James F. Byrnes at the Big Four Ministers Conference in April 1946 at Paris, France.

During the Eightieth Congress (1947–48), Vandenberg became Senate Foreign Relations Committee chairman and steered the Truman Doctrine and the Rio treaty through his committee. The Truman Doctrine, which authorized $400 million in economic and military assistance to Greece and Turkey,

Arthur H. Vandenberg. (National Archives)

especially won Vandenberg's vigorous support. He guided the Greek-Turkish measure through the Senate in April 1947 and inserted an amendment linking the program more closely to the UN. "To repudiate the President of the United States at such an hour," he warned Senate colleagues, "could display a divisive weakness which might involve far greater jeopardy than a steady display of united strength." At the Inter-American Conference on Hemispheric Defense in August 1947, he helped draft the Rio Pact. This regional agreement provided for the collective defense of Western Hemisphere nations.

Vandenberg also enlisted bipartisan Senate support for the Marshall Plan and his own collective security resolution. The Michigan senator persuaded the Truman administration to modify the Marshall Plan so that it would be acceptable to conservative Republican colleagues. Upon his request, the administration agreed to have several top-level business executives testify before congressional committees, delete the specific $17 billion amount from its draft bill, and accept government outsider Paul Hoffman to administer the program. Vandenberg's Foreign Relations Committee reduced the initial authorization to $6.3 billion for the first twelve months. In March 1948 Vandenberg used his legislative skills to secure Senate adoption of the Marshall Plan, which he claimed would "help stop World War III before it starts." Three months later, the Senate overwhelmingly accepted his resolution committing the United States to regional collective defense arrangements within the framework of the UN charter. The Vandenberg resolution laid

the basis for U.S. participation in NATO and other regional collective security pacts.

Vandenberg remained a staunch advocate of containment after Democrat Tom Connally of Texas replaced him in 1949 as Foreign Relations Committee chairman. He resisted efforts by some conservative Republican Senate colleagues to stymie Truman's foreign policy programs. The Michigan Republican helped win Senate ratification of the NATO treaty so as to deter the spread of Soviet aggression into Western Europe. The last important speech of his Senate career in July 1949 came in defense of the NATO treaty. Vandenberg, however, did not always agree with Truman's Asian policies. He questioned American financial and military aid commitments to Nationalist China in the late 1940s and contended that Truman should not have committed U.S. troops in South Korea without a congressional declaration of war. Vandenberg, nevertheless, opposed U.S. recognition of the Communist Chinese government and supported sending UN forces to help South Korea thwart the spread of communism in 1950.

Vandenberg was hospitalized for cancer treatments in Grand Rapids in 1949 and made few Senate appearances thereafter. He suffered a relapse in January 1951 and died three months later. His death left the Senate without its key spokesman for bipartisanship. Vandenberg had worked closely with the executive branch without sacrificing his candor and beliefs and had rallied his party behind Truman's containment policies. He had helped build a solid foundation for America's leadership in world affairs that has continued well beyond his death.

The Arthur H. Vandenberg-Papers are located at the Michigan Historical Collection, University of Michigan, Ann Arbor. For Vandenberg's congressional role, see C. David Tompkins, *Senator Arthur H. Vandenberg: The Evolution of a Modern Republican, 1884–1945* (East Lansing: Michigan State University Press, 1970); Arthur H. Vandenberg, Jr., and Joe A. Morris, eds., *The Private Papers of Senator Vandenberg* (Boston: Houghton Mifflin, 1952); Aurie N. Dunlap, "The Political Career of Arthur H. Vandenberg" (Ph.D. diss., Columbia University, 1956); Newell S. Moore, "The Rise of Senator Arthur H. Vandenberg in American Foreign Affairs" (Ph.D. diss., George Peabody College, 1954); and *Arthur H. Vandenberg: His Career and Legacy* (Ann Arbor: Michigan Historical Collections, 1975). For his biographical background, see *Current Biography*, 1940, pp. 821–23; *Current Biography*, 1948, pp. 637–41; *Dictionary of American Biography, Supplement Five*, pp. 702–4; *New York Times*, 19 April 1951; and *Ann Arbor News*, 4 May 1976.

DAVID L. PORTER

See also Isolationism

Vaughan, Harry H.

(26 November 1893–20 May 1981)

Military aide to President Truman, 1945–53. Harry H. Vaughan, a native of Glasgow, Missouri, graduated from Westminster College in 1916. He met Truman at Fort Sill, Oklahoma, in 1917, where both men were training for duty in World War I. The two served as artillery officers in France during the war, though in different regiments. Their friendship grew in the years after the war, when they regularly attended Officer Reserve Corps summer training sessions at Fort Riley, Kansas.

Vaughan held a series of jobs during the 1920s and 1930s, while Truman began his political career. Their political association began during Truman's 1940 Senate reelection campaign, for which Vaughan served as treasurer. After the election Vaughan joined Truman in Washington as his executive secretary. He went on active duty when World War II began and served as provost marshal in Brisbane, Australia.

Vaughan returned to Washington in 1943 after a plane crash limited his activities. There he became an army liaison to the Truman committee, renewing ties with the senator. When Truman assumed the vice presidency in 1945, he created the new position of military aide to the vice president for Vaughan. After President Roosevelt's death, Vaughan continued as military aide to President Truman.

Seldom does a military aide excite controversy, but Vaughan was an unusual man to hold the position. Precedent dictated selection of a regular officer of exceptional military bearing and impeccable public conduct. Vaughan was a reservist whose antagonistic attitude toward regulars aggravated a delicate situation. Described by an associate as an "unmade bed," Vaughan did not project the military appearance needed to fulfill that part of his responsibilities he himself described as "scenery." Loud and outspoken, his manner invited criticism, and his banter often provided quotable copy for reporters. His demeanor led critics to unfair assessments of his character. Although he was an elder in the Presbyterian church who watched his language and nursed his drinks, his boisterous manner led to criticism for swearing and imbibing. Indiscreet remarks, such as his criticism of Protestant chaplains before a church group, provoked press criticism of Vaughan that continued unabated through the Truman presidency. His proximity to the president made him a target, and his own failure to realize the implications of seemingly innocent comments and actions led to politically damaging incidents.

But the characteristics that made Vaughan controversial endeared him to Truman, who appreciated his quick wit, clever repartee, and high spirits. Vaughan enlivened poker games, and the behavior that led critics to label him a "court jester" enabled Truman to relax and escape the pressures of the presidency. Vaughan bore few responsibilities of importance, and none as a policymaker.

During Truman's first term, Vaughan's imbroglios were inconsequential, if sometimes embarrassing. But after Truman's 1948 election, criticism of Vaughan increased in volume and severity. Charges of improper use of influence appeared. Frequent attacks against Vaughan provoked Truman to denounce columnist Drew Pearson as an "s.o.b."

In the summer of 1949, the Senate Investigations Subcommittee probed the role of influence peddlers known as "five-percenters." Vaughan's name was prominent throughout the inquiry, and his testimony climaxed the hearings. Five-percenters James V. Hunt and John F. Maragon had used Vaughan as a contact for their operations. Maragon ingratiated himself with Vaughan and then traded on his access to the White House staff. With Vaughan's support, Maragon used government transportation and won a spot on an official delegation to Greece.

The most publicized charge against Vaughan criticized his acceptance of a deep freezer from an advertising agent, who sent other freezers to Mrs. Truman and several members of the administration. The unsolicited gift arrived while Vaughan was out of the country, and even though no evidence surfaced to demonstrate that Vaughan had used his influence to reward the donor, the deep freezer became the symbol of corruption in the Truman administration. More serious charges accused Vaughan of diverting scarce building materials for the construction of a race track, releasing controlled materials for private business, and accepting a bribe in a tax evasion case.

In defense, Vaughan claimed that he had merely referred individuals to the proper decision-making authority. The committee was unable to substantiate any charges of illegal activity. Nonetheless, Vaughan was guilty of poor judgment for failing to distinguish between referral and advocacy, naïveté for failing to realize the political implications of his actions, and hubris for falling prey to the flattery of Maragon. Aside from acquiring a freezer of substandard quality, Vaughan had not profited personally from his actions, but he had damaged Truman's presidency and contributed to the environment that would allow Republicans to make corruption a campaign issue in 1952.

Truman never wavered in his support for Vaughan. Advisers suggested that the price of undeserved loyalty was too great and recommended Vaughan's dismissal. Vaughan offered to resign, but Truman refused to consider letting him go. Privately Truman acknowledged his concern; in public he blamed the press and Republican senators on the Investigations Subcommittee for trying to get at the president through his military aide.

Vaughan remained as military aide until the end of Truman's presidency. After January 1953 he lived in Alexandria, Virginia, on his military retirement pay, corresponding regularly with the former president. When Vaughan wrote his memoirs, Truman wrote a stirring foreword defending Vaughan, but later reconsidered and declined permission to include it. The memoir remained unpublished.

Vaughan's memoir, "Whipping Boy First Class," is included among his papers in the Truman Library. His relationship to Truman and to the five-percenter inquiry is examined in Andrew J. Dunar's *The Truman Scandals and the Politics of Morality* (Columbia: University of Missouri Press, 1984).

ANDREW J. DUNAR

See also Scandals

Veterans

During World War II almost 16.5 million men and women donned uniforms and served their country in branches of the armed forces. All but a million later shed their blues and khakis and reentered the civilian world. Potentially, these veterans constituted a powerful pressure group with three established organizations—the Veterans of Foreign Wars (1913), the American Legion (1920), and the Disabled Veterans of America (1920) —and two new organizations—the American Veterans Committee (1944) and the American Veterans of World War II

(1944). Veterans and their organizations following earlier wars, moreover, had played significant political roles during postwar eras. Conflicts between veterans and civilians form one of the many threads in the fabric of U.S. history.

The post–World War II veterans, however, failed to produce controversy or problems. Three interrelated factors explain the success story. First, aware of past history and keenly conscious of the depression of the 1930s, President Franklin D. Roosevelt and Congress enacted legislation that sought to minimize anticipated problems. The Selective Training and Service Act of 1940, which established the nation's first peacetime draft, guaranteed veterans reemployment rights to the jobs they left. In February 1944, largely to weaken the appeal of a bonus for veterans, Roosevelt signed into law the Mustering-Out Pay Act that granted cash payments upon discharge. On 22 June 1944, Roosevelt approved the Servicemen's Readjustment Act of 1944, better known as the G.I. bill.

The most comprehensive and generous veterans legislation ever enacted, the G.I. bill contained three categories of benefits: (1) employment and unemployment, (2) home, farm, and business loans, and (3) training and education of all types on all levels. Whatever the need or interest, the G.I. bill offered help. The multitude of programs were not coercive; they left the initiative with the veteran and blended governmental and private cooperation. The majority of veterans took advantage of their bountiful opportunities.

Passage on 27 June 1944 of the veterans' preference for federal civil service employment completed wartime legislation for them. The law added five points to the scores on competitive civil service examinations of veterans and wives of disabled veterans. Disabled veterans capable of working received a bonus of ten points. Under the law, "five-point" veterans went to the top of the list of all others with the same test scores. Unmarried widows of men killed in action and "ten-point" veterans received additional preference. The Surplus Property Act of October 1944 granted veterans some preferential rights, but the act was not a veterans' benefit measure. Veterans also enjoyed privileged access to benefits under the homestead and reclamation programs. In April 1945, when Roosevelt died, the responsibility of administering the laws and policies passed to Harry S. Truman.

In addition to the factor of legislation, Truman was the second reason for the successful assimilation of veterans back into society, for he viewed veterans sympathetically. A World War I veteran and member of the American Legion, Truman once remarked that "my whole political career is based on my war service and war associates." In 1935 and 1936, Senator Truman had supported immediate payment of a promised World War I bonus, one of the few issues over which he disagreed with Roosevelt.

In August 1945 Truman appointed Gen. Omar N. Bradley as director of the Veterans Administration. Bradley supervised with distinction the array of veterans' programs and ranked as one of Truman's most successful appointments. At its peak in 1948, spending on veterans constituted 20.1 percent of the national budget.

Housing for the millions of veterans who married during or immediately after the war, combined with the absence of wartime construction, proved the most difficult veteran problem Truman faced. On 1 March 1946 Truman asked Congress for authority to spur construction and curb excessive pricing. Congress agreed and on 22 May Truman approved the Veterans'

Emergency Housing Act of 1946 and named Wilson W. Wyatt of Kentucky as housing expediter. In December 1946, a month after voters elected a Republican-controlled Congress, Truman terminated the Veterans' Emergency Housing Act program before it had reached the halfway mark of its two-year operation. He yielded to the national mood that believed government allocations, regulations, and participation were unnecessary in an expanding economy. For several more years the unavailability of housing remained an acute problem, for nonveterans as well as veterans.

The expanding economy with its plenitude of jobs—the third factor accounting for the ease with which veterans resumed their places in society—more than offset the housing shortage and lesser problems. In his annual message to Congress on 6 January 1947, Truman paid "tribute to the fiber of our servicemen and to the flexibility of our economy" that produced an assimilation "so rapidly and so successfully." Indeed, among the successes of the postwar era few equaled the readjustment of veterans.

For a detailed scholarly study of the development of the federal programs and policies for veterans from 1940 to 1946, see David R. B. Ross, *Preparing for Ulysses: Politics and Veterans during World War II* (New York: Columbia University Press, 1969). Another historian, Keith W. Olson, describes the G.I. bill's most popular program in *The G.I. Bill, the Veterans, and the Colleges* (Lexington: University Press of Kentucky, 1974).

KEITH W. OLSON

See also Bradley, Omar Nelson; Demobilization

Veto Power

Of the thirty-eight presidents who served from George Washington through Jimmy Carter, only two—Franklin Roosevelt with 635 vetoes and Grover Cleveland with 584—cast more vetoes than Harry Truman, who disapproved of 250 laws passed by Congress. In his *Memoirs* Truman stated, "I found it necessary to veto more *major* bills [emphasis added] than any other President, with the possible exception of Grover Cleveland." Bills the president vetoed related both to the domestic economy and to internal security.

Most of Truman's vetoes of domestic legislation stemmed from economic problems that developed in the postwar period. With the Emergency Price Control Act due to expire on 30 June 1946, Truman requested a simple extension of the act. Congress instead amended the act so as to restrict the authority of the Office of Price Administration and to permit higher prices on many items to reflect cost increases. On 29 June 1946 the president vetoed the measure, hoping to force Congress to pass a stronger bill. A month later he reluctantly signed a second bill which he said fell short of ensuring stable prices but was better than the first one.

Tax legislation in the postwar period also gave rise to three presidential vetoes, despite the fact that presidents usually defer to Congress on revenue measures. On 16 June 1947 Truman cast his first veto of major legislation passed by the Republican-controlled Eightieth Congress by disapproving a tax reduction bill on the grounds that it was inflationary and that it was unfair in granting too much relief to upper-income taxpayers. A month later the Congress sent up a second bill and Truman vetoed it also, citing the same objections. The next year, however, the Eightieth Congress prevailed: on 1 April 1948 the president vetoed a third bill reducing individual income taxes, but in that election year, both houses easily overrode the veto and the measure became law.

A wave of labor unrest in the immediate postwar period created a demand for legislation that eventually led to two major vetoes by President Truman. Initially, in 1946, he took a get-tough stance toward labor by ordering the federal government to take over coal mines and railroads when workers in those industries went out on strike; he even considered asking Congress to draft the railroad workers into the army. In June of 1946 Congress passed a bill authored by Republican representative Francis Case of South Dakota providing for a thirty-day cooling-off period for strikes in vital industries, but Truman vetoed it on the grounds that it would encourage "quick" strikes. A year later on 20 June 1947 he also vetoed a major bill sponsored by Republican senator Robert Taft of Ohio and Republican representative Fred Hartley of New Jersey that extensively regulated labor unions. Truman went on nationwide radio to brand the bill as "bad for labor, bad for management and bad for the country," but both houses of Congress overrode the veto with many Democrats joining in the override.

In 1948 Truman vetoed bills affecting the coverage of the Social Security program and the administration of the United States Employment Service, as well as the Reed-Bulwinkle Act affecting antitrust actions against railroads; all were overridden by Congress. These vetoes, however, plus those relating to the price control program, tax cuts, and labor-management relations, allowed the president to go to the people in the 1948 campaign as the friend of the "little" person against the "rich and powerful." The veto of the Taft-Hartley Act is also credited with galvanizing the AFL and CIO into concerted action on behalf of Truman and other Democratic candidates and of thwarting Henry Wallace's third-party appeal to labor that year.

Even after the Democrats recaptured control of both houses of Congress, President Truman continued to veto measures he thought benefited vested interests. One was the basing point bill of 1950 relating to setting freight charges affecting the price of steel, which Truman felt endangered the enforcement of the antitrust laws. Another was the Kerr natural gas bill of 1950 exempting independent companies from regulation by the Federal Power Commission, which the president contended would lead to spiraling prices and windfall profits. In his final year in office he vetoed a bill sponsored by Democratic senator Pat McCarran of Nevada that sought to convey to Texas, Louisiana, and California title to offshore oil resources (mistakenly referred to as tidelands oil) the Supreme Court had held belonged to the United States; the president took the position that the legislation would give away a national heritage to citizens of just three states and that it would benefit companies that sought to exploit these oil-rich areas free of federal control and supervision.

Truman's vetoes thus related primarily to domestic economic matters, but he also took a stand against legislation stemming from the red scare in the postwar period. In 1948 he vetoed a bill that authorized certain members of the Senate to direct the FBI to investigate persons appointed to offices established by the Atomic Energy Act of 1946 on the grounds that it permitted an unwarranted legislative encroachment upon the executive branch and was wholly unnecessary and unwise. Two years later he vetoed, as constituting "thought-control," the Internal Security Act sponsored by Senator McCarran that required the registration of Communist and other suspect groups with the attorney general and authorized the detention of persons thought likely to commit espionage and sedition. In 1952 he disapproved the McCarran-Walter Act controlling the immigration and deportation of "subversives" and persons with Communist affiliations, calling it worse than the infamous Alien Act of 1798. Vetoes of the latter two bills were overridden by Congress.

Thus Truman's own assessment of the importance of his vetoes is accurate. It should be noted, however, that he was overridden by Congress on twelve occasions; only Andrew Johnson's fifteen overrides exceeded that number (Gerald Ford also experienced twelve overrides). Moreover, Truman's veto of the offshore oil bill was eventually nullified when President Eisenhower subsequently signed similar legislation granting title to those resources to the states.

Nonetheless, Truman's exercise of the veto power had important consequences for his presidency. His vetoes of legislation passed by the Republican-controlled Eightieth Congress allowed him to frame the issues and gain needed support from labor for his successful 1948 campaign. His vetoes also forced that Congress to modify measures such as Taft-Hartley and tax reduction in order to garner sufficient Democratic support to override his vetoes. Finally, his vetoes helped him delay and blunt Republican attempts to alter some liberal New Deal programs initiated by Franklin Roosevelt.

There is no work that specifically treats Truman's vetoes as such, but Susan Hartmann's *Truman and the 80th Congress* (Columbia: University of Missouri Press, 1971) analyzes his vetoes as part of his general relationship with that Congress. Robert J. Donovan's two volumes, *Conflict and Crisis* and *Tumultous Years* (New York: W. W. Norton, 1977, 1982) treat the major vetoes cast in both his presidential terms. An analysis of Truman's most significant veto is R. Alton Lee, *Truman and Taft-Hartley: A Question of Mandate* (Lexington: University of Kentucky Press, 1966). Truman discusses in depth his 1952 veto of the offshore oil legislation in his *Memoirs*, vol. 2, *Years of Trial and Hope* (Garden City, N.Y.: Doubleday, 1956), Chap. 30.

RICHARD A. WATSON

Vice Presidency

When President Harry S. Truman spoke to newsmen on 13 April 1945, the country was still in a state of shock from the announcement of Franklin Delano Roosevelt's death. Already many questions about the new president had been raised. Who was Harry Truman? Was he capable of the heavy burdens that were so suddenly thrust upon him? Was his brief term as vice president a useful apprenticeship for the assumption of the duties of the presidency? Because historians have investigated Truman's political career mainly in terms of the periods before and after his tenure as vice president of the United States, those eighty-two days have remained obscure. Cabell Phillips, in *The Truman Presidency*, devoted less than a page to the Truman vice presidency, and one of Truman's biographers, Jonathan Daniels, entitled the chapter that dealt with this period "A Brief Interlude." This assumption that Truman's vice presidency was an unproductive time has been accepted by many historians. Nevertheless, it was something more than a mere interruption in Truman's political career.

Roosevelt's advisers skillfully engineered the removal of Vice President Henry Wallace from the 1944 ticket and replaced him with Harry Truman. They did so with the unspoken understanding that Truman would probably succeed to the presidency. Some observers have maintained that Roosevelt did not really care that much who became vice president. Truman himself viewed the office as a dead-end job: "I bet I can go down the street and stop the first ten men I see and that they can't tell me the name of two of the last ten vice-presidents of the United States." Shortly after he received the nomination, one of his Senate colleagues wrote to him that he did not know whether to offer congratulations or commiseration. Once Truman entered the office, however, he took it seriously. In March, he wrote to a friend, "This new job of mine is turning out to be quite a working job in spite of the fact I didn't think it would be." In his *Memoirs*, Truman spoke of the potential power of the vice president:

> The opportunities afforded by the vice presidency, particularly the presidency of the Senate, do not come—they are there to be seized. The man who fills the office can choose to do little or he can do much. The vice-president's influence on legislation depends on his personality and his ability, and especially the respect he commands from the senators. Here is one instance in which it is the man who makes the office, not the office the man.

Truman decided he would concentrate on being "a pipeline for the exchange of information and ideas between the White House and the Senate."

He spoke in his *Memoirs* of another function of the office:

> A good deal of the vice-president's functions are social and ceremonial. . . . Outranking foreign ambassadors, he is almost always the most important guest at a dinner or other social function. Socially the vice-president takes precedence over all other officers of the government except the president. I never cared too much for this aspect of my job as vice-president.

Despite this lack of enthusiasm, however, Truman kept a social schedule that for three months left "Capitol society writers breathless." The Trumans enjoyed parties, and people enjoyed the Trumans.

Truman conscientiously carried out the role delegated to the vice president by the Constitution. In his correspondence, he often told people that he could not attend functions on the days the Senate met: "Since I draw my salary for presiding over the Senate, I try to be here when the Senate is in session." In this capacity, Truman served as a general parliamentarian. As vice president, he could introduce miscellaneous resolutions but not legislation, and he could vote only in the event of a tie. He had one such opportunity. On 10 April the Taft Lend-Lease amendment, which would have prevented the use of Lend-Lease for postwar relief and reconstruction, received a tie vote. Truman broke the tie with a nay vote.

Among the powers delegated to the vice president as presi-

Indiana senator Samuel Jackson holds aloft the arm of Missouri senator Harry S. Truman, the 1944 Democratic National Convention's vice-presidential nominee, 21 July 1944. (Associated Press/Wide World Photos)

dent of the Senate is that of referring a bill to a committee. In one of his most controversial official acts, Vice President Truman referred Montana Democratic senator James Murray's Missouri Valley Authority bill to the Commerce Committee whose chairman, North Carolina democrat Josiah Bailey, was hostile to public power bills. Senator Murray requested that it be sent to the Agriculture Committee which would give the bill a friendlier reception. Despite Murray's protest, Truman did not change his ruling, and Murray introduced an unsuccessful resolution asking the Senate to overrule the vice president. Although the press and the public thought that Truman's move indicated his opposition to the bill, this was not the case. He supported the creation of a Missouri Valley Authority, but had made his decision solely according to Senate rules.

Most of Vice President Truman's activities both inside and outside the Senate centered around the future peace treaty and the San Francisco United Nations conference. Soon after his return from Yalta, Roosevelt announced to the press that Truman "had been asked to serve as Senate–White House go-between on the world security organization charter and other major treaties." Two days after President Roosevelt's death, Harry Hopkins commented that Truman's popularity in the Senate had been the most important factor in his selection as the Democratic nominee for vice president, for, said Hopkins, "the President wanted somebody that would help him when he went up there and asked them to ratify the peace."

The importance of unity in order to win the peace was the central theme in Truman's brief Passover speech broadcast over radio on 26 March 1945. Just as the Jews had suffered for their moral principles, he said, so those who believed in the principles of the United Nations would experience some trials because "all who insist upon fighting for ideals, be they religious or political, must suffer at some time from the intolerance and bigotry of bitter opponents." Truman said that if all men worked together for a lasting peace, the Promised Land where all the world lived together in peace and security could be achieved.

In addition to the legislative and speech-making functions, the routine matters of the vice-presidential office occupied much of Truman's time. His constituency was no longer confined to Missouri but consisted of people from all parts of the United States who wrote to him or called on him to ask for and sometimes give advice. A tremendous volume of mail came through the vice-presidential office, and nearly all letters were answered by Truman or his staff. In a letter to a friend, he wrote, "The difficulty the Vice President has is to keep up with his mail and find time to do the things that are necessary."

Shortly after Truman was inaugurated as vice president, his old political friend, Tom Pendergast, died. Truman flew to Kansas City aboard an army transport plane to attend the funeral and returned to the East Coast for a dinner speech in Philadelphia that night. His actions aroused a storm of public controversy. People objected not only to his attendance at the funeral of a "convicted felon" but to his use of rationed gasoline. To others, Truman's refusal to repudiate his old friendship was considered an act of political courage. In response to a letter that commended his attendance at the funeral, Truman wrote, "There had been so much talking about my connection with him that I just wanted to let them know that they didn't have any effect on me."

Nor was Truman's term as vice president unimportant in the development of his political philosophy. His vice-presidential speeches included ideas that became part of some of his most important policies during his presidential years. Although these ideas may not have had their origin during this period, he at least articulated them now. The Point Four program for example, in which the United States would make available to underdeveloped areas the benefits of its technical knowledge, may have been hinted at in Truman's statement that "enlightened world-wide education may be the lost key to lasting peace." And in a speech delivered at Jefferson City, Missouri, he said, "Either America must be constantly ready to repel *alone* all and any attacks from the rest of the world—or we must be willing to cooperate with friendly states to check the first signs of aggression on the part of any members of the Family of Nations." These words expressed his deep belief in the principle of the United Nations. They also reflected his philosophical approach to what would become the North Atlantic Treaty Organization. On a radio program, Truman spoke of his belief that economic isolation was as impractical as political isolation. His conviction that the United States would have to actively bolster foreign economies was a reaffirmation of his long-standing support for reciprocal trade agreements in the Senate.

Truman's vice presidency, then, was indeed something more than a "brief interlude." In this period, he reinforced his friendships on Capitol Hill and built up vital support for the coming peace treaties and the United Nations. He saw himself as a *political* vice president. In support of Roosevelt's goals he helped shape and steer legislation through the Senate by behind-the-scenes work mending political fences and curbing political feuds. In this way he also saw himself as a champion of the programs of the New Deal. Moreover, he gained experience in dealing with a nationwide constituency. Although short in duration, Truman's vice presidency was an important and constructive apprenticeship for the problems he later faced as president of the United States.

A good general account of Truman's vice presidency is Harold F. Gosnell, *Truman's Crises: A Political Biography of Harry S. Truman* (Westport, Conn.: Greenwood Press, 1980), 209–14. See also Richard Kirkendall, "Truman's Path to Power," *Social Science* 43 (1968): 67–73. The author believes that Truman was acceptable because he was the least divisive candidate in 1944. In Arthur F. McClure and Donna Costigan, "The Truman Vice Presidency: Constructive Apprenticeship or Brief Interlude?" *Missouri Historical Review* 65 (1971): 318–41, the authors argue that Truman's vice presidency was more important than historians have assumed.

ARTHUR F. McCLURE II

See also Election of 1944

Vinson, Frederick M.

(22 January 1890–8 September 1953)

U.S. House of Representatives, 1924–29, 1931–38; associate justice, U.S. Court of Appeals for D.C., 1938–43; director, Office of Economic Stabilization, 1943–45; secretary of the treasury, 1945–46; chief justice, U.S. Supreme Court, 1946–53. Frederick M. Vinson was born in Louisa, Kentucky. His father worked as a county jailer and his mother took in boarders to help put Fred through Kentucky Normal College. Vinson received a B.A. in 1909 and an LL.B. in 1911 from Centre College. While at Centre, Vinson taught mathematics at the college preparatory school, worked in the law library, and was a star player on the baseball team. Admitted to the bar in 1911, he practiced law for two years and after 1913 served as city attorney. Following World War I service, he returned to Kentucky and in 1921 was elected commonwealth attorney for the Thirty-second Judicial District of Kentucky, serving until his election to the House of Representatives in 1924.

In 1931 Vinson was placed on the Ways and Means Committee and won notoriety for his knowledge of financial matters. He played a central role in the creation of New Deal tax legislation and in 1936 became chairman of the Ways and Means Special Subcommittee on Taxation. Vinson was a loyal New Dealer who generally supported Roosevelt's economic legislation. He also backed Roosevelt's Court-packing plan in 1937.

As a reward for his loyalty, Roosevelt appointed him associate justice of the U.S. Court of Appeals for the District of Columbia in December 1937. Serving until May 1943, he was also appointed chief judge of the U.S. Emergency Court of Appeals, which had been established to hear challenges to the regulations of the Office of Price Administration. Vinson's career as a circuit court judge was undistinguished. He participated in about 450 cases, almost all of which were routine. He rarely dissented and did not often write concurring opinions. Themes that were evident during the early court years included a reliance on judicial restraint and the giving of wide latitude to governmental power which often entailed a justification of the infringement of individual civil liberties.

In May 1943, Vinson resigned to become director of the Office of Economic Stabilization, a wartime agency established to control inflation. There his administrative skill became clear. He subsequently was named director of the Office of War Mobilization and Reconversion in 1945. As his career in the executive branch expanded, so did his influence and political contacts. One important friend was Harry Truman, who in July 1945 appointed him secretary of the treasury. Vinson quickly became an influential figure in the Truman cabinet. Truman had great respect for his talents, and the two formed a close friendship.

In June 1946, Truman named Vinson as Chief Justice Harlan Stone's replacement on the U.S. Supreme Court. Intense intracourt antagonisms at the time had forced the president to look outside the Court for a new chief justice. He thought Vinson would be able to unify the Court and reduce tension among the other justices, but Vinson was unable to do so. He lacked the intellectual powers necessary to dominate the Court. In addition, the justices he had to deal with were men of profound convictions and superior intellectual talents. Dissenting opinions persisted as the characteristic feature of the Court. In Vinson's first term, only 36 percent of the decisions were unanimous, and in 1952, the Court hit a record of only 19 percent unanimous decisions.

Although Vinson failed to unite the Court, he did reduce the burden of work for the justices by increasing the number of law clerks and rigorously reducing the Court's caseload. This was in line with his view of judicial restraint, developed as a New Dealer, and also reflected his pragmatism. Uninterested in brooding over the principles of law, he was convinced that the law could be adapted to the felt necessities of almost any human situation if the facts were carefully studied and understood. "Nothing is more certain in modern society," he wrote in the most famous of his opinions, the *Dennis* case (1951), "than the principle that there are no absolutes, that a name, a phrase, a standard has meaning only associated with the considerations which gave birth to the nomenclature. . . . To those who would paralyze our government by encasing it in a semantic straightjacket, we must reply that all concepts are relative." This enabled him to argue for the majority that the "peculiar conditions" of the world, and the nature of the Communist party justified imprisonment of its leaders on the basis of speech alone, even though no evidence of imminent revolution existed.

Dennis was a logical outgrowth of his earlier ruling in *American Communications Association v. Douds* (1950). There Vinson had maintained that although Congress had undeniably discouraged the lawful exercise of political freedom by including a requirement of non-Communist affidavits from union leaders in the Taft-Hartley Act, the abridgement of free speech had to be weighed against the government's power to regulate commerce. He thus upheld the loyalty oath as a valid commercial regulation.

Other reflections of his progovernment position were seen in his opinions in the 1947 John L. Lewis case—*U.S. v. United Mine Workers*, and his dissent in the 1952 steel seizure case—*Youngstown Sheet and Tube v. Sawyer*. There he upheld inherent presidential power to seize industry in alleged emergencies. But whereas in the mining situation he was dealing with defiance of an emergency antistrike injunction, which the majority agreed constituted a genuine emergency, in the steel case his colleagues refused to go along with his extreme construction of inherent presidential power.

Vinson did write unanimous decisions in the civil rights area. In *Shelley v. Kraemer* (1948), he held that judicial enforcement of restrictive covenants was discriminatory state action and violated the equal protection clause of the Fourteenth Amendment. In the 1950 *McLaurin* and *Sweatt* cases, he supported blacks seeking postgraduate training at state universities. His attack on segregation was cautiously made and narrowly conceived, and when pressures mounted to extend the logic of the education cases to the public schools, Vinson fought it by putting off the original hearing, by discouraging Justice Department participation, and by calling for a complete rehearing in the 1953 term. Thus he left Earl Warren to bring the case of *Brown v. Board of Education* (1954) forward.

Despite his Supreme Court record, Vinson's personal popularity remained high with colleagues and national leaders. He was prominently mentioned as a candidate to replace George Marshall as secretary of state, as a dark-horse presidential candidate in 1948, as a top candidate for commissioner of baseball in 1951, and as Harry Truman's choice as the Democratic nominee for president in 1952—an honor he refused, just as he had earlier downplayed Truman's plan to send him to meet with Stalin at Moscow in October 1948. Truman held Vinson in high regard, especially as a political troubleshooter who could move easily into a wide range of fields and do a sound job of solving immediate problems.

A special memorial issue of the *Northwestern University Law Review* 49 (1954) contains valuable essays on Vinson's career. In addition, John P. Frank wrote a perceptive piece, "Fred Vinson and the Chief Justiceship," in *University of Chicago Law Review* 21 (1954): 212, as did Irving F. Lefberg, "Chief Justice Vinson and the Politics of Desegregation," *Emory Law Journal* 24 (Spring 1975): 243. Vinson's career as chief justice is evaluated in James Bolner, "Mr. Chief Justice Vinson: His Politics and His Constitutional Law" (Ph.D. diss., University of Virginia, 1962). C. Herman Pritchett, *Civil Liberties and the Vinson Court* (Chicago: University of Chicago Press, 1954), places his judicial career within the broader context of Vinson Court operations. For a brief overview of the man, see Paul L. Murphy and James McCarthy, "Frederick Moore Vinson," in *Dictionary of American Biography, Supplement 5* (New York: Scribner's, 1977), 711–15.

PAUL L. MURPHY

See also Johnson, Louis Arthur (photograph); Supreme Court, United States (and photograph)

W

Walker, Frank Comerford

(30 May 1886–13 September 1959)

Roosevelt's longtime friend, fund-raiser, and adviser; Democratic national treasurer; New Deal administrator; postmaster general; Democratic national chairman. Born at Plymouth, Pennsylvania, Frank Walker was taken by his devout Roman Catholic, second-generation, Irish-American parents to Butte, Montana, to live where he was given a religious school education which continued at Gonzaga University, Spokane, Washington. He graduated in 1909 from the University of Notre Dame School of Law, practiced law with his brother, a Butte politician, and was elected as a Democrat to one term in the Montana House of Representatives. In 1924 Walker joined his uncle's expanding movie theater business with headquarters in New York City. This gave him eastern connections and made him a multimillionaire.

Frank Walker was always interested in Democratic party politics. He became a major fund-raiser for FDR in 1932 and, as a New Dealer, headed the Executive Council and National Emergency Council until December 1935. Roosevelt appointed him postmaster general to succeed James A. Farley in 1940 and replaced Edward J. Flynn with Walker as Democratic national chairman in January 1943.

To prepare for the wartime election of 1944, Walker fine-tuned the sputtering Democratic machine by streamlining patronage, negotiating with state political leaders, and working for higher voter turnout. He was instrumental in the merger of Minnesota's Farmer-Labor and regular Democratic factions and successfully courted Sidney Hillman's CIO Political Action Committee for voter delivery. Walker then chose Robert Hannegan in early 1944 to succeed him as chairman. Fearing a Roosevelt loss, Walker and Hannegan operated to strengthen the ticket in the South by replacing Vice President Henry A. Wallace with Harry S. Truman. Through effective convention politics, which Harold Ickes half-humorously described as "Hannegan-shenanigans," they produced the "second Missouri Compromise" and helped shape the post-Roosevelt era.

President Truman and Frank Walker remained friends, although Walker in 1945 was the first Roosevelt cabinet member to resign. He had contemplated stepping down well before the advent of Truman's presidency. Truman appointed Walker, a "last hurrah," as alternate delegate to the first United Nations meeting, in London, 1946.

References to Walker are scattered in New Deal literature, but no biography of him exists. Work on one has been started by Dean Kohlhoff. Scholarly publications include Paul L. Simon, "Frank Walker, New Dealer" (Ph.D. diss., University of Notre Dame, 1965) and "Frank Walker: Coordinator of the New Deal, 1933–1935," *Hudson Review* 2 (1969): 75–90. His papers are in the archives at the University of Notre Dame. The Franklin D. Roosevelt Library and the National Archives hold documents relevant to his political career.

DEAN W. KOHLHOFF

Walking

At first a routine mode of transportation for Truman, walking later became a favorite exercise. As a young man living in the countryside at the dawn of the automobile age, Harry Truman customarily walked relatively long distances. He seems frequently to have traveled the one mile between the family farm and the town of Grandview on foot, especially during the years he took the train for regular weekend visits into Independence to court Bess Wallace. Bess herself enjoyed long walks, and the activity became a feature of their romance. After Truman purchased an automobile in 1914, he gave up walking as an ordinary way of getting around, but it continued to be an important part of his life.

Still famous for his daily walks, former president Truman keeps up a brisk pace; one cameraman jokingly dons roller skates to get ahead of him. 1 February 1956. (Associated Press/Wide World Photos)

As an officer he was usually mounted during his World War I service. Nonetheless, in France, he found himself often on foot with his men during difficult forced marches because of the high mortality rate among his regiment's horses or because of a need to give his mount to an injured soldier. Such experiences forged a strong bond between him and his troops.

In later years, he took up the brisk walk, generally at a military pace of 120 steps a minute, as a form of vigorous exercise that kept him fit and helped allieviate the stress that plagued his political career. It was a custom he appears to have begun during his Senate years, perhaps as a means of eliminating the expense of car fares from the tight family budget. As president, he established a routine of early morning walks, flanked by Secret Service men and often accompanied by a few reporters attempting to ask questions and take notes on the run. The custom became his trademark, and he continued it on trips to New York and Washington during the vigorous early years of his retirement.

The best source for the importance of walking in Harry Truman's life is Margaret Truman, *Bess W. Truman* (New York: Macmillan, 1986).

ALONZO L. HAMBY

See also Health

Wallace, Henry Agard

(7 October 1888–18 November 1965)

Early in 1944, Henry A. Wallace became a person of large importance in Harry Truman's life, and until late in 1948, he maintained that position.

By 1944, Wallace was one of the most prominent people in American political life. Born on a farm near Orient, Iowa, he had been raised in Ames and Des Moines and educated in the Des Moines public schools and Iowa State College. Upon graduation, he joined the editorial staff of *Wallaces' Farmer*, and when his father became secretary of agriculture in 1921, H. A. became editor. As a leading agricultural journalist, he was a major participant in the farm politics of the 1920s and a logical choice for secretary of agriculture when Franklin Roosevelt became president. In the next eight years, Wallace provided leadership in the development of a New Deal for agriculture and became a national figure and Roosevelt's choice as his running mate in 1940. During the war, he was an unusually active vice president.

To some people, including the president's wife and the leaders of the Congress of Industrial Organizations, Wallace seemed to be the logical successor to FDR. They applauded his activities as the great champion of a revived New Deal and of

Henry A. Wallace. (The Constant Collection; courtesy of the Franklin D. Roosevelt Library)

the "Century of the Common Man" in which imperial systems would be abolished, trade and investment would flow freely among the nations of the world, and standards of living everywhere would be raised.

Other players in the political game distrusted Wallace. His foes included many southern Democrats, such as Jesse Jones and James Byrnes, and most Democrats from the big-city political machines, including Robert Hannegan, now serving as chairman of the Democratic National Committee. They had an unusually strong interest in the selection of a vice-presidential candidate, for people who were close to Roosevelt recognized that, though he was determined to run for a fourth term, he was suffering from health problems that might end his presidency before that term concluded.

Many of Wallace's enemies campaigned against his renomination for the vice presidency. They sought to persuade Roosevelt that he must not insist upon Wallace as he had in 1940. They portrayed the vice president as too idealistic and impractical. They argued that his presence on the Democratic ticket in the fall election would hurt it. Their pressures on FDR overcame Wallace's own efforts and those of Eleanor Roosevelt on his behalf.

The anti-Wallace campaign came to focus on Truman as the superior alternative. Hannegan and others argued that the Missouri senator had demonstrated his loyalty to the president and the party and was popular with all factions in that organization. Thus, he would strengthen the ticket. The campaign enjoyed considerable success with Roosevelt. While he wrote one

letter to the convention saying that he would vote for Wallace if he were a delegate, he did not insist that Wallace be chosen, and he wrote another letter indicating his willingness to run with Truman. In addition, he pressured Truman to become a candidate.

The outcome was a Truman victory and a Wallace defeat at the Democratic convention. It came even though Wallace was far ahead in the public opinion polls and in the lead at the end of the first ballot. But Truman had hard-working champions, and he was acceptable to the southerners and the liberals, though not their first choice. Each of those factions preferred him to the choice of the rival faction, and he won on the second ballot.

Following Roosevelt's reelection, he selected Wallace as his secretary of commerce, and after FDR died, Truman, believing that he needed the support of the many enthusiastic Wallace supporters, kept him in place. Wallace soon became troubled, however, especially about Truman's apparent hostility toward the Soviet Union, a trait the cabinet officer blamed on advisers such as Byrnes and on the British.

From his post in the cabinet, Wallace pressed the president on Soviet policy, urging him to behave as Roosevelt would, had he lived. The secretary assumed that the Soviets and the Americans could cooperate and emphasized improved trade as a means to that end. He called attention to the Communists' fear of "capitalist encirclement" and rejected the growing tendency to equate Stalin with Hitler and the Soviet Union with Nazi Germany.

On 23 July 1946, Wallace sent the president a long letter. He criticized what he took to be the militarization of American policy, insisting that it would bring war rather than peace. He argued that their history encouraged the Russians to "see themselves as fighting for their existence in a hostile world" and that the U.S. effort to establish "democracy in Eastern Europe, where democracy by and large has never existed, seems to her [the Soviet Union] an attempt to establish the encirclement of unfriendly neighbors which . . . might serve as another effort to destroy her." Truman ignored the advice.

On 12 September, in a major speech at Madison Square Garden, Wallace warned: "The tougher we get, the tougher the Russians will get." He had discussed the speech with the president and had been encouraged to give it, apparently because Truman hoped it would help the Democrats in the congressional elections.

Arousing a storm of controversy, the speech led to a long conversation between Truman and Wallace on 18 September. Explaining that he must support his secretary of state, Truman insisted that Wallace must stop talking about foreign policy. Wallace recognized that more, including a philosophical disagreement, was involved. It was a disagreement between a person whose reading of recent history led him to emphasize the economic factor in international relations, and another who stressed the military element. As Truman expressed this in his diary: "He is a pacifist one hundred percent. He wants to disband our armed forces, give Russia our atomic secrets and trust a band of adventurers in the Kremlin Politburo. I do not understand a 'dreamer' like that." Each man had come to see the other as the kind of person who had produced trouble for the United States in the past, especially the tragedy of World War II, and might lead the nation into a new and even greater horror—atomic war.

Truman felt compelled to fire Wallace, doing so on 20 September and defining the move as necessary to unify the administration on foreign policy. He maintained that there was a "fundamental conflict" between Wallace and the rest of the administration in this area. For his part, Wallace stated that "our present foreign policy does not recognize the basic realities that led to two world wars and which now threatens us with another war."

As the nation's foreign policy moved from "get tough" to "containment" in 1947, Wallace continued to criticize it, and late in the year, recognizing that he had no hope of getting the Democratic nomination for the presidency, he announced his decision to run on a third-party ticket. Supported by both Communists and non-Communist liberals, he criticized the containment policy as a creature of Wall Street and the military, saying it was imperialistic and would lead toward war and away from reform. He called for a reformed capitalist system capable of supplying the material needs of all people. He seemed capable of getting the support of at least 6 percent of the voters, drawing them away from the Democratic candidate and guaranteeing his defeat.

During 1948, Truman campaigned militantly against Wallace as well as the Republicans and obtained help in his anti-Wallace efforts. He condemned Wallace for accepting Communist support. Most labor leaders, fearing the weakening of the Democratic party, the friend of labor, refused to support Wallace, endorsed containment, and began to purge Communists from their ranks. The Americans for Democratic Action, also fearful of a weakening of the Democratic party, denied that liberals and Communists could work together and charged that the Wallace movement was a Communist effort to destroy Truman's foreign policy. And the Soviets, by supporting a Communist coup in Czechoslovakia and blockading Berlin, lent support to the anti-Wallace thesis that liberals and Communists could not cooperate. As most Americans accepted the view that his campaign was Communist-controlled, Wallace began to slip in the polls.

The Wallace movement, now calling itself the Progressive party, suffered further decline when it held its national convention in Philadelphia in July. As expected, the party nominated Wallace for the presidency. His platform endorsed Soviet-American cooperation, criticized Truman's foreign and military policies, and called for domestic reform. Commentators insisted that Communists were in control, even though the party's presidential candidate was a successful participant in the capitalist system, having founded a corporation, the Pioneer Hi-Bred Corn Company, that was the leader in its industry, his platform endorsed capitalism and reform, and his stand on foreign policy was in harmony with the position he had developed well before 1948.

Although his prospects were darkening, Wallace made a strenuous campaign, covering even more ground and making more speeches than Truman. In contrast with the president, who spent almost no time in the South, Wallace campaigned extensively in all parts of the country. He devoted much attention to civil rights, doing so in the South as well as the North, but he emphasized foreign policy, for he regarded it as basic. He encountered much hostility, some of it violent, and dropped still further in the polls.

In spite of his efforts, Wallace placed fourth in the November election, getting 1.1 million popular votes, only 2.7 percent of the total, and no electoral votes and running behind Thurmond as well as Dewey and Truman. Campaigning with considerable effectiveness, the president and his allies had deprived Wallace of hoped-for support from the urban working classes, Jews, and blacks.

Contrary to Wallace's aspirations, the election strengthened the containment policy by suggesting that it had substantial popular support. Three of the four leading presidential candidates—Dewey and Thurmond as well as Truman—had supported it, whereas the candidate who opposed it suffered a humiliating defeat.

The defeat all but ended Wallace's political career. He did speak out against the establishment of NATO in 1949 and in support of Truman's decision to intervene in Korea in 1950, but he devoted his remaining years to scientific experiments on his New York farm.

Wallace's personal papers have been divided among three locations: the library of the University of Iowa, the Franklin D. Roosevelt Library, and the Library of Congress. Those papers and his lengthy oral history interview are also available on microfilm. Some papers remain in his family's possession but should soon be deposited at Iowa State University, and his official papers can be used in the National Archives. An old book, Russell Lord, *The Wallaces of Iowa* (Boston: Houghton Mifflin Co., 1947), remains useful. Edward L. and Frederick H. Schapsmeier provide a more thorough account in *Henry A. Wallace: The Agrarian Years, 1910–1940* (Ames: Iowa State University Press, 1968) and *Prophet in Politics: Henry A. Wallace and the War Years, 1940–1965* (Ames: Iowa State University Press, 1970), but they did not have access to the Wallace papers. Four more specialized studies do draw upon them: Allen Yarnell, *Democrats and Progressives: The 1948 Presidential Election as a Test of Postwar Liberalism* (Berkeley: University of California Press, 1974); Norman D. Markowitz, *The Rise and Fall of the People's Century: Henry A. Wallace and American Liberalism, 1941–1948* (New York: Free Press, 1973); J. Samuel Walker, *Henry A. Wallace and American Foreign Policy* (Westport, Conn.: Greenwood Press, 1976); and Richard J. Walton, *Henry Wallace, Harry Truman and the Cold War* (New York: Viking Press, 1976). And John Morton Blum has edited an important item from the papers: *The Price of Vision: The Diary of Henry A. Wallace 1942–1946* (Boston: Houghton Mifflin Co., 1973). At work on a biography, Richard S. Kirkendall has reported his early findings in several essays: "The Mind of a Farm Leader," *Annals of Iowa* 47 (Fall 1983): 138–53; "ER and the Issue of FDR's Successor," in *Without Precedent: The Life and Career of Eleanor Roosevelt*, ed. John Hoff-Wilson and Marjorie Lightman (Bloomington: Indiana University Press, 1984); "Corn Huskers and Master Farmers: Henry A. Wallace and the Merchandising of Iowa Agriculture," *Palimpsest* 65 (May-June 1984): 82–93; (with Glenda Riley), "Henry A. Wallace and the Mystique of the Farm Male, 1921–1933," *Annals of Iowa* 48 (Summer-Fall 1985): 32–55; and "Henry A. Wallace's Turn toward the New Deal, 1921–1924," *Annals of Iowa* 49 (Winter-Spring 1988): 221–39.

RICHARD S. KIRKENDALL

See also Election of 1948; Progressive Party; Roosevelt, Franklin D. (photograph)

War Crimes Trials

In October 1943 the Allied powers established the United Nations War Crimes Commission. The commission, based in London, immediately started to collect evidence on war crimes. Once in office President Truman acted with his usual dispatch. On 2 May 1945, he appointed Supreme Court Justice Robert H. Jackson as chief counsel to investigate and prosecute major Axis war criminals. "War criminals" were defined as principals of Nazi "criminal organizations" responsible either for specific mass atrocities committed during World War II or for the more general offense—and legally questionable notion—of waging "wars of aggression."

President Truman thought that the "barbaric practices" of these war criminals demanded the unprecedented step of the victors putting the vanquished on trial: "We have a stern duty to teach the German people the hard lesson that they must change their ways before they can be received back into the family of peaceful civilized nations," he wrote in a letter to Gen. Evangeline Booth of the Salvation Army on 25 May 1945.

In August 1945 the Allied powers agreed on the London Charter defining the jurisdiction and powers of the International Military Tribunal, which heard cases from 20 November 1945 till 1 October 1946. It was held in the Nazi stronghold of Nuremberg, "at a time and in a place where one could literally touch the death factories of Auschwitz and Treblinka," as Bradley Smith described it. Only twenty-two defendants were on trial. They represented some of Nazism's most criminal organizations: the party's "leadership corps," the murderous SS and the Gestapo-SD. Hermann Goering was the most notorious man in the stand. The charges were "conspiracy"; "crimes against peace," namely, "the planning, preparation, initiation and waging of wars of aggression"; "war crimes"; and "crimes against humanity." Twelve defendants were given the death penalty. Three life sentences were handed down, among them that of Hitler's deputy, Rudolf Hess, who finally died in Spandau prison in August 1987.

President Truman decided in January 1946 that the Office of Military Government in Germany would handle the "second-string" criminals. The Nuremberg Military Tribunals indicted 185 people through April 1949. In twelve trials famous industrialists like Alfred Krupp and Friedrich Flick as well as high government officials like Ernst von Weizsaecker of the German Foreign Office were convicted. In addition a number of trials in Dachau dealt exclusively with "conventional" war crimes—the most famous among them that of the "Malmedy massacre" of American prisoners by SS troops. The Soviet Union independently conducted war crimes trials against figures such as General Vlasov, who had collaborated with the Germans.

Meanwhile, in Tokyo, the International Military Tribunal Far East lasted from 29 April 1946 till 12 November 1948. Twenty-eight Japanese political and military leaders were convicted, among them four prime ministers. All were found guilty of waging aggressive war in Asia and the Pacific. Seven, including General Tojo, were sentenced to death. In the Western public mind Tokyo has always been overshadowed by Nuremberg even though the Japanese matched the Germans when it came to conventional war crimes. Of the 132,000 British and American POWs taken by the Japanese army, 27 percent died in captivity in contrast to 4 percent taken by the Germans (whereas a staggering three to four million Soviet POWs starved to death in German camps). In addition to the Tokyo trial there were trials in Australia, China, and other locations. General Yamashita's trial held in the Philippines was one of the most controversial of these.

The international military courts had determined "for the first time in history," said President Truman, "the legal culpability of war-makers." The United States alone held about nine hundred war crimes trials in all, in both military and civilian courts. More than three thousand defendants were involved. Yet not all war criminals were apprehended during Truman's presidency. Later cases put on trial involved Klaus Barbie ("the butcher of Lyon") in France and John Demjanjuk ("Ivan the Terrible") in Israel.

On the other hand, in ironic contrast to the trials, it appears that in the emerging cold war the U.S. intelligence services were actively recruiting SS men at the end of hostilities in Europe. And Operation Paperclip brought Nazi scientists to the United States. The fledgling CIA considered Nazi spies—with their superior knowledge of the Soviet Union acquired during the war—useful assets in the fight against communism.

The literature on the war crimes trials is immense. Much was added in the course of the Vietnam War, when many American intellectuals approached the Nuremberg International Military Tribunal very critically for obvious reasons. The best place to start is Norman E. Tutorow's excellent *War Crimes, War Criminals, and War Crimes Trials: An Annotated Bibliography and Source Book* (Westport, Conn.: Greenwood Press, 1986). Here one finds references to the massive documentary collections of proceedings published by the governments involved. For solid studies, see Bradley F. Smith, *The Road to Nuremberg* (New York: Basic Books, 1981) and *Reaching Judgment at Nuremberg* (New York: Basic Books, 1977). Philip R. Piccigallo provides a comprehensive overview of the Far Eastern tribunals in *The Japanese on Trial: Allied War Crimes Operations in the East, 1945–1951* (Austin: University of Texas Press, 1979). The best study of the controversial Malmedy trial is James J. Weingartner, *Crossroads of Death: The Story of the Malmedy Massacre and Trial* (Berkeley: University of California Press, 1979). For a mildly critical approach, see Viscount Maugham, *U.N.O. and War Crimes* (Westport, Conn.: Greenwood Press, 1975). On the postwar U.S. collaboration with Nazis, see Christopher Simpson, *Blowback: America's Recruitment of Nazis and Its Effects on the Cold War* (New York: Weidenfeld & Nicolson, 1988).

GUENTER BISCHOF

See also Jackson, Robert H.

West Germany

See Germany

Wheeler, Burton Kendall

(27 February 1882–6 January 1975)

Democratic U.S. senator from Montana, 1923–47. Born in Hudson, Massachusetts, Burton K. Wheeler received his law degree from the University of Michigan in 1905 and began his practice in Butte, Montana. He served in the Montana legislature from 1911 to 1913 and then as U.S. attorney for Montana from 1913 to 1918, when his concern for civil liberties during wartime hysteria forced him from office. Decisively defeated in the gubernatorial campaign of 1920, he rebounded in 1922 to win election to the U.S. Senate where he became one of the powerful regional barons between the two world wars—a man known for his courage, independence, and concern for farmers and workers. In his first year in the Senate, he rocketed to national prominence as a result of his investigation of the Department of Justice (which led to the resignations of Attorney General Harry M. Daugherty and of William J. Burns, head of the Bureau of Investigation) and of his vice-presidential candidacy on the Progressive party ticket in 1924. He was also a favorite-son candidate for the Democratic presidential nomination in 1940.

The first prominent Democrat to endorse Franklin D. Roosevelt for the Democratic presidential nomination in 1932, Wheeler supported most New Deal legislation despite concern about presidential power. In 1937, such concern prompted him to lead the fight against FDR's Court-packing plan, which Wheeler helped defeat with a letter he solicited from Chief Justice Charles Evans Hughes. Wheeler was also the most powerful senatorial opponent of FDR's foreign policy in 1940 and 1941. To enact peacetime conscription, said Wheeler in August 1940, would "slit the throat of the last democracy," and to enact Lend-Lease, he said in January 1941, would create "the New Deal's triple-A foreign policy; it will plow under every fourth American boy."

Although Wheeler was happiest in opposition and in verbal combat, he was not simply an obstructionist, especially after he became chair of the Senate Interstate Commerce Committee (ICC). In that capacity in 1935, he cordially welcomed freshman Missouri senator Harry S. Truman to the committee. The two were opposites in many ways. Unobtrusive, studious, and seemingly very ordinary, Truman contrasted sharply with the rangy, charismatic, sharp-tongued Wheeler. But they became friends, and Truman remained grateful for the encouragement and opportunities that Wheeler provided.

In particular, Truman became Wheeler's chief lieutenant during the committee's hearings and in sponsoring transportation legislation between 1935 and 1940. When Wheeler appointed a subcommittee in 1935 to investigate railroad financing and determine legislation, Truman was not a member but asked Wheeler if he could attend the hearings. Impressed with Truman's interest, Wheeler appointed him to the subcommittee when a vacancy occurred and then ultimately to vice-chairman. In that capacity, Truman presided during Wheeler's absences, a time-consuming task with few headlines but one that won the respect of his colleagues. When the Senate passed the Civil Aeronautics Act of 1938 and the Transportation Act of 1940, Truman could take satisfaction and, with Wheeler, a good deal of the credit. Wheeler and Truman were also concerned about railway labor. In 1938, for example, when the railroads sought to reduce wages because of the recession, the testimony of both was critical in persuading a presidential emergency board to reject the plea.

Truman's diligence on the ICC probably saved his political career. In grave difficulty in the Democratic primary in 1940, he received endorsements from Wheeler and other senators and indispensable assistance from organized labor, especially the railway brotherhoods who blanketed Missouri with half a million copies of *Labor*, their official publication, endorsing his candidacy. Truman's work on the ICC also undoubtedly played a part in winning senatorial support for his resolution in February 1941 calling for a committee to investigate defense expenditures.

As chair of the Senate Select Committee to Investigate the National Defense Program, Truman's star ascended during the war as Wheeler's declined. Increasingly out of touch with his Montana constituents, especially Roosevelt Democrats, Wheeler found himself in difficulty in the Democratic primary of 1946, much as Truman had in his primary of 1940. Not one to forget a friend and past favors, Truman essentially endorsed Wheeler when he denounced the "smear campaign" that was labeling the Montanan "an enemy of railway labor," which invited newspaper comment about the president's intervention in a party primary.

Following his defeat in the primary, Wheeler opened a law office in Washington, D.C., from which he offered written advice to the president on myriad matters, including appointments, funds for Montana projects, tidelands oil, and overseas communications. An occasional rumor also had Wheeler in line for a significant appointment, which never materialized. Poles apart on foreign policy, they remained friends. As Truman privately wrote in 1951, their views were "almost opposite," but "sixteen years ago" Wheeler was "one of the few Senators . . . who was in any way decent to the Junior Senator from Missouri and I can't forget that. . . . I shall continue to like him as long as I live."

For Wheeler's career to 1940, see Richard T. Ruetten, "Burton K. Wheeler of Montana: A Progressive between the Wars" (Ph.D. diss., University of Oregon, 1961.) For informative recollections, see Burton K. Wheeler with Paul F. Healy, *Yankee from the West* (Garden City, N.Y.: Doubleday, 1962), and Harry S. Truman, *Memoirs* (Garden City, N.Y.: Doubleday, 1955). The few Wheeler papers that survive are located in the Montana Historical Society.

RICHARD T. RUETTEN

See also Senators

White House

Harry S. Truman, though he served nearly two full terms, lived in the White House for only about half of his presidency. Yet he literally and figuratively left a greater mark on it than most of his fellow presidents, if for no other reason that during his term the building was given the most significant restoration-reconstruction treatment in its nearly two hundred years. The result was a blend of history and modernity that made the old house eminently serviceable for his successors in the last half of the twentieth century.

Harry Truman's entry to the White House as president came on one of the grimmest days in America's history, 12 April 1945. Around 5:00 P.M. that afternoon, he was summoned to the White House, where he learned from Mrs. Roosevelt that he had become president. Truman's subdued swearing-in ceremony in the Cabinet Room later that evening launched his tempestuous and eventful presidential service.

By Truman's time, the accumulated effects of a century and a half of additions, renovations, and ill-considered repairs had left the White House in deplorable, even dangerous, structural condition. The very floors were beginning to give way. Truman's sense of history, honed from extensive reading that began when he was a nearsighted lad, contributed to his perspective on the challenge of renovating the home of the nation's chief executive. He rejected radical solutions, preferring to rebuild the White House from within rather than demolish it.

By Thanksgiving 1948, the Trumans were ensconced in Blair House, the presidential guest house. They did not return until March 1952. Tour guide Truman gave the first televised tour of the White House with Walter Cronkite not long after moving back in. The White House had been rebuilt within its historic walls. The three above-ground levels had been removed with exquisite care and two new levels inserted beneath the original basement. A new steel and concrete superstructure reinforced the whole building. The historic portion of the residence was then replaced over the added below-grade facilities. Deemed less successful were Truman's efforts to enlarge the West Wing for offices and the balcony he insisted on placing over the south portico. To many of his numerous critics, those changes seemed to echo in insensitivity the bumbling flaws perceived in his administration.

When Truman went out of office on 20 January 1953 and returned to Independence, he left behind a revamped, enlarged, and modernized—yet still historic—White House that has served its later occupants so well that no major changes have even been proposed for it since his tenure.

Interesting accounts of the reconstruction can be found in Amy LaFollette Jensen, *The White House and Its Thirty-three Families* (New York: McGraw-Hill, 1965), and William Seale, *The President's House: A History* (Washington, D.C.: White House Historical Association, with the cooperation of the National Geographical Society, 1986), 2:1003–57.

JAMES H. CHARLETON

Williamsburg, USS

Built in 1930 as a luxury yacht, then used in World War II as a gunboat, the USS *Williamsburg* became a presidential yacht in November 1945. President Truman rarely used the modestly appointed ship for extended travel, but rather for celebrating holidays and for weekend cruises with friends, staff, and government officials. As he did at the Little White House in Key West, Truman mixed business and pleasure aboard the *Williamsburg*.

Modern communications equipment installed on the yacht kept him informed of daily events. In December 1945, he used this equipment to summon Secretary of State Jimmy Byrnes to what would become one of the most publicized and controversial incidents to take place on the boat. Truman claimed he scolded Byrnes for keeping to himself the progress of negotiations with the Russians (Byrnes later denied the confrontation took place). When not conducting business aboard the *Williamsburg*, Truman relaxed, often with a "slight libation" and an all-night poker game.

The yacht remained in presidential service until July 1953, when President Dwight D. Eisenhower decommissioned what he labeled "a symbol of needless luxury."

For more information, see Lenore Bradley, "The Rise and Fall of the USS *Williamsburg*," *Whistlestop* 16, no. 1 (1988); Harry S. Truman, *Memoirs*, 2 vols. (Garden City, N.Y.: Doubleday, 1955, 1956; and Robert J. Donovan, *Conflict and Crisis: The Presidency of Harry S Truman, 1945–1948* (New York: W. W. Norton, 1977).

LAWRENCE A. YATES

Women

When Harry S. Truman ascended to the presidency in April 1945, American women were entering the final phase of what had constituted a major break from their traditional roles. World War II had disrupted families, withdrawn 16 million men from civilian life, promoted massive internal migration, and launched an unprecedented demand for workers. All these changes dramatically altered women's lives and offered novel opportunities for them in various aspects of public life.

Global warfare produced needs so great that the defense establishment for the first time welcomed women as regular members of the military. The 350,000 female volunteers served in nearly every capacity short of combat, although the majority were engaged in the traditional female areas of office work, communications, and health care. When Truman signed the Armed Services Integration Act of 1948, he affirmed women's continuing presence in the military even in peacetime, although they were restricted to 2 percent of the total strength of the armed forces and advancement was limited.

By far the greatest wartime change was in women's labor force participation. Demands made upon the economy for military and civilian goods created plentiful employment opportunities for women. Between 1940 and 1945, the female labor force grew by more than 50 percent; the more than 18 million women employed represented 37 percent of all women, and they constituted 36 percent of the civilian labor force. The war enabled women to obtain jobs customarily monopolized by men, increased their earnings, lessened discrimination, especially against married and older women, and increased their union membership from 800,000 to more than 3 million.

When Truman took the oath of office, public discussion about women's place in the postwar world had already begun. Underlying that discourse was a pervasive anxiety that the end of defense production and the return of millions of soldiers to

Vice-chairman of the Democratic National Committee India Edwards reaches for another political first for American women—her party's nomination for vice president of the United States. 18 July 1952. (Associated Press/Wide World Photos)

G.I. bill sharply reduced women's presence in the labor force. Women remained at work in larger numbers than in the prewar era, but their share of all jobs fell to 28 percent in 1947. Those who stayed in the labor force were typically forced out of higher-paying jobs and back into industries that had customarily welcomed women.

Truman lent official endorsement to the popular notion that marriage constituted women's primary role and that wives should not take jobs unless absolutely necessary. In 1948, he addressed a conference sponsored by the Women's Bureau to mark the hundredth anniversary of the first American women's rights convention at Seneca Falls, New York. Organizers had entitled the conference, "The American Woman, Her Changing Role: Worker, Homemaker, Citizen," but in his remarks Truman insisted on reversing the order, placing "homemaker" first.

Throughout his presidency Truman confronted demands from women's organizations which had become more assertive on behalf of women's interests during the war. As the war ended, a number of these organizations sought to preserve women's wartime economic gains, but their conferences and data gathering did little to stem the displacement of women. In the postwar years, they focused their efforts in three areas: federal action to improve women's legal status, a national equal pay law, and appointment of women to government positions. Only in the third area did they achieve even marginal success.

In seeking to push their concerns on to the public policy agenda, women faced an uphill struggle. After the uncertainties and dislocations of fifteen years of depression and war, many Americans sought security and comfort in traditional sex roles and family life. These yearnings were reinforced by journalists, mental health specialists, educators, and other experts who upheld marriage and motherhood as women's only meaningful role and who explicitly criticized feminists.

Nor did Truman offer significant encouragement to women seeking larger and more diverse experiences. Reform-minded women had enjoyed a prominent place in his predecessor's political career, and Eleanor Roosevelt had consistently championed a more active role for women in politics and a number of issues of particular concern to women. In contrast, women's presence had been negligible in Truman's political background, and his wife exhibited little public interest in politics or women. Without an advocate in the White House, women's political clout was also attenuated by conflicts among women themselves.

Nowhere was this conflict more apparent than over the issue of an Equal Rights Amendment to the Constitution. Championed by the National Woman's party (NWP) since 1923, the proposed ERA was vigorously opposed by most women's organizations because they feared that it would wipe out special protections that women enjoyed under the law. In response to pressure from Emma Guffey Miller, NWP leader and Democratic national committeewoman, Truman had publicly endorsed an ERA in 1944, and later that year it received approval in the Democratic platform for the first time. His serious consideration of the measure, however, is doubtful. When Miller and other NWP women visited the White House in 1945 to urge his reaffirmation of the ERA, Truman scrawled in his appointment book, "a lot of hooey about equal rights."

Truman never again endorsed the amendment, but he also resisted pressures from its opponents, which included the Women's Bureau and most of the liberal and labor constituency of the Democratic party, to attack it publicly. Rather, he let his

the civilian economy would plunge the nation back into the hard times of the 1930s. Representatives of business, labor, and the government proposed diverse means to ensure full employment, but they all assumed that a partial solution was the retirement of millions of women to domesticity.

In response to public pressure for demobilization and abandonment of the government's wartime controls over the economy, the Truman administration took a number of steps that weakened women's employment situation. It dismantled the National War Labor Board which had supported equal pay for women when that issue arose in labor-management disputes. Black women lost protection against job discrimination when the Fair Employment Practices Commission closed its doors. Victory also brought the demise of the War Manpower Commission and its Women's Advisory Committee which had promoted official attention to the problems of women workers. In 1946, the government discontinued federal funding for child-care facilities. Standing alone to safeguard women's economic status, the Women's Bureau suffered from postwar budget cuts. Although the intention of the Employment Act of 1946 was to promote full employment, it contained neither specific provisions to protect women from job discrimination nor adequate measures to ensure implementation.

The loss of governmental allies combined with the return of servicemen who enjoyed employment preference under the aides respond ambiguously to demands from both sides. The administration remained silent when the ERA reached the floor of Congress for the first time. In 1946, the Senate voted 38–35 in favor, but that majority fell short of the necessary two-thirds. Undoubtedly exasperated by the continuing demands from both sides, Truman wrote Miller in 1951, "It has been my experience that there is no equality—men are just slaves and I suppose they will always continue to be."

In part as a means of defeating the amendment, opponents of an ERA pushed a countermeasure, a women's status bill designed to eliminate "unfair" discrimination and to create a federal Commission on the Status of Women to study and report on women's status and the discriminations they faced. The Women's Bureau and the Department of Labor supported the bill, but Truman made no public comment, and it never reached the floor of Congress. The Truman administration ended with a deadlock on the question of women's legal status, but both the ERA and the commission idea would play large roles in the resurgent feminist movement two decades later.

Federal equal pay policy followed a similar course. A number of women's organizations and labor unions organized a lobbying effort in 1945 and got Truman to endorse the principle of equal pay. While Truman refused to support any particular bill, representatives of the Women's Bureau and the secretary of labor worked with allies in Congress, but the bill fell victim to business opposition, congressional indifference, and the withdrawal of support from the American Federation of Labor which felt that such a measure would encourage women to depend upon government rather than unions.

The third important postwar goal of politically active women in the postwar period was to increase the presence of women in policy-making positions. Owing largely to the efforts of Eleanor Roosevelt and Molly Dewson who headed the Women's Division of the Democratic National Committee, Franklin Roosevelt had appointed unprecedented numbers of women to government positions and federal judgeships. In 1944, Eleanor Roosevelt hosted a conference on women in policy-making, and a coalition of women's organizations formed to develop rosters of qualified women and present them to officials when vacancies arose.

Even more important than this external pressure in persuading Truman to appoint women to high-level posts were the efforts of women activists in the Democratic party. Although pressed by Gladys Tillett, chair of the Women's Division, Truman would not send a letter of support to a group working on behalf of women's appointments, and between 1945 and 1948, Truman named only three women to positions requiring Senate confirmation. His record improved, however, when India Edwards succeeded Tillett as head of the Women's Division.

In contrast to Tillett, whom Truman regarded as a Roosevelt loyalist, Edwards had gone out of her way to promote Truman in publicity materials for the 1944 campaign, and she worked assiduously for him in 1948. In fact, she later recalled that she was "practically the only person who thought he was going to be elected." When asked what she wanted in return for her campaign service, she responded, "Nothing for myself but a lot of jobs for a lot of women." Truman's confidence in and reliance on Edwards were such that some of his male colleagues chafed at her influence. Edwards was the only woman among Truman's trusted advisers; she recalled that he paid her "what

men have always considered the ultimate compliment to a female: that I operated like a man."

Edwards's position as representative of women's concerns to Truman meant that her priority, high-level appointments, claimed more of his support than women's policy interests. By the end of his presidency, he had appointed eighteen women to posts requiring Senate confirmation, one more than Roosevelt had named over his twelve-year presidency. Nine of these appointments were firsts for women. On occasion, Truman stood firm on his choices even when opposition arose. Thus, he insisted on Anna Rosenberg as assistant secretary of defense when opponents resisted because she was female, Jewish, and connected to leftists; and he stood behind Kathryn McHale for the Subversive Activities Control Board over the objections of the chairman of the Senate Judiciary Committee who had heard that McHale was a lesbian.

At the very highest levels, however, Truman resisted the appeals of Edwards and other women. He refused to name a woman to the Supreme Court on the grounds that the other justices did not want to work with a woman. After Frances Perkins resigned as secretary of labor early in his administration, Truman maintained his cabinet as an exclusively masculine domain. Women's most significant progress toward more equal participation in the public sphere during the Truman administration constituted a few more appointments to high-level positions. That spoke as much to the postwar climate which Betty Friedan later characterized as "the feminine mystique" and to the enervation of the women's movement during those years as it did to the social conservatism of the president.

Susan M. Hartmann, *The Home Front and Beyond: American Women in the 1940s* (Boston: Twayne, 1982) provides an overview of the status of women and public policies concerning women. For a detailed account of women's pressures on the Truman administration, especially regarding female appointments, see Cynthia E. Harrison, *On Account of Sex: The Politics of Women's Issues, 1945 to 1968* (Berkeley: University of California Press, 1988). Leila J. Rupp and Verta Taylor, *Survival in the Doldrums: The American Women's Rights Movement, 1945 to the 1960s* (New York: Oxford University Press, 1987), explores postwar women's rights activism, focusing on the National Woman's party. India Edwards, *Pulling No Punches: Memoirs of a Woman in Politics* (New York: G. P Putnam's Sons, 1977), is a first-person account by Truman's closest female political adviser.

SUSAN M. HARTMANN

See also Edwards, India; Roosevelt, Anna Eleanor

World War II

Truman generally shared Franklin D. Roosevelt's views with respect to the coming of World War II and supported his policies. He strove to use the wartime military buildup to further what he took to be the spirit of the New Deal, and he conducted the last five months of the war along lines that had largely been laid out before he assumed the presidency.

Proud of his role in having "whipped the Hun" in 1918,

Truman had no difficulty in identifying the danger that the rise of Hitler's Germany and of an aggressive Japan posed for the United States. Though he voted for the Neutrality Act of 1937 (and, according to his most recent biographer, then kicked himself a hundred times), he was, from his arrival in the Senate in 1935, a vigorous proponent of strengthening and modernizing the army, and of a navy and air force "second to none." When World War II broke out on 1 September 1939, he was among those who urged FDR to call a special session of Congress to revise the Neutrality Act so as to permit arms aid to Great Britain. "We are facing a bunch of thugs," he was soon writing, "and the only theory a thug understands is a gun and a bayonet."

Understandably, Truman had no use for the isolationists—for "Fish and his crowd," as he sometimes put it—and came as close as the president himself to regarding them as un-American and disloyal. Like Roosevelt, too, he believed that by 1940 only Britain remained as a bulwark of democracy and that if it were to go down to defeat, the United States could not survive in a totalitarian world. "Let us prepare," he urged.

By the summer of 1940, Truman worried that America's defense buildup was hampered by inadequate supervision of expenditures and the failure to award contracts to small manufacturers. In February 1941, he expressed his concern to Roosevelt and introduced a Senate resolution calling for an investigative committee. Although established with considerable reluctance and, initially, poorly funded; the committee, which Truman headed until August 1944, uncovered various forms of malfeasance, and claimed credit for saving the nation billions of dollars and even some lives.

It failed to stamp out favoritism in awarding contracts, however, or to safeguard the "economic democracy" its chairman cherished. But, as Truman's visible and valuable contribution to the war effort, it greatly enhanced his reputation as an energetic, incorruptible, but safe New Dealer, and thus made him acceptable for the vice-presidential nomination in 1944.

Heaviest of "the moon, the stars and all the planets" that fell on Truman when FDR died on 12 April 1945 was the burden of bringing World War II to a successful conclusion. Victory in Europe seemed likely within six months, but not in the Pacific. In July, the British and American Chiefs of Staff still set "the planning date for the end of organized resistance by Japan" at 15 November 1946.

It remained for Truman to settle the questions of whether American troops should occupy German territory beyond the Elbe or move on to Prague; whether to use the atomic bomb, of whose existence he learned only after assuming the presidency; and, of course, how the surrenders and the peacemaking were to proceed. Pressed by Winston Churchill on 18 April to occupy and hold as much territory in Central Europe as possible, Truman, true to what he believed to have been Roosevelt's policies, decided instead to abide by the occupation agreements reached in the European Advisory Commission in 1944. Tactical considerations were to continue to guide American troops in Europe, and withdrawal of forces to the designated lines was to follow as soon as militarily possible. Pilsen and Karlsbad were to be the goals in Czechoslovakia, not Prague. The prosecution of the war in Europe and the arrangements for Germany's unconditional surrender, which occurred on 8 May, were thus left in the hands of Gen. Dwight D. Eisenhower, to whom Truman, like Roosevelt before him, gave the fullest support.

As in the final decision of 24 July, to use the atomic bomb against specified targets in Japan, Truman acted pragmatically, giving winning the war with the least expenditure of lives and resources the highest priority. At the Potsdam Conference, some of the accommodations reached with the Soviet Union were clearly influenced by the necessity to continue the war in the Pacific rapidly and at lowest cost, and in the arrangements for Japan's formal surrender on 2 September, Truman was persuaded to leave the emperor in office, once more in the interest of saving lives.

Truman's activities as senator have received less attention than might be expected or that they deserve. They are most fully described in Richard Lawrence Miller's *Truman: The Rise to Power* (New York: McGraw-Hill, 1986). Informative for all of the World War II period, though not to be taken entirely at face value, is the first volume of Truman's *Memoirs, Year of Decisions* (Garden City, N.Y.: Doubleday, 1955).

MANFRED JONAS

See also Atomic and Hydrogen Bombs; Churchill, Winston S.; Commander in Chief; Demobilization; Displaced Persons; Fascism; Germany; Great Britain; Japan; Lend-Lease; Potsdam Conference; Roosevelt, Franklin D.; Soviet Union; Stalin, Joseph; Stimson, Henry L.; Truman Committee; Yugoslavia

Y-Z

Young, Solomon

(24 April 1815–26 January 1892)

The president's maternal grandfather. Solomon Young was the son of Jacob Young (1792–1836) and Rachel Goodnight (+ 1828), both natives of Mecklenburg County, North Carolina, who had early in life moved to Kentucky. Little is known of Solomon's childhood. He married Harriet Louise Gregg (1818–1909) on 9 January 1838. In either 1841 or 1842, the couple moved to Jackson County, Missouri. They had seven children, of which one was Martha Ellen ("Mattie") who married John Anderson Truman in 1881.

Young, whom his grandson Harry described as "a great, big man with a beard" and as "a gentle, very quiet reserved man," accumulated land and at one time owned as much as five thousand acres in southwestern Jackson County. He was evidently a man of both means and enterprise. He traded in feedstock, horses, and cattle. As the westward movement assumed major proportions he organized wagon trains, beginning in 1861, and led them to the West Coast. Although there is no record of the number of wagon trips he took, his wife in later years related that he was often gone for six months out of the year. He also invested in land in California and is reported at one time to have owned much of the land upon which the city of Sacramento now stands. He died in the Truman family home in Grandview.

Margaret Truman relates that her father told her that, in his childhood, he did not like either of his grandfathers very much but that, in his adulthood, his "respect and affection for them grew with every passing year."

There is no organized account of Solomon Young's life. Incidental information is contained in Robert Ferrell, ed., *The Autobiography of Harry S. Truman*, (Boulder: Colorado Associated University Press, 1980); in the president's own *Memoirs*, vol. 1 (Garden City, N.Y.: Doubleday, 1955); in Merle Miller, *Plain Speaking: An Oral Autobiography of Harry S. Truman* (New York: Putnam's, 1973); and in Richard Lawrence Miller, *Truman: The Rise to Power* (New

York: McGraw-Hill, 1986). A privately published volume of some usefulness is Elsie Spry Davis, *Descendants of Jacob Young of Shelby County, Kentucky* (Coronado, Calif.: the author, 1980), a copy of which is on file in the Harry S. Truman Library.

FRANCIS H. HELLER

Yugoslavia

Yugoslavia was the alpha and omega of Harry S. Truman's education in cold war diplomacy. When he took office in 1945, Truman thought of Tito and Yugoslavia simply as extensions of the Soviet Union. By the time he left office, Yugoslavia's break with Russia had disproven the myth of Soviet-dominated monolithic communism.

In the last days of World War II, the Allied command in Italy found itself facing a sharp confrontation with Tito's Communist government. Motivated by economic, ethnic, and strategic factors, the Yugoslavs were determined to absorb Trieste and the so-called Julian hinterland. New to the job and the situation, Truman listened to the State Department, which saw Tito's fervor as a Soviet ploy to expand into territory the Western Allies thought of as their domain. From Truman's vantage, stopping Tito would be synonymous with restraining Russia. An early American insistence that Allied forces retain the entire area soon mellowed into a compromise which ceded much of the hinterland but took a very firm stand on Trieste per se. Getting no support from Moscow, Tito withdrew from Trieste. Thus Truman's introduction to Yugoslavia (and one of his earliest foreign policy decisions) had many of the earmarks of later cold war and containment policies.

There followed three acrimonious years (1945–48) during which the United Nations Relief and Rehabilitation Administration, for which the United States provided the bulk of funds and materials, poured some $400 million of aid into Tito's devastated country while an almost fanatically Communist government did everything imaginable (from shooting down U.S. planes to confiscating American property and haranguing against U.S. policy in the United Nations) to alienate the United States. Truman was particularly displeased by its support for Greek leftists, the fight against whom prompted the 1947 Truman Doctrine.

Convinced, for good reason, that Yugoslavia was Russia's best and brightest postwar ally, Truman and the State Department read reports of a Tito-Stalin split in 1948 with skepticism. But by 1949 they had decided that Yugoslavia really was trying, with great difficulty, to survive as a Communist nation outside (in fact ostracized from) the East bloc. Severe droughts exacerbated economic dislocation caused by the forced severance of ties with the East bloc, and a military attack by Russia and its satellites seemed possible. The United States saw a number of advantages in helping Yugoslavia maintain its rather anomalous independence, including the neutralization of Tito's very large army. An independent, even nonaligned, Communist Yugoslavia was preferable to one wedded to the Soviet Union.

Having decided to help but to do so without, as a February 1949 National Security Council paper put it, making Tito's position any "more difficult by any action on our part," the Truman administration eased trade restrictions and facilitated two "routine" $20 million loans to Yugoslavia from the Export-Import Bank. By 1950 the United States had set in motion a military and economic assistance program which would continue throughout the 1950s. Although this assistance had remarkably few strings attached, a realistic Yugoslav government did stop supporting the Greek revolutionists and did ease up on those of its domestic reforms most repugnant to the West.

Because Yugoslavia remained Communist, this unique cold war success story was one with which the United States always felt a little uncomfortable.

There is not a great deal of material available on U.S.-Yugoslav relations. Although dated, the best full discussion of the early postwar years is John C. Campbell's *Tito's Separate Road: America and Yugoslavia in World Politics* (New York: Council on Foreign Relations, 1967). Truman's Trieste policy and his decision to support Yugoslavia after the Tito-Stalin split are covered, respectively, in Roberto Rabel, "Prologue to Containment: The Truman Administration's Response to the Trieste Crisis of May 1945," *Diplomatic History* 10 (Spring 1986): 141–60, and Lorraine M. Lees, "The American Decision to Assist Tito, 1948–1949," *Diplomatic History* 2 (Fall 1978): 407–22.

LINDA R. KILLEN

See also Cold War; Soviet Union

Zionism

Modern political Zionism is the national liberation movement of the Jewish people. The classical definition proposed by the philosopher and novelist Max Nordau at the First World Zionist Congress (1897) in Basle, Switzerland, states that it is a movement that "seeks to establish for the Jewish people a publicly

recognized, legally secured home in Palestine." There is little evidence that Truman was at the outset of his career a firm Zionist. He did support Zionist positions in the Senate, and in May 1944 he wrote the Zionist Organization of America that when the time came he was willing to help make the fight for a Jewish homeland in Palestine. Still, his major interest in Zionism did not begin until shortly after he assumed the presidency in 1945.

As the Second World War was ending, reports from Europe revealed that upwards of 100,000 Jewish refugees, victims of Nazi persecution and many of them former prisoners in the concentration camps, were still held under guard in Allied internment camps and were suffering under abominable conditions. The mood in the United States was that it had just fought a war against forces of hatred and evil, and these people, the victims of those forces, deserved American help. Public concern for the welfare of the refugees poured forth from many sources as the horrible facts of the death camps became public knowledge. Truman, reflecting the deep emotional and humanitarian commitment of many Americans, determined to take action on behalf of the refugees. He dispatched Pennsylvania Law School dean Earl Harrison, former U.S. commissioner of immigration, to Europe to survey the conditions in the detention centers and report to him.

Harrison reported that conditions were even more grim than had been thought. The overwhelming majority of the refugees were desperate to escape Europe, which was to them a massive charnel house, and they pleaded to be allowed to emigrate to Palestine, which was then under British administration. It was, Harrison urged Truman, the only decent or humane thing to do. Truman pressed the British to admit them as a humanitarian gesture, and at Prime Minister Clement Attlee's suggestion, the two men created the Anglo-American Committee of Inquiry to look into the problems of European Jewry and Palestine.

The committee, a jury of six Americans and six Britons, did not include politicians, Jews, or women, because it was thought that the first two would most likely have already committed themselves on the subject of Zionism and the presence of the last would offend Arab sensibilities. In 120 days the committee collected eyewitness evidence on the conditions and desires of the Jews and Arabs from the United States, London, Jerusalem, Cairo, Saudi Arabia, Lebanon, and the camps of Europe. It became clear that the Jewish community of Palestine was completely prepared for and in favor of taking the refugees in, but the Arabs were opposed.

The committee's lengthy report, published 1 May 1946, began with ten recommendations which the British had assured the committee's members would be carried out if they were unanimous. They all agreed that the 100,000 refugees should be admitted to Palestine promptly, but that there should be in Palestine neither a Jewish state nor an Arab-dominated one. Eight other recommendations concerned administration, control, and other matters. The British, in dread of possible Arab reactions, viewed the committee's report with grave reservations. But Truman, pleased that his concerns for the immediate admission and care of the refugees had been met, praised the recommendation to admit the refugees and left the other matters for further analysis.

Truman and Attlee then convened a second committee in London to arrange implementation of the recommendations, but that committee returned with a reworked British plan that ignored the original recommendations. Truman rejected it. That left Britain in an impossible situation, trying to administer a country with both Arabs and Jews opposed to British rule. In the following year, the problem went to the United Nations Special Committee on Palestine, which recommended partition and the creation of a Jewish state. When the state of Israel became independent on 14 May 1948, Truman overrode the stubborn opposition of his pro-British State Department advisers and insisted on recognizing the state de facto within half an hour of its establishment.

The triumph of the Zionist movement was partly due to the fact that many people confused Zionist-statists, whose goal was a Jewish state, and Zionist-refugeeists, whose goal was merely to help the refugees and who saw in immigration to Israel the likeliest way of doing so. Truman was a refugeeist, not a statist. His concern was to aid the victims of Hitler, not to establish a state, although, of course, if establishing a state was the most reasonable way to help the people, then he would support it. Thus, without quite meaning to, he became a hero of the Zionist movement.

After the establishment of the state of Israel, Truman, tired of incessant Jewish pressures, had little contact with Zionist matters until he left office. In later years he became more supportive of Israel and the United States' special relation with Israel, which further endeared him to American pro-Zionists, Jewish and gentile.

A great deal has been made of the influence on Truman of his former haberdashery partner, Eddie Jacobson, who was Jewish, and of Dr. Chaim Weizmann, renowned Zionist diplomat and later first president of Israel. It is unlikely that Truman was swayed much by either of them, nor was he dictated to in this matter by domestic or Democratic party politics or by the Jewish vote. It is most probable that he considered that he had been given the power to do something decent for helpless people who needed him and that his actions were motivated not by political considerations but by mainly humanitarian ones.

Zvi Ganin, *Truman, American Jewry, and Israel, 1945–1948* (New York: Holmes & Weier, 1979, is an excellent summary and a sound analysis. Peter Grose, *Israel in the Mind of America* (New York: Knopf, 1983), is outstanding both for the high quality of its writing and for its splendid syntheses of different approaches and sources. Frank E. Manuel, *Realities of American Palestine Relations* (Washington: Public Affairs Press, 1949), is a well-rounded early view of Truman's actions. Allen Howard Podet, *Success and Failure of the Anglo-American Committee of Inquiry, 1945–1946* (Lewiston, N.Y.: Edwin Mellen Press, 1987), examines in detail Truman's actions with regard to a key postwar Zionist problem. Howard Morley Sachar, *A History of Israel from the Rise of Zionism to Our Time* (New York: Alfred A. Knopf, 1976), is one of the most interesting, balanced, and helpful works available in this area. Joseph Schechtman, *The United States and the Jewish State Movement: The Crucial Decade, 1939–1949* (New York: Herzl, 1966), is a good general overview. Harry S. Truman, *Memoirs, vol. 1, Year of Decision*, and vol. 2, *Years of Trial and Hope* (Garden City, N.Y.: Doubleday, 1955, 1956), are revealing and forthright.

ALLEN HOWARD PODET

See also Displaced Persons; Israel; Jacobson, Eddie; Jewish-Americans; Palestine; Saudi Arabia

INDEX

Note: Page numbers in italics indicate the subject's major entry.

Abington v. *Schempp,* 61
Acheson, Dean, *1–2,* 44 (photograph), 50, 70, 82, 232
  and atomic policy, 345
  and Formosa issue, 132
  and France, 135
  and Germany, 140–41
  and Kennan, 197
  and Korea, 201, 202
  McCarthy attacks on, 2, 80, 162
  and NSC 68 memorandum, 83, 238–39
  and Truman Doctrine, 365, 366
  See also State, Department of
Act for International Development (1950), 279
ADA. *See* Americans for Democratic Action
Adamson v. *California,* 348
Adenauer, Konrad, 135
Adler v. *Board of Education,* 348
AFL. *See* American Federation of Labor
Africa, 2, *3–4*
Agencies, regulatory, *301–3*
Agricultural Adjustment Acts
  of 1938, *4–5*
  of 1948, 5, 272
  of 1949, 5
Agriculture, *4–5,* 8–9, 35–36, 76, 116
  and Fair Deal proposals, 123, 124
  and Hope, 161
  and Kline, 200
  and Patton, 272
  Truman's Senate record on, 254
Aiken, George, 5
Airlift, Berlin. *See* Berlin airlift
Air Policy Commission, 5
Air power, *5–6,* 34, 350. *See also* Military spending; U.S. Air Force
Albania, 102
Alexander, Sadie T., 59
Altmeyer, Arthur, 330
American Communication Association v. *Douds,* 38, 348, 381
American Communist party. *See* Communist party, American

American Farm Bureau Federation, 35, 200, 272
American Federation of Labor, 206, 251–52, 305, 353
American Friends Service Committee, 268
American Indians. *See* Indians, American
American Medical Association, 251
American Red Cross, 231
Americans for Democratic Action (ADA), *6–7*
  founders of, 33, 164, 309, 322
  as group for anti-Communist liberals, 127, 216, 248
  in 1948 election, 114, 115, 306
  at peak of strength, 92
Ancestry, Truman's, *7–8*
Anderson, Clinton, *8–9,* 35, 345
Anderson, Eugenie, 164
Anglo-American Committee of Inquiry, 95, 181, 269, 393
Anglo-Iranian Oil Company, nationalization of, 53, 179, 266
Anti-Communism, domestic, 67, *72–74,* 75, 298–301
  and Arendt, 9
  and China policy, 2
  and CIA, 46
  and CIO, 248
  and civil liberties, *55–57*
  and civil rights, 31
  and Hoover, 159–60
  and India, 171–72
  and liberals, 216–17
  and Republican party, 303–4
  and Wallace, 385
  See also Americans for Democratic Action; Red scare
Antitrust activity, 39
Arabs. *See* Palestine; Saudi Arabia
Arendt, Hannah, *9–10,* 127
Argentina, 210
Armed Forces, U.S.:
  and air power, 5–6
  and demobilization, 88–90, 271
  racial integration of, *10,* 31, 58, 60, 69, 268
  and Selective Service, 69, 87, 108, 242, 268, 324–25, 377

unification of, *11,* 69–70, 133–34
  See also Military spending; U.S. Air Force; U.S. Army; U.S. Marines; U.S. Navy
Armstrong, Hamilton Fish, 85
Army Corps of Engineers, *11–12,* 241, 297
Assassination attempt, on Truman, *13*
Atomic and hydrogen bombs, *13–16*
  and Britain, 144
  Churchill's view of, 53, 283
  and cold war tensions, 17, 34, 64–65, 66
  control, question of, 176, 323
  dropped on Japan, 68–69, 186–87, 268
  Stimson's recollections of, 342–46 passim
  See also Atomic Energy Commission; Nuclear energy
Atomic Energy Act (McMahon Act, 1946), 15, 16, 69, 97, 263
Atomic Energy Commission, 15, *16–17,* 69, 176, 218, 263, 323
Attlee, Clement, *17–18,* 64, 95, 144, 145, 393
Austin, Warren R., 370
Austria, *18,* 372
Aviation, commercial, *18–19,* 209
Awards, to Truman, *19–20,* 21 (table)
Azerbaijan, 65

Bailey, Josiah, 379
Bailey v. *Richardson,* 55
Baird, Ralph A., 343
Baker v. *Carr,* 61
Baldwin, Raymond, 163 (photograph)
Ball, Joseph, 164, 165
Ball, Robert, 330
Bao Dai, 173
Barkley, Alben W., *22–23,* 44 (photograph), 75
Barnes, Harry E., 180
Baruch, Bernard, *23–24*
Baruch Plan, 15, 23
Battery D, *24,* 45, 185, 236, 276, 277. *See also* Military career, Truman's
Beard, Charles A., 180
Bell, Daniel, 279
Bell, David, 246, 337
Bell Trade Act, 168, 278
Beneš, Edward, 86, 87
Ben-Gurion, David, *24,* 121 (photograph)

Bentley, Elizabeth, 73
Benton, Thomas Hart, 25–26
Beria, Lavrenti, 367
Berlin airlift, 6, 26–27, 53, 66, 70, 98, 140, 231
Bethune, Mary McLeod, 31
Bevin, Ernest, 17–18, 64, 144, 233
Bidault, George, 233
Binaggio, Charles, 86
Biographies of Truman, 28–30
Bisgyer, Maurice, 186
Black, Hugo, 55–56, 57, 136, 347–48
Black Americans, 30–33
    and civil rights, 47, 57–59, 59–60, 75, 91, 124, 331, 349, 381
    and Democratic party, 30, 31, 32, 90, 91, 119
    and Dixiecrats, 7, 32, 58, 91, 96, 115, 116, 118, 331, 356
    exodus of, from South, 90
    and FEPC, 125
    and Hastie, 150–51
    and housing, 164
    and integration of armed forces, 10, 31, 58, 60, 69, 268
    and NAACP, 250
Blockade, Berlin. See Berlin airlift
Blough, Roy, 85
Bob-Lo Excursion Co. v. Michigan, 349
Bogotá Conference (1948), 210–11, 231
Boke, Richard, 297
Bonesteel, Charles, 197
Bosporus Straits, 367
Bowles, Chester, 6, 33, 171, 328
Bowman, Isaiah, 85
Braden, Spruille, 210
Bradley, Omar, 33–35, 141, 191, 377
Brannan, Charles, 4, 9, 35–36, 44 (photograph), 91–92, 200
Brannan Plan, 4, 5, 9, 35–36, 272
Bretton Woods System, 36–37, 296
Bricker, John, 74, 113, 180
Bricker Amendment, 76
Britain. See Great Britain
Brooks, C. Wayland, 179
Brooks, Philip C., 149
Brophy, William A., 172
Brotherhood of Railroad Engineers, 294
Brotherhood of Railroad Trainmen, 293, 294
Brown v. Board of Education, 38, 59, 61, 240, 250, 349, 381
Brussels Pact, 66
Budget, Bureau of the, 37–38, 302
Bulgaria, 102, 143
Bulger, Miles, 184
Bunche, Ralph, 32
Burns, Arthur, 104
Burrus, Rufus, 40
Burton, Harold, 38, 56, 57, 347, 348 (photograph)
Bush, Vannevar, 252, 323, 343
Business-government relations, 38–39, 72
Business ventures, Truman's, 40–41, 129, 185, 193–94
Butterworth, Walton, 132
Byrnes, James, 41–42
    and atomic bomb, 13–15 passim, 343
    and cold war, 64, 65, 102, 143
    considered "soft" on Soviets, 201, 334

and 1944 vice-presidential nomination, 112, 154, 384

Cabinets, 43–45
    meetings of, 343
    See also entries for individual members
Canada, 259
Capper, Arthur, 179
Carey, James B., 7
Catholics, 45–46, 90–91, 119
Catholic Worker Movement, 268
Caudle, T. Lamar, 229
Central Committee for Conscientious Objectors, 268
Central Intelligence Agency, 11, 46, 67, 70, 122
Central Valley Project, 297
Chambers, Whittaker, 73, 154–56, 162, 300
Chapman, Oscar L., 46–47, 172
Chiang Kai-shek, 48, 49, 50, 66, 131–33, 229, 308
China, 2, 48–51, 66, 82, 308
    and Britain, 144–45
    and Formosa, 131–33
    and Korean War, 50–51, 71, 202, 203, 224, 229, 230
    and Lattimore, 211
    and Mao, 229–30
    and NSC 68 memorandum, 261–62
    and Potsdam Conference, 64
    and Taft's views, 80
    and United Nations, 172, 369, 371, 372
China Lobby, 80, 83, 132, 172, 211, 229
China White Paper, 49–50, 229
Chou En-lai, 49, 50 (photograph)
Churchill, Winston, 17, 18, 51–54, 65, 143, 144, 332 (photograph)
    and Iran, 179
    at Potsdam, 282–85
Church-state relations, and Supreme Court, 349
CIA. See Central Intelligence Agency
CIO. See Congress of Industrial Organizations
Citizens Committee on Displaced Persons, 95
Civil Aeronautics:
    Act, 387
    Administration, 18, 19
    Board, 19, 209, 225
Civil liberties, 54–57, 73–74, 347–49
    and Clark, 61
    and loyalty program, 220–21
Civil rights, 30–33, 57–59, 75
    and American Indians, 172
    and Asian-Americans, 188
    and Chapman, 47
    and Dixiecrats, 7, 32, 58, 91, 96, 115, 116, 118, 331, 356
    and Fair Deal, 124
    and integration of armed forces, 10, 31, 58, 60, 69, 268
    and Russell, 317
    Truman's later attitude on, 305
    Truman's Senate record on, 254
Civil Rights, President's Committee on, 10, 31, 58, 59–60, 91, 331
Clark, Bennett Champ, 60–61, 110
Clark, John D., 84, 104, 174
Clark, Mark, 46

Clark, Tom Campbell, 44 (photograph), 56, 57, 61–62, 220, 345, 347, 348 (photograph)
Clay, Lucius D., 26, 134, 140, 231
Clayton, Will L., 231, 232, 343
Clifford, Clark, 62–63, 174
    as drafter of speeches, 37, 337
    and 1946 report on Soviets, 81
    proposes strategy for 1948 campaign, 58, 63, 108, 114, 246
    and Truman Doctrine, 366
Cochran, John J., 110, 293
Coffelt, Leslie, 13
Cohen, Wilbur, 330
Cohn, Roy, 227
COINTELPRO program, 301
Cold war, 63–68, 127
    and Africa, 3
    and Berlin airlift, 6, 26–27, 53, 66, 70, 98, 140, 231
    and Churchill, 51–54
    and containment policy, 80–83
    and Eastern Europe, 102–3
    and France, 135
    and "get tough" policy, 63, 64, 102, 141–43, 148, 334, 384
    and Indochina, 168, 169
    and Italy, 182
    and Korea, 201–2
    and Latin America, 209–11
    and liberals, 215–17
    and United Nations, 176
    and Yugoslavia, 392–93
    See also Marshall Plan; Occupation issues, postwar; Soviet Union; Truman Doctrine
Collazo, Oscar, 13
Colonialism. See Imperialism
Columbia Valley Authority/Administration, 12, 47, 78, 79, 297
Commander in chief, Truman as, 68–72
Commission on Higher Education, 31
Commission on Organization of the Executive Branch of the Government (Hoover Commission), 12, 121, 159
Committee for Economic Development, 72
Committee on Equality of Treatment and Opportunity in the Armed Services, 58, 60
Committee on Government Contract Compliance, 125
Commodity Credit Corporation, 5
Communism and Communists, 72–74. See also Anti-Communism, domestic; China; Cold war; Communist party, American; Red scare; Soviet Union
Communist party, American, 72–74, 300, 301, and Smith Act, 73, 136, 299, 300, 327–28 and Supreme Court, 56–57. See also Dennis v. United States
Compton, Karl T., 343
Conant, James B., 323, 343
Condon, Edward U., 162
Conference on Economic Progress, 199
Congress, United States, 74–76
    and Army Corps of Engineers, 12
    and Bureau of the Budget, 37–38
    distribution of seats in, 1946–52, 118 (table)
    isolationists in, 179–80
    and military spending, 238

Congress, United States (continued)
  See also Democratic party; Eightieth Congress; Republican party; entries for individual members
Congress of Industrial Organizations (CIO), 90, 153–54, 205, 247, 248, 251–52, 299, 305, 322, 353
Congress of Racial Equality (CORE), 268
Connally, Thomas T., 65, 77, 366
Connelly, Matthew J., 77–78
Conscientious objectors, 268
Conscription. See Selective Service
Conservation, 47, 78–79. See also Reclamation
Conservatism, 79–80, 92
  and China, 49, 132
  and civil liberties, 55
  in Congress, 74–76, 303
  and Fair Deal, 124
  and Hoover, 160
  and isolationism, 179–80
  in South, 330–31
  See also Congress, United States; Democratic party; Red scare; Republican party
Containment, 3, 80–84, 85, 103, 176
  and Kennan, 196–97
  and Korea, 201–2, 336–37
  and Vandenberg, 374, 375
  Wallace criticizes, 385
  and World Bank, 37
  See also Cold war
Corcoran, Thomas, 128
CORE, 268
Coughlin, Father Charles, 91
Council of Economic Advisers, 72, 84–85, 104, 174, 199, 261, 302, 328
Council of Foreign Ministers, 64, 65
Council on Foreign Relations, 85
County court judge, Truman as, 121, 151, 170, 184–85, 274
Cramer v. United States, 55, 349
Crime, 85–86
  Kefauver committee on, 195
Crossley, Archibald, 290
Crump, E. H., 195
Culbertson, Jerry, 40
Czechoslovakia, 66, 86–87, 102, 238

Daniel, E. Clifton (son-in-law), 138, 363
Daniels, Jonathan, 88, 314 (photograph)
Dardanelles, 64, 65, 66
Davies, John Paton, 197, 225
Davies, Joseph E., 51–52, 142, 280, 324, 332
Davis, Elmer, 6
Davis, Manvel, 111
Dawson, Donald S., 298
Dawson, William L., 32
Day, Dorothy, 268
Dean, Gordon E., 17
Declaration on Liberated Europe (Yalta), 102, 103, 142
Defense, Department of, 11, 43, 122, 187, 189–90, 239, 262. See also Forrestal, James V.; Johnson, Louis; Lovett, Robert; Marshall, George
Defense Production Acts (1950, 1951), 208, 243
De Gaulle, Charles, 134

Demobilization, 88–90, 271
Democratic party, 74–76, 86, 90–92, 107
  and blacks, 30, 31, 32, 90, 91, 119
  in elections, 110–19
  and the South, 330–31
  See also Americans for Democratic Action; Congress, United States; Dixiecrats; Liberalism; Progressive party
Denham, Robert N., 252
Dennis, Eugene, 73–74
Dennis v. United States, 56–57, 61, 73–74, 99, 136, 183, 240, 300, 327, 348, 381
Desegregation. See Black Americans; Civil rights
Dewey, Thomas E., 92, 92–94, 100, 113, 114–16, 303
Dewson, Molly, 390
Dickman, Bernard, 111
Dies committee, 299
Dilworth, Richardson, 7
Dingell, John, 251
Disarmament Panel, 15, 16
Displaced persons, 18, 94–95, 372, 393–94. See also Israel; Palestine; Zionism
Dixiecrats, 7, 32, 58, 91, 96, 115, 116, 118, 331, 356
Donaldson, Jesse, 44 (photograph)
Douglas, Helen Gahagan, 96–98
Douglas, Lewis W., 98, 371 (photograph)
Douglas, Paul H., 98, 163 (photograph)
Douglas, William O., 7, 57, 99, 347–48
Downey, Sheridan, 297
Draft. See Selective Service
Dubinsky, David, 7, 100
Du Bois, W. E. B., 31
Dulles, John Foster, 83, 100–101, 201–2
Duncan v. Kahanamoku, 38, 349
Dutch East Indies, 168

Eastern Europe, 102–3, 142–43
  Czechoslovakia, 66, 86–87, 102, 238
  Poland, 63–64, 102, 142, 280–81, 283–84
  Yugoslavia, 102, 392–93
  See also Cold war; Germany; Potsdam Conference; Soviet Union
Eccles, Marriner, 103, 105, 328
Echo Park Dam, 47
Economic Cooperation Act/Administration, 156, 233, 234
Economic Stabilization, Office of, 33, 208, 243
Economy, the, 103–6, 174–75
  and business-government relations, 38–39
  and Committee for Economic Development, 72
  and Council of Economic Advisers, 72, 84–85, 104, 174, 199, 261, 302, 328
  and the Fair Deal, 123, 124
  and fiscal and monetary policies, 33, 123, 129–31, 328
  and labor, 206–8
  and regulatory agencies, 301–2
  See also Inflation; Military spending
Eden, Anthony, 52, 179
Education, aid to, proposed, 75
Education, Truman's, 106–7
Edwards, India, 107, 389 (photograph), 390

Eightieth Congress, 37–38, 74, 75, 91, 107–8, 114, 124, 207, 294, 300, 366
Einstein, Albert, 268
Eisenhower, Dwight D., 108–9, 259 (photograph), 260
  and DPs, 95
  and Dulles, 101
  goes to Korea, 35
  heads NATO, 85
  on Joint Chiefs of Staff, 191
  offered Democratic nomination, 7, 92, 114–15, 313
  relationship with Truman, 108–9, 305
  silence on McCarthyism, 108–9, 117, 227, 232
  wins 1952 election, 117, 118
Elections, 110–19
  of 1934, 110–11, 267, 293
  of 1940, 111, 147, 267, 293, 311, 339, 340, 387
  of 1942, 118
  of 1944, 112–13, 118, 267; and contest for vice-presidential nomination, 41, 121, 147, 196, 198, 258, 311–12, 379, 382, 384; Dewey's campaign, 93; labor in, 205, 206, 293; Truman's campaign, 27
  of 1946, 74, 91, 113–14, 118 and table, 120, 124, 207, 216, 304, 354. See also Eightieth Congress
  of 1948, 74, 76, 91–92, 108, 114–16, 118 and table, 124, 125, 127, 216, 267, 304; Barkley on ticket, 22–23; Brannan in, 35, 91–92; Chapman in, 47; Churchill's reaction to, 53; civil rights issue, 7, 10, 32, 58, 116; Clifford's strategy for, 58, 63, 108, 114, 246; Dewey in, 93; and Dixiecrats, 7, 32, 58, 91, 96, 115, 116, 118, 331, 356; and Dulles, 100; Edwards in, 107, 390; Humphrey at convention, 164–65; Ickes in, 166–67; and Israel issue, 180–81; Jewish vote in, 189; and labor, 207, 294, 306, 354; Murphy's strategy for, 246; and polls, 290; Progressive party in, 7, 83, 91, 118, 127, 216, 289–90, 385; radio and TV, use of, 293; reclamation issue in, 296; whistle-stop campaigning, 28, 92, 115, 120, 246, 295, 337
  of 1950, 76, 116, 118 and table, 300, 304
  of 1952, 35, 54, 59, 86, 94, 108, 117, 118 and table, 195, 304, 342
Elsey, George M., 120, 279, 337
Emergency Committee (atomic scientists), 268
Emergency Detention Act, 55, 56
Employment Act of 1946, 84, 104, 105, 120, 199, 216, 272
England. See Great Britain
Equal Rights Amendment, 389–90
European Advisory Commission, 18
European Coal and Steel Community, 234
European Defense Community, 135, 141, 176, 260
European Payments Union, 234
European Recovery Plan. See Marshall Plan
Evans, Thomas L., 120–21
Everson v. Board of Education of the Township of Ewing, 57, 349

Ewing, Oscar, 63, 246
Executive branch, reorganization of, *121–22*
Export-Import Bank, 210, 334, 393

Fahy, Charles H., 10
Fair Deal, 75, 76, 92, *123–25,* 163–64, 199, 216, 217
Fair Employment Board, Civil Service Commission, 58, 60
Fair Employment Practices Committee, 30, 57, *58–59,* 123, 124, *125,* 330
Famine Emergency Committee, 158–59
Farmer, James, 268
Farmer, Truman as, *125–26,* 267
Farming. *See* Agriculture
Fascism, *126–27*
Federal Bureau of Investigation (FBI), *128–29,* 159–61, 228, 299, 300, 301
Federal Housing Administration (FHA), 163, 164, 346, 347
Federal Loyalty and Security Program. *See* Loyalty Program
Federal Power Commission, 302
Federal Republic of Germany. *See* West Germany
Federal Reserve, 105, 131, 328
Federal Trade Commission, 302
Fellowship of Reconciliation, 268
Ferguson, Homer, 163 (photograph)
Finances, Truman's, 40–41, *129*
Finletter Report (on air power), *5–6*
Fiscal and monetary policies, 33, 103–6, 123, *129–31,* 328. *See also* Economy, the
Flick, Friedrich, 386
Flynn, Ed, 112
Flynn, John T., 180
Formosa, 49, 50, 51, 80, 82, *131–33,* 229, 230. *See also* China
Forrestal, James V., 11, 26, 46, 69, *133–34,* 143, 232, 238, 253, 345
Fortas, Abe, 345
"Fortress America" concept, 83
France, 66, *134–36,* 234
   and Indochina, 82, 168, 173–74
   and NATO, 259, 260
   and postwar occupation issues, 65
   and United Nations, 369
Franco, Francisco, 334
Frankfurter, Felix, 57, 136, 347, 348
Freeman, Orville, 164
Fuchs, Klaus, 15, 64–65, 313
Fulbright, William, 321
Full Employment and Balanced Growth Act (1978), 199
Fulton, Hugh A., *136–37,* 364

Galbraith, John Kenneth, 6
Gallup, George, 290
Garner, John Nance, 90, 110, 326
Gates, Marvin, 193
Gates-Wallace-Truman House, *138–39*
Genealogy, Truman's, *7–8*
General Agreement on Tariffs and Trade, 178, 296
George, Walter F., *139*
Germany, 26–27, 68, 102, *139–41*
   and cold war tensions, 64, 65, 66, 70
   and fascism, 126–27

relations with France, 134–36 passim
   and war crimes trials, 386
   See also West Germany
"Get tough" policy, 63–64, 102, *141–43,* 148, 334, 384
G.I. bill, 377, 389
Giboney v. *Empire Storage and Ice Co.,* 55
Goering, Hermann, 386
Gold, Harry, 313
Goldsborough, T. Alan, 214
Good neighbor policy, 209, 210
Gottwald, Klement, 86, 87
Gouzenko, Igor, 64–65, 313
Government-business relations, 38–39, 72
Grady, Henry F., 171
Graham, Wallace H., 321
Granger, Lester, 10
Granoff, A. J., 186
Great Britain, *143–45*
   and Attlee, 17–18
   and Churchill, 51–54
   and DPs, 95, 393–94
   and imperialism, 167, 168
   and Indochina, 173
   and Iran, 178–79, 266
   and Lend-Lease, 64
   and Marshall Plan, 233, 234
   and NATO, 259, 260
   and Potsdam Conference, 282–85
   and United Nations, 369
   withdrawal of, from Greece, Turkey, 66, 145, 232, 365, 370
   and WW II Soviet demands, 338
Greece, 52, 66, 81, 107, 144, *145–46,* 231–32, 307, 365–66
   in NATO, 260
   and UNRRA aid, 372
Green, Thomas, 163 (photograph)
Green, William, 146
Greenglass, David, 65, 313
Groves, Leslie, 13, 14, 342

Hague, Frank, 112
Halvorsen, H. H., 40
Hannegan, Robert E., 22, 45, 111, 112, *147,* 345, 382, 384
Hardy, Benjamin, 279, 337
Harriman, W. Averell, 142, *148–49,* 201, 280
Harrison, Earl, 94–95, 181
Harrison, George L., 343
Harry S. Truman Library, 121, *149,* 171, 304
Hartley, Fred A., 351, 354
Hassett, William D., *150*
Hastie, William H., 32, *150–51*
Haupt v. *United States,* 55, 349
Health, Truman's, *151,* 305
Heart of Atlanta Motel, Inc. v. *United States,* 61
Henderson, Leon, 6
Henderson, Loy W., *152,* 171
Henderson v. *Southern Railway,* 31
Henderson v. *United States,* 38
Hennings, Thomas C., Jr., 152
Hennock, Frieda B., 293, 302
Hess, Rudolf, 386
Highway policy, *152–53*
Hillenkoetter, Roscoe H., 46
Hillman, Sidney, 112, *153–54,* 205

Hirabayashi v. *United States,* 61
Hiroshima, and atomic bomb, 14, 68
Hiss, Alger, 56, 73, *154–56,* 162, 300
Hiss-Chambers case, 128, *154–56,* 162, 300
Ho Chi Minh, 135, 168, 173
Hoffman, Paul G., *156*
Holland, 168
Holland, Louis E., *156–57*
"Hollywood Ten," 56, 245, 300
Hoover, Herbert, 83, 104, 121 (photograph), *157–59,* 180, 203
Hoover, J. Edgar, 73, 128–29, *159–61,* 162, 299
Hoover Commission, 12, 121, 159, 302
Hope, Clifford R., *161*
Hopkins, Harry, 64, *161,* 281, 333
Hornbeck, Stanley K., 168
House Committee on Un-American Activities, 55, 56, 73, 128, 162, 244–45, 300
House of Representatives. *See* Congress, United States
Housing, 75, 123–24, *163–64,* 346–47, 372–73, 377
Housing Act (1949), 163–64, 372–73
Housing and Home Finance Administration, 373
Hughes, Tom, 40
Humphrey, Hubert H., Jr., 7, *164–65*
Hungary, 102
Hunt, James V., 376
Hurley, Patrick, 229
Hydrogen bomb. *See* Atomic and hydrogen bombs

Ibn Sa'ud, Abdul Aziz, 319, 320
Ickes, Harold L., 47, *166–67,* 266, 273, 321
Imperialism, 3, *167–70*
Inauguration, Truman's, *170,* 337
   medal for, 286 (photograph)
Incomes:
   farm, 4, 35–36
   blacks, 32
Independence, Missouri, *170–71,* 276, 304
   Truman's home in, 138–39
India, 144, 168, *171–72,* 307
Indian Claims Commission Act (1946), 172
Indian Reorganization Act (1934), 172
Indians, American, 47, 172
Indochina, 2, 82, 135, 168, 169, *173–74,* 308
Indonesia, 168, 169, 307
Inflation, 103, 104–5, 123, 130–31, *174–75,* 207–8, 243, 341. *See also* Economy, the
Institute of Pacific Relations, 211, 212
Integration, racial. *See* Black Americans; Civil rights
Inter-American Treaty of Reciprocal Assistance, 210
Interim Committee (on atomic policy), 13, 14, 42, 68, 343. *See also* Atomic and hydrogen bombs
Interior, Department of. *See* Chapman, Oscar; Conservation; Ickes, Harold; Reclamation
Internal Revenue, Bureau of, 229, 321
Internal Security Act (McCarran Act, 1950), 56, 74, 75, 127, 225, 300, 378
International Brotherhood of Teamsters v. *Douds,* 55

Internationalism, *175–77*
  versus isolationism, 179–80, 374
  See also United Nations
International Ladies Garment Workers'
  Union, 100
International Monetary Fund, 36–37
International Trade Organization, 178
Interstate Commerce Commission, 357
Interstate Commerce committees (Congress),
  325, 357, 387
Interstate Highway System, 153
Iran, 53, 54, 65, 152, *178–79*, 266, 307
"Iron curtain," 51, 52, 65, 144
Isolationism, 79, 83, 176, *179–80*, 203,
  374
Israel, *180–82*, 307, *393–94*
  vis-à-vis Arabs, 169, 269–70, 320, 370
  and Ben-Gurion, 24
  doubts about creation of, 2, 9, 98, 144
  establishment supported, 63, 186, 256,
    309
  issue of, in United Nations, 370
  and Jewish-Americans, 189
  as refuge for DPs, 18, 94–95
Italy, 52, 64, 66, 127, *182*, 234, 372

Jackson, Robert H., 55, 57, *183*, 347, 348
  (photograph), 386
Jackson, Samuel, 379 (photograph)
Jackson County Court, Truman on, 121,
  151, 170, *184–85*, 274
Jacobson, Eddie, 40, 129, *185–86*, 189, 194,
  394
Japan, 64, 177, *186–88*, 223, 283
  and atomic bomb, 13–15, 68–69
  Stimson's views on, 343–44
  war crimes trials in, 386
Japanese-Americans, 55, *188*
Jenner, William, 74, 80, 180
Jewish-Americans, 119, 180–81, 185–86,
  188–89, 256
Johnson, Alvanley, 294
Johnson, Edwin C., 180
Johnson, Hiram, 179
Johnson, Louis A., 10, 44 (photograph), *189–
  90*, 202
Johnson, Lyndon B., 138, *190–91*, 305
Johnson, Modecai W., 31
Joint Anti-Fascist Refugee Committee v.
  McGrath, 136, 348
Joint Chiefs of Staff, 11, 70, 82, 122, *191–92*
  and Formosa issue, 132
  and Germany, 141
  Leahy as chairman, 213
  and MacArthur, 34–35
Joint Committee on Atomic Energy, 17
Joint Committee on the Economic Report,
  104
Jones, Jesse, 298, 384
Jones, Roger, 38
Joyce, Robert, 197
Judd, Walter, 303
Judge, Truman as. *See* Jackson County
  Court, Truman on
Justice, Department of, 55, 59, 61, 73, 74,
  86, 225, 229, 245
Juvenile delinquency, 85–86

Kansas City, Missouri, *193–94*
Kansas City Star, *194–95*
Kefauver, Estes, 86, 92, 117, *195–96*
Kelly, Edward J., 112, 196
Kennan, George F., *196–97*
  and Formosa issue, 132
  heads Policy Planning Staff, 231
  and Korea, 201
  and the "long telegram," 65, 66, 82
  and the "X" article, 80–81, 83, 85
Kennedy, John F., *197–98*
Kennedy, Joseph P., 80, 180, 197
Kenworthy, E. W., 10
Kerr, Robert, *198–99*
Kerr natural gas bill (1950), 378
Keynes, John Maynard, 104, 130
Keyserling, Leon, 63, 84–85, 104, 124, 174,
  199–200, 261
Key West, Florida, *200*
Kilgore, Harley M., 252, 323
Kim Il Sung, 202
King, Mackenzie, 64
Klemm, Karl D., 193
Kline, Allan B., *200*, 272
Knowland, William, 83, 303
Korean War, 67, 70–71, 82, 92, *200–204*,
  223–24
  and air power, 6
  and blacks, 32
  and Bradley, 34–35
  and China, 50–51, 71, 202, 203, 224, 229,
    230
  and Congress, 75–76
  conservatives' views on, 80
  domestic programs, impact on, 5, 11, 19,
    78, 153
  and draft, 324–25
  economy, impact on, 105, 131
  "Great Debate" about, 336–37
  and India, 172
  and military budget, 239, 262
  and military integration, 10
  mobilization for, 242–43
  NATO, impact on, 259–60
  1952 election, effect on, 117, 118
  pacifists' view of, 269
  and red scare, 300
  and United Nations, 67, 176, 370–71
Krishna Menon, V. K., 171
Krug, Julius, 44 (photograph), 47, 214, 241
Krupp, Alfred, 386
Ku Klux Klan, 57–58
Kuomintang. *See* China
Kuwait, 266

Labor, 120, *205–8*
  and blacks, 32
  effect of WW II on, 90
  and Fair Deal, 123–24
  Green, 146
  Hillman, 112, 153–54, 205
  Lewis, 55, 61, 62, 205, 214, 381
  Murray, 206, 247–48, 306, 322
  and NLRB, 251–52, 353, 354
  and railroad unions, 293–94
  and red scare, 299
  Reuther, 7, 206, 305–6
  Schwellenbach, 73, 206, 306, 322–23
  and steel strike, seizure of mills, 38, 56,
    61–62, 92, 183, 205, 206–7, 243
  Tobin, 45, 356
  Truman's Senate record on, 254
  and Truman vetoes, 378
  and women, 388–90
  See also Taft-Hartley Act; individual
    unions
La Follette, Robert M., Jr., 179, 226
Lamar, Missouri, *208*
Landis, James M., 19, *208–9*
Land Management, Bureau of, 78
Landon, Truman, 83
Langer, William, 179, 180
Latin America, 2, *209–11*, 266, 307
Lattimore, Owen, *211–12*, 228 (photograph),
  225, 227
Lawton, Fred, 37
Leahy, William D., 26, 142, 191, *212–13*, 332
Legislative Reference, Office of, 37
Legislative Reorganization Act (1946), 76
Lehman, Herbert, 100
LeMay, Curtis E., 6
Lend-Lease, 64, *213–14*
Levitt family, builders, 346–47
Lewis, John L., 55, 61, 62, 205, *214*, 381
Liberalism, *215–17*
  and ADA, 6–7, 33, 92, 114, 115
  and Chapman, 47
  and Democratic party, 32
  and Douglas, 96–97
  and Fair Deal, 123–24
  and New Deal, 243
  and 1948 election, 63
Lilienthal, David, 16, 17, *217–18*, 263, 323,
  355
Lindbergh, Charles A., 6
Lippmann, Walter, 81, *218–19*
Literary Digest poll, 290
Lloyd, David D., *219*, 337
Lodge, Henry Cabot, Jr., 179
Loeb, James, Jr., 7
London Conference, Council of Foreign
  Ministers (1945), 64
Lovett, Robert A., 26, *219–20*
Loyalty program, 56, 67, 73, 74, 155, 216,
  220–21, 299–300
Lucas, Scott W., 75, *221–22*

MacArthur, Douglas, 77, *223–25*
  and Formosa issue, 132
  as hero of Truman critics, 180
  in Japan, 69, 186, 187
  and Joint Chiefs, 34–35
  and Korean War, 51, 70–71, 202–3, 231
McCabe, Thomas B., 105
McCarran, Patrick A., 212, *225*, 300
McCarran Act (1950), 56, 74, 75, 127, 300
McCarran-Walter Immigration Act (1952),
  127, 301, 378
McCarthy, Joseph R., 74, *226–28*, 300
  attacks Lattimore, 211–12
  attacks State Dept., 2, 67, 80, 154–55
  as Catholic, 46
  Eisenhower's silence on, 108–9, 227, 232
  FBI leaks to, 128
  Hennings opposes, 152
  Truman opposes, 55

McCloy, John J., 135
McCollum v. Board of Education, 57, 349
McElroy, Henry F., 184, 274
McFarland, Ernest, 75
McGranery, James, 45
McGrath, J. Howard, 45, 228–29, 321
McHale, Kathryn, 390
McKellar, Kenneth, 195
McKim, Edwin, 128
McLaurin v. Oklahoma State Regents for Higher Education, 31, 59, 349, 381
McMahon, Brien, 16, 17
McMahon Act (Atomic Energy Act, 1946), 15, 16
Magnuson, Warren G., 252
Malik, Jacob, 371
Manhattan Project, 13–14. *See also* Atomic and hydrogen bombs
Mao Tse-tung, 49, 50–51, 229–30, 308
Mapp v. Ohio, 61
Maragon, John F., 376
Marin, Luis Muñoz, 47
Marshall, George C., Jr., 230–32, 371 (photograph)
    and armed forces unification, 11
    in cabinet, 43
    in China, 48, 229
    and "get tough" policy, 142
    and Iran, 178
    and McCarthy attacks on, 80, 109, 117, 227
    offers Marshall Plan, 66, 135
    as secretary of defense, 191, 224, 324
    as secretary of state, 197, 220, 365
Marshall Plan, 231, 232–34
    and containment policy, 75, 103, 175, 176
    Hoffman as head, 156
    and individual countries: Austria, 18; Britain, 144; Czechoslovakia, 86, 87; France, 135; Italy, 182
    opposed, 139, 159, 180, 268–69
    scope of aid given, 107, 135, 237, 307
    Stalin denounces, 66
    supporters of, 72, 77, 98, 108, 148, 190, 255, 295, 316, 375
    Taft's ambivalence about, 80
Martin, Joseph, 303
Martin, William M., 105
Masaryk, Jan, 66, 87, 238
Masonic Order, Truman in, 20, 193, 234–35, 240, 277
May, Allan Nunn, 64
Mayerberg, Samuel S., 274
Medina, Harold, 74, 327
Memorials, to Truman, 281
Metzger, Arthur, 40
Mexico, 266
Middle East, 169, 266. *See also* Iran; Israel; Palestine; Saudi Arabia
Military career, Truman's, 24, 45, 121, 134, 185, 193, 235–36, 276–77, 377
Military spending, 5–6, 190, 203, 237–39, and table, 242, 262
Miller, Emma Guffey, 389
Milligan, Jacob L. "Tuck," 110
Milligan, Maurice, 111, 247, 274, 340
Minton, Sherman, 56, 57, 239–40, 347, 348 (photograph)
Missouri, 240–41

Independence, 170–71, 138–39, 276, 304
Kansas City, 193–94
Lamar, 208
Outstate, 267
Missouri River, 241–42
Missouri Valley Authority, 12, 78, 241–42, 297, 379
Mobilization, 242–43. *See also* Korean War; Military spending
Molotov, Vyaschlev, 63–64, 102, 141, 142, 143, 280, 333
Monetary policies. *See* Fiscal and monetary policies
Monnet, Jean, 134, 135
Monnet Plan, 134
Morely, Felix, 180
Morgan, David, 40
Morgan v. Virginia, 38, 349
Morgenthau, Henry, 36, 105
Morgenthau Plan, 18
Morse, Wayne, 163 (photograph), 244
Mossadegh, Mohammad, 53, 54, 152, 179
Movies, movie industry, 244–45, 300
Mundt, Carl, 55
Murphy, Charles S., 63, 246, 327, 337, 341
Murphy, Frank, 247
Murray, James E., 78, 241, 251, 379
Murray, Philip, 206, 247–48, 306, 322
Murrow, Edward R., 181 (photograph)
Music, as Truman's interest, 54, 193, 249
Muste, A. J., 268
Mustering-out Pay Act (1944), 377
Mutual Defense Assistance Act (1949), 50
Mutual Defense Treaty (U.S.-Philippines, 1951), 279
Mutual Security Program (1951), 211, 234
Myer, Dillon S., 47, 172
Myers, Robert, 330

Nagasaki, and atomic bomb, 14, 68
National Association for the Advancement of Colored People, 30, 58, 59, 250
National Committee for Justice, 57
National Congress of American Indians, 172
National Council against Conscription, 268
National Emergency Committee against Violence, 58, 59
National Emergency Council, 30
National Farmers Union, 35, 272
National health insurance, 75, 124, 191, 251
Nationalists, Chinese. *See* China
National Labor-Management Conference (1945), 206
National Labor Relations Act (1947). *See* Taft-Hartley Act
National Labor Relations Board, 251–52, 353, 354
National Military Establishment, 11, 69, 134, 253
National party (South Africa), 3
National Petroleum Council, 266
National Science Foundation, 252, 323
National Security Act (1947), 11, 46, 63, 69, 82, 134, 191, 271
National Security Council, 6, 11, 43, 44, 49, 70, 121, 132, 252–53
National Security Resources Board, 341

National Urban League, 30
National War Labor Board (WW II), 389
National Woman's party, 389
Native Americans. *See* Indians, American
NATO. *See* North Atlantic Treaty Organization
Natural resources, development of, 12, 47, 75, 78–79
Navajo-Hopi Rehabilitation Act (1950), 172
Nazis:
    entrance into U.S., 56, 386
    war crimes trials of, 386
Negroes. *See* Black Americans
Nehru, Jawaharlal, 171, 172
Nelson, Donald M., 157, 364
Netherlands, 168
Neustadt, Richard E., 246, 253, 337
New Deal, 30, 63, 90–91, 118, 121, 215–16, 254–55
    and anti-Communism, 299
    and Communist party, 72–73
    relation to Fair Deal, 123, 124
    Republican responses to, 303
Newell-Weaver Plan, 297
Nichols, John R., 172
Niebuhr, Reinhold, 255
Niles, David K., 59, 95, 189, 256
Nitze, Paul, 83, 197, 238–39, 262
Nixon, Richard, 55, 56, 74, 83, 97, 117, 128, 155, 162, 256–57
Norris, George W., 258
North Atlantic Treaty Organization (NATO), 75, 258–60
    creation of, 66, 103
    Eisenhower heads, 85, 108
    and individual countries: France, 134, 136, 259, 260; Germany, 141; Great Britain, 144, 259, 260; Greece, 145; Turkey, 260, 368
    question of commander, 53
    Taft opposes, 80, 108
    vis-à-vis United Nations, 370
Nosak, Václav, 87
Nourse, Edwin G., 84, 85, 104, 174, 199, 246, 261
NSC. *See* National Security Council
NSC 68 memorandum, 6, 67, 83, 190, 197, 202, 238–39, 253, 261–62
Nuclear energy, 262–64. *See also* Atomic and hydrogen bombs; Atomic Energy Commission
Nuclear weapons. *See* Atomic and hydrogen bombs
Nuremberg trials. *See* War crimes trials

Occupation issues, postwar, 283, 391
    and Austria, 18
    and Japan, 186–88
    and Korea, 70
    and Soviets, 64, 65, 70, 98, 102–3, 140, 280–81, 307
O'Dwyer, William, 86
Oil policy, 78, 265–67
    and Ickes, 166
    and Iran, 53, 54, 178, 179
    and Saudi Arabia, 319–20
    and Truman vetoes, 378
Old Age Assistance, 329–30

Olds, Leland, 302
Oppenheimer, Robert, 13, 15, 16, 301
Ordeal by Slander (Lattimore), 211
Organization of American States, 210
Organized crime, 86
The Origins of Totalitarianism (Arendt), 9, 127
Outstate Missouri, 267. *See also* Missouri
Overton, John, 241

Pace, Frank, Jr., 37
Pacifism, 268–69
Pakistan, 171
Palestine, 95, 98, 144, 266, 269–70, 320, 370, 393–94. *See also* Israel
Palko v. *Connecticut*, 348
Palmer, Dwight R. G., 10
Panel of Consultants on Disarmament, 15, 16
Patterson, Robert P., 11, 232, 270–72
Patterson, Roscoe C., 110
Patton, James G., 35, 272
Pauley, Edwin W., Sr., 112, 166, 201, 266, 272–73, 321, 332
Peacemakers (pacifist network), 269
Pearson, Drew, 128
Pendergast, Thomas J., 273–75
    and Stark, 111, 293, 340
    Truman's association with, 27, 45, 60, 86, 110, 184, 194, 205–6, 247, 380
People's Republic of China. *See* China
Perkins, Frances, 275, 340
Perón, Juan D., 210
Personality, Truman's, 275–77
    various aspects of: 27, 28, 41, 77, 106, 109, 111, 126, 184, 285, 287, 289, 303, 315, 325
Petroleum. *See* Oil policy
Petroleum Administration for Defense, 266
Philippine Islands, 168, 247, 278–79, 307
Pick, Lewis, 241
Pick-Sloan Plan, 78, 241–42, 297
Pine, David A., 243
Pleven Plan, 135, 141
Point Four program, 211, 279–80, 308, 337
Poland, 63–64, 102, 142, 280–81, 283–84
Policy Planning Staff (State Dept.), 197, 231, 233, 238
Polling, public opinion, 28, 287, 290–91
Portraits, of Truman, 25, 281
Postwar occupation. *See* Occupation issues, postwar
Potsdam Conference, 13, 14, 17, 42, 281, 282–85, 333, 339
    Churchill at, 52
    and postwar occupation issues, 18, 64
    and Soviet's entering war on Japan, 64
    Stimson at, 343–45
    Truman's address on, 335
Powell, Adam Clayton, Jr., 32
Presidency, Truman's, 285–87
    cabinet's role in, 43–44
President's Committee on Equality of Treatment and Opportunity in the Armed Forces, 10
President's Committee on Civil Rights, 10, 31, 58, 59–60, 91, 331
Press, the, 287–89
    Kansas City Star, 194–95

Lippmann, 218–19
St. Louis Post-Dispatch, 111, 318–19
Truman's secretaries for, 62, 106, 314–16, 318, 327
Pressman, Lee, 248
Price Administration, Office of, 33, 39, 265
Prices, 33, 104–5
    agricultural, 4–5, 9, 35–36, 76
    control of, 39, 265
    See also Inflation
Prichard, Edward, 128
Progressive Citizens of America, 7, 90, 114, 115, 216, 247
Progressive Era reformers, 215, 217
Progressive party (1948), 7, 83, 91, 118, 127, 216, 289–90, 385
Protectionism. *See* Trade, international
Public reputation. *See* Reputation, public
Public Service Responsibilities of Broadcast Licensees ("blue book"), 293
Puerto Rico, 13, 47
Pulitzer, Joseph, 318

Queuille, Henri, 135
Quirino, Elpidio, 278–79

Racial issues. *See* Black Americans; Civil rights
Radar, 323
Radio, television, 245, 292–93, 300
Railroad unions, strike, 62, 206–7, 293–94, 340–41, 378, 387
Randolph, A. Philip, 10, 30, 31, 268
Rankin, John E., 162
Rayburn, Sam, 75, 294–95
Reading, Truman's, 106, 295–96
Reagan, Ronald, 56, 61
Recession (1949–50), 105, 131
Reciprocal Trade Agreements, 296–97
    and Bretton Woods, 36–37
Reclamation, 297–98
    Bureau of, 12, 47, 241
    See also Conservation
Reconstruction Finance Corporation, 298, 321
Reconversion, of war to peace economy, 103–5, 120, 123–24, 130, 206, 215, 294, 340, 353–54
Red Channels: The Report of Communist Influence in Radio and Television (1950), 293
Red scare, 55–57, 67, 72–74, 91, 92, 102, 207, 298–301
    and broadcasting industry, 293
    and conservatives, 80
    FBI, impact on, 128, 160
    and Hiss-Chambers case, 154–55
    and HUAC, 162
    and India, 171, 172
    and Lattimore, 211–12
    and loyalty program, 220–21
    and McCarran, 225–26
    and McCarthy, 226–28
    and movie industry, 244–45
    and Nixon, 256–57
    and Supreme Court, 348
    and Truman vetoes, 378
    See also Anti-Communism, domestic
Reed, Stanley, 57, 347, 348 (photograph)
Regulatory agencies, 301–3

Reinstein, Jacques, 197
Religion, Truman's, 303
Remington, William, 73
Reorganization Acts (1939, 1945, 1949), 12, 121
Republican party, 74–76, 86, 91, 100–101, 303–4
    in elections, 110–19
    See also Congress, United States; Conservatism; Fightieth Congress; Red scare
Reputation, public, Truman's, 27–28, 287
Retirement, Truman's, 138, 149, 151, 194, 304–5
Reuther, Walter, 7, 206, 305–6
Revenue Acts (1945, 1948, 1950), 130, 131
Revolutions, 306–9. *See also* Imperialism
Rhee, Syngman, 201
Ridgway, Matthew, 203, 224
Riefler, Winfield, 105
Rio Conference (1947), 210, 231
Rio Pact, 75, 210, 374, 375
Roberts, Roy A., 194, 195
Romania, 102, 143
Roosevelt, Anna Eleanor, 6–7, 45, 96, 309–10, 389, 390
Roosevelt, Franklin Delano, 310–12
    and anti-Communism, 299
    and blacks, 30
    and Eastern Europe, 102, 142
    and election of 1940, 111
    imperialism, hostility to, 3
    on Korea, 201
    and Latin America, 209–10
    and liberalism, 215
    and New Deal, 123
    and 1944 vice-presidential nomination, 41, 112, 147, 206, 379
Roosevelt, Franklin Delano, Jr., 7
Roosevelt, James, 109 (photograph), 313
Roper, Elmo, 290
Rosenberg, Anna, 390
Rosenberg, Ethel and Julius, 64–65, 300, 313–14
Rosenberg, Hermann, 185, 186
Rosenman, Samuel I., 314, 337
Ross, Charles G., 62, 106, 314–16, 318
Rowe, James H., Jr., 246
Rural Electrification Administration, 316
Rusk, Dean, 132, 202
Russell, Richard B., Jr., 117, 316–17
Russia. *See* Soviet Union

SAC. *See* Strategic Air Command
St. Laurent, Louis, 259
St. Louis Post-Dispatch, 111, 318–19
Salisbury, Spencer, 40–41
Saudi Arabia, 266, 319–20
Sawyer, Charles, 44 (photograph), 320
Scandals, in Truman's administration, 229, 321, 376
Schenck v. *United States*, 348
Schlesinger, Arthur M., Jr., 127, 321–22
Schoeppel, Andrew F., 47
Schuman, Robert, 135
Schuman Plan, 135
Schwellenbach, Lewis B., 73, 206, 306, 322–23
Science and technology, 252, 323–24

Scientific Research and Development, Office of, 323
Securities and Exchange Commission, 302
Security program. *See* Loyalty program
Segregation, racial. *See* Black Americans; Civil rights
Selective Service, 69, 87, 108, 242, 268, 324–25, 377. *See also* Universal Military Training
Selective Training and Service Act (1940), 337
Senate. *See* Congress, United States
Senate Internal Security Subcommittee, 55, 128, 300
Senator, Truman as, 18, 27, 121, 128, 151, 157, 194, 195, 274, 325–26, 387. *See also* Truman committee
Sengstacke, John H., 10
Service, John Stewart, 225
Servicemen's Readjustment Act (G.I. bill, 1944), 377, 389
Shannon, Joseph, 184, 273
Shaugnessy v. *U.S. ex rel. Mezei,* 56
Shelley v. *Kraemer,* 31, 59, 61, 250, 349, 381
Shipstead, Henrik, 179
Short, Joseph H., 327
Silver, Abba Hillel, 189
Sino-Soviet Friendship Treaty, pact, 51, 65
Sipuel v. *Board of Regents,* 349
Small Business Act (1942), 157
Smaller War Plants Corporation, 157
Smith, Harold, 37
Smith Act, 73, 136, 299, 300, 327–28
Smith v. *Allwright,* 90
Snyder, John W., 44 (photograph), 104, 105, 130, 174, 246, 261, 328–29
Socialist party, American, 355
Social Security, 75, 329–30
Society for Social Responsibility in Science, 268
Somoza, Anastasio, 210
"The Sources of Soviet Conduct" (Kennan), 80–81, 85, 196
South, the, 330–32
   and civil rights, 58, 59, 90
   and Congress, 74–75
   as Democratic, 119
   and Dixiecrats, 7, 32, 58, 91, 96, 115, 116, 118, 331, 356
   flow of labor from, 90
   and George, 138
   and red scare, 91
   and Russell, 316–17
South Africa, 3
Southern Conference Educational Fund, 31
Southern Regional Council, 31
Soviet Union, 332–34
   and Berlin blockade, 6, 26–27, 53, 66, 70, 98, 140, 231
   and Bretton Woods, 36
   and cold war, 63–68
   and containment policy, 80–83
   and Czechoslovakia, 66, 86–87, 102, 238
   and Eastern Europe, 63, 102–3, 280
   and France, 135
   and "get tough" policy, 63–64, 102, 141–43, 148, 334, 384
   and Iran, 178, 179
   and Japan, 187, 188, 343

and Lend-Lease, 64, 213
and Marshall Plan, 66, 233
and NSC 68 memorandum, 6, 67, 83, 190, 197, 202, 238–39, 253, 261–62
and nuclear weapons, 13–14, 15, 69, 345
and Poland, 63–64, 102, 142, 283–84
and postwar occupation issues, 18, 64, 65, 70, 98, 102–3, 140–41, 280–81, 307
and Tito, 392–93
and totalitarianism, 127
and Turkey, 367–68
and United Nations, 369
and U.S. liberals, 215–16
See also Potsdam Conference; Stalin, Joseph
Spain, 334
Sparkman, John, 117
Special Committee to Investigate the National Defense Program. *See* Truman committee
Speeches, speech writing, 28, 62, 115, 120, 246, 253, 292, 335–38, 365–66, 380
Spellman, Francis, 45
Stalin, Joseph, 338–39
   and cold war, 63–68, 102–3, 176
   at Potsdam, 13, 14, 52, 281, 282–85, 332 (photograph), 333
   See also Soviet Union
Stark, Lloyd C., 111, 274, 293, 311, 339–40
State, Department of:
   charges of Communists in, 2, 67, 154–55, 162, 225
   and China, 49–50
   and Greece, 145
   and Japan, 187
   and Kennan, 197
   and Korea, 201, 202, 203
   and Marshall Plan, 231
   and NSC 68 memorandum, 262
   and recognition of Israel, 181, 186, 394
   and Truman Doctrine, 365–66
   and Yugoslavia, 392
   See also Acheson, Dean G.; Byrnes, James; Kennan, George; Marshall, George C.; Stettinius, Edward
States' Rights party. *See* Dixiecrats
Steagall Amendment (1941), 4, 5
Steelman, John R., 95, 174, 246, 327, 340–41
Steel strike, seizure of mills, 38, 56, 61–62, 92, 183, 205, 206–7, 243, 349, 381
Stettinius, Edward R., Jr., 142, 341
Stevenson, Adlai E., 92, 117, 118, 342
Stevenson, William E., 10
Stimson, Henry L., 13–15 passim, 64, 68, 142, 342–43
Stone, Harlan Fiske, 312 (photograph)
Stowe, David H., 337
Strategic Air Command, 6
Stratton, William G., 95
Straus, Michael, 47, 241, 297
Strauss, Lewis L., 15, 17
Stuart, John Leighton, 49, 229
Suburbanization, 164, 346–47
Subversive Activities Control Board, 56
Sundquist, James L., 337
Supreme Court, U.S., 347–50
   and civil liberties issues, 55–57, 74

and movie industry case, 245
and oil jurisdiction cases, 266
and red scare, 301
and steel mills seizure case, 38, 56, 61–62, 92, 183, 243
See also individual cases; individual justices
Sweatt v. *Painter,* 31, 59, 61, 349, 381
Symington, Stuart, 6, 10, 69, 350
Sziland, Leo, 13

Taft, Robert A., 7, 75, 79–80, 91, 117, 118, 202–3, 227, 303, 351–53, 354
Taft-Hartley Act, 353–54
   and CIO, 248, 378
   NLRB created under, 251–52
   as restraint on unions, 55, 108, 207
   and steel strike, 38, 243
   Truman vetoes, 75, 91, 351–52, 378
   and UMW, 214
Taiwan. *See* Formosa
Tansill, Charles C., 180
Tariffs. *See* Trade, international
Taylor, Glen, 290
Taylor, Myron, 46
Technical Cooperation Administration, 279, 337
Television. *See* Radio and television
Teller, Edward, 15
Tennessee Valley Authority, 217–18, 355
Terry v. *Adams,* 240
Texas Railroad Commission, 265
Thomas, J. Parnell, 56, 155, 162
Thomas, Norman M., 6, 355
Thornhill v. *Alabama,* 55
Thurmond, J. Strom, 32, 91, 96, 115, 331, 356
Tillett, Gladys, 390
Tito, Marshal, 392–93
Tobias, Channing, 59
Tobin, Maurice J., 44 (photograph), 45, 356
Tojo, Hideki, 386
Torresola, Griselio, 13
To Secure These Rights, 31, 58, 59–60, 250, 268, 331, 349
Totalitarianism, conceptions of, 126–27
Trade, international, 177–78
   Bretton Woods System, 36–37
   with Latin America, 209, 210–11
   and Reciprocal Trade Agreements, 296
Trans-Arabian Pipeline, 320
Transportation Act (1940), 325, 356–57, 387
Treasury, Department of, 103–5 passim, 131
Tripartite Treaty of Alliance (1942), 178
Trujillo, Rafael, 210
Truman, Elizabeth Virginia Wallace ("Bess," wife), 126, 138, 170, 184, 312 (photograph), 336 (photograph), 357–59
Truman, Harry S., biographical information:
   Attitudes, views on: art, 25; atomic bomb, 14, 53, 69, 186; aviation, 18; blacks, 184; civil rights, discrimination, 30–31, 45, 59, 305; civil liberties, 54–55; commander in chief, his role as, 71; conservation, 78–79; DPs, Israel, 181; feminism, ERA, 389–90; fiscal matters, 130; the French, 134; Germany, WW II, 139–40; isolationists, 391; Japanese, 186; Jews, 189; leadership, 26; presidency,

Truman, Harry S. *(continued)*
22, 285–86; press, 288, 289; religion, 303; southerners, 331; Soviets, 334
Interests, pastimes: cruises on presidential yacht, 388; Key West vacations, 200; Masonic Order, 20, 193, 234–35, 240, 277; music, 193, 248–49; poker playing, 185, 376, 388; reading, 106, 295–96; walking, 382–83; writing, 151, 184, 277–78; veterans' groups, 24, 40, 236, 240
Life events: assassination target, 13; awards, 19–20, 21; business ventures, 40–41, 129, 185, 193–94; chronology of, xix–xx; death, 305; education, 106–7; farming, 125–26, 267; inauguration, 170–337; military service, 24, 121, 134, 185, 193, 235–36, 276–77, 377; retirement, 138, 149, 151, 194, 304–5
Personality, 27, 28, 41, 77, 106, 109, 111, 126, 184, 275–77, 285, 287, 289, 303, 315, 325
Personal life: finances, 40–41, 129; health, 151, 305; homes, 138–39, 170–71; marriage and family, 7–8, 126, 129, 138, 170, 184, 208, 249, 275–76, 303, 357–63, 392; religion, 303
Public offices: county court judge, 121, 151, 170, 184–85, 194, 274; senator, 18, 27, 121, 128, 151, 157, 194, 195, 206, 274, 325–26, 387 (*see also* Truman committee); president, 170, 285–87; vice president, 27, 378–80
Truman, John Anderson (father), 129, 208, 275, 303, 359–60
Truman, John Vivian (brother), 360
Truman, Martha Ellen Young (mother), 126 (photograph), 275–76, 303, 359, 360–62
Truman, Mary Jane (sister), 362
Truman, Mary Jane Holmes (paternal grandmother), 8 (photograph)
Truman, Mary Margaret (Daniel, daughter), 138, 249, 312 (photograph), 336 (photograph), 362–64
Truman committee, 27, 38, 112, 136–37, 154, 194, 206, 236, 270–71, 288, 311, 326, 364, 391
Truman Doctrine, 63, 66, 75, 145, 365–67
amount of aid, 237
and Britain, 52, 144
and Connally, 77
and containment, 81, 82, 103, 107
and Marshall, 230–31
and postwar revolutions, 307
and sidestepping of United Nations, 176, 370
Truman's speech on, 232, 335–36
and Vandenberg, 374–75
Truman Library. *See* Harry S. Truman Library
Tufts, Robert, 197
Turkey, 52, 64, 66, 81, 107, 145, 178, 231–32, 260, 365–66, 367–68
Turner, Robert C., 85
Tydings, Millard, 227, 300

UAW. *See* United Automobile Workers
Ubico, Jorge, 210
Ulam, Stanislaw, 15

UMW. *See* United Mine Workers
Union for Democratic Action, 6, 31
Unions. *See* Labor; Taft-Hartley Act; individual unions
United Automobile Workers, 305
United Mine Workers, 55, 61, 62, 146, 205, 214, 381
United Nations, 2, 23, 32, 77, 97, 175–77, 179, 369–71
and atomic issue, 64, 65, 69
and E. Roosevelt, 309, 310
and Korean War, 67, 201, 202–3
versus NATO, 258
and Spain, 334
Special Committee on Palestine, 394
and Stettinius, 341
and Vandenberg, 374
United Nations Relief and Rehabilitation Administration (UNRRA), 372, 392–93
U.S. Air Force:
and air power, 5–6, 34, 350
and demobilization, 89
and military unification, 11, 133
and racial integration, 10, 69
See also Armed Forces, U.S.
U.S. Army:
and demobilization, 88, 89, 271
and McCarthy's charges, 228
and military unification, 11, 133
and racial integration, 10
See also Armed Forces, U.S.
U.S. Chamber of Commerce, 299
U.S. Coast Guard, 11, 89. *See also* Armed Forces, U.S.
U.S. Marines:
in China, 48, 49
and demobilization, 89
and military unification, 11, 133, 134
See also Armed Forces, U.S.
U.S. Navy, 34
and demobilization, 88–90
and military unification, 11, 133–34
and racial integration, 10
See also Armed Forces, U.S.
United States Relations with China with Special Reference to the Period 1944–1949 (China white paper), 49–50
U.S. Supreme Court. *See* Supreme Court, U.S.
United States v. Carolene Products Co., 347
United States v. Paramount Pictures, Inc., et al., 245
United States v. Rabinowitz, 240
Universal Declaration of Human Rights, 176, 309
Universal Military Training, 69, 82, 90, 107–8, 238, 268, 271, 324–25. *See also* Selective Service
Upper Colorado River Basin project, 47
Urban League. *See* National Urban League
Urban redevelopment, 164, 372–73. *See also* Housing

Vandenberg, Arthur H., 65, 75, 77, 100, 107, 142, 176, 179, 234, 303, 366, 374–75
Vandenberg, Hoyt S., 6
Vardaman, James, 128
Vaughan, Harry H., 128, 321, 375–76
Veterans, 34, 347, 376–77

Veterans Administration, 34, 347, 377
Veterans' Emergency Housing Act (1946), 377
Veto power, Truman's, 76, 286, 377–78
Vice president, Truman as, 27, 378–80
nomination, campaign for, 41, 112–13, 147, 196, 198, 206, 312
Vietminh, 173. *See also* Ho Chi Minh
Vietnam, 168, 173–74
Vincent, John Carter, 225
Vinson, Carl, 190
Vinson, Fred M., 55, 56, 347–50, 380–81
The Vital Center (Schlesinger), 127

Wages and salaries. *See* Incomes
Wage Stabilization Board, 243
Wagner, Robert, 251
Walker, Frank C., 112, 382
Walking, Truman's, 382–83
Wallace, Henry A., 310 (photograph), 383–85
and atomic policy, 345
and crisis in Czechoslovakia, 87, 102–3, 334
dropped from 1944 ticket, 112, 147, 215, 311, 379, 382
in 1948 election, 7, 53, 63, 83, 90, 91, 115, 116, 127, 289–90
pacifists' view of, 269
sees Soviets' viewpoint, 176
Wallace, Madge Gates (mother-in-law), 138, 357, 358
Walsh, David E., 179
Walter-McCarran Immigration Act, 56
War crimes trials, 55, 183, 347, 349, 386
Ward, Angus, 50
War Manpower Commission (WW II), 389
War Mobilization and Reconversion, Office of, 341
War Production Board (WW II), 157
Warren, Earl, 93 (photograph)
Waterman, Alan T., 252
Water Resources Policy Commission, 78, 297
Webb, James, 37, 174, 261, 341
Wedemeyer, Albert C., 48, 49
Weizmann, Chaim, 181, 186, 189, 394
Weizsaecker, Ernst von, 386
Welch, Joseph N., 228
West Germany, 66, 135, 141, 144, 234, 238, 259–60. *See also* Germany
Wheeler, Burton K., 179, 325, 357, 387
Wheeler, Raymond, 241
Wherry, Kenneth S., 179–80
White, Harry Dexter, 155
White, Walter, 31, 59, 250
White House, 387–88
and "Truman balcony," 138
Williamsburg, USS, 388
Willkie, Wendell, 111
Wilson, Charles E., 59, 208, 243
Wise, Stephen, 189
Women, 107, 388–90
Women's Bureau, 389, 390
Women's Division, Democratic National Committee, 107, 390
World Bank, 36–37
World War II, 390–91
and agriculture, 4
and atomic bomb, 13–15, 68–69, 186–87, 268, 342–46 passim

World War II (continued)
    Bradley in, 33–34
    Britain, impact on, 143
    and China, 48
    and Eastern Europe, 102, 280, 283–84
    final months of, 68–69
    and Lend-Lease, 213
    and NATO as response to, 258–59
    and 1944 election, 112–13
    and oil use, 265
    and Patterson, 270–72
    and Potsdam, 282–85
    and science, 323
    and Stalin, 338
    and Stettinius, 341

Truman's views on, 139–40
    war crimes in, 386
    women in labor force during, 388
    and Yugoslavia, 392
    See also Occupation issues, postwar;
        Truman committee
Wright, Fielding, 96, 331, 356
Writings, Truman's, 151, 184, 277–78
Wyatt, Wilson, 7, 163

"X" article (Kennan), 80–81, 85, 197

Yalta Conference, 63, 64, 102, 103, 142,
        280–81, 332, 333
Yamashita, General, 386

Yates v. United States, 300, 328
Young, Harriet Louisa (maternal grand-
        mother), 126 (photograph)
Young, Solomon (maternal grandfather), 392
Youngstown Sheet and Tube Co. v. Sawyer,
        38, 56, 61, 349, 381
Yugoslavia, 102, 392–93

Zionism, 9, 54, 180–82, 186, 189, 393–94.
        See also Israel
Zobrist, Benedict K., 149
Zorach v. Clauson, 57, 349
Zorin, Valerian, 87